Celtic Religions in the Roman Period

CELTIC STUDIES PUBLICATIONS

series editor: John T. Koch

CELTIC STUDIES PUBLICATIONS I

The Celtic Heroic Age: Literary Sources for Ancient Celtic Europe and Early Ireland and Wales, ed. John T. Koch with John Carey (Fourth Edition, revised and expanded, 2003) Pp. x + 440 ISBN 1–891271–09–1

CELTIC STUDIES PUBLICATIONS III

A Single Ray of the Sun: Religious Speculation in Early Ireland, John Carey (Second Edition, 2011) Pp. x + 123 ISBN 978–1–891271–18–2

CELTIC STUDIES PUBLICATIONS IV

Ildánach Ildírech. A Festschrift for Proinsias Mac Cana, ed. John Carey, John T. Koch, and Pierre-Yves Lambert (1999) Pp. xvii + 312 ISBN 1–891271–01–6

CELTIC STUDIES PUBLICATIONS VII

Yr Hen Iaith: Studies in Early Welsh, ed. Paul Russell (2003) Pp. viii + 224 ISBN 1–891271–10–5

CELTIC STUDIES PUBLICATIONS VIII

Landscape Perception in Early Celtic Literature, Francesco Benozzo (2004) Pp. xvi + 272 ISBN 1–891271–11–3

CELTIC STUDIES PUBLICATIONS IX

Cín Chille Cúile—Texts, Saints and Places: Essays in Honour of Pádraig Ó Riain, ed. John Carey, Máire Herbert, and Kevin Murray (2004) Pp. xxiv + 405 ISBN 1–891271–13–X

CELTIC STUDIES PUBLICATIONS X

Arch æologia Britannica: Texts and Translations, Edward Lhwyd, ed. Dewi W. Evans and Brynley F. Roberts (2009) Pp. xii + 262 ISBN 978–1–891271–14–4

CELTIC STUDIES PUBLICATIONS XIII

Tartessian: Celtic in the South-west at the Dawn of History, John T. Koch (second edition 2013) Pp. ix + 332 ISBN 978–1–891271–17–5

CELTIC STUDIES PUBLICATIONS XV

Celtic from the West: Alternative Approaches from Archaeology, Genetics, Language and Literature, ed. Barry Cunliffe and John T. Koch (2010; 2012) Pp. xii + 383 ISBN 978–1–84217–475–3

CELTIC STUDIES PUBLICATIONS XVI

Celtic from the West 2: Rethinking the Bronze Age and the Arrival of Indo-European in Atlantic Europe, ed. John T. Koch and Barry Cunliffe (2013) Pp. viii + 237 ISBN 978–1–84217–529–3

CELTIC STUDIES PUBLICATIONS XVII

Memory, Myth and Long-term Landscape Inhabitation, ed. Adrian M. Chadwick and Catriona D. Gibson (2013), Pp. xi + 347 ISBN 978–1–78297–393–5

CELTIC STUDIES PUBLICATIONS XVIII

The End and Beyond: Medieval Irish Eschatology, ed. John Carey, Emma Nic Cárthaigh, and Caitríona Ó Dochartaigh (2014) 2 vols, Pp. xi + 944 ISBN 978–1–891271–20–5

CELTIC STUDIES PUBLICATIONS XIX

Celtic from the West 3: Atlantic Europe in the Metal Ages: questions of shared language, ed. John T. Koch, Barry Cunliffe, Kerri Cleary, and Catriona D. Gibson (2016), Pp. xii + 539 ISBN 978–1–78570–227–3

CELTIC STUDIES PUBLICATIONS XX

Celtic Religions in the Roman Period: Personal, Local, and Global, ed. Ralph Haeussler and Anthony King (2017), Pp. xiv + 522 ISBN 978–1–891271–25–0

Celtic Studies Publications xx

Celtic Religions in the Roman Period

Personal, Local, and Global

edited by

RALPH HAEUSSLER and ANTHONY KING

Aberystwyth

2017

First published 2017

Cover design by CSP-Cymru Cyf

A Catalogue record for this book is available from the British Library.

ISBN 978-1-891271-25-0

Celtic Studies Publications

for customers in North America:
Casemate Academic
1950 Lawrence Road
Havertown, PA 19083
USA
(phone: 1 610 853 9131)

editorial correspondence:
CSP-Cymru Cyf
Centre for Advanced Welsh and Celtic Studies
National Library of Wales
Aberystwyth, Ceredigion SY23 3HH
Wales

TABLE OF CONTENTS

Balkans & Danube Provinces

Germania Inferior

Cover photo: embossed silver plaque (height 11.3cm) discovered among 3rd-century rubbish at Bewcastle, the Roman *Fanum Cocidi*. Dedicated to a god bearing a Celtic name, Cocidius, the plaque depicts the god standing in a shrine with spear and shield (RIB 986, Tullie House Museum, Carlisle; photo: Anthony King).

CONTRIBUTORS

MIRANDA ALDHOUSE-GREEN
Department of Archaeology, Cardiff University, Humanities Building, Colum Drive, Cardiff, CF10 3EU, Wales, aldhouse-greenmj@cardiff.ac.uk

SILVIA ALFAYÉ VILLA
Ciencias de la Antigüedad, Facultad de Filosofía y Letras, Pedro Cerbuna, 12, Universidad Zaragoza, 50009 Zaragoza, Spain, silvia.alfaye@gmail.com

MANUELA ALVES DIAS
Centro de Estudos Clássicos, Universidade de Lisboa, Lisboa, Portugal, epigraphica@gmail.com

FLORIAN BLANCHARD
Centre de Recherche Bretonne et Celtique (CRBC), Université de Bretagne Occidentale, Faculté des Lettres et Sciences Humaines, 20 Rue Duquesne – CS 93837, 29238 Brest Cedex 3, France, florian3.blanchard@orange.fr

FRANCISCO BURILLO-MOZOTA
Facultad de Ciencias Sociales y Humanas, Universidad de Zaragoza, Teruel, Spain, fburillo@unizar.es

Mª PILAR BURILLO-CUADRADO
Ciencias de la Antigüedad, Facultad de Filosofía y Letras, Pedro Cerbuna, 12, Universidad Zaragoza, 50009 Zaragoza, Spain, mpilar.burillo@gmail.com

MARIA JOÃO CORREIA SANTOS
Centre of Classic Studies (Centro de Estudos Clássicos), University of Lisbon, Portugal, mj.correiasantos@letras.ulisboa.pt

PATRIZIA DE BERNARDO STEMPEL
Departamento de Estudios Clásicos, Universidad del País Vasco / Euskal Herriko Unibertsitatea, Vitoria / Gasteiz, Spain, patrizia.debernardo@ehu.es

ALESSANDRA ESPOSITO
Classics Department, King's College London,

Strand, London WC2R 2LS, England, alessandra.esposito@kcl.ac.uk

ALEXANDER FALILEYEV
Aberystwyth, Wales, a.falileyev@gmail.com

FERNANDO FERNÁNDEZ PALACIOS
Centre for Advanced Welsh and Celtic Studies, University of Wales, Aberystwyth, SY23 3HH, Wales, mbuchanscot@gmail.com

AUDREY FERLUT
Université Jean Moulin Lyon 3, UMR 5189, 69007 Lyon, France, aferlut1@ac-lyon.fr

VOJISLAV FILIPOVIC
Institute of Archaeology, Belgrade, Serbia, vfilipov1@gmail.com

HARTMUT GALSTERER
Institut für Geschichtswissenschaft, Abteilung für Alte Geschichte, Universität Bonn, Bonn, Germany

CRISTINA GIRADI
Università degli Studi di Padova, DISSGEA, Piazza Capitaniato 7, 35100 Padova, cristina.girardi@yahoo.it

Mª CRUZ GONZÁLEZ RODRÍGUEZ
Estudios Clásicos, Universidad del País Vasco/Euskal Herriko Unibertsitatea, Vitoria/Gasteiz, Spain, cruz.gonzalez@ehu.es

RALPH HAEUSSLER
Faculty of Humanities, University of Wales Trinity Saint David, Lampeter, SA48 7ED, Wales, ralph.haussler@uclmail.net

ANTHONY KING
Department of Archaeology, University of Winchester, Sparkford Road, Winchester SO22 4NR, England, tony.king@winchester.ac.uk

JOHN KOCH
Centre for Advanced Welsh and Celtic Studies, University of Wales, Aberystwyth, SY23 3HH, Wales, jtk@wales.ac.uk

DAPHNE NASH BRIGGS
Formerly School of Archaeology, Oxford University, England, d.briggs@classics.oxon.org

WERNER PETERMANDL
Institut für Alte Geschichte und Altertumskunde, Karl-Franzens-Universität Graz, Universitätsplatz 3/II, 8010 Graz, Austria, werner.petermandl@uni-graz.at

VLADIMIR P. PETROVIC
Institut des études balkaniques de l`Académie serbe des sciences et des arts, Knez Mihailova 35/IV, 11000 Belgrade, Serbia, vladimir.arheolog@gmail.com

BLANCA MARÍA PRÓSPER
Departamento de Filología Clásica e Indoeuropeo, Universidad de Salamanca, Plaza de Anaya s/n, 37008 Salamanca, Spain, indoling@usal.es

MANUEL RAMÍREZ SÁNCHEZ
Universidad de Las Palmas de Gran Canaria, Juan de Quesada, 30,
35001 Las Palmas de Gran Canaria, Spain, manuel.ramirez@ulpgc.es

BERNARD REMY
Laboratoire Universitaire Histoire Cultures Italie Europe, Grenoble (LUHCIE)
Centre Camille Jullian, Maison méditerranéenne des sciences de l'homme, 5, rue du Château de l'horloge, BP 647, 13094 Aix-en-Provence, France, bernard.remy07@orange.fr

MARJETA ŠASEL KOS
Institute of Archaeology, ZRC-SAZU, Novi trg 2, 1000 Ljubljana, Slovenia, mkos@zrc-sazu.si

ALFRED SCHÄFER
Römisch-Germanisches Museum der Stadt Köln, Köln, Germany, alfred.schaefer@stadt-koeln.de

PAOLA TOMASI
Dipartimento di Studi Umanistici, Università degli Studi di Pavia, 27100 Pavia, Italy, paola.tomasi@unipv.it

ROGER S. O. TOMLIN
Wolfson College, Oxford University, Oxford, OX2 6UD, England, roger.tomlin@wolfson.ox.ac.uk

JONATHAN WOODING
School of Literature, Arts and Media, University of Sydney, NSW 2006, Australia, jonathan.wooding@sydney.edu.au

STEPHEN YEATES
Wolfson College, Oxford, Oxfordshire, OX2 6UD, England, stephenyeates@pobroadband.co.uk

ABBREVIATIONS

AALR = *Atlas antroponímico de la Lusitania romana*, Mérida & Burdeos, Ausonius Éditions, 2003.

ABC = Cottam, E., P. de Jersey, C. Rudd & J. Sills 2010 *Ancient British Coins*. Aylsham, Chris Rudd.

AC = *Annales Cambriae*, cited from J. Morris (ed. & trans.), *British History and the Welsh Annals/ Nennius*, Arthurian Period Sources 8. London, Phillimore 1980.

AE = *L'Année épigraphique. Revue des publications épigraphiques relatives à l'Antiquité romaine*. Paris 1888–.

AEW = de Vries, J. 2004 *Altnordisches etymologisches Wörterbuch*. Leiden.

AW = Schützeichel, R. 2005 *Althochdeutsches Wörterbuch*. Tübingen.

AIJ = Hoffiller, V. & B. Saria 1938 *Antike Inschriften aus Jugoslawien*. 1: *Noricum und Pannonia superior* (re-print Amsterdam 1970).

ANRW = *Aufstieg und Niedergang der Römischen Welt*. Berlin & New York: Walter de Gruyter 1972–.

Caes. *BGall.* = Caesar, *de bello Gallico*

CAG = *Carte archéologique de la Gaule. Les Alpes-de-Haute-Provence*. Paris, Académie des Inscriptions et Belles Lettres.

CCelt. = Continental Celtic.

CIIC = Macalister, R. A. S. 1996 *Corpus Inscriptionum Insularum Celticarum*. Blackrock, Co. Dublin, Four Courts Press.

CIL = *Corpus Inscriptionum Latinarum*. Berlin. 1861–.

CILCC I = Esteban Ortega, J. 2007 *Corpus de inscripciones latinas de Cáceres. I. Norba*, Universidad de Extremadura, Cáceres.

CIRG I = *Corpus de inscripcións romanas de Galicia*. Santiago de Compostela, Consello da Cultura Galega: vol. I, *Provincia de A Coruña* (1991), vol. II, *Provincia de Pontevedra* (1994).

CPILC = Hurtado de San Antonio, R. 1977 *Corpus Provincial de Inscripciones Latinas de Cáceres*. Cáceres.

CIRP Salamanca = Alonso Ávila, Á & S. Crespo Ortiz de Zárate 1999 *Corpus de inscripciones romanas de la provincia de Salamanca*. Valladolid.

CPILC = Hurtado de San Antonio, R. 1977 *Corpus provincial de inscripciones Latinas de Cáceres, Cáceres*. Cáceres, Diputación Provincial. Servicios Culturales.

CR = *The Cartulary or Redon*, ed. A. de Courson. Paris, 1863.

CSIR = *Corpus Signorum Imperii Romani. Corpus of sculpture of the Roman world*, 18 vols. London or Oxford or Berlin. 1975–2004.

dat. = dative.

DCC/DCCPlN = Falileyev, A. (in collaboration with A. E. Gohil & N. Ward) 2010 *Dictionary of Continental Celtic Place-Names*. Aberystwyth, CMCS.

DE = *Dizionario epigrafico di antichità romane*. Roma : Istituto Italiano per la Storia antica, 1895–1997.

DIL = *(Contributions to a) Dictionary of the Irish Language*. Dublin, Royal Irish Academy, 1913–1976.

DN = divine name.

EDCS = Epigraphik-Datenbank Clauss-Slaby http://www.manfredclauss.de.

EDR = Epigraphic Database Roma.

EE = Ephemeris epigraphica.

ERAv = Hernando Sobrino, Mª R. 2005 *Epigrafía romana de Ávila, Petrae Hispaniarum*, 3/4, Burdeos & Madrid, Ausonius Éditions.

ERCanosa = Grelle, F. & M. Pani 1990 *Le Epigrafia Romane di Canosa*. Bari.

ERPL = Rabanal Alonso, M. A., & S. M.ª García Martínez 2001 *Epigrafía romana de la provincia de León: revisión y actualizaciones*. León.

ERSegovia = Santos Yanguas J. 2005 *Epigrafía romana de Segovia y su provincia*. Segovia.

ERZamora = Bragado Toranzo, J. M.a 1991 *Fuentes literarias y epigráficas de la provincial de Zamora y su relación con las vías romanas de la Cuenca del Duero*. Universidad de León.

Esp. = Espérandieu, E. 1910–1928, *Recueil général des Bas-reliefs, statues et bustes de la Gaule romaine*, vols I-X. Paris, Editions Ernest Leroux; Espérandieu, E. & Lantier, R. 1938–1966 *Recueil général des bas-reliefs, statues et bustes de la Gaule romaine*,vols XI-XV Paris, Editions Ernest Leroux.

Espérandieu, E. 1931 *Recueil général des bas-reliefs, statues et bustes de Germanie*. Paris, Editions Ernest Leroux.

EWD = Pfeifer, W. 2003 *Etymologisches Wörterbuch des Deutschen*. München (1st edition: Berlin, Deutscher Taschenbuch Verlag 1989).

FE = *Ficheiro Epigráfico. Suplemento de Conimbriga*. Coimbra.

FN = family name.

GED = Lehmann, W. P. 1986 *A Gothic Etymological Dictionary. Based on the 3rd edition of Vergleichendes Wörterbuch der Gotischen Sprache by Sigmund Feist*. Leiden.

HAE = *Hispania Antiqua Epigraphica. Suplemento anual de Archivo Español de Arqueología*. Instituto de Arqueología y Prehistoria «Rodrigo Caro». Madrid, Consejo Superior de Investigaciones Científicas.

HB = *The Historia Brittonum of 'Nennius'*, cited from *Monumenta Germaniae Historica, Chronica Minora*, ed. Th. Mommsen. Berlin 1898; also, *British History and the Welsh Annals/Nennius, Arthurian Period Sources* 8, ed. & trans. J. Morris. London, Phillimore, 1980; *The Historia Brittonum 3: The 'Vatican' Recension*, ed. D. N. Dumville. Cambridge, Brewer, 1985.

HD = Heidelberg epigraphische Datenbank, http://edh-www.adw.uni-heidelberg.de/home

HEp = *Hispania Epigraphica. Revista del Archivo Epigráfico de Hispania*. Madrid, Universidad Complutense. Online: http://eda-bea.es/.

Holder = Holder, A. 1896–1910 *Alt-celtischer Sprachschatz*. 3 vols. Leipzig, B. G. Teubner (reprint 1961–1962, Graz, Akademische Druck- und Verlagsanstalt).

ICelt. = Insular Celtic.

IE = Indo European.

IEW = Pokorny, J. 1959–1969 *Indogermanisches etymologisches Wörterbuch*. 2 vols. Bern, Francke.

ILA-Bordeaux = *Inscriptions Latines d'Aquitaine: Bordeaux*, ed. L. Maurin, M. Navarro Caballero, D. Barraud, C. Brial & A. Zieglé, Bordeaux/Paris 2010.

ILER = Vives, J. 1971–1972 *Inscripciones latinas de la España romana*. Barcelona.

ILGN = Espérandieu, É. 1929 *Inscriptions Latines de Gaule Narbonnaise*. Paris, E. Leroux.

ILJug = Šašel, A. & J., *Inscriptiones latinae quae in Iugoslavia inter annos MCMXL et MCMLX repertae et editae sunt* (= Situla 5). Ljubljana 1963; Šašel, A. & J., *Inscriptiones latinae quae in Iugoslavia inter annos MCMLX et MCMLXX repertae et editae sunt* (= Situla 19). Ljubljana 1978; Šašel, A. & J., *Inscriptiones Latinae quae in Iugoslavia inter annos MCMII et MCMXL repertae et editae sunt* (= Situla 25). Ljubljana 1986.

ILLPRON = *Inscriptionum Lapidarium Latinarum Provinciae Norici usque ad annum MCMLXXXIV repertarum indices*. Berlin 1986.

ILN = *Inscriptions Latines de Narbonnaise*. Paris, CNRS éditions (ILN-Die = Rémy, B. *et al.* 2012, *VII, Voconces. VII, 1, Die*; ILN-Vienne = Rémy, B. 2004–2005 *V. Vienne*, 3 vols).

ILS = Dessau, H. 1892–1916 *Inscriptiones Latinae Selectae*, 3 vols. Berlin.

ILSl = *Inscriptiones Latinae Sloveniae*, 1: M. Lovenjak, *Neviodunum*. Ljubljana 1998.

Inscr. Aqu. = J.B. Brusin, J. B. 1991–1993 *Inscriptiones Aquileiae*, 3 vols, Udine.

Inscr.It. = *Inscriptiones Italiae*, Rome 1931–.

IRC I = Fabre, G., M. Mayer & I. Rodà, eds 1984 *Inscriptions romaines de Catalogne*, I, *Barcelone (sauf Barcino)*. Paris, Diffusion de Boccard.

IRG = Bouza Brey, F. & A. D'Ors 1949 *Inscripciones romanas de Galicia*. Santiago de Compostela, Instituto Padre Sarmiento de Estudios Gallegos 1949–.

IRLugo = Arias, F., P. Le Roux & A. Tranoy 1979 *Inscriptions romaines de la province de Lugo*. Paris, Diffusion de Boccard.

IRMN = Castillo, C., J. Gómez-Pantoja & Mª D. Mauleón 1981 *Inscripciones romanas del Museo de Navarra*. Pamplona, Diputación de Navarra.

IRPP = Hernández Guerra, L. 1994 *Inscripciones romanas en la provincia de Palencia*. Valladolid.

JP = catalogue numbers from Johns, C. M. & T. Potter 1983 *The Thetford Treasure*. London, BMP.

LEIA = Vendryes, J., Bachellery, É. & Lambert, P.-Y. 1959– *Lexique étymologique de l'irlandais ancien*. Dublin & Paris, CNRS Éditions.

LHEB = Jackson, K. H. 1994 *Language and History in Early Britain: A Chronological Survey of the Brittonic Languages from the 1st to the 12th c. AD*. 2nd rev. ed. Dublin, Four Courts Press (first published by Edinburgh University Press 1953).

LKA = Sievers, S., O. H. Urban& P. C. Ramsl 2012 *Lexikon zur keltischen Archäologie*, 2 vols. Wien, Österreichische Akademie der Wissenschaften (Mitteilungen der Prähist. Kommission 73).

Lib.Lan. = *The Text of the Book of Llan Dâv: Reproduced from the Gwysaney Manuscript*, ed. J. G. Evans, J. Rhŷs, Facsimile reprint, Aberystwyth, National Library of Wales, 1979; first published, Oxford, J. G. Evans, 1893; datings of the personal names in Lib.Lan. are from W. Davies, *Llandaff Charters*. Aberystwyth, National Library of Wales 1979.

LIV = Rix, H. *et alii* eds [1]1998/[2]2001 *Lexikon der Indogermanischen Verben. Die Wurzel und ihre Primärstammbildungen*. Wiesbaden, Reichert.

LS = Lewis, C. T. & C. Short 1955 *A Latin Dictionary*. Oxford (original edition, 1879).

lupa = http://lupa.at/

MLH IV = Untermann, J. (with D. S. Wodtko) 1997 *Monumenta Linguarum Hispanicarum. IV. Die tartessischen, keltiberischen und lusitanischen Inschriften*. Wiesbaden, Ludwig Reichert.

M.R.M. = Morphological Residual Model.

NPC = Delamarre, X. 2007 *Noms de personnes celtiques dans l'épigraphie classique*. Paris, Errance.

NTS = Hartley, B. R. and Dickinson, B. M. , eds 2008–2012 *Names on Terra sigillata, An Index of Makers' Stamps & Signatures on Gallo-Roman Terra sigillata (Samian Ware)*, 9 vols. London, Bulletin of the Institute of Classical Studies Supplement 102.

NWÄI = De Bernardo Stempel, P. 1999 *Nominale Wortbildung des älteren Irischen: Stammbildung und Derivation*, Tübingen, Max Niemeyer/ W. de Gruyter.

OBret. = Old Breton.

OEng. = Old English.

OHG =Old High German.

OIc. = Old Icelandic.

OIr = Old Irish.

OPEL = *Onomasticon Provinciarum Europae Latinarum*, ed. Lőrincz, B. & Redő, F. ex materia ab Mócsy, A., Feldmann, R., Marton E. et Szilágyi, M. collecta. 4 vols. Budapest, Archaeolingua, 1994 & Wien, Forschungsgesellschaft Wiener Stadtarchäologie, 1999–2002.

PAS = Portable Antiquaties Scheme.

PCelt. = Proto-Celtic.

P.Dura = Bradford Welles, C. *et alii* 1959 *The Excavations at Dura-Europos. Final Report, v, part I, The Parchments and Papyri*. New Haven.

PIE = Proto Indo-European.

pl. = plural.

Plin. *HN* = Plinius, *Historia Naturalis.*

PlN = place name.

PN = personal name.

Pokorny, IEW = Pokorny, J. 1959 *Indogermanisches Etymologisches Wörterbuch*. Heidelberg.

RAP = Garcia, J. M. 1991 *Religiões antigas de Portugal. Aditamentos e observações às «Religiões da Lusitânia» de J. Leite de Vasconcelos. Fontes epigráficas*. Lisboa.

RE = *Paulys Realencyclopädie der classischen Altertumswissenschaft*. 84 vols. Berlin 1894–1978.

RIB = *The Roman Inscriptions of Britain*, 3 vols. Oxford and Stroud.

RIG = *Recueil des inscriptions gauloises*. Paris, CNRS. *I. Inscriptions gallo-grecques* (1985), II.1 *Textes gallo-étrusques, Textes gallo-latins sur pierre* (1988), II.2 *Textes gallo-romains sur instrumentum* (2002).

RINMS = M. Šašel Kos 1997 *The Roman Inscriptions in the National Museum of Slovenia*, Ljubljana.

RSK = B. & H. Galsterer 1975 *Die römischen Steininschriften aus Köln*. Köln, Römisch-Germanisches Museum.

SI = Pais, H. 1884 *Corporis Inscriptionum Latinarum Supplementa Italica, I. Additamenta ad vol. V Galliae Cisalpinae, ex typis Salviucci*. Roma.

Supp.It. = *Supplementa Italica*. Rome 1981–.

Tab. Peut. = Tabula Peutingeriana.

Tab. Sulis = Tomlin, R. S. O. 1988 'The curse tablets', in B. Cunliffe (ed.), *The temple of Sulis Minerva at Bath*, vol. 2. *The finds from the sacred spring*. Oxford, Oxford University Committee for Archaeology, Monograph 16, 1988, 4–277.

Tac. *ann.* = Tacitus, *Annales.*

ThesCRA = *Thesaurus Cultus et Rituum Antiquorum*. Los Angeles, The J. Paul Getty Museum. 5 vols. 2004–2005.

ThLL/TLL = *Thesaurus Linguae Latinae*.

TVindol = Bowman, A. K. & J. D. Thomas, *The Vindolanda writing-tablets* (*Tabulae Vindolandeses*), 4 vols, London 1994– (online: http://vindolanda.csad.ox.ac.uk/).

u.a. = unter anderem.

I

CREFYDDAU CELTAIDD YN Y CYFNOD RHUFEINIG: PERSONOL, LLEOL A BYD-EANG

CELTIC RELIGIONS IN THE ROMAN PERIOD: PERSONAL, LOCAL, AND GLOBAL

Ralph Haeussler & Anthony King

"The inhabitants (of Gaul) are proud and superstitious and once they were that barbaric that they considered man as the best victim and most agreeable to the gods. There are remnants of these savage customs that are today abolished (...)" (Pomponius Mela, *De Chorographia* III 2, 18–9)

F.E.R.C.AN.'s aim is to compile a corpus of the *fontes epigraphici religionum Celticarum antiquarum*, the epigraphic sources for the ancient (i.e. pre-medieval) Celtic religions.[1] The number of pre-Roman epigraphic sources is extremely limited, as most societies did not consider it appropriate to use writing

1 For post-antiquity 'Celtic' inscriptions from AD 400–1000, cf. the *Celtic Inscribed Stones Database*: http://www.ucl.ac.uk/archaeology/cisp/database/ – for the F.E.R.C.AN. project, cf. e.g., Hainzmann & De Bernardo Stempel 2013 and the paper by W. Petermandl in this volume.

"Mae trigolion (Gâl) yn falch ac ofergoelus ac unwaith roeddent mor farbaraidd nes eu bod yn ystyried mai pobl oedd yr ysglyfaeth orau a'r un fwyaf wrth fodd y duwiau. Mae gweddillion yr arferion barbaraidd hyn sydd wedi eu dileu erbyn heddiw (...)" (Pomponius Mela, *De Chorographia* III 2, 18–9)

NOD F.E.R.C.AN. yw llunio corpws o'r *fontes epigraphici religionum Celticarum antiquarum*, sef y ffynonellau epigraffig ar gyfer crefyddau Celtaidd yr hen fyd (h.y. cyn yr Oesoedd Canol).[1] Mae nifer y ffynonellau epigraffig cyn-Rufeinig yn gyfyngedig dros ben, gan nad oedd y rhan fwyaf o gymdeithasau'n

1 Ar gyfer arysgrifau 'Celtaidd' ar ôl cyfnod yr Hen Fyd rhwng OC 400–1000, cf. *Celtic Inscribed Stones Database*: http://www.ucl.ac.uk/archaeology/cisp/database/ – ar gyfer y prosiect F.E.R.C.AN., cf. e.e., Hainzmann a De Bernardo Stempel 2013 a phapur W. Petermandl yn y gyfrol hon.

for religious matters in the Iron Age.[2] Most of the evidence for this project therefore primarily comes from the Roman period. But what can Roman inscriptions really tell us about 'Celtic' religions, if anything? Obviously, the project presumes a certain persistence of Iron Age cults into and throughout the Roman period, which makes sense since the Romans generally did not impose their own cults on the conquered and provincial populations.[3]

2 As we are told by Caesar *BGall.* 6.14. There are some pre-Roman inscriptions, written in Celtic languages (notably Lepontic/Gallo-Etruscan, Gallo-Greek, and Celtiberian inscriptions), but only few refer to the religious sphere. For example, there is the famous bilingual Latin-Celtic inscription from Vercelli/*Vercellae* in Cisalpine Gaul (1st century BC), written in so-called Lepontic script (RIG II.1, E-2). As is common with these early inscriptions, they do not mention any names of deities, but primarily the names of dedicants (also cf. e.g. the dedication from Briona: RIG II.1, E-1). In the case of Vercelli, the inscription does provide some details of the cult: the phrase *campus .... deis et hominbus ... dedit* refers to a 'campus ... given ... to gods and humans' (though P. de Bernardo Stempel 2011 suggests that *deis et hominibus* – a Latin rendering of the Celtic *teuoχtom* – was primarily a legal phrase). In the south of Gaul, we find some Gallo-Greek inscriptions that mention deities (usually not before the 1st century BC), notably Belenos (*RIG* G-28; CAG 13/1 100; CAG 13/1 55; Lejeune, 1968–1969, 61–67, n° 20), Belisama (*RIG* G-153), Matrebo Glanaikabo (*RIG* G-64), Matrebo Namausikabo (*RIG* G-203), Roklosia (*RIG* G-65), Taranoou (Taranis? – *RIG* G-27), and Larasso (*IGF* 207; but for De Bernardo Stempel 2007, 70 an Aquitanian theonym). And in Iberia we find Celtiberian inscriptions mentioning *inter alia* the possible theonyms Neto/Neito and Tokoitos (cf. Abascal 2002).

3 For aspects of continuity and persistence in provincial cults, cf. papers in Haeussler and King (eds) 2007 and 2008). Cf. Festus, s.v. *municipalia sacra* 146L: this passage shows that the Roman *pontifices*, the highest priests of the Roman state, wanted people to worship their ancestral cults, even in the context of a Roman-citizen community.

ystyried ei bod yn briodol defnyddio ysgrifennu ar gyfer materion crefyddol yn yr Oes Haearn.[2] Daw'r rhan fwyaf o'r dystiolaeth ar gyfer prosiect hwn, felly, o'r cyfnod Rhufeinig. Ond beth, os unrhyw beth, y gall arysgrifau Rhufeinig ei ddweud wrthym am y grefydd 'Geltaidd'? Yn amlwg, rhagdybia'r prosiect fod defodau'r Oes Haearn wedi rhyw barhau i'r cyfnod Rhufeinig a thrwy gydol y cyfnod hwn, sy'n gwneud synnwyr gan nad oedd y Rhufeiniaid, fel arfer, yn gorfodi eu defodau eu hunain ar bobloedd orchfygedig yn y taleithiau.[3] A oes

2 Fel yr adroddir wrthym gan Gesar, *BGall.* 6.14. Mae rhai arysgrifau cyn-Rufeinig wedi eu hysgrifennu mewn ieithoedd Celtaidd (yn enwedig arysgrifau Lepontig/Galaidd-Etrwscaidd, Galaidd-Roegaidd, a Cheltiberaidd), ond ychydig iawn yn y cylch crefyddol. Er enghraifft, mae arysgrifen ddwyieithog Ladin a Chelteg o Vercelli/*Vercellae* yng Ngâl Isalpaidd (y ganrif 1af CC), wedi ei hysgrifennu yn yr ysgrifen Lepontig fel y'i gelwir (RIG II.1, E-2). Fel sy'n gyffredin gyda'r arysgrifau hyn, nid ydynt yn crybwyll unrhyw enwau duwiau, ond yn bennaf enwau offrymwyr (hefyd cf. e.e. y cysegriad o Briona: RIG II.1, E-1). Yn achos Vercelli, mae'r ysgrifen yn rhoi manylion y ddefod: cyfeiria'r ymadrodd *campus .... deis et hominbus ... dedit* at 'campus ... a roddwyd ... i dduwiau a phobl' (er yr awgryma P. de Bernardo Stempel 2011 mai term cyfreithiol yn anad dim oedd *deis et hominibus* – ffurf Ladin ar y *teuoχtom* Celtaidd). Yn ne Gâl, ceir rhai arysgrifau Galaidd-Roegaidd sy'n sôn am dduwiau (fel arfer, nid cyn y ganrif 1af CC), yn enwedig Belenos (*RIG* G-28; CAG 13/1 100; CAG 13/1 55; Lejeune, 1968–1969, 61–67, n° 20), Belisama (*RIG* G-153), Matrebo Glanaikabo (*RIG* G-64), Matrebo Namausikabo (*RIG* G-203), Roklosia (*RIG* G-65), Taranoou (Taranis? – *RIG* G-27), a Larasso (*IGF* 207ar gyfer De Bernardo Stempel 2007, 70 enw duw o Acwitania). Ac yn Iberia cawn arysgrifau Celtiberiaidd sy'n sôn *inter alia* am yr enwau duwiau Neto/Neito a Tokoitos (cf. Abascal 2002).

3 Am agweddau ar barhad a dygnwch mewn defodau yn y taleithiau, cf. papurau yn Haeussler a King (gol) 2007 a 2008). Cf. Festus, s.v. *municipalia sacra* 146L: dengys y darn hwn fod y *pontifices*, sef offeiriaid uchaf y wladwriaeth

Can we assess how much of these Celtic 'superstitions' and 'savage customs', as Pomponius Mela pejoratively called them around A.D. 43, survived into the Roman period, and in which form? What exactly was 'abolished',[4] and what are Pomponius Mela's 'remnants'?[5] This also prompts the question whether the Roman conquest initiated a rupture in religious understandings, for instance, if we presume that the druids' alleged eradication had an impact on religious beliefs across the Keltiké.[6] It is also possible that local cults merely adapted gradually to new social needs, new cultural conventions and new media (i.e. writing and sculpture) in a changing world, and thus that there was some persistence of autochthonous religious understandings and practices that Romans pejoratively called 'superstitions'. As we shall see, in most cases one can identify combinations of persistence, transformation, innovation, and rupture, across the Roman West to varying degrees.

The problematic nature of the evidence for 'Celtic religions'

Interestingly, for Julius Caesar the *Galli* had more or less the same beliefs of the gods as the other peoples.[7] Does

4 Perhaps just the alleged human sacrifices, whose existence in the late Iron Age can be disputed.

5 Also cf. Pliny *HN* 30.4 on the rituals that were said to have been abolished: magical art, monstrous rites, and human sacrifice.

6 On the druids' last stand on Anglesey/*Mona*, cf. Tac. *Ann.* 14.29–30.

7 Caes. *BGall.* 6.17: *de his eandem fere, quam reliquae gentes, habent opinionem.* But we

modd i ni asesu faint o'r 'ofergoelion' ac 'arferion barbaraidd' Celtaidd hyn, a defnyddio enw sarhaus Pomponia Mela arnynt tua 43 OC, a oroesodd i'r cyfnod Rhufeinig, ac ar ba ffurf? Beth yn union a 'ddilëwyd',[4] a beth yw 'gweddillion' Pomponius Mela?[5] Mae hyn hefyd yn codi'r cwestiwn a wnaeth y goncwest Rufeinig greu hollt o ran dealltwriaeth grefyddol, er enghraifft, a rhagdybio i ddilead honedig y derwyddon effeithio ar gredoau crefyddol ar draws y Keltiké.[6] Mae hefyd yn bosibl i ffurfiau lleol ar addoli gael eu haddasu yn unig i anghenion cymdeithasol newydd, confensiynau diwylliannol newydd a'r cyfryngau newydd (h.y. ysgrifennu a cherflunio) mewn byd a oedd yn newid, ac o'r herwydd glynodd rhyw ddealltwriaeth o arferion crefyddol brodorol a ddisgrifid yn sarhaus yn 'ofergoelion' gan y Rhufeiniaid. Yn y rhan fwyaf o achosion, fel y gwelwn, gellir nodi cyfuniadau o barhau, trawsnewid, arloesi a rhwygo, ar draws y Gorllewin Rhufeinig i wahanol raddau.

Natur broblemus y dystiolaeth ynghylch 'crefyddau Celtaidd'

Yn ddiddorol, i Iwl Cesar roedd gan y *Galli* yr un credoau am y duwiau

am i bobl addoli duwiau eu hynafiaid, hyd yn oed yng nghyd-destun cymuned o ddinasyddion Rhufeinig..

4 O bosibl yr aberthau dynol honedig, y gellir herio iddynt ddigwydd o ddiwedd yr Oes.

5 Hefyd cf. Pliny *HN* 30.4 ar y defodau y dywedwyd iddynt gael eu dileu: celf hudol, defodau angenfilaidd ac aberthau dynol.

6 Ar safiad olaf y derwyddon ar Ynys Môn/*Mona*, cf. Tac. *Ann.* 14.29–30.

his famous list of the Gaul's main gods – Mercury, Apollo, Mars, Jupiter, and Minerva, as well as Dispater – already lead the way to the local 'panthea' of the Roman period (if we assumed for the sake of argument that his accounts were reliable)?[8] Who is Mercury in Roman Gaul, Britain or Spain: was he ever the Roman god, adopted by the natives or imported by soldiers and colonists, or was this not predominantly a Latin name for an indigenous god whose 'real' name escapes us?[9] And is Caesar's Apollo

â'r bobloedd eraill fwy neu lai.[7] A yw ei restr enwog o brif dduwiau Gâl – Mercher, Apolon, Mawrth, Iau a Minerva, yn ogystal â Dispater – eisoes yn arwain y ffordd at 'panthea' lleol y cyfnod Rhufeinig (a thybio am y tro fod ei adroddiadau'n ddibynadwy)?[8] Pwy oedd Mercher yng Ngâl, Prydain neu Sbaen y Rhufeiniaid: a fu erioed yn dduw Rhufeinig, a fabwysiadwyd gan y brodorion neu a fewnforiwyd gan filwyr a gwladychwyr, neu ai enw Lladin oedd hwn yn bennaf ar gyfer duw brodorol nad yw ei enw 'go iawn' yn hysbys?[9] Ac a yw Apolon Cesar yn

also should take into account that, despite his rather generalizing statements, he also asserts that the Gauls differ by the language, institutions, and laws: *hi omnes lingua, institutis, legibus inter se differunt* (Caes. *BGall.* 1.1.2).

8 Caes. *BGall.* 6.17.1–2; 6.18.1; for general source criticism, cf. Haeussler 2014 with further bibliography. Also cf. Parthenios of Nikaia, in Zwicker 1935, vol. 2, 20 for whom Hercules, not Dispater, was the ancestor of all Gauls, which may explain Hercules' popularity across the Keltiké.

9 Obviously, if we presume the Graeco-Roman concept of polis religion or civic religion, we can hardly assume that anybody in the ancient world would have made a dedication to a Roman Mercury outside Rome or Italy, but even a Roman soldier or magistrate might have worshipped a local 'incarnation' of Mercury (or any other deity). It seems likely that these local Mercuries were becoming increasingly similar across the empire, due to the increasing spatial mobility and exchange of ideas, while taking up more and more substance from their Graeco-Roman counterparts (due to the spread of Graeco-Roman literature, myth, and art); at the same time, we also see the local Mercury with a purse, confirming Caesar's statement that he was considered 'the one to have the greatest strength for the profit of money and trade', *hunc ad quaestus pecuniae mercaturasque habere vim maximam* (...) (Caes. *BGall.* 6.17). And occasionally we find other, non-Classical attributes, such as a tree, like on the votive pillar from Caveirac (Gard) combining Mercury's Classical attributes in a novel way: CIL XII 3090 = 4136 = Esp. I 441. But can we associate these types of 'Romano-Celtic' Mercuries with any pre-

7 Caes. *BGall.* 6.17: *de his eandem fere, quam reliquae gentes, habent opinionem.* Ond er gwaethaf ei sylwadau cyffredinol, dylem gymryd i ystyriaeth ei fod hefyd yn dweud bod y Galiaid yn amrywio o ran iaith, sefydliadau, a chyfreithiau: *hi omnes lingua, institutis, legibus inter se differunt* (Caes. *BGall.* 1.1.2).

8 Caes. *BGall.* 6.17.1–2; 6.18.1; am feirniadaeth ffynhonnell gyffredinol, cf. Haeussler 2014 gyda llyfryddiaeth bellach. Hefyd cf. Parthenios o Nikaia, yn Zwicker 1935, cyf. 2, 20 a gredai mai Ercwlff, yn hytrach na Dispater, oedd hynafiad yr holl Galiaid, a gallai hyn esbonio poblogrwydd Ercwlff ar draws y Keltiké.

9 Os rhagdybir mai'r cysyniad Groegaidd-Rufeinig o grefydd y polisi neu grefydd ddinesig, mae'n amlwg mai go brin y gellir rhagdybio y byddai unrhyw un yn yr Hen Fyd wedi cysegru i Mercher y Rhufeiniaid y tu allan i'r Eidal, ond gallai hyd yn oed milwr neu ynad Rhufeinig wedi addoli 'ymgnawdoliad' lleol o Fercher (neu unrhyw dduw arall). Wrth gwrs, gallwn dybio bod y duwiau Mercher hyn yn ymdebygu'n fwy ac yn fwy ar draws yr ymerodraeth, oherwydd mwy o symudedd gofodol a chyfnewid syniadau, gan fabwysiadu mwy a mwy o sylwedd yr elfennau Groegaidd-Rufeinig cyfatebol (yn sgil lledaeniad llenyddiaeth, chwedlau a chelfyddyd Roegaidd-Rufeinig); ar yr un pryd, gwelir hefyd y Mercher lleol gyda phwrs, gan gadarnhau datganiad Cesar yr ystyrid bod ganddo'r nerth gorau ar er lles arian a masnach', *hunc ad quaestus pecuniae mercaturasque habere vim maximam* (...) (Caes. *BGall.* 6.17). O bryd i'w gilydd, ceir priodoleddau eraill, nad ydynt yn rhai Clasurol , megis coeden, fel yn achos y piler addunedol o Caveirac (Gard) sy'n cyfuno priodoleddau Clasurol Mercher mewn modd

based on his personal knowledge of the Celtic Belenos and Grannus?[10] And who is Caesar's Minerva in Gaul, considering that other goddesses, like Juno, Maia/Rosmerta and the various 'mothers', are more widely attested?[11]

This raises *inter alia* two important questions: Caesar's *interpretationes* reveal the problem of translatability; can there ever be two identical deities in two different cultures or religions? No. Consequently, different people would have made different identifications between Celtic, Greek and Roman deities depending on their personal knowledge of the local cult or deity, on their personal interpretation, and depending on time, since a cult's meaning is bound to change over time. How reliable are Caesar's generalising accounts? Local people made their personal *interpretatio* in the Roman empire, frequently diverging from Caesar's interpretation: for example,

seiliedig ar ei wybodaeth bersonol am Belenos a Grannus y Celtiaid?[10] A phwy yw Minerva Cesar yng Ngwlad Gâl, o ystyried bod mwy o dystiolaeth ynghylch duwiesau megis Iwno, Maia/Rosmerta a'r amryfal 'famau'?[11]

Mae hyn yn codi *inter alia* ddau gwestiwn pwysig: Mae *interpretationes* Cesar yn datgelu problem trosi; a ellir cael dau dduw hollol gyfatebol mewn dau wahanol ddiwylliant neu ddwy wahanol grefydd? Na ellir. O'r herwydd, byddai gwahanol bobl wedi gwneud cysylltiadau gwahanol yn ôl eu gwybodaeth bersonol rhwng y duwiau Celtaidd, Groegaidd a Rhufeinig yn ôl eu gwybodaeth bersonol am yr addoliad neu'r duw lleol, ar eu dehongliad personol, ac yn dibynnu ar amser, gan fod ystyr addoliad yn rhwym o newid dros amser. Pa mor ddibynadwy yw adroddiadau cyffredinoli Cesar? Gwnaed *interpretatio* pobl leol yn

Roman Celtic deity (or are we dealing with a more pacified version suitable for the Roman Principate?). The Berne Scholies on Lucan's *Pharsalia* associate Mercury (and also Mars!) with both Esus and Toutatis (Zwicker 1935, I, 51-2; cf. Duval 1989 for a discussion of ancient sources for Esus, Toutatis, and Taranis). But this raises once again the question whether these Celtic words refer to a god, or whether they are merely used as a surname or epithet with *esus* merely meaning 'god' (cf. Meid 2003) and *toutatis* meaning 'of the people' (Delamarre 2003: 294-5).

10 Apollo is actually rather rare across the Roman West with some notable regional exceptions, like the Apollo Belenos from Aquileia and the Apollo Grannus from Grand: for epigraphic attestations cf. in general Jufer & Luginbühl 2001; also cf. the astrological tablets from Grand: Buisson & Abry 1993.

11 Minerva is comparatively rare, suggesting that Caesar's *interpretatio Romana* did perhaps not usually relate to how many local people saw their own deities.

newydd: CIL XII 3090 = 4136 = yn enwedig I 441. Ond mae modd i ni gysylltu'r mathau hyn o dduwiau Mercher 'Rhufeinig-Geltaidd' ag unrhyw dduw Celtaidd cyn-Rufeinig (neu ai fersiwn fwy heddychol addas ar gyfer y Dywysogaeth Rufeinig sydd gennym?). Mae Scholies Berne ar *Pharsalia* Lucan (a hefyd Mawrth!) yn cysylltu Esus a Toutatis (Zwicker 1935, I, 51–2; cf. Duval 1989 am drafodaeth o ffynonellau hynafol ar gyfer Esus, Toutatis a Taranis). Ond mae hyn yn codi'r cwestiwn unwaith yn rhagor a yw'r geiriau Celtaidd hyn yn cyfeirio at dduw, neu a ydynt yn cael eu defnyddio yn gyfenw neu'n deitl gydag *esus* yn golygu 'duw' yn unig (cf. Meid 2003) a *toutatis* yn golygu 'o blith y bobl' (Delamarre 2003, 294–5).

10 Mewn gwirionedd, mae Apolon braidd yn brin ar draws y Gorllewin Rhufeinig gyda rhai eithriadau rhanbarthol lleol megis yr Apolon Belenos o Acwileia a'r Apolon Grannus o Grand: i gael tystiolaeth epigraffig cf. yn gyffredinol Jufer a Luginbühl 2001; hefyd cf. y llechi seryddol gan Grand: Buisson ac Abry 1993.

11 Mae Minerva yn gymharol brin; efallai nad oedd *interpretatio Romana* Cesar yn adrodd yn aml y modd oedd pobl leol yn gweld eu duwiau eu hunain.

the important god from which all Gauls are said to be descendent, was identified as Dispater by Caesar (*BGall.* 6.18); the evidence suggests that this was the mallet god, well known from iconography; a few worshippers provide us with a Celtic name, Sucellos, 'the good striker',[12] but he is frequently referred to on inscriptions as Silvanus, not Dispater. Local people obviously made different associations and identifications between their own gods and the Roman ones. As a result some deities are rather popular in the Roman West, like Hercules (cf. Paola Tomasi's paper on Hercules in Cisalpine Gaul).[13] Some people might even make more sophisticated *interpretationes*, displaying their intrinsic knowledge of Graeco-Roman culture and mythology; for instance, what is a dedication to Latona, the Greek Letô, doing at Montmirat in Nîmes/*Nemausus'* rather remote hilly hinterland? It probably was an individual's educated explanation for the local mother goddess that went beyond the standard *mater* or Minerva.[14] Another dedicant called

12 Of course, *sucellos*, 'the good striker', might only have been used as an epithet or nickname to describe the major attribute of this important god: the mallet (which in turn might have prompted Caesar's *interpretatio*, comparing him to the Etruscan *Charu* known from gladiatorial games: cf. Haeussler 2012, 152–4). Also cf. the Irish Donn, 'the dark one', and Welsh Beli Mawr, 'Beli the Great', which in turn might relate to the god *Belenos*.

13 For Hercules in Gaul, cf. e.g. Bauchhenß 2008 and Haeussler 2012. For the distribution of Hercules dedications in Cisalpine Gaul, also cf. Haeussler 2015.

14 *AE* 2007, 929; single mother goddesses are quite common in this region, but often referred to as *terra mater* (e.g. at Clarensac: CIL XII 4140) or Minerva (at Combas: ILGN 385–6).

yr Ymerodraeth Rufeinig, gan wyro yn amlwg o ddehongliad Cesar: er enghraifft, nododd Cesar mai'r duw pwysig y dywedid bod pawb yng Ngwlad Gâl yn ddisgynnydd iddo oedd Dispater (*BGall.* 6.18); awgryma'r dystiolaeth mai y duw-ordd oedd hwn, sy'n enwog iawn mewn eiconograffig: gan rai addolwyr ceir enw Celtaidd arno, sef Sucellos, 'yr ergydiwr da', [12] ond ar arysgrifau cyfeirir ato yn aml yn Silvanus, yn hytrach na Dispater. Yn amlwg, gwahanol oedd y cysylltiadau a'r uniaethu a wnâi pobl leol rhwng eu duwiau hwy a rhai'r Rhufeiniaid. O ganlyniad, mae rhai duwiau'n eithaf poblogaidd yng ngorllewin yr Ymerodraeth, megis Ercwlff (cf. papur Paola Tomasi ar Ercwlff yng Ngâl Isalpaidd).[13] Gallai rhai pobl hyd yn oed wneud *interpretationes* mwy soffistigedig, gan arddangos eu gwybodaeth gynhenid am ddiwylliant Groeg a Rhufain a mytholeg; er enghraifft, beth mae cysegriad i Latona, sef Letô'r Groegiaid, yn ei wneud ym Montmirat yng nghefnwlad eithaf mynyddig Nîmes/*Nemausus'*? Mae'n debyg mai cynnig addysgedig unigolyn ar gyfer y fam dduwies leol a aeth y tu hwnt i'r *mater* neu'r Minerva safonol.[14]

12 Wrth gwrs, efallai mai dim ond teitl neu lysenw oedd *sucellos*, 'yr ergydiwr da', i ddisgrifio un o briodoleddau mawr y duw pwysig hwn: yr ordd (a allai yn ei dro wedi sbarduno *interpretatio* Cesar, a'i cymharodd â *charu*'r Etrwsgiaid a oedd yn gyfarwydd o gemau'r cleddyfwyr: cf. Haeussler 2012, 152–4). Hefyd cf. Donn y Gwyddelod, 'yr un du', a Beli Mawr y Cymry, a allai yn ei dro ymwneud â'r duw *Belenos*.

13 Ar gyfer Ercwlff yng Gwlad Gâl, cf. e.e. Bauchhenß 2008 a Haeussler 2012. Ar gyfer dosbarthiad cysegriadau Ercwlff yng Ngwlad Gâl Isalpaidd, hefyd cf. Haeussler 2015.

14 *AE* 2007, 929; mae duwiesau mam sengl yn eithaf cyffredin yn y rhanbarth hwn, y cyfeirir ato yn aml yn *terra mater* (e.e. yn Clarensac:

the local goddess at Lioux (Vaucluse) *[---]ronea*,[15] probably identifying the local goddess with the Italo-Etruscan fertility goddess Feronea. In addition, across the empire our epigraphic record must be the result of countless religious and cultural misunderstandings: how many people – locals, pilgrims, migrants of various origins – might have misunderstood the meaning of a cult, of a theonym, and how to pronounce it? And how many people (and stone masons) were trying to unconsciously 'Latinise' unfamiliar theonyms? Still in today's polytheistic religions, many people travel far to specific shrines, for example to participate in particular festivals or to pray for a good new year, but their knowledge of a deity and his/her myth is often limited to the particular function they are interested in – after all, there are no dogmas, no canonical sacred texts. How much more must this have been the case in Antiquity? At different periods of the year, people visited a sanctuary for particular reasons, and this can result in diverging, or even conflicting, evidence.

Also, we have to ask which deities are attested more frequently, and what this signifies. Taking into account that our available epigraphic testimonies primarily consist of personal ex-votos, we can expect that the deities mentioned reflect people's personal

15 ILN-4, 136: *[]roneai*. Feronea is the only known theonym that would make sense here. The other inscriptions from Lioux refer to M() or M[---], usually interpreted as Mars (ILN-4, 135, 139–40), but other deities, like Mercury and Minerva, are also feasible.

Galwodd cysegrwr arall y dduwies leol yn Lioux (Vaucluse) yn *[---]ronea*,[15] gan uniaethu'r dduwies leol â'r dduwies ffrwythlonrwydd Italig-Etrwsgaidd Feronea. Yn ogystal, ar draws yr ymerodraeth rhaid i'n cofnod epigraffig fod o ganlyniad i gamgymeriadau crefyddol a diwylliannol dirifedi: faint o bobl – pererinion lleol, ymfudwyr o wahanol darddiadau – a allai wedi camddeall ystyr addoliad, enw duw, a sut i'w ynganu? A sut oedd rhai pobl (a seiri cerrig) yn ceisio 'Lladineiddio' enwau duwiau anghyfarwydd? Hyd yn oed heddiw mewn crefyddau polytheistaidd, mae llawer o bobl yn teithio i allorau penodol, er enghraifft cymryd rhan mewn gwyliau penodol neu weddïo am flwyddyn newydd dda, ond yn aml mae eu gwybodaeth am dduw/ies a'i f/myth yn aml yn gyfyngedig i'r swyddogaeth benodol y mae ganddynt ddiddordeb ynddi – wedi'r cyfan, nid oes unrhyw ddogmâu, nac unrhyw destunau sanctaidd canonaidd. Pa faint mwy gwir fyddai hyn wedi bod yn yr Hen Fyd? Ar wahanol adegau o'r flwyddyn, byddai pobl yn ymweld â chysegr am resymau penodol, a gall hyn arwain at dystiolaeth sy'n dargyfeirio neu hyd yn oed sy'n gwrthdaro.

Hefyd, rhaid i ni ofyn pa dduwiau y ceir tystiolaeth iddynt fynychaf, ac arwyddocâd hyn. Gan

CIL XII 4140) neu Minerva (yn Combas: ILGN 385–6).

15 ILN-4, 136: *[]roneai*. Feronea yw'r unig enw duw hysbys a fyddai'n gwneud synnwyr yma. Mae'r arysgrifau eraill o Lioux yn cyfeirio at M() neu M[---], a ddehonglid fel arfer ym Mawrth (ILN-4, 135, 139–40), ond mae duwiau eraill, megis Mercher a Minerva, hefyd yn bosibl.

needs. We should therefore expect an unrepresentative preponderance of deities relating to healing, fertility, and prosperity in our record. In addition there might also be many cults associated with natural features, like springs and mountains, where Latin speakers preserved (a version of) the indigenous name since it could not be translated. 'Pan-Celtic' deities, and those related to myth, might feature less in our inscriptions as these might have been above all important for collective events and rarely resulted in personal ex-votos; Vienne provides us with an exceptional case where civic cults played a rather prominent role and many dedications were set up by magistrates and priests of the *colonia*:[16] accordingly the selection of recorded deities differ, with Mercury and Apollo playing a more conspicuous role, while there is even a unique municipal priesthood for Mars, the *flamen Martis*, showing the importance of his cult for the Allobrogi and entire territory of the *colonia Vienna*, probably going back to pre-Roman times, perhaps as protector of the 'tribe'.[17]

16 On the difference in the epigraphic habit of Vienne and other *ciuitates* and *coloniae* in Gallia Narbonensis, cf. Haeussler 2014b: the evidence from Vienne and her territory seems to have been much more the result of municipal magistrates and priests making dedications on behalf of the community, vicus, or *colonia*. Also, many deities were given the name *augustus*, not just 'Roman' gods, but also e.g. the Matres Augustae, the 'august mothers': ILN-5.1, 13–16.

17 The designation *toutatis*, meaning 'of the tribe/state', might be appropriate here.

gymryd i ystyriaeth fod y tystiolaethau epigraffig sydd ar gael gennym yn cynnwys offrymau personol yn bennaf, gellir disgwyl bod y duwiau a enwir yn adlewyrchu anghenion personol pobl. Dylem, felly, ddisgwyl mwyafrif anghynrychiadol o dduwiau sy'n ymwneud ag iacháu, ffrwythlonrwydd a llewyrch yn ein cofnod. Yn ogystal, gall hefyd fod llawer o ddefodau sy'n gysylltiedig â nodweddion lleol, megis ffynhonnau a mynyddoedd, lle cadwodd siaradwyr Lladin (fersiwn) o'r enw brodorol gan nad oedd modd cyfieithu'r enw brodorol. Gallai duwiau 'Pan-Geltaidd', a'r rheini sy'n gysylltiedig â myth, fod yn llai amlwg yn ein harysgrifau gan ei bod yn bosibl i'r rhain fod yn bwysig yn anad dim ar gyfer digwyddiadau cyffredinol heb arwain yn aml at offrymau personol; yn Vienne ceir achos eithriadol lle chwaraeodd defodau dinesig ran braidd yn amlwg a sefydlwyd nifer o gyflwyniadau gan ynadon ac offeiriaid y *colonia*:[16] o'r herwydd, mae'r detholiad o dduwiau a gofnodir yn amrywio, gyda Mercher ac Apolon yn chwarae rhan amlycach, a hyd yn oed offeiriadaeth ddinesig unigryw ar gyfer Mawrth, y *flamen Martis*, sy'n dangos pwysigrwydd y ddefod hon i'r Allobrogi a holl diriogaeth y *colonia Vienna*, sy'n mynd yn ôl i'r adeg cyn y Rhufeiniaid fwy na thebyg, ac efallai iddo fod yn un o amddiffynwyr y 'llwyth'.[17]

16 Ar y gwahaniaeth rhwng arfer epigraffig Vienne a *ciuitates* a *coloniae* eraill yn Gallia Narbonensis, cf. Haeussler 2014b: ymddengys bod y dystiolaeth o Vienne a'i thystiolaeth yn fwy o lawer oherwydd bod yr ynadon a'r offeiriaid trefol yn gwneud cysegriadau ar ran y gymuned, vicus, neu'r *colonia*. Hefyd, cafodd nifer o dduwiau yr enw *augustus*, nid yn unig dduwiau 'Rhufeinig', ond hefyd e.e. *Matres Augustae*, 'y mamau awstinaidd': ILN-5.1, 13–16.

17 Efallai y byddai'r cysegriad o'r enw *toutatis*, sef

Beyond the epigraphic record

We can counterbalance some of the epigraphic shortcomings by studying iconography, sculpture, and art. Not only was iconography used widely, for example on anepigraphic altars and in rural areas, but iconography might also reveal important and powerful (civic) cults that left hardly any trace in the epigraphic record. Iconography, sculpture, and bas-reliefs can be used in public sanctuaries to present an anthropomorphic representation for a deity or to narrate a myth to the general public. In this respect, we can only speculate on the meaning of the widespread Jupiter giant columns that can be found in public places and at the centre of civic cults,[18] or the representation of Mars and a bull as the local deities from Allones.[19]

We also need to ask whether we can still find any traces of the so-called 'druidic religion' which, having been demonized between Tiberius and Claudius, used to be rather admired by Romans in the late Republic, including Caesar: druids as augurs, philosophers, and 'Pythagoreans'.[20] We might

18 Cf. for example the number of Jupiter columns that were identified on the cathedral mount at Worms/*Borbetomagos*, suggesting a civic cult of the *civitas,* and a similar concentration in Alzey: cf. Haeussler 2008c. Also see Florian Blanchard's paper in this volume.

19 Cf. interpretation of Gury 2012 on the sculpture from the Mars Mullo cult at Allonnes.

20 Cf. Cicero, *De divinatione* I 41 [90] (44 B.C.), on the Aeduan druid Divitiacus, comparing him to Roman augurs and Persian magi: 'He (Divitiacus) claimed to have that knowledge of nature which the Greeks call "physiologia", and he used to make predictions, sometimes by means of augury and sometimes by means of conjecture'. Also cf. Strabo 4.4; Caesar *BGall.*

Y tu hwnt i'r cofnod epigraffig

Gellir goresgyn rhai o'r diffygion epigraffig trwy astudio eiconograffeg, cerflunio, a cherflunio. Yn ogystal â chael ei defnyddio'n eang, er enghraifft ar allorau anepigraffig ac mewn ardaloedd gwledig, ond gallai eiconograffeg hefyd ddatgelu defodau (dinesig) pwysig a phwerus na adawsant fawr ddim ôl yn y cofnod epigraffig. Gellir defnyddio eiconograffeg, cerfluniau, a cherfweddau isel mewn cysegrau i gyflwyno cynrychiolaeth anthropomorffaidd ar gyfer duw neu er mwyn adrodd chwedl i'r cyhoedd. Yn hyn o beth, rhaid dyfalu yn unig beth oedd ystyr y colofnau cawraidd Iau eang y gellir dod o hyd iddynt mewn lleoedd cyhoeddus ac ynghanol defodau dinesig,[18] neu gynrychioliadau o Fawrth ar ffurf tarw yn yr un modd â'r duwiau lleol o Allones.[19]

Mae hefyd angen i ni holi sut y gallwn ni ddarganfod unrhyw olion o 'grefydd y derwyddon' a gollfarnwyd rhwng Tiberius a Claudius, ond a edmygid gan Rufeiniaid yn y Weriniaeth hwyr, gan gynnwys Cesar: derwyddon yn ddaroganwyr, athronwyr a 'Pythagoreaid'.[20] Yma gellir cyfeirio at

'gan y llwyth/y wladwriaeth', yn briodol yma.

18 Cf. er enghraifft nifer y colofnau Iau a nodwyd ar fryn y gadeirlan yn Worms/*Borbetomagos* gan awgrymu addoliad dinesig y *civitas,* a ffocws tebyg yn Alzey: cf. Haeussler 2008c. Hefyd gweler papur Florian Blanchard yn y gyfrol hon.

19 Cf. dehongliad Gury 2012 ar y cerflun o addoliad Mars Mullo yn Allones.

20 Cf. Cicero, *De divinatione* I 41 [90] (44 B.C.), ar dderwydd Aeduan Divitiacus, gan gymharu daroganwyr Rhufain a doethion Persia: 'Honnodd (Divitiacus) fod ganddo wybodaeth am natur sef yr hyn a eilw'r Groegiaid yn "ffysiologia", ac arferai ragddweud, weithio trwy ddaro-

allude here to the famous calendar of Coligny of the late 2nd century AD, a major epigraphic source for our understanding of 'Celtic' religion and major seasonal events.[21] This leads us to the role of astronomy: the paper by Burillo-Mozota and Burillo-Cuadrado on the latest excavations of the Celtiberian sanctuary at Segeda reveals once more the importance of cosmological aspects in pre-Roman cults. We can identify such aspects, in various forms, also in other regions of the Keltiké, for example in the popularity of gods, such as Sol and Luna (though rarely with Celtic name), as well as in the astronomical orientation of temples, sanctuaries, houses, and tombs throughout the Roman period.[22]

To understand 'Celtic' cults therefore goes beyond the names of deities. Bone evidence, too, can reveal a cult's religious calendar with animal sacrifice taking place at particular points in the calendar; certain pre-Roman and Roman-period deities, for example, might require sacrifices at *samonios/Samhain*, for example at Hayling Island and Acy-Romance, others at *Bealtaine* or *Lughnasa*.[23] It is remarkable to see the persistence of such rituals into the Roman period, even though a cult might have acquired a more 'Roman' appearance in time.

6.14; Amm. Marc. 15.9.8; for an overview, cf. Haeussler 2014, 48.

21 For a critical edition of the calendar of Coligny, see RIG-3; also cf. Swift 2002.

22 Cf. C. Haselgrove 1995 with further bibliography.

23 Cf. Green 1992, 42, s.v. Beltene; 136, s.v. Lughnasad; 185–6, s.v. Samhain. For Hayling Island, cf. King 2005, 363, for Acy-Romance, cf. Lambot 2006, 185.

galendr enwog Coligny ar ddiwedd yr 2il ganrif OC, ffynhonnell epigraffig bwysig ar gyfer ein dealltwriaeth o'r grefydd 'Geltaidd' a digwyddiadau tymhorol o bwys.[21] Mae hyn yn ein harwain ni at rôl seryddiaeth: mae'r papur gan Burillo-Mozota a Burillo-Cuadrado ar y cloddiadau diweddaraf yn y gysegrfa Geltiberaidd yn Segeda yn egluro unwaith eto bwysigrwydd agweddau cosmolegol ar ddefodau cyn-Rufeinig. Gallwn nodi'r agweddau hyn, ar wahanol ffurfiau, hefyd mewn rhanbarthau eraill o'r Keltiké, er enghraifft poblogrwydd y duwiau, megis Sol a Luna (er yn anaml gydag enw Celtaidd), yn ogystal â gogwydd seryddol temlau, cysegrau, tai a beddau gydol y cyfnod Rhufeinig.[22]

Mae deall defodau 'Celtaidd', felly, yn mynd y tu hwnt i enwau'r duwiau. Gall tystiolaeth esgyrn, hefyd, ddatgelu calendr defod gydag aberthau anifeiliaid yn digwydd ar adegau penodol yn y calendr; gallai fod gofyn i rai o dduwiau'r cyfnod cyn-Rufeinig a Rhufeinig gael aberthau yn *samonios/Samhain*, er enghraifft ar Ynys Hayling ac Acy-Romance, ac eraill yn *Bealtaine* neu *Lughnasa*. [23] Mae'n rhyfedd gweld parhad y defodau hyn yn y cyfnod Rhufeinig, hyd yn oed pe bai defod wedi magu gwedd fwy 'Rhufeinig' gydag amser. Yn absenoldeb arysgrifau, y

gan ac weithiau trwy ddyfalu'. Hefyd cf. Strabo 4.4; Cesar *BGall.* 6.14; Amm. Marc. 15.9.8; i gael trosolwg, cf. Haeussler 2014, 48.

21 Am argraffiad beirniadol o galendr Coligny, gweler RIG-3; hefyd cf. Swift 2002.

22 Cf. C. Haselgrove 1995 gyda llyfryddiaeth bellach.

23 Cf. Green 1992, 42, s.v. Beltene; 136, s.v. Lughnasad; 185–6, s.v. Samhain. Ar gyfer Ynys Hayling Island, cf. King 2005, 363, ar gyfer Acy-Romance, cf. Lambot 2006, 185.

In the absence of inscriptions we can often only speculate about the deity (or deities) that received particular sacrifices at particular times of the year, but it would be interesting to see if patterns can be identified across the Keltiké; after all, a certain standardisation of cult architecture in the Roman period (the so-called *Romano-Celtic temple*, *Umgangstempel* or *fanum*, relatively square temples, usually with an ambulatory, quite unlike a Roman temple) shows an astonishing degree of religious communication across the provinces. And we may wonder whether we are merely dealing here with an architectural 'fashion' or whether this was the result of the continued perseverance of a priestly 'caste'?).[24]

With respect to the druids, the graffito DRU on a 2nd-century AD incense burner from Chartres is equally intriguing as it may have referred to *druids* – and if so, we have to ask what such a find really testifies: the persistence (or 'revival'?) of druids and druidic religion (cf. paper by Miranda Aldhouse-Green)? Can we really assume that all traces of 'druidism' were eradicated in the 1st century AD? Many pre-Roman priesthoods might have been transformed into Roman-style priesthoods, like the *flamen Martis* of the Allobrogi (*v. supra*); in other cases, personal names might reflect people's religious role, like the *cognomen* bardus, 'bard(?)', as in Lucius

24 For 'Romano-Celtic temples', cf. King 2007 for the origin of this architectural form; for a survey of all potential Romano-Celtic temple sites, cf. Fauduet 2010.

cyfan y gellir ei wneud yw dyfalu am y duw (neu'r duwiau) a gafodd aberthau penodol ar adegau penodol yn ystod y flwyddyn, ond byddai'n ddiddorol gweld a ellir nodi patrymau ar draws y Keltiké; wedi'r cyfan, mae rhywfaint o safoni o ran pensaernïaeth y cyfnod Rhufeinig (sef y *–deml Rhufeinig-Geltaidd, Umgangstempel* fel y'i gelwir neu'r *fanum*, temlau cymharol sgwâr, fel arfer gyda rhodfa, yn wahanol iawn i deml Rufeinig) yn dangos gradd syfrdanol o gyfathrebu crefyddol ar draws y taleithiau. Ac efallai y gellir holi ai dim ond 'ffasiwn' pensaernïol a geir yma neu a oedd hyn o ganlyniad i barhad 'cast' offeiriadol?).[24]

O ran y derwyddon, mae'r graffito DRU ar losgydd thus o'r 2il ganrif OC o Chartres yr un mor ddiddorol gan ei fod wedi cyfeirio'n wreiddiol at *dderwyddon*, o bosibl – ac os felly, rhaid gofyn beth a ddangosir gan y canfyddiad hwn: parhad (neu 'adfywio'?) derwyddon a chrefydd y derwyddon (cf. papur gan Miranda Aldhouse-Green)? A ellir rhagdybio'n wir y dilëwyd holl olion 'derwyddiaeth' yn y ganrif 1af OC? Mae'n bosibl i nifer o fathau cyn-Rufeinig o offeiriadaeth gael eu trawsnewid yn rhai ar ddull Rhufeinig, megis *flamen Martis* yr Allobrogi (*v. supra*): mewn achosion eraill, gallai enwau personol adlewyrchu rôl grefyddol pobl, megis y *cognomen* bardus, 'bardd(?)', megis yn Lucius Erax Bardus a wnaeth gysegriad i Apolon Belenos yn Bardonecchia.[25] Fel

24 Ar gyfer 'temlau Rhufeinig-Geltaidd', cf. King 2007 ar gyfer tarddiad y ffurf bensaernïol hon: ar gyfer arolwg o holl ddarpar safleoedd temlau Rhufeinig-Geltaidd, cf. Fauduet 2010.

25 Yn yr Alpes Cottiae; cf. AE 1959, 170 = AE 2005,

Erax Bardus who made a dedication to Apollo Belenos at Bardonecchia.[25] Otherwise, we might look at traces of 'magic' in our search for survival of Iron Age rituals in the Roman period – but then we have to wonder whether 'druidism' had anything to do with magic, and if so, how can we distinguish Celtic, Roman, Greek, Egyptian magical traditions within an increasingly cosmopolitan Roman empire?

Celticity & Translatability

From its outset, the scope of F.E.R.C.AN. has always been much wider than just inscriptions for an obvious reason. Though there is a wealth of epigraphic evidence, we can only aspire to understand it if we take into account the wider context, like iconography and our archaeological knowledge of cult places, ritual practices, and sacred landscapes. Since its launch in 1998, fifteen workshops, organised locally by the F.E.R.C.AN. coordinators of the project's European members (see Table 1), have provided an important venue to exchange ideas and enhance our methodology regarding 'Celtic' religions during the Iron Age and the Roman period. Needless to say that the definitions of 'Celtic' and 'Celticity' have always been a challenging issue.[26] On the one hand, hundreds of deities have names in a Celtic language.[27] It is

25 In the Alpes Cottiae; cf. AE 1959, 170 = AE 2005, 961. Also cf. e.g. Q(uintus) Cassius Bardus (ILAfr 166, 8).

26 Cf. Sims-Williams 1998 on Celtomania and Celtoscepticsm.

27 Cf. in general the repertoire of Celtic deities in Jufer and Luginbühl 2001.

arall gallem ni nodi rhai olion o 'hud' wrth chwilio am oroesiad defodau Oes Haearn yn y cyfnod Rhufeinig – ond wedyn rhaid i ni holi a oedd a wnelo 'derwyddiaeth' unrhyw beth â dewiniaeth, ac os felly, sut y gellir gwahaniaethu traddodiadau Celtaidd, Rhufeinig, Groegaidd, Eifftaidd mewn ymerodraeth Rufeinig a oedd yn fwy ac yn fwy cosmopolitan?

Celtigrwydd a Throsiadwyedd

O'r cychwyn cyntaf, mae cwmpas F.E.R.C.AN. wedi bod erioed yn ehangach o lawer nag arysgrifau yn unig, a hynny am resymau amlwg. Er bod cyfoeth o dystiolaeth epigraffig, yr unig obaith sydd gennym o'i deall yw trwy gymryd i ystyriaeth y cyd-destun ehangach, yn yr un modd ag eiconograffig a'n gwybodaeth archeolegol am fannau addoli, arferion defodol a thirweddau cysegredig. Ers ei lansio yn 1998, mae tri ar ddeg o weithdai, a drefnwyd yn lleol gan gydlynwyr F.E.R.C.AN. ar gyfer aelodau Ewropeaidd y prosiect (gweler Tabl 1), wedi darparu lleoliad pwysig i wella ein methodoleg ynghylch crefyddau 'Celtaidd' yn ystod yr Oes Haearn a'r cyfnod Rhufeinig. Afraid dweud mai pwnc heriol fu diffinio 'Celtaidd' a 'Celtigrwydd' erioed.[26] Ar y naill law, mae gan gannoedd o dduwiau enwau mewn iaith Geltaidd.[27] Mae'n debyg y gallai rhai o'r rhain fod yn gysylltiedig

961. Hefyd cf. e.e. Q(uintus) Cassius Bardus (ILAfr 166, 8).

26 Cf. Sims-Williams 1998 ar Geltomania a Cheltosgeptiaeth.

27 Cf. e.e. cyfres y duwiau Celtaidd yn Jufer a Luginbühl 2001.

feasible that some of them might have related to religious understandings and myths that might have their roots in pre-Roman times. But most of all, they illustrate that people still spoke Celtic dialects across the Roman West, enabling them to use (and hypothetically also *create*) theonyms and epithets in a Celtic language.[28] In other words, Celtic theonyms may not necessarily indicate a pre-Roman 'Celtic' deity, especially when they just have rather literal meanings, like 'mighty' or 'powerful' (*mogons / mogetios*, *vernostonos*, etc.),[29] and can therefore be associated as unspecific epithets to different gods.[30]

We have to be aware that the story is extremely complex: Celtic terms were used to describe deities in various forms, not just as theonyms, but also as epithets, epicleses, and cognomina; some names might make a reference to a deity's particular function or characteristic, or to a mythical event. For instance, (Mars) Nabelcus, 'The Wounder of Heaven' or (Mars) Divannos, 'The Great Destroyer' might refer to creation myths.[31] Similarly,

â dealltwriaeth grefyddol ac efallai y gallai gwreiddiau rhai o'r chwedlau fynd yn ôl i amserau cyn-Rufeinig. Ond yn bennaf, dangosant fod pobl yn dal i siarad tafodieithoedd Celtaidd ar draws y Gorllewin Rhufeinig, gan eu galluogi nhw i ddefnyddio (ac mewn theori *creu* hefyd) enwau duwiau theitlau mewn iaith Geltaidd.[28] Mewn geiriau eraill, efallai nad yw enwau duwiau, o reidrwydd, yn arwydd o dduwdod 'Celtaidd' cyn-Rufeinig, yn enwedig os ystyron braidd yn llythrennol sydd iddynt, megis 'grymus' neu 'pwerus' (*mogons / mogetios*, *vernostonos*, ac ati),[29] ac o'r herwydd gellir eu cysylltu'n deitlau amhenodol ar gyfer gwahanol dduwiau.[30]

Rhaid i ni fod yn ymwybodol bod yr hanes yn un hynod gymhleth: defnyddid termau Celtaidd i ddisgrifio duwiau ar amrywiol ffurfiau, nid yn unig enwau duwiau, ond hefyd teitlau, arddeisyfiadau, a llysenwau; gallai rhai enwau gyfeirio at swyddogaeth neu nodwedd benodol rhyw dduw neu'i gilydd, neu at ddigwyddiad mytholegol. Er enghraifft, gallai (Mawrth) Nabelcus, 'Clwyfwr y Nefoedd' neu (Mawrth) Divannos, 'Y Dinistriwr Mawr' gyfeirio at chwedlau creu.[31] Yn yr un modd,

28 Cf. introduction to the 2005 F.E.R.C.AN. workshop in London: Haeussler and King 2007.

29 For the problem of terminology, see De Bernardo Stempel 2008b .

30 Cf. example *mogons* which appears on its own as singular and plural, male and female, since it is merely a reference to the 'mighty' god(s)/ goddess(es); there is also a dedication to the 'mighty god V.' (*deo mogont(i) Vitire(!)*, from Netherby, RIB 971) and to the 'mighty god C.' (*[d]eo mogonito(!) Cad()*, from Risingham/ *Habitancum*, RIB 1225). For the term 'unspecific epithet', cf. e.g. De Bernardo Stempel 2008b, 69.

31 Compare for example Shiva in Hinduism as the destroyer and creator of the world.

28 Cf. cyflwyniad i weithdy 2005 F.E.R.C.AN. yn Llundain: Haeussler a King 2007.

29 Ar gyfer y broblem, erminoleg De Bernardo Stempel 2008b .

30 Cf. yr enghraifft *mogons* sy'n ymddangos ar ei phen ei hun ar ffurf unigol neu luosog, yn wrywaidd ac yn fenywaidd, gan mai cyfeiriad yn unig yw at y duw(iau)/duwies(au) 'nerthol'; mae hefyd gyfeiriad at y 'duw nerthol V.' (*deo mogont(i) Vitire(!)*, o Netherby, RIB 971) ac at 'y duw nerthol C.' (*[d]eo mogonito(!) Cad()*, o Risingham / *Habitancum*, RIB 1225). Ar gyfer y term 'teitl amhenodol', cf. e.e. De Bernardo Stempel 2008b, 69.

31 Cymharer, er enghraifft, Shiva mewn Hindŵaeth yn ddinistrydd a chreawdwr y byd.

names like Uxovinus, 'The Very White',[32] might just refer to a white deity – or his sculpture – but could equally refer to a particular myth, perhaps reflecting the god's purity and/or supreme knowledge.

We constantly need to re-think our interpretations, and the larger our data base, the better our methodology might become. Moreover, we need to bear in mind that a clear attribution is not always possible: some 'Celtic' theonyms have equally been interpreted as Germanic, Aquitanian, or pre-Celtic.[33] Some reason for this confusion is of course our source material: we primarily know these names from a Latin-speaking context, and usually only in the dative; hence also the difficulty whether to reconstruct a Latin nominative in *-us* or a Celtic nominative in *-os*: should we

32 ILN-4, 124 = ILS 4694 from Apt; translation suggested by De Bernardo Stempel 2007.

33 There are different interpretations, e.g. for the Almahae (Celtic, Germanic, or Gallo-Latin, cf. Haeussler 2008 with further bibliography), or the deities in Aquitania (Celtic for De Bernardo Stempel 2008, Aquitanian for Gorrochateguí 2008; 2013). Finally, there is also the question of deonomastic names, i.e. theonyms or epithets named after a locality, town, river, mountain, *ethnos*, person, etc., sometimes preserving pre-Celtic toponyms in the theonym. But the question is of course what came first: e.g., is the god *Nemausus* named after the city *Nemausus* (Nîmes) or vice versa? The god Vintur in Gallia Narbonensis, for example, seems to be the personification of the Mont Ventoux: consequently we might label Vintur a 'deonomastic' theonym, but this does not deny that people in the Roman period (and surely also in the late Iron Age) were worshipping and appeasing the god Vintur (similar to other mountainous deities, like Poeninus), i.e. the dedications in his honour are evidence for 'Celtic' (i.e. indigenous, local) religion (ILN-Apt, 17 (Apt), ILN-Apt, 143 (Goult), CAG-26, p. 421 (Mirabel-aux-Baronnies)).

mae'n bosibl bod enwau megis Uxovinus, 'Y tra gwyn', [32] yn cyfeirio at ryw dduw gwyn – neu gerflun ohono – ond mae'r un mor bosibl ei fod yn cyfeirio at chwedl benodol, gan adlewyrchu, o bosibl, purdeb y duw a/neu ei wybodaeth aruchel.

Mae angen yn barhaus i ni ailfeddwl ein dehongliadau, a pho fwyaf y gronfa ddata sydd gennym, gorau oll fydd ein methodoleg. Hefyd, mae angen i ni gofio nad yw priodoli clir bob amser yn bosibl: mae rhai enwau duwiau 'Celtaidd' wedi eu dehongli i'r un graddau yn rhai Germanig, Acwitanaidd neu gyn-Geltaidd.[33] Un rheswm dros y dryswch, wrth gwrs, yw ein ffynonellau: yn bennaf, rydym yn adnabod yr enwau hyn o gyd-destun Lladin, ac fel arfer ar y ffurf dderbyniol yn unig; o ble daw hefyd yr anhawster a ddylid ail-greu ffurf enwol Ladin gydag

32 ILN-4, 124 = ILS 4694 o Apt; y cyfieithiad wedi ei awgrymu gan De Bernardo Stempel 2007.

33 Mae gwahanol ddehongliadau, e.e. ar gyfer yr Almahae (Celtaidd, Almaenig, neu Galaidd-Ladin, cf. Haeussler 2008 gyda llyfryddiaeth bellach), neu'r duwiau yn Acwitania (Celtaidd ar gyfer De Bernardo Stempel 2008, Acwitanaidd ar gyfer Gorrochateguí 2008; 2013). Yn olaf, mae hefyd gwestiwn enwau deonomastig, h.y. enwau duwiau neu deitlau wedi eu henwi ar ôl ardal leol, tref, afon, *ethnos*, person, ac ati, sydd weithiau'n cadw enwau lleoedd cyn-Geltaidd yn enw'r duw. Fodd bynnag, y cwestiwn, wrth gwrs, yw pa un a ddaeth yn gyntaf: e.e., a yw'r duw *Nemausus* wedi ei enwi ar ôl y ddinas *Nemausus* (Nîmes) neu'r gwrthwyneb? Ymddengys mai personoli'r Mont Ventoux a wna'r duw Vintur yn Gallia Narbonensis, er enghraifft: o'r herwydd, byddai modd labelu Vintur yn enw duw 'deonomastig', ond nid yw hyn yn golygu nad oedd pobl yn y cyfnod Rhufeinig (ac ar ddiwedd yr Oes Haearn hefyd, mae'n rhaid) yn addoli ac yn heddychu'r duw Vintur (yn debyg i dduwiau mynyddig eraill, mae Poeninus), h.y. mae'r cysegriad er anrhydedd iddo yn dystiolaeth o grefydd 'Geltaidd' (h.y. brodorol, lleol) (ILN-Apt, 17 (Apt), ILN-Apt, 143 (Goult), CAG-26, t. 421 (Mirabel-aux-Baronnies)).

say, for instance, Cocidius or Cocidios? Moreover, the paper by Alves Dias and Correia Santos reminds us that not every Celtic name, like *Danceroi* and *Aro*, was necessarily a theonym – instead, a critical contextual analysis is essential to re-think traditional assumptions.

On the other hand, we can also recognise further testimonies for these 'indigenous', 'Celtic' religions, as manifested in the Roman period. Mother goddesses, like the *matres*, *matronae*, Iunones, *proxsumae*, or single mothers, like *terra mater* or *regina*, despite their Roman name, clearly relate to local religious understandings, not Greek or Roman ones.[34] Sometimes this becomes more

34 For Matres, Iunones, etc. cf. overview in Haeussler 2008b with further bibliography; cf. Delamarre 2013 for the case of the Matronae *Andrusteihae* within a Dumezilian tripartite division of the world. There are also 'pre-Roman' attestations in Gallo-Greek, probably dating no earlier than the 1st century BC, e.g. the mothers from Glanum and Nimes (*v. supra*); approximately 500 years ealier is the Tartessian inscription from southern Portugal that contains the divine name ek^{u}rine; John Koch has identified this as *Epona regina* or 'horse queen' (Koch 2013, 43–4, J.4.1; for Epona, *v. supra*). For the evidence on Juno Regina and Regina, cf. Haeussler 2008b, 26–7: e.g., altars to Regina from Leamington (Glos.) (RIB 125 = CSIR-GB I.7, 94: *Dea Regina* – in the nominative – with rather crude representation of the goddess) and Lanchester/*Longovicium* (RIB 1084: *Reginae votum Misio v.l.s.*), and *regina* was also associated with other Celtic names, e.g. with Candida: *dea regina Candida* (at Osterburken: AE 1985, 685, 695; Candida is considered a calque of a Celtic theonym for Lejeune 1981); on a graffito in Celtic from Lezoux, we also find the term *rigani*, now associated with *Rosmerta*, who is widely attested on Roman inscriptions: *e ieuri Rigani Rosmertiae* – for a discussion whether this is a dedication to 'Queen Rosmerta' or to the 'Purveying Queen', see Lejeune 1981; for *Rosmerta* as 'La Pourvoyeuse' cf. De-

-*us* neu ffurf enwol Geltaidd gydag -*os*: a ddylid dweud, er enghraifft, Cocidius neu Cocidios? Yn ogystal, mae'r papur gan Alves Dias a Correia Santos ein hatgoffa ni nad yw pob enw Celtaidd, megis Danceroi ac Aro, o reidrwydd yn enw duw – yn hytrach, rhaid wrth ddadansoddi cyd-destunol beirniadol i ailfeddwl rhagdybiaethau traddodiadol.

Ar ben popeth arall, gellir hefyd gydnabod tystiolaeth bellach ar gyfer y crefyddau 'brodorol', 'Celtaidd' hyn a welwyd yn y cyfnod Rhufeinig. Mae mam-dduwiesau, megis y *matres*, *matronae*, Iunones, *proxsumae*, neu famau sengl, megis *terra mater* neu *regina*, er gwaethaf eu henw Rhufeinig, yn cyfeirio'n glir at ddealltwriaeth grefyddol leol, yn hytrach na rhai Groegaidd neu Rufeinig.[34] Weithiau

34 Ar gyfer Matres, Iunones, ac ati cf. y trosolwg yn Haeussler 2008b gyda llyfryddiaeth bellach; cf. Delamarre 2013 ar gyfer achos Matronae *Andrusteihae*, o fewn rhaniad triphlyg y byd gan Dumézil. Mae hefyd dystiolaeth 'gyn-Rufeinig' mewn Galaidd-Roeg, nad yw'n debygol o fod yn gynharach na'r ganrif gyntaf C.C. e.e. y mamau o Glanum a Nîmes (*v. supra*); tua 500 mlynedd ynghynt yn yr arysgrifen Dartesaidd o dde Portiwgal sy'n cynnwys yr enw dwyfol ek^{u}urine; mae John Koch wedi nodi mai *Epona regina* neu 'farch-frenhines' (Koch 2013, 43–4, J.4.1; ar gyfer Epona, *v. supra*). Ar gyfer y dystiolaeth ar Juno Regina a Regina, cf. Haeussler 2008b, 26–7: e.e., allorau i Regina o Leamington (Caerloyw) (RIB 125 = CSIR-GB I.7, 94: *Dea Regina* – yn yr enwol – gyda chynrychiolaeth braidd yn amrwd o'r dduwies) a Lanchester/*Longovicium* (RIB 1084: *Reginae votum Misio v.l.s.*), ac roedd *regina* hefyd wedi ei gysylltu ag enwau Celtaidd eraill, e.e. gyda Candida: *dea regina Candida* (yn Osterburken: AE 1985, 685, 695; ystyrir Candida yn ddynwarediad ar enw duw Celtaidd gan Lejeune 1981); mewn graffito Celteg o Lezoux, cawn hefyd y term *rigani*, sydd bellach wedi ei gysylltu â *Rosmerta*, y mae tystiolaeth eang iddo ar arysgrifau Rhufeinig: *e ieuri Rigani Rosmertiae* – am drafodaeth ai cysegriad i'r 'Frenhines Rosmerta' neu i'r

apparent when Celtic epithets are used, like the 'well-leading mother goddesses', the *Matres Suleviae*,[35] or the *Matronae Dervonnae* (from Celtic *dervos*, 'oak').[36] And in this 'global' world of the Roman empire, we can sometimes see how people reflect on the divine variations they encounter across the empire, like soldiers from Britain making dedications to the *matres transmarinis*,[37] 'the mothers from overseas', or to *Mat(ribus) Af(ris) Ita(lis) Ga(llis)*, 'the African, Italic, and Gallic mothers'.[38]

Iconography also reveals other 'indigenous/Celtic' deities and believes across the Keltiké in Roman times, like the mallet god, the wheel god, the various tree and warrior gods, and of course the 'Jupiter Giant Rider' (*Jupitergigantenreiter* or *cavalier à l'anguipède*), particularly typical for

lamarre 2003, 276, *smer, smerto-*.

35 Usually, people only referred to them as *Suleviae* – the *Matres* was probably implied – but there are dedications to the *Matres Suleviae*, notably from Rome and Colchester: cf. Jufer & Luginbühl 2001, 64, s.v. *Suleviae*. This epithet was also used for single goddesses, like the Sulevia Edennica Minerva from Collias (Gallia Narbonensis): CIL XII 2974.

36 *Matribus Dervonnibus* at Milan/*Mediolanum* (CIL V 5791) and from nearby Brescia/*Brixia*, the deity's name was 'Latinised' to Fatae whilst preserving the Celtic epithet/cognomen: *Fatis Dervonibus* (CIL V 4208 = Inscr.It. 10.5, 813 = ILS 3762). For *dervos*, cf. Delamarre 2003, 140, s.v. *dervos*. Also cf. other 'tree deities', like the *Matres Baginatiae* in the Drôme (AE 2000, 884–886).

37 RIB 919, 920, 1030, 1224, 1318, 1989 from Old Penrith, Newcastle, Risingham, Binchester, and Castlesteads.

38 RIB 653 = ILS 4787 from York, set up by the legionary Marcus Minucius Audens. The 'Italic mothers', probably referring to Cisalpine Gaul, are also evoked in a dedication of an altar from Dover: RIB III 3031, set up by a *st(rator) co(n)[s(ularis)]* named *Ol(us) Cor[---] Candid(us)*.

daw hyn i'r amlwg wrth ddefnyddio teitlau Celtaidd, megis 'y mam-dduwiesau ffynnon-arweiniol', y *Matres Suleviae*,[35] neu'r *Matronae Dervonnae* (o'r gair Celtaidd *dervos*, 'derwen').[36] Ac yng nghyd-destun 'byd-eang' yr Ymerodraeth Rufeinig, weithiau gellir gweld sut mae pobl yn adfyfyrio ar yr amrywiadau dwyfol y maent yn dod ar eu traws ledled yr ymerodraeth, megis milwyr o Brydain sy'n cysegru i'r *matres transmarinis*[37] 'y mamau o dramor', neu i *Mat(ribus) Af(ris) Ita(lis) Ga(llis)*, 'y mamau Affricanaidd, Eidalaidd a Galaidd'.[38]

Trwy eiconograffi daw hefyd dduwiau a chredoau 'brodorol/Celtaidd' eraill i'r amlwg ar draws y Keltiké adeg y Rhufeiniaid, megis y duw-ordd, y duw-olwyn, y gwahanol dduwiau-goed a duwiau-ryfelwyr, ac

'Frenhines sy'n Darparu' sydd dan sylw, gweler Lejeune 1981; ar gyfer *Rosmerta* yn 'La Pourvoyeuse' cf. Delamarre 2003, 276, *smer, smerto-*.

35 Fel arfer, ni fyddai pobl ond yn cyfeirio atynt yn *Suleviae* – mae'n debyg bod *Matres* ymhlyg – ond mae cysegriadau i'r *Matres Suleviae*, yn bennaf o Rufain a Colchester: cf. Jufer a Luginbühl 2001, 64, s.v. *Suleviae*. Rhoddwyd y teitl hwn hefyd i dduwiesau unigol, megis y Sulevia Idennica Minerva o Collias (Gallia Narbonensis): CIL XII 2974.

36 *Matribus Dervonnibus* ym Milan/*Mediolanum* (CIL V 5791) ac o Brescia/*Brixia* gerllaw, 'Lladineiddiwyd' enw'r duw yn Fatae gan gadw'r teitl/cyfenw Celtaidd: *Fatis Dervonibus* (CIL V 4208 = Inscr.It. 10.5, 813 = ILS 3762). Ar gyfer *dervos*, cf. Delamarre 2003, 140, s.v. *dervos*. Hefyd cf. 'coed-dduwiau' eraill, megis y *Matres Baginatiae* yn y Drôme (AE 2000, 884–886).

37 RIB 919, 920, 1030, 1224, 1318, 1989 o Old Penrith, Newcastle, Risingham, Binchester, a Castlesteads.

38 RIB 653 = ILS 4787 o Gaerefrog, a sefydlwyd gan y llengfilwr Marcus Minucius Audens. Gelwir hefyd ar y 'mamau Italig', gan gyfeirio fwy na thebyg at Gâl Isalpaidd, mewn cysegriad allor o Dover: RIB III 3031, a sefydlwyd gan *st(rator) co(n)[s(ularis)]* o'r enw *Ol(us) Cor[---] Candid(us)*.

eastern Gaul, whose relationship to Gallo-Roman religions is analyzed by Florian Blanchard in this volume. Though sometimes associated with theonyms (or epithets) in a Celtic language, like *sucellos* ('the good striker') or *taranis* ('the thunderer'), many of these popular (and therefore presumably powerful and commanding) deities have generally been the first victims of *interpretatio*: in other words, the local people referred to them by an appropriate Latin name when setting up Latin inscriptions. We are therefore predominantly dealing with 'native' variations of Jupiter, Juno, Mars, Mercury, Minerva, Silvanus, etc., that continued to evolve in the Principate, creating deities that were neither 'Roman' nor (pre-Roman) 'Celtic', but typical for their time, their local setting, and local society.

Finally, we need to consider the wider archaeological context. Are we dealing with 'Celtic' or 'Romano-Celtic' religion when we find votive inscriptions in a Gallo-Roman or Britanno-Roman sanctuary with non-Roman architecture and cult practices? For example, the sanctuary in Uley (Gloucestershire) is rather 'non-Roman' in origin and character, despite the cult statue to Mercury, and the finds from Uley ought to feature in a corpus of the *fontes* of Celtic religions. The archaeological evidence reveals an enormous continuity of ritual practices from the late Iron Age down to the mid-4th century AD.[39] At some stage during the sanctuary's existence, somebody

39 King 2005, 332–4.

wrth gwrs 'Iau-y-Cawr-o-Farchogwr' (*Jupitergigantenreiter* neu *cavalier à l'anguipède*), a oedd yn enwedig o nodweddiadol yn nwyrain Gâl, a dadansoddir eu perthynas â'r crefyddau Galaidd-Rufeinig gan Florian Blanchard yn y gyfrol hon. Er eu bod weithiau'n gysylltiedig ag enwau duwiau (neu deitlau) mewn iaith Geltaidd, megis *sucellos* ('yr ergydiwr da') neu *taranis* ('y taranwr'), yn gyffredinol roedd nifer o'r duwiau poblogaidd (ac o'r herwydd, pwerus a llywodraethol, fwy na thebyg) gyda'r cyntaf i ddioddef oherwydd *interpretatio*: mewn geiriau eraill, cyfeiriodd y bobl leol atynt wrth enw Lladin priodol wrth osod arysgrifau Lladin. Felly, rydym yn ymdrin yn bennaf ag amrywiadau 'brodorol' ar Iau, Iwno, Mawrth Mercher, Minerva, Silvanus, ac ati, a barhaodd i esblygu yn y Dywysogaeth, gan greu duwiau nad oedd yn 'Rhufeinig' nac yn 'Rhufeinig' na 'Cheltaidd' (cyn-Rufeinig), ond yn nodweddiadol o'u hamser, eu cyd-destun lleol a'r gymdeithas leol.

Yn olaf, mae angen i ni ystyried y cyd-destun archeolegol ehangach. Ai crefydd 'Geltaidd' neu 'Geltaidd-Rufeinig' sydd dan sylw pan geir arysgrifen addunedol mewn cysegr Galaidd-Rufeinig neu Brythonig-Rufeinig gyda phensaernïaeth an-Rufeinig ac arferion defodol? Er enghraifft, nid yw'r cysegr yn Uley (Swydd Caerloyw) yn 'Rhufeinig' iawn ei darddiad na'i nodweddion, er bod cerflun addoli i Mercher, a dylai canfyddiadau Uley fod yn rhan o gorpws *fontes* crefyddau Celtaidd. Mae'r dystiolaeth archeolegol yn datgelu parhad nifer helaeth o arferion defodol o ddiwedd yr Oes Haearn i first made the association of the local deity with Mercury and somebody else, perhaps when the Romano-Celtic temples was constructed, set up a statue of Mercury. These individual acts set in motion long-term processes and we can presume that in the long term this was probably changing people's understanding of their local god: a hybridised, local deity develops that taken up additional features, while other aspects of his cult or myth might have become forgotten, even in oral tradition. Uley, like other Romano-Celtic sanctuaries, also shows how writing could be adopted and adapted to serve an 'autochthonous' cult. Here, the use of curse tablets, similar to Bath, but different from many continental *defixiones* (cf. Roger Tomlin's paper), could perhaps be an expression of the *superstitio* of the local people that Romans remarked upon. In other sanctuaries, like Glanum/Glanon in Southern Gaul, writing had already been adopted in the late Iron Age, and one Gallo-Greek inscription mentions the god Belenos.[40] But his name is no longer attested in Roman Glanum. Instead, Hercules was worshipped at the sacred spring, as a healing god:[41] did he replace Belenos here, rather than the commonly assumed counterpart, Apollo (cf. paper by Ralph Häussler in this volume)?[42] All

40 RIG G-63.

41 For Glanum, and the role of Hercules in particular, cf. Roth Conges 1997.

42 Apollo Belenos/Belinus is attested at Bardonecchia (*v. supra*) and notably at Aquileia in the Roman period. Belenos has been traditionally translated as 'brilliant' or 'luminous', but X. Delamarre (2003, 71–2, s.v. *belo-*) has convincingly shown that this name is likely to

ganol y 4edd ganrif OC.[39] Ar ryw adeg yn ystod bodolaeth y cysegr, gwnaeth rhywun y cysylltiad rhwng duw lleol a Mercher a chododd rhywun arall, efallai adeg adeiladu'r temlau Rhufeinig-Geltaidd, gerflun Mercher. Cychwynnodd y gweithredoedd hyn brosesau hirdymor a gellir rhagdybio mai'r tebygrwydd oedd bod hyn yn newid dealltwriaeth pobl o'u duw lleol: mae duw lleol ar ffurf hybrid yn datblygu nodweddion ychwanegol, wrth i agweddau eraill ar ei addoliad neu ei fyth gael eu hanghofio, o bosibl, hyd yn oed mewn traddodiad llafar. Mae Uley, yn yr un modd ag addoliad Rhufeinig-Geltaidd arall, yn dangos sut y gellid mabwysiadu ysgrifennu a'i addasu at ddiben addoliad 'brodorol'. Yma, gallai defnydd llechi melltithio, tebyg i Gaerfaddon, ond yn wahanol i lawer o *defixiones* (cf. papur Roger Tomlin), fod yn arwydd o *superstitio* y bobl leol y gwnaeth y Rhufeiniaid sylw arno. Mewn cysegrau eraill, megis Glanum/Glanon yn ne Gâl, mabwysiadwyd ysgrifennu eisoes tua diwedd yr Oes Haearn, a chyfeiria un arysgrifen Galaidd-Roegaidd at y duw Belenos.[40] Ond bellach nid oes sôn amdano yn Glanum Rhufeinig. Yn hytrach, addolwyd Ercwlff yn y ffynnon gysegredig honno, yn dduw iacháu: [41] a ddisodlodd Belenos yma, yn hytrach na'r duw cyfatebol a ragdybir yn gyffredinol, sef Apolon (cf. papur gan Ralph Häussler yn y gyfrol hon)?[42]

39 King 2005, 332–4.

40 RIG G-63.

41 Ar gyfer Glanum, a rôl Ercwlff yn enwedig, cf. Roth Conges 1997.

42 Mae tystiolaeth i Apolon Belenos/Belinus yn Bardonecchia (*v. supra*) ac yn enwedig yn Acwileia yn y cyfnod Rhufeinig. Yn draddodiadol, cyfieithwyd Belenos yn 'ddisglair' neu

this shows the all-pervading problem of translatability between different cultures and religions.

We therefore need to ask whether we are really having thousands of 'Celtic' gods or whether people just employed different names and labels for the same deity or divine concept, emphasising particular aspects of a local divine embodiment that was important to them. It is feasible that the same goddess was called 'Mother (Earth)' (*mater, terra mater*), 'The Purveyer' (*rosmerta*), 'The Queen' (*regina*, perhaps also *Juno Regina*), 'The Well-leading (Goddess)' (*sulevia*), 'The Very Powerful (goddess)' (*belisama*), or 'of the sacred grove' (*nemetona*), while other people preferred to make a comparison with Graeco-Roman deities in their Latin dedications, like Minerva, Juno Regina, Maia, Letô, and Fortuna, and perhaps also Bona Dea or Magna Mater. We find similar phenomena in many cultures and religions; also, god's 'real' name might have become a taboo name, prompting the creation of a range of alternative designations to address a deity.

Others' name of choice may relate to the locality, for example by using a particular topographical epithet, such as perhaps *Sulevia Edennica Minerva,* 'the well-leading Minerva of Eyssène'.[43] And sometimes we seem

mean 'Maître de la Puissance'. Though Hercules and Silvanus/Sucellos clearly dominate Glanum's epigraphic record, there is some rather uncertain evidence for Apollo: CIL XII 99 and IGF 51.

43 From Collias (Gard), discovered at the *L'Ermitage-de-Laval* Chapel: CIL XII 2974 (*add.* p. 832) = ILGN 398 = ILS 4662 = CAG 30/2, n° 085, 8*; Delamarre 2003.

Y cyfan y mae hyn yn ei ddangos yw problem hollbresennol trosi rhwng gwahanol ddiwylliannau a chrefyddau.

Felly, mae angen i ni ofyn a yw'n wir bod gennym filoedd o dduwiau 'Celtaidd' neu a oedd pobl yn defnyddio gwahanol enwau a labeli ar gyfer yr un duw neu gysyniad dwyfol, gan bwysleisio agweddau penodol ar ymgorfforiad dwyfol lleol a oedd yn bwysig iddynt. Mae'n bosibl y cyfeirid at yr un dduwies o dan yr enw 'Mam(-Ddaear)' (*mater, terra mater*), 'Y Darparwr' (*rosmerta*), 'Y Frenhines' (*regina*, efallai hefyd *Juno Regina*), 'Y (dduwies) arweiniol' (*sulevia*), 'Y (dduwies) dra phwerus' (*belisama*), neu 'o'r gelli sanctaidd' (*nemetona*), wrth i eraill ddewis gwneud cymhariaeth â duwiau Groegaidd-Rufeinig yn eu cysegriadau Lladin, megis Minerva, Juno Regina, Maia, Letô, a Fortuna, ac efallai hefyd Bona Dea neu Magna Mater. Cawn ni ffenomena tebyg mwn nifer o ddiwylliannau a chrefyddau; hefyd, gallai enw 'go iawn' fod yn enw tabŵ, gan ysgogi creu ystod o ddynodiadau amgen wrth gyfarch duw.

Gallai'r enw a ddewisa eraill fod yn gysylltiedig â'r ardal, er enghraifft trwy ddefnyddio teitl topograffaidd penodol, megis, o bosibl, *Sulevia Edennica Minerva,* 'Minerva ffynnon-arweiniol Eyssène'.[43] Ac weithiau,

'oleuol', ond mae X. Delamarre (2003, 71–2, s.v. *belo-*) wedi dangos yn argyhoeddiadol ei bod hi'n debyg mai ystyr yr enw hwn yw 'Maître de la Puissance'. Er ei bod yn debyg mai Ercwlff a Silvanus/Sucellos sy'n cael y prif sylw yng nghofnod epigraffig Glanum, mae peth tystiolaeth ansicr ar gyfer Apolon: CIL XII 99 ac IGF 51.

43 O Collias (Gard), a ddarganfuwyd yng Nghapel *L'Ermitage-de-Laval*: CIL XII 2974 (*add.* t. 832) = ILGN 398 = ILS 4662 = CAG 30/2, n° 085, 8*;

to be dealing with a personification, either of a particular function (similar to the Roman Fortuna, Abundantia, Ops, Pax, Salus, etc.), or of a town, river, or mountain. We need to be aware that opposing interpretations are frequently possible, like a deonomastic and a functional one: for example, the goddess Segomanna is traditionally associated with the river Seynes, but she could also have been a supra-regional, powerful goddess: 'Great-by-her-Victories'.[44] Certain male names, too, like 'the Divine' (*divanno*), 'the All-mighty' (*lanovalus*),[45] 'the Master of Force' (*belenos*), or the 'Powerful' (*vernostonos*), seem rather interchangeable and non-specific, while 'surnames' like 'the thunderer' (*taranis*) or 'the good striker' (*sucellos*) are already less interchangeable as they relate to a deity's particular function or myth. But none of them is necessarily the 'real' name of a god. And then there are of course the eight Celtic epithets (e.g., *Andicrosos, Ausecos, Medugenos*) that served to convey the meaning of a god called *Faunus* from the 4th-century hoard discovered near the then abandoned Iron Age sanctuary of Thetford; in her paper, Daphne Nash-Briggs also argues for 'speculative etymologizing, verbal and visual riddles, and cryptic allusions' in the religious sphere, i.e. an educated elite who was capable to make up new theonyms and epithets.

44 E.g., ILGN 393; ILS 9311; CAG 30/3, n° 319, 1*, p. 686; CAG-30/2, p. 353; for the etymology of Segomanna, cf. Delamarre 2003, 268, s.v. *sego-* 'victoire, force': 'Grand-par-ses-Victoires'.

45 Delamarre 2003, 196, 305 for Lanovalus as 'Tout-Puissant' or 'Plein Prince'.

ceir yr argraff mai'r hyn sydd gennym yw personoli, boed yn swyddogaeth benodol (debyg i Fortuna, Abundantia, Ops, Pax, Salus Rhufain ac ati), neu'n dref, yn afon, neu'n fynydd. Mae angen i ni fod yn ymwybodol bod dehongliadau cyferbyniol yn aml yn bosibl, megis un deonomastig ac un swyddogaethol: er enghraifft, cysylltir y dduwies Segomana yn aml ag afon Seynes, ond gallai hefyd fod yn dduwies bwerus, uwch-ranbarthol: 'Mawr-trwy-ei-Champau'.[44] Ymddengys fod rhai enwau, dwyfol, hefyd, megis 'y Dwyfol' (*divanno*), 'yr Holl-alluog' (*lanovalus*),[45] 'Meistr Grym' (*belenos*), neu'r 'Pwerus' (*vernostonos*), braidd yn gyfnewidiol ac amhenodol, a 'chyfenwau' megis 'y taranwr' (*taranis*) neu'r 'ergydiwr da' (*sucellos*) eisoes yn llai cyfnewidiol am eu bod yn ymwneud â swyddogaeth neu fyth penodol y duw. Ond nid enw 'go iawn' rhyw dduw yw'r un o'r rhain o reidrwydd. Ac wedyn, wrth gwrs, yr wyth teitl Celtaidd (e.e. *Andicrosos, Ausecos, Medugenos*) a oedd yn fodd i gyfleu ystyr o'r enw *Faunus* o gelc o'r 4edd ganrif a ddarganfuwyd ger cysegr o'r Oes Haearn yn Thetford a oedd wedi ei adael erbyn hynny; yn ei phapur, dadleua Daphne Nash-Briggs hefyd am 'etymoleiddio dyfaliadol, posau llafar a gweledol, a chyfeiriadau cryptig' yn y maes crefyddol, e.e. elit addysgedig a oedd yn gallu bathu enwau duwiau a theitlau newydd.

Delamarre 2003.

44 E.e., ILGN 393; ILS 9311; CAG 30/3, n° 319, 1*, t. 686; CAG-30/2, t. 353; am darddiad Segomanna, cf. Delamarre 2003, 268, s.v. *sego-* 'victoire, force': 'Grand-par-ses-Victoires'.

45 Delamarre 2003, 196, 305 ar gyfer Lanovalus yn 'Tout-Puissant' neu 'Plein Prince'.

Local, personal, global

Significant for the advancements since 1998 have been three crucial aspects of the F.E.R.C.AN. Project: its diachronic perspective, the pan-European viewpoint, and the multidisciplinary approach, involving *inter alia* archaeologists, historians, philologists, and linguists from across Europe. Among others, this has exposed both striking parallels and profound divergences in our evidence across the Celtic world, both in the Iron Age and during the subsequent transformation of cults in the Roman period. This recognition already prompted a minor change of the project's title ten years ago from 'Celtic' *religion* to *religions* since we are certainly dealing, despite all superficial resemblances, with rather localised religious understandings and cult practices, and it seems hardly feasible that they all derive from a 'common proto-Celtic religion' from which all Iron Age and Roman cults derive; many of the parallels between Celtic regions do not necessarily attest a common 'Celtic ancestry', as we can also find parallels with other Indo-European and non-Indo-European cultures. Despite certain analogies, diversity seems to dominate, suggesting that we are dealing with many localised phenomena. Consequently, we need to ask whether there ever there any pan-Celtic deities or pan-Celtic myths and believes, or whether they are all a reconstruction based on feeble evidence (see for example the paper by John Koch and Fernando Fernández

Lleol, personol, byd-eang

Rhan arwyddocaol o'r datblygiadau er 1998 fu tair agwedd hollbwysig ar Brosiect F.E.R.C.AN.: ei bersbectif diachronig, y safbwynt pan-Ewropeaidd, a'r dull amlddisgyblaethol, sy'n cynnwys *inter alia* archeolegwyr, haneswyr, ieithegwyr ac ieithyddion o bob cwr o Ewrop. Ymhlith eraill, mae hyn wedi datgelu cyfochredd trawiadol a gwahaniaethau mawr o ran ein tystiolaeth ar draws y byd Celtaidd, yn yr Oes Haearn ac yn ystod gweddnewidiad dilynol y defodau yn ystod y cyfnod Rhufeinig. Arweiniodd y gydnabyddiaeth hon eisoes at fân newid yn nheitl y prosiect ddeng mlynedd yn ôl o'r *grefydd* 'Geltaidd' i *grefyddau* gan ei bod yn sicr ein bod yn ymwneud, er gwaethaf pob tebygrwydd arwynebol, â dealltwriaeth grefyddol leol ac arferion addoli, a go brin fod pob un yn deillio o 'grefydd gyffredin broto-Geltaidd' sydd wrth wraidd holl ddefodau'r Oes Haearn a'r Cyfnod Rhufeinig: nid yw nifer o'r adleisiau rhwng rhanbarthau Celtaidd o reidrwydd yn brawf o 'linach Geltaidd' gyffredin, mae adleisiau i'w cael ymhlith diwylliannau Indo-Ewropeaidd ac an-Indo-Ewropeaidd eraill. Er gwaethaf rhai cymariaethau, ymddengys fod amrywiaeth wedi mynd â hi, gan awgrymu ein bod ni'n ymwneud â llawer o ffenomenâu. O ganlyniad, mae angen i ni holi a fu unrhyw dduwiau pan-Geltaidd neu fythau a chredoau pan-Geltaidd, neu a yw pob yn ymgais i ail-greu ar sail tystiolaeth wan (gweler, er enghraifft, y papur gan J. Koch ac F. Fernández am astudiaeth i'r duw pan-Geltaidd Lugus

for a study of the elusive pan-Celtic god Lugus who gave rise to so many toponyms, notably *Lugdunum*/Lyon).[46]

This leads to the theme of this volume: *Celtic religions: local, personal, global.* On the one hand, we can see certain features that seem to reappear across the Keltiké, such as theonyms like Epona, Esus, Rosmerta, and Toutatis, though we should not ignore subtle (and sometimes less subtle) differences in time and space.[47] So-called 'Celtic' religions, like contemporary Greek and Roman cults, always seem to have been tied to the locality and integrated into the local landscape: it is the religion of the local *ethnos* ('polis' or 'tribe'), and many cults and myths were connected to local springs, rivers, lakes, and mountains, often connecting and adapting mythical accounts to particular locations (cf. Marjeta Šašel Kos' paper on river deities). This helps to explain the myriad of local deities: how many hundreds of unique Celtic theonyms/epithets are known, and how many orthographic variations?[48]

46 For Lugus in general and for the various towns called *Lugdunum*, cf. the study by Hily 2007.

47 And we should not ignore the possibility that some 'theonyms' are merely surnames, epithets, epicleses, and not the actual name of a god – *v. infra*.

48 The best overview is still Jufer & Luginbühl 2001. For orthographic variations, cf. for example divine names like *Abianus* – *Abianius* – *Avianus*, *Accorus* – *Adcorus*, *Esus* – *Aesos*, *Belenos* – *Belinus*; *Belatucadros* – *Baliticaurus* – *Belautairus*, etc., and there are of course the multiple variations for the enigmatic 'Veteres' on Hadrian's Wall, attested both as singular and plural (e.g., *Vitiribus*, *Hvitiribus*, *Vetiri*, *Vetri*, *Vitire*, *Votrim*, *Vheteri*, etc.), perhaps reflecting different attempts by individuals to render the pronunciation of a name as they perceived it

sy'n llawn dirgelwch a oedd wrth wraidd cynifer o enwau lleoedd, yn enwedig *Lugdunum*/Lyon).[46]

Arweinia hyn at thema'r gyfrol hon: *Crefyddau Celtaidd: lleol, personol, byd-eang.* Ar y naill law, gallwn weld rhai nodweddion sy'n ymddangos eu bod yn ailymddangos ar draws y Keltiké, er enghraifft, enwau duwiau megis Epona, Esus, Rosmerta, a Touatis, er na ddylem anwybyddu mân wahaniaethau (ac weithiau rhai llai mân) o ran amser a lle.[47] Ymddengys fod crefyddau 'Celtaidd', yn yr un modd â defodau Groegaidd a Rhufeinig, bob amser yn gysylltiedig â'r ardal leol ac yn rhan annatod o'r dirwedd leol: crefydd yr *ethnos* ('polis' neu 'lwyth') lleol ydyw, ac roedd nifer o ddefodau a mythau'n gysylltiedig â ffynhonnau, afonydd, llynnoedd a mynyddoedd lleol, sydd yn aml yn cysylltu ac yn addasu adroddiadau chwedlonol i leoliadau penodol (cf. Marjeta Šašel Kos' papur ar dduwiau afon). Helpa hyn i esbonio'r myrdd o dduwiau lleol: faint o gannoedd o enwau duwiau/teitlau Celtaidd unigryw sy'n hysbys, a faint o amrywiadau orthograffig?[48] Yn

46 Ar gyfer Lugus yn gyffredinol a'r gwahanol drefi o'r enw *Lugdunum*, cf. yr astudiaeth gan Hily 2007.

47 Ac ni ddylem anwybyddu'r posibilrwydd mai llysenwau, teitlau, arddeisyfiadau yn unig yw rhai 'enwau duwiau' yn hytrach nag enw go iawn y duw – *v. infra*.

48 Y trosolwg gorau o hyd yw Jufer a Luginbühl 2001. Ar gyfer amrywiadau orthograffig, cf. enwau dwyfol megis *Abianus* – *Abianius* – *Avianus*, *Accorus* – *Adcorus*, *Esus* – *Aesos*, *Belenos* – *Belinus*; *Belatucadros* – *Baliticaurus* – *Belautairus*, ac ati, ac mae, wrth gwrs, llu o amrywiadau ar gyfer y term enigmatig 'Veteres' ar Fur Hadrian, a geir ar ffurf unigol a lluosog (e.e., *Vitiribus*, *Hvitiribus*, *Vetiri*, *Vetri*, *Vitire*, *Votrim*, *Vheteri*, ac ati), gan adlewyrchu, o bosibl, ym-

In addition, in Roman times, we need to take into account how societal and cultural developments across the empire must have influenced local religious understanding.[49] This led to local people redefining their cults and cult practices, not just vis-à-vis Graeco-Roman cults, but also in response to Graeco-Oriental 'mystery' cults that spread throughout the Keltiké, challenging people's traditional religious understandings.

This also leads us to the theme of personal religion: certainly in the Roman empire, the individual social agent could make personal choices in the sphere of religion, more than ever before (accelerated by staggering migration, societal complexity, and increased cultural interaction). It is also these individuals that are responsible for the bulk of our sources: the countless votive inscriptions. Addressing a deity by a Celtic, Roman, or Greek name, choosing a particular form of ex-voto, or anthropomorphic representation seems to have increasingly become a personal choice that ran parallel to and complemented the civic cults of the local community: how many cult places can be found in suburban and rural locations, frequently of minuscule size, far away from the sway of the local *ordo*?[50]

into Latin characters; cf. Birley 1980, 107–8; Jufer & Luginbühl 2001, 71–3.

49 Cf. papers on continuity and innovation between Iron Age and Roman period in Haeussler and King (edd.) 2007–2008.

50 Cf. Haeussler 2008a; 2014b for examples of numerous small-scale cult places in Southern Gaul, like Lioux, Les Milles (Aix-en-Provence), and many more; for 'peri-urban' cult places of varying size and monumentality, cf. the study

ogystal, adeg y Rhufeiniaid, mae angen i ni gymryd i ystyriaeth y modd y mae'n rhaid bod datblygiadau cymdeithasol a diwylliannol ar draws yr ymerodraeth wedi dylanwadu ar ddealltwriaeth grefyddol leol.[49] Arweiniodd hyn at bobl leol yn ailddiffinio eu defodau a'u dulliau addoli, nid yn unig ynghylch defodau Groegaidd-Rufeinig, ond hefyd mewn defodau 'dirgelwch' Groegaidd-Ddwyreiniol a ledodd ar draws y Keltiké, gan herio dehongliadau crefyddol traddodiadol pobl.

Mae hyn hefyd yn ein harwain ni at thema crefydd bersonol: yn sicr, yn yr ymerodraeth Rufeinig, gallai'r asiant cymdeithasol unigol wneud dewisiadau personol yng nghylch crefydd, yn fwy nag erioed o'r blaen (rhywbeth a gyflymwyd trwy allfudo graddol, cymhlethdod cymdeithasol, a chynnydd o ran rhyngweithio diwylliannol). Yr unigolion hyn hefyd sy'n gyfrifol am y rhan fwyaf o'n ffynonellau: yr arysgrifau addunedol diddiwedd. Ymddengys fod cyfarch duw wrth enw Celtaidd, Rhufeinig neu Roegaidd, dewis ffurf arbennig ar offrymau llw, neu gynrychiolaeth anthropomorffig wedi mynd yn fwy ac yn fwy yn ddewis personol a oedd yn cydredeg â defodau dinesig y gymuned leol ac yn ategu'r defodau hynny: faint o leoedd addoli y gellir dod o hyd iddynt mewn maestrefi a lleoliadau gwledig, yn aml o faint bach, bach ymhell i

drechion gan unigolion i gyfleu ynganiad enw fel y'i clywsant i gymeriadau Lladin; cf. Birley 1980, 107–8; Jufer a Luginbühl 2001, 71–3.

49 Cf. papurau ar barhad ac arloesi rhwng cyfnod yr Oes Haearn a'r cyfnod Rhufeinig yn Haeussler a King (gol.) 2007–2008.

This personal religion is nowhere more obvious, and more enigmatic, than in the case of Hadrian's Wall: while the army calendar prescribed certain sacrifices to emperors and festivals for Roman state gods,[51] the individual soldier must have been free to worship whatever deity he wished, resulting in countless altars to deities bearing Celtic names, like Belatucadros, Cocidios, Veteres, and many more (but of course also deities like Mithras). But are we dealing with autochthonous deities or imported deities from the Continent? Imported deities are more obvious in the case of 'Germanic' theonyms, like Thincsus, worshipped by people who frequently identified themselves as coming from Germania Inferior.[52] But who, for example, was

by Pechoux 2010.

51 As in the case of the *Feriale Duranum*: P.Dura 54; cf. Herz 1998.

52 A very interesting example for this Germanic diaspora identity comes from Housesteads on Hadrian's Wall; set up by the *Germani* from Twent, they not only worship Mars Thincsus, but also the 'two Alaisiagae': *Deo | Marti | Thincso | et duabus | Alaisiagis | Bed(a)e et Fi|mmilen(a)e | et n(umini) Aug(usti) Ger|m(ani) cives Tu|ihanti | v(otum) s(olverunt) l(ibentes) m(erito)* (RIB 1593 = CSIR-GB I.6, 159 = ILS 4760). In a similar dedication from Housesteads, the same *Germani cives Tuihanti* (this time additionally identified as *cunei Frisiorum Ver(covicianoum)*) only made a dedication to Mars and the two Alaisiagae (RIB 1594 = CSIR-GB I.6, 160 = ILS 4761): surely, they must have just left out the epithet and the same Mars Thincsus was implied; the nature of the two Alaisiagae is still problematic: probably 'Germanic'? The situation is complex due to these Alaisiage being called Beda and Fimmilena on RIB 1593 and Baudihillia et Friagabis on RIB 1576. But what about the dedication to *deus Mars* by *Calve() Ger(manus)* at Housesteads: did he worship Mars Thincsus, Mars Cocidius, or perhaps the Roman Mars? At Ebchester/*Vindomora*, a certain Virilis Ger(manus) made a dedication *deo Vernostono*

ffwrdd o batrwm yr *ordo* lleol?[50]

Nid yw'r grefydd bersonol hon yn fwy amlwg yn unman, nac yn fwy enigmatig, nag yn achos Mur Hadrian: er mai calendr y fyddin oedd yn pennu rhai aberthau i ymerawdwyr a gwyliau duwiau'r wladwriaeth Rufeinig,[51] rhaid bod y milwr unigol yn rhydd i addoli pa dduw bynnag a fynnai, gan arwain at allorau ar gyfer duwiau sydd ag enwau Celtaidd, megis Belatucadros, Cocidios, Veteres, a llawer rhagor (ond hefyd duwiau megis Mithras). Ond ai duwiau brodorol sydd dan sylw neu rai a fewnforiwyd o'r Cyfandir? Mae duwiau a fewnforiwyd yn amlycach yn achos enwau duwiau 'Germanig', megis Thincsus, a addolwyd gan bobl a nodai yn aml eu bod yn hanu o Germania Leiaf.[52] Ond pwy, er enghraifft, oedd

50 Cf. Haeussler 2008a; 2014b am enghreifftiau o nifer o leoedd addoli ar raddfa fach yn ne Gâl, megis Lioux, Les Milles (Aix-en-Provence), a llawer rhagor; ar gyfer lleoedd addoli 'peri-trefol' o amrywiol faint a choffadwyedd, cf. yr astudiaeth gan Pechoux 2010.

51 Megis yn achos y *Feriale Duranum*: P.Dura 54; cf. Herz 1998.

52 Daw enghraifft ddiddorol iawn o hunaniaeth y diaspora Germanig hwn o Housesteads ar Fur Hadrian; sefydlwyd y rhain gan y *Germani* o Twent, maent yn addoli nid yn unig Mars Thincsus, ond hefyd y 'ddwy Alaisiaga': *Deo | Marti | Thincso | et duabus | Alaisiagis | Bed(a)e et Fi|mmilen(a)e | et n(umini) Aug(usti) Ger|m(ani) cives Tu|ihanti | v(otum) s(olverunt) l(ibentes) m(erito)* (RIB 1593 = CSIR-GB I.6, 159 = ILS 4760). Mewn cysegriad tebyg o Housesteads, gwnaeth yr un *Germani cives Tuihanti* (y tro hwn, nodir yn ychwanegol eu bod yn *cunei Frisiorum Ver(covicianoum)*) gysegriad yn unig i Fawrth a'r ddwy Alaisiaga (RIB 1594 = CSIR-GB I.6, 160 = ILS 4761): rhaid eu bod wedi hepgor y teitl a'r un Mars Thincsus a olygid; erys natur y ddwy Alaisiaga yn broblem o hyd: 'Almaenig' fwy na thebyg? Mae'r sefyllfa yn un gymhleth am mai'r enw a roddir ar yr Alaisiagae yw Beda a Fimmilena a RIB 1593 a Baudihillia a Friagabis ar RIB 1576. Beth am y cysegriad i *deus Mars* gan *Calve() Ger(manus)*

Coventina at Carrawburgh (*Brocolita*, an auxiliary fortress): was she really an autochthonous 'Romano-Celtic goddess of water and springs', and do these inscriptions reveal a pre-existing sacred site at Carrawburgh, prior to the Claudian invasion (cf. paper by Fernando Fernández)? The enigma becomes even larger when we look at Britain as a whole: whilst most 'Celtic theonyms' are attested on inscriptions from the North, in the south we find a large number of sanctuaries that were in use from the late Iron Age into the Principate: cult practices there often only evolved gradually, suggesting an enormous degree of religious 'persistence',[53] but interestingly most of these sanctuaries, where cult practices hardly changed over many generations, usually yield no inscription at all (see for example

Cocidio (RIB 1102), using a 'Celtic' formula; and at Brampton, the *Germani* Duio, Ramio, Trupo and Lurio fulfilled their vow to a god with a Celtic name, *deus Maponus* (RIB 2063 – CSIR GB I.6, 158 = ILS 4640); *Labareus Ge(rmanus)* worshipped *dea Setlocenia* at Maryport/Alauna (RIB 841), and Aurelius Crotus German(us) and Maduhus Germ(anus) worshipped Coventina: *die(!) Coventine(!)* and *dea nimfa(!) coventine(!)* respectively, at Carrawburgh/*Brocolita* (RIB 1525–6 = CSIR GB I.6, 144–5) (for Coventina, see paper by Fernando Fernández in this volume). Those 'Germans' equally worshipped established cults in Roman Britain and their own, imported deities, like Thincus and the *matres Germaniae* (worshipped by *M(arcus) Senec[ia]nius V[---]* at Housesteads, RIB 652; the *vex(illatio) Germa[no]r(um) V[o]r[e]d(ensium)* worshipped the *deae matrae transmarinis* at Old Penrith/*Voreda*: RIB 920).

53 For example, bone evidence shows an enormous degree of continuity over generations, even centuries, from the late Iron Age (1st century BC) well into the post-invasion period, sometimes up to the 2nd–3rd century AD; cf. King 2005.

Coventina yn Carrawburgh (*Brocolita*, caer gynorthwyol): ai duwies frodorol Rufeinig-Geltaidd dŵr a ffynhonnau oedd hi, ac a yw'r arysgrifau hyn yn datgelu safle cysegredig blaenorol yn Carrawburgh cyn yr ymosodiad o dan Claudius (cf. papur gan F. Fernández)? Cynyddu a wna'r dirgelwch pan edrychwn ni ar Brydain yn ei chyfanrwydd: er bod tystiolaeth i'r rhan fwyaf o 'enwau duwiau Celtaidd' ar arysgrifau o'r Gogledd, yn y de gwelir bod nifer fawr o gysegrau yn cael eu defnyddio o ddiwedd yr Oes Haearn hyd y Dywysogaeth: yn aml esblygu yn raddol yn unig a wna'r arferion addoli, gan awgrymu gradd fawr o 'barhad' crefyddol,[53] ond yn ddiddorol, yn achos y rhan fwyaf o'r cysegrau hyn, fel arfer

yn Housesteads: a addolai Mars Thincsus, Mars Cocidius, neu o bosibl Mawrth Rhufain? Yn Ebchester/*Vindomora*, gwnaeth rhyw Virilis Ger(manus) gysegriad i *deo Vernostono Cocidio* (RIB 1102), gan ddefnyddio fformiwla 'Celtaidd'; ac yn Brampton, Cyflawnodd y *Germani* Duio, Ramio, Trupo a Lurio eu hadduned i dduw oedd ag enw Celtaidd, *deus Maponus* (RIB 2063 – CSIR GB I.6, 158 = ILS 4640); addolodd *Labareus Ge(rmanus) dea Setlocenia* ym Maryport/Alauna (RIB 841), ac addolodd Aurelius Crotus German(us) a Maduhus Germ(anus) Coventina: *die(!) Coventine(!)* and *dea nimfa(!) coventine(!)* yn eu tro, yn Carrawburgh/*Brocolita* (RIB 1525–6 = CSIR GB I.6, 144–5) (ar gyfer Coventina, gweler y papur gan Fernando Fernández yn y gyfrol hon). Roedd y 'Germaniaid' hynny yn addoli i'r un graddau defodau a oedd wedi ennill eu plwyf ym Mhrydain y Rhufeiniaid a'u duwiau eu hunain a fewnforiwyd, megis Thincus a'r *matres Germaniae* (a addolid gan *M(arcus) Senec[ia]nius V[---]* yn Housesteads, RIB 652; addolai'r *vex(illatio) Germa[no]r(um) V[o]r[e]d(ensium)* y *deae matrae transmarinis* yn Old Penrith/*Voreda*: RIB 920).

53 Er enghraifft, dengys tystiolaeth yr esgyrn fod gradd fawr o barhad dros genedlaethau, hyd yn oed canrifoedd, o ddiwedd yr Oes Haearn (y ganrif gyntaf C.C.) ymhell i mewn i'r cyfnod ar ôl yr ymosodiad, weithiau hyd at y 2il–3edd ganrif O.C.; cf. King 2005.

Steven Yeates' paper for the newly discovered cult place at Abingdon); this is not limited to rural cult places, but includes civic cults: for instance, Verulamium's important sanctuary of Folly Lane equally revealed not a single inscription during its 200 years existence. This contrasts sharply, of course, with sanctuaries like Uley and Bath with a myriad of inscribed *defixiones* (see paper by Roger Tomlin).

In order to understand the epigraphic evidence, a contextual analysis is absolutely essential. How significant is the text of an inscription on its own? Case studies, like Glanum and Châteauneuf, serve to illustrate how crucial it is to locate inscriptions as precisely as possible within a sanctuary or town (cf. paper by Ralph Haeussler). It warns us not to associate just any ex-voto or dedication from the same locality to a particular cult, but to take more care about the separate assemblages ('Vergesellschaftung') that might have belonged to distinct cult places or ritual activity zones; since most inscriptions come from archaeological excavations, Glanum also allows us to explore the positioning of religious inscriptions and how people experienced them: what was visible to the general public, and what was restricted to initiates? We also need to take care of ex-votos being moved; small votive offerings, like bronze figurines (with or without inscriptions), might have been moved over long distances across the empire before being deposited as ex-voto in a local sanctuary; even small stone altars might have been moved from a

ni cheir unrhyw arysgrifen o gwbl (cf. er enghraifft papur Steven Yeates ar gyfer y lle addoli sydd newydd ei ddarganfod yn Abingdon); nid yw hyn yn gyfyngedig i leoedd addoli gwledig, ond mae'n cynnwys defodau dinesig: er enghraifft, yng nghysegr pwysig Folly Lane yn Veralamium ni welwyd yr un arysgrif yn ystod 200 mlynedd ei fodolaeth. Mae hyn yn wahanol iawn, wrth gwrs, i gysegrau megis Uley a Chaerfaddon a'u myrdd o *defixiones* anysgrifenedig (gweler y papur gan Roger Tomlin).

Er mwyn deall y dystiolaeth epigraffig, mae dadansoddiad cyd-destunol yn gwbl anhepgor. Pa mor arwyddocaol yw testun arysgrifen ar ei ben ei hun? Mae astudiaethau achos megis Glanum a Châteauneuf, yn helpu i ddangos pa mor bwysig yw lleoli arysgrifau mor fanwl ag y bo modd mewn cysegr neu dref (cf. y papur gan Ralph Haeussler). Mae'n ein rhybuddio ni rhag cysylltu unrhyw offrwm neu gyflwyniad o'r un ardal â defod arbennig, ond i fod yn fwy gofalus ynghylch y cynulliadau ar wahân ('Vergesellschaftung') a oedd, o bosibl, yn perthyn i leoedd addoli neu barthau gweithgarwch defodol penodol; gan fod y rhan fwyaf o arysgrifau'n deillio o gloddiadau archeolegol. Mae Glanum hefyd yn caniatáu i ni archwilio lleoliad arysgrifen grefyddol a phrofiad pobl o'r rhain: beth oedd yn weladwy i'r cyhoedd, a beth a oedd yn gyfyngedig i rai a oedd wedi eu cyflwyno i'r ddefod? Pwyll piau hi hefyd wrth ystyried offrymau llw sydd wedi eu symud; gellid bod wedi symud offrymau bach, megis ffigurynnau efydd (gydag arysgrifau

building to a seasonal makeshift cult place in the course of a year, as we can see in Anthony King's paper. We also should not disregard standardized production, for example, of the Minerva votive leafs from the sanctuary at Ashwell which were used as ex-votos for the goddess Senuna,[54] which raise so many questions: for example, why did the local people choose the image of Minerva to represent their goddess? Which aspect of Minerva did they relate to? Did they have a more intrinsic knowledge of Minerva's myth or did her image of a powerful, seemingly bellicose goddess in armour simply appeal to them? Alternatively, we might want to see a pattern here considering that, also in Britain, in Bath/*Aquae Sulis*, we find Minerva again: Sulis Minerva.

While writing became an intrinsic part of certain 'native' sanctuaries in the Roman period, we should not forget that across the Roman West, we find a vast number of sanctuaries of Iron Age origin where inscriptions were generally not used. And if we find one or two inscriptions, we should question their meaning. At the (otherwise 'anepigraphic') sanctuary of Hayling Island, for example, the only inscription was set up by a legionary.[55] Is this merely the soldier's personal *interpretatio* of a local cult that had started a century prior to the Claudian invasion and only changed gradually? To what extent can such sporadic inscriptions, notably set up by

54 Cf. Jackson and Burleigh 2007.
55 *[Na]evian[us(?)]* from the *legio VIII[I]* – RIB III 3042.

neu hebddynt), dros bellteroedd maith ar draws yr ymerodraeth cyn eu gosod yn offrwm llw mewn cysegr lleol; byddai modd hefyd symud allorau cerrig bach o adeilad i le addoli tymhorol dros dro yn ystod blwyddyn, fel y gwelir ym mhapur Anthony King. Hefyd ni ddylem ddiystyru cynhyrchiad safonol, er enghraifft, dail addunedu Minerva o'r cysegr yn Ashwell a ddefnyddid yn offrymau addunedu i'r dduwies Senuna,[54] sy'n codi cynifer o gwestiynau eraill: er enghraifft, pam dewisodd y bobl leol ddelw Minerva i gynrychioli eu duwies? Â pha agwedd ar Minerva oedd y rhain yn gysylltiedig? Oedd ganddyn nhw wybodaeth fwy hanfodol am chwedl Minerva neu a oedd ei delwedd hi o dduwies rymus ryfelgar mewn arfwisg at eu dant? Fel arall, efallai yr hoffem weld patrwm yma o ystyried hefyd ym Mhrydain, yng Nghaerfaddon/*Aquae Sulis*, ein bod yn darganfod Minerva unwaith eto: Sulis Minerva.

Er i ysgrifennu fynd yn rhan annatod o rai cysegrau 'brodorol' yn y cyfnod Rhufeinig, ar draws y Gorllewin Rhufeinig, ni ddylid anghofio y ceir nifer fawr o gysegrau o'r Oes Haearn lle na ddefnyddid arysgrifau fel rheol. Ac os ceir un neu ddwy arysgrifen, dylid cwestiynu eu hystyr. Yn y cysegr (heb epigraffeg fel arall) ar Ynys Hayling, er enghraifft, llengfilwr oedd yr unig un i osod arysgrifen.[55] Ai *interpretatio* personol y milwr o ddefod leol a oedd wedi dechrau ganrif cyn ymosodiad Claudius ac na newidiodd ond yn raddol, sydd dan sylw? I ba raddau

54 Cf. Jackson a Burleigh 2007.
55 *[Na]evian[us(?)]* o'r *legio VIII[I]* – RIB III 3042.

outsiders, reflect the religious meaning of a cult? In any case, it provides an epigraphic testimony for one of the *cultores* that frequented a sanctuary that goes back to a pre-Roman Iron Age cult place. Then there are also unusual cases like Woodeaton: there, we do not find any inscriptions *per se*, but there is a mysterious series of bronze letters that do not make up any meaningful word: were they used for ritual activities or were they attached to a cult or votive object?[56]

One important question remains: why did people use Celtic theonyms and epithets in otherwise (more-or-less) perfectly written Latin inscriptions? And how does this use of Celtic names change in the course of time and in the various parts of the Roman West? For example, the Celtic theonyms attested on the Parisian *pilier de nautes* ('pillar of the boatmen') during Tiberius' reign, like Smert[ri]os, [C]ernunnos, Tarvos Trigaranus, and Esus, reflect rather different choices and modalities compared to the 2nd–3rd century AD when the majority of votive inscriptions were set up. The Celtic theonyms from Paris are hardly ever attested. Have they all been replaced by Latin names? But what about all these diverse Celtic names of imperial times? Since it seems unlikely that all Celtic divine names were actually names of deities, then the use of these Celtic names must have served a certain purpose. First, it is feasible that these are designations or epithets that cannot be easily translated into

y gall yr arysgrifau ysbeidiol hyn, yn enwedig gan ddieithriaid, adlewyrchu ystyr grefyddol addoliad? Beth bynnag, darpara dystiolaeth epigraffig am un o'r *cultores* a fynychodd gysegr sy'n mynd yn ôl i le addoli Oes Haearn cyn-Rufeinig. Mae hefyd achosion anarferol megis Woodeaton: yno nid oes unrhyw arysgrifau fel y cyfryw, ond mae cyfres ryfedd o lythrennau efydd nad ydynt yn creu unrhyw air ystyrlon: a ddefnyddid y rhain ar gyfer gweithgareddau defodol neu oeddent yn gysylltiedig â gwrthrych defodol neu offrymol?[56]

Erys un cwestiwn pwysig: pam y defnyddiodd pobl enwau a theitlau Celtaidd ar gyfer duwiau mewn arysgrifau Lladin ysgrifenedig graenus (fwy neu lai) fel arall? a sut mae'r defnydd hwn ar enwau Celtaidd yn newid gydag amser ac mewn amrywiol rannau o'r Gorllewin Rhufeinig? Er enghraifft, mae'r enwau Celtaidd ar dduwiau ar *pilier de nautes* ('piler y cychwyr') Paris yn ystod teyrnasiad Tiberius, megis Smert[ri]os, [C]ernunnos, Tarvos Trigaranus ac Esus, yn adlewyrchu dewisiadau braidd yn wahanol a ffurfiau o'u cymharu â'r 2il a'r 3edd ganrif OC pan osodwyd y rhan fwyaf o'r arysgrifau offrwm. Does braidd dim tystiolaeth o enwau duwiau Celtaidd o Baris. A yw'r enwau Lladin wedi disodli pob un? Ond beth am bob un o'r gwahanol enwau Celtaidd hyn o adeg yr ymerodraeth? Gan ei bod yn ymddangos yn annhebygol mai enwau duwiau oedd pob enw dwyfol Celtaidd, rhaid bod yr enwau Celtaidd wedi eu defnyddio at ryw ddiben penodol. Yn

56 For Woodeaton, cf. Goodchild & Kirk 1954; RIB 236–239e.

56 Ar gyfer Wood Eaton, cf. Goodchild a Kirk 1954; RIB 236–239e.

Latin. Is there a good Latin translation for *cocidios*, 'the blood-reddened' god?[57] It is also possible that there were linguistic misunderstandings: while local people might have referred to a god, for example, as *mogons*, the 'mighty, powerful (god)', a Latin-speaking soldier, magistrate, trader, or colonist might have mistaken this as a god's theonym, resulting in one of the many votive inscription. But within the increasingly connected and globalizing world of the Roman empire, it will also be necessary to demarcate different 'native' cults and deities from each other, for example by creating stronger local identities and particularities.

The F.E.R.C.AN. project's focus on the epigraphic record also meant a continuous examination and re-thinking of the etymology of the various divine names, theonyms, epithets, and epicleses in Celtic. Since 1998, many linguists have scrutinised the etymology in the context of F.E.R.C.AN. workshops, like Wolfgang Meid, Xavier Delamarre, Pierre-Yves Lambert, Patrick Sims-Williams, and Patrizia de Bernardo Stempel.[58] We have seen many new exciting, and sometimes controversial, translations for theonyms, like Belenos not as healing or spring god, but as 'Maître de la Puissance', or Sulis Minerva as 'One-Eyed Minerva', Iboita as 'drinking goddess', and the god Lucuttectos was recently suggested to be not a Celtic god

gyntaf, mae'n bosibl na ellir cyfieithu'r dynodiadau neu'r teitlau hyn yn hawdd i'r Lladin. Oes cyfieithiad Lladin da ar gyfer *cocidos* y duw 'gwaedgoch'?[57] Gall hefyd fod camddeall ieithyddol: tra byddai pobl leol wedi cyfeirio at dduw, er enghraifft, o dan yr enw *mogons*, y 'pwerus, grymus (duw)', gallai fod milwr, ynad, masnachwr, neu wladychwr Lladin ei iaith, wedi camgymryd hwn am enw'r duw, gan arwain at un o'r arysgrifau addunedol niferus. Fodd bynnag, oddi mewn i sefyllfa gynyddol gysylltiedig a byd-eang yr ymerodraeth Rufeinig, bydd hefyd angen tynnu'r ffin rhwng gwahanol ddefodau a duwiau 'brodorol', er enghraifft, trwy greu hunaniaethau a nodweddion lleol cryfach.

O ganlyniad i bwyslais prosiect F.E.R.C.AN. ar y cofnod epigraffig, bu hefyd arholi ac ailfeddwl parhaus ar darddiad y gwahanol enwau dwyfol, enwau duwiau, teitlau, arddeisyfiadau yn y Gelteg. Er 1998, mae llawer o ieithyddion wedi craffu ar darddiadau'r geiriau yng nghyd-destun gweithdai F.E.R.C.AN., megis Wolfgang Meid, Xavier Delamarre, Pierre-Yves Lambert, Patrick Sims-Williams a Patrizia de Bernardo Stempel.[58] Mae gennym lawer o gyfieithiadau cyffrous newydd, ac weithiau dadleuol, ar gyfer enwau duwiau, megis Belenos nid yn dduw iacháu na gwanwyn, ond yn 'Maître de la Puissance', neu Sulis Minerva yn 'Minerva

57 If we accept P. de Bernardo Stempel's (2008) translation for Cocidios; also for Delamarre (2003, 120), Cocidius derives from *cocos, coccos*, 'écarlate, rouge'.

58 See Table 1 for the F.E.R.C.AN. proceedings.

57 Os derbynnir cyfieithiad P. de Bernardo Stempel (2008) ar gyfer Cocidios; hefyd ar gyfer Delamarre (2003, 120), daw Cocidius o *cocos, coccos*, 'écarlate, rouge'.

58 Gweler Tabl 1 ar gyfer trafodion F.E.R.C.AN.

(like 'son/descendant of Lugus'),[59] but an epithet for Apollo: a 'mice-catching Apollo'.[60] Also presumed deities, like *Mogons*, are now considered to be mere epithets that can be attributed to different gods. The idea of a secondary theonym is interesting: epithets were increasingly used as the proper name for a god, as in the case of (Mars) Cocidios and (Apollo) Maponos.[61] And finally, there has been some thought about the origin of some of these Celtic-language theonyms and epithets.[62] It is important to rethink existing paradigms, but all new interpretations equally need to be scrutinised thoroughly.

All this has led to a better understanding. We are able today to recognize different categories of 'divine names', and thus being able to recognise more complex divine formulae. An important observation relates to multiple theonyms, like Apollo Maponus or Mars Cocidios. Rather than to interpret them as 'conflations' of two comparable or even identical deities, a Celtic and a Roman one, many of these combinations suggest that the Celtic word is merely a kind of epithet: in this case Apollo 'the son of god (i.e. Zeus)' and 'the blood-reddened' Mars respectively.[63] Another interesting example is this dedication from Noricum: *Marti | Latobio | Marmogio*

59 *ILN*-3, 203.
60 De Albentiis Hienz & De Bernardo Stempel 2013.
61 Cf. De Bernardo Stempel 2008 for the term *secondary theonym*.
62 Cf. e.g. De Bernardo Stempel 2007, 2008; De Albentiis Hienz & De Bernardo Stempel 2013.
63 Following De Bernardo Stempel 2008; Delamarre 2003.

Unllygeidiog', Iboita yn 'dduwies yfed', ac yn ddiweddar awgrymwyd nad duw Celtaidd oedd Lucuttectos (megis 'mab/disgynnydd Lugus'),[59] ond teitl ar gyfer Apolon: 'Apolon y daliwr llygod'.[60] Hefyd bellach ystyrir bod duwiau rhagdybiedig, megis *Mogons,* bellach i'w hystyried yn deitlau i'w priodoli i wahanol dduwiau. Mae syniad enw duw eilaidd yn ddiddorol: yn fwy ac yn fwy, defnyddid teitlau'n enw priod ar gyfer duw, megis yn achos [Mawrth] Cocidos ac [Apolon] Maponos.[61] Ac yn olaf, bu peth meddwl am darddiad yr enwau duwiau a theitlau Celteg.[62] Mae'n bwysig ailfeddwl paradeimau presennol, ond mae hefyd angen craffu ar yr holl ddehongliadau newydd yn drylwyr.

Mae'r cyfan wedi arwain at well dealltwriaeth. Heddiw mae modd i ni gydnabod gwahanol gategorïau 'enwau dwyfol', a thrwy hynny y gallu i adnabod fformiwlâu dwyfol mwy cymhleth. Mae sylw pwysig yn ymwneud â nifer o enwau duwiau, megis Apolon Maponus neu Mawrth Cocidios. Yn hytrach na dehongli'r rhain yn 'gyfuniadau' o ddau dduw cymharol neu hyd yn oed cyfystyr, y naill yn Geltaidd a'r llall yn Rhufeinig, awgryma nifer o'r cyfuniadau hyn mai math o deitl yn unig yw'r enw Celtaidd: yn yr achos hwn, Apolon 'mab duw (h.y. Zeus)' a Mawrth 'y gwaedgoch' yn eu tro.[63] Enghraifft ddiddorol

59 ILN-3, 203.
60 De Albentiis Hienz a De Bernardo Stempel 2013.
61 Cf. De Bernardo Stempel 2008 gyfer y term enw duw eilaidd (*secondary theonym*).
62 Cf. e.e. De Bernardo Stempel 2007, 2008; De Albentiis Hienz a De Bernardo Stempel 2013.
63 Yn dilyn De Bernardo Stempel 2008; Delamarre 2003.

| *Toutati* | *Sinati Mog|[e]tio C(aius) Val(erius)* | *[V]alerinus* | *ex voto*. Gaius Valerius Valerinus did not worship a long list of six deities, but in view of what we have seen so far in this paper, there are obviously at most two gods involved: Mars and Sinatis, i.e. the very mighty (*marmogios*) Mars Latobios ('of the plain'?) and the mighty (*mogetios*) Sinatis of the people/*touta*.[64]

The case of Apollo Maponus also leads us to another important theme: the medieval Welsh and Irish literature. After all, the Britanno-Roman Maponus seems to have become Mabon in the Welsh Mabinogi; and the name Mabon, son of Mellt (i.e. 'Lightning'), seems appropriate to identify the son of a weather god. But we cannot just create one-to-one equivalents between ancient and medieval sources. With the organisation of the XIIIth F.E.R.C.AN. Workshop in Lampeter, the meeting was hosted for the first time in a Celtic-speaking country which provided the incentive to explore in more detail the evolution of medieval Welsh and Irish myths and to critically review their usefulness for the study of Iron Age and Romano-Celtic cults (see paper by John Koch and Fernando Fernández, and for the 'Anti-Nativism' debate see Jonathan Wooding's paper).[65] This is important for our methodology since there are a number of similarities between our Romano-Celtic evidence and the Welsh and Irish mythologies. What is the relationship between Lugus, the Irish Lugh, and the Welsh Llew? Are

64 CIL III 11721 = ILS 4566; cf. De Bernardo Stempel 2005 for etymological discussion.

65 Also cf. Wooding 2009.

arall yw'r cysegriad hwn o Noricum: *Marti* | *Latobio* | *Marmogio* | *Toutati* | *Sinati Mog|[e]tio C(aius) Val(erius)* | *[V]alerinus* | *ex voto*. Nid oedd Gaius Valerius Valerinus yn addoli rhestr hir o chwe duw, ond o ystyried yr hyn yr ydym eisoes wedi ei weld yn y papur hwn, mae'n amlwg mai dau dduw sydd o dan sylw ar y mwyaf: Mawrth a Sinatis, h.y. Tra nethol (*mormogis*) Fawrth Latobios ('y gwastadedd'?) a nerthol (*mogetios*) Sinatis y bobl/*touta*.[64]

Mae achos Apolon Maponus hefyd yn ein harwain ni at thema bwysig arall: llenyddiaeth Gymraeg a Gwyddeleg yr Oesoedd Canol. Wedi'r cyfan, mae lle i gredu mai Maponus y Brythoniaid Rhufeinig sydd wrth wraidd Mabon yn y Mabinogi: a'r enw Mabon, mab Mellt yn ymddangos yn briodol ar gyfer dynodi mab un o dduwiau'r tywydd. Ond ni allwn ni greu cyfatebiaethau fesul un rhwng yr hen ffynonellau a rhai'r oesoedd canol. A XIIeg Gweithdy F.E.R.C.AN. yn Llanbedr Pont Steffan, hwn oedd y tro cyntaf i'r cyfarfod gael ei gynnal mewn gwlad lle siaredir iaith a oedd yn gymhelliad i archwilio'n fanylach esblygiad chwedlau Cymraeg a Gwyddeleg yr Oesoedd Canol ac adolygu eu defnyddioldeb ar gyfer defodau'r Oes Haearn a'r cyfnod Rhufeinig-Geltaidd (Gweler y papur gan John Koch a Fernando Fernández, ac ar gyfer y ddadl 'Gwrth-Frodoriaeth' gweler papur Jonathan Wooding).[65] Mae hwn yn bwysig i'n methodoleg gan fod nifer o bethau cyffredin rhwng

64 CIL III 11721 = ILS 4566; cf. De Bernardo Stempel 2005 am drafodaeth etymolegol.

65 Hefyd cf. Wooding 2009.

there any differences between Irish *Samhain* and the *samonios* on the calendar from Coligny? How useful is the Rhiannon myth from the Mabinogi to understand (and reconstruct) the Romano-Celtic goddess Epona?[66] And to what extent was Welsh mythology also the product of over 350 years of Roman 'occupation' in Britain? It will be important to explore further the transitional period between late Antiquity and the early Middle Ages, and how, despite Christianity, 'Celtic' myths and cults continued to evolve; after all, certain (Britanno-Roman) cult aspects seem to have flourished down to the 4th century in Britain, judging from the Romano-Celtic temples and sanctuaries in Caerwent, Lydney Park, Maiden Castle, Thetford, and many other sites. What was their impact on early medieval institutions, practices, and folklores?

We hope that this overview provides some insight into the vast methodological problems that one encounters in the study of Celtic religions and deities. The papers in this volume each reflect a large variety of methodological approaches to the topic, reflecting different disciplines and traditions and discussing a multitude of evidence.

y dystiolaeth Rufeinig-Geltaidd a'r chwedlau Cymraeg a Gwyddeleg. Beth yw'r berthynas rhwng Lugus, Lugh y Gwyddelod, a Llew'r Cymry? A oes unrhyw wahaniaethau rhwng *Samhain* y Gwyddelod a *samonios* ar y calendr o Coligny? Pa mor ddefnyddiol yw chwedl Rhiannon y Mabinogi er mwyn deall (ac ailadeiladu) y dduwies Rufeinig-Geltaidd Epona?[66] Ac i ba raddau roedd chwedlau Cymraeg hefyd yn gynnyrch dros 350 mlynedd o reolaeth Rufeinig ym Mhrydain? Bydd yn bwysig archwilio ymhellach y cyfnod pontio rhwng diwedd cyfnod yr Hen Fyd a dechrau'r Oesoedd Canol a sut, er gwaethaf Cristnogaeth, y parhaodd y chwedlau 'Celtaidd' i esblygu: wedi'r cyfan, ymddengys fod rhai agweddau defodol (Brythonig-Rufeinig) wedi ffynnu tan yn 4edd ganrif ym Mhrydain, a barnu wrth y temlau a'r cysegrau Rhufeinig-Geltaidd yng Nghaerwent, Parc Lydney, Castell Maiden, Thetford a llawer o safleoedd eraill. Beth oedd eu heffaith neu ar sefydliadau, arferion, a chwedlau cynnar yr oesoedd canol?

Gobeithio y bydd y trosolwg hwn yn rhoi rhyw gipolwg ar y problemau methodolegol enfawr sy'n dod i'n rhan ni wrth astudio'r crefyddau a'r duwiau Celtaidd. Mae pob un o bapurau'r gyfrol hon yn adlewyrchu amrywiaeth fawr o ddulliau methodolegol at y pwnc, gan adlewyrchu'r gwahanol ddisgyblaethau a thraddodiadau a thrafod llu o dystiolaeth.

66 Cf. e.g. Haeussler 2008b with further bibliography.

66 Cf. e.e. Haeussler 2008b gyda llyfryddiaeth bellach.

BIBLIOGRAPHY — LLYFRYDDIAETH

Abascal, J. M. 2002 'Téseras y monedas. Iconografía zoomorfa y formas jurídicas de la Celtiberia', *Palaeohispanica* 2, 9–35.

Bauchhenß, G. 2008 'Hercules in Gallien: facts and fiction', in: Haeussler and King (eds) 2008, vol. 2, 91–102.

Birley, A. R. 1980 *The People of Roman Britain*, London: Batsford.

Buisson A. & Abry J.-H. (eds.) 1993 *Les tablettes astrologiques de Grand (Vosges) et l'astrologie en Gaule romaine, Actes de la table ronde du 18 mars 1992, Université de Lyon III*. Paris, De Boccard (Coll. du Centre d'études romaines et gallo-romaines, nouvelle série, 12).

De Albentiis Hienz, M. & P. de Bernardo Stempel 2013 'Apolls Epitheta – griechisch, lateinisch, keltisch bzw. keltorömisch. Eine Typologie der Beinamen klassicher Gottheiten'. *Geistes-, sozial- und kulturwissenschaftlicher Anzeiger* 148 (1-2), 7–126.

De Bernardo Stempel. P. 2005 'Die in Noricum belegten Gottheiten und die römisch-keltische Widmung aus Schloß Seggau',*Keltischer Götter im Römischen Reich*, ed. W. Spickermann & R. Wiegels, 15–28. Möhnesee, Bibliopolis.

De Bernardo Stempel, P. 2007 'Einheimische keltische und keltisierte Gottheiten der Narbonensis im Vergleich',*Auf den Spuren keltischer Götterverehrung. Akten des 5. F.E.R.C.AN.-Workshop, Graz 9.–12. Oktober 2003*, ed. M. Hainzmann, 67–80. Wien, Österreichische Akademie der Wissenschaften Wien (Mitteilungen der Prähistorischen Kommission, volume 64).

De Bernardo Stempel, P. 2008a 'Strato teonimici nelle provincie romane (con esempi prevalentemente aquitani)'. In D'Encarnação, J. (ed.) 2008, 145–50.

De Bernardo Stempel, P. 2008b 'Continuity, *translatio* and *identificatio* in Romano-Celtic religion: The Case of Britain', in Haeussler and King (eds) 2007, vol. 2, 67–82.

De Bernardo Stempel, P. 2011 'Il testo pregallico della stele di Vercelli', *Finem dare: il confine, tra sacro, profano e immaginario. A margine della stele bilingue del Museo Leone di Vercelli. Convegno internazionale, 22–24 maggio 2008*, ed. G. Cantino-Wataghin, A. Rosso & F. M. Gambari, 67–79. Vercelli.

Delamarre, X. 2003 *Dictionnaire de la langue gauloise* (2nd revised edition). Paris, Éditions Errance.

Delamarre, X. 2013 'La structuration verticale de l'espace chez les Anciens Celtes et les déesses rhénanes *Matronae Andrusteihae*', *Théonymie celtique, cultes, interpretatio / Keltische Theonymie, Kulte, interpretatio*. A. Hofeneder & P. de Bernardo Stempel (eds), 97–9. Wien, Österreichische Akademie der Wissenschaften.

D'Encarnação, J. (ed.) 2008 *Divindades indígenas em análise. Divinités pré-romaines - bilan et perspectives d'une recherche. Actas do VII workshop F.E.R.C.AN., Cascais, 25-27.05.2006 Cascais*. Coimbra/Porto.

Duval, P.-M. 1989. 'Teutates, Esus, Taranis' In: *Travaux sur la Gaule (1946-1986)*, 275–87. Rome, École Française de Rome (Publications de l'École française de Rome, 116).

Fauduet, I. 2010 *Les Temples de tradition celtique en Gaule romaine* (2nd revised edition). Paris, Editions Errance.

Goodchild, R. & J. R. Kirk 1954 'The *Romano Celtic Temple* at Woodeaton', *Oxoniensia* 19, 15–37.

Gorrochategui, J. 2008 'Hacia el corpus de divinidades indígenas de la Novempopulana', in: D'Encarnação, J. (ed.) 2008, 272–3.

Gorrochategui, J. 2013 'Linguistisque et peuplement en Aquitania'. *L'âge du Fer en Aquitaine et sur ses marges. Mobilité des hommes, diffusion des idées, circulation des biens dans l'espace européen à l'âge du Fer. Actes du 35e Colloque international de l'AFEAF (Bordeaux, 2–5 juin 2011)*, ed. A. Colin & F. Verdin, 17–32. Bordeaux (Aquitania Supplément 30).

Green, M. 1992 *Dictionary of Celtic myth and legend*. London, Thames and Hudson.

Gury, F. 2012 'Mars et le taureau: à propos du bloc sculpté provenant du sanctuaire de Mars Mullo à Allones (Sarthes)'. *Mediterraneo antico* 15/1–2, 175–98.

Jackson, R. & G. Burleigh 2007 'The Senuna treasure and shrine at Ashwell (Herts)', in Haeussler & King (eds), vol. 1, 37–54.

Haeussler, R. & A. C. King (eds) 2007–2008 *Continuity and Innovation in Religion in the Roman West*. 2 vols., Portsmouth, RI, Journal of Roman Archaeology (Supplementary Series 67).

Haeussler, R. & A. C. King 2007 'Introduction: The formation of Romano-Celtic religion(s)'. In Haeussler and King (eds) 2007, vol. 1, 7–12.

Haeussler, R. 2008a 'Pouvoir et religion dans un

paysage gallo-romain: les cités d'Apt et d'Aix-en-Provence', *Romanisation et épigraphie. Études interdisciplinaires sur l'acculturation et l'identité dans l'Empire romain*, ed. R. Haeussler, 155–248. Montagnac, Éditions Monique Mergoil (Archéologie et Histoire Romaine, 17).

Haeussler, R. 2008b. 'How to identify Celtic religion(s) in Roman Britain and Gaul', in: D'Encarnação (ed.) 2008, 13–63.

Haeussler, R. 2008c. 'A new sacred landscape at the fringes of the Roman Empire: the civitas Vangionum', in: Haeussler & King (edd.) 2008, vol. 2, 185–216.

Haeussler, R. 2012 '*Interpretatio indigena.* Re-inventing local cults in a global world', *Mediterraneo Antico* 15 (1–2), 143–74.

Haeussler, R. 2014 'Manipulating the past. Re-thinking Graeco-Roman accounts on "Celtic" religion'. *Fraude, mentiras y engaños en el mundo antiguo*, ed. F. Marco Simón, F. Pina Polo & J. Remesal Rodríguez, 35–54. Barcelona, Edicions de la universitat de Barcelona.

Haeussler, R. 2014b 'Differences in the epigraphic habit in the rural landscapes of Gallia Narbonensis', *Öffentlichkeit – Monument – Text. XIV Congressus Internationalis Epigraphiae Graecae et Latinae 27–31 Augusti MMXII*, ed. W. Eck, P. Funke & M. Dohnicht, 323–45. Berlin, de Gruyer.

Haeussler, R. 2015 'A landscape of resistance? Cults and sacred landscapes in Western Cisalpine Gaul', *Trans Padum ... Vsque Ad Alpes. Roma tra il Po e le Alpi: dalla romanizzazione alla romanità. Atti del convegno Venezia 13–15 maggio 2014* (Studi e ricerche sulla Gallia Cisalpine, 26), ed. G. Cresci Marrone, 261–86. Roma, Edizione Quasar.

Hainzmann, M. & P. de Bernardo Stempel 2013 'Interpretatio Romana vel indigena im Spiegel der Götterformulare', *Théonymie celtique, cultes, interpretatio / Keltische Theonymie, Kulte, interpretatio: X. workshop F.E.R.C.AN., Paris 24.–26.Mai 2010*, ed. A. Hofeneder & P. de Bernardo Stempel, 193–220. Wien: Österreichische Akademie der Wissenschaften.

Haselgrove, C. 1995. 'Social and symbolic order in the origins and layout of Roman villas in Northern Gaul', *Integration in the early Roman West. The role of culture and ideology*, ed. J. Metzler, M. Millett, N. Roymans, & J. Slofstra, 65–76. Luxembourg, Dossiers d'Archéologie du Musée d'Histoire et d'Art IV.

Herz, P. 1998 'Feriale Duranum', *Der Neue Pauly* IV, 480–1.

Hily, G. 2007 *Le dieu celtique Lugus* (PhD thesis). Paris, Ecole pratique des hautes etudes – EPHE, Humanities and Social Sciences.

Jackson, R. & G. Burleigh 2007 'The Senuna treasure and shrine at Ashwell (Herts.)' in: Haeussler & King (eds), vol. 1, 37–54.

Jufer, N. & T. Luginbühl 2001 *Les dieux gaulois: répertoire des noms des divinités celtiques connus par l'épigraphie, les textes antiques et la toponymie.* Paris, Errance.

King, A. C. 2005 'Animal remains from temples in Roman *Britain'*, *Britannia* 36, 329–70.

King, A. C. 2007. 'Romano-Celtic temples in Britain: Gallo-Roman influence or indigenous development?', in: Haeussler & King (eds.), vol. 1, 13–8.

Koch, J. 2013. *Tartessian. Celtic in the South-west at the Dawn of History.* 2nd revised and expanded edition. Aberystwyth, Celtic Studies Publications.

Lambot, B. 2006. 'Religion et habitat. Les fouilles d'Acy-Romance', *Religion et société en Gaule*, ed. G. Goudineau, 177–90. Paris, Editions Errance.

Lejeune, M. 1981 'En marge d'une rigani gauloise', *Comptes rendus des séances de l'Académie des Inscriptions et Belles-Lettres*, 125/1, 29–30.

Meid, W. 2003 'Keltische Religion im Zeugnis der Sprache.' *Zeitschrift für Celtische Philologie* 53, 20–40 (= Gorrochategui, P. & de Bernardo Stempel, P. 2004, *Die Kelten und ihre Religion im Spiegel der Sprache*, Vitoria 2004, 175–95).

Pechoux, L. 2010 *Les sanctuaires de périphérie urbaine en Gaule romaine*2010, Montagnac, Éditions Monique Mergoil (AHR-18).

Roth Congès, A. 1997 'La fortune éphémère de *Glanum* : du religieux à l'économique (à propos d'un article récent)', *Gallia* 54, 157–202.

Sims-Williams, P. 1998 'Celtomania and Celtoscepticism', *Cambrian Medieval Celtic Studies* 36, 1–36.

Swift, C. 2002 'Celts, Romans and the Coligny calendar'. *TRAC 2001. Proceedings of the Eleventh Annual Theoretical Roman Archaeology Conference, Glasgow 2001*, ed. M. Carruthers *et al.*, 83–95. Oxford, Oxbow Books.

Wooding, J. 2009 'Reapproaching the Pagan Celtic Past – Anti-Nativism, Asterisk Reality and the Late-Antiquity Paradigm', *Studia Celtica Fennica* 6, 51–74.

Zavaroni, A. 2007 *On the structure and terminology of the Gaulish calendar*, British Archaeological Reports British Series.

Zwicker, J. 1934–1936. *Fontes historiae religionis celticae*. Berlin: de Gruyter.

TABLE 1 - F.E.R.C.AN. WORKSHOPS

Workshop	Year	Location	Conference Proceedings
I	1998	Vienna, Austria	not published
II	1999	Luxembourg	not published
III	2000	Vitoria/Gasteiz, Pays Basque, Spain	J. Gorrochategui & P. de Bernardo-Stempel (eds.), *Los Celtas y su religión a través de la epigrafía, Actas del III Workshop F.E.R.C.AN.* Vitoria-Gasteiz 2004.
IV	2002	Osnabrück, Germany	R. Wiegels & W. Spickermann (eds.), *Keltische Götter im Römischen Reich. Akten des 4. internationalen Workshops "Fontes Epigraphici Religionis Celticae Antiquae" (F.E.R.C.AN.) vom 4.-6.10.2002 an der Universität Osnabrück.* Möhnesee, Bibliopolis. 2005.
V	2003	Graz, Austria	M. Hainzmann (ed.), *Auf den Spuren keltischer Götter-verehrung. Akten des 5. F.E.R.C.AN.-Workshop, Graz 9.-12. Oktober 2003*, Wien/Vienna, Österreichische Akademie der Wissenschaften Wien (Mitteilungen der Prähistorischen Kommission, volume 64). 2007.
VI	2005	London, England	R. Haeussler & A. C. King (eds.), *Continuity and Innovation in Religion in the Roman West*, Portsmouth, Rhode Island (JRA Supplements 67 & 67.2), vol. 1 & vol. 2. 2007 & 2008.
VII	2006	Cascais, Portugal	J. d'Encarnação (ed.), *Divindades indígenas em análise. Divinités pré-romaines - bilan et perspectives d'une recherche. Actas do VII workshop F.E.R.C.AN., Cascais, 25-27.05.2006 Cascais.* Coimbra/Porto. 2008.
VIII	2007	Gargnano, Italy	A. Sartori (ed.), *Dedicanti e cultores nelle religioni celtiche : 8. workshop F.E.R.C.AN., Gargnano del Garda, 9–12 maggio 2007.* Milano, Cisalpino. 2008.
IX	2008	Molina, Spain	J. Arenas Esteban (ed.), *Celtic Religion across Space and Time.* Molina de Aragón & Toledo, 2010.
X	2010	Paris, France	A. Hofeneder & P. de Bernardo Stempel (eds.), *Théonymie celtique, cultes, interpretatio / Keltische Theonymie, Kulte, interpretatio.* Wien, Verlag der Österrechischen Akademie der Wissenschaften, 2013.
XI	2011	Erfurt, Germany	W. Spickermann (ed.), *Keltische Götternamen als individuelle Option? Celtic Theonyms as Individual Option? Akten des 11. internationalen Workshops „Fontes Epigraphici Religionum Celticarum Antiquarum" vom 19.-21. Mai 2011 an der Universität Erfurt.* Osnabrück (Osnabrücker Reihe zu Altertum und Antike Rezeption, vol. 19). 2013.
XII	2012	Berlin, Germany	Published as part of: W. Eck & P. Funke (eds.), *Öffentlichkeit - Monument - Text. XIV Congressus Internationalis Epigraphiae Graeca et Latinae, 27.-31. Augusti MMXII. Akten* (Corpus Inscriptionum Latinarum, Auctarium, series nova, XIV). Berlin: De Gruyter.
XIII	2014	Lampeter, Wales	This volume.
XIV	2015	Trier, Germany	*Kelto-römische Gottheiten und ihre Verehrer. Akten des 14. F.E.R.C.AN.-Workshops Trier 12.-14. Oktober 2015* (Pharos 39). Rahden/Westf : VML, Verlag Marie Leidorf GmbH, 2016.
XV	2016	Lisbon, Portugal	Forthcoming.

II

SOME EPIGRAPHIC COMPARANDA BEARING ON THE 'PAN-CELTIC GOD' LUGUS

John T. Koch & Fernando Fernández Palacios

As the subject of Celtic mythology developed over the 20th century, the methodology combined ancient Celtic and Romano-Celtic epigraphic evidence together with early Welsh and Irish literature with the objective of recovering ideas about pre-Christian gods. In our current work, it is perhaps no longer safe to assume that the pre-Christian Celtic-speaking peoples (even) shared a common mythology, however one could go about recovering it from surviving material. At the same time, a larger body of ancient epigraphic evidence is now available for the traditional comparative procedure. Against this background, the presentation will consider possible implications of expanded onomastic comparanda from ancient inscriptions relevant to tales from the Welsh Mabinogion and Old and Middle Irish sagas. The focus will be on some narratives that have been seen as reflections of the myth of the 'pan-Celtic god Lugus'. Some recent alternative interpretations will also be weighed in light of detailed epigraphic parallels.

Die Grenzen meiner Sprache bedeuten die Grenzen meiner Welt.[1]

The very first thing that strikes one, in reading the Mabinogion, is how evidently the medieval story-teller is pillaging an antiquity of which he does not fully possess the secret; he is like a peasant building his hut on the site of Halicarnassus or Ephesus; he builds, but what he builds is of materials of which he knows not the history, or knows by glimmering tradition merely;—stones not of this building, but of an older architecture, greater, cunninger, more majestical.[2]

COMPARABLE names found in Romano-Celtic epigraphy recur in supernatural narratives of medieval Ireland and Wales. From the point of view of linguistics, this shared onomastic stock can be treated as a discreet subset among the more than a thousand cognate words and names that can be attributed to the common source of the attested Celtic languages. This material is therefore susceptible to the core methodology of Celtic studies—i.e. the systematic comparison of the Brythonic, Goidelic,

1 Wittgenstein, *Tractatus Logico-Philosophicus* 5.6.
2 Arnold 1867, 61.

and Continental Celtic languages—as this technique has advanced incrementally since launched by Lhuyd in 1707. As Celtic studies developed through the 20th century, this subset of Common Celtic names has been of special interest not only as linguistic evidence *per se* but in promising a 'Jacksonian' (1964) window onto the mythology and religion of the pre-Roman, pre-Christian, and mostly preliterate Celts of the Iron Age. In work in the field of Celtic mythology, for which Mac Cana's 1968 book of that name remains an influential example, an eclectic evidence base and synthetic methodology have been employed. The approach brought together the evidence of cognate names with a comparison of themes seen as reflecting myths or religious beliefs branching from a common tradition. This method often went beyond direct evidence from the inherited Celtic lexicon as might establish the distinctively Celtic identity of recurrent ideas. The work of the Rees brothers in particular emphasized the international character of concepts surfacing in the Celtic literatures.[3]

The methodology of the present case study is more narrowly linguistic. As anticipated by Dillon,[4] Lugus can be considered a Pan-Celtic god in that reflexes of his name occur for a divine or mythological figure in all sub-branches of Celtic. The present paper focuses on the ancient attestations and cognate forms in the medieval Irish and Welsh tales, together with some associated forms in those tales for which there are counterparts in ancient epigraphy. This might be seen as an exercise in paring down and purifying, so that what we have left will be less than what was given credence a generation ago, but more secure.

However, the 'language alone' side of the balance has continued to grow and solidify. Ancient epigraphic evidence in particular has been greatly augmented by new discoveries, as well as better readings, interpretations, and more accessible resources for previously known inscriptions. The field of Celtic historical lexicography progresses continually, with new etymologies accepted and faulty ones identified and remedied or replaced. The sound laws that account precisely for the relationship of the cognates are constantly honed. The earlier meanings of shared items are augmented and refined as work goes ahead on the primary evidence of texts in the Celtic languages, as well as fuller and more accurate meanings of the cognate forms in other Indo-European languages.

On the level of ideas rather than words, we have no established procedure for recovering pagan gods and myths, or even to say for certain whether this is how the *dramatis personae* of, say, the Mabinogi originated. It will be essentially impossible to make such comparisons scientific, eliminating subjectivity and speculation. On the other hand, despite the intervening centuries and enormous social and cultural as well as linguistic changes, there is a very precise method for deriving medieval from Ancient Celtic forms. The sound laws are regular. They operate invariably in the same way and in the same order. Each successive generation of linguists understands these rules better than the generation before. Historical and comparative lexicography provides a

3 Rees & Rees 1961.
4 1948, 51.

steadily better grasp of the earlier meaning of words. Although we have only occasional flashes of insight into how the thoughts of Celtic-speaking communities evolved across the maelstrom of the post-Roman Migration Period, we can track many, many specific details of language across this gulf.

The attributes and acta that *Celtic Mythology* assigned to the Pan-Celtic Lugus relied heavily on a passage from Caesar's *Bellum Gallicum* that contained no Celtic names or words.

> *Deum maxime Mercurium colunt. Huius sunt plurima simulacra: hunc omnium inventorem artium ferunt, hunc viarum atque itinerum ducem, hunc ad quaestus pecuniae mercaturasque haber vim maximam arbitrantur.* (BGall. VI 17)
>
> Of the gods they worship Mercury most of all. Of him there are the most images. They hold him to be the inventor of all the arts, the guide in journeys and travelling, and they consider him to have the greatest potency for seeking wealth and in commerce.

Although this passage is brief, if its 'Mercury' is accepted as coterminous with Lugus, it expands that Celtic god's dossier enormously, taking in every dedication to, Celtic or Latin epithet or by-name for, and image of Mercury in Gaul and the other Celtic-speaking provinces. The words *itinerum dux* and *inventor omnium artium* in particular invite comparison with Lug's central role in *Cath Maige Tuired* as a traveller from afar and the omnicompetent master of all crafts amongst the *Tuath Dé* 'Tribe of the gods'. This rôle is echoed in his recurrent epithet *Samildánach* 'equally endowed with many arts'.

There are further suggestive parallels among the Welsh figures with cognate names. For example, Lleu-elys in *Cyfranc Lluδ and Lleuelys* returns from overseas to deliver his people from supernatural oppression (*gormes*) by using specialist knowledge. More pointedly, Lleu in the Fourth Branch of the Mabinogi acquires his name and epithet (*Lleu Llaw-gyffes*, 'Lleu of the Deft Hand') in an episode in which he was making gold-ornamented shoes. For this episode, comparison is often made to a dedication commissioned by a guild of shoemakers in the Celtiberian town Uxama Argaela. This Romano-Celtic inscription invokes a group of deities called the *Lugoues*, i.e. the plural of *Lugus*:

LVGOVIBVS SACRVM L. L(...) VRCICO COLLEGIO SVTORVM D. D.[5]

The plural is also found in Gaul, in an inscription consisting merely of the nominative LVGOVES.[6]

Combining these attributes of Lug and Lleu(elys) in the tales with Caesar's 'Mercury' suggests that Lugus was the genius of the class of peripatetic artisans, for whom *aes dáno* 'people of gifts, arts' is the Old Irish term. However, this equivalence

5 CIL II 2818 — Osma, Soria.
6 CIL XIII 5078 — Avenches [Aventicium], Switzerland.

and the value of Caesar's testimony were questioned as long ago as 1940 by Sjoestedt: 'In view of the profound divergence in the mentality and social structure which we observe as between Romans and Celts, one must wonder at such a similarity in their religious ideas...'.[7] Likewise, Dillon and Chadwick's *Celtic Realms* makes the key point: 'But [Caesar] is simply equating Gaulish deities with his own Roman gods. He does not give us a single Gaulish name'.[8]

Years later, a more thorough refutation of Lugus='Mercury' was Maier's, concluding:

> ... like all classical authors writing about foreign religions, Caesar assumes that it is only man-made institutions which differ from one people to another, whereas the gods everywhere were the same. According to this scheme of thought, no matter how numerous the Celtic gods may be, they are never anything but manifestations of the deities known from classical mythology'.[9]

Caesar was not averse to writing Gaulish (or Ancient Brythonic) names. *Bellum Gallicum* fairly bristles with the native names of individuals, groups, and places. His representation of Celtic names in Roman letters is more phonologically accurate than the norm. He had spent many years in Celtic lands, shrewdly fashioning military alliances and establishing Roman administration. There was, therefore, no reason for Caesar not to have given the Gaulish names for 'Mercury' and the other gods if this strengthened the point he was making, as it would have done if the god he described was coterminous with the god called *Lugus*. It does not necessarily follow that none of what Caesar says of 'Mercury' reflects a native god (sometimes) called *Lugus*.

But the extent to which Caesar and the other classical authors are stuck in their own culture's religious terminology and conceptual framework devalues their testimony on Celtic religion. We should not assume that this pitfall simply disappeared with Greco-Roman paganism; for modern researchers, familiarity with the Olympians continued to condition the expectations in investigations of gods of other Indo-European religions. For example, de Vries related 'Mercury'=Lugus to an explicit concept of cognate Indo-European pantheons.[10]

On a second point, Maier's reinterpretation has been challenged. He argues that many examples of the Ancient Celtic names with *Lugu-* are not evidence for a god of this name, but corresponded to a homophonous Old Irish word *lug*, meaning 'lynx', which could be used as a kenning for 'warrior, hero'. Carey (2010) has since reviewed the relevant examples, and reached the opposite conclusion: 'Medieval Irish literature does not provide us with any persuasive indications of a word *lug* meaning "lynx"' (166). The examples once adduced for it are, in their contexts, better understood as meaning '(the god) Lug' or, metaphorically, 'Lug-like hero', the Irish supernatural figure being a renowned warrior. Consistent with this conclusion, there is an entry in the *Etymological Dictionary of Proto-Celtic* '**Lugu-* "god Lug", perhaps originally "the shiny one", but

7 Trans. Dillon 1949, 33.
8 Dillon and Chadwick 1967, 13.
9 Maier 1996, 135.
10 De Vries 1977, 58–63.

no **lugu-* "lynx"'.[11] While effectively rescuing the Lugus=Lug=Lleu equation, Carey's intervention leaves Caesar's 'Mercury' approximately where Maier left him: though not safely ignored altogether in the Lugus question, we cannot, on the other hand, simply insert the *Bellum Gallicum* passage into the semantic field of the Proto-Celtic item **Lugu-*.

The inscription of Uxama Argaela naming the Lugoues and the shoemakers' guild has long been known. Rhŷs saw the parallel to Lleu and Gwydion's guise as shoemakers in the Mabinogi.[12] But the fuller extent of the Palaeohispanic evidence was not widely recognized until Tovar (1982). He drew special attention to the long Celtiberian inscription in Roman script of Peñalba de Villastar:

> ENIOROSEI | VTA · TIGINO · TIATVMEI | TRECAIAS · TOLVGVEI | ARAIANOM · COMEIMV || ENIOROSEI · EQVOISQVE | OGRIS OIOCAS · | TO·GIOAS · SISTAT · LVGVEI · TIASO | TOGIAS.[13]

Although there is no general agreement about the interpretation of the text overall, most commentators, including Tovar, have seen both occurrences of LVGVEI as datives singular of the divine name *Lugus*.[14]

Tovar also brought in epigraphic evidence from north and west of the Celtiberian area in the eastern Meseta. These texts invoke the Lugoues as a group in the dative plural, as at Uxama. Some use an indigenous case ending rather than Latin *-bus*:

> LVGVBO ARQVIENOBO C(AIVS) IVLIVS HISPANVS V.S.L.M.;[15]
> LVCOBO | AROVSA(ECIS) | V. S. L. M. | RVTIL[IA] | ANTIANIA;[16]
> DIBVS M[.] LVCVBO;[17]
> LVCOVBV[S] ARQVIENI[S] SILONIVS SILO EX VOTO.[18]

In the first and last example, the Lugoues' by-name *Arquien-* begins with the element that occurs frequently as the Palaeohispanic personal name *Arquius*, feminine *Arcea*. This name derives from Western Indo-European and means 'archer, bowman', cf. Latin *arquus*, *arcus* 'bow, arch', Gothic *arƕazna* 'arrow'.[19] What follows *Arqui-* could be a nasal suffix, but more probably the common compound-name second element **genos* 'born from' with loss of *g*, cf. MEDVGENVS[20] versus CAVNVS MEDVENI.[21] There are many Palaeohispanic examples both with and without *-g-* in this Common Celtic compound name, which means 'mead/honey' + 'born'.

Another point raised by Tovar was that the Hispanic evidence for Lugus was an

11 Matasović 2009.
12 Rhŷs 1892, 424–5.
13 MLH IV, K.3.3 — Peñalba de Villastar, Teruel.
14 Cf. Wodtko 2000, 234–7.
15 Cf. HAE 1957–60, 1718; IRLugo 67; Búa 2000 ; Vallejo 2013 — Liñarán, Sober, Lugo.
16 HEp 11, 313; Vallejo 2013 — Lugo.
17 Búa 2003 , 153–4; Marco 2005, 301 — Peña Amaya, north of Burgos.
18 AE 1957, 93; Búa 2000; IRLugo, 68; IRG II, 18 — Sinoga, Rábade, Outeiro do Rei, Lugo.
19 Koch 2016, 438–42.
20 HEp 5, 946 — Messejana, Aljustrel, Beja.
21 HEp 1, 181 — Plasenzuela, Cáceres.

Fig. 1. Geographical distribution of forms of the name *Lugu-* in the Iberian Peninsula mentioned in the text.

argument against the prevalent idea that the cult had spread to Britain and Ireland from Gaul towards the end of the pre-Roman Iron Age, a traveller from afar in fact and not merely in the tales. As Tovar argued, because Celtiberian preserved archaic linguistic features lost in the other Celtic languages and full La Tène Celtic culture never reached the Iberian Peninsula, it was unlikely that a new Celtic god had been imported into Spain in the Seconnd Iron Age. Lugus was more probably an inheritance, predating the separation of Gaulish and Celtiberian. Though Tovar did not use these terms, his conclusion was that Lugus was a Proto-Celtic, rather than a Pan-Celtic, god. This is, as noted above, the conclusion reached by Matasović along different lines.

On the configuration of the Celtic family tree, Tovar anticipated current doctrine. There is general agreement that the first split divided Hispano-Celtic, on the one hand, from the proto-language of Gaulish-Brittonic-Goidelic, McCone's 'Gallo-Insular'.[22] A Gaulish-Brittonic-Goidelic commonality following the Hispano-Celtic split is implied by linguistic innovations shared by this subgroup, such as the uninflected enclitic relative pronoun **io*. But Lugus occurs on both sides, going back to the common ancestor.

Palaeohispanic epigraphy is a field in which the present authors have lately worked as part of the Atlantic Europe in the Metal Ages (AEMA) project, funded by the UK's Arts and Humanities Research Council (AHRC), and one of us previously with the Hesperia

22 McCone 1996; cf. Isaac 2005.

Fig. 2. Predominantly Indo-European and non-Indo-European pre-Roman onomastic zones of the Iberian Peninsula, as characterized by place-names in *briga* and *il(t)i*, respectively. *Briga* and *brig-s* are Celtic or both Celtic and Lusitanian.

Their original meaning was 'height, hill', subsequently 'hillfort', and apparently simply 'major town' in the Roman period. The dashed green line represents the approximate boundary between the zones. Indo-European (mostly Celtic) outliers in the *il(t)i* zone are printed in green italic type.

project in Spain. In refocussing presently on comparanda for *Lugus* and associated names from the Iberian Peninsula, a few points may be noted: (1) The material is relatively extensive. (2) Much of it is linked primarily or exclusively with Brythonic and/or Goidelic comparanda with less close, less numerous, or simply no analogues in Gaul. (3) Much of that Palaeohispanic comparanda was found in the west and north of the Peninsula, rather than the Celtiberian region in the eastern Meseta. This pattern could be a mere accident of survival, but there are other possibilities. The distribution could have to do with survivals in marginal areas, whereas cultural innovations emanating from the La Tène core region had transformed or obliterated older Common Celtic traditions. It could also be that the Atlantic seaways played more of a rôle in the spread of Celtic-language culture than has been generally recognized.

There are Palaeohispanic forms of the god's name with a nasal suffix, e.g.: BANDE LVGVNO.[23] The god's multiforms in the Iberian Peninsula include one probably feminine and one surely feminine example: LVGGONI ARGANTICAENI;[24] LVGVNIS | DEABVS | AVR(ELIVS) CEL(ER) | V.S.L.M.[25] The nasal suffix can be paralleled in Ogamic Primitive Irish personal names: MODDAGN[I] MAQI GATTAGN[I] MUCOI LUGUNI;[26] COVAGN[I]

23 HEp 17, 230 — Vale de Prazeres, Fundão, Castelo Branco.
24 Búa 2000, 274 — Villaviciosa, Oviedo.
25 HEp 6, 167; Beltrán, Jordán, Marco Simón 2005, 920 — altar in Atapuerca, Burgos.
26 CIIC 307 — Windgap, Waterford.

MAQ[I MU]C[OI] LUG[U]N[I];[27] VEQIKAMI MAQI LUGUNI;[28] [..]CANAVVI MAQ L[UGU]N[I].[29] The corresponding Old Irish name is *Luigne*. The epithet or second name in LVGGONI ARGANTICAENI is the exact cognate of the Early Breton woman's name *Argantken* 'beautiful in silver'.[30] It is also remarkable, in considering the Fourth Branch of the Mabinogi, to have a form of the name *Lugus* juxtaposed in this way with a compound beginning with the Proto-Celtic word for 'silver' **arganto-* < PIE **H_2erĝn̥to-*.

During the 1980s, significant progress was achieved on the decipherment of the South-western or 'Tartessian' inscriptions of the Early Iron Age, notably the pioneering work of J. A. Correa. He identified several probably Celtic elements in the SW corpus, most of which have won wider acceptance in subsequent scholarship. Most relevant to the present study is what was, until September 2008, the longest known SW inscription, J.1.1 'Fonte Velha 6' (Fig. 3):

> lok^{o}ob^{o}o niirab^{o}o t^{o}o aŕaia|i k^{a}alt^{e}e lok^{o}o|n ane naŕk^{e}e k^{a}ak^{i}iśiin|k^{o}olob^{o}|o ii t^{e}e·ro-b^{a}ar|e (b^{e})e t^{e}a|siioonii.

Correa[31] compared the opening words **lok^{o}ob^{o}o niirab^{o}o** with LVGVBO ARQVIENOBO and similar pared theonyms from the Roman Period inscriptions cited above, explaining **lok^{o}ob^{o}o** as the dative plural of the Celtic god's name *Lugu-* and deriving **niirab^{o}o** from PIE √*ner-* 'man, hero', also occurring in the group name Νεριοι in the north-west of the Peninsula. He proposed that the written form **lok^{o}ob^{o}o** probably represented */lugubo/* in light of the fact that the grapheme u was wholly absent from the 72-sign text. In all of this, Correa was followed by Untermann, Villar, Guerra, Koch and Jordán.[32] The **lok^{o}ob^{o}o niirab^{o}o** text is especially significant in that it probably dates to the 6th or 7th century BC, and is thus several centuries earlier than any other attestation of *Lugu-*. It also shows that the god had been worshipped as a group as early as this and using a pattern of diction essentially the same as that found formulaically in inscriptions of the Roman Period, e.g. LVGVBO ARQVIENOBO.

Although Correa's argument that **lok^{o}ob^{o}o** transcribes */lugubo/* is plausible, another possibility is that **Lugu-* had once had ablaut in its paradigm and that **lok^{o}ob^{o}o** reflects the full grade. As Kaufman argues,[33] it is more likely that the SW inscriptions conventionally write the diphthong */ou/* as simplex o than that the language had simplified the sound to */ō/* as early as the First Iron Age. The likelihood of full-grade form of *Lugu-* is suggested by several Palaeohispanic personal names, especially from Burgos: AMBATAE AIONCAE LOVGEI F.;[34]

27 CIIC 41 — Castlekeeran, Meath.
28 CIIC 113 — Knockshanawee, Cork.
29 CIIC 112 — Knockshanawee, Cork.
30 Cartulary of Quimperlé, AD 1126; Evans 1988, 549.
31 Correa 1981, 208; 1992, 99–100.
32 Untermann 1995, 255; Villar 2004, 261–3, 268; Guerra 2010; Koch 2013, 197–8; Jordán 2015, 309, 318, cf. also Jordán 2006.
33 Kaufman 2015, 60, 74.
34 Abásolo 1974a, 185 — Lara de los Infantes, Burgos.

[CA]LPVRNIAE AMBATAE LOVGEI F.;[35] ELAESVS PETOLVS LOVGEI PETRAIOCI F.;[36] AEMILIA LOVGO C. F. CLVNIENSIS;[37] BRVTTIA FESTA LOVGEIDOCVM;[38] LOVGESTERI CARANICVM;[39] SEGIO LOVGESTERICO AIONIS F.[40]

There is frequent overlap between the stock of divine names and personal names. As McManus points out,[41] a productive category of compound personal names in the Ogam inscriptions has divine names for their first element. These include: LUGUQRIT MA[QI] QRITT[I];[42] LUGUQRIT[TI MAQI] [ADDI]LONAS;[43] --] ECC MAQI L[UGUQ]RRIT[44] > OIr. *Luccreth*, for the second element cf. Welsh *prydydd* 'poet' < *k^{u}ritios* 'maker of forms', in which case these same ideas are found juxtaposed again in VELITAS LUGUTTI,[45] cf. OIr. *file*, gen. *filed* '(high-ranking) poet' and *Luigtheg*, gen. *Luigthig*[46] < **Lugutīko-*; CATVVIRR MAQI LUGUVVE[C];[47] LUGUVVECCA MAQI[--][48] > OIr. gen. *Lugech*, *Lugach*; LUGUDECCAS MAQI [...MU]COI NETA-SEGAMONIAS DOLATU BIGA-ISGOB[...];[49] [CU]NAMAQI LUGUDECA MUC[OI] CUNEA;[50] LUGUDUC MΛQI MAQIOC[--]CI[--].[51]

Personal names commencing with **Lugu-* also occur in the other early Celtic languages. Thus, in Gaulish: D M IVL(IAE) LVGVSELVAE VXORIS;[52] ELVONTIV IEVRV · ANEVNO OLICNO · LVGVRIX ANEVNICNO.[53] In Brythonic: *Louocatus* AD 509 x

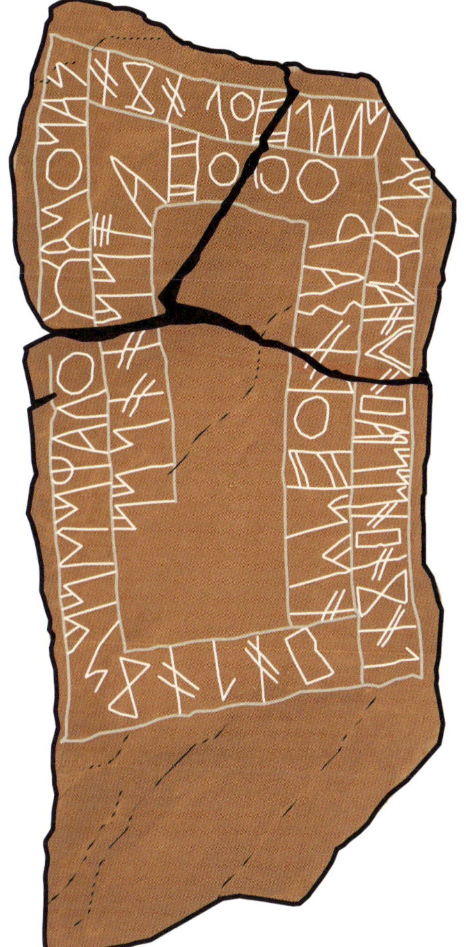

Fig. 3. South-western ('Tartessian') inscription 'Fonte Velha 6' (J.1.1 — Bensafrim, Lagos) 136 x 73 x 15cm.

35 AE 1980, 587 — Lara de los Infantes, Burgos.
36 Abásolo 1974a, 70 — Lara de los Infantes, Burgos.
37 AE 1973, 298 — Braga.
38 CIL II 3121; González Rodríguez 1986, nº 133 — Uclés, Cuenca.
39 CIL II 2849 = CIL II 5797; HEp 10, 589 —Pozalmuro, Soria.
40 Palol & Vilella 1987, 81; HEp 2, 141; HEp 13, 202 — San Juan del Monte, Burgos.
41 McManus 1991, 103.
42 CIIC 146 — Reask, Kerry.
43 CIIC 68 — Kilcaskan, Cork.
44 CIIC 207 — Kilcoolaght, Kerry.
45 CIIC 251 — Crag, Kerry.
46 McManus 1991, 108.
47 CIIC 221 — An Drom Loiscthe [Dromlusk], Kerry.
48 CIIC 140 — Áth an Charbaill [Aghacarrible], Kerry.
49 CIIC 263 — Ardmore, Waterford.
50 CIIC 286 — Kilgrovan, Waterford.
51 CIIC 108 — Kilcullen South, Cork.
52 CIL XIII 996; Raybould & Sims-Williams 2007, 65 — Périgueux.
53 RIG II.1, L-4 — Genouilly.

521[54] < **Lugu-catu-s*, OW *Louhelic*,[55] *Loumarch*,[56] Old Cornish *Loumarch* Bodmin Manumissions (twice) also once written *Leumarch* < **Lugu-marco-s* 'stallion of Lugus', *Leucum* Bodmin Manumissions < **Lugu-coimo-s* 'dear to Lugus', cf. the place-name *Lugu-ualium* > Old Welsh *Cair Ligualid* 'Carlisle'.[57]

**Lugu-* also occurs in other name-formation types in the various early Celtic languages. It is the second element in a recurring compound name in the Ogam corpus: NETTAVROECC [KOI] MAQI MUCCOI TRENALUGGO;[58] TTRENALUGOS,[59] cf. OIr. *Trianlug*. The following Gaulish examples probably show suffixed forms of *Lugu-* rather than compounds: NAMNIA SVLLA LIVI LVGAVN[I] A(AVLI) LIVI VIND[I]LICIANI LIVIVS LVGAVNVS POSVIT;[60] LVGIOLAE;[61] LVGISSIV[S;[62] cf. also CVM LVGARIO SEPTANII F. / LVGARIVS SEPTANII F.[63] The simplex occurs as a woman's name in the west and centre of the Iberian Peninsula: LVGVA CADDECVN;[64] [A]TTA LVGVA CARAECICVM EBVRENI VXOR.[65]

In the lists above, the name recurring in Ogam forms as LUGUDECCAS, LUGUDECA, and LUGUDUC can be etymologized as **Lugu-dek-* 'serving the god Lug'.[66] The same compound name is found in Gaulish and Hispano-Celtic: D M LVGVDECA(E) PIAE(?) C[O] NIVG(I) GRAT(A)E [ET] GRAECINO FILI[S] PO[S(VIT)];[67] VALERIO ANNONI LVGVADICI F. VXAMENSIS.[68] The Old Irish form of this name is *Luguid* or *Lugaid*, gen. *Luigdech*, fairly common in Early Irish literature. *Lugaid Mac Con* is the name of an important and ambivalent figure in Irish legendary history, a king of Ireland reckoned to have ruled a few centuries before St Patrick's time. This Lugaid is the central figure of the lengthy Old Irish tale *Cath Maige Mucrama* ('The Battle of Mag Mucrama'). One key episode in this narrative can be understood as motivated by beliefs associated with the hero's name, *Lugaid* < **Lugu-dek-s*. In this part of the tale, Lugaid and his warband have left Ireland in exile and receive hospitality from the king of Alba (Britain or north Britain). They seek to conceal which one of them is Lugaid, their leader. To force this information out of them, their host offers them a meal of mice with their pelts on. Somehow, Lugaid's identity is uncovered through his men's behaviour in this memorably revolting, but poorly motivated episode. As argued in Koch 1999, the original point, which the handlers of the extant *Cath Maige Mucrama* had lost sight of, was not that eating mice was disgusting,

---

54 LHEB 14; Lapidge & Sharpe 1985 it. 823.
55 Lib. Lan. 249.
56 AC 903.
57 HB §66a.
58 CIIC 26 — Donaghmore, Kildare.
59 CIIC 120 — Montaggart, Cork.
60 CIL XIII 804 — Bordeaux.
61 CIL XIII 3043 — Paris.
62 CIL XIII 11313 — Trier.
63 AE 1983, 477 — Vila Nova de Gaia, Pontevedra.
64 HEp 1, 400; ERPL, 395 — La Remolina, León.
65 FE 340; ERAv 134; HEp 13, 71 — Narros del Puerto, Ávila.
66 Uhlich 2002, 409.
67 CIL XIII 5926 — Bourbonne-les-Bains.
68 CIL II 2732, 142 — Segovia.

but that someone named *Lugaid* < **Lugu-dek-s* 'serving the god Lugus' could not eat *lochaid* 'mice' < **lukotes* (nom. sg. *luch* < **lukot-s*), because his name was too similar to the animal's. He would insult a king and risk his life rather than eating his totem. This example is a reminder that, when we compare various kinds of evidence associated with Lugus, the domains of etymological meaning, traditional narrative, and the phonological surface of the language are intertwined and do not evolve independently.

Koch (1992) draws attention to further pivotal episodes in Irish and Welsh tales in which words sounding like *Lug* and *Lleu* are conspicuously avoided. In the Ulster Cycle, there is a recurrent oath, the form of which varies somewhat, but is basically *tongu do dia toinges mo thuath*, meaning 'I swear to the god to whom my people swear' or, as a headless relative, 'I swear to god what my people swear'. Old Irish *tongu* 'I swear' is a suppletive verb. Its verbal noun is *lugae* 'oath' (later *luige*), and that is the word that is avoided here in a roundabout way. The supernatural character Lug has a special rôle in the Ulster cycle as the otherworldly father of the central hero Cú Chulainn in the complex, and textually early birth tale *Compert Con Culainn*. Lug also reappears at a dramatic turning point in the Ulster Cycle's lengthy central saga *Táin Bó Cúailgne*. The reader will therefore think that it is Lug that Cú Chulainn has in mind when he swears the oath as a challenge, gearing up for heroic exploits, in the 'boyhood deeds' section of the first recension of TBC. The wording there is *tongu do dia toingte Ulaid* 'I swear to the god by whom the Ulster folk swear'.

In the Fourth Branch of the Mabinogi, a large chunk of the action turns on three episodes in which the protagonist Lleu's mother Ar(y)anrot swears prohibitive destinies on her son. With these, she seeks to thwart him in attaining full adult personhood, by denying him a name, arms, and a wife. Each time the wording of the oath is almost verbatim: *mi a dynghaf dyghet iδau...* 'I swear a destiny on him...' It is the first of these oaths, intended to prevent Lleu from getting his name, that makes the underlying wordplay apparent: *mi a dynghaf dyghet iδau, na chaffo enw yny caffo y genhyf i* 'I swear a destiny on him, that he not get a name until he gets it from me'. Later, Ar(y)anrot is tricked into giving the boy the name *Lleu*, as the outcome of the shoemaker episode. A malveolent mother attempting to thwart her child's destiny to get his name *Lleu* could hardly do so formalizing her curse with words that included the nearly homophonous *llw* 'oath', the usual object of *tyngaf* 'I swear'. The audience will have felt the tension slyly built by not saying *mi a dyngaf lw i Leu* 'I swear an oath to Lleu'. But Ar(y)anrot is finally outsmarted, so that the name she has carefully avoided slips out. Putting the oaths of the Ulster Cycle and the Fourth Branch together, what is pointedly not being said is word-for-word the same, implying a common source: **toṇgū (do) Luguei lugi̯om* 'I swear an oath to Lugus'.

Cognates of OIr. *tocad* gl. 'fors', MW *tynghet* 'fate, destiny, luck'[69] occur as personal names in Goidelic, Brythonic, and most abundantly across the centre-west of the Indo-European zone of the Iberian Peninsula : Ogam TOGITTAC[C] MAQ[I] SAGARET[TOS],[70]

69 Matasović 2009 sn. **tonketo-*.
70 CIIC 172 — Ballywiheen [Baile Uí Bhaoithín], Kerry.

cf. OIr. nom. *Toicthech*, TVNCCETACE VXSOR DAARI HIC IACET,[71] both TOGITTAC[C] and TVNCCETACE are genitives meaning 'Fortunate'; IVLIA L. F. TONCETA;[72] TONCETA MATER;[73] IVLIA C. F. TONCETA;[74] TONGETA BOVTI F.;[75] TONGETA TANCINI F.;[76] TONGETA PROBINAE LIB.;[77] TONGETAE PITINNAE;[78] TONGETA TVLORI F.;[79]] TONGETERI F. CLVN(IENSIS);[80] TONGETAE RVFI;[81] TONGETA PETOBI;[82] TONGETAE ALVQVI F.;[83] TONGETO ARANTO;[84] IVLIA TONGETA;[85] IVLIA RVFA TONGETI F.[86]

Palaeohispanic *Toncetamos* can be understood either as a superlative 'most fortunate' or based on the ordinal numbers, 'sequenced auspiciously', cf. ROTAMVS TRI[T]EI CAT[---][87] ~ Vedic *prathamá* first', *pratamá* 'foremost', *prathama-já* first-born': [T]ONCIVS [T]ONCETAMVS F. MILES SIGNIFER COH. II LVS.;[88] TONGETAMVS CAVNI F.;[89] ARA(M) POS(VIT) TONCIVS TONCETAMI F. ICAEDIT(ANVS) MILIS TREBARVNE L.M.V.S.;[90] TALAVS TONCETAMI F. BOVTIE(CVM);[91] OVRISONI TONCETAMI F.;[92] RVFINA RVFI TONGETAMI F.[93]

From the preceding list, it appears that Palaeohispanic *Toncius/Tongius* could occur in the same families as *Toncetamus* and used in ways consistent with being a different formation from the same root: TONCIVS ANDAI[--- F.];[94] TONGIVS;[95] TONGIV[S];[96] TONGI;[97] BOVDICAE TONGI F. MATRI;[98] CELTIVS TONGI F.;[99] TONGIVS BOVTI F.;[100]

---

71 CIIC 451 — St Nicholas, Pembrokeshire.
72 CIL II 295 — Odrinhas, Lisbon.
73 AE 1971, 164c — Collipo, Leiria.
74 CIL II 296 418 — Torres Vedras, Lisbon.
75 CIL II 620; CPILC 524; CILCC I, 101; HEp 3, 122 — Brozas, Cáceres.
76 CIL II 5349; CPILC 80 — Belvís de Monroy (Cáceres).
77 AE 1967, 172 — Idanha-a-Velha, Idanha-a-Nova, Castelo Branco.
78 FE 402 — Torre de Coelheiros, Évora, Évora.
79 FE 107; HEp 2, 828 — Amieira do Tejo, Nisa, Portalegre.
80 HEp 13, 1003; AE 2004, 708 — São Salvador de Aramenha, Marvão, Portalegre.
81 HEp 2, 904 — Cárquere, Resende, Viseu.
82 HEp 2, 896 — Lamas de Moledo, Castro Daire, Viseu.
83 CIL II 5248 — Región de Lamego, Viseu.
84 HEp 7, 1286 — Cárquere, Resende, Viseu.
85 Vasconcellos 1913, 455–7 — Cárquere, Resende, Viseu.
86 HEp 5, 55 — Badajoz.
87 AE 1986, 293 434 — São Martinho de Mou, Viseu.
88 AE 1896, 1418 — Fundão, Castelo Branco.
89 HEp 1, 207 — Villamiel, Cáceres.
90 EE VIII 15; ILER 941 — Idanha-a-Velha, Idanha-a-Nova, Castelo Branco.
91 Albertos 1975a, 2. 212. nº 234 — Yecla de Yeltes, Salamanca.
92 ERZamora, 171 — Domez, Zamora.
93 CIL II 447 — Idanha-a-Velha, Idanha-a-Nova, Castelo Branco.
94 EE VIII 10; Encarnação 1984, 574 — Elvas, Portalegre.
95 CPILC 738 — Calzadilla de Coria, Cáceres.
96 CPILC 592 — Valencia de Alcántara, Cáceres.
97 Almeida 1956, 227, nº 135 — Idanha-a-Velha, Idanha-a-Nova, Castelo Branco.
98 AE 1967, 170; Albertos 1983, 872 — Telhado, Fundão, Castelo Branco.
99 AE 1934, 22; Encarnação 1984, 638 — Montalvão, Nisa, Portalegre.
100 CPILC 47; CILCC I, 71 — Arroyo de la Luz, Cáceres.

Fig. 4. Geograhical distribution of names in *Tonc-* and *Tong-* in the Iberian Peninsula.

TVOVTAE TONGI F.;[101] CATVENVS TONGI F.;[102] CILVRA TONGI;[103] MAELONI TONGI F.;[104] ALEINIVS TONGI F(ILIVS) GENIO AMMAIENCIS;[105] MAELO TONGI F. / TONGIVS;[106] AVITAE TONGI F.;[107] C. IVLIVS TONGIVS;[108] CAMIRA TONGI F.;[109] RVFVS TONGI F.;[110] TITANVS TONGI F.;[111] FLACCO TONGI F.;[112] TONGIO TANCINI F.;[113] TONGIVS SVNVAE F.;[114] TONGIVS VIROTI;[115] [T]ONGIVS L. GOVTI;[116] A. C. NORBANI TONGI F.;[117] MATERNVS TONG[I];[118] NIGER TONGI F.;[119] TONGIVS TANGINI F.;[120] TANGINVS TONGINAE F.;[121]

101 HAE 1172; Almeida 1956, 133 — Idanha-a-Velha, Idanha-a-Nova, Castelo Branco.
102 CPILC 221; HEp 8, 77 — Coria, Cáceres.
103 AE 1967, 167 — Idanha-a-Velha, Idanha-a-Nova, Castelo Branco.
104 AE 1977, 364 — Fundão, Fundão, Castelo Branco.
105 HEp 13, 1001; AE 2004, 706 — São Salvador de Aramenha, Marvão, Portalegre.
106 CIL II 749; CPILC 89; CILCC I, 107 — Brozas, Cáceres.
107 AE 1967, 167 — Idanha-a-Velha, Idanha-a-Nova, Castelo Branco.
108 CIL II2/7, 956; HEp 7, 147 — Monterrubio de la Serena, Badajoz.
109 CIL II 757; CPILC 25; Albertos 1977b, 38; CILCC I, 26 — Alcántara, Cáceres.
110 CIL II 729; AE 1968, 214; CPILC 586 = CPILC 596 — Valencia de Alcántara, Cáceres.
111 CIL II 795 & *add.* p. 826; CPILC 202; M. Beltrán 1975–76, 26; Melena 1985, 498; AE 1977, 388 — Ceclavín, Cáceres.
112 AE 1967, 167 — Idanha-a-Velha, Idanha-a-Nova, Castelo Branco.
113 CIL II 5310; CPILC 269 — Hoyos, Cáceres.
114 CIL II 757; CPILC 25; Albertos 1977, 38; CILCC I, 26 — Alcántara (Cáceres).
115 CPILC 221; HEp 8, 77 — Coria, Cáceres.
116 CIL II 840; CPILC 188 = CPILC 662 — Cáparra, Cáceres.
117 CPILC 734; CILCC I, 371 — Valdefuentes, Cáceres.
118 AE 1985, 529; FE 67 — Proença-a-Velha, Idanha-a-Nova, Castelo Branco.
119 HAE 1173 — Idanha-a-Velha, Idanha-a-Nova, Castelo Branco.
120 AE 1967, 181 — Idanha-a-Velha, Idanha-a-Nova, Castelo Branco.
121 HEp 4, 1051; HEp 5, 1019 — Condeixa-a-Velha, Condeixa-a-Nova, Coimbra.

PROCVLO TONG(I)NI F.[122]

Uncertainty over the first element of the name of Lleu's mother in the Fourth Branch, *Ar(y)anrot*, was canvassed by Williams.[123] It has never been fully resolved subsequently whether this is a reflex of PC **arganto-* 'silver' or a term now limited to place-names.[124] The two Middle Welsh manuscript copies consistently spell the name *Aranrot*, which most translators have modernized as *Aranrhod*. However, the form *Aryanrot* occurs in the Welsh Triads and some medieval poetry, that is, Modern Welsh *Arianrhod* 'silver' + 'wheel'. It is at any rate apparent that some of the medieval Welsh poets and scribes, working within the framework of their language and tradition, thought that first element of Lleu's mother's name was 'silver'. Early forms of the name of one of the female saints of Brycheiniog favour the 'silver' interpretation or at least confirm that it is phonologically possible. The most archaic spelling for this name occurs in the *Cognatio Brychan* text, spelled *Arganwen*,[125] which clearly contains PC **arganto-* 'silver' and must go back to a written source of the Old Welsh period. In *De Situ Brecheniauc*, which survives in a manuscript of *c.* 1200, the same figure is *Aranwen*.[126] In the *Plant Brychan* tract, she is *Aryanwen*.[127] These variants can be explained as follows. As the first element of a compound, and thus not accented in Old Welsh, *argan(t)-* 'silver' regularly became *aran-*, i.e. the lenited *g-* simply disappeared. However, this sound shift tended to be reversed to *aryan-* as the compounds were correctly understood to contain the common word, the high-frequency isolated form of which was *aryan(t)* silver, which had always been fully accented and therefore less prone to phonetic reduction. An analogous development is found with the word for 'iron', which was also found in Brythonic names. In Old Breton, one finds *Iarn-* as an unaccented first element and *hoiarn* in final position under the accent. This distribution is probably the phonologically regular one, and examples with *Hoiarn-* as first element involve an analogical restoration of the most common form of the common word to all positions, e.g.: *Iarnuueten*;[128] *Hoiarnuueten*.[129]

The Palaeohispanic divine name and epithet LVGGONI ARGANTICAENI was mentioned above. Similarly, 'silver' is found as the first element of a compound name in the bilingual Latin–Cisalpine Gaulish inscription of Vercelli: ARGANTOCOMATERECVS / ARKATOKO⟨K⟩MATEREKOS.[130] Simplex 'silver' is found several times as a personal name in the Celtiberian area, notably as a feminine name in the third long inscription from Botorrita:[131] **arkanta mezukenoskue abokum**;[132] **arkanta loukanikum**;[133] **arkanta**

122 EE IX 127; CPILC 644; Melena 1985, 489 — Villamiel, Cáceres.
123 Williams 1930, 269.
124 Cf. Hughes 2000, xxiii–xxvii.
125 Bartrum 1966, 18.
126 Bartrum 1966, 15.
127 Bartrum 1966, 82 & n.
128 CR §86 AD 865, §169 AD 863, §170 AD 866.
129 CR §97 AD 842/8.
130 RIG II.1, E-2.
131 K.1.3 – Botorrita, Zaragoza.
132 III-11.
133 K.1.3.

Figure 5. Geograhical distribution of names in *Arganto-* 'silver' in the Iberian Peninsula.

teiuantikum tirtunos;[134] **arkanta toutinikum**;[135] **arkanta ailokiskum**;[136] **arkanta**;[137] SEMPRONIA ARGANTA;[138] ARGANTO MEDVTICA MELMANIQ(VM).[139] Cf. the Old Breton simplex personal name *Argant*.[140] The simplex also occurs as a Celtiberian kindred name with a velar sufix: [T]OVTONI ARGANTIOQ(VM) ABALI F.[141]

In the western Peninsula, the oldest example of 'silver' in a personal name, or anywhere, is the suffixed form Ἀργανθωνιος,[142] the name of the beneficent philo-Greek king of the silver-based polity of Ταρτησσος (very probably centred on present-day Huelva). His phenomenal 80-year reign notionally spanned *c.* 625–*c.* 545 BC. This name recurs in the Roman Period, again in the west: FLACCVS ARGANTON(I) MAGILANCVM MIROBRIGENSIS.[143]

In Old Breton, compound personal names beginning with 'silver' are common: *Arganthael*,[144] *Argantlon*,[145] *Argantlouuen*,[146] *Argantmonoc*.[147] *Argantken* was mentioned above. Amongst the Old Cornish names of the Bodmin Manumissions, one finds *feminam Arganteilin* and *Argantmoet*.

134 III-21.
135 III-44.
136 III-53.
137 IV-20.
138 HEp 8, 275; HEp 10, 291 — Saelices, Cuenca.
139 AE 1916, 73; Abascal 1983, 22 — Riba de Saelices, Guadalajara.
140 CR §109, AD 869.
141 IRPP 42; HEp, 6, 578 — Palencia.
142 Herodotus 1.163–5.
143 CPILC 34; HEp 13, 232; CILCC I, 200 — Garrovillas, Cáceres.
144 CR §176, AD 841–51.
145 CR §189, AD 841–48; §131, AD 821/27/32.
146 CR §136, AD 842.
147 CR §255, AD 820/26.

Much of the action in the Fourth Branch of the Mabinogi is directed by character who acts as the foster-father for young Lleu. In Middle Welsh sources his name is spelled *Guydyon*, *Gwydyon*, amd *Gwytyon*. The modernization is *Gwydion*. Rhŷs recognized an earlier tradition in the Old Welsh genealogies of British Library MS 3859 in the sequence:[148] ... *Lou Hen map Guidgen map Caratauc map Cinbeli*n *map Teuhant* ... This series represent rulers of the remote past. The first three are historical, belonging to the time of the Claudian invasion of Britain and the end of the pre-Roman Iron Age: Caratācos †AD 58, his father Cunobelinos †*c.* AD 41, and Cunobelinos's father Tasciouanos, who ruled *c.* 20 BC–AD 10. The first two are attested in both Roman histories and pre-Roman coin legends. Tasciouanos is known only from coinage and Welsh genealogies.[149] *Lou* is the Old Welsh form of *Lugus*. Like its Old Irish cognate *sen*, Welsh *hen* 'old' usually precedes its noun. Where *hen* follows a name in genealogies, this may indicate an ancestor figure. *Guidgen* therefore appears to be the Old Welsh form of *Gwydion*. This is not a regular phonological development; rather, the old name has been assimilated to the pattern of names of supernatural figures in Welsh tales, such as *Riannon*, *Teirnon*, *Mabon*, and *Modron*. This suffix goes back to that found in Gaulish and Brythonic divine names of the pagan period, such as *Epona*, as well as *Maponos* and *Mātrona* which correspond to the last two Welsh names. It is interesting to note that this name type appears to have been expanding productively in medieval Welsh literature. OW *Guidgen* is a compound of words derived from the Proto-Celtic roots **u̯idu-* 'wood' and **geno-* 'be born', both of which are productive in onomastics, though this compound name itself is not common. Another possible example is the Goidelic or Gaelicized *Fedgenus*, the name of the brother of an abbot of Iona, Uirgnou the Briton, who died in 623.[150]

As proposed by Wodtko,[151] the Palaeohispanic dedication MVNIDI FIDVENEARVM HIC[152] 'can plausibly be connected to PIE **wid^{h}u-* "tree, wood"'. As explained above in connection with the examples MEDVGENVS and MEDVENI, *-g-* was frequently lost at the beginning of the second element of Palaeohispanic compound names, much of the evidence being from the western Peninsula and involving specifically **geno-* 'be born' as the second element and following a first element ending in *-u-*. Therefore, Wodtko's proposal allows that FIDVENEARVM possibly reflects a native divine name which was originally (nominative) **U̯idugeniās*, meaning '(goddesses) associated with *U̯idu-genos' or specifically '(divine) daughters of *U̯idu-genos'. With a little imagination, the *Fidueneae* could be 'goddesses conjured from the wood', reminiscent of Blodeuweδ conjured from flowers by Math and Gwydyon to create a bride for Lleu, in the Fourth Branch. In short, we might be dealing with the cognate of Old Welsh *Guidgen*, the precursor of *Gwydyon* in the Mabinogi.

However, this is uncertain. Wodtko scrutinized the Paços de Ferreira inscription

148 Rhŷs 1892, 551 n. 1.
149 Koch 1987.
150 Herbert 1988, 39.
151 Wodtko 2009, 32.
152 CIL II 5607; HEp 10, 2000, 742— Paços de Ferreira, Eiriz, Porto.

because it might be considered evidence for Lusitanian or Lusitanian-Callaecian. The Indo-European sources of the consonant(s) written F in Lusitanian remain unresolved. If PIE **bh* had regularly become Lusitanian F in all environments, we would expect more examples, as **bh* had occurred frequently in the proto-language. If, on the other hand, the F- in FIDVENEARVM is parallel to the development in Goidelic (e.g. OIr. *fid* 'wood, tree' < PC **u̯idu* < PIE **u̯idhu-*), its rarity could be explained by the lateness of the change, just beginning to make its appearance when the pre-Roman language(s) of the western Peninsula died out.

This paper closes turning to the second epigram at the top, Matthew Arnold's well-known metaphor for the profound and mysterious mythological roots of the Mabinogi. It hardly needs pointing out how passé its attitude to the subject is. Nonetheless, the up-to-date scepticism over 'Mercury'=Lugus has more in common with Arnold's thinking than with some of the approaches to Celtic myth and religion pursued in the meantime. Where we have perhaps come full circle is that Celtic researchers today, like Arnold, do not expect big ideas to have survived coherently from Celtic religion into the Christian Middle Ages, with ancient gods and myths fully recoverable by way of the Irish and Welsh tales. Instead, we sift through what is called in Wales *glo mân*, the 'fine coal' or nitty-gritty, meaning here, the words and names, their meanings, and immediate associations, where these show a long-lasting and widespread currency. Today, Arnold's imagery is strikingly romantic and value-laden. But it is little more than a mystification of basic historical linguistics. Every human being in using language is 'pillaging an antiquity of which he does not fully possess the secret'. In their changing forms and meanings, the words used today had formerly been arranged to express innumerable now-lost ideas. For the Celtic languages and Celtic-speaking societies a transformative discontinuity coincided with the Conversion, end of the Western Empire, and Migration Period. The Continental Celtic languages that once stretched from Portugal to central Asia Minor disappeared. The Neo-Celtic that persisted in Ireland, Britain, and Brittany suddenly appeared very different from its ancient forerunners. Whether or not the thoughts articulated before this seismic fault-line were actually 'greater, cunninger, more majestical' than what followed, they were surely different.

BIBLIOGRAPHY

Abascal, J. M. 1983 'Epigrafía romana de la provincia de Guadalajara', *Wad-al-Hayara*, 49–115.

Abásolo Álvarez, J. A. 1974a *Epigrafía romana de la región de Lara de los Infantes*. Burgos, Diputación Provincial.

AEMA project: www.aemap.ac.uk

Albertos Firmat, M.ª L. 1975a *Organizaciones suprafamiliares en la Hispania antigua*, Studia Archaeologica 37, Valladolid.

Albertos Firmat, M.ª L. 1977 'Correcciones a los trabajos sobre onomástica indígena de M. Palomar Lapesa y M.ª Lourdes Albertos Firmat', *Emerita* 45, 33–54.

Albertos Firmat, M.ª L. 1983 'Onomastique personelle indigène de la Péninsule Ibérique sous la domination romaine', ANRW II 29.2, 853–92, Berlin.

Almeida, D. Fernando de 1956 *Egitânia. História e arqueologia*, Lisboa.

Arnold, M. 1867 *On the Study of Celtic Literature*. London. Smith, Elder and Co.

Beltrán Lloris, F., C. Jordán Cólera, & F. Marco Simón 2005, 'Novedades epigráficas en Peñalba de Villastar (Teruel)', *Palaeohispanica* 5, 911–56.

Bartrum, P. C. 1966 *Early Welsh Genealogical Tracts*. Cardiff, University of Wales Press.

Beltrán Lloris, M. 1975–76 «Aportaciones a la epigrafía y arqueología romana de Cáceres: 1. Epigrafía romana inédita de Cáceres», *Caesaraugusta* 39-40, 19–101.

Búa Carballo, J. C. 2000 'Estudio lingüístico de la teonima lusitano-gallega', Tesis Doctoral, Salamanca.

Búa Carballo, J. C. 2003 *Cosus. Una exemplo da epigrafía e relixíon*, Boletín Avriense.

Carey, J. 2010 'Celtic **lugus* "lynx": A Phantom Big Cat?', *Celtic Language, Law and Letters: Proceedings of the Tenth Symposium of Societas Celtologica Nordica*, Meijerbergs Arkiv för Svensk Ordforskning 38, ed. F. Josephson, 151–67.

Correa Rodríguez, J. A. 1981 'Nota a la inscipción tartesia GM.II', *Archivo español de arqueología* 54, 203–9.

Correa Rodríguez, J. A. 1992 'La epigrafía tartesia', *Andalusien zwischen Vorgeschichte und Mittelalter*, eds. D. Hertel & J. Untermann, 75–114. Cologne, Böhlau.

Dillon, M. 1948 *Early Irish Literature*. Chicago, University of Chicago Press.

Dillon, M. & N. K. Chadwick 1967 *The Celtic Realms*. New York, New American Library.

Encarnação, J. d' (1984) *Inscrições romanas do Conventus Pacensis* I-II, Coimbra.

Evans, C. 1988 'Women's Names in Early Brittany', *Proc. First North American Congress of Celtic Studies, Ottawa 1986*, ed. G. W. MacLennan, 545–53. Ottawa, Chair of Celtic Studies.

González Rodríguez, M.ª C. 1986 *Las unidades organizativas indígenas del área indoeuropea de Hispania*, Veleia Anejo 2. Vitoria/Gasteiz.

Guerra, A. 2010b 'Algumas observações sobre a escrita do Sudoeste', *Xelb 10: Actas do 7º Encontro de Arqueologia do Algarve. Silves – 22, 23 e 24 Outubro 2009*. Silves, Museu Municipal de Arqueologia de Silves.

Herbert, M. 1988 *Iona, Kells, and Derry: The History and Hagiography of the Monastic Familia of Columbia*. Oxford, Clarendon (reprinted, Blackrock, Four Courts Press, 1996).

Hesperia project: http://hesperia.ucm.es/consulta_hesperia/access.html

Hughes, I. 2000 *Math Uab Mathonwy: Pedwaredd Gainc y Mabinogi*. Aberystwyth, Adran y Gymraeg, Prifysgol Aberystwyth.

Isaac, G. R. 2005 'Insular Celtic vs Gallo-Brittonic: an Empirical and Methodological Question', *Celtic Connections: Papers from the Tenth International Congress of Celtic Studies, Edinburgh, 1995, 2. Archaeology, Numismatics, Historical Linguistics*, ed. W. Gillies & D. W. Harding, 190–202. University of Edinburgh Archaeology Monograph Series 2.

Jackson, K. H. 1964 *The Oldest Irish Tradition: A Window on the Iron Age*. Felinfach, Llanerch, 1999. First published, Cambridge, Cambridge University Press.

Jordán Cólera, C. 2006 '[K.3.3]: Crónica de un *teicidio* anunciado', *Estudios de lenguas y epigrafía antiguas – ELEA* 7, Real Academia de Cultura Valenciana, sección de Estudios Ibéricos "D. Fletcher Valls", 37–72.

Jordán Cólera, C. 2015 'Presente, pasado y futuro de la Paleohispanística', *Studia Classica Caesaraugustana. Vigencia y presencia del mundo clásico hoy: XXV años de Estudios Clásicos en la Universidad de Zaragoza*, Monografías de Filología Griega 25, eds. J. Vela Tejada, J. F. Fraile Vicente, C. Sánchez Mañas, 301–38. Zaragoza, Prensas de la Universidad de Zaragoza.

Kaufman, T. 2015 *Notes on the Decipherment of Tartessian as Celtic*, Journal of Indo-European Monograph Series 62. Washington DC, Institute of the Study of Man.

Koch, J. T. 1987 'llawr en asseδ "the Laureate Hero in the War-chariot" (*C*[*anu*] *A*[*neirin*] 932): Some Recollections of the Iron Age in the Gododdin', Études Celtiques 24, 253–78.

Koch, J. T. 1992 'Further to *tongu do dia toinges mo thuath*, &c.', *Études Celtiques* 29, 249–61.

Koch, J. T. 1999 'A Swallowed Onomastic Tale in *Cath Maige Mucrama*?', *Ildánach Ildírech: A Festschrift for Proinsias Mac Cana*, Celtic Studies Publications 4, ed. J. Carey, J. Koch, P.-Y. Lambert, 63–80. Aberystwyth, Celtic Studies Publications.

Koch, J. T. 2013 (1st edn. 2009) *Tartessian: Celtic in the South-west at the Dawn of History*, Celtic Studies 13. Aberystwyth.

Koch, J. T. 2016 'Phoenicians in the West and Break-up of the Atlantic Bronze Age', *Celtic from the West 3. Atlantic Europe in the Metal Ages: questions of shared language*. Celtic Studies Publications XIX, eds J. T. Koch, B. Cunliffe, C. D. Gibson, K. Cleary, 431–76.

Oxford, Oxbow Books.

Lapidge, M. & R. Sharpe 1985 *A Bibliography of Celtic-Latin Literature 400–1200*. Dublin, Royal Irish Academy.

Lhuyd, E. 1707 *Archaeologia Britannica, Giving some Account of the Languages, Histories and Customs of the Original Inhabitants of Great Britain: from Collections and Observations in Travels through Wales, Cornwal, Bas-Bretagne, Ireland and Scotland. Vol. I. Glossography.* Oxford, The Theater.

Mac Cana, P. 1970 *Celtic Mythology*. Library of the World's Myths and Legends. London, Chancellor, 1996. First published, Feltham, Hamlyn.

McCone, K. R. 1996 *Towards a Relative Chronology of Ancient and Medieval Celtic Sound Change.* Maynooth Studies in Celtic Linguistics I. Department of Old and Middle Irish, St Patrick's College, Maynooth.

McManus, D. 1991 *A Guide to Ogam*. Maynooth Monographs 4. Maynooth, An Sagart.

Maier, B. 1997 'Is Lug to be Identified with Mercury (Bell.Gall. VI 17, 1)? New Suggestions on an Old Problem', *Ériu* 47, 127–35.

Marco Simón, F. 2005 'Religion and Religious Practices of the Ancient Celts of the Iberian Peninsula', *e-Keltoi* 6: *The Celts in the Iberian Peninsula*, 287–345.

Matasović, R. 2009 *Etymological Dictionary of Proto-Celtic*, Leiden Indo-European Etymological Dictionary Series 9. Leiden/ Boston, Brill.

Melena, J. L. 1985 'Salama, Jálama y la epigrafía latina del antiguo Corregimiento', J. L. Melena (ed.), *Symbolae L. Mitxelena*, I, 475–530, Vitoria.

Palol, P. de & J. Vilella 1987 *Clunia II. La epigrafía de Clunia* [EAE 150]. Madrid.

Raybould, M. E. & P. Sims-Williams 2007 *The Geography of Celtic Personal Names in the Latin Inscriptions of the Roman Empire.* Aberystwyth, CMCS.

Rees, A. D. & B. Rees 1961 *Celtic Heritage: Ancient Tradition in Ireland and Wales.* London, Thames & Hudson.

Rhŷs, J. 1892 *Lectures on the Origin and Growth of Religion as Illustrated by Celtic Heathendom.* London, Williams and Norgate.

Sjoestedt, M.-L. 1994 *Gods and Heroes of the Celts*, trans. M. Dillon. Blackrock, Co. Dublin, Portland, OR, Four Courts Press, 1994. English trans. first published, London, Methuen, 1949.

Tovar Llorente, A. 1982 'The God Lugus in Spain', *Bulletin of the Board of Celtic Studies* 29, 591–9.

Uhlich, J. 2002 'Verbal governing compounds (synthetics) in Early Irish and other Celtic languages', *Transactions of the Philological Society* 100/3, 403–33.

Untermann, J. 1995 'Zum Stand der Deutung der "tartessischen" Inschriften', *Hispano-Gallo-Brittonica: Essays in Honour of Professor D. Ellis Evans on the Occasion of his Sixty-Fifth Birthday*, eds J. F. Eska, R. G. Gruffydd, & N. Jacobs, 244–59. Cardiff, University of Wales Press.

Vallejo Ruiz, J. M.ª 2013 'Hacia una definición del Lusitano', *Acta Palaeohispanica* XI / *Palaeohispanica* 13, 273–91.

Vasconcellos, J. Leite 1913 *Religiões da Lusitania* III, Lisboa.

Villar Liébana, F. 2004 'The Celtic Language of the Iberian Peninsula', *Studies in Baltic and Indo-European Linguistics in Honor of William R. Schmalstieg*, eds. P. Baldi & P. U. Dini, 243–74. Amsterdam, John Benjamins.

de Vries, J. 1977 *La religion des Celtes.* Paris, Payot. First published as *Keltische Relgion*, Stuttgart, Kolhammer Verlag, 1961.

Williams, I. 1930 *Pedeir Keinc y Mabinogi.* Caerdydd, Gwasg Prifysgol Cymru.

Wodtko, D. S. 2000 *Monumenta Linguarum Hispanicarum* 5.1, *Wörterbuch der keltiberischen Inschriften*, ed. J. Untermann. Wiesbaden, Ludwig Reichert.

Wodtko, D. S. 2009 'Language Contact in Lusitania', *International Journal of Diachronic Linguistics and Linguistic Reconstruction* 6, 2009, 1–48.

III

TYRANNIES OF DISTANCE? MEDIEVAL SOURCES AS EVIDENCE FOR INDIGENOUS CELTIC AND ROMANO-CELTIC RELIGION

Jonathan Wooding

Evidence from medieval Insular (British and Irish) sources has traditionally featured in discussions of Celtic religion in the Roman period and earlier. Methodological issues arise from the comparison of the main data-sets for Romano-Celtic religion with later sources, from what had been a far corner of the Roman world; these include issues of possible anachronism and regional difference, as well as differences of priority between Classical and medieval studies.

THE study of Celtic religion, as is well-known, presents challenges that arise from limited data, but also their concentration in different periods in widely-separated locations. One solution is to treat religion mainly as a phenomenon local to the different Celtic-speaking regions—an approach that in some ways converges with recent trends in studies of Celtic identity, as well as Roman provincial religion.[1] To limit our interest only to the widely-separated contexts of our sources, however, runs the risk of treating absence of evidence as evidence of absence. Remaining at issue in this case, moreover, is a substantial body of literary evidence from Insular (medieval British and Irish) sources that appears to refer, not just to local indigenous deities and institutions, but to ones shared with the Continental Celts. The evidence, dating mostly from the medieval period, has often been treated, with varying degrees of restraint, as an inheritance from a unitary 'Celtic' religious system in Antiquity.[2] Such treatment is qualified by some particular revisionist trends that developed across the second half of the twentieth century. One of these was a focus on local sources of cultural innovation that was a response to earlier 'diffusionist' or 'migrationist' models of later prehistory; it tends to highlight the separateness of Britain and Ireland from other regions in which

1 Sims-Williams 2013; Haeussler 2012; Ando 2005; Webster 2015.
2 For example: Ross 1967, 42–4; Green 1990. Useful summary in Hutton 2011, 59–60.

Celtic languages were spoken in Antiquity.[3] Another trend, arising from medieval Celtic studies, was against 'nativism'—the desire to recover data concerning earlier culture, including pre-Christian religion, from medieval Irish and Welsh narratives. This critical trend has placed a strong emphasis on the Christian context of writing of these narratives, diminishing their claims to represent legacies of pre-Christian culture. Notwithstanding the sometimes polemical force of these revisionist trends—or perhaps because of it—there is a general lack of clear consensus in the resultant positions. The main issues should be familiar to scholars working in the field of Insular Celtic Studies—but, as Mark Williams has recently observed, we might be unwise to take even that for granted.[4] The very sporadic theoretical discussion of these issues is certainly an obstacle to those whose interest in this evidence is more religious than literary. In this short discussion, which will inevitably be a somewhat personal reflection on the debates, I will attempt to map some changing perceptions in criticism, as well as point up some important recent contributions.

As an aid to focusing a reflection on a very diverse debate, I will centre my approach on a single theme: distance.[5] There are a number of different ways that distance is at issue in the revisionist debates and their aftermath. One conception of distance here is the distance in time which we envisage between medieval sources and the actual currency of pre-Christian religion. There is also a cultural distance envisaged between the mentalities of 'Christian' writers and their 'pagan' ancestors. Another conception of distance is the physical distance presumed between the Insular (British and Irish) cultures and those of the Continent. Historiography, also, may be interrogated in terms of distance. What Owen Chadwick, writing on the study of Christianity in the Celtic nations, termed the 'remarkable assumption of difference' is actually a broader problem in studies of Insular religious culture.[6] Revisionist critics have, for example, been surprisingly slow to reach outside the local context to compare the historical experience of conversion and contextualisation in other countries. Tacit assumptions of isolation haunt many of the approaches.

Let us first, however, look briefly at the key data-sets that are at issue. Hiberno-Latin authors such as, for example, Tírechán, Augustinus Hibernicus, Cogitosus, and Muirchú have left a substantial body of seventh-century narratives that make very brief, but plausible, allusions to pre-Christian beliefs in Ireland. These allusions include ideas that might appear to be shared with Continental Celtic beliefs, such as transmigration of souls and belief in 'otherworlds'.[7] Some religious or ceremonial titles are shared between Classical and medieval sources; for example, Latin *druides*/Old Irish *druíd*; Greek *bardoi*/Welsh *beirdd*.[8] A phrase such as 'women's magic', is found in

3 James 1998, 17, 34-42; Raftery 1994; cf. Megaw & Megaw 1992, 258-9; Sims-Williams 1998a, 32.
4 Williams 2016, 45, responding to Wooding 2009, 61.
5 *Viz.* my title, which borrows a famous phrase from the Australian historian Geoffrey Blainey.
6 Chadwick 1954, 175.
7 Patrick, *Confessio* ch. 41; Tírechán, *Collectanea* 26 (on the *síde*), 42 (on *magi*); Augustinus, *De mirabilibus* I.17 (on transmigration as a doctrine of the Irish *magi*).
8 Slavin 2018 (forthcoming).

similar form in Gaulish (*bnano[m] bricte*) and Old Irish (*brichta ban*). These apparent correspondences offer the possibility that similar conceptions of the supernatural existed across a considerable distance of time and space.[9] In Irish and Welsh vernacular literature, generally of a somewhat later date, the names of certain characters appear to be cognate with theonyms from Classical sources—for example, Lugus/Lugh/Lleu and Nodens/Nuadu/Nudd, amongst a number of others.[10] Such characters are sometimes overtly positioned in the sources so as to be understood as figures from pre-Christian eras—for example the conversations between characters of different eras in *Acallam na Senórach* (Colloquy of the Ancients), *Síaburcharpat Con Culaind* (Phantom Chariot of Cú Chullain), and *Immram Brain maic Febuil* (Voyage of Bran son of Febul), or the positioning of the Tuatha Dé Danann as penultimate settlers of Ireland in *Lebor Gabála Érenn* (Book of the Settlements of Ireland).[11] Most of the medieval references are not explicitly to gods *qua* gods, but to heroes, of whom some present plausible signs that they might be euhemerised gods—John Carey and Mark Williams, in important studies, argue that early Irish writers evince a uniquely thorough form of contextualisation.[12] Only a handful of sources appear to ascribe to early literary heroes, for example Labraid Loingsech and Mannanán Mac Lir, actual veneration as 'gods'—and these attributions are open to considerable interpretation.[13]

The correspondences in names and other features between Continental and Insular sources nonetheless are such that it does not require wild flights of the imagination to make connections here. This is worth saying, lest the weight of recent criticism incline us to see the older nativist interpretations as simply foolish or naïve. Naturally a great many alternative explanations can be, and now are, posited for the apparent convergences between Continental and Insular indigenous Celtic religions. As there is a shared basis in language, names of gods and heroes could be derived independently from the same, or similar, roots.[14] This might also be true for titles, such as '*druid/ druí*', without the requirement of this having been a shared institution across separate regions.[15] A concept such as 'women's magic'—already in Roman Gaul showing some resemblances to the witchcraft of the Middle Ages—may belong to a much wider paradigm which inspired similar names across a number of language groups.[16] The 'otherworlds' of the Classical-era druids, on examination, are not a particularly close match to those of medieval literature.[17] It is, nonetheless, important to observe here that offering viable alternative explanations does not itself amount to disproof.[18] In Augustinus Hibernicus' account of Irish beliefs regarding transmigration, for example,

9 Mees 2009, 55-6; cf. Maier 2013, 112–3.
10 For recent comment: Williams 2016; Sims-Williams 2011, 7–15; Hutton 2011, 64–8.
11 See especially Nagy 1983; Nagy 1997; Carey 1995; Carey 2015.
12 Williams 2016, 490–3; Carey 1999, 32.
13 Carney 1989, 50; cf. Breatnach 1992, 120; Carey 2008, 3–8; Williams 2016, 63–8.
14 Sims-Williams 2011, 10–1; Maier 1996, 128–9.
15 Hutton 2009, 32–3.
16 Maier 2013, 117.
17 Sims-Williams 2011, 54–5.
18 Cf. also McCone 2000, 57.

the parallels with Continental beliefs are notable.

The tone of the debate may be an obstacle here. It is hard not to see the more extreme expressions of scepticism regarding connections and continuities as deriving additional force from overreaction to the romantic populism that surrounds many Celtic topics. It is admittedly confusing that works aimed at a general audience persist in identifying medieval narratives as 'myths';[19] as Williams has recently noted: 'the nativist position in any simple form is long out of date in the academy ... many readers will recognize that a version of it continues to be recycled by popular writers on Celtic religion'.[20] What may indeed be puzzling to many outsiders is the polarized, even zero-sum, quality of the debate. Even within the academy, anyone wanting to gain a balanced view of what has replaced 'simple nativism' will find themselves struggling to reconcile views of dense, sometimes obscure, publications—while, as Williams observes, being offered more digestible fare that seems to ignore the revisionist debates altogether.[21] Nativism may be out of date, but what has replaced it is far from identifiable as a consensus—unless it be, as Seán Ó Coileán once said about the related debate concerning orality, a negative consensus 'of justified ignorance and bewilderment in the face of conflicting attitudes and theories'.[22]

Nativism and Archaism: Tyrannies of Distance in Time

Accordingly, at risk of going into too much of the backstory, it is probably helpful if we first unpack the nativism debate a bit here, to identify why the matter is so confusing. In the mid-twentieth century, approaches to the study of the medieval Irish and Welsh literature tended to a consensus that much of it was 'archaic' in content. It was also assumed that the extant medieval literature from Ireland and Wales—even that written in Latin—had a close proximity to an oral tradition that itself was the nearer end of a long continuum into prehistory. The 'passion for orality', as David Dumville terms it, had actually intensified from its Victorian origins by the mid-twentieth century; it may be seen as historically-situated in a nationalism in which formerly colonialist ideas concerning native peoples were subsequently adopted by the colonised themselves as a tool for decolonisation. At the centre of this process was a romantic belief in the exceptional conservatism of tradition in remote places and the purity of 'native tradition' in contrast to worldly culture.[23] The particular circumstances of nationalism in Celtic countries probably ensured the persistence of this conservative model there beyond its general currency elsewhere—long enough to gain renewed force from the

19 MacKillop 2005, xxiv–xxvii.

20 Williams 2016, 45–6.

21 As foundational reading, two lengthy book-reviews by Sims-Williams (1996) and Dumville (1996) are usefully read in conjunction with their subject: McCone 1990. Williams (2016, 38–71) is a recent helpful survey. Wooding (2009) reviews the issues in the light of cultural politics. Indispensible is Ó Cathasaigh 1984 (usefully reprinted in Ó Cathasaigh 2014, 35–50).

22 Ó Coileáin 1977, 7.

23 Dumville 1996, 390; Meek 2000, 57–9; O'Leary 1994, 14–52; Said 1988, 14–5.

mythologisms which emerged in the 1930s through '50s, in the work of scholars such as Georges Dumézil, Mircea Eliade, Lord Raglan, and the Welsh brothers Alwyn and Brinley Rees.[24] As late as the 1960s Kenneth Jackson, in influential studies of the Irish Ulster Cycle tales and of early Welsh poetry, was comfortable in seeing these as substantially preserving a snapshot of society hundreds of years previous to the extant versions.[25]

A very few examples of nativism, out of many, may also be useful here. In Wales in the 1920s through '50s, W. J. Gruffydd's foundational studies of the Four Branches of the *Mabinogi* identified a substratum of considerably older narrative—including euhemerised deities—in these eleventh-century Welsh tales.[26] In Ireland in the same period T. F. O'Rahilly was especially inclined to find deities lurking behind heroic protagonists of medieval narratives.[27] D. A. Binchy, studying medieval Irish law texts that comprise text and commentary of varying date, believed that he could idenitfy not only very early medieval strata in the laws, but even a discrete stratum that was composed before the advent of Christianity.[28] Alongside these attempts to reach into the nearer zones of prehistory, other Irish and Welsh scholars, enthused by the newer mythological theories, were using the medieval Celtic tradition as a source for myths of social structure from a much earlier, Indo-European, past.[29] If these debates have moved on, we should not see all of this as failed scholarship. It is fair to say that many critics have found synchronic use of theories of myth—what Tom Sjöblom terms the 'weak' form of the mythologist critique—to be productive in criticism of medieval literature.[30] Through the vagaries of selective reprinting, the monographs of O'Rahilly and the Rees brothers survive in print as one-sided conversations with mostly-forgotten adversaries, but they are not without value to informed readers. The idea that poetry with conservative metres could have a long life in oral tradition is still guardedly given considerable weight, as it is in other fields.[31]

Criticism in Insular Celtic Studies from the 1960s to present has, however, tended against both the idea of mimetic survivals from recent prehistory and mythological survivals from deeper prehistory.[32] What was at the beginning a grinding debate gained sudden traction in the 1980s with some notable empirical case-studies. In 1986 Jim Mallory's study of material representations in the Ulster Cycle tales indicated that the *mise-en-scène* of the world of Cú Chullain was more that of the late first millennium than the Iron Age, consistent with the date of composition of the extant tales.[33] In 1984 Liam Breatnach demonstrated that Binchy's archaic stratum in the laws included phrases translated from Latin Canon Law—at very least showing that this stratum was

24 Sjöblom 2004; Rees & Rees 1963.
25 Jackson 1963; cf. Sims-Williams 2012, 6–8; Sims-Williams 2016.
26 Jones 1975, 196–9; cf. Sims-Williams 2011.
27 O'Rahilly, 1953, 260–71.
28 Breatnach 1984, esp. 458–9.
29 Rees & Rees 1961.
30 Sjöblom 2004, 63–4; Nagy 2007, 8—also Nagy 2011 for a fine example.
31 Greene 1971; Sims-Williams 2016.
32 On mimetic and mythological survivals see Ó Cathasaigh 2014, 40, 42–3.
33 Mallory 1986, Mallory 1992.

not wholly pre-Christian in content.[34] These straightforward demonstrations were, however, followed by a somewhat factional polemic, which appropriated the more theoretical critique of literary 'nativism' that had been propounded by James Carney since the 1950s.[35] A 1990 monograph by Kim McCone was the only sustained attempt to define the extent of the debate—and it arguably failed to do this.[36] There was also only a limited response at this time from scholars of religion.[37] A direct approach by James Mackey at the time failed to gain much momentum, though it raised significant questions concerning the narrowness of the terms of the debate (see below).[38]

One of the reasons for these failures was perhaps that too much was lumped under the 'nativist' tag for the purposes of criticism. Carney's position against nativism was primarily a stand against the tendency to interpret early Irish literature as evidence of a long 'tradition', to the exclusion both of acknowledgment of the genius of individual authors and of comparability to contemporary literatures; in the words of Rachel Bromwich, failing to 'give to the mature literature and culture of the medieval Celtic nations the recognition to which it is entitled'.[39] The 'anti-nativism' of the 1980s and '90s, however, was more closely concerned with questions of the intent of 'Christian' writers in representing the 'pagan' past. It also engaged with theories of mythology which putatively reach into a deeper, pre-Celtic, Indo-European, past. A sharp criticism by Donnchadh Ó Corráin of this preoccupation with mythology provoked dissent amongst the main protagonists of the debate, arguably because it exposed the eclectic character of the debate.[40]

I hope this brief account has at least helped to contextualise the nativism debate. The productive legacies of anti-nativism are not in doubt. There has been a much sharper focus on Celtic narratives as literate works. New studies on the Patristic sources of Insular culture can be said to have revolutionised our understanding of the intellectual environment through which the earliest Insular Christians would have encountered their 'pagan past'.[41] Of more mixed value, perhaps, has been the tendency to place a stronger emphasis on texts in their immediate context, revaluing texts as medieval, rather than relics of a more ancient mythology. Here it is worth observing that the answer to nativism may not be to reclassify all our sources as 'medieval'. Elva Johnston, in an important study, has recently highlighted the fact that the Christianity that arrived in Ireland was late-Antique rather than medieval in cultural terms and that this has important implications for how we approach the question of religious change.[42] Even the earliest Irish hagiographies, whose models are often Patristic, might be seen

34 Breatnach 1984.
35 Carney 1955, 276, 298, 305.
36 Dumville 1996; Sims-Williams 1996; Ó Corráin 1994.
37 A welcome development now is a generation of scholars of religion credentialed in both in the philological disciplines and Religious Studies: Stausberg 2008, 32; Ritari & Bergholm 2015.
38 Mackey 1992a; Mackey 1992b.
39 Minutes of Cambridge Senate 1967 in Lapidge 2015, 256.
40 Ó Corráin 1994, 25.
41 See, especially, Borsje 1996; Carey 1999; O'Loughlin 1999.
42 Johnston 2013, 10–21.

as 'late-Antique'.[43] We need to assimilate fully the changes to our view of the conversion process. Up to the 1960s it was generally assumed that the 'Celtic' churches of Britain and Ireland were the product of a late, fifth to sixth century, process of Christianisation. We would now see the process as having begun substantially earlier, with the churches both of Britain and Ireland being extensions of a continuing Romano-British church.[44] Anthony Harvey and Cathy Swift, in studies from the 1980s and '90s respectively, drew attention to the evidence for late-Antique literacy, in the form of ogham, which may be continuous with medieval literacy in Ireland and Celtic Britain. If the anti-nativist critique initially invited us to retreat from associations of medieval literature with prehistoric tradition, there is a need now to return some of the evidence to a literate, late-Antique context, shaking off the legacy of a model in which Christian culture began suddenly in the fifth century.

To do this we need both clear dates and some ability to assess the extent of literacy. The survival of Insular manuscripts, or manuscripts containing texts of Insular origin, is mostly clustered into particular periods. Manuscripts of vernacular literature from Ireland and Wales, with the exceptions of some Latin manuscripts with marginalia, are all post-1000 AD; this likely represents a natural limit on the survival of materials rather than the floruit of composition of texts. Scholars such as Richard Sharpe, Breatnach, and Sims-Williams have cautiously sought to return to our consideration the existence of an early-medieval written, rather than oral, tradition—which might offset what Sims-Williams once described as an 'over-cautious positivism'.[45] There are new indicators we can draw upon to consider what has been lost of the early written tradition.[46] If we envisage earlier influences of literate culture this may also have implications for reassessing as literary, data that were once only envisaged in terms of oral transmission.[47]

Dating of extant texts presents many issues for both specialists and users of texts.[48] As McCone observed in 1996, with respect to Old Irish texts: 'a basic Old Irish date is all that can usually be aspired to except in the rare event that firm external dating criteria can be invoked'.[49] This view contrasts sharply with the confidence with which earlier scholars assigned dates. Accordingly, a scholar of religion approaching the text *Immram Brain maic Febuil* (the voyage of Bran son of Febul)—with its interesting references to a pre-Christian deity, Manannán—may be bemused to find it claimed for a seventh-century (Meyer), eighth-century (McCone), and even ninth/tenth-century date (Mac Mathúna).[50] Similar disagreement may be seen in recent treatment of Welsh

43 Harvey 1987, 13–4; Swift 1997—also see Sims-Williams (1998, 17–8) on the tendency to artificially separate Celtic epigraphy from other literacy.

44 Sharpe 2002, 94–105.

45 Sharpe 2010, 48–55; Breatnach 1992, 120–2; Sims-Williams 1998b, 32–3 and quote at 15.

46 Charles-Edwards & McKee 2018 (forthcoming).

47 E.g. Koch 1987; Koch 1990; Ó Riain 1982.

48 A very welcome initiative is the Chronologicon Hibernicum project, at Maynooth, led by Prof. David Stifter: https://www.maynoothuniversity.ie/chronologiconhibernicum.

49 McCone 1996, 31.

50 Meyer 1895, xv–xvi; Mac Mathúna 1985, 417; McCone 2000, 44, 66; on Manannán as a'god' see Meyer 1913, 78—also MacQuarrie 2004.

literature.[51] This matter is made more confusing for the non-specialist on account of the fact that many important sources are available only in pre-modern editions, whose apparatus, if not the text itself, are no longer state of the art. These will evince dates and interpretations at variance with modern studies.

The anti-nativist's attention to the extant text as a literary work also may unhelpfully converge with a conservative tendency of Celtic scholarship to confine attention to problems of extant texts. In his informative response to McCone's monograph Dumville noted the tendency in early Irish studies, linked to anti-nativism, in which a medieval text is read as 'utilitarian in character and propagandist in intent ... required to explain itself within narrow political and chronological frames'.[52] Often historical studies in Celtic nations are concerned with the editorial problems of individual texts.[53] The danger here is that we lose interest in history as it exists outside the most certain context of the sources;[54] whereas arguably it is also the task of the historian to find ways to give voice to people and topics who are not fully represented by documentary history. Conversion is one such topic, where histories are often written after the event, by servants of the incoming church. It is encouraging to see this topic returning to historical attention.[55]

Tyrannies of Distance: Space

The second category of distance evinced in our debates is distance in space. The trend against unitary conceptions of 'Celtic' has made much of the difference of British Celtic-speakers from Gauls,[56] and Irish archaeologists have made much of the limited impact of external influences in late Iron-Age Ireland.[57] Also of note here for religion scholars is the basic assumption of difference found in the once popular thesis that Irish indigenous religion was essentially 'magic' rather than religion.[58] Inherent in these conceptions is the idea that, in prehistory, the regions that would become the medieval Celtic world were remote and different from the larger nations that caught the attention of Classical writers.

In comparing Classical-era culture on the Continent with medieval Insular sources, Sims-Williams observes that 'a problem for rational people is the geographical distance between the ancient and modern Celtic-speaking peoples who are being compared'.[59] The distances involved are not, however, exactly eye-watering—especially when we consider the distances spanned by some early cultures. The English Channel, separating

51 Rodway 2013, 1–34.
52 Dumville 1996, 395.
53 Davies 1983, 67; Byrne, 1971, 2.
54 See Ó Cathasaigh (2014, 43–4) on 'textualism'.
55 Flechner & Ní Mhaonaigh 2016—unfortunately this book appeared too late for me to take account of its treatment of a number of points treated here.
56 James 1998.
57 Raftery 1980; Raftery 1994.
58 For summary and critique see Mackey 1998b; Hutton 2009, 33–5; Maier 2013, 117.
59 Sims-Williams 2012, 43.

Celtic Britain from Gaul, is 30kms across at its narrowest point. Holyhead, in Wales is around 100kms from the coast of Ireland. Ireland is, admittedly, around 1600kms from the parts of Gaul whence come Posidonius' sources of Celtic culture. Yet we would probably not question the connection of cultures in the north and south of Gaul, which are around 800kms apart. Travel by sea in this era was, if anything, likely to have been more convenient than travel overland.[60] The literary evidence for shipbuilding gives no particular cause to doubt the possibility of regular contact across seas.[61]

This subject calls for more holistic study. 'Isolation' models are arguably a legacy of Edwardian theories of culture-history that still haunt interpretations.[62] Recent theories of Celtic origins have re-valued sea-travel, but the 'seaways' are invoked unevenly as a *deus ex machina* in theories of culture.[63] A tendency to search for discrete 'events' of contact across the sea—La Tène, Roman, etc.—may be seen as a legacy of Edwardian diffusionism.[64] What we need to appreciate is the fact of adjacency, which may have led to multiple events of sharing.

Let us use a short case-study to explore the possible complexities of contact a bit further. Sources such as the seventh-century Lives of St Brigit use the term (*druí/druíd*) as synonymous with Latin *magus/-i*. We are naturally tempted to see these 'druids' as essentially the same as those described by Caesar in the first century BC. As Catherine McKenna rightly observes, however, we thus 'may uncritically import into the *Vita Prima* [of Brigit] notions of the 'druid' derived from Posidonius, Caesar, Pliny, Lucan and Tacitus'.[65] The Irish 'druids' have quite different characteristics and functions in Irish sources to their Classical counterparts—albeit this may be exaggerated by the different genres in which they are represented.[66] We should not assume similarity.

If we imagine that druids had a cognate origin, inherited from a 'common Celtic' past, this would allow for institutions with a common origin in Gaul and Ireland—perhaps amounting to little more than a common name—at a long remove in time and space from each other. But we must be wary of exaggerating the distances. Roman writers placed druids in their own era very close to Ireland. Caesar (*Gallic War* VI.13) tells us that druids from Gaul regularly travelled to Britain for their studies. Anglesey, where Tacitus located a centre of the druids in Britain (*Annals* XIV.30), is around 1,000 kms from the main druidic centre in Gaul, but only 200 kms from Kildare (where the Lives of Brigit are set). Between Tacitus and the early Lives of Brigit lies around 550 years in time, but again we can overestimate distance in time here. As Ausonius in Gaul and Augustinus in Ireland show, we cannot assume that Roman-era druids just disappeared

60 Campbell (2001, 291) offers the suggestion that pre-Roman polities existed across seas, rather than separated by them.

61 A preliminary sketch of evidence for the Irish Sea in Wooding 2018 (forthcoming). Also see Caesar, *B.Gall.* III.8-13 on the indigenous ships of the Veneti.

62 See e.g. Wooding 1996, Ch. 1; also Sharpe 2010, 46; Handley 1999, 166.

63 Cunliffe & Koch 2010; Wooding 1996, 6; Isaac 2004; Campbell 2001, 286.

64 Cf. Swift (2003, 59–61) who suggests Roman vectors for Celtic cults in Ireland—though I applaud the broad approach of the study.

65 McKenna 2002, 68.

66 Hutton 2009, 32.

or were forgotten after the time of Tacitus.[67] We should hence set aside assumptions of shared origins followed by relative isolation, along with essentialist assumptions of 'Celticity'. There may be no more reason to imagine that the advent of druids in Ireland, or even of some Continental cults, is a matter of deep Celtic origins than, for example, regional exchanges or periodic renewals.[68]

Historiographical Distance

We turn briefly to my third iteration of distance—historiographical distance. Here there is space for only a few simple observations. In an early response to McCone's monograph, Mackey, one of the few scholars of religion at the time to respond to McCone's thesis of minimal survivals from pre-Christian belief, observed: 'the success of such displacement is usually partial and temporary, as any religionist's analysis of modern Africa can show'.[69] The experience of conversion in Africa—and one could add here the African disapora in the Americas—provides many examples of lived and historical experience of conversion and contextualisation in which aspects of earlier religion persist long after the conversion period. Such comparisons need not only be sourced from outside Europe. In his review of McCone's monograph, Dumville observes that McCone's scepticism concerning the presence of pre-Christian gods in Irish genealogies ('he seems to regard admitting their presence there as a descent into nativism') contrasts with the practice of closely neighbouring European cultures.[70] Martin Carver, taking an archaeologist's long view of a continuum of material culture across the conversion period in Scotland, rightly questions the emphasis placed on 'the revolutionary and revelatory character long credited to Christianity'.[71] Such broader views, as well as some recent studies comparing the Insular and the African experiences of conversion,[72] are welcome steps in subverting the assumption of difference.

Conclusion

Where does this leave the medieval evidence for indigenous and Romano-Celtic religion? We can no longer go to the Insular sources and expect to find simple mimetic survivals of prehistoric society, or discrete mythic legacies from a distant past. The type of scepticism evinced in 1990s anti-nativism has, however, received only uneven support. Recent studies suggest that Irish assimilation of the 'pagan' past was unusual and complex; Sims-Williams suggests that the study of putative Welsh legacies is

67 Ausonius, *On the Professors of Bordeaux* IV (Attius Patera); on Augustinus see note 7 *supra*.
68 Compare, *mutatis mutandis*, the comments of Sims-Williams' (2011, 8–16) on Irish influence on Welsh literature.
69 Mackey 1992, 287.
70 Dumville 1996, 393.
71 Carver 2009, 334.
72 McCrae 2000; Elawa 2016.

dependent on the Irish in complex ways.[73] There are no simple legacies here, but at least rich ones in which study of processes offers potential to recover detail of pre-Christian religious culture. Subverting 'tyrannies of distance' here to envisage a more connected, and earlier, culture of religious transmission and change, will also help to achieve this.[74]

BIBLIOGRAPHY

Ando, C. 2005 '*Interpretatio Romana*', *Classical Philology* 100, 41–51

Binchy, D. A. 1943 'The linguistic and historical value of the Irish law tracts', *Proceedings of the British Academy* 29, 195–227.

Borsje, J. 1996 *From Chaos to Enemy: Encounters with Monsters in Early Irish Texts.* Turnhout, Brepols.

Borsje, J. 2009 'Monotheistic to a certain extent: the "good neighbours" of God in Ireland', *The Boundaries of Monotheism: Interdisciplinary Explorations into the Foundations of Western Monotheism*, ed. A.-M. Korte & M. de Haardt, 53–82. Leiden and Boston, Brill.

Breatnach, L. 1984 'Canon and secular law in early Ireland: the significance of *Bretha Nemed*', *Peritia* 3, 439–59.

Breatnach, L. 1992 Review of Tranter and Tristram, *Early Irish Literature*, *Cambridge Medieval Celtic Studies* 23, 120–2

Breatnach, L. 2006, Satire, praise and the early Irish poet', Ériu 56, 63–84.

Byrne, F. J. 1971 'Ireland before the Norman invasion', *Irish History 1945–70*, ed. T. W. Moody, 1–15. Dublin, Irish Historical Studies.

Campbell, Ewan 2001 'Were the Scots Irish?', *Antiquity* 75, 285–92

Carey, J. 1995 'Native elements in Irish pseudohistory', *Cultural Identity and Cultural Integration*, ed. D. Edel, 45–60. Dublin, Four Courts.

Carey, J. 1999 *A Single Ray of the Sun. Religious Speculation in Early Ireland.* Andover MA, Celtic Studies Publications, 1999.

Carey, J. 2008 'From David to Labraid: sacral kingship and the emergence of monotheism in Israel and Ireland', in *Approaches to Religion and Mythology in Celtic Studies*, ed. K. Ritari & A. Bergholm, 2–27. Newcastle, Cambridge Scholars.

Carver, M. 2009 'Early Scottish monasteries and prehistory: a preliminary dialogue', *Scottish Historical Review* 88, 332–35.

Carney, J. 1955 *Studies in Irish Literature and History*. Dublin, Dublin Institute for Advanced Studies.

Carney, J. 1989 'The dating of archaic Irish verse', *Early Irish literature: Media and Communication,* ed. S. N. Tranter & H. L. C. Tristram, 39–55. Tübingen, Narr.

Chadwick, Owen 1954 'The evidence of dedications in the early history of the Welsh church', in *Studies in Early British History*, ed. Nora K. Chadwick. Cambridge, CUP, 173–88.

Charles-Edwards, G. & McKee, H. forthcoming 2018 'Papyrus in the early Insular world', *From the East to the Isles: Approaches*

73 Williams 2016, 490-3; Sims-Williams 2009, 1–8.

74 I would like to thank Ralph Häussler, Tony King, and John Koch for the invitation to make this short methodological contribution to the F.E.R.C.AN. volume and also to thank them for their abundant patience.

to the Eastern Connections of the Early Churches of Britain and Ireland, in Memory of Donald Allchin, ed. J. Wooding. Oxford, Sobornost.

Cunliffe, B. W. & Koch, J. T. *Celtic from the West: Alternative Perspectives from Archaeology, Genetics, Language and Literature.* Oxford, Oxbow.

Davies, Wendy 1983 'An historian's view of Celtic archaeology', *25 Years of Medieval Archaeology*, ed. D. Hinton, 67–73 Sheffield, Society for Medieval Archaeology.

Dumville, D. N. 1996 Review of K. McCone, *Pagan Past and Christian Present, Peritia* 10, 389–98.

Elawa, Nathan Irmiya 2016 The Significance of the Cultural Context in the Christianization Process: A Comparative Study of Religious Change among the Jukun in British Colonial Nigeria and the Irish in Early Ireland. PhD dissertation, University of Wales.

Flechner, R. & M. Ní Mhaonaigh (eds.) 2016 *Converting the Isles 1: the Introduction of Christianity into the Early Medieval Insular World.* Turnhout, Brepols.

Green, M. 1986 *The Gods of the Celts.* Stroud, Sutton.

Green, M. 1990 'Pagan Celtic religion: archaeology and myth', *Transactions of the Honourable Society of Cymmrodorion*, 13–28.

Greene, David 1971 'Considerations in the dating of early Welsh verse', *Studia Celtica* 6 (1971), 1–11.

Häussler, R. 2012 '*Interpretatio indigena:* re-inventing local cults in a global world', *Mediterraneo Antico* 15, 143–174.

Handley, M. 1999 'The British Isles and the Mediterranean world: contact and exchange AD 400–700', in *Origins and Revivals: Proceedings of the First Australian Conference of Celtic Studies,* ed. G. Evans, B. K. Martin & J. Wooding, 159–85. Sydney, Sydney Series in Celtic Studies.

Harvey, Anthony, 'Early literacy in Ireland: the evidence from Ogam', *Cambridge Medieval Celtic Studies* 14 (Winter 1987), 1–15.

Hutton, R. 2009 *Blood and Mistletoe: the History of the Druids in Britain***.** New Haven, Yale University Press.

Hutton, R. 2011 'Medieval Welsh literature and pre-Christian deities', *Cambrian Medieval Celtic Studies* 61, 57–86.

Isaac, G. 2004 'The nature and origins of the Celtic languages: Atlantic seaways, Italo-Celtic and other para-linguistic misapprehensions, *Studia Celtica* 38, 49–58.

James, S. 1998 *The Atlantic Celts: Ancient People or Modern Invention.* London, British Museum.

Johnston, E. 2013 *Literacy and Identity in Early Medieval Ireland*. Woodbridge, Boydell.

Jones, G. E. (1975) 'Early prose: the Mabinogi', in *A History of Welsh Literature,* ed. A. O. Jarman & G. Rees, 189–202. Cardiff, University of Wales.

Lapidge, M. (ed.) 2015 *H. M. Chadwick and the Study of Anglo-Saxon, Norse and Celtic in Cambridge*. Aberystwyth, *CMCS* 69/70.

Jackson, K. H. 1963 *The Oldest Irish Tradition: A Window on the Iron Age,* Cambridge, CUP.

Koch, J. T. 1987 'A Welsh window on the Iron Age: Manawydan, Mandubracios', *Cambridge Medieval Celtic Studies* 14, 17–52

Koch, J. T. 1990 'Brân, Brennos: an instance of early Gallo-Brittonic history and mythology', *Cambridge Medieval Celtic Studies* 20, 1–20.

Mackey, J. P. 1992a 'Christian past and primal present', Études celtiques 29, 285–97.

Mackey, J. P. 1992b 'Magic and primal religion', *Zeitschrift für celtische Philologie* 45, 66–83.

McKillop, J. 2005 *Myths and Legends of the Celts.* Harmondsworth, Penguin.

Mac Mathúna, S. 1985 *Immram Brain: Bran's Journey to the Land of the Women,* Tübingen, Niemeyer.

Mac Néill, M. 1962 *The Festival of Lughnasa*. Oxford, Oxford University Press.

Macquarrie. C. 2004 *The Biography of the Irish God of the Sea from The Voyage of*

Bran (700 A.D.) to Finnegans Wake (1939): the Waves of Manannán. Lewiston NY, Edwin Mellon.

Maier, Bernhard 1996 'Is Lug to be identified with Mercury (Bell. Gall. VI.17, 1)? New suggestions on an old problem', Ériu 47, 127–36.

Maier, Bernhard 2013 'Dead men don't wear plaid: Celtic myth and Christian creed in medieval Irish conceptions of the afterlife', *Writing Down the Myths,* ed. J. F. Nagy, 105–31. Turnhout, Brepols.

Mallory, J. P. 1986 'Silver in the Ulster Cycle of tales', *Proceedings of the Seventh International Congress of Celtic Studies,* ed. D. Ellis Evans, 33–65. Oxford, Celtic Studies.

Mallory, J. P. 1992 'The world of Cú Chulainn: the archaeology of *Táin bó Cúailnge*', *Aspects of the Táin,* ed. J. P. Mallory, 103–59. Belfast, December Publications.

McCone, K. 1990 *Pagan Past and Christian Present in early Irish Literature*. Maynooth, Dept of Old Irish.

McCone, K. 1996 'Prehistoric, Old and Middle Irish', *Progress in Medieval Irish Studies,* ed. McCone and K. Simms, 5–53. Maynooth, Dept of Old Irish.

McCone, K. 2000 *Echtrae Chonnlai and the Beginnings of Vernacular Narrative Writing in Ireland*. Maynooth, Dept of Old Irish.

McKenna, C. 2002 'Between two worlds: Saint Brigit and pre-Christian religion in the *Vita Prima*', *Identifying the 'Celtic'*, CSANA Yearbook 2, ed. J. F. Nagy, 66–74. Dublin, Four Courts Press.

McCrae, C. 2000 *The Sacred Tree: Divinities and Ancestors in Encounter with Christianity in the Religious Experience and History of the Early Irish and the Akan People of Ghana.* Cardiff, Cardiff Academic Press.

Meek, Donald 2000 *The Quest for Celtic Christianity.* Edinburgh, Handsel.

Mees, Bernard 2009 *Celtic Curses.* Woodbridge, Boydell.

Megaw, R. & V. 1992 'The Celts, the first Europeans?', *Antiquity* 66, 254–60

Meyer, K. & A. Nutt (eds) 1895–7 *The Voyage of Bran Son of Febal to the Land of the Living*. London, Nutt. 2 vols.

Meyer, K. 1913, *Sanas Cormaic. An Old-Irish glossary*. Halle and Dublin, Anecdota from Irish Manuscripts 4, 1–128.

Nagy, J. F. 1983 'Close encounters of the traditional kind in medieval Irish literature, *Celtic Folklore and Christianity: Studies in Memory of William W. Heist*, ed. Patrick Ford, 129–49. Santa Barbara, CA, McNally.

Nagy, J. F. 1997 *Conversing with Angels and Ancients: Literary Myths of Medieval Ireland*. Dublin, Four Courts.

Nagy, J. F. 2007 'Introduction', in *Myth in Celtic Literatures, CSANA Yearbook* 6. Dublin, Four Courts.

Nagy, J. F. 2011 *Mercantile Myth in Medieval Celtic Traditions.* Cambridge, ASNAC.

Ó Cathasaigh, T. 1984 'Pagan survivals: the evidence of early Irish narrative', *Irland und Europa: Die Kirche im Frühmittelalter,* ed. P. Ní Chatháin & M. Richter, 291–307. Stuttgart, Klett-Cotta.

Ó Cathasaigh, T. 2014 *Coire Sois—the Cauldron of Knowledge: a Companion to Early Irish Saga.* South Bend IN, Notre Dame.

Ó Coileáin, S. 1977 'Oral or literary: some strands of the argument', *Studia Hibernica* 17–18 (1977–78), 7–35.

Ó Corráin, D. 1994. 'Early Irish history: some points for debate', *Newsletter of the School of Celtic Studies of the Dublin Institute for Advanced Studies* 7, 25–7.

O'Leary, P. 1994 *The Prose Literature of the Gaelic Revival.* University Park PA, Penn State University.

O'Loughlin, T. 1999 *Celtic Theology: Humanity, World and God in Early Irish Writings.* London, Continuum.

O'Rahilly, T. F. 1946 *Early Irish History and Mythology*. Dublin, Dublin Institute for Advanced Studies.

Ó Riain, P. 1982 'Towards a methodology in early Irish hagiography', *Peritia* 1, 146–59.

Raftery, B. 1994 *Pagan Celtic Ireland: The Enigma of the Irish Iron Age.* London, Thames and Hudson.

Raftery, Joseph 1980 'Mainland Europe and the offshore islands, *Archaeologia Atlantica* 3, 1–7

Rees, A. & B. 1961 *Celtic Heritage: Ancient Tradition in Ireland and Wales.* London, Thames and Hudson.

Rodway, Simon 2013 *Dating Medieval Welsh Literature: Evidence from the Verbal System,* Aberystwyth, CMCS.

Ritari, K. & A. Bergholm (eds) 2015 *Understanding Celtic Religion—Revisiting the Pagan Past.* Cardiff, University of Wales.

Ross, Anne 1967 *Pagan Celtic Britain.* London, Routledge.

Said, E. 1988 *Nationalism, Colonialism and Literature: Yeats and Decolonization.* Derry, Field Day.

Sharpe, R. 2002 'Martyrs and local saints in late Antique Britain', *Local Saints and Local Cults in the Early Medieval West,* ed. A. Thacker & R. Sharpe, 75–154. Oxford, OUP.

Sims-Williams, P. 1996 Review of McCone 1990, *Éigse* 29, 179–196.

Sims-Williams, P. 1998 'Celtomania and Celtoscepticism', *Cambrian Medieval Celtic Studies* 36, 1–35.

Sims-Williams, P. 1998b 'The uses of writing in early-medieval Wales', *Literacy in Medieval Celtic Societies,* ed. H. Pryce, 15–38. Cambridge, CUP.

Sims-Williams, P. 2011 *Irish Influence on Medieval Welsh Literature.* Oxford, OUP.

Sims-Williams, P. 2012 'Celtic civilization: continuity or coincidence?' *Cambrian Medieval Celtic Studies* 64, 1–45.

Sims-Williams, P. 2013 'Post-Celtoscepticism: A personal view', *Saltair, Saíochta, Sanasíochta agus Seanchais: A Festschrift for Gearóid Mac Eoin*, ed. D. Ó Baoill *et al.*, 422–8. Dublin, Four Courts.

Sims-Williams, P. 2016 'Dating the poems of Aneirin and Taliesin', *Zeitschrift für celtische Philologie* 63, 163–234.

Sjöblom, T. 2004 'Mind stories: a cognitive approach to the role of narratives in early Irish tradition', *Cambrian Medieval Celtic Studies* 47, 59–72.

Slavin, Bridgette, forthcoming 2018 *Druídecht: Perceptions of Magic and Druidry in Medieval Irish Texts.* Cardiff, University of Wales.

Stausberg, M. 2007 'Western Europe', *Religious Studies: A Global View*, ed. G. D. Alles, 14–49. London, Routledge.

Swift, C. 1997 *Ogam Stones and the earliest Irish Christians*, Maynooth, Dept of Old Irish.

Swift, C. 2003 'The gods of Newgrange in Irish literature and Romano-Celtic tradition', *Stones and Bones: Formal Disposal of the Dead in Atlantic Europe during the Mesolithic-Neolithic Interface*, ed. G. Burenhult & S. Westergaard, 53–63. Oxford, BAR.

Webster, J. 2015 'A dirty window on the Iron Age? Recent approaches to Romano-Celtic religion', Ritari & Bergholm 2015, 121–54. Cardiff: University of Wales.

Williams, Mark 2016 *Ireland's Immortals: A History of the Gods of Irish Myth.* Princeton: Princeton UP.

Wooding, J. M. 1996 *Communication and Commerce along the Western Sealanes.* Oxford, British Archaeological Reports.

Wooding, J. M. 2009 'Reapproaching the pagan Celtic past: anti-nativism, asterisk reality and the Late-Antiquity paradigm', *Studia Celtica Fennica: Finnish Journal of Celtic Studies* 6, 61–73.

Wooding, J. M. forthcoming 2018 'Literary evidence for early Medieval Welsh seafaring', in *Reclaiming History from the Sea: Maritime Archaeology around Wales,* ed. A. Aberg *et al.* Aberystwyth, RCAHMW.

IV

A FOURTH-CENTURY 'CURSE TABLET' FROM ULEY

Roger S. O. Tomlin

The temple of Mercury on West Hill, Uley (Glos.), was excavated in 1977–79 and published by the excavators, Ann Woodward and Peter Leach, in The Uley Shrines *(1993). The finds include a masterpiece of Romano-British sculpture, the cult-statue head, and a unique written 'archive', 140 lead tablets, 86 of which are inscribed. They are 'curse tablets' like the well-known Bath Tablets, petitions addressed to Mercury by the victims of theft and anti-social behaviour, which uniquely document a Romano-British rural community. I present the 14 texts which have been fully published, and a fifteenth (no. 68, inv. no. 3652) which is unpublished. Unusually, it names the thief, and is inscribed in New Roman Cursive unlike the majority of the Uley tablets, which are in capitals or Old Roman Cursive.*

ULEY, near Stroud in Gloucestershire, is a village tucked into the westward escarpment of the Cotswolds, and above it is West Hill, which is the site of a Romano-Celtic temple between a large hill-fort (Uley Bury) and a well-preserved long barrow (Hetty Pegler's Tump). The temple was excavated in 1977–79 by Ann Woodward and Peter Leach, who published the results in 1993.[1] They show that the site was probably sacral in the pre-Roman period, and afterwards occupied by a sub-Roman Christian church, but the only written documents come from the stone-built temple of the second century, which was demolished towards the end of the fourth. This was dedicated to the god Mercury, who received letters inscribed in Latin on sheets of lead, much like the letters written to the goddess Sulis Minerva at Bath which were found in the Hot Spring, coincidentally in 1979 when the Uley excavation ended.[2] But unlike the Bath Tablets, the Uley Tablets were not found where they were deposited, but either unstratified or 'in the deposits of votive material spread over the demolished and robbed remains' of the temple.[3] We do not know how they were originally deposited, nor can we date them archaeologically; but their handwriting, unless it is in capitals, ranges from Old Roman Cursive (ORC) of the second and third centuries to New Roman Cursive (NRC) of the fourth.

1 Woodward & Leach 1993.
2 Tomlin 1988.
3 Woodward & Leach 1993, 112.

The Bath Tablets have recently entered the Unesco 'Memory of the World', along with the plays of Shakespeare, and the Uley Tablets have an equal claim. The two sites are the richest source of 'manuscripts' from a civilian context in Roman Britain, and Uley is exceptional for also being non-urban. When fully published, its tablets will write a new chapter in the social and economic history of the Romano-British countryside. 140 were found in the excavation, but about 50 were not inscribed, whether they were 'blanks' intended for use later, or were inscribed in ink which has since disappeared, or simply accompanied the verbal messages of illiterates. But 86 were inscribed, and are summarised in the interim report.[4] Five are fully published there, and nine others have been published since. These fourteen may now be tabulated, numbered as in the report.

Uley tablets already published

Uley 1 (ORC) (Woodward and Leach 1993, 118–20). Cenacus complains of the theft of a draught animal (*iumentum*) and asks Mercury to deny the named thieves health until they return it and pay to the god the devotion (*devotionem*) which he has demanded.

Uley 2 (capitals) (*ibid.*, 120–22). Memorandum (*commonitorium*) of Saturnina concerning a stolen piece of linen. The thief is to have no rest until he brings it to the temple of Mercury, when a third of it will be given to the god for exacting it (*ita ut hoc exsigat*).

Uley 3 (capitals) (*ibid.*, 123, with *Britannia* 22 (1991), 307–8). Fragmentary text relating to the theft of a gold ring from a house (*de hos[pitiolo]*).

Uley 4 (capitals) (*ibid.*, 124–6). Biccus curses the health of a thief until he brings the stolen property to the temple.

Uley 5 (ORC) (*ibid.*, 126–7). The name of the thief of a bridle is given (*nomen furis ... donator*).

Uley 33 (capitals) (*Britannia* 26 (1995), 378, No. 4). List of names.

Uley 43 (capitals) (*Britannia* 20 (1989), 329, No. 3). Docilinus asks Mercury to inflict the greatest death (*max[i]mo [le]to adigas*)[5] upon three named persons who have done harm to his farm animal (*pecus*), and to deny them health until they redeem themselves.

Uley 49 (capitals) (*Britannia* 26 (1995), 376, No. 3). Another list of names.

Uley 50 (capitals) (*Britannia* 29 (1998), 433, No. 1). Fragmentary text relating to the theft of silver plate and four gold rings.

Uley 55 (ORC) (*Britannia* 26 (1995), 371, No. 1). Rufus gives (*donavi*) the thief of cloak-material.

Uley 72 (ORC) (*Britannia* 23 (1992), 310, No. 5). Honoratus complains of losing two wheels and four cows from his house (*de hospitiolo meo*). The thief is not to enjoy health until he has returned them.

Uley 76 (ORC) (*Britannia* 26 (1995), 373, No. 2). The anonymous writer complains to Mercury of malicious persons (*de illis qui mihi male cogitant et male faciunt*) who are to enjoy no health until they pay for it.

---

4 Tomlin 1993

5 This unusual phrase occurs elsewhere only in *Tab. Sulis* 10, 11–12, where it is corrupted to *maximo letum [a]digat*, which raises the question of what shared sources of reference, whether verbal or written, were available to petitioners at Bath and Uley.

Uley 80 (ORC) (*Britannia* 27 (1996), 439, No. 1). This page (*carta*) is given to Mercury, that he punish a glove-thief.

Uley 86 (capitals) (*Britannia* 24 (1993), 310, No. 1). The name 'Petronius'.

Uley 68, published here

Some of the tablets are displayed in the British Museum, which is supporting their full publication, still in progress. Uley 68 is one of eight NRC texts. Its publication may be prefaced by some general remarks. Conventionally these documents are called 'curse tablets', but note the inverted commas. Scholars often use the Latin word *defixio*, although it has almost no ancient warrant. When Tacitus refers to 'curse tablets', he uses circumlocution: 'spells and devotions, the name of Germanicus written on lead tablets ... and other evil devices by which it is believed that souls are consecrated to the infernal powers'.[6] He uses the synonymous terms *devotio* and *sacrari*, and one of the Bath tablets uses the verb *devoveo* from which the noun *devotio* is derived.[7] *devotio* itself is used in Uley 1, but in a somewhat different sense. None of the Uley Tablets calls itself a *devotio*, let alone a *defixio*. When they refer to themselves, they call themselves variously a 'complaint', a 'request', a 'petition' or 'prayers', a 'page', a 'memorandum', a 'donation'.[8]

Note in particular the terms 'complaint', 'request', and 'petition'. These are not just curses, like the tablet from London which says quite frankly: 'I curse Tretia Maria' (*defico*, whence *defixio*).[9] They are what Henk Versnel calls 'judicial prayers', petitions from the victims of theft and anti-social behaviour in an under-policed world addressed to a superhuman patron, our Godfather which art in Heaven.[10] Markus Scholz has recently catalogued Latin curse tablets prompted by theft, 95 in all.[11] No fewer than 78 are British: does this mean that Roman Britain was full of thieves, or did it simply have a well-developed sense of justice? At all events, the total does credit to British archaeologists.

The petitioner typically addresses the god by name, often naming himself as well, rather like someone writing a letter.[12] Often tablets are rolled up, before being buried or thrown into water. Sometimes they are enciphered, by reversing the letter-order, even by mirror-image script; one Uley tablet (52, unpublished) is transliterated into Greek letters. Clearly they were not intended for human eyes, and it would be wrong to 'rationalise' them by saying that they worked psychosomatically because the thief *knew*

6 *Annales* II 69, *carmina et devotiones et nomen Germanici plumbeis tabulis insculptum ... aliaque malefica quis creditur animas numinibus infernis sacrari*.

7 *Tab. Sulis* 10, 5. For *devotio* as a formal curse, see Macrobius, *Saturnalia* III 9.

8 Respectively *queritur* (Uley 1), *conqueror* (Uley 72), and *queror* (Uley 76); *rogat* (Uley 1), *rogo* (Uley 43), and *rogaverim ... rogo* (Uley 72); *petitio* and *iteratis precibus* (Uley 72); *carta* (Uley 8); *commonitorium* (Uley 2); *donat* (Uley 2), *dat* (Uley 4), *donator* (Uley 5), and *donavi* (Uley 55).

9 RIB 7.

10 Versnel 1991 and 2010.

11 Scholz 2011.

12 Tomlin 2002.

(having been told) that he had been cursed; but he might sometimes *wonder* if he had been cursed – especially if he happened to fall ill.[13] The converse of this thought is in Uley 76: the writer knows he has been cursed, but not the persons responsible, since he has done nothing to provoke such malice.

The language of the tablets is formulaic, often at the cost of syntax.[14] The thief, for obvious reasons, is hardly ever named; Uley 1 is exceptional in naming him, and Uley 43 is precious for its glimpse of village politics since the writer knows which neighbours have bewitched his animal. Instead, the thief's 'name' (*nomen*) is surrogate for him, as in Uley 5; and at Bath one tablet is inscribed with no more than 'the name of the thief who has stolen my bracelet'.[15] Most often the nameless thief is identified by means of mutually exclusive clauses, 'whether male or female' (etc.), as in Uley 2, 4, 5, 55, 72, 76.[16] The god is asked to destroy his health and well-being – often there will be more of these mutually exclusive clauses, 'neither eating nor drinking', as in Uley 72 and 76 for example[17] – until the stolen property is returned; incidentally to the temple, emphasising that the god is the agent.[18] His interest may even be engaged, as well as his sense of justice, by offering him a commission: one-third in Uley 3 and 5, one-half at Lydney Park and Pagans Hill, two-thirds in the London amphitheatre, but only one-tenth at Ratcliffe-on-Soar.[19]

The new tablet, Uley 68, is exceptional in naming the thief. It is also unusually small. It was cut from lead sheet, only 47 by 38 mm, and is complete except for loss to the top edge of face (*a*) and the bottom edge of face (*b*), but it was badly stressed by being folded twice after it was inscribed. Face (*b*) is heavily coated with corrosion products in which the writing is rather faint. Both faces are inscribed in fluent NRC with a broad nib-like point.

Translation

'To the holy god Mercury. I, ?Carinus, ?implore you concerning the theft which has been done to me (by) Primanus. And Mercury is neither to permit him ... nor ... nor ... neither sun nor moon, neither ... of an infant ... fulfil vengeance with his blood.'

13 Tomlin 1988, 101–5. A 'psychosomatic mechanism for curse tablets' is developed by Kiernan 2004, with anthropological parallels.
14 Tomlin 1988, 63–8. Adams 1992.
15 *Tab. Sulis* 15, *nomen rei qui destrale involaverit.*
16 For Bath and other sites, see Tomlin 1988, 67–8.
17 For Bath and other sites, see Tomlin 1988, 66–7.
18 Tomlin 1988, 68.
19 Respectively RIB 306; *Britannia* 15 (1984) 339, No. 7; *Britannia* 34 (2003), 362, No. 2; *Journal of Roman Studies* 53 (1963) 123.

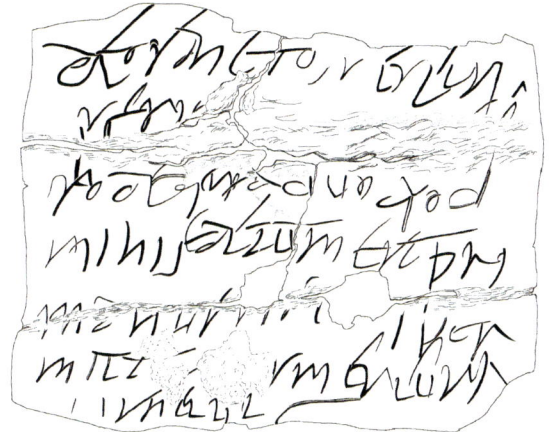

30 mm

Transcript, face (*a*)

deo sancto Ṃercuriọ
Cạriṇ[ ]ẹc̣-
ro de fuṛṭo{uo} quod
mihi factum est Pri-
manus ṇẹc̣ [e]i per-
mitt[ ]s Mercurius
{-ụṣ} nec *traces*

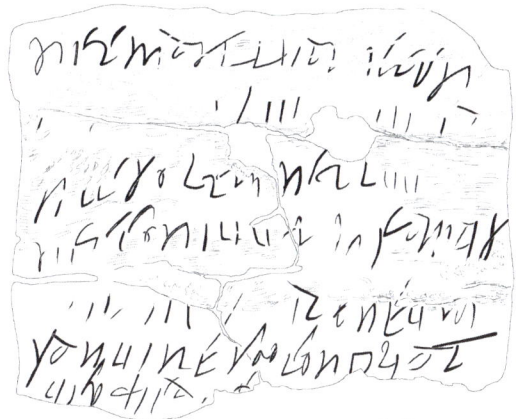

30 mm

Transcript, face (*b*)

nec mas *traces*
traces
nẹc soleṃ neç lụṇ[am]
nec coniuu.. infaṇtis
traces neum
san(g)uine sụo conp̣liat
veṇdica[tionem?]

Notes (*a*)

2. The petitioner's name has been damaged by the fold, but if the stroke above the second letter is only a repetition of the second element of initial *c*, his name can be restored as *Carin[us]* or *Carin[ianus]*, depending on the space available. It was followed by a verb in the first-person indicative, as shown by the termination *-ro* in 3. At the end of 2, only the top of the two previous letters survives, but the elements are compatible with *e* and *c*. Since the context is one of 'complaint', the verb is likely to have been *execro* (active, as in *Tab. Sulis* 99, 1) or *[obs]ec|ro*, probably preceded by *tibi* or *te* respectively.
3. The scribe seems to have treated the *o* of *furto* as the first element of *q*, by adding a downstroke, and continuing with *uo*. Then he realised his mistake, and wrote *quod* again, the *u* (exceptionally in this hand) being *v*-shaped.

3–4, *Pri|manus*. In the context, *Primanus* although nominative must be the name of the thief. Grammatically, either *fecit* (instead of *factum est*) or *a Primano* (instead of *Primanus*) would be required, but the scribe wrote one formula (*factum est*) and proceeded as if he had written the other (*fecit*). Neither is actually attested in Britain, but *fraudem fecit* is used in Uley 3 as well as twice at Bath (Tomlin 1988, 64), and *quot mihi furtum factum est* is used in the Mérida tablet (Audollent 1904, no. 122, with Tomlin 2010, 247–9).

5–6, *nec [e]i per|mitt[ ]s*. The formula of not 'permitting' the thief is frequent (Tomlin 1988, 65–6). *Mercurius* is nominative, so *permitt[at]* in the third person is required, not *permitt[a]s*, for which any way there is too much space. The verb was followed by a word ending in *s*, perhaps *[nato]s*, although it would be rather cramped; for the formula *nec natos nec nascentes* ('children neither now nor in the future'), compare *Tab. Sulis* 10, 13–15.

6, *Mercurius*. The final *s* has been interlineated above *r*, since there was no room for it at the end of the line.

7. *us* seems to have been repeated at the beginning of the line, since *nec* (if correctly read) marks a new word. The rest of the line is damaged, and it is unclear whether the line below *mer* is meant as a letter or only to fill space.

Notes (*b*)

1, *nec*. The sense evidently continues from (*a*), but the rest of the line has been crossed out by a series of more or less horizontal lines.

3, *nec solem nec lun[am]*. *nec* and *nec* are damaged, but they would imply two more alternatives to be denied to the thief. There are good traces of *solem* and *lun[am]*, the 'sun' and the 'moon', contrasting sources of light, but the formula has not been found before.

4. The word after *nec* looks rather like *coniugis*, but *g* cannot be read. The concluding *infantis* also suggests a family context.

5. Badly damaged, with just a possibility that the end-word is *[ba]leneum* (for *balineum*, 'bath').

6–7, *san(g)uine suo conpliat / vendica[tionem]*. The idea of 'paying' with one's blood is frequent (Tomlin 1988, 67), but this formula is new. After *vendica-* the surviving letter-tips do not strongly support the restoration suggested, but the context makes it inevitable.

The spelling is 'Vulgar', that is, influenced by the pronunciation. In *san(g)uine*, *g* has been lost by lenition; compare *sanuene sua* in *Tab. Sulis* 46, 7. *conpliat* is for *conpleat*, unstressed short *e* and *i* often being confused. This is not the case with *vendica[tionem]*, but the form *vendicas* for *vindicas* is found three times in the London Bridge tablet (*Britannia* 18 (1987), 360, No. 1), where it is suggested that it anticipates the change found in some, but not all, Romance languages: compare Italian *vengiare*, French *venger*, Spanish *vengar*, but note Sardinian *vindicare*, Portuguese *vingar*, and see Meyer-Lübke 1935, s.v. *vindicare*.

BIBLIOGRAPHY

Adams, J. N. 1992 'British Latin: the text, interpretation and language of the Bath curse tablets', *Britannia* 23, 1–26.

Audollent, A. 1904 *Defixionum Tabellae*. Paris.

Kiernan, P. 2004 'Did curse tablets work?' *TRAC 2003: Proceedings of the Thirteenth Annual Theoretical Archaeology Conference* (Leicester 2003), ed. B. Croxford, H. Eckardt, J. Meade, J. Weekes, 123–34. Oxford, Oxbow Books.

Meyer-Lübke, W. 1935 *Romanisches Etymologisches Wörterbuch*. Heidelberg, 3rd edition.

Tomlin, R. S. O. 1988 *Tabellae Sulis: Roman inscribed tablets of tin and lead from the Sacred Spring at Bath*. Oxford = Part 4 (The curse tablets), *The Temple of Sulis Minerva at Bath, II: Finds from the Sacred Spring*, ed. B. Cunliffe. Oxford.

Tomlin, R. S. O. 1993 'The inscribed lead tablets: an interim report', in Woodward and Leach 1993, 113–30.

Tomlin, R. S. O. 2002 'Writing to the gods in Britain', in *Becoming Roman, Writing Latin? Literacy and Epigraphy in the Roman West*, ed. A. E. Cooley, 165–79. Portsmouth, RI.

Tomlin, R. S. O. 2010 'Cursing a thief in Iberia and Britain', *Magical Practice in the Latin West*, ed. R. L. Gordon & F. Marco Simón, 245–73. Leiden.

Scholz, M. 2011 'Verdammter Dieb – Kleinkriminalität im Spiegel von Fluchtäfelchen', *Gefährliches Pflaster: Kriminalität im Römischen Reich*, ed. M. Reuter & R. Schiavone, 89–103. Mainz.

Versnel, H. S. 1991 'Beyond cursing: the appeal to justice in judicial prayers', *Magika Hiera: Ancient Greek Magic and Religion*, ed. C. A. Faraone & D. Obbink, 60–106. Oxford.

Versnel, H. S. 2010 'Prayers for justice in east and west: recent finds and publications', *Magical Practice in the Latin West*, ed. R. L. Gordon & F. Marco Simón, 275–354. Leiden.

Woodward, A. & P. Leach 1993 *The Uley Shrines. Excavation of a ritual complex on West Hill, Uley, Gloucestershire: 1977–9*. London.

V

SOMETHING OLD, SOMETHING NEW: THE NAMES OF FAUNUS IN LATE-ROMAN THETFORD (NORFOLK) AND THEIR IRON-AGE BACKGROUND

Daphne Nash Briggs

This paper revisits the late-fourth-century Roman treasure found in 1979 on Gallows Hill, Thetford (Norfolk) – a place of long-term ceremonial and funerary significance that straddles the Icknield Way close to where it crosses an important prehistoric, Roman, and post-Roman tribal boundary. A review of Latin traditions concerning deus Faunus, *who is named on silver spoons in the treasure, and detailed discussion of the eight non-Latin theonyms coupled with his, suggest a high degree of correspondence, with multiple lines of historical and material connection, between well-researched pre-Roman activity in that same place, aspects of the known pre-Roman history of the Iceni, and some less generally familiar first-century BC/AD Icenian coin images that may account for the association of Faunus' name with what must have been a powerful ancestral* genius loci *long associated with one of the territory's ruling clans. It also suggests the relevance of this, and late-Roman Bacchic spirituality, to the late-Roman people represented in the treasure. The paper concludes with a speculative sketch of some historical circumstances that might help to explain why this treasure was assembled and buried where and when it was.*

AROUND or soon after the end of the 4th century AD a gold and silver treasure was buried on Gallows Hill in the northern outskirts of Thetford (Norfolk). This place had a peculiar public history, and the treasure was placed in the footprint of a recently dismantled late-Roman timber structure. Inscribed silver spoons and some other contents suggest that it once belonged to a small group of wealthy, well-connected, and very well educated late-Roman people and to a *deus Faunus* linked with eight Brittonic theonyms. Although its known contents are incomplete and much of its immediate context was destroyed by building works before it could be explored, enough relevant archaeology has been rescued to convey some sense of the very long-term significance of a sacred place in a commanding position on the Icknield way, close to a long-term tribal and *civitas* boundary.[1]

1 For detailed publication of the treasure and discussion see Johns & Potter 1983, cf. Henig 1995, 218–24. Chadburn (1995) identified some missing items: see n. 13. 1.

Thetford itself was never in Antiquity a focal town settlement – these were rare in ancient East Anglia – but it was in a populous environment with farms and larger estates, some rural settlements, and several important ceremonial centres, any of which may have hosted manufacturing activities, markets, and periodic fairs. The Icknield Way, a prehistoric pathway along the chalk escarpment from the Channel coast in Dorset to the North Sea, passed through Thetford (Figs. 1 and 6). Thetford Castle, a 6-ha unoccupied Iron-Age enclosure on one of Thetford's three low hills, overlooked the place where the rivers Thet and Little Ouse could be forded. North of the Thet, the path crossed Gallows Hill, a visible landmark in an otherwise sparsely wooded lowland heath. Several Bronze-Age barrows would still have been upstanding there in the late second century BC, when one in particular seems to have been the focal point for a late-Iron-Age ceremonial complex, commonly known as the Fison Way monument from its location in a modern industrial estate.

The history of this site must have been related to its command of an important road near a border crossing in a social environment exceptionally rich in evidence for horsemanship and charioteering. It is in exactly the sort of place where travellers into and out of a territory could be obliged to present their credentials and pay their respects: late phases of the complex actually obstructed the track. Its pre-Roman development has been thoroughly discussed elsewhere.[2] Two aspects are especially relevant to the present discussion: its non-domestic, specialized, funerary character and its apparent political status.

Briefly, the complex first took shape between the 2nd century BC and the AD 40s (Fig. 2) in a period of political change that was ultimately driven by expansion of the Roman empire into Gaul and Britain. Always culturally somewhat different from their neighbours, the Iceni probably had some Germanic clans, they never imported wine at a time when nothing other than their own policies could have prevented them from doing so, and they seem always to have invested an unusually high proportion of their wealth in ceremonial activities. A rich northern centre funded a highly distinctive gold coinage during and after Julius Caesar's invasions in 55 and 54 BC (Fig. 2. 1–2), which probably bankrupted them, and the Icenian peoples' subsequent development was shaped by interaction, sometimes conflict, amongst themselves and with powerful neighbours. Land in Suffolk across the Little Ouse and between the rivers Yare and Alde may have been disputed with Catuvellauni and Trinovantes respectively. Archaeology and coinage together suggest piecemeal formation of a tripartite regional union of semi-autonomous district élites in *c.*20 BC–AD 10, cohering around periodic activities at various centres: in effect, they formed an amphictyonic league. By the time of Claudius' invasion in AD 43 the main district centres were in the Fens around Stonea, in the Breckland around Ashill and Saham Toney (probably the federal centre), and around Crownthorpe and Norwich in the east, whilst Thetford and a cluster of sites on the Fen edge guarded access from

2 See Gregory 1992 for the site and finds, Bradley 2005, 184–87 for its funerary aspects, and Nash Briggs 2012 for fuller discussion of the Iron-Age site and its significance.

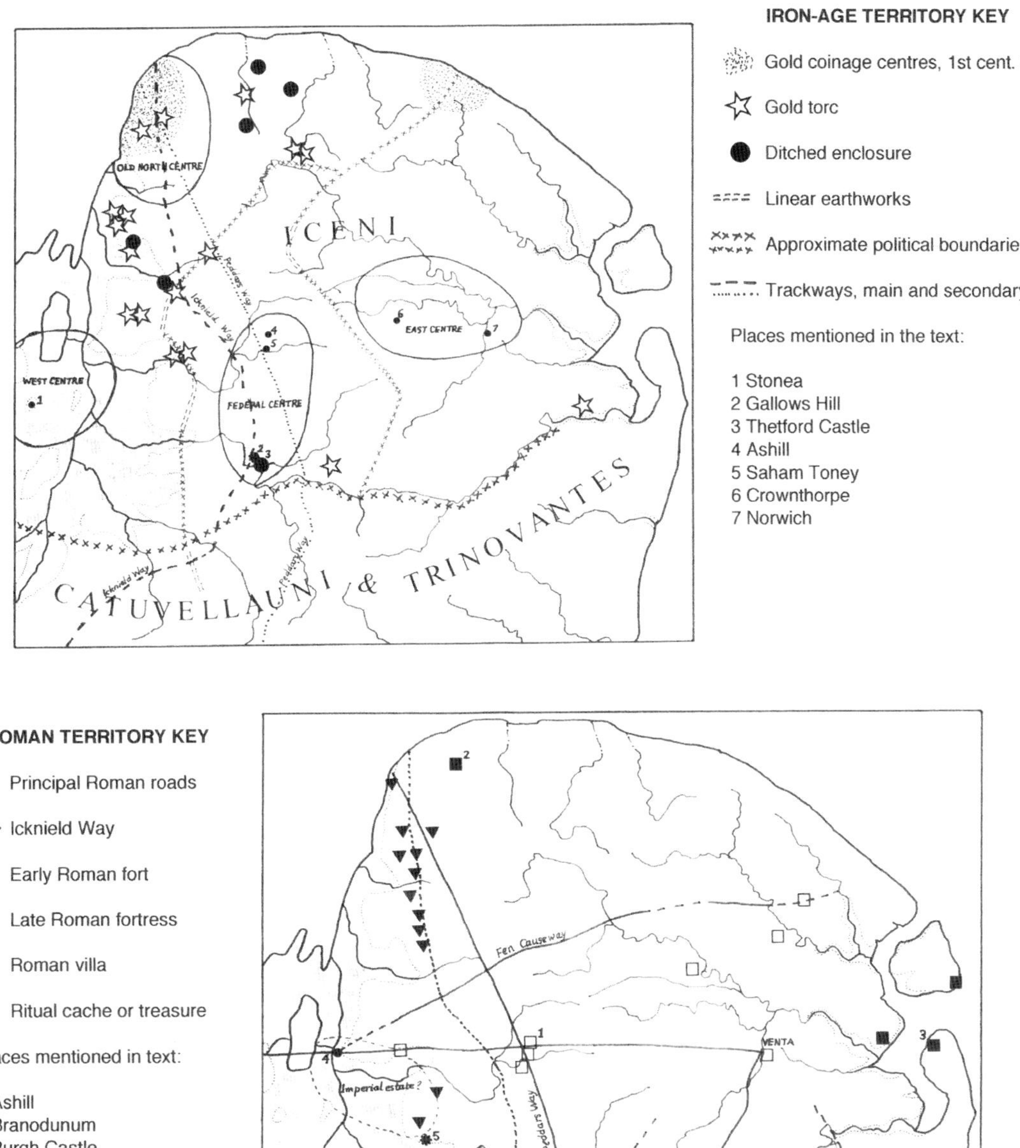

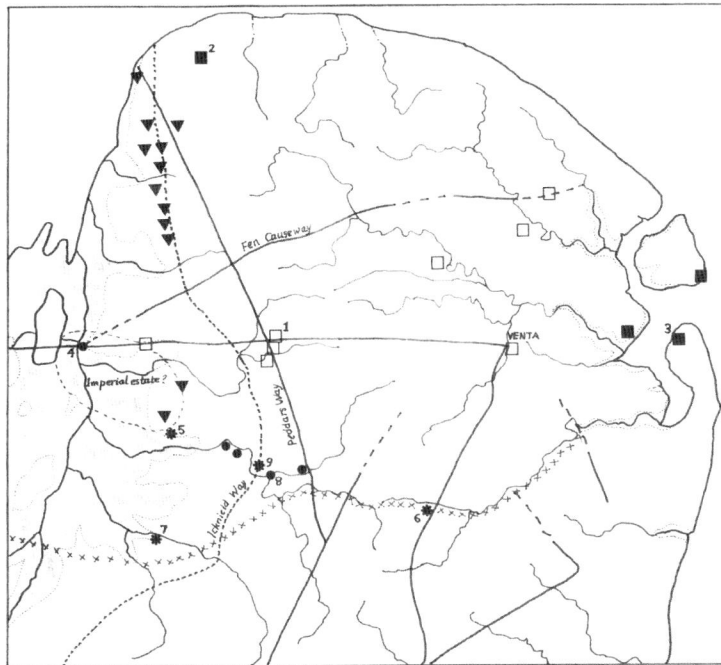

Fig. 1. Icenian Lands. Source: Davies 2009 and various, with approximate ancient coastlines. Shaded areas represent fens and wetlands,with standang water, marshes, seasonal flooding, and islands of higher, reliably dry land, especially around Stonea and the Isle ol Ely (Cambs.).
*Hockwold: temple with late Roman cache of ritual paraphernalia and headgear.

inland (Fig. 1).[3]

Claudius left the Iceni free when he conquered Britannia and founded a Roman colony at Camulodunum. He evidently trusted Prasutagus, *rex Icenorum*,[4] and may even have known him personally if they had been raised together in the Imperial household in Rome. They must have been of much the same age, and heirs to rulerships in important allied territories were often educated in that way, even sometimes awarded citizen rights. As a privileged neighbour of Claudius' new province, Prasutagus would have been obliged to hold things together and minimize conflict, and he seems to have achieved a long and prosperous reign not as a paramount war-lord, like Cunobelinus over the Catuvellauni and Trinovantes, but as a sacral head of state or chief officer of a league of territorial clans: in Roman terms, more like the early City's second king, Numa Pompilius, than their warrior founder, Romulus. The relevance of this comparison, with which anyone given a Latin education would have been familiar, will emerge, and might explain the only two, partially Latin, names or titles that we have for what must be the same individual: Prasutagus (secular: "presiding magistrate") and Esuprastus (sacral: Fig. 3. 8–9): "priest of Esus", cf. Roman *Pontifex Maximus*.[5]

Around this time, the site on Gallows Hill was completely redesigned and rebuilt (Fig. 3). A large central enclosure now featured an enormous round building with a second storey or tower, not apparently for domestic use or feasting, but with various empty pits and non-structural holes that might once have held such things as cult images or military standards. Outside the ditch, the north and west retained a funerary character with some actual graves but many more token burials or complete cenotaphs, some enclosed, some not, as if assembling the notable dead of many different clans.[6] A semi-detached southern annex enclosed what seems to have been a shallow pond, possibly sometimes heated, with a drain and two large internal post-holes (see **Tugios*).

Creation of this complex, now a gateway to the Roman Empire, is exactly the sort of community-building exercise that rulers are apt to conduct when political institutions change, including Claudius in Colchester. Romulus, for instance, founding Rome under ritual supervision, was said to have begun by digging a circular trench into which samples of produce and everything useful or necessary were placed, and to which every man in the founding population finally cast a little soil from his homeland, that was mixed in to represent the union of people of diverse origins.[7]

One enclosure in the Phase II funerary zone was used for metal working, and 109 fragments of clay moulds for silver pellets were found. If these represent an Icenian coin mint, it can only have been for their last possible coinage, inscribed *SUB ESUPRASTO / ESICO FECIT* (Fig. 3), struck either whilst the site was being rebuilt, or conceivably in

3 See Davies 2009, Chadburn 2006, Nash Briggs 2011 and 2012.
4 Tacitus *Annales* 14.31
5 Nash Briggs 2011, 94–5.
6 Perhaps as multiple *herôa*: cf. Haeussler 2010.
7 Plutarch *Romulus* 1.11. Two unexplained trenches close to where the previous focus had been (Fig. 3, F) might have served a purpose similar to Romulus' *mundus* when the site was rebuilt, and the position of the western one was respected when the site was rebuilt (Fig. 4).

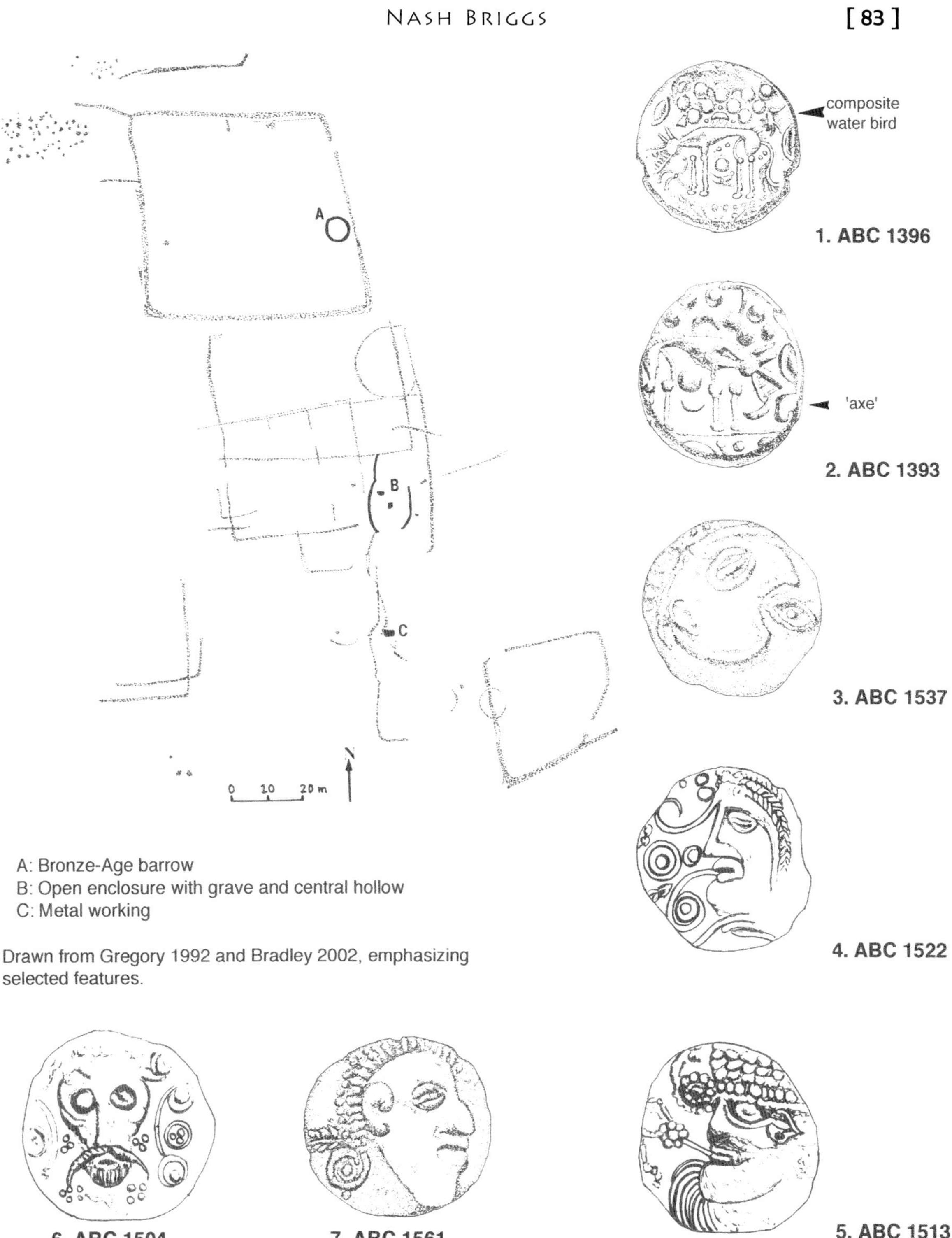

Fig. 2. Iron-Age site phase I (2nd century BC – *c.* AD 40) and Icenian coins contemporary with phase I

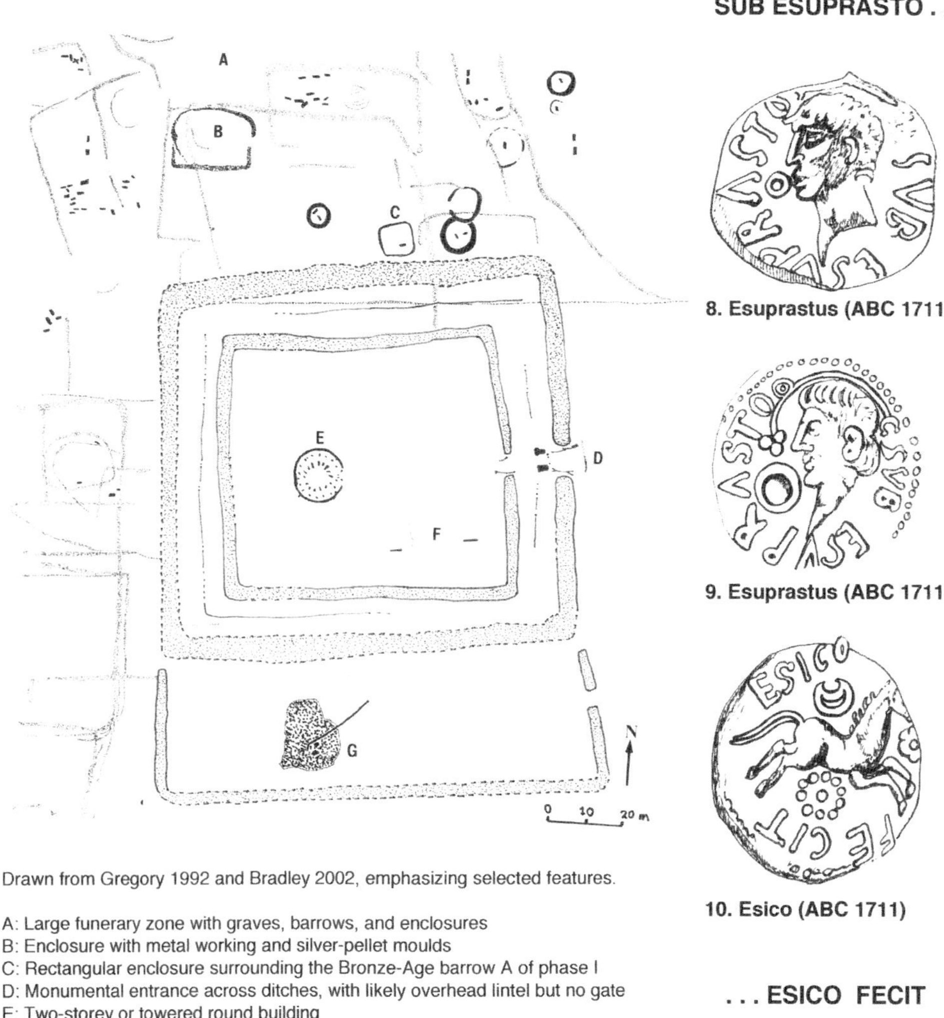

Fig. 3. Iron-Age site phase II (*c.*AD 40–50) and last Icenian coinage *c.* AD 35–45.

connection with the AD 47 uprising, which a Roman governor ill-advisedly provoked and only defeated after a costly campaign in the Fens. Prasutagus cannot have been held responsible for the violence, as he continued in office. Perhaps Esico had to pay an indemnity.

Subsequent events on Gallows Hill seem to reflect further tightening of the tribal union. Soon after AD 47 or around the time of Claudius' death and Nero's accession, the entire site was demolished and rebuilt, perhaps partly funded with money that Seneca is said to have foisted on the Iceni, presumably for pro-Roman projects (Fig. 4).[8] This

8 Dio Cassius *Roman History* 62.2.

time a vast, unified structure occupied the entire site. The existing central building was given a second, western entrance in whose shelter meadow hay and samples of the most recent harvest were stored to wait out the winter. Two matching but one-storeyed buildings now flanked it, each approached through an open compound in front, with a central grave-like hollow and an actual grave to one side, resembling the central compound in the phase I complex. It was a strange, spooky place, with restricted use, but some foreign visitors. Its new format seems to express cyclical concepts of death and renewal – of the sun, of vegetation, and, probably, of human life itself. It also reflects the mature territory's political structure, whose three districts were nominally equal, but one stood above the others. Timber for the nine serried ranks of tree-sized posts that enclosed the place – in effect, a permanently winter-dormant grove of oaks and ashes – must have come from all over the territory.

Prasutagus himself must have overseen such an imposing, expensive, act of landscape theatre, like Roman king Numa who was said to have called on the gods to help him civilize the stubborn, warlike people Romulus had left behind. This he was said to have done by leading the people in sacrifices, processions, and religious dances and by creating priesthoods.[9] All these things, in hindsight, could also have been ascribed to Prasutagus, who died in AD 60 or 61. Famously, he had wanted the kingdom shared between his own heirs and Nero, but Nero seized it all, and his soldiers' insulting treatment of Prasutagus' family and other prominent Iceni provoked such destructive reprisals that Nero is said to have considered abandoning Britain altogether.

The Romans did, of course, stay, and almost immediately after the AD 61 rebellion the Phase III monument was completely and, it seems, respectfully dismantled under military supervision. The administrative centre of the Roman *civitas,* Venta Icenorum, was located in the eastern district at Caistor St Edmund. In the west, extensive drainage was undertaken on the Fens, and there was a big Imperial estate with salterns and potteries around Denver, probably on land confiscated from Iron-Age leaders. The Roman *civitas* was a prosperous civilian environment with a thriving rural economy. In northern Norfolk almost everything still depended on landowing families, eventually in comfortable villas, notably along the Icknield Way (Fig. 1). Many must have descended from Iron-Age ruling clans, with tales of great deeds before the Romans. Activity and investment in religious life and skilled manufacturing was sustained at an exceptionally high level.[10]

For nearly three peaceful centuries Thetford was simply a convenient stopping-place on one of several major transport routes in Roman East Anglia. Control of the Icknield Way had lost its former political significance, whilst the road still linked the fen-edge estates, and, crucially, led to the part of the coast where marine currents must have made access to and from north Germany and Denmark exceptionally easy, even in small boats. On Gallows Hill, the vast bare ditches of the Iron-Age shrine, still a visible crop-mark in the 1980s, stood open where the road passed through, as though this

9 Plutarch *Numa* 7.
10 See e.g. Davies 2009 *passim*.

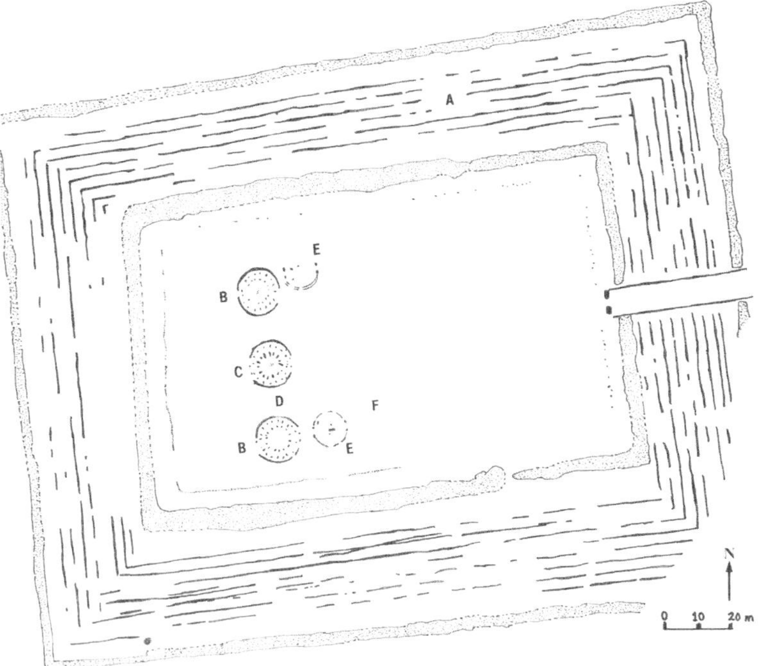

Drawn DNB from Gregory 1992 and Bradley 2002, emphasizing selected features.

A: Between massive ditches, 8 or 9 parallel rows of furrows planted with hundreds of felled trees, some still with branches.
B: New single-storeyed buildings.
C: Altered two-storey or towered building from phase II.
D: Area with numerous non-structural small pits and stake-holes.
E: Open compounds with grave-like centre hollow and prossible side graves.
F: Position of enclosure B of phase I; the western 'unexplained trench' from Phase II enters the southern compound just inside the north terminal of its entrance.

Silver coins of the Iceni, *c.*AD 10–35 and Verica Rex Commi f. (Regini and Atrebates, *c.* AD 10–40)

Fig. 4. Iron-Age site phase III (*c.*AD 50–61) and silver coins of the Iceni, *c.*AD 10–35 and Verica Rex Commi f.

place was *sacer* and best positively left wild. The ancient complex was never rebuilt – it was probably too identified with its specific role in the independent tribal kingdom – and Roman activities focussed elsewhere (Fig. 6). There was early Roman material on the line of the bypass, north-west of the ditches, and buildings were later erected to their south-west. Intensive activity by metal detectorists in the late 1970s produced copious finds, including an inscribed lead tablet,[11] probably several thousand mainly late Roman coins, allegedly several hoards of late Roman silver siliquae, and the 1979 treasure. Archaeological field work supervised by Tony Gregory in 1980 produced an additional 110 coins whose chronological distribution provides a credible profile of the likely overall pattern of Roman activity on the site, suggesting that it peaked in the later 4th century AD and continued at a high level until the end of Roman coin supply in Britain.[12] These developments coincide with officially sanctioned changes in *civitas* self-determination, reflected in various items in the Thetford treasure described below, and must relate to more pressing concerns than in the recent past about security on the Icknield way.

The 1979 Thetford treasure and its bilingual inscriptions

The treasure found in 1979, published in 1983, and now in the British Museum comprised a lathe-turned shale box with gold jewellery and gems and silver strainers and spoons, the latter in well-matched sets for 5 or 6 people that readily fall into three groups, like the layout of a grand late-Roman dining-room. Sadly, the current inventory is incomplete: some small items were probably not recovered when the treasure was unearthed, other objects were definitely parted from it, and it is impossible to establish how many other Roman finds from the site and its surroundings may once have related to it.[13] Nonetheless, the treasure is reassuringly self-consistent and suggests a collection that was very carefully assembled with some specific purpose in mind; a suggestion will be made in the Discussion.

The Bacchic orientation of the whole ensemble must represent the spiritual outlook of the people to whom it once belonged, and was widespread in late Roman Britain as an alternative to Christianity.[14] Bacchus, too, was a saviour god, and his cult is peculiarly well suited to this particular spot, representing, as Bacchus did, the triumph of life over death. More surprising is the prominence of a *deus Faunus*, so far unparalleled in Britain, and the eight non-Latin appellations coupled with his name.

To approach this, it helps to consider two contrasting strands in conventional

11 Hassall & Tomlin 1982, 410.
12 Gregory 1992, 119–20.
13 Contents now in the British Museum = Gold: 1 belt buckle, 22 finger rings, 4 bracelets, 5 necklaces, 2 loose pairs of clasps, 5 pendants (2 earrings, 1 amulet, 2 mounted gems), 1 unmounted gem and 4 loose beads. Silver: 3 strainers and 33 spoons (16 cygni, of which one was plain and uninscribed, and 17 cochlearea, 3 of which had parcel-gilt pictures); Chadburn 1995 identified a few missing items: ten freshly minted gold solidi of Magnus Maximus (AD 383–388), another ring like *JP* 19, and a small gold bust of a woman.
14 Henig 1995, 200–5; Toynbee 1962, 128–30.

Roman views of Faunus. One is more folkloric, representing him since Republican times as a pastoral *numen* and spirit of wild places, almost totally identified with Arcadian Pan Lykaios, and hence with the Bacchic scene. The names "Pan" and "Faunus" were freely interchanged, especially in verse. In standard 4th-century iconography, Pan with his companion flock of satyrs and fauns was a stock member of Bacchus' ecstatic and disorderly entourage, and the Thetford Faunus must have been pictured as present, with his own set of spoons, at a Bacchic feast (*lectisternium*). An exceptional little Pan-like mask found near Thetford could well represent the face of this particular divinity (Fig. 5.17).[15]

Faunus' other aspect had political connotations. Indigenous Latin Faunus was a powerful, quasi-historical entity, integral to the legendary history of Rome, and this, I think, was what made him so useful to the people represented by the Thetford treasure. In the early days of empire, the Romans had appealed to Arcadian Pan to bring an ancient, parochial, state cult into a grander Hellenistic and Classical present. In just the same way and for similar reasons, some Iceni seem to have appealed to Roman Faunus–Pan to give respectable 4th-century shape to a pre-Roman *numen* on Gallows Hill whose cult must have taken on fresh significance as they stepped forward to take charge of their own affairs in the twilight of effective Imperial governance. What links all the divinities concerned is their promotion of fertility, their special connection with fields, flocks, woods, and wild places, their perception as ancestral figures ready to advise on occult ritual matters, and their association with revered ancient kings like Roman Numa Pompilius and Icenian Prasutagus. Like the great god Pan, the resident spirit of Gallows Hill was decidedly not dead.[16]

The bilingual inscriptions[17]

1. ****ANDICROSOS*** *DEI FAV ANDICROSE* (*JP* 53) *AN* (*JP* 81)

'Unwilted, not drained, ithyphallic', hence, probably, 'evergreen' – a word-form like 'undeflated', from Gallo-Brittonic *an-* (=negative particle, 'not') + *dī-* (a prefix denoting negation or undoing, cf. Latin *dis-* or *de-*) + **cros[s]os* ('hardened, fleshed-out', *sc.* with blood).[18]

15 Davies 2009, 156.

16 There was a story, that appealed to Christians, that a sailor in Tiberius' reign had heard people on an Aegean island lamenting that the great god Pan was dead (Plutarch *Moralia* 5. 17). Thetford spoons inscribed *RESTITUTI VIVAS* and *VIR BONE VIVAS* could have been selected for a dual application to human celebrants and to the divinity whose cult was reinstated. The sulphur-filled amulet *JP* 30 has been related to the oracle of Faunus at Zolforata in Latium, an area of suphurous springs (Johns & Potter 1983, 50). Cf. the pond in the phase II complex on Gallows Hill (Fig. 3 site G). Prasutagus may have been responsible for the first links between Roman Faunus and the ancestral *numen* of Gallows Hill.

17 For previous discussions see Jackson 1983; De Bernardo Stempel 2008; Nash Briggs 2012.

18 Paul Kavanagh (*pers. comm.* 2010), whom I heartily thank for help with the Thetford inscriptions. Jackson (1983, 47) suggested < Gallo-Brittonic *andi-* (='in, into', or an intensifier) + *crose* which he did not recognize. De Bernardo Stempel (2007, 79) suggested < *andi-* + Gaulish *crosa* ('cave'), meaning 'of the deep cave'. *Crosa* = 'cave' is difficult to substantiate with Delamarre (2003) and the University of Wales Proto-Celtic Wordlist. A cave does indeed feature in relevant Roman *Faunus*-related stories,

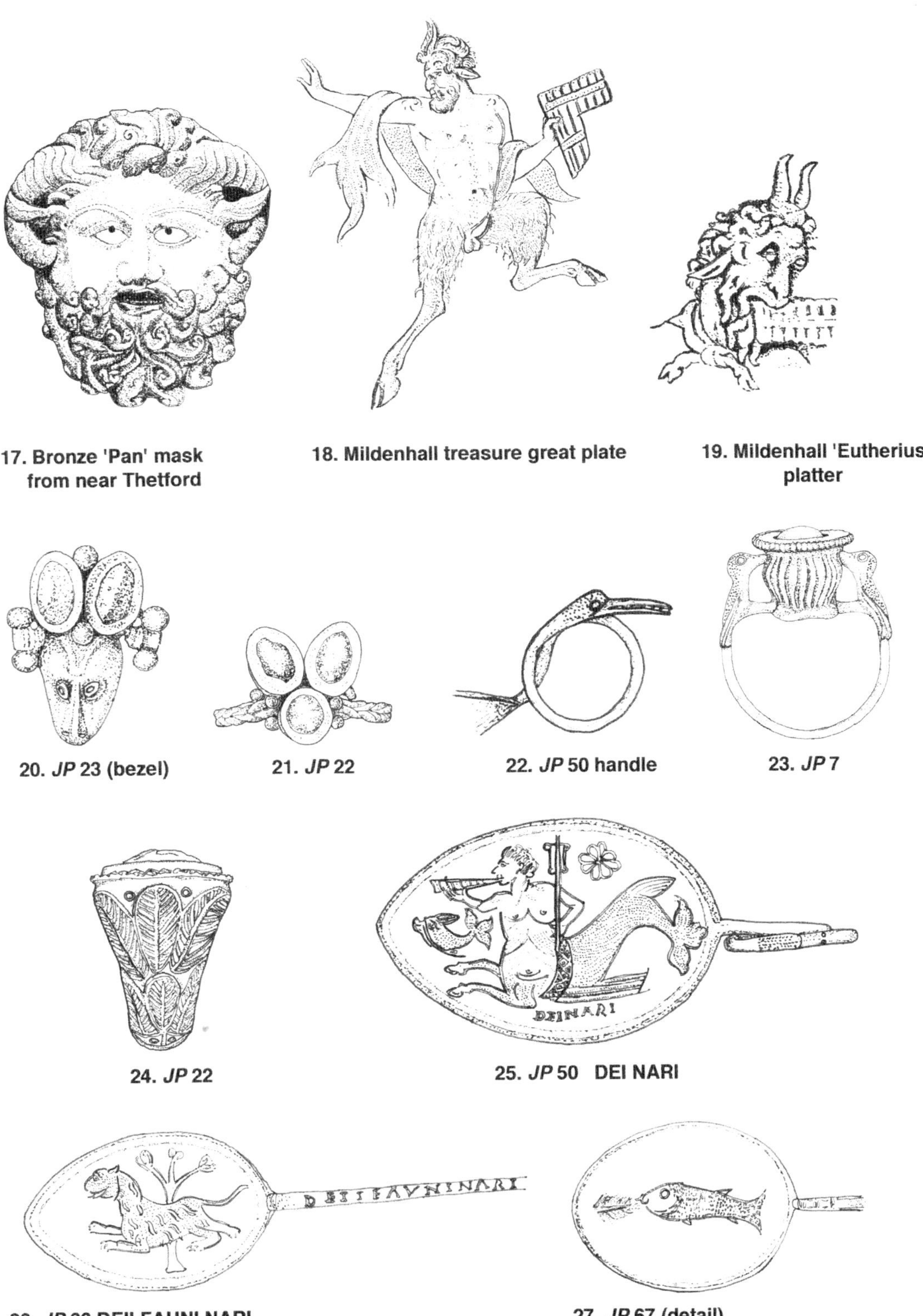

Fig. 5. 4th-century Faunus at Thetford.

*Faunus *Andicrosos* would be the libidinous Pan of the Bacchic scene on the Mildenhall (Suffolk) great dish (Fig. 5.18). In a popular fable that connects with several items in the Thetford treasure, Ovid tells of Faunus' lust for Hercules' royal Lydian mistress.[19] The pair were walking to a cave in a grove sacred to Bacchus, where they had rites to perform, when Faunus spotted the queen from a high ridge and lit up with desire (*vidit et incaluit* . . . '*hic meus ardor erit*'). The couple then exchanged clothing, jewellery, and equipment before retiring to separate beds for the night. At midnight, whilst they slept – *quid non amor improbus audet?* – Faunus crept in and groped around until he felt what he took to be the queen in her silky garments, and climbed into the bed with an erection harder than horn (*tumidum cornu durius inguen erat* = **andicrosos*). He had, of course, found Hercules, who shoved him onto the floor. When torches were lit and the truth was revealed, everyone laughed, and that, dear reader, is why Faunus hates deceptive clothing and summons people naked to his rites.[20]

More seriously, indigenous Roman traditions connected Faunus with the Lupercalia, a rowdy street festival of purification, fertility, and affirmation of the city boundaries on February 15 when winter had ended and the first lambs had been born.[21] It was still being celebrated in the 6th century AD, and was generally thought to be in Faunus' honour, which is what matters here. In the classic rites, a goat was sacrificed, and aristocratic young men from two colleges of Luperci, clad only in girdles cut from strips of the goat's skin, ran through the city streets, striking out with more of the skin. Women in the crowd who wished to get pregnant positioned themsleves for a propitious slap. Ovid explained that when wives in Rome were barren in Romulus' time, they had supplicated Juno in her sacred grove under the Esquiline hill, and she told them to "let the sacred he-goat go in to the Italian mothers".[22] Hence Faunus, as *Inuus*, was supposed to 'go in' to make all female creatures bear young – **andicrosos*, indeed. It may be relevant that several items in the Thetford collection do actually suggest an élite 4th-century wedding, and allude to the union of Venus and Mars.

Whilst the emphasis here is upon animal vigour, several of the Thetford divinity's other epithets also reflect the vegetal sphere, and **andicrosos* might reasonably include evergreen plants – including Bacchus' own ivy, that flowers in late autumn, survives the dead of winter unwilted, and fruits in late winter, typically in February.

---

but Norfolk has no natural caves, whilst the phallic interpretation matches Pan–Faunus stereotypes in Latin literary narratives and Bacchic iconography.

19 *Fasti* 2. 308–358: Hercules had to serve queen Omphale ('belly-button') of Lydia for a year, so she was his *domina* (*ibid.* 2. 305). A 4th-century noble lady was also a *domina*. Could this relate to the missing small gold bust of a woman (n. 12): cf. the 'empress' pepper-pot in the contemporary Hoxne treasure (Johns 2012, 78–85)?

20 Ovid *Fasti* 2. 358: *et nudos ad sua sacra vocat*. This tale could actually have been dramatized as entertainment at a nuptial feast: with the exception of one old ring, none of the Thetford jewellery, even the great gold buckle, seems ever actually to have been worn. References to Hercules include 2 club-shaped pendants (*JP* 28, 29), and to a marriage include the clasped-hands engagement ring *JP* 10.

21 A number of wolf-related themes link Roman Faunus and Rome's origin-legend with élite iconography in this part of East Anglia from the Iron Age well into the Anglo-Saxon period, but these lie outside the scope of this paper.

22 '*Italidas matres*', *inquit*, '*sacer hircus inito*': Ovid *Fasti* 2.425–452.

2. ***AVSECOS*** *DEI FAVNI AVSECI (JP 55) DEI FAV*[23] *AVSECI (JP 73)*

'Ear-ish', 'prick-ear', or 'of the ears'. **Ausicos* = **ausi-* ('ear') < I-E **aus-i-* or **aus-es-*, 'ear', as in Old Irish *au*, later *ó* 'ear', + adjectival suffix *-ico-* (cf. O.I. adj. *óach*).[24]

**Ausecos* may refer to the common image of Pan–Faunus with features resembling a goat or sheep (Fig. 5.17–21), but it also describes one with big ears who listens and hears everything – a trait shared by several of the heads on Icenian Iron-Age coins (Fig. 2.5–7). Latin Faunus also had an intrinsic connection with the sort of farming economy that typified ancient East Anglia. In times of great distress sacral rulers everywhere must be seen to be doing something constructive, so when a succession of disastrous droughts and floods had ruined harvests and caused livestock to abort, king Numa is said to have retired to a wholly wild grove, and after performing preliminary rites, sacrificed two ewes, one to Faunus and one to Sleep, and slept on their skins in quest of a remedy.[25] Faunus came to him in his sleep, and asked him for sacrifice (of a cow in calf).

Occult divination of exactly this sort could in principle have been performed in the Iron-Age 'grove' on Gallows Hill, perhaps in its various grave-like hollows. Certainly, the only domestic animal bones identified were some sheep's lower leg bones and feet, as if from headless skins. If **ausecos* can also mean 'of the corn ears', it has vegetal resonance that evokes the the annual store of semi-cleaned barley in the phase III site and connects with many coin images of an Icenian grain-god (see **Saternios* and Figs. 2.4, 5, 7; 4.11–14).

3. ***BLOTVCOS*** *DEI FAV BLOTUCI* (*JP* 57) *BLO* (*JP* 64, 75, 80)

'Of the blossom', 'blooming'. Late version with */-o-/* of **blātucos*, from Gallo-Brittonic **blātu-* or **blāto-* 'flower, blossom', as in Welsh *blawd*, cf. Latin *flos*, and/or perhaps **blāti-* or **blāto-* 'flour', as in the other Welsh *blawd* or French *blé,* + adjectival-formative suffix *-uco-*.[26]

This would be a potent vegetal spirit, akin to **Andicrosos*, bringing Spring and making woods and meadows bloom. Classical comparanda for a *Faunus* **Blātucos* are less compelling than others from the local Iron Age. On Icenian coins contemporary with phase I of the Fison Way complex, heads may breathe tendrils and flowers and the tribal boar has sprouts among the bristles on his back (Figs. 2 & 4). Fresh hay with meadow flowers and summer fruits were stored for the winter in the phase III shrine, whilst a 4th-century **Blotugus*' blossom would enable bees to make honey for mead (see **Medugenus*).

23 Ligatured letters in inscriptions are underlined. *AV* may also be read as *AVN*.

24 Cf. Gaulish woman's name *Suausia* 'with beautiful ears' or Latin *auris*, 'ear', *ausculto*, 'I listen' (Jackson 1983, 47; De Bernardo Stempel 2007, 78). Latin *lupercus*, 'wolfish', is a grammatically similar formation.

25 Ovid *Fasti* 4. 650–72.

26 Jackson (1983:47); De Bernardo Stempel (2008, 78). For /ā/ becoming /o/ cf. a late Gaulish god *Bloturix* (for *Blaturix*, King of Blossom) in Lorraine (Kavanagh, *pers. comm.*).

4. ***CRANOS** *DEI FAVNI * CRANI* (JP 52, 74, both times with leaf-shaped word separator).[27]
CRA (JP 82)
**Cranos* makes potential sense in at least three relevant languages and must be a cross-cultural instance of the well-known ancient fascination with speculative etymologizing, verbal and visual riddles, and cryptic allusions, especially in the realms of politics and religious mystery. **Saternios* (below) is a transparently bilingual example on another Thetford spoon. Here we encounter:

1. Brittonic 'of the stores, barn, or treasury', cf. Welsh *crawn*, 'accumulated treasure' < PIE **krā[u]*-, 'put together in a heap, conceal' + suffix *-*nos* denoting 'master of' or 'concerned with', as in several other Indo-European theonyms.[28] **Cranos* would be patron of landowners, farmers, and estate-managers by guarding haystacks, granaries, and stores, as for instance in the central building on the Iron-Age site. He would also guard any revenues derived from managing transport across the *civitas* border, likely to have been of heightened interest in the late 4th century AD. The recently demolished timber structure by which the Thetford treasure was actually buried could perfectly well have been a store-house or barn. PIE **krā[u]*- also gives Old Irish *cráu*, *cró*, 'stall, hut, shed', Welsh *craw,* Cornish *crow*, and Breton *kraou,* 'animal stall',[29] compatible with Classical *Faunus'* pastoral responsibilities.

2. 'The head'. '*FAUNUS CRANOS*, obviously representing the real Greek epithet κράνος, "with a ram's head"',[30] might describe the Latin poets' *Faunus bicornis* of the Mildenhall plates or the little ram-horned mask from near Thetford (Fig. 5).[31] These educated people may well have been playing with Greek here, but κράνος ('helmet'), κρανίον ('[upper] head [of men and animals]', 'crown of the head', or 'skull'), and various other related words, all denote heads without horns.[32] However, **cranos*, simply as a head, could apply to a revered ancestral figure. 'Old gods', deified legendary figures, and family ancestors had for centuries been represented both in Insular and Continental iconography by their heads alone, often ascribed the power of inspired speech. Old images must have helped to keep stories alive, if not always faithfully transmitted. The Icenian figures represented by the 'head' ring in the treasure and by the central 'head' emblem in the design of contemporary *civitas* military insignia (Fig. 6) must be of this kind.[33]

3. 'The Voice (in the marshes)'. In northern East Anglia, Germanic vocabulary would

27 This feature, perhaps simply a decorative choice by the engraver, is unique here to the pair of *CRANI* spoons and to *JP* 59, *VTI * FELIX*, whose duck has the same eye detail as the *CRANI* duck *JP* 52, but is not carrying a cake.
28 Jackson 1983, 47 (a more promising lead than he seems to have thought); on *-*nos* see West 2007, 137.
29 Jackson 1983, 47; Pokorny 1959, 616.
30 De Bernardo Stempel 2008, 78.
31 Ovid *Fasti* 2. 268, cf. 3. 312, *'sic quatiens cornua Faunus ait...'*
32 Nussbaum 1986, 228. Nothing justifies *CRANI* meaning 'horn', which would require the /a/ and /r/ of a horn-word to be reversed in a way that would be equally anomalous in Latin, Brittonic, and Germanic. See Fig. 2.6 for an Iron-Age skull-like image.
33 E.g. Ross 1998 Cf. Fig. 4.16, on a silver coin of Verica, king of the Regini and Atrebates *c.* AD 10–40; the head on a thin pillar apparently stuck in the ground, as items in the Fison Way shrine may have been, must be an *imago* of Commius, Verica's dynastic ancestor (not literally his father).

never have been out of place, especially in the late 4th century AD. PIE **grā* > Proto-Gmc. **kranōn* name the crane and other large birds of wetlands and marshes, giving OE *cran (<kranaz)* 'crane' and O.Sax. *krano*, 'heron, stork'. **Kranōn* is derivationally close to Greek γέρανος, Gaulish *(tri)garanos* ('crane', cf. *Gariennus*, Norfolk's River Yare, and *Gariannum*, the late Roman coastal fort of Burgh Castle). It also relates to Gmc. **kerranan*, 'to creak' or cackle, cf OE verb *crāwan* 'to crow' like a cock, or 'cry' like a bird.[34] The common crane has a loud, piercing cry. **Cranos* would then be one whose voice is heard in the fens and marshes, like *Faunus Fatuus* and *Pan*, whose voices spooked travellers in lonely places. The little ram-horned mask from near Thetford is in fact uttering, as were several heads on relevant Icenian coinage (cf. **Cranos* (2) and Figs. 2.3–5; 3.8; 4.11). Roman Faunus was said to be son of Picus, the green woodpecker (cf. woodpecker ring Fig. 5.23), and if the Gallows Hill *numen* had his own avian *alias*, a crane, bittern, or heron are plausible candidates. For centuries on end, from late prehistory until long after the Romans had left, East Anglian élites employed water-bird imagery as signifiers, perhaps of clan identity. This is seen, for instance, in a composite lapwing–bittern–avocet device on 1st-century BC Icenian gold staters (Fig. 2.1), the emphatically duck-billed dolphins of the late-Roman Icenian *civitas* insignia and two of the Thetford rings (Fig. 6. 28–30), and the unusually detailed modelling of the treasure's duck-handled spoons, notably the toothed and snarling crane-like head on *Deus *Narios*' (q.v.) own spoon (Fig. 5. 22, 25).[35]

4. 'The tree', cf. Greek κράνος and κράνον, Latin *cornus, cornum*, the Mediterranean cornel-cherry, which, like ivy, flowers in February, has wood so favoured for spear-shafts that κράνον could actually mean 'spear', and has useful fruit for grazing swine. This *Faunus *Cranos* would be a *Silvanus* or, like *Dionysus* (*Bacchus*), δενδρίτης or ἔνδενδρος.[36] It would relate to Latin Faunus' woodland character and also connect with the leaf-shaped word-separator on the *CRANI* spoons and the leaf-decoration on three gold rings in the treasure (*JP* 2, 3, 4) and in the manes of the fighting horses on the great gold buckle (*JP* 1). The woodpeckers of ring *JP* 7 (Fig. 5.23) point to Faunus' father Picus and the woodpeckers that helped to feed the infants Romulus and Remus. The ancient Latin royal line boasted a succession of Silvii, most famously the mother of Romulus and Remus, and in the 4th-century treasure a Silviola is honoured on two of the spoons.[37]

34 Orel 2003, 220, 213; Pokorny 1959, 384.

35 For the composite bird see Kretz 1999. *Picus viridis*, the green woodpecker, is commonly known as the yaffle from its distinctive, haunting call: like *Faunus–Pan*, this typical bird of woodland edges and sheep-grazed clearings is more often heard than seen.

36 Hidden faces appear in the foliage on the large ring *JP* 2 (Fig. 5.24), whose gem shows cupid riding a lion, a Bacchic device. In Celtic, PIE **kwres-*, 'wood, copse, tree (?)' > Old Irish *crann* ('tree' < proto-Celtic **kwresno* or *kwranno: University of Wales Proto-Celtic Wordlist). In Brittonic, a word on this root should have initial */p-/*, as in Gaulish *prenne* ('large tree': Delamarre 2003, 251; cf Greek πρῖνος, 'holm-oak'), so for **cranos* to mean 'tree' in a Celtic language, it would have to represent a fossilized relic of proto-Celtic vocabulary for some particular kind of tree that escaped the Brittonic shift of **kw* > **p*, or else be an outright loan-word from Irish, by no means unthinkable in Britain at this time.

37 She could have been the bride of the man with the enormous, official, Roman military-Mars ring *JP* 16, for whom the great buckle may also have been made (as part of her dowry?) and have been related to the Silvicola at Hoxne – there is no need to invoke a spelling mistake; cf. in the Iron Age, the Germanic

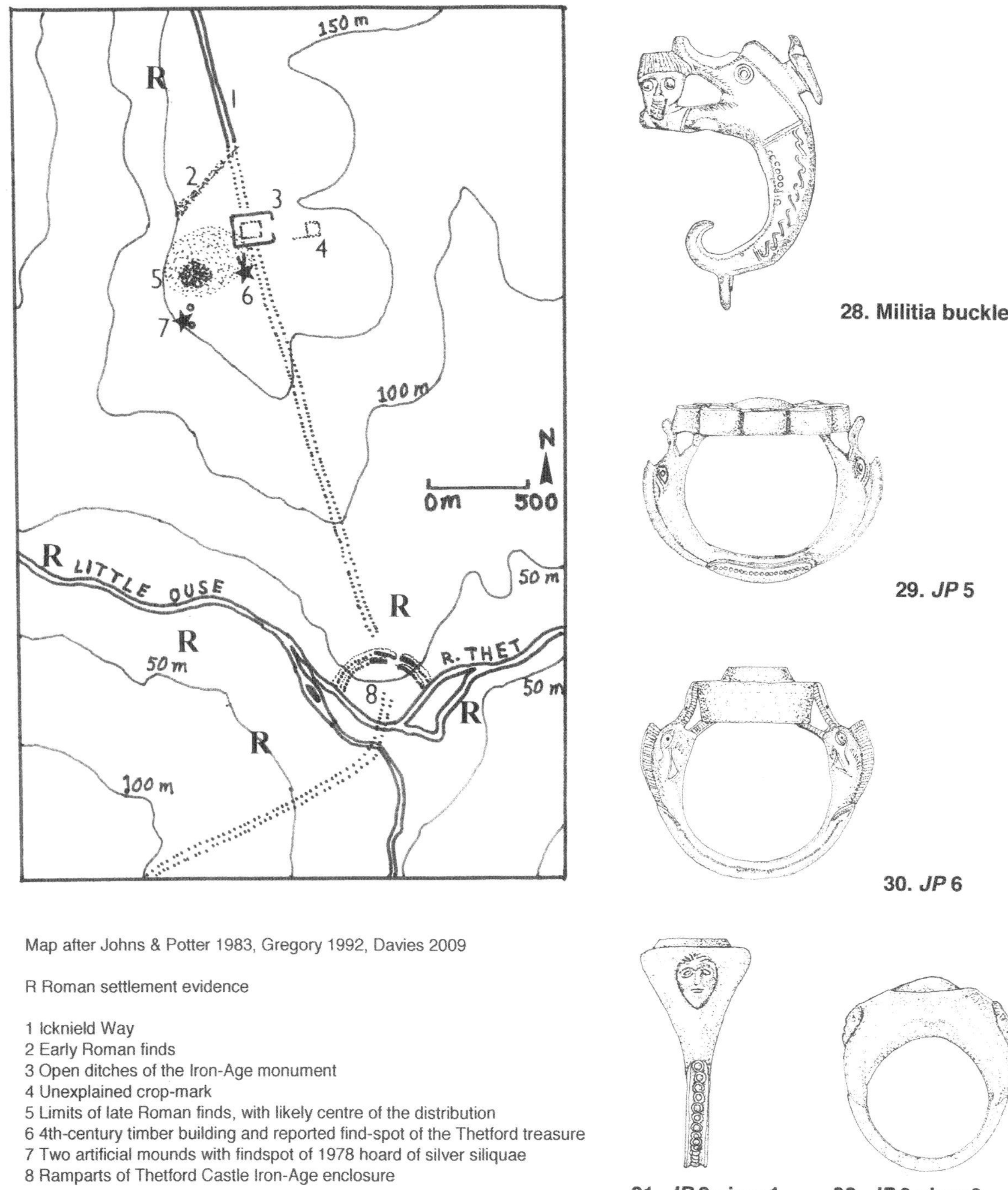

Fig. 6. Gallows Hill, phase IV: AD 61–*c*.400 and late 4th-century Icenian *civitas* insignia. Line drawings DNB: 28 half of an Icenian bronze militia buckle found by the Icknield Way near Tring in 2008 (private collection); 29–32 after Johns & Potter 1983.

On Gallows Hill, a vast grove of symbolic winter-dormant trees had surrounded the last version of the Iron-Age complex.

5. ***MEDVGENOS, *MEDIGENOS** *DEI FAV MEDVGENI (JP* 54) *DEII FAVNI MEDIGENI (JP 56) DEI FAV MEDIGENI (JP* 71) *MED (JP* 79)
'Mead-begotten', from Celtic *medu* (mead) + *genos* ('clan, family' < **gen-*, 'to beget, give birth to').

**Medugenos* is linguistically straightforward but culturally startling. Bacchus, Pan, and Faunus were involved exclusively with wine, of which not even Bacchus was said to have been literally begotten. It is true that in Roman tradition king Numa was said to have captured Faunus and Picus by getting them drunk (for his motive, see **Tugios*), but he did this with wine (*pocula Bacchi; mero*), of which the woodland spirits were innocent. Late-Roman banqueters did commonly drink *mulsum*, a potent intoxicant made from wine with honey added in the cup – for instance with the eminently practical implement *JP* 49 – and some later writers did say Numa used *mulsum* as bait.[38] But *mulsum* is still wine, and mead had very different connotations. From any late Roman's point of view, it was the quintessential drink of nobles and heroes outside the Roman empire, in the mead-halls of contemporary north Germany and Scandinavia. **Medugenos* is an élite, obliquely theophoric, name-form like Brittonic *Bodvogenus* (who was a superb 2nd- or 3rd-century AD metal-smith in the Fens), or 3rd/4th-century Germanic *Aessicunia* at Bath, and suggests a lost origin-myth for the *genius loci* of Gallows Hill that had useful Germanic resonance, in the spirit of *Cranos* (3).[39] Like Classical Pan and Faunus – even aspects of Bacchus himself – the ancient *numen* of Fison Way could certainly be described as aboriginal and powerful, was probably likewise semi-divine, and very possibly, like Pan and Bacchus in Italy or Roman Faunus in Britain, was considered an honoured outsider from overseas (cf. **Narios*). It is also entirely possible that one way to contact such a spirit on weighty public business was to induce a ritual stupor with an intoxicant based on mead – and that this is what is seen in some first-century Icenian coin images with heads speaking from a death-like state of apparently visionary trance (Fig. 2.3–5, 7). A god thus summoned might be loosely described as mead-begotten.

6. ***NARIOS** *DEI NARI (JP* 50: parcel-gilt picture spoon with Triton) *DEII FAVNI NARI (JP* 66: parcel-gilt picture spoon with Bacchic tigress) *DEII FAVNI NARI (JP* 51)
'The Hero', 'the Lord', 'the powerful, noble, great-hearted Man', cf. Gaulish *Narius*, f. *Naria*, *Deae Nariae*. If **Nārius*, cf. Old Irish *nár* ('man, person'); if with a short /*a*/, cf. early Welsh *nar*, < IE **ner-* 'man, hero, virile strength' > proto-Celtic **nero-* (?), 'hero' > Welsh *ner*, 'hero', Old Irish *ner*, 'boar', hence 'the manly, boar-like [Faunus]'.[40]

élite name or title ECEN ('oaken': Nash Briggs 2011, 86–7) authorizing one of the most extensive 1st-century Icenian silver coinages, as it happens from this central canton (Chadburn 2006, 484).

38 Wine: Ovid *Fasti* 3.301, 304; *mulsum*: Plutarch *Numa* 15.4 (put wine & honey in their water); Arnobius *Adversus Gentes* 5.1 (*mulsum*).

39 On Aessicunia, which would be *Esugenos in Brittonic, see Nash Briggs 2011, 89.

40 Jackson 1983, 47; Delamarre 2003 s.v. *nerto-*, 'strength, vigour, power'; Pokorny 1959, 765; cf. Ger-

This, on the god's own spoons, may well be his primary, public title in Thetford: cf. the Man on the ring (**Cranos* (2)) and the acclamation VIR BONE VIVAS of *JP* 60. The name of Faunus himself was considered a euphemistic contraction of *Favonius*, for a potentially very dangerous spirit whose secret name was unspoken.

**Narios* has some martial overtones, implicit in the boar-connotation and reflected in the emphatically boar-crested, duck-billed dolphins of the late Icenian *civitas* insignia (Fig. 6. 28–30). The 'Norfolk god' depicted on the 1st-century coinage, probably a Mars-type Teutatis, wears a boar's-skin headdress or can swap places entirely with a boar (Fig. 4. 11).[41] *Deus *Narios*' own parcel-gilt spoon (Fig. 5. 25) depicts a Triton, a conventional figure from Oceanus' retinue in Bacchic iconography, except that this one is amphibious and equestrian. He has a horse's forelegs (abnormal for a Triton, but related to the fighting horses on the treasure's great gold buckle, *JP* 1), he wears a cavalry belt with the same gaudy aesthetic as some jewels in the treasure, including the dolphin-boar rings; he holds his steering oar like a military standard, has a back body modelled like a boat, and blows his conch like a commander. Even the spoon's handle is modelled as an aggressive crane-like bird baring a row of teeth (Fig.5. 22 ; cf **Cranos* (3)). **Narios* here points to other well-known outsiders in the Roman legendary past, like Aeneas, a putative ancestor of the Julian line, or Arcadian Evander (another 'Good Man' with a golden reign) who arrived in Latium as an exile with his prophetess mother to be welcomed by Faunus, king of the *Aborigines*, and allegedly introduced the rites of Pan Lykaios. A parallel Icenian narrative about Prasutagus, Claudius, and the coming of Faunus to Thetford could easily have been woven during the centuries when they were Romans.[42]

7. ****SATERNIOS*** *DEO FAVNI SATERNIO* (*JP* 58)

'Giver of plenty', 'sower of seeds'. From PIE **sā-/ sa-* ('plenty, swarm', cf. Latin *satis*) + suffix *-erno-* > 'giver of plenty' or proto-Celtic **satā* ('seed') + derivational suffix **-ernj-*, as in proto-Celtic **tigerno-* or **tegernjo- (?)* "ruler", "lord" < **tegos*, "house" (cf. Lat. *dominus* < *domus* and 5th-century British *Vortigern*).[43]

A *deus *Saternios* would guarantee abundance – flocks of animals, swarms of bees, shoals of coins and glittering treasure, and especially the collection and sowing of seeds (cf. **Andicrosos, *Blotugos,* and **Cranos* (1)). Many images on 1st-century Icenian silver coinage represent a guardian of the seed-corn and harvest. Heads have seeds for hair or a barley-beard; the federal god's emblematic boar (cf. **Narios*) has sprouts amongst his

manic goddess *Nerthus* (Tacitus *Germania* 40.2). Italic Mars – similar to the Icenian Iron-Age tribal god – had a consort, *Nerio* ('Valour'). Hero: University of Wales Proto-Celtic wordlist; boar: Pokorny 1959, 765 and De Bernardo Stempel 2008, 79, who regards *Blotugos, Medugenos* and *Narios* as coined on Greek epithets usually associated with Dionysus.

41 See Nash Briggs 2012 for details and *ead.* 2014 for a 5th-century sequel in Thetford.

42 Esico who struck coins *sub Esuprasto*, possibly actually in the second Gallows Hill complex, has a good German name, and the house-mice in the phase III grain store were genetically German (Nash Briggs 2012, 44). Faunus was a minor divinity (*habent fines numina nostra suos*: Ovid *Fasti* 3. 314). Evander: Ovid *Fasti* 2. 279; Faunus as King of *Aborigines*: Dion. Hal. 1.31.2.

43 Jackson 1983, 47; University of Wales Proto-Celtic Lexicon; Kavanagh *pers. comm.* 2010.

bristles; the tribal mare, perhaps his mate, sheds grain from her body and may have a leaf for a tail (Figs. 2. 7, 4. 11–14). Semi-cleaned barley was amongst the harvest stored in the central building in the phase III shrine on Gallows Hill.

**Saternios* has additional chthonic and political connotations. It has long been observed that it must play on the name of Roman Saturn. In some versions of Faunus' doubtful origins his father was (Martius) Picus, son of Saturn, with whom both Faunus and the Icenian god certainly shared attributes.[44] This was a grand and propitious lineage: Mars was also said to have fathered the founders of Rome, a legend referenced elsewhere in the Thetford treasure, and in addition to potent agrarian functions, was, of course, a horse-connected god of war (cf. **Narios*). In Roman Imperial legend, Saturn, identified with Greek Kronos, was said to have come to Italy long before Evander and established himself on the Capitol hill where he founded a fortified village reputedly called *Saturnia*. He gave a wild people their first laws, taught them to till the land and cultivate the vine, and in historical times his temple was the Roman state treasury: cf. **Cranos* (1). Saturn's consort was Ops ('Plenty'), and for Romans, 'Saturn's reign' was a by-word for an ideal state of peace, order, and plenty.[45] There had certainly been revenues, metal-working, and a coin mint during the lifetime of the Iron-Age site on Gallows Hill. **Saternios* hints that its ancient *numen*, whose character overlapped with that of Faunus, may have been ascribed a similar lineage, which would then connect with the final appellation in the series in the Thetford treasure.

8. ****TVGIOS*** *DEI TVGI* (*JP* 78)

'Striker', 'Blade' < **touga*, 'axe': a striking, reaping, or cutting blade.[46] Cf. compound aristocratic names *Togimarus, Togirix, Togodumnus*.

Not inscribed in the bowl of any spoon, nor coupled with the name *Faunus,* but simply *DEI TVGI* on the handle of one cochleare with straight, undecorated stem, resembling *JP* 76, 77 *RESTITVTI*, 79 *MED*, 80 *BLO*, and 82 *CRA* (with which it might make a set of 6), and the two parcel-gilt cochlearia: 66 tigress with *DEII FAVNI NARI* and 67 fish with feather, uninscribed.

If **Tugios* relates to Faunus at all, it might allude to the sacrificial knife with which the officiating priest at the Lupercalia smeared the foreheads of the leading pair of *Luperci* with blood from the goat he had just sacrificed, whereupon the lads were obliged to laugh. **Tugios* describes one who cuts or strikes, and good gods also destroy, like Esus of the Paris monument laying an axe to a willow tree.[47] Without autumn and winter there would be no Spring; without night there can be no dawn; without death

44 Faunus and Saturn: Virgil *Aen.* 7. 47–49. Saturn's own name was sometimes said to be derived from 'sowing': Macrobius *Saturnalia* 1.10.19. Macrobius, together with Virgil and Ovid, are invaluable sources for what educated Romans may have thought.

45 E.g. Virgil, whose words in *Ecl.* 4.7, *redeunt Saturnia regna,* were indexed in place of a London mint-mark on coins of Carausius (AD 286–293: de la Bédoyère 2005).

46 Delamarre 2003, 298.

47 *Tarvos trigaranos* on another of its faces might connect with **Cranos* (3). Cf. Saturn's reputation for teaching the art of grafting shoots and managing trees: Macrobius, *Saturnalia* 1.7.25.

there cannot be renewal – central themes in Bacchic spirituality but also implicit in the funerary character and seasonal reference of successive Iron-Age monuments on Gallows Hill, themselves repeatedly demolished, renewed, and demolished again. Saturn's most enduring symbol was a great bill-hook or sickle, still pictured with the Grim Reaper, and Romans celebrated the vastly popular Saturnalia in December, after the rustic Faunalia and just before the winter solstice.

Tugios also raises the prerogatives of kings and rulers, and here it may be significant that this name, alone in the collection, is not coupled with Faunus'. The axe was a widespread ancient symbol of rule, representing sacrificial obligations and a godlike right to enforce executions. An axe, bundled with rods (*fasces*), was emblematic of a Roman consul's supreme authority, whilst axes, or axe-like symbols, are represented on a number of Iron-Age coin types in Gaul and Britain. In the design of early Icenian gold staters (mid-1st century BC) one such device accompanies a monstrous water-wolf eating the moon (Fig. 2.2).[48]

Many ancient civilizations were uncomfortably aware that their otherwise admired ancestors had practised human sacrifice to placate dangerous gods, and had legends to explain how some celebrated figure had successfully negotiated substitutes with the deity in question. These stories occur in both Greek and Latin literature to explain various peculiar features of cult practices, and one in particular is relevant to the Thetford treasure. In a popular story held up to ridicule by the 4th-century Christian apologist, Arnobius of Sicca, Roman King Numa captured Faunus and Picus by getting them drunk. He needed their help to call Jupiter out of the sky to instruct him how to expiate angry red lightning-bolts. It is implicit in what ensued that Jupiter actually wanted human sacrifice by decapitation, for which Numa improvised cunning substitutes. Jupiter said, "cut off a head". Numa said he would cut an onion from his garden. Jupiter said, "a man's". Numa said he would get (the) hair. Jupiter said, "a life" (*anima*); Numa said he could have a fish's [*anima*]. Jupiter laughed (cf. Luperci laughing when their brows were wiped with the bloodied blade), accepted these offerings to expiate his weapons, complimented Numa's courage in speaking with a god, and went on to affirm his rulership, and the future glory of his city, by promising to send a public pledge of empire the next day, which he duly fulfilled.[49]

These were iconic scenes in the legendary history of early Rome, for which Faunus as well as Numa could be thanked, and may help to explain not only this inscription, but also the selection of an uninscribed spoon with a fish in the set of three parcel-gilt spoons – the others were *JP* 50 (*DEI NARI* and Triton), and *JP* 66 (*DEII FAVNI NARI* and Bacchic tigress) – probably for the *numen* himself at the feast (Fig. 5.27). Fish were often pictured on late-Roman tableware, and can be variously understood, but this one nibbles something like the silver-foil votive plaques – themselves symbolic substitutes for other sorts of sacrifice – that were commonly used as thank-offerings in the 4th century AD, even by Christians. Its presence suggests this fish is alive, as Numa promised Jupiter

48 On this Iron-Age myth see Nash Briggs 2010.
49 Ovid *Fasti* 3.339–344.

that his victim would be.

Roman Iceni must also have had to explain what their own forebears had put in place of human sacrifice, since there can be little doubt that they, and countless others in Britain, *had* formerly sacrificed human victims in circumstances deemed appropriate.[50] This would have had to stop in a privileged territory adjacent to Claudius' new province, perhaps as a condition of being left free. In this, as in many other respects, Prasutagus' record would have been easy to match in hindsight with the reputation of the Romans' own king Numa. Both were said to have had long and prosperous reigns as lawgivers and sacral kings, both kept formerly bellicose populations occupied building monuments and celebrating festivals, and the artificial (fish-?) pond in the second-phase enclosure on Gallows Hill could even have been the setting for symbolic enactments of surrogate sacrificial hangings or drownings from a structure set in its pair of post-holes, analogous with the annual 'drownings' of straw 'men' that the Romans themselves cast into the Tiber from a bridge.[51]

Discussion

Enough has now been said to suggest a high degree of correspondence between some local Iron-Age cult traditions, with which the non-Latin theonyms in the treasure connect, some Classical narratives concerning Faunus that may account for the association of his name with theirs, and the relevance of late-Roman Bacchic spirituality to the people represented in the treasure. I would like to conclude with a speculative sketch of some historical circumstances that might help to explain why this treasure was assembled and buried where and when it was.

I begin with the premise that descendants of several pre-Roman ruling clans were still amongst the big landowners in the area, some indeed senior office-holders in the *civitas*, and others perhaps with hereditary priesthoods. Like aristocrats anywhere they would all have had more or less credible family traditions about notable ancestors that could be called upon, embellished, and reinvented to suit their purposes as history rolled on. It is most unlikely that Prasutagus' clan, for instance, would have forgotten or forgiven Nero's treatment of his widow and daughters or his confiscation of their property in the Breckland and Fens.

At some point in the later 4th century, a number of southern British *civitates* seem to have formed what must have been officially sanctioned local militia, rather like mounted police, whose distinctive belt-buckles have geographical distributions that almost exactly match those of late-Iron-Age coinages.[52] Rings in the Thetford treasure

50 Iron-age anthropoid swords (one was found at Shouldham, west Norfolk) and a specific sort of large, shallow, bronze spoon with internal markings and a small hole through which a viscous liquid can drip (one was found at Ditchingham, east Norfolk: John Davies, *pers. comm.*), have been recognized as specialized equipment for blood sacrifice and divination (Fitzpatrick 1996).

51 Argei: e.g. Ovid *Fasti* 5. 625–634, cf. Macrobius *Saturnalia* 1.7.30–31: Saturn and Dis were said to have received human sacrifice in Italy until Hercules made substitutes.

52 See the classic study by Laycock 2008.

shed unexpected light on this initiative amongst the Iceni, whose specific signifier was a pair of duck-billed, boar-crested, military dolphins exactly like those modelled on one pair of Thetford rings, upholding a bare (divine or civilian) head, resembling the heads on another ring in the treasure and some Iron-Age coinages (Fig. 6; cf. 4. 15). Julian Caesar's *magister militum*, Lupicinus, may well have taken steps to formalize these units when he was in London in AD 360 on business connected with the provinces' security. The Mildenhall great plate and matching platters – almost certainly his own – would have made handsome and well-selected gifts to an Icenian official of curial class charged with commissioning the local militia and with regulating, even taxing, traffic on the Icknield Way. Personal loyalty of such people to Lupicinus may have been what made Julian so nervous after the army in Trier had declared him Augustus, that he had Lupicinus recalled and arrested before he had time to react to the news.[53] Lupicinus' arrangements in Britain apparently held, and the visible surge in activity on Gallows Hill would be compatible with its having had, for instance, a guard-house, assembly-ground, and storage facilities, whilst under Julian a shrine to the old presiding spirit of the place could have been openly restored, coupled with the name of Roman Faunus. This match – not, for instance, with rustic Silvanus[54] – might first have been made centuries before, and afforded the old spirit of the place a politically safe ongoing identity in Bacchus' retinue, but his own appellations in the Thetford treasure suggest that his Iron-Age character as *deus *Narios* and **Tugios* was stirring. The indigenous *numen* had been there long before the Romans first arrived, just as Faunus had been king in Latium long before Rome was founded, and, what is more, was ancestral to the Roman royal line. Children born around this time were given personal names that seem to celebrate both the reinstated cult in Thetford and this thread in Roman legendary history – to which, I think, they were relating a view of their own pre-Roman past: Silviola, Agrestis, Auspicius, Primigenia, Ingenua, Restitutus.

Some time later, a young couple from this generation were engaged and married with Deus (Faunus) *Narios' (and Bacchus') blessing — a rich, civilian bride, perhaps from the family that owned the Mildenhall treasure, to a Herculean cavalry officer with gaudy military tastes, perhaps commanding the *civitas* guard; much of the Thetford treasure could have been from her own handsome dowry, made with bullion from Imperial donatives her father had received, and was afterwards preserved, untouched, for decades as treasure in itself and as valued keepsakes from her wedding.[55]

53 On this episode see Painter 1977; Salway 1993, 255–6, cf. Laycock 2008, 108–34. Painter conjectured that the platters had belonged to Eutherius, Julian's chamberlain, a powerful Imperial official and an Armenian eunuch. This inspired suggestion seems reflected in the 'Good Beast' on his plate (Fig. 5.19), demure and flop-eared, playing his pipes, not the ithyphallic Pan of the great plate (Fig. 5.18), which, if bestowed by Lupicinus, is actually 'signed' with a conceit on his own name: the central image of Oceanus has a wolf's eyes and whiskers, and a pair of dolphins set upright like pricked ears (*lupus*), whilst all the dolphins look feathered and have the distinctive cheek markings of a green woodpecker (*picus*). They also have duck bills and short boar-crests: Lupicinus' diplomatic gifts, designed to go on display, were well chosen.

54 Silvanus occurs in at least 25 British inscriptions, Faunus only here (De la Bédoyère 2007, 273–4).

55 The gold body chain in the Hoxne treasure was probably made, and kept, in exactly this way (Johns

It is not known what part, if any, Icenians may have played in the shockingly well coordinated Barbarian conspiracy of 367, but there must from then onwards have been heightened concern for security on the Icknield Way as well as with coastal defence. The intensified activity on Gallows Hill fits with this, and the owner of the broken Icenian militia buckle that matches the Thetford rings must have met a violent death away from home, as it was found beside the Icknield way near Tring (Buckinghamshire). Julian died in AD 363 and under some of his successors pagan worship would have had to be discreet. It would have been easy to conceal treasures such as these, and only keep on open display those items that would not attract adverse attention. Silviola, indeed, may even have been baptised. Life went on.

Between 383 and 388 Magnus Maximus gave someone the freshly minted solidi found with the treasure. He was highly regarded in some parts of Britain, is known to have employed many *foederati*, and the owner(s) of the Thetford treasure were rich and well-connected people in a part of Britain from which, for instance, Anglian and Saxon soldiers could very easily be sourced. Maximus is often held responsible for withdrawing the official Imperial army from Britain. This view has very reasonably been questioned, but even if true, its main impact on the Iceni, who had never hosted more than a nominal Roman garrison, would have been to increase the status and responsibilities of resident community leaders and commanders of local militia, who must between them have taken charge early in the 5th century when the provincial economy collapsed. It was probably during those years that the Thetford treasure, containing a small and carefully structured selection of meaningful heirlooms and a few items still in current use, finally went to ground, with a box made of Kimmeridge shale, from the Dorset end of the Icknield Way. Roman treasure was buried for many different reasons, and caches not recovered either because the owners never came back for them, or could not find them – or else because they were votive offerings and not supposed to be unearthed. It is tempting to think that that was why this particular treasure was buried where it was, and when it was, probably after AD 400, by people in need of all the divine support they could get as they jostled for position in unsettled times.[56] That they were not unhopeful is reflected in the choices they made – the image of an amphibious, equestrian Deus *Narios; the union of civil, religious, and military functions; allusions to their own distinguished past, their Germanic connections, and above all to their Roman inheritance, with tacit references to Romulus' conception, good king Numa, and other origin-myths of the city of Rome. Recurrent themes of secular and religious power, fertility, and renewal seem reflected in its contents and the confident, ambitious tenor of some of its Latin acclamations, as though to a once and future king. *Vir bone, vivas*!

2010, 23–9); for Hoxne's Silvicola see n. 37. Donatives: Nearly all the spoons, certainly, come from a single batch of silver, and the solidi must have been from a subsequent donative to the bridegroom himself. Some of the bracelets and rings could, equally, be gifts from bridegroom to bride.

56 For what it is worth, the Anglo-Saxon Chronicle records for AD 418: 'In this year the Romans collected all the treasures which were in Britain and hid some in the earth so that no one afterwards could find them, and some they took with them into Gaul'.

BIBLIOGRAPHY

Bradley, R. 2005 *Ritual and Domestic Life in Prehistoric Europe*. London, Routledge.

Chadburn, A. 1995 'More artefacts from the Thetford Treasure?', *Britannia* 26, 323.

Chadburn, A. 2006 *Aspects of the Iron-Age coinages of northern East Anglia with especial reference to hoards*. Unpublished Ph.D. thesis, University of Nottingham.

Davies, J. A. 2009 *The Land of Boudica: Prehistoric and Roman Norfolk*. Oxford, Oxbow.

De la Bédoyère, G. 2005 'Carausius, Virgil and the marks RSR and INPCDA', *Image, Craft and the Classical World: Essays in Honour of Donald Bailey and Catherine Johns*, ed. N. Crummy, 187–95. Montagnac, Mergoil.

De la Bédoyère, G. 2007 *Gods with Thunderbolts. Religion in Roman Britain*. Stroud, Tempus.

De Bernardo Stempel, P. 2008, 'Continuity, translatio and identificatio in Romano-Celtic religion: the case of Britain', *Continuity and Innovation in Religion in the Roman West*, ed. R. Haeussler & A. C. King, vol. 2, 67–82. Portsmouth, RI, JRA supplementary series 67.

Delamarre, X. 2003 *Dictionnaire de la Langue gauloise. Une approche lingistique du vieux-celtique continental* 2nd edition. Paris, Errance.

Fitzpatrick, A. P. 1996 'Night and day: the symbolism of astral signs on later Iron-Age anthropomorphic short swords', *Proceedings of the Prehistoric Society* 62, 373–98.

Green, M. J. 1997 *Exploring the World of the Druids*. London, Thames & Hudson.

Gregory 1992 *Excavations in Thetford, 1980–1982, Fison Way*. Dereham, Norfolk Museums Service (East Anglian Archaeology 53).

Haeussler, R. 2010 'From tomb to temple. On the rôle of hero cults in local religions in Gaul and Britain in the Iron Age and the Roman period', *Celtic Religion across Space and Time*, ed. J. Alberto Arenas-Esteban, 200–27. Junta de Comunidades de Castilla-la Mancha (IX Workshop F.E.R.C.AN.).

Hassall, M. W. C. & R. S. O. Tomlin 1982 'Roman Britain in 1981', *Britannia* 13, 410.

Henig, M. 1995 *Religion in Roman Britain*. London, Batsford.

Jackson, K. 1983 'The inscriptions on the silver spoons', in Johns & Potter 1983, 46–8.

Johns, C. 2010 *The Hoxne Late Roman Treasure: Gold Jewellery and Silver Plate*. London, British Museum.

Johns, C. & T. W. Potter 1983 *The Thetford Treasure: Roman Jewellery and Silver*. London, British Museum.

Kretz, R. 1999 'On the track of the Norfolk Wolf', *Chris Rudd List* 48, 3–9.

Laycock, S. 2008 *Britannia the Failed State. Tribal Conflicts and the End of Roman Britain*. Stroud, Tempus.

Nash Briggs, D. 2010 'Reading the Images on Iron-Age Coins: 3. Some Cosmic Wolves', *Chris Rudd List* 110, 2–4.

Nash Briggs, D. 2011 'The language of inscriptions on Icenian coinage', *The Iron Age in Northern East Anglia: New Work in the Land of the Iceni*, ed. J. A. Davies, 83–102. Oxford, BAR British Series 549.

Nash Briggs, D. 2012 'Sacred image and regional identity in late-prehistoric Norfolk', *Art, Faith and Place in East Anglia*, ed. T. A. Heslop, E. Mellings, M. Thøfner, 30–49. Woodbridge, Boydell.

Nash Briggs, D. 2014 'An emphatic statement: the Undley-A gold bracteate and its message in fifth-century AD East Anglia', *Wonders Lost and Found. A Book to Celebrate the Archaeological Work of Professor Michael Vickers*, ed. N. Sekunda (forthcoming). Gdańsk, Monograph Series Akanthina.

Nussbaum, A. J. 1986 *Head and Horn in Indo-European*. Berlin/New York, Walter de Gruyter.

Orel, V. 2003 *A Handbook of Germanic Etymology*. Leiden, Brill.

Painter, K. S. 1977 *The Mildenhall Treasure: Roman Silver from East Anglia*. London, British Museum.

Pokorny, J. 1959 *Indogermanisches etymologisches Wörterbuch*. Tübingen, A. Francke.

Ross, A. 1998 'Celtic heads and holy waters', *Chris Rudd List* 32, 2–4.

Salway, P. 1993 *The Oxford Illustrated History of Roman Britain*. Oxford, Oxford University Press.

Toynbee, J. M. C. 1962 *Art in Roman Britain*. London, Phaidon.

West, M. L. 2007 *Indo-European Poetry and Myth*. Oxford, Oxford University Press.

VI

THE ROMAN RELIGIOUS LANDSCAPE OF ABINGDON, OXFORDSHIRE

Stephen Yeates

Excavations were carried out in 2010 at the site of the Old Gaol in Abingdon by John Moore Heritage Services as part of a developer funded project. This paper provides a brief description of the features identified and an assessment of the site as part of an identifiable religious complex, even though so little of the site survived. The site contained the remains of a horseshoe-shaped ditch with a central standing post. Subsequently a small square shrine was constructed, with later robbing in the medieval period. The nature of the artefacts found suggested that the site was highly likely to be a temple site; these included items such as spearheads, and the small bronze figurine of a water bird. It is argued that various features on the site have their parallels on other religious sites. Horseshoe-shaped features of the Iron Age have been recognised at the religious complex of Marcham-Frilford, Oxfordshire, and at Wanborough, Surrey, besides other sites. The Roman period development of the site, with a temenos enclosure and two internal temples, can also be recognised at Marcham-Frilford and Wanborough, as well as at Woodeaton, Oxfordshire. There are indications that the Old Gaol Roman religious site was established at around AD 60–80, a date at which there is conformity with a number of other sanctuaries in the southeast of England. Finally, it is argued that a religious site of this type (a horseshoe ditch with post, followed by a double temple complex) is recognisable as a specific Atrebatic monument.

ABINGDON is a town now located in Oxfordshire, although historically part of the County of Berkshire, with Abingdon acting as its county town during the Middle Ages. These shires lie in the Thames Valley in central southern England (Fig. 1). Abingdon is the site of both a medieval and a post-medieval town, but a town that appears to have earlier origins with key components beneath it dating from the Iron Age, Roman, and early medieval periods.

Archaeological work was carried out by John Moore Heritage Services at the Old Gaol site, Abingdon, during the latter part of 2010. The development site was located in an area of the town between Bridge Street on the northeast side, East Saint Helen's Street on the northwest and west sides and the River Thames on the southeast side. It is located on a slightly elevated part of the river's flood plain at about 50m to 54m Ordnance Datum. The underlying geology is Ampthill and Kimmeridge Clay strata

Fig. 1. Location of Abingdon and other sites mentioned in the text (S. J. Yeates).

formed in the Jurassic period.[1] This is capped here by the Wolvercote Sand and Gravel Member laid down in the Quaternary period.

Britannia's *civitas* territories were developments of earlier tribal systems that evolved in British prehistory.[2] The town of Abingdon undoubtedly lay in the territory of a tribal group known as the Atrebates, evident from analysis of the extent of that tribe's Iron Age coinage.[3] The Atrebates were a tribe that belonged to a larger ethnic group known as the Belgae. Although the Belgic tribes are considered in many modern academic studies to have been a 'Celtic' people, Roman and Greek ethnographers and geographers and other contemporary sources indicated quite clearly that they were Germanic, or predominantly Germanic.[4] Caesar stated that the Belgae and Celtae were different peoples with different languages, institutions and laws.[5] He also stated that the Belgae were predominantly German in origin.[6]

In earlier studies there had been a tendency to conflate findings from widely dispersed sites from many disparate tribal territories to come up with a homogenised view that completely ignored many substantial differences between those tribal groups.

1 mapapps.bgs.ac.uk/geologyofbritain/home.html.
2 Yeates 2012, 116–44.
3 Bean 2000.
4 Yeates 2012, 48–115.
5 Caesar, *BGall.* 1.1 (Edwards 1963).
6 Caesar, *BGall.* 2.4, 3.11.

Later studies in Britain have focussed on analysing the religious activity within tribal groups. Some of the earliest studies using this approach were those on the Brittonic tribal group called the Dobunni.[7] These studies were able to elucidate, for the first time, specific religious cults and activities, and deities that were probably only worshipped in this tribal group. The mother goddess of the Dobunni does in one respect fit into the wider Roman tradition of the Matres or Matronæ, a broad system of representation derived from Juno; but best employed with reference to distinctive local variations. Subsequent discussion and interpretation here considers the analysis from the Old Gaol in Abingdon evidence with other sites identified as belonging to the Atrebates.

One aspect revealed in the Dobunnic studies was to recognise long periods of homogenous social development amongst these communities through the presence of replicated archaeological sites.[8] We can recognise that the *civitas* territories of the Roman period were derived from earlier Iron Age tribal areas, and that certain early medieval kingdoms evolved from *civitas* territories,[9] and further it is possible to recognise long-term processes taking place within smaller political units. Roman *civitas* territories were divided into *vici* or towns, which developed into the early medieval *parochia* established for folk-groups or communities. Likewise, the *vici* territories must have been created from smaller sub-tribal political components amongst the Iron Age tribes, called here communities. It was thus possible, for specific archaeological sites, to start showing the long-term communal development in process, by recognising that a set of specific archaeological monuments existed that were important to the folk-groups and were replicated from one community to the other. The analysis of this long term communal development fits into wider anthropological traditions addressed by Giddens's structuration and Ingold's taskscapes.[10]

The archaeological features recognised amongst the Dobunni, from the later Bronze Age, included a series of extensive and relocated large settlements, along with a series of hilltop enclosures, some of which were hill-forts. By the Roman period each of the *vici* territories had a nucleated Roman settlement. In the early medieval period, a minster church was established and a new lay manor with a lay church. There were also a series of attached chapels, some of which could be recognised as serving a specific function in the wider territory. Thus, it was possible to recognise similar sites performing similar functions across the *parochia* in the area under study. These traditions enable us to discuss activities and sites that are recognisable amongst sub-tribal groups and it will be something that will be returned to later in the discussion on the Atrebatic religion.

7 Yeates 2006; 2008; 2009.
8 Yeates 2006, 57–66; 2008, 59–89; 2010.
9 Dark 1994; 2000.
10 Giddens 1984, 110–62; Ingold 2000, 194–200.

The wider landscape of Abingdon

The landscape of Abingdon developed over a long period of time. Analyses from archaeological excavations and watching briefs across the town have shown that a major settlement was established on the site at least as early as the Middle Iron Age. The remains of a Late Iron Age *oppidum*, or town, were initially recognised at the Vineyard site, which was excavated in the 1970s.[11] This showed that Abingdon had a dense settlement surrounded by a multiple ditch system. Further parts of this ditch system and settlement were recognised in archaeological observations in Station Road,[12] and the area of West Saint Helen's Street, near the Shireborne Ditch.[13] Whilst Iron Age hilltop enclosures or hill-forts are a significant feature of neighbouring Dobunnic areas of settlement, only one potential hill-top enclosure in the territory of Abingdon has been identified at Milton Hill,[14] at the south end of the folk-group territory.

The Iron Age *oppidum* subsequently developed into a Roman *vicus*, but the location of its infrastructure has previously been poorly understood.[15] The Roman *vicus* has been detected in excavations between Abbey Gardens and West Saint Helen's Street.[16] The remains of a ditch have been identified in West Saint Helen's Street.[17] Tradition has it, from medieval sources, that the town was previously called *Seuekesham,* no significant analysis of the name has occurred but it could be derived from an earlier name for the town.[18] A number of outlying cemeteries have been recognised as satellite sites. These include burials sites to the northwest of the Roman settlement,[19] and at Barrow Hills.[20]

In the early medieval period a minster was established, probably in the 7th century AD.[21] The lay authorities abandoned the Roman *vicus* at this time leaving the town in the hands of a priest. The lay authority established a new settlement with a lay mother church at Sutton Courtenay. By the 10th century it seems that a further church was established in Abingdon at Saint Helen's.[22] Saint Helen's, as with other churches dedicated to Saint Helen for example at Worcester, appear to have been established in a larger monastic enclosure to provide for the general population of the *parochia*, and to separate it from the territory of the religious order.

What can also be noted in the case of Abingdon is that the stream that once ran through the prehistoric settlements under central Abingdon, and which was later diverted to fill the *oppidum* ditch, was subsequently diverted into a culvert on the edge of the monastic complex. The stream was known as the Sunningwell. The name is

11 Allen 1989.
12 Moore 2003.
13 Brady *et al.* 2007.
14 Hart *et al.* 2012, 212–18.
15 Henig & Booth 2000, 71–2.
16 Allen 1997; Biddle 1968.
17 Miles 1975, 82–3.
18 Stenton 1913; Lambrick 1968a; Myres 1968.
19 Devaney 2007.
20 Chambers & McAdam 2007, 13–54.
21 Biddle *et al.* 1968, 26–69.
22 Lambrick 1968a.

documented from 811 in the form of *Sunnigwellan,* and again in 821 as *Sunningauuille*; with the subsequent forms *sunningawylles broc* and *sunninga wylle broces* from 956.[23] The etymology of the name is the w(i)ella of the *Sunningas*; associated with a folk-group called the *Sunningas*. Amongst the Dobunni it was apparent that significant prehistoric and Roman settlement was focussed along the banks of rivers or streams that are associated with folk-names.[24] This example seems to be a similar case, and further examples can be found in the Thames Valley.

The temple site and the internal landscape of Abingdon

Although Iron Age and Roman activity in Abingdon has been recognised, little has been written about the internal dynamics of the small town. The excavations at the Old Gaol have enabled us for the first time to start identifying the internal design, and where certain religious sites may have been located.

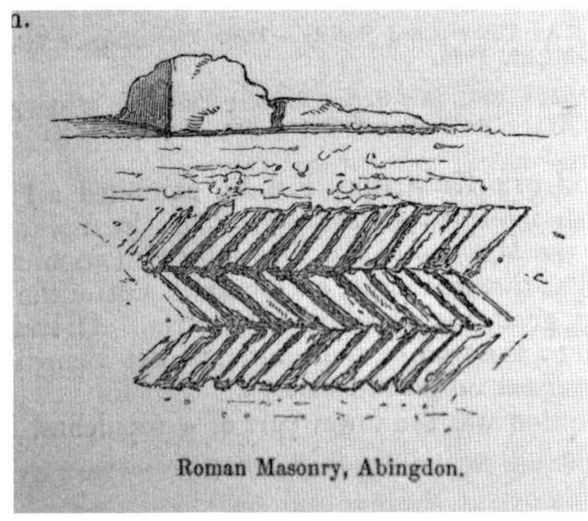

Fig. 2. Sketches of the stonework noted in 1865 (Akerman – Society of Antiquaries).

Our knowledge of the Old Gaol site did not, however, start in 2010 but much earlier than this, in 1865. Akerman made a short report that was published in the Proceedings of the Society of Antiquaries.[25] The initial report mentioned massive foundations at the north end of Fore Street, now called East Saint Helen's Street, and the subsequent account provided unscaled sketches of stonework (Fig. 2), along with a text mentioning demolition of the Roman upper layers of this structure. The finds included pottery, bones, a denarius of Philip, and a small coin of Constantine. Akerman's interpretation of the site is as follows:

> A great number of animal bones were also found, which, coupled with the massive character of the masonry, lead to the inference that a temple has occupied this spot, which commands a view of the Thames, and its valley.[26]

In later accounts reporting this find, for example in the Oxfordshire Historic Environment Record, the claimed Roman temple was recorded simply as a Roman building.[27]

Excavations were carried out at the Old Gaol Leisure Centre in 1972–75, where the remains of a Roman period pit were identified.[28] Further excavations took place at Twickenham House, which identified stone wall footings claimed to date to the 2nd

23 Gelling 1974, 459.
24 Yeates 2006, 57–66; 2008, 59–89.
25 Winter Jones 1865, 145; Franks 1865, 202–3.
26 Franks 1865, 203.
27 Oxfordshire HER, PRN2518.
28 Parrington 1975.

Fig. 3. Photograph of terminus on Iron Age horseshoe shaped feature (John Moore Heritage Services).

century AD.[29]

The excavations in 2010 recognised the remains of a complicated landscape. There were indications of activity from the later part of the prehistoric period, culminating in the digging of a small horseshoe-shaped ditch with bulbous terminals (Figs. 3–4). Set centrally to this was a posthole that would have contained an upright post. The ditch was sealed by deposits that contained pottery datable to *c.* AD 50–70.

The site does not appear to have gone out of use but the ditch was replaced by a building (Figs. 5–6). However, only one wall of this

Fig. 4. Drawing of the Iron Age horseshoe-shaped feature (David Gilbert).

29 Wilson & Wallis 1991.

structure survived, as the rest of the structure had been systematically robbed during the medieval period. The surviving wall of the building was straight; it can be deduced from this, and other factors, that there was probably square or rectangular structure. The surviving wall was on the south side of an area of robbing that indicates that the structure was approximately 5 m across. One other factor was that the construction of the wall could be dated from pottery finds to AD 60-80. There were also certain artefacts from the vicinity of the building that have been suggested that the building was a temple or shrine. These include: four coins, fragments of broken brooches, and two spearheads. But perhaps one of the most significant find was a small cast bronze of a water bird. All of these are the sort of objects often deposited as votive materials. The water bird, probably representing a goose, is probably of 2nd century AD date.

Fig. 5. Photograph of the surviving Roman wall (John Moore Heritage Services).

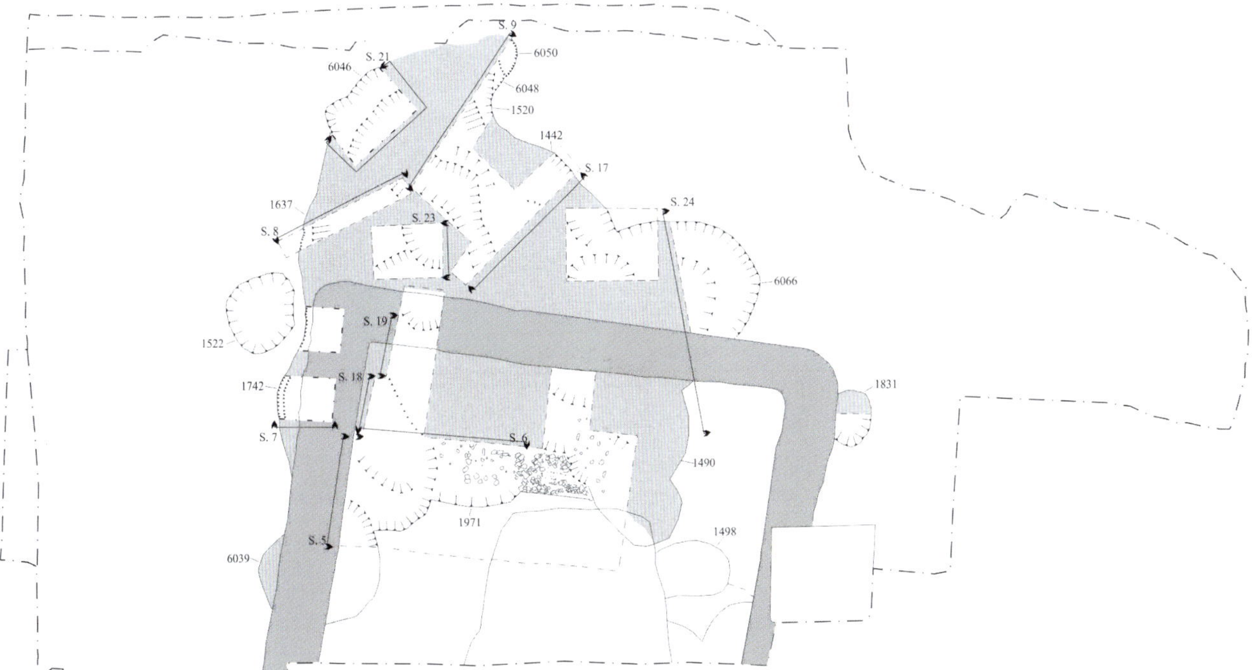

The structure was systematically robbed in the medieval period, probably in the 12th and 13th centuries AD. The reason for this can only be surmised, but

Fig. 6. Drawing of the surviving Roman feature and later medieval pitting (David Gilbert).

the most likely interpretation is due to the presence of quantities of resources such as metal and stone that could be recycled. Another possibility is that the finds of sculpture and bronze with pre-Christian images were recognised as subversive by the Church in Abingdon and hence the putative temple was destroyed.

Although only fragmentary pieces survive from the Iron Age and Roman site, what has survived is significant enough to enable the site to be identified as the location of a religious precinct.

Atrebatic posts

The late Iron Age feature, horseshoe ditch with bulbous terminals and a central standing post, recognised on the site is similar to other religious sites recognised in the *civitas* of the Atrebates, but also to sites in those of the Belgae and Reg(i)ni (Fig. 7).

The nearest examples can be seen at the temple complex of Marcham-Frilford, lies some 4.5 kilometres to the west of Abingdon, and at the Wanborough temple in Surrey. Under the smaller circular shrine at the site of Marcham-Frilford there was an irregular horseshoe-shaped feature, excavated initially by Bradford and Goodchild.[30] The feature was treated as having a single phase, but due to its shape, and the two raised areas in the line of the ditch, it is possible that the feature was dug and re-dug on at least one occasion, and that this factor was missed by the original excavators. It is only re-cutting that the peculiar shape of the ditch might be explained. Internally, a number of postholes were noted and it is feasible that when the ditch was re-dug a new post was erected.

The Wanborough temple site also preserved the remains of a horseshoe-shaped gully located under a circular temple. At the centre of the gully were the remains of a posthole that would have contained a standing central post.[31] The temple site at Farley Heath, Surrey, should also be noted, as to the north of this temple the remains of a curving ditch were noted that was considered to be part of a horseshoe or penannular shaped feature.[32] The full extent of this feature was not excavated.

At the site of the temple at Lancing Down, West Sussex, amongst the tribe of the Reg(i)ni, the earliest feature at the site was a more circular than elliptical horseshoe-shaped feature that also had a central standing post.[33] Therefore, although the remains under the Old Gaol are fragmentary it is possible to contextualise this late Iron Age feature, due to its similarity to the other examples cited amongst the Atrebatic peoples and their southern neighbours.

The next question is surely the significance of the central standing post in the ditch. Here, we should perhaps consider the significance of a gold coin, attributed to

30 Bradford & Goodchild 1939; Kamash, Gosden & Lock 2010.
31 Williams 2007.
32 Poulton & Bird 2007.
33 Bedwin 1981.

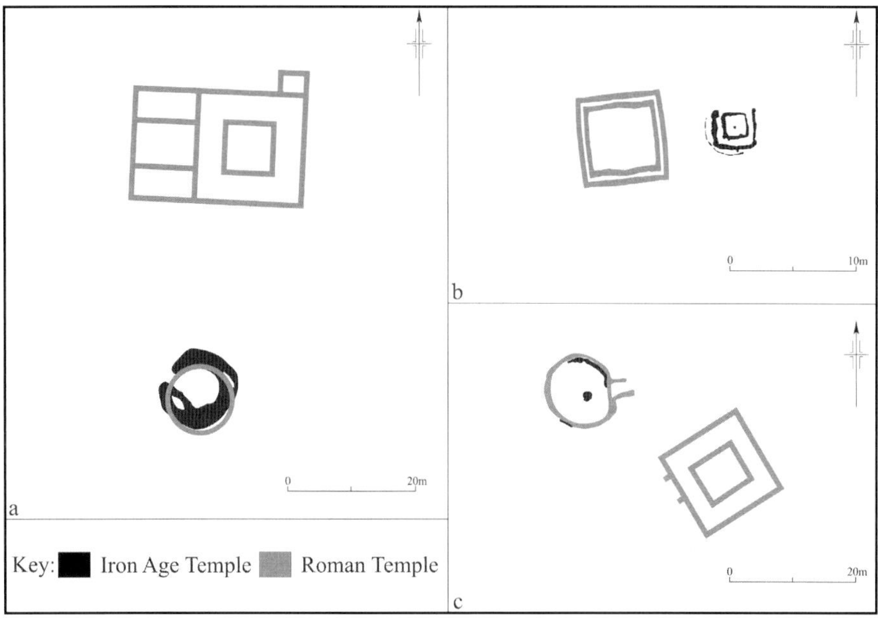

Fig. 7. Comparable sites to the Abingdon religious complex (Andrej Čelovský): a) Marcham-Frilford, Oxfordshire; b) Lancing Down, West Sussex; c) Wanborough, Surrey.

the Belgae people, now called the Cogwheel Smiler.[34] One of the coin's sides appears to show a standing post wrapped with bands of ribbons or streamers of fabric (Fig. 8). At the base there is a curving feature that could feasibly represent a bank of an earthwork running around the exterior of the ditch, a possible early representation of an early type of May Pole.

Atrebatic temple complexes

The excavations at the Old Gaol identified the remaining wall of a Roman building, which could be dated to about AD 60-80. It was apparent from the area of systematic robbing that this structure had to be a building of a square shape roughly 5 m across. It can be determined from the date of the construction, and its probable shape, that the structure was a small square shrine (Fig. 7).

The development of simple square Iron Age buildings as religious structures can be seen from excavations across southeast Britain. The most noted example occurs at Danebury in Hampshire, where there was probably a group of four such

Fig. 8. The Cogwheel Smiler ABC770 (Chris Rudd www.celticcoins.com).

34 ABC 2010, ABC 770.

square trench structures that lay in the centre of the hill-fort and dating to before the 2nd century BC.[35] Other prehistoric religious structures of this shape have been found at the temple site of Hayling Island, Hampshire, dating to the 1st century BC.[36] There were also features of this type at Westhampnett, West Sussex, where four quadrangular shrines were identified.[37] Sussex examples of small square prehistoric shrines have been noted at Lancing Down, associated with a Phase 2 structure, and at Chanctonbury and Bow Hill, West Sussex.[38] At Slonk Hill, West Sussex, there were also three square structures associated with two specific prehistoric phases.[39] Other Iron Age shrines have been found in excavations amongst the Trinovantes to the north of the river Thames at Little Waltham, Essex, and dated to the 3rd to 2nd centuries BC;[40] at Stansted (Airport Catering facilities), Essex, dated to the 1st century BC;[41] at Heathrow, Middlesex;[42] and building A at Balkerne Lane in Colchester, Essex.[43]

To the north of Abingdon the remains of a further square structure was noted during the laying of a pipeline.[44] The feature was dated to the middle to late Iron Age, and although there was nothing found during the excavations to associate the building with religious activity an adjacent feature was described as a small enclosure with a central sump or well. This type of feature was also recognised at a site in Gloucestershire known as the Farnworth Gravel Pits, at Lower Slaughter.[45] Such features appear to be a votive well in an enclosure and to be associated with river of water shrines.

Simple square shrines continued to be built into the Roman period, and perhaps the closest example locally is that at Woodeaton, Oxfordshire.[46] Here, a simple square shrine was constructed c AD 60–80, at about the same time that the building at the Old Gaol was constructed. Other square buildings were also built in the Roman period across the region.

The date at which the Old Gaol building was rebuilt appears to be significant and to relate to a time when temple structures were either constructed or re-constructed in stone. It was noted that this was the case at Woodeaton for the first Roman re-build.[47] Similar dates for construction appear to have been identified at temple sites across the Atrebatic territory: for example at Wanborough in Surrey,[48] and in neighbouring but affiliated tribal groups such as that of Hayling Island in Hampshire.[49] There were

35 Cunliffe 1984, 81–87, 187.
36 Downey *et al.* 1980, 289; King 2007, 16; King & Soffe 2013.
37 Fitzpatrick *et al.* 1997, 178, 180.
38 Bedwin 1980; 1981; Rudling 2001.
39 Hartridge 1978.
40 Drury 1978, 24–5, 124.
41 Brooks 1989, 322–5.
42 Grimes & Close-Brooks 1993.
43 Crummy 1980, 268–72.
44 Cullen *et al.* 2004.
45 Timby 1998, 384–89.
46 Goodchild & Kirk 1954.
47 Goodchild & Kirk 1954, 18–25.
48 Williams 2007.
49 Downey *et al.* 1980, 289.

also Roman temples constructed at this time at Harlow in Essex,[50] and two temples at Colchester.[51] The temple site at Stonea in Cambridgeshire also appears to have a contemporary construction date for one of its phases.[52]

These *c.* AD 60-80 dates are also significant because it has resonance with Roman ethnographic textual sources. Tacitus, in the *Agricola*, introduces a *topos* that described the construction of temples and shrines as part of a civilising Roman action.[53] These activities he claimed were carried out in the winter of AD 79 in a non-campaigning period. The text probably overplays the civilising effect as many of the sites were often reused.

It is possible to point out further similarities that confirm the nature of the Abingdon complex and other Atrebatic sites. Akerman described the uncovering of a significant masonry structure to the rear of one of the houses fronting onto Fore Street (or East Saint Helen's Street as it is now called) in 1865 (Fig. 2). Here, the masonry was so massive that the work to remove part of the structure took over a month, and Akerman interpreted the site as part of temple for this reason. Akerman did not actually state that this was a massive Roman podium, but this seems to be the implication. Excavations to the south of the 1865 site at the Old Gaol noted a second smaller adjoining shrine; this time a probable square feature some 5 m across.

The earliest recognised example was that located at Marcham-Frilford where an extensive rectangular religious enclosure or *temenos* was located that contained a relatively central Romano-Celtic temple and a smaller circular shrine under which was the horseshoe-shaped Iron Age feature discussed above.[54] Similar interpretation can be made for the Roman temple complex at Wanborough, where there was certainly a *temenos* enclosure, but this time of an irregular design.[55] In that enclosure were two temples, the larger a Romano-Celtic temple and a smaller circular east-facing structure, underneath which was the remains of a horseshoe-shaped ditch with central standing post (see above). Although the temples are similar, the detailed designs do differ; that at Abingdon being a Roman podium design and a small square shrine.

There are parallels at the temple site at Woodeaton. Here, it is possible to recognise a similar Roman period phase of a large *temenos* enclosure with the remains of two Roman temples located internally.[56] It is only the larger temple here that has been excavated, and this started off as a square structure only being transformed later into a Romano-Celtic temple. The smaller temple in the complex has never been excavated but has shown up on aerial photographs. If it is a similar type of complex, then the temple would have replaced a horseshoe-shaped feature with a standing post of Iron Age date.

50 France & Gobel 1985, 21–35.
51 Crummy 1980, 248–56.
52 Jackson 1996, 214–20.
53 Tacitus, *Agricola* 21 (Hutton *et al.* 1970).
54 Bradford & Goodchild 1939.
55 Williams 2007.
56 Goodchild & Kirk 1954, 18–25; RCHME. NMR 15284/54, 14.6.1995.

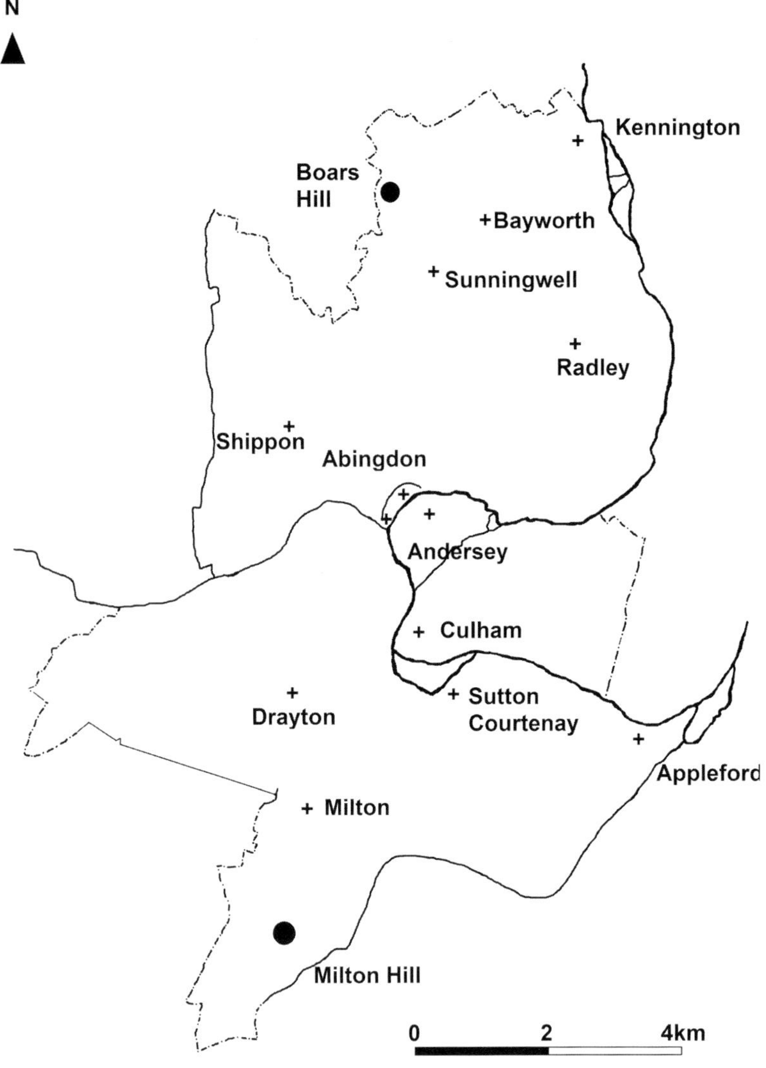

Fig. 9. *Parochia* of Abingdon showing oppidum and temple location (S. J. Yeates).

Discussion

The features identified at the Old Gaol site include the remains of a horseshoe-shaped ditch of a late Iron Age date with bulbous terminals and a central standing post. The ditch was filled by AD 50–70, and a building was constructed over the site in the period AD 60–80. It is argued that this feature can be compared to the other Atrebatic sites at Marcham-Frilford and Wanborough, and it possesses some similarities to features at Farley Heath and Woodeaton. It should be noted that this type of temple complex (two shrines over a horseshoe ditch) is not found throughout Britain but is one of a number of types used specifically by the Atrebates.

Study of the neighbouring Dobunni has shown how it is possible to look at the broader transformation in the landscape over a longer period, from the Iron Age to the early medieval period.[57] Here, it was evident that the landscape was structured and that each large early medieval parish contained the remains of specifically identifiable features. Thus, it was possible to see the transformation of a smaller Iron Age folk-group providing the basis for a Roman *vicus*, a component of a *civitas*, and for the origins of the earliest parishes. In the case of Abingdon the site was located in a relatively central position (Fig. 9). The early parish associated with the church of Marcham was also extensive, but at that site the temple was not central to the known parochial limits (Fig. 10). It may, however, have been considered as a symbolic central religious site. In the case of Wanborough it is more difficult to reconstruct the early medieval parochial system. The parish of Wanborough is considered to have been part of the earlier parish of Puttenham. The earlier parochial system around Woodeaton is also more difficult to re-construct, although Islip to the north was part of an earlier Christian parish. It is possible that a series of later medieval parishes on the south edge of Otmoor previously belonged to this territory. If this was the case, then it might be argued that the Woodeaton temple was located on a hill where two spurs of this territory come together.

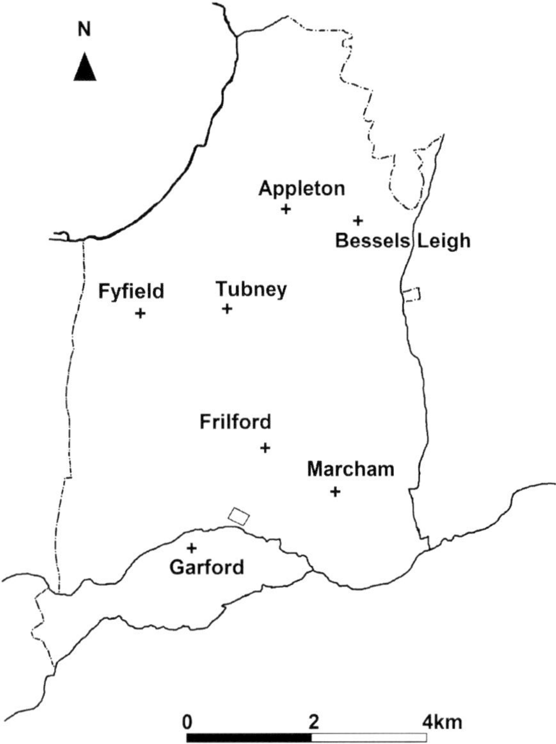

Fig. 10. *Parochia* of Marcham showing the temple site (S. J. Yeates).

If it was indeed the case that each *vicus* had such a feature it is possible to imply that the late Iron Age standing post in the horseshoe was highly symbolic for the communities to which they belonged. In Germanic traditions, and we should remind ourselves that the Belgic peoples were called Germanic by the Roman ethnographers, the standing post was used to mark the centre of a territory. This is most notable with the case of the German Irminsol where the post was associated with a god and a territory. The Belgae coin with the twisted bands of textile appears to represent an early form of May Pole, and it is likely that these sites represented a specific and important gathering point, perhaps at May for the people of the Iron Age folk-group or community.

We should perhaps envisage that in the Roman period it was the case that these

57 Yeates 2006; 2008; 2009; 2010.

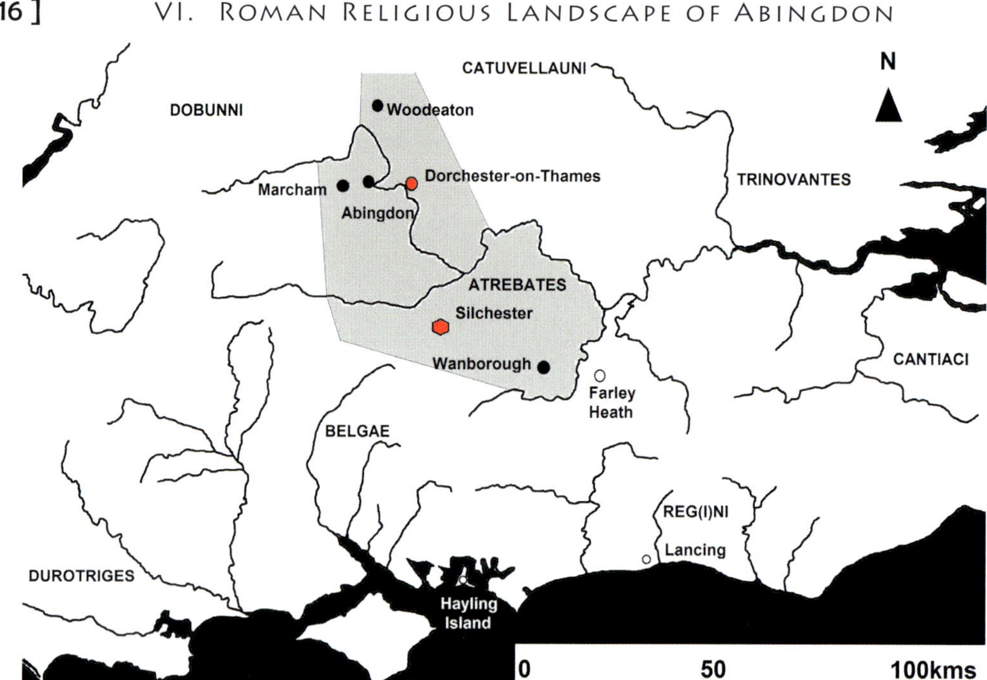

Fig. 11. An assessment of the location of the Atrebatic territory (S. J. Yeates).

sites were completely reworked with the addition of recognisable shrines and temples. It has not yet been confirmed if these larger double temple complexes themselves retained a further standing post or totem associated with the tribal deity or folk-group deity. However, this is feasible, as we know that standing columns, often of stone, were constructed in *temenos* enclosures, often in line with and on the main axis of the main temple. In this way we can recognise a type of evolving site that was specifically Atrebatic and which can now serve to identify the possible boundaries of their *civitas* territory (Fig. 11). We should expect to see an example of this type of structure in every *vicus* of the *civitas*. These sites can therefore be seen as significant on at least a regional scale and should be given better protection.

This paper has approached the subject in a more regional or local approach. Although certain aspects of Roman-period religious culture are evident on a broader Empire-wide level, these aspects were also being introduced into local and regional systems, each of which was adapting to the Roman traditions in their own way.

Acknowledgements

I would like to thank John Moore Heritage Services for allowing me to discuss this unpublished site at the conference and submit this paper. I would also like to thank David Gilbert and Andrej Čelovský for information about the site and working on some of the submitted illustrations. A thank you will also go to Liz Cottam and Chris Rudd of Ancient British Coins for the use of the Cogwheel Smiler image. Martin Henig and David Yeates read copies of the text prior to submission, and also thank you to an un-named assessor.

BIBLIOGRAPHY

Allen, T. 1989 'Abingdon – Vineyard development', *South Midlands Archaeology* 19, 44–6.

Allen, T. 1997 'Abingdon – West Central Redevelopment Area', *South Midlands Archaeology* 27, 47–53.

Bean, S. 2000 *Coinage of the Atrebates and Regni.* Oxford, Oxford University School of Archaeology Monograph 50.

Bedwin, O. 1980 'Excavations at Chanctonbury, Wiston, West Sussex 1977', *Britannia* 11, 173–222.

Bedwin, O. 1981 'Excavations at Lancing Down, West Sussex – 1980', *Sussex Archaeological Collections* 119, 37–56.

Biddle, M. 1968 'The excavations at Abingdon Abbey', in Biddle *et al.* 1968, 60–7.

Biddle, M., H. T. Lambrick & J. N. L. Myres 1968 ed. 'The early history of Abingdon, Berkshire, and its abbey', *Medieval Archaeology* 12, 26–69.

Bradford, J. S. P. & R. G. Goodchild 1939 'Excavations at Frilford, Berkshire, 1937–8', *Oxoniensia* 4, 1–70.

Brady, K., A. Smith & G. Laws 2007 'Excavations at Abingdon West Central Redevelopment: Iron Age, Roman, medieval and post-medieval activity in Abingdon', *Oxoniensia* 72, 107–202.

Brooks, H. 1989 The Stansted Temple. *Current Archaeology* 117, 322–5.

Chambers, R. A. & E. McAdam 2007 *Excavations at Barrow Hills, Radley, Oxfordshire, 1983–5 – volume 2: The Romano-British cemetery and Anglo-Saxon settlement.* Oxford, Oxford Archaeology / Thames Valley Landscape monographs 25.

Crummy, P. 1980 'The temples of Roman Colchester', *Temples, Churches and Religion. Recent research in Roman Britain with a gazetteer of Romano-Celtic temples in Continental Europe*, ed. W. Rodwell, 243–83. Oxford, British Archaeological Report British Series 77 (2 volumes).

Cullen, K., J. Webster, E. R. McSloy, S. Inder, C. Highbee & T. Gilmore 2004 'Abingdon pipeline', *South Midlands Archaeology* 34, 55–8.

Cunliffe, B. 1984 *Danebury. An Iron Age hillfort in Hampshire. Volume 1 – The excavations 1969–1978: the site.* London, Council of British Archaeology.

Dark, K. R. 1994 *Civitas to Kingdom. British political continuity 300–800.* Leicester, Leicester University Press.

Dark, K. R. 2000 *Britain and the End of the Roman Empire.* Stroud, Tempus.

Devaney, R. 2007 'The excavation of Iron age, Roman, medieval and Civil war features south of the Vineyard, Abingdon, Oxfordshire', *Oxoniensia* 72, 74–106.

Downey, R., A. King & G. Soffe 1980 'The Hayling Island temple and religious connections across the Channel', *Temples, Churches and Religion. Recent research in Roman Britain with a gazetteer of Romano-Celtic temples in Continental Europe*, ed. W. Rodwell, 289–304. Oxford, British Archaeological Report British Series 77 (2 volumes).

Drury, P. J. 1978 *Excavations at Little Waltham 1970–71.* London, Council for British Archaeology.

Edwards, H. J. (Trans.) 1963 *Julius Caesar: The Gallic War*, London, Loeb Classical Library

Fitzpatrick, A. P., A. B. Powell & M. J. Allen 1997 *Archaeological Excavations on the Route of the A27, Westhampnett Bypass, West Sussex, 1992. Volume 1: Late Palaeolithic – Anglo-Saxon.* Salisbury, Wessex Archaeology Monograph 12.

France, N. E. & B. M. Gobel 1985 *The Romano-British Temple at Harlow.* Gloucester, West Essex Archaeological Group.

Franks, A. W. 1865 'Thursday December 21st 1865', *Proceedings of the Society of Antiquaries* 2nd Series, 3, 201–6.

Gelling, M. 1974 *The Place-names of Berkshire. Part 2: The Hundreds of Kintbury Eagle, Lambourn, Shrivenham, Ganfield, Ock, Hormer, Wantage, Compton, Moreton, Index to Parts 1 and 2.* Cambridge, Cambridge University Press/English Place-Name Society Volume 50.

Giddens, A. 1984 *The Construction of Society.* Oxford, Polity Press.

Goodchild, R. & J. R. Kirk 1954 'The Romano-Celtic temple at Woodeaton', *Oxoniensia* 19, 15–37.

Grimes, W. F. & J. Close-Brooks 1993 'The excavations of Caesar's Camp, Heathrow, Harmondsworth, Middlesex, 1944', *Proceedings of the Prehistoric Society* 59, 303–60.

Hart, J., E. R. McSloy & M. Alexander 2012 'The Archaeology of the Cleeve to Fyfield Water

Main, South Oxfordshire: Excavations in 2006–7', *Oxoniensia* 77, 199–266.

Hartridge, R 1978 Excavations at the Prehistoric and Romano-British site on Slonk Hill, Shoreham. *Sussex Archaeological Collections* 116, 69–141.

Henig, M & P. Booth 2000 *Roman Oxfordshire.* Stroud, Alan Sutton Publications.

Hutton, M., W. Peterson, R. M. Ogilvie, E. H. Warmington, & M. Winterbottom (trans.) 1970 *Tacitus: Agricola, Germania and Dialogus*, London, Loeb Classical Library.

Ingold, T. 2000 *The Perception of the Environment: essays in livelihood, dwelling and skill.* London, Routledge.

Jackson, R. P. J. 1996 'Excavations at Stonea Grange', *Excavations at Stonea, Cambridgeshire 1980-85*, ed. R. P. J. Jackson & T. W. Potter, 61–668. London, British Museum Press.

Kamash, Z, C. Gosden & G. Lock 2010 Continuity and religious practices in Roman Britain: The case of the rural religious complex at Marcham / Frilford, Oxfordshire, *Britannia* 41, 95–125.

King, A. C. 2007 'Romano-Celtic temples in Britain: Gallic influence or indigenous development?' *Continuity and Innovation in Religion in the Roman West, volume 1*, ed. R. Haeussler & A. C. King, 13–8. Portsmouth, RI, Journal of Roman Archaeology Supplement Series 67.

King, A. C. & G. Soffe 2013 *A Sacred Island: Iron Age, Roman and Saxon temples and ritual on Hayling Island.* Winchester, Hayling Island Excavation Project.

Lambrick, G. 1968a 'The foundation tradition of the Abbey', in Biddle *et al.* 1968, 26–34.

Lambrick, G. 1968b 'Buildings of the monasteries at Abingdon from the late 7th century to 1538', in Biddle *et al.* 1968, 42–59.

Miles, D. 1975 'Excavation at West Saint Helen Street, 1972', *Oxoniensia* 40, 79–101.

Moore, J. 2003 'Abingdon – former Station Inn, Station Yard', *South Midlands Archaeology* 33, 59–60.

Myres, J. N. L. 1968 'The Anglo-Saxon cemetery', in Biddle *et al.* 1968, 35–41.

Parrington, M. 1975 'Excavations at the Old Gaol', *Oxoniensia* 40, 59–78.

Poulton, R. & J. Bird 2007 'Farley Heath Roman temple', *Surrey Archaeological Collections* 92, 1–147.

Rudling, D 2001 Chanctonbury Ring revisited: the excavations of 1988-1991, *Sussex Archaeological Collection* 139, 75–121

Stenton, F. M. 1913 *The Early History of Abingdon Abbey.* Oxford, Clarendon Press.

Timby, J. R. 1998 *Excavations at Kingscote and Wycomb, Gloucestershire. A Roman estate centre and small town in the Cotswolds with notes on related settlements.* Cirencester, Cotswold Archaeological Trust.

Williams, D. 2007 'Green Lane, Wanborough: excavations at the Roman religious site 1999', *Surrey Archaeological Collections* 92, 149–265.

Wilson, R. & J. Wallis 1991 'Prehistoric activity, early Roman building, tenements, yards and gardens behind Twickenham House, Abingdon', *Oxoniensia* 56, 1–15.

Winter Jones, J. 1865 'Tuesday June 15th 1865', *Proceedings of the Society of Antiquaries* 2nd Series, 3, 143–54.

Yeates, S. J. 2006 *Religion, Community and Territory. Defining religion in the Severn Valley and adjacent hills from the Iron Age to the Early Medieval period.* Oxford, British Archaeological Report British Series 411 (3 volumes).

Yeates, S. J. 2008 *The Tribe of Witches. The religion of the Dobunni and Hwicce.* Oxford, Oxbow Books.

Yeates, S. J. 2009 *A Dreaming for the Witches. A recreation of the Dobunni primal myth.* Oxford, Oxbow Books.

Yeates, S. J. 2010 Still living with the Dobunni, in H. Lewis & S. Semple (eds) *Perspectives in Landscape Archaeology. Papers presented at Oxford 2003-5,* 78–93. Oxford, British Archaeological Reports International Series 2103.

Yeates, S. J. 2012 *Myth and History. Ethnicity and politics in the first millennium British Isles.* Oxford, Oxbow Books.

VII

CARRYING THE GODS WITH THEM? PROVENANCE AND PORTABILITY OF ALTARS TO ROMANO-CELTIC DEITIES IN BRITAIN

Anthony C. King

This study of complete altars from Roman Britain shows that just 18% come from good provenances, and only 5% from temple sites, mainly military shrines in the vici *of northern Britain. The presence of altars in Romano-Celtic temples in Britain is very limited indeed. Another 5% come from wells or pits, including Coventina's Well, Carrawburgh, and represent the structured deposition of altars in carefully selected ritual locations. A small number are found* in situ *in what are usually regarded as secondary positions, such as barrack rooms or houses. Some of these are small, 40 cm or less in height, and may have been transported to these locations quite easily. When the heights of altars are analysed further, certain deities such as Belatucadrus or Vitiris are strongly represented in a small size range of 21–30 cm, and it leads to the inference that the so-called secondary positions may in fact have been primary locations for veneration of these deities, and that portable altars were the norm..*

Provenance

OF the 444 complete altars in RIB I, RIB III and *Britannia* 2007–2015, 82 (18.5%) have a good or reasonably secure excavated provenance. Of these, 22 of the 82 (26.8%) are from or near temple buildings, *in situ* (mainly *mithraea* or military *vicus* shrines), 8 (9.8%) are *in situ* in other positions, e.g. in barrack rooms or houses, 24 (29.3%) are from wells or pits, including 11 from Coventina's Well, Carrawburgh, 5 (6.1%) are from fort headquarters strongrooms, 23 (28.0%) are reused, or from rubble, ruins, etc. Examples from Romano-Celtic temples are very rare, but include the large uninscribed altar from Springhead Temple 1, found in the *cella* of the temple.[1] Uley has three damaged uninscribed altars with Mercury iconography, from destruction levels over the temple site.[2] In the Bath temple precinct, an altar to Sulis, dedicated by a *haruspex,* was found *in situ.*[3]

1 Appendix 2, no. 63; *CSIR Britain* 1.10.117; Penn 1959. See below n. 32.
2 Appendix 2, nos. 36 & 68; Woodward & Leach 1993, 94–7.
3 Appendix 1, no. 298; RIB 3049; Cunliffe & Davenport 1985, 36–7. For recent consideration of the contexts of Roman altars, see Busch & Schäfer 2014.

Fig. 1. An example of a small altar in the 21–30 cm height range, from High Rochester (RIB 1269; Appendix 1, no. 86). Ht 30 cm, width 20 cm. *Dis / Mounti/bus Iul(ius) / Firmin/us dec(urio) f(ecit)* — 'To the Mountes (Moguntes?) gods, Iulius Firminus, Decurion, made this'. Newcastle Museums..

Unsurprisingly, larger altars tend to be found *in situ* or close to their apparent original position to a greater extent than those of smaller size and bulk. Indeed, the largest certain altar from Roman Britain, 163 cm high, was found in position in a circular shrine to Vinotonus, in a remote location on Bowes Moor, North Yorkshire, together with a smaller altar from the adjacent rectangular shrine to Vinotonus Silvanus.[4] Two large altars to Anociticus/Antenociticus were found in the eponymous shrine at Benwell, apparently positioned to either side of the cult statue in the apse of the temple.[5] The majority of altars found in temples are from *mithraea* in northern Britain and Wales,[6] but others to non-local deities include one to the Nymphs from a shrine adjacent to the Carrawburgh *mithraeum*, one to Jupiter Dolichenus from *Vindolanda* and one to Nemesis from the Chester amphitheatre.[7]

For altars located in non-temple positions, but nevertheless indicating use as an altar, there are two interesting examples from military barrack blocks. One is the smallest from Roman Britain, at only 5 cm high, anepigraphic, found on the surface of a low masonry platform (altar base?) in the *contubernium* of a barrack in the *classis Britannica* fort at Dover.[8] The other is from Chester, possibly a small statuette base to Genius rather than an altar, from barrack block, site XV, Deanery Field.[9] A final example is from a house in Caerwent, to Mars Ocelus, found standing upright against the south wall of the central block of House XVIs.[10] The first two of these can be linked to private devotion by military personnel, but the Caerwent altar is more enigmatic and cannot easily be interpreted as being a house-shrine.

The deliberate placing of altars in special depositional contexts, such as wells and shafts, is in effect, a secondary location, but one of interest because of the deliberate nature of the deposition. The well-known example of the altars in Coventina's Well, appear to have been deliberately placed in groups, possibly in a series of separate

4 Appendix 1, nos 444 & 361; Wright 1946. The largest 'altar' in Appendix 1, from Housesteads (no. 445), is more plausibly an inscribed door jamb from a temple.
5 Appendix 1, nos 390, 426; Breeze 2006, 155–7.
6 Appendix 1, nos 121, 152, 170, 349, 357, 366, 367, 384, 409, 410, 427, 439.
7 Carrawburgh: Appendix 1, no. 354; Vindolanda: Appendix 1, no. 352; Birley & Birley 2010; Chester: Appendix 1, no. 156; RIB 3149.
8 Appendix 2, no. 1; RIB 3032; Philp 1981, 53.
9 Appendix 1, no. 1; RIB 451.
10 Appendix 1, no. 217; RIB 310.

episodes.[11] This would suggest the periodic clearance of the shrine, but conservation of the altars in a sacred context. Geographically, most other examples come from north of Hadrian's Wall, from pits and wells at Newstead, Auchendavy, Bar Hill, Birrens, and most recently, a pair of Mithraic altars face down in a shallow pit at Inveresk.[12] These may be deposition in advance of evacuation of the garrison to the Hadrian's Wall area.

Such deposits are much rarer in southern Britain; apart from altars from wells at Farnworth, Gloucestershire, and, less certainly, from Hughtown, Isles of Scilly,[13] the main exemplar is the inscribed plaque to Mars Camulus, probably from an altar or statue base, from Tabard Square, London.[14] It was carefully placed in a pit or shaft during the late 4th century, just to the south of the northern Romano-Celtic temple in the ritual precinct. The inscription itself would have been up to 200 years old when deposited.

Provenance, therefore, is of great importance for understanding the use to which altars were put, and the case of altars in barrack blocks is particularly interesting in indicating a non-temple location for making offerings. Significant, too, is deliberate deposition when altars were no longer needed, or the site was threatened in some way. However, the majority of known altars have no provenance data, usually because they were found up to four centuries ago, and their provenance was poorly recorded. Included in this majority are large numbers of quite small altars, to which our attention will now turn.

Altar size and dedication

The second aim of this paper is a more detailed analysis of the sizes of complete altars. A significant number are quite small, in the 21–30 cm height range, and are of interest for their relative ease of portability (Fig. 1). This raises the question of their possible transport by dedicants, either to take to shrines or for use in more informal settings such as domestic or military space, such as a barrack room. Another, and related factor, is the possibility that the dedicant's wealth and status, and the size of an altar were intertwined in some way. Were small altars personal dedications, or simply produced for poorer dedicants? As the final line in Fig. 1 indicates, the use of *fecit* may imply literally that the dedicant made the altar, and therefore that some altars were 'home-produced' rather than the product of a professional stone mason's workshop.

The bar chart of altar sizes (Fig. 2; Appendices 1 & 2) gives the distribution of heights for all altars, including anepigraphic, weathered and illegible examples. There is a group in the size range 10 to 50 cm and then a drop to a slightly lower number in the size range 51 to 60 cm. A rather larger group of more substantial altars runs from 61 cm up to *c.* 140 cm in height. The smaller size range are those which are possibly portable, at

11 Allason-Jones & McKay 1985, 8.

12 Appendix 1, nos 277, 287, 311, 325, 393, 414. For Inveresk, see *Britannia* 42, 2011, 441–4. Cf. also Clarke 1997.

13 Appendix 2, nos 15 and 64.

14 Appendix 1, no. 103; RIB 3014; Killock 2015, 66–7, 192–3.

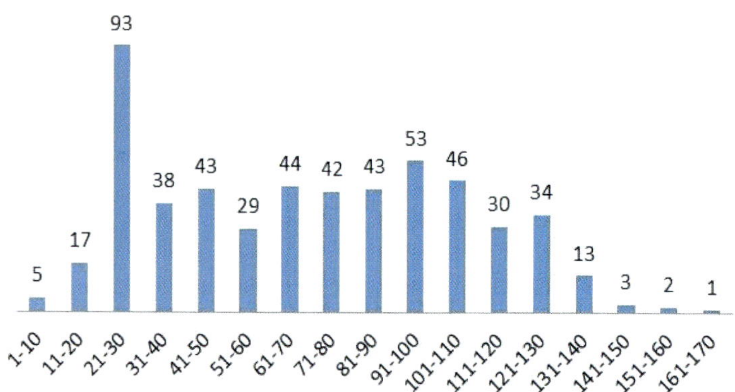

Fig. 2. Bar chart of all complete altar heights from Roman Britain. Data from Appendices 1 and 2.

least for those up to *c.* 30 cm in height and weighing *c.* 20/25 kg.[15] This group is dominated by a very large number (93, i.e. 17.4% of the total on Fig. 2) in the size range 21–30 cm.[16] The larger size range represents those which are presumably more permanently located, and not moved around very much. They can be regarded as more conventional altars, the largest of which being substantial blocks of stone. The highest of this group, in the range 161–170 cm are physically difficult

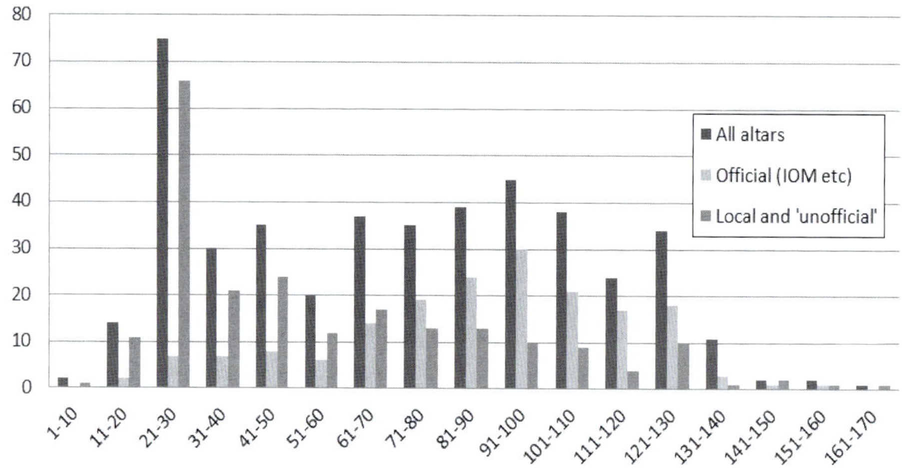

Fig. 3. Bar chart, as Fig. 1, with separate indication of official cults, e.g. IOM, Fortuna, etc., and local cults, e.g. Cocidius, Belatucadrus, etc. Data from Appendix 1 (i.e. only inscribed altars). Altars to eastern cults are included in the bars giving heights for 'All altars', but are excluded from both the 'Official' and 'Local' bars in the chart.

15 It has not been possible to weigh any altars directly, but estimates of stone density used in modern quarrying give *c.* 2600 kg per cubic metre for limestone and *c.* 2300 kg per cubic metre for sandstone (http://simetric.co.uk/si_materials.htm). This means that an altar 30 x 15 x 15 cm would weigh *c.* 16–18 kg.

16 This total is probably boosted to a small (but unquantifiable) extent by differential bias in favour of the preservation of complete small altars, in contrast to the greater likelihood of break-up for secondary usage in the case of larger altars.

to use in terms of making an offering in the *focus* on top of the altar.

Further analysis of this size distribution (Fig. 3; Appendix 1) demonstrates that 'official' cults, e.g. IOM, make up the bulk of the altars centred on the 90–100 cm height range, while local and Romano-Celtic deities, such as Belatucadrus or Vitiris form the vast majority of the small altars, with very few in the larger size range. When individual cults are picked out, three groupings of Romano-Celtic deities can be discerned, on the basis of altar heights. Those that are most like the larger group of 'official' cults are composed of Silvanus[17] and Sulis (Fig. 4), the latter in particular having conventionally-sized altars, nearly all coming from Bath. The second group, the Matres and Cocidius (Fig. 5), is more relevant in respect of potential portable altars, since the bar chart has a peak in the 41–50 cm range. This is probably too large for easy portability, but demonstrates the dedication of relatively small altars compared to the overall range in Fig. 2.

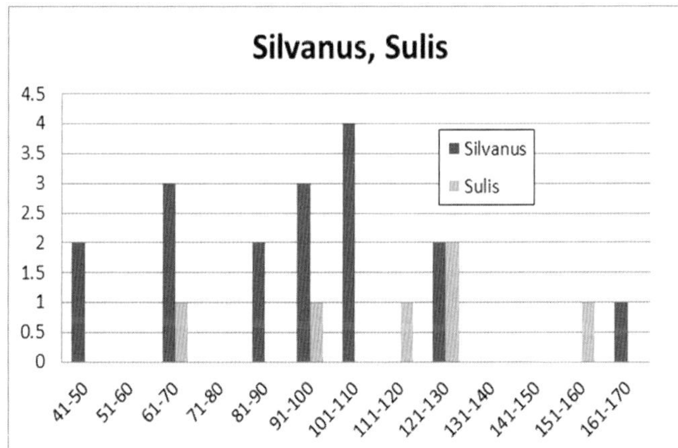

Fig. 4. Bar chart of heights of altars to Silvanus and Sulis.

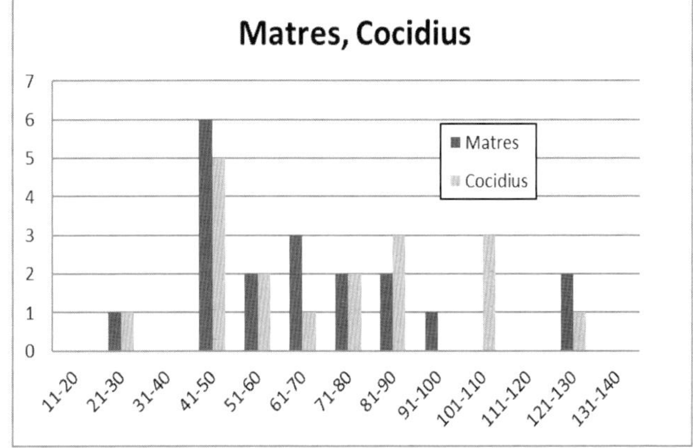

Fig. 5. Bar chart of heights of altars to the Matres and Cocidius.

17 Although a Latin deity, a good case can be made for Silvanus being consistently equated with local woodland/wildland deities in Britain, e.g. Cocidius, Vinotonus. Cf. Fairless 1984, 230; Wright 1946; Henig 1984, 174.

Fig. 6 (Left). Altar to Cocidius (RIB 1683; Appendix 1, no. 342), found in modern foundations at Hardriding, 3 km SW of Chesterholm (Vindolanda). Ht 102 cm, width 43 cm, depth 39 cm. *Deo / Cocidio / Decimus / Caerelli/us Victor / pr(aefectus) coh(ortis) II Ner(viorum) / v(otum) s(olvit) l(ibens) m(erito)* 'To the god Cocidius, Decimus Caerellius Victor, prefect of Cohors II of the Nervii, willingly and deservedly fulfilled his vow'. Chesters Museum (Photo A. C. King).

Fig. 7 (Middle). Altar to Cocidius (RIB 1577; Appendix 1, no. 135), found in the vicus of Housesteads just to the east of the mithraeum. Ht 43 cm, width 23 cm. *Cocidio [et] / Genio pr[ae]/sidi Vale/rius m(iles) l[e]/g(ionis) VI V(ictricis) P(iae) F(idelis) v(oto) p(osuit)* 'To Cocidius and the Genius of the garrison, Valerius, soldier of Leg VI Victrix PF, set this up as his vow'. Newcastle Museums.

Fig. 8 (Right). Altar to Cocidius (RIB 1633; Appendix, no. 37), from foot of crag below Hadrian's Wall, Milecastle 37 (Housesteads). Sufficient remains of the base of this altar to estimate its original height. Ht c. 24 cm, width 18 cm. *Deo / Cocidio / Vabrius / [v(otum)] s(olvit) l(ibens) m(erito)* 'To the god Cocidius, Vabrius willingly and deservedly fulfilled his vow'. Chesters Museum (Photo A. C. King).

Three altars to Cocidius bring out a correlation between size and the status of the dedicant. An officer, the *praefectus cohortis* of *Coh II Nerviorum*, dedicates an altar of 105 cm height, probably at a shrine at Vindolanda (Fig. 6). Under half this size, at 43 cm, is the altar to Cocidius and the Genius of the garrison, dedicated by a *miles* of *Leg VI Victrix*, presumably involved in construction work on Hadrian's Wall (Fig. 7). It comes from the *vicus* of Housesteads fort, near the *mithraeum*, and is a well-carved stone, with *patera* and jug on the sides. It was possibly a personal offering at a shrine in the *vicus*. The third example is more crudely lettered, and comes from near Milecastle 37 on Hadrian's Wall, near Housesteads (Fig. 8). At *c.* 24 cm, this stone is certainly portable, but its provenance does not give any information about its location when in use. The dedicant, Vabrius, was a *peregrinus*, and probably not directly connected with the military, unlike the majority of Cocidius dedications.[18] Such differentiation of altar size and social status can be seen elsewhere, and of itself, is not surprising. However, when the third group is considered, the higher-status dedicants are no longer present and nearly all the altars are of relatively small size.

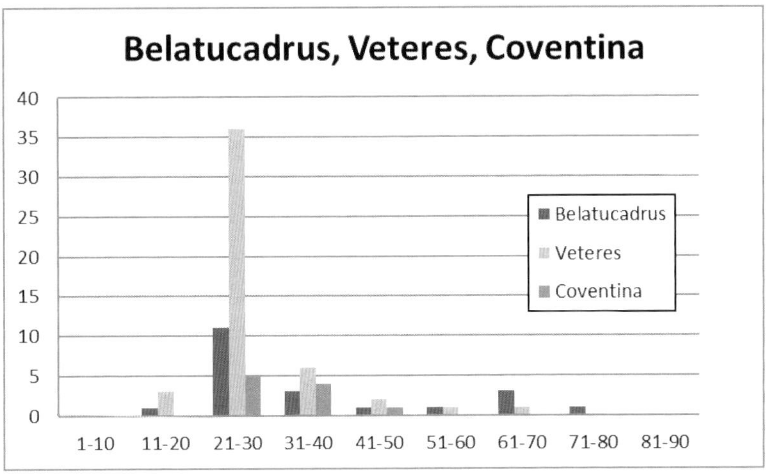

Fig. 9. Bar chart of heights of altars to Belatucadrus, Vitiris and Coventina.

The third group consists of Coventina, Belatucadrus and Vitiris (or the Veteres). The bar chart (Fig. 9) shows a strong representation of small and very small altars. The altars to Coventina are all in the size range 21–50 cm, and are fairly standardised. However, they may be a special case since all examples come from Coventina's Well.[19] Greater variety is seen in the more widespread altars to Belatucadrus, which are also found in the Penrith/Brougham area as well as the western sector of Hadrian's Wall.[20] A personal dedication by a *peregrinus* 'for his own welfare' from Brougham (Fig. 10) is a typical example in not having a military association.[21] It has lettering of variable quality, and the name of the god displays one of the many spelling variations that are a characteristic of this deity.[22] Another example, from the *vicus* of Old Penrith fort (Fig. 11) has poorly executed lettering and omits the name of the dedicant.[23] Other altars to this god also omit the name of the dedicant,[24] including a crudely carved and possibly 'home-produced' example from Carvoran, definitely portable at 25 cm height (Fig. 12).

18 Fairless 1984, 232; Birley 1986, 59.
19 Allason-Jones & McKay 1985. For discussion of the Germanic dedicants at this shrine, and the possibility of a Germanic serivation for Coventina, see Clay 2007, 52–3; 2008, 147; Fernández (this volume).
20 Fairless 1984, Fig. 13.1.
21 Fairless 1984, 226–7; Birley 1986, 60–1.
22 Fairless 1984, 225.
23 Its unusual shape, with a base extension seems to indicate that this stone was dug directly into the ground. The altar is also unusual in being flat, with a depth of only 9 cm.
24 E.g. RIB 1776, 1784, both from Carvoran. This fort has many small-sized altars to Belatucadrus and the Veteres; Goldberg 2015, 200.

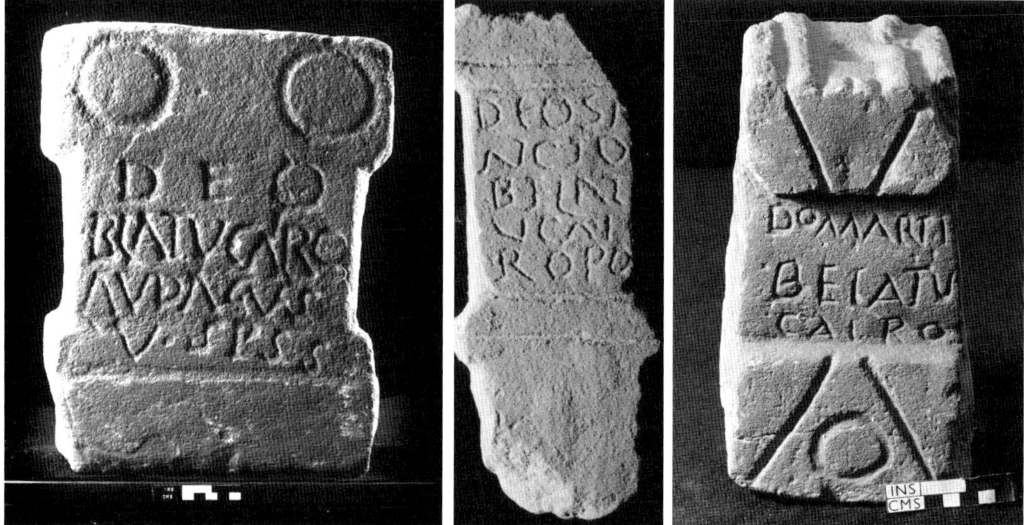

Fig. 10 (Left). Altar to Belatucadrus (RIB 774; Appendix 1, no. 115), found built into a stable wall at Brougham Castle. Ht 38 cm, width 29 cm. *Deo / Blatucairo / Audagus / v(otum) s(olvit) p(ro) s(ua) s(alute)* — 'To the god Blatucairus, Audagus fulfilled his vow for his own welfare'. Newcastle Museums.

Fig. 11 (Middle). Altar to Belatucadrus (RIB 3229; Appendix 1, no. 138), found unstratified in excavation of vicus to south of Old Penrith Roman fort. Ht (including base extension) 43 cm, width 16 cm, depth 9 cm. *Deo sa/ncto /Belat/ucai/ro po(suit)* — 'To the holy god Belatucairus, ... set this up'. Tullie House Museum, Carlisle.

Fig. 12 (Right). Altar to Belatucadrus (RIB 1784; Appendix 1, no. 51), from Carvoran, Hadrian's Wall. Ht 25 cm, width 13 cm. *D(e)o Marti / Belatu/cairo* — 'To the god Belatucairus'. Newcastle Museums.

The dedications to Vitiris, or the Veteres,[25] are an interesting group, and have the greatest concentration of any deity in the 21–30 cm height range (Fig. 9). They also display a wide range in terms of quality, varying from the delicately carved example from Netherby (Fig. 13), which has the Erymanthian boar on one side and the tree of the Hesperides on the other, thus linking the cult to Hercules,[26] to the miniature altar, 16.5 cm high, found reused in a road level at Corbridge (Fig. 14). This has very crude lettering, but does have a *focus*, and the name of the dedicant: it is one of best examples of a truly portable personal altar from the Hadrian's Wall area. A third example, from Chester-le-Street, displays another feature of some of the altars in northern Britain (Fig. 15). The altar is well-carved, with careful detailing, probably having been produced by a professional workshop.[27] However, the lettering is jarringly crude and ill-formed by comparison, and was probably added by unskilled craftsmen to the blank shaft of the altar.

25 For discussion of the name and its variants, see Goldberg 2015, 198–203; De Bernardo Stempel 2008, 75. The latter suggests that the H in Hveteris represents Henos ('old'), and is not evidence of Germanic association.

26 Birley 1954, 37–8; Goldberg 2015, 199, 204. Cf. also Birley 1986, 62–4.

27 Kewley 1974, 58, no. 1.

Fig. 13. Altar to Vitiris (RIB 973; Appendix 1, no. 19), from Netherby. Ht 23 cm, width 13 cm. *Deo / H(eno) Ve/tiri* — 'To the god Henos Vetiris'. On the right side the Erymanthian Boar, on the left side the tree of the Hesperides. Tullie House Museum, Carlisle (Photo as in Birley 1954, Fig. 6; scale in inches).

Fig. 14 (Right). Altar to Vitiris (RIB 1141; Appendix 1, no. 6), found in excavation of late Roman road-level east of site XXXIX, Corbridge. Ht 16.5 cm, width 9.5 cm, depth 9 cm. *Vit(iri) / M/iti(us) [---]* — 'To Vitiris, Mitius (set this up)'. Corbridge Museum. (Photo A. C. King)

Fig. 15 (Far Right). Altar to Vitiris (RIB 1046; Appendix 1, no. 172), found in a Roman well, c. 200 m north-west of Chester-le-Street fort. Ht 56 cm, width 22 cm. *Deo / Viti/ri D/uih/no v(otum) s(olvit)* — 'To the god Vitiris, Duihno fulfilled his vow'. Newcastle Museums.

There was clearly a preference for small altars in the worship of these deities, especially so in the case of the third group, and they do not have clear provenances in temple sites, with the exception of Coventina's Well and those to Sulis at Bath. Even in the latter case, while most of the altars come from the Sulis temple precinct or adjacent baths, some were recovered from elsewhere in the town. Other explanations must therefore be sought for the ritual contexts in which these small altars were dedicated. Some of the altars are very crudely carved, and may have been produced by the dedicants

Fig. 16. Anepigraphic altar, from Waltham Roman villa excavations, Whittington, Gloucestershire. Ht 10 cm, width 6.5 cm, depth, 4.4cm. Photos showing front face and top, from Henig 2013, by kind permission.

themselves.

The analysis represented by the bar charts only includes inscribed altars. There are also a number of anepigraphic examples (Appendix 2),[28] on average smaller in size than the inscribed altars, especially if weathered stones in Appendix 2 are omitted as being of uncertain status in terms of whether they once carried an incised inscription. Some of the anepigraphic altars are very small, such as the one excavated at Waltham villa, Whittington, Gloucestershire, in 2000 (Fig. 16).[29] This is only 10 cm high, 6.5 cm wide and 4.4 cm deep, with simple linear incised lines for decoration, including a simple saltire cross on what was presumably the front, and a clear *focus* indicating its intended function as an altar. Martin Henig's discussion of this piece also refers to similar examples from Chedworth and Cirencester, both in Gloucestershire,[30] and in at least two cases also with saltire crosses, which may have been solar wheel symbols,[31] and in one case with a simple carved figure of a warrior god. Another anepigraphic altar comes from the *cella* of Springhead, Kent, Temple I, found *in situ*.[32] Interestingly, it is in a stone type, millstone grit, that indicates transport over a considerable distance, since the nearest sources are in the northern parts of Britannia.

Conclusion

Inscriptions up to 30/40 cm height (*c.* 20 kg) were fairly easily transportable. But did this actually happen? The type of stone at nearly all sites is local or regional, e.g. red sandstone in the western sector of Hadrian's Wall and buff sandstone in eastern sector.

28 The biggest single group comes from Coventina's Well, and may originally have had painted inscriptions to the goddess. Cf. Allason-Jones & McKay 1985, 18–9.

29 Henig 2013. Not included in Appendix 2.

30 Chedworth: Henig 1993, no. 126. Cirencester, *ibid.*, no. 129. For further discussion of examples from Goucester, Caerleon and Augst, see Henig & Adcock 2016, 40–1.

31 Aldhouse-Green 1984, 346.

32 *CSIR Britain* 1.10.117. Inf. Martin Henig, Penny Coombe and Kevin Hayward, at a lecture to the Institute of Classical Studies, London, 2015. At 79 cm high, this altar is too large for transport as personal luggage, and presumably was carried in a cart or similar means of transport. For recent evaluation of the Springhead sanctuary, see Andrews *et al.* 2011, 209–13. There is a smaller uninscribed millstone grit altar from Stanwick, Northants; inf. Martin Henig, from a report in preparation.

This would imply that, if altars were moved about, they were not transported over very long distances. However, there are exceptions to this, such as the millstone grit altar from Springhead, mentioned above. It may be relevant that this is a southern British temple site, on a major Roman road from London to Richborough and Dover. The altar may have been dedicated by a traveller passing through the sanctuary, or by a pilgrim to this important cult centre, with the means to transport a relatively large altar.

The dominance of Vitiris and Belatucadrus in the small size range, and the lack of evidence (thus far) for their presence in shrines, suggests worship at a more personal level. It is possible that temples or shrines in the formal sense (e.g. *fana*) were not a requirement for these cults, and that they were more domestic and military/domestic (i.e. military *vici*) in nature and location. They may have been placed inside buildings or possibly in exterior 'informal' locations. Many small altars are also of a production quality that suggests that they are 'home-produced' and not 'professional' in terms of their carving and lettering. Was there a stratum of identity formation and reinforcement, especially in the army, through non-official 'local' deities in non-official locations?

Preliminary analysis of the status of the dedicants shows that men and junior officers form the main group of dedicants of small altars, whilst more senior officers, often with *tria nomina*, are linked to larger sizes. This is to be expected, but does indicate a significant element of worship was 'unofficial', associated with local Romano-Celtic deities, and personal in nature.

A last comment is that this study has concentrated on Britain, but it is very likely that a similar situation existed in Gaul and other regions of the Roman Empire. This is demonstrated by a recent find of a small altar, 9.1 cm high, to a previously unknown local deity, Dagiata or Agiata, from a domestic settlement context at Bétheny (Marne).[33] Other examples can readily be seen in museum collections,[34] often classified as 'miniature' altars, but they are fully functional, with a *focus,* and as such should preferably be regarded as ordinary, albeit small-sized, versions of larger altars.

Acknowledgements

I am very grateful to Martin Henig and Martin Goldberg for their comments and the provision of additional information and photographs. Photography of altars at Chesters and Corbridge Museums was enabled by kind arrangement with museum staff, and other photographs were provided by Newcastle Museums and Tullie House Museum, Carlisle. This paper was originally given at the Lampeter F.E.R.C.AN. Workshop, and subsequently at RAC 2016, at La Sapienza University, Rome.

33 Lefebvre *et al.* 2014.

34 For instance: from Vertault, anepigraphic, Musée du Pays Châtillonais, inv. 905.15.1; from Autun, to Anvallus, dedicated by a *gutuater*, Musée Rolin, CIL XIII 11225, inv. M.L.1570 (cf. Bulliot 1901; Green 1997, 115); from Segovia, to Epona, Museo de Segovia inv. A-12233; from Duratón, three altars to Matres and Minerva, Museo de Segovia inv. A-7350, Museo Arq. Nac. Madrid inv. A-37801, Col. Fontaneda Castillo de Ampudia Palencia (cf. Martinez Caballero & Vilches Crespo 2015, 140, 148, 150-1); three on display in the Musée Gallo-Romain, Lyon.

Appendix 1

List of inscribed altars from Roman Britain, from smallest to largest in height. Data from RIB I (2nd edition), RIB III and *Britannia* volumes 40 to 46. Key to stone types: BS buff sandstone; G gritstone; L limestone; MG millstone grit; O oolite; RS red sandstone; S sandstone; WM white marble.

No.	*Place*	*Details*	*Deity*	*H (cm)*	*W (cm)*	*D (cm)*	*Stone*	*RIB/Brit*
1	Chester	statuette/altar base in barrack block, site XV, Deanery Field	Genius signiferorum	10	13	13	WM	451
2	Burgh-by-Sands	3 miles SW of fort	Latis	10	6		RS	2043
3	Corbridge	surface cleaning	Diana	14	11		BS	1126
4	Burgh-by-Sands		Belatocadrus	14	10		RS	2039
5	Chesterholm	on road in vicus	Moguns & Genius loci	16	11	10	BS	3334
6	Corbridge	in late road level E of Site XXXIX	Vitiris	16.5	9.5	9	BS	1141
7	Chedworth		Lenus Mars (?)	18	11		O	126
8	Housesteads	on floor in block XIII in NW corner of fort	Mars	18	11		RS	1597
9	Chesterholm	unstratified in rubble at S gate	illeg	18	11	7	BS	3346
10	Chesterholm	in excavation (no details)	Dea .... (illiterate)	19	15	15	BS	B40.5
11	High Rochester		Hercules	20	17		BS	1264
12	Benwell	in N part of fort	Mars	20	13		BS	1332
13	Housesteads	on roadway S of S gate	Veteres	20	15		BS	1606
14	Chesterholm		Neptune	20	13		lost	1694
15	Chesterholm	in fort	Veteres	20	11		lost	1699
16	Birdoswald		Latis	20	10		BS	1897
17	Piercebridge	in stokehole of hypocaust, Tofts Field	Veteris	22	15	11	BS	3254
18	Chesterholm	found with no. 79	Veteres	22	13	7	BS	3339
19	Netherby		Hveter (Hercules imagery)	23	13		RS	973
20	Chester-le-Street	N side of fort	Deae Vitires	23	13		BS	1047
21	Benwell	in N part of fort	Vitires	23	13		BS	1336
22	Chesters		Votris	23	13		BS	1458
23	Carrawburgh	in Coventina's Well	Coventina	23	18		BS	1528
24	Housesteads	reused in building II of vicus	Veteres	23	13		BS	1607

No.	Place	Details	Deity	H (cm)	W (cm)	D (cm)	Stone	RIB/Brit
25	Chesterholm	unstratified on rampart N of W gate	Veteris	23	13		BS	1697
26	Carvoran		Vitiris	23	13		BS	1799
27	Carvoran		Veteres	23	15		BS	1803
28	Carvoran		Veteres	23	11		BS	1804
29	Carvoran		Vitires	23	13		BS	1805
30	Birdoswald		Ratis	23	10		BS	1903
31	Burgh-by-Sands		Belatucadrus	23	15		RS	2044
32	Hadrian's Wall	possibly Carvoran	Hvitires	23	17		BS	2069
33	Brougham	on river bank N of fort	Belatucabrus	23	14		RS	3230
34	Chesterholm	fallen from fort wall	Vitires	23	12	11	BS	3341
35	Corbridge	Site XI	VMD (Vitiris?)	24	14		BS	1145
36	Chesters	E gate	Veteres	24	15		BS	1456
37	Hadrian's Wall	near MC 37	Cocidius	24	18		BS	1633
38	Burgh-by-Sands		Belatucadrus	24	13		lost	2038
39	Old Penrith	unstratified in excavation of S vicus	Balatocaurus	24	15	13	BS	3228
40	Risingham		Nymphae	24	12		grey S (not local)	3489
41	Chesterholm	in intervallum road of fort	Hveteres	24	13	13	BS	B41.7
42	Durham area		Vitiris	24	15	13	BS	B46.10
43	Daglingworth	near villa	Cuda	25	23	6	O	129
44	York	Micklegate	Matres Afr Ital Gall	25	14			653
45	Chester-le-Street	N side of fort	Digenis	25	17		BS	1044
46	Lanchester		Regina	25	13		BS	1084
47	Benwell	in N part of fort	Vetris	25	13		BS	1335
48	Carrawburgh	in Coventina's Well	Dea Nimfa Coventina	25	14		BS	1526
49	Carrawburgh	in Coventina's Well	Covetina	25	13		BS	1532
50	Great Chesters		Veteres	25	13		BS	1729
51	Carvoran		Mars Belatu-cairus	25	13		BS	1784
52	Birrens		Fortuna	25	15		RS	2095
53	Chesterholm	in rubble in vicus	Hvitiris	25	12	10	BS	3335
54	Chesterholm	in rubble in vicus	Vetiris	25	18	10	BS	3337
55	South Shields	reused in 4th c. ditch of fort	Vitiris	26	17	12	BS	3268

No.	Place	Details	Deity	H (cm)	W (cm)	D (cm)	Stone	RIB/Brit
56	Chesterholm	in 3rd c, building in vicus	Vitires	26	16	11	BS	3342
57	Lemington		Regina	27	19	9	O	125
58	Castlesteads		Belatugagrus	27	11		RS	1976
59	Chester	1 mile E of The Cross	Genius centuriae Aureli Verini	28	15			447
60	York	St Mary's Convent	Veter	28	13			660
61	Brougham	from S moat	Belatucadrus	28	18		RS	775
62	Piercebridge		Mars Condates	28	20		lost	1024
63	Lanchester		Mars	28	14		BS	1079
64	Lanchester		Mars	28	18		BS	1081
65	Corbridge	E of Site XI	Veteris	28	18		BS	1139
66	Benwell	in N part of fort	Mars Victor	28	18		BS	1333
67	Chesters		Dea Ratis	28	18		BS	1454
68	Carrawburgh		Belleticaurus	28	15		BS	1521
69	Carrawburgh	in Coventina's Well	Coventina	28	15		BS	1525
70	Carvoran		Veteris	28	15		BS	1793
71	Carvoran		Vetiris	28	18		BS	1796
72	Castlesteads		Belatucadrus	28	20	13	RS	1977
73	Carrawburgh	in Coventina's Well	Coventina	29	17		BS	1529
74	Housesteads		Mars	29	17		BS	1592
75	Carvoran	N side of fort	Baliticaurus	29	19		BS	1775
76	Carvoran		Veteris	29	19		BS	1794
77	Kirkbride		Belatocairus	29	23		RS	2056
78	Chesterholm	in Severan wall	Hvvtris	29	14	13	grey S	3336
79	Chesterholm	in 4th c, storehouse in vicus	Veteres	29	20	18	BS	3338
80	York	relief + altar	Mercury	30	25			655
81	Old Penrith		Mountis (Mogons)	30	18		BS	922
82	Lanchester		Mithras, Cautopates, Sol Invictus	30	18		BS	1082
83	Lanchester		Vitiris	30	25		BS	1087
84	Ebchester		Mars & Num Aug	30	25		BS	1100
85	Ebchester		Vitiris	30	15		BS	1104
86	High Rochester		Di Mountes (Moguntes)	30	20		BS	1269
87	Chesters		Vitiris	30	15		BS	1455

No.	*Place*	*Details*	*Deity*	*H (cm)*	*W (cm)*	*D (cm)*	*Stone*	*RIB/Brit*
88	Housesteads	in angle tower of fort	Hveteris	30	18		BS	1602
89	Great Chesters		Veteris	30	15		BS	1728
90	Carvoran		Epona	30	15		lost	1777
91	Carvoran		Deum (?)	30	18		BS	1806
92	Tilston	unstratified in Roman settlement site	Genius loci	31	24	11	RS	3167
93	York	St Mary's Convent	Mars	33	20			650
94	Old Carlisle		Belatucaurus	33	20		RS	889
95	Carlisle	Annetwell Street	Genius centu-riae	33	20		whitish S	944
96	Lanchester	near fort	Mars	33	19		BS	1078
97	Corbridge		Vitiris	33	23		BS	1140
98	Carrawburgh	in Coventina's Well	Minerva	33	18		BS	1543
99	Housesteads	in room in block VI in SW corner of fort	Hvitris	33	18		BS	1603
100	Carvoran		Blatucadrus	33	18		BS	1776
101	Hadrian's Wall	possibly Houses-teads	Nemesis	33	18		BS	2065
102	Croy Hill	100 m S of fort	Mars	33	20		BS	2159
103	Southwark	in pit between 2 Romano-Celtic temples, Tabard Street	Num Augg & Mars Camulus	33	29		WM stone panel	3014
104	Benwell	in fort SW of prae-torium	Minerva	34	18	13	BS	3285
105	Adel		Brigantia	36	23		S	630
106	Greta Bridge		Mars	36	25			743
107	Chester-le-Street		Deae Vitires	36	18		BS	1048
108	Carrawburgh	in Coventina's Well	Coventina	36	18		BS	1524
109	Carrawburgh	in debris in room B of bath-house W of fort	Fortuna	36	20		BS	1537
110	Carvoran		Hammia	36	15		BS	1780
111	Carvoran		Vitiris	36	23		BS	1800
112	Carrawburgh	in Coventina's Well	Covventina	37	19		BS	1535
113	Carvoran		Veteris	37	23		BS	1795
114	Caernarvon	in 3rd c, debris in strong-room of praetorium	Minerva	38	18		S	429

No.	*Place*	*Details*	*Deity*	*H (cm)*	*W (cm)*	*D (cm)*	*Stone*	*RIB/Brit*
115	Brougham		Blatucairus	38	29		RS	774
116	Piercebridge	in NE angle of fort	Jupiter	38	25		BS	1021
117	Carrawburgh	in Coventina's Well	Conventina	38	20		BS	1522
118	Carrawburgh	in Coventina's Well	Convetina	38	23		BS	1523
119	Hadrian's Wall	near spring S of MC 42	Apollo	38	15		BS	1665
120	Chesterholm	near Romano-Celtic temple in vicus	Veteres?	38	18	17	BS	3343
121	Caernarvon	in nave of mithraeum, with 3 small uninscribed altars	illeg	40	15	14	G	3146
122	Netherby		IOM & Hveteris	41	20		RS	969
123	Lanchester		Vitiris	41	19		BS	1088
124	Ebchester		Vitiris	41	20		BS	1103
125	Newcastle		Silvanus	41	25		BS	1321
126	Castlesteads		illeg	41	18	13	RS	1996
127	Chester-le-Street	in fort area	uninscribed	41	18		S	2333
128	Lanchester		Victoria	42	20		BS	1086
129	Chesterholm	found near no. 352	illeg	42	23	17	BS	B41.6
130	Adel	N side of church	Matres	43	23			629
131	York	St Mary's Convent	Matres Domesticae	43	25		L	652
132	Netherby		E... (Epona?)	43	20		whitish S	967
133	Netherby		Silvanus	43	25		RS	972
134	Carrawburgh	reused in mithraeum	Matres	43	23		BS	1540
135	Housesteads	E of mithraeum	Cocidius & Genius praesidis	43	23		BS	1577
136	Stanwix		Matres Domesticae	43	28		RS	2025
137	Dover	N of classis fort	Matres Ital	43	20	16	cream L	3031
138	Old Penrith	found near no. 39	Belatucairus	43	16	9	RS	3229
139	Caerwent	from centre of town opposite temple insula	Genius loci	45	23	16	RS	3076
140	Catterick	inside S wall of town	Matres Domesticae	45	23	21	BS	3210
141	Custom Scrubbs	from Roman Tump	Romulus	46	38	13	O	132
142	Old Carlisle		Brigantia	46	22		RS	902
143	Carlisle	English Street	Mars Barrex	46	28		BS	947

No.	Place	Details	Deity	H (cm)	W (cm)	D (cm)	Stone	RIB/Brit
144	Carvoran		IOM Heliopolitanus	46	23		BS	1783
145	Hadrian's Wall	near MC 60	Cocidius	46	30		RS	2020
146	Hadrian's Wall	near MC 65	Mars Cocidius	46	20		RS	2024
147	Greetland	Thick Hollins	Victoria Brigantia & Num Aug	48	36			627
148	Castleford	in River Calder	Victoria Brigantia	48	25			628
149	York	City Art Gallery	Mars	48	25			651
150	Netherby		Apollo	48	25		whitish S	965
151	Carrawburgh	in Coventina's Well	Covontina	48	23		BS	1533
152	Housesteads	in mithraeum	IOM, Cocidius & Genius huius loci	48	25		BS	1583
153	Birdoswald		IOM	48	28		BS	1877
154	Castlesteads		Mars & Num Aug	48	18		RS	1987
155	Hadrian's Wall	in wall structure W of MC 59	Mars Cocidius	48	20		RS	2015
156	Chester	in shrine in amphitheatre	Nemesis	48	33	26	RS	3149
157	Winchester	Jewry Street	Matres Ital Germ Gall	51	33		S	88
158	Custom Scrubbs	from Roman Tump	Mars Olludius	51	38	13	O	131
159	Brough-on-Noe	in strong room of praetorium	Arnomecta	51	30		G	281
160	Brougham	0.5 maile SE of fort	Balatucadrus	51	30			772
162	Bewcastle	0.5 mile S of fort	Cocidius	51	23		BS	985
163	Risingham	in river	Mogons Cad... & Num Aug	51	36		BS	1225
164	Carrawburgh	reused in structure in centre of fort	Genius huius loci	51	20		BS	1538
165	Birdoswald		Mars & Victoria	51	25		BS	1899
166	Castlecary	near W rampart	Mercury	51	23		BS	2148
167	Bewcastle	in river	Cocidius	53	33		whitish S	988
168	Chester-le-Street	300 m N of fort	Mars Condates	53	28		BS	1045
169	Hadrian's Wall	MC 3	Digenis (?)	53	28		BS	1314
170	Housesteads	in mithraeum	Sol	53	25		BS	1601
171	Lancaster	Vicarage Fields	illeg	56	25		S	603
172	Chester-le-Street	in Roman well 200 m NW of fort	Vitiris	56	22		BS	1046

No.	*Place*	*Details*	*Deity*	*H (cm)*	*W (cm)*	*D (cm)*	*Stone*	*RIB/Brit*
173	High Rochester	in strong room of praetorium	Genius DN & Signi coh	56	43		BS	1262
174	Cirencester	NW sector of town	Suleviae	58	30			105
175	Carlisle	English Street	Parcae	58	30		RS	953
176	Newcastle	County Council offices	IOM	58	25		BS	1316
177	Bath	debris in spring of Hot Bath near St John's Hospital	Sulis Minerva	61	28		O	150
178	Lincoln	1 mile ENE of cathedral	Genius loci	61	25		L	246
179	York,	St Dennis, Walm-gate	Arciaco & Num Aug	61	30			640
180	Brougham		Balatucairus	61	38			773
181	Brougham		Mars	61	30		white S	780
182	Netherby		Mogons Vitiris	61	33		RS	971
183	Carvoran		Nymphae	61	38		BS	1789
184	Heronbridge	in 2nd c. level (Matres shrine?) on Roman industrial site	Matres Ollototae	64	38		RS	574
185	Kirkby Thore		Belatucadrus	64	38		RS	759
186	Great Chesters	in bath house SE of fort	Fortuna	64	48		BS	1724
187	Carvoran	in apodyterium of bath house inside SW angle of fort	Fortuna Aug	64	36		BS	1778
188	Castlesteads	0.5 mile W of fort	IOM	64	38		RS	1979
189	Castlesteads		IOM	64	33		RS	1980
190	Duntocher	near fort	IOM	64	30		BS	2201
191	Westerwood	90 m W of fort	Silvanus & Quadriviae	64	26	27	BS	3504
192	Bath	in ruins of Hot Bath	Diana	66	36		O	138
193	Wroxeter	near forum	illeg	66	46		BS	286
194	Michaelchurch	in church	Tridamus	66	38		S	304
195	Chester	in cathedral close	Matres	66	30			456
196	Lancaster	N of the Castle	Mars Cocodius	66	41		S	602
197	York	Bishophill	IOM Dis Dea-busque, Penates	66	41		L	649
198	South Shields	inside fort near E gate	Aesculapius	66	33		BS	1052
199	Chesterholm		Silvanus	66	28		BS	1696
200	Birdoswald	inside fort	Silvanus	66	46		BS	1905
201	Castlesteads	300 m N of fort	Num Aug & Vanauns	66	36		RS	1991

No.	*Place*	*Details*	*Deity*	*H (cm)*	*W (cm)*	*D (cm)*	*Stone*	*RIB/Brit*
202	Newstead	200 m E of fort	Campestres	66	30		RS	2121
203	Newcastle	Castle excavations	illeg	66	36	17	yellow S	3283
204	Chesterholm	vicus excavations	uninscribed	66	32	24	BS	B43.7
205	Caerleon	reused as channel in bath house	Fortuna	69	23	20	O	317
206	Manchester	close to river near fort	Fortuna Conservatrix	69	41	29	RS	575
207	York	reused in Roman baths, Old Railway Station	Fortuna	69	43			644
208	Greta Bridge		Mars	69	30		S	742
209	Maryport	200 m E of fort	illeg	69	43		RS	836
210	Old Carlisle	1 mile SW of fort	Belatucadrus	69	36		RS	887
211	Risingham		Matres Tramarinae	69	33		BS	1224
212	Birrens		Harimella	69	36		whitish S	2096
213	Camelon	i km W of fort	illeg	69	26	22	BS	3510
214	Risingham		Di Cultores huius loci	71	36		BS	1208
215	Hadrian's Wall	MC 52	Cocidius	71	28		BS	1956
216	Lincoln	just inside E wall of lower town	Mars	74	26		L	248
217	Caerwent	standinf against S wall in House XVIs	Mars Ocelus	74	28		S	310
218	Chester	unstratified near cathedral	Genius centuriae	74	33			446
219	Chester	Bridge Street Row	Minerva	74	36			457
220	Doncaster	St Sepulchre Gate	Matres	74	38			618
221	Ilkley	Congregational Church	illeg	74	41			634
222	Bowes		Fortuna	74	43			730
223	Maryport		Setlocenia	74	38		RS	841
224	Binchester		Fortuna	74	46		BS	1029
225	Ebchester	0.25 mile SW of fort	Vernostonus Cocidius	74	41		BS	1102
226	Hadrian's Wall	MC 19, 2nd c. level	Matres	74	30		BS	1421
227	Carrawburgh		Minerva	74	43		BS	1542
228	Birrens		Viradecthis	74	46		RS	2108
229	Castlecary	in bath house of fort	Fortuna	74	36		BS	2146
230	Auchendavy	in pit just SW of fort	Diana & Apollo	74	30		BS	2174
231	Balmuildy	on S wall of bath house inside fort	Fortuna	74	33		BS	2189

No.	*Place*	*Details*	*Deity*	*H (cm)*	*W (cm)*	*D (cm)*	*Stone*	*RIB/Brit*
232	Bath	Lower Stall Street	Loucetius Mars & Nemetona	76	43		O	140
233	Kirkby Thore		illeg	76	38		S	766
234	Old Carlisle		IOM	76	53		RS	897
235	Old Penrith	inside fort	Mars Belatu-cadrus & Num Augg	76	48		BS	918
236	South Shields	W of fort	Mars Alator	76	30		BS	1055
237	Risingham	near spring on E side of Dere Street	Nymphae	76	28		BS	1228
238	Carvoran		Dea Syria	76	43		BS	2175
239	Auchendavy	in pit just SW of fort	Genius Terrae Britanniae	76	38		buff G	2175
240	Maryport		IOM	78	38		RS	818
241	Chesters	in bath house	Fortuna Con-servatrix	78	30		BS	1449
242	Maryport	Camp Farm exca-vations	IOM	78	35	33	RS	B44.3
243	Maryport	350 m NE of fort	IOM	79	41		RS	826
244	Benwell		Lamii tres	79	41		BS	1331
245	Birdoswald		Fortuna	79	36		BS	1873
246	Castlesteads		IOM & Genius loci	79	43		RS	1984
247	Birrens	in ruins outside fort	Mercury	79	46		BS	2102
248	Birrens		Num Aug & Mercury	79	38		RS	2103
249	Caerleon	in churchyard	Salus Regina	81	51		O	324
250	Chester	Eastgate Street	Genius centu-riae	81	28			448
251	Chester	in situ in Eastgate Street	Genius loci	81	48			450
252	Ribchester		Matres	81	56			586
253	York	The Mount	Silvanus	81	33		L	659
254	Maryport		IOM	81	48		RS	834
255	Netherby		Cocidius	81	36		whitish S	966
256	South Shields		illeg	81	38		BS	1058
257	Wallsend		illeg	81	38		BS	1302
258	Carrawburgh		Fortuna	81	43		BS	1536
259	Chesterholm	120 m W of fort	IOM	81	38		BS	1689
260	Chesterholm		Sattada	81	48		BS	1695
261	Birdoswald		IOM	81	41		BS	1875
262	Aldborough	1 mile NW of town	illeg	81	48		S	2347

No.	Place	Details	Deity	H (cm)	W (cm)	D (cm)	Stone	RIB/Brit
263	Birdoswald	from parade ground area near MC 49	IOM	81	46	18	BS	3438
264	Birrens		Di & Deae omnes	83	38	15	RS	2109
265	Maryport	350 m NE of fort	IOM & Num Aug	84	38		BS	824
266	Bewcastle		Cocidius	84	46		whitish S	989
267	Corbridge		Silvanus	84	51		BS	1136
268	Birdoswald		IOM	84	36		BS	1874
269	Auchendavy	in pit just SW of fort	Mars, Minerva, Campestres, Hercules, Epona, Victoria	84	30		buff G	2177
270	Moresby	W of fort	IOM	86	36			797
271	Maryport	350 m NE of fort	Mars Militaris	86	46		RS	838
272	South Shields	100 m S of fort	Brigantia	86	41		BS	1053
273	Ebchester		Genius ...	86	51		BS	1099
274	Whitley Castle	near NE corner of fort	Hercules	86	46		BS	1199
275	Housesteads	Chapel Hill	Alaisiagae, Baudihillia, Friagabis, Num Aug	86	36		BS	1576
276	Hadrian's Wall	possibly Housesteads	Matres Germ	86	28		BS	2064
277	Newstead	in mid 2nd c. pit 83 in S annexe	Apollo	86	38		RS	2120
278	Mumrills	1 mile SE of fort	Hercules Magusanus	86	30		BS	2140
279	Lympne	in E gate	Neptune	89	39		L	66
280	Bitterne	in Roman defensive wall	Ancasta	89	30		L	97
281	Bath	debris in Lower Stall Street	Locus religiosus, Virtus & Num Aug	89	46		O	152
282	Maryport	350 m NE of fort	IOM	89	33		RS	819
283	Corbridge	reused as kerb in road S of Site XI	Jupiter Dolichenus, Caelestis Brigantia & Salus	89	41		BS	1131
284	Chesterholm	120 m W of fort	Domus Div & Num Augg	89	58		BS	1700
285	Birdoswald		Cocidius, replaced by IOM	89	33		BS	1885
286	Birdoswald		Pro salute d n ... imp	89	46		BS	1911
287	Auchendavy	in pit just SW of fort	IOM & Victoria	89	38		BS	2176

No.	Place	Details	Deity	H (cm)	W (cm)	D (cm)	Stone	RIB/Brit
288	Dorchester, Oxf.	Bishop's Close	IOM & Num Aug	91	84		lost	235
289	Maryport	350 m NE of fort	IOM & Num Aug	91	41		light S	825
290	Carlisle	Whiteclosegate	Mercury	91	30		BS	952
291	Bollihope Common		Num Augg & Silvanus	91	41			1041
292	Risingham	in bath house in SE angle of fort	Fortuna Redux	91	48		BS	1212
293	Risingham		illeg	91	51		BS	1230
294	High Rochester	in large building near S gate	Minerva	91	38		BS	1266
295	Wallsend	300 m W of fort	IOM	91	43		BS	1299
296	Croy Hill		Nymphae	91	43		BS	2160
297	Bar Hill	240 m E of fort	Silvanus	91	43		BS	2167
298	Bath	in situ in temple precinct	Sulis	92	88	52	O	3049
299	Carriden	140 m E of fort	IOM	92	41	23	BS	3503
300	Slack	1.5 miles E of fort	Bregans & Num Aug	94	48		S	623
301	Clifton	possibly from Brougham	IOM & Genius loci	94	38			792
302	Maryport	350 m NE of fort	IOM	94	38		RS	830
303	Maryport		Mars Militaris	94	46		RS	837
304	Maryport	350 m NE of fort	Victoria Aug	94	41		RS	842
305	High Rochester		Roma	94	51		BS	1270
306	High Rochester	near NW angle of fort	Silvanus	94	33		BS	1271
307	Carrawburgh		Dea Matris Deum	94	43		BS	1539
308	Chesterholm		IOM	94	42		BS	1688
309	Castlesteads		Discipulina Auggg	94	56		RS	1978
310	Castlecary	W side of fort	Neptune	94	33		BS	2149
311	Bar Hill	in well of praetorium	possibly Signis	94	43		BS	2169
312	Chichester	North Street/West Street junction	Genius	97	53			90
313	Cirencester	Sheep Street	Genius	97	48	38		102
314	Lincoln	near SE angle of lower town	Parcae & Num Aug	97	53		L	247
315	Littleborough		illeg	97	56		S	277
316	Chester	Foregate Street	IOM Tanarus	97	46		RS	452
317	Greta Bridge	in ruins of possible shrine near fort	illeg	97	33		lost	745

No.	*Place*	*Details*	*Deity*	*H (cm)*	*W (cm)*	*D (cm)*	*Stone*	*RIB/Brit*
318	Old Carlisle	near fort	Bellona	97	43		RS	890
319	Old Carlisle		IOM	97	58		RS	898
320	Corbridge		Maponus Apollo	97	53		BS	1122
321	Wallsend		IOM	97	45	34	BS	1300
322	Castlesteads		Mithras	97	51		RS	1993
323	Bar Hill		Apollo	97	43		S	2165
324	Manchester	in pit if vicus	Matres Hananef-tae & Ollototae	97	38	26	RS	B40.3
325	Birrens	in well in prae-torim	Discipulina Aug	98	58		RS	2092
326	Maryport	350 m NE of fort	IOM	99	43		RS	817
327	Maryport	350 m NE of fort	IOM	99	43		RS	828
328	Maryport	350 m NE of fort	IOM	99	64		RS	831
329	Carlisle	Scotch Street	Genius loci	99	43		RS	945
330	High Rochester	in bath house	Genius & Signi coh	99	53		BS	1263
331	South Shields	60 m NE of fort	illeg	99	43	39	BS	3270
332	Chesterholm	reused in 4th c. commandant's house	IOM & Genius praetorio	100	51	27	BS	3333
333	Hereford	St John Street	Silvanus	102	43			303
334	Maryport	350 m NE of fort	Victoria Aug	102	36		RS	843
335	Lanchester	probably in bath house of comman-dant's house	Fortuna Aug	102	36		BS	1073
336	Lanchester		IOM	102	36		BS	1076
337	Corbridge		Heracles of Tyre (Greek letter-ing)	102	53		BS	1129
338	Corbridge		IOM	102	43		BS	1130
339	Risingham		Cocidius & Silvanus	102	53		BS	1207
340	Risingham	in bath house in SE angle of fort	Fortuna	102	51		BS	1210
341	Housesteads		IOM	102	43		BS	1589
342	Chesterholm		Cocidius	102	48		BS	1683
343	Chesterholm	in hypocaust in fort	Fortuna populi romani	102	61		BS	1684
344	Great Chesters	reused in room added to comman-dant's house	IOM Dolichenus	102	53		BS	1725
345	Hadrian's Wall	E of MC 55	Cocidius	102	36		RS	1961
346	Hadrian's Wall	near Brampton	Maponus & Num Aug	102	33		RS	2063

No.	*Place*	*Details*	*Deity*	*H (cm)*	*W (cm)*	*D (cm)*	*Stone*	*RIB/Brit*
347	Halton	3 miles NE of Lancaster	Mars	104	51		S	601
348	Bewcastle	reused; in 4th c. fill of strong room of praetorium	Discipulina Aug	104	43		BS	990
349	Rudchester	in mithraeum	Sol Invictus	104	53		BS	1396
350	Chesters	0.25 mile W of fort	Bona Dea Regina Caelestis	104	48		BS	1448
351	Castlehill	a few hundred m to E of fort	Campestres & Britannia	104	41		BS	2195
352	Chesterholm	in situ in shrine	IOM Dolichenus	105	49	48	BS	B41.4
353	Lanchester	65 m S of fort	IOM	106	37	46	BS	3262
354	Carrawburgh	in situ in shrine near mithraeum	Nymphae & Genius loci	106	55	40	BS	3316
355	Maryport	NW of fort	IOM	107	56		MG	813
356	Maryport		Jupiter Aug	107	41		RS	814
357	Carrawburgh	in situ in mithraeum	Mithras	107	47		BS	1545
358	Housesteads		Hercules	107	53		BS	1580
359	Hadrian's Wall	central sector	illeg	107	48		BS	2073
360	Cramond		IOM	107	43		BS	2134
361	Bowes Moor	in situ in rectangular shrine	Vinotonus Silvanus	109	55		MG	732
362	Maryport	350 m NE of fort	IOM & Num Aug	109	46		RS	815
363	Maryport	350 m NE of fort	IOM	109	41		RS	816
364	Maryport		IOM	109	46		RS	823
365	Netherby		Fortuna Conservatrix	109	43		RS	968
366	Rudchester	in mithraeum	Mithras	109	53		BS	1395
367	Housesteads	in mithraeum	Sol Invictus Mitras	109	41		BS	1600
368	Newstead	65 m SE of fort	Silvanus	109	48		BS	2124
369	Brough-on-Noe	225 m from SE side of fort, found with small uninscribed altar	Hercules Augustus	109	48	43	buff G	3181
370	Birdoswald		IOM?	110	55	23	BS	3439
371	Bath	in cistern of Cross Bath	Sulis Minerva & Num Aug	112	46		O	146
372	Maryport		Dis Deabusque (Mars & Hercules imagery)	112	58		RS	810
373	Maryport	350 m NE of fort	IOM	112	46		RS	822
374	Maryport	350 m NE of fort	IOM	112	46		light S	827
375	Old Carlisle		IOM	112	53		RS	894

No.	Place	Details	Deity	H (cm)	W (cm)	D (cm)	Stone	RIB/Brit
376	Chesters		IOM	112	66		BS	1450
377	Housesteads		IOM & Num Augg	112	56		BS	1587
378	Birrens		Ricagambeda	112	43		RS	2107
379	Maryport		Virtus Aug	114	46		RS	845
380	Corbridge	in strong room of Site XLV compound headquarters	Discipulina Augg	114	58		BS	1127
381	High Rochester	in large building near S gate	Minerva	114	51		BS	1267
382	Housesteads	S of fort	IOM & Num Augg	114	51		BS	1585
383	High Rochester	in large building near S gate	Minerva & Genius collegiae	117	53		BS	1268
384	Carrawburgh	in situ in mithraeum	Mithras	117	53		BS	1544
385	Housesteads	Chapel Hill	IOM & Num Augg	117	51		BS	1584
386	Housesteads	Chapel Hill	IOM & Num Augg	117	56		BS	1586
387	Birdoswald		IOM	117	38		BS	1894
388	Chester	1.2 miles E of The Cross	Nymphae et Fontes	119	61	48	RS	460
389	Risingham		Hercules	119	66		BS	1215
390	Benwell	in temple	Anociticus	119	51		BS	1329
391	Housesteads	S of fort	IOM & Num Augg	119	56		BS	1588
392	Birdoswald		IOM	119	53		BS	1889
393	Newstead	in well in praetorium	IOM	119	48		BS	2123
394	Newstead	in ditch of E annexe	illeg	119	51		RS	2125
395	Newcastle	site of Roman bridge	Neptune	122	51		BS	1319
396	Housesteads	in SW corner of fort	Silvanus Cocidius	122	38		BS	1578
397	Chesterholm	in ruins of probable commandant's house	Genius praetorii	122	56		BS	1685
398	Birrens		Fortuna	122	46		RS	2093
399	Newstead	in ditch of E annexe	Diana Regina	122	53		BS	2122
400	London	reused in riverside wall	Domus Div & Isis	122	60	43	O (Lincolnshire)	3001
401	Bath	Stall Street	Sulis	123	64		O	147

No.	*Place*	*Details*	*Deity*	*H (cm)*	*W (cm)*	*D (cm)*	*Stone*	*RIB/Brit*
402	Colchester	just W of toen wall	Matres Suleviae	123	69	58	green S	192
403	Bakewell	Haddon Hall grounds	Mars Braciaca	123	48		G	278
404	Inveresk	found with no. 414	Sol	123	55	31	BS	B42.6
405	Bath	Pump Room	Sulis	124	66		O	144
406	Corbridge		Astarte (Greek lettering)	124	58		BS	1124
407	Risingham		Mars Victor	124	53		BS	1223
408	Newcastle	Swing Bridge	Ocianus	124	51		BS	1320
409	Rudchester	in mithraeum	Deus (mithraic symbols)	124	46		BS	1398
410	Carrawburgh	in situ in mith-raeum	Mithras	124	46		BS	1546
411	Housesteads		Mars, Victoria, Num Augg	124	51		BS	1596
412	Castlesteads		IOM & Num Aug	124	56		RS	1983
413	Birrens	from W of fort	Minerva	124	43		BS	2104
414	Inveresk	in pit, deliberately buried	Mythras	126	55	26	white S	B42.5
415	Eastgate		Silvanus	127	53		MG	1042
416	South Shields		Di Conservatori	127	61		BS	1054
417	Corbridge		Apollo Maponus	127	51		BS	1120
418	Housesteads	Chapel Hill	Mars	127	51		BS	1591
419	Housesteads	Chapel Hill	Mars, duae Alaisiagae, Num Aug	127	56		BS	1594
420	Chesterholm	in ruins of prob-able comman-dant's house	IOM, Genius et Custodes coh	127	53		BS	1687
421	Birdoswald	280 m E of fort	IOM	127	56		BS	1880
422	Castlesteads	in river	IOM	127	64		RS	1981
423	Birrens		IOM	127	51		RS	2097
424	Binchester	80 m S of fort	IOM, Matres Ollototae sive Transmarinae	130	36		BS	1030
425	High Rochester	3 miles N of fort	Victoria & Pax	130	56		G	1273
426	Benwell	in temple	Antenociticus & Num Augg	130	51		BS	1327
427	Rudchester	in mithraeum	Sol, Apollo, Ani-cetus Mithras	130	51		BS	1397
428	Hadrian's Wall	possibly Houses-teads	sive Deus sive Dea	130	46		BS	2071
429	Old Kilpatrick	in ditch of fort	IOM	131	48	41	BS	3509
430	Great Chesters		Deus ...	135	43		BS	1732
431	Hadrian's Wall	Kirksteads	illeg	135	58		RS	2034

No.	Place	Details	Deity	H (cm)	W (cm)	D (cm)	Stone	RIB/Brit
432	Birrens		Mars, Victoria Aug	135	58		RS	2100
433	Old Penrith	100 m N of fort	Omnes Dii, Unseni Fersomeri	137	64		RS	926
434	Lanchester	270 m NNW of fort	Garmangabis, Num Gordiani	137	61		BS	1074
435	Corbridge		Apollo Maponus	137	64		BS	1121
436	Corbridge	in S entrance to W granary, Site X	illeg	137	53		BS	1143
437	Chesterholm	in ruins of probable commandant's house	IOM, ceteri dii, Genius praetorii	137	61		BS	1686
438	Whitley Castle	100m NE of fort	Apollo	140	53	38	BS	1198
439	Housesteads	in mithraeum	Sol Invictus Mytras	140	53		BS	1590
440	Caerleon	outside E angle of fortress	Fortuna, Bonus Eventus	142	61		O	318
441	Ilkley		Verbeia	145	46		G	635
442	Bath	Pump Room	Sulis	152	71		O	143
443	Maryport	in NW angle of fort	Genius loci, Fortuna Redux, Roma Aeterna, Fatus Bonus	152	66		RS	812
444	Bowes Moor	in situ in circular shrine	Vintonus	163	74		S	733
445	Housesteads	Chapel Hill;; possibly a door jamb not an altar	Mars Thincsus, duae Alaisiagae, Beda, Fimmilena, Num Aug	183	58		BS	1593

Appendix 2

List of anepigraphic and weathered (illegible) altars from Roman Britain, from smallest to largest in height. Data from *CSIR*; NB coverage of Britain by *CSIR* is not yet complete. Key to stone types as Appendix 1.

No.	*Place*	*Details*	*Comment*	*H (cm)*	*W (cm)*	*D (cm)*	*Stone*	*CSIR*
1	Dover	from contubernium of barrack = RIB 3032	uninscribed	5	3	3	hard chalk	1.10.118
2	Cdehworth	near villa	geometric design	8	5	5	O	1.7.128
3	Netherby		weathered	10	7	5	RS	1.6.325
4	Cirencester	The Avenue	male figure	13	8	5	O	1.7.129
5	Chedworth	villa	Lenus Mars (?)	16	9	7	O	1.7.127
6	Bisley		snake & altar	16	9	6	O	1.7.169
7	Chesters		uninscribed	21	16	11	BS	1.6.283
8	Carrawburgh		illeg	21	17	11	BS	1.6.292
9	Hadrian's Wall	area	weathered	21	15	10	BS	1.6.326
10	Carrawburgh		uninscribed	22	14	11	BS	1.6.290
11	Carrawburgh		uninscribed	22	14	10	BS	1.6.291
12	Chesters		uninscribed	23	12	10	BS	1.6.282
13	Carlisle	Warwick Road	uninscribed	23	11	12	BS	1.6.507
14	Carrawburgh		uninscribed	25	19	11	BS	1.6.289
15	Farnworth	from well	Mercury	25	16	11	O	1.7.76
16	Chesterholm	on floor of building in vicus	uninscribed	26	15	9	BS	1.6.307
17	Housesteads		uninscribed	26	19	15	BS	1.6.298
18	Housesteads		uninscribed	26	20	12	BS	1.6.296
19	London	St Bartholemew's Hospital	Mercury	26	14	14	O	1.10.61
20	Chesters		weathered	27	17	15	BS	1.6.281
21	(Newcastle)	uncertain prov.	uninscribed	28	14	13	BS	1.1.344
22	Chesters		weathered	28	19	13	BS	1.6.280
23	Ancaster	SE corner of churchyard	uninscribed	30	13	11	L	1.8.69
24	Bowness-on-Solway		weathered	31	14	10	cream S	1.6.324
25	Housesteads		uninscribed	32	16	13	BS	1.6.295
26	(Newcastle)	uncertain prov.	uninscribed	35	15	11	BS	1.1.346
27	Dunnington		weathered	36	22		S	1.3.35
28	(Newcastle)	uncertain prov.	uninscribed	36	25	15	BS	1.1.343
29	York		Jupiter	37	13	22	S	1.3.5
30	York	Station Road	weathered	37	21	21	S	1.3.87
31	Camelon		weathered	39	15	15	BS	1.4.160
32	Bisley Common	in tumulus?	Mars	39	20	13	O	1.7.55

No.	*Place*	*Details*	*Comment*	*H (cm)*	*W (cm)*	*D (cm)*	*Stone*	*CSIR*
33	(Newcastle)	uncertain prov.	phallus	41	18	17	BS	1.1.341
34	Carrawburgh		burnt	43	22	17	BS	1.6.288
35	Sea Mills		Jupiter	44			L	1.2.106
36	Uley	from temple	Mercury	44	24	15	O	1.7.72
37	Castlesteads		weathered	45	29	18	BS	1.6.318
38	Wike		Fortuna (rudder)	47	31	21	S	1.3.14
39	King's Stanley		Mars	48	26	10	O	1.7.49
40	Hazelwood		Mars	50	25	15	O	1.7.52
41	Wilderspool		uninscribed	52	36	27	RS	1.9.117
42	(Newcastle)	uncertain prov.	uninscribed	56	23	16	BS	1.1.345
43	London	Goldsmiths Hall	hunter god	58	29	20	O	1.10.73
44	King's Stanley		Mars	59	28	18	O	1.7.50
45	Bisley Common	in tumulus?	Mars	59	27	15	O	1.7.53
46	Bisley Common	in tumulus?	Mars	59	29	13	O	1.7.54
47	King's Stanley		Mars	60	27	17	O	1.7.48
48	King's Stanley		Mars	60	29	16	O	1.7.58
49	Cherington		Cotswold hunter god	60			O	1.7.113
50	York	S of Holgate Road	Matres	61	42	32	S	1.3.26
51	Bisley-with-Lypiatt	in church fabric	Cotswold hunter god	61	32	15	O	1.7.112
52	Carlisle	Grapes Inn	Mercury	62	28	21	RS	1.6.482
53	Helsby		sacrifical instruments	64	43	31	RS	1.9.116
54	(Gloucester)	uncertain prov.	Mars	65	28	18	O	1.7.51
55	Bisley-with-Lypiatt	in church fabric	warrior god on horse	65	34	13	O	1.7.123
56	Bablock Hythe	in River Thames	Genius	69	27	11	O	1.7.35
57	Chesterholm		Hercules	71	36	26	BS	1.6.32
58	(Newcastle)	uncertain prov.	weathered	73	25	33	BS	1.1.340
59	London	Bartholemew Lane	uninscribed	75	20	26	Barnack stone	1.10.118
60	Bath	Cross Bath	Bacchus & Aesculapius (/)	76	46	25	O	1.2.3
61	Uppington	in church	uninscribed	76	35	28	G	1.9.154
62	King's Stanley		Genius	77	32	14	O	1.7.37
63	Springhead	in situ in Temple 1 cella	sacrificial instrument	79	41	40	MG	1.10.117
64	Hughtown	from well	sacrificial instruments	81	43		granite	1.7.II.4
65	Hadrian's Wall	area	weathered	89	47	37	BS	1.6.301
66	Hadrian's Wall	reused in stile	weathered	90	40	33	BS	1.6.287

No.	*Place*	*Details*	*Comment*	*H (cm)*	*W (cm)*	*D (cm)*	*Stone*	*CSIR*
67	Birrens	in strong room of praetorium	uninscribed	91	51	34	RS	1.4.17
68	Uley	from temple	Mercury	93	43	33	O	1.7.73
69	Chesterholm		weathered	94	45	25	BS	1.6.305
70	Castlesteads		weathered	95	47	42	BS	1.6.317
71	Bampton		Fortuna	95	33	22	O	1.7.28
72	Ilkley	in church	weathered	97	35	40	S	1.3.36
73	Carlisle	below the Castle	weathered	98		28	cream S	1.6.506
74	Birdoswald	probable prov.	weathered	100	55	31	BS	1.6.314
75	Drumburgh		weathered	101	41	29	BS	1.6.323
76	High Rochester	above door of cottage	weathered; inscription chiselled off	101	46		BS	1.1.311
77	Great Chesters	S gate	weathered	104	60	53	BS	1.6.310
78	Dorn		Genius	107	36	24	O	1.7.39
79	Housesteads	c. 260 m E of SE corner of fort	Hercules	108	55	36	BS	1.6.30
80	Housesteads		weathered	109	49	45	BS	1.6.300
81	Ilkley	in church	Verbeia (?)	109	37	45	L	1.3.31
82	Birdoswald	probable prov.	Neptune	111	53	22	BS	1.6.89
83	Hadrian's Wall	area	uninscribed	114	61	40	BS	1.6.316
84	Dorn		Genius	115	49	27	O	1.7.38
85	Halton Chesters	in church yard	weathered	116	66	43	BS	1.1.307
86	Stone-in-Oxney	in church (from Lympne fort?)	uninscribed	117	63	50	Kentish ragstone	1.10.120
87	Newcastle		weathered	119	71	41	BS	1.1.303
88	Housesteads	SE of fort	weathered	121	63	50	BS	1.6.294
89	Great Chesters		weathered	133	43	29	BS	1.6.309
90	Chesters	probable prov.; used as cross base	weathered	141	61	40	BS	1.6.279
91	Rudchester		uninscribed	142	51	42	BS	1.1.305

BIBLIOGRAPHY

Aldhouse-Green, M. 1984 *The Wheel as a Cult-Symbol in the Romano-Celtic World.* Brussels, Collection Latomus 183.

Allason-Jones, L. & McKay, B. 1985 *Coventina's Well. A Shrine on Hadrian's Wall.* Chesters, Trustees of the Clayton Collection, Chesters Museum.

Andrews, P., Biddulph, E., Hardy, A, Brown, R. 2011 *Settling the Ebbsfleet Valley. High Speed 1 excavations at Springhead and Northfleet, Kent. The Late Iron Age, Roman, Saxon, and Medieval landscape, volume 1: the sites.* Oxford & Salisbury, Oxford Wessex Archaeology.

Birley, A. & Birley, A. 2010 'A Dolichenum at Vindolanda', *Archaeologia Aeliana* 5th series, 39, 25–51.

Birley, E. 1954 'The Roman fort at Netherby', *Transactions of the Cumberland and Westmorland Antiquarian and Archaeological Society* 2nd series, 53, 6–39.

Birley, E. 1986 'The deities of Roman Britain', *ANRW* II, 18, I, 3–112.

Breeze, D. J. 2006 *J. Collingwood Bruce's Handbook to the Roman Wall,* Newcastle upon Tyne, Society of Antiquaries of Newcastle upon Tyne (14th edition).

Bulliot, J. G. 1901 'Découverte de deux inscriptions romaines et d'un casque votif à Autun', *Bulletin Monumental* 65 (ser. 7, 5), 30–6.

Busch, A. W. & Schäfer, A. 2014 (eds) *Römische Weihealtäre im Kontext,* Friedberg, Likias.

Clarke, S. 1997 'Abandonment, rubbish and 'special' deposits at Newstead', *TRAC 96: Proceedings of the Sixth Annual Theoretical Roman Archaeology Conference*, ed. K. Meadows *et al.*, 73–81. Oxford, Oxbow Books.

Clay, C. 2007 'Before there were Angles, Saxons and Jutes: an epigraphic study of the Germanic social, religious and linguistic relations on Hadrian's Wall', *Pagans and Christians – from Antiquity to the Middle Ages. Papers in honour of Martin Henig, presented on the occasion of his 65th birthday,* ed. L. Gilmour, 47–63. Oxford, BAR Int. Ser. 1610.

Clay, C. 2008 'Developing the 'Germani' in Roman studies', *TRAC 2007. Proceedings of the seventeenth annual Theoretical Roman Archaeology Conference*, ed. C. Fenwick *et al.*, 131–50. Oxford, Oxbow Books.

Cunliffe, B. & P. Davenport 1985 *The Temple of Sulis Minerva at Bath I: the site.* Oxford, Oxford University Committee for Archaeology.

De Bernardo Stempel, P. 2008 'Continuity, *translatio* and *identificatio* in Romano-Celtic religion: the case of Britain', *Continuity and Innovation in Religion in the Roman West*, ed. R. Haeussler & A. C. King, vol. 2, 67–82. Portsmouth, RI, Journal of Roman Archaeology Supplement 67.

Fairless, K. J. 1984 'Three religious cults from the northern frontier region', *Between and Beyond the Walls: essays on the prehistory and history of North Britain in honour of George Jobey,* ed. R. Miket & C. Burgess, 224–42. Edinburgh, John Donald Publishers.

Fernández Palacios, F. 2017 'The theonym *Conventina', *Celtic Religions in the Roman Period. Personal, local, and global*, ed. R. Haeussler & A. C. King. Aberystwyth, Celtic Studies Publications.

Goldberg, M. 2015 'The cult of Vitiris and Ptolemy's *Votadini:* vernacular religion in northern Britain', in *Understanding Roman Frontiers. Papers offered to Professor Bill Hanson on the occasion of his retirement*, ed. D. J. Breeze *et al.*, 196–211. Edinburgh, John Donald.

Green, M. J. 1997 *Exploring the World of the Druids,* London, Thames & Hudson.

Henig, M. 1984 *Religion in Roman Britain,* London, B. T. Batsford.

Henig, M. 1993 *Corpus Signorum Imperii Romani, I.7, Roman Sculpture from the Cotswold Region,* Oxford, British Academy.

Henig, M. 2013 'A miniature altar from Waltham villa, Whittington', *Glevensis* 46, 1–2.

Henig, M. & K. Adcock 2016 'New finds from Gloucester (*Colonia Nerviana Glevensium*)', *Association for Roman Archaeology News* 36, 38–41.

Kewley, J. 1974 'A Roman stone-masons' workshop at Chester-le-Street and Lanchester', *Antiquaries Journal* 54, 53–65.

Killock, D. 2015 *Temples and Suburbs. Excavations at Tabard Square, Southwark.* London, Pre-Construct Archaeology Monograph 18.

Lefebvre, A., M.-T. Raepsaet-Charlier & W. Van Andringa 2014 'Un autel miniature consacré à une déesse locale chez les Rèmes', *Gallia* 71.2, 329–34.

Martinez Caballero, S. & S. Vilches Crespo (ed.) 2015 *Imago Urbis Romae. Ciudades romanas de Segovia*. Segovia, Museo de Segovia.

Penn, W. S. 1959 'The Romano-British settlement at Springhead: excavation of Temple 1, Site C', *Archaeologia Cantiana* 73, 1–61.

Philp, B. 1981 *The Excavation of the Roman Fort of the* Classis Britannica *at Dover, 1970–1977,* Dover, Kent Archaeological Rescue Unit.

Woodward, A. & P. Leach 1993 *The Uley Shrines. Excavation of a ritual complex on West Hill, Uley, Gloucestershire: 1977–9.* London, English Heritage.

Wright, R. P. 1946 'A Roman shrine to Silvanus on Scargill Moor, nr. Bowes', *Yorkshire Archaeological Journal* 26, 383–6.

VIII

TALKING TO THE GODS
EVIDENCE FOR RELIGIOUS PROFESSIONALS AND RELIGIOUS PATTERNS IN ROMAN BRITAIN

Alessandra Esposito

This paper considers the distribution of different archaeological markers related to priestly roles in Roman Britain. Epigraphic and iconographic evidence are often considered the main resources to study religion, but when its number is limited, it is crucial to consider other elements. Tools and elements of religious apparels are fairly common in the province and their study provides an insight on the performative aspect of these religious personnel.

To paint a religious landscape of Britain it is necessary to consider briefly the socio-ethnic composition of the province. For long after the Roman conquest in AD 43, a number of different communities, usually addressed in the literature as 'tribes' or peoples, characterised its territory. Their names derive from classical sources, and are regarded as 'Celtic'.[1] They might have been convenient labels used by the Roman historians to sort and unify a reality that appeared to them confused and highly fragmented. It has been argued consequently that these communities, rather than being 'ethnic' tribes sharing a set of cultural and religious traditions,[2] would have merged upon the occurrence of an occasional danger, uniting around a charismatic figure, a leader or king. In this sense, they represent groupings of people that could present themselves as rather fluid.[3] For the purpose of this article, it will suffice to note that both theories underline that the diversification of local communities in Britain, that undoubtedly had its roots in the Late Iron Age, clearly continued after the Roman conquest. Focusing on religion and ritual practices, a natural consequence of this fragmentation of the local population is its differentiation in 'cult communities'.[4] The identification of these communities allows an analysis of the diversified outcome of the meeting between Roman religion(s) and native/local beliefs and consequently their ritual practices, suggesting different responses to the

1 Haeussler 2008.
2 Cunliffe 2005.
3 Millett 1995; James 1999.
4 Derks 1998.

introduction of the Roman element where 'resistance, adaptation, and acceptance (...) may occur simultaneously'.[5]

To trace these cultural changes, this paper considers the spatial distribution of different archaeological markers connected to ritual activities. These include evidence for religious performers, places of cult and objects involved for religious activities. The spatial relationship between the distribution of temple sites and inscribed altars is well-known;[6] inscribed altars are more common in the north of the province, specifically at military sites, mainly clustering around the lines of Hadrian's and the Antonine Wall and other major military settlements. The evidence from southern Britain is less abundant. The situation remains unchanged if the rare carved altars without inscriptions are included (*c.* 100 identified in CSIR). If southern Britain presents a rather low number of inscriptions, Romano-Celtic temple-sites are far more common. It has been argued that this difference between the two regions might be due to the characteristics of the local cults 'where Latin epigraphy and Roman architecture were not considered appropriate or were beyond the means of the indigenous population'.[7] A further characteristic of this area is the highest evidence for curse tablets in the province, the majority, if not all, of them concerned with curses against thieves.[8]

These elements have led to the consideration of southern Britain as an area different from the rest of the province in terms of ritual practices and responses to the elements of Roman religious practice. To these archaeological markers, the evidence for priestly regalia is added. Priests would wear these objects, consisting mainly of headdresses and sceptres, during religious ceremonies.[9] Britain in general is an interesting case-study for the analysis of this evidence. Similar objects are found in Gaul and Germany among the western provinces, but the quantity attested here is noteworthy. The interest in this evidence is increased by the scarcity in Britain of more 'classical' evidence (epigraphy and iconography) for priestly roles. This suggests social implications about the public visibility and the self-representation of these roles.[10] The epigraphic and literary evidence connected to priestly figures, although limited, shows the presence of those priestly roles connected to the 'classic' Roman organization of the *coloniae*, but what happens beyond their boundaries? Priestly regalia appear are found at rural temple sites both as single objects and in deposits, while few of them are found isolated from shrines, temples or religious complexes. This might be the result of our incomplete archaeological knowledge of the landscape. It might also mean, though, that they were used for a different type of celebrations that did not require the fixed structure of a temple. The analysis of the geographical distribution of these finds compared with the distribution of temples, using GIS plotting of the precise location of sites and finds, allows further considerations.

5 Webster 1997, 167; on the same concept also Millett 1995.
6 Millett 1995; Mattingly 2004; Haeussler 2008.
7 Haeussler 2008, 44.
8 Tomlin 2002; Mattingly 2004.
9 Henig 1984; Bird 2011.
10 General considerations about these topics in Rüpke 2011.

Epigraphic and iconographic evidence

The *corpus* of the epigraphic evidence for priestly roles in the province is limited and accounts for ten occurrences (Table 1), of which only four come from the area considered in this article.

It is usually argued that among the first consequences of the Roman 'occupation' was the introduction of official priestly *collegia*. The organization of a *colonia* involved the creation of municipal priesthoods (*flamines* and *augustales*) as stated in the *Lex Coloniae Genetivae* from the Caesarian colony Urso in Spain.[11] The cult of the Deified Emperor was the first to be officially introduced in Britain after the Roman conquest and it is attested by a high number of inscriptions. Its main centre was Camulodunum, where the altar and the temple of Claudius were built to match the aims of those from Lugdunum (Lyon) and from Ara Ubiorum (Cologne) as cores of the so-called imperial cult in the province.[12] Substantial information concerning these colleges found in literary sources together with a solid *corpus* of inscriptions, at least in other provinces, has led some scholars to claim that these sacerdotal *collegia*, together with those of other civic cults like that of Jupiter Optimus Maximus, are the only ones that allow detailed study. The scarcity of inscriptions and material evidence for those *collegia* related to non-civic or minor cults would not allow a similar analysis.[13] The presence of a *collegium* of priests of the imperial cult in Britain is traceable in the written sources but is only

Table 1. Occurrences of priestly titles in Britain.

TITLE	PLACE	REFERENCE	NAME	SUPPORT
archiereia	Corbridge	RIB I 1129	Diodora	altar
haruspex	Bath	RIB III 3049	Lucius Marcius Memor	statue-base
magister sacrorum	Greetland	RIB I 627	Titus Aurelius Aurelianus	altar
praepositus religionis	Lydney Park	RIB II 2448.03	Titus Flavius Senilis	mosaic
sacerdotes delecti	Colchester	Tac. *Ann.* 14.31		
sacerdos of Sulis Minerva	Bath	RIB I 155	Gaius Calpurnius Receptus	funerary inscription
sacerdos of Dea Nemesis	Hadrian's Wall	RIB I 2065	Apollonius	altar
sacerdos	Vindolanda	TVindol. 313		tablet
sacerdos	Wallsend	RIB I 1314	Iulius Maximus	altar
sevir augustalis of York and Lincoln	Bordeaux	Fellows-Jensen *et al.* 1998	Marcus Aurelius Lunaris	altar
sevir augustalis of York and Thérouanne	York	RIB I 678	Marcus Verecundius Diogenes	coffin

11 Rüpke 2006.
12 Fishwick 1961.
13 Van Andringa 2002.

partially supported by the archaeological record. Tacitus records the building of the temple of Claudius at Camolodunum, for which he notes that *sacerdotes delecti* had to collect contributions.[14] The use of the word *sacerdotes* instead of *flamines* suggests that the cult of the deified emperors also included Claudius, still alive at the time. *Delecti* probably refers to a choice of particular figures, following an election by the early provincial council.[15]

The only two *seviri augustales* recorded in stone for the province, both held their office in two *coloniae* at the same time, but none in the area here considered. A stone coffin, probably from York but now lost,[16] had an inscription recording Marcus Verecundius Diogenes, *cives* of Bourges who had been *sevir* of both the *coloniae* of *Eburacum* (York) and of the *Morinorum* (Tarvenna, modern Thérouanne, according to Tomlin),[17] while a different reading implies that Diogenes was *sevir* at York and also a *moritex*.[18] Marcus Aurelius Lunaris is recorded as a *sevir augustalis* of both the *coloniae* of *Eburacum* (York) and *Lindo* (Lincoln) on an altar found in Bordeaux, where it was dedicated in AD 237.[19]

The best attested priestly title in the province is that of *sacerdos*. A funerary inscription was set by Calpurnia Trifosa for her husband Gaius Calpurnius Receptus, former *sacerdos* of Sulis Minerva, the titular deity of the religious complex at Bath, where the inscription was found.[20]

Again from Bath is the only record of a *haruspex* from Britain. A statue-base was dedicated to Sulis by the *haruspex* Lucius Marcius Memor as a gift to the goddess, probably at the beginning of the 4th century AD.[21] The way in which the title was inscribed, with the letters *HAR* being in a central position and the final *USP* apparently added later by a second hand,[22] provides some more information on the identity of this character. It has been argued that the letters 'HAR' on their own might have been mistaken for *hariolus*, a fortune-teller of some sort and of a lower status than the *harsupex*, thus the urge for an expansion, or that the office was generally unintelligible in the way it was abbreviated

14 Tac. *Ann.* 14.31.
15 Fishwick 2002, 89.
16 RIB I 678.
17 RIB I 678 *Addenda.*
18 Fellows-Jensen, Gore & Rollason 1998, 114. After Delamarre, *Dictionnaire de langue gauloise*, this is a Celtic word meaning 'navigator, marine'. The first to suggest to read '*moritex*' was Mann, translating it as 'shipper' (comment reported in Birley 1966, 208). The Gallic title of *moritex* is uncommon but has two other instances. Of these, one is found on the slab from Tabard Street, London, dedicated by Tiberinus Celerianus, a civis Bellovacus, recording himself as a *moritex Londiniensium*. The role of *moritex* seems to be that of a representative or delegate of the (likely not only commercial) interests of British communities on the continent (Dondin-Prayer & Loriot 2008, 144). Similar to his colleague Celerianus representing the Londinienses, Verecundius Diogenes would have represented a British community, likely the colonia of York. His role as *moritex*, a delegate rather than a mere merchant, fits well together with his role of *sevir* of the colonia of York, as the role was considered to be a prestigious office, especially for a freedman.
19 Courteault 1921; Fellows-Jensen, Gore & Rollason 1998, 90.
20 RIB I 155.
21 RIB III 3049.
22 Roman Britain in 1965, *Journal of Roman Studies* 56, 1966, 217.

because unusual. The *haruspex* was probable not a permanent figure at the temple, but a member of the governor's staff, recording his visit at the site.[23]

Finally, one inscription from the temple in Lydney Park records the restoration of a mosaic floor made by Titus Flavius Senilis *pr rel*, using the offerings from the temple (*ex stipibus*), assisted by Victorinus *interp(r)[e]tiens*.[24] The role of Senilis has been expanded by Tomlin as '*pr(aepositus) rel(igionis)*', and translated 'superintendent of the cult',[25] based on the opinion that the archaeological context of the inscription would suggest a religious function of this title. As was also noticed by Fulford,[26] the expansion of PRREL as *praepositus religionis* would provide a *unicum* for this title, as it is not attested in any other text. A better documented expansion of PRREL is the one already proposed by Mommsen, '*pr(aepositus) rel(iquationis)*',[27] a military officer in charge of detachments of ground units or marine ones.[28] Although not common, the title is attested on four other inscriptions, all datable to various periods in the 3rd century AD.[29] The presence of such an officer fits in the reconstruction that sees the *II Legio Augusta* active in the fort at Cardiff or the fortress at Carleon in the 4th century AD, although garrisoned at a reduced level in this period, exploiting natural resources, mainly wood and iron, from the Lydney area.[30] Birley believes that Lydney could have been a pilgrimage site, meaning that the fleet did not have to be stationed near the temple (i.e. in the Bristol Bay) to justify the presence of Senilis at the temple site.[31]

Following on the interpretation of Senilis as a religious officer, Hassall considered Victorinus' title as '*interpretiante*' (nom. *interpretans*), translated by Frere and Tomlin as 'interpreter (of dreams)'.[32] The role of Victorinus as an interpreter of dreams is based on the consideration that the temple of Mars Nodens at Lydney Park was a healing place.[33] Here, incubation techniques might have been practiced, making the interpretation of dreams a fitting activity requiring the constant presence of a professional on site.[34] The

23 Cunliffe & Davenport 1985, 36–7; Tomlin 2009, 64. He could have been a member of the governor's staff (Cunliffe & Davenport 1985, 36–7; Tomlin 2009, 64, as attested in Numidia); in chapter 62 of the Lex Ursonensis, both duoviri and aediles each had among their staff a haruspex and a tibicen. The *haruspices* would have operated on the holidays established in the civic calendar, for example the foundation date of the colonia (or of the municipium), supervised the foundation of public temples, and acted as counsellors in case of exceptional circumstances (Haack 2003, 111). It is also possible that he was a *haruspex* active in the army, a rare but not unknown role in the imperial provinces (Haensch 1997, 722; Wheeler 2008). However, what is missing here, as also noted by Haack (2006, 82–3), is the legion to which Memor would have been attached, a mention present in the other inscriptions.

24 RIB II 2448.03.

25 Frere & Tomlin 1992, 84. Follow this interpretation: Fulford 2002, 100 and Ling 2007, 69.

26 Fulford 1996, 26–7.

27 CIL VII 137.

28 Reddé 1986; Kissel 1995.

29 CIL VIII 14854; AE 1981, 134; ILS 9221; CIL X 3345.

30 Fulford 1996, 24–6.

31 Richmond 1963, 112; Birley 1986, 70.

32 This reading has since encountered a certain favour in the literature (Hassall 1980: *loc. cit.*; Frere & Tomlin 1992, 84; Allason-Jones 2011.

33 Henig 2001, 12.

34 Henig 1984.

role of professional interpreters of dreams is well known in the Mediterranean world.[35] Nonetheless, a recent analysis of the term 'interpreter' occurring in a Vindolanda tablet sheds a different light on the possible occupation of these figures, likely to be translators or middlemen in commercial transactions.[36] It is also important to consider at this point the indirect evidence for religious specialists whose specific status can be difficult to define. In particular, this would include the authors of curse tablets and phylacteries (latest example from London).[37] The phylacteries might have been made outside the province, but the curse tablets must be made locally.

The iconographical evidence for the activities performed by these figures in the province is also rather scarce. Only one stone-relief, a slab from Bridgeness, on the eastern end of the Antonine Wall[38] shows the performance of a sacrifice with actual people. A consistent number of dedicatory reliefs and altars show deities or Genii pouring libations on altars, like the ones from Cirencester and Carlisle,[39] British examples of stereotyped representations well known in other provinces.

In the Bridgeness relief, a *suouetaurilia* is being performed. The celebrant is apparently not veiled, as one would have expected for a Roman cult, but wears the toga. He is pictured with a ceremonial bowl (*patera*) in his right hand, pouring its content on an altar, an action prior to sacrifice itself.[40] Four figures are behind him, probably the soldiers of the *legio II Augusta.* Two more figures join the picture; a player of double pipes in a short tunic and a man crouching next to the animals, likely the *victimarius.* Who is the celebrant in this scene? He is usually interpreted as the *legatus legionis* or even the governor of the province,[41] here performing an official rite.

Metal figurines showing 'people' performing mainly libations *velato capite* from Britain are usually considered in the publications as 'priest' and 'priestess'.[42] Both male and female wear a toga and are pictured pouring libations with the right hand and holding a variety of objects, mainly scrolls, in their left, or praying.[43] The intention of the iconographical choice is truly to underline the ritual action performed but the modern conventional indication of 'priest/priestess' may be misleading. These figurines might more likely depict a dedicator or worshipper and not a professional figure[44] or a deity.

35 For example, the sanctuary of Serapis at Memphis counted in its staff interpreters that were structured religious personnel at least from the 2nd century BC (Vinagre 2000, 141).
36 Mairs 2012.
37 Tomlin 2013.
38 RIB I 2139; Phillips 1972–4 and previous bibliography.
39 RIB I 102 and 944.
40 Henig 1984, 86; Bianchi Bandinelli 2002, 205.
41 Henig 1984, 86.
42 Toynbee 1962; Bird 2011, 274.
43 Toynbee 1962; Green 1976; Durham 2012.
44 Durham 2012.

Epigraphic evidence of ritual ceremonies: the inscribed altars

Inscriptions connected to religious performances are generally referred to as 'sacred dedications'. They are based on the 'principle of reciprocity' between the dedicator and the god (*do ut des)* and express not only a religious but also a legal commitment.[45] They record different acts, mainly the fulfilling of vows made to a deity, but also thanksgivings or commands received by the gods through visions or dreams. This particular case is attested in several inscriptions from Britain and is characterized by the use of expressions like *monitu, ex uisu/visu, iussu/ex iussu, ex imperio, ex nuntio, ex responsu, somnio praemonitus.*[46] Moreover, while there are no records of the early stage of a vow (the *nuncupatio*) in stone from the area considered (the only clear example from Britain being an inscription from Bowness-on-Solway, Cumberland),[47] the extensive evidence for curse tablets in the same area can be considered here. In terms of ritual, they approximate more to the *nuncupatio* element of a dedication than its solution, as they establish the terms of engagement with a god.

The evidence of the altars provides an insight into the display of both private and public religion. Overall, the dedication of these objects does not involve, apparently, the presence of a professional priest, nor in fact is the placement of the altar in a sanctuary mandatory, as some are found in areas not apparently connected to religious structures.[48] The altar performs in this case a dual function. On the one hand, it represents the very *object* dedicated to the deity. On the other, it is also the place where the ritual of the dedication is performed.

Nonetheless, the setting of these altars required at least three binding elements. Firstly, the choice of a place consecrated by men through the ritual of *consecration*, or chosen by the deity him/herself, perhaps through an extraordinary act. This is, for example, the case attested by a slab from the fort at Halton Chesters recording the striking of a thunderbolt – *fulgur diuom.*[49] Secondly, a specific time, according to an official calendar for festivities (i.e. *Feriale Duranum*), the prescriptions for a particular deity, a personal 'deadline' established during the *nuncupatio* or a combination of them. This information can sometimes be obtained from the British inscriptions. It is the case of around twelve inscriptions recording the setting of an altar to celebrate the fulfilment of a vow on a specific day, i.e. 21st of April[50] or the 1st of January.[51] Other examples from Britain do or seem likely to correspond to known festival dates (e.g. *Matronalia* in the tablet n. 581 from Vindolanda). Finally, the actual dedication, a ritual involving libations, music, food and, eventually, animal sacrifice.[52] Sometimes a whole community

45 Bodel 2009, 20.

46 *monitu* (RIB I 320), *ex uisu/visu* (RIB I 153, 3149, 760), *iussu/ex iussu* (RIB I 1022, 1024, 1131), *ex imperio* (RIB I 2091), *ex nuntio* (RIB III 3499), *ex responsu* (RIB I 587), *somnio praemonitus* (RIB I 1228).

47 RIB I 2059.

48 Bodel 2009, 23–34.

49 RIB I 1426; Brunelli 2004; Van Andringa, Creissen & Chevalier 2010.

50 RIB I 1270.

51 RIB I 1983; Henig 1982; Isserlin 1994.

52 Rüpke 2009, 33.

or a restricted group of people fulfils a vow and appoints a specific person to handle the practical aspect of actual setting the altar (as in the case of the *vicani Vindolandesses curam agente [...]*).[53]

We have already noted how inscribed altars are documented far less frequently in southern Britain than the rest of the province. To be more specific, out of 992 inscriptions connected to religious matters (not only vows but also renovations or dedications of buildings and statues), only 91 were found in the counties of south and south-east England. Of these, less than half (*c.* 47%) are inscribed altars. This also appears to be a characteristic of the area. Among the religious inscriptions from the rest of the province, inscribed altars cover about the 77% of the evidence.

Rather than a local scarcity of stone,[54] the limited number of inscriptions in the area has been related to a difference in religious practice.[55] In this part of the province, epigraphy was apparently not considered a necessary means to express devotion. However, it is important to bear in mind how the extensive reuse of inscriptions starting from the Middle Ages might have affected the evidence we have today. Dedicatory inscriptions are indeed found on a different set of objects in the region: everyday objects, like metal plates and metal and ceramic vessels and rings. Adding the consistent habit of deposition of curse tablets[56] offers more considerations about the use of writing for religious purposes.

Deposits of 'regalia'

Of the range of deposits containing ritual objects, this paper only considers those of priestly regalia, as they provide direct evidence for priestly activities. Their addition to the epigraphic and iconographic evidence provides a more comprehensive picture in order to identify the characteristics of ritual practices and the location of their performance.

Priestly regalia consist mainly of head-dresses and sceptres. Diadems are considered items of distinction (ornamental jewellery) or symbols of consecration (religious gear). Common attributes of goddesses in general,[57] particularly the half-moon examples, they also became an element of the empresses' hairstyle, starting with the portrait of Drusilla[58] until the early Byzantine period.[59] During religious performances, the diadem would have been worn over the *infula*, a woollen band circling the head to which attach the *vittae* falling on the shoulders. The same arrangement was intended for the animals to be sacrificed.[60]

53 RIB I 1700.
54 Millett 1995.
55 Woodward 1992; Mattingly 2004; Haeussler 2008.
56 Tomlin 1999.
57 Boucher & Tassinari 1976, 41–5.
58 Rose 1997, 76–7.
59 Breglia 1966; Inan & Rosenbaum 1966.
60 Rose 1997, 77.

Fig. 1. Deposit of regalia from Bury St Edmunds (© Suffolk County Council: Photo by A. Brown).

The different types of head-dresses, like crowns and diadems, are usually connected to Romano-Celtic[61] or oriental cults. Southern Britain provides a conspicuous quantity of evidence in this sense. The assemblage from Hockwold cum Wilton, Norfolk[62] offers an interesting sample of headdresses, including both diadems and a 'crown'. It has been argued that these objects might be the personal property of a professional priest.[63] However they sometimes show signs of repair, which might be connected to the value coming from their 'life' as ritual objects.[64] Some diadems, like those found at Hockwold, also appear to have been adjustable in size, thus allowing them to be used by different people. This characteristic is also common to other types of head-dresses like those worn by priests of the imperial cult in the Eastern provinces.[65]

Sceptres from Britain include extraordinary finds like the group of almost twenty

61 Bird 2011, 274.
62 Roman Britain in 1956. Eastern Counties, *Journal of Roman Studies* 47, 1957, 211, pl. IX.
63 Allason-Jones 2011.
64 Bird 2011.
65 Rumscheid 2010.

found at Wanborough.[66] Generally, the sceptre-heads are in the form of animals or human/divine figures. The iconographical evidence shows the sceptre as a short staff held by emperors as a symbol of power on gems[67] and on reliefs.[68] They apparently fall in the category of the 'Insignien-Zeichen' and are specific to the task of the priest.

The presence of some of these objects at temple sites, both in deposits and as single finds, fits with the presence of religious professionals involved in managing the sacred buildings and their facilities. But some of them appear to be isolated in the rural landscape. An intriguing example is the group from Bury St. Edmunds, Suffolk, found in 2010 by a metal-detectorist.[69] It contains many of the finds typically considered under the heading of 'regalia' with the addition of votive objects. 61 objects were organized in two separate groups: some were deposited in a grey ware vessel while the others have been placed beneath or around it (Fig. 1). Buried within the vessel were one iron and 15 copper-alloy objects. At the base of the vase were the staff terminals shaped as birds, a triangular staff terminal, then a folding strap or belt. On the top was the crown, whose discs were piled on each other. The last objects were three copper-alloy metal plaques shaped as 'feathers', folded to fit into the top of the vessel. The second group comprises a copper-alloy tankard (in several fragments including the handle and two nails) and a copper-alloy crest, both buried under the vessel. The others objects include a bone fragment, 3 nails (an iron one and two in copper-alloy), a fragment of an iron blade and more than 20 fragments of sheet copper-alloy. A part from the crest, probably belonging to a Corinthian helmet, part of a cult-image of Minerva[70] or a curved headdress,[71] most of the other objects fall in the category of priestly regalia.

This type of chain-linked headdress is known from other sites in Britain like Cavenham Heath,[72] Hockwold,[73] Stony Stratford,[74] Farley Heath,[75] and Wanborough.[76] The copper-alloy discs were held together by small chains and possibly attached to a leather cap.

Staff terminals shaped as birds are present in the deposits from Felmingham Hall, Norfolk,[77] Willingham Fen, Cambridgeshire,[78] and Woodeaton, Oxfordshire.[79] The triangular staff terminal ends with a small sphere and has two holes pinched at the base that likely hold small rings so to produce a rattle-like sound. Similar examples in copper-

66 Bird 1994.
67 Meagow 1987, Taf. 2.5, 3, 4.2.
68 Koeppel 1983; 61, Kat.13.
69 Worrell *et al.* 2011; Esposito 2016.
70 Worrell *et al.* 2011.
71 PAS database, record SF-D4D044.
72 Layard 1925.
73 Roman Britain in 1956. Eastern Counties, *Journal of Roman Studies* 47, 1957, 198–234.
74 Lysons 1817.
75 Poulton 2007.
76 O'Connell & Bird 1994; Bird 2007.
77 Gilbert 1978.
78 Alföldi 1949.
79 Kirk 1949.

alloy and iron are found in Brigstock, Northamptonshire[80] and in iron from London.[81] The importance of this deposit compared to others lies in the number of objects retrieved and also in their variety. Usually these type of deposits contain exclusively (Cavenham Heath, Hockwold and Wanborough) or mainly (Deeping St James) head-dresses or exclusively sceptres (Willingham Fen). They rarely contain so many different objects and never reach the same number or variety (i.e., the Felmingham Hall Hoard contains 11 objects and the Stony Stratford hoard contains 5 objects plus 30 fragments of silver votive plaques).

The Bury St Edmunds find has been convincingly interpreted as an intentional deposit of votive and priestly material, but the reasons for burying it, whether for safekeeping or ritual/votive are unknown at the moment.

Conclusions

The interest in studying ritual practices in Britain during the Roman rule lies in analysing how ritual practices traditionally considered the prerogative of specific cultural groups and stressed in the dichotomy Roman/native appear to overlap in the reality of the religious experience and involve different people, bearing different cultural identities. These practices are strongly influenced by the cultural background of communities and are possibly traceable in their different geographical patterns (presence/absence of temples and sacred dedications; evidence for priestly activities).

We might argue, for example, that in the areas where the network of temples was denser, religious professionals were needed to manage these religious complexes and perform rituals; when the network disappears, as in north-central Britain, Romans had to rely on self-performed rituals (the use of an altar). A concern with this reconstruction seems to rise when looking at the evidence for regalia. The deposit found at Bury St Edmunds joins a consistent group of similar assemblages from the same region. This may lead to the consideration that the deposition of regalia might have a specific ritual significance in this area of the province. Regalia, mainly sceptres, are in fact found in other regions of the province but not in deposits. Only further research will eventually decode this intricate mosaic of ritual behaviours.

80 Greenfield 1963.
81 *London in Roman times* 1930, 108.

BIBLIOGRAPHY

Alföldi, A. 1949 'The bronze mace from Willingham Fen', *Journal of Roman Studies* 39, 19–22.

Allason-Jones, L. 2011 'Priests and priestesses in Roman Britain', *Priests and State in the Roman World*, eds. J. H. Richardson & F. Santangelo, 429–44. Stuttgart, Franz Steiner Verlag.

Allason-Jones, L. & R. F. Miket 1984 *Catalogue of the Small Finds from South Shields Roman Fort.* Newcastle upon Tyne, The Society of Antiquaries of Newcastle upon Tyne, Monograph 2.

Ando, C. 2008 *The Matter of the Gods.* Berkeley, University of California Press.

Bianchi Bandinelli, R. 2002 *Roma: La fine dell'arte antica.* Torino, Biblioteca Universale Rizzoli.

Bird, J. 2007 'Catalogue of Iron Age and Roman artefacts discovered before 1995', in Poulton 2007, 34–69.

Bird, J. 2011 'Religion', *Artefacts in Roman Britain: their purpose and use*, ed. L. Allason-Jones, 269–92. Cambridge, Cambridge University Press.

Birley, E. 1986 'The Deities of Roman Britain', *Aufstieg und Niedergang der römischen Welt*, II. 18.1, 3–112.

Bodel, J. 2009 'Sacred dedications: a problem of definition', *Dediche sacre nel mondo greco-romano: diffusione, funzioni, tipologie*, ed. J. Bodel & M. Kajava, 17–30. Rome, Institutum Romanum Finlandiae.

Booth, P., T. Champion, S. Foreman, P. Garwood, H. Glass, J. Munby & A. Reynolds 2011 *On Track. The Archaeology of High Speed 1 Section 1 in Kent.* Oxford, Oxford Wessex Archaeology Monograph 4.

Boucher, S. & S. Tassinari 1976 *Bronzes antiques du Musée de la Civilisation gallo-romaine à Lyon, vol. 1: Inscriptions, statuaire, vaisselle.* Lyon, Musée de la Civilisation gallo-romaine.

Breglia L. 1966 'Diadema', *Enciclopedia dell'arte antica, classica e orientale*, 85–9. Rome, Istituto della Enciclopedia Italiana.

Brunelli S. 2004 'Il 'fulgur' nelle epigrafi della Cisalpina e delle Gallie', *Epigraphica* 66, 185–215.

Burleigh, G. 2008 'Pre-Roman gods, goddesses and shrines in the *territorium* of Baldock, England', *Divinidades indígenas em análise, Actas do VII workshop FERCAN, Cascais, 25–27.05.2006*, ed. J. d'Encarnação, 189–219. Coimbra/Porto, CEAUCP.

Corder, P. & I. A. Richmond 1938 'A Romano-British interment, with bucket and sceptres, from Brough, East Yorkshire', *Antiquaries Journal* 18, 68–74.

Corteault, P. 1921 'An Inscription recently found at Bordeaux', *Journal of Roman Studies* 11, 101–7.

Cunliffe, B. 2005 *Iron Age Communities in Britain.* London, Routledge.

Cunliffe, B. & P. Davenport 1985 *The Temple of Sulis Minerva at Bath*, I. *The Site.* Oxford, Oxford University Committee for Archaeology Monograph 7.

Derks, T. 1998 *Gods, Temples and Ritual Practices.* Amsterdam, Amsterdam University Press.

Durham, E. 2012 'Depicting the gods: metal figurines in Roman Britain', *Internet Archaeology* 31. http://intarch.ac.uk/journal/issue31/durham_index.html

Esposito A. 2016, 'A Context for Roman Priestly Regalia: Depositional Practices and Spatial Distribution of Assemblages from Roman Britain', *TRAC 2015. Proceedings of the Twenty-Fifth Annual Theoretical Roman Archaeology Conference, Leicester 27–29 March 2015*, 92–110. Oxford-Philadelphia, Oxbow.

Fellows-Jensen, G., D. Gore & D. Rollason, D. 1998 'Sources for York history to AD 1100', *The Archaeology of York*, 1. York, York Archaeological Trust.

Fishwick, D. 1961 'The Imperial Cult in Roman Britain', *Phoenix* 15, 159–73.

Frere, S. S. & R. S. O. Tomlin 1992 *Roman Inscriptions of Britain, volume 2, fasicule 4,* Instrumentum Domesticum. Stroud, Sutton.

Fulford, M. G. 1996, *The second Augustan Legion in the West of Britain, the ninth annual Caerleon lecture in honorem aquilae legionis II Augustae*, Cardiff.

Fulford, M. G. 2002, 'Chapter 5. The Second Augustan Legion in the West of Britain', Brewer R.J. (ed.), *The Second Augustan Legion and the Roman Military Machine*, Cardiff, 83–102.

Gilbert, H. 1978 'The Felmingham Hall Hoard, Norfolk', *Bulletin of the Board of Celtic Studies* 28, 159–87.

Green, M. J. 1976 *A Corpus of Religious Material from the Civilian Areas of Roman Britain.* Oxford, British Archaeological Reports, British series 24.

Green, M. J. 1983 *The Gods of Roman Britain.* Aylesbury, Shire Publications.

Greenfield, E. 1963 'The Romano-British shrines at Brigstock, Northants', *Antiquaries Journal* 43, 228–63.

Haeussler, R. 2008 'How to identify Celtic religion(s) in Roman Britain and Gaul', *Divinidades indígenas em análise, Actas do VII workshop FERCAN, Cascais, 25–27.05.2006*, ed. J. d'Encarnação, 13–63. Coimbra/Porto, CEAUCP.

Henig, M. 1982 'Seasonal feasts in Roman Britain', *Oxford Journal of Archaeology* 1, 213–23.

Henig, M. 1984 *Religion in Roman Britain.* London, Batsford.

Inan, J. & E. Rosenbaum 1966 *Roman and Early Byzantine Portrait Sculpture in Asia Minor.* London, British Academy.

Isserlin, R. 1994 'An archaeology of brief time: monuments and seasonality in Roman Britain', *TRAC 94, Proceedings of the Fourth Annual Theoretical Roman Archaeology conference, Exeter*, ed. S. Cottam, D. Dungworth, S. S. & J. Taylor, 45–56. Oxford, Oxbow Books.

Jackson, R. & G. Burleigh 2007 'The Senuna treasure and shrine at Ashwell (Herts.)', *Continuity and Innovation in Religion in the Roman West Vol. 1*, ed. R. Haeussler & A. C. King, 37–54. Portsmouth, RI, Journal of Roman Archaeology Supplementary Series 67.

James, S. 1999 *The Atlantic Celts. Ancient People or Modern Invention?* London, British Museum Press.

Kirk, J. 1949 'Bronzes from Woodeaton', *Oxoniensia* 14, 1–49.

Kissel, T.K. 1995, *Untersuchungen zur Logistik des römischen Heeres in den Provinzen des griechischen Ostens (27 v. Chr.–235 n. Chr.)*, Pharos 6, St. Katharinen, Scripta Mercaturae Verlag.

Koeppel, G. M. 1983 'Die Historischen Reliefs der Römischen Kaiserzeit. VI: Reliefs von bekannten Bauten der augusteischen bis antoninischen Zeit', *Bonner Jahrbücher* 189, 61–143.

Künzl, E. 1997 'Römische Tempelschätze und Sakralinventare: Votive, Horte, Beute', *Antiquité Tardive* 5, 57–81.

Layard, N. 1925 'Bronze crowns and a bronze head-dress from a Roman site at Cavenham Heath, Suffolk', *Antiquaries Journal* 5, 258–65.

Ling, R. 2007, 'Inscriptions on Romano-British Mosaics and Wall-Paintings', *Britannia* 38, 63–91.

Lysons, S. 1817 *Reliquiae Britannico-Romanae, Containing Figures of Roman Antiquities Discovered in Roman Britain*, Volume II. London, Cadell & Davies.

London in Roman Times 1930. London, London Museum catalogue no. 3.

Mairs, R. 2012 '"Interpreting" at Vindolanda: commercial and linguistic mediation in the Roman army', *Britannia* 43, 17–28.

Mattingly, D. J. 2004 'Being Roman: expressing identity in a provincial setting', *Journal of Roman Archaeology* 17, 5–25.

Mattingly, D. J. 2011 *Imperialism, Power, and Identity. Experiencing the Roman Empire.* Princeton, Princeton University Press.

Meagow, W.-R. 1987 *Kameen von Augustus bis Alexander Severus.* Berlin, Walter de Gruyter.

Millett, M. 1995 'Rethinking religion in Romanization', *Integration in the Early Roman West. The role of culture and ideology*, ed. J. Metzler, M. Millett, N. Roymans & J. Slofstra, 93–100. Luxemburg, [publisher?].

O'Connell, M. G. & J. Bird 1994 'The Roman temple at Wanborough, excavation 1985–1986', *Surrey Archaeological Collections* 82, 1–168.

Phillips, E. J. 1972–4 'The Roman distance slab from Bridgeness', *Proceedings of the Society of Antiquaries of Scotland* 105, 176–82.

Poulton, R. 2007 'Farley Heath Roman temple', *Surrey Archaeological Collections* 93, 1–147.

Reddé, M. 1986, *Mare nostrum: les infrastructures, le dispositif et l'histoire de la marine militaire sous l'Empire romain*, Rome-Paris.

Richmond, I.A. 1963, *Roman Britain*, London.

Rose, C. B. 1997 *Dynastic Commemoration and Imperial Portraiture in the Julio-Claudian Period.* Cambridge, Cambridge University Press.

Rudling, D., ed. 2008 *Ritual Landscapes of Roman South-East Britain.* Oxford, Oxbow Books.

Rumscheid, J. 2000 *Kranz und Krone.* Tübingen, Istanbuler Forschungen 43.

Rüpke, J. 2006 'Urban religion and imperial expansion: priesthood in the *Lex Ursoniensis*', *The Impact of Imperial Rome on Religions, Ritual and Religious Life in the Roman Empire*, ed. L. De Bois, P. Funke & H. Hahn, 11–23. Leiden, Brill.

Rüpke, J. 2009 'Dedications accompanied by inscriptions in the Roman Empire: functions, intentions, modes of communication', *Dediche sacre nel mondo greco-romano: diffusione, funzioni, tipologie*, ed. J. Bodel & M. Kajava, 31–41. Rome, Institutum Romanum Finlandiae.

Rüpke, J. 2011 'Different Colleges – Never Mind!?', *Priests and State in the Roman World*, ed. J. H. Richardson & F. Santangelo, 25–38. Stuttgart,

Franz Steiner Verlag.

Smith, A. 2001 *The Differential Use of Constructed Sacred Space in Southern Britain, from the Late Iron Age to the 4th Century AD*, Oxford, British Archaeological Reports British Series 318.

Tomlin, R. S. O. 2002 'Writing to the gods in Britain', *Becoming Roman, writing Latin? Literacy and Epigraphy in the Roman West*, ed. A. E. Cooley, 165–79. Portsmouth RI, Journal of Roman Archaeology, Suppl. 48.

Tomlin, R. S. O. 2009 *The Roman inscriptions of Britain. Vol. 3, Inscriptions on stone found or notified between 1 January 1955 and 31 December 2006.* Stroud, Alan Sutton.

Tomlin, R. S. O. 2013 'III. Inscriptions', *Britannia* 44, 381–96.

Toynbee, J. M. C. 1962 *Art in Roman Britain.* Oxford, Phaidon.

Valensi, L. 1967 *Römer in Gallien: Romanisierung Aquitaniens am Beispiel von Bordeaux.* Munich, Musée d'Aquitaine de la ville de Bordeaux.

Van Andringa, W. 2002 *La Religion en Gaule romaine: Piété et politique, Ier–IIIe siècle apr. J.-C.* Paris, Errance.

Van Andringa, W. 2011 'New combinations and new statues. The indigenous gods in the pantheons of the cities of Roman Gaul', *The Religious History of the Roman Empire*, ed. J. A. North & S. R. F. Price, 109–38. Oxford, Oxford University Press.

Van Andringa, W., T. Creissen & C. Chevalier 2010 'Pompéi: Le *fulgur conditum* de la Maison des Quatres Styles, I, 8, 17 (campagne 2008)', *The Journal of Fasti Online.* http://www.fastionline.org/docs/FOLDER-it-2010-208.pdf

Vinagre, M.A. 2000, 'Los intérpretes de sueños en los templos de Serapis, Arys', *Antigüedad, religiones y sociedades* 3, 129–41.

Webster, J. 1997 'A negotiated syncretism: readings on the development of Romano-Celtic religion', *Dialogues in Roman Imperialism. Power, discourse, and discrepant experience in the Roman Empire*, ed. D. J. Mattingly, 165–84. Portsmouth RI, Journal of Roman Archaeology Suppl. 23.

Whittaker, C. R. 1997 'Imperialism and culture: the Roman initiative', *Dialogues in Roman Imperialism. Power, discourse, and discrepant experience in the Roman Empire,* ed. D. J. Mattingly, 143–61.

Williams, D. 2008 'The Wanborough temple', *Ritual Landscapes of Roman south-east Britain,* ed. D. Rudling, 87–93. Oxford, Oxbow Books.

Woodward, A. 1992 *Shrines and Sacrifice.* London, Batsford.

Woolf, G. 1997 'Beyond Roman and natives', *World Archaeology* 28.3, 339–50.

Woolf, G. 2009 'The religion of the Roman diaspora', *Ritual Dynamics and Religious Change in the Roman Empire: proceedings of the eighth Workshop of the International Network Impact of Empire (Heidelberg, July 5–7, 2007),* ed. O. Hekster, S. Schmidt-Hofner & C. Witschel, 239–52. Leiden, Brill.

Worrell, S., J. Pearce, S. Moorhead & P. Walton 2011 'II. Finds Reported under the Portable Antiquities Scheme', *Britannia* 42, 399–437.

IX

THE THEONYM *CONVENTINA

Fernando Fernández Palacios

*The paper seeks to shed some light regarding the etymology of the theonym *Conventina, which occurs on thirteen inscriptions from* Brocolitia *(Carrawburgh, Northumberland, England). After revising the context and the associations in which the epigraphs were recovered, a forma plena is proposed from which all the different readings can be explained. The etymologies that have been offered for the original meaning of the theonym *Conventina are analysed, which includes a discussion on the etymology of the Venta place-names of ancient Britain.*

Introduction

THE theonym **Conventina* occurs in Britain on thirteen inscriptions (Table 1), all from the site known as Coventina´s Well, at *Brocolitia* (Carrawburgh, Northumberland), a Roman fort on Hadrian´s Wall.[1] The well was discovered in October 1876, situated in the *vicus* adjacent to the fort. It produced the thirteen inscriptions, almost all on stone altars,[2] together with approximately 14,000 Roman coins, bronze statuettes of horses, jewellery, votive images of heads, and other miscellaneous cult-related items.[3]

Two inscriptions are evidence of the treatment of **Conventina* as a *nympha*: Table 1, no. 13 records a vow [NY]MPHAE COVENTINAE made by a *decurio*, and no. 6 is a dedication DEAE NIMFAE COVENTINE. The association with the well, and on at least one altar the depiction of the goddess resembling the standard Graeco-Roman representation of nymphs (Fig. 1),[4] has led scholars to think that the goddess was an

1 The inscriptions can be read in, e.g., Irby-Massie 1999, 286–8 (nos. 440–453), though the most consulted version is Allason-Jones & McKay 1985, the only monograph devoted entirely to the Coventina´s Well (for the readings, 13–17 and 41–47a). The inscriptions are held in Chesters Museum. In coming from a single site, **Conventina* is similar to *Sulis* (see further below). It has no relationship at all with the inscriptions from Spain and France that have traditionally been linked to **Conventina*, cf. Prósper 2002, 244–7, *pace* de Bernardo Stempel 2008.

2 10 stone altars, 1 pedimented stele, 1 dedication slab, and 1 pottery incense burner.

3 See *Archaeologia Aeliana* 8 (1880); Allason-Jones & McKay 1985. A Bronze Age axe-hammer was one of the more unusual finds.

4 Table 1, no. 1; cf. Allason-Jones; McKay, 1985, Pl. VI. The goddess is represented in relief above the

no.	RIB	Inscription	Format of inscription	no. in Allason-Jones & McKay 1985	attributed dates, AD
1	1534	*Deae / Covventinae / T D(---) Cosconia/nus pr(aefectus) coh(ortis) I Bat(avorum) l(ibens) m(erito)*	Pedimented stele	4	*c.*140 prob. 3rd c.
2	1524	*Deae Co/ventine coh(orti) I Cube/rnorum / Aur(elius) Camp/ester / v p l a*	Altar	5	late 2nd c.
3	1525	*Die Cove/ntine A/urelius / Crotus / German(us)*	Altar	10	late 2nd c.
4	1523	*De(ae) Conveti(ne) / v(otum) ret(t)u/lit Maus / optio c(o)ho(rtis) / p(rimae) Frixiau(onum)*	Altar	6	2nd-3rd c.
5	1529	*Deae Coven/tine P[---]a/nus m(i)l(es) c(o)ho(rtis) [--- / ---TTOIN--- / ---] v(otum) [li]/bes animo / r(eddidit) et posivit*	Altar	7	late 2nd c. 2nd-3rd c.
6	1526	*Deae Nim/fae Coven/tine Mad/uhus Germ(anus) / pos(uit) pro se et suis / v s l m*	Altar	9	late 2nd c. 2nd-3rd c.
7	1528	*D(e)ae Coven(tine) / Vinomath/us v s l m*	Altar	8	2nd-3rd c.
8	1532	*Deae Co/vetine Cr/otus v(o)t(um) l(i) b/e(n)s s[o]lui pro m(ea) sa(lute)*	Altar	11	2nd-3rd c.
9	1533	*Deae sanc(tae) / Covontine / Vincentius / pro salute sua / v(oto) l(aetus) l(ibens) m(erito) d(edicavit)*	Altar	12	2nd-3rd c.
10	1531	*Cove/tina(e) A(u)/gusta(e) / votu(m) / man/ibus suis / Satu/rni/nus / fecit / Gabi/nius*	Incense burner	142	2nd-3rd c. 3rd c. or later
11	1535	*Covven[ti(nae)] / Aelius [---] / pius p[ref(ectus)] / coh(ortis) I Bat(avorum) / v s l m*	Altar	11	3rd-4th c.
12	1522	*Deae / Conventi/nae / Bellicus / v s l m p*	Altar	12	
13	1527	*[Ni]mphae Coventinae / [---]tianus dec[u]ri(o) / ---] SLE[.]V / [---] m(erito)*	Dedication slab	13	

Table 1. Catalogue of **Conventina* inscriptions, all from Carrawburgh, Hadrian's Wall.

aquatic one. Green, for example, speaks of 'the personified spirit of a spring that welled up out of the ground to feed a pool'.[5] She remarks that the pool or well was enclosed by a high sanctuary wall, 'and the pool forms a replacement for the *cella* or inner sanctum in a normal Romano-Celtic shrine'.[6] This aquatic aspect could imply an association with

inscription leaning back with a branch in her right hand, cf. Maxfield & Dobson 1995, no. 242 (p. 127).

5 Green 1995, 99. Similarly, Green 1992, 67. Elsewhere Green describes 'the Romano-British goddess Coventina', which 'presided over a natural spring and well at Carrawburgh; she is named and is depicted as a single or a triple water-nymph, reclining on water-lilies and pouring water from a vessel; and she had a temple built in her honour' (Green 2004, 138).

6 Green 1992, 67.

healing powers, although no medicinal properties have been detected.[7] The cult has parallels with other sites of Britain where the worship was closely focussed on specific wells (such as *Mars Nodens* at Lydney, Gloucestershire, and Cockersand Moss, Lancashire, and *Sulis* in Bath).[8]

A relief found in Coventina´s Well seems to represent three water-nymphs of equal importance (see Plate 1).[9] If this is not entirely a product of assimilation to Roman beliefs, it could be connected to Indo-European ternary cults,[10] some of which are specifically Celtic (Macha, the three Brigits, *Taruos Trigaranos* the three-horned bull, the *Matres*, some triple attributes of horse-goddess Epona).[11] Miranda Green speaks of the Celtic indigenous personification of the local spring.[12]

As to chronology, it seems that the pool or well at the *vicus* of Carrawburgh was constructed as a functional cistern early in the 2nd century AD, but soon became a focus of religious practices. The deposition of the dedicatory inscriptions into the well is explained as the result either of an intentional attack on the cult site or as consequence of simple disuse.[13]

Fig. 1. **Conventina* depicted as a reclining nymph, from Coventina's Well, Hadrian's Wall. See Table 1, no. 1 for the inscription.

The correct form for *Conventina

Over the course of what is now more than a century since the discovery of the Coventina's Well, the etymology of **Conventina* has been the subject of several proposed derivations, some of them

7 Green (2004, 143–4) thinks that 'the votive pins and dog-figurine suggest a healing role for the goddess', maybe in relation to childbirth. Cf. Green 1989, 41; 1992, 67.

8 Cf. Irby-Massie 1999, 99.

9 Allason-Jones & McKay 1985, 13, Pl. V.

10 For discussion of whether it is **Conventina* being depicted here in triple form see Allason-Jones & McKay 1985, 13. Green (1992, 68; 2004, 77) says; 'at Carrawburgh, the shrine of Coventina, a local goddess of springs has produced one depiction of a trio of Nymphs, presumably a version of the deity herself', offering several archaeological parallels (in Green 1989, 156).

11 Irby-Massie 1999, 148. In fact, Epona and the Matres can be related to the underworld (Green 1976, 14). A silver ring that may come from Coventina's Well possesses an inscription with the word *Matres* (Allason-Jones & McKay 1985, no. 32 (p. 20), Pl. XII: RIB II 2422.28). Cf. in general Vendryes 1952 (originally published in 1935).

12 Green 1989, 156.

13 See, for example, Green 1989, 40; 1992, 67; 1995, 99.

Form	Cat. No.
CONVENTINAE	12
CONVETI(ne)	4
COVVENTINAE	1
COVVEN[TI(nae)]	11
COVENTINAE	13
COVEN(tine)	7
COVENTINE	2
COVENTINE	5
COVENTINE	6
COVENTINE	3
COVONTINE	9
COVETINE	8
COVETINA	10

Table 2. Attested forms of **Conventina.*

Form	Cat. no.	Dating
CONVENTINAE	12	?
CONVENTINA(e)	10	2nd-3rd c./3rd. c. or later
CONVENTI(ne)	4	2nd-3rd c.
COVVENTINAE	1	*c.*140 / prob. 3rd c.
COVVEN[TI(nae)]	11	3rd-4th c.
COVENTINAE	13	?
COVENTINE	2	late 2nd c.
COVENTINE	5	late 2nd c. / 2nd-3rd c.
COVENTINE	6	late 2nd c. / 2nd-3rd c.
COVENTINE	3	late 2nd c.
COVEN(tine)	7	2nd-3rd c.
COVONTINE	9	2nd-3rd c.
COVETINE	8	2nd-3rd c.

Table 3. Dates attributed to **Conventina* inscriptions.

quite bizarre.[14] Before entering into the debate, it is worth justifying what it seems the correct name of the goddess, **Conventina*, which appears under the following forms (see Table 2): *Covetina*, *Covetine*, *Coventine*, *Covontine*, *Coventinae*, *Covventinae*, *Convetinae* and *Conventinae*. Although the different spellings have been explained as the result of 'perhaps a mixture of Celtic and Germanic backgrounds' in a context of oral communication,[15] or as mere whims,[16] I think that we can find a better explanation. But before that, we must acknowledge the difficulties in any attempt to construct a chronology for the inscriptions. Most of them have not been accurately dated, having received only a tentative date (see Table 3).

The *forma plena* seems to be **Conventina,*[17] which we have attested in the dative case in no. 12. The development of this form is first to one in which the *n* originally in *Con-* has ceased to be nasal, but continues to be represented as a segment in **Covventina* (e.g. nos 1, 11).[18] In these, the assimilation with the nasal in the cluster *nv* is in progress. This process is fully complete in the other forms of the name. The absence of the second *n* in some forms is due to dissimilation, and the same process of assimilation can be said with respect to the second *o* of the form **Covontina*.

14 For a historiography of the proposals see Allason-Jones & McKay 1985, 3–6. Henig 1984, 47 says that it is a Celtic name, but he does not offer arguments, and likewise Green 1995, 99.

15 Raybould 1999, 28. It has been assumed that the dedicants came mainly from Gaul and Germany and were mostly associated with the army (Green 1995, 101). About these see further below.

16 Irby-Massie, 1999, 288 refers to Clayton who stated that the double "v" of Table 1, nos 1 and 11 could be explained as 'an accident' or 'to give greater emphasis to the syllable', cf. Clayton 1880, 9. Clayton also suggested the ignorance of the sculptor as the probable explanation of the form *Conventinae* (Clayton 1880).

17 Jackson 1953, 481 thought that what we have called *forma plena* occurred 'perhaps out of etymological consciousness or perhaps by Latinising orthography' (*-nv-* > *-v-* in Vulgar Latin). Indeed, it is possible that **Conventina* be a back formation or hypercorrection or Latinization.

18 Maybe *Covventina* could stand for [koβwentina] < **Com+ventina.*

Reviewing the etymology

If we take it as established that *Conventina* is the 'correct' (or full) name of the goddess (although see further below),[19] we are in a better position to attempt an etymology. **Conventina* is an adjectival formation in **-inā*. *Con-* is explained as the Proto-Indo-European preposition **kom-* 'so an etwas entlang, daß Berührung damit stattfindet: neben, bei mit',[20] which is the source of the Proto-Celtic prefix **kom-* 'zusammen', cf. *Convenae*, a *populus* of Aquitania, the Celtiberian nominal compounds kombalkez, kombalkores, and the same preposition probably used as a preverb in konbouto,[21] Latin *cum*, etc.

Nevertheless, the majority of the forms are COVENTINA rather than CO<u>N</u>VENTINA. In Welsh, Gaulish and British *com-* often appears as **co-* before *v-* [w] and so this *co-* could be considered a byform of *com-* (in other words, it could be old) or it could be a sound change. Tacitus uses the word *covinnus* for Caledonian chariots.[22] The correspondent Middle Welsh word is *kywein* meaning 'convey', the Latin source of *convey* probably being the cognate of Welsh *cywain.*[23]

As to *-vent-*, it is necessary to discuss a series of place-names that contain the word *Venta*. It occurs in several place-names of Roman Britain: *Venta Belgarum*, *Venta Icenorum*, *Venta Silurum,*[24] and as the second element in *Bannaventa*[25] and *Glannoventa.*[26] To judge from the places with these names, *Venta* comes to signify an important town, for it is the main place of three *civitates*. With respect to *Venta Belgarum*, the place was the capital of the *Belgae* and in Roman times an important city (today Winchester, Hampshire). *Venta Icenorum*, for its part, was a place probably established by the Romans as the main town of the Iceni after the defeat of Boudica (today Caistor St Edmund, Norfolk).

The proper etymology of *Venta* has been very much discussed. There is in France a place-name *Ouíntion* > *Vence*, and *Vens*, near Seyssel,[27] which can be compared with the personal names *Vintelius*, *Vintidia*, *Vintinus* and *Vintius.*[28] In France, Holder cites

19 Cf. also Jackson, *Konwentina* > *Kowentina*, though giving an explanation through Celtic (**kom-* > *kow* + noun- and adjective-forming suffix *-in-* + nominative singular feminine suffix *-a*) that leaves *–vent-* unsolved and unidentified (Allason-Jones & McKay 1985, 4).

20 Pokorny, *IEW* 612.

21 Wodtko 2000, 186–91. In Britain we have **kom-* in the divine name *Condatis* (on the god see Fairless 1984, 235–8), cf. Gaulish *condate* 'confluence of streams or rivers'.

22 Tacitus, *Agricola* 35, *couinnarius eques. Couinnus* is attested several times in the *Vindolanda* letters (nos. 597–9), frequently associated with the adjective *pensilis* (Bowman & Thomas 2003, 58–62, especially p. 59). By the late first century AD the chariot was used for civilian purposes (Martial 12.24).

23 Cf. Welsh *cywir* < **kom-wīr-*. Incidentally, *mynwent* 'graveyard' < Latin *monumentum* could very well have been influenced by *Bannaventa*.

24 References in Rivet & Smith 1979, 492–3. *Venta Belgarum* survives in *Winchester*, Anglo-Saxon *Wintan-ceaster* (Jackson 1970, 80). According to Jackson (*ibid.*), in the case of *Venta Silurum* '*Venta* here survives in the Welsh name of the place, *Caer Went*; and in *Gwent*, part of Monmouthshire, the old kingdom-name clearly derived from that of the Roman town', cf. Old English *Wente* 'the people of Gwent', *Went-sǣte* 'the inhabitants of Gwent'.

25 Rivet & Smith 1979, 262–5. A second *Bannaventa* (*Bannaventa Berniae*) has been proposed in relation to St Patrick (Rivet & Smith 1979, 511–2).

26 Rivet & Smith 1979, 367.

27 Ptolemy 3.1.37. See Falileyev 2010, 239.

28 Delamarre 2007, 201.

Ventadour (Corrèze) < **Ventadornum* and Rostaing *Ventabrun*.[29] Furthermore, although Welsh *Gwent* derives from *Venta*, it has been said that its Celticity is not demonstrated.[30] In fact one would be inclined to think that the exceptions that Jackson pointed out, of Romano-British names not developing Indo-European *e* before a nasal plus stop to *i* in Common Celtic,[31] could be explained through an Indo-European pre-Celtic *stratum* akin to the one found by Nicolaisen in hydronyms.[32] Precisely the first exception named by Jackson was *Venta*, to which he added **Gabrosentum* (Moresby, Cumberland).[33] Nonetheless, it must be said that */-ent-/* and */-int-/* alternated in Celtic, as Sims-Williams pointed out to me,[34] and furthermore we find, for example, Celtiberian personal names with */-ent-/*: turenta and *Uxenti f(ilius)*.[35]

In drafting this paper I tried to exploit the Indo-European non-Celtic idea by searching for *Venta* as a Proto-Indo-European root with the meaning of 'source' or similar, but all my hunts were in vain. Although Indo-European **ued* 'sources'[36] + adjectival suffix **-nt-* could seem attractive on this point at a first sight, there are many problems, for example, how to fully explain the falling out of *-d* in **wed* and, moreover, the highly unusual use of an adjectival suffix **-nt-* with a noun. Olmstead thinks that maybe it is a nasalized form of Indo-European **ued-* 'wet', as in Germanic **uent-*, English *winter* 'the wet season'.[37] He translates the theonym, with question marks, as 'with Waters', with a second element from Indo-European **auent-* 'to wet; a spring' (river goddess *Aventia*, the *Ant* in Norfolk). The *A-* would have been lost by haplology/syncope. Prósper speaks of this etymology as highly unlikely.[38] De Bernardo Stempel, for her part, thinks that 'Coventina' is a personification of a non-Celtic river name **Couentina* from earlier **Cosuentina* pointing out as parallels the Italian hydronym *Casuentus* and the theonyms *Cohuetena* < **Cosuentina* (from Hispania) and *Casuontanus* < **Cosuentanus* (from Noricum).[39]

Sims-Williams states that *Ventā* is a Celtic word and he speculated with a meaning

29 Holder 1.174. Hilsberg 2009, 48 discusses the hydronym *The Solent* in southern England (attested as *Soluente*, c. 731 (manuscript from the 9th), c. 1000; *Sol(w)ente, (utt on) solentan* in 948), and points out that 'The Solent is assumed to consist of a suffix *–wente* which is a known form of Old European river names and is, therefore, a very ancient name example'. Nevertheless, I cannot find such a form in Old European river-names and it seems to me that an easier solution for the etymology of that river-name is to think in the present participle of Latin *solvere* 'to dissolve', 'to destroy', 'to free', *solvente*, word that continues in use at least in Italian and Spanish.

30 Coates 2007, 19 asks why the apparently non-Celtic names, among them *Venta*, are not readily explainable as Germanic. *Gwent* does not exist as a common noun in Welsh, which is consistent with that form existing only in names borrowed for places (Gwent, Llinwent, Ardduwent). Notice that although the *Geiriadur Prifysgol Cymru* has no entry for it, it analyses *cadwent* as *cad* + *gwent* and *gosgrynwent* as containing *gwent* 'maes' ('field').

31 Jackson 1953, 278.

32 See, for example, Nicolaisen 1982.

33 For the sources cf. Rivet & Smith 1979, 364–5.

34 Cf. McCone 1996, 55–6, who specifically treats *Coventina* and *sent-/hynt*.

35 Bronze of Botorrita III; *Tabula Contrebiensis.*

36 Wodtko *et al.* 2008, 706–15.

37 Olmstead 1994, 427–8.

38 Prósper 2002, 245.

39 De Bernardo Stempel 2008. Nonetheless, these linguistic developments need further evidence.

'market'.[40] This opinion seems to go back to Ifor Williams, who concluded that *venta* was ´field´ in Celtic and perhaps had a secondary meaning ´market-place´, finding a similar sense-development in *magus*.[41] Recently Matasović has reconstructed in Proto-Celtic a noun **wentā* 'place, town' (Middle Welsh *cad-went* 'battlefield') from Proto-Indo-European **$h_1$wen-* 'place' (?) (Greek eunh, Albanian *vend* 'place'), taking into account also the *Venta* toponyms from ancient Britain[42]. From the Welsh point-of-view can be added *gosgrynwent*,[43] the mid-Wales place-name *Llinwent* ´? flaxfield´[44] and *Ardduwent* 'Arddun´s field'.[45] *Llinwent* is a farmstead in Powys that had a medieval hall-house and *Arddunwnent* a township of Flintshire.[46] In fact *cadwent* is attested several times and seems to have different meanings: 'battle-field', 'battle', 'attack', 'onslaught', 'assault'; *gosgrynwent*, for its part, is translated as 'battle, fight, onslaught', and it occurs in *Llawysgrif Hendregadedd* along with *cadwent*: 'Gosgrynwent cadwent ked wallaw (Cynddelw)'. However, it seems clear that for the meaning Matasović has relied on Kenneth Jackson, who on this matter wrote: 'One may well *guess* that it means something like "town", but this can be nothing but a speculation', disagreeing with Ifor William´s proposal above.[47]

Previously van Hamel had proposed a Welsh **gwent* 'worry, excitement', thinking that it was a word evocative of military atmosphere, and in that way related to Welsh *gwanu*, translated into French as 'percer', and *ymwan* 'se battre'.[48] The correspondent form of **gwent* in Irish would be *fét*, which is only found – like the Welsh one – as an element of compound words, and both go up to **uentā* 'warlike action', a derivative in -*tā* (cf. Welsh *aberth*, Irish *edbart* < **ati-ud-bhertā*)[49] from the stem **wen-* 'to vanquish', also 'battre, blesser'.[50]

The meaning 'market' assigned to *Venta* as a Celtic word brings to mind the medieval Latin *venta* 'market', ultimately a derivation from Latin *vendita*.[51] In Vulgar Latin the loss of syllable-final nasals is attested.[52] Gutenbrunner tried to relate **Conventina* to Latin *conventus* 'assembly' but strangely enough he saw the divinity as a Germanic

---

40 Sims-Williams 2006, 118. I follow the Sims-Williams criteria to reject, as not related to our *Venta*, place-names from outside Roman Britain as *Beneventum* (in southern and northern Italy in ancient times), *Benavente* (Zamora and Asturias, Spain, from medieval times), *Benavent* (Lérida, Spain) and *Benavente* in Portugal near the mouth of the Tagus (Sims-Williams 2006, 119–20).

41 Williams 1949.

42 Matasović 2009, 413. *Cad-went* is translated as 'battle, effort, activity' in van Hamel 1937, 106.

43 Van Hamel 1937, 106, 'une scène agitée'.

44 See Sims-Williams 2006, 334; 2007, 334.

45 Rivet & Smith 1979, 263.

46 The *Geiriadur Prifysgol Cymru* s. v. *cadwent* writes an '&c.' which seems to point out to the existence of more examples.

47 Jackson 1970, 80.

48 Van Hamel 1937, 106.

49 Van Hamel 1937, 107.

50 Van Hamel 1937, 103–5 and 107. At first it would mean 's´efforcer, aspirer', later 'travailler, souffrir' and in Celtic the most common meaning would be 'percer, couper' (van Hamel 1937, 108).

51 For the details see Rivet & Smith 1979, 262–3, who reject the possibility that Latin *venita* might be the correct etymology for the British *Venta* place-names.

52 *Appendix Probi* and inscriptions.

goddess of the Thing.[53] Nevertheless, it would be satisfactory to think of *conventus* because of its relationship to social intercourse. One of the most recent publications on the etymology of **Conventina* suggests that there may be a relationship with Latin *conventio*,[54] but this is highly unlikely from the semantic point of view because with the meaning 'meeting, assembling' it is very rarely used. Even morphologically Latin used other diminutive forms (*conventiculum*, *conventiuncula*) and moreover the word is of the third declension.[55]

**Conventina* ends in the adjectival suffix *-ino-*, *-inā*, frequently found in both Celtic and Latin.

German etymology?

In principle one would be tempted to agree with de la Bédoyère when he points out that it is 'extremely unlikely that the First Cohort of Batavians based here brought Coventina with them since she is unknown anywhere else; instead they probably found the traces of a native shrine and adopted her'.[56] In this respect Webster was reasonable in the supposition that the spring 'was known and venerated long before Hadrian´s Wall was built';[57] it was longer than even Webster had in mind, because as Fairless pointed out in his study on *Belatucadrus*, *Cocidius* and *Conditis*, 'although apparently Celtic deities are in question, they themselves may possess more archaic pre-Celtic features'.[58]

Nonetheless, it seems pertinent to relate the divine name **Conventina* to two personal names attested in *Germania Superior*: *Coventalis* (from ancient *Tabernae*, modern Rheinzabern), written on *instrumentum domesticum*, in particular *terra sigillata*,[59] and *Coventi* (gen.) (from Gundershoffen).[60]

In addition, in two of the Coventina's Well inscriptions dedicated to **Conventina* it is stated that the dedicant is German: *Crotus German(us)* (Table 1, no. 3), and *Maduhus Germ(anus)* (no. 6); in the latter also with what seems a German personal name, *Maduhus*. Both dedicants wrote the goddess name as *Coventine*. There is another inscription with a possible German personal name: *Vinomathus* (no. 7), who presumably wrote the theonym in the same way: *Coven(tine)*.[61] *Coventine* is also the form used by the member of the *Cohors I Cubernorum* (no. 2), and in the same way *Coventine* can be read in no. 5, *miles* of a cohort, presumably of Germanic origin. Another case of *Coventine* is that of no.

53 Gutenbrunner 1936, 49–50 (*non vidi*).
54 Busse 2006.
55 LS 463.
56 De la Bédoyère 2015, 102.
57 Webster 1986, 78. It is presented as a local cult in Irby-Massie 1999, 213–4.
58 Fairless 1984, 224. We do not go as far as Ó Catháin 1995, 91, who suggested that a number of wells in Ireland and Scotland that are named after a trio of holy women would be common reflexes of pre-Indo-European culture among the peoples of north-western Europe.
59 AE 2003, 1265e; Gavrielatos 2012, 256, without a precise date, but not later than the 3rd century.
60 CIL XIII 6028, inscription devoted to Mercurius.
61 There is the possibility that *Vinomathus* is Celtic (substantive *matu* 'bonum' from the adj. *mati-* 'good' present for example in the place name *Andomatunnon*, Upper Germany, cf. de Bernardo Stempel 2005, 89), if we follow de Bernardo Stempel´s glottalization of dental stops, cf. for example de Bernardo Stempel 2013, 77, n. 100 and 79.

8, probably corresponding to a soldier, asking for his health, which gives us some reason to think that no. 4 must be interpreted as *Coventi(ne)* because it belongs to a member of the *Cohors I Frixiavonum*. In the cases of the Batavians, both no. 1 and no. 11 write the name of the goddess as *Covventinae*.

With respect to the denomination *Germanus*, Clay has reached the following conclusion:

> In Britain the term '*Germanus*' seems to have been associated with military units of the Batavi, Cuberni, Frisiavones, Frisii, Tuihanti and Vangiones, who had been initially permitted into the Roman empire in order to participate in military defence. The term is occasionally given to persons of suspected social and economic importance within militarised contexts but exact martial positions are never provided.[62]

It has been pointed out that the fact that *Crotus* and *Maduhus* specify the ethnic affiliation 'may indicate that they were in a minority',[63] but I think that it has to do more with the observation of 'a communal consciousness of themselves'.[64] Therefore, there is perhaps room for a German etymology.

Conclusions

Summarizing, we seem to have the following possibilities:

a) Indo-European non-Celtic **ued* 'sources' + adjectival suffix **-nt-*.

b) Indo-European non-Celtic **Conventina* 'with Waters'?, from **auent-* 'to wet; a spring' with loss of a- by haplology/syncope.[65]

c) Indo-European non-Celtic 'Coventina' as a personification of a non-Celtic river name **Couentina* from earlier **Cosuentina*.[66]

d) Celtic **gwent* 'worry, excitement', related to Welsh *gwanu*, translated into French as 'percer', and ymwan 'se battre'.[67] Delamarre, not knowing van Hamel´s article, proposes *-ventā*, *-venton*, Gallo-Brittonic **wentā* 'place of slaughtering (for animals)', from the economic point of view, or 'place of sacrifice (of animals)' from the religious point of view < Proto-Celtic **g^{w}entā* < Indo-European **g^{wh}en-*tā, **g^{wh}en-ton*.[68]

e) Celtic *Venta* > *Gwent*, meaning *gwent* in Welsh 'field'. *-went* can mean 'field', and so *ventā* was ´field´ in Celtic and perhaps had a secondary meaning ´market-place´, finding a similar sense-development in *magus*. This is followed with some reservations by Sims-Williams, who places *Ventā* among the Celtic-looking strings and elements, and gives with a question mark the meaning 'market'.[69] Sims-Williams also speaks of an

62 Clay 2008, 147.
63 Fairless 1989, 528.
64 Clay 2008, 139.
65 Olmstead 1994, 427–8.
66 De Bernardo Stempel 2008.
67 Van Hamel 1937.
68 Delamarre 2010–2012, 126–9; 2012, 27.
69 Sims-Williams 2006, 118–20.

element *went-* which seems to mean 'field'.[70]

f) Celtic. Matasović has reconstructed in Proto-Celtic a noun **wentā* 'place, town'.[71]

g) Latin *convenire* 'to meet with', 'to speak to'. *Pax convenit vel conventa est* 'peace is agreed upon'.

h) Latin *conventus* 'meeting, assembly'.[72]

i) Latin *conventio* 'meeting, assembling'.[73]

j) Latin *vēndĭta* 'market', feminine participle of Latin *vendere* 'to sell' (**vēnum dare* 'to put up for sale'), Vulgar Latin *venta* 'place of rendezvous for market-people' (attested also in several Romance languages).

k) German.

For reasons given above, a), b) and c), that is, an Indo-European non-Celtic etymology, seems not to work due to morphological issues. The Celtic etymologies proposed up to now, d), e) and f), seem to rely on several not proven semantic changes. Regarding g), h), i) and j), all of them solutions through Latin, i) is the weakest, the other ones could be possible in terms of morphology and semantics. Finally, the German answer is beyond our scope.

BIBLIOGRAPHY

Allason-Jones, L. & B. McKay 1985 *Coventina's Well. A shrine on Hadrian's Wall.* Gloucester, The Trustees of the Clayton Collection.

Busse, P. E. 2006 'Coventina', *Celtic Culture. A Historical Encyclopedia*, ed. J. Koch, 494–5. Santa Barbara, California, ABC-Clio.

Clay, C. L. 2008 'Developing the 'Germani' in Roman Studies', *TRAC 2007: Proceedings of the Seventeenth Annual Theoretical Roman Archaeology Conference*, ed. C. Fenwick *et al.*, 131–50. Oxford, Oxbow Books.

Coates, R. 2007 *Linguistic light on the birth of England*, Bristol (Inaugural professorial lecture, University of the West of England) (http://www.uwe.ac.uk/hlss/llas/bcl/5resources/Inaugural_coates_061207.pdf)

De Bernardo Stempel, P. 2005 'Ptolemy´s evidence for Germania Superior', *New Approaches to Celtic Place-Names in Ptolemy´s Geography*, ed. J. de Hoz *et al.*, 71–94. Madrid, Ediciones Clásicas.

De Bernardo Stempel, P. 2008 'Continuity, Translatio and Identificatio in Gallo-Roman Religion: the case of Britain', Haeussler & King, eds, 67–82.

De Bernardo Stempel, P. 2013 'The phonetic interface of word formation in Continental Celtic', *Continental Celtic Word Formation. The Onomastic Data*, ed. J. L. García Alonso, 63–83. Salamanca, Ediciones Universidad de Salamanca.

De la Bédoyère, G. 2015 *The Real Lives of Roman Britain.* New Haven-London, Yale University Press.

Delamarre, X. 2007 *Noms de personnes celtiques dans l'épigraphie classique.* Paris, Errance.

Delamarre, X. 2010–2012 'Notes d'onomastique vieille-celtique', *Keltische Forschungen* 5, 99–137.

Delamarre, X. 2012 *Noms de lieux celtiques de l'Europe ancienne.* Paris, Errance.

Fairless, K. J. 1984 'Three religious cults from the

70 Sims-Williams 2007, 334.
71 Matasović 2009.
72 Gutenbrunner 1936.
73 Busse 2006.

northern frontier region', *Between and Beyond the Walls. Essays on the prehistory and history of North Britain in honour of George Jobey*, ed. R. Miket & C. Burgess, 224–42. Edinburgh, John Donald Ltd.

Fairless, K. J. 1989 *Aspects of the Archaeology of the Brigantes*, Durham theses, Durham University. Available at Durham E-Theses Online: http://etheses.dur.ac.uk/6643/

Falileyev, A. 2010 *Dictionary of Continental Celtic Place-Names*. Aberystwyth, CMCS.

Gavrielatos, A. 2012 *Names on Gallo-Roman Terra Sigillata (1st – 3rd c. A.D)*, Leeds (doctoral thesis, School of Classics, University of Leeds).

Green, M. J. 1989 *Symbol & Image in Celtic Religious Art.* London, Routledge.

Green, M. J. 1992 *Dictionary of Celtic Myth and Legend.* London, Thames & Hudson.

Green, M. J. 1995 *Celtic Goddesses. Warriors, Virgins and Mothers.* London, British Museum.

Green, M. J. 2004 *The Gods of the Celts.* Stroud, Sutton.

Gutenbrunner, S. 1936 *Die germanischen Götternamen der antiken Inschriften.* Halle, Verlag Max Niemeyer.

Haeussler, R. & A. C. King, eds 2008 *Continuity and Innovation in Religion in the Roman West (6th International FERCAN Workshop, London, 2005).* Portsmouth, RI: Journal of Roman Archaeology Supplementary Series, 67, vol. 2.

Henig, M. 1984 *Religion in Roman Britain.* London, Routledge.

Hilsberg, S. 2009 *Place-Names and Settlement History. Aspects of Selected Topographical Elements on the Continent and in England*, University of Leipzig (Wissenschaftliche Arbeit zur Erlagung des akademischen Grades Magister Artium).

Irby-Massie, G. L. 1999 *Military Religion in Roman Britain.* Leiden-Boston-Köln, Brill.

Jackson, K. H. 1953 *Language and History in Early Britain*. Edinburgh, Edinburgh University Press.

Jackson, K. H. 1970 'Romano-British names in the Antonine Itinerary', *Britannia* 1, 68–82.

Matasović, R. 2009 *Etymological Dictionary of Proto-Celtic.* Leiden-Boston, Brill.

Maxfield, V. A. & B. Dobson 1995 *Inscriptions of Roman Britain*, 3rd edition. London, London Association of Classical Teachers.

McCone, K. 1996 *Towards a Relative Chronology of Ancient and Medieval Celtic Sound Change.* Maynooth, Department of Old and Middle Irish, St Patrick's College.

Nicolaisen, W. F. H. 1982 '"Old European" names in Britain', *Nomina* 6, 37–42.

Ó Catháin, S. 1995 'The holy women of Teelin, Mímisbrunnr and the Akkas', *10mh Co-Labhairt Eadar-Naiseanta na Ceiltis. 10th International Congress of Celtic Studies* (synopses of papers), 91. Edinburgh.

Olmstead, G. 1994 *The Gods of the Celts and the Indo-Europeans.* Budapest, Archaeolingua.

Prósper, B. M. 2002 *Lenguas y religiones prerromanas en la Península Ibérica.* Salamanca, Ediciones Universidad de Salamanca.

Raybould, M. E. 1999 *A Study of Inscribed Material from Roman Britain. An inquiry into some aspects of literacy in Romano-British society.* Oxford, Archaeopress, BAR British Series 281.

Rivet, A. L. F. & C. Smith 1979 *The Place-Names of Roman Britain.* London, Batsford.

Sims-Williams, P. 2006 *Ancient Celtic Place-Names in Europe and Asia Minor.* Oxford, Blackwell.

Sims-Williams, P. 2007 'Common Celtic, Gallo-Brittonic and Insular Celtic', *Gaulois et Celtique Continental*, ed. P.-Y. Lambert & G.-J. Pinault, 309–54. Geneva, Droz.

Van Hamel, A. G. 1937 'La racine *uen-* en celtique et en germanique', *Mélanges linguistiques offerts à M. Holger Pedersen à l'occasion de son soixante-dixième anniversaire, 7 avril 1937*, 103–9. Copenhagen, Levin & Munksgaard.

Vendryes, J. 1952 'L'unité en trois personnes chez les Celtes', *Choix d'études linguistiques et celtiques*, ed. J. Vendryes, 233–46. Paris, Klincksieck.

Webster, G. 1986 *The British Celts and their Gods under Rome.* London, Batsford.

Williams, I. 1949 [linguistic notes to the study by Richmond & Crawford], *Archaeologia* 93, 1–50.

Wodtko, D. 2000 *Monumenta Linguarum Hispanicarum. Band V.1. Wörterbuch der keltiberischen Inschriften.* Wiesbaden, Reichert.

Wodtko, D. S. *et al.* 2008 *Nomina im Indogermanischen Lexikon.* Heidelberg, Universitätsverlag Winter.

X

MATRES ENDEITERAE, DEUS SANCTUS ENDOVELECOS, DEA NAVE, AND OTHER INDIGENOUS AND CLASSICAL DEITIES IN THE IBERIAN PENINSULA

Patrizia de Bernardo Stempel

This paper discusses the linguistic as opposed to the geographical classification of the votive strings attested in the Iberian peninsula, shows their links with Central Europe and accounts for the scarce occurrences of interpretatio Romana*. Besides highlighting the difference between divine names and deities and between invocations and proper theonyms, the study shows how* ENDÉITERAE *matches Narbonensic Ανδοουνναι and* ENDOVELECOS *(later* ENDOVELLICOS*) may describe Apollon's prophetic numen. It also identifies a Gaulish iconographic parallel for the 'Fonte do Idolo' (Braga / P), where the watering goddess* NABIA*, also invoked as* DEA NAVE*, is involved.*

WHILE discussing some of the better documented divine names attested in the Iberian Peninsula, a couple of which I have recently seen myself in the 'Museo de Burgos', the present paper[1] draws attention to the general problems that make the analysis of the Hispanic theonymic corpus more difficult.

1. The Linguistic classification of Hispanic divine names

The most prominent problem in the current state of the art is the purely geographic classification of the cults documented in the Iberian Peninsula. Although geographical distribution and linguistic and cultic features do not necessarily agree,[2] there is much

1 I warmly thank the organizers of our XIIIth workshop, Dr Ralph Häussler and Prof. Tony King, and all colleagues who contributed to the discussion on 18th October 2014. I am also deeply indebted to Drs Alonso Domínguez Bolaño (the archaeologist of Archeos S.L. who discovered the verraco of Muelas del Pan), Rosario García Rozas (director of the Zamora Museum), Marta Negro Cobo (director of the Burgos Museum), José María Saiz (member of the Diputación de Burgos), and Francisco Tuset Bertran (professor at the Universitat de Barcelona), who kindly provided me with unpublished materials (see note 61 below), photographs, and other important information.

2 As the distribution of the actually Roman cult of the originally Indo-Iranian god *MITRA* certainly shows (see, among others, Hensen 2013, 7 and 21ff.).

confusion about what are called 'Celtiberian' and 'Lusitanian' cults.

1.1. Thus, the adjective 'Lusitanian' ought almost always to be understood in a geographical sense, given that several of the divine names attested in that (western) region, and even in those inscriptions which are ascribed to the linguistically Lusitanian corpus, show clearly Celtic isoglosses.

Examples of this kind are: ***BANDUS / BANDUA***, whose cultual affinity with the Roman *TUTELA* speaks in favour of a deified Celtic concept *$b^h nd^h us$, related to Old Indian *bandhu-* 'relationship, association' and to which various types of epithets of appurtenance to the respective communities could be added;[3] ***ICCONA***, akin to the Celtic theonyms *ICOVELLAUNA*, *IHAMNA-GALLA*, and *ICAUNA*, and also describing a health goddess or *SALUS*[4]; ***TREBARUNA***, on account of its characteristically Celtic ending.[5]

Few, by contrast, are the divine names such as ***DEA NEFA*** in Portugal, that is, containing specifically Lusitanian, 'anti-Celtic' sound-changes like the transformation of an inherited *b^h into *f*.[6]

1.2. The same applies to the adjective 'Celtiberian', which is also often used erroneously in order to refer to any kind of Hispanic Celticity.

Thus, the divine names ***ABIONA*** and ***VLADOS*** found in Gallaecia are indeed Celtic, but simply Celtic with no specific dialectal characteristics and not in the least 'Celtiberian':[7] in that case, one ought to expect ***AIBONA* and ***VLATOS*.

1.3. It is clear by now that even in the Iberian Peninsula there were different levels of Celticity,[8] which, not unlike as it has been shown for Aquitania and Italy, were also represented among divine names.[9] To a remarkably archaic lexical layer belongs the name of the oak-goddesses ***PERKUNETAS*** contained in the name of the border sanctuary called 'trikanta Perkunetaka' at Botorrita, given that it still preserves the Indo-European **p-* in initial antevocalic position.[10] Furthermore, it is archaic because its *-n-* has not yet been assimilated to the preceding *-r-* as it happened later in the Central European theonym *HERQURA* from *$Per k^w un\bar{a}$.[11]

---

3 See de Bernardo Stempel 2003; 2010c, 24, with discussion of more recent studies by other scholars.
4 More details in de Bernardo Stempel 2013e, 81–2.
5 The Celtic ending *-una* implies, at least before a proper homophonous suffix *-una* came into being, the existence of a preceding Celtic nasal stem with nominative singular *-u* < *-ō#. This means, for example, that a Celtic theonym **SENU* (probably the British *DEUS VETER*) ought to have existed before *SENUNA* was coined.
6 It can, indeed, be traced back to the Indo-European root *neb^h- 'feucht, Wasser' (*IEW* 315f., *LIV*² 448), cf. Tovar 1983, 270 and Bayer 1999, 124. Tovar's classification as 'Precelta' (*l.c.*) is, however, obsolete.
7 As they have been called, for example, by Beltrán Lloris (2011, 43).
8 See de Bernardo Stempel 2002. Multiple evidence to this effect can also be found in de Bernardo Stempel 2007; 2009b, de Bernardo Stempel *et al.* 2011; 2012, 168–73.
9 See de Bernardo Stempel 2008a and, respectively, *eadem* 2013e, 73 and *passim*.
10 De Bernardo Stempel 2008/2010, 125–6 and 141; 2009a, 693–4.
11 The theonym probably referred to the deity of the life tree, cf. the discussion in de Bernardo Stempel 2013e, 80–1. Falileyev's contribution (2008) leaves out part of the evidence (I am deeply indebted to my husband, Reinhard Stempel, for a translation of the Russian original).

Totally unsure is, by contrast, the existence of a particularly archaic invocation ‡***Drusuna*** supposed to represent the regular feminine derivation of a thematic compound **Dru-sun-o-s* 'son of the oak' containing the inherited Indo-European and Old Celtic lexeme *(-)sunus* 'son'.[12] While Francisco Marco Simón reported a numen of such a name to be attested twice at Soria and once at Segobriga,[13] the (only?) unshortened votive string engraved in the dative case on a small altar from the 2nd century AD found in the proximity of Soria is now read *Drubune / Nesad*[by Juan Carlos Olivares Pedreño.[14]

With the Gaulish type represented by the various Hispanic instances of ***Epona*** < **Ekwo-nā*[15] one may compare the older Celtiberian type ***Equoisos*** < **Ekwo-s(o)-yo-s*, attested at Peñalba, but matching in its word-formation the theonym *Etnosos* < **Petno-so-s* at Bourges.[16] Therefore, the invocations *Epona* and *Equoisos* represent two different stages in the development of the voiceless labiovelar.

Besides, a dialectal Hispanic development is to be observed in the votive string *Louter(o) d(eo)* from the province of Guadalajara. There, the nexus **-kt-* in the name of the carpenter god **Leug-ter-o-s* > **Loukteros*, akin to the *Luchtar* (later *Luchta*) of the Old Irish mythological tradition, has been simplified to *-t-* (***Louteros***) as usual in the Iberian Peninsula.[17]

1.3.1. It is in fact a regional isogloss that can now account for the newly found votive inscription *dea / Na/ve* at Vicinte near Lugo.[18] The regional Hispanic development *ya* > *ye* > *e* which has been observed in several territories in and outside the Iberian Peninsula[19]

---

12 See de Bernardo Stempel 2013a, 284–5 with further bibliography. The Celtic divine name *Ex-p(e)rc-ennios* attested in Aquitania might be a synonym. Note that it was quite normal to extract from a Celtic male divine name a corresponding female form, cf. de Bernardo Stempel 2006, esp. 35–6 and 38; 2013a, 285 n. 143.

13 Marco Simón 2003, 133 with n. 21. See also Gómez-Pantoja & García Palomar (1995), who also edit a second votive inscription in which the name of the goddess is shortened.

14 Olivares Pedreño 2015, 187–90 with photographs. *Dubruna* <**Dubrunā* ?

15 From Lara de los Infantes near Burgos (seen at the 'Museo de Burgos' on the 5th September 2014) to Isturgi in the province of Jaén, see Arenas-Esteban & López-Romero 2010, 158 with map no. 5, 159. Hernández Guerra 2004, 165.

16 See de Bernardo Stempel 2008, 183–4 n. 11, 191; 2003a, 49.

17 See Arenas-Esteban *et al.* 2003, to which Sergent 2012 has to be added. The latter now compares with the Celtic carpenter god (*Louteros* etc.) the divine carpenter called in Vedic *Viśvakarman* 'He who makes everything', thereby showing how the epithet *Sucellos* 'the good striker' may have replaced in Gaul the ancient Celtic theonym **Lukteros* 'He who bends (the wood > everything)'. I should like to add in passing that the work by Arenas-Esteban and myself has not been correctly quoted by Gamo Pazos (2012, 56–9), who disregards the free space, sufficient for one letter, left at the end of the first line, ignores the ligature <et> which can be seen at the beginning of the 2nd line, and consequently reverts to the old assumption of a female dative form ***Louterde* even if no parallels are known for the hypothetic divine name ‡*Louterda*. On the isogloss de Bernardo Stempel 2002, 102.

18 Acuña Castroviejo 2013. I thank Mª Cruz González Rodríguez for providing me with a copy of this article.

19 The first step of this isogloss, namely the development of unstressed **yo/ya* to (*y*)*e*, can be appreciated, among many others, in the ethnic name *Nitielii*, the mountain name *Berigiema*, the toponyms *Alixie* and *Turibrie*, and the gen. sing. *Coties* of a woman's name. The second step can be seen, among others, in the singular idionymic genitives *Avites* and *Boudes* (from **Avityās* and **Boudyās*); in the toponyms *Sentice* < **Senti-k(a)-yā*, O.r.e /Ωρία, Ta.r.m.e.s.Tu.Te.z / *Termestudia*; in the ethnonyms a.r.Ke.Tu.r.Ki < **Argyoturkī*, s.e.Ko.Pi.r.i.Ke.z < **Segobrigyōs*, and in the ethnonymic plural genitives

permits us to trace the involved theonym back to a nominative singular ***Nave***, and this to a variant **Navie*,[20] originating in the well-known nominative singular form *Navia*.

Interestingly, the monophthongization of the ascending diphthong *-ie* points now to a Celtic origin of the name and thus to ***Nabia*** as the original form of the theonym, which resulted from a protoform **Nōbʰ-yā* referring to a 'Watering' deity,[21] as is indeed suggested by some homophonous hydronyms.[22]

Therefore, the *-v-* contained in the later variants *Navia* > *Navie* > *Nave* of the theonym's original form *Nabia* was evidently due to the Celtic intervocalic lenition of the voiced labial stop.[23]

In the same direction points the votive string *tongoe Nabiagoi* found in the monumental complex of 'Fonte do Idolo' at Braga,[24] which has a perfectly Celtic explication.[25] In it, the diphthong *-oi* of the Latinized Old-Celtic dative singular of the thematic declension appears still preserved in absolute final position (*Nabiagoi#*), but transformed into *-oe* when followed by a nasal consonant inside the syntagma (**tongoi Na~* > *tongoe Na~*). This sequence of substantive and attribute in the dative case is mostly assumed to invoke the oath god *Tongos*[26] as related to the water goddess *Nabia* and therefore described as **Nabia-ko-s* (that is, *Nabiagos* with the Britannic-type lenition very common in the North-West Hispanic Celticity).[27] However, both the female

---

Po.l.s.Ke.n / o.l.s.Ke.n < **Wolskyom*, n.e.r.o.n.Ke.n < **Ner-ón-ik-yom*, s.e.l.o.n.Ke.n < **Sel-ón-ik-yom*. See for details Bernardo Stempel 2006a, with previous bibliography; 2012a; 2014a.

20 Not to be confounded with the form *Navie* in the votive inscription *IRL* Nr. 71 found nearby at San Martín de Monte de Meda/ Guntín (but originating from the *O Picato*-hillfort), which is just the contracted variant of *Navia*'s usual dative singular *Naviae*.

21 From the same verbal root **nebʰ-* meaning 'humid' and also 'water' mentioned in note 6 above. Further Celtic word-formations in *-yo-/-yā* with lengthened root grade and agentive meaning are listed in *NWÄI*, 204–8.

22 See Melena 1984, 243–4.; Marco Simón 2008, 280. A connection with Greek νάπη 'wooded valley' as proposed by Melena (1984, 244) is at odds with Celtic phonetics and, moreover, unconvincing. Also no longer suitable is the etymology connecting the goddess' name with Sp. *nava* 'valley' and favoured, among others, by Prósper 2002, 189–95. Also cf. Olivares Pedreño 1998–1999; 2002, 233–40; Barberarena 2005, 716–7. See, moreover, § 5.3.2 below.

23 As e.g. in the personal names *Dubius*, *Dubia*, which in the Narbonensis are also written as *Duvius*, *Duvia* (*OPEL* II, 110 and 112).

24 The photographs in Olivares Pedreño 2002, 220, 221, 227 show that the reading '*Tongenabiagoi*' given by Richert (2005, 7 and 22) is wrong. See also Rodríguez Colmenero 2002; Tranoy 2002.

25 There is no linguistic reason whatsoever to ascribe, with Prósper 1997, the votive string *tongoe Nabiagoi* to the Lusitanian language.

26 As stated by Kelly (1988, 199 with n. 60), 'The terminology connected with the swearing of oaths is extensive', so that he is able to list no less than thirteen different Old Irish substantives denoting various types of oaths. Seven of them are derived from the same verbal stem *tong-* (Matasović 2009, 383) and its compounds, being itself 'The verb most commonly used for "swears"' (Kelly, *ibid.*). This accounts for verbal nouns derived at a later, post-Indo-European stage, such as e.g. ContCelt. *tó**n**gos* with nasal infix included or its synonym *tó**n**c**na**man* with additional nasal suffix at Chamalières. We may recall that also a substantive like *la**n**cea*, a Gaulish loanword in Latin, contradicts Prósper's claim that 'transfer of the nasal infix in the present tense of an Indoeuropean verbal formation to a thematic noun must be rejected as a morphological rarity' (1997, 163).

27 For the adjectival expression of a relationship between two deities postulated by this hypothesis compare the theonymic string *Vesuna Erinia*, translated into Italian as '*Vesona* qui onorata insieme con *Erinis*' by Campanile (2008, II, 869). The same kind of relationship is expressed by means of a different pattern in the theonymic string *deus Mercurius Mithrae* (details in Hensen 2013, 57).

figure sculpted in the left part of the sacred area and the fact that 'Old Irish sagas make numerous references to the practice of swearing by the elements'[28] make me think that the formula rather addresses an oath (*tongos*) sworn by or in the presence of the aforesaid water-deity *Nabia*.[29]

Also in a Celtic perspective, I would like to draw attention to the existence, in the sacred area of Fonte do Idolo and close to the aforesaid formula for (the taking of?) the ***Tongos Nabiagos***, of an aedicula containing a man's head which has a striking structural and iconographic parallel[30] in the Gaulish inscription of Saint-Germain-Source-Seine,[31] which is, by the way, dedicated to the deity dwelling in the river *Sequana*.[32] It is conceivable that, beside the man's head and the fluvial context, the dedication at Saint-Germain-Source-Seine might share with Fonte do Idolo a connection to oath-taking practices.[33]

2. Links with Central Europe: Matres Endeiterae and other deities

2.1. More or less close links with Central Europe can be observed also with regard to several Hispanic divine names. An evident relationship with the Central European population of the *Boii*[34] bears the name of the goddess ***Boiogena*** found at Lara de los Infantes in a dedication *Boiogenae / Numerius | v(otum) s(olvit) l(ibens) m(erito)*,[35] kept at the 'Museo de Burgos' (Fig. 1).

Although the inscription dates from the 2nd or 3rd century AD, the theonym seems to be comparatively archaic from a lexical point of view, given that it probably meant something like 'Mother of the Boii' rather than **'daughter of the Boii'. It would then

---

28 Kelly 1988, 198: 'anyone who broke such an oath could expect to be punished by the elements themselves. [...] It is likely that such forms of oath-taking were used in early Irish law, though no direct evidence has survived.' He exemplifies this statement with a passage out of *Comthoth Lóegairi* (*LU* 9794–9815, cf. also Plummer 1884, 162–72) See also Cross 1969, *passim,* on perjury punished by drowning in literary texts.

29 This alternative also agrees with the existence of one or more settlements called *Tongobriga*. For toponyms of this kind cf. *DCCPlN*, 219 and Prósper 1997, 166. It may be added in passing that, besides the linguistic problems, a dedication such as Prósper's 'to the lake in the valley' (1997, 163) would not suit the monument itself and its French comparandum.

30 Another iconographical coincidence between Hispania and the Gauls has been investigated by Marco Simón 2003.

31 See the photographs in Rodríguez Colmenero 2002, 26; Tranoy 2002, 31; and, respectively, in *RIG*-2/1, 143 and 145; Meid 1989, 43f.; 2014[3], 38.

32 The Gaulish dative singular *Aresequani* points to a deity named *Aresequana* or *Aresequanis*.

33 We may recall that below the tympanon with the main Gaulish dedication in Latin characters, the frame of the French aedicula contains an additional sentence meaning something like 'good (δαγο-) libations/offerings (-λιτους) he made (αυουωτ)'. The verb is actually written <αυοωυ|τ>. See for more details the discussion in de Bernardo Stempel forthcoming: § 2.2.1 with n. 25.

34 On their documentation see now Hainzmann 2015. The goddess is also described by Hernández Guerra 2004, 165, as a 'divinidad de carácter étnico'. The analysis of *Boiogena* as 'nacida del combate' (Prósper 2007, 170), seems rather inadequate now, because it is linked to an obsolete etymology of the ethnic name.

35 No. 11 in Crespo Ortiz de Zárate & Alonso Ávila 1999, 24–5. I warmly thank my friend and colleague J. Arenas-Esteban for providing me with photographs of the inscriptions seen on the 5th September 2014 at Burgos Museum.

have a parallel in personal names like the Norican *Adginna* and *Adginnos*,[36] that is, names belonging to the prototype **Ad-gén(n)o-s*, which is best translated as 'The great procreator' or 'Begetter of a great progeny',[37] particularly on account of the compound Αδγεννοριγ(ος) at Vaucluse, 'The king among the begetters of great progenies': this onomastic type is relatively well preseved in *Adgénnus* and *Adgénnius* (which later became *Adgínnus* and *Adgínnius*[38]), together with its *i*-stem and *n*-stem derivatives *Adgénnis* and *Adgénno*.[39] It should be noted that the archaism postulated for the theonym *BOIOGENA* as opposed to personal names such as *Cintugenos* 'First born' is matched by a ceramic graffito reading Βοιος in Greek characters which has recently been found near Gerona in the Catalan region and is dated already to the 6th century BC.[40]

Fig. 1. Dedication to the goddess *BOIOGENA* (Museo de Burgos, Junta de Castilla y León). Photo: J.A. Arenas-Esteban.

2.2.1. Further links with Central Europe are to be found among the epithets of the Hispanic *MATRES*. First of all, the Hispanic ***MATRES VETERES*** at Porcuna[41] match exactly the *VETERES* aka *SENAE* known from Britain and Noricum as well as, in the singular number, from Aquitaine.[42] In this context one should also recall the semantic affinity between the Hispanic ***SENAICOS*** < **Sena-k(o)-yo-s* and the British *DEUS VETER* or *HENOS*, which was already pointed out on previous occasions.[43]

2.2.2. Most strikingly, also the Hispanic ***MATRES ENDEITERAE***[44] at Clunia[45] can now be

36 Listed by Kakoschke 2012, 232–3.

37 It should, nevertheless, be mentioned that a different translation ('zum Geschlechte gehörig') is offered by Schmidt (*KGPN*, 112).

38 Also written *Aginius*.

39 Listed by Raybould & Sims-Williams 2009, 191–2; *KGPN*, 112f.

40 Published by Casas Genover & de Hoz 2011.

41 See, among others, Núñez Marcén & Blanco 2002, 60; Hernández Guerra & García Martínez 2002, 150.

42 See now de Bernardo Stempel 2008, with older bibliography. The Norican inscription was published by Dolenz *et al.* 2004.

43 As in de Bernardo Stempel 2008b, 75, for example.

44 The Gaulish accentuation implied by the diachronical reconstruction of this epithet (see below) indicates that the nominative plural was not ***ENDEITERAS* with the archaic Celtiberian ending as assumed by Beltrán Lloris & Díaz Ariño 2007, 49–50.

45 There are actually two inscriptions from Clunia, dated to the 1st cent. AD, which contain the same votive string *Matribus endeiteris*, namely no. 62 and no. 63 in Crespo Ortiz de Zárate & Alonso Ávila 1999, 54 and 55, corresponding to no. 6.b and no. 6.c in Gómez-Pantoja 1999, 423. The first dedication is Inv. no. 4600, 'Museo de Burgos', where I saw it on 5th September 2014 [Fig. 2]. The second

shown to be a semantic equivalent of the Narbonensic (ματρες) Ανδοουνναι at Collias (*RIG*-G-183). It is possible to trace back the hitherto unexplained epithet[46] *ENDEITERAE* to a protoform **andoterai* 'the deeper ones' by way of **ande*^{i}*térai* > **endeitérai*. Both sound changes assumed are not infrequent, namely the assimilation of (both) pretonic vowels to the vowel of the stressed syllable on the one hand,[47] and the typically Celtic (pre-)palatalization of consonants in palatal environments on the other. The latter sound change is particularly frequent in several dialectal areas of the Iberian Peninsula.[48] Also the usage of the inherited oppositional suffix *-*tero*- for deriving divine names is well known in Spain, where it is found in the name of the goddess *DUITERA* from a protoform **DUBITERA* 'The dark(er) one', possibly representing an epithet of the night-goddess called in Celtic *ATAECINA*.[49]

Fig. 2. Dedication to the *MATRES ENDEITERAE* (Museo de Burgos, Junta de Castilla y León). Photo: J.A. Arenas-Esteban.

As to the Gaulish pendant (ματρες) Ανδοουνναι of the Hispanic *MATRES ENDEITERAE*, their relationship to the underworld, called in Welsh *annwfn* > *annwn*, was unearthed by myself in 1989. On account of the Welsh comparandum, namely *annwfn* < **an(de)-dúbno-*, the most adequate reconstruction for the Gaulish epithet Ανδοουνναι still seems that of a pluralized *ā*-stem theonymic derivative **Andedúbn-ā* or else **An(de)dúbn-ā* with haplology. The attested form correponds, however, to a nom. plur. [andounnai],[50] written <andoounnai> because of the Greek orthographic convention of noting the diphthong [ou] with <oou>, as in the inscriptions *RIG* G-153, G-154, and G-163.

is at Clunia in the museum at the excavation site [Fig. 3]. The reasons for reading *endeiteris* also in the first of them are explained in particular by Beltrán Lloris & Díaz Ariño 2007, 36–7, 49–50, fig. 11–13). It should be noted in passing that Hernández Guerra 2004, 162, still retains the wrong reading ***Tendeiteris* for the first inscription although the form had been duly corrected in *idem* & García Martínez 2002, 150.

46 With respect to its interpretation, Núñez Marcén & Blanco consider that 'habida cuenta del lugar de procedencia y la variedad de epítetos documentados, parece poco probable poder atribuirle el "habitual" valor tópico' (2002, 57).

47 See de Bernardo Stempel 2013b, 44 with further bibliography, and 79. The derivational basis *ande-*, also contained in Gaul. *andero-* 'inferior', *andernados* 'below', *andamico-* 'of lowest quality' (DLG^2 s.vv.) has been discussed in de Bernardo Stempel 1987, 73–5.

48 For an actualized study of the various outcomings and of the processes involved see now de Bernardo Stempel 2011.

49 See Chapter XII in this volume.

50 That is, if the Collias inscription is not an isolated instance of redundant writing <{o}ου> representing a simple vowel [u] and the divine name was actually *ANDUNNAI* in the nominative plural.

Fig. 3. Dedication to the *Matres endeiterae*
(Museo de Clunia, Junta de Castilla y León). Photo: F. Tuset Bertran.

There are therefore two alternative possibilities:

A. Unlike the Welsh comparandum, the Continental Celtic divine-name may have not yet been reduced by haplology. In this case, a nominative plural **Andedúbnai* would have developed to **Anðeðúβnai* >**Anðoðúβnai* > **Andoúnnai* with (i.) rounding of the pretonic vowel before the vowel *u* of the stressed syllable; (ii.) early dissimilatory loss of the second (voiced) dental fricative; (iii.) assimilation of *-βn-* to *-nn-*.

B. If, however, the Continental Celtic divine-name underwent the same reduction by haplology as the Brittonic form, one would have to assume that the etymological vowel **-u-* had been dissimilated to *-o-*, i.e. lowered before the lenition product *-wn-* < **-βn-* Under this phonetically somewhat less plausible hypothesis, the nasal consonant's gemination would have to be attributed to its posttonic position, thus suggesting that the votive string was still pronounced [an'dounnabo].[51]

2.2.3. One may note in passing that the new interpretation offered here for the Hispanic *Matres endeiterae* might shed new light also on an epithet of the ***Matres*** found in the Rioja. It is the epithet ***useae***, which results from the alternative reading as *Matribus / Useis* of the votive string in a Laguardia inscription.

It ought to be noted, firstly, that although a reading '*Matribus / Festis*' has been meanwhile proposed by Núñez Marcén and Blanco, the reason behind such a proposal was, nevertheless, not purely epigraphical.[52] Secondly, that the epithet '*festae*' proposed by Núñez Marcén and Blanco would be quite unparalleled and is not recorded in the

51 See de Bernardo Stempel 1989 and 2010a, 76 with the improvements contributed by Lindeman 1991, 146 and Eska 1992.

52 Núñez Marcén & Blanco 2002, 51–3.

large F.E.R.C.AN.-list of epithets and epicleseis.[53] Thirdly, that a second instance of the traditional reading may lie behind an another Riojan votive string, namely *Mat(ribus) U(seis?)* from Canales de la Sierra.

If *useis* and not ‡*festis* were the proper reading also at Laguardia, the underlying epithet *USEAE* would represent the antonym of the mother-goddesses of the underworld, called *ENDEITERAE* in ancient Spain and Ανδοουνναι in Narbonensis. The epithet, at first spelt *USIAI*, may indeed have been derived from an archaic comparative **upsis* 'upper', the *MATRES USEAE* (< **upsyai*) thus being the 'Mother goddesses of the upper world', that is, of our world.[54] The Celtic languages are indeed known for preserving archaic comparatives formed by adding the inherited comparative morpheme **-yōs/-yos/-is* to a 'slim' derivational base lacking the characteristic suffixes of the positive grade.[55] It would therefore be advisable to take another look at the stone which is now owned by a private citizen.

2.3. It is also worth mentioning that the goddesses ***RIXAMAE***, found on a *tabula aenea ansata* at Arucci in the province of Huelva (Baeturia Celtica),[56] but ascribed by Martial to his Celtiberian homeland when he speaks of *choros(que) Rixamarum*,[57] share their divine name with the epithet *RIGISAMOS*, 'king-like' and hence 'most kingly' of a British and Aquitanian *MARS*.[58] Interestingly however, the Hispanic **Rigisamai* presents a slightly modernized variant of the latter, with unmistakably 'Gaulish' stress and pretonic syncope in the form of the nominative plural: **rig(i)sámae* > *RIXÁMAE*.

2.4. Another Gaulish deity that also seems to have been venerated in Spain is ***DAMONA***, the 'divine cow'.[59] The name of this goddess is matched by the personal name ***Damunia***, embedded, in the form of the dative singular, in a funerary inscription engraved on the right flank of a *verraco* found in the wall of the hillfort of San Esteban at Muelas del Pan and exhibited at the at the 'Museo de Zamora' (Fig. 4). [60] According to Domínguez

53 Also *HEp* 12 (2002) 3 no. 1 qualifies it as 'inusitado'.

54 On the Celtic upper and nether world see, for example, Delamarre 1999.

55 *NWÄI*, 423–424. See *CCCGr*, 184, and also *GOI*, 236 § 375 and 527 § 850, for the 'irregular' comparatives meaning 'higher'.

56 *Iunia · Avita / Rixamis / a(nimo)·l(ibens)·d(edit)*; see Gimeno Pascual & Rothenhöfer 2012. Bermejo 2014 is quite weak on the philological side.

57 *Epigrammata*: IV, 55, 16, see Shackleton Bailey 1993, 302–3.

58 On the invocation *MARS RIGISAMOS*, corresponding to Latin *MARS REX*, see *NWÄI* 392–3 with n. 12, and 429–30, as well as de Bernardo Stempel 2008b, 79; 2014, 18.

59 See Jufer & Luginbühl 2001, 36–7; Fauduet 2007, 180; *DLG*[2], 135; *DCML*, 75–6.

60 Inventory number MZA 93/25/C/21/67. The term *verraco* is used for a mostly pre-Roman sculpted bull or boar usually placed along the routes along which the shepherds drove their cows to pasture. Their functions are resumed as follows by Marco Simón: 'Estas esculturas de toros y jabalíes [...] tienen un significado religioso y cultual ampliamente reconocido [...] y diversamente concretado, así como una significación funeraria especialmente manifestada en época romana; pero pueden tener también un valor simbólico y funcional como delimitadores de áreas de pasto y expresión de estatus social de [...]los "señores del ganado" [...]' (2008, 284). Álvarez Sanchís (2003, 102) speaks of a 'función apotropaica [de las esculturas] como defensoras del poblado y el ganado', while a good survey can be found in Álvarez Sanchís 2008; see also Álvarez Sanchís 2005.

Bolaños & Nuño González,[61] this *verraco* represented a bull with his usual attributes, and the full inscription reads *D(is) M(anibus) Damunie an(norum) XVI.*

Given that the vowel labialization in labial environment, leading from *-mo-* to *-mu-*, is a well-known feature of the Hispanic Celticity (as well as of other areas of the Keltiké),[62] and that the derivational morpheme *-yā* is also contained in the Norican divine name *[C]ARVONIA* for 'The divine deer',[63] it is possible to trace the personal name *Damunia* back to the theonym *DAMONA*, which is what the very form and the main function of a verraco may suggest.[64] We may recall that at Boubonne-les-Bains the author of a dedication to the goddess *DAMONA* bears the theophoric name *Daminius*,[65] which is also attested in Belgica and Britain as well as among the potters at Lezoux, while at La Graufesenque, in Aquitania, and in Lugdunensis there are instances of the more archaic theophoric personal name *Damonus*.[66]

Fig. 4. Verraco with funerary inscription for *Damunia* (Museo de Zamora, Junta de Castilla y León). Photo: R. García Rozas.

On account of the above-mentioned Norican theonym, the theophoric personal name *Damunia* engraved on the Muelas del Pan-verraco because of its earlier funerary employment may even have been based on an expanded variant (that is, determined by means of the suffix **-yā*) of the divine name itself. In either case, the Zamora find points to the existence of a Hispanic cult of the goddess *DAMONA* on the Iberian Peninsula.

2.5. One finds, moreover, Hispanic divine names that are, if not formally, at least semantically similar to Central European ones. Of the first type is the affinity, already remarked upon several times,[67] between *NEMETONA* in Belgica, possibly the *MATRAE NEMETIALES* at Grenoble,[68] and the Hispanic divine names ***NEMEDOS*** and ***NIMMEDOS*** at Mieres and Segovia.

61 Domínguez Bolaños & Nuño González 1994, 167–8. I thank Alonso Domínguez Bolaños who kindly sent me the relevant pages of their unpublished excavation report.

62 See Eska 1995; de Bernardo Stempel 2015.

63 See the evidence in Hainzmann *et al.* 2017. This integration seems more likely than ***[T]ARVONIA* on account of the plastic representations of deers found in the area, as in the Strettweg cult-chariot.

64 See note 60 above.

65 The various aspects of Celtic theophoric names have been studied by de Bernardo Stempel 2008c.

66 *NPC* 81; *OPEL* II, 92; Kakoschke 2006, 157; 2011, 91; *NTS* 3, 240–51.

67 Firstly by Marco Simón 1993; see also *idem* 2003, 133.

68 On account of the votive string MATRIS | NEMETIALI, Rémy (2008, 219) wonders whether the dedication was a complex one instead and invoked a god *NEMETIALIS* besides the generic *MATRES*.

A solely semantic affinity seems to exist, by contrast, between *Videtillos* in Dijon on a bronze mask dated to ca. 150 AD[69] and the Riojan theonym ***Dercetios*** [70] 'The seeing one', provided that the Latinized oronym *Dercetius* was not the origin of the god called *Dercetios*, as has been sometimes assumed, but just a secondary formation, that is, a place name due to the veneration of the homonymous god on that Spanish mountain.[71] The first divine name is a mixed-language theonym which appears to be derived from the Latin verb *vidēre*,[72] and both invocations contain the same agentive suffix *-etios*.

2.5.1. I should add that, whenever the divine names belonging to this second type express the same meaning through different languages, the Celtic ones may be replicas of classical attributes of so-called 'Mediterranean' deities.[73] Accordingly, it is not impossible that the two last-mentioned divine names were actually descriptions, albeit used *sine dei nomine*, of the Graeco-Roman *Apollo* whose excellent sight was recorded by no less than eight Greek epithets.[74]

2.5.2. This is even more probable in the case of the deity originally called ***Endovelecos*** in Portugal.[75] His name, recently attested in the votive string *Endove[l]eco d(eo)*,[76] apparently goes back to an agentive velar derivative **Endo-wéle-ko-s* 'He who sees inside/in the deep'.[77] The original form of the god's name became regularly *Endovélicos* by vowel weakening in unstressed position, and, at times, *Endovólicos* with vowel labialization behind *-w-*[78] or even *Ennovólicos*[79] by assimilation of the etymological *nd*-nexus. The variant *Endovólicos* led, in its turn, regularly to *Endovóllicos*, and in the same way a theonymic variant *Endovéllicos* was regularly developed from the original form *Endovélicos*.[80]

We may hence compare it[81] with those Greek epithets of the classical *Apollo*

69 See Delamarre 2007, 199; Rapsaet-Charlier 2012, 54, 61, 72.
70 See Olivares Pedreño 2002, 117.
71 Mentioned by Marco Simón 1998, 79; Olivares Pedreño 2002, 117.
72 Note that Fauduet, in her London F.E.R.C.AN. lecture 2005, showed a Gaulish dedication *deo Videtio* with an eye engraved below the name of the god.
73 On the huge problem of recognizing which deities are not indigenous see also § 5 below.
74 See de Albentiis Hienz *et al.* 2013, 53. More details in § 2.5.2.
75 A history of the archaeological investigation is given by Schattner *et al.* 2005, while Olivares Pedreño 2002, 228ff., lists the older interpretations proposed for the god, to which Grenier 1953–1954 ought to be added. On the cult of the classical *Apollo* in Portugal see Gil Mantas 2002.
76 The inscription itself is edited by Guerra *et al.* 2003, 460–1.
77 As in the clearly Celtic 'function name' of the prophetess *Veleda* (Birkhan 1997, 897–8.; Egeler 2013, 29. For the transmission of the name and the historical details cf. Hofeneder 2005–2011, II, 475–8). On the Insular Celtic verbs from the same root see *DKP*, 609–75.
78 Perhaps prompted by the proximity of a velar *-l-*, see de Bernardo Stempel 2015.
79 The inscription itself is edited by Guerra *et al.* 2003, 459–60.
80 On posttonic gemination, see de Bernardo Stempel 2010a. Later variants of this divine name are *Enobólicos*, with assimilation to *n(n)* of the etymological nexus *nd* as well as the hypercorrect writing <b> of the labiodental consonant *-v-*, and the Latinate *Indovéllicus*. For a list of the various attested forms see Cardim Ribeiro 2002, 88, as well as Olivares Pedreño 2002, 229, with some additions in Guerra *et al.* 2003, 457–61; cf. also Guerra 2008. Rather speculative are the etymologies hitherto proposed for the divine name and the variants at study. The same is true for Cardim Ribeiro 2009.
81 This does, however, not apply to the divine name *Velicos*, which, notwithstanding Calado 1996, is just a monophthongized variant of the indigenous theonym *Vaelicos*, whose cult at Postoloboso appears

which describe his outstanding sight, such as εὔσκοπος 'well-sighted', ὠκύσκοπος 'sharp-sighted', and τηλέσκοπος 'far-sighted', together with πανδερκὴς ἔχων ὄμμα, εἰσορόων πάντα, ἐπόψιος, ἐπόπτης, and πανόψιος, all of them describing an 'all-seing' god.[82] Of these epithets *Endovelecos* may very well have been a replica by *explication vel translatio Celtica*, that is, in the same way in which the Gaulish (*Apollo Grannos*) *amarcolitanos* is a Celtic rendering of Greek (Ἀπόλλων) τηλέσκοπος.[83]

The assumption that *Endovelecos*' name with all its later phonetic variants was just a secondary theonym, originating from a Celtic epithet used *sine dei nomine* of the Graeco-Roman *Apollo*, can be traced back, in nuce, to Antonio Martínez de Quesada in the 18th century,[84] before being favoured in modern times by Olivares Pedreño.[85] It is even more plausible if we take into account that the god venerated as *Endovelecos* is not only a *deus sanctus* and a benevolent deity invoked to recover one's health (as documented by the dedications *pro salute(m!)*[86]), but also an oracular deity (as attested by the dedications *ex responsu(m!), (ex) iussu numinis* besides *iussu ipsius*, and also *ex visu*), which is, above all, described as a *praestantissimum numen*: one shall recall that *Apollo* himself was called both *sanctus* and *praestantissimus* (as also περικαλλής and κάλλιστος in Greek),[87] and that he was a healer and a prophet as stated by at least 12 and, respectively, 45 different classical epithets. Even the fact that one of his dedications was offered *ex imperato Averno* tallies with Apollo's chthonian aspect documented by the Greek epithet χθόνιος. Last but not least, all we know about *Endovelecos*'cult is Roman, including his iconography.[88]

3. Hidden Hispanic theonyms

3.1. The case of *Damunia* just discussed in § 2.4 shows that one must not forget the evidence provided by theophoric personal and family names whenever one wants to trace a reliable panorama of the cults present in a certain region.

Analogously, the genitival clan-name *Ateroecon* engraved as the only word on the right flank of another verraco seems to imply the veneration of a group of 'Fathers' or

---

to have been completely different from that of the god described as *Endovelecos* at San Miguel da Mota: see on *Vaelicos* Cardim Ribeiro 2002, 80; Marco Simón 2008, 278.

82 As discussed in de Albentiis Hienz *et al.* 2013, 53.

83 See de Albentiis Hienz *et al.* 2013, 93, 96.

84 *Pace* Cardim Ribeiro 2005, 723, 754, who thinks of *Endovelecos* as a kind of *Silvanus* or *Faunus*.

85 'El carácter oracular y salutífero del dios *Endouellicus* apunta, en nuestra opinión, un carácter apolíneo claro' (Olivares Pedreño 2002, 231).

86 For this and the following dedications to *Endovelecos* see Cardim Ribeiro 2002, 88–9; d'Encarnação 2008.

87 For this and the following epithets of *Apollo* see de Albentiis Hienz *et al.* 2013, 43, 57, 59, 69–70, 73, 76–8.

88 'L'iconographie d'*Endouellicus* évoque celle des divinités classiques: il est représenté nu, avec le manteau sur le dos' (Guerra 2008, 166). Cardim Ribeiro (2002, 80) moreover stresses that 'à excepção do teónimo em si mesmo, tudo o mais que se conhece acerca desta divindade apresenta um cunho perfeitamente "clássico", de feição plenamente romana: a iconografia do deus; as estátuas dos devotos; os monumentos epigráficos e os elementos rituais; a linguagem e os formulários neles expressos; os relevos simbólicos patentes em certas aras; a quase totalidade dos respectivos dedicantes'.

Ateres as in Brittany at Plumergat,[89] given that it may be traced to a former **(P)atero-k(o)-yo-m*.[90]

3.2.1. Often forgotten is the presence of the god ***Belenos*** in the Iberian Peninsula. His cult can not only be assumed on the basis of the probably theophoric personal name *Belenos* painted on two ceramic vessels traditionally classified as Iberian and found along the Catalan coast,[91] but is also documented by the family name *Belainocum* in a Roman inscription from Ablanque in the province of Guadalajara.[92] Going back to **Belán-yo-kōm*, this genitival 'family name' refers either to a group (collegium?) of priests or cultores of *Bélenos* in its later variant *Bélanos* (i.e., with weakened posttonic vowel), or else to the clan descending from a man who bore the theophoric name *Bélainos* < **Bélan-yo-s*.[93]

3.2.2. The widely-known Celtic spring-god *Belenos*[94] may also be hidden in the Iberian Peninsula behind the tabuistic theonymic label *Airu*. It has been remarked several times that the name of a deity, far from revealing the actual complexity of his, her or their *vires*, just gives us a glimpse at his, her or their original function. However, not even this is always true.

Although we know that a springs or water god was venerated in the Iberian Peninsula under the Celtic name ***Airu***,[95] and that a particularly deep well is still known in Spanish as *pozo airón*,[96] various Celtic cognates make clear that *Airu* < **ary-ō(n)* is not a proper theonym,[97] but just a taboo name, a synonym of the various *Maglos*, *Rego*, *Veroris* < **Upero-rik-s*, and *Vlatos*.[98] Old Irish *aire* means indeed 'noble, chief', and Gaulish *ariios* at Saint-Germain-Source-Seine (*RIG* *L-12) seems to indicate a high priest or magistrate, while a plural *arioune*s 'lords' (written as <ariuones>, i.e. with inversion

89 *RIG* L-15 = M8 in Davies *et al.* 2000, 237–44, with comments by Sims-Williams 2003, 78–9. On its interpretation see de Bernardo Stempel 1997, 101–3.

90 Although the latter has been classified as a genitival family-name, the fact that it is the only word on the right flank of a verraco together with its semantics ('of The fatherly') may suggest at least a relationship to a plural divine name. For more details, cf. Álvarez Sanchis 2008, 174 and de Bernardo Stempel 2011, 182 with n. 42.

91 See the discussion in de Bernardo Stempel 2002, 90; cf. also Arenas-Esteban *et al.* 2011, 123.

92 No. 3 in Gamo Pazos 2012.

93 The various forms of the god's name and its etymology are discussed en detail in de Bernardo Stempel 2013e, 78–80.

94 See the bibliography in note 93 above.

95 González Rodríguez & Marco Simón 2009, 68, 78.

96 See Abascal Palazón 2011.

97 Contrary to what is suggested e.g. by Abascal Palazón, who interprets '*Airo* o *Aironis*' as 'formado a partir de un nombre común desconocido para nosotros', 'es decir, como un teónimo formado a partir de una voz común de la lengua céltica prerromana que identificaba un manantial o lugar en que brotaba el agua' (2011, 255 and 254).

98 De Bernardo Stempel 2010b, 106–8. Cf. in this sense already García Alonso 2007.

of the digraph <ou>[99]) is attested in the Lepontic inscription of Prestino.[100] In addition, a close cognate of those *ARIOUNES VOLTIAVI* is apparently represented by the theonymic formula *ARIOUNI MINCOSEGAEIGI* 'The much seezing/ frequently winning lords', attested in Orense.[101]

There is also no room for doubt about the literal meaning 'The Lord' of the Hispanic divine name *AIRU*. This, however, does not necessarily imply the existence of a spring or water god solely named '*AIRU*' and necessarily distinct from the widespread Celtic *BELENOS*. The invocation *AIRU* was, in any case, just a tabuistic substitute for the actual theonym.

4. The Hispanic types of 'Interpretatio Romana'

At this point, I should like to offer some remarks about the types of *interpretatio Romana* actually documented on the Iberian Peninsula, putting some order into what has been said on the topic by various authors.

4.1. First of all, it is not adequate to speak of *interpretatio Romana* whenever we find a Graeco-Roman/Mediterranean or else oriental theonym accompanied by a detoponymic epithet of appurtenance.

A theonymic string such as, among many others, ***SALUS UMERITANA*** 'The Salus from Emerita' (with *Emeritana becoming ***Um****eritana* on the Otañes patera[102]) is actually not different from a theonymic string of the type of *SULEVIAE NANTUGACAE*,[103] 'The *SULEVIAE* of the valleys' at Condado (Orense). Even if the essence of the original cult will have slightly changed according to the various places of worship, the mere addition of an epithet of appurtenance does not respond to an intent of interpreting the deity involved by linking it to a different cultual environment.[104]

4.2. Real instances of *interpretatio Romana* are those documented in the theonymic strings which we now call *identificationes Romanae vel indigenae*, namely where two

99 The digraph <ou> was used for representing /u/ in several Old Celtic texts, not only in the Gallo-Greek and occasionally in the Celtiberian corpus, but even in some Gallo-Latin documents such as the gold lamina of Baudecet or the big brick inscription of Châteaubleau. On the digraph in Palaeohispanic texts cf. now my contribution in *Acta Palaeohispanica XII* (forthcoming).

100 Which may be translated into Latin as 'Summus hospes, Blialeti (filius), dominis Voltiavis sedes dedit', cf. de Bernardo Stempel 2014b, 94–5.

101 See the discussion in de Bernardo Stempel 2010b, 107 n. 6; 2011, 187; 2016, 197–8.

102 See note 62 above and Olivares Pedreño 2002, 126–7.

103 The dialectal palatalization (see note 49 above) in the attested votive string *Sule(vi)is nantug****aic****is* (cf. Olivares Pedreño 2002, 97) may have been prompted by the dative-plural ending *-is*. Therefore, it seems probable that the involved epithet was not the usually restituted ‡*NANTUGAICAE* with threefold suffixation (that is, the feminine nominative plural of a supposed polyderivative **{*nantu+-k(o)-+-ak(o)-+-yo-*}), but simply *NANTUGACAE*, namely the plural of an original name **Nantu-kā* redetermined with a second velar suffix after lenition affected the former one.

104 Compare what is said in Kuhnen 1996, 142, on behalf of the Trier *LARES*: 'Eine Gleichsetzung der Laren mit keltischen Gottheiten fand nicht statt. Funde von Larenstatuetten in Gallien setzen also entweder einen hohen Grad der Romanisierung von Einheimischen voraus oder gehörten Römern aus anderen Reichsgebieten, die hier lebten'.

deities belonging to different Panthea and with completely different names[105] are (partially) equated.[106] To this type belongs e.g. ***Apollo Grannos*** at Astorga.[107]

4.3. By contrast, what really is almost absent from the theonymic corpus of the Iberian Peninsula is not *interpretatio Romana* altogether, but votive strings of a kind well attested in Gaul and Central Europe (as has been hinted at by Olivares Pedreño, albeit in a general and unspecific way[108]), namely those in which the name of a Graeco-Roman deity is accompanied by a Gaulish description of the very same deity. This is the case for ***Hermes devoris*** at Chaves,[109] for example, which refers in Celtic to the same classical god elsewhere known as *Mercurius deorum rex*, thus belonging to the category we now call *explicationes vel translationes Celticae*.[110] A further instance of this procedure may have been the *praestantissimus* (*Apollo*?) *Endovelecos* discussed above in § 2.5.2.

The utter scarcity of such Celtic and actually Gaulish descriptions for the classical deities in the Iberian Peninsula is, however, hardly surprising, given that the Gaulish language was never widely spoken in the Hispanic provinces, at least not in the centuries in which our Roman votive inscriptions were written.

4.3.1. The same reason may also account for the denomination ***matres*** not being replaced by that of *matronae* in the Iberian Peninsula: there, the invocation *matres* was certainly felt as truly Roman and not as linguistically Celtic (that is, as if it were the result of a syncopated archaic Celtic nominative plural **máteres*) so that there was no need for a replacement. Accordingly, the lack of familiarity with the Gaulish language explains why in the Iberian Peninsula – other than, for example, in both Germaniae – there are no instances of the invocation *matres* being substituted by an unambiguously Roman term such as the elsewhere much used classifier *matronae* for the mother-goddesses.[111]

5. Indigenous Hispanic divine names?

5.1. Another point which I would like to stress is that one should not classify automatically as 'indigenous' any unfamiliar divine name.

In the case of the dedication in the Portuguese rock sanctuary of Panóias, for example, there are several reasons for reverting to a classical explication of the votive string *Diis Deabusque ... omnibusque Numinibus et* (scil. *numinibus*) *Lapitearum*.[112]

105 That is, different both in form and in semantic content.
106 See most recently de Bernardo Stempel 2014, 33–5; 2013d, 31–2.
107 Richert 2005, 48 no. 37; Olivares Pedreño 2008, 245. A further example is the Identificatio mentioned by Macrobius (Hofeneder 2005–2011, III, 124 T 1) between *Mars* and *Netos* (venerated in Celtiberian as *Neitos*, and in the Hispanoceltic corpus as *Netu*); Marco Simón 2012, 220.
108 Olivares Pedreño 2008; see also Marco Simón 2010; 2012; 2013.
109 Richert 2005, 46; Olivares Pedreño 2008, 245.
110 See the bibliography in note 144 below.
111 On the reasons for such a substitution, cf. also de Bernardo Stempel & Hainzmann 2009, 81; 2010, 32.
112 The whole inscription reads *Diis Deabusque aeternum lacum omnibusque Numinibus et Lapitearum*

Even if not favoured in modern times, the analysis of the theonymic string **(*NUMINA*) *LAPITEARUM*** as referring to the mythological Greek Λαπίθαι,[113] is indeed the most powerful both for linguistic and cultual reasons:[114]

1) The Λαπίθαι were an originally Thessalian population, partly historical and partly mythological, members of which were also found in other Greek regions. Some of them boasted of their descent from a Thessalian river god and a nymph by way of Apollo, and they were also involved in combats with Heracles, defeated the Centaurs, and took part in the quest of the Argonauts.[115] Legends regarding the Λαπίθαι were represented in the temple of *APÓLLON EPIKOÚRIOS* at Bassai in Arkadia, and of Zeus at Olympia.[116]

And in Panóias rock sanctuary, at only a small distance from the aforementioned inscription,[117] the very same dedicant *G(aius) C. Calp(urnius) Rufinus v(ir) c(larissimus)* offered two dedications to *SERAPIS*, a Graeco-Aegyptian god of ultimately Greek origin.[118] The first of them[119] is in Latin and includes *ISIS*;[120] the second is even written in Greek (with the exception of the dedicant's name), and includes besides 'Serapis, the Highest' also 'Kore, the Earth',[121] thereby expressly mentioning the celebration of mysterical rytes as the aim of the place (και μυσταριοις).

There is, on the contrary, no specific reason for supposing an indigenous deity in this same cult context.[122]

2) The adaptation of the Greek substantive Λαπίθαι to Latin phonetics and morphology would have automatically produced *LAPITAE* in old times, and hence

cum hoc templo sacravit G(aius) C. Calp(urnius) Rufinus v(ir) c(larissimus), in quo hostiae voto cremantur, see now also Correia Santos *et al.* 2014, 210–2; I am deeply indebted to Maria João Correia Santos for sending me this publication.

113 Proposed by Jerónimo Contador de Argote already in the year 1732, and followed by José d'Encarnação 1975, cf. *ibid.* at p. 250 and p. 252–3: 'Ora acontece precisamente que os Lapíteas se podem filiar – com muita probabilidade – nos *Lapithae* da Tessália; seriam, portanto, não autóctones ou pelo menos, não pertencentes a um estrato étnico suficientemente recuado para os considerarmos indígenas. De resto, tal hipótese encontra apoio no facto de haver na mesma «cidade» de Panoias uma inscrição em grego'.

114 Note that even Untermann, although favouring a different explanation, reckons with an influence of the Greek name Λαπίθαι: 'Wie eine griechische Inschrift im Heiligtum zeigt, waren Sprecher dieser Sprache am dortigen Kultleben beteiligt, und es ist nicht auszuschliessen, dass diese etwas von dem sagenhaften Volk der Λαπίθαι – *Lapithae* – Lapithen in Thessalien gewusst haben' (2006, 256).

115 More details in *DMGR*, 252–3. See also Graves 2004, 353–5, who mentions orgiastic rites and a connection with the Eleusian mysteries.

116 See Larson 2009, 99; Dowden 2010, 42.

117 For the placement of the various inscriptions, see Rodríguez Colmenero 1995, 173; Alföldy 2002, 211.

118 See Dunand 2010, 259–61; van Andringa 2011, 85; *DMGR s.v.* 'Apis'.

119 See the new reading by Correia Santos *et al.* 2014, 205–10.

120 'Isis, comme mère des dieux, comme victorieuse des puissances de la nuit, posséda très vite des mystères, et c'est sous cet aspect qu'elles se prêta à diverses identifications dans la religion hellénique.' (*DMGR*, 238). See also Alvar Ezquerra & Muñiz Grijalvo 2002.

121 One of the two new readings proposed by Correia Santos *et al.* 2014, 213–8, gives the votive string of the involved dedication as Υψισ(τω) τω Σεραπιδι συν Γα Κορα.

122 As has been done, among others, by Blázquez: 'aquí el consagrante ha introducido un elemento local' (1975, 112); Rodríguez Colmenero: 'los *Lapitae*, sin duda el grupo gentilicio poseedor del lugar' (1993, 64); Blázquez: 'probablemente, el nombre del pueblo' (1995, 54); Alföldy 2002, 12.

possibly, instead of the more regular ***Lapitarum*, an analogical genitive **Lapitaerum*, written *Lapitearum* by simple graphical transposition.

The theonymic string *NUMINA LAPITEARUM* implies that the genitive plural *Lapitearum* is a substantive, as e.g. in *et numinibus Augustorum*.[123] It is rather awkward to trace it back, with some authors, to an adjective, and in particular to Lat. *lapideus*.[124]

The explanation favoured here is also more straightforward than to postulate a hypercorrect writing of an unparalleled indigenous variant of the frequent Latin genitive *lapidum* 'of the stones'.[125]

3) Last but not least, the explanation favoured here is the only one that accounts for the 1st-declension genitive plural,[126] which can be satisfactorily explained only by means of an originally Greek ethnic name whose nominative plural ended in -αι.

It is, in fact, not feasible to reconstruct a totally unparalleled theonymic string ***NUMINA FATARUM LAPITEARUM* in order to account for the *primo visu* feminine gender of the genitive referring to *numinibus* in the inscription at study: one did normally not use more than one theonymic classifier belonging to the same linguistic milieu. If such had been the case, the rarely used classifier *NUMEN* which, moreover, mostly referred to male divine powers,[127] would have been perfectly redundant.

Also the cruel character of the rites to be performed at Panóias[128] seems to agree better with the orgiastic Λαπίθαι than with the *NYMPHAE* or *MATRES* postulated by several scholars.[129] Accordingly, the *NUMINA LAPITEARUM* appear to have been neither indigenous nor Latin, but Greek in origin.[130]

5.2. At Évora, in Portugal, the theonymic string ***CARNEUS CALANTICE(N)SIS*** has been analysed by Prósper as if containing a Celtic theonym *KARNIOS* referring to an indigenous god of the cairns and followed by a Latinized epithet *CALANTICE(N)SIS*.[131] Although such an analysis is not implausible, what we know at the moment may suggest that the god involved was the Graeco-Roman *APOLLO*, as very probably also in the case of the

123 *RIB* III 3180, from Nettleham. There is therefore no need to take, with Untermann 2006, 254, *Lapitearum* as referring to the following *cum hoc templo*.

124 In this sense Guerra: 'It is suggested, at least as an alternative to the traditional interpretation, that the name *Lapitearum* could correspond to an adjective, associated with the Latin word *lapis*, with the *t* being a hypercorrection.' (2002, 157–8 and 147).

125 As is done by Untermann 2006, 255 and 251, according to whom the alleged 'adjective' 'contain[s] a word of the Preroman language of Galicia with the meaning "stone, rock", related to Lat. *lapis*'.

126 The incongruence of the *primo visu* female gender seems to have excaped most scholars, with the exception of Carlos Búa, see Guerra 2002a, 63; Untermann 2006, 254.

127 Untermann 2006, 255 n. 16, recalls its usage instead of *DEUS* or *GENIUS* and also in theonymic formulae such as *NUMEN AUGUSTI* and the likes.

128 Cf. in particular ... *cum hoc templo... in quo hostiae voto cremantur* in the very same inscription, and *Hostiae, quae cadunt, hic immolantur. Exta intra quadrata contra cremantur. Sanguis laciculis iuxta superfunditur* in the first inscription of the sanctuary; Correia Santos *et al.* 2014, 210–2, 204–5.

129 Among them Untermann 2006, 254–5, with further bibliography.

130 More examples of Greek divine names embedded in indigenous dedications can be found in de Bernardo Stempel forthcoming.

131 Prósper 2002, 173–5. In the same sense also Lajoye 2008, 169–70, who proposes a similar reading for another inscription.

PRAESTANTISSIMUS (*APOLLO*?) *ENDOVELECOS* discussed above in § 2.5.2.

Indeed, as was recently suggested by de Albentiis Hienz and myself,[132] the theonymic string *CARNEUS CALANTICE(N)SIS* may simply refer to the well-known 'Apollo of the ram', who was venerated in Greece, among others, under the more or less homophonous names κάρνειος, καρνεῖος, and καρνῆιος (besides κάρνος, καρνίας, and τράγιος). Accordingly, the attested votive string *Carneo Calantice(n)si* may just represent the regular dative of a Latinate (*APOLLO*) *CARNEUS* followed by an equally Latinate albeit indigenous epithet of appurtenance.[133]

5.3. A classical deity may also lie behind the votive strings *Cornuto Cordono* and *deo Cordono* attested at Peñalba in two of the additional four inscriptions discovered ten years ago by Francisco Beltrán, Francisco Marco, and their team.[134] Given that a ***IUPPITER CORNUTUS*** is attested in the Narbonensic votive string *Iovi corn*[*uto*],[135] the longer one of the aforesaid two strings can easily contain an epithet of the same *IUPPITER* invoked *sine dei nomine* and followed by an indigenous epithet of appurtenance,[136] perhaps in the form of a genitive plural *CORDONO(M)*.

Accordingly, the shorter votive string *deo Cordono* would simply consist of the theonymic classifier *DEUS* plus the epithet of appurtenance of the classical *IUPPITER CORNUTUS*, here in the genitival form *CORDONO(M)*, or else as a congruent attribute *CORDONUS* in the dative singular. This is a votive sequence for which there are several parallels, among them *deae sanctae Turibrigensi*, also in Spain.[137]

5.3.1. I have already remarked on other occasions that genitival attributes are often not recognized as such, as in the notorious case of the Mars of Rigonemeton, that is the *MARS RIGONEMETI* referred to in the Britannic dedication *Marti Rigonemeti*: his epithet of appurtenance is most likely to be just the genitive of a toponym *Rigonemeton* matching *Augustonemeton*.[138]

A similar case may be appreciated in the dedication *I.O.M. anderon* found at an imprecise location in the North-West of the Iberian Peninsula.[139] Although it is often integrated as ***I(ovi) o(ptimo) m(aximo) anderon(i)* by its editors,[140] the theonymic

132 De Albentiis Hienz *et al.* 2013e, 74–5, 85.

133 Namely *CALANTICE(N)SIS*.

134 Nos. 3 and 2 in Beltrán Lloris & Marco Simón 2008.

135 See the bibliography in Jufer & Luginbühl 2001, 36, who alternatively propose *Iovi Corn[igero]*.

136 Some suggestions regarding its referent are offered by Beltrán Lloris & Marco Simón 2008, 175, who, however, regard it as a proper theonym. This would, however, disagree with the normal order of constituents in Roman votive inscriptions, in which the theonym comes first and the epithet or epithets follow(s).

137 See, among others, Olivares Pedreño 2002, 248.

138 *RIB* III 3180: *deo Marti Rigonemeti et Numinibus Augustorum Q. Nerat(ius) Proximus arcum de suo donavit*. The reasons for rejecting a functional epithet ‡ *RIGONEMETIS* meaning 'Mars of the sacred grove' instead of an epithet of appurtenance have been discussed in de Bernardo Stempel 2008b, 78 with n. 96; 2010c, 23 with n. 47–8.

139 Richert 2005, 48 no. 39.

140 Prósper 2002, 487; Delamarre 2007, 21.

string we have here is, in my opinion, not *I.O.M.* ‡*ANDERU* (or *I.O.M.* ‡*ANDERO* if Latinized), but rather ***I.O.M. ANDERON***, the epithet *ANDERON* representing the same genitive plural *anderon* of Gaulish type attested in the syntagma *brixtia anderon* 'the magic of the **(a)nd^{h}eroi*, that is, the netherworld' at Chamalières.[141] Therefore, an adequate Latin translation of this Hispanic dedication would rather be 'Iovi optimo maximo inferum'[142] than **'Iovi, optimo, maximo, inferno' as is usually assumed.

5.3.2. A further genitival epithet which has been misunderstood in the Hispanic corpus of divine names is the form *coronae* which follows the theonymic dative *Nabiae* in the often discussed dedication from Marecos near Porto.[143] The underlying theonymic string is, in fact, hardly ***NABIA CORONA* with a deonomastic epithet referring either to a parhedros god ***CORONOS* or to a related territory, as has generally been assumed,[144] but rather ***NABIA CORONAE***, that is, with the genitive of the Latin word *corona* 'crown' as an epithet. Accordingly, *NABIA CORONAE* simply refers to a crowned avatar of the goddess *NABIA* > *NAVIA* discussed in § 1.3.1 above, much in the same way of the equally genitival epithets of the *Vergine* **del diadema** *azzurro / della rosa / dell'usignolo / della sedia* painted by Raphael.

6. Deities as opposed to divine names

6.1. A last caveat I should like to utter is that, although scholars all over the world often attribute to a deity the same classification that applies to its name, divine names cannot be equated with deities. Neither with regard to their number, because, on the one hand, several names can be used to refer to one and the same deity while, on the other, the same taboo or antonomastic theonym can be used to address different deities. Nor with regard to their classification, because although it is possible, at least in most cases, to identify the language of a divine name, it is rarely possible to ascertain the milieu in which the involved cult actually originated.

6.2. The latter problem is particularly excruciating in the case of eponymous deities, not to speak of the various Latin renderings of indigenous theonyms, and of the many indigenous renderings of Latin and Greek divine names.[145]

---

141 The compelling reasons for not taking this as **'the women's magic' have been explained in de Bernardo Stempel 2014c, 52 § 1.5:
'a. In der besagten magischen Inschrift werden ganze sechs Männer, aber keinerlei Frauen erwähnt. Männlichen Geschlechts ist selbst die angerufene Gottheit, nämlich der göttliche(*DIÍUIO-S*) Sohn (*MAPO-S*) [Apoll], der Übelabwehrer(*AR-VER-IÍATI-S*).
b. Jede magische Handlung erfordert einen präzisen Sprachgebrauch. Man darf deswegen annehmen, daß die magischen Prozeduren des *brictom banom*, 'des Frauenzaubers', das nicht umsonst im air. *bricht ban* unverändert weiterlebt, und der *brixtia anderon*, zueinander in Opposition standen. Folglich ergibt sich für den – im Determinatum modernisierten – Terminus *brixtia anderon* 'die Magie der Unterweltlichen [Götter]' zwangsläufig als die bessere Übersetzung'.
142 I.e. 'To Juppiter, the best and greatest, of the netherworld'.
143 See Richert 2005, 21 no. 49; González Rodríguez 2008, 90 n.10; 98 no. 9a.
144 See, among others, Blázquez 1975, 130; Olivares Pedreño 1998–99, 231, 233f.; 2002, 76; 2006, 152.
145 That is, the various *explicationes vel translationes Latinae* and, respectively, *Celticae* highlighted, most

A cult may, in fact, have come into being much later than when the toponym or ethnonym it refers to was coined. This happened unambiguously in the case of Salzburg, whose older name **Ív(v)avon*, later **Ivvávon*, was Celtic and meant 'The yew-tree settlement', but was not venerated until Roman times as shown by the Latinate name of the god *Iuvávus*: indeed, his name originated in the modernized toponym *Iuvávum*, a paretymological Latinization of the original Celtic place-name.[146]

Therefore, an eponymous deity ought always to be classified independently from the actual language of the toponymical or ethnical derivational basis of its name. In more general terms, the classification of any deity ought not to be equated with the linguistic classification of its name or names.

6.2.1. In this context, I would like to cast a fresh look at the Lusitanian rock inscription at Lamas de Moledo.[147] Remarkably, its votive dedication *magareaigoi Petranioi*, leading us to a theonymic string *MAGARIAIGOS PETRANIOS*, uses a mixture of languages to address the deity, which appears to have been originally a **makar-iakios Petra-nios*, that is, 'the blessed God from the stone'. Although usually unrecognized,[148] its first element consists of the Greek loanword μάκαρ 'blessed',[149] which has been adapted here by adding the Celtic suffix **-yako-*, and redetermined, as often, by means of the suffix *-yo-*. Both suffixes blended together in the ending **-iaicos* > *-eaigos* typical of the western regions of the Iberian Peninsula.[150] The same lenition of the velar stop (*-k-* > *-g-*) observed in the originally Greek qualifier[151] has also taken place in the accusative *porgom* < **porcom* 'pig' of Italic stock in l. 10 of the same inscription.

Of linguistically Italic stock is, morever, the determinatum *PETRANIOS*, which, even if used instead of a theonym, is itself an epithet in *-yos*, referring to 'the(*-yos*) god(*-no-*) of the stone(*petra*)'.[152]

If we now take into account, together with the location of the inscription,[153] (1) that the god is venerated together with the 'stony' goddess *CROUGIA* (invoked here in the orthographic variant *CROUGEA*); (2) that 'the blessed God from the stone' and 'the Stone' are venerated together with a type of Jupiter, the dative votive string *Iove A(ugusto?) Caeilobrigoi* referring either, as usually assumed, to a detoponymic Juppiter or else to a Juppiter 'strong in the sky' (from a derivative of Lat. *caelum* and Celt. *brigo-* 'strength');[154]

---

recently, in de Bernardo Stempel 2014.

146 Hainzmann *et al.* 2011–2012.

147 *MLH*-L-2.1. See also Rodríguez Colmenero 1993, 99–103; 1995, 216–20; Untermann 2002, 68–9; Curado 2002, 73–4.

148 Among others by Villar 1999, 293; Vaz 2002, 40; Curado 2002, 74.

149 On Greek and Latin elements in the religion of the Keltiké cf. de Bernardo Stempel forthcoming.

150 A systematic study of these kinds of blended velar suffixes is offered by de Bernardo Stempel 2011, 177–87.

151 Note, however, that some other scholars read the dative of the epithet as *macareaicoi* without lenition, and others even as *magareaicoi* with asymmetrical lenition.

152 Here with the classical, i.e. non dialectal, treatment of the nexus {Cons+*-yo-*}.

153 *MLH* IV, 750–2.

154 Several epithets describing various kinds of Jupiter in the sky are collected in de Bernardo Stempel 2013c.

(3) that it cannot be excluded that the animal to be offered to 'the blessed God from the stone' might have been a bull, that is, if the word across lines 9 and 10 of the inscription originally read *taurom*,[155] we may wonder whether the deity venerated at Lama de Moledo was really a truly indigenous Lusitanian one, as has been automatically assumed up to now, or if the inscription of Lamas de Moledo was rather one of the Portuguese dedications of the Mithraic type.[156]

It is, in fact, well known that the originally oriental god *Mitra* (later written *Mithras*) was *rupe natus*,[157] that his *petra genetrix* was also itself the object of some dedications,[158] that the sky-god *Iuppiter* belonged to the classical deities coopted into the Mithraic cult,[159] which often took place in rock sanctuaries, and that the bull played a central part in it.[160] Besides, the Belgian Baudecet inscription, for example, shows us that *Mitra* could be invoked together with all kinds of deities from different panthea.[161]

I am obviously very far from being able to prove such a daring hypothesis, and it is anyhow impossible to confirm or refute it on purely linguistic grounds. My sole aim in this last section was just to insist that one cannot *a priori* assume that the language of a votive dedication coincides with its cultual and cultural environment.

Index of main divine names and/or deities discussed

155 Cf. also the comments by Curado 2002, 73, 76.
156 See Álvar 2002, 206f.; Rodríguez Álvarez 2007; and the map in Hensen 2013, 23.
157 See, among others, Hensen 2013, 53.
158 'Gelegentlich ist die *petra genetrix*, der Geburtsfelsen, selbst Gegenstand von Weihungen' (Hensen 2013, 53).
159 See Hensen 2013, 31, 49.
160 See Hensen 2013, 48ff.
161 A revised analysis of the (numbered) list of twelve very different deities inscribed on the gold tablet of Baudecet is offered by de Bernardo Stempel forthcoming, § 1.1.

BIBLIOGRAPHY

Abascal Palazón, J. M. 2011 'Airones y aguas sagradas', *Aquae Sacrae: Agua y sacralidad en la Antigüedad*, ed. A. Costa, Ll. Palahí Grimal & D. Vivó, 249–56. Girona, Universitat, Institut de la Recerca Histórica.

Acuña Castroviejo, F. 2013 'Unha nova inscrición votiva do Convento Lucense en Vicinte (Outero de Rei, Lugo)', *Croa: Boletín da Asociación de Amigos do Museo do Castro de Viladonga* 23,18–21.

Alfayé, S., P. de Bernardo Stempel, M. C. González Rodríguez & M. Ramírez Sánchez 20XX 'La diosa *Du(v)itera* en una inscripción de Tejeda de Tiétar (Cáceres, *HEp* 3/1993, 139)' in this volume.

Alföldy, G. 2002 'Panóias: o santuário rupestre', *Religiões da Lusitânia: loquuntur saxa*, ed. J. Cardim Ribeiro, 211–14. Lisbon, Museu Nacional de Arqueologia.

Álvar, J. 2002 'Cultos orientais e mistéricos na província da Lusitânia', *Religiões da Lusitânia: loquuntur saxa*, ed. J. Cardim Ribeiro, 205–10. Lisbon, Museu Nacional de Arqueologia.

Alvar Ezquerra J. & E. Muñiz Grijalvo 2002 'Testimonios del culto a Isis en Hispania', *Ex Oriente lux: las religiones orientales antiguas en la Península Ibérica* (Spal monografías no. 2), ed. E. Ferrer Albelda, 245–58. Sevilla, Universidad, Fundación El Monte.

Álvarez-Sanchís J. R. 2003 'Límites y fronteras de la Edad del Hierro en la Meseta Occidental', *Boletín Auriense* 33, 95–113.

Álvarez-Sanchís, J. R. 2005 *Verracos: esculturas zoomorfas en la provincia de Ávila*. Ávila, Diputación Provincial and Institución Gran Duque de Alba (Cuadernos de Patrimonio Abulense no. 1).

Álvarez-Sanchís, J. [R.] 2008 'Simbolismo y función de los verracos en la cultura vettona', *De dioses y bestias: Animales y religión en el Mundo Antiguo* (Spal monografías no. 11), ed. E. Ferrer Albelda, J. Mazuelos Pérez & J. L. Escacena Carrasco, 163–82. Sevilla, Universidad, Servicio de asistencia religiosa.

Arenas-Esteban, J. A. & P. de Bernardo Stempel 2003 'Ein zweiter Blick auf einen unbekannten hispanischen Gott', *Anzeiger der Philosophisch-historischen Klasse der Österreichischen Akademie der Wissenschaften* 138, 83–8.

Arenas-Esteban, J. A. & P. de Bernardo Stempel

2011 'Celtic dialects and cultural contacts in protohistory: the Italian and Iberian peninsulas', Études celtiques 37, 119–39.

Arenas-Esteban, J. A. & R. López-Romero 2010 'Celtic divine names in the Iberian Peninsula: towards a territorial analysis', *Celtic Religion across Time and Space (IXth Workshop F.E.R.C.AN., Molina de Aragón 2008)*, ed. J. A. Arenas-Esteban, 148–79. Toledo, Diputación.

Barberarena Núñez, M. L. 2005 'Las manifestaciones religiosas en el *conventus Emeritensis* (parte española) a través de los documentos epigráficos', *Palaeohispanica* 5 (= *Acta Palaeohispanica IX*, Barcelona 2004), 709–20.

Bayer, W. 1999 'Botorrita I. Semantische und etymologische Interpretationen: ein Beitrag zu den Deutungsmöglichkeiten der Inschrift', *Veleia* 16, 109–35.

Beltrán Lloris, F. 2011 'Lengua e identidad en la Hispania romana' *Palaeohispanica* 11, 19–59.

Beltrán Lloris, F. & B. Díaz Ariño 2007 'Altares con teónimos hispano-célticos de la Meseta norte', *Auf den Spuren keltischer Götterverehrung (5. F.E.R.C.AN-Kolloquium, Graz 2003)*, ed. M. Hainzmann, 29–56. Vienna, Österreichische Akademie der Wissenschaften (Mitteilungen der Prähistorischen Kommission 64).

Beltrán Lloris, F. & F. Marco Simón 2008 'New inscriptions in the sanctuary of Peñalba de Villastar (Teruel)', *Continuity and Innovation in Religion in the Roman West* (6th F.E.R.C.AN. Workshop, London 2005), ed. R. Haeussler & A. C. King, vol. II, 168–84. Portsmouth, Rhode Island, Suppl. series no. 67 to the *Journal of Roman Archaeology*.

Bermejo, J. 2014 'Un santuario a las *Matres* en el foro de *Arucci*: la constatación de las *Rixamae* en la *Baeturia Celtica*', *Onoba* 2, 107–25.

Birkhan, H. 1997 *Kelten: Versuch einer Gesamtdarstellung ihrer Kultur*. Vienna, Österreichische Akademie der Wissenschaften.

Blázquez, J. M. 1975 *Diccionario de las religiones prerromanas de Hispania*. Madrid, Ediciones Istmo.

Blázquez, J. M. 1995 'Algunos dioses hispanos en inscripciones rupestres', *Saxa scripta (inscripciones en roca): Actas del simposio int. ibero-itálico (Santiago de Compostela 1992)*, ed. A. Rodríguez Colmenero & L. Gasperini, 47–59. Sada/A Coruña, Ediciós do Castro (Anejo de *Larouco* nº 2).

Calado, M. 1996 'Endovélico e Rocha da Mina: o contexto arqueológico', *Ophiussa* zero (1996), 97–108.

Campanile, E. 2008 'Note sulle divinità degli Italici meridionali e centrali', *Latina & Italica: Scritti minori* [di E. Campanile] *sulle lingue dell'Italia antica*, vol. II, 853–71. Pisa and Rome, Fabrizio Serra Editore.

Cardim Ribeiro, J. 2002 'Endovellicus', *Religiões da Lusitânia: loquuntur saxa*, ed. J. Cardim Ribeiro, 79–90. Lisbon, Museu Nacional de Arqueologia.

Cardim Ribeiro, J. 2005 'O *deus sanctus Endovellicus* durante a romanidade: ¿uma interpretatio local de Faunus/Silvanus?', *Palaeohispanica* 5 (= *Acta Palaeohispanica IX*, Barcelona 2004), 721–66.

Cardim Ribeiro, J. 2009 '¿Terão certos teónimos paleohispânicos sido alvo de interpretações (pseudo-)etimológicas durante a romanidade passíveis de se reflectirem nos respectivos cultos?', *Palaeohispanica* 9 (= *Acta Palaeohispanica X*, Lisboa 2009), 247–70.

Casas Genover & M. P. de Hoz 2011 'Un grafito del siglo VI a.C. en un vaso cerámico de Mas Gusó (Gerona)', *Palaeohispanica* 11, 231–48.

Correia Santos, M. J., H. Pires & O. Sousa 2014 'Nuevas lecturas de las inscripciones del santuario de Panóias (Vila Real, Portugal)', *Sylloge epigraphica Barcinonensis* 12, 197–224.

Crespo Ortiz de Zárate, S. & Á. Alonso Ávila 1999 *Las manifestaciones religiosas del mundo antiguo en Hispania romana: el territorio de Castilla y León*. Valladolid, distr. by Pórtico Librerías.

Cross, T. P. 1969 *Motif-Index of Early Irish Literature*. New York, Kraus Reprint.

Curado, F. P. 2002 'A "ideologia tripartida dos Indoeuropeos" e as religiões de tradição paleohispânica no ocidente peninsular', *Religiões da Lusitânia: loquuntur saxa*, ed. J. Cardim Ribeiro, 71–7. Lisbon, Museu Nacional de Arqueologia.

Davies, W., J. Graham-Campbell, M. Handley, P. Kershaw, J. T. Koch, G. le Duc & K. Lockyear 2000 *The Inscriptions of Early Medieval Brittany / Les inscriptions de la Bretagne du haut moyen âge*. Oakville/CT and Aberystwyth, Celtic Studies Publications.

De Albentiis Hienz, M. & P. de Bernardo Stempel 2013 'Apolls Epitheta — griechisch, lateinisch, keltisch bzw. keltorömisch', *Geistes-, sozial- und kulturwissenschaftlicher Anzeiger der Österreichischen Akademie der Wissenschaften* 148.1–2 (= *Graekorömische und keltorömische Theonymik und Religion, XII. Workshop F.E.R.C.AN., Berlin 2012*), 7–126.

De Bernardo Stempel, P. 1987 *Die Vertretung der indogermanischen liquiden und nasalen Sonanten im Keltischen*. Innsbruck, Innsbrucker Beiträge zur Sprachwissenschaft 54.

De Bernardo Stempel, P. 1989 'A Welsh Cognate for Gaul. ανδοουνναβο?', *Bulletin of the Board of Celtic Studies* 36, 102–5.

De Bernardo Stempel, P. 1997 'Spuren gemeinkeltischer Kultur im Wortschatz: 6. Der irische "Pfeiler der Sippe" und das *nt*-Verbaladjektiv in der gallischen Inschrift von Plumergat', *Zeitschrift für celtische Philologie* 49–50, 101–6.

De Bernardo Stempel, P. 2002 'Centro y áreas laterales: la formación del celtibérico sobre el fondo del celta peninsular hispano', *Palaeohispanica* 2, 89–132.

De Bernardo Stempel, P. 2003 'Los formularios teonímicos, *Bandus* con su correspondiente *Bandua* y unas isoglosas célticas', *Conimbriga* 42, 197–212.

De Bernardo Stempel, P. 2003a: 'Die sprachliche Analyse keltischer Theonyme', *Zeitschrift für celtische Philologie* 53, 41–69.

De Bernardo Stempel, P. 2006 'Theonymic gender and number variation as a characteristic of Old Celtic religion', *Anthropology of the Indo-European World and Material Culture (5th Colloquium of Anthropology of the Indo-European World and Comparative Mythology, Santiago de Compostela 2004)*, ed. M. V. García Quintela, F. J. González García & F. Criado Boado, 31–47. Budapest, Archaeolingua Series maior, 20.

De Bernardo Stempel, P. 2007–2008 'The "old" Celtic goddess *Sena*: a new testimony from Aquitania', *Veleia* 24–25, 1203–6 (= *FS Ignacio Barandiarán Maestu*, ed. J. Eraso & J. Santos, vol. 2, 1203–6).

De Bernardo Stempel, P. 2008 'Cib. *TO LVGVEI* "hacia *Lugus*" vs. *LVGVEI* "para *Lugus*": sintaxis y divinidades en Peñalba de Villastar', *Emerita* 76.2, 181–96.

De Bernardo Stempel, P. 2008a 'Strati teonimici nelle provincie romane (con esempi prevalentemente aquitani)', *Divindades indígenas em análise / Divinités pré-romaines – bilan et perspectives d'une recherche (VII Workshop FERCAN, Cascais 2006)*, ed. J. d'Encarnação, 145–50. Coimbra and Porto, Centro de Estudios Arqueológicos das Universidades de Coimbra e Porto.

De Bernardo Stempel, P. 2008b 'Continuity, *translatio* and *identificatio* in Gallo-Roman religion: the case of Britain', *Continuity and Innovation in Religion in the Roman West* (6th F.E.R.C.AN. Workshop, London 2005), ed. R. Haeussler & A. C. King, vol. II, 67–82. Portsmouth, Rhode Island, Suppl. series no. 67 to the *Journal of Roman Archaeology*.

De Bernardo Stempel, P. 2008c 'I nomi teoforici del celta antico', *Dedicanti e* cultores *nelle religioni celtiche (VIII Workshop F.E.R.C.AN., Gargnano 2007)*, ed. A. Sartori, 73–104. Milan, Cisalpino (Quaderni di *Acme* 104).

De Bernardo Stempel, P. 2008[CD]/ 2010 [book] 'La ley del 1er Bronce de Botorrita: uso agropecuario de un encinar sagrado', *VI Simposio sobre Celtíberos: Ritos y Mitos (Daroca/ Zaragoza, Noviembre 2008)*, ed. F. Burillo Mozota, Chapt. 11, 123–45. Zaragoza, Centro de Estudios Celtibéricos and Fundación Ségeda.

De Bernardo Stempel, P. 2009a 'La gramática celtibérica del primer bronce de Botorrita: nuevos resultados', *Palaeohispanica* 9 (= *Acta Palaeohispanica X*, Lisboa 2009), 683–99.

De Bernardo Stempel, P. 2009b 'El nombre —¿céltico?— de la *Pintia* vaccea', *Boletín del Seminario de Estudios de Arte y de Arqueología: Arqueología* 75, 243–56.

De Bernardo Stempel, P. 2010a 'Die Geminaten des Festlandkeltischen', *Akten des 5. Deutschsprachigen Keltologensymposiums (Zürich, September 2009)*, ed. K. Stüber, Th. Zehnder & D. Bachmann, 65–87. Vienna, Praesens Verlag (Keltische Forschungen–Allgemeine Buchreihe 1).

De Bernardo Stempel, P. 2010b 'Celtic taboo-theonyms, *GÓBANOS/ GOBÁNNOS* in Alesia and the epigraphical attestations of *AISOS/ ESUS*', *Deuogdonion (FS Claude Sterckx)*, ed. G. Hily, P. Lajoye, J. Hascoët, G. Oudaer & Ch. Rose, 105–32. Rennes, Tir.

De Bernardo Stempel, P. 2010c 'Method in the Analysis of Romano-Celtic Theonymic Materials: Improved Readings and Etymological Interpretations', *Celtic Religion across Time and Space (IX Workshop F.E.R.C.AN., Molina de Aragón 2008)*, ed. J. A. Arenas-Esteban, 18–27. Toledo, Junta de Comunidades de Castilla-La Mancha.

De Bernardo Stempel, P. 2011 '*Callaeci*, *Anabaraecus*, *Abienus*, *Tritecum*, *Berobriaecus* and the new velar suffixes of the types -*ViK*- and -*(y)eK*-','Αντίδωρον *(FS Juan José Moralejo)*, ed. M. J. García Blanco, T. Amado Rodríguez, M. J. Martín Velasco, A. Pereiro Pardo &

M. E. Vázquez Buján, 175–93. Santiago de Compostela, Universidad.

De Bernardo Stempel, P. 2012 'Reinterpreting some documents of the Celtiberian and other Palaeohispanic corpora', *Palaeohispanica* 12, 51–71.

De Bernardo Stempel, P. 2013a 'Celtic "son", "daughter", other descendants, and *sunus in Early Celtic', *Indogermanische Forschungen* 118, 259–97.

De Bernardo Stempel, P. 2013b 'The Phonetic Interface of Word Formation in Continental Celtic', *Continental Celtic word-formation data (Simposio Salamanca 2011)*, ed. J. L. García Alonso, 63–83. Salamanca, Universidad.

De Bernardo Stempel, P. 2013c 'Iuppiter in der Höhe, seine klassischen und keltischen Beinamen', *Carnuntum Jahrbuch* Jg. 2013, 93–8.

De Bernardo Stempel, P. 2013d 'Individuality in Celtic divine names: theonyms, epithets and theonymic formulae', *Keltische Götternamen als individuelle Option? / Celtic Theonyms as an Individual Option? (11. Workshop F.E.R.C.AN., Erfurt 2011)*, ed. W. Spickermann, 25–37. Rahden/Westfalen, Verlag Marie Leidorf (Osnabrücker Forschungen zu Altertum und Antike-Rezeption 19).

De Bernardo Stempel, P. 2013e 'Celtic and other indigenous divine names found in the Italian Peninsula', *Théonymie celtique, cultes,* interpretatio */ Keltische Theonymie, Kulte,* interpretatio *(X. Workshop F.E.R.C.AN., Paris 2010)*, ed. A. Hofeneder & P. de Bernardo Stempel, 73–96. Vienna, Österreichische Akademie der Wissenschaften (Mitteilungen der Prähistorischen Kommission 79).

De Bernardo Stempel, P. 2014 'Keltische Äquivalente klassischer Epitheta und andere sprachliche und nicht-sprachliche Phänomene im Rahmen der sogenannten *interpretatio Romana*', *Zeitschrift für celtische Philologie* 61, 7–48.

De Bernardo Stempel, P. 2014a 'Tipología de las leyendas monetales célticas. La Península Ibérica y las demás áreas de la Céltica antigua', *VII Simposio sobre Celtíberos: Nuevos descubrimientos – Nuevas interpretaciones (Daroca 2012)*, ed. F. Burillo Mozota & M. Chordá Pérez, Chapt. 20, 185–201. Teruel, Centro de Estudios Celtibéricos de Segeda (Daroca) and Institución Fernando el Católico (Zaragoza).

De Bernardo Stempel, P. 2014b 'Livelli di celticità linguistica nell'Italia settentrionale', *Les Celtes et le Nord de l'Italie: Premier et Second Âges du fer / I Celti e l'Italia del Nord: Prima e Seconda Età del Ferro (XXXVIe colloque de l'AFEAF, Vérone 2012)*, ed. Ph. Barral, J.-P. Guillaumet, M.-J. Roulière-Lambert, M. Saracino & D. Vitali, 89–102. Dijon, *Revue archéologique de l'Est*, 36e Supplément.

De Bernardo Stempel, P. 2014c 'Indogermanisch *$h_2$end^{h}e(s)-ro-s/-rā/-ro-m, *neig^{w}-sk-ā und ihre Fortsetzungen im Keltischen und den Nachbarsprachen', **Wék^{w}os, revue d'études indo-européennes* 1, 47–74.

De Bernardo Stempel, P. 2015 'Labialisierung und Velarisierung festlandkeltischer Vokale', *Mélanges en l'honneur du professeur Pierre-Yves Lambert*, ed. H. Le Bihan, G. Oudaer & G. Hily, 191–214. Rennes, Tir.

De Bernardo Stempel, P. 2016 'Celto-Roman and Other Divine Names Found in NW Spain (*Conventus Asturum*, *Lucensis*, and *Bracarensis*)', *Gallo-Römische Gottheiten und ihre Verehrer (14. F.E.R.C.AN.-Workshop, Trier 2015)*, ed. K. Matijević, 189-228. Rahden/Westf., Marie Leidorf (Pharos 39).

De Bernardo Stempel, P. forthcoming ‚Die Sprache der keltischen Religion als Zeugnis für Kontakte mit Griechen und Römern', *Kelten, Römer, Griechen: Sprache und Kulturkontakte im Römischen Reich und seinem Umfeld / Celts, Romans, Greeks: Language and cultural contacts in the Roman Empire and associated areas (Kolloquium Heidelberg 2014)*, ed. G. Kloss, G. Broderick & L. Willms. Heidelberg.

De Bernardo Stempel, P. & M. Hainzmann 2009 'Die Namenformulare mit *sive* in römischen Inschriften', *Anzeiger der Philosophisch-historischen Klasse der Österreichischen Akademie der Wissenschaften* 144, 5–20.

De Bernardo Stempel, P. & M. Hainzmann 2010 '*Sive* in theonymic formulae as a means for introducing explications and identifications', *Celtic Religion across Time and Space (IXth. Workshop F.E.R.C.AN., Molina de Aragón 2008)*, ed. J. A. Arenas-Esteban, 28–39. Toledo, Diputación.

De Bernardo Stempel, P., F. Romero Carnicero & C. Sanz Mínguez 2012 'Grafitos con signario celtibérico en cerámicas de *Pintia* (Padilla de Duero-Peñafiel, Valladolid)', *Palaeohispanica* 12, 157–94.

De Bernardo Stempel, P., C. Sanz Mínguez & F. Romero Carnicero 2011 'Nueva fusayola con inscripción en signario celtibérico de la necrópolis vaccea de Las Ruedas de *Pintia*

(Padilla de Duero, Valladolid)', *Palaeohispanica* 10, 405–26 (*Festschrift Javier de Hoz*).

Delamarre, X. 2007 *Noms de personnes celtiques dans l'épigraphie classique*. Paris, Éditions Errance.

D'Encarnação, J. 1975 *Divindades indígenas sob o dominio romano em Portugal: subsidios para o seu estudo*. Lisbon, Imprensa nacional – Casa da moeda.

D'Encarnação, J. 2008 'Dédicants et *cultores*: quelques aspects ... dans la Lusitanie romaine: Le cas d'*Endovellicus*', *Dedicanti e* cultores *nelle religioni celtiche (VIII Workshop F.E.R.C.AN., Gargnano 2007)*, ed. A. Sartori, 61–71. Milan, Cisalpino (Quaderni di *Acme* 104).

Dolenz, H. & P. de Bernardo Stempel 2004 '*Sena*[*bos*]. Eine norische Gottheit aus Tiffen', *Ad Fontes! (Festschrift Gerhard Dobesch)*, ed. H. Heftner & K. Tomaschitz, 737–46. Vienna, Wiener Humanistische Gesellschaft & Die Herausgeber.

Domínguez Bolaños, A. & J. Nuño González 1994 *Castro de San Esteban (Muelas del Pan, Zamora): Excavación arqueológica 1993. Vol. II: Inventario de Materiales.* Informe inédito de los trabajos de excavación depositado en el Servicio territorial de Cultura en Zamora de la Junta de Castilla y León (unpublished excavation report, deposited at the Zamora's offices of the *Servicio territorial de Cultura* belonging to the administrative region of Castilla & León).

Dowden, K. 2010 'Olympian Gods, Olympian Pantheon', *A Companion to Greek Religion*, ed. D. Ogden, 41–55. Chichester, Wiley-Blackwell.

Dunand, F. 2010 'The religious system at Alexandria', *A Companion to Greek Religion*, ed. D. Ogden, 253–63. Chichester, Wiley-Blackwell.

Egeler, M. 2013 *Celtic Influences in Germanic Religion: a survey*. Munich, Herbert Utz Verlag.

Eska, J. F. 1992 'Further to ανδουνναβο', *Journal of Celtic Linguistics* 1, 119–25.

Eska J. F. 1995 'Two notes on phonology in Continental Celtic', *Studia Celtica Japonica* 7, 9–19.

Falileyev, A. I. 2008 'Aericura', repr. in *idem* 2012 *Selecta Celto-Balcanica*, 133–41. Saint Petersburg, Nestor-Istorija.

Fauduet, I. 2007 'Divinités celtiques sur les objets métalliques en Gaule', *Continuity and Innovation in Religion in the Roman West* (6th F.E.R.C.AN. Workshop, London 2005), ed. R. Haeussler & A. C. King, vol. I, 177–87. Portsmouth, Rhode Island, Suppl. series no. 67 to the *Journal of Roman Archaeology*.

Gamo Pazos, E. 2012 *Corpus de inscripciones latinas de la provincia de Guadalajara*. Guadalajara, Diputación.

García Alonso, J. L. 2007 'Etimología: Pozo Airón, Deo Aironi', *Pasado y presente de los estudios celtas*, AA.VV., 137–46. Ortigueira, Fundación Ortegalia and Instituto de Estudios Celtas.

Gil Mantas, V. 2002 'Na mira da perfeição das artes e dos homens: *Apollo* e seu filho *Aesculapius*', *Religiões da Lusitânia: loquuntur saxa*, ed. J. Cardim Ribeiro, 125–30. Lisbon, Museu Nacional de Arqueologia.

Gimeno Pascual, H. & P. Rothenhöfer 2012 'Eine neue Weihung an die *Rixamae* in der *Baeturia Celticorum* und Martial IV 55', *Veleia* 29, 435–9.

Gómez-Pantoja, J. 1999 'Las madres de Clunia', *Pueblos, lenguas y escrituras en la Hispania prerromana (VII Coloquio sobre lenguas y culturas paleohispánicas, Zaragoza 1997)*, ed. F. Villar & F. Beltrán Lloris, 421–32. Salamanca, Universidad (Acta Salmanticensia, Estudios filológicos 273).

Gómez-Pantoja, J. & F. García Palomar 1995 'Nuevas inscripciones latinas de San Esteban de Gormaz (Soria)', *Boletín del Seminario de estudios de Arte y Arqueologia* 61, 185–96.

González Rodríguez, M. C. 2008 'Noms des divinités préromaines du Nord-Ouest hispanique: bilan provisoir', *Divindades indígenas em análise / Divinités pré-romaines – bilan et perspectives d'une recherche (VII Workshop FERCAN, Cascais 2006)*, ed. J. d'Encarnação, 81–104. Coimbra and Porto, Centro de Estudios Arqueológicos das Universidades de Coimbra e Porto.

González Rodríguez, M. C. & F. Marco Simón 2009 'Divinidades y devotos indígenas en la *Tarraconensis*: las dedicaciones colectivas', *Palaeohispanica* 9 (= *Acta Palaeohispanica X*, Lisboa 2009), 65–81.

Graves, R. 2004 *Los mitos griegos* (*The Greek Myths*, Spanish transl. by E. Gómez Parro). Barcelona, Círculo de Lectores.

Grenier, A. 1953–1954 'Le dieu lusitanien Endovellicus', *Études celtiques* 6, 195–7.

Guerra, A. 2002 '*Omnibus Numinibus et Lapitearum*: algumas reflexões sobre a nomenclatura teonímica do Ocidente peninsular', *Revista portuguesa de Arqueologia* 5.1, 147–59.

Guerra, A. 2002a 'Teónimos paleohispânicos e antroponímia', *Religiões da Lusitânia: loquuntur saxa*, ed. J. Cardim Ribeiro, 63–5. Lisbon, Museu Nacional de Arqueologia.

Guerra, A. 2008 'La documentation épigraphique sur *Endouellicus* et les nouvelles recherches dans son sanctuaire à S. Miguel da Mota', *Continuity and Innovation in Religion in the Roman West* (6th F.E.R.C.AN. Workshop, London 2005), ed. R. Haeussler & A. C. King, vol. II, 159–67. Portsmouth, Rhode Island, Suppl. series no. 67 to the *Journal of Roman Archaeology*.

Guerra, A., Th. Schattner, C. Fabião & R. Almeida 2003 'Novas investigações no santuário de Endovélico (S. Miguel da Mota, Alandroal): a campanha de 2002', *Revista portuguesa de Arqueologia* 6.2, 415–79.

Hainzmann, M. 2015 'Zur epigraphischen Hinterlassenschaft der Boier', *Boier zwischen Realität und Fiktion* (Internationales Kolloquium: Český Krumlov 2013), ed. M. Karwowski, V. Salač & S. Sievers, 103–13. Bonn, Römisch-germanische Kommission des Deutschen Archäologischen Instituts (Kolloquien zur Vor- und Frühgeschichte 21).

Hainzmann, M. & P. de Bernardo Stempel 2011–2012 '*Iuvavus* und Verwandte: Überlieferung, linguistische Kommentierung, Gesamtbeurteilung', *Römisches Österreich* 34/35, 51–62.

Hainzmann, M., P. de Bernardo Stempel (mit einem Beitrag von G. Bauchhenß) 2017 *Corpus F.E.R.C.AN. Vol. I. Provincia Noricum. Fasc. 1. Die Gottheiten in ihren sprachlichen und kultischen Erscheinungsformen*. Vienna, Österreichische Akademie der Wissenschaften.

Hensen, A. 2013 *Mithras. Der Mysterienkult an Limes, Rhein und Donau*. Darmstadt: Theiss (Die Limesreihe – Schriften des Limesmuseums Aalen 62).

Hernández Guerra, L. 2004 'Pequeños altares en el área de la Meseta septentrional', *Hispania antiqua* 28, 153–68.

Hernández Guerra, L. & S. M. García Martínez 2002 'Nueva aportación al culto a las *Matres* en *Hispania*', *Hispania antiqua* 26, 147–55.

Hofeneder, A. 2005–2011 *Die Religion der Kelten in den antiken literarischen Zeugnissen*. 3 vols. Vienna, Österreichische Akademie der Wissenschaften (Mitteilungen der Prähistorischen Kommission, Bde. 59, 66, 75).

Jufer, N. & Th. Luginbühl 2001 *Répertoire des dieux gaulois*. Paris, Éditions Errance.

Kakoschke, A. 2006 *Die Personennamen in den zwei germanischen Provinzen*, Vol. 1: *Gentilnomina*. Rahden/Westfalen, Verlag Marie Leidorf.

Kakoschke, A. 2011 *Die Personennamen in der römischen Provinz Britannien*. Hildesheim *et al.*, Olms.

Kakoschke, A. 2012 *Die Personennamen in der römischen Provinz Noricum*. Hildesheim *et al.*, Olms.

Kelly, F. 1988 *A Guide to Early Irish Law*. Dublin, D.I.A.S. (Early Irish Law Series 3).

Kuhnen, H.-P. 1996 *Religio Romana: Wege zu den Göttern im antiken Trier*. Trier, Schriftenreihe des Rheinischen Landesmuseums.

Lajoye, P. 2008, 'Un monstre gaulois: Cernunnos, le dieu aux bois de cerf', *Divindades indígenas em análise / Divinités pré-romaines – bilan et perspectives d'une recherche (VII Workshop FERCAN, Cascais 2006)*, ed. J. d'Encarnação, 165–72. Coimbra and Porto, Centro de Estudios Arqueológicos das Universidades de Coimbra e Porto.

Larson, J. 2009 (2007) *Ancient Greek Cults: a guide*. New York and London, Routledge.

Lindeman, F. O. 1991 'Varia III: 2. Gaulish ανδοουνναβο', Ériu 42, 146.

Marco Simón, F. 1993 'Nemedus Augustus', *Studia Palaeohispanica et Indogermanica* (*FS Jürgen Untermann ab amicis Hispanicis oblata*), ed. I. J. Adiego Lajara, J. Siles & J. Velaza, 165–77. Barcelona, Universitat.

Marco Simón, F. 1998 *Die Religion im keltischen Hispanien*. Budapest, Archaeolingua Series Minor 12.

Marco Simón, F. 2003 '*Signa deorum*: comparación y contexto histórico en Hispania y Galia', *Arqueología e iconografía: indagar en las imágenes*, ed. T. Tortosa & J. A. Santos, 121–36. Rome, Bretschneider.

Marco Simón, F. 2008 'El horizonte simbólico: dioses y espacios de culto', *Arqueología vettona: la meseta occidental en la Edad del Hierro*, AA.VV., 277–88. Alcalá de Henares, Museo Arqueológico regional (Zona arqueológica 12).

Marco Simón, F. 2010 'Rethinking *interpretatio* as a key factor in the religious Romanisation of the west', *Deuogdonion (Festschrift Claude Sterckx)*, ed. G. Hily, P. Lajoye, J. Hascoët, G. Oudaer & Ch. Rose, 413–31. Rennes, Tir.

Marco Simón, F. 2012 'Patterns of *interpretatio* in the Hispanic provinces', *Mediterraneo antico* 15.1–2, 217–31.

Marco Simón, F. 2013 'Local cult in global context: *interpretatio* and the emergence of new divine identities in the *provincia Tarraconensis*', *Théonymie celtique, cultes,* interpretatio / *Keltische Theonymie, Kulte,* interpretatio *(X. Workshop F.E.R.C.AN., Paris 2010)*, ed.

A. Hofeneder & P. de Bernardo Stempel, 221–32. Vienna, Österreichische Akademie der Wissenschaften (Mitteilungen der Prähistorischen Kommission 79).

Matasović, R. 2009 *Etymological Dictionary of Proto-Celtic*. Leiden and Boston, Brill.

Melena, J. L. 1984 'Un ara votiva romana en El Gaitán, Cáceres', *Veleia* N.S. 1, 233–60.

Núñez Marcén, J. & A. Blanco 2002 'Una nueva propuesta de lectura y contextualización de la conocida ara votiva a las "Matribus useis" de Laguardia (Álava)', *Iberia* 5, 49–64.

Olivares Pedreño, J. C. 1998–1999 'El culto a *Nabia* en *Hispania* y las diosas polifunctionales indoeuropeas', *Lucentum* 17–18, 229–41.

Olivares Pedreño, J. C. 2002 *Los dioses de la Hispania céltica*. Madrid and Alicante, Real Academia de la Historia and Universidad.

Olivares Pedreño, J. C. 2006 'Cultos romanos e indigenismo: elementos para el análisis del proceso de romanización religiosa en la Hispania céltica', *Lucentum* 25, 139–57.

Olivares Pedreño, J. C. 2008 '*Interpretatio* epigráfica y fenómenos de sincretismo religioso en el área céltica de Hispania', *Hispania antiqua* 32, 213–47.

Olivares Pedreño, J. C. 2015 'Nueva interpretación de cuatro inscripciones votivas de Soria y La Rioja', *Palaeohispanica* 15, 187–98.

Plummer, Ch. 1884, 'Irish miscellanies: The conversion of Loegaire, and his death', *Revue Celtique* 6, 162–72.

Prósper, B. M. 1997 '*Tongoe nabiagoi*: la lengua lusitana en la inscripción bracarense del ídolo de la fuente', *Veleia* 14, 163–76.

Prósper, B. M. 2002 *Lenguas y religiones prerromanas del occidente de la Península Ibérica*. Salamanca, Universidad.

Prósper, B.M. 2007 'Varia Celtica epigraphica: 3. Tres divinidades de la Hispania celta: Aeiodaicino, Aiioragato, Boiogenae', *Palaeohispanica* 7, 168–74.

Rapsaet-Charlier, M.-Th. 2012 'Les cultes de la cité des Lingons: l'apport des inscriptions', Étudier les lieux de culte de Gaule romaine (Table-ronde, Dijon 2009), ed. O. de Cazanove & P. Méniel, 37–73. Montagnac, Éditions Monique Mergoil (Archéologie et histoire romaine 24).

Raybould, M. E. & P. Sims Williams 2007 *A Corpus of Latin Inscriptions of the Roman Empire Containing Celtic Personal Names*. Aberystwyth, *Celtic Medieval Celtic Studies* Publications.

Raybould, M. E. & P. Sims-Williams 2009 *Introduction and Supplement to 'A Corpus of Latin Inscriptions of the Roman Empire Containing Celtic Personal Names'*. Aberystwyth, *Celtic Medieval Celtic Studies* Publications.

Rémy, B. 2008 'Les *cultores* des divinités indigènes dans la colonie de Vienne', *Dedicanti e* cultores *nelle religioni celtiche (VIII Workshop F.E.R.C.AN., Gargnano 2007)*, ed. A. Sartori, 195–223. Milan, Cisalpino (Quaderni di *Acme* 104).

Richert, E. A. 2005 *Native Religion under Roman Domination: deities, springs and mountains in the north-west of the Iberian Peninsula*. Oxford, BAR Int. Series 1382.

Rodríguez Álvarez, P. 2007 'Los cultos orientales en la epigrafía gallega', *El mundo religioso hispano bajo el imperio romano: pervivencias y cambios*, ed. L. Hernández Guerra, 273–82. Valladolid, Universidad (Centro Buendía 83).

Rodríguez Colmenero, A. 1993 *Corpus-catálogo de inscripciones rupestres de época romana del cuadrante noroccidental de la Península Ibérica*. Sada/A Coruña, Ediciós do Castro (Anejo de *Larouco* 1).

Rodríguez Colmenero, A. 1995 'Corpus de inscripciones rupestres de época romana del cuadrante NW de la Península Ibérica', *Saxa scripta (inscripciones en roca): Actas del simposio int. ibero-itálico (Santiago de Compostela 1992)*, ed. A. Rodríguez Colmenero & L. Gasperini, 157–259. Sada/A Coruña, Ediciós do Castro (Anejo de *Larouco* 2).

Rodríguez Colmenero, A. 2002 'Deuses na planície: *Nabia* e assimilados', *Religiões da Lusitânia: loquuntur saxa*, ed. J. Cardim Ribeiro, 25–9. Lisbon, Museu Nacional de Arqueologia.

Schattner, Th. G., A. Guerra & C. Fabião 2005 'La investigación del santuario de Endovelico en São Miguel da Motta (Portugal)', *Palaeohispanica* 5 (= *Acta Palaeohispanica IX*, Barcelona 2004), 893–908.

Sergent, B. 2012 'Sucellus et Viśvakarman', *Études celtiques* 38, 175–95.

Shackleton Bailey, D. R. 1993 *Martial: Epigrams, edited and translated*. Vol. I. Cambridge/Mass., Harvard University Press.

Sims-Williams, P. 2003 Review of 'Davies *et al.* 2000', *Celtic Medieval Celtic Studies* 45, 78–80.

Tovar, A. 1983 'Etnia y lengua en la Galicia antigua: el problema del celtismo', *Estudios de cultura castrexa e de historia antiga de Galicia*, ed. G. Pereira Menaut, 247–82. Santiago de Compostela, Universidad.

Tranoy, A. 2002 'A "Fonte do ídolo"', *Religiões da Lusitânia: loquuntur saxa*, ed. J. Cardim Ribeiro, 31–2. Lisbon, Museu Nacional de Arqueologia.

Untermann, J. 2002 'A epigrafía em lingua lusitana e a sua vertente religiosa', *Religiões da Lusitânia: loquuntur saxa*, ed. J. Cardim Ribeiro, 67–70. Lisbon, Museu Nacional de Arqueologia.

Untermann, J. 2006 '*Lapatiaci*, *Lapiteae*, *Lapateni* – gallaekische Namenprobleme', *Beiträge zur Namenforschung* N.F. 41.3, 251–8.

Van Andringa, W. 2011 'Religions and the integration of cities in the empire in the second century AD: the creation of a common religious language', *A Companion to Roman Religion*, ed. J. Rüpke, 83–95. Chichester, Wiley-Blackwell.

Vaz, J. L. I. 2002 'Tipologia dos santuários rupestres de tradição paleohispânica em territorio portugués', *Religiões da Lusitânia: loquuntur saxa*, ed. J. Cardim Ribeiro, 39–42. Lisbon, Museu Nacional de Arqueologia.

Villar, F. 1999 'Sobre la inscripción lusitana de Lamas de Moledo: la divinidad Crougia', *AIΩN sezione linguistica* 21, 247–301.

XI

TWO DIVINITIES OF THE CELTIC CANTABRI
1) ERVDINO, DIVINITY OF THE YEARLY CYCLE
2) CABVNIAEGINO, THE CELTIC FATE OF IE *KAP- AND THE GAULISH SPINDLE WHORL FROM SAINT-RÉVÉRIEN

Blanca María Prósper

The Cantabri have usually been held to be Celtic populations to judge from their personal names. This contribution aims to show that their few preserved divine names have good Celtic etymologies and interesting Indo-European connections.

THE *Cantabri* were an indigenous population of northwestern Spain whose realms covered the best part of western Cantabria, eastern Asturias and northwestern León and Palencia.[1] They fall into several groups, *Vadinienses*, *Orgenomescī*, *Avariginī*, *Camaricī*, etc., the first of which has left us a most interesting set of funerary stelae. No text in their indigenous language has survived, but their onomastics are more informative than traditionally believed. After a century-long discussion on the ethnic and linguistic ascription of these populations, which have even been claimed to be mixed with Basque and Iberian strata, we can safely conclude that, as far as their onomastics are concerned, they are of Celtic ancestry. A transparent example is the PlN of the spot where this inscription was found: *Dobra* continues the Celtic feminine adjectival form **dubrā*, which means 'dark', presumably owing to the thick forests covering the mountain.

Inscriptions usually lack an archaeological context. Dating them is often a strenuous

1 This work has been financed by the Spanish Government (MINECO *FFI*2012-30657: *La antroponimia indígena indoeuropea de Hispania: Estudio comparativo*). I am indebted to David Stifter for his knowledgeable comments on a previous version of this work.

task. We have to bear in mind that the Cantabri and the Astures were the last focus of resistance against the Roman power in ancient Hispania. Epigraphic activity must consequently have begun only after the Cantabrian wars were over (after 16 BC). Although some criteria for dating the inscriptions have been advanced, they usually apply to funerary inscriptions and leave us in the dark as regards DNN. In this work, I shall endeavour to clear up the etymology of two epigraphically attested divine names of ancient Cantabria. As we will see, the first of these votive inscriptions is extraordinary in that the exact date on which it was written or consecrated is made explicit.

1. Deus Erudinus: 'deus quondam deusque futurus'?

The inscription containing this unknown but perfectly readable DN *Deus Erudinus*, was found in 1925 by the archaeologist Hermilio Alcalde del Río in Mount Dobra (Torrelavega, Cantabria). Iglesias Gil & Ruiz Gutiérrez propose the following reading:[2]

CORNE(LIVS) VICANVS
âVNIGAINV̂M
FESTI* F(ILIVS) ARA(M)
POSSVIT DEO
ERVDINO X K(ALEND)IS
âVGV(STIS) M(ARCO) A(NTONINO) VÊ(RO) CO(N)S(VLIBVS)

*v.l. CESTI

The person who made the votive offering was probably of indigenous origin, but he was given a Latin name. Thus, the onomastic formula CORNE(LIVS) VICANVS | AVNIGAINVM | FESTI F(ILIVS) is partly indigenous: It consists of a gentilic + cognomen + indigenous FN (gen. pl.) + father's PN (gen.). The FN in the gen.pl. AVNIGAINVM is paralleled (with some variants) by a number of FNN in the northwest: ELESIGAINVM, ARGANTICAENI.[3]

This DN is unparalleled, and has never been paid attention from the linguistic point of view. Most surprising is the fact that, in spite of the chronological uncertainties besetting most of the Hispanic votive and funerary epigraphy, this one is dated precisely on 23rd/24th July. García y Bellido advanced an interpretation of the consular names as MA(NLIO) EV(TROPIO) CO(N)S(VLIBVS) and concluded they refered to the consuls of 399 AD,[4] but some specialists now agree on a slightly different reading and a much earlier date, namely AD 161.[5] This has the obvious advantage of placing this dedication long before Theodosius' decree that rendered it virtually impossible to exhibit public

2 1998, nr. 4.
3 The occurrence of the digraph <AI> is only amenable to explanation if *-ik-ino-* has undergone a secondary insertion of /a/, possibly intended to counteract the tendency towards palatalization of /i/.
4 García y Bellido & González Echegaray 1949, 214–7.
5 Cf. Iglesias Gil & Ruiz Gutiérrez 1998, 67, following a suggestion of Armin Stylow. In their view, the date corresponds to the consulate of M. Aurelius Antoninus III y L. Aurelius Verus II. Jenaro MacLennan 1996, 314 has proposed an alternative reading MA(TER) E(I)V(S) C(VM) O(MNIBVS) S(OLVIT) or perhaps MA(TER) E(X) V(OTO) CO(N)S(ECRAVIT).

dedications to the pagan gods.

The etymology of ERVDINO is obscure thus far: Only one has been proposed to my knowledge. García y Bellido traced it back to Celtic **rud-* 'red' with a prothetic vowel, on the grounds that this is typical of Basque words beginning by *r-*. This idea tacitly rests on the hypothesis, long discredited but still hovering over the minds of many amateurs, that the Basque language was once spoken all over northern Hispania and was secondarily restricted to its present location in the Basque country. Predictably, the existence of four altars devoted to a *Mars Rudianus* (Narbonensis) has been erroneusly connected with *Erudinus* and used as welcome evidence in favour of the ungrounded idea that Hispano-Celtic deities are related to battle and their names often allusive to the red colour of blood.

In my view, ERVDINO goes back to the IE adjective **perutino-* 'the one of last year'. It shows regular Celtic loss of word initial /p/, which is attested all over Hispania including the western regions, as in OLCA (from **polkā* 'fertile field'), ARCELTIVS (from **pr̥h*$_2$*i-*), etc. Additionally, this form has undergone voicing of the intervocalic stop /t/, which happens to be well attested in the PNN of the Cantabri: CLVDAMVS (**klutamo-*); AMBADVS (**amba(x)to-*), TRIDIO (**triti̯o-*), CALAEDICON, CALEDIGE (**kaleto-*). The chronology is unclear, but the change seems to have set in by the end of the second century;[6] it may have been later if the stop was followed by *-i̯-*.

The form **perut(-i)* forming the base of **perutino-* is an adverb of time meaning 'last year' and attested in most IE languages, as in Attic Greek πέρυσι (Doric πέρυτι), OIr. ónn uraid, gl. 'ab anno priore', MIr. *inn-uraid*, Skt. *parút*, Arm. *heru*, ON. *fjorð*, MHG. *vert*. This form can be analyzed as a very primitive prepositional compound **pér-ut(i)*. Nussbaum has conducted an interesting study of this formational scheme.[7] He reckons with original /e/ grade locatives of root nouns, which undergo a secondary reduction when they enter composition with an accented governing preposition. The original locative with the full grade of the root is preserved in the Hittite dative-locative form of the root noun *uitti* (< **u̯eti*). Only Sanskrit *parút* continues an endingless locative **u̯et*.

Its original meaning is not obvious, however. According to Dočkalová and Blažek it meant 'over the year',[8] but on another syntactic interpretation one may equally translate 'in the previous year'. The suffixless hypostatic class as a whole may have come into being through a reanalysis of the *entheos* type.[9] This may be the case with **per-uti* '(in) the year (that is) before', which would provide the adverbial basis for an exocentric *entheos* compound **per-uti̯-o-* that would acquire a relational, not possessive meaning 'related to the year before'. If this adjective ever existed it was early replaced by the form **per-uti-(i)no-* now found in three branches.[10]

6 Stelae from the 2nd century exhibit inconsistent renditions of CCelt. /t/: CLVDAMVS vs. ANDOTO, TRIDI vs. ANDOTI.

7 Nussbaum 1986, 82–4.

8 Dočkalová & Blažek 2011, 425.

9 Sadovski 2000.

10 Albeit this point cannot be further substantiated, it is worth mentioning an isolated PN MOLAECVS SAMVTI (Germania Superior). The father's name could be traced back to a thematic derivative of an

The list of compounds of this kind is now and then enriched by new examples which, given their very archaic nature, are often refashioned or even hypostasized as adjectives which occasionally survive only as PNN. Additionally, they sometimes contain prepositions never attested as independent forms in any IE language, as in the case of **me-*: **$h_1$en-g(e)uH* 'in hand' > Gk. ἐγγύ- 'near', **pro(s)-ǵn(e)u* 'on, to the knees' > Gk. πρόχνυ, Skt. *prajñu*, **h_1n̥-dom* 'in house' > Hitt. *andan*, Lyc. *nte*, Gk. *ἔνδον*, Lat. *endo*, OIr. *and*; **me-ǵʰsr-i* 'to/in hand' > Gk. *μέχρι* 'until', Arm. *merǰ* 'near'; **me-bdi* 'on foot' > PN MEBDIVS (Bracarensis).[11]

A delocatival adjective **perutino-* may have existed in IE side by side with the adverb to judge from Myc. *pe-ru-si-nu-wo-* demanding a Proto-Gk. **perutin-u̯o-* which is seemingly continued in Attic Gk. περυσινός and in Armenian *hervänig*. Myc. *pe-ru-si-nu-wo-* goes back to **perutin-u̯o-* shows an intrusive labial glide and is obviously related to *περυσινός*, but not necessarily identical. **perutino-* may be analyzed as **perut-ino-* or **peruti-(i)no-*, and then similar to Gk. ἑαρινός 'related to spring time' (note the striking formational coincidence with Skt. *paryār-íṇī* 'cow calved after a year', lit. 'afteryear-ly', Lat. *hornus* 'produced this year', from **gʰo(i̯)-i̯ōr-ino-*).

Vine has recently sought to show that the base of the Mycenaean adjective is an ablatival adverbial **perutim* '(from) last year', which was endowed with the 'oppositional' suffix **-u̯o-*.[12] True, many primitive adjectives bearing a suffix *-u̯o-* are deadverbial, like **pro-u̯o-*, **ḱei̯-u̯o-*, and delocatival; but addition of **-u̯o-* to secondarily resuffixed adverbials like the proposed **peruti-m* remains unattested. Therefore the Mycenaean form stands a good chance of being the product of contamination with such adjectives as **deḱsi-u̯o-* after all. Vine would have a good comparative case, however, if OIr. *ónn uraid*, where *uraid* has been taken from an ancient accusative in view of the definite article,[13] actually *looked* like one because it went back to **peruti-m*. The Hispano-Celtic adjective would be an exocentric thematic derivative of a dialectal variant **perutin*, which poses some questions concerning the inconveniently late chronology required for the use of such an archaic derivational device, however. The Irish form may have been erroneously interpreted as an accusative of time after apocope, which eliminates the problem.

But what is a 'last year's' divinity? It is a common place of the history of religions that many divinities are associated with fertility and the everlasting natural cycle of death-and-return. Some of them even bear names derived from an IE word for 'year', such as the Roman goddess *Anna Perenna*, usually taken from **per-atnā*, or the Umb. *Vesuna*, if from **u̯etsōnā*.

The crucial clue to the meaning of this particular divinity probably resides in the explicit date of the inscription: 24th July is a moment in which the cereals (probably

adverb **sm̥-ut(i)*, and would possibly mean '(born) in the same year'. Cf. Hitt. *sāudist-* 'suckling animal', from **sm̥-u̯etes-t-*, Homeric οἰέτεας 'of the same year', and Mycenaean *au-u-te* if it means 'this same year' (Vine 2009b). These forms continue the genitive of a root stem, and accordingly the locative form would be copying the locative ending of **peruti*.

11 Prósper 2014c.

12 Vine 2009a.

13 Schrijver 1995, 257.

rye and barley) are beginning to be harvested, and that must have been a good year for agriculture. The divinity that made it possible through sufficient rain and a good climate is that of the last year or last season, and is subjected to renewal himself, as far as he takes part in a cycle of death and rebirth typical of male divinities of Greece, the middle East, Egypt, etc..[14] Suffice it to say that Dionysos is the typical example, but there are other IE divinities associated to fertility and sharing the property of death and rebirth, sometimes bearing a name that is indicative of this: Cf. the Slavic spring-god *Jarilos* and Lithuanian *Jõris*, whose names belong to the same stem as English *year*. Avestan has a divinity *maiδiiōi-šəma-* 'god of the second season'. However, most theories of ancient religion have long abandoned the view of a divinity periodically dying and resurrecting unchanged, so that we are at a loss about what lies specifically behind our DN, whether death and rebirth of a god, or an epithet of a well-known divinity, or simply a generic association with the cycle of life. An adjective *φeruti-*no-* may have come to mean 'one year old' as in Armenian, or 'belonging to the yearly cycle'. In Ireland, the *Lugnasad* marked the beginning of the harvest season on August 1st. This festival was celebrated in honour of Lugus, it was typically held on heights, and it is known to have been held also in Lugdunum in honour of Augustus.[15] This is only one week after the date of our inscription, so that the connection cannot be ignored. Jenaro MacLennan has pointed out that this is the exact day on which the Roman *Neptunalia* were celebrated, during which Neptunus was conciliated as a water god in order to secure the fertility of the fields.[16]

On the other hand, *Erudinus* may have been an epithet of Lugus himself, and then no ancient, inherited *φeruti-*no-* would have to be reconstructed. Still, if this were the case I would expect a local formation **erut-i̯ai̯kino-*, **erut-ikino-*, which would match other DNN of the Cantabri which are originally epithets, such as CABVNIAEGINO and OBBELLEGINO (Palencia). Finally, the social implications of these ideas are unclear: Maybe the dedicant was a chieftain or ruler of the community. There is no positive indication that this is a strictly private cult and that *Erudinus* is the protector of a particular family or *cognatio*, the *Aunigaini*. Consular dating was ruled out by Jenaro MacLennan on the grounds that this is very unusual in private dedications, which may point to a collective dedication in a broader sense.[17]

2. Deus Cabuniaeginus

2.1 The inscription

Another altar devoted to the unparalleled divinity *Deus Cabuniaeginus* was unearthed in 1891 forming the walls of the hillfort of Monte-Cildá, Palencia:[18]

14 The classical reference is Frazer 1894.
15 Koch 2006, 1201–2, MacNeill 1962.
16 Jenaro MacLennan 1996.
17 Jenaro MacLennan 1996.
18 Hernández Guerra 1994, nr. 1.

CABVNIAEGINO
DOIDER[A TRIDIA
[-]M PRO SALVT[E]
[?D]VRATIONIS FI(LII)
[P]OLECENSIVM
L(IBENS) M(ERITO) S(OLVIT)

Although there are some doubts as to the correct reading of the dedicant's PN and that of her son,[19] the DN is clear. They are indigenous persons, the mother possibly belonging to the *Tridiavi* and bearing a typical Cantabrian name whose original form was *Dovidera*.

CABVNIAEGINO is an adjectival form, but in this case we may be dealing with a divine epithet that relates the divinity to the area he protects. It obviously contains the suffixal chain **-i̯ai̯k-ino-* and is based on a form **kabuno-* which has no direct cognates.[20] Whether this underlying form is of onomastic or appellative nature is unknown. **kabuno-* has been traced back to the same root as the PN CABVRVS, which is superficially attractive but inconclusive and starts from the implicit assumption that an adequate analysis may be attained by simply attaching an unexplained suffix to a sequence that looks like a root, without ever assessing its verbal or nominal status. In other words, no compatibility is expected to exist between the root and its derivational formants, and no Common Celtic, let alone IE noun or adjective is expected to result from the analysis. I will seek to show that the distribution of apparently metanalyzed suffixes such as *-aro-* or *-uro-* is not haphazard; there is a reason for the exclusion of some variants when attached to specific roots, and for their spatial distribution. In other words, it is sometimes preferable not to ascribe these forms to the realm of onomastics if their ultimately appellative nature can be accounted for in phonetic terms. There are cases for which a secondary suffix *-aro-*, *-uro-*, etc. must be assumed that additionally may have been used exclusively to derive proper names; but, as we are going to see, when the original sequence *-CrV-*, *-ClV-* was preserved in CCelt., Hispano-Celtic often shows a special evolution, not shared by the rest of the Celtic dialects, which set us on the right track and allows to identify the Hispanic outcome of an older layer of nouns and adjectives.

What is more, there are reasons to doubt the existence of some derivational stems.

19 Cf. a detailed revision of former readings in Ramírez Sádaba & Campo Lastra 2010. [-]VRATIONIS is an isolated name. The elongated <T> may stand for <T+I>, not <I+T> as assumed by the latest editors among others. They deny that the first symbol is <D>, but this would make sense if we are dealing with a cognate of Gaul. DVRATVS, DVRATI, which are probably provided with a suffix **dus-*. Since there is little (but by no means insuffcent) room at the beginning of the line and the stone is badly chipped out, VRATIONIS could be a complete form going back to **u̯erāti̯ū* and this, *e.g.*, to **uφerā-to-* (cf. Lat. *superāre*, OHG. *oberon*, K.1.1. *urantiom*). The gentilic *Veratius*, which is mostly but not only attested in Celtic speaking areas (besides Rome and southern Italy) and in Celtiberian gen. sg. VERATI, could perhaps be of Celtic origin and the isolated VERANTIVS (Stolac, Dalmatia) would be the Celtic counterpart of *(Ex-)superantius*.

20 Other formations containing this suffix in the area are: SDVBLEGINO, BIRACIDEGINO, ALISSIEGINI, PENDIEGINO, ARONIAECINORV(M), OBBELLEGIN[O] (*-i̯ai̯-* > *-i̯ɛ:-*).

For instance, a base **kabu-* has been posited for *Caburus*;[21] but the alleged cognate OIr. *cab* 'mouth, muzzle' does not exist.[22] A preform **g^hab^{h}u-* which would match Lith. *gabùs* 'clever, skilful' could form the base of **kabu-no-* and **kabu-ro-*, but I find no compelling reason for the remodelling of its initial consonant. Consequently, CABVRVS calls for an explanation. As I have advanced, the structure of CABVNIAEGINO is equally unparalleled, and no *-u-* or nasal stem is available that would account for it.

2.2 Some thoughts on Celtic *kaφ-, *gab-... and *kab-

The Celtic root **gab-* 'to take, seize' is only preserved with certainty in OIr. *gaibid*. Its only cognates are Italic, specifically Latin *habeo*, Umb. *habia*, *hahtu*, etc. In view of this, a Late-IE **g^h(e)Hb^h-* is usually reconstructed.[23] The original present stem is **gab-(e)i-* according to Schrijver.[24] Surprisingly, this root structure may not be preserved in Hispano-Celtic at all. Jordán has studied the 3rd person plural verb CABINT in an unpublished Celtiberian bronze tablet in the Latin alphabet, and concluded it is suggestive of Hispano-Celtic having **kab-* instead of inherited **gab-*.[25] He tentatively relates it to the phonetically ambiguous *kabizeti* in Botorrita-I.[26] In sum, confusion with **keh$_2$p-* 'take'[27] must have occurred somewhere down the line. Schumacher has already posited a similar refashioning to account for Brittonic **kab-* in MW. *kaff*, etc. (favouring a confusion with **kag^h-*).[28] The whole material must be consequently reconsidered.

In my view, the secondary root **kab-* is also contained in the rare PNN CABITVS and CABVTA, CABVTI, CABVTONIS attested in Gaul and Alpes, alongside a *-n-*stem *Kabutu* in Botorrita-III. Their immediate antecedent is attested in the Gaulish PN CAXTOS (Paris),[29] OIr. *cacht* 'servant', MW. *caeth* 'slave', Lat. *captus*. In CABITVS, **kabi-* owes its extension to the present stem, like *kabizeti*. CABVTI/*Kabutu* possibly reflect a thematicized amphikinetic **kap-ōt-* (cf. **med-ōt-* 'ruler' in OIr. *coimdiu*, Hispano-Celtic PN MEDVTVS). The phonetic outcome **ka.ūt-* (> **kau̯t-*) of PCelt. **kaφ-ūt-*, acc. **kaφ-ot-m̥* may be attested in CAVTVS, CAVTIVS (Pannonia, Noricum), CAVTONI (Lusitania). Since the original gen. sg. was **kax-t-ós*, a morphophonetic alternation persisted and a paradigm remodelling gave rise to **kab-ūt-*, which has inserted the labial by analogy with CABITVS, etc. Furthermore, a PN

21 Delamarre 2003, 432.
22 In fact it is a modern form also attested in Scots Gaelic, and probably a loanword from English *gap* and *gab* 'chatter'. Cf. MacBain 1982, s.u. A slab of sandstone reading SVCABO CVNOVENDV[S] found near Northumberland contains a possibly related compound, but everything indicates SVCABO is the dative of a thematic word. Delamarre's translation 'good mouth' crucially depends on the Gaelic form, and is in any event unrelated to our example, like the dative IOTACABO in the Lugdunensis. CABVCA and CABVSA are exclusively attested as potter's names and probably contain the well known metanalyzed suffixes *-uko-*, *-uso-*. The underlying **kab-(o)-* may be of verbal origin, which we might speculatively relate to the Latin compounds containing *-kap-* 'seizing' (see below).
23 But **g^heHb-* in LIV, 195.
24 Schrijver 2003, 68–85.
25 Jordán 2014.
26 An aorist subjunctive built to the present stem, analyzed as **gab-i-s-e-ti* in Prósper 2008, 39–40.
27 LIV 344-5, cf. Lat. *capio*, Goth. *haban*.
28 Schumacher 2004, 320–1.
29 Delamarre 2003, 112.

CABEDVS is attested once among the Cantabri and once in Lara (Burgos). Since this name is unparalleled, the attractive reconstruction **kab-et-o-* (thematicized agent noun) or **kab-eto-* (verbal adjective) can only be sustained at the cost of accepting that /t/ has undergone voicing.

The root **kab-* must have come into being by crossing of **gab-* and **kaφ-*, either independently, which is difficult to believe, or because the confusion is older than previously believed, perhaps comprising most of the Celtic territory like the phonetic change *-mn-* > *-u̯n-*. But how did the confusion precisely come about? I suspect it is usually the old deverbative formations derived from **kap-* (prototypically those containing *-t-*) that took on a form **kab-*. The process may have been triggered by forms suffixed by *-t-*, in which the preceding *-b-* and *-p-* were neutralized, and subsequently spread to the rest of the (mostly prevocalic) forms. A verb **gab-* was afterwards ousted by the newborn **kab-*. Such names as GABILVS, as well as OBret. *ad-gabael*, MW. *gafael* (vs. remodelled *caffael*), OIr. *gabál* 'seizing', simply remained untouched by this chain of events. Note that, if it is a modified version of **kap-* that actually survived, the whole process can be projected further back in time, since different dialects or groups of dialects simply had to select **gab-* (Goidelic) or **kab-* (the rest). The Gaulish name CABILVS, CABILO is especially interesting, since it is similar to ᴮToch. *kapille* 'fever' (**kap-i̯e-li̯o-* and Lat. *capulus* 'handle' (and then **kapi-lo-*, not **kap-elo-* with a rather doubtful instrumental suffix). If related, the Gaulish PN CABIRVS is another case of secondary verbal **kabi-*.

If the Gaulish forms CABVTONIS, CABITVS, CAXTOS, Hispano-Celtic *Kabutu*, CABEDVS, MW. *caffat* < past participle **kabato-* and the finite forms MW. *caff* (present stem **kab-ī-*), Celtib. CABINT, *kabizeti* are directly related, we may conclude that the only obstacle to the reconstruction of a root **kab-* that would have ousted **gab-* in all branches except Goidelic is a small number of Gaulish forms: The doubtful GABXSITV (Lezoux;[30] L. Fleuriot's reading has never reached general consensus, and the expected imperative is **gab-i-tūd* or **ga(x)s-tūd*), GABAS[31] (context unclear, often held to be a preterite) and most importantly GABI (spindle whorl of Saint-Révérien, Nièvre),[32] unanimously translated as an imperative 'take!' thus far.

2.3 Another interpretation of Saint-Révérien

Just for the sake of argument, one could eliminate GABI from the discussion by abandoning its traditional interpretation and translating the text MONI GNATHA GABI | BVÐÐVTTON IMON differently from the generally accepted 'come, girl, take my kiss'.[33] Meid compares BVÐÐVTTON to the rare MIr. *bus* 'lip', which entails a subtle shift from the original meaning, besides the fact that its stem is unknown; Watkins translates 'penis' and compares OIr. *bot*, which is implausible if the Gaulish reflex of CC. **bozdo-* were

30 RIG II.2, L-101.
31 RIG II.2, L-55.
32 RIG II.2, L-119.
33 Meid 1980, 15–6.

**botto-* as in ICelt.[34] An inverse meaning 'give!' for GABI is out of the question. There is wide consensus about the status of BVÐÐVTTON IMON as the DO of GABI. In my view, however, GNATHA GABI could be a noun phrase meaning 'captivating girl' and comparable to Gaul. NATA VIMPI 'beautiful girl', and GABI would go back to *g^hab^h-ī, *-i̯ās*. According to Neumann, the same inflection would be present in the Germanic dedications to the MATRIBVS GABIABVS, GARMANGABI (Britain), etc., in which the meaning would be 'giver' for reasons internal to Germanic.[35]

This would go some way towards explaining the doublet DNN OLLOGABIABVS (Mainz, Germania Superior) vs. ALAGABIAE (Germania Inferior), the first of which has at least one Celtic component. The traditionally assumed meaning 'all-giving', presumably generated in a Germanic compound, is problematic, however: If the Germanic verb 'give' goes back to *g^heb^h-,[36] and is then different from Italic and Celtic *g^heHb^h- 'take', we would have to posit an /o/-grade form *g^hob^h-ī. Still, Goth. *gabei* 'riches' goes back to *g^hab^h-ī(-n-)* like the OHG. dat. pl. *kepim* translating *opibus* and possibly the DN GABINIS (Germania Inferior), and its original meaning may have been 'having, possession' rather than 'dowry, endowment'. This isolated Germanic remnant of our root might have survived in DNN fully synonymous with their Celtic counterparts or may have succumbed to the early influence of the nearly homonymous forms meaning 'give', whatever their subsequent relation to Celtic. On a different account, Celtic **ollo-gab-ī* 'all-embracing, plentiful' and possibly the other onomastic items were secondarily nativized in Germanic.

The same idea could now be extended to Umbrian HABINA/*hapina*, a sacrificial animal, which otherwise remains unexplained. It has been linked to Lat. *agnus*.[37] Nonetheless, that an alleged preform *$ag^{u̯(h)}$nī-nā* should have evolved into *χabinā by dissimilation and addition of initial aspiration simply begs the question, and is further questioned by 'central Italic' AVNOM HIRETVM. If, as Nieto Ballester has cogently observed,[38] this sequence is mirrored by Umbrian *unu erietu*, and if *unu* goes back to *$ag^{u̯h}$no-* 'lamb',[39] it is unlikely that *$ag^{u̯(h)}$nī-nā* should have given anything other than **au̯nīnā*, with a stable syllable structure and preservation of the natural connection with the masculine form. HABINA/*hapina* seems synchronically related to the subjunctive *habia*, etc., and further to Lat. *habeo* 'to have, carry', and accordingly is more likely to refer to a pregnant animal, possibly a ewe, as opposed to GOMIA/*kumia*, which designates a pregnant sow (compare Latin *forda bos* vs. *sus gravida/praegnans*). Assuming it goes back to *$g^hab^{(h)}$-ī-nā*, its inner-Italic derivation is trivial. To sum up, the reconstruction of a *devī*-stem *$g^h\mathring{H}b^h$-ih_2* for Celtic, Italic and Germanic is worth considering.

34 Watkins 1999, 542.
35 Neumann 2008, 365–6. A state of the art in French 2014, who traces back the OIc. DN *Gefjun* to Gmc. **gabī* enlarged by a Hoffmann suffix.
36 LIV 193.
37 De Vaan 2008, 30.
38 Nieto Ballester 1993.
39 A preform *$ag^{u̯}$no-*, as suggested by the other IE languages, is not excluded, since the outcome *-bn-* is often conditioned by paradigmatic pressure, as in Oscan *kúmbened* vs. CEBNVST.

If GNATHA GABI in Saint-Révérien is a noun phrase, the whole sentence hinges on the meaning and syntax of the first imperative: The form MONI, which by Meid's account is superfluous and belongs to a poorly attested root meaning 'go', as in OIr. *muinithir* 'go around' (though one could argue that it was partly grammaticalized as an extra-sentential element, like Sp. *venga*, Eng. *come*), would accordingly be a transitive imperative and continue the original causative **mon-e̯ie/o-* of **men-* 'to think', in OIr. *muinithir* 'to think, meditate', OBret. *guo-monim* gl. 'polliceri', Celtib. MONIMAM. Its actual structure was consequently **mon-ī* (identical to Lat. *mon-ē*). An additional advantage of this alternative interpretation would be the possibility of reading the text upside down, shared by virtually all these spindle whorls.

For phonetic as well as comparative reasons, IMON is not certain to be a possessive adjective **emo-* as usually claimed (whose best comparanda are Gk. ἐμόν and Hitt. *ammuk* 'me', *ammel* 'of me'), and neither a direct cognate of Skt. *im*-ám 'this'.[40] It might go back, e.g., to **Hēm-o-* 'affectionate', mechanically built (in analogy to the scheme **aḱr-i-*: **aḱr-o-*) to a noun **Hēm(H)-i-*, possibly preserved in South-Picene ímih.[41]

BVÐÐVTTON is a derivative of a noun going back to **b^hud^h-tu-* 'offering' (in the sense of the root **b^he̯ud^h-* 'to be aware, wake', inherited by G. *bieten* 'offer', MW. *bodd* 'good will, favour', OIr. *buide* 'satisfaction', ^A^Toch. *pota*, ^B^Toch. *pauta* 'flatter, honour') and in spite of scholarly tradition is entirely unrelated either to lips or to penises.[42] The commonly adduced Gaulish PN BVSSVMARVS would mean 'rich in presents, great by his presents' rather than 'having big lips (or penis)'. It is worth mentioning that the first term of the *-māro-* compounds is usually an abstract (often a *-tu*-stem!), not a body part; and these formations are likely to designate properties/qualities that one has a good share of, rather than 'big things' that a person possesses. Additionally, bahuvrihis show the inverse word order: inverse bahuvrihis refer to inherent physical properties, like 'broad-chested'. But in this case it is far from certain that the adjective *-māro-* has been used: See the Cantabrian EN PEMBELORVM (a tribe of the *Orgenomescī*, CIL II 5729), which goes back to **k^ưenno-belo-* 'big headed'. The PN BVSSVGNATAE (Noricum) and especially the DNN DEO BVSSVMARO in Dacia and BVSSVRIGIO (Dacia) and Ζεύς Βουσσουρίγιος (Galatia), leave little room for doubt as to their meaning, which is reminiscent of other 'fortune dispensing' divinities like Skt. *Bhaga-*, Russ. *dažь-bog*, Gk. δαίμων (and conversely adjectives and names evoking a 'godsend', like Skt. *deva-datta-* 'given by the divinity', Slavic *Bogdan*, Gk. θεόδοτος, Luwian *Tiwata-wiya*, Persian *Baghdad*). Note that

40 A suggestion by S. Schumacher *apud* Stifter 2011a, fn. 19. In that case I would expect IMON to precede the noun. Furthermore, addition of *-om* is very productive in Indo-Iranian. It remains unattested in Celtic to my knowledge.

41 See Vine 2006; if his explanation of Lat. *amī-cus* as containing an instrumental ultimately related to this noun is right, Italic simply had recourse to external derivation to meet the same goal. A cognate of Lat. īmus and perhaps Oscan *imad-en* (abl.fem. + postp.) 'deep, last, intimate; small?' is semantically conceivable but phonetically uncertain; a demonstrative **esmo-* would confront the same syntactic problems as **i-m-óm* and is phonetically implausible. Both have occasionally been related to SP. ímih.

42 The suffix remains unclear: although a diminutive may be the prefered option, we cannot reject out of hand the possibility that it is a deinstrumental possessive formation of the type *acūtus*, meaning 'related to offering' or the like.

the root *b^hag- 'divide, attribute' may be marginally attested in Celtic or 'Pannonian' onomastics if two instances of a PN BAGETONIS (gen. sing., Pannonia Superior) go back to an agent noun *b^hag-et- 'distributor of riches' (or more likely *bāget- from *b^heh_2g-et- under acceptance of Lubotsky's Law for Indo-Iranian). Finally, this view is supported by the Gaulish PN DANNOMARVS, which obviously does not mean something as foolish as 'rich in magistrates' or 'possessing big civil servants', but 'rich in gifts', like DANNORIX is 'prince of gifts' (*deh_3-no- *in* MW. *dawn*, OIr. *dán* 'gift', secondarily transferred to the -*u*- stems, but the change is probably underway in other dialects, as shown by the PN DANNVMARA, Belgica).

A derived PN BVSSVRO in Pannonia Superior definitely speaks in favour of an inherited -*tu*- stem. And this type of structure is unlikely to designate a body part like 'lip'. Finally, the very acceptance of a meaning 'present' would make the traditional interpretation of GABI lose ground: One does not expect the offerer of a talking object to keep telling the recipient to take it forever. My tentative translation of Saint-Révérien is 'keep in mind, ravishing girl, (this) little token of affection', obviously referring to the spindle whorl itself.[43]

Interestingly, Vine's idea casts some light on the syntactic and phonetic difficulties of another spindle whorl reading GENETA IMI DAGA VIMPI (Sens, Yonne, L-120; the alternative reading GENETTA presupposing a ligature of <E+T> can be dispensed with), which has been translated as 'I am a girl, good, beautiful' (L-120) or 'girl mine, good, beautiful'.[44] If we take IMI to reflect the feminine form of IMON, the word order has nothing anomalous: as usual in these artifacts, a man is addressing his beloved one[45] and a sequence of noun + adjective(s), this time to be translated as 'girl affectionate, good, beautiful', is found.[46]

---

43 Note that, if the first syllable of BVÐÐVTTON were scanned short (that is, if 'tau gallicum' systematically rendered an affricate /t^s/), and the first vowel of GNATHA is equally short, and this word is a *nominativus pro vocativo*, we would obtain a catalectic iambic trimeter with a dieresis dividing the two lines (see Stifter 2011a, 174–5 for a different arrangement and translation).

44 Meid 1980, 21.

45 This is probably the case even in more uncertain cases, like the text usually read as VEADIA TVA | TENET, which is more likely to read AVE ADIATV | GENETA (as per L-116). I have additional misgivings on some allegedly mixed texts, like GENETA VIS CARA (L-114), which in my view contains an adjective VISCARA and is merely descriptive in nature, not urging anybody to do anything and accordingly constitutes a sort of message intended to last in time.

46 And then IMI is to be separated from sentence final ιμμι 'I am' in the dish of Escengolatus (from *esmi* via *emmi*, while IMI shows no gemination). An instrumental *ēm-ī 'with love' looks less likely. There is no convincing explanation of why IMI and VIMPI are -*ī* stems, but it has been argued that they are substantivized adjectives, in which case they would respectively mean 'darling, love' and 'beauty'; Lambert recently proposes a special suffixation comparable to the German weak form of the adjective and the French use of the article, as in 'la belle', which was specifically used phrase-finally, so that words in -<I> are allowed to accompany nouns («une extension de son emploi», see Feugere & Lambert 2010). This is in line with what we find in Yonne, namely two combinations of -<A> + -<I>. Still, some adjectival endings remain constant in whatever position, like DAGA in L-141, unless we have to understand this case as predicative and then 'strong'. This seems to be the case if the whole sequence, perhaps to be read as CERVESA PO(TA) TAVRILLA BISIETVTO DAGA means 'drink beer, Taurilla, be kind'.

2.4 A phonetic solution for CABVRVS and CABVNIAEGINO

Returning to CABVRVS and CABVNIAEGINO, I assume they go regularly back to **kap-* and are by no means the product of the early merger of two IE roots as depicted above, though they might have provided some indirect input for it. The Celtic outcome of IE /p/ has not been lost in medial syllables when a liquid follows, and is phonologized as /b/ in most Celtic dialects; because of its comparatively poor attestation, and because the onomastic material at issue comes mostly from the western regions, Hispano-Celtic has been very superficially studied. I believe there are objective reasons to reconstruct an intermediate stage in which this labial was still a voiceless fricative in this context. If such a stage can be posited, it is conceivable that there exists a Celtic dialect in which the outcome of this cluster differs from those of Gaulish and Insular Celtic.

This provides a suitable phonetic explanation of the PN CABVRVS as opposed to Gaulish GABRVS: In Hispano-Celtic, heterosyllabic clusters of *muta cum liquida* have been regularly broken by an anaptyctic vowel causing resyllabification, probably in order to optimize the unnatural syllabic structure containing a coda stronger than the ensuing onset.[47] Anaptyxis must have taken place when the stop was still voiceless, which, as we will see below, accounts for the quality [u] of the prop-vowel. Upon resyllabification, the voiceless fricative became phonetically voiced [*β*] and was phonologized as /b/, since CCelt. intervocalic [φ] from IE /p/ had long been lost. See more on the actual process below.

If we extend the hypothesis of vowel insertion in clusters of *muta cum liquida* to those containing nasal segments, which are comparatively stable but not immune to this phenomenon, we must posit a process **-φ.n-* > **-φun-* > *-βun-* to account for CABVNIAEGINO, which could thereby be derived from a noun **kap-no-* 'harbour' (ultimately from **kh̥*$_2$*p-*). **kaφno-* eventually resulted in **kau̯no-* in the rest of the Celtic branches, as in OIr. *cúan*, and might form the base of the DN CAVNONNAE (Narbonensis). As for the actual meaning or specific functions of these divinities, we are still and probably will always be in the dark: CABVNIAEGINO may refer to the protector of a place or region called something like **Cabuno-*, and in that case the underlying PlN would not be related to the divinity itself, and was probably called 'the harbour' because it was well protected or sheltered. The PlN *Cabueñes* (Asturias) may have the same origin. The PN CAVNVS (Gaul, Lusitania, etc.) may go back to a *-n*-stem **kam-ū*, **kam-n-ós*, which has the advantage of explaining CAMONIVS, CAMVNIA (Dalmatia, Umbria) as derived from the nom.-acc. stem.

Many Hispanic names beside the aforementioned are illustrative of this tendency. What is more, there are by now many indications of a neat context-bound distribution of the prop-vowels, depending on whether they follow a voiceless or a voiced stop. In the first case, as claimed above, we find a vowel /u/, and in the second case we find /a/ or no prop-vowel. The reason for this may have to do with the intrinsically

47 Cf. the Preference Law for Syllable Structure in Vennemann 1988; for Hispano-Celtic see Prósper 2014a.

longer duration of voiceless, especially voiceless fricative segments, which may have generated the intrinsically shortest prop-vowel. An early shift in the syllable boundaries accounts for the homogeneous tautosyllabic outcome in the rest of Celtic. To conclude, morphological boundaries play a decisive role in some clusters of *muta cum liquida* being unexceptionally tautosyllabic, like *(-)*brig*- 'high place, hillfort', *(-)*treb*- 'settlement', as opposed to breaking of initial **Cl*-.[48] Other exceptions occur in *inherited* compounds, e.g. ethnonyms: longer words are often prone to resyllabification, and consequently may not undergo anaptyxis. Finally, forms containing -*VRCR*- seem to be syllabified as -*VRC.R*-, perhaps because they retain the original PCelt. syllabification, when the first sonorant formed the nucleus (-*R̥C.R*-). The same applies to complex nuclei in the sequence -*Vi̯/u̯C.R*-. Alternatively, a CCelt. cluster -*(V)RCRV*- was syllabified as -*(V)R.CRV*-. Thereupon, a prop vowel was inserted yielding -*VR.C*$_ə$*RV*-, which is reminiscent of the 'Sievers' effect (in Edgerton's specific formulation).

2.5 Resyllabification of Hispano-Celtic clusters of 'muta cum liquida'

2.5.1 Clusters of voiceless stop + liquid

**-t.r/l- > *-tur/l-*:

**kat-ro-/*katu-ro-*? 'battling' > Hispano-Celtic CATVRVS; CATRVS (Belgica), CATRONI (Noricum), pseudo-gentilic CATRONIVS.

**ai̯t-ro-* 'bitter, harsh' > Hispano-Celtic PN AETVRVS, AETVRA, AETVRIQVM, cf. Lith. *aitrùs* 'harsh'.[49] A -*ro*- derivative of an action noun **ai̯tu-ro-* 'giving' is equally possible.

**mut-ro-* 'dark' > Celtib. FN *Muturiskum*, PN MVTVRRA < **mutur-i̯ā*, Madrid,[50] OIr. *mothar* 'marsh'.

**φā-tlo-* 'drinking vessel' > Hispano-Celtic **ātulo-*, with a nasal derivative **ātul-ū*, **ātul-n-os* > Celtib. FN *Atulikum* (K.0.6); in that case, identical to Lat. *pōculum*; OIr. *ól* 'act of drinking' shows an unexpected short vowel. The PN ATVLLVS commonly adduced as its derivational basis is especially well attested in Latium and Campania and rare in Celtic speaking areas and accordingly not even certain to be Celtic.

**sta-tlo-* 'place' > Hispano-Celtic **statulo-*, with a nasal derivative **Statul-ū*, **Statul-n-os* > Celtib. *Statulu*, *Statulos*, STATVLICI (Castelo Branco, Portugal); Gaul. STATLIAE (Narbonne), OIr. *sál* gl. 'calx'.

**trito-tl-o-* > Hispano-Celtic **tritotulo-*, with a nasal derivative Celtib. *Tirtotulu* (Iniesta), perhaps a thematicized compound of the numeral 'third' and the root **telh*$_2$- 'to stand, suffer', cf. Gk. πολύ-τλα-ς. A nomen instrumenti seems less likely. **trito-* might be replacing **tri-* for all we know about compounds of whatever meaning containing a numeral + a root noun. Still, the FN *Tirtobolokum*, containing an agent noun **g*^{u}*olh*$_1$*ó*- 'launching' leads me to think that the first member is not a numeral but a substantivated past participle, where the root is in turn compatible with several etymologies, like **t(e)rK-* or **tr(e)i̯-*.

**-kl- > *-kul-*:

?**u̯ok*^{u}*-tlo-* 'word' > CCelt. **u̯oxtlo-*: Celtiberian FN *Ukulikum* (Botorrita-III), PN VQVLANCA (Burgos) may contain a -*n*-stem **u̯okul-ū*, **u̯okull-os* derived from **u̯ok(k)lo-* with early loss or assimilation of -*t*- (followed by late contextual raising of /o/, well attested in the vicinity of labials); OIr. *foccul/focal* may have undergone a similar process (original **u̯oklo-* would

48 Prósper 2014b.

49 Pokorny 1959, 17.

50 On the resyllabification and glide absorption **-r.i̯- > -r.ri̯- > -rr-* see Prósper 2014a.

result in †*fól*); MW. *gwaethl* 'dispute' either reflects a different evolution or analogical restoration of the suffix. It is directly related to Skt. *vaktram* 'mouth'.

Late-IE **-pr/l-* > CCelt. **-φ.r/l-* > Hispano-Celtic **-φur/l-* > *-βur/l-*:

**ap-lo-* 'strength' > CCelt. **aφ-lo-* > Celtiberian **aβulo-*; cf. Gaulish EN *Di-ablintes* 'the weak ones' vs. its 'Illyrian' antonym MAGAPLINVS 'very strong' (< **m̥ǵh̥₂-*): The basic form is attested in the compound *(Likine) Abulorau̯ne* (Andelos, Navarra; an iberized PN on a mosaic inscription) from Hispano-Celtic **Likin-os Aβulo-u̯lau̯n-os* 'ruling by strength'.[51] Its nasal derivative **Aβul-ū*, **Aβul-n-os* yields Celtiberian *Abulu*, *Abulos*, FN *Abulokum*.[52]

**ep-ro-* 'boar' > CCelt. **e-φro-* might be reflected in Hispano-Celtic as **eβuro-* in a PN *Eburṡunos* (Botorrita-III), if from **eφro-sū-* 'boar-pig' (cf. OCS. *veprĭ* 'boar' < **u̯eprio-*, Latv. *vepris*, Thrac. *ἔβρος* 'buck' (Hesych), OHG. *ebur*, OE. *eofor* < PGm. **eburo-* 'boar'; for the compound, Gk. σῦς κάπρος). The variants are probably due to tabooistic reasons. **Eburo-* is otherwise attested in Celtic only with the meaning 'yew': OIr. *ibar*, MW. *efwr*. I no longer suscribe to my former analysis of *Eburṡunos* as 'son of the yew/boar'.

**alp-ro-* 'weak' > PN ALBVRVS (Lusitania), cf. Lith. *alpùs*, Skt. *alpa-*.

rep-ro-* 'seizing' > 'furious', (western-)Hispano-Celtic PN REBVRRVS (via **reφro-* > **reφuro-* > **reβuro-* → **reβur-i̯o-* > **reβurri̯o-*) vs. the latinized cognomen REBVRINVS (reβur-ino-*); Gaul. PN REBRICVS. Cf. Skt. *rapas-* 'wound', **rep-tu-* in OIr. *rext* 'paroxysm', MW. *anreith* 'booty', perhaps Lat. *rapio*, Gk. ἐρέπτομαι.

**kap-ro-* 'goat' > **kaφ-ro-* > Hispano-Celtic **kaβuro-* in Celtiberian FN *kaburikum* (Botorrita-III), western-Hispano-Celtic CABVRVS. The PNN CABRVS and CABRILLVS are attested in Gaul or Britannia, but are unknown in Hispania except for a number of problematic forms (see below).

How can we come to terms with the initial voiced velar of Gaulish and ICelt. **gabro-*? Isaac's reconstruction **kpro-* > **gbro-* > **gabro-* is untenable.[53] First, **kapro-* is widely attested, as in Gk. κάπρος or Lat. *caper*, and a CCelt. form with an initial voiceless stop must have existed for the Gaulish and Brittonic PNN going back to **kabro-* to be possible. See Stifter in defense of the idea that «before resonants, the newly developed **φ* acquired a voiced allophone [*β*], which was subsequently re-interpreted as the phonetically lenited allophone of **b*» (ICelt. forms show lenition of /b/ in this context).[54] I basically agree on this, except that a prior stage **kaφro-* must have survived into Hispano-Celtic. The voiced Anlaut of the appellative form **gabro-* is secondary, perhaps analogical on **gʰai̯do-* 'goat', but the archaism **kabro-* was occasionally preserved unaltered as a PN. The voicing never reached the immediate ancestor of Hispano-Celtic: **gaβro-*/**kaβuro-* are therefore not expected to coexist in the same dialect.

Several western-Hispano-Celtic compounds contain a sequence <CABRV>-, not

51 With dissimilation of laterals, as in Lat. **sol-alis* > *solaris* and the hybrid Celtiberian PlN (on coins) *Olka-iŕun* 'field-city', containing Basque *ilun* 'city'.

52 In all likelihood a possessive formation, like *Statulu*. Still, this form shows the Ablaut originally corresponding to the original individualizing suffix, directly applied to adjectives and nouns. Otherwise, the expected outcome would be *Abulu*, †*Abulunos*, and if there had been no anaptyxis in the base form we would expect **apl-V-* vs. **apl̥-C-* to yield *Abulu*, †*Abalos*. I believe both types to have coexisted until they were levelled out in Celtiberian: upon progressive loss of the semantic distinctions, two new morphological types came into being: The usual declension *-C-ū*, *-C-ūn-os* (possibly due to the spread of the thematic derivative **-o-h₃ō(n)*, **-o-h₃n-ós*), and the conservative one with the form *-VR-ū*, *-VR-n-os*. See Prósper 2014a, 143.

53 Isaac 2007, 68–71.

54 Stifter 2011b.

<CABRO>-, which is by all accounts strongly anomalous unless we posit a dialectal, unmotivated *-u*-stem. Accordingly, I contend *-ur-* was metathesized into *-ru-* after **kaβuro-* underwent regular syncope of the thematic vowel in compounds.[55] In other words, secondary *-Cur.R/*$^{?}$*C-* was dispreferred in medial syllables, as in the dvandva **tūro-mogo-* > EN *Turmogus* vs. FN *Turumokum* /trumogu:m/ (Botorrita-III), OEng. *þurh* > *through*, Oscan **(k*^{u}*)turto-* > *trutos* 'fourth', as opposed to preservation or fortition and glide absorption of the word-final string *-ur.i̯V-* (as in the ENN SEVRRVS < **segur-i̯o-* and GIGVRRVS < **gigur-i̯o-*; cf. REBVRRVS, MVTVRRA below). This seamlessly accounts for the extant evidence:[56]

CABRVMVRIA (PlN, Valladolid): **kaβuro-mur-i̯o-* > **kaβur-mur-i̯o-* > **kaβru-mur-i̯o-* 'goat-swamp(-place)'.[57] Cf. Gaul. *Gabro-mago*, *Gabro-sentum*.

CABRVAGENIGORVM (FN, León): **kaβuro-u̯o-geno-* 'caprigenus' > **kaβur-u̯a-geno-* > **kaβr(u)-u̯a-geno-*.

CABRVIAMI (PN, Castelo Branco): **kaβuri̯-amo-* 'most goat-like' > **kaβrui̯-amo-* (DEO VACOCABVRIO in Astorga). The superlative suffix **-m̥Ho-* is very common in the peripheral areas of IE Hispania.

CABRVNI (Castelo Branco, Badajoz): **kaβurno-* (PNN CABVRN[- Bragança, CABVRNIANVS Lamego) from the gen. of the individualizing nasal stem **kaβur-ū*, **kaβur-n-os*; cf. Lat. *caprō*, *-ōnis* and Oscan καπροιννα[ι, epithet of Mefitis, from **kaproni̯ā*.

CABRVLEICI (León), CABRVLA (Castelo Branco) goes back to the diminutive **kaβuro-lo-* > **kaβur-lo-* > **kaβru-lo-* (Celtiberian PEDOLVS, AGOLIECA, AVROLVS, western TVROLVS).

This material confirms that the *appellative* form for 'goat' still contained **k-* in Hispano-Celtic, but the Hispano-Celtic PlN VAGABROBENDAM (Fuentes de Ropel, Zamora) seems problematic for my chronology: Its Anlaut **g-* is conducive to the conclusion that **gaβro-* is pan-Celtic after all. However, VAGABRO- does not belong here at all. It is the match of the seemingly umlauted Gaulish FVRNO VOGEBRICO (La Graufesenque)[58] going back to a compound **uφo-gabro-* 'sustaining, sustained$^{?}$', which probably has nothing to do with goats, but designates some sort of construction or bricklaying technique.[59] In fact, a very archaic deverbative adjective ***$g^{h}ab^{h}$*-ro-* underlies Latin *manubrium* 'handle, held-by-hand', *enubrō* 'prohibiting'.[60] **gaβro-* 'goat' remains consequently unattested in Hispania. Finally, it can hardly be due to chance that the Roman cognomen *Capratinus* has a cognate in two Vetton FNN in the gen. pl. CABVRATEIQVM (Ávila), where the possessive morpheme *-(ā-)to-* is indicative of the appellative nature of the base **kaβuro-*. Whether the *Caburriates* located in Piedmont by Pliny (with a number of *variae lectiones*) have to be included here is uncertain. This is my schematic reconstruction of the process:

55 Prósper 2014c.

56 The same probably applies to the (mostly) western-Hispanic PN ABRVNVS, ABRVNAENI. If it is identical to ABVRNVS, attested in Hispania and elsewhere in Europe, it may have undergone local metathesis for the same reason. Alternatively, it would be non-Celtic and comparable to Lat. *aper* 'boar', Umb. *abrunu*, Lat. *Apronius*, and the dialectal form *apruno* (Varro). Two examples of *Abronius* in Braga and Mainz (a person of Lusitanian provenience) are probably nothing but attempts at latinization or local reflexes of *Apronius*.

57 For **mu(H)-ro-* 'swamp' see Pokorny 1959, 741.

58 RIG II.1 L-30e.

59 RIG II.1, p. 109 tentatively translates 'l'endroit sous les chevrons', understanding the underlying syntax of the compound as prepositional.

60 From Proto-Italic **n̥-χafro-*; cf. De Vaan 2008, 190–1, 278.

IE *kap-ro- 'goat' > CCelt. *kaφro-:
> ICelt., Gaul. *gaβro- (noun, PN GABRIVS, GABRILLVS, Ubian DN GEBRINIO?), archaic *kaβro- (PN CABRVS)[61]
> Hispano-Celtic *kaβuro- (PN CABVRVS, FN *kaburikum*)

Late IE *kap-ero- 'goat' > CCelt. *kaφero-:
> ICelt., Hispano-Celtic *kaero- with regular loss of /p/ in OIr. *cauru*, gen. *cáerach* 'sheep',[62] W. *caeriwrch* 'roebuck'; a primary derivative is preserved in the Hispano-Celtic PNN CAERIA, CAERIVS (Lusitania), CAERRI (Palencia, Valladolid, Vaccaei; with resyllabification).

The Gaulish EN *Caerosī* (Gallia Belgica, Caesar *B.Gall.* 2.4.10; v. l. *Caeroesi*) may be analyzed as a compound (as if from) *$kapero\text{-}sth_2o$-* which matches the first term of the Galatian PN Ἐποσόγνατος, interpreted by Delamarre as *$(h_1)eḱu̯o\text{-}sth_2o$-* 'qui se tient à cheval'.[63] The DN IBOSO (Aquitania) might be a similar compound (as suggested by the clearly compounded IBOIT(A)E in Aquae Sextiae, which may contain *$h_1oi̯\text{-}to$-* 'way'?, thus providing a related structure). Specifically, this kind of compounds, when their first term is a noun, usually consists of neuters designating *places*, as in OHG. *ewist* 'sheepfold' from *$h_2ou̯i\text{-}sth_2o$-* or Celtib. *boustom* "cow stall" from *$g^uou̯\text{-}sth_2o$-*. Accordingly, I would translate Ἐποσόγνατος as 'born in a horse pen' and EPOTSOROVIDI (gen. sing., Aquitania)[64] as 'taking care of the horse pen', in which an underlying *φro-u̯id- would preserve, whatever the subsequent semantic changes in the preverb, the exact match of the base of Lat. *providus* (originally not an adjective in *-idus*, and not derived from *providere*; cf. Skt. *aśva-vid-* and especially Lat. *invidus*, Gk. νῆϊς 'nescius', OIr. *noidiu* 'infant'). I propose to understand the EN *Caerosī* in the same way, with a slight shift in the meaning of *-sth_2o-*, from object noun 'sheep enclosure/protection' to agentive noun 'sheep protectors', which was possibly favoured by compounds of *-sth_2o-* whose first term is an adverb or a locative; the resulting name is typical for a pastoralist population.[65]

IE *$g^hH̥b^h$-ro- 'held/holding' > CCelt. *(uφo-)gabro-:
> Gaulish adjective VOGEBRICO
> Hispano-Celtic PlN VAGABROBENDAM

2.5.2 CCelt. Clusters of voiced stop + vibrant

*-d.r- > *-dar-:
*kad-ro- 'beautiful' > MARTI BELATVCADRO (Britannia), western-Hispano-Celtic PN CADROIOLONIS, but usually attested as *kadaro-: Celtiberian FN *kazarokum*, PlN CADARNAVAEGIVM < *kadaro-nāu̯ā-(a)iko- 'beautiful valley' (Zamora), PN CADARVS (Lusitania), CADARIG(VM) (Cantabri).[66]

61 For *kabrosto- 'honeysuckle' cf. Bertoldi 1947.
62 From *ka.erūχs < *$kapero\text{-}h_3k^u$-s according to Stifter 2011b, 8. He favours late contraction of the hiatus after loss of the CC. outcome of IE /p/. The Gaulish ethnonym *Caeracates* would be a derivative of the oblique stem *ka.erāk- after the velar stem had been generalized.
63 Delamarre 2012, 122.
64 CIL XIII 1036.
65 Prósper 2012.
66 See Prósper 2014c. The dedications to BELATVCAVRO and BALATOCAVRO (for -<CADRO>) in Britannia reflect the same need to optimize the syllable structure by a different means.

*-b.r- > *-bar-:

**ai̯b-ro-* 'harsh' > Hispano-Celtic PN AEBARVS, OEng. *āfor*, OHG. *eibar* 'horrid, violent', from **h$_2$ei̯b^h-ro-*, ^{A}Toch. *ewär*.[67]

**abro-* 'strong'? > Hispano-Celtic ENN *Cant-abrī*, *Art-abrī*; the western PNN TALABARVS/-A 'strong-forehead?' may reflect the simplex **abaro-*.

**sam(b)-ro-* > Hispano-Celtic PN SAMBARO (Baetica), possibly origonym SAMBRVCOL(ENSI) (Aquae Flaviae, if from **sambr(o)-okelo-*)[68] could go back to **sm̥-ró-* or **sn̥g^u-ró-* 'falling, sinking, shallow?'; cf. SAMBRACIONI (Rome).

**treb-ro-* 'wise' > possibly in the western DN (dat.) TREBARVNE, TREBARONE, attested in short votive texts and in Lusitanian (Cabeço das Fráguas) and in the PN TREBRIA (Samnium), OIr. *trebar* 'wise', from **treb-* 'settlement'[69]

**dub-ro-* 'dark' (> 'water') > western PN (hápax) DVBRA, mount and river *Dobra*. If Celtic at all (this form is widespread: cf. Lith. RN *Dubravá*, OCS. *dŭbrŭ* 'valley', Illyrian *Dubris*, etc.), this form is exceptional, possibly resyllabified early because of the preceding *-u-*. In any event this is also a special context giving rise to special phonetic changes, as in **kup-no-* and **kup-ro-* (see below 2.7.).

I have excluded CAMB(A)RVS and LAB(A)RVS from consideration since the medial vowel is also attested elsewhere, and consequently may be reflective of an older remodelling. Hispano-Celtic PN CABARCVS (Asturias), CABARI (Lusitania), may be the product of nasal omission for CAMBARVS; but a *Valerius Cabarus* is mentioned by Caesar in Gaul, so **kab-aro-* may be old.

*-g.r- > *-gar-:

**lang^u-ro-* 'agile, swift' > **lang-ro-* > western-Hispano-Celtic PN LANGARI 'swift, light' (Évora), Gk. *ἐλαφρός, OHG. lungar*, from **h$_1$ln̥g^{uh}-ró-*.[70]

**sag-ro-* 'savage' > maybe **sagaro-* in Celtiberian *Sakarokas*, SACARICI (Lara, Burgos);[71] Ogamic *Sagro-*, OIr. *sár* 'strong'.

**lug-ro-* 'sad' > PN LVGARIVS (Vila Nova de Gaia, Porto); PN LVGRACVS (Carlisle, Britannia), Gk. *λυγρός*, ^{B}Toch. *läkle* 'pain' (with assimilation?)

2. 5. 3. CCelt. clusters of voiced stop + lateral were resyllabified early without anaptyxis:

*-b/g.l- > *-(V).bl-/-(V).gl-:

**mag-lo-* 'prince' > Celtib. PN MAGLAENA, Ogamic *Cunamagli*, Gaul. MAGLOMATONIVS, from IE **m̥ǵ-lo-* (cf. Lat. *magnus*, from **m̥ǵ-no-*). A similar formation MAGALVS (Dalmatia, Germania Superior) possibly goes back to **m̥ǵh̥$_2$-lo-* or has been redone.

**abol-*, *ablos* 'apple' → **abl-ū*, **abl̥-n-os* 'apple tree' > PNN ABLO, ABLONIVS and FN *Abiliqum*/ABLIQVM: consequently not to be confused with *Abulu*, *Abulokum* any more. Thematic **abl̥-n-o-* > **aballo-* > Celtib. PN *Abalos*, derivative *Abaliu* (Botorrita-III).

---

67 Pokorny 1959, 11; Pinault 2001, 128.

68 Note that IE words for 'summer' like OIc. *sumar*, Arm. *samarn* and possibly the first term of the Gaulish PlN *Samaro-briva* may all point to an IE adjective **sm̥h$_2$-éro-*. In my present state of knowledge, I believe this sequence would have given nothing in Hispano-Celtic but †SAMARVS and <SAMAR>- in compounds.

69 My interpretation of this DN as a compound in Prósper 1994 was based on the existence of another DN TREBOPALA (Cabeço das Fráguas).

70 The RN *Lambre* < **Lambris* (Galicia) is accordingly non-Celtic.

71 In the photograph provided by HEp-online, the first <C> looks different from the second; consequently I favour a reading SAGARICI. The widespread form *sagarius* is Latin, even when used as a PN.

2.6 Resyllabification of Hispano-Celtic clusters of 'muta cum nasali'

2.6.1 Clusters of voiceless stop + nasal

Late-IE **kap-no-* 'harbour' > CCelt. **kaφ.no-* > **kaφuno-* > **kaβuno-* > western-Hispano-Celtic CABVNIAEGINO; **-φ.n-* > **-u̯n-* in the other Celtic branches.

2.6.2 CCelt. clusters of voiced stop + nasal

**du̯i-gno-* 'twin' > **u̯ĭ/īgno-* > Celtiberian PNN VIGANVS, VIGGANO, VIGANICA, FN *uikanokum* Botorrita-I-B.41; Gaul. PNN VIGNVS, VIGNIDIVS, Lat. *bignae* 'twins', OI. *dvi-jā-* 'twice born'. This presupposes that the compound could no longer be analyzed.[72]

**abno-* > Hispano-Celtic PN ABANVS; Lat. *agnus*, Lusitanian acc. sg. ANGOM (Lamas de Moledo), ANCNVN (Freixo de Numão),[73] Gk. *ἀμνός*, OCS. *agnę* with Winter's law, from **h₂egᵘno-*; OIr. *úan* is problematic.

?**mag-no-* 'big' > PN MAGANVS (Lusitania) if equatable to Lat. *magnus*. The original form is held to have been **m̥ǵh̥₂-nó-*, which should have evolved into PLat. **ingă-no-* (cf. Gk. *ἀγανός* 'magnificent' > 'pleasant') and Celtic **angano-* (Schrijver's rule predicts *R̥DC-* > Italo-Celtic *RaDC-*, which suggests that *mag-* contains no laryngeal).

?**u̯id-no-* 'seeing' > PN VIDANVS (Palencia). This isolated name is amenable to several explanations; it could be based on the original oblique stem of a holokinetic nasal stem appellative **u̯ei̯d-ū* attested in OIr. *fíadu* 'witness'. A past part. comparable to Skt. *-vinna-*, Gk. *-ιδνός* is only reconstructable on the assumption that the allegedly CCelt. **u̯indo-* 'white, brilliant' is an infixed form and then not the product of early metathesis. Finally, it could be similar to a very rare PN VITANI (Aquitania) with intervocalic voicing.

2.7 Yes, but... what about the (Hispano-)Celtic outcome of IE *kup-ro-?

This particular sequence is said to have followed a different evolutionary path, specifically through the stages IE **kup-ro-* 'desirable, full of desire'? > CCelt. **kou̯ro-* > **kobro-* in OIr. *accobor* 'desire, will' and a number of Gaulish compounds with a first term **kobro-*.[74] If Hispano-Celtic had inherited a word **kobro-*, I would expect to find †COBARVS, but neither this form nor †COBVRVS is attested. Interestingly, a Carpetanian (southern Celtiberian) inscription containing the onomastic formula MONIS BOCOVRIQ(VM) ALLONIS F(ILIVS) (I C.) has been uncovered some years ago.[75] In my view, the unparalleled FN BOCOVRIQ(VM) simply continues a compound of a type well attested in Goidelic, in which **kobro-* has agentive sense: *milchobar* 'desiring honey' > 'bear'; *Conchobar* 'desiring dogs'; PN *Ólchobar* 'desiring ale'. The underlying PN **bō-kou̯ro-* is therefore a compound (as if from) IE **gᵘou̯-kupro-* 'wishing for cattle' which needs no further substantiation, as it reproduces a well known feature of nomadic societies heavily relying on livestock for living and often stealing it as transpires from many cattle raids in IE myth and folklore. In point of fact, this very semantic content is preserved in Skt. *gav-íṣ-*, *paśv-íṣ-*, *gavyayú-*, etc.

72 In fact it is quite old; see for the Latin and Sanskrit cases Nussbaum 2003.

73 Prósper 2010, 69.

74 Delamarre 2003, 120. Cf. the Umb. DN *Cupras matres*, South-Picene *kuprí*, *qupíríh*, the Sicilian nymph Κύπαρα, Sab. *ciprum* 'bonum', Ven. PN *Kuprikonioi*.

75 *HEp* online, *AE* 1990, 579.

From the phonetic point of view, our form attests the intermediate step *kou̯ro- and makes an evolution *kup-ro- > *kuφ-ro- > *koβro- with unmotivated lowering of medial /u/ unnecessary.[76] But why was bou̯- monophthongized earlier than kou̯ro-? There are several possible answers to this question. To begin with, there are many indications that primitive /o/ tended to raising in the initial syllables of polysyllabic words, especially when flanked by labial and velar sounds, which might have a counterpart in the monophthongization of /ou̯/; second, dissimilation of /ou̯/ in contiguous syllables is conceivable; and third, it might be the case that the compound goes back to *g^{u}ou̯o-, where dissimilatory loss of medial /u̯/ is equally possible. Finally, it may be the case that the phonetic segments, ex hypothesi [o:] and [ʊu̯] (see below) reflected a residual phonemic opposition /o:/ vs. /ou̯/ that may have been restricted to some areas: this would presuppose an earlier, structurally different opposition in which there were still two phonemic diphthongs with a different degree of opening in the first element and in turn opposed to /u:/, and cannot be substantiated for such a late date; the actual pronunciations, ex hypothesi [ɔu̯] and [ʊu̯], had probably merged long ago when the Latin alphabet was eventually imposed (but see below on the alternative possibility).

This interpretation in turn may illuminate a hitherto obscure votive inscription from Lusitania, allegedly reading: ARABO | COROBE|EICOBO | TALVSICO|BO. | M. T. B. | . D. M. | . L. A. (Arroyomolinos de la Vera, Cáceres).[77] ARABO is an unlikely masculine DN; accordingly, we may alternatively read ARA(M?) BOCOROBREICOBO TALVSICOBO, that is, altar devoted to the group of divinities protecting a place called †*Bōcōro-bri-s*, where the first term shows monophthongization of both diphthongs, *-bri-* is the typical outcome of *-brig-* in western Hispano-Celtic, and the relationship of the hillfort at issue to the unnamed divinity is established by way of a velar suffix, probably *-*ai̯ko-*, regularly yielding *-ei̯ko-* in a sequence *-bri̯-ai̯ko-*. -<BO> unequivocally continues an indigenous dative plural ending *-b^ho.

In that case, a phonetic evolution *kupro- > *kuφ.ro- > *kʊu̯.ro- > *koβ.ro- has reached its last-but-one stage in Common Celtic in contradistinction to those cases of IE /p/ in the coda following /a/ and preceding a nasal or liquid segment that I have reviewed above, in which the fricative stage [φ] of IE /p/ in a heterosyllabic cluster lasted longer and an approximant arose after the split-up of Common Celtic. If related to *kupro-, some infrequent Gaulish PNN like COVRA do not bear witness to the existence of the previous stage, but are mere attempts to improve the syllabic structure (see fn. 16 for British BELATVCAVRO). All this also applies to the sequence *-pn-* when preceded by a back high vowel, as in *kupno- 'desire' > *kou̯no-,[78] attested in the PN COVNVS and therefore unrelated to CAVNVS; cf. Celtiberian FN COVNEIDOQVM, whose base is identical to OIr. *cúandae* 'beautiful' (alternatively from IE *ḱou̯no-). Another likely example

76 This change is known to happen occasionally in a similar context, e. g. in <DOMNO> for <DVMNO>, implausibly put down to the influence of Latin *domnus*.

77 It has been variously interpreted; the account and translation by *HEp* on line are absurd. This is a refined version of Prósper 2002.

78 Schrijver 1995, 348, fn. 1.

is **supno-* 'dream' > **so̯uno-*, and this change has often been held to account for OIr. *clúain* 'meadow', Celtib. *kolounioku* (A.67), PlN *Clunia*, if from **ḱlop-ni-* 'damp area'. Interestingly, the blatant difference between the Celtiberian PlNN *Clunia* < **klou̯n(i)i̯ā* and *Rauda* < **rou̯dā* 'red' (nowadays *Coruña del Conde* and *Roa*, both in Burgos) would seem to suggest that as late as the 2nd century BC there actually was a phonemic difference between /ʊu̯/ and /ou̯/ (possibly [ɔu̯]) depending on the origin of the diphthong, and that it was interpreted by the Romans in their own terms respectively as /u:/ and /au̯/, since /ou̯/ no longer existed in contemporary Latin. If this holds true, the actual functional load of the opposition must have been very low and was never reflected in writing, at least in the Iberian script.

BIBLIOGRAPHY

Bertoldi, V. 1930 'Gallico **cabrostos* 'ligustro' (da **cabros*, il corrispondente gallico del greco κάπρος, ecc.)', *Revue Celtique* 47, 184–196.

Delamarre, X. 2003 *Dictionnaire de la langue gauloise*. Paris, Errance.

Delamarre, X. 2012 'Notes d'onomastique vieille-celtique', *Keltische Forschungen* 5, 99–137.

Dočkalová, L. & V. Blažek 2011 'The Indo-European year', *Journal of Indo-European Studies* 39, 414–95.

Feugere, M. & P.-Y. Lambert 2010 'Une belle gauloise... A propos d'une fibule inscrite de Laon', *Études celtiques* 37, 147–52.

Frazer, J. 1894 *The Golden Bough: A Study in Comparative Religion*. London, MacMillan.

French, K. 2014 *We need to talk about* Gefjun. *Toward a new etymology of an Old Icelandic theonym*. MA Dissertation, Reykjavík.

García y Bellido, A. & J. González Echegaray 1949 'Tres piezas del Museo Arqueológico Provincial de Santander', *Archivo Español de Arqueología* 22, 214–17.

Hernández Guerra, L. 1994 *Inscripciones romanas en la provincia de Palencia*. Valladolid, EUV.

Iglesias Gil, J. M. & A. Ruiz Gutiérrez 1998 *Epigrafía romana de Cantabria*. Bordeaux-Santander, Ausonius.

Isaac, G. 2007 *Studies in Celtic Sound Changes and their Chronology*. Innsbruck, IBS.

Jenaro MacLennan, L. 1996 'Nota sobre la inscripción latina del ara votiva a *Erudino* de la Cantabria romana', *Archivo Español de Arqueología* 69, 311–4.

Jordán, C. 2014 'La forma verbal *cabint* del bronce celtibérico de Novallas (Zaragoza)', *Emerita* 82, 329–45.

Koch, J. T. 2006 *Celtic Culture. A Historical Encyclopaedia*. Oxford, ABC-Clio.

MacBain, A. 1982 *An etymological dictionary of the Gaelic language*. Glasgow, Gairm.

MacNeill, M. 1962 *The festival of Lughnasa*, Oxford, OUP.

Meid, W. 1980 *Gallisch oder lateinisch? Sozio-linguistische und andere Bemerkungen zu populären gallo-lateinischen Inschriften*. Innsbruck, IBS.

Neumann, G. 2008 *Namenstudien zum Altgermanischen*. Berlin-New York, De Gruyter.

Nieto Ballester, E. 1993 '*Aunom hiretum* (Ve 227)', *Sprachen und Schriften des antiken Mittelmeerraums*, ed. F. Heidermanns, H. Rix and E. Seebold, 281–92. Innsbruck, IBS.

Nussbaum, A. J. 1986 *Head and Horn in Indo-European*. Berlin-New York, De Gruyter.

Nussbaum, A. J. 2003 'A benign interpretation: Latin *benignus* and the *bonus*-rule', talk held at the 23rd *East Coast Indo-European Conference*, Harvard, June 2003.

Pinault, G.-J. 2001 'Nouveautés lexicales et morphologiques dans le manuscrit de Yanqi du Maitreyasamiti-Nāṭaka en tokharien A', *Akten des 27. deutschen Orientalistentages*, ed. S. Wild and H. Schild, 121–36. Würzburg, Ergon.

Pokorny, J. 1959 *Indogermanisches etymologisches Wörterbuch*. Bern, Francke.

Prósper, B. M. 1994 'El teónimo paleohispano

Trebarune', *Veleia* 11, 187–96.

Prósper, B. M. 2002 *Lenguas y religiones pre-romanas del Occidente de la Península Ibérica*. Salamanca, EUSAL.

Prósper, B. M. 2008 *El bronce celtibérico de Botorrita* I. Rome-Pisa, Fabrizio Serra.

Prósper, B. M. 2010 'Cabeço das Fráguas y el sacrificio indoeuropeo', *Iberografías* 6, 63–70.

Prósper, B. M. 2012 'Indo-European divinities that protected livestock and the persistence of cross-linguistic semantic paradigms: *Dea Oipaingia*', *Journal of Indo-European Studies* 41, 46–58.

Prósper, B. M. 2014a 'Time for Celtiberian dialectology: Celtiberian syllabic structure and the interpretation of the bronze tablet from Torrijo del Campo, Teruel (Spain)', *Keltische Forschungen* 6, 115–55.

Prósper, B. M. 2014b 'Some considerations on metathesis and vowel epenthesis in Hispano-Celtic', *Wek^{w}os* 1, 207–18.

Prósper, B. M. 2014c 'Sifting the evidence: New interpretations on Celtic and Non-Celtic personal names of western Hispania in the light of phonetics, composition and suffixation', *Continental Celtic Word Formation. The Onomastic Evidence*, ed. J.-L. García Alonso, 181–200. Salamanca, EUSAL.

Ramírez Sádaba, J. L. & R. Campo Lastra 2010 'Cautela sobre los nombres personales documentados una sola vez: El ara dedicada a *Cabuniaegino*', *Palaeohispanica* 10, 447–59.

Sadovski, V. 2000 'Die exozentrischen Zusammensetzungen mit Vorderglied Präverb-Präposition im R̥gVeda: Entheos-Komposita und präpositionale Rektions-Komposita', *Indoarisch, Iranisch und die Indogermanistik*, ed. B. Forssman and R. Plath, 455–74. Wiesbaden, Reichert.

Schrijver, P. 1995 *Studies in British Celtic Historical Phonology*. Amsterdam, Rodopi.

Schrijver, P. 2003 'Athematic *i*-presents: The Italic and Celtic evidence', *Incontri Linguistici* 26, 59–86.

Schumacher, S. 2004 *Die keltischen Primärverben. Ein vergleichendes, etymologisches und morphologisches Lexikon*. Innsbruck, IBS.

Stifter, D. 2011a 'The textual arrangement of Alise-Sainte-Reine [L-13]', *Zeitschrift für Celtische Philologie* 58, 165–81.

Stifter, D. 2011b Review of: G. R. Isaac 2007, on line: http://www.univie.ac.at/ lexlep/ images/4/4b/Stifter_Review_of_Isaac_2007. pdf

Vaan, M. de 2008 *Etymological Dictionary of Latin and the other Italic Languages*. Leiden, Brill.

Vennemann, Th. 1988 *Preference Laws for Syllable Structure and the Explanation of Sound Change*. Berlin-New York, De Gruyter.

Vine, B. 2006 'South Picene ímih', presented in Montreal at the 137th meeting of the American Philology Association.

Vine B. 2009a 'Att. *περυσινός* (Myc. *pe-ru-si-nu-wo*) «last year's»', *Alessandria* 3, 3–12.

Vine, B. 2009b 'A yearly problem', *East and West*, ed. K. Yoshida and B. Vine, 205–24. Bremen, Hempen.

Watkins, C. 1999 'Two Celtic notes', *Studia Celtica et Indogermanica. Festschrift für Wolfgang Meid zum 70. Geburtstag*, ed. P. Anreiter and E. Jerem, 539–43. Budapest, Archaeolingua.

XII

LA DIOSA DU(V)ITERA EN UNA INSCRIPCIÓN DE TEJEDA DE TIÉTAR (CÁCERES)

Silvia Alfayé Villa, Patrizia de Bernardo Stempel, Mª Cruz González Rodríguez, Manuel Ramírez Sánchez

*New reading and interpretation of a votive inscription kept at Tejeda de Tiétar, in the province of Cáceres (HEp 3, 1993, 139). After examining the inscription, the authors SAV, MªCGR y MRS recognize a hitherto unknown divine name Duitera and propose a new interpretation of the iconography. The linguistic analysis carried out by PdBSt identifies an archaic Celtic epithet *Dubitera meaning 'The dark(er) one' and used in opposition to another deity. Derived in accordance to Caland's law, it may have characterized the night goddess otherwise known as Ataecina. The paper also includes an analysis of the theophoric personal names of the series Dobiterus, Dovitena and the like in Western Hispania.*

1. Introducción[1] (SAV, MªCGR y MRS)

EN la Iglesia de San Miguel Arcángel de la localidad de Tejeda de Tiétar (provincia de Cáceres), en el muro sur y situada a la izquierda de la puerta de entrada, junto al primer contrafuerte (hilada cuarta, a unos 86 cm del suelo) se encuentra empotrada una inscripción votiva, dispuesta en posición horizontal (Fig. 1). La inscripción fue conocida y publicada por vez primera a mediados de los años cuarenta del pasado siglo[2] y, desde esta fecha, ha sido objeto de diversos estudios. A partir del examen directo del epígrafe[3], ofrecemos una nueva lectura del nombre de la divinidad y una nueva valoración de la representación iconográfica.

1 Este trabajo se enmarca en el Proyecto de Investigación I+D+i HAR2011-25370 financiado por el Ministerio de Ciencia e Innovación del Gobierno de España; en el Grupo de investigación *Hiberus* (Universidad de Zaragoza); en el Grupo Consolidado del Sistema Universitario Vasco (IT 698-13); en la UFI 11/14.

2 Ramón y Fernández-Oxea 1944–45, 91–2, lám. IV.

3 La autopsia de la pieza fue realizada por Silvia Alfayé Villa, Mª Cruz González Rodríguez y Manuel Ramírez Sánchez el 16 de mayo del 2013.

Figura 1. Localización del epígrafe en el muro sur de la iglesia de San Miguel Arcángel (Tejeda de Tiétar, Cáceres, España). Fotografía de los autores.

2. Estudio de la inscripción (SAV, MªCGR y MRS)

La pieza (Fig. 2), de granito, mide [87 cm] x 38 cm que corresponden a la cabecera y al cuerpo central del ara, que se conservan completos, faltando únicamente el basamento[4]. Debido a su reutilización, para encajarla en la pared y acoplarla a los sillares contiguos, ha sido recubierta, en los laterales, por cemento. La superficie está deteriorada y muestra numerosos golpes, como consecuencia del apedreamiento del que ha venido siendo objeto[5].

El campo epigráfico está dividido en dos por la escena decorativa. La parte superior, con tres líneas, mide 27 cm x 38 cm y la inferior, justo debajo de la escena, con una sola línea, mide [8 cm] x 38 cm. Por su parte la decoración, rehundida, ocupa un espacio de 48 x 25 cm, y está rodeada por una moldura de unos 6 cm.

El texto dice:

VOTVM
FECIT LIBE
S FLÂVS DVI
TẸ RA

Votum | fecit libe(n)|s Flâus Dui|tẹra.

'El voto lo hizo de buen grado Flaus a Duitera.'

4 Según Beltrán Lloris 1975–76, 72, nº 51, la pieza es "conocida vulgarmente en la localidad como la piedra de la 'muerte pelona', sin duda a causa de la figura esculpida en su parte central".

5 Domínguez Moreno 1987–88, 39–40.

La letra es una capital muy descuidada, con un tamaño bastante desigual, incluso dentro de una misma línea. Así, en la l. 1 el tamaño de las letras oscila entre 4 cm (O) y 6 cm (V y M), mientras que en la l. 2 varía entre 6 (F) y 7 cm (L); por su parte, en la l. 3 el tamaño de las letras oscila entre 5 (L) y 6 cm (F), mientras que en la l. 4 mantiene un tamaño uniforme de 5 cm. El ancho del interlineado no llega a 1 cm. El grabado de las letras es muy profundo. Los vértices de unión entre los trazos oblicuos de las letras están redondeados. La M es muy abierta y la A carece de trazo horizontal. La L tiene el trazo horizontal ligeramente inclinado y la segunda S de la l. 3 presenta unos trazos más rectos que la misma letra en el comienzo de la línea.

En la tercera línea hay un nexo entre las letras A y V. No hay signos de interpunción.

Las variantes de lectura del texto se repiten desde la *editio princeps*:

Figura 2. Inscripción votiva de Tejeda de Tiétar (Cáceres, España). Fotografía de los autores.

Ramón y Fernández-Oxea 1944–45, 91–2, lám. IV a, l. 3:
Selaisdui | OVTI... | A... | TARA[6].

Soria Sánchez 1975a, 284, y 1975b, 1150, ll. 3, 4: *Libenter | Deae*[7].

Beltrán Lloris 1975–76, XXX, nº 51, fig. 44, ll. 3, 4, 5 y 6:
S Fiais Du[- - -] | [B-, C-]outi f(ilius)| IV...S S|AT...BA.

Albertos, *sched.* ll. 3, 4, 5 y 6: *SELAISDVI | Clouti f (¿) | AVRI | ATABA*[8].

Hurtado de San Antonio 1977, XX, nº 72, ll. 2 y 3: *Libenter | Deae*[9].

Soria Sánchez 1983, 208, ll. 3, 4 y 5: *Fecit sibi | Seiniso | oviit | Iulius.*

Domínguez Moreno 1987–88, 34, ll. 3, 4 y 5: *Selais Duil(lis) | Dulius | Iulius.*

---

6 Ramón y Fernández-Oxea 1944–45, 91–2, ya advierte del desgaste de las letras en las líneas 4, 5 y 6. En referencia a esta última, sin lugar a dudas la más deteriorada, indica: "Bajo los pies de la figura, en otra estrecha faja de piedra, que le sirve de base parece leerse algo así como ...TARA". En la fig. 3 se pueden observar claramente tres de estas letras: la T, la R y la A.

7 Soria Sánchez 1975a, 1150, señala que "hay algunas letras indescifrables".

8 La lectura de Albertos, realizada a partir del examen de la fotografía publicada por Beltrán Lloris, procede de una ficha autógrafa inédita que se conserva en el fichero epigráfico del Centro *CIL* II-UAH. Cf. Albertos, *sched.*

9 Hurtado de San Antonio 1977, 305, considera que la diosa a la que está dedicada la inscripción es *Ataecina*: "la diosa por excelencia es Adaegina Turibrigense".

Soria Sánchez 1994, 454, l. 3: FLAVSDVI.

HEp 3, 1993, 139, l. 3: *Dui* o *Dul*[10]; l. 6 (muy desgastada debajo de la figura):

¿+TVRA o TVRD?.

Soria Sánchez 1995, 386, ll. 3, 4 y 5: *SFLAVSDVI.*

Bonnaud 2002, 85, ll. 1 a 4:

[...] | votum fecit libe(nter) | Selais Duil(lis) / Dulius Iulius.

Olivares Pedreño 1999, 110–1, l. 3: *Selais Duillis*[11].

Vallejo Ruiz 2005, 323, ll. 3 y 4: *Flaus DV...| Ilucius Bouti f.*

Como se observa, los problemas de lectura e interpretación surgen, de forma mayoritaria[12], a partir de la línea 3 (última línea del campo epigráfico superior) y afectan al nombre del dedicante y de la divinidad.

Comenzando por este último, consideramos que el nombre divino que se proponía hasta ahora, *Selais Duillis,* basado en la lectura de las líneas 2 y 3, debe ser corregido ya que, como se puede ver en la fotografía que adjuntamos (Fig. 2) y la lectura que proponemos, es claro que la primera S, del inicio de l. 3, corresponde al final del vocablo *Libe(n)s* de la fórmula votiva bien conocida; la E corresponde a una F (inicial del nombre del dedicante), y las letras leídas como AI se identifican de forma clara con el nexo AV con lo que estamos ante el nombre *Flaus*, el del dedicante, y no ante el primer elemento del nombre de la divinidad. Este figura a continuación, tras las letras de la parte final de la l. 3: DVI – tal y como se han venido leyendo –, y sigue no en el recuadro central de la escena decorativa, sino bajo esta (Fig. 3), al final de la inscripción y donde, ya desde la *editio princeps,* por parte de algunos investigadores se habían visto 4 letras (*TARA*) que nosotros también hemos identificado y que, salvo en el caso de la segunda (que debido a su desgaste y al mal estado de conservación ha sido interpretada también como V en *HEp* 3, 1993, 139), coinciden con nuestra propuesta. El problema de esta línea es, justamente, su deterioro, que hace que unicamente el examen directo y cuidadoso de la pieza permita observar e identificar un trazo horizontal y parte de otro vertical que, en nuestra opinión, corresponden al ángulo superior de una E[13]. De esta forma, la invocación a la divinidad local[14] sería *Duitẹra,* documentado por vez primera en este

10 En el comentario que Stylow realiza en *HEp* 3 (1993, 139) a partir de los datos proporcionados por Gamallo Barranco y Gimeno Pascual, quienes hicieron el examen directo de la pieza en noviembre de 1990, señala, por vez primera, el nexo AV de la línea 3 e identifica el nombre del dedicante de forma correcta como *Flaus*. Esta es la lectura seguida también por Gallego Franco 2002, 82, n. 71.

11 Olivares Pedreño 1999, 111, puntualiza que se trata de una "lectura dudosa" .

12 El único autor que añade una línea, presumiblemente perdida, al inicio del texto es Bonnaud 2002, 86, aunque ya Beltrán Lloris (1975–76, 76) había señalado que "falta por la parte superior el texto".

13 Al mal estado de la línea se suma el hecho de que en ella hay más espacio que en el resto de las líneas entre una letra y otra, especialmente entre las letras segunda y tercera (entre E y R). La reproducción fotográfica de esta línea (Fig. 3) no permite conclusiones seguras para la identificación de la segunda letra. Como ya hemos indicado, la identificación de los rasgos paleográficos de una E en este lugar sólo es posible con el estudio *in situ* de la pieza. En cualquier caso, la invocación *Duitẹra* no es ajena al repertorio onomástico ya conocido de la zona (véase §4).

14 Cf. Domínguez Moreno 1987–88, 34–6; Olivares Pedreño 1999, 110 y 2002, 38 indica que la lectura es dudosa; Bonnaud 2002, 85–6.

texto (sobre su análisis lingüístico véase *infra* §4).

El nombre que porta el dedicante, *Flaus*, está bien atestiguado en toda la península[15] y, muy especialmente, en la mitad norte de *Lusitania*[16]. Aquí figura como nombre único, sin filiación, característica que se repite en la fórmula onomástica de la mayor parte de las inscripciones votivas de la misma provincia de Cáceres[17].

También destaca la fórmula votiva utilizada — *votum fecit libe(n)s* — ya que no es la más usual[18]. De hecho, en la base de datos EDCS se recogen sólo cuatro ejemplos más con esta variante: *vot(um) f(ecit) lib(ens)* en un epígrafe de Óbuda (Budapest), procedente de *Aquincum* (*AE* 2008, 1140) y que no conserva el nombre de la divinidad; *votum fecit libe(n)s animo* en Mantiel (Guadalajara) en una dedicación a Hércules (*AE* 2008, 711); *votum fecit animo libe(n)s* en un ara de Narros del Puerto (Ávila) dedicada a Júpiter (*ERAv* 131; *HEp* 13, [2003/04 (2007)], 73; *AE* 2004, 729; *AE* 2005, 771); y *v(otum) f(ecit) v(otum) s(olvit) l(ibens) m(erito)* en Artés (Barcelona), en un texto en el que el nombre de la divinidad se ha perdido (*IRC* I, 25).

Figura 3. Detalle de la última línea de la inscripción de Tejeda de Tiétar (Cáceres, España). Fotografía de los autores.

Junto a la escasa frecuencia en la utilización del verbo *facere* asociado al término *votum* se añade, en nuestro caso, lo inusual de su ubicación en el texto, ya que aparece en primer lugar mientras que el nombre de la divinidad figura en la última línea.

Respecto a la cronología, a pesar de los problemas que presenta la datación de un epígrafe fuera de contexto arqueológico y en ámbito rural, ante la fórmula votiva desarrollada y la ausencia del término latino *dea* asociado al nombre de la divinidad[19], proponemos fechar la inscripción entre el s. I y mediados del s. II d. C.

15 Abascal Palazón 1994, 368. Véase también en § 4.1.

16 Gallego Franco 2002, 82, n. 71.

17 Véase al respecto *CPILC* así como Esteban Ortega 2007 y 2012. De unos 160 epígrafes votivos recogidos en *CPILC*, sólo en unos 32 casos los dedicantes de epígrafes votivos indican la filiación.

18 Por su parte, la fórmula *votum fecit* se documenta en unos 33 ejemplos repartidos por todo el Imperio Romano, tal y como recoge EDCS (consulta: 18/07/2014).

19 Véanse para las Galias y Germanias los trabajos de Raepsaet-Charlier (1993; 2001).

3. Propuesta de lectura iconográfica (SAV, MªCGR y MRS)

3.1 Descripción del bajorrelieve y su problemática

La imagen antropomorfa que acompaña el texto epigráfico es una figura humana de pie, grabada tosca y esquemáticamente, rehundida y que presenta cabeza ovalada (de 12, 5 cm de diámetro x 11 cm de altura), rasgos del rostro apenas perceptibles, hombros cuadrados, brazos hacia abajo pegados al torso, antebrazos abiertos en ángulo recto y piernas de unos 12 cm de altura (Figs. 2 y 4).

La figura ha sido interpretada por Beltrán Lloris y Domínguez Moreno[20] como la representación del dedicante, ya fuera en actitud de orante, en el caso del primero, o como bailarín travestido ritualmente a imitación de la diosa, en opinión del segundo, resultando esta última interpretación, al igual que la de Bonnaud, excesivamente imaginativa[21].

Figura 4. Detalle de la decoración de la inscripción de Tejeda de Tiétar (Cáceres, España). Fotografía de los autores.

Ciertamente, parece tratarse de la imagen del *cultor*, pero también podríamos estar ante la representación de la diosa a la que se dedicó esa pieza, ya que existen paralelos iconográficos peninsulares para ambas posibilidades (Fig. 5), algunos de los cuales ya fueron señalados por el propio Beltrán Lloris.

3.2 Paralelos en inscripciones religiosas

Los paralelos de carácter religioso se localizan en la misma provincia de Cáceres. El primero de ellos es una pieza hallada en Talaván y, lamentablemente, hoy desaparecida. En este epígrafe el campo epigráfico ocupa la parte inferior con el texto siguiente: *Munidi Ebe|robrigae | Toudopala|ndaigae Am|maia Boutea* (*CPILC* 471), mientras que en la superior, dentro de una hornacina, se representa una figura humana frontal y de pie, vestida con túnica larga, que tiene la mano izquierda sobre el pecho y la derecha sobre el vientre (Fig. 5a)[22].

20 Beltrán Lloris 1975-76, 73-5, nº 51, fig. 44; Domínguez Moreno 1987-88, 40.

21 Alfayé Villa 2011, 87. Por su parte, Bonnaud 2002, 85-6, había señalado que "en ce qui concerne la figure anthropomorphe, il pourrait s'agir d'un individu, peut-être armé, exécutant une danse rituelle comme cela se pratiquait dans diverses régions de la péninsule dans l'Antiquité".

22 Sobre esta pieza, *vid.* también García y Bellido 1976, 116-7, nº 8, fig. 8; Cerrillo Martín de Cáceres & Cruz 1993, 165-6, nº 2, lám. II.2; Olivares Pedreño 2002, 29, n. 67 y 36. Para Esteban Ortega 2007, 233-4, nº 340, se trata de la imagen de la divinidad invocada por medio de la forma *Munidi*, a la que estaría dedicada el ara, aunque también podría interpretarse como la representación de la dedicante,

El segundo paralelo, cuyo carácter es más controvertido, es un epígrafe hallado en la 'Dehesa Zafrilla', en Malpartida de Cáceres, que se conserva en estado pésimo dado que ni la parte inferior ni la superior están completas debido a la rotura de la pieza (Fig. 5b). Según Abascal Palazón[23], se trata de una dedicación a *Ataecina*, con la lectura *[---]/+A+++/ d(eae) d(ominae) s(anctae) pos/u^erun^t*, en la que aparecería representado de forma esquemática un devoto de la diosa en actitud orante. Este investigador relaciona esta pieza con la existencia de un lugar de culto en el sitio del hallazgo, la 'Dehesa Zafrilla', del que también procederían dos cabritas votivas de bronce dedicadas a la mencionada diosa, conocidas desde 1885 y que presentan un texto votivo similar, y otra ara de lectura problemática[24].

Figuras 5a-e. 5a) Inscripción de Talaván (Cáceres), fotografía del Archivo de *Hispania Epigraphica*; 5b) Inscripción de Malpartida de Cáceres (Cáceres), dibujo de J. M. Abascal Palazón 1995, fig. 54; 5c) Estela de Coria (Cáceres), fotografía del Archivo de *Hispania Epigraphica*; 5d) Inscripción de Vigo (Pontevedra), fotografía de D. Juliá 1971, nº 17, fig. 8b; 5e) Inscripción de Căşeiu (Rumanía), fotografía de L. Bianchi 1985, nº 176, fig. 104.

Por su parte, Beltrán Lloris[25] clasificó esta pieza como funeraria, ofreciendo la lectura *...[f(ilius)] an(norum) i...| d(onum) d(e) s(uo) pos|u^erun^t*, e interpretando los trazos grabados en la zona inferior como "una decoración antropomorfa de carácter

Ammia Boutea. La primera hipótesis sería posible siempre y cuando tuviésemos la certeza de que la inscripción está dedicada a una sola divinidad, ya que la interpretación del formulario votivo *Munidi Eberobrigae Toudopalandaigae* como alusivo a una única deidad no es totalmente segura.

23 Cf. Abascal Palazón 1995, 87–8 y 95, fig. 54, nº 7.

24 Cf. Abascal Palazón 1995, 88 y 94, para la posible existencia en la 'Dehesa Zafrilla' de "un santuario de segundo rango o un centro de culto de tipo familiar dedicado a esta divinidad". Por su parte, García-Bellido 2001, 67–8, considera, "dado lo anómalo de una imagen de la divinidad y la carencia de nombre divino en la dedicatoria", que "es preferible pensar que estamos ante un voto de otras gentes". La misma autora (2001, 67, n. 66) plantea la posibilidad de que pudiera tratarse de la dedicación de gentes de origen púnico a su divinidad y que la representación pudiera ser la de *Tanit* en avanzado estado de antropomorfización, igual a las muchas halladas en el norte de África.

25 Beltrán Lloris 1975–76, 58–9, nº 37, fig. 31.

muy sumario, limitada a un trazo vertical rematado en un botón y dos brazos acodados y hacia arriba, todo ello con evidente tosquedad", identificando esta figura como una esquemática imagen frontal del difunto de pie y con los brazos hacia arriba en actitud orante[26].

En nuestra opinión, la lectura e interpretación de Abascal Palazón resulta la más probable; no obstante, estimamos que no habría que descartar la posibilidad de que el grabado respondiera a una reutilización posterior de la pieza. E, incluso aún en el caso de que epígrafe e imagen sean contemporáneos[27], creemos que no se debe obviar el hecho de que la imagen está incompleta debido a la fractura de la pieza, observándose restos de trazos que continuarían en la zona perdida y que conformarían una figura distinta a la que ahora percibimos.

3.3 Paralelos en inscripciones funerarias

Los paralelos en inscripciones funerarias (Fig. 5) se localizan también en la provincia de Cáceres, en dos epígrafes procedentes, respectivamente, de Plasenzuela (*CPILC* 397) y de Coria (*CPILC* 218)[28], y en un tercero, de carácter más controvertido, hallado en una zona más alejada geográficamente, en el noroeste, concretamente en Vigo (Pontevedra, *IRG* III, supl. 18)[29].

La primera de las piezas, la de Plasenzuela, fechada por Esteban Ortega[30] en el siglo I d.C., es una estela funeraria rectangular en cuya fragmentada parte superior se localiza, dentro de una cartela, el epígrafe. Debajo del campo epigráfico, y dentro

26 Al igual que Beltrán Lloris, también Esteban Ortega & Salas Martín 2003, 90, nº 89, fig. 89, descartan la interpretación de la pieza como votiva y la consideran de carácter funerario (------*]et m++| d(onum) d(e) s(uo) pos|u^erun^t)*, sugiriendo, incluso, que la imagen podría haberse realizado con posterioridad a la factura del epígrafe. Sin embargo, estos investigadores descartan la interpretación de Abascal Palazón como una pieza votiva por razones que no resultan suficientemente sólidas. Por un lado, aluden a la morfología del soporte y argumentan que el carácter rectangular de la pieza se corresponde con el que presentan las estelas funerarias de la zona, pero también en ese territorio se conocen inscripciones votivas en soportes prácticamente idénticos. Por otro lado, señalan que los epítetos de *Ataecina* aparecen al final del texto, y esto resultaría, en su opinión, inhabitual. No obstante, hay que tener en cuenta que el texto es casi idéntico al documentado en las cabritas votivas halladas en ese mismo lugar de 'Dehesa Zafrilla' y dedicadas también a la diosa *Ataecina* (sobre dichas cabritas votivas cf. Abascal Palazón 1995, 89–90 y 95–6, nº 10–11. En un trabajo posterior, Esteban Ortega 2007, 166, nº 291, describe esta inscripción como "de carácter incierto, posiblemente funeraria", fechándola a finales del siglo II o en el III d.C., y sugiere leer en la l. 2 *m(ater)*.

27 En este sentido, la existencia del mismo esquema compositivo en otra pieza, hallada en Malpartida de Cáceres, con texto en la parte superior y decoración geométrica grabada en la parte inferior (véase Esteban Ortega & Salas Martín 2003, nº 91), podría interpretarse como un argumento a favor de la contemporaneidad de epígrafe y figura, aunque, debido al desgaste de la inscripción, no sabemos si nos encontramos ante una pieza votiva o funeraria.

28 Sobre la iconografía de estos dos epígrafes cacereños, su interpretación como la representación estilizada del difunto y sus paralelos en otros epígrafes funerarios peninsulares véase, en último lugar, el reciente trabajo de Tantimonaco & Gimeno Pascual 2014, en especial 219–20 y n. 27.

29 Además de este epígrafe, la figura de Tejeda encuentra ciertas similitudes en representaciones antropomorfas de otras inscripciones funerarias del área galaica. Destacan, sobre todo, cinco piezas más de Vigo (Juliá 1971, figs. 9a y b; 10a y b y 11), una de Mazarelos (Oza dos Rios, A Coruña, *CIRG* I, nº 63), y otra de San Tirso de Cando (Outes, A Coruña, *CIRG* I, nº 74). Ya Beltrán Lloris 1975–76, 73, señaló paralelos con "determinadas estelas en las que aparecen esculpidas las figuras de los difuntos".

30 Esteban Ortega 2012, 181–2, nº 648.

de una hornacina, se ha representado una figura humana frontal, de pie, con los ojos y la boca toscamente señalados, con los brazos hacia arriba y las manos extendidas. Callejo Serrano[31] identifica esta imagen como la representación del cadáver de una niña desnuda y "en decúbito supino". En cambio, para Cerrillo Martín de Cáceres y Cruz[32] se trataría de una figura masculina representada en posición de orante. Además, hay que añadir que en las caras laterales de esta pieza se han representando sendos brazos humanos, con las manos extendidas hacia abajo, que, tanto para Callejo Serrano como para Beltrán Lloris, estarían abrazando y protegiendo a la figura humana (difunta) representada frontalmente en la cara principal. De hecho, para este último autor[33] estaríamos ante la representación de un dios del panteón local que protege al fallecido, una iconografía que, como acertadamente señala, presenta similitudes con otras dos piezas, una de Coria y otra de Vigo.

En la segunda pieza de este grupo, de nuevo una inscripción cacereña, de Coria (*CPILC* 218), se ha representado una cabeza humana en la parte superior y, a cada lado de esta, un brazo terminado en manos abiertas y extendidas que pertenecerían a una figura que no se ha conservado debido a la rotura de la estela por su parte superior (Fig. 5c). Para Beltrán Lloris[34] se trataría de la imagen de la divinidad local que acoge en sus brazos al muerto, representado *pars pro toto* mediante la testa. Una interpretación similar ofrece este autor para la escena representada sobre la tercera de las piezas mencionadas, una estela rectangular hallada en Vigo, que ha sido identificada como funeraria pese a que las letras conservadas resultan ilegibles (*IRG* III, supl. 18)[35]. En la zona superior de esta última pieza se ha representado el tronco superior de una figura humana con los brazos abiertos, debajo del cual aparecen otras dos figuras humanas de menor tamaño, de pie y uniendo las manos sobre un ara, situándose una a cada lado del altar (Fig. 5d). Dado el supuesto carácter funerario de la pieza, la mayor parte de la historiografía interpreta esta escena como la representación de una divinidad que acoge y protege entre sus brazos a esos dos individuos, que no serían sino los difuntos a quienes se dedicaría la pieza, pese a que, como ya hemos comentado anteriormente, no se conserve el epígrafe que así lo pruebe y, por tanto, no se puede afirmar con seguridad que la pieza sea de carácter funerario. En cambio, para Acuña Castroviejo y Casal García[36] se trataría de la diosa *Iuno Pronuba* o *Concordia* presidiendo la *dextrarum iunctio*, "el acto nupcial representado por los dos jóvenes esposos uniendo sus manos derechas sobre un altar", aunque no precisan si atribuyen un carácter votivo o funerario a esta escena. Cabe destacar el hecho de que la figura presumiblemente divina de la pieza viguesa comparte la morfología geometrizante de la cabeza con la imagen de Tejeda, y es posible que, aunque de forma más tosca, la figura cacereña pudiera estar

31 Callejo Serrano 1967, 112–3, nº 19, lám. 15.
32 Cerrillo Martín de Cáceres & Cruz 1993, 165, nº 1, lám. II.1.
33 Beltrán Lloris 1975–76, 68.
34 Beltrán Lloris 1975–76, 51–2, nº 29, fig. 25.
35 Anati 1968, 118, fig. 134; Beltrán Lloris 1975–76, 68; Rodríguez Lage 1974, 48; *CIRG* II, nº 55; Acuña Castroviejo & Casal García 2010, 389, fig. 5.
36 Acuña Castroviejo & Casal García 2010, 389, fig. 5.

representada en una actitud similar a la viguesa, con los brazos dispuestos para acoger a sus devotos (Fig. 2). De ser cierta esta posibilidad, estaríamos ante la representación de la diosa a la que se dedicó esa ara y no ante la imagen del *cultor* en posición oferente.

3.4 Una nueva valoración

Sobre la base de las piezas señaladas como paralelos para la figura de Tejeda, esta podría interpretarse como la representación frontal y de pie del oferente, del *cultor* que aparece representado detrás de una gran mesa de ofrendas[37], tal y como interpretamos, por las medidas (26 x 14 cm) y proporción respecto a la imagen antropomorfa, el rectángulo que corta la figura humana (Fig. 4). En esta mesa rectangular, grabada en perspectiva cenital, debieron representarse las ofrendas y presentes destinados a la divinidad, y de los que quedarían algunos restos apenas perceptibles (Fig. 4), que son los que, habitualmente, se han venido interpretando como letras en ll. 4 y 5. De ser plausible esta hipótesis[38] se trataría de ofrendas vegetales, del tipo, por ejemplo, de los *liba*. Este tipo de ofrendas, bien documentadas también en otras religiones antiguas como la umbra y romana, podían hacerse solas o en combinación con un sacrificio animal[39].

Los paralelos iconográficos de mesas representadas cenitalmente como la de Tejeda (Fig. 4), para mostrar los objetos que están sobre ellas, se encuentran fuera

37 Macrobio, *Sat.* III, 11: "*Ut in templo, inquit, Iunonis Populoniae augusta mensa est. Namque in fanis alia vasorum sunt et sacrae supellectilis, alia ornamentorum: quae vasorum sunt instrumenti instar habent, quibus semper sacrificia conficiuntur, quarum rerum principem locum optinet mensa in qua epulae libationisque et stipes reponuntur. Ornamenta vero sunt clypei coronae et huiuscemodi donaria. Neque enim dedicantur eo tempore quo delubra sacrantur, at vero mensa arulaeque eodem die quo aedes ipsae dedicari solent, unde mensa hoc ritu dedicata in templo arae usum et religionem optinet pulvinaris*".

38 Por su parte, los gestos de la figura de Tejeda de Tiétar recuerdan los de las figuras de los ex votos ibéricos. Véase, por ejemplo, Calvo y Sánchez & Cabré Aguiló 1917. Menos acertada es la posibilidad que la representación corresponda a la imagen de la diosa a la que se dedica la inscripción representada frontalmente sobre un trono en el que estaría apoyando las manos; como paralelo, aunque en este caso en una pieza funeraria, debe señalarse una estela de Gastiain (Navarra, *IRMN* 42, lám. XLII), véase Marco Simón 1976, 192–3, fig. 27. Si la figura estuviera de pie, la postura de los brazos podría indicar la actitud de acogida y protección de los devotos, como parece suceder en la estela de Vigo mencionada en el texto (Fig. 5d), en la que la presumible deidad ha sido representada, como ya se ha señalado, con una cabeza similar a la de la figura de Tejeda y también con una postura parecida del tronco superior, con los brazos extendidos y abiertos. Esta posición es también la que encontramos representada metonímicamente en los brazos con las manos extendidas de la estela funeraria de Plasenzuela, o en los brazos que protegen a la cabeza de la pieza ya descrita de Coria (Fig. 5c). Los problemas que presenta esta interpretación de la figura de Tejeda como la imagen de la diosa representada frontalmente sobre un trono son: (1) la dimensión de los tronos, que pueden ser altos y estrechos o a veces cuadrados (es decir, cúbicos), pero nunca tan bajos y, a la vez, alargados como en la pieza de Tejeda (Fig. 4), que, en nuestra opinión, parece corresponder, en consecuencia, a la representación de una mesa; (2) que en las representaciones iconográficas de tronos, ya sea en inscripciones votivas (como sucede, por ejemplo, con las representaciones de la diosa *Nehalennia* en Germania inferior) o funerarias (como la que acabamos de citar de la provincia de Navarra), los tronos aparecen siempre grabados detrás de la figura antropomorfa; y, (3) que, por regla general, dicha figura antropomorfa aparece sentada.

39 Sobre las ofrendas vegetales en la religión romana véase Delgado Delgado 2005 y Scheid 2011, así como Lacam 2014 para la religión umbra. Para la iconografía de las escenas de sacrificios pueden verse, entre otros, Turcan 1988; Greenland 2007 y *ThesCRA* II, III y V.

de la península Ibérica, concretamente en Dacia[40] (Fig. 5e) y en Italia, en la zona del Piamonte[41], en escenas de banquetes funerarios.

La representación del *cultor* resulta acorde con lo que se conoce de las escasas representaciones antropomorfas en inscripciones votivas hispanas dedicadas a divinidades de nombre indígena[42], y de las que hemos visto ya un ejemplo en el epígrafe de Malpartida de Cáceres (Fig. 5b) dedicado, muy probablemente, a la diosa *Ataecina* con la que, según la propuesta etimológica de P. de Bernardo Stempel, podría estar relacionada la diosa de Tejeda.

4. Estudio lingüístico (PdBSt)

4.1. Peculiaridades de la inscripción y forma originaria del nombre divino

La inscripción cacereña de Tejeda de Tiétar nos enseña, en sus cinco palabras, hasta cuatro peculiaridades lingüísticas. La primera es la asimilación producida en el nexo *ns*, por lo que el participio *libens* ha llegado a pronunciarse y escribirse *libes*. Se trata de un cambio fonético muy frecuente en latín, donde refleja incluso una pronunciación culta[43] y da cuenta a la vez de la abreviación <COS> por *cons(ul)* y de variantes como *Inseques* para el cognomen *Insequens*[44]. Asimismo, un cambio fonético *ns* > (*s*)*s* es regular en celta, donde afecta – entre otros – los acusativos plurales como p.ej. el galo *mnas* y el irl.a. *mná* < ie. *g^{w}*nH-ns* 'a las mujeres'[45].

La segunda peculiaridad de la inscripción cacereña es que el nombre del dedicante, que en realidad corresponde a *Flavus*, aparece escrito como <FLAVS>, es decir con la simplificación de la secuencia gráfica <VV> que se observa en muchos otros casos, como p.ej. en los cognomina <PRIMITIVS> en lugar de *Primitivus*[46] y <BOLERIAVS> de **Boleriavus* (o quizás **Valeriavus*) y también en el dativo teonímico <OLLODEV> que representa *Ollodevu*[47]. Esta misma peculiaridad, al lado de variantes como <IVENALIS> en lugar de *Iuvenalis*[48], nos permite pensar que también el formulario votivo[49] <DVITERA> de la inscripción de Tejeda de Tiétar haya sufrido una reducción a partir de un *<DVVITERA> más antiguo.

Además, si tenemos en cuenta que la lenición de las oclusivas sonoras estaba ya

40 Bianchi 1985, nº 152, 163, 176 y 209.
41 Mercando & Paci 1998, nº 60.
42 Cf. Alfayé 2011, 65–103; 2013.
43 Véase ahora Poccetti 2007, 29–31.
44 Kakoschke 2012, 458–9.
45 Véase, entre otros, De Bernardo Stempel 1987, 83 y 94.
46 Kakoschke 2012, 578–9.
47 Ambos en Hainzmann *et al.* 2007.
48 Kakoschke 2012, 471.
49 Con este término solemos indicar todo el tramo ('string' en inglés) de una dedicación / invocación que contiene – sin modificar – los nombres y los atributos de una o más divinidades. Si por contra lematizáramos sus componentes, poniéndolos en nominativo, obtendríamos lo que solemos llamar 'formulario teonímico'.

operativa dentro del celta común[50] y que en este tipo de textos latinos la grafía <V> puede representar el desarrollo fonético de una *-*b*- intervocálica (como p.ej. en el nombre personal *Duvius* que a veces reemplaza el más transparente *Dubius*[51]), cabe suponer que la <-V-> que ha desaparecido en <DVITERA> representara el producto fonético [β] de la lenición pancéltica de una *-*b*- intervocálica originaria. Más abajo, en los §§ 4.3–5, veremos que la reconstrucción de una forma originaria **DUBITERA* no es sólo viable, sino se revela más bien acertada, en virtud de la estructura y de la etimología de la palabra, encajando – además – en el marco de la onomástica personal derivada del nombre divino.

La reducción que acabamos de postular – y que podría explicar también el nombre de agrupación <DVITIQ(VM)> (gen.pl.) en una inscripción romana procedente del territorio celtibérico[52]– parece haber sido de tipo exclusivamente gráfico. Sin embargo, se comentará en margen que (1) la pronunciación paroxítona que se aprecia en la capa modernizada del celta de la Península Ibérica[53] y que es evidente también en el genitivo idionímico sincopado *Dobteri*[54], podría conjeturarse, igualmente, para el nombre divino (**DUVITÉRA* ?), dado que la posición ante vocal átona era al parecer favorecedora de la caída de *-*v*-[55]; (2) la cercanía de una -*i*- semivocálica o vocálica también propiciaba la caída de *-*v*-[56].

La cuarta y última peculiaridad de la dedicación cacereña es de tipo morfológico y no fonético: la forma de dativo singular utilizada para un tema en -*ā* femenino acaba en -*ā* y no, como sería normal, en -*ae*. Es esta una variante de dativo de tipo latino-dialectal e itálico regularmente descrita en las mejores gramáticas[57] y no es nada infrecuente en las cercanías de la inscripción estudiada aquí[58]. A partir del dativo singular femenino

50 *LKA*, 910–4, *s.v.* «Keltische Grundsprache» (esp. 912). El hecho de que la lenición céltica haya tenido lugar en tres olas diferentes fue resaltado ya por Sims-Williams 1990, 233, y McCone 1996, 96 s. En De Bernardo Stempel 2006, 12 dichas olas se ponen en relación con las demás isoglosas que se desarrollaron en las diferentes etapas formativas de las lenguas célticas.

51 Atestiguado cada uno cinco veces en la Narbonense, mientras que la forma base *Dubius* se documenta también en Bélgica, Germania Inferior y Panonia (*pace OPEL* 2, 112, *NPC*, 90, Meid 2005, 269–70). Un ejemplo hispánico de *Dubius* en *HEp* 11 (2001 [2005]), nº 202.

52 Nº 114 de Cabeza de Griego / Cuenca en González Rodríguez 1986, 129.

53 Véase la tabla nº 5 en Arenas-Esteban *et al.* 2011, 126, donde se recogen los resultados de De Bernardo Stempel 1995, 2002 y, con más detalles, 2007.

54 Recogido en *AALR*, 161, para el idiónimo teofórico *Dob(i)terus*, cuya vocal centralizada -*o*- también se explica a partir de una forma original **Dubitéros* (véase la discusión del tipo 1.2 en el § 4.5 abajo).

55 Según se observa en De Bernardo Stempel 1994, 23 y 30; veáse p.ej. el ordinal galo *nametos* < **navamétos*. El mismo desarrollo conjetura Prósper 2002, 409, para explicar los idiónimos discutidos abajo en el § 4.5.

56 Véanse los ejemplos en Delamarre 2009, 356–7.

57 Cf. además Villar 1986 y De Bernardo Stempel 2000, 55–6: "Bei den *ā*-Stämmen [...] findet sich der *ā*-Dativ im Latein der Peripherie einschl. Faliskisch, im Pälignischen, Marsischen und Marruzinischen [47]. Folglich erweisen geographische Ausdehnung und sich abzeichnende relative Chronologie zumindest den geneuerten Singular als späte Konvergenz zwischen Latein und Teilen des Kernitalischen", aquí en la p. 56. Sin embargo, dicha desinencia secundaria de dativo singular es una variante a veces ignorada por los epigrafistas, como Olivares & Ramajo 2013, 194, en su reciente edición de otra inscripción votiva cacereña, y Rodríguez Colmenero 2010, 181–4.

58 Véanse dativos teonímicos como *Bandua*, *Iccona* o *Nabia* – De Bernardo Stempel 2003, 202–3, *ead.* & García Quintela 2008, 263 y 267–8 y también Prósper & Villar 2009, 30.

Duiterā que tenemos atestiguado, restituiremos, por lo tanto, un nominativo **DUITERA*, es decir **DU(V)ITERA*, para el nuevo nombre divino.

4.2 El sufijo contrastivo ie. -tero- en celta arcaico

La terminación en *-terā* coincide con el femenino del sufijo contrastivo-oposicional indoeuropeo *-*(t)eros*/-*(t)erā* que llegó a aprovecharse con regularidad para formas de comparativo en indoiranio y griego, dejando tan sólo restos en el celta antiguo[59]. Luego, el sufijo se aprovechará, si bien modificado, en goidélico, para dar una forma nueva a la categoría céltica del ecuativo[60].

La historia de dicho sufijo en las lenguas célticas atraviesa, por lo menos, seis fases. En la primera lo vemos, todavía sin dental, añadirse a adverbios para conferirles el valor contrastivo heredado del indoeuropeo, como en el celta continental *andero-* 'inferus' < **nd^h(e)-ero-* con su antónimo *uero-* 'superus' < **up-ero-*.

En la segunda fase, el sufijo siguió añadiéndose a adverbios, pero interponiendo una *-t-* como en en las parejas irl.a. *centar* 'este mundo' vs. *alltar* 'el otro mundo' o *airther* 'este' (*'lo que está delante') vs. *íarthar* 'oeste' (*'lo que está detrás'); también se añade a unos temas pronominales.

En la tercera fase, el sufijo empezó a añadirse a adjetivos: en británico quedan unos neutros singulares substantivados como abstractos, como galés *gwynder* 'blancura' (*'lo que es blanco en oposición a lo que es obscuro': **windo-tero-m*) o bretón *braster* 'grandeza' (*'lo que es grande en oposición a lo que es pequeño': **g^{w}rHsto-tero-m*). Como decíamos arriba, dicha fase fue compartida con el indoiranio y el griego, donde los adjetivos así derivados se aprovecharon como verdaderos comparativos.

En la cuarta fase, para formar comparativos, se añadía el sufijo contrastivo al viejo comparativo en *-is*, como en los antónimos irl.a. *ósar* 'iunior' < **yow-is-tero-s* y *sinser* 'senior' < **sen-is-tero-s*[61].

La quinta fase es una innovación exclusiva del goidélico y consiste en el aprovechamiento del sufijo adjetival, tras adaptarlo a los temas en *-i-* breve, para expresar comparativos de equivalencia o ecuativos, a partir de casos como *gilithir snechta* 'blanco como la nieve', desarrollado de un originario *'más blanco que la nieve'.

La sexta fase, finalmente, se puede considerar un desarrollo de la tercera y consistió en añadir el sufijo *-teros*/*-terā* a bases sustantivales, a menudo para indicar un

59 Cf. De Bernardo Stempel 1997, 721–3 y *NWÄI*, 425–426. Una discusión reciente de dicho sufijo a nivel indoeuropeo ha sido ofrecida por Luján 2000, 84 ss., si bien su reconstrucción glotogónica separaría el tipo en *-*tero-* de aquello, al parecer, más arcaico en *-*ero-*.

60 Más detalles en Meid 1967 y De Bernardo Stempel 2013a, 33.

61 Una ampliación sufijal del mismo tipo da cuenta, entre otros, del lat. *magister* < **mag-is-tero-s* y su correspondiente femenino umbro *mestru*, véase ahora García Ramón 2013, 111–2. Dado que su etimología sigue siendo obscura (Vallejo Ruiz 2005, 318–9), no se puede afirmar con certeza que el genitivo idionímico hispanocéltico *Elguisteri* pertenezca a este mismo grupo de derivados (en ese sentido Luján [2000, 82–3] por el posible paralelo estructural del gen.pl. de agrupación *Elguismiq(um)*). Puede que la base derivacional de ambos se esconda detrás del nom.sg. /elguiz/ que parece subyacer – con asimilación de sonoridad de la *-*s* final originaria – bajo la forma celtibérica e.l.Ku.e.i.z (véase Wodtko 2000, 109–12 con la bibliografía anterior).

acercamiento semántico de la nueva palabra a su base derivacional: p. ej. en el caso de irl.a. *muinter* 'familia', que, derivado como **moni-terā* de la base **moni-* continuada en el irl.a. *muin* 'protección', señala la familia como el segmento social más protegido[62].

A continuación veremos que el nombre divino *Duitera* apunta a una base derivacional de tipo adjetival y al comienzo de lo que acabamos de definir como fase tercera dentro del aprovechamiento céltico del sufijo *-teros*, *-terā*.

4.3 La ley indoeuropea de Caland y el céltico *dubu-/dubi- 'oscuro'

Pasando ahora a observar la base derivacional del nombre divino, veremos que el *Dui-* de *Duitera* no sólo puede, sino incluso debe continuar una secuencia más antigua **Dubi-*. Ésto es lo que implican los personales (teofóricos) del tipo *Dobitérus* > *Dovitérus* > *Doitérus* que vamos a analizar en detalle en el § 4.5. Contrariamente a lo que se ha dicho en investigaciones acerca de esos nombres[63], dicha forma **dubi-* no tiene por que proceder de **{*dubu-* + *-i-*}, sino se explica simplemente como antigua 'variante de Caland' del adjetivo protocéltico tradicionalmente reconstruido como **dubu-* 'oscuro > negro'[64].

Lo que se conoce hoy como 'Ley de Caland' fue denominado en origen "Calandsche Regel" por J. Wackernagel[65], que identificó como indoeuropea común una regularidad que W. Caland había observado en avéstico (1892) y luego en indo-iranio (1893). El término define la regularidad con la cual un conjunto – al que se suele llamar 'sistema de Caland'[66] – de morfemas declinacionales (*-u-*, *-i-*) y sufijos derivativos (*-ro-*, *-ont-*; *-mo-*, *-no-*)[67] alternan entre sí a la hora de formar nuevas palabras de una misma base[68]. Entre otros, unas cuantas bases nominales "which have inherently adjectival semantics"[69] pasan a ser temas en *-i-* cuando se emplean como primeros miembros de compuestos[70].

Al estudiar la vigencia de esta regla en celta, se ha visto que hay evidencia tanto a través de alternancias entre las lenguas célticas y varias ramas del indoeuropeo, como a través de alternancias en el interior de la misma rama céltica, lo que sin duda constituye un notable arcaismo de este grupo lingüístico[71]. En la misma dirección apunta el hecho de que la mayoría de las variantes de Caland irlandesas sean temas en *-u-* o en *-i-*[72].

62 Más detalles acerca de los ejemplos citados se hallan en Meid 1967 y *NWÄI*, 425–6.
63 Véanse abajo las notas 77, 82 y 90.
64 *LEIA*-D, 223; *NWÄI*, 91–2; Matasović 2009, 108.
65 Wackernagel 1897=1969, 770.
66 Como en Meißner 1998, *passim*.
67 "Überhaupt läßt eine Gesamtbetrachtung erkennen, daß es gerade die Stammbildungen bzw. Ableitungen auf Sonant oder *-s-* sind, die an dem Calandschen System bzw. Wechsel partizipieren": *NWÄI*, 530.
68 Cf. Nussbaum 1976 y Collinge 1985, 23–7.
69 Nussbaum 1976, 6. Acerca de las relaciones adjetivales en el marco del sistema de Caland véase también Balles 2009, 9–12.
70 Un ejemplo donde el primer elemento es un adjetivo con tema en *-i-* (en vez de *-ro-* u *-o-*) es el idiónimo irlandés *Ruidgal* 'Valor rojo' (es decir 'sangriento' > 'fuerte'), cf. Uhlich 1993, 121 y 295.
71 *NWÄI*, 529-37.
72 *NWÄI*, 531–2.

De particular importancia para nuestra argumentación es, asimismo, el hecho de que unos cuantos adjetivos irlandeses antiguos forman su comparativo a partir de un tema alternativo en *-i-*, como p.ej. *remor* 'grueso, gordo', cuyo morfema derivacional **-ro-* ha sido sustituido por *-i-* en el ecuativo *remithir* así como en el comparativo *reime*, y por otros sufijos en unos derivados substantivales[73].

En consecuencia, un tema en *-i-* en una formación de palabra arcaica, y en particular en una formación de comparativo en *-tero-*, nos puede remitir a un lexema que normalmente se conoce como tema en *-u-*, así como a una palabra afín que sea derivada en *-no-* o en *-ro-*. En celta, éste es – entre otros – el caso del hidrónimo *Dubis*, antiguo nombre del río Doubs, un afluyente del río Saône[74], que remite, como tema en *-i-*, al adjetivo **dubu-* 'oscuro'. El mismo hidrónimo **Dubi-s* está, además, contenido en el adjetivo de pertenencia **Dubi-askā* que contribuye a formar el topónimo *vallis Dubiasca*[75], donde se puede todavía apreciar la función, a menudo deonomástica, que el sufijo **-askā* realiza en celta antiguo. El adjetivo **dubu- /dubi-* está, asimismo, relacionado con el célt. **dubro-* que, a partir del sentido de 'oscuro', ha pasado a designar unos tipos de agua; incluso puede, a pesar de un par de problemas de detalle, que haya también relación con el adjetivo céltico **dubno-*, cuyo sentido de 'profundo' podría haberse desarrollado a partir de 'obscuro'[76], dado que a veces se aprovechan variantes de Caland para conferir nuevos sentidos a la palabra originaria.

No hay, por lo tanto, ninguna razón para dudar que la base *du(b)i-* del nombre divino *DU(V)ITERA* sea la variante de Caland que corresponde al adjetivo céltico **dubu-*[77].

4.4. La etimología de DU(V)ITERA y la diosa detrás del nombre

Por lo que acabamos de ver, el nombre divino *DUITERA* representa el desarrollo de **DUVITERA*, a su vez procedente de una forma céltica originaria **DUBITERA*, con toda probabilidad proparoxítona al inicio (/du'ßitera/) y luego paroxítona (/dußi'tera/)[78].

Si bien dicho nombre divino está empleado aquí de forma independiente, es decir como si fuera un teónimo, su base derivacional y sufijo apuntan más bien a un adjetivo, es decir a un epíteto teonímico 'la oscura', utilizado para caracterizar a la diosa involucrada en oposición a otra, clara, cuyo nombre hispánico de momento desconocemos[79].

---

73 *NWÄI*, 533–4.

74 Véanse Falileyev *et al.* 2010, 18 y 115 con los testimonios latinos y griegos, y Billy 2011, 237–8. Igualmente, Delamarre (2012, 142) menciona, entre otros, un hidrónimo *Duina* (AD 875) también afluente del río Saône y reconducible a una protoforma **Dubí-nā*, así como un superlativo hidronímico **Dubis(s)amā* 'La muy oscura', que se continúa en el nombre de otros dos ríos.

75 En un testamento del año 739 incluido en el cartulario de la catedral de Grenoble: Holder 1, 1355.

76 En este sentido *LEIA*-D, 210–1.

77 Nótese que la reconstrucción de un supuesto adjetivo protocélt. "*dovi-s* 'stark, gut'" por parte de Stokes y Bezzenberger en el lejano1894 (150), si bien acogida por unos autores españoles modernos, radica en el malentendido de un sintagma irlandés antiguo en el cual figuraba, en realidad, el lexema irl.a. *doë* 'antebrazo, brazo, mano' (*DIL*-D, col. 243 *s.v.* «1 doé» [*sic*]; véase, además, *LEIA*-D, 133 *s.v.* «1 dóe»). Eso explica la falta de una entrada correspondiente en las obras lexicográficas posteriores, tanto indoeuropeísticas (*IEW*, De Vaan 2008, 73 s.) como celtológicas (*LEIA*, Matásović 2009).

78 Véase arriba en el §4.1 con las notas 53–55.

79 En Galia, Italia y Nórico se atestigua *ĐIRONA* > *SIRONA* como invocacíon a una divinidad de las estrellas,

Cabe, por lo tanto, preguntarse si acaso estamos en presencia de una caracterización de la misma diosa de la noche que se venera en esta misma área de la Hispania occidental bajo el nombre céltico de *Atacina* > **Ataicina* > *Ataecina* y otras variantes fonéticas desarrolladas a partir de la protoforma **Atakī-nā*, 'La noche divina'[80]. De hecho, según he indicado en varios de mis trabajos acerca de la teonimia céltica, los numerosísimos nombres divinos atestiguados en la Céltica antigua parecen encubrir un número mucho más pequeño de divinidades[81].

4.5 Los nombres personales teofóricos referentes a la diosa

No por último, la identificación del nuevo nombre divino *Du(v)itera* arroja luz sobre una serie onomástica muy frecuente en la Península Ibérica, sobre todo en la mitad occidental. De hecho, nombres personales del tipo de *Dobiterus* y afines, que antes de la identificación de la forma *Duitera* en la inscripción de Tejeda de Tiétar habían sido explicados de varias maneras[82], resultan ahora ser teofóricos.

La nueva lectura de la inscripción cacereña nos permite, en particular, aclarar la historia de la serie onomástica en cuestión y reconducir las variantes atestiguadas a los niveles correspondientes de desarrollo fonético (tabla 1):

Según indicaba con acierto Moralejo Laso, "el número de variantes y sus particulares diferencias fonéticas [...] hacen suponer un uso de estos nombres muy largo en el tiempo, como también amplio en el espacio, para explicar la evolución de las primeras formas hasta las demás" (1978, 450)[83].

Al lado de los nombres personales que reproducen sin más el epíteto de la diosa, se hallan también otros, derivados del nombre divino, como es – de hecho – normal dentro de la onomástica teofórica[84].

Hay, pués, unos nombres femeninos derivados por medio de sustitución sufijal.[85] En los ejemplos que se atestiguan en el conjunto de nuestra serie onomástica, la

---

o quizás incluso de la luna, con una posible variante *Serana* en Panonia (más detalles en De Bernardo Stempel 2013b, 80).

80 La presente etimología de *Ataecina* representa una modificación y puesta al día de la interpretación de Luján Martínez (1998): véanse la discusión de su análisis en *NWÄI*, 80–1 (junto con 581 n. 97), y más recientemente De Bernardo Stempel (2013b, 80), así como, por lo que respecta el desarrollo fonético del teónimo, De Bernardo Stempel 2011, 79 con la n. 20.

81 Véase ahora De Bernardo Stempel 2014 con la bibliografía anterior.

82 Por Moralejo Laso 1978, Luján 2000, Prósper 2002 y 2007, 111 ss., y Vallejo Ruiz 2005, cuyos datos acerca de los testimonios individuales de las variantes no consideramos necesario repetir aquí. Wodtko (2010, 251–4) se limita a referir las interpretaciones de los tres últimos investigadores citados. Véase también *AALR*, 160–1 con el mapa 112.

83 Sin embargo, su reconstrucción de los hechos se ha quedado obsoleta. Lo mismo vale para Vallejo Ruiz (2005, 304–10), que le sigue muy de cerca, con *-te(i)na* como forma obligatoria de femenino, las variantes con *Doui-* como originarias y la reconstrucción *ad hoc* de célt. ***douis* (véanse lo dicho arriba en la nota 77 y lo explicado a continuación). Prósper parece oscilar entre dos posturas (2002, 409 vs. 417 y 420), y su reconstrucción, tanto fonética como morfológica, es innecesariamente compleja. La reconstrucción más acertada es la de Luján (2000, 83), si bien no explica ni la vocal *-i-* que precede el sufijo *-tero-*, ni la terminación en *-tena*, que él llama "sufijo", de algunos de los nombres femeninos.

84 Una tipología de los nombres teofóricos célticos se dibuja en De Bernardo Stempel 2008.

85 Es decir 'Suffixersatz', un procedimiento de formación de palabra que se ilustra en *NWÄI*, 557–65.

Tabla 1

1.1	**Dubiterā* y **Dubiterus*
	el original, puede que a restituir en unos cuantos casos de *Dubit[ ]* [a]
1.2	**Dobitera, Dobiteria* y *Dobiterus, Dobterus* [b]
	con centralización de la vocal (¡átona!) de la cuarta sílaba desde el final (y hasta con síncopa en la antepenúltima)[c] y grafía original para las consonantes

2.1	**Duvitera* y **Duviterus*
	con vocalismo original y lenición de la oclusiva sonora intervocálica
2.2	**Dovitera* y *Doviterus* [d]
	con lenición de la oclusiva sonora intervocálica y centralización de la vocal (¡átona!) de la cuarta sílaba desde el final
2.3	**Dovidera* y *Doviderus* [e]
	como el anterior, pero con el añadido de la 2ª lenición céltica para la oclusiva sorda

3.1	*Duitera* y **Duiterus*
	con vocalismo todavía original y simplificación del nexo gráfico <vv> tras la lenición de la oclusiva sonora intervocálica
3.2	**Doitera* y *Doiterus* [f]
	con centralización de la vocal (¡átona!) de la cuarta sílaba desde el final tras la eliminación de la *-*v*-
3.3	*Doidera, Doiderus* y nombre de agrupación familiar *Doiderigum* [g]
	como el anterior, pero con el añadido de la 2ª lenición céltica para las oclusivas sordas

a *OPEL* 2, 110.

b *OPEL* 2, 104; Abascal Palazón 1994, 345; *HEp* 1 (1989), nº 153, y *HEp* 18 (2009 [2012]), nº 295; *AALR*, 160 s., nº 39, 63, 144, 203, 417, 428 y 584.

c Conviene recordar que las vocales átonas pueden o estrecharse o centralizarse, y de hecho el paso de topónimos como Ἔβουρα a Ebora (sin explicar en Falileyev *et alii* 2010, 117) nos proporciona un paralelo para poder retrotraer el nombre personal *Dobiterus* a un más antiguo **Dubiterus*. Por lo que respecta la síncopa de la antepenúltima sílaba, De Bernardo Stempel (1994, 22) recoge ca.18 ejemplos galos.

d *OPEL* 2, 108; Abascal Palazón 1994, 348; *HEp* 3 (1993), nº 466, y *HEp* 6 (1996), nº 632; *AALR*, 160 s., nº 203 y 578.

e *OPEL* 2, 108; Abascal Palazón 1994, 347; *HEp* 1 (1989), nº 408.

f *OPEL* 2, 108; Abascal Palazón 1994, 346; *HEp* 5 (1995), nº 623.

g *OPEL* 2, 108; Abascal Palazón 1994, 346; *HEp* 1 (1989), nº 381 y 382, y *HEp* 4 (1994), nº 961; González Rodríguez 1986, C 19.

terminación en *-ra* de unas variantes onomásticas femeninas (¡y no su entero sufijo **-terā*!) fue reemplazada por el morfema *-na* que contribuía a formar diminutivos[86]. Derivados secundarios obtenidos con ese procedimiento son *Dobitena*[87] (a partir del tipo 1.2: **Dobitera*), *Dovitena*[88] (a partir del tipo 2.2: **Dovitera*), *Dovidena*[89] (a partir del tipo 2.3: **Dovidera*), *Doitena*[90] (a partir del tipo 3.2: **Doitera*) y *Doidena*[91] (a partir del tipo 3.3: **Doidera*). En cuanto a *Dovidona*[92] y *Doidina*[93], parecen corresponder, más bien que a simples variantes fonéticas del tipo *Dovidena* que acabamos de citar, a otros dos subtipos de derivados por sustitución sufijal: en estos, los conocidos morfemas derivacionales onomásticos *-ona* e *-ina* sustituyeron a la terminacíon *-era* de **Dovidera* (tipo 2.3), dado que, tras la sonorización debida a la lenición de la **-t-* original, la secuencia *-dera* ya no gozaba de transparencia semántica.

Muy común es la formación de idiónimos derivados en **-yā*. El *Dobiter[i]a* citado arriba (tipo 1.2) es sólo un ejemplo, mientras que en la zona en cuestión este tipo de derivados tiende a asumir la apariencia de los temas en *-ā*. Éste es el origen de los femeninos *Dobiteina*[94] (con *Dobit-* como en el tipo 1.2) y *Doviteina*[95] (con *Dovit-* como en el tipo 2.2), que, por proceder de **Dobiten-yā* y – respectivamente – de **Doviten-yā*, se formaron a partir de los derivados con la sustitución sufijal que acabamos de comentar, perteneciendo, por lo tanto, al grupo de los hiperderivados. Se notará que también los diminutivos femeninos irlandeses en *-ne* proceden de la unión de **-yā* con un sufijo con nasal.

A una protoforma derivada de la base adjetival **dubi-* podría remontarse también el nombre de agrupación *Duitiq(um)* mencionado arriba[96], si bien – a diferencia de la serie onomástica formada por *Dubiterus* y sus variantes – su formación de palabra no nos proporciona pistas precisas para su análisis.

En este contexto hay que mencionar, finalmente, el pseudo-cognomen romano *Dubitatus*, *Dubitata*: "der Form nach klarerweise ein lateinischer Name, dessen seltsame Semantik aber für einen zugrunde liegenden keltischen Namen spricht, wahrscheinlich ebenfalls auf der Basis von **dubu-* 'Schwarz'"[97]. El hecho de que su terminación en *-tatus*/*-tata* se parezca *primo visu* a aquella del superlativo griego[98] podría quizás sugerir que los *Dubitatus*, *Dubitata* y sus derivados pseudo-gentilicios *Dubitatius*, *Dubitatia*, tan

86 Como, p.ej., en los conglutinados que se describen en *NWÄI*, 321–26, 351–2 y 361–70.
87 *HEp* 14 (2005 [2008]), nº 40; *AALR*, 160 nº 203.
88 *OPEL* 2, 108; Abascal Palazón 1994, 348; *HEp* 11 (2001 [2005]), nº 380; *AALR*, 160 nº 75 y 161 (s.n.).
89 *OPEL* 2, 108; Abascal Palazón 1994, 347.
90 *OPEL* 2, 108; Abascal Palazón 1994, 346.
91 *OPEL* 2, 104; Abascal Palazón 1994, 346; *HEp* 12 (2002 [2006]), nº 539.
92 *OPEL* 2, 108; Abascal Palazón 1994, 347.
93 Abascal Palazón 1994, 346.
94 *OPEL* 2, 103; Abascal Palazón 1994, 345; *HEp* 13 (2003/04 [2007]), nos. 571 y 909; *AALR*, 160, nº 203, 208 y 320.
95 *OPEL* 2, 108; *AALR*, 160 nº 435.
96 En la nota 52. — Por otro lado, ante los muchos siglos que los separan, no procede hablar en este lugar de nombres personales irlandeses y británicos que se asemejan más o menos lejanamente a nuestra serie hispanocéltica en *-tero-*/*tera*.
97 Así Meid 2005, 269 como ya Lochner v. Hüttenbach 1989, 194.
98 Surgido del cruce de dos sufijos elativos todavía atestiguados en celta (*NWÄI*, 427).

frecuentes en provincias de habla céltica[99], sustituyeran específicamente los personales teofóricos indígenas que acabamos de describir, relacionados con la diosa descrita por medio del epíteto 'contrastivo' **Dubitera* 'La (más) oscura (de las dos)' > **Duvitera* > *Duitera*.

BIBLIOGRAFÍA

Abascal Palazón, J. M. 1994 *Los nombres personales en las inscripciones latinas de Hispania*. Murcia, Universidad Complutense de Madrid & Universidad de Murcia.

Abascal Palazón, J. M. 1995 'Las inscripciones latinas de Santa Lucía del Trampal (Alcuéscar, Cáceres) y el culto de Ataecina en Hispania', *Archivo Español de Arqueología* 68, 31–106.

Abascal Palazón, J. M. 2002 'Ataecina', *Religiões da Lusitania. Loquuntur saxa*, ed. L. Raposo, 53–60. Lisboa, Museu Nacional de Arqueologia.

Acuña Castroviejo, F. & R. Casal García 2010 'Revisitando la plástica galaico-romana', *Escultura romana en Hispania 6 (Actas de la 6ª Reunión Internacional de escultura romana en Hispania celebrada en el parque arqueológico de Segobriga los días 21 y 22 de octubre de 2008)*, ed. J. M. Abascal Palazón & R. Cebrián Fernández, 385–402. Murcia, Tabularium.

Albertos, *sched.* = *Schedae epigraphicae, quas* Mª L. Albertos Firmat *de inscriptionibus Hispanis ad nomina vernacula praesertim spectantibus ex im. phot. ab amicis missis, permultis oculatim descriptis sibi paraverat; quarum exempla, paulo antequam mortem obiit a.* 1986, *CIL* II^2 *dedit*.

Alfayé Villa, S. 2011 *Imagen y ritual en la Céltica peninsular*. A Coruña, Toxosoutos.

Alfayé Villa, S. 2013 'Sobre iconografía y teonimia en el noroeste peninsular', *Palaeohispanica* 13, 189–208.

Anati, E. 1968 *Arte rupestre nelle regioni occidentali della Penisola Iberica*. Capo di Ponte, Edizioni del Centro.

Arenas-Esteban, J. A. & P. de Bernardo Stempel 2011 'Celtic dialects and cultural contacts in protohistory: the Italian and Iberian peninsulas', *Études celtiques* 37, 119–39.

Balles, I. 2009 'The Old Indic cvi construction, the Caland system, and the PIE adjective', *Internal Reconstruction in Indo-European. Methods, Results, and Problems (Section Papers from the XVI Intern. Conference on Historical Linguistics: Copenhagen, August 2003)*, ed. J. E. Rasmussen & Th. Olander (en colab. con A. R. Jørgensen), 1–15. Copenhague, Museum Tusculanum Press.

Beltrán Lloris, M. 1975–1976 'Aportaciones a la epigrafía y arqueología romana de Cáceres', *Caesaraugusta* 39–40, 19–111.

Bianchi, L. 1985 *Le stele funerarie della Dacia. Un'espressione di arte romana periferica*. Roma, Giorgio Bretschneider Editore (Archaeologica 45).

Billy, P.-H. 2011 *Dictionnaire des noms de lieux de la France*. París, Errance.

Bonnaud, Ch. 2002 'Les divinités indigènes de Vettonie sous le Haut-Empire Romain: essai d'inventaire et interprétation', *Conimbriga* 41, 63–103.

Callejo Serrano, C. 1967 'Cédulas epigráficas del Campo Norbense', *Zephyrus* 18, 85–120.

Callejo Serrano, C. 1977 'Simbología funeraria romana de la alta Extremadura', *Revista de la Universidad Complutense de Madrid* 36 (nº 109) (= *Homenaje a A. García y Bellido* III), 145–61.

Calvo y Sánchez, I. & J. Cabré Aguiló 1917 *Excavación en la Cueva y Collado de los Jardines (Sta. Elena, Jaén). Memoria de los trabajos realizados en 1916*. Madrid, Junta Superior de Excavaciones y Antigüedades.

Cerrillo Martín de Cáceres, E. & M. Cruz 1993 'La plástica indígena y el impacto romano en la Lusitania', *Actas de la I Reunión sobre escultura romana en Hispania*, coord. T. Nogales Basarrate, 159–78. Madrid, Ministerio

99 Kakoschke 2006, 165–6, 2007, 313–4, 2009, 164, 2010, 315, 2011, 345–6, 2012, 96 y 394; *OPEL* 2, 110; *NTS* 3, 336–9.

de Cultura.

Cibu, S. 2003 'Chronologie et formulaire dans les inscriptions religieuses de Narbonnaise et des provinces alpines (Alpes Graies et Poenines, Cottiennes et Maritimes)', *Revue archéologique de Narbonnaise* 36, 335–60.

Collinge, N. E. 1985 *The Laws of Indo-European*, Amsterdam, Benjamins.

De Bernardo Stempel, P. 1987 *Die Vertretung der indogermanischen liquiden und nasalen Sonanten im Keltischen*. Innsbruck, Innsbrücker Beiträge zur Sprachwissenschaft 54.

De Bernardo Stempel, P. 1994 'Zum gallischen Akzent: eine sprachinterne Betrachtung', *Zeitschrift für celtische Philologie* 46, 14–35.

De Bernardo Stempel, P. 1995 'Gaulish accentuation. Results and outlook', *Hispano-Gallo-Brittonica: Essays in Honour of D.E. Evans*, ed. J. F. Eska, R. G. Gruffydd & N. Jacobs, 16–32. Cardiff, University of Wales Press.

De Bernardo Stempel, P. 1997 'Celtico e antico indiano: in margine alle più recenti teorie', *Bandhu: Scritti in onore di C. Della Casa*, ed. R. Arena, M. P. Bologna, M. L. Mayer Modena & A. Passi, vol. II, 717–34. Alessandria, Edizioni Dell'Orso.

De Bernardo Stempel, P. 2000 'Kernitalisch, Latein, Venetisch: ein Etappenmodell', *125 Jahre Indogermanistik in Graz*, ed. M. Ofitsch & Ch. Zinko, 47–70. Graz, Leykam.

De Bernardo Stempel, P. 2002 'Centro y áreas laterales: la formación del celtibérico sobre el fondo del celta peninsular hispano', *Palaeohispanica* 2, 89–132.

De Bernardo Stempel, P. 2003 'Los formularios teonímicos, *Bandus* con su correspondiente *Bandua* y unas isoglosas célticas', *Conimbriga* 42, 197–212.

De Bernardo Stempel, P. 2006 'Las lenguas célticas en la investigación. Cuatro observaciones metodológicas', *Cuadernos de filología clásica. Estudios griegos e indoeuropeos* 16, 5–21.

De Bernardo Stempel, P. 2007 'Varietäten des Keltischen auf der Iberischen Halbinsel: Neue Evidenzen', *Kelten-Einfälle an der Donau (Akten des 4. Symposiums deutschsprachiger Keltologinnen und Keltologen: Linz /Donau, Juli 2005)*, ed. H. Birkhan (en colab. con H. Tauber), 149–62. Viena, Österreichische Akademie der Wissenschaften (Denkschriften der Philos.-hist. Klasse 345).

De Bernardo Stempel, P. 2008 'I nomi teoforici del celta antico', *Dedicanti e* cultores *nelle religioni celtiche (VIII workshop internazionale F.E.R.C.AN.: Gargnano, Maggio 2007)*, ed. A. Sartori, 73–104. Milán, Cisalpino (Quaderni di *Acme*, 104).

De Bernardo Stempel, P. 2011 '*Callaeci, Anabaraecus, Abienus, Tritecum, Berobriaecus* and the new velar suffixes of the types *-ViK-* and *-(y)eK-*', Ἀντίδωρον: *Homenaje a Juan José Moralejo*, ed. Mª J. García Blanco, T. Amado Rodríguez, Mª J. Martín Velasco, A. Pereiro Pardo & M. E. Vázquez Buján, 175–93. Santiago de Compostela, Universidade de Santiago de Compostela.

De Bernardo Stempel, P. 2013a 'From Indo-European to the individual Celtic languages', *Saltair saíochta, sanasaíochta agus seanchais: A Festschrift for Gearóid Mac Eoin*, ed. D. Ó Baoill, D. Ó hAodha & N. Ó Muraíle, 25–42. Dublín, Four Courts Press.

De Bernardo Stempel, P. 2013b 'Celtic and other indigenous divine names found in the Italian peninsula', *Théonymie celtique, cultes,* interpretatio */ Keltische Theonymie, Kulte,* interpretatio *(X. Workshop F.E.R.C.AN.: París, 24.-26. Mai 2010)*, ed. A. Hofeneder & P. de Bernardo Stempel (en colab. con M. Hainzmann & N. Mathieu), 73–96. Viena, Österreichische Akademie der Wissenschaften (Mitteilungen der Prähist. Kommission 79).

De Bernardo Stempel, P. 2014 'Keltische Äquivalente klassischer Epitheta und andere sprachliche und nicht-sprachliche Phänomene im Rahmen der sogenannten *‚interpretatio Romana'', Zeitschrift für celtische Philologie* 61, 7–48.

De Bernardo Stempel, P. & M. V. García Quintela 2008 'Población trilingüe y divinidades del castro de Lansbriga (prov. Ourense)', *Madrider Mitteilungen* 49, 254–90.

Delamarre, X. 2009 'Iria (**Īryā*) "L'opulente, la fertile" (Ligurie, Galice, Dalmatie)', *Veleia* 26, 355–8.

Delamarre, X. 2012 *Noms de lieux celtiques de l'Europe ancienne*. París, Errance.

Delgado Delgado, J. 2005 'La ritualización del reino vegetal: los *liba*', *Paraíso cerrado, jardín abierto. El reino vegetal en el imaginario religioso del Mediterráneo*, ed. R. Olmos, P. Cabrera & S. Montero, 189– 206. Madrid, Ediciones Polifemo.

De Vaan, M. 2008 *Etymological Dictionary of Latin and the Other Italic Languages.* Leiden & Boston, Brill (Leiden Indo-European Etymological Dictionary Series, 7).

Domínguez Moreno, J. M. 1987–1988 'El ara votiva

de Tejeda de Tiétar y su información sobre una danza prerromana', *Norba* 8–9, 33–41.

Esteban Ortega, J. 2007 *Corpus de inscripciones latinas de Cáceres. I. Norba*. Cáceres, Universidad de Extremadura, Servicio de Publicaciones.

Esteban Ortega, J. 2012 *Corpus de inscripciones latinas de Cáceres. II. Turgalium*. Cáceres, Universidad de Extremadura, Servicio de Publicaciones.

Esteban Ortega, J. & J. Salas Martín 2003 *Epigrafía romana y cristiana del Museo de Cáceres*. Cáceres, Editora Regional de Extremadura.

Falileyev, A., (en colab. con A. E. Gohil y N. Ward) 2010 *Dictionary of Continental Celtic Place-Names*. Aberystwyth, *Cambrian Medieval Celtic Studies Publications*.

Gallego Franco, H. 2002 'El *cognomen Flaus* en Hispania romana: significado onomástico y reflejo social', *Scripta Antiqua in honorem A. Montenegro Duque y J. Mª Blázquez Martínez*, ed. S. Crespo Ortiz de Zárate & A. Alonso Ávila, 429–41. Valladolid, Universidad de Valladolid.

García-Bellido, Mª P. 2001 '*Lucus Feroniae Emeritenses*', *Archivo Español de Arqueología* 74, 53–72.

García Ramón, J. L. 2013 'Italische Personennamen, Sprachkontakt und Sprachvergleich. I. Einige oskische Namen. II. Altlatein *Ferter Resius* / *rex Aequeicolus*', *Linguarum varietas* 2, 103–17.

García y Bellido, A. 1967 'Sobre un tipo de estela funeraria de togado romano bajo hornacina', *Archivo Español de Arqueología* 40, 110–20.

González García, F. J. 2010 'Hábito epigráfico, decoración plástica e interacción cultural en el noroeste hispano en época romana. Análisis de las estelas funerarias de Vigo (Pontevedra)', *Madrider Mitteilungen* 51, 397– 418.

González Rodríguez, Mª C. 1986 *Las unidades organizativas indígenas del área indoeuropea de Hispania*. Vitoria-Gasteiz, Universidad del País Vasco / Euskal Herriko Unibertsitatea (Anejos de *Veleia*, Series Maior 2).

Greenland, F. A. R. 2007 'Table for one. Drinking alone on women's grave monuments from Roman Celtiberia', *Ancient East & West* 6, 113–34.

Hainzmann, M. & P. de Bernardo Stempel 2007 'Zwei neue altkeltische Gottheiten. *Ollodevos* und *Acinoris*', *Auf den Spuren keltischer Götterverehrung (Akten des 5. F.E.R.C.AN-Kolloquiums: Graz, Oktober 2003)*, ed. M. Hainzmann, 139–46. Viena, Österreichische Akademie der Wissenschaften (Mitteilungen der Prähistorischen Kommission 64).

Juliá, D., 1971 *Étude épigraphique et iconographique des stèles funéraires de Vigo*. Heidelberg, F. H. Kerle.

Kajanto, I., 1982 *The Latin Cognomina*. Roma, Giorgio Bretschneider Editore.

Kakoschke, A. 2006 *Die Personennamen in den zwei germanischen Provinzen. 1. Gentilnomina*. Rahden / Westfalen, Verlag Marie Leidorf.

Kakoschke, A. 2007 *Die Personennamen in den zwei germanischen Provinzen. 2,1. Cognomina Abaius-Lysias.* Rahden / Westfalen, Verlag Marie Leidorf.

Kakoschke, A. 2009 *Die Personennamen in der römischen Provinz Rätien*. Hildesheim *et al.*, Olms-Weidmann.

Kakoschke, A. 2010 *Die Personennamen in der römischen Provinz Gallia Belgica*. Hildesheim *et al.*, Olms-Weidmann.

Kakoschke, A. 2011 *Die Personennamen in der römischen Provinz Britannien*. Hildesheim *et al.*, Olms-Weidmann.

Kakoschke, A. 2012 *Die Personennamen in der römischen Provinz Noricum*. Hildesheim *et al.*, Olms-Weidmann.

Lacam, J.-Cl. 2012 'La gourmandise des dieux: les gâteaux sacrés des Tables de Gubbio (IIIe–IIe s. av. J.-C.)', *Mélanges de l'École française de Rome - Antiquité* [En línea], 124. 2, Publicado el 23 julio 2013, consultado el 18 julio 2014. URL: http://mefra.revues.org/886.

Lochner von Hüttenbach, F. 1989 *Die römerzeitlichen Personennamen der Steirmark. Herkunft und Auswertung*. Graz, Leykam.

Luján Martínez, E. R. 1998 'La diosa Ataecina y el nombre de la noche en antiguo irlandés', *Emerita* 66 (2), 291–306.

Luján [Martínez], E. R. 2000 'Sobre los orígenes de los comparativos indoeuropeos en **-teros*', *Revista Española de Lingüística* 30 (1), 77–102.

McCone, K. 1996 *Towards a Relative Chronology of Ancient and Medieval Celtic Sound Change*. Maynooth, St. Patrick's College, The Department of Old Irish (Maynooth Studies in Celtic Linguistics 1).

Marco Simón, F. 1976 *Las estelas decoradas de los conventos Caesaraugustano y Cluniense*. Zaragoza, Institución Fernando el Católico.

Matasović, R. 2009 *Etymological Dictionary of Proto-Celtic*. Leiden & Boston, Brill (Leiden Indo-European Etymological Dictionary Series, 9).

Meid, W. 1967 'Zum Aequativ der keltischen

Sprachen, besonders des Irischen', *Beiträge zur Indogermanistik und Keltologie: Festschrift Julius Pokorny*, ed. W. Meid, 223–42. Innsbruck, Innsbrucker Beträge zur Kulturwissenchaft 13.

Meid, W. 2005 *Keltische Personennamen in Pannonien*. Budapest, Archaeolingua (Series Minor 20).

Meißner, T. 1998 'Das "Calandsche Gesetz" und das Griechische – nach 100 Jahren', *Sprache und Kultur der Indogermanen. (Akten der X. Fachtagung der Idg. Ges.: Innsbruck 1996)*, ed. W. Meid, 237–54. Innsbruck, Innsbrucker Beiträge zur Sprachwissenchaft 93.

Mercando, L. & G. Paci 1998 *Stele romane in Piemonte*. Roma, Giorgio Bretschneider Editore (Serie Miscellanea, vol V).

Moralejo Laso, A. 1978 'Sobre los nombres *Doviterus, Dovitena*', *Actas del V Congreso Español de Estudios clásicos (Madrid, 20–25 de abril de 1976)*, Madrid, Sociedad Española de Estudios Clásicos, 449–54.

Nussbaum, A. J. 1976 *Caland's "Law" and the Caland System*. Ph.D. Diss. Harvard University, Cambridge/Mass., Harvard Reprints.

Olivares Pedreño, J. C. 1999 'El panteón religioso indígena en el área extremeña', *Hispania Antiqua* 23, 97–118.

Olivares Pedreño, J. C. 2002 *Los dioses de la Hispania Céltica*. Madrid & Alicante, Real Academia de la Historia & Universidad de Alicante.

Olivares Pedreño, J. C. & L. Mª Ramajo Correa. 2013 'Un altar votivo procedente de Cilleros dedicado a los dioses lusitanos *Arentia* y *Arentius* y precisiones sobre otra inscripción votiva de Villamiel (Cáceres)', *Veleia* 30, 193–203.

Poccetti, P. 2007 'Notes de linguistique italique. Nouvelle série. 3. L'attestation osque du terme pour 'consul' et le traitement de [ns] avec ses reflets latins et romans', *Revue des Études latines* 84, 27–36.

Prósper, B. Mª 2002 *Lenguas y religiones prerromanas del occidente de la Península Ibérica*. Salamanca, Ediciones Universidad.

Prósper, B. Mª 2007 *Estudio lingüístico del plomo celtibérico de Iniesta*. Salamanca, Ediciones Universidad.

Prósper, B. Mª & F. Villar. 2009 'Nueva inscripción lusitana procedente de Portalegre', *Emerita* 77 (1), 1–32.

Raepsaet-Charlier, M.-Th. 1993 Dis deabusque sacrum: *Formulaire votif et datation dans les Trois Gaules et les deux Germanies*. París, Diffusion De Boccard.

Raepsaet-Charlier, M.-Th. 2001 'Le formulaire des dedicaces religieuses de Germanie superieure', *Religion in den germanischen Provinzen Roms*, ed. W. Spickermann, 135–71. Tubinga, Mohr Siebeck.

Ramón y Fernández-Oxea, J. R. 1944–1945 'Antigüedades cacereñas VIII', *Boletín del Seminario de Estudios de Arte y Arqueología* 11, 81–95.

Rodríguez Colmenero, A. 2010 'De nuevo sobre la supuesta *Bandua Lansbrica* [sic!] y otras divinidades del Castro de San Cibrán das Lás [...]', *Larouco* 5, 179–85.

Rodríguez Lage, S. 1974 *Las estelas funerarias de Galicia en época romana*. Ourense, Instituto de estudios orensanos Padre Feijóo.

Scheid, J. 2011 'Les offrandes végétales dans les rites sacrificiels des Romains', *«Nourrir les dieux ?» Sacrifice et représentation du divin (Actes de la VIe Rencontre du Groupe de recherche européen 'FIGURA. Représentation du divin dans les sociétés grecque et romaine': Université de Liège, 23–24 octobre 2009)*, ed. V. Pirenne-Delforge & F. Prescendi, 105–17. Lieja, Centre International d'Étude de la Religion Grecque Antique.

Sims-Williams, P. 1990 'Dating the transition to Neo-Brittonic: phonology and history, 400–600', *Britain 400–600: Language and History (Proceedings of an International Symposium: Eichstätt, October 1988)*, ed. A. Bammesberger & A. Wollmann, 217–61. Heidelberg, Carl Winter.

Soria Sánchez, V. 1975a 'Descubrimientos arqueológicos de Extremadura', *Revista de Estudios Extremeños* 31(2), 279–85.

Soria Sánchez, V. 1975b 'Nuevas aportaciones a la arqueología extremeña', *XIV Congreso Nacional de Arqueología (Vitoria, 1975)*, ed. Secretaría General de los Congresos Arqueológicos Nacionales, 1143–52. Zaragoza, Universidad de Zaragoza.

Soria Sánchez, V. 1983 'Armas en la Edad del Bronce en Extremadura', *Gladius* 16, 201–8.

Soria Sánchez, V. 1994 'Diccionario epigráfico de inscripciones de Extremadura', *Coloquios Históricos de Extremadura XX. Homenaje a Francisco Pizarro en el 450 aniversario de su muerte (1477–1541)*, ed. Centro de Iniciativas Turísticas de Trujillo, 448–59. Cáceres, Diputación provincial de Cáceres.

Soria Sánchez, V. 1995 'Catalogación de inscripciones recientes de Extremadura', *Actas del XXII Congreso Nacional de Arqueología (Vigo, 1993), vol. II*, 383–9. Vigo, Xunta de Galicia. Consellería de Cultura, Comunicación Social e Turismo.

Soria Sánchez, V. 1999 'Inscripción y noticias arqueológicas de Extremadura', *XXIV Congreso Nacional de Arqueología, vol. IV. Romanización y desarrollo urbano en la Hispania republicana (Cartagena 1997)*, 791–8. Murcia, Comunidad Autónoma de la región de Murcia. Dirección general de Cultura. Instituto de Patrimonio Histórico.

Stokes, W. & A. Bezzenberger 1894 *Wortschatz der keltischen Spracheinheit*. Reimpresión de la 4ª edición de 1894, Gotinga, Vandenhoeck & Ruprecht, 1979 (= 2ª parte del *Vergleichendes Wörterbuch der indogermanischen Sprachen* de A. Fick).

Tantimonaco, S. & H. Gimeno Pascual 2014 'Un nuevo epitafio de una esclava en *Toletum*', *Veleia* 31, 213–26.

Turcan, R. 1988 *Religion romaine. II. Le culte*. Leiden & Nueva York, Brill (Iconography of Religions XVII, 1).

Uhlich, J. 1993 *Die Morphologie der komponierten Personennamen des Altirischen*. Witterschlick, M. Wehle.

Vallejo Ruiz, J. Mª 2005 *Antroponimia indígena de la Lusitania romana*. Vitoria-Gasteiz, Universidad del País Vasco/Euskal Herriko Unibertsitatea (Anejos de *Veleia*, Series Minor 23).

Villar, F. 1986 'El dativo latino epigráfico en *-ā*', *Emerita* 54 (1), 45–62.

Wackernagel, J. 1897 = 1969 'Vermischte Beiträge zur griechischen Sprachkunde: 3. Αργικεραυνος und Genossen', reimprimido en idem, *Kleine Schriften*, vol. 1, Gotinga, Vandenhoeck & Ruprecht, 769–75.

Wodtko, D. S. 2000 *Wörterbuch der keltiberischen Inschriften*. Wiesbaden, Reichert (= *Monumenta Linguarum Hispanicarum*, ed. J. Untermann, V/1).

Wodtko, D. S. 2010 'The problem of Lusitanian', *Celtic from the West*, ed. B. Cunliffe & J. T. Koch, 335–67. Oxford, Oxbow Books.

XIII

LOOKING AT COSMOLOGY THROUGH THE LENS OF HERMENEUTICS AND SEMANTICS

Maria Pilar Burillo-Cuadrado
& Francisco Burillo-Mozota

The main source for understanding Celtiberian religious ideas is iconography. Unlike many other cultures, the iconography seems to focus on one main motif, the sun. This paper proposes three different iconographic syntaxes, realistic and abstract ones, that were intended to tell the same story, the solar myth. For example, on monochrome pottery, the sun is depicted as a left-facing or right-facing swastika, associated with a horse and an anthropomorphic figure with equine head. Based on structuralist and phenomenological theoretical approaches, and a 3D analysis of the pottery, this paper suggests a cosmogonical interpretation of Celtiberian iconography in which the sun appears as the highest deity. To explain its diurnal motion, radiant circles or right-facing swastikas are used, and circles with no rays and left-facing swastikas for its nocturnal return. The horse figures carry the sun and are in themselves identified with the solar deity. The sun would return through an aquatic sphere situated in the upper cosmos, and the figure of the fish depicted on Numantine vessel no. 2308 is particularly important on its return journey. It would be a means of transport or an enemy to be vanquished so that the sun could return to its place of origin and rise again.

Introduction[1]

THE cosmos is the great mystery that has always amazed and continues to amaze humanity. The sun, symbol of life, is the most important heavenly body. In the pre-scientific age its diurnal motion was an enigma, crossing the universe from sunrise to sunset, prompting the question of where it went at night, its unknown path to a new dawn each day. The wonder was repeated each night, in all its immensity, with the continuing cycle of the moon and the stars, with the planets standing out as the brightest.

The identification of the most important heavenly bodies with deities has been one of the constants in the religions of antiquity. Thus in Greek religion we find the Sun identified with Helios, the Moon with Selene and the planets with gods whose Roman

1 This study has been undertaken within the Iberus Research Group (H08), financed by the Government of Aragon and the European Social Fund, and R&D&i project: HAR2015-68032-P, 'La Serranía Celtibérica y Segeda, el Patrimonio Histórico como motor de desarrollo rural', financed by the Spanish Ministry of Economy and Competitiveness and ERDF funds.

names survive today: Mercury, Venus, Mars, Jupiter, Saturn. The Greek texts that have survived recount the myths associated with each of these deities, but these myths can be depicted in another way: through iconography. Text and art generate two forms of language, and their inter-relation helps scholars of today understand these deities, their manifestations and their relationships with human beings.

For the researcher the problem arises when a culture, the Celtiberian being one, has left no texts describing their myths and rituals.[2] In this case iconography will thus be the principal, if not the only, way of reconstructing the cosmological aspects of their religion.[3] So it is important to develop an adequate theoretical and methodological framework for understanding the religious significance of much of Celtiberian iconography. But this approach presents a major challenge, given the inscrutable nature of the signs and symbols that we need to interpret. So we need to analyse this iconography using a hermeneutic and pragmatic approach, the only way of channelling and reawakening our dormant senses in order to feel and understand the supernatural reality that pervaded, as absolute truth, the Celtiberian society we are studying and which can only be apprehended through its iconography.

Theory and method

Studies in social anthropology and the history of religions demonstrate the power of religious sentiment in ancient societies to be a fact that can be considered universal.[4] In the Celtiberian world, therefore, as in all ancient societies, the presence of the supernatural was unquestionable. The gods transcended human existence as the 'great truth', in a universe superior to the visible world and everyday life, which it permeated and endowed with meaning.

The first problem posed when it comes to understanding religion are the religious sentiments, mentality and principles of the researcher. We, researchers in the twenty-first century, come up against a number of important limitations for understanding religious sentiment in ancient societies. In Western culture science dominates as the most certain form of knowledge, rationalism as the only way of approaching the truth. In addition, the education we have received has distanced our deepest feelings from a belief in the supernatural as a supreme vital reality. We currently live in an agnostic and secular society in which spirituality has been eroded. Added to this is the fact that for those of us who have been brought up from childhood, as in our case, in the Catholic church, rational truth as a form of knowledge is reinforced, because God, and a belief of his actual existence, can only be approached through faith, and this can only be

2 In the Celtiberian area only one sanctuary has been identified with a solar alignment, the so-called Segeda Sanctuary of the Sun. It is a horizontal monumental construction, aligned with prominent points on the horizon where the sun sets at the equinoxes and the summer solstice (Burillo & Pérez 2015).

3 Studies of Celtiberian religion, including Sopeña 1995, Alfayé 2009, Burillo-Cuadrado & Burillo-Mozota 2010, Marco 2010, Burillo-Cuadrado 2015b, are based on an interpretation of the iconography that has survived into the present.

4 Morris 1994.

achieved with divine grace. So it is necessary to deconstruct the religious mentality of the researcher in order to empathise with the religious sentiments and values of human beings in Antiquity.

Phenomenology and hermeneutics

Phenomenology is the philosophical approach used to channel this difficult investigative task, since it allows the researcher to adopt a dialectical approach to the subject matter of investigation.[5] The transcendental phenomenology of Edmund Husserl is a theory of knowledge that unifies the real world and the ideal, the existential and the essential. It consists of becoming aware of an object subjectively, so that the free fantasy or creativity of the researcher is given greater weight than his or her perceptions. It works towards universal knowledge through 'eidetic reduction', which dispenses with individual acts in order to reach the *eidos*, universals or archetypes.[6] That is, the essences that are constantly repeated in time and space, whether there is a direct relationship or if there is none. The meaning of things is evident in each archetype as the structure of the unconscious of every human being.[7] It is therefore the identification of the *eidos* or archetypes, which in our case we need to identify in Celtiberian iconography, that will allow us to transcend the individual in our research to reach the universal.

Hans-Georg Gadamer developed the philosophy of Husserl and Wittgenstein in his later period and incorporates the Greek thought of Plato and Aristotle to raise phenomenology to a new philosophical, hermeneutic, form of knowledge in which subject and object interact in a process of reciprocal mediation, a dialectic between the subject that understands and the 'thing itself', which asserts itself as something preferable in the context of the possible and the probable and adopts the so-called 'hermeneutical circle'[8] as an explanatory resource. Which in our case means studying Celtiberian iconography directly in its original medium and not from a secondary, decontextualized and previously interpreted source, such as tracings.

Pragmatism as the integration of semiotics and semantics

In the search for a universal ontological model, Gadamer finds the ideal of scientific objectivity in language as a means of understanding, as the primary place of hermeneutics, in line with the theories of the Swiss linguist Ferdinand Saussure in the early twentieth century.[9]

5 The philosopher Husserl was the founder of phenomenology, a critical response to the naturalistic empiricism and positivism of the natural and exact sciences that had excluded the humanities from the sphere of the sciences (Medina 2001).

6 Husserl's concept of *eidos* is developed by Jung (1981) under the term 'archetype'.

7 Ortiz-Osés 1988.

8 Gadamer uses game theory to explain hermeneutical knowledge, where the subject is not the players but the game itself, which moves constantly back and forth without ending, and that movement contains subject, activity and content (Gadamer 1992).

9 Saussure's only work, *Course in General Linguistics*, was published posthumously by his students from the lectures he gave between 1907 and 1911 (Saussure 1985). It states that language is a system of arbitrary signs, consisting of a signifier, or material component of the linguistic sign, and meaning,

However, it was in 1869 in the United States of America that the philosopher Charles S. Peirce[10] defined the sign as a means of communication between an object and its interpreter. To study a sign, the subject matter of semiotics, he establishes three steps: the syntactic, the semantic and the pragmatic. The syntactic refers to the study of the relationship between the different signs, in our case iconographic representations. The semantic analyses the signs and their meaning. Finally, the pragmatic studies the relationship between signs and the context in which they are used. However, his work took a long time to become known, and it was the Italian Umberto Eco[11] who brought together the two currents of thought, European and American, and in 1976 he published his *Treatise on General Semiotics*, in which he develops a comprehensive theory of all meaning systems based on signs.[12] In the realm of philosophy it was Jürgen Habermas who asserted the validity of pragmatic approaches in the nineteen-eighties.[13]

Our aim is to understand Celtiberian religion from the way in which Celtiberian society communicated, evidenced by the language of its iconography. Semantics is therefore inseparable from phenomenology and hermeneutics. We must articulate icons by means of their 'iconographic syntax' in order to understand the meaning of the signs and symbols, and the scene or scenes they form, which will only be possible if we can make analogies with other scenes, both contemporary or synchronic, and from different cultural or diachronic stages. Only in this way can we begin to understand the *eido*, universal or archetype that the Celtiberians share with other cultures and define what is peculiar or specific to the Celtiberian culture.

Celtiberian iconography

The Celtiberians, unlike the Iberians of the Upper Guadalquivir, had no monumental buildings in their cities, sumptuous burials in their cemeteries or life-sized statues. This is because the dominance of a social structure based on the blood ties of the extended family generated a society in which wealth was shared and constrained the appearance of a prominent aristocracy responsible for monumentalising and embellishing their cities and tombs.[14] However, the Celtiberians had a rich artistic tradition of small objects,

which is the mental component or subjective idea that is associated with the sign. This posthumous work would become the basis of semiotics and structuralism, and had a major impact on the field of the social sciences and humanities.

10 Barrena & Nubiola (2013) state that the American philosopher Charles S. Peirce published three papers between 1868 and 1869, on the basis of which he is considered the father of semiotics. However, his work did not become known until Charles W. Morris published *Foundations of the Theory of Signs* in 1938.

11 Eco 1977.

12 In Spain, Ricardo Olmos (1996) is the leading exponent of the application of semiotics to Iberian iconography. The most highly regarded representative of his school is Trinidad Tortosa (2006) who, following Eco, has established 'the iconographic code' that takes into account the morphology of signs, syntactical aspects and themes of the icon.

13 Habermas is considered one of the most important philosophers of the second half of the twentieth century and is highly regarded for his interdisciplinary thinking (Guerra 2015).

14 See Burillo-Mozota (2010) for an analysis of the social structure of the Celtiberians in terms of their peasant way of life.

a

b

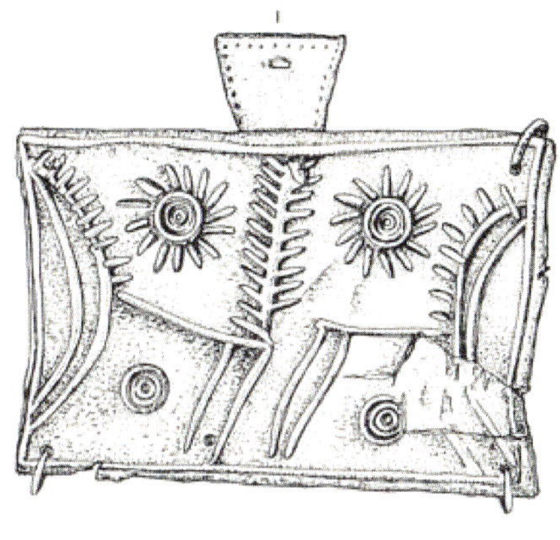
c

Fig. 1. Horses and concentric circles depicted on: a) ceremonial staff with two horses and a horseman from Numantia (Jimeno 2005, 495), b) horse fibula from Herrera de los Navarros (Burillo-Mozota), c) articulated plaque from Arcóbriga (Lorrio & Sánchez, 2009, 223).

mainly fashioned from bronze or ceramic.[15] So it is on objects of bronze and ceramic as an artistic medium that we find the icons, signs and symbols that shape the scenes that help us understand the religious feelings of the Celtiberians.

Interestingly, a chronological sequence is found in the aesthetic manifestation of scenes, which go from a realistic phase to another that was more schematic which, using the theoretical and methodological approaches referred to above, has allowed us to analyse it as a system and infer diachronic relationships in order to interpret the icons and scenes depicted. These two phases are characterised in the following way:

First phase (fifth to second century BCE)

This is characterised by objects made of bronze (Fig. 1): fibulas, ceremonial staffs and embossed plaques decorated with realistic scenes. Fibulae in the shape of a horse with or without rider and frequently impressed with concentric circles.[16] The finials of ceremonial staffs take the form of two horses, facing outwards on each side, with or without a horseman between them, and always with concentric circles along the entire body of the horses.[17] The embossed plaques have a flat surface that is decorated with more complex images depicting a scene. The horse is the animal most frequently depicted on these flat plaques, accompanied by concentric circles, both radiant and non-radiant, or zig-zag and ladder-like shapes. The human image only appears on a single plaque found in Alpanseque.[18]

15 Foradada *et al.* (2015) demonstrate that the Celtiberians made unique and innovative contributions in the field of world aesthetics. Examples are their polyhedral hospitality tesserae, foreshadowing works of art produced in the twentieth century by sculptors such as Pablo Serrano and Eduardo Chillida.

16 Horse fibulae, interpreted as a manifestation of equestrian elites, in the monograph by Almagro-Gorbea & Torres 1999.

17 Ceremonial staffs have been analysed, together with depictions of standards and insignia, in Pastor 1998, as *signa equitum* in Almagro-Gorbea 1998 and Lorrio 2010.

18 See Jimeno *et al.* 2010 for a synthetic study of embossed plaques, with special attention to those that

Second phase (second to first century BCE)

In the second phase, ceramic is the Celtiberians' preferred material.[19] The scenes depicted on pottery are more complex than those of the previous phase, so they provide more data for studying Celtiberian religion. Although we find decorated ceramics throughout Celtiberian territory, it is the city of Numantia that provides the largest number of examples. Those from Numantia fall into two distinctive groups in terms of their colouring and iconographic style (Fig. 2).

One group is characterized by the use of a single colour to decorate the pottery. Suns are depicted schematically, in the form of swastikas or tetraskelions facing left or right. The horse is still the animal most frequently depicted but is usually found in the form of a protome, associated with tetraskelions, in some cases forming fantastic anthropomorphic figures. The scenes are usually simple, often duplicated around an axis, as if reflected in a mirror. That is, they are designed to be seen without the person looking at or holding the piece having to move.

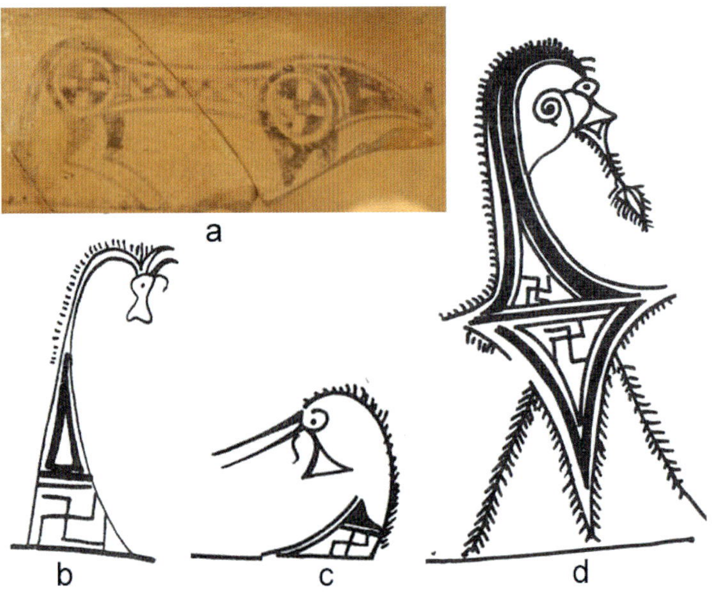

Fig. 2. Numantine pottery: a) Horse with images of crosses inside it, polychrome Numantine ceramics nº 1998 (Burillo-Cuadrado), b) and c) Tetraskelion inside a protome of a horse: monochrome pottery from Numantia (Wattenberg 1993, Lam. VI, 1-1202 and Lam. II, 2-1194), d) tetraskelion within an anthropomorphic figure: monochrome pottery from Numantia (Wattemberg 1963, Lam. VII, 13-1216).

Another group, found only in the city of Numantia, is characterized by polychrome decoration. The horse is depicted as a complete animal and there are no protomes. Tetraskelions are very scarce and suns are depicted as concentric circles and radiant symbols. The figures are realistic, occupying the entire surface of the vessel so that, except for the plaques, the ceramic vessel has to be rotated for the scene to be seen.

The important thing is that both monochrome and polychrome ceramics and bronzes depict the same concepts in different ways, and this provides a basis for understanding the meaning that lies beyond the icons and scenes depicted.

appeared at the Numantine necropolis, and Lorrio & Sánchez 2009 for those found in the necropolis of Arcóbriga, with references to the ones that are known. For the one from Alpanseque, see Cabré & Morán 1975.

19 The city of Numantia has produced the largest number of decorated ceramics in the whole of Celtiberia. Wattenberg (1963) offers a corpus with the most outstanding decoration and Romero 1976, a study of the pottery with polychrome decoration.

The dual solar iconography: the mystery of the Sun's return

Joseph Dechelette has pointed out that all the concentric circles that appeared on the Celtic fibulae represented the sun,[20] although it has been suggested that the non-radiant circles depicted on embossed plaques could represent the full moon or the stars, in the case of the smaller ones.[21]

While we agree that not all the non-radiant concentric circles are suns, and the stars are also depicted, we differ in the identification of the full moon. Hermeneutics says that signs and symbols must have a clear and obvious meaning for the society that uses them, since they form a language that conveys an unmistakeable message. But whether we can succeed in discovering their real meaning is another matter, so we need to know the archetype or graphic universal that, in this case, is used to represent the moon by examining closely how this has been resolved graphically in other cultures.

In all periods the Moon is usually depicted waxing or waning so that it cannot be confused with the Sun, which is depicted as round. It is only shown as being circular in a few cases where polychromatic decoration is used, when it given a uniform colour, white or silver. A factor that all the images of the moon have in common is that their outline is drawn with a single line, or at most with one more line around it to indicate the light it emits. This is because, unlike the Sun, one can stare at the Moon and see its contours perfectly. To avoid any iconic ambiguity the Sun is painted yellow, orange or red, and these colours are often combined in concentric circles, indicating different intensities of light at its core and the halos radiating around it, since it is this variability that is perceived when looking at the sun directly, always with great difficulty: we see that ball of incandescent fire as having an indefinite and radiant outline. So we need to ask ourselves, if the largest non-radiant concentric circles do not represent the Moon, which heavenly body do they represent?

As stated above there are two successive phases of Celtiberian iconography. In the first two, the symbols used are radiant and non-radiant concentric circles associated with the horse. In the context of phenomenology, entropathy allows us to assert with confidence that the radiant concentric circles represent the sun, but we lack the criteria for determining the meaning of the non-radiant concentric circles. In the second phase, in monochrome ceramics, these realistic representations disappear and in their place we find another iconic duality consisting of tetraskelions turning in a clockwise or anticlockwise direction, which are also associated with equine figures. These schematic motifs have been identified with the sun in motion, as the Executive Committee for excavations in Numantia has argued.[22]

20 Dechelette 1909.

21 Jimeno *et al.* (2010, 386) suggest that the large, non-radiant concentric symbols on the embossed plates from Numantia should be identified with the full moon.

22 The identification of the tetraskelions that decorate Numantine ceramics with the Sun was proposed by Mélida (1912, 34): 'Some scholars believe that several ornamental motifs on Numantine pottery are true symbols. The principal among them is the *swastika* or gammata cross, whose original meaning was the sun in motion', citing Dechelette 1910, 453–62, as reference.

To understand the meaning of non-radiant concentric circles we need to relate the images of the sun of both iconographic phases. In our deductive reasoning, we use 'iconographic syntax' in the temporal dimension of 'iconographic diachrony'. These analytical strategies allow a connection to be made between images that we assume to be related because they belong to the same culture and a significant context connects them, in this case the astral world associated with the figure of the horse, whose grapheme has changed over time, but not its meaning. In this way a relationship can be established between images that are closely linked in meaning, but are depicted differently because of the aesthetic and cultural changes that take place in a society with the passage of time. Our theory is that this is an 'iconographic syntax' of successive periods of Celtiberian culture that reflect the same cosmological ideas but which are depicted in different ways because of conceptual changes in the iconography over the course of time.

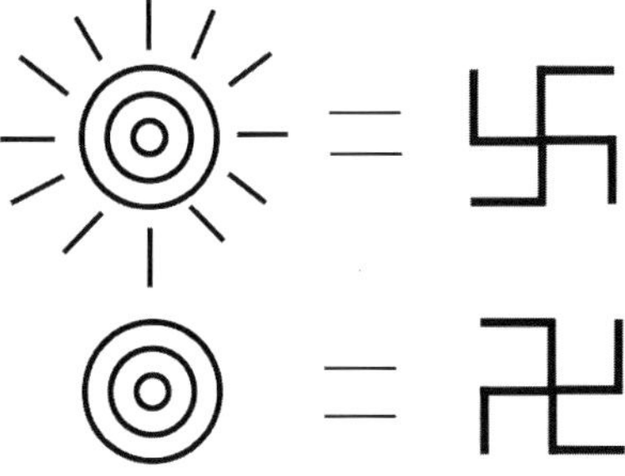

Fig. 3. Example of "Diachronic iconographic syntax": Relationship of radiant concentric circles with anticlockwise tetraskelions and concentric circles with clockwise tetraskelions (Burillo-Cuadrado).

The second stage provides a reference that supports this interpretive code, since it uses the same symbol, the tetraskelion, to represent the Sun but moving in two different directions, giving it a dual meaning. The two ways of depicting the sun in the first phase, in the form of radiant and non-radiant concentric circles, need to be connected with this duality. Thus it can be deduced that one of the two tetraskelions would be similar to the radiant symbol representing the Sun and the other, also a solar image, with the non-radiant concentric circles. The two tetraskelions are, after all, the same solar symbol but are moving in two different directions, that is, the Sun is moving but in the opposite direction. This reasoning is an example of applying the 'hermeneutical circle' in which the dialogue between the subject and the different representations reaches the point when its solution takes the form of an equation, consisting in this case of four variables, that is used to unveil an unknown factor, an image whose meaning we do not know or that we do not know for certain, in this case the non-radiant concentric circles, which in this deductive field we can confirm is a symbol of the Sun (Fig. 3).

But we need to ask ourselves why the Sun is depicted in two ways in each of the Celtiberian iconographic phases. In order to provide a solution to this enigma we have to try to get as close as possible to our ancestors' beliefs and way of thinking, and search for the 'universals' or 'archetypes' that will help answer this question.

Three 'universal' explanations of the enigma of the nightly return of the Sun

We can say that the perception of the Sun's daily path, from when it rises until it sets, is one of the few 'truths' on which human beings agree regardless of the period or place in which they live. It is this is one of the 'archetypes' that all humanity has perceived in the same way, throughout its entire existence. But this daytime, observable path is not the only one travelled by the sun. The mythology of most ancient religions has attempted to explain the path followed by the sun at night after it disappears over the horizon, and imagine the hidden night road it takes before reappearing at dawn the following day on the opposite side from where it dropped out of sight. That is, there is an invisible nocturnal sun that is the counterpart of the visible Sun of the day.

The hermeneutic approach leads to the initial conclusion that there cannot be many answers that will explain the unknown path followed by the Sun each night before dawn. The nightly return of the Sun, since it cannot be observed, is susceptible to imaginative explanations of its invisible path. However, hermeneutics tells us that the explanations given in different cultures have to be limited. This is because the Sun has to reappear every day at the same geographical point, preceded by the dawn.

In the first period of Egyptian culture the Sun god Ra crossed the sky to descend beyond the 'western horizon' to the underworld, which he crossed during the night illuminating the dead and giving them life. It was a path fraught with dangers he had to escape from, the most deadly of which was the serpent Aapep. In this way, overcoming these perils, he returned to the east and reappeared the next morning, on the 'eastern horizon'.[23]

But in the late Egyptian world, we find a different explanation for the Sun's journey, in which the solar disk is depicted travelling amongst stars at night in the body of Nut, the goddess of the Sky.[24] The implication in this case is that the world of the dead through which the Sun-god Ra's solar boat travels is above, not below in the underworld.

In Greek religion, the Sun is the god Helios. Robert Graves[25] synthesizes the movement of the sun in this way: 'Helios drives his four-horse chariot daily across the Heavens from a magnificent palace in the far east, near Colchis, to an equally magnificent far-western palace, where his unharnessed horses pasture in the Islands of the Blessed. He sails home along the Ocean stream, which flows around the world, embarking his chariot and team on a golden ferry-boat'. In this case the underworld of the dead is untouched by the motion of the sun, which only touches the surface of the earth at one point, the Islands of the Blessed, reserved for those who have been born three times, and have three times been worthy of Elysium, residence of the virtuous in the Beyond.

In the case of the Celtiberian world we have no hieroglyphics, such as those of the Egyptians, or written descriptions, like those of the Greeks. The only way left to us is the hermeneutical interpretation of images of the sun. In Celtiberian iconography the radiant solar image of the first phase represents the Sun that the Celtiberians and all

23 Burkard 1997, 445.

24 On the ceiling of the Chapel of the New Year in the temple of Hathor in Dendera, dating to the first century BCE, the goddess is depicted about to swallow the setting Sun and giving birth to the rising Sun (Burkard 1997, fig. 41). A similar depiction of the goddess Nut, from the Book of Amduat, decorates a sarcophagus from the necropolis of Sakkara belonging to the Ptolemaic period (Lull 2006, 44, fig. 11).

25 Graves 1984, 154.

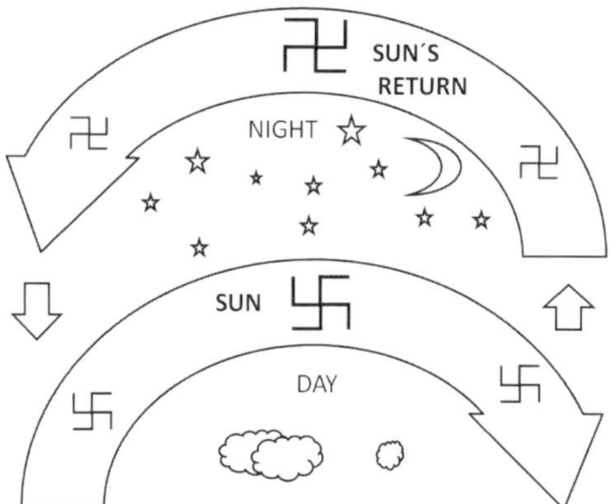

Fig. 4. Diagram of the movement of the Celtiberian sun, based on an interpretation of Numantine iconography (Burillo-Cuadrado).

humanity see each day. In the second phase this image is replaced by the clockwise schematic tetraskelion that adds movement to the image of the sun. That is, it is an image that depicts the movement of the sun during the course of the day. Thus, the anticlockwise tetraskelion must indicate the movement of the Sun in the opposite direction, its necessary return through the night to repeat the eternal mystery of its daily reappearance at dawn at the point opposite where it was hidden from view (Fig. 4).

The anticlockwise triskelion is a Celtiberian iconographic device that represents one of the mysteries contemplated in most religions, the movement of the sun, visible by day but not at night, when human beings cannot see it, as it takes the daily journey many mythologies explain, describing the dangers that could lie in wait for it. In their first iconographic phase, the Celtiberians solve the problem of representing the nightly wanderings of the Sun by removing the rays from the concentric circles. Thus the radiant concentric circles represent the Sun during day and the unadorned concentric circles the Sun during the night. In the first phase the Sun is depicted static, not moving, but in the second the symbol used, the swastika, contains within it the image of the Sun's movement in both directions: clockwise during the day, anticlockwise at night. The anticlockwise tetraskelions, dynamic graphemes, and concentric circles, a static image, graphically depict the Sun's return through a higher realm of the heavens that could not be seen by the human eye, a solution similar to that found in the later phase of Egyptian religion. We can conclude that there were three possible solutions or 'archetypes' for the Sun's return in the cosmologies of antiquity.[26]

1. In the ancient Egyptian world, the Sun's movement was circular, crossing the heavens in his boat in the course of the day and returning through the underworld.
2. In the Greek world Helios returns in his golden boat on the waters surrounding the earth, after crossing the sky in his chariot.
3. The third possibility is that proposed by the Celtiberian world and which we also find in the final period of Egyptian culture. The sun would move across the sky during the day and return at night through a higher realm of the sky that could not be observed.

26 Burillo-Cuadrado 2015a.

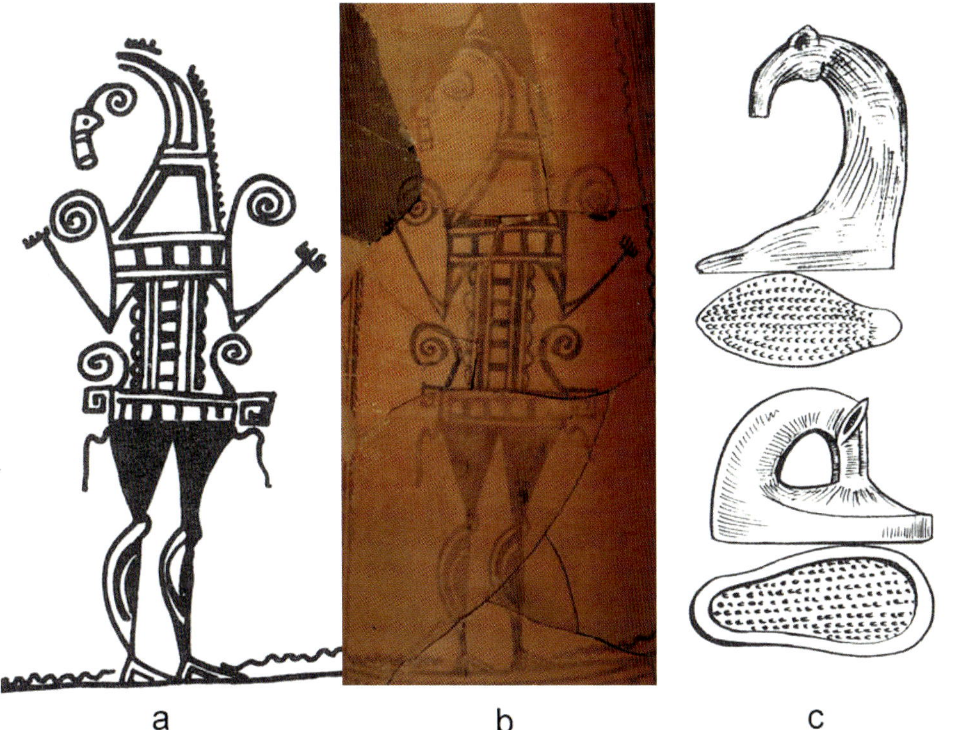

Fig. 5. a) Anthropomorphic horse painted on a frustum from Numantia (Wattenberg 1993, Lam. VI, 2-1203), b) photo of the same piece, c) Horse protomes in terracotta (Wattenberg 1963, 91, 457 and 458).

The horse as a solar divinity

Solar symbols are usually associated with the figure of the horse in both phases of Celtiberian iconography. In the first phase the horse forms part of the scene but is separate from images of the Sun, whereas in the second the tetraskelion appears within the image of the horse. In this way the Sun is integrated into the horse, which elevates this animal to the status of a solar deity, which distinguishes this Celtiberian religious manifestation from those found in the Graeco-Roman world, where horses did no more than pull the chariot carrying the sun god, Helios.

As we have demonstrated,[27] in Celtiberian culture the horse is represented as a solar divinity in three different ways: with the complete figure, in the form of a protome, and as an anthropomorphic being with the head of a horse. Curchin[28] calls it a 'reverse centaur',

27 For a discussion of the various depictions of the horse as a solar deity in Celtiberian pottery, see Burillo-Cuadrado & Burillo-Mozota 2010; Burillo-Cuadrado 2015b.

28 It was Ortego (1975) who first proposed that this semi-zoomorphic figure version was a version of the fabulous centaur conceived in reverse, with the humanoid standing. Curchin (2003–2004, 186–9), who accepts this interpretation, has made a study of it and says that it was originally a mythological invention of the Celts. Wattenberg (1963, 215) had already proposed that it should be identified with a divinity. Paulsen (1931, 223–81) also identified this figure as a god or goddess of horses, similar to the Celtic goddess Epona. It has been suggested that this female deity appears in four Roman representations in Celtiberia, but as Alfayé (2009, 349) says, they should not be interpreted as such. The anthropomorphic Celtiberian figure should not be associated with it either, as it repre-

a Hellenistic term we consider inappropriate for describing this semi-zoomorphic figure, because in the Greek world the centaur has the body of a horse and the head, torso and arms of a man. That is, what is important about the centaur is human and the animal aspect is secondary. This scale of values extends to other fantastic animals in Greek mythology, such as the sphinx, satyr and siren, with the exception of the Minotaur, but this relates to an archaic myth. In contrast, the Celtiberian anthropomorphic figure gives greatest importance to the horse's head, the human body serving merely as a carrier.

The proposition that horse protomes are a simplified representation of an equine deity with an anthropomorphic body is based on the fact that the base of the protome is a human foot, as we can see in two terracottas found in Numantia, where the sole of the foot has been made into a grater (Fig. 5). Therefore, the image in the form of a protome would be synthesizing the two elements that define the anthropomorphic figure: the head of the horse and the human foot. When this syncretic figure is observed in the ceramic iconography, the equine figure stands out as the most important and significant element, the human reference being relegated to a line at the bottom that only a knowledge of this Celtiberian symbol could interpret as a human foot. Unravelling this symbol at this distance in time has only been possible thanks to the preservation of the two terracottas referred to above because, since they are three-dimensional, the foot can be seen. However, when depicted in two dimensions it virtually disappears.

This solar deity would be common to all the Celtiberians since, although most of the images that represent it come from Numantian monochrome ceramics, the horse protome has been found in various parts of Celtiberia and is in fact the only zoomorphic representation we find in other Celtiberian sites. So it is one of the few elements that gives substance to Celtiberian culture on the basis of this peculiar religious manifestation.

The situla with a fish intent on devouring a horse with a tail attached to the head of a bovid[29]

The iconography of Celtiberian pottery is not usually studied directly on the object that is used as its medium of expression, but from tracings made of the designs depicted on the surface of the vessels. This significantly limits our understanding of them. On one hand, the scene is seen in two dimensions, like a painting; it gives an inaccurate rendering by separating the pictorial scene from its three-dimensional, volumetric support (Fig. 6).

---

sents a male deity.

29 The situla listed as number 2308 Numancia is known from its photograph and a tracing of 1912 that appeared in the report submitted to the Ministry of Public Instruction and Fine Arts by the Executive Committee responsible for excavating Numantia (Mélida 1912, Pl. XLIII & XLIV). Subsequently, Wattenberg (1963, Pl. XVII, 1-1297 & Ph. Pl. XIV, 1) included it in his monograph on indigenous ceramics from Numantia, even though the tracing separates the head of the bovid in the depiction of the scene. Finally, Romero Carnicero (1976, fig. 6, 22 & Pl. III. 22) presents a new tracing in his book on polychrome Numantine ceramics. Its analysis has also been the subject of a case study in Burillo-Cuadrado 2015b.

Fig. 6. Ceramic nº 2308 held by the Numantine Museum:
a) Tracing (Álvarez in VV.AA., 1912, XLIV), b) Consecutive photos (Burillo-Cuadrado).

It should be noted that in the case of most decorated Celtiberian pottery, especially globular shapes and jugs, at least half of the scene is obscured at any given time, because it is on the opposite side from the one being observed. On the other hand, most of the tracings have been made in black and white and therefore the colours and details – some of them minute – decorating the vessel disappear, so a substantial part of the pictorial information decorating the pot is lost when they are studied. However, we have studied the actual Numantine situla decorated with a fish about to devour a horse with a tail that ends in the head of a bovid, integrating the scene with the three-dimensional character of the vessel and observing that only by rotating it, i.e. including this fourth dimension, is it possible to really understand its iconography.

An analysis using hermeneutics

Studies of iconography based on tracings pose the problem that, by removing the direct relationship of the subject with the object, the information it contains is impaired and decontextualized. To overcome these analytical deficiencies this vessel was studied on the basis of Gadamer's hermeneutics[30] in order to establish a direct relationship between the researcher and the ceramic vessel, a strategy of dialectical analysis that uses the 'hermeneutical circle'. To this end, the piece was studied directly and scanned by 3D laser, thanks to the collaboration of Luis Peña Serrano, which allowed us to continue a dialogue with vessel after examining it in person at the Numantine Museum.

Being able to hold in one's hands this unique example of Celtiberian art, replete with symbols posing enigmas to be deciphered, both individually and in terms of the way they work together to create the 'iconographic syntax' of the scene, was an extraordinary feeling, quite different from the coldness and apparent objectivity with which we had previously analysed the tracings, photos and commentaries of the scene depicted. This process allowed us to assimilate hermeneutics' argument for comprehending an observable reality from the direct relationship that is established between the subject and the object. The latter acquires a value and life of its own that allows it to be questioned dialectically, until the message we think it contains can be unravelled. It was an open reading and like all readings, susceptible to future reinterpretation, like a musical score when it is played again.

The 'fourth dimension' of movement offers evidence of the ritual use of the vessel

Our first impression when holding this vessel was that our aesthetic perception of its decoration far exceeded that we had gained previously from tracings and photos. One of the most striking aspects was that, since the scene occupied the entire surface of the piece, the whole of the scene could not be seen from any one position, which invalidated our previous perception obtained from the tracings that had been made of it. The vessel has to be rotated for the scene to be dynamically created in the observer's brain. One thing was clear: the two-dimensional character of the tracings showing a complete scene, which could be seen in its entirety at a glance, did not reflect the true picture, whose fragmented parts were distributed over the entire body of the vessel, around its three-dimensional surface. It had to be rotated through 360 degrees in order to see the whole scene. That is, the decoration of this vessel is deliberately designed to conceal part of the scene depicted, so that a motionless observer at a distance from the vase would not see the whole scene and therefore would not understand it. The observer or someone else had to rotate it.

Movement is necessary in order to understand the iconography decorating this vase. That is, a ritual is required that involves rotating it through 360 degrees so that the scene depicted on its surface can be seen and understood. In fact, the shape of the vase has been created for this ritual function, as it is a situla that, since it has a handle over the mouth, could easily be rotated.[31]

The act of rotating the situla invokes a new concept that as far as we know has

30 Gadamer 1992.

31 In Romero (1976, Pl. III, 22) it can be seen that this handle was added in the initial restoration of the vase, but it has now been removed to return it to the form in which it was found.

not been taken into consideration when analysing ceramic iconography: the 'fourth dimension', consisting of the movement of the object and the time necessary to rotate it.[32] It also indicates that two agents were necessary: one, an individual who would carry the situla or act as officiant, and the other, the group of those present at the ritual, contemplating the scene as the vase is rotated through 360 degrees, the symbol is unveiled and the compression of the myth it represents is achieved.

A fantastic scene that takes place in water

Direct contact with the vase made it possible to see the detail in the drawings, the distribution of the scene on the surface, and also something else that had not been evaluated and that has proved critical for understanding its meaning: the colour of the figures.

The scene, framed by wavy lines, covers the whole of the body of piece. It is a unique and unparalleled scene. It shows a very large and menacing fish, with its mouth open to reveal a row of sharp teeth, that is trying to devour a horse, whose tail ends in a bovid's head, something that is rather surprising and which differs from the typical horsetail found in other Numantine representations.[33] Around the two animals are three short, wide waves. The semiotics should enable us to distinguish signs and symbols in this representation, and establish an 'iconographic syntax' in order to decipher the meaning of the scene and enable us to reconstruct Celtiberian religion.

The two-headed beast displays a graphic syncretism of a horse and a bovid.[34] As already noted in the previous section, in Celtiberian iconography horses should be identified with a solar deity. However, bovids are related with the lunar deity in many cultures, including those of the Indo-European world, because of the similarity between their horns and the Moon in its fourth quarter.[35] The association of the horns of bovids with the Moon probably reflects a Celtiberian 'archetype'. So this Celtiberian composition would depict a fantastic two-headed animal that would synthesise in a single individual the two most important heavenly bodies in the cosmos, the Sun and the Moon.

The other main character is the giant fish that, because it is the same size as the horse, can also be categorised as an imaginary animal. It should be remembered that the Celtiberians lived in the heart of the Iberian Peninsula, so any contact with a fish of this size must have been purely legendary, since the fish found in rivers and inland lakes would never have reached the abnormal size of the one depicted on this vase.[36]

32 Foradada *et al.* (2015) proposed the concept for the first time at the 7th Symposium on the Celtiberians.

33 Wattenberg 1963, Pl. XII. 1-1260.

34 It should be noted that this is not a unique case in Celtiberian iconography since a bronze spear from a chariot was found in the Castro de Las Arribillas of Prados Redondos in Molina de Aragón (Guadalajara), which has a double Protome of a horse and a bull, although in that case they were superimposed (Galan 1989–1990).

35 Sergent 2005, 350.

36 Delgado's study (2008) of the fish depicted in polychrome Celtiberian ceramics does not include the

The three short waves situated at significant points of the scene have been studied by Jose Manuel Pastor[37] within what he calls 'graphic cadence symbols' present in Iberian and Celtiberian iconography. These signs are not mere decoration: they indicate movement, which gives dynamism to the scene and help us understand it. Two of the waves are behind the fins of the fish, emphasizing that it is advancing rapidly on its prey. These two marks intensify the threatening appearance of the fish, with its mouth wide open to expose its sharp teeth, and show that it is swimming rapidly towards the two-headed beast, clearly intent on devouring it. The third wave is situated below the head of bovid, a graphic expression of the desperate flight of the two-headed beast, in which the horse is shown galloping away from the fish and the tail, with the bovine head at the end of it, which has been given life a life of its own and is trying to escape from the danger, and even overtake the animal to which it is attached. The movement of the predatory fish and the panic of the two-headed animal with the head of bovid are graphically accentuated by the position of the 'S' shapes beside the fins and under the head of the bovid, indicating movement.

This representation prompts two questions: Where is the scene set? and What does it represent? We shall try to answer these questions.

Coelum Aqueum, or the existence of a realm of celestial water in Celtiberian mythology

In our view, a series of graphic indicators show that the scene depicted on the situla takes place in a watery realm. The first is the important role of the fish in the scene depicted. The second is the delimitation of the scene by means of two wavy lines situated both along the rim and at the bottom of the vessel, the upper line beginning at the first dorsal fin of the fish. The wavy lines are a graphic representation of water and their arrangement creates a frame for what is happening in a watery setting. The third is the blue-green colour used to decorate the fish and also the figure of the two-headed animal. It should be remembered that river fish are generally of earthy colours and their varied colouring helps to camouflage them against possible predators, so the blue-green colour used for the bodies of fish and the two-headed figure is an extrapolation by the Celtiberian artist of the colouring given to water. Therefore this colour unifies the imaginary space in which the scene is set, the watery realm. This colour is exceptional in Celtiberian, and also Iberian, iconography, and in fact this pigment should be analysed to discover its characteristics. The colour was, therefore, deliberately chosen to emphasise the idea that the action depicted is taking place in water.

Another question arises: how can the horse, with its bovine syncretism in this case, be situated in a watery realm, when it is associated with a deity that lived in the Heavens? Could it be that Celtiberian mythology included the belief that there was a large body of water in the firmament? The answer is Yes.

---

one that decorates this situla. He identifies the other fish depicted with specific species, all of which are river fish: trout, catfish, salmon, stickleback and carp.

37 Pastor (2010) expounded his theory, already published in a previous study (Pastor 1998), at the Sixth Symposium on Celtiberians and it was unanimously accepted by the scholars present.

To explain the rain and snow many cultures believed that there was a sea or ocean in the sky that was the source of water. This is another 'archetype' configured by one of the universal myths. It is masterfully synthesized in the biblical account of the creation of the universe:[38] 'And God said, Let there be a firmament in the midst of the waters, and let it divide the waters from the waters. And God made the firmament, and divided the waters which were under the firmament from the waters which were above the firmament: and it was so. And God called the firmament Heaven.'

This Judeo-Christian conception of the cosmos survived in Western thought into the Modern Age, mixed with Graeco-Roman interpretations.[39] Until recently the idea persisted that the Earth was at the centre of the universe, surrounded by various spheres, the nearest being that of the most important heavenly bodies. But for the purposes of this study what is most striking is that in the medieval period, on the basis of previous traditions, the ninth sphere was called the *Coelum Aqueum*; it was above the sphere of the fixed stars and below the *Primum Mobile.*[40]

Another example of this 'archetype' can be found in Egyptian religion. There are many scenes in which all the Egyptian gods travel across the sky in boats, reflecting the same cosmic idea of the existence of a large body of water in the sky that was the source of rain.[41]

This was therefore a 'universal' that existed in various cultures and it helps us understand that the Celtiberians shared this belief that there was a large body of water within the firmament.

Are we looking at a picture of an eclipse?

Analysing the image that concerns us it looks as if the fish is an enemy from which the Sun and the Moon, represented by the two-headed beast, have to escape. In our opinion this would be the mythological representation of an eclipse, as we will try to explain using the hermeneutical method and searching for this 'archetype' in other mythologies.

A study by Daphne Nash Briggs on the iconography of Gaulish coins[42] has looked at various scenes of eclipses in which wolves or imaginary beasts try to devour the Sun and the Moon, an interpretation supported by Dominique Hollard.[43]

In Norse religion the sun goddess, *Sól*, and the moon god, *Mani*, were pursued by

38 The Bible, King James version (Genesis 1, 6–8)

39 Godwin 2009.

40 Jerónimo Muñoz, a sixteenth century humanist, when interpreting the Second Book of Pliny's Natural History, emphasizes the idea that the rain from the clouds was insufficient to cause the flood, hence the necessary existence of an aquatic realm known as *Coelum Aqueum* (Navarro & Rodríguez 1988, 383)

41 The sky goddess Nut, whose body consisted of water, is of uncertain etymology but her name could mean 'she of the waters' (Lull 2006).

42 Nash Briggs (2012) has based her research on the iconography of Celtic coins.

43 A coin from the late third–early second century BCE from the Calvados area of France depicts an animal, identified as a wolf, with its mouth open to devour the Sun, represented in the form of a wheel. In another of similar characteristics the same kind of beast can be seen trying to devour a wheel, a symbol of the sun, and another icon in the form of a quarter circle, which would be the Moon (Hollard 1999).

the wolves Sköll and Hati, which tried to devour them. When they succeeded in doing so an eclipse occurred, but the deities were able to escape, and this marked the end of the astronomical event. The chase would end on Ragnarök, the day of the end of the world, when the wolves would succeed in consuming the deities without the Sun or Moon being able to escape.[44]

In the collective religious imagination of China, the Sun and the Moon were devoured by a dog or a wild beast, and this resulted in an eclipse. The Chinese used the sound of bells to frighten the beast so the Sun and the Moon could escape. An eclipse was a bad omen, and it was customary to fast when one occurred to prevent it happening again in the future.[45]

These are just a few examples of the myths found behind an eclipse, an astronomical event of great importance in antiquity. They all share the idea of a beast intent on devouring the sun, the moon, or both. We think this universal idea is also depicted on the Numantine situla we have studied, where a big fish (imaginary beast) is attempting to devour the two-headed beast that synthesizes the sun in the form of a horse and the Moon in the form of a bovine head at the end of a horse's tail. This is, then, a graphic interpretation of a universal myth, the eternal struggle between good and evil in which, if the fish succeeds in catching the two-headed beast, an eclipse will occur, which will end when the solar and lunar deities succeed in overcoming the danger and manage to escape.

This vase is also exceptional for its form, since in the polychrome pottery of Numancia, there is only one other situla, No. 1,998, that depicts a sacrificial scene. We need to ask ourselves whether the ritual in which this vessel was used, so that those who watched it and the officiant himself could see the scene was connected with the subject of the scene depicted. That is, a magic ceremony to prevent the eclipse occurring and allow the Sun and Moon to flee from the looming danger of the beast pursuing them.

44 See the 'Dan McCoy' website for tales of Norse mythology in their original language and English translations: Skoll and Hati 2015.

45 Rana 1995 analyses the conception of the eclipses in various ancient religions, including those of China.

BIBLIOGRAPHY

Almagro-Gorbea, M. & Torres, M. 1999 *Las fíbulas de jinete y de caballito*. Aproximación a las elites ecuestres y su expansión en la Hispania céltica, Institución Fernando el Católico.

Alfayé-Villa, S. 2009 *Santuarios y rituales en la Hispania Céltica*. Oxford, BAR International Series no. 1963.

Barrena, S. & J. Nubiola 2013 *Charles S. Peirce (1839–1914): un pensador para el siglo XXI*. Pamplona, Ediciones Universidad de Navarra S. A.

Burillo-Cuadrado, Mª P. 2015a 'Coelum aqueum, aproximación al Cosmos celtibérico a partir del análisis de la cerámica no. 2308 del Museo de Numancia', *VII Simposio sobre Celtíberos Nuevos Hallazgos, Nuevas Interpretaciones*, ed. F. Burillo & M. Chordá, 303–11. Zaragoza, Fundación Segeda-Centro de Estudios Celtibéricos & Instituto de investigación y Desarrollo Rural. Serranía Celtiberica.

Burillo-Cuadrado, M.ª P. 2015b 'A myth in Celtiberian astronomy', *SEAC 2011 Stars and Stones: Voyages in Archaeoastronomy and Cultural Astronomy*, ed. F. Pimenta, N. Ribeiro, F. Silva, N. Campion, A. Joaquinito & L. Tirapicos, 252–5. Oxford, Archaeopress, BAR International Series 2720.

Burillo-Mozota, F. 2010 'Aproximación a la estructura social del campesinado celtibérico', *Coloquio Internacional de Arqueología Espacial. Arqueología de la Población, Arqueología Espacial*, 28, 135–54. Teruel, Seminario de Arqueología y etnología turolense.

Burillo-Mozota, F. & M. Pérez-Gutiérrez 2015 'The astronomical sanctuary of the Celtiberian town of Segeda (Mara, Zaragoza, Spain)', *SEAC 2011 Stars and Stones: Voyages in Archaeoastronomy and Cultural Astronomy*, ed. F. Pimenta, N. Ribeiro, F. Silva, N. Campion, A. Joaquinito & L. Tirapicos, 228–31. Oxford, Archaeopress, BAR International Series 2720.

Burkard, G. 1997 'Las concepciones del Cosmos: los edificios del mundo', *Egipto el Mundo de los Faraones*, ed. R. Schulz & M. Seidel, 445–9. Colonia, Könemann.

Cabré, E. & J. A. Morán 1975 'Una decoración figurativa abstracta en la Edad del Hierro de la Meseta Oriental Hispánica', *Crónica del XIII Congreso Arqueológico Nacional*, ed. A. Blanco, L Pericot & A. Beltrán 605–10. Zaragoza, Universidad de Zaragoza & Seminario de Arqueología.

Curchin, L. A. 2004–2005 'Mitología Celtibérica: El problema de las bestias fantásticas', *Kalathos*, 22–23, 183–9. Teruel, Campus Universitario de Teruel.

Dechelette, J. 1909 'Le culte du soleil aux temps préhistoriques', *Revue archéologique*, T. XIII, 305–57. Paris, Presses Universitaires de France.

Dechelette, J. 1910 *Manuel d'archéologie préhistorique celtique et gallo-romaine. Tome 2. Archéologie celtique ou protohistorique, Age du bronze*. Paris, Librairie Alphonse Picard et fils.

Delgado Lozano, S. 2008 'Sobre las representaciones de peces en las cerámicas polícromas celtibéricas', *Oppidum* 4, 13–34. Segovia, IE Universidad.

Eco, U. 1977 *Tratado de Semiótica General*. Barcelona, Editorial Lumen.

Foradada, C., F. Burillo, M.ª P. Burillo & J. J. Luis 2015 'La cuarta dimensión en las téseras de hospitalidad poliédricas', *VII Simposio sobre Celtíberos Nuevos Hallazgos, Nuevas Interpretaciones*, ed. F. Burillo & M. Chordá, 311–20. Zaragoza Fundación Segeda-Centro de Estudios Celtibéricos & Instituto de investigación y Desarrollo Rural. Serranía Celtiberica.

Gadamer, H. G. 1992 *Verdad y Método II*. Salamanca, Ediciones Sígueme.

Galán Domingo, E. 1989–1990 'Naturaleza y cultura en el mundo celtibérico', *Kalathos* 9–10, 175–204. Teruel, Campus universitario de Teruel.

Godwin, J. 2009 *Armonía de las esferas*. Gerona, Atalanta.

Graves, R. 1984 *Los Mitos Griegos*. Barcelona, Ariel.

Guerra Palmero, Mª. J. 2015 *Habermas. La apuesta por la democracia*. Bonalletra Alcompas S. L, Barcelona.

Hollard, D. 1999 'Le cheval solaire et le loup mangeur de lune: à propos d'un exemplaire du type BN 7229 trouvé en forêt de Saint-Germain-en-Laye', *Cahiers Numismatiques, Revue trimestrielle de la Société d'études numismatiques et archéologiques*, 36.142, 11–23.

Jimeno, A., J. I. De la Torre & A. Chain 2010 'Ritos funerarios y Mitos Astrales en las necrópolis celtibéricas del Alto Duero', *VI Simposio sobre Celtíberos. Ritos y Mitos*, ed. F. Burillo, 369–90. Zaragoza, Fundación Segeda-Centro de Estudios Celtibéricos.

Jung, C. G. 1981 *Arquetipos e inconsciente colectivo.* Barcelona, Paidos Ibérica.

Lorrio, A. 2010 'Los signa equitum celtibéricos: origen y evolución', *Serta Palaeohispanica in honorem Javier de Hoz, Palaeohispanica* 10, 427–46. Zaragoza, Institución Fernando el Católico.

Lorrio, A. & Mª. D. Sánchez 2009 *La necrópolis celtibérica de Arcóbriga. Monreal de Ariza, Caesaraugusta* 80. Zaragoza, Institución Fernando el Católico.

Lull, J. 2006 *La astronomía en el antiguo Egipto.* Valencia, Universidad de Valencia.

Marco Simón, F. 2010 'Dioses, espacios sagrados y sacerdotes', *VI Simposio sobre Celtíberos. Ritos y Mitos*, ed. F. Burillo, 11–25. Zaragoza, Fundación Segeda-Centro de Estudios Celtibéricos.

Medina Cepero, J. M. *2001 El pensamiento de Husserl en 'La crisis de las ciencias europeas y la fenomenología trascendental'.* Madrid, Ediciones Apóstrofe.

Mélida, J. R. 1912 *Excavaciones en Numancia, Memoria presentada al Ministerio de Instrucción pública y Bellas Artes por la Comisión Ejecutiva.* Madrid, José Blass.

Morrris, C. W. 1994 *Fundamentos de la teoría de los signos.* Barcelona, Planeta Agostini.

Nash Briggs, D. 2010 'Reading the Images on Iron-Age Coins: 3. Some Cosmic Wolves', *Chris Rudd List* 110, 2–4.

Navarro, V. & E. Rodríguez 1998 *Matemáticas, Cosmología y Humanismo en la España del siglo XVI. Los Comentarios al Segundo Libro de la Historia Natural de Plinio de Jerónimo Muñoz.* Valencia, Universitat de Valencia.

Olmos, R. (ed.) 1996 *Al otro lado del espejo. Aproximación a la imagen ibérica.* Madrid, Colección LYNX.

Ortego, T. 1975 'Caballos ritos y ultratumba en los pueblos celtibéricos', *Revista de Soria* 25, unpaginated.

Ortiz-Osés, A. C. G. 1988 *Jung Arquetipos y Sentido.* Bilbao, Universidad de Deusto.

Pastor, J. M. 1998 'Ideogramas musicales onomatopéyicos y animistas de las punturas figurativas ibérica y celtibéricas', *Kalathos* 17, 91–129. Teruel, Campus Universitario de Teruel.

Pastor, J. M. 2010 'Doble espiral y eses en serie: símbolos gráficos de cadencia en las culturas ibérica y celtibérica', *VI Simposio sobre Celtíberos. Ritos y Mitos*, ed. F. Burillo, 473–84. Zaragoza, Fundación Segeda-Centro de Estudios Celtibéricos.

Paulsen, R. 1931 'Die Funde von Numantia', *Numantia II: Die Stadt Numantia*, ed. A. Schulten,223–81. München, F. Bruckmann.

Rana, N. C 1995 *Myths and Legends Related to Eclipses.* New Delhi, Vigyan Prasar.

Romero Carnicero, F. 1976 *Las cerámicas polícromas de Numancia.* Soria, Centro de Estudios Sorianos.

Saussure, F. 1985 *Curso de lingüistica general.* Barcelona, Planeta Agostini.

Sergent, B. 2005 *Les Indo-Européens.* Paris, Payot.

Skoll and Hati – Norse Mythology for Smart People 2015 *http://norse-mythology.org/skoll-hati/*

Sopeña-Genzor, G. 1995 Ética y ritual, Aproximación al estudio de la religiosidad de los pueblos celtibéricos. Zaragoza, Instituto Fernando el Católico.

Tortosa Rocamora, T. 2006 *Los estilos y grupos pictóricos de la cerámica ibérica figurada de la Contestania*, Anejos de AESPA XXXVIII. Mérida, Instituto de Arqueología.

Wattenberg, F. 1963 *Las cerámicas indígenas de Numancia.* Madrid, Consejo Superior de Investigaciones Científicas: Instituto Español de Prehistoria & Diputación Provincial de Valladolid.

XIV

THE GODS THAT NEVER WERE

NEW READINGS OF THE INSCRIPTIONS OF PENEDO DE REMESEIROS (CIL II 2476), PENEDO DAS NINFAS (CIL II 5607), CUEVA DEL VALLE (CIL II2.7, 932) AND CASTRO DAIRE (CIL II 5247)

Manuela Alves Dias & Maria João Correia Santos

This paper discusses the theonyms of four controversial inscriptions: Penedo de Remeseiros (CIL II 2476), a long juridical text invoking a Deus Adiutor; Penedo das Ninfas (CIL II 5607), in which it is finally possible to identify the name of the summoned deities as Munidi Fiduenearum and Cosuneae; the rock-inscription of Cueva del Valle (CIL II2.7, 932), thought to be dedicated to Iuppiter and that clearly does not mention any deity at all; and finally, the votive altar of Castro Daire (CIL II 5247), where both the names of the dedicant and of the divine entity are missing.

Introduction

THE rough nature of the inscriptions of Penedo das Ninfas and Penedo de Remeseiros, carved in bare granite out-crops and far away from Roman cities, led to the assumption that they should be both dedicated to indigenous deities. Likewise, the rock inscription of Cueva del Valle, next to the entrance of a natural cave used as a sanctuary during the Republican Period led to a search for the name of the supposed deity that should, theoretically, be mentioned. Something similar occurred with the votive altar of Castro Daire, on which appear the carved figures of an animal and a man with a long spear. However, not everything is always as it seems.

For Penedo das Ninfas and Penedo de Remeseiros, in order to confirm certain features, we used a new tool for epigraphic research, the Morphological Residual Model – M.R.M.,[1] especially useful in severely eroded surfaces, as it allows to perceive all the faint traces of carving and even to capture the non-visible marks that still exist. The restitution of the original traces happens in two stages: firstly, the measuring of the

1 Correia Santos *et al.* 2014, 202–3; Correia Santos and Pires 2014; Correia Santos *et al.* 2014; Pires *et al.* 2014.

epigraphic field's relief; and then, the calculation of the M.R.M. This method is based on the assumption that in the same object coexist multiple scales of relief, from the general shape of the rock itself to the morphology of its microscopic crystals, allowing to contrast the subtle differences of relief at multiple scales and to calculate the difference between them.[2]

The revision of all the four inscriptions allows us to correct former readings and to 'erase' four gods that were never in those texts: *Danceroi* in Penedo de Remeseiros; *Nimid* or *Numid* in Penedo das Ninfas; *Deus Arus* in the altar of Castro Daire and *Iovi* in Cueva del Valle. The Portuguese altar of Castro Daire is the most striking example, since it is a votive inscription without the names of both the dedicant and the deity, which draws attention to the risk involved in expecting to identify these elements in all votive inscriptions.

In search of the Gods that never were

Penedo de Remeseiros, Montalegre, Vila Real (CIL II 2476)

The inscription of Penedo de Remeseiros is engraved in a small granite outcrop of 1.20 by 2.33 m dominating a meadow and shows a profusion of abbreviations that made the reading of some parts a true challenge, hence generating different interpretations.[3]

Fig. 1. Penedo de Remeseiros (M. J. Correia Santos).

2 Pires *et al.* 2014.

3 See also Fontes 1980, 11; Rodríguez Colmenero 1981, 141–50; 1995, 136; Silva 1986, 286–7, n. 309. Epigraphic field: 2,50 x 0,75 m; l.1: 9; l.2: 10; l.3: 9,5; l.4: 8,5; l.5: 11; l.6: 10 cm

According to Argote:[4] *Allius Reburri rogo deu(m) adiutorem | in (h)a(e)c conducta conservanda | si q(u)is in (h)a(e)c conducta p(ossessionem) mici aut meis | involaverit si R(.) quaecunquae res at(?) mi(h)i | [.]A[.]S si L si qui ea res V S L V F | Danceroi*

The proposal of Dopico Caínzos and Pereira-Menaut[5] is quite similar: *Allius (vel os) Reburri . rogo . Deu (m) . adiutorem | in . (h)a(e)c . conducta . conservanda | s[i] q(u)is . in . (h)a(e)c . conducta. p(ossessionem). mici. aut. meis | involaverit. si . R . quaecunquae res . at. mii | [.] . A . S. SI . L . Siquit. ea. res . V . S . L. V . F | Danceroi.*

On the other hand, for Búa Carballo,[6] the text should go as follows: *Alli [...] Reburri. Rogo. Deu. Adiutorem | in . ac . conducta. conservanda | s[i]qis. in . ac . conducta. P . Migi. aut . meis | [I]nvolaverit . si . R . quaecunquae res . at. miis | [.] . A . S . SI . L . Siquit. ea. res . V . S . L . V . [.]| [.]anceroi.*

More recently Rodríguez Colmenero[7] considered an alternative: *Callida Reburri (filia). rogo. Deu(m). Adiutorem Dan(cerum?)| in ac(tam). conducta(m) conservanda (m)| q(uis)q(u)is. in ac(ta). conducta P(artem). migi aut meis| I(?)nvolaverit. Si. R(etineretur). Quaecumquae. Res. F(urtatum). Miis(?)| O(?)(mnino). A(pportabit). Si S(entit). Si. L(iquet). Si Quit ea pr(a)es(ens) . V(otum). S(olvit). L(ibens). V(olenti). D(eo).| Danceroi.*

The result of the M.R.M allowed us to confirm certain aspects and to clarify others that are not so clear. It is possible to read:

> *Allius L. Reburri (filius). rogo. Deu(m). Adiutorem | in. ac . conducta . conservanda. | siqis. in . ac . conducta . p(ossessionem). mici . aut. meis .| invidia verit. si . r(estituerit). quaecunquae . res. at . mii.|. A. N. S. si. L. siquit. ea . res . V. S. L. V. S vel P. | Banceroi.*[8]

In general, it appears to refer to a rented property, summoning a deity to assure the observance of a contract of *locatio-conductio*, in a particular way that reminds the *tabula execrationis* of Mérida.[9] This type of contract was generally made *in perpetuum*, as long as the one who rents pays

Fig. 2. Monochromatic M.R.M. of Penedo de Remeseiros (H. Pires).

---

4 Argote 1732–1734, 1325; *apud* CIL II 2476.

5 Dopico Caínzos & Pereira-Menaut 1993, 633–41.

6 Búa Carballo 2000, 407–12.

7 Rodríguez Colmenero 2010, 134–5.

8 Correia Santos *et al.* forthcoming.

9 CIL II 462: *Dea Ataecina Turi|brig(ensis) Proserpina| per tuam maiestatem| te rogo oro obsecro| uti vindices quot mihi| furti factum est quisquis | mihi im(m)u(t)avit involavit | minusve fecit eas [res] q(uae) i(nfra) s(cripta) s(unt) | tunicas VI[p]aenula | lintea II in[dus]ium I cu/ius [.] IOM[.]M ignoro | IA[.]ius | VI.* See Pereira-Menaut & Almeida 1981, 142–5.

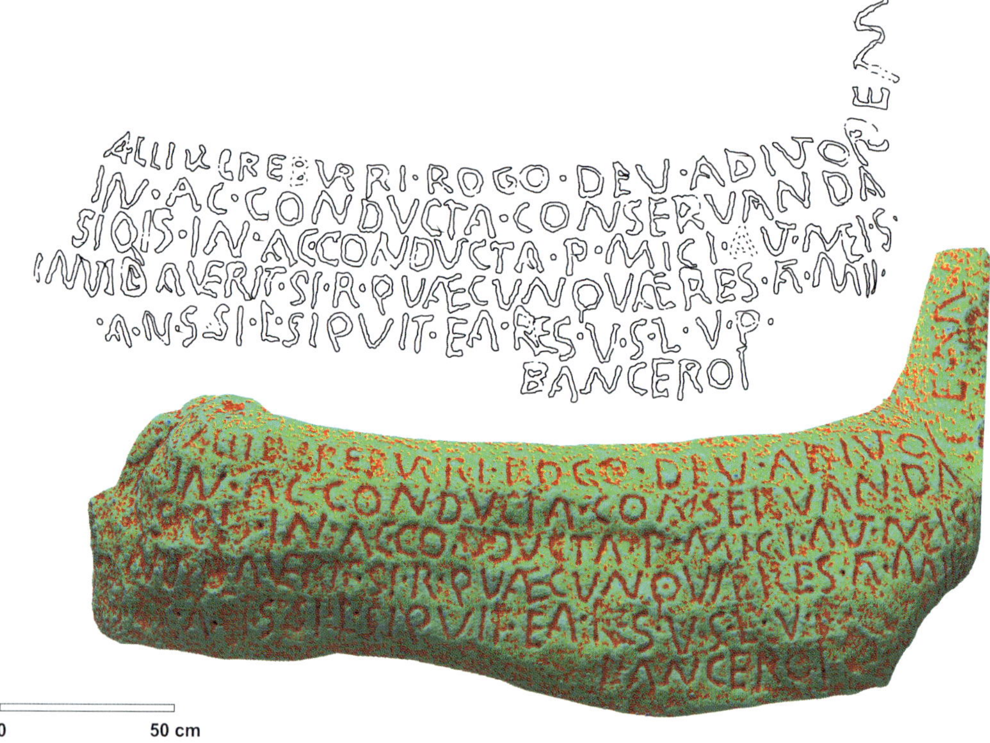

Fig. 3. Tracing over polichromatic M.R.M. of Penedo de Remeseiros (M. J. Correia Santos & H. Pires).

his *vectigal*, which lead Dopico Caínzos and Pereira-Menaut[10] to read in l.4 *involaverit*, meaning the *possessio* was of hereditary right and the dedicant would be pleading to a god to avoid anyone from usurping his property.

Nevertheless, in l.4, instead of *involaverit*, it is written *invidia verit*. Another possibility could be to read *verb(o)* instead of *verit*: in this case, the expression could correspond to *absit invidia verbo*, which is 'be the jealousy be absent from these words', since it was believed that excessive good fortune caused envy to the unseen powers.[11] However, it is written *verit*, with a clear 'T' at the end, and so, *invidia ve(r)it* is the correct reading.

The expression *invidia*, mostly related to epitaphs, is also found in a juridical Italian inscription from Canosa di Puglia.[12] In the particular case of Remeseiros, it seems to be the indicative present or perfect of the verb *verrere*, eventually meaning to 'sweep the jealousy away'. Therefore, what *Allius*, son of *Reburrus* seems to plead for, is protection against jealousy and, in the case something happened to his property, that his rights might be restored.

But to which god does he plead? To *Deu(m). Adiutorem*. Could this god be *Banceroi*,

10 Dopico Caínzos & Pereira-Menaut 1993, 638–9.
11 Livy 9.15.
12 *ERCanosa* 11; *AE* 1984, 250; *AE* 2003, 359; *AE* 2008, 417.

with which ends the inscription? A former interpretation of Rodríguez Colmenero[13] suggested the reading of *D(eo) Danceroi* both in l.1 and l.6, which the author thought to be a deity equivalent to *Silvanus*, indicating the presence of an indigenous sacred place. In support of his thesis, the author refers that the rock itself should be the altar, given the existence of cup-marks and draining channels in the upper part. However, it is impossible to identify such elements: the naturally eroded surface of the rock surely was mistaken as anthropic marks. Regarding the proposed reading of *Deu(m). Adiutorem Dan(cerum?)* in l.1 and of *Danceroi* in l.6, both must be discarded, since what is written is, respectively, *Deu(m). Adiutorem* and *Banceroi*.

Another aspect worthy of attention is that *Banceroi* seems to correspond to an indigenous plural form, similar to the ethnic names *Magariaicoi* and *Caelobrigoi* of Lamas de Modelo[14] or *Vesucoi* of Barcelos,[15] which doesn't seem to match the singular *Deu(m). Adiutorem*. It appears, then, reasonable that *Banceroi* could be an ethnic name, to which eventually belonged *Allius* and would, somehow, be sanctioning the action described in the text.

On the other hand, it is rather interesting that there is not one single example of the epithet *adiutor* associated with Roman or indigenous deities. Instead, it appears as a profession[16] as well as an anthroponym.[17]

The expression *deus adiutor*, very rare in itself, is documented epigraphically in a Christian religious context in *Africa Proconsularis* Haidra[18] and in Sicily,[19] as well as in Psalm 77, 35 and Psalm 51, 9.[20] If we turn to the linguistic features of the text, it seems clear a Late Antiquity chronology, for instance, in the use of *ac* instead of *hac* and *mici* instead of *mihi;* as well as in the use of the preposition *in* regarding the idea of an end, an objective, as shows *in ac conducta conservanda.*[21] Hence, it seems reasonable to think

---

13 Rodríguez Colmenero 2010, 134–5, 137–8.

14 CIL II 416.

15 *HEp* 4, 1994, 1003; Búa Carballo 2000, 79.

16 Some examples, in Zagarolo, *Latium et Campania*: [*D(is) M(anibus)] | [-3-]si M(arci) [f(ilii)] | Bassi | decurialis | armamentari(i) et | architecti et | plebei adiutori[s] | procurationis | alabarchiae Pelusi* (*AE* 1999, 418); in Lopate, *Moesia superior*: *D(is) M(anibus) | Valer(ia) Filete | vix(it) an(nos) LX[1] | et Serg(ius) Sul[ti]/tus [I]unior vix(it) | an(nos) XXV h(ic) s(iti) s(unt) | Serg(ius) Sultitia/nus mil(es) leg(ionis) VII | Cl(audiae) P(iae) F(idelis) adiutor | prior cornicular(iorum) co(n)s(ularis) | matri | et fratri | b(ene) m(erentibus) f(aciendum) c(uravit)* (*AE* 2004, 1227); Ostia Antica, *Latium et Campania*: *[.]| Tr[om(entina?) -3-]as | sevir August(alis) | idem q(uin)q(uennalis) item | q(uin)q(uennalis) ordinis | Augustalium | et patronus | corp(oris) mens(orum) fr(umentariorum) | Ost(iensium) adiutor(um) | Laurens Lavin(as) | comparavit sibi | vi<v=B>us* (*AE* 2009, 192); Turda/Potaissa, Dacia: *I(ovi) O(ptimo) M(aximo) | Paterno | Aurel(ius) Vet/us adiutor | offici(i) corni/culariorum e | v(oto) l(ibens) m(erito) p(osuit)* (CIL III 894); in Rome: *D(is) M(anibus) | Cn(aei) Iuli Cn(aei) fil(ii) | Domati Prisci | ex(ornati) equo public(o) | adiutoris | haruspicum | Imperatoris | pontificis | Albani* (CIL VI 216).

17 Kajanto 1980.

18 *Deus in adiutorium meum intende domine ad adiuvandum me festina* (*AE* 2001, 2076d).

19 *[I(n) n(o)m(ine) d(omi)ni] salv(atoris) [n(ostri) Ih(su) Chr(ist)i hic requiescit [---|----] n[o]t(arius) Eutych[i]anae qui vixit annos | quinquaginta sept(em) ereptus sep|timo decimo die mensis Maii indicti]|one sexta qui legis ora pro eo | sic deum [h]abeas adiutorem* (*AE* 2008, 600).

20 Respectively, '*et rememorati sunt quia Deus adiutor est eorum et Deus excelsus redemptor eorum est*', and '*Ecce homo qui non posuit Deum adiutorem suum sed speravit in multitudine divitiarum suarum et praevaluit in vanitate sua*'.

21 A similar construction is the documented in the *Thesaurus Linguae Latinae* (col. 790): "Vulg. Sirahc

that this *deum adiutorem* could actually be the Christian god, making *Danceroi* the god that never was.

Penedo das Ninfas, Sanfins de Ferreira, Porto (CIL II 5607)

The inscription of Penedo das Ninfas is located at the very base of an important Romanized hillfort and is also carved on a small granite outcrop of approximately 2.40 x 3.60 x 1.20 m, in this case, on both east and west faces of the rock.[22]

The first reference to this inscription was published by Argote,[23] who read in the eastern face *Cos . neae| P. S.* and in the western, *Fidu [...] hic.* Later on, Hübner,[24] first including it in the group of Iberian inscriptions and only afterwards in CIL II 5607. Sarmento[25] mentions the doubt of reading, in the western side, *Niminid* or *Nimid,* which he relates with the Irish *nemed*, concluding that this inscription refers to a sanctuary of the *Fidueneas* deities.

In the opinion of Vasconcelos,[26] the first word should be the name of a deity, *Cosuneae*, hence it would be more reasonable to read in the western side *numinib(us)*, except for the last letter, which indeed is a D instead of a B. The author proposed, nevertheless to read both texts as *Cosuneae | F(idem) S(olvit) numinib(us)* and *Fidu [...] Hic.*

Even so, only in the 1970's would this inscription attract again the interest of researchers: Encarnação[27] refers the opinion of Almeida, to whom the epigraph would probably be a medieval landmark, given the existence of two crosses by the side.
On the other hand, for Silva[28] it would mark a sanctuary dedicated to *Cosunea* of the *Fiduenae,* and both the inscriptions would be part of the same text: *Numidi | Cosuneae | Fiduenarum | hic | l(ibentes?) | f(idem?) s(olverunt).*

Another alternative was proposed by Tranoy,[29] who reads *Munidi Fiduenarum | hic* and, on the other side of the rock, *Cosuneae*. Instead, in the opinion of Rodríguez Colmenero[30] it is more plausible to read: *Munidi | Fiduene aram | hic | l(ibens) [p(osuit)]*, on one side, and *Cosuneae | F(ideuene) s(olvit votum)*, on the other one.

According to the proposal of Búa Carballo,[31] the text facing west presents *Nimidi Fiduenearum hic (finis)*; and the one facing east, *Cosu Ne(meaeco) Ae(dem) F(..) [(...)] S(acrauit).* That author believes it could mark the limit of the sanctuary precinct dedicated to the *Fidueneae*, following the hypothesis of Sarmento and Silva, relating

13, 18: *invoca deum in salute tua".* See Correia Santos & Gaspar *forthcoming.*

22 Granite; Side W: 55–80 x 59 cm; l.1: 12, l.2: 10; l.3: 26 cm; Side E: 75 x 145 cm; l.1: 10, l.2: 28 cm.
23 Argote 1732–1734, 768.
24 Hübner 1890, 258–9.
25 Sarmento 1896, 147.
26 Vasconcelos 1905, 188, 326–7.
27 Encarnação 1975, 171.
28 Silva 1980, 80–2; 1986, 300.
29 Tranoy 1981, 273.
30 Rodríguez Colmenero 1993, 80–1; 1995, 194–6.
31 Búa Carballo 2000, 382–3.

this site also to two votive altars found at Santo Tirso, around 5 km to W, dedicated respectively to *Dom(ino) Deo Nemedec[o]*[32] and *Deo Domeno Cusu Nemedeco,*[33] as already proposed by Vasconcelos.[34]

More recently, Silva[35] published again the same inscription, giving an alternative reading: *Munidi| Fiduenearum| Hic* and *Cosuneae . | Hic S.*

Both texts are deeply carved and are easy to read, seeming to have been carved at the same time, as indicated by their paleographic characteristics. The result of the M.R.M only confirmed in detail the last reading of Silva, allowing to read in Face W, *Cosuneae . | hic s* and in Face E: *Munidi | Fiduenearum| hic.*[36]

Fig. 4. Monochromatic M.R.M. of East and West side of Penedo das Ninfas (H. Pires).

The principal doubts regarding this inscription referred to the names of the deities. One of them was read as *Niminid, Nimid,*[37] *numinib(us),*[38] *Numidi,*[39] *Munidi,*[40] and related by several authors to *nemed, nemeton,* from which this inscription should mark the place of an open-air sanctuary.[41]

However, what is written is indeed *Munidi*, with the two occurences of I clearly marked, which invalidates the readings that supposed an N at the beginning and its relation with *nemed* and *nemeton.* So far, we know four dedicatories to *Munidi*, two of them associated with ethnic names, such as *Mun[i]di Igaed(itanorum)* of Monsanto,[42] and *Munidi Eberobrigae Toudopalandaigae* of Talaván.[43] The same form and construction

32 *ILER* 896; *RAP* 51; Búa Carballo 2000, 391–2.
33 CIL II 2375, 5552; *ILER* 796; *HEp* 9, 1999, 757; *AE* 1957, 315; *RAP* 50.
34 Vasconcelos 1905, 326–7.
35 Silva 2007.
36 Correia Santos *et al.* forthcoming.
37 Argote 1732–1734, Sarmento 1895.
38 Vasconcelos 1905.
39 Silva 1980.
40 Tranoy 1981; Rodríguez Colmenero 1993, 1995.
41 Sarmento 1895, 147; Silva 1986, 300; Marco Simón 1993, 319.
42 *AE* 1967, 142.
43 Fita y Colomer 1914, 304–13; *CPILC* 471; *AE* 1915, 8; *HAE* 2393; *AE* 1956, 154; *HEp* 6, 1996, 246. The other two dedications are from Celorico da Beira, Guarda - *[...] | [...] | [...] [M]alceini | [sac]rum | [M]unidi* (CIL II 424; *HEp* 2, 1990, 792) and Vila Pouca de Aguiar, Vila Real - *[Mu]nidi | v(otum) l(ibens) [...]* (Rodríguez Colmenero 1997, nº 199; *HEp* 7, 1997, 1258).

occurs here: *Munidi Fiduenearum.*

Concerning *Cosunea,* Búa Carballo[44] suggests instead *Cosu Ne(meaeco) Ae(dem),* given the existence of the two altars already mentioned dedicated to *Cosu Nemeoeco* in Santo Tirso. But it is also possible that it is a single word, eventually corresponding to a feminine deity that could be related with the god *Cosu.*[45]

The reading of Búa not only is highly hypothetical, but also breaks the syntactical order that both texts present: the simple invocation of the god, to which follows the expression *hic*, which ends with an S only in the eastern side, possibly an abbreviation of *s(tatuit)* or something alike.

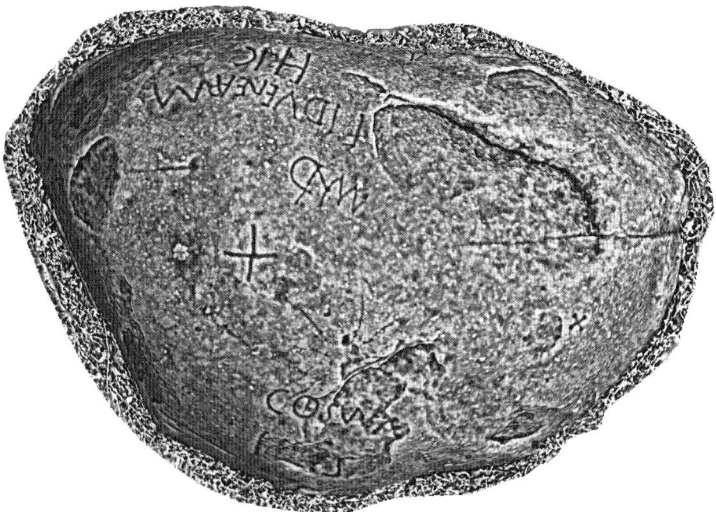

Fig. 5. Monochromatic M.R.M. of the upper part of the rock of Penedo das Ninfas (H. Pires).

The text itself suggests being a landmark and this is even more inviting when we observe that in the upper part of the rock, on an artificially flattened surface, is carved a cross orientated precisely according to the four cardinal points. This cross is very similar to a *decussis*,[46] and it matches perfectly the urban organization of the hillfort nearby, whose streets are disposed according to the *kardo* and *decumanus*.[47]

However, in this case, it should not be a mark of Roman centuriation, but a landmark between two ethnic entities: the settlement of Sanfins appears to be abandoned after the 2nd century AD and no Roman city was identified in its proximity. Although the site seems to have been occupied since the 5th century BC, the urban settlement was built at the very end of the 2nd century BC,[48] which suggest that it could be a situation of grouping and relocation of indigenous communities following the Roman conquest.

44 Búa Carballo 2000, 382–3.

45 So far, there are twelve references to this deity, mentioned as *Cosu/Cosue/Coso*: Viana del Bollo, Ourense (*IRG* IV, 113; *HEp* 2, 1990, 601); Caldas de Reis, Pontevedra (*CIRG* II, 12); Portas, Pontevedra (*CIRG* II, 128; *HEp* 6, 1996, 762; *AE* 1994, 959; *HEp* 13, 2003/2004, 505); Zas, Brandomil, La Coruña (CIL II 5071; CIL II 5628; *IRG* I, 7; *CIRG* I, 39; *AE* 1952, 113; *AE* 1955, 257); Sada, Meirás, La Coruña (*AE* 1955, 257; *CIRG* I, 9); Negreira, Logrosa, La Coruña (*CIRG* I, 22; *HEp* 4, 1994, 333); Coristanco, Torres de Nogueira, La Coruña (*CIRG* I, 68; *HEp* 4, 1994, 327); Laxe, La Coruña (Castillo y D'Ors, 1959: 152 nº 9; *CIRG* I, 70); Monte Mozinho, Penafiel, Porto (HEp 8, 1998, 611); São Pedro do Sul, Viseu (*HEp* 7, 1997, 1299); Peal de Becerro, Jaén, Andalucía (*HEp* 5, 1995, 520a); Levroux, Aquitania (CIL II, 2418).

46 In fact, very similar crosses are documented in the centuriation marks of Felgueira and Pinhel, within the territory of *Bracara Augusta:* Carvalho & Clavel-Lévêque 2008, 159; Carvalho 2012, 158.

47 The settlement of Sanfins is clearly organized according to the *kardo* and *decumanus,* with the principal axis respecting the appropriate dimensions (Hyginus, *De Limitibus Constituendis*, La 111, 12–5).

48 Paço & Jalhay 1955; Paço 1968; Silva 1986, 46–7, 53.

Also, given the existence of cup-marks connected by little draining channels on the upper part of the rock and its location next to a water source, it is possible that this rock already had symbolic value in former times, making sense not only its use as a landmark, but also the invocation of two indigenous tutelary deities.

Cueva del Valle, Zalamea de La Serena, Badajoz (CIL II².7, 932)

Another example is the one of Cueva del Valle, a small natural cave of no more than 58 m², in which were found more than 500 fragments of anthropomorphic terracotta *exvotos*, as well as miniaturized vases, dated from the 1st century BC to the 1st century AD.[49]

Fig. 6. General view of Cueva del Valle's inscription (M. J. Correia Santos) (detail www2.uah.es:CILII7,0923.jpg).

At about 10 m from its entrance, along the same rock surface, there is another natural cavity, with 2 x 3 m, above which was carved the inscription. The text is clearly carved: *Q. Cornelius Quartio / V I.*[50]

García y Bellido and Menéndez Pidal[51] first refer to the place as a Romanized indigenous sanctuary but it is Álvarez Martínez[52] who mentions the rock inscription, which, in his opinion, was dedicated to *Iuppiter*. On the other hand, Moneo[53] defends it could be dedicated to a solar indigenous god, lately assimilated to *Iuppiter*; while Celestino Pérez and Cazorla Martín[54] believe it is possibly related to a chthonic deity, proposing to expand the last two letters as *V(oto) I(unoni)*. More recently, the reading admitted by *CIL* II².7, 932 is *Q(uinto) Cornelio Quart(...) Io/vi.*

Now, all these interpretations pose the same problem. If it is strange that a Roman deity, invoked by a dedicant with a Roman name is abbreviated, while the dedicant, with the full name, takes the leading role; what is even more suspicious is the reading of *Quart(...) Io/vi,* since *Quartio* is the nominative of a well-documented Roman name

49 Celestino Pérez 1997, 374; Cazorla Martín & Celestino Pérez 2008, 215–24; Correia Santos 2015.
50 Epigraphic field: 160 x 25 cm; letters: l.1, 7–12.5 cm and l.2, 7.5 cm.
51 García y Bellido & Menéndez Pidal 1963, 3.
52 Álvarez Martínez 1986, 146.
53 Moneo 2003, 83.
54 Celestino Pérez & Cazorla Martín 2010, 89.

that never appears abbreviated in such manner.[55] Moreover, given the association of this inscription with a cave, it would be more reasonable to presume its relation with chthonic entities, instead of solar deities.

At the end, this inscription shows the risk of trying to identify the name of a deity in a text that we suppose to be a votive inscription, in this case, a god that was never there. Hence, the previous readings should be corrected to *Q(uintus). Cornelius Quartio| v(oto) i(ussit)*.[56] The dedicant presents the *tria nomina* and belongs to the *gens Cornelia*, but the most interesting is that he is the only dedicant which name is carved in the rock, in spite of the great amount of *exvotos* found in this cult place, what would suggest this inscription as an expression of the evergetism of *Cornelius Quartio*.

The date proposed by *CIL* II^2.7, 932 for this inscription, between AD 30 and 70, should also be revised. If we look at the archaeological record of the surrounding landscape, it is noteworthy that the human occupation was more intense during the republican period.[57] Two Roman settlements are located at no more than 1 km from Cueva del Valle, being contemporary with the material found in the cave: Cerro Borreguero and El Tesoro,[58] as well as the *villae* of Traseras del Cementerio and Las Cañadas,[59] located respectively at 3.5 and 5 km.[60]

Therefore, the inscription of Cueva del Valle should be interpreted as a testimony of devotion and possible evergetism from an individual named *Q. Cornelius Quartio*, to a god that remains unknown.

The altar of Castro Daire, Viseu (CIL II 5247)

Finally, another case of an inscription with a god that never was, is the altar of Castro Daire. From the time of Hübner, it is thought to be dedicated to *Deus Arus*, an opinion that was mostly favored by Vasconcelos,[61] in spite of being the only testimony of this so-called deity.

It is a small votive altar that presents engraved texts in two faces and a third one with a sculpted anthropomorphic figure. In the front side, besides a zoomorphic representation, it is possible to read VOTV || AROL|A S, which led to different interpretations: Figueiredo[62] read it as *Votu(m) Arol a(ra) s(alutis);* Vasconcelos,[63] *Votu(m) Aro l(ibens) a(nimo) s(olvit)*.

---

55 In *Baetica*, Cádiz (CIL II 1906); Alcolea del Río, Sevilla (CIL II 4968, 8); Burguillos del Cerro, Badajoz (*HEp* 4, 1994, 139); Talavera la Real, Badajoz (*HEp* 6, 1996, 145a); Valverde de Júcar, Cuenca (*AE* 1984, 590); Santanyi, Mallorca (Veny, 1965; nº 111); Peñalba de Castro, Burgos (CIL II 2772); Tarragona (CIL II 6091); and in *Lusitania*, Herdade da Camugem, Elvas (*IRCP* 597).

56 See CIL III 5565; CIL X 444; *CIRP* Salamanca; *ERSegovia* 175.

57 Rodríguez Díaz & Ortiz Romero 1989; 2003; Mayoral Herrera *et al.* 2011.

58 Ortiz Romero, 1991; Rodríguez Díaz & Ortiz Romero, 2003

59 Cazorla Martín & Celestino Pérez 2008, 215.

60 It is also worth mentioning the proximity of Zalamea de la Serena, traditionally identified with *Iulipa*. For further discussion regarding *Iulipa* see Stylow 1991, 12, 21.

61 Vasconcelos 1892, 6; 1905, 314.

62 Figueiredo 1887, 52–7.

63 Vasconcelos 1905, 314.

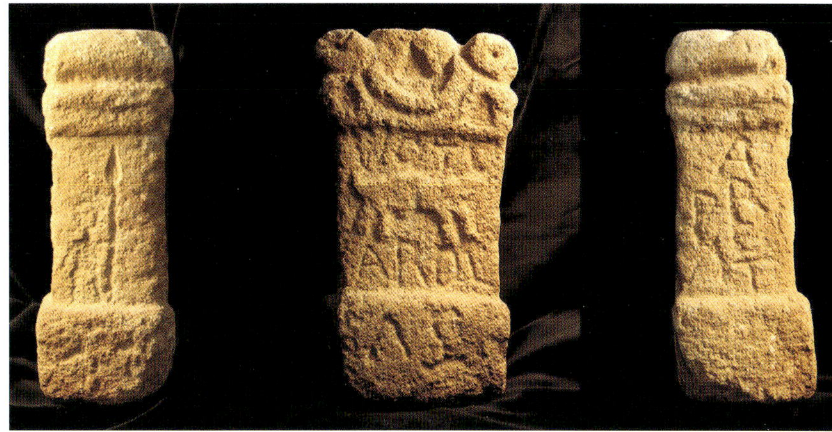

Fig. 7. Votive *arula* of Castro Daire (M. J. Correia Santos).

On the left side of the altar, there is another inscription: A| P R| E| A | T. Figueiredo[64] supposed it could be the initials of the dedicant's name, while Hübner uttered two possibilities: *aparet votu(m) Aro l(ibens) a(nimo) s(olvit)*; and *votu(m) Aro L A S Aprae T*, keeping the last letter without resolution. On the other hand, Untermann[65] proposed an alternative: that *Aro* could be *Ar(r)o,* the nominative of the dedicant's name, an anthroponym well documented in the Iberian Peninsula.

However, another interpretation is possible if we consider both texts as one: *Votu(m) arola s(olvit),*[66] with *arola* instead of *arula*, which is perfectly admissible;[67] and on the other side, *patera*, written in such a manner that the letters, disposed clockwise, seem to substitute the usual iconographic representation.

Regarding the sculpted representations, the zoomorphic figure seems to be a pig and it could be the representation of an animal offering; while the human figure that appears on the right side of the altar, holding a spear in the left hand, could perhaps be a representation of the dedicant himself, as already assumed Hübner and Vasconcelos. It is interesting that the spear itself seems to detain the main role of the scene, located at the very center of the surface, with much more detail than the human figure. But even more curious is the infraction of the usual iconographic representation of armed figures that always hold the spears in the right hand: would it be the representation of a left handed dedicant?

This *arula* states the fulfilment of a vow made to a god whose name we do not know, on behalf of someone we do not know either. If we assume that this altar was placed in a shrine of a known god, the name of the deity was dispensable for the contemporary reader visiting the shrine, which may explain its absence on the altar. As for the nonexistent dedicant, it is not unprecedented. It seems that what really mattered was the fulfillment of the vow and the ritual involved: the mention of libations, conveyed in the text *patera* and a possible animal sacrifice, represented by the pig.

64 Figueiredo *op. cit.*
65 Untermann 1985, 344–5; 1965, 60–1.
66 Alves Dias 1991.
67 Carnoy 1906, 59–60.

Final remarks

Epigraphists and religion scholars usually seek the formal perfection of a votive text, ignoring the circumstances of its specific context, as if such texts were written to be read by us, out of context, as if they were merely a displayed item in our museums. This 'necessity' of identifying the gods in votive inscriptions, leads many times to create gods by convenience, gods that never were.

When confronted with names that do not occur elsewhere, such as *Danceroi* or *Aro*, we should be methodologically suspicious and avoid their immediate classification as theonyms. Similarly, there are several kinds of votive inscriptions and, in spite of being chronologically distant, Penedo das Ninfas, from the 1st century BC and Penedo de Remeseiros, probably of the 5th–6th century AD, both texts summoned the gods to ensure the reliability of a non-religious situation: the first one, a territorial division; and the second one, the possession of land. On the other hand, the inscriptions of Cueva del Valle and of Castro Daire, are entirely different: the first one, probably from the 1st century BC, testifying a possible act of evergetism, with no mention of any deity at all; and the second one, from the 1st century AD, with no theonym or dedicant, in which the fulfillment of the vow is what seems to have mattered.

If only we could understand their specific contexts as a whole, certainly it would explain the formal specificities they denote. Surely, for these ancient societies, gods were much more and beyond the rules of what we think should be the case for a votive inscription.

BIBLIOGRAPHY

Álvarez Martínez, J. M. 1986 'La presencia romana en la Baja Extremadura', *Historia de la Baja Extremadura*, ed. M. Terán, I, 88–185. Badajoz, Real Academia de Extremadura de las Letras y las Artes.

Alves Dias, M. M. 1991 'O Deus *Arus*(?) de Castro Daire, Viseu, Portugal (*CIL* II 5247)', *Actas das IV Jornadas Arqueológicas* (Lisboa, 1980), 361–5. Lisboa, Associação dos Arqueólogos Portugueses.

Argote, J. C. 1732–1734 'Da cidade de Panóias e das antiguidades e vestígios que actualmente existem dela', *Memórias para História Eclesiástica do Arcebispado de Braga*, Primaz das Hespanhas. Lisboa, Régia Officina Sylvianna.

Búa Carballo, J. C. 2000 *Estudio Linguístico de la Teonímia Lusitano-Gallega.* Unpublished Thesis, Universidad de Salamanca.

Carnoy, A. J. 1906 *Le Latin d'Espagne d'après les Inscriptions.* Bruxelles.

Correia Santos, M. J. 2015 *Los santuarios rupestres de la Hispania Indoeuropea*, Doctoral Dissertation, University of Zaragoza, http://zaguan.unizar.es/record/31628/files/TESIS-2015-069.pdf

Correia Santos, M. J. & Gaspar, C. *forthcomming* 'Las inscripciones tardoantiguas en el Norte de Portugal: Dios, los hombres y el territorio', *V Coloquio Internacional Nuevas Perspectivas sobre la Antigüedad Tardía*, 'La pérdida de las Hispanias: Ideología, Poder y Conflicto', Universidad Complutense (3–5 Fevereiro de 2016) Madrid.

Correia Santos, M. J. & H. Pires 2014 'A estela funerária de Capela, Penafiel', *Ficheiro Epigráfico* 119, Coimbra.

Correia Santos, M. J., O. Sousa & H. Pires 2014 'Nuevas lecturas de las inscripciones del santuario de Panóias (Vila Real, Portugal)', *Sylloge Epigraphica Barcinonensis* 12, 197–224.

Correia Santos, M. J., O. Sousa, H. Pires, J. Fonte & L.

Gonçalves-Seco 2014 'Travelling back in time to recapture old texts.', *Information Technologies for Epigraphy and Cultural Heritage, Proceedings of the First EAGLE International Conference* (29–30 September 2014, Paris), ed. S. Orlandi, R. Santucci, V. Casarosa & P. M. Liuzzo, 437–54. Roma, Sapienza Università Editrice.

Encarnação, J. 1975 *Divindades indígenas sob o domínio romano em Portugal: subsídios para o seu estudo*. Lisboa, Imprensa Nacional Casa da Moeda.

Figueiredo, A. C. B. 1887 'Ara descoberta em Castro Daire', *Revista Archeologica e Historica* 1, 52–7.

Fita y Colomer, F. 1914 'Nuevas inscripciones romana y visigótica de Talaván y Mérida', *Boletín de la Real Academia de la Historia* 64, 304–13.

García y Bellido, A. & Menéndez Pidal, J. 1963 *El distylo sepulcral romano de Iulipa (Zalamea)*, Anejos de Archivo Español de Arqueología III. Madrid.

Mayoral Herrera, V., S. Celestino Pérez, E. Salas Tovar & M. Bustamente Álvarez 2011 'Fortificaciones e implantación romana entre La Serena y la Vega del Guadiana: el Castejón de las Merchanas (Don Benito, Badajoz) y su contexto territorial', *Archivo Español de Arqueología* 84, 87–118.

Paço, A. & E. Jalhay 1955 'Tesouro monetário da citânia de Sanfins', *Anais da Academia Portuguesa da História* 6, 189–275.

Paço, A. 1968 'Citânia de Sanfins, VIII – fragmentos de estátuas de guerreiros galaicos', *Broteria* 76, 710–25.

Pires, P., J. Fonte, L. Gonçalves-Seco, M. J., Correia Santos & O. Sousa 2014 'Morphological Residual Model – a tool for enhancing epigraphic readings of highly erosioned surfaces', *Information Technologies for Epigraphy and Cultural Heritage, Proceedings of the First EAGLE International Conference* (29–30 September 2014, Paris), ed. S. Orlandi, R. Santucci, V. Casarosa & P. M. Liuzzo, 133–4. Roma, Sapienza Università Editrice.

Rodríguez Colmenero, A. 1993 *Corpus-Catalogo de inscripciones rupestres de época romana del cuadrante Noroeste de la Península Ibérica*. A Coruña, Edicios do Castro.

Rodríguez Colmenero, A. 1995 'Corpus de inscripciones rupestres de epoca romana del quadrante noroeste de la Península Ibérica', in A. Rodríguez Colmenero & L. Gasperini (ed.), 'Saxa Scripta (Inscripciones en Roca), Actas del Simposio Internacional Ibero-Itálico sobre Epigrafia Rupestre, Santiago de Compostela Y Norte de Portugal', *Anejos de Larouco* 2, 117–259.

Rodríguez Colmenero, A. 2010 'El dios *Dancerus* de la Cañada de Remeseiros (Vilar de Perdizes, Montalegre, Portugal), un Silvano indígena protector de los contratos de arrendamiento', *Serta Palaeohispanica J. de Hoz, Palaeohispanica* 10, 133–46.

Rodríguez Díaz, A. & Ortiz Romero, P. 1989 *Poblamiento prerromano y recintos ciclópeos de La Serena, Badajoz*, Cuadernos de Prehistoria y Arqueología de la Universidad Autónoma de Madrid.

Rodríguez Díaz, A. & Ortiz Romero, P. 2003 'Defensa y territorio en la Beturia: castros, *oppida* y recintos ciclópeos', *Defensa y territorio en Hispania de los Escipiones a Augusto: espacios urbanos y rurales, municipales y provinciales*, ed. A. Morillo, F. Cadiou & D. Hourcade, 219–52. León, Universidad de León-Casa de Velásquez.

Sarmento, F. M. 1896 'Materiais para a arqueologia do concelho de Guimarães', *Revista de Guimarães* 13–14, 149–68.

Silva, A. C. F. 2007 *A Cultura Castreja no Noroeste de Portugal*. Paços de Ferreira, Câmara Municipal de Paços de Ferreira.

Silva, A. C. F. 1980 'Organizações gentilícias entre Leça e Ave', *Portugália* 1, 79–90.

Silva, A. C. F. 1986 *A Cultura Castreja no Noroeste de Portugal*. Paços de Ferreira. Museu Arqueológico da Citânia de Sanfins e Câmara Municipal de Paços de Ferreira.

Stylow, A. U. 1991 'El *Municipium Flavium V(...)* de Azuega (Badajoz) y la municipalizacion de la *Baeturia Turdulorum*', *Studia Historica. Historia Antigua* 9, 11–27.

Tranoy, A. 1981 *La Galice Romaine. Recherches sur le Nord-Ouest de la Péninsule Ibérique dans l'Antiquité*. Paris, Diffusion de Boccard.

Untermann, J. 1985 'Teónimos de la región lusitano-gallega como fuente de las lenguas indígenas', *Actas del III Coloquio sobre Lenguas y Culturas Paleohispanicas*, 343–364.

Untermann, J. 1965 'Misceláneas epigráfico-lingüísticas', *Archivo Español de Arqueología* 38, 8–25.

Vasconcellos, J. L. 1892 *Sur les Religions de lu Lusitanie*, Lisboa, Imprensa Nacional da Casa da Moeda.

Vasconcellos, J. L. 1905 *Religiões da Lusitânia*, vol. II. Lisboa, Imprensa Nacional da Casa da Moeda.

XV

LES DIEUX AU NOM INDIGÈNE ET LEURS CULTORES CHEZ LES VOCONCES DE VAISON-LA-ROMAINE D'APRÈS LES INSCRIPTIONS*

Bernard Rémy

Dans cette cité latine bien 'romanisée' aux deux capitales (Die et Vaison), les habitants ont continué à prier des dieux au nom indigène, parfois latinisé ou grécisé, qui occupent une place non négligeable dans le panthéon des Voconces méridionaux. Dix-neuf inscriptions honorent ou remercient huit divinités de ce type : Albarinus (deux occurrences), Baginus (une) et les Baginatiae/ Baginiatiae (trois), Belesema (une), Boutrix (une), Dulovius/Dullovius (deux), Graselos (une), Vasio (sept occurrences), Vintur (une). Deux sont des inscriptions gallo-grecques ; les autres sont rédigées en latin. Leurs attributions étaient diverses (divinité éponyme, d'une source, des hauteurs [?], des hêtres…). Je n'ai pas pris en compte les dieux au nom latin pourvu d'un surnom indigène, tel Mars Albiorix. L'arc chronologique des documents est large : du IIe siècle av. J.-C. ou de la première moitié du Ier siècle avant notre ère (inscriptions gallo-grecques) à la fin du Haut-Empire. Ils proviennent de Vaison (dix occurrences) et d'autres localités des départements de la Drôme et du Vaucluse (neuf occurrences : campagnes et « agglomérations secondaires »). La plupart ont été retrouvés hors de leur contexte originel, ce qui nous interdit ordinairement de localiser les sanctuaires avec quelque précision.

PENDANT longtemps, les historiens des religions ont distingué trois catégories divines dans le panthéon gaulois de l'époque romaine : les dieux indigènes, les dieux 'gallo-romains' et les dieux 'orientaux'. En fait, comme l'ont montré John Scheid, Marie-Thérèse Raepsaet-Charlier, William Van Andringa et Ralph Häussler,[1] cette vision n'est pas exacte, au moins pour les dieux 'gallo-romains'.[2] En effet, si nous admettons que la conquête romaine a provoqué une assimilation organisée et volontaire des cités gauloises, éventuellement avec des variantes liées à des territoires précis (par exemple, chez les Trévires), il faut aussi admettre qu'il n'existe pas de véritable différence

---

* Réalisée dans le cadre de la préparation du volume VII.2, *Voconces de Vaison* des *Inscriptions Latines de Narbonnaise (ILN)*, cette étude doit beaucoup à la relecture de l'état actuel des notices par Xavier Delamarre. Plusieurs des notices utilisées ont été écrites en collaboration avec Henri Desaye, Patrice Faure, David Lavergne, Jean-Marc Mignon, Nicolas Mathieu et Benoît Rossignol. Merci à N. Mathieu de sa relecture critique, à Fabrice Delrieux de sa réalisation de la carte et à Julien Charles de ses clichés photographiques.

1 Scheid 2006a ; 2006b ; Raepsaet-Charlier 2006a ; 2006b ; Van Andringa 2006 ; Häussler 2008 ; 2012.

2 Voir aussi le livre lumineux de J. Scheid (2013) : *Les dieux, l'État et l'individu.*

entre des dieux qui seraient romains et des dieux qui seraient indigènes. Ils sont tous un peu des deux. Les divinités honorées par les 'Gallo-Romains' — ou plus exactement les Gaulois romanisés — ne sont pas de simples transpositions de dieux superficiellement romanisés, car remplacer le nom indigène d'un dieu par un nom latin indique un degré décisif d'intégration dans la religion romaine des divinités et des *cultores*. Même si les divinités 'interprétées' ont conservé une certaine dimension locale, il est probable qu'elles avaient en fait des personnalités et des fonctions très proches de celles des dieux gréco-romains du même nom, ne serait-ce que par leurs origines indo-européennes communes. Comme leurs dévots, elles s'étaient romanisées. Ainsi que le remarque R. Häussler (à paraître), 'ces cultes reflètent leurs croyances religieuses et leurs préférences, surtout le choix personnel de nommer et de représenter un dieu ou une déesse'.

Il n'en va peut-être pas de même des divinités qui ont conservé sous l'Empire un nom gaulois (Belado, Boutrix, Subronis Sumelis, Vasio...), parfois latinisé (Albarinus, Alaunius, Dulovius/Dullovius...) ou grécisé (Belesama, Graselos...), même s'il n'est évidemment guère possible de connaître leur véritable identité. Toutefois, au vu de leur dénomination, nous pouvons penser qu'elles avaient conservé, au moins en partie, leur nature et leurs attributions originelles.

Les divinités

Chez les Voconces de Vaison,[3] j'arrive au total, assez modeste, de vingt-cinq inscriptions qui honorent ou remercient douze divinités de ce type. Deux (n° 8, 17) sont des inscriptions gallo-grecques ; les autres sont rédigées en latin. Je n'ai pas retenu les déesses Mères, car ces divinités plurielles universelles sont tantôt honorées sous leur nom latin de *Matres*,[4] tantôt sous leur nom indigène latinisé de *Matrae*,[5] qui n'est qu'une variante de la forme latine. De même, je n'ai pas pris en compte les dieux au nom latin pourvu d'un surnom indigène, tel Mars Albiorix.

Dans la mesure du possible, car il est assez souvent difficile de les appréhender, j'ai essayé de classer ces divinités en fonction de leurs attributions supposées, ce qui m'a conduit à distinguer sept catégories :

1. Une divinité éponyme : Vasio

Pourvue d'un nom indigène,[6] *Vasio* était sans doute une divinité ancestrale des Voconces méridionaux, mais R. Häussler envisage la possibilité que 'le culte de *Vasio* ait été créé, autour de la période augustéenne, par l'*ordo* avec le but de promouvoir l'identité locale'.[7] En tout cas, au moins sous l'Empire, elle était la divinité éponyme de la

3 Sur le statut complexe de la cité voconce, qui comptait deux capitales (Pline l'Ancien, *Histoire naturelle*, 3, 4, 37), voir l'introduction aux *ILN, Die*.
4 *CIL* XII 1303, 1305, 1307, 1308, 1699, *ILGN* 193.
5 *CIL* XII 1302, 1306, 1309, 1310.
6 Delamarre 2007, 190.
7 Pour Delamarre (2003, 300), *Vasio* serait 'le dieu qui vient en dessous'. Häussler (à paraître) envisage que *Vasio* puisse être un dieu chtonien ou le dieu honoré dans la plaine et l'oppose à Vintur, le dieu du

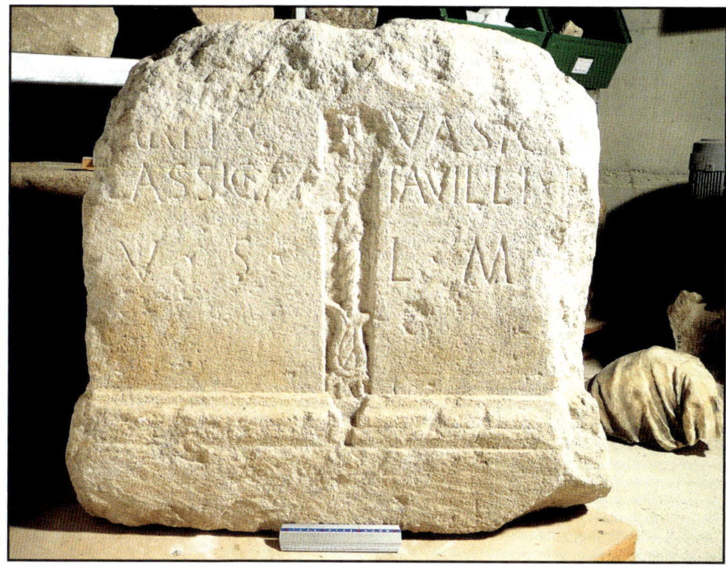

Fig. 1. Vaison : Dédicace votive fragmentaire à Mars (?) et à *Vasio* par un pérégrin. Vaison, musée Théo-Desplans (cliché : Julien Charles, Service du Patrimoine de Vaison-la-Romaine).

ville de Vaison et même de la partie méridionale du territoire voconce qui protégeait la communauté civique, comme le faisaient *Vienna*, *Axima* et bien d'autres. Sept, peut-être huit, dédicaces (n° 1–8) lui sont adressées. La déesse est honorée seule à trois reprises (n° 1–2, à Vaison ; 3, à Mérindol-les-Oliviers), peut-être quatre (n° 4, à Vaison), mais, dans cette dernière inscription, à la ligne 1, le nom de la divinité est largement mutilé (*[---]ni*). En dehors de Vaison, la restitution la plus probable serait *[Iunio]ni*, que l'on ne peut d'ailleurs pas exclure, mais, ici, le nom de *Vasio* est sans doute plus plausible.

Une fois (n° 5), elle est remerciée en compagnie de Mars qui n'est évidemment pas le Mars guerrier, mais très vraisemblablement un dieu protecteur. Le contexte civil de l'inscription laisse penser que pendant la 'paix romaine' la divinité guerrière de l'époque gauloise a glissé de sa fonction protectrice de la sphère guerrière à la sphère civile. Georges Dumézil l'avait déjà bien établi dans son commentaire de la prière que Caton propose de faire réciter au *uillicus*. Celui-ci s'adresse à Mars *pater*, afin, dit-il, que 'tu arrêtes, repousses et boutes dehors les maladies visibles et invisibles, la disette et la désolation, les calamités et les intempéries [...]' *(ut tu morbos uisos, inuisosque uiduertatem, uastitudinemque calamitates intemperiasque prohibessis defendas auerruncesque...)*.[8] S'appuyant sur cette démonstration, qu'il considère comme définitive, John Scheid montre que, par exemple, le Mars Lénus de Trêves ne peut pas être considéré comme un simple dieu guérisseur, 'car c'est par son action agressive envers toutes les forces menaçantes que Mars défend ceux qui l'implorent'.[9] Même si Mars avait conservé une certaine dimension locale, sa personnalité et ses fonctions étaient donc très proches du Mars gréco-romain. Nous retrouvons très probablement cette association divine dans une dédicace votive fragmentaire (n° 6). Toujours, à Vaison (n° 7), *Vasio* pourrait être

Ventoux.

8 Caton, *De l'agriculture*, 141. Dumézil 1966, 232 = 1987, 241.

9 Scheid 1992, 38.

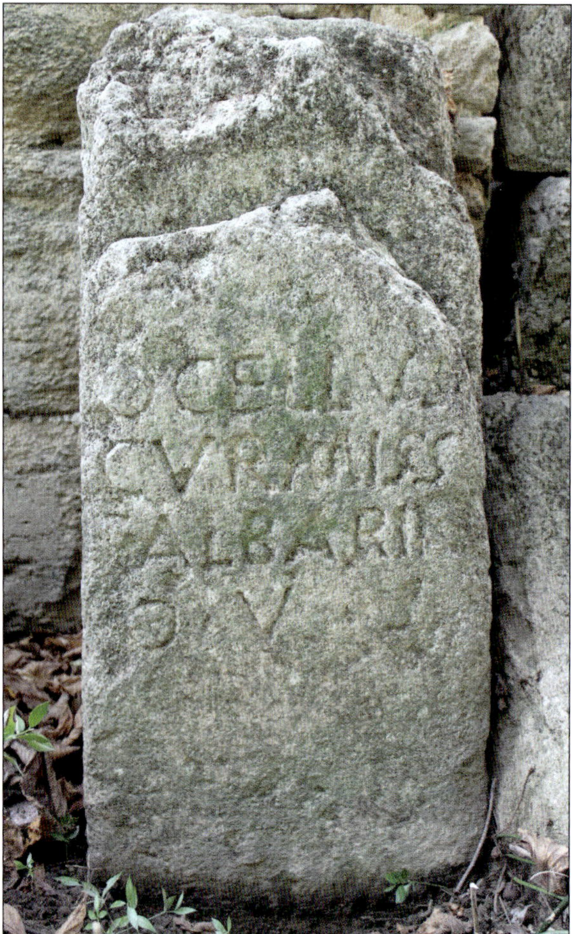

Fig. 2. Le Barroux (Vaucluse). Dédicace votive à Albarinus par Ocellus, fils de Curmissus, Caromb collection particulière (cliché : Julien Charles).

honorée avec une autre divinité, mais la lacune du texte n'est pas certaine. S'il manque bien une ligne au début du texte, la restitution du nom de Mars est au moins plausible, puisque, en l'état actuel de nos connaissances, *Vasio* n'est peut-être associée à aucun autre dieu. Enfin, il est quasiment certain que nous devons accepter la lecture par Suarès du nom de *Vasio* à la ligne 2 d'une inscription fragmentaire perdue de Piégon, Drôme (n° 8). On peut donc raisonnablement envisager que le nom d'une autre divinité était gravé à la première ligne. Faut-il retenir une des leçons de Suarès :[10] Dulovius, une divinité au nom indigène qui est attestée deux fois à Vaison?[11]

2. La divinité de la source du Groseau : Graselos

À Malaucène (Vaucluse), où la dédicace votive gallo-grecque (n° 9) a été retrouvée dans les environs de la source du ruisseau du Groseau, Graselos était très probablement la divinité topique et protectrice de la source, d'où part un aqueduc, assez bien identifié, pour Vaison.

3. Une divinité des hauteurs(?) : Albarinus

Attesté dans deux dédicaces votives fragmentaires à Saint-Hippolyte-le-Graveyron (n° 10) et au Barroux (n° 11; Fig. 2), dans le Vaucluse, Albarinus, nom gaulois latinisé,[12] pourrait être une divinité des hauteurs qui sont nombreuses dans la région. Il n'est guère possible d'être plus précis.

4. La divinité du Ventoux (?) : Vintur

À Mirabel-aux-Baronnies, dans la Drôme (n° 12), est remercié un dieu, dont le nom a

10 *Codex Vaticanus* 9141, f° 30.
11 *CIL* XII 1279, 1280 ; voir *infra.*
12 Delamarre 2007, 16.

été mal conservé par la tradition manuscrite, mais la proposition d'Otto Hirschfeld dans le *CIL* XII de lire *Vinturi* ne fait guère de doute, d'autant que *Vintur* est connu par deux inscriptions de la cité d'Apt.[13] M. Clerc supposait que *Vintur* était 'la divinité générale des montagnes de toute la région provençale',[14] mais il faut peut-être plutôt considérer que ce nom gaulois[15] désignait le mont Ventoux divinisé (*Ventour* en occitan).

5. Des divinités des hêtres(?) : Baginus et les Baginatiae/Baginiatiae[16]

Baginus et les *Baginatiae* (n° 13) sont attestés à Bellecombe-Tarandol (Drôme), mais la pierre pourrait éventuellement avoir été déplacée depuis Sainte-Jalle (Drôme), où ont été retrouvées trois dédicaces, deux aux *Baginatiae* (n° 14–15) et une aux *Baginiatiae* (n° 16). Suffixée en *-iatia* au lieu de *-atia*, cette dernière leçon, 'paraît être seconde par rapport à la première du point vue philologique',[17] ce qui n'implique pas qu'elle soit chronologiquement postérieure. Cette unique version peut éventuellement être le résultat d'une simple erreur du lapicide, mais elle peut aussi avoir un sens linguistique. À Sainte-Jalle, trois autres autels sont dédiés *Matribus Bagininiensib(us)*, *Matribus B[a]g(in-)* et sans doute *M(atribus) B(agin-)*.[18]

Il est évident que Baginus et les *Baginatiae/Baginiatiae* sont les 'versions' masculine et féminine d'une même divinité parfois assimilée aux Mères. Elles portaient un nom gaulois latinisé, dérivé du mot **bagos*, le hêtre.[19] Au vu de ce nom, faut-il penser, à l'origine, à un culte du hêtre[20] plutôt qu'à un culte topique ? La première hypothèse semble être renforcée par le fait que nous connaissons dans la cité de Vienne, à Morestel (Isère), une dédicace privée à Jupiter *Baginas*,[21] où le qualificatif de Jupiter est évidemment de la même famille que celle des divinités 'voconces'. On connaît aussi en Comminges — dans les Pyrénées — trois dédicaces *deo Fago*,[22] au dieu hêtre, et des autels décorés de motifs végétaux ou d'un arbre.[23] Robert Sablayrolles et Jean-Luc Schenck considèrent que 'la relation entre ces décors et le dieu hêtre paraît évidente'.[24] Enfin, un dieu Bacos (forme de **Bagos* ?) est attesté à Chalon-sur-Saône.[25]

Pour sa part, Xavier Delamarre envisage aussi que **bagos* puisse signifier chêne-

13 *ILN, Apt* 17, d'Apt ; 143 de Goult.
14 Clerc 1906, 272.
15 Delamarre 2007, 201.
16 Pour plus de détails, voir Rémy 2013.
17 Desaye *et al.* 2000, 185.
18 *AE* 2000, 884 ; 885 ; 890. Remarquons que la seule épiclèse écrite en entier de ces déesses Mères est encore différente : *Baginiensis/ses*, avec le suffixe *-ensis* qui s'applique ordinairement aux noms de lieux. Dans les deux autres dédicaces aux Mères, le qualificatif est largement abrégé, ce qui nous interdit d'être certain de son développement, même si l'abréviation implique un adjectif très connu dans la région.
19 Delamarre 2003, 64.
20 Häussler 2008, 173–5 ; Lambert 2013, 119.
21 *Ioui / Baginati / Corinthus / Nigidi Aeliani / ex uot[o]. ILN, Vienne* 572.
22 *CIL* XIII 33, près de Saint-Béat ; *CIL* XIII 223–225 ; Sablayrolles & Schenck 1988, n° 29–30, près de Saint-Bertrand-de-Comminges (Haute-Garonne).
23 Sablayrolles & Schenck 1988, n° 102–104, à Tibiran-Jaunac (Hautes-Pyrénées).
24 Sablayrolles & Schenck 1988, 40.
25 *CIL* XIII 2603.

vert.[26] C'est une hypothèse moins convaincante, puisque l'on retrouve **bagos* dans les régions septentrionales de la Gaule, par exemple à Bavay, dont le nom est issu du celtique **Bagacos*[27]. Or le chêne-vert ne pousse pas dans cette région. Le linguiste remarque également qu'il y a une autre étymologie possible pour les *Baginatiae* par la souche verbale celtique **bāg-* 'combattre', irlandais *bág* 'combat'. Dans le contexte de la 'paix romaine', c'est peut-être une hypothèse moins probable, sauf à envisager la même évolution du rôle de ces divinités que pour Mars.

6. Une divinité protectrice des petites gens et des artisans(?) : Belesema

À Vaison (n° 18), une inscription gallo-grecque commémore la donation à Belesema d'un enclos sacré. Le nom gaulois de Belesema, la 'très puissante'[28] se retrouve comme épithète de Minerve dans une inscription latine trouvée à Saint-Lizier, Ariège (*Minerua Belisama*).[29] Le rapprochement de Belesama/Belisama avec Minerve laisse penser que cette déesse gauloise pourrait avoir été la protectrice des petites gens et des artisans, puisque c'est le rôle attribué par César à Minerve dans sa rapide présentation du panthéon gaulois.[30]

7. Les divinités aux attributions indéterminées ou incertaines : Alaunius, Belado, Boutrix, Dulovius/Dullovius et Subronis Sumelis

7.1 Alaunius : Divinité au nom indigène,[31] elle se retrouve seulement à Mannheim en Germanie supérieure,[32] où elle est attestée comme épithète de Mercure (*Genio Mercuri Alauni*). À Lurs (Alpes-de-Haute-Provence), Alaunius est le dieu éponyme d'un mamelon (Pied d'Aulun) et d'*Alaunium*, une station routière de la voie *Domitia (?)*, attestée dans les principaux itinéraires antiques,[33] qui était peut-être une agglomération urbaine,[34] située à proximité du château et de la chapelle de Notre-Dame-des-Anges. Ailleurs, c'est le nom de rivières et de localités.[35] Il pourrait aussi être un dieu nourricier.[36]
7.2 Belado : divinité indigène, 'la puissante'.[37] Elle est assez bien attestée dans la partie sud de la cité[38] et en Provence, où elle est parfois associée à Mars.[39]
7.3 Boutrix : cette divinité masculine[40] n'est apparemment connue dans le monde

26 Delamarre 2003, 64.
27 Sergent 1990, 247–61.
28 Häussler (à paraître) la rapproche de Belenos 'le maître de la puissance' (Delamarre 2003, 71–2).
29 La finale du datif *-ai* est devenue *-i*. *CIL* XIII 8.
30 *Guerre des Gaules* 6.17.2.
31 Delamarre 2007, 16.
32 *CIL* XIII 6425.
33 Gobelets de Vicarello, *Table de Peutinger*, *Itinéraire d'Antonin*.
34 Leveau 1993, 283.
35 Delamarre 2003, 37.
36 *Ibid.*
37 Delamarre 2007, 18.
38 Trois occurrences : deux à Limans chez les Voconces : *ILGN* 219, 220 ; une à Lardiers: *CAG, 04*, n° 101, p. 250, 3*.
39 *AE* 1991, 1197, à Plaisians, dans le *Vocontium* ; *ILN, Aix-en-Provence*, 190, à La Tour-d'Aigues.
40 Delamarre 2007, 47.

romain que par une dédicace de Vaison (n° 18). Selon X. Delamarre,[41] nous pouvons penser à la syncope d'un **Bouti-rix* (voir la souche **Bout(o)-* dans les noms propres : *Boutus, -ius, -a* qui est fréquente : *Bouti m(anu)*,[42] *Bouteriō*,[43] probablement dérivé de **bou-to-*, de la souche **bō(u)-* 'boeuf, vache'.

Fig. 3. Beaumont-du-Ventoux (Vaucluse). Donation à Subronis Sumelis par Voretovirius, un pérégrin, d'un monument indéterminé. Malaucène, collection particulière (cliché : Julien Charles).

7.4 Dulovius/Dullovius : avec un ou deux L, Dul(l)ovius est un dieu au nom indigène latinisé,[44] qui, en dehors du territoire de Vaison, est seulement attesté à deux reprises dans la péninsule Ibérique.[45] Nous le retrouvons deux fois à Vaison (n° 19, 20) et peut-être une fois à Piégon, Drôme (voir *supra* et n° 8). Delamarre envisage qu'il puisse être un antonyme de 'la déesse *Suleuia*, la (déesse) qui conduit bien' ;[46] Dul(l)ovius serait 'le (dieu) qui égare'.[47]

7.5 Subronis Sumelis : celtique, *Subronis*, 'Bonne-Poitrine',[48] cette divinité ne semble pas être connue ailleurs qu'à Beaumont-du-Ventoux, Vaucluse (n° 21; Fig. 3), mais on connaît *Ver-bronara*, 'Super-Poitrine', à Buoux,[49] et *Co-bronia*, 'sœur de lait' ('du même sein'), à Milan.[50] Sumelis est aussi un nom indigène.[51] Il est à rapprocher de *Sumeliu* et de Sumelo en Norique,[52] de *Sumela* à Bieno.[53] Pour **Su-mel(i)o-*, il faut comprendre ' (qui a un) bon *melo-*' (sens inconnu du thème *melo-*). Plutôt que celui d'une divinité, il faut plutôt penser que ce nom est une épithète de la déesse Subronis.

Enfin, il convient de signaler — sans pouvoir aller plus loin — les divinités, au nom

41 Lettre.
42 *CAG, 59/2*, 321, à Bavay.
43 *CIL* III 11520, à Zollfeld, en Norique.
44 Delamarre 2007, 91.
45 *AE* 1900, 119 ; 1965, 109.
46 Delamarre 2003, 287.
47 Faut-il penser à un nom prophylactique, comme Sapricius?
48 Delamarre 2003, 92 ; 2007, 173.
49 *ILN, Apt* 122.
50 *CIL* V 5997.
51 Delamarre 2003, 223 ; 2007, 174.
52 *CIL* III 5604 ; 5639.
53 *CIL* V 6640.

très mutilé, honorées au Pègue avec Diane Tifatina,[54] car, au vu du datif pluriel — *[---] cis* — conservé à la fin de la ligne 3, il convient sans doute, avec Jacques Gascou, de penser à des divinités collectives gauloises 'qui avaient une fonction voisine de la Diane chasseresse'.[55]

Le support

Les épigraphistes commencent enfin à prendre conscience qu'il est important de prendre en compte le support des inscriptions, car il fournit des renseignements non négligeables, notamment sur les moyens financiers des *cultores* et sur les ateliers de lapicides. Nous ignorons la nature de quatre monuments qui sont perdus (n° 3, 5, 7, 8). Quatorze textes ont été gravés sur des autels (n° 1, 2, 6, décoré très probablement d'un candélabre, 9, 11?, 12, 13, 14, 15, 16, 22, 23?, 24, 25) ; trois sur des plaques (n° 4, 10, 17) ; deux sur des bases (n° 19, avec un personnage assis entouré de palmes, sur une des faces, 20) ; un sur un bloc (n° 18) et un (n° 21) sur une stèle(?). La présence d'un candélabre sur un autel de Vaison constitue un des rares exemples d'association figurée explicite entre la dédicace votive et l'allumage d'une chandelle, pratique évoquée dans la littérature, notamment dans l'*Anthologie Palatine*,[56] dédiée à L. Calpurnius Piso.

Le matériau utilisé n'est pas toujours connu (n° 3, 5, 7, 8, 19, 20, 23, 24). On retrouve du marbre (n° 12), du calcaire coquillier de Beaumont-du-Ventoux (n° 2, 4, 6, 13, 18, 21), de la mollasse de Caromb (n° 11) et différents types de calcaire (n° 1, 9–10, 14–17, 22, 25).

Les différents types d'inscriptions

Dans les inscriptions mentionnant des divinités au nom indigène, nous pouvons distinguer deux types de documents :

1. Deux donations

Une, en grec, à Belesama (n° 17) d'un lieu sacré (*nemeton*). La plaque commémorative de cette donation, dont les raisons ne sont pas indiquées, par un pérégrin devait être intégrée dans un monument assez important, peut-être un pilier qui délimiterait le terrain donné à cette divinité dans la ville de Vaison. Une, en latin, à Subronis Sumelis (n° 21) d'un monument indéterminé, à Beaumont-du-Ventoux par Voretovirius, un pérégrin.

2. Vingt-trois dédicaces

Les autres *cultores* ont honoré ou remercié 'à la romaine' par des dédicaces les divinités au nom indigène. Ils avaient donc bien intégré les complexes pratiques cultuelles

54 *Dianae / [Ti]fatinae / [---]IN[---]CIS, / M(arcus) Iccius Mummius. CIL* XII 1705.
55 Gascou & Guyon 2005, 17–8, n° 9.
56 *Anth. Pal.* 6.249.

romaines. Nous ignorons par quelles voies les populations gauloises avaient eu accès à cette connaissance. Comme l'utilisation des *Antiquités religieuses* de Varron, le seul 'manuel' connu sur le 'système' religieux romain, est peu probable, il faut sans doute envisager une transmission orale.

Sept fois (n° 3, texte fragmentaire, 5, 7, 8, texte fragmentaire, 18, 19, 22, texte fragmentaire), nous ignorons si le document est une 'simple' dédicace aux dieux ou une dédicace votive. Dans tous les autres cas, les *cultores* ont attendu la satisfaction de leur demande — plus exactement l'exécution par le dieu invoqué de sa part du contrat qu'il est réputé avoir accepté — pour s'acquitter de leur vœu, car si la demande n'était pas exaucée dans le délai imparti, le contrat était caduc. Ils ont utilisé le formulaire votif traditionnel *u(otum) s(oluit) l(ibens) m(erito)*, une fois abrégé en *u(otum) l(ibens) m(erito)* [texte n° 6] et une fois en *u(otum) s(oluit)* [texte n° 11]. Les deux frères *[---]eilei* (n° 4) ont choisi une formule proche : *ex uoto*. [---]us Tacitus (n° 25) a peut-être tenu à préciser qu'il avait fait graver la dédicace à ses frais.

Répartition géographique des inscriptions (Fig. 4)

Dix documents ont été retrouvés à Vaison (n° 1, 2, 4–7, 17–20). Quinze proviennent de Mérindol-les-Oliviers (n° 3), Piégond (n° 8), Mirabel-aux-Baronnies (n° 12), Bellecombe-Tarandol (n° 13) et Sainte-Jalle (n° 14–16), dans le département de la Drôme, Malaucène (n° 9), Saint-Hippolyte-le-Graveyron (n° 10), Le Barroux (n° 11) et Beaumont-du-Ventoux (n° 21), dans celui du Vaucluse, Lardiers (n° 22), Limans (n° 23, 24) et Lurs (n° 25) dans les Alpes-de-Haute-Provence.

À Vaison, aucun texte n'a été retrouvé dans son contexte originel,[57] sauf, semble-t-il, la donation à Belesema (n° 17). L'enclos sacré (*nemeton*)[58] de la divinité pourrait être le sanctuaire découvert par Yves de Kisch au sud de l'Enclos des Cordeliers.[59] Il n'est donc guère possible d'envisager de localiser avec quelque précision les sanctuaires. Tout au plus, pourrait-on considérer que celui de *Vasio* pourrait avoir été situé au voisinage de la chapelle de Saint-Quenin, puisque deux dédicaces (n° 1, 5) ont été retrouvées dans ce secteur et qu'une troisième (n° 4) — dont l'attribution à *Vasio* n'est pas certaine — provient des fouilles de Bernard Liou et Y. de Kisch, au nord de la cathédrale qui n'est pas très éloignée de Saint-Quenin.

Dans les campagnes, les lieux de découverte des pierres sont tout aussi imprécis, sauf à Malaucène, à Sainte-Jalle et à Lardiers. À Malaucène (n° 9), plausible agglomération, la dédicace gallo-grecque à Graselos a été retrouvée près de la source du Groseau, non loin de la chapelle de Notre-Dame-du Groseau. Faut-il envisager la christianisation du lieu de culte de cette divinité des eaux ? À Sainte-Jalle (n° 14–16), centre assuré du *pagus Bag(inensis ?)*,[60] toutes les dédicaces ont été découvertes à proximité immédiate de

57 Voir, en dernier lieu, les notices de la *CAG, 26*, de la *CAG, 84/1* et de la *CAG, 04*.
58 Voir Delamarre 2003, 232–3.
59 Goudineau & de Kisch 1999, 69.
60 *CIL* XII 1377. Voir Desaye, Lurol & Mège 2000, 190–2.

l'angle nord-ouest de l'église actuelle, ce qui atteste très probablement la présence d'un sanctuaire païen à l'emplacement de l'église. Peut-être pourrions-nous même envisager que ce lieu de culte existait déjà à l'époque de l'indépendance. La localisation d'un hêtre remarquable pourrait avoir déterminé le lieu d'implantation du centre cultuel et peut-être politique[61] de cette communauté rurale. Puis, au Ve ou au VIe siècle, le temple païen paraît avoir été remplacé par une première église, où sainte Galle/Jalle aurait été ensevelie, s'il faut en croire le récit de la vie de cette sainte. À Lardiers (n° 22), la découverte a été faite dans le sanctuaire du Chastelard.

À l'époque romaine, les dieux au nom indigène sont donc honorés ou remerciés aussi bien à Vaison que dans les campagnes. Ils ne sont en rien des survivances rurales.

Datation

En dépit de quelques progrès,[62] la datation des inscriptions 'religieuses' reste très délicate. Nous devons nous borner à dater du Haut-Empire onze textes (n° 1–3, 8, 12, 16, 18, 19, 22, 23, 24). Les deux inscriptions gallo-grecques (n° 9, 17) ont très vraisemblablement été gravées au IIe siècle av. J.-C. ou dans la première moitié du Ier siècle avant notre ère.[63] Les duo nomina première manière des deux frères [---]eilei (n° 4) attestent une datation de l'époque julio-claudienne, ce que pourrait confirmer l'écriture. Comme la probable épitaphe de M. Licinius Goas[64] date du Ier siècle après J.-C., il va de soi que sa dédicace à Dullovius (n° 20) a été gravée à la même époque. Les dédicaces à Albarinus de Saint-Hippolyte-le-Graveyron (n° 10) et du Barroux (n° 11), ainsi que celles à Baginus et aux Baginatiae de Bellecombe-Tarandol (n° 13) et à Alaunius de Lurs (n° 25) pourraient dater du Ier siècle, où le nom du cultor précède souvent celui de la divinité.[65] La dédicace (n° 7) de l'affranchi M. L(-) Homullus laisse aussi penser au Ier siècle en raison de l'abréviation l(ibertus),[66] mais ce critère de datation n'est peut-être pas pertinent dans le cas de ce document, car l'indication de l'affranchissement ne fait pas partie de la dénomination d'Homullus. Les cinq inscriptions (n° 5, 6, 14, 15, 21) gravées au nom de pérégrins sont antérieures à 212, date de l'édit de Caracalla, ou de peu postérieure.

Les 'cultores'

L'auteur(e) de la dédicace à Boutrix (n° 18) n'a pas mentionné son nom, car il faut admettre que lorsque le support — un bloc rectangulaire, en mollasse de Beaumont — a été retaillé de partout, en vue d'un remploi, le texte n'a pas été mutilé. Sinon, il faudrait supposer un très important espace vacant, soit avant le début de l'inscription, soit entre

61 Il semble possible de faire un rapprochement du culte des divinités de ce *pagus* voconce avec le culte, sans doute public et officiel, de Vintius dans le *pagus Dia[---]*, chez les Allobroges de la cité de Vienne (voir Rémy 2008, 237–51).

62 Voir notamment Cibu 2003 ; Dondin-Payre & Raepsaet-Charlier 2001 ; 2006.

63 *RIG* I, p. 3.

64 *CIL* XII 1420.

65 Cibu 2003, 353–5.

66 Dondin-Payre & Raepsaet-Charlier 2001, XI.

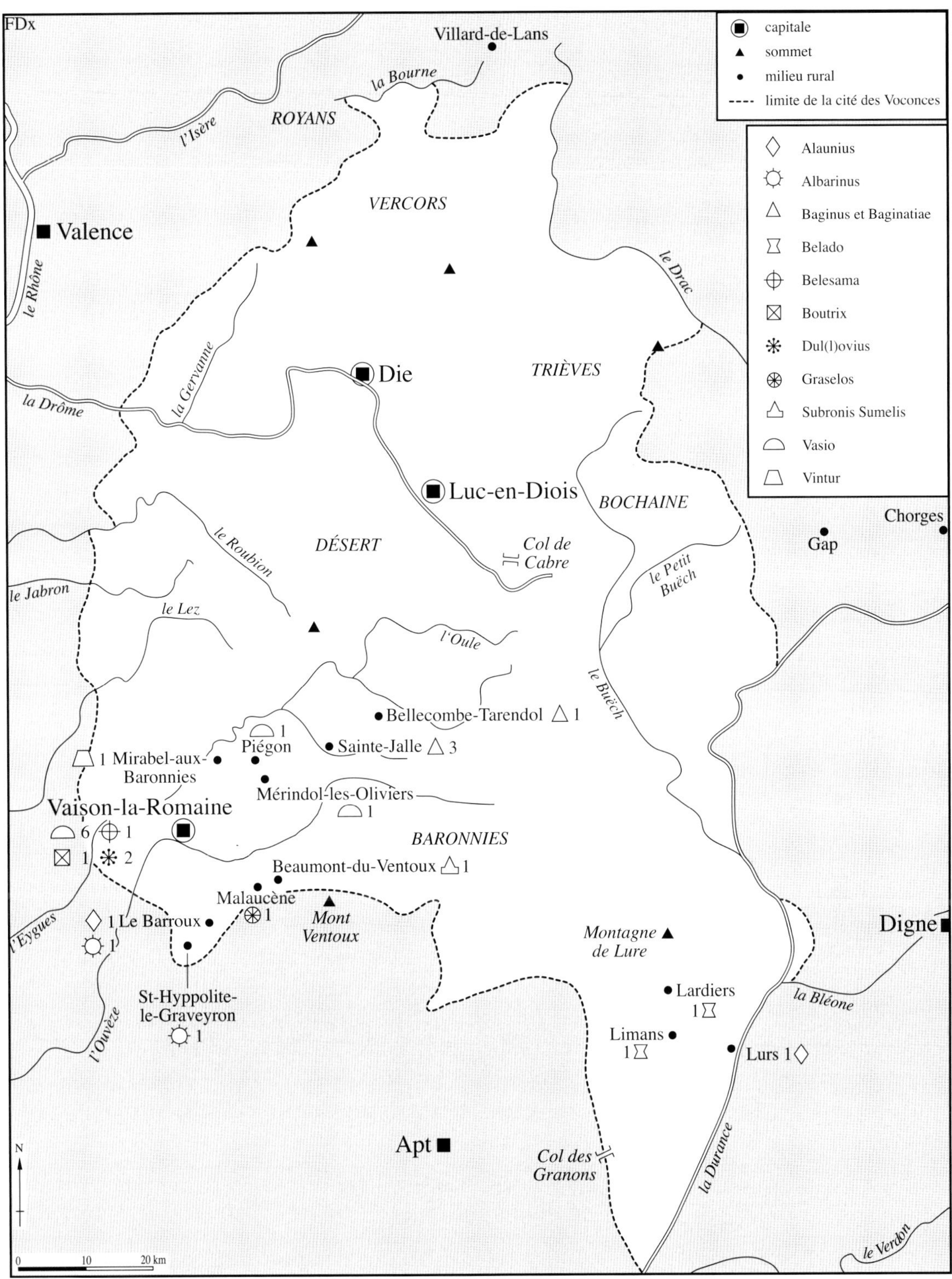

Fig. 4. Les dieux au nom indigène dans le territoire des Voconces de Vaison (conception : B. Rémy, Fabrice Delrieux ; réalisation : F. Delrieux, Université de Savoie).

le nom du dieu et celui du dévot. La première dédicace à Dulovius (n° 19) ne comporte très probablement pas non plus de dévot(e). Nous ignorons tout du ou des *cultor(es)* des textes n° 8 et 22. Les vingt et une autres inscriptions mentionnant des divinités au nom indigène ont été gravées à l'initiative d'une (?) collectivité, les *Cadienses* (n° 12), et d'au moins vingt-deux *cultores* privés, car le texte n° 4 émane de deux frères.

Les Cadienses

La nature de cette collectivité pose problème. À valeur toponymique, la désinence *-ensis* sert à désigner les habitants d'un lieu. Reste à savoir quel lieu précis ou à défaut quel type de lieu. Nous pouvons penser à un *uicus*, à un lieu-dit ou à un domaine. Dans le cas d'un *uicus*, on aurait sans doute employé, comme pour Buis-les-Baronnies ou Nyons,[67] le terme de *uicani* ; pour un domaine, on aurait plutôt utilisé un adjectif dérivé d'un nom en *-ana/um* ou en *-acum*. Dans ces conditions toute identification reste incertaine.

La plupart des auteurs, notamment Michel Lejeune,[68] considèrent que Segomaros, fils de Villu (n° 17), était un citoyen de Nîmes — *tooutios Namausatis*[69] — et que la forme *tooutios* (citoyen) est incorrecte ; il aurait fallu écrire *toutios*. Pour sa part, Pierre-Yves Lambert estime 'qu'il y a peut-être ici un exemple de l'instrumental-sociatif pluriel thématique indo-européen *-ois>-us*'.[70] Il faudrait alors traduire 'avec les concitoyens de Nîmes'. Segomaros aurait ainsi associé de manière informelle ses concitoyens nîmois à sa donation. Quoi qu'il en soit, il faut envisager des rapports encore très mal connus entre Vaison et Nîmes.[71]

Les particuliers

Les inscriptions ont livré les noms plus ou moins complets de vingt-deux *cultores*. Sauf Primula, fille de Quintus (n° 15), tous sont des hommes. Un des dévots, C. Birrius Fuscus (n° 1), a aussi fait graver à Vaison une dédicace votive à Mercure (*ILGN* 194).

A. Statut juridique

J'ai recensé neuf citoyens romains : C. Birrius Fuscus (n° 1), L. Messius Rhodinus (n° 2), les deux frères *[---]eilei*, fils de Manius (n° 4), C. Girubius Cato (n° 16), M. Licinius Goas (n° 20), T. Ven[---] Cila[---] (n° 24), [---]us Tacitus (n° 25) et M. L(-) Homulus (n° 7), un affranchi — huit pérégrins : Cassicus (?), fils de Tavilus (n° 6), un anonyme, fils d'un anonyme (n° 9), un anonyme, fils de [---]marus (n° 10), Ocellus, fils de Curmissus (n° 11), Felix, fils de Smerus (n° 13), Ioventius, fils de Lemiso (n° 14), Primula, fille de Quintus (n° 15), Segomaros, fils de Villu (n° 17) — et cinq *incerti* : [---]essius (n° 3), Tacitus (n° 5), Voretovirius (n° 21), [---]urum (n° 22) et Co[---] Urs[---] (n° 23). Toutefois, Tacitus et Voretovirius étaient probablement des pérégrins, vivants dans cette cité de droit latin,

67 *ILN, Vienne* 303.
68 *RIG* I, G-153.
69 *Namausatis* est un ethnique formé sur le nom indigène de Nîmes.
70 Lambert 2003, 87.
71 Voir Béraud, 2014.

qui n'ont pas mentionné, comme c'est courant, leur patronyme, même si l'hypothèse d'un affranchi de pérégrin, voire d'un esclave, bien que ces derniers aient fort peu de lisibilité épigraphique, ne soit peut-être pas à exclure totalement pour Tacitus. Le nom indigène de Voretovirius exclut quasiment cette hypothèse.

Sans surprise, nous pouvons remarquer que les citoyens romains, en principe plus romanisés, honorent presque aussi souvent des dieux au nom indigène que les pérégrins et les *incerti* de cette cité de droit latin.

B. Statut social

Aucun *cultor* n'a mentionné la moindre fonction (magistrature, prêtrise...). Il faut donc très probablement en conclure qu'ils étaient de simples particuliers, mais ils appartenaient au moins aux couches moyennes de la société voconce, car faire graver une inscription impliquait quelques moyens financiers et un certain niveau culturel.

C. Dénomination

Il faut évidemment distinguer les citoyens romains des pérégrins/citoyens de droit latin.

Les citoyens romains

Sept citoyens romains sont désignés par les classiques *tria nomina* ; les deux frères *[---]eilei* portaient les *duo nomina* première manière (prénom + gentilice), suivis de leur filiation indiquée par le prénom du père, Manius. En effet, la lacune de la ligne 2 du texte n° 4 permet d'intégrer le gentilice *[---]eilei*, au nominatif pluriel (en facteur commun), précédé des deux prénoms, mais il est impossible de placer deux surnoms dans la lacune de la ligne 3. Il est sans doute beaucoup moins pertinent de penser que les *cultores* étaient des pérégrins désignés par leur nom unique, car un nom au pluriel ne se justifierait pas, puisque chaque homme avait son propre nom.

Les gentilices

Nous disposons de quatre gentilices utilisables, car il est impossible de retrouver le gentilice réduit à l'initiale 'L' d'Homullus (n° 7) et ceux, trop fragmentaires, des deux frères (n° 4) et des n° 24 et 25. Deux, voire trois, citoyens romains portaient un gentilice indigène : Birrius (n° 1), rarissime en Narbonnaise; Messius (n° 2), commun dans la Province. Girubius (n° 16) n'est pas attesté ailleurs dans les inscriptions sur pierre des provinces occidentales, mais X. Delamarre[72] le range parmi les noms indigènes (voir les thèmes Geru-, Giro-, on aurait ici un composé **Giru-biyo-*). Enfin Licinius (n° 20) est un gentilice latin 'italien', fréquent en Narbonnaise.

Les surnoms

J'ai recensé quatre *cognomina* latins : Fuscus (n° 1), assez bien attesté dans la Province ;

72 Delamarre 2007, 104.

Homullus (n° 7), Cato (n° 16), Tacitus (n° 25), très peu fréquents ou peu fréquents en Narbonnaise, où le seul surnom grec, Rhodinus, ne se retrouve qu'une autre fois. *Hapax* dans le monde romain,[73] Goas n'est ni grec, ni latin, ni indigène. P.-Y. Lambert[74] considère qu'il pourrait être un nom italique, peut-être vénète. Faut-il en déduire que Marcus Licinius Goas n'était pas un Voconce?

Les pérégrins/citoyens de droit latin

Sauf Tacitus(?) [n° 5] et Voretovirius, probables pérégrins, désignés respectivement par un unique nom latin, rarissime et par un nom indigène qui est un *unicum* en Narbonnaise,[75] les huit pérégrins/citoyens de droit latin certains ont une dénomination complète (nom unique + filiation), mais deux sont anonymes (n° 9, 10, dont le père avait un nom gaulois fragmentaire). Cassicus (?), fils de Tavilus (n° 6), Ocellus, fils de Curmissus (n° 11) et Segomaros, fils de Villu[76] (n° 17), un Nîmois, avaient une dénomination rare entièrement indigène, même si le nom Segomaros a été grécisé dans cette inscription gallo-grecque. Il en allait peut-être de même de Ioventius, fils de Lemiso (n° 14), encore que ce patronyme, rarissime dans les provinces occidentales, pourrait être un nom latin 'régional'. Primula, fille de Quintus (n° 15), associait deux noms 'latin régionaux' de traduction, bien présents en Narbonnaise. Enfin, Felix, fils de Smerus (n° 13), avait un nom unique latin très commun, qui pourrait très éventuellement être un nom 'latin régional' de traduction, et un patronyme indigène, qui semble être un *hapax* dans la Province comme nom unique ou *cognomen*.

Les noms à connotation indigène sont de loin les plus nombreux parmi les *cultores*, mais ce corpus documentaire est beaucoup trop restreint pour qu'il soit possible d'en tirer une conclusion fondée sur la préférence donnée aux dieux au nom indigène par les *cultores* attachés à leur passé voconce, comme l'atteste le choix de leur dénomination.

Conclusions

Au terme de cette analyse, nous pouvons constater que les divinités au nom indigène occupent une place non négligeable dans le panthéon des Voconces méridionaux, au moins pendant tout le Haut-Empire. Elles ont des attributions variées et sont honorées ou remerciées à Vaison comme dans les agglomérations et les campagnes par leurs *cultores*, dont la dénomination a une forte connotation indigène. Citoyens romains ou pérégrins, ces derniers appartenaient aux couches moyennes de la société voconce.

73 Fabri de Pereisc, *Codex Parisinus Latinus* 8957, f° 219 et Suarès, *Codex Vaticanus* 9141, f° 13', n° 17, qui dépend probablement de Pereisc, donne la lecture CONS qui serait un nom abrégé, ce qui est assez peu probable.

74 Lettre du 25 octobre 2001 à J. Gascou.

75 Delamarre 2003, 227 ; 2007, 205.

76 La filiation est indiquée par l'adjectif indigène patronymique Villoneos, avec suffixation en *-eo-* de Villu, qui semble être un *hapax* en Narbonnaise.

Appendice : catalogue des inscriptions

Ce catalogue est un simple instrument de travail. Il a pour but d'éviter au lecteur de retourner aux sources pour vérification. Nous avons donné les références les plus aisément accessibles. Les lemmes sont génétiques.

1 - Vaison. Dédicace votive à *Vasio* par Gaius Birrius Fuscus, un citoyen romain.

Autel, en calcaire, avec base et couronnement moulurés. Le sommet est dépourvu de foyer, le *puluinus* gauche est cassé. La pierre est creusée en forme de sarcophage sur la face opposée à l'inscription.
Découvert, avant 1902, à Vaison, dans un champ, près de la chapelle de Saint-Quenin. Conservé à Montélimar, dans la collection Vallentin du Cheylard.
Dimensions : 123 x 52/60 x 35/45 cm.
Texte de quatre lignes. H. d. l. : l. 1 : 9 ; l. 2 : 7,5 ; l. 3 : 6,5 ; l. 4 : 7,5 cm. Séparation par points triangulaires peu marqués.
ILGN 201 (*CAG, 84/1*, p. 349–50, n° 480*).

> *Vasioni / G(aius) Birrius / Fuscus / u(otum) s(oluit) l(ibens) m(erito).*
>
> À *Vasio*, Gaius Birrius Fuscus s'est acquitté de son vœu volontiers et à juste titre.

Date : Ier–IIIe siècles.

2 - Vaison. Dédicace votive à *Vasio* par Lucius Messius Rhodinus, un citoyen romain.

Autel, en mollasse de Beaumont, avec base et couronnement moulurés.
Découvert, en 1917, à Vaison, dans un champ, au-dessous de la voie ferrée, sur l'emplacement d'un cimetière mérovingien. Conservé à Vaison, dans une collection particulière.
Dimensions : 91 x 45/47 x 28/30 cm.
Texte de quatre lignes. Champ épigraphique : 15,5 x 45 cm. H. d. l. : l. 1 : 4,5–6 ; l. 2 : 5–5,2 ; l. 3 : 4,5–4,7 ; l. 4 : 4 cm. Points triangulaires de séparation.
ILGN 202 (*CAG, 84/1*, p. 359, n° 529*).

> *Vasioni / L(ucius) Messius / Rhodinus / u(otum) s(oluit) l(ibens) m(erito).*
>
> À *Vasio,* Lucius Messius Rhodinus s'est acquitté de son vœu volontiers et à juste titre.

Date : Ier–IIIe siècles.

3 - Mérindol-les-Oliviers (Drôme). Dédicace fragmentaire à *Vasio* par un i*ncertus*, quasi anonyme.

Support fragmentaire indéterminé.
Signalé, au XVIIe siècle, à Mérindol-les-Oliviers, sans autre précision. Perdu.
Dimensions indéterminées.
Texte, mutilé, de deux lignes. H. d. l. inconnue.
CIL XII 1338, d'après Suarès, *Codex Vaticanus* 9141, f° 12 (*CAG, 26*, p. 419, n° 180).

> *Vasion(i) / [---]essius / ---*
>
> À *Vasio*, [---]essius [---].

Date : Ier–IIIe siècles.

4 - Vaison. Dédicace votive fragmentaire à *Vasio* (?) par deux frères, citoyens romains.

Plaque rectangulaire moulurée, en mollasse de Beaumont, brisée en haut et à gauche.
Trouvée, en 1972, à Vaison, lors des fouilles au nord de la cathédrale. Conservée à Vaison, au musée Théo Desplans (inv. n° 990.51.003, réserves).
Dimensions : 45 x 46,5 x 14 cm.
Texte mutilé à gauche de trois lignes entouré d'un cadre mouluré. Champ épigraphique : 38 x 42 cm. H. d. l. : l. 1 : 8 ; l. 2 : 6–8 ; l. 3 : 6,8–7,5 cm. Séparation par *hederae*.
AE 1992, 1202 (*CAG, 84/1*, p. 146, n° 129*).

> *[Vasio ?]ni / [---]eilei M(ani) f(ilii ?) / [ex uo]to fec(erunt).*
>
> À *Vasio* (?) [--- et ---], fils de Manius [---] ont placé (ce monument) à la suite d'un vœu.

Date : les *duo nomina* (première manière) des dédicants attestent l'époque julio-claudienne.

5 - Vaison. Dédicace à Mars et à *Vasio*, par Tacitus, un pérégrin (?).

'Grande pierre'.
Signalée, en 1717, à Vaison, 'au voisinage de l'église Saint-Quenin'. Perdue.
Dimensions indéterminées.
Texte de trois lignes. H. d. l. inconnue.

CIL XII 1301, d'après Martène & Durand 1717, 293 (*CAG, 84/1*, p. 146, n° 130*).

Marti / et Vasioni / Tacitus.

À Mars et à *Vasio*, Tacitus.

Date : si le *cultor* était bien un pérégrin, nous pouvons proposer pour cette dédicace une date antérieure à 212 ou de peu postérieure.

6 - Vaison. Dédicace votive fragmentaire à Mars (?) et à *Vasio* par Cassicus (?), fils de Tavilus, un pérégrin. Photo 1.

Autel mouluré, en mollasse de Beaumont, dont la partie supérieure a été brisée. Sont conservées la base moulurée et une partie du dé. Le champ épigraphique est divisé en deux par un candélabre.
Signalé, en 1929, à Vaison, sans autre précision. Conservé à Vaison, au musée Théo Desplans (inv. n° 990.51.008, réserves).
Dimensions : 70 x 70/78 x 32 cm.
Texte de trois lignes. Champ épigraphique : 38 x 64 cm. H. d. l. : l. 1 : + 3,5 ; l. 2 : 4-4,5 ; l. 3 : 5,5-6 cm. Points triangulaires de séparation.
AE 2003, 1085 (*CAG, 84/1*, p. 122, n° 78*) ; B. Rémy & N. Mathieu, avec la collaboration de H. Desaye et B. Rossignol, 'Deux inscriptions revues de Vaison-la-Romaine (Vaucluse) : une nouvelle occurrence de l'association Mars/*Vasio* ? - une épitaphe d'authenticité douteuse', *Bulletin Archéologique de Provence*, 36, 2014.

[M]arti ? Vasion[i] / Cassicus (?) Tauili f[il(ius)] / u(otum) s(oluit) l(ibens) m(erito).

À Mars (?) (et) à *Vasio*, Cassicus (?), fils de Tavilus s'est acquitté de son vœu volontiers et à juste titre.

Date : avant 212 ou de peu postérieure.

7 - Vaison. Dédicace à *Vasio* et peut-être à une autre divinité (Mars ?) par Marcus L(-) Homullus, un citoyen romain affranchi.

Support indéterminé, brisé en haut (?).
Signalé, au XVIIe siècle, à Vaison, '*in aedibus Seguini*'. Perdu.
Dimensions inconnues.
Texte, sans doute mal lu, de trois lignes. H. d. l. inconnue. Points de séparation et *hederae*.
CIL XII 1336, d'après Suarès, *Codex Vaticanus* 9141, f° 28, n° 1 (*CAG, 84/1*, p. 112, n° 11*).

[Marti et ?] / Vasion(i) / M(arcus) L(-) Hom[ul]/lus l(ibertus).

[À Mars ? et ?] à *Vasio*, Marcus L(-) Homullus, affranchi.

Date : Ier siècle (?).

8 - Piégon (Drôme). Dédicace fragmentaire à *Vasio* et à une autre divinité (Dulovius ?).

Support indéterminé.
Signalée, au XVIIe siècle, '*in Podio Guigonis*' (Suarès), qui désigne le village de Piégon (*CAG, 26*). Perdu.
Dimensions indéterminées.
Texte fragmentaire de trois lignes, difficile à interpréter. H. d. l. inconnue.
CIL XII 1337, d'après Suarès, *Codex Vaticanus* 9141, f° 12' et 30 (*CAG, 26*, p. 482).

[---]VLAV / Vasioni / [--- ?]RIVII / ---- ?[1]

[---] et à Vaison [---].

Date : Ier-IIIe siècles.

9 - Malaucène (Vaucluse). Dédicace votive à Graselos par un pérégrin anonyme.

Autel, en calcaire, sans base, avec couronnement retaillé.
Trouvé, avant 1810, près de Malaucène, dans les environs de la source du Groseau, puis, à partir de cette date, utilisé comme piédestal de la croix qui se trouve devant la chapelle de Notre-Dame-du-Groseau et enfin placé à l'intérieur de la chapelle. Conservé au même endroit.
29,2 x 23 x 25 cm.
Texte, difficile à lire, de cinq lignes. H. d. l. : 2,3-2,5 cm. Vu.
CIL XII, p. 824, d'après un moulage (*CAG, 84/1*, p. 439, n° 069,17*) ; *RIG* I, 148.

[---]λουσ | [---]ναλιακοσ | [Γ]ρασελου | [β]ρατουδε | καντενα.

[---]lus, fils de [ ] s'est acquitté volontiers de son vœu à Graselos.

Date : IIe siècle-première moitié du Ier siècle av. J.-C.

1 L. 1 : [---]VLAV, Suarès, *Codex Vaticanus* 9141, f° 12', avec une annotation dans la marge : '*forte Dulouio*' ; DVLOVIO, Suarès, *Codex Vaticanus* 9141, f° 30, avec le commentaire d'Hirschfeld : '*haud dubie coniectura*'.

10 - Saint-Hippolyte-le-Graveyron (Vaucluse). Dédicace votive fragmentaire à Albarinus par un pérégrin anonyme, fils de [---]marus.

Plaque, en calcaire, brisée à gauche.
En 1888, O. Hirschfeld signale que cette inscription était dans la cathédrale de Carpentras jusqu'en 1850, date où elle a été transférée à la bibliothèque Imguibertine. En 1921, J. Hannezo indique qu'elle provient de Saint-Hippolyte-le-Graveyron, sans localisation précise. En 1922, E. Lepaule donne la même provenance, 'sur un linteau de porte'. Conservé à Carpentras, au musée lapidaire.
Dimensions : 93 x 47 x 14 cm.
Texte, mutilé à gauche, d'une ligne. H. d. l : 6 cm. Points de séparation.
CIL XII 1157 (*CAG, 84/1*, p. 460, n° 109,3*) ; Christol & Janon 2004, 272–8.

> *[---]mari f(ilius) Albarino u(otum) s(oluit) l(ibens) m(erito).*

> [---], fils de [---]marus s'est acquitté de son vœu à Albarinus, volontiers et à juste titre.

Date : Ier siècle.

11 - Le Barroux (Vaucluse). Dédicace votive à Albarinus par Ocellus, fils de Curmissus, un pérégrin. Photo 2.

Autel, en mollasse de Caromb. L'ensemble est très dégradé et la face arrière est peut-être retaillée. Le plausible couronnement s'est délité. Le fût est profondément enfoncé dans le sol, ce qui nous interdit de savoir si la base est conservée.
Signalé, en 1936, au Barroux, à la Grange de l'Hôpital, 'engagé comme linteau de porte' (Sautel). Conservé à Caromb, au domaine des Pradets, par les familles Grangier-Bressieux.
Dimensions : 97 x 37,5 x 30 cm.
Texte de quatre lignes. H. d. l. : l. 1: 4,5–5 ; l. 2–4 : 4,8–5 cm. Points triangulaires de séparation.
Sautel 1936, 63 (*AE* 1940, 159 ; Sautel 1939, 39, n° 83) ; Barruol 1963, 368 ; Rémy B., N. Mathieu, P. Faure & J.-Cl. Meffre, 'Inscriptions latines nouvelles ou révisées de Vaison-la-Romaine et de ses environs', à paraître.
Voir Christol & Janon 2004, 276.

> *Ocellus / Curmiss(i) / f(ilius) ? Albarin/o u(otum) s(oluit).*

> Ocellus, fils de Curmissus, à Albarinus s'est acquitté de son vœu.

Date : Ier siècle.

12 - Mirabel-aux-Baronnies (Drôme). Dédicace votive au dieu *Vintur* par les *Cadienses.*

Autel, en marbre, dont la partie supérieure avait disparu.
Découvert, au XVIIIe siècle, à Mirabel-aux-Baronnies, où il supportait alors le bénitier, dans la chapelle Notre-Dame-de-Beaulieu. Perdu.
Dimensions inconnues.
Texte de trois lignes. H. d. l. inconnue. Pas de points de séparation.
CIL XII 1341, d'après Moreau de Vérone 1837, 161 (*CAG, 26*, p. 421, n° 182).

> *Vinturi / Cadienses / u(otum) s(oluerunt) l(ibentes) m(erito).*

> À *Vintur*. Les *Cadienses* se sont acquittés de leur vœu volontiers et à juste titre.

Date : Ier–IIIe siècles.

13 - Bellecombe-Tarandol (Drôme). Dédicace votive au dieu *Baginus* et aux déesses *Baginatiae* par Felix, fils de Smerus, un pérégrin.

Autel, en mollasse de Beaumont, avec couronnement mouluré, surmonté d'une cimaise épaufrée ; la base a disparu.
Découvert, en 1889, à Bellecombe-Tarandol, sans localisation précise. Il n'est peut-être pas exclu que la pierre ait été déplacée depuis Sainte-Jalle, qui est très proche. Conservé à Valence, au musée (inv. n° AR. 206, réserves).
25 x 24 x 15 cm.
Texte de cinq lignes. La dernière, presque illisible, a été mutilée depuis la mise au jour de l'inscription. H. d. l. : l. 1–5 : 3 cm. Points triangulaires de séparation.
ILGN 251 ; *CAG, 26*, p. 182, n° 46,2*.

> *Felix Sme/ri f(ilius) Bagino / et Bagina/tiabus / u(otum) s(oluit) l(ibens) m(erito).*

> Felix, fils de Smerus, s'est acquitté de son vœu à *Baginus* et aux *Baginatiae* volontiers et à juste titre.

Date : Ier siècle.

14 - Sainte-Jalle (Drôme). Dédicace votive aux *Baginatiae* par Ioventius, fils de Lemiso, un pérégrin.

Autel, en calcaire à grains fins, avec base et couronnement moulurés. Le couronnement

comporte à son sommet des *puluini* et un *focus* ombiliqué.
Découvert, en 1999, à Sainte-Jalle, lors de travaux exécutés à proximité de l'angle nord-ouest de l'église. Conservé à Sainte-Jalle, dans l'église.
Dimensions : 64 x 33/34 x 22 cm.
Texte de quatre lignes. H. d. l. : l. 1–4 : 4 cm. Points triangulaires de séparation.
AE 2000, 889 ; *CAG, 26*, p. 544, n° 306a.

> *Baginatiabus | Iouentius | Lemisonis f(ilius) | u(otum) s(oluit) l(ibens) m(erito).*
>
> Aux *Baginatiae*, Ioventius, fils de Lemiso, s'est acquitté de son vœu volontiers et à juste titre.

Date : antérieure à 212 ou de peu postérieure.

15 – Sainte-Jalle (Drôme). Dédicace votive aux *Baginatiae* par Primula, fille de Quintus, une pérégrine.

Autel, en calcaire granuleux, avec base et couronnement (brisé à gauche) moulurés. Sur le sommet de l'autel, *puluini* décorés et *focus* ombiliqué (fleuron) ; celui de gauche a disparu. Dans le champ épigraphique, patère ombiliquée en dessous de l'inscription.
Découvert, en 1999, à Sainte-Jalle, lors de travaux exécutés à proximité de l'angle nord-ouest de l'église. Conservé à Sainte-Jalle, dans l'église.
Dimensions : 80 x 39/40 x 31 cm.
Texte de trois lignes. Champ épigraphique : 18,5 x 31 cm. H. d. l. : l. 1 : 4 ; l. 2–3 : 3 cm. Points ronds de séparation.
AE 2000, 887 ; *CAG, 26*, p. 544, n° 306b.

> *Baginatiab(us) | Primula Quinti f(ilia) | u(otum) s(oluit) l(ibens) m(erito).*
>
> Aux *Baginatiae*, Primula, fille de Quintus, s'est acquittée de son vœu volontiers et à juste titre.

Date : antérieure à 212 ou de peu postérieure.

16 – Sainte-Jalle (Drôme). Dédicace votive aux *Baginiatiae* par Caius Girubius Cato.

Autel, en calcaire granuleux, avec base moulurée, dont le couronnement a été brisé. On voit encore les traces sur la face supérieure d'une *lysis* à trois acrotères reliée par une moulure centrale au *focus*.
Découvert, en 1999, à Sainte-Jalle, lors de travaux exécutés à proximité de l'angle nord-ouest de l'église. Conservé à Sainte-Jalle, dans l'église.
Dimensions : 117 x 46 x 38/39 cm.
Texte de cinq lignes. Champ épigraphique : 44 x 37 cm. H. d. l. : l. 1 : 6 ; l. 2 : 4,5 ; l. 3 : 4 ; l. 4 : 3,5 ; l. 5 : 4 cm. Séparation par *hederae* et palme (l. 5).
AE 2000, 886 ; *CAG, 26*, p. 544, n° 306c.

> *Bagini|atiabus | C(aius) Girubiu | Cato | u(otum) s(oluit) l(ibens) m(erito).*
>
> Aux *Baginiatiae*, Caius Girubius Cato s'est acquitté de son vœu volontiers et à juste titre.

Date : Ier–IIIe siècles.

17 – Vaison (Vaucluse). Donation, en grec, à Belesama d'un lieu sacré (*nemeton*) par Segomaros, fils de Villu, un pérégrin, citoyen de Nîmes.

Plaque rectangulaire, en calcaire à grain très fin, retaillée de partout.
Découverte, vers 1835/1840, à Vaison, 'au sud et à 100 ou 200 pas, de l'enclos des Cordeliers'. Conservée à Avignon, au musée Calvet (n° inv. E 25).
25 x 31 x 6,5 cm.
Texte de sept lignes. H. d. l. : 2–4 cm.
CIL XII, p. 162 ; *RIG* I, G-153 : *CAG, 84/1*, p. 288, n° 137, 326* ; Gascou & Guyon 2005, 3–4, n° 1.

> Σεγομαρος | Ουιλλονεος | τοουτιους | Ναμαυσατις | ειωρου Βηλη|σαμι σοσιν | νεμητον
>
> Segomaros, fils de Villu, citoyen de Nîmes, a offert à Belesama cet enclos sacré.

Date : IIe siècle–première moitié du Ier siècle av. J.-C.

18 – Vaison. Dédicace à Boutrix.

Bloc rectangulaire, en mollasse de Beaumont, retaillé de partout, en vue d'un remploi.
Signalé, en 1962, à Vaison, au quartier de Théos, en remploi. Conservé à Vaison, au musée Théo Desplans (inv. n° 990.51.001, réserves).
Dimensions : 54 x 41,5 x 8 cm.
Texte de deux lignes. H. d. l. : l. 1 : 6,2–6,9 ; l. 2 : 6,8–7,2 cm.
AE 1992, 1204 ; *CAG, 84/1*, p. 341, n° 427*.

> *Sacrum | Boutrici.*
>
> Consacré à Boutrix.

Date : Ier–IIIe siècles.

19 – Vaison. Dédicace fragmentaire (?) à Dulovius.

'*Basis exigua*'. Sur le devant est sculpté un personnage assis entouré de palmes ; l'inscription est gravée sur l'autre face.
Signalée, au XVIIe siècle, à Vaison, dans l'évêché. Une origine vaisonnaise est donc très probable. Perdue.
Dimensions indéterminées.
Texte d'une ligne. H. d. l. inconnue.
CIL XII 1279, d'après Suarès, *Codex Vaticanus* 9141, f° 13', n° 15 (*CAG, 84/1*, p. 115, n° 31*).

Dulouio.

À Dulovius.

Date : Ier–IIIe siècles.

20 – Vaison. Dédicace votive à Dullovius par Marcus Licinius Goas, un citoyen romain.

'*Basis*'.
Signalée, au XVIIe siècle, à Vaison, chez Robert Blégier, l'actuel château de La Villasse. Perdue.
Dimensions indéterminées.
Texte de quatre lignes. H. d. l. inconnue. Points de séparation.
CIL XII 1280, d'après Fabri de Pereisc, *Codex Parisinus Latinus* 8957, f° 219 et 8958, f° 240 (*CAG, 84/1*, p. 114–5, n° 30*).

Dullouio / M(arcus) Licinius / Goas / u(otum) s(oluit) l(ibens) m(erito).

À Dullovius, Marcus Licinius Goas s'est acquitté de son vœu, volontiers et à juste titre.

Date : Ier siècle.

21 – Beaumont-du-Ventoux (Vaucluse). Donation à Subronis Sumelis par Voretovirius, un pérégrin, d'un monument indéterminé. Photo 3.

Stèle (?), en mollasse de Beaumont, brisée en haut et assez largement ébréchée à droite.
Signalée, en 1848, à Beaumont-du-Ventoux, 'dans la maison Saint-Bonnet' (Deloye). Conservée à Malaucène, dans la collection Chastel.
Dimensions : 49 x 32,5 x 11,5 cm.
Texte de quatre lignes. H. d. l. : 5,1–5,3 cm. Séparation par *hedera* (l. 2) et par losange (l. 4).
CIL XII 1351, d'après Deloye 1847–1848, 326 + 825 ; *CAG, 84/1*, p. 415, n° 015, 9*, avec fig. 729.

Subroni / Sumeli / Voreto/uirius f(ecit).

À Subronis Sumelis, Voretovirius a fait (ce monument).

Date : antérieure à 212 ou de peu postérieure.

22 – Lardiers (Alpes-de-Haute-Provence). Dédicace fragmentaire à Belado (?) par un *incertus* anonyme.

Autel, en calcaire, brisé en deux fragments non jointifs. De la partie supérieure (A), il reste la partie droite du dé et du couronnement, dont la moulure semble avoir été arasée ; la base moulurée (B) est fragmentaire et anépigraphe. Il manque toute la partie centrale du dé.
Partie A : découverte, en 1961, à Lardiers, dans le sanctuaire du Chastelard, lors des fouilles de G. Barruol, entre les niches I et II de la voie sacrée ; partie B : retrouvée, en 1962, dans la niche II de la voie sacrée. Conservées à Apt, au musée.
Dimensions : partie A : 47 x 31 x 22,5 cm ; partie B : 77 x 64 x 40 cm.
Texte, mutilé à gauche et en bas, de trois lignes. H. d. l. : l. 1 : 10 ; l. 2 : 7,5 ; l. 3 : (?) cm.
Rolland 1962, 655 ; Barruol 1990, 56–7 (*CAG, 04*, n° 101, p. 250,3*).

[Bel]adon(i) ? / [---]urum / [---]++ / ---

À Belado (?),[---].

Date : Ier–IIIe s.

23 – Limans (Alpes-de-Haute-Provence). Dédicace votive fragmentaire à Belado par un *incertus* quasi anonyme.

Autel (?), retaillé en vue d'un remploi en haut (couronnement), en bas (base) et à droite, ce qui a fait disparaître la partie droite du texte.
Signalé, en 1904, à Limans, où il servait 'de montant à la porte d'entrée de l'habitation de M. Charles Canard'. Conservé à Mane, au musée-conservatoire de Salagnon.
Dimensions : 50 x 15 x (?) cm.
Texte de quatre lignes. Point triangulaire de séparation.
É. Espérandieu, *Revue Épigraphique*, V, n° 111, octobre–décembre 1903, p. 49, n° 1557, d'après une copie de Lieutaud (*AE* 1904, 143 ; *ILGN* 219 ; Barruol, 1990, p. 56–7, avec une photo ; *CAG, 04*, p. 253, n° 104,2*).

Bela[doni] / Co+[---] / Vrs[---] / u(otum s(oluit) [l(ibens) m(erito)].

À Belado, Co[---] Urs[---] s'est acquitté de son vœu, volontiers et à juste titre.

Date : Ier–IIIe s.

24 – Limans (Alpes-de-Haute-Provence). Dédicace votive fragmentaire à Belado par un citoyen romain.

'Autel brisé de tous les côtés, sauf à gauche'.
Signalé, en 1904, à Limans, où 'il servait de chambranle à une fenêtre de l'habitation de M. Mary Testanière'. Pourrait être conservé sous l'épais crépi de la maison.
Dimensions : 69 x 22 x 13 cm.
Texte, sans doute mal lu par l'inventeur, de quatre lignes. H. d. l. : 4, 5 cm. Points de séparation.
É. Espérandieu, *Revue Épigraphique*, V, n° 111, octobre–décembre 1903, p. 49, n° 1556, d'après une copie de Lieutaud (*AE* 1904, 142 ; *ILGN* 220).

Bela[doni] | u(otum) s(oluit) [l(ibens) m(erito)] | T(itus) Ven+ [---] | Cila I[---].

À Belado, s'est acquitté de son vœu Titus Ven[---] Cila[---].

Date : Ier–IIIe siècles, peut-être avant *ca* 150 en raison des *tria nomina* du *cultor*.

25 – Lurs (Alpes-de-Haute-Provence). Dédicace votive fragmentaire à Alaunius par un citoyen romain.

Autel, en calcaire, brisé en bas, à gauche et à droite, avec couronnement mouluré.
Découverte, en 1730, par le père Palun, lors de fouilles, à Lurs, à 'cent pas' de la chapelle Notre-Dame-des-Anges (Abbé Millou, *Man. 1850–1854*, p. 7–8). Conservé à Lurs, dans le mur nord de la chapelle Notre-Dame-des-Anges.
Dimensions : 50 x 30 cm.
Texte, mutilé à gauche (l. 1 et 3) et à droite (l. 3), de trois lignes, peut-être entouré d'un cadre mouluré.
CIL XII 1518, d'après Arbaud, *Bulletin du Var*, 1, 1868, p. 195 et Laurière 1878, 475 (*CAG, 04*, p. 259–60,13*) ; Barruol & Martel 1962, 162–3.

[---]us Tacitus | Alaunio | [---] s(ua ?) p(ecunia ?). V(otum) s(oluit) l(ibens) [m(erito)].

[---]us Tacitus, à ses frais (?), s'est acquitté de son vœu volontiers et à juste titre.

Date : la forme de la dédicace pourrait permettre de dater le texte du Ier siècle, où le nom du *cultor* précède souvent celui de la divinité (Cibu 2003, 353–5).

BIBLIOGRAPHIE

Barruol, G. 1963 'Mars *Nabelcus* et Mars *Albiorix*', *Ogam* 15, 4–5, 345–68.

Barruol, G. 1990 'Cultes et sanctuaires : autres témoins', *Archéologie au pays de Forcalquier : radioscopie d'un territoire rural.* Mane, Les Alpes de Lumière.

Barruol, G. & P. Martel, 1962 'La voie romaine de Cavaillon à Sisteron sous le Haut-Empire', *Revue d'Études Ligures* 28, 125–202.

Béraud, M. 2014 'Ventidia Nice et Ventidia Primula : une affranchie et sa patronne à Nîmes au début du IIe s. ap. J.-C.', *Domitia* 13, 61–82.

Christol, M. & M. Janon, 2004 '*Albarinus*, dieu indigène dans la cité de Carpentras (Gaule Narbonnaise)', *Zeitschrift für Papyrologie und Epigrafik* 146, 272–7.

Cibu, S. 2003 'Chronologie et formulaire dans les inscriptions religieuses de Narbonnaise et des provinces alpines (Alpes graies, pœnines, cottiennes et maritimes)', *Revue Archéologique de Narbonnaise* 36, 335–60.

Clerc, M. 1906 *La bataille d'Aix.* Paris, Fontemoing.

Delamarre, X. 2003 *Dictionnaire de la langue gauloise*, 2e éd. Paris, Errance.

Delamarre, X. 2007 Nomina Celtica Antiqua Selecta Inscriptionum. *Noms de personnes celtiques dans l'épigraphie classique.* Paris, Errance.

Deloye, A. 1847–1848 'Inscriptions grecques et latines découvertes à Vaison', *Bulletin de l'École des Chartes* 2e sér., 4, 305–38.

Desaye, H. 1999 'Le territoire des Voconces et ses subdivisions aux Ier et IIe siècles', *Terres voconces* 1, 17–24.

Desaye, H., J.-M. Lurol & J.-Cl. Mège 2000 'Découverte d'autels aux déesses *Baginatiae* à Sainte-Jalle (Drôme)', *Revue Archéologique de Narbonnaise* 33, 178–93.

Dondin-Payre, M. & M.-Th. Raepsaet-Charlier 2001 'Critères de datation épigraphique pour les Gaules et les Germanies', *Noms, identités culturelles et romanisation sous le Haut-Empire*, éd. M. Dondin-Payre & M.-Th. Raepsaet-Charlier, IX-XIV. Bruxelles, Le livre Timperman.

Dondin-Payre, M. & M.-Th. Raepsaet-Charlier 2006 'Critères de datation des inscriptions religieuses', *Sanctuaires, pratiques cultuelles et territoires civiques dans l'Occident romain*, éd. M. Dondin-Payre & M.-Th. Raepsaet-Charlier, XIII. Bruxelles, Le livre Timperman.

Dumézil, G. 1966 *La religion romaine archaïque.* Paris, 2e éd., Paris, Payot, 1987.

Fabri de Pereisc, N.-Cl. *Codex Parisinus Latinus* n° 8957, conservé à Paris, à la BNF.

Gascou, J. & J. Guyon 2005 *La collection d'inscriptions gallo-grecques et latines du Musée Calvet.* Paris, de Boccard.

Goudineau, Chr. & Y. de Kisch 1999 *Vaison-la-Romaine.* Paris, Ministère de la Culture.

Häussler, R. 2008 'Pouvoir et religion dans un paysage gallo-romain : les cités d'Apt et d'Aix-en-Provence', *Romanisation et épigraphie. Études interdisciplinaires sur l'acculturation et l'identité dans l'Empire romain*, dir. R. Häussler, 155–248. Montagnac, éd. M. Mergoil.

Häussler, R. 2012 '*Interpretatio indigena.* Re-inventing local cults in a global world', *Mediterraneo Antico* 15, 1–2, 143–74.

Lambert, P.-Y. 2013 'Le statut du théonyme gaulois', *Théonymie celtique, cultes,* interpretatio. *Keltische Theonymie, Kulte,* interpretatio. *X. Workshop F.E.R.C.A.N., Paris, 24–26 mai 2010*, éd. A. Hofeneder & P. de Bernardo Stempel, avec la collaboration de M. Hainzmann & N. Mathieu, 113–24. Vienne, Verlag der Österreichischen Akademie der Wissenschaften.

Laurière, J. de 1878 'Quelques inscriptions romaines du département des Basses-Alpes', *Bulletin Monumental* 44, 474–85.

Leveau, Ph. 1993 'Agglomérations secondaires et territoires en Gaule Narbonnaise', *Revue Archéologique de Narbonnaise* 26, 277–99.

Martène, Dom Éd. & Dom U. Durand 1717 *Voyage littéraire de deux religieux bénédictins de la congrégation de Saint-Maur*, vol. 1. Paris.

Moreau de Vérone, M. J. B. 1837 'Mémoire sur les Voconces par M. de Vérone', publié après sa mort par J. Ollivier, *Bulletin de la Société d'Archéologie et de Statistique de la Drôme* 1, 70–96 et 129–65.

Raepsaet-Charlier, M.-Th. 2006a 'Les dévots dans les lieux de culte de Germanie supérieure et la géographie sacrée de la province', *Sanctuaires, pratiques cultuelles et territoires civiques dans l'Occident romain*, éd. M. Dondin-Payre & M.-Th. Raepsaet-Charlier, 347–435. Bruxelles, Le livre Timperman.

Raepsaet-Charlier, M.-Th. 2006b 'Les *cultores* de Mars en Gaule Belgique', *Mars en Occident. Actes du colloque international 'Autour d'Allones (Sarthe). Les sanctuaires de Mars en Occident', Le Mans, Université du Maine, 4–5–6 juin, 2003*, éd. V. Brouquier-Reddé, E. Bertrand, M.-B. Chardenoux, K. Gruel & M.-Cl. L'Huillier, 45–62. Rennes, PUR.

Rémy, B. 2008 'Borvo, Vintius et Coriotana dans la cité de Vienne', *Divindades indígenas em análise. Divinités pré-romaines. Bilan et perspectives d'une recherche. Actas do VII Workshop FERCAN, Cascais, 25–27.05.2006*, dir. J. d'Encarnaçao, 237–51. Coimbra-Porto.

Rémy, B. 2013 '*Baginus*, les déesses *Baginatiae* et les déesses mères *Baginienses* chez les Voconces, Jupiter *Baginas* dans la cité de Vienne', *Keltische Götternamen als Individuelle Option? Akten des 11. internationalen Workshops 'Fontes Epigraphici Religionum Celticarum Antiquarum' vom 19.–21. Mai 2011 an der Universität Erfurt*, éd. W. Spickermann, avec la collaboration de L. Scheuermann, 213–21. Rahden, Verlag Marie Leidorf.

Rolland, H. 1962 'Informations archéologiques, Circonscription d'Aix-en-Provence (secteur nord)', *Gallia* 20, 2, 655–63 (Basses-Alpes).

Sablayrolles, R. & J.-L. Schenck 1988 *Collections du musée archéologique départemental de Saint-Bertrand-de-Comminges*. I, *les autels votifs.* Saint-Bertrand-de-Comminges, Conseil général de la Haute-Garonne.

Sautel, J. 1936 'Découvertes gallo-romaines de M. Marius Sage à Caromb et dans ses environs', *Rhodania*, 57–64.

Sautel, J. 1939 Forma Orbis Romani. *Carte archéologique de la Gaule romaine. Carte et texte du département du Vaucluse.* Paris.

Scheid, J. 2006a 'Les dévotions en Germanie inférieure : divinités, lieux de culte, fidèles', *Sanctuaires, pratiques cultuelles et territoires civiques dans l'Occident romain*, éd. M. Dondin-Payre & M.-Th. Raepsaet-Charlier, 297–346. Bruxelles, Le livre Timperman.

Scheid, J. 2006b 'Réflexions sur le Mars trévire', *Mars en Occident. Actes du colloque international 'Autour d'Allones (Sarthe). Les sanctuaires de Mars en Occident', Le Mans, Université du Maine, 4–5–6 juin, 2003*, éd. V. Brouquier-Reddé, E. Bertrand, M.-B. Chardenoux, K. Gruel & M.-Cl. L'Huillier, 35–44. Rennes, PUR.

Scheid, J. 2013. *Les dieux, l'État et l'Individu : réflexions sur la religion civique à Rome*. Paris, Les éditions du Seuil.

Sergent, B. 1990 'Les origines sacrées de Bavay', *Mythologie en Nord. Actes du IV*e *Congrès international de Mythologie, Lille, août 1989*, éd. Société de Mythologie française, 247–61. Beauvais, Société de Mythologie française.

Suarès, J.-M. de *Codex Vaticanus* 9141, Manuscrit ayant été la propriété du cardinal F. Barberini; déposé ensuite à la Bibliothèque du Vatican.

Van Andringa, W. 2006 'Nouvelles combinaisons, nouveaux statuts. Les dieux indigènes dans les panthéons des cités de Gaule romaine', *Celtes et Gaulois face à l'histoire. La romanisation et la question de l'héritage celtique. Actes de la table ronde de Lausanne, 17–18 juin 2005*, dir. D. Paunier, 193–218. Glux-en-Glenne, Centre archéologique européen.

XVI

DE TARANIS AU JUPITER CAVALIER À L'ANGUIPÈDE : RÉFLEXIONS AUTOUR DU SUBSTRAT CELTIQUE DANS LA RELIGION GALLO-ROMAINE

Florian Blanchard

From the inventory of Gallo-Roman images of Jupiter, the author reflects on the links between Taranis and Jupiter. This is to define the nature and role of the Celtic substratum in the Gallo-Roman religion.

RÉCEMMENT encore, historiens et chercheurs mettaient en exergue la prégnance et l'influence d'un substrat culturel et religieux celtique dans le culte de Jupiter pendant la période romaine[1]. Celui-ci était souvent décrit comme l'abâtardissement plus ou moins volontaire et conscient d'une divinité celtique aux fonctions proches de Jupiter, Taranis, dont le culte aurait subsisté à l'époque romaine notamment à travers les images du dieu à la roue et du cavalier à l'anguipède. Depuis plus d'un siècle, linguistes, historiens, archéologues, chercheurs comparatistes tentent de mettre en évidence les liens unissant Taranis et Jupiter, notamment lorsque ce dernier arbore une roue en s'appuyant sur l'unique source littéraire où Taranis est cité comme une divinité gauloise majeure, le texte de Lucain. Les termes du débat historique et de ses postulats sont demeurés invariables : quelle était la personnalité de Taranis ? Quelle était la réalité de son culte ? Quel poids a eu ce dernier dans le phénomène complexe et multiforme de l'*interpretatio romana* ? Ce questionnement a été derechef alimenté par les spécificités iconographiques jupitériennes en Gaule, ce dieu ayant parfois comme attribut une roue ou étant représenté à partir de la première moitié du IIe siècle comme un cavalier terrassant un ou des anguipèdes. Celles-ci ont été le plus souvent interprétées comme le signe tangible d'un héritage celtique prégnant dans le culte de Jupiter. Ainsi, la question de l'impact d'un substrat religieux gaulois, et surtout celui du culte de Taranis, dans la façon qu'ont eue les Gallo-romains, du Neckar à la Garonne, de se représenter

1 Deyts 1992, 97–101 par exemple.

Jupiter que ce soit à travers son iconographie, sa nature et ses fonctions, a polarisé la recherche parfois au détriment de notre connaissance de la religion gallo-romaine.

Cette communication ne se fixe pas pour ambition de renouveler fondamentalement les problématiques car les sources à notre disposition restent maigres, voire indigentes, et de nombreux chercheurs ont eu l'occasion de les interroger. Il s'agit plus d'ici de mesurer l'acquis de nos connaissances sur les liens unissant Taranis et Jupiter, le substrat celtique et la religion gallo-romaine. Notre propos traitera pour une large part de la question de l'iconographie singulière de Jupiter en Gaule : est-elle le refuge du conservatisme religieux gaulois et le signe de la résistance du culte de Taranis comme cela a été si souvent avancé ? La réalité semble plus nuancée. Le réexamen des sources antiques et l'histoire de l'art sont en mesure d'apporter quelques éléments susceptibles à la fois d'enrichir notre appréhension de la religion gallo-romaine et de ses images inconnues dans l'art gréco-romain.

A la recherche de Taranis et du substrat celtique

Malgré la multitude d'études se référant aux vers de Lucain, mener une réflexion sur le substrat gaulois ne peut faire l'économie d'un réexamen de ceux-ci. Hormis l'*excursus* ethnographique de César au livre VI de *La Guerre des Gaules*, notre principale source littéraire sur les dieux gaulois demeure *La Guerre Civile*, appelée communément et par erreur *La Pharsale*, rédigée par Lucain[2]. Ce texte est celui qui a suscité le plus grand nombre d'exégèses et de recherches. Dans un des passages du poème consacré à la description de la Gaule (I.392–466), il dresse la liste les peuples celtes à l'époque de César (I.444–446) et parlant de ceux-ci, il écrit : « et ceux qui apaisent par un sang détestable le féroce Teutatès, le hideux Esus sur ses foyers cruels et Taranis, autel non moins inhumain que celui de la Diane de Scythie ». Ces quelques vers traitent des dieux vénérés par les Gaulois, de leur culte et des pratiques rituelles associées. Deux autres hypertextes apportent des indications supplémentaires sur la personnalité de ces trois dieux[3]. Un commentateur des vers de Lucain dans un manuscrit daté du Xe siècle dont les parties les plus anciennes pourraient dater du IVème siècle note :

> Mercurius est dans le parler des Gaulois nommé Teutates, lequel était honoré chez eux de sang humain. Teutates-Mercurius chez les Gaulois est apaisé ainsi : dans un cuveau empli, un homme est plongé par la tête, pour y être asphyxié. Esus-Mars est apaisé ainsi : un homme est suspendu à un arbre jusqu'à ce que, par suite de l'effusion de son sang, il ait laissé aller ses membres. Taranis-Ditis pater est apaisé chez eux de la façon suivante : dans une cuve de bois, un certain nombre d'hommes sont brûlés.

Le rédacteur poursuit en parlant d'autres témoignages :

> Nous avons trouvé de même par la suite des témoignages variant selon les auteurs. [...]. Et pour Jupiter, le maître des guerres et le plus grand des dieux Taranis,

2 Lucain, *La guerre civile* I–IV 2003, éd. Bourgery.
3 *Scholies de Lucain* 1869, éd. Usener.

> habitué jadis à être apaisé par des têtes humaines, aujourd'hui à se réjouir de têtes de bétail[4].

L'auteur a visiblement compilé de nombreux témoignages sur les divinités citées par Lucain pour rendre ces vers plus accessibles à ses lecteurs. Nous ignorons les sources auxquelles lui-même a eu recours mais il faut remarquer que celui-ci met avant tout en exergue les modalités rituelles pratiquées lors des cultes par les Gaulois. Si l'on suit les commentateurs de Lucain, à l'image des sacrifices humains qui ont cédé la place à celui du bétail, le culte de Jupiter s'est substitué à celui de Taranis.

Bien que cela paraisse incohérent de prime abord, cet extrait, si souvent pris en référence, suscite plus d'interrogations qu'il n'apporte de réelles connaissances sur les équivalences entre les divinités gauloises et romaines si on le confronte à un examen critique. Il est nécessaire de s'interroger sur la finalité poursuivie par l'auteur dans ce passage, sur son choix de nommer trois divinités gauloises au contraire de César qui soulignait les accointances entre les panthéons gaulois et romain, sans les citer. Plus encore, c'est la réalité chronologique des sources employées par Lucain et ses commentateurs qui doit être examinée car elle fonde tout l'intérêt et la portée de ce témoignage littéraire. Lucain a-t-il recueilli lui-même ces informations par une observation directe ou rapporte-t-il des faits anciens ? A l'image d'autres auteurs de cette période, Lucain a probablement puisé dans des œuvres existantes diverses informations nécessaires à sa description des Gaulois et de leurs mœurs. La composition du passage qui nous intéresse, dans lequel César rappelle ses légions de Gaule, illustre la multiplicité des recours de l'auteur à des écrits antérieurs qu'il synthétise et réactualise. En effet, le texte associe des relevés géographiques du territoire gaulois, la description des peuples qui y vivent mais également des considérations sur l'origine des marées avant de conclure par l'évocation des divinités gauloises et du rôle des druides[5]. Certains faits cités dans ces passages nous éclairent potentiellement sur la nature et la datation des ouvrages sur lesquels ces passages s'appuient. Ainsi, l'intérêt pour l'origine des marées renvoie à une question largement débattue par les savants grecs notamment Timée de Taormine ; Lucain compile les différentes hypothèses apportées au fil des siècles (rôle des fleuves, des vents, des astres...) avant d'indiquer que personnellement, il y voit la volonté des dieux[6]. De plus, nous savons qu'une partie des informations géographiques mais surtout les éléments ethnographiques traitant des druides sont en fait une reprise plus ou moins partielle d'écrits de Poseidonios d'Apamée[7]. Comme l'a mis en exergue Jean-Louis Brunaux à propos des auteurs traitant des druides en Gaule, César, Strabon, Diodore et Lucain, pour ne citer que ceux-ci, compilent le texte de Poséidonios[8]. Ce savant grec voyage en Gaule au début du Ier siècle av. J.-C., son récit est constitué d'observations mais également de références à d'autres ouvrages antérieurs des IIe et

4 Heichelheim 1932 ; Duval 1958–1959, 41–8.
5 Pichon 1912, 23–34.
6 'Timaios', RE VI.2 (1936), 1076–1203.
7 *Posidonius*, I *The Fragments* (1972), II *The Commentary* (1988), III *The Translation* (1999), éd. Kidd I. G.. Cambridge, Cambridge University Press.
8 Brunaux 2006, 199–219.

IIe siècles av. J.-C. Il faut donc relativiser l'historicité des informations apportées par Lucain. Les cultes et les rituels décrits en Gaule sont-ils pratiqués à l'époque césarienne par l'ensemble de ces peuples ? Cette assertion est à considérer avec circonspection. Bien que nous sachions par l'archéologie que les Gaulois érigeaient lors de certains conflits des trophées humains pouvant être rapprochés des rituels décrits, la pratique exceptionnelle des sacrifices paraît toutefois s'estomper partir du IIIe siècle av. J.-C. Ceci accrédite d'ailleurs l'ancienneté des sources utilisées par Lucain[9]. De plus, cette évocation des dieux gaulois et de leur culte sanguinaire est un *topos* fréquent et attendu dans la littérature gréco-latine. Lucain y exacerbe volontairement dans le registre épique le contraste entre la sauvagerie des cultes gaulois et la culture méditerranéenne. Enfin, Lucain est peu disert sur la diffusion géographique de ces cultes. Nous ignorons si ces divinités sont honorées partout en Gaule ou sont celles de certains peuples. La formulation de ces vers est absconse. Cette indication paraît ne pas concerner la totalité des Gaulois à l'époque de César mais s'appliquer à quelques peuples sans que l'on puisse déterminer s'il s'agit des Trévires et les Ligures cités précédemment ou d'autres populations[10]. Surtout aucun indice ne nous est apporté sur leur essence. Ces observations sur la composition du passage de Lucain démontrent que ce témoignage littéraire synthétise des informations d'époques et d'origines diverses. Il faut donc rester prudent sur la réalité chronologique et la diffusion géographique des cultes gaulois cités. Gardons-nous de généraliser la valeur de cette source et d'ériger ces divinités en triade nationale gauloise à l'époque de la conquête césarienne.

Ajoutons, par ailleurs, que face au laconisme de ce passage, nous ne nous pouvons que nous référer aux équivalences tardives des commentateurs. Il paraît également nécessaire de s'interroger sur l'établissement de telles correspondances et sur la nature des matériaux mythologiques employés. Les commentateurs et les scholiastes n'ont-ils pas simplement procédé à un rapprochement étymologique entre Jupiter et la racine *taran* pour établir une corrélation entre deux dieux tonnants, Taranis et Jupiter en dévidant les renseignements compilés au sein de sources variées[11]. Par ailleurs, ces renseignements sur les identités divines et les équivalences sont mal-assurées voire contradictoires dans les différentes occurrences : Taranis est rapproché de Jupiter et de Dis Pater alors que Teutates et Esus sont rapprochés de Mars et Mercure. La définition de Taranis vaut explication de son équivalence avec Jupiter, les commentateurs indiquent que Taranis est le plus grand des dieux du ciel et le maître des guerres. Il faut souligner que la séparation entre Jupiter maître des guerres et Mars dieu du combat sur le terrain, tradition purement romaine, est appliquée ici au panthéon gaulois. Cette répartition purement romaine des fonctions guerrières et la précision « *caelestium deorum maximum* » nous éclairent sur la méthode employée par le commentateur pour définir la personnalité de Taranis. N'a-t-il pas voulu justifier l'équivalence entre Taranis et Jupiter en apposant les principales fonctions joviennes à la personnalité de

9 Brunaux 1995.
10 Duval 1958–1959, 41–2.
11 Vendryes 1997, 32 ; Lambrechts 1942, 65.

Taranis ? Le syncrétisme mis en lumière entre les deux divinités semble provenir d'une *interpretatio romana* bien tardive, à une époque où la religion polythéiste disparaît et où le souvenir de la religion gauloise s'est largement perdu. Pour les scholiastes, il est important d'établir une équivalence entre les divinités citées par Lucain et celles que César a listées et ordonnancées dans *De Bello Gallico*[12]. Force est de constater, une fois ces faits mis en évidence, que l'équivalence entre Jupiter et Taranis n'offre qu'une vision tronquée, voire contradictoire, de la réalité religieuse de la Gaule indépendante où l'ethnocentrisme romain et la volonté syncrétique ne laissent que peu de place à la nuance et à un approfondissement des essences divines. Face à l'aporie de ces sources et à la multiplicité de leur origine, mener une recherche systématique des équivalences entre deux panthéons à partir d'une simple correspondance étymologique ou de commentaires impose de rester lucide et circonspect devant la tentation de faire de Taranis une divinité honorée par tous les Gaulois et le parfait pendant de Jupiter. Ces indices littéraires ne sont pas probants pour suggérer un puissant substrat celtique et un syncrétisme dans lequel Jupiter aurait recouvert et supplanté Taranis, divinité principale des Gaulois.

Toutefois, il faut porter au crédit de Lucain la citation de théonymes attestés par la toponymie, l'anthroponymie et l'épigraphie notamment[13]. Ainsi, une inscription en alphabet grec mise au jour à Orgon en Narbonnaise mentionne explicitement *Taranus* (Taranis). Pourtant, ce dernier ne semble avoir que peu subi l'*interpretatio romana* en Gaule puisqu'à ce jour sa personnalité n'est pas associée à celle de Jupiter. Le seul exemple attesté d'une épiclèse formée sur la racine *taran-* est celui de Skradin en Dalmatie où Arria Successa invoque *Iovi Taranuco*[14]. A Chester en Bretagne, c'est l'épiclèse *Tanaro* qui est associée à la titulature capitoline dans l'invocation. En Germanie Supérieure, dans les localités de Böckingen et de Godramstein, deux dédicaces sont adressées au *Deo Taranucno* comme une divinité à part entière selon les normes religieuses gréco-romaines[15]. Si l'on y retrouve la racine *taran-*, le suffixe terminal *–cnus* renvoie ici à une filiation (fils de *Taranus* ? dieu engendré par le tonnerre ?). On peut se demander si ces deux témoignages, découverts à une centaine de kilomètres l'un de l'autre, ne sont pas dédiés à une divinité topique car ils sont réalisés *ex iussu*, sur l'ordre du dieu. A Godramstein, le formulaire dédicatoire, datable de la fin du IIe ou du IIIe siècle, mentionne le théonyme de manière tronquée (seule la traverse du T apparaît au-dessus du A) et précise que cet autel et peut-être d'autres offrandes ont été financés par l'entremise d'une collecte. Les circonstances des dédicaces et cette alternance *Taranus/Tanarus/Taranucnus* dans un corpus déjà très réduit amène à s'interroger sur l'appartenance de ces trois formes linguistiques à un seul théonyme, et donc à une seule divinité. S'agit-il d'une métathèse linguistique issue de formes archaïques ou est-ce l'indice d'une absence d'équivalence religieuse[16] ? Même si l'on retient l'hypothèse de la

12 Sjoestedt 2009, 35.
13 Le Roux 1958, 30–5.
14 CIL III, 2804.
15 CIL XIII, 6094 et 6478.
16 Le Roux 1958, 38–9. Green 1982, 38–9. Haeussler 2008, 24–5.

métathèse, ce théonyme serait certes commun à plusieurs provinces de l'ère celtique[17] mais ces témoignages demeurent ambivalents. En effet, si l'on compare le nombre de ces occurrences avec celles des autres divinités gauloises, on s'aperçoit que ce dernier ne devait pas être un culte au premier plan dans le monde celtique. En effet, Belenus a reçu une cinquantaine de dévotions et Teutates (Toutatis) une quinzaine pour ne citer qu'eux[18]. Ainsi, le rayonnement de celui-ci dans le panthéon celtique semble limité au regard de ces occurrences épigraphiques. Cela d'autant plus que deux témoignages traditionnellement recensés par les études consacrées à Taranis sont à écarter. Sur l'autel de Thauron en Aquitaine, le mot *Tarunuen* placé sur la dédicace après l'invocation à Jupiter et au *numen* impérial est plus probablement un anthroponyme qu'une épiclèse au regard de la formule dédicatoire[19]. La situation semble similaire à Amiens où la graffite *Taranuos* inscrite sur le col d'un vase fait penser à un nom de propriétaire ou d'artisan, plutôt qu'à une dédicace[20].

Quelles fonctions pouvaient avoir ces épiclèses et plus généralement ces formulaires d'invocation ? S'agissait-il d'associer deux essences divines ou d'insister sur le caractère tonnant de Jupiter, sur sa fonction de dieu du tonnerre, par le truchement d'un théonyme ou d'un surnom vernaculaire ? Ces remarques touchent le nœud du problème. Ces dédicaces s'adressent-elles à un dieu spécifique perçu de manière équivalente par l'ensemble des *cultores* ou ces témoignages renvoient-ils plus simplement à une divinité du tonnerre dont l'essence est parfois mal individualisée ? Les éléments manquent pour trancher et le dossier épigraphique se révèle bien mince après examen.

Pendant de nombreuses années, les écrits de Lucain et les témoignages épigraphiques sont demeurés les seules sources que l'historien pouvait interroger alimentant l'essentiel des exégèses sur la place du culte de Taranis en Gaule indépendante. Cependant, les perspectives se sont élargies dans la seconde moitié du XXe siècle avec la traduction en français des textes mythologiques irlandais par Christian Guyonvarc'h renouvelant en profondeur notre appréhension des mythes celtiques[21]. Fruit d'un travail de compilation des légendes mythologiques celtiques par des moines chrétiens irlandais durant le haut Moyen Âge, ces récits, consignés dans le but de les conserver et de les christianiser, évoquent les actions héroïques de plusieurs divinités celtes connues par ailleurs. Il faut noter que le théonyme de Taranis n'y apparaît nullement. L'absence d'un dieu de la foudre témoigne dûment que ce culte n'avait probablement pas un rôle primordial dans le panthéon celtique contrairement à ceux de Lug, Esus, Ogmios et d'autres dont les Irlandais ont tenu à conserver le souvenir. Mais plus que l'absence de Taranis dans ces récits mythologiques, il est difficile de distinguer une divinité dont les fonctions sont équivalentes à celles indiquées par les commentateurs de Lucain pour Taranis ou ayant des accointances avec celles de Jupiter. Malgré l'évhémérisme qu'ont subi ces traditions

17 Gricourt 1990, 292 ; Jufer & Luginbühl 2001, 65–6.
18 Jufer & Luginbühl 2001, 28–9 et 66–7 ; Lacroix 2007, 180–2.
19 Perrier 1960.
20 AE 1966, 269.
21 Guyonvarch 1980.

religieuses, les populations celtiques d'Irlande ne possédaient pas de divinité céleste à part-entière commandant les phénomènes célestes et météorologiques à l'image de Jupiter en Gaule. C'est un élément supplémentaire allant à l'encontre de l'hypothèse communément reproduite qui fait de Taranis, une divinité de premier plan et le prédécesseur de Jupiter. Finalement, les liens historiques et religieux entre les deux divinités sont pour le moins ténus.

D'autres figures divines sous-jacentes : Dagda et Teutates.

Face aux difficultés que revêt l'assimilation Taranis-Jupiter, certains historiens ont mis en évidence des liens unissant Jupiter et d'autres divinités celtiques sous-jacentes. Certains chercheurs comparatistes ont émis l'hypothèse que le dieu Dagda serait dans la religion celtique irlandaise le pendant du Taranis gaulois et du Jupiter romain par l'analogie de certains traits de sa personnalité et de ses fonctions[22]. En effet, Dagda signifie littéralement le « dieu bon ». Or Jupiter est invoqué dans la plus grande partie des inscriptions suivant sa titulature capitoline *Iovi Optimo Maximo* comme « un dieu très bon et très puissant ». D'ailleurs dans les épopées, Dagda porte un surnom *Eochu Ollathir Ruadrofessa*, c'est-à-dire « le père de l'univers chevauchant, le Rouge (soleil) qui sait tout »[23]. On retrouve dans cette titulature des caractères communs avec Jupiter : la place suprême du panthéon comme créateur de l'univers, omniscient et omnipuissant. Mais la comparaison ne peut aller plus loin et Dagda n'est pas l'exact équivalent du Jupiter gallo-romain. Ceci est renforcé par les recherches récentes de Bernard Sergent qui conclut de sa comparaison entre le panthéon celte et grec :

> S'ensuit-il que Zeus, apparenté au Jupiter des Latins, est l'équivalent du Dagda ? Sur un plan théologique général, oui, en ce que l'un et l'autre expriment la sphère de la souveraineté. Ils sont dieux célestes, maîtres de la foudre et du tonnerre. Mais c'est à peu près tout : aucun des mythes et des aspects du Dagda, si l'on excepte son caractère séducteur, ne se retrouve autour de la figure du grand dieu souverain grec[24].

Son aspect physique et son attribut sont à cent lieues du raffinement de l'apparat jupitérien : ventru, hideux, vêtu d'une tunique courte et de bottes fourrées. Il traîne derrière lui une énorme massue montée sur roue et il est le maître de l'abondance nourrissant les hommes de son chaudron inépuisable « que nul ne quitte non repu »[25]. Ceci n'est pas sans rappeler les attributs du dieu au maillet *Sucellus*, le bon frappeur défenseur et nourricier, armé d'une massue et d'un chaudron. La correspondance entre Jupiter et Dagda se cristallise donc sur quelques points de convergence trop incertains et restreints.

La mise au jour de seize autels découverts à Bölcske et au Mont Gellért (Aquincum), sur les anciens territoires des Celtes danubiens, dans la province de Pannonie et datés

22 Sterckx 1992 ; Sergent 2005, 128–9 ; Raydon 2013.
23 De Vries, 46–7.
24 Sergent 2004, 11.
25 Sjoestedt 2009, 50.

des IIe et IIIe siècles, dédiés à *Iuppiter Teutanus* interpelle du fait de l'épiclèse attribuée à ce dieu dans cette cité. Cette dernière n'est pas sans rappeler le dieu Teutatès évoqué par Lucain. Dans ce cas particulier, *Teutanus* se réfère-t-il à Teutatès, dieu du peuple et de la tribu ? Il est difficile de se prononcer tant les dédicaces sont laconiques. Ici, l'épiclèse *Teutanus* pourrait être de nature topique car les autels proviennent d'un sanctuaire public situé sur le territoire du *municipium* puis de la *colonia* d'*Aquincum*. De plus, ceux-ci ont été érigés pour huit d'entre eux le 11 juin pour commémorer des *vota* publics pour la *salus* des Empereurs et l'*incolumitas* de la cité des Eravisques[26]. L'épiclèse semble alors moins évoquer l'assimilation de Jupiter à Teutatès que renvoyer au lieu et à la fonction poliade de ce sanctuaire de la cité des Eravisques. Déjà en 1948, Joseph Vendryes avançait l'idée « que Teutates n'était en somme qu'un adjectif désignant le dieu de la tribu sans qu'il fût nommé autrement ; du moins l'appelait-on ainsi quand on ne voulait pas lui assigner une fonction spécialisée »[27]. A l'instar du cas particulier de Jupiter Teutanus, on peut se demander si, selon les régions du monde celtique, le théonyme Taranis ne renvoie pas à des divinités différentes dont la nature et les fonctions sont diverses.

Une nouvelle fois, la recherche d'une superposition entre Jupiter et une divinité celtique primordiale qu'il aurait supplantée s'avère infructueuse. Il n'y a pas d'adéquation, d'équivalence entre les dieux celtiques et les dieux romains : toute tentative de rapprochements, de chercher des équivalents et des antécédents aux divinités romaines, est illusoire[28]. L'équivalence avec Dagda et Teutatès est tout aussi fragile et inconsistante qu'elle l'était avec Taranis. Il n'existe manifestement pas de divinités indigènes gauloises et/ou celtiques qui préfigurent les divinités romaines du fait de la non-correspondance des panthéons et des pratiques cultuelles de chaque côté des Alpes. Les exemples précédents démontrent que derrière l'unicité supposée de la religion celtique, c'est la différenciation des panthéons locaux qui prime. De là proviennent les perpétuelles hésitations, imprécisions et difficultés des historiens dans cette recherche des prédécesseurs celtiques aux cultes gallo-romains. Cette méthode de recherche ne peut à l'évidence que mener à des contresens, à des rapprochements artificiels et limités qui privent les dieux gallo-romains d'une personnalité autonome. Cette recherche du substrat celtique prend ainsi le pas sur la réalité de la religion gallo-romaine. Prisonnier du poids de la tradition littéraire gréco-romaine, des finalités toutes personnelles de ces auteurs et des équivalences insolubles, le chercheur ne peut se départir de la délicate question de l'héritage celtique. Car bien que le théonyme Taranis soit attesté par nos sources à l'époque impériale et peut-être dans les siècles précédents, le substrat gaulois dans le culte jupitérien ne se résume pas à l'influence de ce dernier mais est plus nuancé et protéiforme à l'instar de ce que d'autres historiens ont pu relever pour d'autres dieux[29].

---

26 Szabo 2006.
27 Vendryes 1997, 33.
28 Thévenot 1957, 37–8 ; Moitrieux 2002, 195–6.
29 Duval 2002, 119–23 ; Lavagne 1979 ; Moitrieux 2002, 171–96.

Ainsi, il est indéniable que Jupiter possède une originalité dans son iconographie, sa personnalité et son culte dans les provinces des Gaules et des Germanies. Par exemple, de nombreuses représentations joviennes gallo-romaines substituent ou associent une roue à la foudre. Celle-ci est souvent considérée comme un attribut provenant d'une divinité gauloise sous-jacente, ne pouvant être autre que Taranis. Ce postulat, établi comme un système de lecture, fait qu'elles ne sont jamais rattachées pleinement à Jupiter. Elles sont soit classées comme des images de Taranis soit comme celles du dieu à la roue[30]. Ces dernières datent toutes de la période gallo-romaine et aucun argument ne permet de définir la roue comme l'attribut d'une divinité à l'époque de l'indépendance. L'unique image datée de l'époque de l'indépendance qui pourrait représenter un dieu à la roue est gravée sur le chaudron cultuel du Gundestrup dont le postulat tient à la présence d'une roue. Les hypothèses sur ce chaudron que ce soit sur sa datation, sur son lieu de fabrication et son rôle cultuel sont aussi nombreuses que les publications qui le concernent[31]. Nous ne reprendrons pas ici le débat sur cet artefact. Ce chaudron figure un peuple, peut-être en guerre ou victorieux, dont les cavaliers et des fantassins en marche sont entourés de leurs divinités et héros. Certaines plaques figurent aussi des sacrifices rituels. L'agencement des plaques martelées suggère l'écoulement d'un cycle dans lequel s'insère la bataille.

La plaque qui nous intéresse montre au centre un dieu dont seul le buste est visible, la barbe et les cheveux tressés. Il dresse ses deux bras, une de ses mains serre une roue à moitié visible soutenue par un guerrier agenouillé vêtu d'une cotte de maille et d'un casque à corne de bovins. Les deux personnages sont entourés d'un bestiaire associant trois griffons, un serpent à tête de bélier et deux carnassiers (félidés ?). Le seul lien supposé entre cette divinité et Taranis serait donc la roue saisie par le dieu. Pour autant, la signification de cette scène et l'identité du dieu nous sont inaccessibles. Est-ce Taranis ou une divinité céleste particulière à un peuple qui est intégré(e) aux scènes mythologiques du chaudron ? Le dieu est associé à un guerrier : doit-on y voir un épisode mythologique, d'un dieu et d'un intercesseur? Faute d'inscriptions ou d'éléments probants, le rapprochement entre Taranis et cette image n'est qu'une association empreinte de doutes. Il faut aussi mettre en balance une autre réalité soulignée par Miranda Green: le théonyme de Taranis n'est jamais associé sur aucun monument (autels, images,...) où le symbole de la roue est figuré[32]. A l'inverse, on peut ajouter que sur les quelques autels où celui-ci est mentionné, cet attribut n'est jamais associé au théonyme. Enfin, la roue apparaît dans des contextes très divers (armes halstattiennes, monuments funéraires...)[33]. L'équivalence n'est donc pas logique, et encore moins étayée, entre Taranis et le dieu à la roue. Le problème est inextricable : ne connaissant rien sur la nature de ce dernier, on lui prête des fonctions jupitériennes et l'attribut indigène qu'est la roue fonde la ressemblance et l'équivalence sans preuve

30 Lambrechts 1942, 64–80 ; Hatt 1989, 182–203 ; Gricourt & Hollard 1990–1991.
31 Hatt 1989, 74–80 ; Goudineau 2006, 71–7.
32 Green 1984, 254–7 et 1986a, 66-7.
33 Lambrechts 1942, 67–70.

tangible ; c'est le serpent qui se mord la queue. Nous serions avisés de suivre le conseil de Montaigne, repris par Henri Lavagne : « La ressemblance ne fait pas tant une comme la différence fait autre »[34]. Le fait que Jupiter ait bénéficié dans son iconographie d'apports indigènes ne signifie pas *ipso facto* que celui-ci ait assimilé la personnalité d'une divinité antérieure, strictement équivalente dans son essence, à laquelle le dieu aurait prêté ses atours. L'équivalence n'est que le mirage du système introduit à dessein par César qui voulut que les dieux gaulois soient les équivalents des dieux de Rome. Poussés par le même but, les scholiastes de Lucain ont forgé des équivalences séduisantes mais qui ne résistent pas à l'analyse car les réalités religieuses en Gaule romaine ne sont pas réductibles à l'ordonnance littéraire, aussi poétique et épique soit-elle.

Les Jupiter à la roue, le substrat culturel et la religion gallo-romaine

Adaptation d'un type iconographique classique qui conserve ses caractéristiques principales avec de simples variations, les Jupiter à la roue montrent ainsi le dieu portant cet attribut inusité dans les autres provinces. Création iconographique spécifiquement gallo-romaine, cette série est à la fois diffusée dans toutes les provinces gallo-romaines, de la Narbonnaise à la Germanie Inférieure, et à la fois très dispersée. Dernière particularité, la roue est un attribut répertorié parmi les trois grandes familles de représentations jupitériennes en Gaule : dix-huit pour les figurations jupitériennes classiques[35], huit pour les Jupiter accosté d'un anguipède[36], onze pour les cavaliers à l'anguipède[37] et trois statuettes en bronze[38]. Avec un total de quarante témoignages, ceux-ci ne représentent qu'une portion réduite des 484 œuvres joviennes inventoriées. D'autres supports explicitent ce lien entre Jupiter et la roue : des autels mis au jour essentiellement en Narbonnaise, une rouelle en bronze au sanctuaire de Matagne-la-Petite, des figurines en terre blanche et un panneau de mosaïque à Saint-Romain en Gal[39].

Le fait que ces deux attributs, le foudre et la roue, soient interchangeables ou cumulables prouve qu'ils avaient pour les Gallo-romains une signification très proche[40]. Mais culturellement, il est très probable que le foudre romain à six rais ne recouvrait aucune réalité tangible et ne renvoyait pas à une représentation culturelle de la foudre

34 Lavagne 1979, 156.
35 Jupiter classique influencé par le poncif capitolin : Alise-Sainte-Reine, Alzey, Aschaffenburg et Tongres. Jupiter en pied : Anais, Bordeaux, Bridiers, Escorneboeuf, Laudun, Mandeure, Nîmes, Odernheim, Séguret, Tholey, Vaison (2), Varennes-Reuillon et Wiebelskirchen. Blanchard 2015, 89–91 et 164–171.
36 Champagnat, Dompierre-Les-Eglises, Eymet, La Jonchère-Saint-Maurice, Néris-les-Bains, Saint-Pantaléon-les-Vignes et Mouhet. Blanchard 2015, 183–4.
37 Quémigny-sur-Seine, Meaux, Luxeuil-les-Bains, Montiers-sur-Saulx, Trêves-Euren, Eckartswiller, Eckelsheim, Meddersheim, Butterstadt, Obernburg-am-Main et Weissenburg. Blanchard 2015, 114–5 et 172–82.
38 Chew 2008. Landouzy-la-Ville où la dédicace s'adresse explicitement à *I(ovi) O(ptimo) M(aximo)*, Le Châtelet-de-Gourzon où Jupiter porte le foudre, une roue ainsi que des esses et peut-être Rontecolon.
39 *Esp.* 524, 832, 2881, 6849 et 7201 ; Picard 1974 ; Chew 2008, 38–40 ; Blanchard 2015, 127–37.
40 CIL XII 3023. Par exemple, la roue associée au *fulgur conditum* à Montmirat.

ou des pouvoirs célestes de Jupiter pour une partie de la population des Gaules. Il faut admettre que la coexistence des deux attributs est révélatrice d'une différenciation dans l'acculturation des différentes composantes de la population : certaines étaient initiées à la culture classique et à sa stylisation des éléments naturels tandis que d'autres catégories de la population restaient attachées à leur tradition culturelle gauloise de la stylisation des phénomènes naturels célestes comme la foudre.

Les conceptions du ciel et de la foudre diffèrent entre les civilisations méditerranéennes et la civilisation gauloise en cours d'acculturation. Les éléments constitutifs du foudre romain expriment deux manières divergentes de concevoir la foudre qui déchire le ciel. Dans les civilisations méditerranéennes, le foudre est considéré comme une arme de jet lancé par Jupiter à l'instar d'une javeline. Cela est sensible dans l'élément qui joue le rôle de corps central du foudre à six rais souvent plus massif que les rais latéraux. Ceux-ci sont la transposition des arcs électriques qui zèbrent et déchirent le ciel. Les arcs électriques sont symbolisés ici par les segments disruptifs des rais. Les Romains accordent donc la prééminence iconographique au phénomène lumineux, à l'éclair moins qu'à la foudre et ses aspects sonores. Les Gaulois, quant à eux, semblent avoir eu une autre vision du ciel et de la foudre. Leur symbolique idéographique particulière est l'héritière d'un art gaulois où la stylisation des phénomènes naturels est complexe et extrêmement réfléchie[41]. La roue témoigne d'une conception et une représentation mentale différentes de celles du foudre romain. Elle peut être ainsi comprise comme un pendant de l'astre solaire, une boule de feu lancée à vive allure vers la Terre par Jupiter ; ses rayons seraient autant d'éclairs déchirant le ciel comme le propose Jean-Jacques Hatt. Ceci explique l'aspect circulaire et le choix d'un objet connu de tous pour symboliser ce phénomène naturel. La roue illustre l'étendue du pouvoir de Jupiter sur le ciel par le lien supposé entre celle-ci, l'astre solaire et les phénomènes célestes à l'instar d'un relief votif en plomb de Plessis-Barbuise où Jupiter tenant le foudre se trouve à l'intérieur d'une roue qui pourrait symboliser la sphère céleste[42]. Aux conceptions culturelles divergentes répondent de ce fait deux attributs, qui malgré une signification proche, sont culturellement éloignés. Il est probable que la roue recouvrait des fonctions, des pouvoirs célestes et protecteurs bien plus généraux (tonnerre et foudre, contrôle de l'astre solaire, rotation des astres et cycles saisonniers ?) que la seule possession de la foudre, exprimant mieux la manière dont certains Gallo-romains se représentaient culturellement l'immensité des fonctions et pouvoirs de Jupiter sur l'univers[43]. Le choix de la roue s'est donc naturellement imposé aux sculpteurs locaux car culturellement cet attribut avait un sens immédiatement identifiable par l'ensemble de la population gallo-romaine tandis que la stylisation du foudre à six rais correspondait à une conception mentale et culturelle mal connue et incomprise par une partie de la population. La roue n'a pas vocation de rappeler le culte de Taranis mais marque plus probablement la survivance, voire la vigueur, d'une culture et d'une conception du

41 Hatt 1966, 11–31.
42 Thévenot 1968, 25 ; Hatt 1989, 188–92.
43 Thévenot 1968, 37–45 ; Green 1986b.

monde différente, que la culture romaine enrichit progressivement par ses dieux, sa religion et ses apports culturels.

Le cavalier à l'anguipède : une nouvelle image jupitérienne, vecteur de nouvelles identités culturelles et religieuses.

Fig. 1. Colonnes jupiteriennes de Heidelberg (a), Mosbach-Diedesheim (b), Wiesbaden-Schriestein (c), and Frankfurt-Heddernheim (d), DAO F. Blanchard.

Apparus dans les provinces rhénanes, probablement à Mayence, dans la première moitié du IIe siècle, les cavaliers à l'anguipède sont une deuxième série de témoignages spécifiquement gallo-romains (Fig. 1). Ces œuvres ont particulièrement focalisé le débat historique depuis la seconde moitié du XIXe siècle, certains chercheurs y ont vu un culte nouveau où se mêlent culte jupitérien et culte impérial en réponse aux troubles du IIIe siècle. D'autres ont relié l'apparition de ces groupes au même contexte troublé ou au recours plus courant des civils à des réalisations monumentales alors que jusqu'à cette période, elles étaient surtout le fait des militaires et des autorités locales. Ceci aurait conduit les Gallo-Romains à un revenir à certaines croyances de l'époque de l'indépendance notamment au culte de Taranis caché sous l'apparat du cavalier romain mais visible dans la roue, attribut porté par certains d'entre eux[44]. Pourtant, ces groupes ont été mis au jour dans des contextes archéologiques très divers (les camps militaires, les temples, les villes, les agglomérations secondaires ainsi que les domaines agricoles) témoignant des différents statuts de ce culte (familial, communautaire, public et civique) selon les cités.

Bien plus qu'un retour à des conceptions religieuses celtiques plus d'un siècle et demi après la conquête romaine, force est de constater que l'iconographie renouvelée du cavalier à l'anguipède, qui combine poncifs iconographiques méditerranéens et conception culturelle gallo-romaine, illustre plusieurs transformations religieuses nées au cours du IIe siècle. Le premier élément qui distingue celui-ci de nombre d'autres cultes vient du fait qu'il s'est focalisé autour des monuments eux-mêmes, des

44 Lavagne 2001 ; Blanchard 2015, 104–5.

colonnes du cavalier à l'anguipède et non d'un mythe cosmologique[45]. Les dévots ont cherché à exprimer à travers ces colonnes des croyances qu'ils ne pouvaient exprimer par les mythes et les rites attachés aux représentations classiques de Jupiter. En effet, c'est ce que l'on peut avancer par l'étude du symbolisme des éléments iconographiques qui constituent l'image du Jupiter cavalier.

Fig. 2. Cavalier à l'anguipède de Merten, Cliché L. Kieffer et J. Munin, Musée de La Cour-d'Or, Metz Métropole.

Ainsi, le choix d'un dieu cavalier est à chercher au cœur même de la culture gallo-romaine, dans sa manière d'exprimer des valeurs de pouvoir et d'autorité reliée chez les Gallo-romains à la cavalerie. Contrairement aux représentations classiques, la puissance du dieu est agissante lancée dans l'action d'une chevauchée contre un ennemi. Ceci rappelle très probablement la prépondérance sociale des *equites* dans l'organisation sociale et dans la culture gauloise ainsi que l'attachement des habitants aux valeurs martiales dans ces provinces où l'art de la cavalerie était resté un marqueur social de pouvoir, cultivé et reconnu. Ces caractéristiques et vecteurs culturels empreints de l'héritage gaulois se sont combinés avec des thèmes iconographiques et culturels gréco-romains, notamment le thème de la gigantomachie, faisant du cavalier à l'anguipède le témoin privilégié de l'identité gallo-romaine et de la provincialisation de la religion romaine[46].

Mais plus important encore, l'apparition d'images et de monuments inconnus dans le reste de l'Empire indique probablement une évolution dans la manière de se représenter en Gaule l'ordre cosmique et la puissance de Jupiter. Ainsi, les fonctions du cavalier à l'anguipède semblent considérablement s'élargir si l'on analyse la symbolique des colonnes et l'environnement archéologique de celles-ci. Les divinités de la semaine souvent figurées sur le socle intermédiaire et les bustes des Saisons sculptées sur les chapiteaux montrent que Jupiter garantit l'écoulement éternel des cycles ordonnant la temporalité du monde au profit de la vie et des hommes. De plus, les pierres à quatre dieux semblent placer l'action des principales divinités du panthéon sous son patronage ; celles-ci agissent par délégation de son pouvoir[47]. On y décèle la recherche

45 Woolf 2001.
46 Blanchard 2015, 104–26.
47 Bauchhenß & Noelke 1981, 31–84 ; Blanchard 2015, 47–54.

d'une rationalisation du panthéon autour d'une divinité suprême, non encore unique, commandant à la destinée du monde céleste et mortel. Ce culte pourrait représenter une étape vers l'hénothéisme ou du moins vers une unicité plus forte déjà perceptible dans la popularité de certains cultes comme celui de Mithra par exemple. Loin d'être une simple variante iconographique ou encore la résurgence d'un culte celtique, le cavalier à l'anguipède illustre la force de l'identité culturelle et le dynamisme religieux gallo-romain entre le IIe et le IVe siècle ap. J.-C.

Conclusion

Au terme de ces quelques observations sur les liens unissant Taranis et Jupiter, le substrat celtique et la religion gallo-romaine, on mesure les moyens imparfaits de l'enquête au regard de l'aporie de nos sources. De nombreuses hypothèses, souvent érigées en concept et système de lecture notamment dans l'historiographie française, montrent leurs limites face à l'analyse factuelle et critique. Pour autant, il faut se prémunir de la tentation inverse qui consisterait à minimiser le substrat celtique car il fonde la singularité des cultes en Gaule à l'époque romaine. Toutefois, ce substrat celtique n'est pas celui que l'on nous a esquissé, c'est-à-dire la survivance et la résistance du panthéon gaulois, ceci pour deux raisons. La première tient à la faiblesse et à l'origine de nos sources, nous connaissons trop peu de choses sur les dieux gaulois de l'époque impériale pour être en mesure de définir des équivalences entre les deux panthéons, celui précédant la conquête et le panthéon gallo-romain. Tenter de le faire ne sert en rien la recherche historique mais vient renforcer la vision ethnocentrique de César et Lucain niant l'altérité gauloise. La seconde, et la plus importante, vient de la nature de ce substrat celtique. Il est probablement plus culturel que religieux, au sens strict du terme contrairement à ce que l'on a tant écrit. Car la principale rupture apportée par la conquête romaine est moins l'arrivée de nouveaux cultes que l'effacement des cadres religieux gaulois au profit des pratiques cultuelles romaines. Cette rupture a été appréhendée ces dernières années par les recherches menées autour du modèle de la *polis religion* en Gaule dont la réalité reste difficilement perceptible en dehors des colonies[48]. Comme l'ont souligné C. Guyonvarc'h et F. Le Roux, comment la religion gauloise aurait-elle pu survivre à la disparition de son clergé, aux bouleversements de ses traditions, à l'affaiblissement de sa langue et à la force de l'acculturation latine ?[49] La vigueur du substrat celtique dans la religion gallo-romaine est surtout le miroir de la verdeur de la culture gauloise puis gallo-romaine. Ce qui est le plus remarquable dans le processus d'acculturation en Gaule, notamment dans le domaine religieux et particulièrement dans l'iconographie, c'est la capacité des Gallo-Romains à conserver, redéfinir et combiner leur culture, leur vision singulière du monde divin aux poncifs iconographiques gréco-romains[50]. C'est ainsi que la roue s'est imposée comme un

48 Haeussler 2011, 391–8.
49 Guyonvarc'h & Le Roux 1986, 445–55.
50 Moitrieux 2014 par exemple.

attribut de Jupiter à l'échelle des différentes provinces et qu'au cours du IIe siècle, la culture gallo-romaine a été en mesure de forger son propre poncif et un monument associé, vecteur des bouleversements religieux de cette époque : les colonnes du Jupiter cavalier à l'anguipède.

BIBLIOGRAPHIE

Bauchhenß, G. & P. Noelke 1981 *Die Jupitersäulen in den germanischen Provinzen* (Bonner Jahrbücher des Rheinischen Landesmuseums, Beiheft 41). Köln, Rheinland-Verlag.

Blanchard, F. 2015 *Jupiter dans les Gaules et les Germanies. Du Capitole au cavalier à l'anguipède*, Rennes, PUR.

Brunaux, J. L. 1995 'Religion gauloise et religion romaine. La leçon des sanctuaires de Picardie', *Cahiers du Centre Glotz* 6, 139–61.

Brunaux, J. L. 2006 *Les druides. Des philosophes chez les Barbares*. Paris, Editions du Seuil.

Chew, H. 2008 'Un nouveau Jupiter à la roue en bronze au musée d'Archéologie. Criciro, *saltuarius* dans le Mâconnais', *Antiquités nationales*, 25–43.

De Vries, J. 1977 *La religion des celtes*. Paris, Payot.

Deyts, S. 1992 *Images et dieux de la Gaule*. Paris, Errance.

Duval, P. M. 1958–1959 'Teutates, Esus, Taranis', *Etudes Celtiques* 8, 41–58.

Duval, P. M. 2002 *Les dieux de la Gaule*. Paris, Payot.

Green, M. 1982 'Tanarus, Taranis and the Chester Altar', *Journal of the Chester Archaeological Society* 65, 37–44.

Green, M. 1984, *The Wheel as cult-symbol in the Romano-Celtic World, with special Reference to Gaul and Britain* (Revue d'Études Latines, 183). Bruxelles, Latomus.

Green, M. 1986a *The Gods of the Celts*. Gloucester, Sutton.

Green, M. 1986b 'Jupiter, Taranis and the Solar Wheel', *Pagan Gods and Shrines of the Roman Empire*, éd. M. Henig & A. C. King, 65–75. Oxford, Oxford University Committee for Archaeology.

Gricourt, D. & D. Hollard 1990 'Taranis, dieu celtique à la roue, remarques préliminaires', *Dialogues d'Histoire Ancienne* 16-2, 275–320.

Gricourt, D. & D. Hollard 1991 'Taranis, caelestium deorum maximus', *Dialogues d'Histoire Ancienne* 17–1, 343–400.

Guyonvarc'h, C. 1980 *Textes mythologiques irlandais* I, Rennes, Ogam.

Guyonvarc'h, C. & F. Le Roux 1986 'Remarques sur la religion romaine : rupture et continuité', *Aufstieg und Niedergang der Römischen Welt* II 18.1, 423–55.

Hatt, J.-J. 1966 *Sculptures gauloises, Esquisse d'une évolution de la sculpture en Gaule depuis le VIe siècle avant J.-C. jusqu'au IVème siècle* après *J.-C.* Paris, Éd. temps.

Hatt, J.-J. 1989 *Mythes et dieux de la Gaule, les divinités masculines*. Paris, Picard.

Haeussler, R. 2008 'How to identify Celtic religion(s) in Roman Britain and Gaul', *Divindades indigenas em anàlise. Divinités pré-romaines-bilan et perspectives d'une recherché. Actas do VII workshop F.E.R.C.A.N*, éd. J. d'Encarnaçao, 13–63. Coimbra/Porto.

Haeussler, R. 2011 'Beyond *polis Religion* and sacerdotes publici in Southern Gaul', *Priests and States in Roman World*, éds. J. Richardson and F. Santangelo, 391–428. Stuttgart, Steiner.

Heichelheim, H. 1932 'Taranis', RE IV A.2, 2274–2284.

Jufer, N. & Luginbühl, T. 2001 *Les dieux gaulois. Répertoire des noms de divinités celtiques connus par l'épigraphie, les textes antiques et la toponymie*. Paris, Errance.

Lacroix, J. 2007 *Les noms d'origine gauloise. La Gaule des dieux*. Paris, Errance.

Lambrechts, P. 1942 *Contributions à l'étude des divinités celtiques*, Bruges, De Tempel.

Lavagne, H. 1979 'Les dieux de la Gaule Narbonnaise : romanité et romanisation', *Journal des savants* 3, 155–97.

Lavagne, H. 2001 'Les ambivalences d'une image du pouvoir impérial : le cavalier à l'anguipède en Gaule romaine', *Images et représentations du pouvoir et de l'ordre social dans l'Antiquité. Actes du colloque, Angers, 28–29 mai 1999*, éd. M. Molin, 37–43. Paris, Boccard.

Le Roux F. 1958 'Taranis, Dieu celtique du ciel et de l'orage', *Ogam* 10, 30–9 et 11, 307–24.

Moitrieux, G. 2002 *Hercules in Gallia, Recherches sur la personnalité et le culte d'Hercule en Gaule.* Paris, De Boccard.

Moitrieux, G. 2014 'L'iconographie lapidaire des périphéries est-elle le signe d'une résistance à la romanisation de la Gaule ?', *Confinia, Confins et périphéries dans l'Occident romain*, éd. R. Bedon, 135–56. Limoges, PULIM.

Perrier, J. 1960 'L'autel de Thauron (Creuse)', *Gallia* 18-2, 195–7.

Picard, G.-C. 1974 'Une offrande à Jupiter sur la mosaïque calendrier de Saint-Romain-en-Gal', *Bulletin de la Société Nationale des Antiquaires de France* (séance du 27 novembre), 127–37.

Pichon, R. 1912 *Les sources de Lucain.* Paris, Leroux.

Raydon, V. 2013 'Le Dagda, le dieu de l'orage du panthéon irlandais ? Un écueil du comparatisme interceltique', *Dialogues d'Histoire Ancienne* 39.1, 75–105.

Sergent, B. 2004 *Le livre des dieux. Celtes et Grecs II.* Paris, Payot.

Sergent, B. 2005 'Taranis', *Le site du Mont Bégo : de la protohistoire à nos jours*, éd. Jérôme Magail & Jean-Marc Giaume, 119–34. Nice, Serre Editeur.

Sjoestedt, M. L. 2009 *Dieux et héros des Celtes.* Dinan, Terre de Brume.

Sterckx, C 1992 'Le cavalier et l'anguipède, Partie II', *Ollodagos, Actes de la société belge d'études celtiques* 4.1, 1–126.

Szabo, D. 2006 'Par Taranis ? Par Toutatis ? Par Teutanus ? Le culte de Jupiter Teutanus chez les Celtes danubiens', *Religion et société en Gaule*, éd. C. Goudineau, 203–6. Paris, Errance.

Thévenot, E. 1957 'A propos des Mars celtiques', *Ogam* 9, 37–40.

Thévenot, E. 1968 *Divinités et sanctuaires de la Gaule.* Paris, Fayard.

Vendryes, J. 1997 *La religion des Celtes.* Spézet, Coop Breizh.

Woolf, G. 2001 'Representation as cult: the case of the Jupiter columns', *Religion in den germanischen Provinzen Roms*, éd. W. Spickermann, 117–34. Tübingen, Steiner.

XVII

THE MAGICIAN'S HOUSE DRUIDS, PRAYERS AND MAGIC IN ROMAN GAUL

Miranda Aldhouse-Green

In 2005 a strange basement room was discovered beneath a Gallo-Roman house in Chartres. The cellar was found to have been a secret underground shrine, full of ritual objects, including a set of incense-burners. These large pottery vessels bore inscribed prayers and incantations, together with lists of Gallic spirit-names. One of these names was 'Dru'. The name of the presiding priest was Caius Verius Sedatus, a Roman citizen. What was going on here, in the middle of a Roman city in the late first–early second century AD? Did 'Dru' refer to Druids? Did the cellar reflect a secret, magical cult hidden from Roman authority? And, if so, how come a Roman citizen was involved? This paper examines the Chartres find and seeks to put it into the broader context of complex cultural interaction, subversion and Gallic religious survival.

DRUIDS are difficult! There exists for them the conundrum of a plethora of evidence and no evidence at all. On the one hand, there is a noisy clamour of Classical literature on a subject essentially foreign to its perpetrators' experience, for its authors hailed from the Mediterranean world whilst the Druids belonged to regions to the north and west of that arena. I recall Carlo Ginzberg's statement at the Harvard Witchcraft seminar held in August 2009: 'there is no innocent eye'.[1] This is so true of the Greek and – especially – Roman reportage of Druidism which, at best, must have contained ignorance, supposition and unwitting bias and, at worst, colonial spin and barbarising invention. On the other hand, the 'evidence' consists of mute archaeological artefacts, things, animal and human remains that appear to have been associated with ritual action or its results at about the time that the Druids were thought to have been active in Britain and Gaul: between about 200 BC and AD 400.[2] The principal problem lies in the failure in our ability to knit together these two skeins of data. It is well-nigh impossible to separate fact from fiction in the ancient texts and, although particular elements of apparently sacral material culture *might* be connected with Iron Age or Roman-period Druids, there is no reason to cite this group rather than

1 Aldhouse-Green in Mitchell *et al.* 2010a, 872.
2 Aldhouse-Green 2010b, 13–7.

Fig. 1. Map of the tribes of Gaul. Illustrator: Ian Dennis.

any other band of religious officials that may have been operational during this time. So is there any way of cutting the Gordian knot? How closely and effectively can we marry material culture to contemporary literature? Do recent discoveries help us in the quest for real Druids?

Focus on Chartres

Autricum (modern Chartres) was the political capital of the Carnutes, whom Caesar, writing his *De Bello Gallico* in the fifties BC, identified as occupying territory south-west of Paris (Fig. 1). The Carnutes enjoyed an uneasy and fluctuating relationship with Caesar's forces: the Roman general had been firm friends with a high-ranking individual called Tasgetius but after he was assassinated by fellow Carnutians, Caesar took immediate action against his murderers.[3] Thereafter, relations between Rome and this polity deteriorated and the Carnutes were one of the first tribal groups to engage with the pan-Gallic uprising led by the Arvernian chieftain Vercingetorix.[4] The Carnutes appear to be a classic example of an Iron Age polity torn asunder by pro- and anti-Roman factions that could split families down the middle. This kind of inter-tribal division is graphically illustrated elsewhere in Gaul, for instance among the Aedui of Burgundy when Caesar was governor (and conqueror), and later in Britain, notably among the Iceni under Prasutagus and Boudica,[5] and the Brigantes, ruled by Cartimandua and Venutius during the mid-later first century AD.[6]

Caesar's friend Tasgetius may have been one of the *obsides* recorded in Roman literature, the child of a Gallic nobleman sent to Rome to learn Roman *mores* and governance in order to return ready to apply sophisticated systems of *romanitas* at

3 Caes. *BGall.* 5.25.
4 Caes. *BGall.* 7.2.
5 Tac. *Ann.* 14.31.
6 Tac. *Ann.* 12.40.

home, a practice not always appreciated by those left behind.[7] If so, his close alliance with Rome may have led both to his assassination and to later Carnutian hostility towards Caesar. Tasgetius is important in the present context, for it may have been one of his descendants whose activities in early Roman Chartres led to the writing of this paper.[8] This latter individual's name was Caius Verius Sedatus, and his possession of *tria nomina* (in particular his *cognomen* Sedatus) during this period meant that he was almost certainly a Roman citizen. It may be no coincidence, too, that he shared his *praenomen* and *nomen* with Caius Julius Caesar, perhaps a reflection of longstanding amity between his family and the Roman government. His *cognomen*, however, is Gaulish, deriving from *sed* and *sedd*, meaning 'sit' or 'seat'. Sedatus and cognate names, such as Sedatianus and Assedomarus are by no means uncommon in Roman Gaul. For instance, the name appears on tombstones as far afield as Bordeaux[9] and Dagsburg in the Vosges,[10] occurring, too, in Burgundy, at Langres, Dijon and Autun.[11] An Alpine settlement named Sedunum is recorded among the Helvetii (or their sub-polity the Nantuates).[12] Interestingly, Sedatus is also attested as a divine name, among the Aquitani, where his name is coupled with that of the Italian rural deity Silvanus.[13]

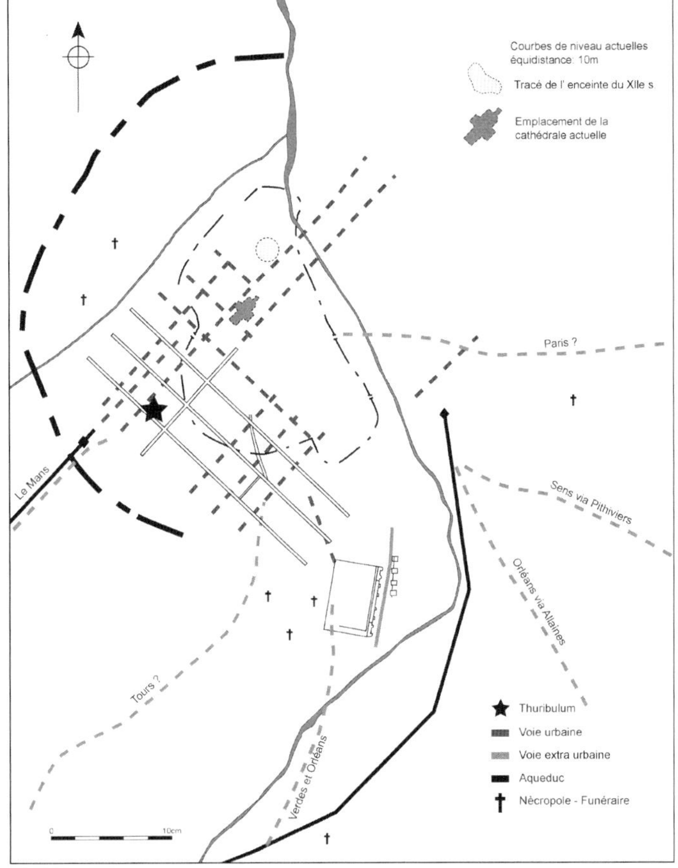

Fig. 2. Site plan of Roman *Autricum* (Chartres) showing the position of Sedatus' cellar-shrine. Illustrator Ian Dennis (after Gordon *et al.* 2010).

According to Caesar, the Carnutes occupied key lands within Gaul, for it was in Carnutian territory, he comments, that the annual pan-Gallic Druidic assembly was

7 Creighton 2000, 92–4.
8 The nucleus of the present paper, under the same title, was delivered by the author for the 2011 Professor John Mulvaney Lecture at the Australian National University, Canberra on June 1st, 2011.
9 *CIL* XIII 846.
10 *CIL* XIII 5988.
11 *CIL* XIII 11587; XIII 5551; XIII 2706.
12 Koch 2007, map 17.5.
13 *CIL* XIII 11024; Evans 1967, 56–7, 253–4; Whatmough 1949–51, 17, 243, 1249; Raybould & Sims-Williams 2007, 12.

held, 'in a consecrated place'.[14] This is a significant passage for it suggests that Druidism formed an organised network that bound together enormous tracts of land. Moreover, Caesar states that this event took place 'on a fixed date each year'[15] which, if it were truly so, carries implications concerning the capacity of the Druids to make precise calendrical computations from the observation of heavenly bodies. However, for present purposes, the key point is that the location of Caesar's Druidic assembly is likely to have been the Carnutian capital of Chartres, and that is precisely whence comes new evidence suggesting the presence of Roman-period Druids. However, when this new material is examined in detail, it is clear that all was not as it appears but that something much more complicated was going on than simply a Druidic survival into Roman Gaul.

Sedatus the Magician

On 20th July 2005, work on the construction of an underground carpark in the centre of Chartres (Fig. 2) was interrupted by the unearthing of Roman remains dating to the early second century AD.[16] These comprised the debris of a burnt-out house whose collapse preserved what appears to have been a tiny underground shrine (1.7 x 2 m) in the basement of its premises. When the cellar was in active use, a wooden ladder resting on stone steps was used to access the shrine. At some point, perhaps for secrecy or when the rituals there ceased, the liturgical material – including incense-burners, pots with snake-decorated handles, ceramic lamps and a broad-bladed 'sacrificial' knife – had been hidden away beneath the stairs.

It is the group of *turibula* – censers – that supplies clues both as to what was going on in this subterranean space and as to the identity of the person in charge. They also provide evidence, of a kind, for the presence of Druids. Remains of three incense-burners were found, and there may once have been a fourth (for reasons that will presently become apparent). Of the three, one is virtually complete, and most of its surface is covered with cursive writing, scratched on to the leather-hard surface of the pot prior to its firing (Fig. 3) The inscriptions are in four blocks, each of which is self-contained and almost identical to its fellows, and each panel is headed with the name of a cardinal point: *oriens, meridie, occidens* and *septentrio.*[17] These headings lead to the inference that there may once have been four censers, each placed to mark out one of the compass points (Table 1).

And now Caius Verius Sedatus makes his entrance. Each of the four inscriptions on the *turibulum* consists of a prayer directed to the *omnipotentia numina*[18] by Sedatus, who proclaims himself *vester custos*[19]. There follows a list of names, most of whose meanings (if any) are impenetrable: words like 'Echar', 'Stna', 'Bru' and 'Halcemedme'

14 Caes. *BGall.* 6.13, trans. Wiseman & Wiseman 1980, 121.
15 Caes. *BGall.* 6.13.
16 Gordon *et al.* 2010; Joly *et al.* 2010; Marco Simón 2015.
17 'East', 'south', 'west' and 'north'.
18 'Omnipotent spirits'.
19 'Your Guardian'.

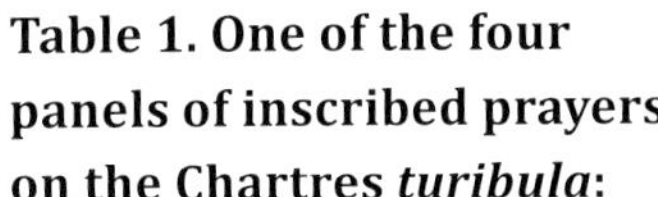

Table 1. One of the four panels of inscribed prayers on the Chartres *turibula*:

Meridie
Vos rogo omnipotentia
numina ut omnia bona
conferatis C(aio) Verio
Sedato quia ille est
vester custos
Echar Aha
Bru Stna
Bros Dru
Chor Drax
Chos
Halcemedme
Halcehalar

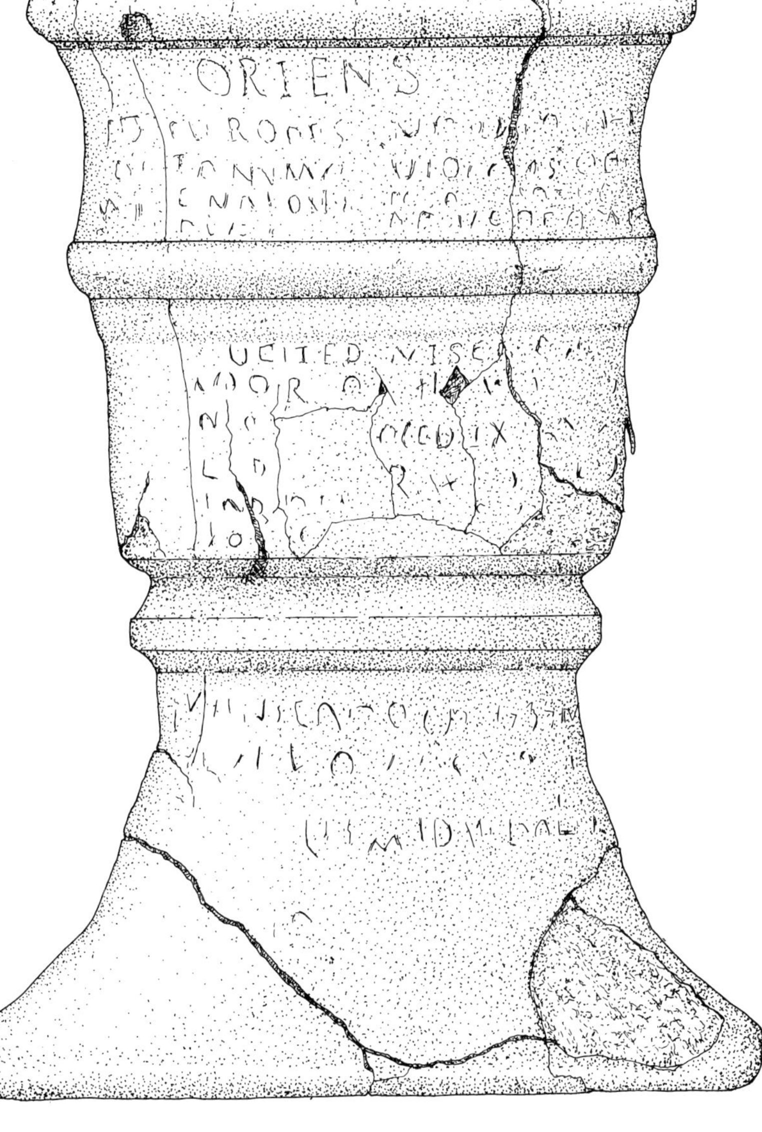

Fig. 3. The complete *turibulum* from the Chartres cellar-shrine. Illustrator Ian Dennis (after Gordon *et al.* 2010)

(Table 1). But one word, 'Dru', causes a stir of interest because it appears to refer to the Druids; if so, the Chartres *turibulum* represents the only known inscribed reference to this religious leadership and, indeed, our sole irrefutable archaeological evidence for them. If the list of names inscribed on the incense-burner does represent Sedatus' *omnipotentia numina*, though, the inclusion of the word Druid suggests that what Caesar, Strabo, Lucan, Tacitus and numerous other ancient writers identified as a title for a Gallo-British religious official had undergone a change of status for the Gallo-Roman

Sedatus. For him, then, Druids had transmogrified from priests to gods, one of many to whom he directed his prayers. It is even more peculiar that his tone is not so much that of a suppliant but of a controller of spirits. He calls himself their guardian and, by implication, he is in charge: they are summoned to do his bidding. He is a magician, a person imbued with the power to conjure tenebrous forces.

The list of obscure words on the Chartres *turibula* chimes with the secret names that appear in Graeco-Egyptian magical texts, although the latter are usually later in date than the *Autricum* shrine.[20] It is likely that most of the words were 'mumbo-jumbo', made-up words designed to heighten Sedatus's power as a keeper of cosmic knowledge and the 'secret' names of the spirits whom he summons. Sedatus – an educated, literate man – certainly appears to have wished to create magical names for the spirits he was conjuring in his prayers, for it is surely significant that he failed to include in his list any of the Gallic deities known from Roman literature or inscriptions: names such as Taranis, Epona, Esus or Teutates. It seems as though Sedatus' aim was to confound, to create a deliberate counterpoint not only to established Roman religion but also to the recognised pantheon of local deities, only some of whom were syncretised with those bearing Roman names.

The second element of the Chartres prayers, argued as lending itself to thoughts of eastern influence,[21] is the reference to the cardinal points. Directional alignments also played a significant role in the layout and use of sacred spaces in Iron Age and Roman-period Gaul and Britain, for instance at Acy-Romance, Ardennes, Gournay-sur-Aronde, Oise, and Great Chesterford, Essex.[22] Directionality was also endemic within Roman ritual practice: from the carefully planned layout of towns[23] to the scratching out of cardinal points by the Roman *Augur* with his *lituus* prior to divination.[24] And, of course, it is possible that the enigmatic pairs of bronze spoons found placed in graves or deliberately deposited in bogs in late Iron Age Britain also bear witness to the importance of compass points: one of each pair has its inner surface marked in four quadrants.[25]

Words: sound, power and magic

> A number of those who practised magic collected their books and burned them publicly; when the value of these books was calculated, it was found to come to fifty thousand silver coins.[26]

The context of this New Testament passage is St Paul's visit to the Ionian Greek city of Ephesus in Asia Minor, famous for its great library and the monumental temple to Diana.

20 Gordon 2002.
21 Gordon *et al.* 2010, 499.
22 Lambot 2000; Brunaux 1996; Medlycott 2011, 75.
23 Woodward & Woodward 2004.
24 Beard *et al* 1998, 22.
25 Aldhouse-Green 2010b, 163, fig. 53; Fitzpatrick 1997, 20.
26 *Acts of the Apostles* 19, v 19.

The purpose of quoting it is simply to illustrate the prevalence of magic in the eastern Mediterranean provinces of the Roman Empire and the sheer value placed on written magical words. The Ephesian magicians had just witnessed Paul's miracles and had encountered a power so great that the cloth he had touched retained the capacity to heal even without Paul's physical presence. The act of book-burning was an acknowledgment of a vastly superior spirit force.

The 'magical words' listed in Sedatus's repeated prayer were carefully chosen to be effective in dramatic proclamation aloud, for they are full of 'plosives' and repetitious alliterations. Speaking aloud is important in a ritual context for words are closely associated with power. Oratory is persuasive and so is religious sermonising. In chanting his prayer aloud in the reverberative confines of the sacred cellar, Sedatus was taking charge of the situation and acting as both the mouthpiece/commander of the spirit world and the controller of his 'congregation', if such there were (given the small size of the cellar-shrine). Once spoken and heard, words – whether said, chanted or sung – take on an independent persona, capable of echo, distortion and of being driven deep into the consciousness of both speaker and listeners. Words spoken aloud also become collective, allowing a simultaneous shared experience. Indeed Sedatus' choice of an underground space in which to conduct his rituals may have been as much about its qualities as an echo-chamber as about secrecy.

There is a sense in which the inscriptions on the Chartres incense-burners could be interpreted as spells as well as prayers and, thus, the chanting of the names, perhaps over and over again, might have had a hypnotic effect upon those present in the shrine. Properties intrinsic to the *turibula* themselves perhaps encouraged the 'magical' effect of the alien chanted words, for is it not feasible that the material burned in these censers included psychotropic substances – such as *artemisia*, or convolvulus seeds, both of which (along with many others) are recorded in the archaeological record of the Iron Age?[27] Rather in the manner of sweat lodges used in the inducement of trance among some Plains Indians communities,[28] the devotees who participated in Sedatus's rituals in the dark cellar, filled with smoke and, maybe, drug-laden fumes, and with sonorous repetitive and alliterative chanting, may well have experienced weird, out-of-body trance states. There is likely to have been a close physical connection between what was smouldering *inside* and what was inscribed on the *outside* of the Chartres vessels. The words mingled with the incense so that it would seem as if the *turibula* actually contained the spirits conjured by Sedatus, and were instruments used by him – perhaps – in 'emotive divination'.[29] This is a ritual process in which the celebrant makes direct contact with the spirits he has conjured. It may even be that, like the *śakti*

27 A clump of *artemesia* was found in a spouted bowl placed in the 'Doctor's Grave' at Stanway, Colchester, Essex (Crummy *et al.* 2007, 207); the gilded bronze leaves forming part of the religious sceptre found at Manching (Bavaria) have been identified as convolvulus (Perrin 2000, 22). *Artemesia* is a well-documented herbal remedy (Wiltshire 2007, 394) but it is also used as a hallucinogenic substitute for cannabis (Schultes *et al.* 1992, 98).

28 St Pierre & Long Soldier 1995, 19.

29 Carr 2002, 64.

karakam of rural Indian Hindu practice,[30] the *turibula* at Chartres were vessels of transformation, power-houses in which the process of divine possession took place, a possession manifested in the written words inscribed on its outer surface.[31] The sounds and intoxicating fumes may have combined with the strict control of light in a dark place, where torches or smoking oil-lamps were placed so as to cast giant shadows on the walls, as if to give the impression that the conjured spirits were present in the room. As the celebrant and summoner of spirits, we can imagine that Sedatus dressed the part. What did he wear, I wonder? Perhaps he donned special robes, maybe a headdress, like the decorated head-band worn by the 'priest' buried at Deal in Kent in about 100 BC (Fig. 4),[32] or like the diadems from Romano-British temples, such as Wanborough in Surrey and Hockwold in Norfolk.[33] He probably carried a magician's wand (Fig. 5): the group of sceptres from Wanborough in Britain and Villeneuve-Saint-Germain (Aisne) in Gaul exemplify their use in the western Roman provinces.[34]

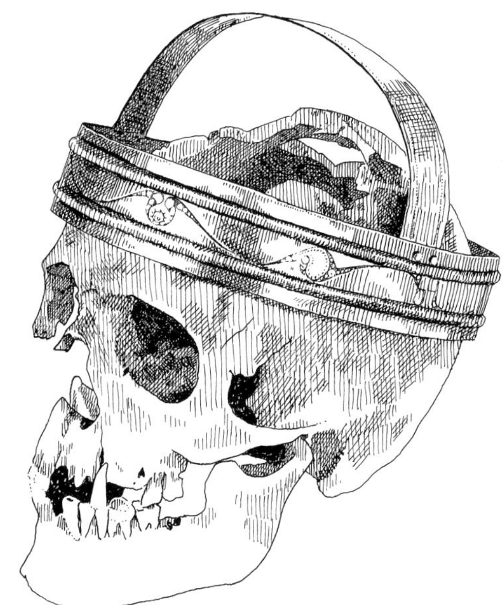

Fig. 4. The skull of a man buied at Deal in Kent in about 100 BC wearing a decorated ceremonial headband. llustrator: Paul Jenkins.

The spell-like properties of the Chartres prayer lead to consideration of its relationship to coeval written chants, notably those inscribed on Gallo-British *defixiones* or curse tablets. Like the Chartres inscription, many of these curses, written in cursive script on lead or pewter, were meant to be spoken, or even sung. The transmission of sound was clearly key to the efficacy of the spell. Chanting the spell aloud enabled it to be shared by those other than the spell-caster and, of course, the spoken or sung words make direct connections with the object (or the victim) of the prayer or curse. In the context of ancient Athenian cursing rituals, Ralph Anderson has considered the nature of the relationship between the spell-binder and the recipient, pointing out the essentially active, if not aggressive, character of the former and the passive helplessness of the

30 Foulston 2002, 164.

31 The *śakti karakam* is a ceramic vessel that is first purified in a sacred tank or river outside a village Hindu temple, and then filled with rice or other foods and borne into the shrine. It is the act of submergence in the water that causes it and its attendant worshippers, to be possessed by the local deity. The pot thus acts as a 'power-house', an agent for transformation, enabling people to be imbued with spirit force.

32 Parfitt 1995, 13, 155.

33 Aldhouse-Green 2010, 154–7; O'Connell & Bird 1994, 93–6.

34 O'Connell & Bird 1994, 106–11; Debord 1982, 213, 245.

Fig. 5. Reconstruction of a priest, from regalia discovered at the Wanborough Roman temple, Surrey. © Surrey Archaeological Society.

latter.[35] Despite the fact that the Chartres inscriptions appear to be neither harming spells nor directed at a victim, it is valid to imagine the same kind of relationship between Sedatus, the guardian and mouthpiece of his controlled spirits and those listening to his utterances, a connection forged by the passage of words from mouth to ear. In his treatise on judicial *defixiones* in the ancient world, John Gager refers to 'the coercive power of words'.[36] In the case of the Chartres prayers, the recipients of the magical spoken words were the *omnipotentia numina* called upon by Sedatus who refers to himself as *vester custos*. The inference is that Sedatus' power over these spirits, including those whom he termed Druids, is his ability to bring them to life with speech.

So can we imagine close associations between the prayers on the Chartres *turibula* and the much more common *defixiones*? Two clear connections can be made: firstly in the direct evidence, present in certain of the curse-tablets, for use of the projected voice, in the allusion to singing; secondly, one of the Gallic curses, the tablet from Larzac in southern France (Fig. 6) makes specific reference to a seeress, using the native term *uidlua*, which is etymologically related to the word for Druid.[37] An *uidla* is a 'seeing one' or 'knowing one'. The long and highly complex Larzac curse has been admirably dissected and re-interpreted by Bernard Mees.[38] It is full of darkness and steeped in magico-religious potency. It is also saturated in femininity: the deity, Adsagsona, the religious practitioner (or magician), Severa Tertionicna ('Daughter of Tertiu'), and all the named victims are not only themselves women but they are paired: mother and daughter or mother and foster-daughter. Indeed, the inscription itself refers to 'this enchantment of women'. Furthermore, the Larzac *defixio* was placed in the tomb of a woman called Gemma, whose remains were interred, in a pot inscribed with her name, in a large cemetery along with over a hundred other burials. The curse appears to have been placed there not because she was part of the magical rituals conducted by Tertionicna but in order to facilitate the transference of the written message to the infernal regions in company

35 Anderson 2002, 221.
36 Gager 1992, 120.
37 Meid 1992, 40–6; Mees 2009, 67
38 Mees 2009, 50–69.

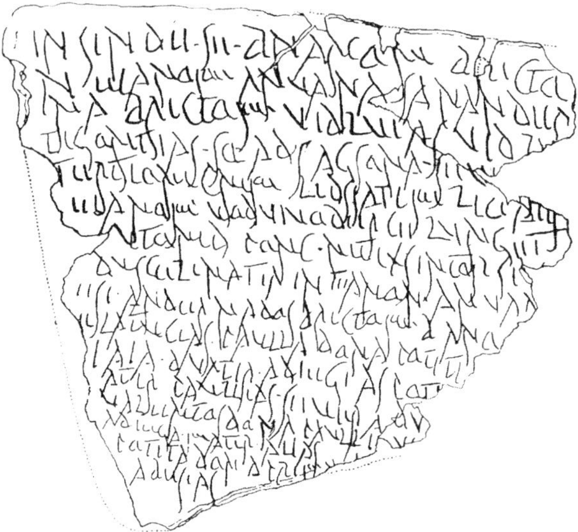

Fig. 6. Part of the lead *defixio* from Larzac in southern France. © Paul Jenkins (after Meid 1992).

with the dead woman, where it would be activated.

Gaius Verius Sedatus's name and his use of Latin situate him firmly within Roman Gaul. The same is true of Severa Tertionicna, who bears both a traditional Roman name, Severa, and a local one ('Tertiu's daughter'). Mees points to 'Severa Tertionicna, then to have been a Gaulish woman, a seeress who was at home writing and speaking Latin',[39] whilst her mother, whose name is wholly indigenous, may not have had the same cross-cultural connections nor the same level of education. Like the Chartres *turibulum* prayers, the Larzac curse contains regular rhythms and alliterations suggesting that it was chanted aloud. There is even a reference, within the inscription, to the curse as a *duscelinata* ('an evil death-song').[40] The seeress Severa Tertionicna herself has two alliterating Gaulish-language titles: *lidsatim* (learned or knowing) and *liciatim* (binding, skein, thread), the latter a common theme in Gallo-Roman curses, where the victim is fixed or bound by the curse and whose fate is sealed by the spinning threads of destiny, severed by the Fates. The certainty that many inscribed prayers, spells and magical curses like those from Chartres and Larzac were uttered aloud is reinforced by others from Roman Gaul, such as the *defixio* from Chamalières in the Auvergne, which is described as an *ison canti* (a 'magical song'), or the one from a well within a late Iron Age *oppidum* at Montfo, only 50 km from Larzac, that contains an allusion to itself as a *necracantum* or 'death song'.[41] Thus Sedatus's chant at Chartres may be firmly contextualised within a magical tradition current in the first and second centuries AD within Roman Gaul. What makes the Chartres prayers so special is their specific mention of Druids.

According to ancient authors, notably Julius Caesar,[42] the Druids were religious practitioners with a range of influences and responsibilities far outside the node of ritual authority, including justice, healing, natural philosophy, astronomy and curation of oral tradition. None of the many classical writers[43] allude to the Druids as other than grounded in mortality and as high-ranking politico-religious leaders with pronounced powers of prophecy. But here, in the early second century AD, is Caius Verius Sedatus,

39 Mees 2009, 57.
40 Mees 2009, 196.
41 Mees 2009.
42 Caes. *BGall.* 6.13.
43 At least thirty-five can be identified (Chadwick 1997, xxii–xxx).

inscribing ritual censers with lists of secret, magical names, to whom he refers as *omnipotentia numina,* among whom are Druids. According to Sedatus's prayers, the Druids have become part-and-parcel of the spirit-world.

The Magician's House

What was going on in the dark cellar at Chartres? How did Gallic religious officials become spirits? Was Sedatus ignorant of genuine Druidism, subjugated as it undoubtedly was by *romanitas*? Did he, instead deliberately manipulate a resonant, iconic word in order to lend *gravitas* and authenticity to a new religious movement that was, in essence, a palimpsest or mish-mash of traditions, widely ranging in space and time, reinvented by a wily Gallo-Roman wielder of 'magic'? I wonder whether it is permissible to take an even closer look at Sedatus himself, focusing on his very name, his *cognomen*. Earlier in this paper, I referred to the name Sedatus as that of a deity, coupled with Silvanus in Aquitania. This fragmentary inscription on a piece of marble comes from the Roman town of Auci. Sedatus means 'the seated one', and therefore could be regarded as a title rather than a name *per se*. It is not impossible that Caius Verius chose his own *cognomen* in order to convey self-empowerment and religious credibility. For Roman magistrates, their judicial authority was symbolised by their right to preside while seated in a *sella curulis*, a folding chair, rather like the canvas seat favoured by modern film directors. The remains of such furniture have been found in very late Iron Age high-status tombs in southern Britain, for instance in the Lexden tumulus just outside Camulodunum (Colchester), probably in the grave of a British ruler who died in about 10 BC,[44] and in the broadly coeval 'chieftain's burial' at Folly Lane, Verulamium.[45] The repertoire of religious iconography of late Iron Age and Roman-period Gaul and Britain reveals a link between rank and seated positions. A group of Gallic images, mainly of stone, depicts persons wearing torcs (themselves indicative of high status) and seated in the yogic cross-legged position.[46] Most prominent of these are representations of people wearing antlers or antler-headdresses. The best-documented example is the image on the Gundestrup cauldron, a highly-decorated gilded silver vessel found in a Danish peat-bog and dating to the first century BC[47] but most images of this type come from Roman Gaul and occur occasionally also in Britain.[48] It is not impossible, therefore, that Caius Verius picked a *cognomen* for himself that chimed with a self-image of high status and religious authority.

The key to gaining any understanding of the shrine at Chartres is the character of Sedatus himself and the nature of syncretised Gallo-British religion within the Roman Empire. If Sedatus was a Roman citizen, as his triplefold name suggests, then we might surely have expected him to have played a prominent role in *Autricum*'s society It would

44 Foster 1986; Creighton 2000, 181–3.
45 Niblett, 2001, 60, fig. 27.
46 Aldhouse-Green 2004, figs. 2.7, 2.8, 2.9.
47 Kaul 1991, 21, pl. 15; Aldhouse-Green 2004, fig. 6.2.
48 Green 1989, figs. 37–40.

seem then, on the face of it, unlikely that he spent his time skulking in cellars of private houses, babbling subversive magical doctrines. But if his 'surname' were self-styled, it becomes more plausible that he was operating as a quasi-shaman, within a sub-text of mainstream religion. For some Carnutians, the Druids still may have held resonance and it is quite possible that Druidism continued subliminally in many Roman towns in Gaul and Britain, just as Russian shamans did within the repressive contexts of Soviet religious persecution.[49] We know from late Roman texts, such as the Augustan Histories, that Druids remained in the consciousness of Gaul three hundred years after their official demise, for in these documents, Gallic Druidesses are credited with predicting future emperors, including Diocletian and Aurelian.[50] According to Ausonius, an academic from Bordeaux, by the fourth century AD, Druids formed family dynasties.[51] It is tempting to think of Sedatus as a highly-educated, widely-read and urbane Roman citizen, a pillar of his community who, perhaps, pursued a public career by day but, under cover of darkness, repaired to the subterranean shrine beneath his house where his followers gathered and wove his magic: a magic in which an ancient and powerful priesthood had been transformed into spirits under his control. Could it even be that the magician's house was burnt down by those opposed to his 'un-Roman' practices? After all, sorcery was frowned upon and the practice of magic was looked upon as an offence to Roman civil authority.[52] Sedatus may have represented the first of many new religious movements in which Druids played ever-shifting roles. He might have been very at home at Stonehenge on a twenty-first century midsummer morning.

BIBLIOGRAPHY

Aldhouse-Green, M. J. 2004 *An Archaeology of Images. Iconology and cosmology in Iron Age and Roman Europe*. London: Routledge.

Aldhouse-Green, M. J. 2010a 'Reading prehistoric religion', in S. Mitchell, N. Price, R. Hutton, D. Purkiss, K. Patton, C. Raudvere, C. Severi, M. Aldhouse-Green, S. Semple, A. Pluskowski, M. Carver & C. Ginzberg, 'Witchcraft and Deep Time – a debate at Harvard', *Antiquity* 84, 864–79.

Aldhouse-Green, M. J. 2010b *Caesar's Druids. Story of an Ancient Priesthood*. New Haven and London, Yale University Press.

Anderson, R. 2002 'Kill or cure: Athenian judicial curses and the body in fear', *Practitioners, Practices and Patients. New Approaches to Medical Archaeology and Anthropology*, ed. P. Baker & G. Carr, 221–37. Oxford, Oxbow Books.

Beard, M., J. North & S. Price 1998 *Religions of Rome. Volume 1. A History*. Cambridge, Cambridge University Press.

Brunaux, J.-L. 1996 *Les religions gauloises. Rituels celtiques de la Gaule indépendante*. Paris, Errance.

Carr, G. 2002 'A time to live, a time to heal and a time to die: healing and divination in later Iron

49 Pentikäinen 1998, 8, 99; Hutton 1993, 7; 2001, 25; Aldhouse-Green 2010b, 101–4.
50 Chadwick 1997, 81.
51 Ausonius, *Commemoratio Professorum Burdigalensium*; Chadwick 1997, 82.
52 Graf 1999, 36.

Age and early Roman Britain', *Practitioners, Practices and Patients. New Approaches to Medical Archaeology and Anthropology,* ed. P. Baker & G. Carr, 58–73. Oxford, Oxbow Books.

Chadwick, N. 1997 *The Druids.* Cardiff, University of Wales Press (2nd edition: first published 1966).

Creighton, J. 2000 *Coins and Power in Late Iron Age Britain.* Cambridge, Cambridge University Press.

Crummy, P., S. Benfield, V. Rigby & D. Shimmin 2007 *Stanway: An Elite Burial Site at Camulodunum.* London, Society for the Promotion of Roman Studies, Britannia Monograph Series No. 24.

Debord, J. 1982 'Premier bilan de huit années de fouilles à Villeneuve-Saint-Germain'. *Révue Archéologique de Picardie,* Numéro spécial, 1: *Vallée de l'Aisne : cinq années de fouilles protohistoriques,* 213–64.

Evans, D. Ellis 1967 *Gaulish Personal Names. A Study of some Continental Celtic Formations.* Oxford, Clarendon Press.

Fitzpatrick, A. P. 1997 *Who were the Druids?* London, Weidenfeld and Nicolson.

Foster, J. 1986 *The Lexden Tumulus: A Re-appraisal of an Iron Age Burial from Colchester, Essex.* Oxford, British Archaeological Reports British Series 156.

Foulston, L. 2002 *At the Feet of the Goddess. The Divine Feminine in Local Hindu Religion.* Brighton, Sussex Academic Press.

Gager, J. G. 1992 *Curse Tablets and Binding Spells from the Ancient World.* New York/Oxford, Oxford University Press.

Gordon, R. 2002 'Shaping the text: theory and practice in Graeco-Egyptian malign magic', *Kykeon: Studies in honour of H. S. Versnel,* ed. H. E. J. Horstmannhoff, H. W. Singer, F. T. van Straten, J. H. M. Strubbe, 69–111. Leiden, Brill.

Gordon, R., D. Joly & W. Van Andringa 2010 'A prayer for blessings on three ritual objects discovered at Chartres-*Autricum* (France, Eure-et-Loir)', *Magical Practice in the Latin West. Papers from the International Conference held at the University of Zaragoza 2005,* ed. R. Gordon & F. Marco Simón, 487–518. Leiden, Brill.

Graf, F. 1999 *Magic in the Ancient World.* Cambridge, Mass., Harvard University Press.

Green, M. J. 1989 *Symbol and Image in Celtic Religious Art.* London, Routledge.

Hutton, R. 1993 *The Shamans of Siberia.* Glastonbury, Isle of Avalon Press.

Hutton, R. 2001 *Shamans. Siberian Spirituality and the Western Imagination.* London, Hambledon.

Joly, D., W. Van Andringa & S. Willerval 2010 'L'attirail d'un magicien rangé dans un cave de Chartres (*Autricum*)', *Gallia* 67.2, 125–208.

Kaul, F. 1991 *Gundestrupkedlen.* Copenhagen, Nationalmuseet Nyt Nordisk Forlag Arnold Busck.

Koch, J. T. 2007 *An Atlas for Celtic Studies. Archaeology and Names in Ancient Europe and Early Medieval Ireland, Britain and Brittany.* Oxford, OxbowBooks.

Lambot, B. 2000 'Victimes, sacrificateurs et dieux', *Les Druides,* ed. V. Guichard & F. Perrin, 30-6. *L'Archéologue* Hors Série 2.

Marco Simón, F. 2015. 'Discrepant behaviour: on magical activities in Hispania and Gallia', *Religion in the Roman Empire: The Dynamics of Individualisation,* ed. R. Haeussler, T. King, F. Marco Simón and G. Schörner, in press. Oxford: Oxbow Books.

Medlycott, M. 2011 *The Roman Town of Great Chesterford.* Chelmsford, East Anglian Archaeology Report No. 137, Historic Environment Essex County Council.

Mees, B. 2009 *Celtic Curses.* Cambridge, Boydell and Brewer.

Meid, W. 1992 *Gaulish Inscriptions.* Budapest, Archaeolingua Alapítvány.

Niblett, R. 2001 *Verulamium. The Roman City of St Albans.* Stroud, Tempus.

O'Connell, M. G. & J. Bird 1994 'The Roman temple at Wanborough, excavation 1985–1986', *Surrey Archaeological Collections* 82, 1–168.

Parfitt, K. 1995 *Iron Age Burials from Mill Hill, Deal.* London, British Museum Press.

Pentikäinen, J. 1998 *Shamanism and Culture.* Helsinki, Etnika.

Perrin, F. 2000 'Le Gui', *Les Druides,* ed. V. Guichard & F. Perrin, 21–2. *L'Archéologue* Hors Série 2.

Raybould, M. E. & P. Sims-Williams 2007 *The Geography of Celtic Personal Names in the Latin Inscriptions of the Roman Empire.* Aberystwyth, CMCS.

St. Pierre, M. & T. Long Soldier 1995 *Walking in the Sacred Manner. Healers, Drummers and Pipe Carriers – Medicine Women of the Plains Indians.* New York, Touchstone/Simon and Schuster.

Schultes, R. E., A. Hofmann & C. Rätsch 1992 *Plants of the Gods. Their Sacred, Healing and Halluinogenic Powers.* Rochester, Vermont, Healing Arts Press.

Whatmough, J. 1949–51 *The Dialects of Ancient*

Gaul. Privately printed by J. Whatmough.

Wiltshire, P. E. J. 2007 'Palynological analysis of the organic material lodged in the spout of the strainer bowl', in P. Crummy *et al.*, 394–8.

Wiseman, A. & P. Wiseman 1980 *Julius Caesar. The Battle for Gaul*. London, Chatto and Windus.

Woodward, P. & A. Woodward 2004 'Dedicating the town: urban foundation deposits in Roman Britain', *World Archaeology* 36.1, 68–86.

Woolf, G. 1998. *Becoming Roman. The Origins of Provincial Civilization in Gaul*. Cambridge, Cambridge University Press.

XVIII

THE IMPORTANCE OF LOCATION:
RELIGIOUS INSCRIPTIONS FROM ARCHAEOLOGICAL CONTEXTS

Ralph Haeussler

There are many cult places where ritual activities continued virtually unchanged from the late Iron Age to the Roman period. Some of these might yield inscriptions, perhaps attesting a Celtic or Roman theonym. But a Celtic theonym or epithet on its own can hardly provide an insight into 'Celtic' religions. And a Roman theonym might merely be one worshipper's personal interpretation of a cult. Inscriptions provide a rather biased image of a cult, especially in the context of indigenous cults where the use of epigraphy might have appeared alien to many worshippers. Only a contextual analysis that takes into account archaeological and sculptural evidence can provide a wider picture of an ancient cult. A series of case studies (Glanum, Châteauneuf, Lydney Park) aims to show where in a sanctuary inscriptions were set up, who could have seen them, how they might have related to other cult features, and how this affects our interpretation of cults and deities. We see the importance to identify the original location of an inscription as precisely as possible.

IT is vital to look at the wider context when studying the texts of religious dedications. A large proportion of inscriptions derive from non-archaeological and non-stratigraphic contexts. Many had been re-used as building material, from late Antiquity when altars and *stelai* were recycled to construct houses and fortifications, and subsequently churches. This causes numerous problems for our analysis of ancient cults: if we find a series of altars built into a church, this does not necessarily mean that they all came from the same cult complex. As an example, the village of Suno, in Cisalpine Gaul, is generally considered to be a major rural cult place, a regional or extra-urban religious hub, dedicated to a series of deities typical for this part of sub-Alpine Gaul: Matronae, Mercury, Hercules, as well as Jupiter, Victoria, and the rare epitaph of a *haruspex*.[1] Unfortunately, virtually all the inscriptions come from the church of San Genesio. In other words, this allegedly important sanctuary might never have existed, since the inscriptions might have been collected from a number of different sites in and around Suno. This can therefore change the way in which we interpret the nature of the cults.

1 Cavalieri 2012; Haeussler 2015.

The number of non-stratigraphic inscriptions has often been over-estimated in scholarship. A large number have been discovered during archaeological excavations and many inscriptions were discovered *in situ*, in their original position. These inscriptions raise important questions. For example: Where were these inscriptions placed, how did one experience them, who could actually see them, how long were they on display, and what purpose did they have? How do inscriptions relate to a particular cult and which inscriptions belong together? The latter is a rather problematic issue, as we have already seen in the case of Suno. Since the first guidelines for the Corpus-F.E.R.C.AN., devised in Luxembourg in 1999, it was recognised that we are faced with a problem: if we imagine, for example, a sanctuary dedicated to Apollo Grannus, like Grand, it was decided that all Apollo dedications from this sanctuary need to be taken into account, even if the Celtic name *Grannus* was left out. Similar cases would be Apollo Maponus, Mars Cocidios, or Sulis Minerva. Whether people called the goddess of Bath's sacred spring Sulis, Sulis Minerva, or just Minerva, they all worshipped the same deity. And in the concept of 'polis religion', in which deities were predominantly considered local deities, associated with particular geographical features, local identity, and/or a cult organised and financed by the local community or municipality, many of these deities would have been considered embedded in local topography, culture and society (in a manner of speaking, 'indigenous' in origin), and only when we consider all the varieties of naming practices may we really understand their function and character. This is particularly important if we want to analyse the *cultores* who frequented a sanctuary: we obviously should not leave out a large proportion of the *cultores* who did not address a god by his/her full name (after all, some theonyms might even have been taboo names)[2] or perhaps even choose a different name that suited their personal *interpretatio*. If a large number of deities from one site is attested, both in epigraphy and sculpture, we need to look at evidence for a more precise location and for a contextual analysis.

Glanum: local, personal and global

Let us take the example of the Iron Age oppidum Glanum (Saint-Rémy-de-Provence) in Roman times. Though there had been some previous sporadic finds from the area, the vast majority of inscriptions and votive offerings derive from the ongoing excavations since 1921, which makes it an ideal case study (see Fig. 1 for overview). But again, we need to be alert: while some inscriptions seem to have been found *in situ*, others had already been 'recycled' during Glanum's lifetime or after its abandonment in the mid-3rd century AD.

Glanum's sacred spring: Glanicae, Glanis and Hercules

Several of Glanum's cult places provide a wide range of evidence. At the heart, there is the sacred spring that had already been monumentalised in the 3rd century BC. In

2 Well-known is the taboo to pronounce YHWH in Judaism; alternative denomination, not just in Judaism but all religions, can also become theonyms and eventually even taboo names.

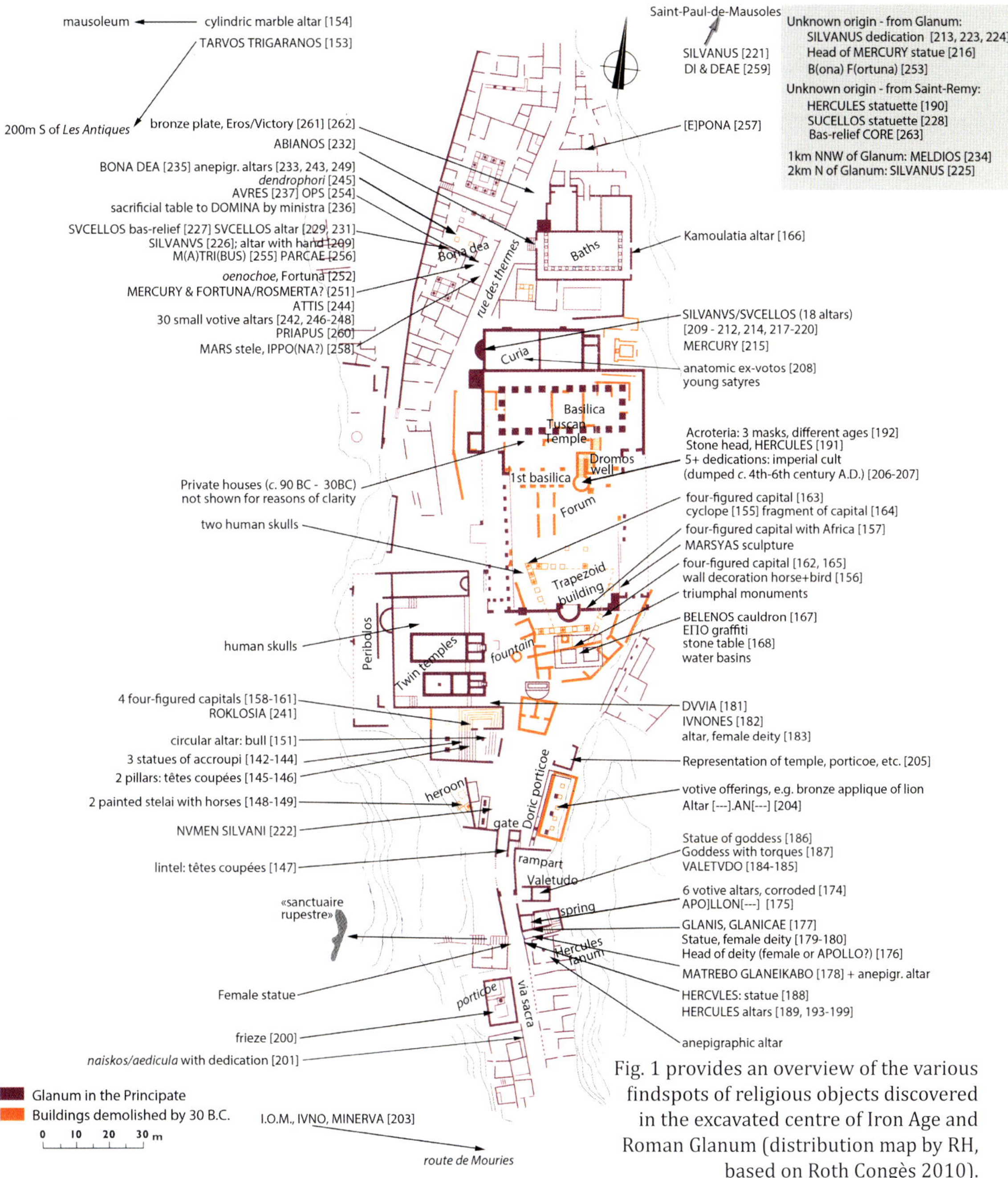

Fig. 1 provides an overview of the various findspots of religious objects discovered in the excavated centre of Iron Age and Roman Glanum (distribution map by RH, based on Roth Congès 2010).

Roman times, it presents us with a conundrum. One often presumes that the toponymic god Glanis and the Glanic mother goddesses were worshipped here.[3] But the evidence from the Roman period appears rather complex and confusing since so many different deities are attested (Fig. 1).[4]

3 For Glanum, cf. Rolland 1946, 1958; Roth Conges 1997, 2010.

4 For the cults of Glanum, cf. Roth Congès 1997.

Let us look at the picture that worshippers must have been experienced in the 1st-3rd century. How did one approach the sacred spring? The *cultores* came from the large open space in front of the twin temples and passed the Doric portico that probably had a religious function (perhaps a place for the pilgrims' preparation and purification). Having entered the 'sacred way' through a small gate, they followed the narrow sacred way that was surrounded by mountainous slopes on either sides and dominated by the impressive Mont Gaussier, whose potential sacred role has often been ignored. We can only speculate how this street might have appeared: it was probably decorated during religious festivals and we can imagine all possible noises and smells that were contained north of the Iron Age rampart, not least from the so-called 'wine smokery' a few metres after the spring.

Unless we presume the display of numerous perishable materials as votive offerings, the most visible sign of a religious site is the assemblage of Hercules altars next to the spring's entrance. These altars were all set up in the actual street, together with a statue of the god, visible to the passing public. Hercules must have been a healing deity in this context; like other sculptures in Glanum, his statue shows him holding a vessel.[5] Moreover, the *rogans/rogare* formula on several inscriptions may indicate that people might have put questions or petitions to the god, perhaps implying an oracular deity (which could be connected to *aures* and *roklosia*: *v. infra*). But as one entered the narrow passageway that led towards the spring, one passed another series of monuments, predominantly female: first, the statue of a goddess, carrying a plate with fruits, discovered *in situ* in a cult niche in the left wall at a height of 1.15 m.[6] There is space for a second figure, but it must have been removed or destroyed prior to Glanum's abandonment; perhaps the fragment of a female statue – in 'archaic Greek' posture found opposite the via sacra (building XXXV) – might have belonged here.[7] There is also a Gallo-Greek altar to the Glanic mothers (*matrebo Glaneikabo*), discovered at the entrance together with an anepigraphic altar,[8] and a Latin dedication to Glanis, the Glanicae and Fortuna Redux,[9] discovered next to the cult niche. Apart from six corroded votive altars,[10] there are also two possible finds relating to Apollo, all of which were found in the nymphaeum's basin;[11] they might have been on display together with other ex-votos. There is also the representation of a goddess wearing a torque on an

5 For discussion of Hercules' role, cf. Roth Congès 1997 (vs. Gros 1995 who prefers to see this as a sanctuary for sheep transhumance). Calling Hercules with drinking vessel a Hercules *bibax* may miss the point: not a drunken god, but a reference to the sacred water: we can also see other deities holding a *patera* or bowl at Glanum (not least, Silvanus-Sucellos). The idea of a 'fanum' – a temple or shrine – for Hercules has nowadays been largely discarded since the presumed building faces south and there is no direct connection to the Hercules altars.

6 Rolland 1958, 87 (plate 30, 2).

7 Rolland 1958, 87 (plate 29,2).

8 *C.* 2nd–1st century BC: *RIG* G-64 (fig. 69); *CAG* 13/2, n° 100, p. 297 (fig. 236); Mullen 2008.

9 AE 1954, 103; Rolland 1958, 87–9 (plate 30,3); AE 1964, 146; CAG 13/2, n° 100, p. 296 (fig. 235).

10 CAG 13/2, n° 100, p. 304.

11 A Greek dedication to [Απο]λλων (CAG 13/2, n° 100, 44, p. 304; IGF 51, fig. 60) and the archaic representation of an Apollo head: Roth Congès 1997. We do not have a precise origin for the third item, a small fragment with the badly written text *Apol(l)i/ni* — CIL XII 991; CAG 13/2, no. 100, p. 265.

acroterion discovered in the Valetudo temple.[12] In pre-Roman Glanum, there used to be lots of representations of deities and deified ancestors with torques, notably in the trapezoid building and the 'heroon', some of them female, but this seems to be the only one that was still visible in imperial times. The Valetudo temple overlooks the whole 'nymphaeum'; the spring was instrumentalized by Marcus Agrippa who constructed the Valetudo temple, probably *c.* 19 BC, bringing its healing power in the service of the Roman empire, and notably for Augustus who had suffered a severe illness in 23 BC.[13]

How can we interpret this seemingly random assortment of deities at the sacred spring? Here we see the interaction of local, personal and global understandings that shaped people's religious understandings. First, there is the local cult place focussing on the spring – a site that did not change its appearance from the 3rd century BC until Glanum's abandonment. Most of our epigraphic evidence reflects personal choices and personal *interpretations*: some people interpreted the local deities as mother goddesses, others as Hercules or Glanis, and Marcus Agrippa understood – or redefined – her as the Roman Valetudo. We do not have a single 'official' inscription at the spring, neither from any of Glanum's decurions or priests.[14] The global understanding is evident: Agrippa inserts the local spring into the worship of the Roman goddess Valetudo – this must have been a very conscious decision: Agrippa considered the main deity to be female when he visited the shrine.

This raises the question about Hercules, the main visible divine power at the spring; even more than Valetudo, Hercules was a deity acknowledged across the Mediterranean and widely attested across the Keltiké (attested in Glanum since the 2nd century BC).[15] We also find some tenuous evidence for Apollo. How can we have Apollo and Hercules at the same shrine? First, it is possible that they were not worshipped at the same time, judging from the condition of the Apollo finds. Second, we also need to take into account a large stone cauldron from Glanum from *c.* 100 BC that might provide the missing link: a Gallo-Greek dedication to Belenos,[16] a strong, powerful deity ('Maître de la Puissance'),[17] but also a healing god, sometimes worshipped as Apollo Belenus/Belinus in imperial times.[18] And as a strong god, it is feasible that people might have interpreted Belenos as Hercules, especially in a place like Glanum: after all, Hercules is said to have passed the region (there is the 'Heraklean Way' and the 'Stony Plain', the Crau, created when

12 Rolland 1958, 104 (plate 36,2).
13 Unlike Salus, Valetudo is the deity for personal health; this may reflect a re-interpretation of Glanum's cult as a personal healing cult.
14 There were dedications to the imperial cult that were set up by the *Glanienses*, the people of Glanum, probably displayed on the forum, but dumped into the well under the forum. Agrippa also does not mention his titles, but this does not imply that we are dealing with an act of personal philanthropy; the title *co(n)s(ul)* could theoretically be reconstructed.
15 2nd-century BC bronze figurine of Hercules, naked and beardless, carrying a drinking vessel (*rhyton*), discovered in Saint-Rémy-de-Provence: Rolland 1958, 109 (plate 39.2).
16 It was re-used as building material in the Augustan period: RIG G-63 (fig. 68); CAG 13/1, nº 100, 58*, 1.
17 Delamarre 2003, 72, s.v. *belo-*, *bello-*.
18 Notably in Aquileia, but also at Bardonecchia: to *deo Apollini Beleno* by L(ucius) Erax Bardus, *ex respon(so)*: AE 1959, 170 = AE 2005, 961.

Zeus assisted Hercules).[19] It is possible that people's personal *interpretatio* reflects the particular local character of the god: a powerful therapeutic deity that took up features from Belenos and was subsequently also influenced by Apollo, like his possible oracular capacity, while at the same time being inserted in the local mythical landscape, i.e. Hercules' travels. The god Glanis is mentioned in only one inscription: is this just an attempt by the worshipper to give the god a local name, or did he have any deeper insight when he made a dedication to Glanis and the Glanicae?[20] After all, this combination of one male god and plural mother goddesses is quite common in Gallia Narbonensis.

This leads us to the female deities. There is lots of evidence for the presence of a female goddess, notably in sculpture and iconography. But apart from Valetudo and the Glanic mother goddesses, we cannot put a name to her (or them). If we are really dealing here with mother goddesses, their relative rarity in the epigraphic record in Glanum would be rather unusual since the *matres* are otherwise extremely common in Southern Gaul, together with other single goddesses, like Minerva or Terra Mater, that are equally elusive in Glanum.

We are dealing with a sanctuary that gradually evolved from the Iron Age through the late Republican period to the imperial period: we can expect a certain level of persistence and continuity. And yet, the choice of deities in Glanum seems particular within the religious landscapes of Southern Gaul. If we want to understand the further development of these originally 'Celtic' cults, then we need to insert our jigsaw puzzle into different environments, e.g. at the sacred spring itself, within Glanum, and within Gallia Narbonensis, as well as chronological developments: the transformation of a powerful male healing god from Belenos, to Apollo and finally Hercules is only one possible scenario to account for sociocultural and political developments. What rituals took place at the sacred spring and how does this site relate to the rest of Glanum? Hercules is only attested at the sacred spring, but evidence for healing deities also comes from other parts of Glanum, like the countless anatomic representations discovered under the *curia*. Focussing on a Celtic theonym, like Glanis, is not helpful to understand a cult or religion. We need to look at the whole picture if we want to understand Celtic and Gallo-Roman cult activities. Let us just hypothesize that the pair Glanis/Glanicae might reflect a similar divine concept as other 'Celtic' couples, like Belenos/Belisama,[21] or perhaps Mercury/Rosmerta that we will discuss below.

Epona & Bona Dea – disentangling Glanum's pantheon

Another interesting constellation of finds can be found further north in Glanum's town centre, indicating an array of deities of diverse origins and meanings that needs to be

---

19 Strab. 4.7.

20 AE 1964, 146; CAG 13/2, n° 100, p. 296 (fig. 235): He also dedicated this to Fortuna Redux which may reflect his background: a Roman citizen and veteran of the *legio XXI Rapax*.

21 Belisama is attested on a rare Gallo-Greek dedication from Vaison-la-Romaine: RIG G-153; for Delamarre (2003, 72) 'La Très Puissante'.

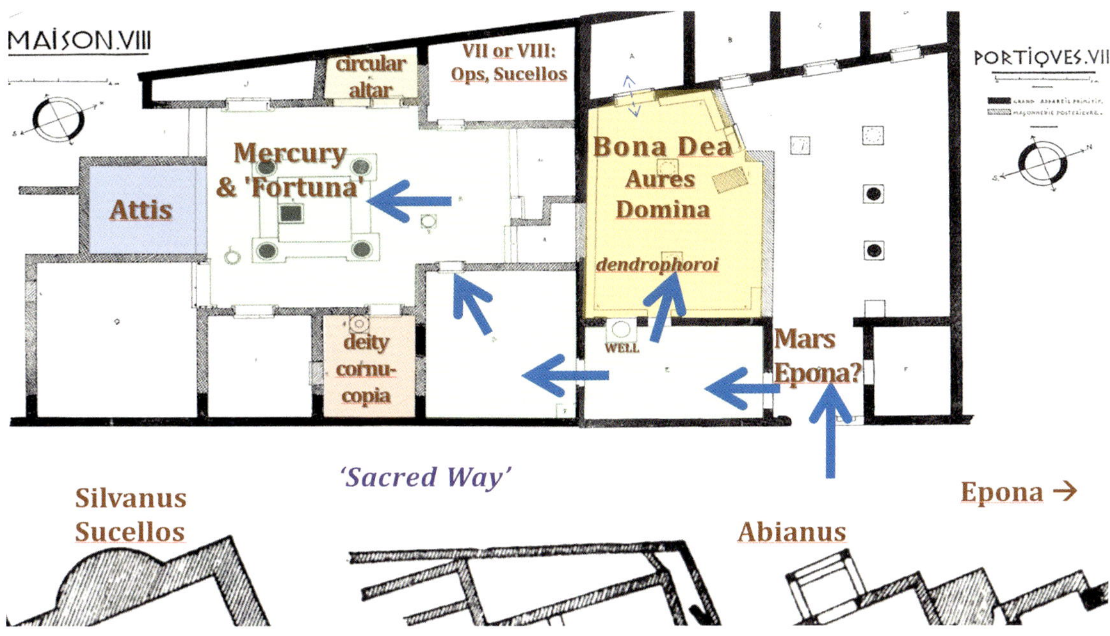

Fig 2. Reconstruction of the distribution of finds in the Bona Dea temple and House VIII (based on Rolland's excavation reports).

disentangled: Bona Dea, Epona, Fortuna, Matres,[22] Ops,[23] Parcae,[24] but also Attis, Mercury and Sucellos/Silvanus. At the heart of this religious 'hub', there is the so-called Bona Dea temple which can be clearly recognized: part of the Hellenistic market ('House VII') had been separated by a wall to create a dedicated cult place in Roman times that must have been out of view of the public; there does not seem to be any direct access from the street (Fig. 2). The finds relating to the cult of Bona Dea, also addressed as *domina* and *aures*,[25] were all discovered within the so-called '*cella*',[26] like an impressive altar, a sacrificial table, and also an altar depicting a bust of a woman holding a *patera* in her right hand and a shaft or sceptre in her left.[27]

But what is Bona Dea doing in this ancient Celto-Ligurian oppidum? The 'Good

22 CAG 13/2, n° 100, 74*, p. 356, inscription n° 4: MTPI = *M(a)tri(bus)*?

23 AE 1946, 157; CAG 13/2, n° 100, p. 356 (fig. 339).

24 *Parcis / trebus / sororibus* (AE 1946, 158; CAG 13/2, p. 356 (fig. 340)); the Parcae are not usually called 'three sisters', but we find a comparable find from Ladenburg, though called 'the well leading sisters', with a Celtic divine name: *Sulevis sororibus* (CIL XIII 11740 = ILS 9323).

25 Bona Dea: AE 1946, 155; CAG 13/2, n° 100, p. 355 (fig. 337); sacrificial altar by the *ministra* to Dom(i) na: AE 1946, 154; Brouwer 1989, p. 136, n° 134; CAG 13/2, n° 100, p. 354 (*domina* is also used as epithet for Isis and Venus, and we find dedications to Domina alone, for example, in the Baetica, Pannonia, Moesia and Dacia). The elegant *aures* altar with wreath, ribbons and ears: AE 1946, 153; Brouwer 1989, pp. 135–6, n° 133; CAG 13/2, n° 100, p. 354; the latter is almost identical to a Bona Dea altar from Arles, dated to AD 25–50 (Brouwer 1989, no. 130; CIL XII 654 (add. p. 817); ILS 3496; CAG 13/5, p. 318). Other finds from the 'Bona Dea temple' include an anepigraphic circular altar, discovered next to the Aures altar: Rolland 1946, 98.

26 But the nature of this cult place is rather 'un-Roman': it is no temple and therefore the term 'cella' is problematic. What does this tell us about the identity of Bona Dea or about the status of her cult?

27 CAG 13/2, p. 378, fig. 378; from House VII or VIII, there is also an altar with the bust of a female person holding her hair half-long: could this be Glanum's Bona Dea?

Goddess' is a very enigmatic Roman goddess since her cult was forbidden to men which means that her 'real' name was unknown. Already Classical authors hypothesized about her identity.[28] We therefore need to ask what people in Glanum could have possibly known about her cult. Is this still the Roman goddess or one particular for Glanum or the Gallia Narbonensis?[29] The Bona Dea temple and the neighbouring House VIII provide an interesting assemblage of finds. But we need to identify the individual findspots as precisely as possible: which altars, ex-votos and sculptures were placed in which room, which were visible from the street, and what was only accessible to initiates?

House no. VIII is called *Maison d'Atys* because of some 30 small votive altars for the Phyrgian god.[30] A large cult relief of Attis probably constituted the centre of worship, perhaps in House VIII, one of its rooms, though the dedication by Attis' worshippers, the *dendrophoroi*, was found in the Bona Dea temple. This could point toward a cult of Attis' consort, Magna Mater Cybele, but she is not attested. It may also imply that some (male) *cultores* identified Bona Dea with Magna Mater in Glanum. This combination is rare in material evidence, but alluded to by some ancient authors, however speculative.[31] Many of the anepigraphic votive altars from House VIII are rather small, less than 20 cm tall. Some of the finds can be attributed to different parts of House VIII: for example, a large relief with a rather 'provincial' representation of Mercury and a goddess with cornucopia and rudder (Fortuna?) was found at the centre, in the *impluvium*; votive altars, some with pinecone (i.e. for Attis), were found in room H, south of the *impluvium*; an anepigraphic circular altar in form of a column, with hollow top, was found in room K to the west of the *impluvium*. And to the east, in a well in room E, an elaborate bronze jug with a depiction of a deity with cornucopia[32] on the handle was found. For a number of finds, the older excavation reports only provide an imprecise reference, House VII or VIII, like for numerous altars with female representations, perhaps Bona Dea,[33] a dedication to 'Plenty',[34] and also an altar with a male standing god, with *patera* and long shaft (mallet?),[35] and a similar, but very crude, representation of a god.[36]

The latter two seem to be representations of the mallet god, 'the good striker' (Sucellos/Silvanus), and create a connection to the countless small votive altars discovered across the road, in the so called *'curia'*, the north-west corner of the forum. But it is difficult to say whether the latter were on public display, either in the *curia* or along the *rue de thermes*. It is equally possible that they were merely stored here in the

28 Cf. in general Brouwer 1989.
29 We also find her cult at Arles and Narbonne: Brouwer 1989.
30 All non-epigraphic except for inscription of the *dendrophoroi*, which was discovered in house VII near the Bona Dea altar: For the Attis finds, cf. CAG 13/2, no 100, 71*, p. 352-3; For the inscriptions *dendro/fori / Glanici*: Rolland 1946, 12–3 (fig. 7); AE 1946, 156; CAG 13/2, n° 100, 71*, p. 352 (p. 353, fig. 332).
31 E.g., Macrobius *Saturnalia* 1.12.16–33.
32 CAG 13/2, n° 100, p. 351 (fig. 329): Fortuna?
33 Esp. 7871.
34 *Opibus / Optata / v(otum) s(oluit) l(ibens) m(erito)* — AE 1946, 157; CAG 13/2, n° 100, p. 356 (fig. 339).
35 Esp. 7870 (plate XIII); CAG 13/2, n° 100, p. 356–7.
36 Esp. 7862 (plate XI); CAG 13/2, p. 356.

basement: the forum level would have been several metres higher; also, a direct access from the *rue de thermes* to the curia seems unlikely. We are dealing here with lots of small altars reflecting the 'religiosity' and gratitude of poorer people: is it possible that ex-votos were systematically removed from public display?

What kind of place are we dealing with? House VIII can hardly have been a residential house in Roman times. But was it a cult place or merely a treasure house? And, in the latter case, would it have been the treasure house for one specific or for several cult places in the vicinity? It is feasible that this place contained many more votive objects and that those in bronze and precious metals were probably salvaged when Glanum was abandoned in the 3rd century (the bronze jug from the well, *supra*, might have been overlooked). The excavations also suggest that the Bona Dea temple and House VIII somehow belonged together. House VIII might have been a space accessible to men and women, and hence yields a different selection of artefacts. Perhaps one had to enter via the former Hellenistic market to access both Bona Dea and House VIII. There, different rooms might have served different purposes: some places might have served for banqueting of *collegia*, like the *dendrophoroi*, others could have served as treasure rooms, religious consultants, oracular activities, and the actual worship. House VIII might have been a kind of multi-purpose cult place.

Some inscriptions were probably positioned outside the buildings, in the street, similar to the Hercules altars at the spring. For example, a votive altar to Abianus was discovered opposite House VII/VIII to the right of the entrance to the baths:[37] Abianus – a Celtic theonym meaning 'Sacred Water'[38] – seems quite appropriate for the bath complex and might indicate that the baths might have retained some religious functions in the Roman period; after all, this is close to the 2nd-century BC temple with dromos well. Another interesting find is an unconventional stele (Fig. 3).[39] It was discovered in House VII and contains two superimposed inscriptions. The earlier one, probably dating to the 1st century AD, is dedicated to Mars: 'Sextus Tiberius Ver() *missicus* has deposited an aureus to Mars in the altar at the entry of the temple(?)'.[40] The stele has indeed three '*loculi*' to receive offerings by the worshippers. It is possible that it was placed at the entrance to the temple, perhaps in the forecourt or in the street, so that *cultores* could easily make their offerings day and night. In this respect, this is an interesting stele, though the name Mars is unexpected since he is otherwise not attested in Glanum. Probably during the 3rd century AD, the stele seems to have been recycled, perhaps moved to another location, and inscribed with a new dedication:

37 Height 65cm: *Abian/o / Caeci[li]/us Firmus v.s.l.m.* — AE 1937, 143; AE 1946, 159; CAG 13/2, n° 100, p. 377 (fig. 377).

38 The theonym derives from the root **ab-ya* 'l'eau', thus probably 'sacred water': cf. De Bernardo Stempel 2007; Delamarre 2003, 29-30, s.v. *abona, abu-*, 'rivière'.

39 205 by 33 by 17 cm — AE 1946, 151; CAG 13/2, p. 355.

40 *Sex(tus) Tib(erius) Ver() missici/us aureum / Marti pos[uit] / [i]n ara ad pri[m]/as heius* PICLV.

IIX M IP PO	*Ex m(onitu) (H)ippo(nae)*	'On instruction by Epona(?),
L C VIATO	*L(ucius) C() Viato(r)*	Lucius Cornelius Viator,
IID DIS OMN	*(a)ed(ituus?) dis omn[i]-*	custodian(?), (made a
BVS	*bus.*	donation?) to all gods.'

This might show the all-embracing role of this cult place, notably at the time of this dedication.[41] It goes beyond the worship of just one or two deities, like Bona Dea and Attis. The fact that the temple custodian was instructed by Epona to make a dedication to all gods sounds intriguing. But the reconstruction *(a)ed(ituus)* is unfortunately rather precarious: two letters are barely sufficient to reconstruct a relatively uncommon word; a simple *(d)ed(it)* (or *(d)ed(dicavit)*) might be more likely; if it was a title, it could equally have been an *(a)ed(ilis)*. Also, the spelling *(H)ippona* is unique; Epona is also attested on another altar in Glanum, conventionally dated to *c.* 100-50 BC, which was recycled as building stone in House II north of the baths already in Roman times. Epona is otherwise extremely rare in Southern Gaul, perhaps an early victim of *interpretatio*.[42] Considering the late date, *Hippona* might well have been a sophisticated reconstruction by an educated citizen, perhaps attempting to elucidate the Celtic theonym Epona whose original meaning might have been partially lost.

Epona brings us back to the question about the meaning of this cult place, and perhaps of Glanum in general. This goddess was often reduced to a mere patron for horses and travellers in the Roman empire. But we can reconstruct some of her complexity in a Gallic context: her complex iconography and the many similarities with Rhiannon (**Rīgantōna*, 'divine queen') in the Welsh Mabinogi point towards an eminent mother goddess, indeed as *terra mater*; she is a chthonic goddess, responsible for the fecundity of the world.[43] Is Epona the missing link to understand Glanum's cults? Though very hypothetical, one could argue that these two inscriptions to Epona might just be the tip of the iceberg.

Trying to understand the nature of Glanum's female goddess, we need to remember that, first, there are some parallels with the goddess(es) from the sacred spring (e.g., healing, mother goddesses/*matres*, Fortuna, etc.). It therefore seems possible that these two cult places were linked. Second, we seem to be dealing with one or more goddesses providing prosperity and fertility; this is something also associated when Classical authors compared Bona Dea with Ops, Maia, Demeter,[44] Terra Mater, and many more.

41 There is also another alter *v.s.l.m. dibu(s) de(a)b[u(s)?]*, discovered just outside the archaeological park in 1927: ILGN 149; De Brun 1935, 21; Rolland 1936, 136; CAG 13/2, n° 100, p. 379 (fig. 381). Rolland suggested to read Budenicus; a name generally presumed to originate in *budina*, 'troops', and attested as Mars Budenicus – in almost visible distance – on the oppidum Collias (Gard): CIL XII 2973 (*add.* p 832); ILS 4549; CAG 30/2, p. 332; AE 2007, 927.

42 In a wall separating House II '*Maison d'Epona*' from the baths: Rolland and Rolland 1933, 3 and 27 (fig.); Rolland 1934, 53 (fig.); De Brun1935, 9; RIG pp. 74–5 (fig. 67) (no n°); CAG 13/2, n° 100, 79*, pp. 360–1.

43 For Epona, cf. Euskirchen 1993, Haeussler 2008; for the reconstruction *Rhiannon* < **Rigantōna*, cf. Koch 2006, vol. 4, 1499. Here, we should remember that Epona, too, was called Regina (e.g., CIL III 7750, Apulum) and that, just like the *matres*, there seems to be a plural version (e.g., *Eponab(us)*: CIL III 7904 = ILS 2417).

44 A large high-quality relief (today in Munich), interpreted by some as Kore, was discovered in Saint-

Here, we should remember the importance of Terra Mater in regional dedications, notably from Nîmes.[45] And, as in other places in the region, we find once again a goddess with cornucopia, a goddess of abundance. The choice of deities in Glanum could therefore fit quite well into the South Gaulish 'pantheon'. Both Epona and Bona Dea can be seen as mother goddesses representing earth and fertility. Indeed, at a fundamental level, Epona, Terra Mater, Bona Dea, Ops, Rosmerta/Maia, and the *matres* all represent the primordial concept of a mother goddess.[46] Some inscriptions from Glanum may have merely provided names for specific aspects, like *ops* as divine personification of 'abundance' and 'plenty', while the Celtic word *rosmerta* ('Good Purveyor') might be considered as suitable epithet. Religion is closely linked to social and cultural developments: through time, people's perception of a deity is bound to change. Here we might take into account an earlier Gallo-Greek inscription dedicated to 'Roklosia' by a certain Cornelia: it was found reused in the southern *peribolos* of the Augustan twin temples which provides a *terminus ante quem*.[47] Lejeune, Roth Congès, and Blétry already suggested that Aures and Rokloisia are identical; like *ro-smerta*, *ro-kloisa* also start with *ro-* 'very': depending on our interpretation Rokloisiabo can mean 'aux Très Écoutantes', which would create a direct link to Bona Dea and her *aures*, 'ears', or it could mean 'aux Très Renommées'.[48] Again, we need to be careful: a Celtic word, but perhaps just one of many names how *cultores* might have addressed the deity, here perhaps as the 'Very Renowned (Mother?) Goddesses'. Like Epona, the theonym/epithet

Fig. 3. The Mars/Epona stele with the three 'loculi' from Glanum (photo: Henri Rolland, SRA DRAC PACA).

Rémy-de-Provence in the 17th century: cf. Picard 1963, fig. 18.

45 Terra Mater, notably worshipped together with the 'wheel god' who was addressed as Jupiter on Southern Gaulish inscriptions, e.g. at Clarensac and Nîmes: CIL XII 4140 (*add.* p. 342) and 3071.

46 And we should bear in mind that the name Bona Dea is actually only attested once in Glanum: the other two dedications refer to the Aures and to Domina: *v. supra*. Moreover, we sometimes find Epona together with other healing deities, like Asclepius and Salus on an altar from Sarmizegetusa (AE 1998, 1101).

47 κορνηλια | κλοισαβο | βρατουδεκαντ – Rolland 1958, 54–5 (plate 17,4); Szemerényi 1974, 249; RIG G-65 (fig. 70); Lambert 1994, 87–8.

48 Lejeune, in RIG; Roth Congès 1997; 2010; Delamarre 2003, 260, s.v. *ro*, 'très, trop'; 261, s.v. *rocloisia-bo*, 'aux très écoutantes' ou 'aux Très-Renommées'; Blétry 1998; De Bernardo 2007.

Roklosia might have lost (some of) its importance in the Augustan period.

Why Bona Dea? As mentioned earlier, Marcus Agrippa promoted the cult of Valetudo at the spring, clearly inserting an important indigenous cult centre – and also a centre for the anti-Roman allegiance of the Salluvi – into Roman/Mediterranean understanding. The (hypothetical) *interpretatio* of an important local goddess by means of Bona Dea might derive from a similar initiative, and obviously not only in Glanum, but also in the important *coloniae* Arles and Narbonne (perhaps also under Augustus?). Was it a Roman initiative? Impossible to tell, but it seems likely since, unlike Ceres and Maia, Rome's Bona Dea festivals were rather peculiar,[49] and would have been on the mind of a Roman immigrant; even an educated Gaul would probably have had a different perception of Bona Dea. Perhaps there were some similarities in the nature of the festivals, both in Rome and Glanum; judging from the female dedicants in Glanum, both cults were exclusive to women. To some extent the establishment of her cult might have sparked off other developments, such as a form of organisation increasingly similar to Rome, or the introduction of the cult of Attis as male counterpart. Here we need to ask to what extent Attis could have been worshipped on his own as deity of vegetation and as god who triumphs over death. But why is Attis so important, while there is no evidence for his counterpart, Magna Mater? The mentioning of the 'Glanic dendrophoroi', discovered together with the Bona Dea altar, seems to suggest that his cult followed standard conventions.

And yet it seems that there is more to Bona Dea than just a Roman goddess. The multi-cultural origin of the *cultores* resulted in a unique cult that built on Glanum's 'Celtic' Iron Age foundations, re-shaped indigenous cults, and created, as so often in Gaul, something completely new. Bona Dea was probably well integrated in her environment, closely integrated to Glanum's sacred sites. The local worshippers might not have seen our problems to 'categorize' a deity: the distinction between Roklosia, Epona, Fortuna, Bona Dea, and Ops might just be in our way of thinking. For instance, the 'provincial' relief of Mercury and the goddess with cornucopia and rudder must have been a prominent feature of 'House VII'. But why is Mercury's emblematic consort in Gaul, Maia/Rosmerta (the 'Great Purveyor'), depicted here with a rudder? It does not have to be Fortuna, but could theoretically represent some worshippers' view of the local goddess (*bona dea, aures, roklosia, ops*, etc.). As with Epona and Rhiannon, Terra Mater and Jupiter/Taranis (and perhaps Glanis and Glanicae?), the relief of a 'Gallic' Mercury and his consort represents the union of male and female forces frequently depicted in Gaul.[50] Mercury might have been more important than generally suggested: among the finds from the so-called 'Mas Tardieu' (i.e. the site later identified as the Roman curia/forum), there is also a dedication to Mercury.[51] We need to take extra care when discussing sporadic finds from non-archaeological contexts: there is also an

49 Brouwer 1989; Versnel 1992.

50 Mercury's consort in Gaul is Rosmerta — or, using a Latin name, Maia who is often considered identical to Bona Dea (also see paper by Ferlut in this volume).

51 AE 1925, 35; ILGN 145; De Brun 1935, 16; CAG 13/2, n° 100, p. 338.

unusual depiction of Mercury as a veiled pontifex, wearing his wings under the veil.[52] We should not forget the ex-votos for Silvanus/Sucellos: most of them were of rather 'crude' in nature, and many were anepigraphic or had bad lettering; this may suggest a socially different group of *cultores*, though equally associated with a healing deity, as we have seen earlier. Just hypothetically, we might be dealing here with the couple Silvanus and Silvana:[53] after all, Silvanus is very close to Faunus, and Bona Dea was frequently identified as Fauna.[54] We thus repeatedly the pairing of deities in Glanum that provides food for thought: Glanicae & Glanis, Fauna & Faunus, Silvana & Silvanus, Maia/Rosmerta & Mercury, Bona Dea/Cybele & Attis, Bona Dea & Hercules,[55] Belisama & Belenos, Terra Mater & Jupiter (wheel god), Epona & Jupiter (Rhiannon & Pwyll?).[56]

As so often, we can see that traditional categories, like 'Roman', 'Greco-Oriental', 'Celtic' and 'indigenous' are not useful to understand local cults and people's religious understandings in Roman times. How people called a deity depended on their status, gender, language, education, origin, etc. Altogether, a contextual analysis might indicate that Glanum's town centre was more like one huge sacred space that had different activity zones. As we have seen in Fig. 1, there are lots of finds between Bona Dea and the sacred spring. Even if cults and rituals had evolved since the Iron Age, there is still a continued sacredness in this part: the forum might still have a played a certain role in the cult, just like the two Roman podium temples; for the latter, no evidence was discovered *in situ*, but a number of discarded altars, buried in front of the temples, equally relate to female deities (Iunones, Duvia, Roklosia, and many more).

Nuncupatio & ex-voto: the Limetus sanctuary of Châteuneuf (Savoy)

The evidence from the 'Gallo-Roman' sanctuary at Châteauneuf in Savoy, dedicated to Limetus, Mercury and Maia, is quite different in nature.[57] The excavations from 1978 to 1986 have yielded an astonishing 77 graffiti. 59 graffiti were engraved on the actual walls of the double-cella temple, notably from inside the ambulatory (Fig. 4). It is feasible that worshippers wrote their graffiti as a personal message to the gods; the ambulatory must have been heavily used by worshippers since its floor shows significantly more

52 Esp. IX 6697; Roth Conges 1997, 183–4.
53 This couple is attested nearby at Roussillon: ILN-Apt, 130.
54 Macrobius *Saturnalia* 1.12.22; see my discussion in Haeussler 2017.
55 One may also consider the potential relationship between Hercules and Bona Dea in Roman myth, as reported by Macrobius, *Saturnalia* 1.12.28 and Propertius 4.9.21–70. There is also an altar to Bona Dea, Hercules, and Silvanus from Rome: *Sanct[o Silvano] / Herculi [---] / et Bon[ae Deae(?)] / aedicul[am et] / aram [---]* – Brouwer 1989, 24, AE 1946, 93.
56 Epona is usually attested alone, but this reflects the nature of the evidence (protector of horses) and perhaps a memorable scene of her (or rather, Rhiannon's) myth, i.e. riding in a kind of side saddle, reproduced countlessly in Roman sculpture. But in Noricum, for example, we find a dedication to IOM and Epona (CIL III 5192 [*add.* p. 1830] = ILS 4859; also in Dalmatia as IOM Eponae Reginae — CIL III 12679 = ILS 4837) – a combination that resembles the Jupiter and Terra Mater dedications from the Narbonensis.
57 On the Châteauneuf excavation, cf. Mermet 1993.

usage than the floors in the two cellae.[58] The act of writing one's vow onto the temple wall seems to have been part of the ritual at Châteauneuf. The diversity of lettering style and the number of variant spellings suggest that the majority of inscriptions were engraved by the *cultores* themselves. It is important to remember that such graffiti generally provide a different form of religious communication compared to votive altars in stone. They are usually more personal: instead of the standardised *votum solvit* one also finds rare expressions, like 'with prayers to the gods'.[59] At Châteauneuf the graffiti also provide an insight in the value of the donations and votive offerings – values seem to range from a few *asses* to 35 *denarii*. Other graffiti were engraved on other materials, like the unique deposit of 18 tiles that was found against the ambulatory's southern wall: Mermet suggests that there might have been a status or altar on the outside and that worshippers deposited their offerings and ex-votos here (all inscribed on *tegula* or *imbrex*, mainly mentioning *Augustus* and *Caesar*).[60]

A particular find is the dedication to a god bearing a seemingly Celtic name, *Limetus. It was engraved on a square plaque of grey schist, 48 by 48 cm, that was discovered *in situ* in the floor at the geometric centre of the temple between the two *cellae*, facing the visitors who entered the temple from the east; it roughly dates to the Julio-Claudian period and may indicate the deity to whom this temple was dedicated originally. It was set up by the sons of Atepo, [Pr]im[us] and Quartio.[61] The graffiti from the temple walls also contain a series of short dedications to the god *Limetus;[62] there is also this short votive inscription: *[-----] u(otum) a(nimo) l(ibens) m(erito) [s(oluit)] / Neroni / Limet[o]*.[63] How does this combination of Nero and Limetus came about? There are many possible scenarios. We could perhaps also envisage that these dedications and offerings were the result of seasonal festivals that must have taken place at Châteauneuf, like at the other sanctuaries; some festivals honoured the local gods, others the emperor, for example when celebrating the emperor's birthday. Some graffiti from the 'fanum' refer, among others, to the goddess Roma and the emperor (just *Caesari* or *Augusto*). In the context of a public cult, we should perhaps expect the permeation of the imperial cult in most local sanctuaries. This may show people's personal devotion to the emperor, but above all that Limetus was a cult financed by the community or municipality, in this case the *colonia Vienna*.

Most graffiti are rather short (see Fig. 4), but there are also some longer texts, like a *votum* to Mercury that reveals the worshipper's intention if and when the god fulfils his

58 Mermet 1993, 102.

59 *[---] diis preci[bus---]*: CAG 73, n° 079, 8*, p. 146; AE 1999, 1027; ILN-Vienne-2, 477.

60 Mermet 1993, 126–7.

61 It is not certain whether we are dealing with two dedicants since the text is damaged, but Primus and Quartio both suggest a single names: *[--Pr]im[us et?] / Quartio / Atepon(is) / [f]i(lii) Limet[o] / u(t) u(ouerant) s(oluerunt) l(ibentes) [m(erito)]*, 'Primus et Quartio, sons of Atepo, have willingly and deservedly fulfilled their vow to Limetus as they had vowed' (AE 1999, 1027; CAG 73, n° 079, 7*, p. 144; ILN-Vienne, 462). For the Celtic origin of the father's name, Atepo, cf. Delamarre 2003, 57, s.v. *ate-*, *at-*; this name is also attested at Nîmes.

62 E.g., *Lim[eto]* — AE 1993, 1118; Rémy 1999, 31–8; CAG 73, p. 144, n° 079; ILN-Vienne, 464.

63 AE 1993, 1152; Rémy 1999, 31–8; AE 1999, 1027; ILN-Vienne, 463; CAG 73, p. 144, no. 079 — for Mermet 1993, 130: *v(ovit)*.

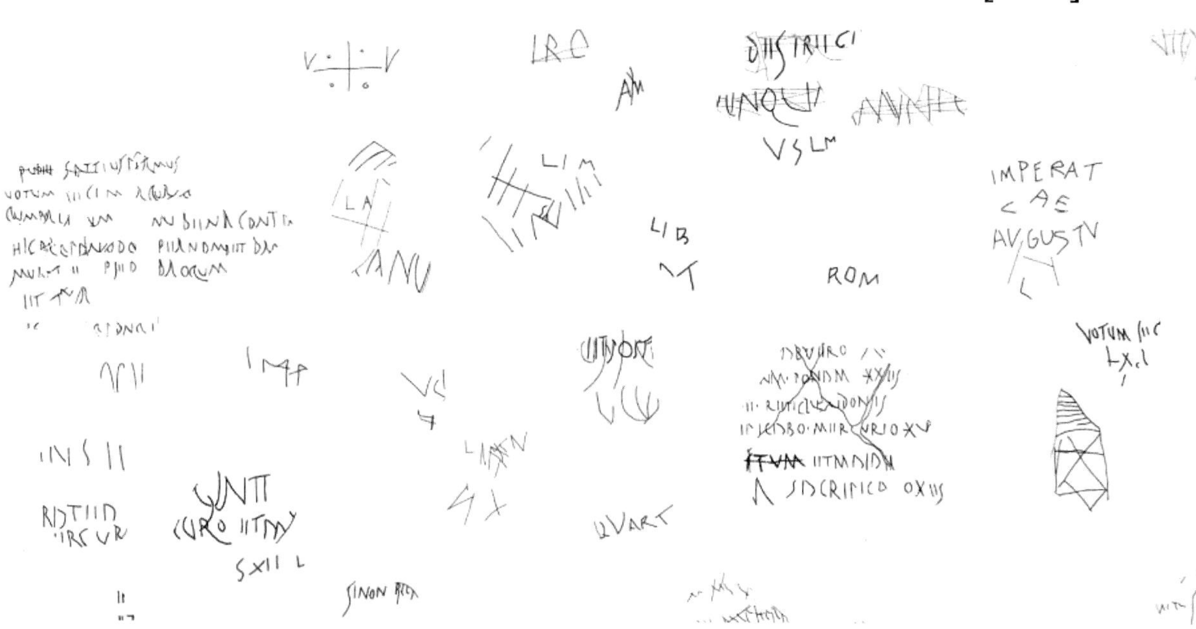

Fig. 4. A selection of the various graffiti and how they might have appeared on Châteauneuf's ambulatory walls — arbitrary arrangement, based on the drawings of Mermet 1993.

wish. This seems to be a *nuncupatio*, a public pronouncing of vows, instead of the usual fulfilment of a vow. We should not forget that these inscriptions must have been visible not only to the gods and the priests, but also to other *cultores* and visitors to the temple.

Publi[u]s Attius Firmus
uotum feci Merqur[i]o (!)
qum primum [---]NV bene conti[ngit mihi(?)]
hic profano do[num] per NOM et DRO[---]
mulsi e[t] pie D[---]D RO <c=q>um [---]
et t[e]r [---]V[---]
IC[---]M FONAI[---].

'Publius Attius Firmus, I have made a vow to Mercury, as soon as something good happened (to me?), I sacrifice here a gift of [---] and piously [---].[64]

One almost gets the impression that this was a legal text. Inscribing it onto the temple wall might have constituted a vital element of making a vow at Châteauneuf. The following vow provides a comparable scenario: in case the dedicant became rich, he/she promised donations of 20 denarii:

[--- cum primum(?) h]abuero (denarios) V[---]
[--- tum don]um ponam (denarios) XII s(emissem)
*[---]*E *retic(u)lu[m(?)] idon(e)is(!)*
[--- sacr]ificabo Mer[c]urio (denariis) V[---]
et Maiae
sacrifica[b]o (denariis) II s(emisse).

64 Mermet 1993, 108, no. 2; AE 1993, 1113; CAG 73, n° 079, 8*, p. 145; AE 1999, 1027; ILN-Vienne-2, 466.

> 'If I have 45 (or more?) *denarii*, I will set up as offering a gift (statue?) for 12½ *denarii*,... sufficient to (repair?) the enclosure (of the temples)... I will sacrifice to Mercury 5 (or more?) *denarii* and to Maia I will sacrifice 2½ *denarii*.'[65]

We have moved from the theonym *Limetus to the Latin theonyms Mercury and Maia. Maia takes the place of Rosmerta across Vienne's territory. One could advocate that Limetus and Mercury are two completely distinct deities, or alternatively that the Roman Mercury gradually took over the role of the indigenous Limetus. But one might also argue that Limetus and Mercury are closely related to that extent that the name Limetus might just be an epithet to describe Mercury's function.

We need to bear in mind that *Limetus is to date a unique theonym. Our graffiti only provide us with LIMET. Other reconstructions, like *Limetanus, are therefore equally possible.[66] It has widely been advocated that we are dealing with a Celtic, perhaps even pre-Roman deity.[67] But it is equally possible that this word is based on the Latin word *limes*; a frontier deity would be very appropriate considering Châteauneuf's location between the *colonia* of Vienne (Allobrogi) and the Alpes Cottiae and Alpes Graiae.[68] For Bernard Rémy, Limetus was an epithet to describe Mercury as frontier deity since Mercury in Gaul is considered 'le gardien des frontières', making this 'le dieu protecteur des frontiers et par extension la divinité garante de la prospérité du territoire'.[69] We should, however, also take into account that the term *limes* predominantly means a road, path or passage in the 1st century AD, but then again, Châteauneuf could have been frequented on the way from Gaul to Italy.

By contrast, Limetus was merely a 'divinité topique' for Sorrel.[70] But is Limetus really just a deonomastic name? The word is likely to be Celtic: after Xavier Delamarre, Limetus, like comparable personal names,[71] derives from the Celtic word *lemo-*, *limo-* for 'elm'.[72] An 'elm god' would, of course, suggest a tree deity comparable to other theonyms from Gallia Narbonensis, like Baginas / Baginatiae, Buxenus, etc. Interestingly, a certain Ioventius, son of *Limiso*, made a dedication to the 'beech deities', Baginatiae, at Saint-Jalle.[73] Moreover, Limetus as 'tree god' fits quite well to the South Gaulish Mercury who is frequently associated with trees: for example, we see Mercury walking towards a tree on an altar from Saint-Bauzély (Gard),[74] and trees feature prominently on the

65 Mermet 1993, 106–7, graffito n° 1 (fig.); AE 1993, 1112b; CAG 73, n° 079, 8*, p. 144 (fig. 82); AE 1999, 1027; ILN-Vienne-2, 471.

66 As a theonym, Limetus is unique, but we find, for example, a Quintus Limetus in Haltern (Galsterer 1983, 151: *Q(uinti) Limeti)*) and a Gaius Mamilius Limetanus at Cerveteri (CIL I 2765 (*add.* p. 1054, 1066) = ILLRP 1148 = AE 1961, 207).

67 Cf. Mermet 1993; Rémy 1999; *CAG 73*, n° 079.

68 Mermet 1993.

69 Rémy 1999, 33.

70 Sorrel 2006.

71 E.g., Limetius, Limenius, Limo, Lemisunia, and Lemiso.

72 Delamarre 2003, 198, s.v. *lemo-*, *limo-*, 'orme'.

73 CAG-26, p. 544 = AE 2000, 889: *Baginatiabus / Ioventius / Lemisonis f(ilius) / v(otum) s(olvit) l(ibens) m(erito).*

74 Discovered in 1972 north of the village of Saint-Bauzély, cf., with further bibliography, *CAG* 30/3, n° 233, pp. 564–5, 8*, fig. 662.

Mercury altar from Caveirac (Gard).[75] This may suggest that the tree must have played a certain role in people's understanding of their local 'Mercuries'. We can also allude to the god Esus (for many, based on the Berne scholiast, a possible equivalent to Mercury): Esus is depicted cutting down a tree on the *pilier des nautes* from Paris, once again indicating that the tree must have played a certain role in local myth and religious understanding.[76] The role of the 'elm', however, is more enigmatic, but this tree must have had some significance considering how many names contained the word *lemo/limo-*, including the Lemovices, 'the people of the elm'; perhaps one can allude here to the creation of Ask and Embla from ash and elm tree in Old Norse anthropogenic myth. And in Greek myth there is the nymph Πτελέα, 'elm', one of the eight hymadryads; we also find nymphs planting elms on the tombs of Trojan heroes, like Eëtion.[77]

We should not forget that these dedications to Limetus, Mercury, Maia, Nero, Caesar, Augustus and Roma were all visible at the same time, prior to the sanctuary's abandonment in the Flavian period. It is possible that people recorded their personal devotion to a god in the temple at different periods of the year – at various religious festivals – during the relatively brief existence of the Châteaunneuf sanctuary. Together, they can provide an insight in the nature of the local 'Gallo-Roman' cult.

Temple inscriptions from Britain

We find similar scenarios in other sanctuaries across the Celtic-speaking regions of the Roman empire. But despite certain similarities, we should not forget that each case is absolutely unique. Another interesting case is of course the sanctuary of Uley in Britain where 140 lead tablets were discovered. A number of these tablets were discovered in the *cella* of the temple; the others unfortunately come from later demolition and rubble layers, making it virtually impossible to identify their original place of deposition in the sanctuary.[78] In the case of curse tablets, it is obvious that they were not on display, but we also find lots of other finds, like silver leafs, to a serious of deities, like Senuna and Toutatis, that must have been visible at sanctuaries in Roman Britain.

On a clear day, there is inter-visibility between Uley and the sanctuary of Lydney Park, overlooking the River Severn.[79] Lydney, dedicated to Nodons, seems superficially similar to an Asklepeion containing a serious of small rooms where pilgrims would have spent the night expecting a divine dream (*enkoimesis*); there was also a bath and a large guest house. Lydney is important due to its large number of small finds. Apart from more than 8,000 coins, up to the 5th century AD, there are some 300 bronze bracelets,

75 CIL XII 3090 = Esp. I 441. There is also an altar from Vernègues (Bouches-du-Rhône) which shows the three 'icons' *wheel, mallet* and *tree*, that might represent the thundering god, Jupiter/taranis, the mallet god *sucellos* and a tree god (Esus/Mercury?).

76 Cf. Esus cutting a tree on the *pilier des nautes*: Haeussler 2012.

77 Hom. Il. 6.419–20.

78 Cf. Woodward 1993, 127. For the inscribed curse tablets, cf. R. S. O. Tomlin in this volume, and Tomlin 1993.

79 Aldhouse-Green 2004, 208.

Fig. 5. The inscribed mosaic from the cella of the Nodons sanctuary in Lydney (after Bathurst & King 1879, plate VIII).

320 pins, nine bronze and stone representations of dogs, and a bronze plaque. Having been constructed in the 3rd century AD, it has yielded inscriptions *in situ*, notably this large mosaic which was found inside the temple/*cella* in 1805. The formula *ex stipibus* shows that it was funded by the collective of worshippers, probably by contributions from local communities into the 'temple treasure' (Fig. 5):

> *D(eo) M(arti?) N(odenti) T(itus) Flavius Senilis pr(aepositus) rel(igionis?) ex stipibus pos{s}uit | o[pitu]lante Victorino | interp(r)[e]tiante.*
>
> 'To the god Mars(?) Nodens Titus Flavius Senilis, superintendent of rites(?), had this laid from offerings, with the assistance of Victorinus the interpreter (of dreams?).'[80]

Traditionally it has been suggested that Nodons has a 'hunting aspect' and that this mosaic, with 'sea monsters and fish' suggest 'some connection of Nodens with the sea'.[81] But all these interpretations are hypothetical. The mosaic may theoretically suggest a deity similar to Neptune, though we should not forget that even the Greco-Roman Poseidon/Neptune is more complex than just a god of the sea and patron of sailors. But if Nodons was akin in nature, then why would he be associated with Mars? Rather than just some 'fishing' associations, the mosaic might represent, for example, a primeval myth. Across the Roman provinces, people used – and adapted – Greco-Roman iconography

80 CIL VII 137; RIB II.4, 2448, 3; Ling 2007, 68–9 (fig. 4); AE 2007, 858.
81 Lewis 1966, 89; cf. Bathurst & King 1879, 22–3 for comparison between Nodons and Glaucus.

Fig. 6. Bronze arm from the Lydney Park sanctuary (photo: RH).

to represent and re-invigorate their own myths and legends. We can compare this to other snake-like creatures in 'Celtic' and 'Gallo-Roman' iconography, like Smertrios killing a serpent (or 'hydra') on the Parisian *pilier des nautes*, and other myths representing the '*Chaoskampf*' between a 'culture hero god' and a chaos monster;[82] this *Chaoskampf* is probably also represented in the Gaulish *Jupitergigantenreiter*. And this 'monster' could, theoretically, also lead us to other supernatural beings, notably the so-called Formorians (*Fomhóraigh)* in Irish mythology, as we shall see next.[83]

Who is Mars Nodons? The most obvious parallels are the Welsh god Nudd/Lludd Llaw Ereint ('Lludd of the Silver Hand') and the Irish god Nuadu. Apart from linguistic affinity, there is also a surprising parallel: the god Nuadu lost an arm during his first battle.[84] Having been protected by god Dagda, he survived the battle, but could no longer be a king as he was no longer physically perfect; he was replaced by Bres, a half-Fomorian. The Fomorians are similar to the Greek Titans: primeval beings coming from the sea or underground. As opponents of the *Tuatha Dé Danann*, the 'good' supernatural beings, they represent the destructive powers and the personification of chaos and darkness. After the god of healing, Dian Cécht, had replaced Nuadu's lost arm with a working silver arm, Nuadu could finally dispose of Bres and his oppressive rule and restore his place as ruler.[85] Is it just a coincidence that a bronze left arm, which used to be displayed standing upright, was discovered at Lydney (Fig. 6)?[86] This may suggest that the myth of Nuadu's lost arm and its silver replacement – or a variation thereof – was already known in 4th-century Britain and/or originated here before spreading to Ireland. Both Nuadu's role in a battle and as protector of the *populus/tuath* may also help to understand why the people in Roman Lydney associated Nodons with Mars.

Under this assumption, Nodons/Nuadu must have been a very powerful god.[87] And like so many powerful deities, people also attributed healing powers to him. Most of

82 Watkins 1995.
83 Carey 2012, 355.
84 *The First Battle of Mag Tuired* 48. Cf. Carey 1984.
85 *Lebor Gabála Érenn* 64; *The Second Battle of Mag Tuired* 27–35; *Annála na gCeithre Máistrí* M3304-10.
86 Of course, this could just have been an anatomic ex-voto.
87 For Jouët 2007, 36 the 'original prototype' of Nuadu was 'un dieu ciel-diurne déclinant, analogue au dieu latin Vedius'; of interest for Lydney: Vedius/Vejovis was also associated with Asclepius, i.e. a healing deity.

our evidence is biased as it mainly consists of ex-votos. Hence throughout the Roman provinces, most deities are primarily attested in their role of healing deity, while other functions are more difficult to prove. The evidence from Lydney shows Nodons' varied functions. A number of artefacts must have been on display in the temple: bronze tablets must have been nailed to the temple walls, like Blandinus' votive tablet to DM NODONTI,[88] the little votive tablet by Pectillus, dedicated to DEO NUDENTE M, with the image of a canid (to which we can add the dog figurines),[89] or the bone plaque representing a woman with her hands on her waist that was probably fixed to the wall by a worshipper who may have survived childbirth. There is also a curse tablet to DEVO NODENTI that explicitly mentions *templum [No]dentis.*[90] Moreover, a large number of individual bronze letters that could make up the word NODENTI SACRUM might have been fixed to the temple wall or a votive object. The different media allow more easily to record slight variations in pronunciation and spelling: Nodons, Nodens and Nudens (with the last form we are seeing the development towards Welsh Nudd). It becomes apparent that no inscription from Lydney makes any explicit mentioning of Mars. M could equally stand for Mercury and D.M. for *deus maximus*. There is only one inscription, on a Mars statuette, from Cockersand Moss in Lancaster that mentions Mars,[91] and we should take into account that the context – and local demography –is different.

Conclusions

These are just a few examples of inscriptions from archaeological contexts in which we can see the importance of location and contextual analysis. Location can provide different interpretations, revealing the interaction between different artefacts, and their place in rituals and people's experiences. One could add countless more examples. The positioning of an altar in the landscape can be important. For instance, at Maryport, the Roman Alauna,[92] recent excavations by Ian Hayes and Tony Wilmott have significantly revised our understandings: the idea that more than 20 Jupiter altars were placed on the military parade ground and subsequently buried during periodical *lustra*, has to be jettisoned.[93] At the site of the inscriptions, to the east of the fort, two adjacent temples, facing east-north-east, seem to point to a particular sacred place on a nearby elevation, some 150 m away. The whole situation should make us question

88 RIB 305 = ILS 4729: *D(eo) M(arti) Nodonti / Flavius Blandinus / armatura / v(otum) s(olvit) l(ibens) m(erito).*

89 RIB 307 = ILS 4729a: *Pectillus / votum quod / promis{s}it / deo Nudente(!) / M(arti) dedit.*

90 RIB 306 = ILS 4730 = AE 2000, 804: *Devo / Nodenti Silvianus / an<e=i>l(l)um perdidit / d<i=e>m<i=e>-diam partem / donavit Nodenti / inter quibus nomen / Seniciani nollis / pe<r=t>mittas sanita/tem donec perfera(t) / usque templum [No]/dentis. // Rediviva.*

91 RIB 616 = AE 1958, 95a: *Deo Marti Nodonti Aur/elius [---]cinus sig(illum).* The other inscription from Cockersand Moss also uses DMN (RIB 617).

92 N.B. This is also a river name, today the river Ellen. But there are also theonyms, e.g., Alaunus (CIL XIII 6425), or in variations of the dedication *Bedaio Augusto et Alounis sacrum* (CIL III 5572, 5581): Delamarre 2003, 37, s.v. alaunos, -a, as epithet meaning 'nourricières'.

93 Haynes & Wilmott 2012, 28; for the Roman Temples Project Maryport cf. http://www.ncl.ac.uk/historical/research/project/5116.

the nature of Maryport's Jupiter: in the main, these altars do not derive from the kind of military ceremony which, for example, the Feriale Duranum prescribes.[94] The shape of the temples (one circular, the other one similar to a Roman temple, but both without the mandatory Roman-style podium) indicate a more indigenous context; also, most of Maryport's Jupiter altars do not mention the emperor's *numen* which seems to have been almost compulsory in British military dedications.[95] The recent excavation might even suggest a Jupiter column, perhaps similar to eastern Gaul. Even though we are in a military context, Jupiter seems to represent the divine force of the *locus*. Again, location is important, like the contextualisation of finds as well as alignment of sites; moreover, inside and outside of the fort and the vicus is crucial: on one hand, the typical range of dedication we expect in a military community, like Fortuna Redux; on the other hand, a particular cult place within the local sacred landscape.

In fact, a number of cult places across the Roman provinces were not placed at the focal sacred site itself, but within visible distance: in Gallia Narbonensis, for example, a number of cult places dedicated to the god Vintur were located in considerable distance from, but in clear visibility of the Mont Ventoux.[96] A similar scenario can be found across the Alps: the god Poeninus – sometimes associated with Jupiter – was not worshipped at the peak of the mountain, but at a sanctuary along the Great St Bernard pass. Cult places can often be related to geographical features at a certain distance; in some cases, this may indicate that the sacred place itself was actually a taboo place.

Location can also inform us about a deity's functions. In the Luberon region, north of the Roman colony Aquae Sextiae (Aix-en-Provence), we find the goddess Dexiva, 'The Favourable (Goddess)', and her cult within the ramparts of the then abandoned Iron Age hilltop site ('oppidum') of Le Castellar.[97] And just at the foot of the hill, we find altars to the god Lanovalus, 'The All Mighty (God)'.[98] These apparent oppositions – male and female, 'Favourable' vs. 'Powerful', inside and outside of the rampart, top and bottom of the hill – may have mirrored the interplay between the two deities, a relationship that might also have been reflected in local myths, legends and festivals.

We have seen the limitations in studying a Celtic theonym or epithet in isolation, ignoring the wider context. What can the text alone tell us about 'Celtic' religions and the persistence and transformation from Iron Age to late Antiquity? We know of so many cult places where rituals continued virtually unchanged from the late Iron Age

94 There is one inscription to Jupiter Capitolinus and two for Mars *militaris*, but again, we must be aware that inscriptions from Maryport must have originated from different locations in the fort, the vicus, and the attested cult places. For the Feriale Duranum, cf. P.Dura 54.

95 Jupiter dedications from Maryport: RIB 816–819, 821–823, 828–831, 833–835: IOM; RIB 814: Jupiter Augustus; RIB 815, 824–826: IOM et numen Augusti; RIB 820: IOM Capitolinus.

96 For Vintur: ILN-4, 17; ILN-4, 143; CIL XII 1341 (add. p 825) = CAG-26, p. 421.

97 For Dexiva cf. Delamarre 2003, 142–3.

98 Delamarre's interpretation seems rather convincing (2003, 196–7, s.v. *lano-*, 306, s.v. *ualos*):'Tout-Puissant', 'Plein-Prince'. The altars were found near the river Laval, but as so often, we have to ask what came first (the chicken or the egg): was Lanovalus named after the river, or the river after the god or local cult place.

to the 3rd/4th century AD.[99] This implies that also the raison-d'être of such a sacred site only evolved gradually, even if the indigenous, Celtic theonyms are not attested. The votive offerings of different worshippers stem from diverse interpretations of a cult. And whether they refer to the deity or deities by a Celtic, Latin or Greek name and whichever language the devotees used to record their religious experience, each tiny testimony provides an important piece in a jigsaw puzzle that we need to put together if we want to learn more about the local cult in its entirety.

BIBLIOGRAPHY

Aldhouse-Green, M. 2004 'Gallo-British deities and their shrines', *Companion to Roman Britain*, ed. M. Todd, 193–219. Oxford, Blackwell.

Bathurst, W. H. & C. W. King 1879 *Roman Antiquities at Lydney Park, Gloucestershire*. London: Longmans, Green, and Co.

Blétry, S. 1998 'L'autel de Loreia Pia à Glanum et les «divinités écoutantes»', *Revue archéologique de Narbonnaise* 31, 155–7.

Brower, H. J. 1989 *Bona Dea, The Sources and a Description of the Cult* (Études préliminaires aux religions orientales dans l'Empire romain, 110). Leiden, Brill.

Carey, J. 1984 'Nodons in Britain and Ireland', ZCP 40, 1–22.

Carey, J. 2012 'Fomoiri', *The Celts: History, Life, and Culture*, ed. J. T. Koch, 355. ABC-CLIO.

Cavalieri, M. 2012 Nullus locus sine genio. *Il ruolo aggregativo e religioso dei santuari extraurbani della Cisalpina tra protostoria, romanizzazione e piena romanità.* Bruxelles, Éditions Latomus.

De Bernardo Stempel, P. 2007 'Einheimische, keltische und keltisierte Gottheiten der Narbonensis im Vergleich', *Auf den Spuren keltischer Götterverehrung: Akten des 5. int. F.E.R.C.AN-Workshops, Oktober 2003 in Graz,* ed. M. Hainzmann, 67–79. Wien, ÖAW.

De Brun, P. 1935 'Les dieux de Glano et de Glanum près de Saint-Rémy-de-Provence (Bouches-du-Rhône)', *Provincia* 15, 247–64 (also as offprint, pages 1–31).

Delamarre, X. 2003 *Dictionnaire de la langue gauloise: une approche linguistique du vieux-celtique continental.* 2nd revised edition. Paris, Errance.

Euskirchen, M. 1993 'Epona', *Berichte der RGK* 74, 609–850.

Galsterer, B. 1983 *Die Graffiti auf der römischen Gefäßkeramik aus Haltern*. Münster, Aschendorff.

Gros, P. 1995 'Hercule à Glanum. Sanctuaires de transhumance et développement „urbain"', *Gallia* 52, 311–31.

Haynes, I. and T. W. Wilmott 2012 'The Maryport Altars. An archaeological myth dispelled', *Studia Universitatis Babes-Bolyai, Historia* 57.1, 25–37 (http://www.studia.ubbcluj.ro/download/pdf/728.pdf).

Haeussler, R. 2008 'How to identify Celtic religion(s) in Roman Britain and Gaul', *Divindades indígenas em análise. Divinités pré-romaines – bilan et perspectives d'une recherche*, ed. J. d'Encarnação, 13–63. Coimbra, Centro de estudos Arqueològicos.

Haeussler, R. 2012. 'Interpretatio indigena. Re-inventing local cults in a global world', *Mediterraneo Antico* 15 (1-2), 143–74.

Haeussler, R. 2015 'A landscape of resistance? Cults and sacred landscapes in Western Cisalpine Gaul', *Trans Padum ... Vsque Ad Alpes. Roma tra il Po e le Alpi: dalla romanizzazione alla romanità. Atti del convegno Venezia 13–15 maggio 2014* (Studi e ricerche sulla Gallia Cisalpine, 26), ed. G. Cresci Marrone, 261–86. Roma, Edizione Quasar.

Haeussler, R. 2017 'Review of "Attilio Mastrocinque, Bona Dea and the Cults of Roman Women. Stuttgart: Steiner"', *Bonner Jahrbücher* 215 (2015 [2017]), 543–9.

Jouët, Philippe 2007 *L'Aurore celtique dans la mythologie, l'épopée et les traditions.* Fouesnant, Yoran embanner.

99 Cf. King 2005 for the persistent nature of animal sacrifice in Romano-British temple sites.

King, A. C. 2005 'Animal Remains from Temples in Roman Britain', *Britannia* 36, 329–69.

Koch, J., ed. 2006 *The Historical Encyclopaedia of Celtic Culture, 5 volumes. Santa Barbara, Denver & Oxford, ABC-CLIO.*

Lambert, P.-Y. 1994 *La langue gauloise.* Paris, Errance.

Lewis, M. J. T. 1966 *Temples in Roman Britain. Cambridge, Cambridge University Press.*

Ling, R. 2007 'Inscriptions on Romano-British Mosaics and Wail-Paintings', *Britannia, 38,* 63–91.

Mermet, C. 1993 'Le sanctuaire gallo-romain de Châteauneuf (Savoie)', *Gallia* 50, 95–138.

Picard, C. 1963 'Les religions étrangères à Glanum: le quartier cultuel hellénistique', *Revue archéologique du Centre de la France* 2 (2–3), 179–202.

Rémy, B. 1999 'Religion populaire et culte impérial dans le sanctuaire indigène de Châteauneuf (Savoie)', *Revue archéologique de Narbonnaise* 32, 31–7.

Rolland, H. 1936 'Note sur un autel votif découvert à Glanum', *Provincia* 26, 136–7.

Rolland, H. 1946 *Fouilles de Glanum (Saint-Rémy-de-Provence)* (*Gallia*, supplément 1). Paris.

Rolland, H. 1958 *Fouilles de Glanum. 1947–1956* (*Gallia*, supplément 11). Paris.

Roth Congès, A. 1997 'La fortune éphémère de Glanum: du religieux à l'économique', *Gallia* 54, 157–202.

Roth Congès 2010. *Glanum. De l'oppidum salyen à la cité romaine* (2nd augmented, revised edition). Paris, Éd. du Patrimoine.

Sorrel, C. 2006. *Histoire de la Savoie en images: images et récit.* Montmélian, Fontaine de Siloé.

Szemerényi, O. 1974. A Gaulish dedicatory formula. *Zeitschrift für vergleichende Sprachforschung (KZ)* 88, 246–86.

Tomlin, R. S. O. 1993 'Votive objects: the inscribed lead tablets', *The Uley Shrines. Excavation of a ritual complex on West Hill, Uley, Gloucestershire, 1977–79*, ed. A. Woodward & P. Leach, 113–30. London, English Heritage.

Versnel, H. S. 1992 'The Festival for Bona Dea and the Thesmophoria', *Greece & Rome*, 2nd Series, 39.1, 31–55.

Watkins, C. 1995 *How to Kill a Dragon: Aspects of Indo-European Poetics.* London, Oxford University Press.

Woodward, A. 1993. 'Votive objects: the inscribed lead tablets', *The Uley Shrines. Excavation of a ritual complex on West Hill, Uley, Gloucestershire, 1977–79*, ed. A. Woodward & P. Leach, 127. London, English Heritage.

XIX

CELTIC GODDESSES FROM GALLIA BELGICA AND THE GERMANIAE: CHARACTERISTICS, DEDICANTS AND RITUAL PRACTICES

Audrey Ferlut

In the three provinces of Gallia Belgica, Germania Superior and Germania Inferior, about 70 goddesses can be recognised as Celtic and Germanic. These deities had very different functions: protection, fecundity, development of nature, goddesses of water spring and waters, protection of travellers, and so on. Identifying them as 'Celtic' is quite difficult, apart from the linguistic study of the gods' names and the analysis of the location of the discoveries of the monuments dedicated to them. Some had a few – even only one – altars or inscriptions, others had more than hundred. Those deities who had many worshippers were integrated into specific forms of cult. Most of the time, the forms of cults were Roman but it was possible to establish continuity with the rituals from pre-Roman Gaul. Roman cult practices, such as the uotum, *were not completely new for Celtic peoples living in the northern areas of the Roman Empire. In Germania Inferior, a form of Celtic cult could also be noticeable in the formula of the inscriptions with the expression* ex imperio ipsarum, *which seemed to be the persistence of some form of Celtic cult performed before the Roman conquest. The men and women who worshipped these goddesses were not usually people with Celtic names. They were far less numerous than those who had the Roman citizenship and Roman* tria nomina. *The worshippers belonged to groups that could afford inscriptions and altars. Moreover, some cults were widespread because of the mobility of groups such as merchants and Roman soldiers. The worshippers and those who were vectors of the cult differed from one province to another. Indeed, Gallia Belgica seemed to have a very different profile from the two Germaniae, focusing more on Celtic goddesses than the two others and having a larger number of deity names.*

IN the Roman period, a large number of gods and goddesses became physically visible across the Keltiké. Roman expressions of worship, such as anthropomorphic sculpture and epigraphy, brought to light deities that people had probably worshipped for decades, possibly centuries prior to Roman rule. Among the rich evidence from Gallia Belgica and the two Germaniae, it is a difficult task to identify which deities were really 'Celtic' in origin. It is necessary to use a large variety of sources to determine a deity's ancestry; archaeology and epigraphy provide us with the largest body of evidence. Literary sources can also be useful, but they must be confronted with the archaeological and epigraphic material. Indeed, regarding Celtic goddesses in Gallia

Belgica, Germania Inferior and Germania Superior, literary sources remain quite silent, apart from Caesar's famous passage about the Gallic Minerva (*De Bello Gallico* 6.16–18). Based on archaeology and epigraphy, we can identify up to seventy Celtic goddesses in those three provinces. Another difficulty is to determine whether the goddesses were 'Celtic ' or not in regions with lots of Germanic settlers, notably in Germania Inferior. At the same time, it is important to remember that these territories faced the Celtic immigrations from late Iron Age period and into the Roman period so that a certain 'Celtic' influence is quite certain. Moreover, linguistic studies help us to prove that many goddesses must have had a 'Celtic' origin.

Identifying their 'Celtic' nature is not enough to understand the cults associated with each goddess. It is imperative to take into account ritual practices, their Roman or Celtic elements, and the demography and identity of the worshippers as well as the wider pantheons of the provinces. The nature of ritual practices for Celtic goddesses, as far as it can be recognised, seem to have been mainly Roman in nature, largely resulting from Roman (and 'Romanised') worshippers. But to be really aware of those aspects of those goddesses' cults, we must present the criteria that help us to scrutinize a goddess' 'Celticity' and her functions. Moreover, we have to focus on ritual practices to analyse the impact of *Romanitas* and the possibility of continuity with the pre-Roman late Iron Age. Finally, the portrait of worshippers and of the pantheons in each province allow us to show the diverse impact of 'Romanity' among the local people and the Celtic nature of each pantheon.

Celtic goddesses: criteria and functions

In the three provinces under study, a list can be compiled of almost seventy goddesses that could be considered Celtic or possibly Celtic, i.e. goddesses whose names are Celtic, worshipped in territories influenced by Celtic migrations and culture, or Roman goddesses interpretated as a 'Celtic' deity by dedicants (Table 1). Three main criteria are used to identify the Celtic nature of each goddess: the linguistic roots in the goddess' name, the association with a Celtic consort,[1] and the local nature of the deity.

Celtic roots are found in the theonyms of seventeen goddesses (Table 2). Such linguistic criteria are important, but it only helped to define a quarter of the total godesses given in Table 1. In the case of some goddesses, the consort can be very helpful. Indeed, if the consort was recognised as a Celtic god, we could assume that the goddess might equally have been Celtic in nature (Table 3). The first two goddesses' names in the Table do not occur in Table 2, but the others are already identified as Celtic deities. The fact they had a Celtic consort reinforces this, and confirms that an association with a Celtic consort could be an important criterion to define the Celtic nature of a goddess.

These two criteria identify only nineteen of the list in Table 1 as Celtic. A closer

1 Ferlut 2015. Some Goddesses were systematically worshipped with one particular god, her consort. If the god had a 'Celtic' origin visible in the Celtic roots in his name and if the goddess' name had Celtic roots too in her name, it is quite certain that they were both of 'Celtic' origin.

look at the local nature of the deity will provide us with answers for the rest of the feminine divinities. Two ways can be explored to satisfy the definition of a local goddess: a match between the goddess' name and the locational name, and the concentration of dedications in a small area. One *caveat* should be made however: it is not simply because a location –mountains, springs, forests, and sites of *ciuitates* – hosted a divinity that the goddess was local. Indeed, in the Germaniae and in Gallia Belgica, some springs belonged to *Apollo*, *Hercules*, *Sirona* and *Rosmerta* and these deities are not local.[2]

Table 1: List of the Celtic and possibly Celtic goddesses from Gallia Belgica and the Germaniae

Abnoba, Alauna et Boudina, Ammaca et Gamaleda, Ancamna, Anixilomara, Apadeua, Arcanua, Ardbinna, Argenta, Artio, Atesmerta, Auentia, Aueta, Brixta, Burorina, Caiua, Camloriga, Candida, Damona, Epona, Exomna, Hariasa, Herecura, Hludana, Hurstrga, Icouellauna, Idbans Gabia, Inciona, Iseneucaega, Lucena, Lucreta, Magisena, Maia, Mairae, Maluisae, Matres, Matronae, Meduna, Mogontia, Nantosuelta, Naria Nousantia, Nehalennia, Nemetona, Obela, Quadruuiae – Triuiae et *Biuiae –, Ritona Pritona, Rosmerta, Sandraudiga, Sequana, Sibulca, Sirona, Suleuae, Sunuxsalis, Titaca, Traualalhae, Vercana, Vihansa, Vincia, Viradecdis, Viroddis, Visucia, Visuna.*

Notes: Many *Matronae* had an epithet, which would enlarge this list; see Ferlut 2011, chapter 5. *Hurstrga*; see Delamarre 2003 for linguistic commentary. *Maia* is often interpreted as a form of *interpretatio indigena. Quadruviae*; see Ferlut 2011; 2012a. *Viradecdis* is also known under the names *Viradechtis, Virathetis, Virodacthis, Virodactis*; see Ferlut 2011, annexes.

The match between the deity's name and the name of the location allows us to identify three local deities: *Auentia, Mogontia* and *Sequana*. For the first, the dedications were discovered in Aventicum (Avenches), three in the heart of the *ciuitas* and the last in the present city of Payern. *Auentia* is the local and tutelary goddess from Aventicum. Moreover, it seems that *Auentia* was a goddess protecting the *incolae* and the *fiscus.*[3] The second, *Mogontia*, was the tutelary goddess of Mogontiacum (Mainz), even if the inscription was discovered in Metz. But, the dedicant probably was from Mogontiacum and he was *tabellarius*, an army messenger. He probably thanked her when he arrived safely in Divodurum. The Celtic nature of that goddess is however questionable. Indeed, there was no ethnos or pre-Roman settlement where Mainz was built during the Roman period but, the inscription was found close to Metz in a region deeply touched by the Iron Age 'Celtic' settlements so the dedicant may have decided to create a theonym in the Roman period, based on his link with Mogontiacum and Metz. It is difficult to have a clear answer for that goddess anyway. Finally, the last one was *Sequana*. She was the goddess of the River Seine at its spring.

2 Ferlut 2011, chapter 3.

3 Ferlut 2012a, 798–800. The dedicants were all *incolae* but they also were *curatores* from the colony and its fiscus. They probably took care of the recollection and the repartion of the *munera* among the *incolae*. The systematic link between *Auentia's* worshippers and the fiscus allows the hypothesis that *Auentia* was a goddess protecting the fiscus as well as the *incolae*.

Table 2: List of goddesses with Celtic names

Name	Reference and comment
Alauna	Delamarre 2003, 37; Lambert 2003, 37, 44
Boudina	Delamarre 2003, 83; Lambert 2003, 148
Artio	Delamarre 2003, 55–6
Aueta	Delamarre 2003, 60–1
Auentia	Delamarre 2003, 60–1
Brixta	Delamarre 2003, 90. She was also systematically associated with the Celtic god from Luxueil-les-Bains, *Luxouius* whose name based on the Celtic word meaning 'lame man'; Delamarre 2003, 208.
Camloriga	Delamarre 2003, 101
Damona	Delamarre 2003, 134–5. She was the consort of many gods but especially of *Boruo.*
Epona	Delamarre 2003, 163
Hludana	Delamarre 2003, 210–1
Lucena	Delamarre 2003, 209
Meduna	Delamarre 2003, 221–2
Nemetona	Delamarre 2003, 232–3
Obela	Delamarre 2003, 242
Ritona	Delamarre 2003, 238–9; Lambert 2003, 29; Schwinden 1996
Sibulca	Delamarre 2003, 94; Lambert 2003, 192
Suleuae	Delamarre 2003, 286

Table 3: List of goddesses with their Celtic consorts (see Ferlut 2015)

Goddess name	Celtic consort's name
Nantosuelta	*Sucellus*
Inciona	*Veraudnus*
Damona	*Boruo*
Alauna and *Boudina*	*Voroius*
Brixta	*Luxouius*

Thus, a perfect match between the goddess' name and the location is quite rare, so we now need to look at the weaker criterion of the number of dedications to a goddess in a very small area. Many can be identified in this way (Table 4). Most of them had only one or two dedications in a very specific area as the table demonstrates, but there are some concentrations with a high number of inscriptions and sculpture, such as *Nehalennia* or the *Matronae*. In the particular case of the *Matronae*, the Celtic nature of the goddesses can be also reinforced by an analysis of the epithets (Table 5). Indeed, even if the dedications are mainly concentrated in Ubian[4] territory, which is already an indicator of the regional aspect of the deities, some epithets are also local.

4 Scholars has debated for a long time about the Celtic or Germanic origin of the Ubian population. The question is about the transfer from the Germanic region to the Roman provinces on the other bank of the Rhine river. If this debate has not been close for now, it is obvious that the goddesses called the *Matronae* were Celtic in many ways (name, epithets, some types of the ritual practices with the expression *ex imperio ipsarum*, and so on).

Table 4: Local goddesses, number of dedications and location

Goddess	No.	Location
A. Gallia Belgica		
Alauna et *Boudina*	2	Pantenburg
Ammaca et *Gamaleda*	1	Maastricht
Atesmerta	1	Le Corgebin
Burorina	1	Domburg
Caiua	2	Pelm; other inscriptions were discovered in Budesheim, *Germania superior,* 10 km from Pelm; see below
Camlorigae	1	Soissons
Icovellauna	6	Sanctuary of the Sablon (Metz); one inscription in Trier {by someone from Metz)
Inciona	1	Niederanven
Mogontia	1	Sanctuary of the Sablon (Metz)
Nantosuelta	1	Sarrebourg
Obela	1	Trier, in the basilica
Sequana	1	Salmaise
Ritona	4	Trier and Pachten
B. Germania Superior		
Anixilomara	1	Avenches
Auentia	4	Avenches
Brixta	2	Luxueil-les-Bains
Caiua	2	Budesheim; see above
Damona	9	Bourbonne-les-Bains
Lucena	1	Mainz
Magisena	1	Strasbourg
Naria Nousantia	2	Bern and Cressier
Viroddi	1	Kalbertshausen
Visuna	1	Baden-Baden
C. Germania Inferior		
Apadeua	1	Cologne
Arcanua	2	Born-Buchten
Ardbinna	1	Gey
Exomna	1	Alem
Hariasa	1	Cologne
Hurstrga	1	Kapel-Avezaath
Idbans Gabia	1	Pier
Iseneucaega	2	Zennewijnen
Lucreta	1	Cologne
Nehalennia	255	Domburg and Colijnsplaat, three sanctuaries in a 30 km radius
Sandraudiga	1	Zundert

Sibulca	1	Bonn
Sunuxalis	11	Inscriptions located in a 50 km radius around Cologne.
Travalalhae	1	Cologne
Vihansa	1	Tongres
Vincia	1	Jülich

Table 5: List of Celtic epithets associated with the *Matronae*
(Ferlut 2011; Spickermann & de Bernardo Stempel 2005)

Abiamarcae, Albiahenae, Almavihenae, Amrahenae, Amfratninae, Berguiahenae, Bouduneihae, Brittae, Canstrusteihiae, Eburnicae, Gabiae, Gesahenae, Leudinae, Masanae, Mediotautehae, Noricae, Octocannae, Senonae, Suebae, Treuerae, Vacallinehae, Veterahenae, Vesuniahenae.

Indeed, epithets such as *Treuerae, Seno, Suebae*, and *Eburnicae* created a correspondence between a Celtic people and the goddess. Moreover, some scholars, such as Lehner, Rüger and Alföldy,[5] suggested that some epithets are representative of the name of a *curia* from a *pagus*, a *vicus*, a *ciuitas* or a sanctuary. This is clear for *Albiahenae, Amfratninae, Austriahenae, Aruagastae, Gesahenae* and *Vacallinehae*, respectively from *Albianacum, Amarates, Austriates, Aruagastes, Gesationes* and *Vacalli*, but enlarging that hypothesis to include all of the *Matronae*'s epithets could be risky.

The local aspect of the goddesses seems to be the most certain way to determine if a goddess was 'Celtic' or at least 'local'. It is possible to object that being located in a Celtic area does not mean that the deity was Celtic, but it could be a clue. Moreover, we can see in several cases a conjunction between the linguistic root of the name, the location and even the consort.

'Interpretatio Romana' and 'interpretatio Gallica'

Tacitus was the first to talk about *interpretatio Romana.*[6] That notion, together with its counterparts, *interpretatio Gallica* and *interpretatio indigena* (created by modern scholarship), generated fierce debates, first to prove their existence and then to determine the deities that underwent such *interpretationes.*[7] For the Romans themselves, *interpretatio Romana* consisted in giving Latin names to exogenous gods, here Celtic gods; Tacitus and Caesar[8] demonstrated that the Romans often practised such an interpretation. On the opposite side of the equation, for the local population, *interpretatio*

5 Lehner 1910; Rüger 1970; Alföldy 1968.
6 Tacitus, *Germania* 53.3.
7 Dunand & Lévêque 1973; Lévêque 1973; Scheid 2010; Haeussler 2008; 2012; Charles-Laforge 2014; Ferlut 2011, chapter 6.
8 Caesar, *De Bello Gallico* 6.16-18; Tacitus, *Germania* 53.3.

Table 6: Evidence for *interpretatio Gallica*

Goddess	Date	Criteria for *interpretatio gallica*	Reference in Ferlut 2011
Anixilomara	*c.* 101–250	Celtic name; Dedicant with a Celtic *cognomen*; Uncertainties about the *interpretatio gallica* because of the absence of figurative sculpture.	22
Atesmerta	*c.* 201–300	Celtic name; Dedicant with a Celtic *cognomen*; Uncertainties about the *interpretatio gallica* because of the absence of figurative sculpture.	33
Brixta	*c.* 41–215	Celtic name; Dedicant with a Celtic *cognomen*; Uncertainties about the *interpretatio gallica* because of the absence of figurative sculpture.	53
Sibulca	*c.* 150–250	Celtic name; Dedicant with a Celtic *cognomen*; Uncertainties about the *interpretatio gallica* because of the absence of figurative sculpture.	1816
Suleuae	*c.* 1-100	Celtic name; Dedicant with a Celtic *cognomen*; *Suleuae* was an epithet associated with the *Matronae* and the *Iunones*; Representation in triplicate with the attributes for abundance.	1844
Sunuxsalis	*c.* 151–250	Celtic name; Dedicant with a Celtic *cognomen*; Representation with the Roman attributes for fertility.	1849
Maia (in this case, it is not *interpretatio gallica* but *interpretatio indigena*)	*c.* 100	Roman name; Dedicant with a Celtic *cognomen*; Caduceus which is the same attribute as her consort Mercurius.	886
	c. 101–250	Roman name; Dedicant with a Celtic *cognomen*; Caduceus as her consort Mercurius also represented on the altar.	887
	142	Roman name; Dedicant with a Celtic *cognomen*; Caduceus as her consort Mercurius mentioned in the inscription.	880
	c. 150–250	Roman name; Dedicant with a Celtic *cognomen*; Mercurius is her consort in the inscription.	883
Matronae Aufaniae	*c.* 171–255	Celtic name; Dedicant with a Celtic *cognomen*; Roman attributes for fecundity: *cornucopia*, fruit baskets and children.	1077
	c. 164–255	Celtic name; Dedicant with a Celtic *cognomen* according to *CIL*; Roman attributes for fecundity: *cornucopia*, fruit baskets and children. Germanic attributes: Ubian hat.	1350

Matronae Alaferhuiae	*c.* 150–255	Celtic name; Hybrid *praenomen* showing the dedicant's Celtic origin; Roman attributes for fecundity: *cornucopia*, fruit baskets and children. Germanic attributes: Ubian hat.	1134
Nehalennnia	*c.* 101–250	Celtic name; Dedicant with a Celtic *cognomen*; Roman attributes for fecundity. (See Note below)	1621, 1626
	c. 101–250	Celtic name; Dedicant with a Celtic *cognomen*; Roman attributes for fortune and luck, i.e. a rudder.	1627
	c. 151–250	Celtic name; Dedicant with a Celtic *cognomen*; Roman attributes for fecundity.	1631
Rosmerta	*c.* 101–250	Celtic name; Dedicant with a Celtic *cognomen*; Roman attributes mainly used for spring and water goddesses.	1773, 1777, 1781
	c. 201–250	Celtic name; Dedicant with a Celtic *cognomen*; Roman attributes mainly used for spring and water goddesses.	1799

Note : Some scholars, such as Wolfgang Spickermann, assert that Nehalennia is a goddess from a Germanic origin, but others, like Patrizia de Bernardo Stempel (cf. Spickermann & de Bernardo Stempel 2005, 141), disagree. Many incertainties remain considering this goddess' origin but many elements in the cult, the representations, the name of the dedicants let us assume that it is a goddess from a Celtic origin. Moreover, the regions where the cult is very developed had mainly a Celtic pre-Roman settlement and some dedicants came from Britannia which can reinforce the plea about a Celtic origin. Because of the incertainties, we chose to maintain Nehalennia in the list of the Celtic goddesses.

Gallica, a notion employed by many French scholars, consisted in giving a Gaulish name to a deity. Three criteria are necessary for this scheme of *interpretatio*: the dedicant should have a Gaulish name, the deity's name should be Gaulish as well and the god should have the same characteristics as a Roman god, characteristics identified within the gods' attributes visible on sculptures and lateral representations on the votive altars. English-speaking scholars also highlighted the phenomenon of *interpretation indigena*[9] regarding the way people of indigenous origin adapted the Roman habits and Roman forms of cult sometimes by giving a Latin name to goddesses they knew – *Maia* seems to be interpreted that way several times, representing the native goddess Rosmerta (Table 6). The analysis of the data using these criteria of *interpretatio Gallica* showed that Roman goddesses were rarely interpreted that way, apart from *Maia* but it is more a question of *interpretatio indigena* here.[10] Among almost eight hundred inscriptions, only eighteen – fourteen with certainty – were manifestations of *interpretatio Gallica* (Table 6). The rarity of *interpretatio Gallica* shows that people from Gallia Belgica and the Germaniae decided to worship goddesses according to their original nature: Celtic, Roman or even "Oriental". Celtic goddesses were more visible because of Roman ways of

9 See notably Haeussler 2008; 2012.
10 Clifford 2012.

worship (see below), but they kept their Celtic nature and the worshippers made vows to them for their specific functions.

Function and attributes

In the region under study, worshippers addressed their vows to mother goddesses to obtain fecundity and to protect themselves in life and death, to spring and water goddesses, sometimes but not always for health purposes, to goddesses protecting travelers and finally to goddesses protecting the Empire borders and its integrity.[11]

Seventeen feminine deities could be considered as goddesses of nature and fecundity bringing abundance, fecundity and protection in life and death to the dedicants (Table 7). Other goddesses had attributes linked to water and springs. Some already had the characteristic of being a goddess of nature and fecundity, such as *Rosmerta* or *Maia*[12], which means that those feminine deities did not have a unique function. But there is a *caveat* in determining if a goddess was a deity of springs and water or not. It is not because a sanctuary was built close to a spring or a river that the goddess was necessarily a deity of springs and water: 'A sanctuary, as a village or a farm, must be built close to a water supply. So, the link between sacred and vital can be used as a postulate'.[13] At least twelve Celtic goddesses were water and spring deities (Table 8). But they did not have the same manner in which they used water as an attribute. Some can be considered as nymphs, such as *Maia*.[14] They lived in the area of the spring or the water source, and this was the expression of their divine presence in the area. Others, like *Damona*, *Brixta*, *Rosmerta*, *Sirona*, and *Visucia*, were worshipped because they healed. In these instances, they frequently had a consort, like *Apollo* or *Mercurius*, who was the healer god, as *Asclepios;* and the goddesses were the impersonations of recovered health, as *Hygia* when linked with *Asclepios*. Finally, some were the eponymous or local goddesses responsible for the existence of a river or a spring and their characteristics, such as *Aueta, Icovellauna, Inciona, Sequana, Vercana* and *Visuna.*

Some goddesses from Gallia Belgica and the Germaniae were responsible for the protection of travellers during their journey. For many of them, it is linguistic analysis that provides us with their function in the absence of figurative representation, i.e. *Alauna* and *Boudina, Hludana, Ritona, Obela, Nehalennia* and *Viradecdis*. Obviously, in the Celtic language, their name rarely signified 'protection for travellers'. But, their names associated the deities with specific domains or locations that help to link them with protection for the travelers. For example, *Alauna* whose name means 'river' or 'something with a nomad nature',[15] was always associated with *Boudina* in the

11 Ferlut 2011, chapters 1 to 5.
12 *Maia* is often represented with fruits or a cornucopia, attributes linked to nature and fecundity.
13 Deyts 1986, 19; Ferlut 2011, chapter 2.
14 Ferlut 2015. In some sanctuaries and regions, *Maia* seems to have taken on the role and functions of a nymph. This implies that we can list her in the same category of goddesses that had the same roles as the nymphs.
15 Delamarre 2001, 37; Lambert 2003, 37, 44.

Table 7: The goddesses of nature and fecundity, their attributes and functions

Goddess	Attributes	Function
Artio	Bear, fruits, *cornucopia*	Goddess about nature (bear), abundance of Earth (*cornucopia* and fruits)
Atesmerta	Purse, caduceus.	Abundance of Earth (purse), properity and peace (caduceus)
Camloriga	Purse	Abundance of Earth (purse).
Damona	Ear of wheat, snake	Abundance of Earth (ear of wheat), protection of the living people (snake).
Epona	Fruits, *cornucopia*, horse.	Abundance of Earth and fertility (fruits, *cornucopia*) and psychopomp deity (horse).
Herecura	Fruit basket	Abundance of Earth and fertility. Queen of the death realm (Celtic form of Proserpina).
Hludana	Laurel	Abundance of Earth.
Hurstrga	?	Batavian goddess of abundance.
Lucreta	Fruits, *cornucopia*	Abundance of Earth and fertility.
Maia	*Cornucopia*, rooster, goat, patera, fruits, caduceus.	Abundance of Earth and fertility (Fruits, *cornucopia*), prosperity and peace (caduceus).
Matres, Matronae	Fruits, *cornucopia*, thread, roll and children.	Human fecundity (children), protection in life and death (roll and thread), fertility (Fruits, *cornucopia*).
Nantosuelta	Beehive, house on the top of a pole, crow.	Abundance of Earth and fertility (beehhive), goddess of life and death (crow), domestic cult (house on the top of a pole).
Naria Nousantia	?	Pastoral deity.
Nehalennia	Fruits, *cornucopia*, laurel, round loaf, bow.	Abundance of Earth and fertility (Fruits, *cornucopia*, laurel, round) and protection of maritime and river navigation (bow).
Rosmerta	*Cornucopia*, rooster, goat, patera, fruits, caduceus.	Abundance of Earth and fertility (Fruits, *cornucopia*), prosperity and peace (caduceus).
Sandraudiga	Fruits, *cornucopia*	Abundance of Earth, fecundity and fertility.
Viroddis	Roses, fruits (mainly apples).	Abundance of Earth and fecundity

Table 8: Spring and water goddesses

Goddess	Consort	Main characteristics	Water sanctuary
Aueta	None	Linguistic root: close to *Auantia* or *Auentia* meaning 'spring or river'.	No dedicated sanctuary, but an *aedes* in the sanctuary of the Altbachtal. Location of dedications: Mont Afrique; Altbachtal. Springs: Mont Afrique; spring in the vicinity of the Altbach River.
Brixta	*Luxouius*	Her consort is a Celtic water god *Luxouius*.	Sanctuary with Roman baths in Luxueil.

Damona	Apollo *Boruo*	Her consort is *Boruo*, water and healer god.	Sanctuary with Roman baths in Bourbonne les Bains.
Icovellauna	None		Sanctuary of the Sablon, Metz, with a bipartition of space: water spurted out in the sacred space and was used in the profane space.
Inciona	*Veraudnus*		Fanum type destroyed by quarrying. Doubt on the existence of temple with bipartition of space.
Maia	*Mercurius*	Goddess protecting from disease who, with her consort Mercurius, was present in water sanctuaries.	Her presence was noticed in many sanctuaries even if they were not directly dedicated to her.
Rosmerta	*Mercurius*	Goddess protecting from disease who, with her consort Mercurius, was present in water sanctuaries.	Her presence was noticed in the santuary of Deneuvre, Moselle, even if it was not her own sanctuary.
Sequana	None	Eponymous goddess from the Seine River.	Sanctuary of the springs of the Seine River.
Sirona	*Apollo*	Goddess associated to Apollo. Healer deity, goddess of purification able to practice divination.	Present in many water sanctuaries, notably Wallenborn.
Vercana	None	Goddess whose name means 'the one who lives close to the river, here with no doubt the Rhine River'.	No sanctuary. Goddess worshipped at the moment of the creation of the aqueduct from Ernstweiler by the soldiers responsible for its construction.
Visucia	*Mercurius*	Probably a similar role as *Rosmerta*	Her presence was noticed in many sanctuaries even if they were not directly dedicated to her.
Visuna	None	Goddess who name can mean 'water'.	A dedication was uncovered in the Roman baths in Baden Baden, but no proved sanctuary.

inscriptions, whose name means 'victory, advantage, profit'.[16] So, both deities' functions can be combined, i.e. protection during the journey on rivers and profits. The dedicant would have made a vow to both of them to obtain fortune – on the ancient meaning of the word, i.e. luck – during a journey on the river. *Hludana* could be another example of a goddess protecting travellers. Her name means 'swamp, swampy, muddy'.[17] It probably meant that she protected anyone who crossed swamp and muddy areas.[18] Evidence of the protection of travellers can also be seen in the formula the vows made by worshippers, as in the case of the Nehalennia inscriptions (Table 9):

16 Delamarre 2001, 83; Lambert 2003, 148.
17 Delamarre 2003, 210–1.
18 Ferlut 2011.

Table 9: *Nehalennia* and the protection of travellers

Formula	Date	Reference in Ferlut 2011
Expression of thanks: *ob merces recte conservatas*. The dedicant's position: *Negotiator cretarius Britannicianus*	*c.* 101–250	1543
The dedicant's position: *actor navis*	*c.* 101–250	1551
Expression of thanks: *ob merces recte conservatas*. The dedicant's position: *Negotiator cretarius Britannicianus*	*c.* 151–250	1655
The dedicant's position: *Nautis*, Sequani citizen	*c.* 151–250	1664
Expression of thanks: *ob merces conservatas.*	*c.* 151–250	1662
Expression of thanks: *pro mercibus conservandis.*	*c.* 151–250	1557, 1588, 1619
The dedicant's position: *negotiator Britannicianus.*	*c.* 151–250	1669
Expression of thanks: *Pro navibus.*	*c.* 151–250	1561
Expression of thanks: *Ob merces bene conservatas.* The dedicant's position: *negotiator Britannicianus.*	*c.* 151–250	1553
The dedicant's position: *negotiator Britannicianus.*	*c.* 151–250	1640

Other goddesses offered protection to travellers but also to the Imperial borders and their integrity: the *Quadruuiae*, the *Triuiae* and the *Biuiae.*[19] Some could question the Celtic nature of those goddesses but the study of the site of origin in Pannonia and the systematic association with the *Siluanae* in that region confirms that they were really of Celtic origin.[20]

In this survey of *Gallia Belgica* and the *Germaniae*, we have been able to identify almost seventy Celtic goddesses using the linguistic roots of their names, their location and the correspondence with the name of *ciuitates*, *uici* and *pagi*. Moreover, those deities were mainly divinities from the pre-Roman period who appeared on religious landscape thanks to Roman modes of expression, such as sculpture and epigraphy. *Interpretatio Gallica* was indeed quite rare compared with *interpretatio indigena*. They also had multiple functions among which the dedicants could choose to obtain abundance, fertility, prosperity, health, and protection during their journey, and even protection of the Empire. But determining the functions and the Celtic nature of those goddesses is not enough to understand the ritual practices. We need to focus on the way the dedicants worshipped the divinities, if they used Roman rites or Celtic rites and if some sort of continuity can be found with the pre-Roman period.

Ritual practices

Over the centuries, during the expansion of their Empire, the Romans left imprints of their religion in all the territories they conquered. However, they had to take into account the religious 'substratum' that already existed in those territories. Most of the time, the

19 For the origin of the goddess, see Ferlut 2011, chapter 4; Ihm 1963.
20 Ferlut 2011, chapter 4; Heichelheim 1963; Dorcey 1992; Kandler 1985.

Roman authorities accepted the ways the ritual practices worked, tolerated and used the local pantheons. They also brought new ritual practices in the new provinces such as the *uotum* and new forms of religious expression such as anthropomorphic sculpture and epigraphy; practices and modes of expression which were quickly adopted by the new peoples of the Empire. Roman rites and Roman forms of temples – few were purely Roman, the majority were Romano-Celtic temples created during the imperial period as a new model of temple adopted in the Gallo-Roman provinces – were largely adopted in the northern provinces, notably for the Celtic goddesses.

The 'uotum' and usage of Roman rites

For the Celtic goddesses, we can assert that almost all ritual practice was linked to the *uotum*. Indeed, it was a full rite followed by worshippers in order to fulfill the vow once granted, i.e. libation, sacrifice of animals, plant offering and *ex-uoto*. The *uotum* was generally practiced in a sanctuary, within the enclosure of a temple.[21] It was quite rare to know the nature of the sacrifice or the offering, except when the dedicant represented it on the lateral faces of the altar offered when the vow was fulfilled. It had the objective to prove that the dedicant fulfilled the vow. That act was addressed both to the goddess and to the worshippers at the sanctuary. It also proved that the goddess was favourable to the worshipper, proclaimed her powers and showed to the rest of the community that the dedicant had the ear of the gods. The altar also perpetuated the transient offering, by naming or representing it.

Van Andringa believes that the *uotum* made no sense outside of public ceremonies,[22] being part of the collective practices of the civic community. Le Bohec and other historians,[23] however, believe that it was a contract with the divinity in which the dedicant asked the goddess for a precise and occasional demand and it could be perfectly practised in private and domestic ceremonies. Some dedications with the specific formula of the *uotum* discovered in the private sanctuary of Niedaltdorf confirmed the latter hypothesis.[24]

In the three provinces studied for this paper, 50% of the known dedications to Celtic goddesses were based on the *uotum*. The fulfillment had several forms: sacrifice of an animal, plant offering (the most common case), libations, temple offering, and statue offering. The evidence for these includes the formula of the inscription, sculptures on the altars (Tables 10–12) and discoveries such as animal remains, made during excavations.[25] Archaeological researches on the sanctuaries and on the rites in *Gallia Belgica* and the *Germaniae* demonstrate that the forms of sacrifices were quite close to those practiced in Rome. Representations of fruits, *cornucopia*, trees and laurel branches on the lateral faces of the altars confirm that this kind of offering was quite

21 De Sury 1994, 169–70.
22 Van Andringa 2002, 20, 118–23.
23 Le Bohec 2008; González Rodríguez & Marco Simón 2009, 71–2; De Sury 1994, 169–70.
24 Ferlut 2011, chapter 2. This sanctuary was found in a Roman villa, thus giving it private status.
25 Scheid 2000; Lepetz & Van Andringa 2008; Méniel 2008.

commonplace in the region. The ex-voto could also take the form of a libation (Table 11). Sometimes, in the case of the *Quadruuiae*, worshippers offered temples, *aedes* or to repair such a building.

Table 10: Scenes of sacrifice and banquet

Goddess	Date	Evidence	Appendix
Matronae	*c.* 150–225	Sacrificial banquet	5
	c. 164–255	Scene of sacrifice on the lateral faces of the altar	13, 15, 16
	c. 164–255	Table of a sacrificial banquet on the lateral faces of the altar.	6
	c. 164–255	Scene of sacrifice	9, 11, 14, 19
	c. 164–255	*Praefatio.*	10, 18
Nehalennia	*c.* 101–250	Table of a sacrificial banquet on the lateral faces of the altar.	20
	c. 164–255	Scene of sacrifice	21

Table 11: Libations

Goddess	Date	Evidence	Appendix
Matronae	*c.* 164–255	Vase with handle and tumbler	12
	c. 164–255	Scene of libation	11, 14-16
Nantosuelta	*c.* 101–250	The goddess is practising a libation	1537 (see note)
Nehalennia	*c.* 164–255	Scene of libation	21
Visuna	*c.* 101–250	Libation equipment (*prefericulus, patera*).	24

Note: This reference is not in the Appendix but in Ferlut 2011, annexes.

Table 12: Offerings

Goddess	Date	Evidence	Appendix
Ancamna	*c.* 150–250	Skin of the victim of a sacrifice on the top of the altar.	1
Apadeva	*c.* 150–250	Skin of the victim of a sacrifice on the top of the altar.	2
Lucreta	*c.* 101–200	Fruits and *cornucopiae.*	3, 4
Matronae	164	A man and a woman are making a plant offering	8
	c. 164–255	Pig head	12
	c. 164–255	Fruits and *cornucopiae.*	6
	c. 164–255	Fruits.	7, 17
	c. 164–255	Animal offering on the lateral faces of the altar.	10
Quadruuiae	*c.* 150–250	Reconstruction of an altar and a temple.	22
	c. 150–250	Construction of a temple.	23

All these ritual practices are a Roman form of expression of worship, but there may be indications that some rituals had a pre-Roman form. Inscriptions have revealed a particular ritual practice, in which dedicants acted on the godesses' orders to make and/or to fulfill the vow. The formula of the inscriptions contains the expression *ex iussu*, *ex imperio ipsarum* and related formulas.[26] Apart from six exceptions,[27] the inscriptions with *ex imperio ipsarum* are concentrated in a very small area; east of Cologne to Jülich, and south to Zülpich and Pesch. They are mainly dedicated to the *Matronae*, and most of them are from Germania inferior. According to the meaning of that expression, the goddess ordered the dedicant to perform the vow. Alföldy[28] thought that it was all the goddess' manifestations that could broadcast the message. He also suggested that the expression *ex imperio ipsarum* was not Roman but Celtic. The expression *ex imperio ipsarum* appears to have been only used for Celtic goddesses, even if receiving an order from a goddess to perform a sacrifice was not specifically Celtic. An inference from this is that the formula highlights some specific rites from the pre-Roman period; close to the Roman rite but different enough to be expressed in a different way in the inscriptions.

Following on from this, we can speculate whether, in the way the vow was performed during the Gallo-Roman period, it was specifically Roman or if the Gauls practiced similar rites before the Conquest. Brunaux[29] demonstrated that Gauls shared the habit of the vow with almost all the Indo-European populations. For them, the vow was an oral practice, the most solemn announcement made among an entire community where men and gods were assembled. It was possibly because of the existence of such practices, that the *uotum* was so well accepted and used after the Conquest. As an example, Brunaux[30] categorised plant offerings into two types: freshly harvested cereals, fruits or branches, and seconly loaves, cakes, crushed cereals and beverages. The latter confirms that the Gauls practiced libation.

The dedicants

Spickermann[31] has shown that women were not very common among the overall dedicants in the Galliae, the Germaniae and Raetia. In respect to goddess cults, we may speculate that women could be more strongly represented among the dedicants than in other cults. However, only 17 goddesses out of the 67 identified in Table 1 had women's dedications (Table 13). Women made only 9.5 % of the total of dedications. So, they were not the most common kind of dedicants, even for goddesses. It also seems that, when they offered a dedication, they mainly did it alone.

The analysis of their names shows that 90 % of them belonged to families of Roman citizens. Thus, it means that women who participated in these cults, and made epigraphic dedications, belonged to families where *romanitas* was deeply integrated.

26 Detailed tables are available in Ferlut 2011.
27 Kapersburg, Wesselig and Heddernheim in *Germania Superior*, Niederemmel and Trier in *Gallia Belgica* and inscriptions to *Nehalennia* in *Germania inferior*.
28 Alföldy 1968.
29 Brunaux 2000.
30 Brunaux 2000, 147–9, based on evidence from Mirebeau.
31 Spickermann 1994.

So, the women who made the vows were from families that were largely educated in the Roman manners and habits. That idea is reinforced by the fact that the inscriptions from women were mainly uncovered in the great *ciuitates* as Cologne, Bonn or in the largest sanctuaries as those for the *Matronae*. Dedicating an altar and making a sacrifice was also very expensive, which means that the women should have a high standard of living, high enough to be financially independent in some ways.

However, we know that dedications in the form of altars are only one element, since only the richest could afford to pay for such a monument. Having a few altars made by women did not mean that they did not participate in the cult and its rituals. Most of the time, in a Roman family – and there is no clue that it was different in Gallia Belgica and the Germaniae – it was the *pater familias* that performed any actions linked to religion, as his role of leader of the family obliged him to do.

For a more complete picture, we need to examine which goddesses they mainly made dedications to. Table 13 shows that it was the *Matres* and *Matronae* that attracted most of them, and it is likely that the attributes of these goddesses' functions made them more relevant for women.

Table 13: Dedications to goddesses made by women

Goddess	**Number of dedications**
Artio, Caiua, Epona, Mairae, Nehalennia, Sirona, Suleuae, Viradecdis and Viroddi	1 each = 9
Rosmerta	2
Bellona, Herecura and Sunuxalis	9
Matres and Quadruuiae	8
Damona	6
Matronae	43
Total	87

Table 14: Celtic goddesses worshipped by men, by rank and role

Status	**List of goddesses**
Men from the equestrian order and senators	Auentia, Epona, Iseneucaega, Matres, Matronae, Nemetona, Quadruuiae.
Municipal magistrates	Auentia, Epona, Matronae, Naria Nousantia, Nehalennia, Rosmerta, Sirona, Titaca, Viradecdis, Visucia.
People in *vici*	Epona, Matronae, Quadruuiae, Viradecdis (1 each), Rosmerta (2).
Priests	Epona, Matronae, Nehalennia, Nemetona, Rosmerta.

Dedicants, therefore, were mainly men, but were they of Celtic or non-Celtic origin? Only 91 inscriptions were dedicated by people with a Celtic origin in their names (mostly the *nomen* or *cognomen*), i.e. 11 % of the dedications. However, the epigraphic evidence mainly dates to the 2nd and 3rd centuries AD, and it is thus not surprising to see few people with a demonstrable Celtic origin among the dedicants, as many people had become Roman citizens. An additional observation is that people with Celtic origins in their names did not only make dedications to Celtic goddesses: *Iuno* or *Minerua* also had a few dedicants.[32]

In so far as most of the male dedicants had Roman names and were Roman citizens, it is possible to look deeper into the participation of priests, the municipal elite, *vicani*, and men from the Equestrian order and senators (Table 14). Dedications from the upper classes of Roman imperial society and of Roman *ciuitas* society were quite rare. The same conclusion can be made for the *uicus*, and we have no sign at all of an official dedication made by a colony or any other kind of *ciuitas* in the three provinces studied.

What are the reasons for such a lack of inscriptions to the Celtic goddesses among those people and communities? The first hypothesis could be that they were more attracted by Roman goddesses and, as far as we know, it was the case.[33] The second hypothesis is that they preferred gods to goddesses. The number of senators and members of the equestrian order were not numerous enough in these provinces to have much presence in the goddesses' cults, but the municipal elite were far more numerous. It is worth noticing that the latter group concentrated their dedications on Graeco-Roman goddesses and on tutelary goddesses from their *ciuitas* as *Auentia*.[34]

In the case of cult servants and priests, dedications were quite rare, and in fact 80% of those in Table 14 were by *seviri augustales*. We can assume that the Celtic feminine divinities were quite rare in public and civic cult, so they probably decided to focus on other gods, more integrated to that cult, especially male divinities.

A last group of men among the worshippers were the military. In Gallia Belgica, they were not many but in the Germaniae they had a real impact on society, and especially on religion.[35] Military dedications to the godesses number 59; not a very high number out of the 802 total inscriptions to Celtic goddesses, but far more than the previous groups discussed above. The *Quadruuiae* and *Matres/Matronae* were the most attractive for them.

Table 15: List of Celtic goddesses in *Gallia Belgica* and *Germania Superior*

Gallia Belgica: *Alauna, Ammaca, Ancamna, Artio, Atesmerta, Aueta, Boudina, Burorina, Caiua, Camlorigae, Damona, Epona, Gamaleda, Icouellauna, Inciona, Maia, Matronae and Matres, Mogontia, Nantosuelta, Obela, Ritona Pritona, Rosmerta, Sirona, Suleuae, Vercana and Meduna, Vihansa, Visucia* and *Xulsigiae.*

Germania Superior: *Abnoba, Anixilomarae, Artio, Aventia, Aueta, Brixta, Caiua, Damona, Epona, Herecura, Lucena, Lucreta, Magisena, Maia, Maluisae, Matronae, Matres, Naria Nousantia, Quadruuiae, Rosmerta, Sequana, Sirona, Suleuae, Titaca, Vercana and Meduna, Viradecdis, Viroddis, Visucia* and *Visuna.*

32 Ferlut 2011, chapter 21.
33 Ferlut 2011, 322–5.
34 Ferlut 2012a.
35 Ferlut 2011, 326–35; 2012b.

Different patterns between provinces

Celtic goddess did not have the same importance in the three provinces (Table 15).[36] In Gallia Belgica, the Celtic goddesses were largely dominant in the pantheon and numerically greater than for the other two provinces. In Germania Inferior, the number of inscription is in excess of 600, but almost all were to the *Matronae* (411) and Nehalennia (255). In Germania Superior, even if the number of Celtic goddesses is similar to Gallia Belgica – 30 to 49 – the total number of inscriptions did not exceed 150. Moreover, the overall statistics for the three provinces for the feminine pantheon[37] shows that the Celtic goddesses represented 83% of the dedications. In Germania Inferior, the number of dedications to Celtic feminine divinities was quite close with 85%, but as stated above, only for two deities: the *Matronae* and *Nehalennia*. By contrast, in Germania Superior, Celtic goddesses represented only 24% of the entire number of inscriptions.[38]

Conclusion and summary

Celtic goddesses in Gallia Belgica and the Germaniae are quite numerous, but their identification is not easy. Several can be considered as Celtic because their names had Celtic linguistic roots but it was mainly because of their local nature that we can determine that the deities were Celtic, or at least, local or autochthonous. Moreover, they mainly presided over domains such the abundance of nature, fecundity, protection in life and death, travellers and water and springs. Rites to worship them were mainly the *uotum* and its linked ritual of the ex-voto: animal sacrifice, plant offering, libation and so on. Some rites from the pre-Roman period became visible through the epigraphy, such the command issued by some goddesses using the formula *ex imperio ipsarum*.

The dedicants included women and people of Celtic origin, but they were very few. Most of the worshippers were men, most of the time Roman citizens, with a deep knowledge of *romanitas*. A lot were also soldiers and seemed to have a significant involvement with some cults, on the contrary to men from social groups such as municipal elites, senators, members of the equestrian orders and priests who were not involved a lot in the cults to Celtic goddesses. Finally, a very different pattern appeared in each province, Gallia Belgica with a large number of Celtic goddesses contrary to the other two provinces in which the pantheon was quite different: dominated by the *Matronae* and *Nehalennia* in Germania Inferior and dominated by the Graeco-Roman goddesses in Germania Superior.

36 Ferlut 2011, chapter 18.
37 Ferlut 2011, 265–6.
38 See Ferlut 2011, chapter 18, for further explanation.

Appendix: Sources for Tables 10-12

1. Feyen *AE* 1916, 27 = Finke 12
Altar in red sandstone. The victim's skin is represented on the top of the altar. Date: probably 2nd or 3rd centuries AD.
In h(onorem) d(omus) d(iuinae) Marti | et Ancamnae | C(aius) Serotini|us Iustus ex uoto / posuit.
For Serotinius: Solin-Salomies 1988, 169. For Iustus: Kajanto 1982, 252; Solin-Salomies 1988, 347.

2. Köln Ness-Lieb 206 = *AE* 1956, 247 = *RSK* 3
Altar in limestone. Height: 51.5 cm, width: 31 cm, depth: 17 cm. The top of the altar contains pediment and volutes. The victim's skin is engraved on top of the altar. The lateral faces are decorated with little trees. Decoration of the altar and its form date it from the 2nd or the 3rd century AD.
Deae | Apadeuae | T(itus) Ver(inius) Sene(cio) | l(ibens) m(erito)
The *nomen* Verinius is Latin: Solin-Salomies 1988, 203. For Senecius: Kajanto 1982, 301; Solin-Salomies 1988, 400.

3. Köln *RSK* 77
Altar with pediment and base in limestone. Height: 39.5 cm, width: 34 cm. Each lateral face is decorated with *cornucopia* and fruits and a tenon of pine. The top is adorned with volutes and fruits. Date: 2nd century AD.
Lucretis | A[...] | pro se | et suis | u(otum) s(oluit) l(ibens) m(erito)
The *cognomen* has been restored as Anaillus but without any certainty. In this case, it is not Latin but Celtic, cf. Delamarre 2003, 20.

4. Köln CIL XIII 8171 = *RSK* 78
Altar with pediment and base in limestone. Height: 31 cm, width: 16 cm, depth: 10 cm. Each lateral face is decorated with a *cornucopia* full of fruits. The top of the altar is adorned with grapes and an apple. Date: probably 2nd or 3rd centuries AD.
Deabus | Lucretis | Iulia Mate|rna uotum | soluit libens | merito Drou|sa filia [res(tituit)]
For Iulius: Solin-Salomies 1988, 98. For Maternus: Kajanto 1982, 303; Solin-Salomies 1988, 360.

5. Eschweiler-Fronhoven *AE* 1984, 690 = C.B. Rüger 2, n° 31
Altar in rose sandstone broken in the middle. Height: 72 cm, width: 46 cm, depth: 22 cm. The left lateral face is decorated with a table holding grapes, dates, ears of wheat, quince, pine cone and unidentified fruits. The dedicant already dedicated altars to the *Matronae Vatuiae* in Rödingen. Date: *c.* 150–225 AD.
M(atronis) Amratnin|[e]his T(itus) Iulius | Vitalis pro | se [et suis] u(otum) | s(oluit) l(ibens) m(erito)
For Iulius: Solin-Salomies 1988, 98. For Vitalis: Kajanto 1982, 274; Solin-Salomies 1988, 424.

6. Pier Clauss no. 7 = *AE* 1977, 549
Altar in sandstone. Height: 92 cm, width: 60 cm, depth: 28 cm. Fruits decorate the top of the altar. On the right face, a *cornucopia*. At the base of it, two flowers and two birds. On the left face, a table with a flagon/bottle under it. On the table, a flower, a pitcher, a cake and pig's head, and a vessel. Date: *c.* 180–200 AD.
Matronis | Alusneihis | T(itus) Tattianus | Eranus pro | se et suis l(ibens) m(erito)
For Tattianus: Solin-Salomies 1988, 182. For Eranus: Holder, vol. I, 1457; Delamarre 2003, 97.

7. Nideggen-Embken CIL XIII 7909 = Lehner 515
Altar in sandstone. Height: 75 cm, width: 48 cm, depth: 18 cm. Fruits decorate the top of the altar. On the left face, a vase with fruits. On the right face, a *cornucopia* and a fruit. Date: *c.* 164–255 AD.
Matronis | [V]eteranehis | Tertinius | [F]irmanus pro | se et suis u(otum) s(oluit) l(ibens) m(erito)
For Tertinius: Solin-Salomies 1988, 184. For Firmanus (Firminus): Kajanto 1982, 258; Solin-Salomies 1988, 332.

8. Bonn *AE* 1930, 19 = Lehner, *BJ* 135, no. 19 = Nesselhauf 165 = Esp. XI 7761
Aedicula flanked by two pillars with an inscription below. Height: 107 cm. In the *Aedicula*, the

Matronae are represented wearing the common costume of Germania Inferior. They sit on a bench. The one in the middle, the smallest, puts her feet on a little bench and holds fruits on her knees. Behind the bench, three people can be recognised: a woman, a girl and a young boy. In front of the left flanking pillar, it is possible to distinguish the lower body of a man. Opposite, on the right pillar, there is probably a woman. All of them may compose the family of the dedicant. On the left lateral face, a servant from the temple is standing up. In his left hand, he holds a plate with fruits and, in the other hand, a garland of flowers. A tree is behind him. The other lateral face side is adorned with a branch of a tree with a garland. Date: *c.* 164 AD.
Matronis | Aufaniabus | Q(uintus) Vettius Seuerius | quaestor C(oloniae) C(laudiae) A(rae) A(grippinensis) | uotum soluit l(ibens) m(erito) | Macrino et Celso co(n)s(ulibus)
For Vettius: Solin-Salomies 1988, 206. For Severius: Kajanto 1982, 256; Solin-Salomies 1988, 402.

9. Bonn *AE* 1930, 21 = Esp. XI 7777
Aedicula. The altar is composed of a representation of the *Matronae* in the *Ubii* costume and in triplication. They hold fruit baskets on their knees. A young boy, probably one of the dedicants, is on their left. A scene of offering is represented below the triplication. A sacrificiant performed the offering and the dedicants are on either side of the altar. The scene seems to represent a libation. Date: *c.* 164–255 AD.
Matronis | Aufaniabus | Q(uintus) Caldinius Celsus | l(ibens) m(erito)
For Caldinius: Solin-Salomies 1988, 42. For Celsus: Kajanto 1982, 230; Solin-Salomies 1988, 312.

10. Bonn CIL XIII 8042 = Lehner, *BJ* 135, no. 20 = Esp. XI 7762
Aedicula. Height: 119 cm. The main face is engraved with a representation of the *Matronae* in triplication between pilasters decorated with tendril scrolls and grapes. The three goddesses hold fruit baskets on their knees while sitting on a bench. Two feminine entities are close to them and they stand on globes. Under the inscription, a sacrifice scene, in which a young man holds a little box, a man plays a double flute and a servant holds a pot and a saucepan. On the right lateral face, remnants of a male character. It is possible to see a *cornucopia.* Below, a servant stands in front of a large cooking pot on a hearth, held in place by a hook. On the left lateral face, a woman wears a coat and priestly scarf. In her left hand, she holds a little fruit basket and in the other hand, a cloth. Below, a young boy carries a pig on his back. Date: *c.* 164–255 AD.
Aufanis | C(aius) Candidinius Verus | dec(urio) C(oloniae) C(laudiae) A(rae) A(grippinensium) pro se et suis | u(otum) s(oluit) l(ibens) m(erito)
For Candidinius: Solin-Salomies 1988, 45. For Verus: Kajanto 1982, p. 253 and Solin-Salomies 1988, p. 420.

11. Bonn Lehner, *BJ* 135, no. 28 = Nesselhauf 172 = Esp. XI 7760
Aedicula. Above the inscription, three *Matronae* hold fruit baskets in their hands. Below the inscription, a scene of sacrifice, in which a servant pours the content of a patera on the altar. The left face is adorned with a tree. The right face has a man holding unidentified objects in his hands. Date: *c.* 164–255 AD.
[Matronis Auf]anis | [.] Iul(ius) Pomponianus et | Bassiana Gaillu pro se et suis | l(ibentes) m(erito)
For Iulius and Bassianius: Solin-Salomies 1988, 98, 32. For Pomponianus: Kajanto 1982, 153; Solin-Salomies 1988, 381. For Calla: Holder, vol. I, 700; Delamarre 2003, 53.

12. Müddersheim CIL XIII 7855 = Lehner 261 = Esp. IX 6567
Aedicula in sandstone. Height: 90 cm, width: 55 cm, depth: 25 cm. A plate with fruits is engraved on the top of the altar. The triple *Matronae* are flanked by two pillars. The goddesses hold fruit baskets on their knees. On the left lateral face, a table with three feet, on which a pig head, a vase and a goblet are represented. On the right face, a *cornucopia* and a bird. Date: *c.* 164–255 AD.
Matronis | Aruagastis | Aul(us) T(i)tius Victor | [u(otum) s(oluit)] l(ibens) [m(erito)]
For Titius: Solin-Salomies 1988, 187. For Victor: Kajanto 1982, 278; Solin-Salomies 1988, 422.

13. Düren CIL XIII 7864 = ILS 4805 = *AE* 2001, 1437 = Esp. IX 6569
Aedicula, within which are triple seated *Matronae.* Scenes of sacrifices are engraved on the lateral faces. Date: *c.* 164–255 AD.
Matronis Hama|uehis C(aius) Iulius | Primus et C(aius) Iulius | Quartus ex i[m]perio | ipsarum I I

l(ibentes) m(erito).
For Iulius: Solin-Salomies 1988, 98. For Primus and Quartus: Kajanto 1982, 291, 293; Solin-Salomies 1988, 384, 388.

14. Jülich CIL XIII 7895 = Lehner 326 = ILS 4802 = Esp. VIII 6349
Aedicula uncovered in Bettenhofen. Triple *Matronae* in a panel in the middle of the inscription. A scene of *praefatio* is represented below this, in which two *Matronae* and two dedicants are around the altar. Date: *c.* 164–255 AD.
Matronis | Ettra|henis | et | Gesa|henis | M(arcus) Iul(ius) Amandus
For Iulius: Solin-Salomies 1988, 98. For Amandus: Kajanto 1982, 360; Solin-Salomies 1988, 291.

15. Rödingen CIL XIII 7889 = Lehner 332 = ILS 4803 = Esp. VIII 6336
Aedicula. The *Matronae* are represented in triplication holding fruit baskets on their knees. The lateral faces contain representations of a man and a woman performing a libation. Date: *c.* 164–255 AD.
Matr(o)n(is) Gesaienis | M(arcus) Iul(ius) Valentinus | et Iulia Iu[lia]nna | ex imperio ipsarum l(ibentes) m(erito)
For Iulius: Solin-Salomies 1988, 98. For Valentinus and Iulliannus: Kajanto 1982, 247, 148; Solin-Salomies 1988, 417, 346.

16. Nideggen-Embken CIL XIII 7907 = Lehner 522 = Esp. VIII 6355
Aedicula. Three *Matronae* in individual roundels, holding a sacred vase and a patera are positioned below the first line of the inscription. On the right lateral face, a man is performing a sacrifice, holding a vase in his hand. On the other face, a woman, holding a vase, pours the content of a patera on the floor. Date: *c.* 164–255 AD.
M(atronis) Veteranehis | C(aius) Matrinius | Primus ex imp(erio) | ip(sarum) pro se et | suis l(ibens) m(erito)
For Matrinius: Solin-Salomies 1988, 115. For Primus: Kajanto 1982, 291; Solin-Salomies 1988, 384.

17. Nideggen-Embken CIL XIII 7908 = Lehner 516 = Espérandieu, VIII 6350
Aedicula. Height: 85 cm, width: 61 cm, depth: 30 cm. Two pillars flank triple *Matronae,* who are wearing the *Ubii* costume and a pendent in the form of a *Lunula.* They hold fruit baskets on their knees. On the left lateral face, a table with a fruit basket on it. On the right face, a *cornucopia* full of ears of wheat and fruits. Date: *c.* 164–255 AD.
Matron[is] | Veteran[ehis] | C(aius) Prmini[us] | Sap[pienus]
For Priminius: Solin-Salomies 1988, 144. For Sappienus: Delamarre 2003, 160 s.v. Sapienus.

18. Zülpich CIL XIII 7923 = Lehner 323 = Esp. VIII 6358
Aedicula in sandstone. Height: 85 cm, width: 53 cm, depth: 14 cm. A scene of *praefatio* is represented under the inscription. On the right, a soldier dedicant wearing a *paenula*, holding a sword in his left hand and a plate in his right. On the left, a *Matrona*, wearing the *Ubii* costume, is holding a flower in her hands. The soldier makes her an offering. On the left lateral face, a laurel branch. The right face is empty. Date: *c.* 164–255 AD.
Matronis Cuche|nehis L(ucius) Marcius Ae|toni(u)s F(irminus) Verecundus | mil(ites) leg(ionis) I M(ineruiae) P(iae) F(idelis) u(otum) s(oluerunt) l(ibentes) m(erito)
For Marcius and Firminus: Solin-Salomies 1988, 112, 79. For Verecundus: Kajanto 1982, 264; Solin-Salomies 1988, 420. For Aetoni(u)s: Delamarre 2003, 14.

19. Antweiler CIL XIII 7952 (lost; illustrated in an engraving in *CIL*)
Aedicula. Triple *Matronae* with fruit baskets on their knees. Under the inscription, a scene of sacrifice with a servant holding an incense box in his hand, on the left of the altar. A woman is behind the altar, and on the left, a *Matrona* is watching the sacrifice. Date: *c.* 164–255 AD.
Matronis Vacalli|nehis Tib(erius) Claudi(us) *| Maternus imp(erio) ipsa(rum) | l(ibens) m(erito) | p(osuit)*
For Claudius : Solin-Salomies 1988, 56. For Maternus: Kajanto 1982, 303; Solin-Salomies 1988, 360.

20. Domburg CIL XIII 8786 = HC 6 = Esp. IX 6645
Altar composed of 30 assembled fragments. The goddess is seated on a large throne standing on

a platform under a shell canopy. Two ends of the canopy are held by cupids, with a palm leaf in their hands. On her right, a dog is looking at her. A bowl full of apples is on her left. On the right lateral face, Neptune is represented with his foot on a ship bow. He is holding a trident in his right hand. A vase full of apples is engraved under him. On the left face, Hercules is shown with the lion skin and his club. Two columns with plants encircle him. In a panel beneath, a tripod sacrificial table with an animal head on of it between two loaves. Under the table, a basket and vases. Date: 2nd or 3rd centuries AD.
Deae | Nehalleniae | Flettius Gennalonis | pro se et suis | u(otum) s(oluit) l(ibens) m(erito)
For Flettius: Delamarre 2003, 100. For Gennalonis: no mention in Solin-Salomies 1988, Kajanto 1982 or Delamarre.

21. Domburg CIL XIII 8798 = HC 16 = Esp. IX 6658
Altar in common stone. Height: 76 cm, width: 46 cm, depth: 21 cm. Three goddesses are sat on a large throne, with fruit baskets on their knees. Under the inscription, a scene of sacrifice shows two people making a libation, a priest and a servant, a *camillus*. Each lateral face is decorated with a *cornucopia* full of fruits. Date: *c.* 150–250 AD.
Nehalleniae.| ...ine ini f(ilius)

22. Strasbourg CIL XIII 5971
Altar with unidentified decoration above the inscribed face. Date: *c.* 150–250 AD.
Quadr(iuis) | Septimini|us Victor | ar(am) cum tem|plo rest(ituit) u(otum) s(oluit) l(ibens) l(aetus) m(erito)
For Septiminius: Solin-Salomies 1988, 168. For Victor: Kajanto 1982, 278; Solin-Salomies 1988, 422.

23. Xanten CIL XIII 8638
Altar. Date: *c.* 150–250 AD.
Quadru[u(is)] | et Genio lo|ci Flauiu[s] | Seueru[s] | uet(eranus) leg(ionis) X[XX] | V(lpiae) V(ictricis) templum | cum arborib(us) | constituit | u(otum) s(oluit) l(ibens) m(erito)
For Flavius: Solin-Salomies 1988, 80. For Severus: Kajanto 1982, 256; Solin-Salomies 1988, 402.

24. Baden-Baden CIL XIII 11714 = *AE* 1907, 110 = Esp. *Germanie*, 449
Altar in red sandstone. Height: 61 cm, width and depth: 16 cm. A *patera* and a *prefericulus* are engraved above the lowest line of the inscription. Date: *c.* 101–250 AD.
Visunae | L(ucius) Saluius | Similis S(alui) | Similis | fil(ius) Medi|omat(ricus) | u(otum) s(oluit) l(ibens) m(erito)
For Salvius: Solin-Salomies 1988, 161. For Similis: Kajanto 1982, 280; Solin-Salomies 1988, 404.

25. Bonn Esp. XI 7774
Fragment of a *tabula* in limestone. Height: 34 cm, width: 70 cm, depth: 13 cm. The sculpture shows three *Matronae Aufaniae* seated on a throne on a pedestal, wearing the *Ubii* costume, holding fruit baskets on their knees. They are positioned between two groups of female worshippers, each holding a fruit basket. This sculpture represents the procession prior to the sacrifice itself. Date: *c.* 164–255 AD.

BIBLIOGRAPHY

Alföldy, G. 1968 'Epigraphische aus dem Rheinland III', *Epigraphischen Studien* 5, 33–92.

Brunaux, J.-L. 2000 *Les religions gauloises, nouvelles approches sur les rituels celtiques de la Gaule indépendante*. Paris, Errance.

Charles-Laforge, M.-O. (ed.) 2014 *Les Religions dans le monde romain. Cultes locaux et dieux romains en Gaule de la fin de la République au IIIe siècle après J.-C.*. Arras, Artois Presses Université.

Clauss, M. 1976 'Neue Inschriften im Rheinischen Landesmuseums Bonn', *Epigraphische Studien* 11, 1–42

Clifford, A. 2012 ‚Die Riten der Anderen', *Mediterraneo Antico*, 15, 31–50.

Delamarre, X. 2003 *Dictionnaire de la langue gauloise*. Paris, Errance. 2nd edition.

De Sury, B. 1994 'L'ex-voto d'après l'épigraphie, contribution à l'étude des sanctuaires', *Les sanctuaires de tradition indigène en Gaule romaine, actes du colloque d'Argentomagus, octobre 1992*, ed Ch. Goudineau, I. Fauduet & G. Coulon, 165–90. Paris, Errance.

Deyts, S. 1986 'Cultes et sanctuaires des eaux en Gaule', *Archeologia* 37, 9–30.

Dorcey, P. F. 1992 *The cult of Silvanus: a study in Roman folk religion*. New York, Columbia Studies in the Classical Tradition.

Dunand, F. & Lévêque, P. 1973 *Les syncrétismes dans les religions grecque et romaine. Colloque de Strasbourg, 9–11 juin 1971*. Paris, PUF.

Ferlut, A. 2011, *Le culte des divinités féminines en Gaule Belgique et dans les Germanies sous le Haut Empire romain*, PHD Dissertation, université Lyon (available online at: http://theses.univ-lyon3.fr/documents/lyon3/2011/ferlut_a#p=0&a=top).

Ferlut, A. 2012a 'Le culte de *Dea Auentia*, déesse tutélaire de la Colonia Pia Flavia Constans Emerita Heluetiorum Foederata (Aventicum)', *Visions de l'Occident romain, hommages à Yann Le Bohec*, B. Cabouret, A. Groslambert et C. Wolff (dir.), vol. 2, 793–815. Paris, CEROR.

Ferlut, A. 2012b 'Les soldats et les divinités féminines sous le Haut-Empire romain', *Le métier de soldat, Actes du 5ème congrès international sur l'armée romaine*, ed C. Wolff & Y. Le Bohec, 203–45. Lyon, CEROR.

Ferlut, A. 2015 'Goddesses as consorts of the healing Gods in *Gallia Belgica* and the *Germaniae. Healing gods and heroes in the Graeco-Roman World,* ed. P. Pachis. Open Library Humanities, Url: https://olh.openlibhums.org/articles/10.16995/olh.43/

Finke, H. 1927 'Neuen Inschriften', *BRGK* 17, 1–107 & 198–231.

González Rodríguez, C. & Marco Simón, F. 2009 'Divinidades y devotos indígenas en la *Tarraconensis:* las dedicaciones colectivas', *Acta Palaeohispanica* 9, 71–2.

Haeussler, R. 2008 'How to identify Celtic religion(s) in Roman Britain and Gaul', *Divindades indígenas em análise. Divinités pré-romaines – bilan et perspectives d'une recherche. Actas do VII workshop F.E.R.C.AN., Cascais, 23–25.05.2006 Cascais*, 13–63. Coimbra/Porto, ed J. d'Encarnação.

Haeussler, R. 2012 'Interpretatio indigena. Re-inventing local cults in a global world', *Mediterraneo Antico* 15 (1–2) 143–74

Heichelheim, F. M. 1963 *s. v. Quadruviae*, *RE* 24, 1963, col. 711–9.

Hondius-Crone, A. 1955 *The Temple of Nehalennia at Domburg*. Amsterdam, J. M. Meulenhoff (HC in the Appendix).

Ihm, M. 1963 *s. v. Quadriviae*, *Ausführliches Lexikon der griechischen und römischen Mythologie*, vol. IV, col. 1–7.

Kajanto, I. 1982 *Latin Cognomina*. Helsinki, Societas Scientiarum Fennica.

Kandler, M. 1985 'Das Heiligtum des Silvanus und der Quadriviae im Petroneller Tiergarten', *JOEAI* (*Jahreshefte des Österreichischen Archäologischen Institutes in Wien*) LVI, 143–68.

Lambert, P.-Y. 2003 *La Langue gauloise*. Paris, Errance. 2nd edition.

Le Bohec, Y. 2008 'Romanisation ou romanité au temps du principat : question de méthodologie', *REL* 86, 127–38.

Lehner, H. 1910 Das Heiligtum der *Matronae Aufaniae* bei Nettersheim, *BJ* 119, 301–21.

Lehner, H. 1918 *Die antiken Steindenkmäler der Provinzialmuseums*. Bonn, Kommission der Buchhandlung F. Cohen (Lehner in the Appendix).

Lepetz, S. & Van Andringa, W. (eds) 2008 *Archéologie du sacrifice animal en Gaule Romaine, Rituels et pratiques alimentaires*, Montagnac, APA.

Lévêque, P. 1973 'Essai de typologie des syncrétismes', *Les Syncrétismes dans les religions grecque et romaine, Actes du Colloque de Strasbourg, 9–11 juin 1971*, 179–87. Paris, PUF.

Méniel, Ph. 2008 'Sacrifices d'animaux, traditions gauloises et influences romaines, *Archéologie du sacrifice animal en Gaule Romaine, Rituels et pratiques alimentaires,* 147–54. Montagnac, APA.

Nesselhauf, H. 1937 'Neue Inschriften aus dem römischen Germanien und dem angrenzenden Gebieten', *BRGK* 27, 51–134 (Nesselhauf in the Appendix).

Nesselhauf, H. & Lieb, H. 1959 ,Dritter Nachtrag zu CIL XIII, Inschriften aus dem Germanischen Provinzen und den Trevergebiet', *BRGK* 40, 120–9 (Ness-Lieb in the Appendix).

Rüger, C. B. 1970 'Gallish-Germanischen Kurien', *Epigraphischen Studien* 9, 251–60.

Rüger, C. B. 1981 'Inschriftenfunde der Jahre 1975-1979 aus dem Rheinland', *Epigraphische Studien* 12, 1981, 287–309.

Rüger, C. B. 1983 'Römische Inschriftfunde aus dem Rheinland 1978-1982', *Epigraphische Studien* 13, 1983, 111–66.

Scheid, J. 2000 'Réflexions sur la notion de lieu de culte dans les Gaules romaines', *Archéologie des sanctuaires en Gaule romaine*, ed. W. Van Andringa, 19–21. Saint-Etienne, Presses universitaires de Saint-Etienne.

Scheid, J. 2010 *La religion des Romains*. Paris, Cursus.

Schwinden, L. 1996 'Der römische Tempelbezirk von Niedaltdorf/Ihn – Kultzentrum oder Villenheiligtum?', *Trierer Zeitschrift* 58, 511–23.

Solin, H. & Salomies, O. 1988 *Repertorium nominum gentilium et cognominum latinarum*. Hildersheim-Zürich-New-York, Olms-Weidmann.

Spickermann, W. 1994 Mulieres ex voto: *Untersuchungen zur Götterverehrung von Frauen in Römischen Gallien, Germanen und Rätien (1.–3. Jahrhunderts n. Chr)*. Bochum, Bochumer historische Studien, Alte Geschichte Nr. 12.

Spickermann, W. & P. de Bernardo Stempel 2005 'Keltische Götter in der Germania Inferior', *Keltische Götter in Römischen Reich, Akten des 4. Internationalen Workshops F.E.R.C.AN., 4.–6.10.2002, Universität Osnabrück*, ed. W. Spickermann & R. Wiegels, 125–48. Möhnesee, Bibliopolis.

Van Andringa, W. 2002 *Piété et religion en Gaule*. Paris, Errance.

XX

SULLE TRACCE DEI LUOGHI DI CULTO DELLE DIVINITÀ PLURALI IN GALLIA CISALPINA

Cristina Girardi

The phenomenon of plural deities is widespread across Gallia Cisalpina and the theonymic panorama is rather varied: Matronae, Iunones, Fatae, Dominae, Fortunae, Dianae, Martes, Lymphae, Parcae, Silvanae, *and many more. The Cisalpina is an ethnically diverse area and not all plural deities can therefore be labelled as 'Celtic'. The aim of this paper is to identify some of the cult places were plural deities were worshipped: some inscriptions mention sacred structures, like* templum, fanum, aedes, compitum, *or* ara *(e.g.,* aedes *and* signa III *for the* Iunones *at Aquileia, CIL V 781). It is also possible to suggest cult places when we find concentrations of votive inscriptions and votive deposits, as in the case of Suno (*Novaria ager*). A Latin inscription, showing clear signs of pre-Roman linguistic influence, attests female plural deities at the sanctuary of Monte San Martino, situated on a 1,075 high mountain near Riva del Garda (Trento) and frequented from the Iron Age until medieval times.*

Introduzione

LE attestazioni epigrafiche di divinità plurali in *Cisalpina* sono numerose[1], i teonimi sono in prevalenza femminili (*Iunones, Matronae, Fatae, Parcae, Vires, Dominae,* per citare quelli più ricorrenti), ma non mancano alcuni esempi di teonimi maschili (*Martes* e *Nixi)*, e un unico caso evidente di genere duplice (*Fati* e *Fatae)*[2]. Il quadro etnico-culturale della *Gallia Cisalpina* è stratificato e complesso[3]: ad aree occupate da popolazioni celtiche – quali Piemonte, Lombardia e in parte Liguria e Friuli, e quindi profondamente 'celtizzate' – si contrappongono le aree abitate da Veneti e Reti (Veneto, Trentino, Istria), che furono celtizzate solo attraverso contatti culturali. Pertanto non tutte le divinità plurali dell'area *Cisalpina* possono essere ricondotte al sostrato celtico facilmente, ogni singolo caso andrà inserito e analizzato nel suo contesto etnico-geografico. Poiché a fronte di una ricca e articolata documentazione epigrafica le testimonianze di luoghi di culto attestati

1 Alcune opere d'insieme che trattano le divinità plurali della Cisalpina sono: Pascal 1964; Landucci Gattinoni 1986; Landucci Gattinoni 1994; Zaccaria 2001–2002; Mennella & Lastrico 2008; Häussler 2015.

2 Sul problema del genere delle divinità plurali si veda Girardi 2015, con bibliografia precedente.

3 Zaccaria 2001–2002, 131; Mastrocinque 1991, 217; Häussler 2013, 35–70; Murgia 2013, 7–9.

archeologicamente sono scarse, si cercherà di rintracciare i luoghi di culto partendo dai dati offerti dalle iscrizioni, considerando, in primo luogo, quelle che menzionano strutture sacre come *aedes, compita, teguria, aediculae, arae.*

I luoghi del sacro nelle iscrizioni

L'iscrizione[4] alle *Divae Matronae*, rinvenuta a Foresto, frazione del comune di Bussoleno (Torino), menziona la riedificazione di un *compitum*[5] crollato a causa delle ingiurie del tempo; i *compita* erano delle piccole cappelle poste all'incrocio di strade, dove non solo venivano venerati i *Lares Compitales*, ma anche altre divinità. Nel 1977, nell'area del cimitero del paese, fu rinvenuto un frammento di trabeazione decorato con cinque ordini di motivi a fasce sovrapposti, che può essere, con buona probabilità, ricondotto all'*epistylium* del *compitum*[6]. Il ritrovamento di questo frammento e l'individuazione di un passo in un opuscolo del 1868[7], sfuggito al Mommsen, indicante il luogo di ritrovamento dell'epigrafe, ha permesso a Silvana Finocchi[8] di stabilire una relazione tra il frammento di trabeazione e l'iscrizione e di riconoscere l'area dell'attuale cimitero con annessa pieve risalente all'XI secolo, come la zona dove originariamente sorgeva il *compitum*. Provengono probabilmente dal medesimo luogo anche le altre quattro[9] iscrizioni sacre, menzionanti le *Matronae*, rinvenute nella prima metà dell'Ottocento. Due di queste contengono il teonimo *Matronae* in forma estesa, mentre le altre due presentano la sola iniziale. Quattro delle cinque dediche alle *Matronae* sono incise su delle lastrine di piccole dimensioni, supporto che lascerebbe presupporre la loro apposizione ai lati esterni del *compitum* oppure alle pareti del recinto sacro. L'abbreviazione o la totale omissione del teonimo nelle dediche sacre rinvenute all'interno di santuari è da considerarsi prassi piuttosto comune in quanto la titolazione del santuario era certamente nota.

Un aspetto peculiare della zona Piemontese è la presenza, lungo gli itinerari vallivi intensamente trafficati a fini commerciali, di tutta una serie di sacelli votivi dedicati alle *Matronae*[10]. Sulla sommità del colle Monginevro 'furono rilevate mura di pietra squadrate connesse con grappe di piombo e ferro, forse pertinenti a un tempio dedicato alle *Matronae*'[11], e l'effettiva presenza di una cultualità dedicata alle divinità madri sembrerebbe comprovata anche dalla menzione dell'oronimo *Mons Matronae* nell'*Itinerarium Burdigalense*, in Ammiano Marcellino e in Ennodio[12]. Poco

4 *CIL* V, 7228: *Divis Matronis / T(itus) Vindonus Ieranus / compitum vetustate / conlabsum*(!) *ex voto / restituit l(ibens) l(aetus) m(erito).*
5 De Ruggiero 1900b; Wissowa 1900.
6 Finocchi 1978, 5.
7 La menzione di questo opuscolo "La Dora. Memorie di G. Regaldi, II ed., 1867, p. 77" si trova in Finocchi 1978, 9, nota 10.
8 Finocchi 1978.
9 Le iscrizioni *CIL* V, 7226, 7227, 7224 sono state rinvenute nel 1827, mentre non è conosciuta la data di rinvenimento dell'iscrizione *CIL* V, 7241.
10 Le iscrizioni lungo le strade 'raggiungono il centinaio ed equivalgono a circa la metà del totale generale delle iscrizioni sacre restituite dalla *Cisalpina* occidentale' (Mennella 1998, 167).
11 Banzi 1999, 40.
12 Banzi 1999, 41.

lontano da Foresto, ad Avigliana, nella *statio Fines Cotti*, insediamento strategico della *Quadragesima Galliarum*, posta a 16–18 miglia da *Augusta Taurinorum*, al confine con le *Alpes Cottiae*, sono state rinvenute due dediche alle *Matronae*[13], una delle quali arricchita da una decorazione ad altorilievo raffigurante cinque figure femminili che si tengono per mano, con le braccia incrociate 'a catena'[14]. La *statio* svolgeva un importante ruolo di tipo emporico-commerciale, in questo punto confluivano infatti tutta una serie di itinerari minori[15] ed è probabile che in questo punto stradale nevralgico sorgesse anche un edificio sacrale dedicato alle *Matronae*, di cui però finora, non sono state rinvenute tracce archeologiche.

Un'altra iscrizione[16] menzionante un *compitum* è quella rinvenuta a Piacenza[17] nel 1934 durante lo scavo di Piazza Cavalli[18]; si tratta di una porzione dell'*epistylium* di un *compitum* dedicato alle *Matronae* e ai *Lares*. A differenza dell'iscrizione di Foresto, qui le *Matronae* vengono affiancate ai *Lares*, divinità protettrici dei crocicchi.

Da un'iscrizione[19] proveniente da Verona abbiamo notizia del rifacimento di un *compitum* consacrato ai *Lares* da parte di sei donatori, tre *magistri*[20] di condizione ingenua e tre *ministri* di condizione servile. I donatori restaurarono a loro spese il tempietto, provvedendo al consolidamento del tetto e delle pareti, e donando *valvae* (porte d'ingresso a doppio battente) e l'ingresso[21]. Un'altra dedica[22] veronese ai *Lares* menziona invece l'edificazione di un'*aedicula*[23] per la salvezza dell'imperatore Antonino Pio. Moltissime iscrizioni sacre veronesi provengono purtroppo da contesti di reimpiego[24] e risulta pertanto impossibile stabilire se le divinità menzionate dalle numerose iscrizioni fossero venerate in strutture cultuali loro dedicate o se la devozione avvenisse in piccoli sacelli disseminati lungo le strade della città. La formula *l(ocus) p(ublicus) d(atus) d(ecreto) d(ecurionum)*[25] che compare al termine dell'iscrizione alle

13 *CIL* V, 7210; Cimarosti 2012, n. 13: *Matronis / T(iberius) Iulius Prisci l(ibertus) / Aceste*; *CIL* V, 7211; Cimarosti 2012, n. 16: - - - - - - / *+[- - -] / Caes[ar(is)] / ser(vus) vi[licus] / station(is) [XL], / Matron(is) [v(otum) s(olvit) l(ibens) m(erito)].*

14 Cimarosti 2012, 131.

15 Banzi 1999, 33, 154 nota 17.

16 *AE* 1937, 15 = *AE* 1964, 211: *M(arcus) De[- - -] Memu[- - -]anu[s] / Matronis et Laribus / compitum v(otum) s(olvit) l(ibens) m(erito);* Rigato 2008, 232–3.

17 *Placentia, Regio VIII.*

18 Marini Calvani 2000, 339.

19 *CIL* V, 3257; *Pais*, SI 614; *ILS* 3610; EDR130863 (F. Boscolo Chio): *Magistri: / M(arcus) Licinius M(arci) f(ilius) Pusillio, / Sex(tus) Vipsanius M(arci) f(ilius) Clemens, / Q(uintus) Cassius C(ai) f(ilius) Niger. / Ministri: / Blandus C(ai) Afini Asclae ser(vus), / Murranus P(ubli) Clodi Turpionis ser(vus), / Auctus M(arci) Fabrici Hilari ser(vus) / compitum refecerunt, tectum / parietes allevarunt, valvas / limen de sua pecunia, Laribus dant. / Cosso Cornelio Lentulo L(ucio) Pisone Augure co(n)s(ulibus)*; Buonopane 1987, 297; Bolla 2009, 7; Boscolo 2013, 443.

20 Boscolo 2013.

21 Buonopane 1987, 297.

22 *CIL* V, 3258: *Laribu[s Augustis pro salute] / Imp(eratoris) Caesar[is divi Hadriani f(ilii) divi Traiani] / Parthici ne[p(otis) divi Nervae pron(epotis) Antonini Aug(usti) Pii] / aediculam [- - -] / M(arcus) Seius M(arci) f(ilius) FI[- - -] / opus proba[verunt - - -]*; Buonopane 1987, 296.

23 De Ruggiero 1895a.

24 Bolla 2009, 7.

25 Pistarino 2014, cap. 2 'le iscrizioni di ambito sacro'.

Parcae[26] – probabilmente una base di statua, in quanto sono visibili i segni delle grappe a cui era fissata la statua delle divinità – ci trasmette un'importante informazione sulla concessione di uno spazio pubblico per l'erezione di un monumento sacrale e potrebbe forse anche alludere a una sorta di legittimazione, da parte dell'*ordo decurionum,* del culto delle *Parcae*.

Numerose sono le iscrizioni dedicate a divinità plurali rinvenute ad Aquileia, purtroppo però, come la maggior parte delle iscrizioni sacre, non sono contestualizzabili, poiché i materiali provengono quasi sempre da contesti di reimpiego, da sterri o recuperi occasionali. Pertanto, nonostante l'imponente mole di materiale relativa al sacro rinvenuta, 'delineare una vera e propria topografia del sacro risulta un'operazione quasi improponibile'[27]; solo per alcuni culti (Mitra, Asclepio, Igiea, Iside, Serapide, *Magna Mater*, Beleno) è stato possibile proporre una localizzazione dei luoghi di culto sulla base della frequenza delle relative iscrizioni[28]. Rimane quindi sconosciuta[29] l'esatta collocazione all'interno della colonia dell'*aedes*, ubicato su suolo privato[30] ed eretto in onore delle *Iunones*[31], come adempimento di un voto, dal seviro *M. Magius Amarantus*[32], da sua figlia *Vera* e dalla liberta *Ilias*. L'*aedes*[33], da intendersi probabilmente come una struttura di modeste dimensioni, era dotato di tre statue raffiguranti le *Iunones*, di un portico con muro di cinta e di una *culina*, un locale per la preparazione dei pasti sacrificali o dei banchetti pubblici[34].

L'iscrizione trentina posta da *Druinus*, *actor* di *M. Nonius Arrius Mucianus*, console del 201 d.C., commemora invece l'erezione *a solo,* a sue spese, di un *tegurium*/*tugurium*[35] per i *Fati* e le *Fatae*[36]. Si tratta dell'unica[37] attestazione in *Cisalpina* dell'elargizione di una somma di denaro, 200 sesterzi, per il mantenimento di una struttura sacra. Nel commento del *Corpus* il termine *tegurium* viene comparato a una struttura di età moderna, il ciborio, 'un tempietto sostenuto da quattro colonne, aperto per ogni lato'[38]. La lastra è murata nel portico del cortile interno di Castel Toblino (Trento) ed

---

26 *CIL* V, 3281; EDR093798 (C. Girardi): *Loco public(o) dat(o) d(ecreto) d(ecurionum). | Parcis Aug(ustis) sacr(um). | L(ucius) Cassius Vervici f(ilius) | Nigrinus, VIvir Aug(ustalis) v(otum) s(olvit) l(ibens) m(erito);* Modonesi 1995, 32, n. 26.

27 Fontana 2004, 401.

28 Bertacchi 2003, 45.

29 L'epigrafe era reimpiegata nel pavimento della basilica di Aquileia: *InscrAq* 236.

30 Raoss 1964–1967, 1696–1697.

31 *CIL* V, 781; *ILS* 3119; *InscrAq* 236; EDR093887 (F. Mainardis): *Iunonibus sacrum. | M(arcus) Magius M(arci) l(ibertus) Amarantus | IIIIIIvir et | Magia M(arci) f(ilia) Vera, Magia M(arci) l(iberta) Ilias | aedem, signa III, portic(um) cum marceriis et | culina(m) et locum in quo ea sunt | votum solverunt. | Loco privato.*

32 Buonopane 2001, 358, n. 46.

33 De Ruggiero 1895a.

34 De Ruggiero 1900a.

35 Bruns 1934.

36 *CIL* V, 5005; *ILS* 3761; *InscrIt*, X, 5, 1098; *SuppIt* 8, 1991, p. 183; EDR091098 (D. Fasolini): *Fatis Fata[bus], | Druinus M(arci) No[ni] | Arri Muciani c[larissimi v(iri)] | actor praediorum | Tublinat(ium), tugurium | a solo, impendio suo, fe|cit, et in tutela eius | ((sestertios)) n(ummos) CC conlustrio | fundi Vettiani dedit*; Landucci Gattinoni 1994, 85–95; Chisté 1971, 28–32.

37 Zerbini 1990, 25.

38 Cfr. Mommsen in *CIL* V, 5005; Bruns 1934, 780.

è mutila della parte superiore destra; può essere inoltre interessante notare che a pochi chilometri a nord, nel comune di Vezzano (Trento), fu rinvenuta[39] una dedica alla versione maschile di queste divinità: *Fati Masculi.*

Luoghi di culto di modeste dimensioni, probabilmente piccoli recinti con un'*ara*[40] devozionale posta all'interno, vengono menzionati in tre iscrizioni, due delle quali dedicate alle *Vires*. La prima[41], proveniente da *Opitergium*, menziona la dedica di un altare come scioglimento di un voto, la seconda[42], da Aquileia, ricorda invece la ristrutturazione di un'ara, mentre la terza iscrizione[43], rinvenuta nei dintorni di Correggio[44] (Reggio Emilia), presenta una particolare struttura del testo: a una prima parte in cui compaiono gli elementi onomastici della dedicante, *Aninia Sex(ti) l(iberta) Ge*, segue una seconda parte dove si trova l'indicazione del teonimo *Iunones* e la dedica dell'ara e del luogo sacro sulla base di precise norme giuridiche. L'iscrizione si conclude con una dettagliata descrizione dell'utilizzo da parte di terzi del luogo sacro: è possibile effettuare restauri ed abbellimenti, praticare sacrifici, a patto che non siano compiuti atti empi o frodi ai danni delle divinità lì venerate.

I complessi santuariali

I santuari archeologicamente attestati in cui si trovano elementi della devozione a divinità plurali nell'area cisalpina sono solamente due, una ulteriore area di culto è stata invece supposta sulla base di una serie di indizi.

Il primo santuario (fig. 1) è quello di Forum Cornelii[45] (Imola), individuato nell'area del Cinema Teatro Modernissimo, già negli anni 20 del '900, anni in cui venne alla luce un'ara dedicata alla *Bona Dea* e un cippo ai *Fauni*[46]. E' però durante le ultime campagne di scavo (2003–2005), che è stato rinvenuto un pezzo di fondamentale importanza: un piccolo gruppo statuario bronzeo, raffigurante due[47] figure maschili inginocchiate nell'atteggiamento del parto, corredato dall'iscrizione *Nixibus. Lucania Fadilla v(otum) s(olvit) l(ibens) m(erito)*[48]. L'ex-voto, databile sulla base delle caratteristiche paleografiche

39 '*Reperta Vezzani*', cfr. Mommsen in *CIL* V, 5002; EDR091095 (G. Migliorati); *ILS* 3759, *InscrIt*, 10, 05, 1095; *SuppIIt*, 08, 1991, p. 183, ad nr. (A. Garzetti) : *Fatis Mas/culis sacr(um). / Staumus Ve/sumi Britti et / Cornelia Sex(ti) fil(ia) / Prisca / ex voto posuer(unt) / [- - - - - -].*

40 De Ruggiero 1895b.

41 *CIL* V, 1964; EDR098202 (S. Nicolini): *Q(uintus) Carminius Q(uinti) l(ibertus) Phileros / Viribus aram v(otum) s(olvit) l(ibens) m(erito).* Forlati Tamaro 1958, 23.

42 *CIL* V, 8247; *InscrAq*, 367; EDR117019 (F. Mainardis): *Viribus Fes/tus Ursioni/s Aug(usti) lib(erti) / ser(vus) / ara(m) vot(o) rest(ituit).*

43 *CIL* XI, 944; *ILS* 4909: *Aninia Sex(ti) l(iberta) Ge. Iunonibus hanc / aram locumque iis legibus dedicavit. / Si quis sarcire reficere ornar(e) coronar(e) volet licet / et si quit sacrifici quo volet ferre et ibi ubi volet uti sine / scelere sine fraude lic[et]*; Tarpini 2002; Rigato 2008, 230–1.

44 Le ricerche d'archivio di Calzolari hanno evidenziato che il luogo di rinvenimento dell'iscrizione è Fabbrico oppure Correggio. Bormann, nel *Corpus*, inseriva invece l'iscrizione tra quelle di *Carpi et viciniae*: Calzolari 1984; Tarpini 2002, 54.

45 *Regio* VIII.

46 *AE* 1927, 106 = *AE* 1945, 48: *P(ublius) Sextilius / Th(r)eptus / v(otum) s(olvit) / sanctissim(is) Faunib(us) / c(um) s(uis).*

47 La terza figura maschile è purtroppo perduta.

48 Rigato 2008, 239–41.

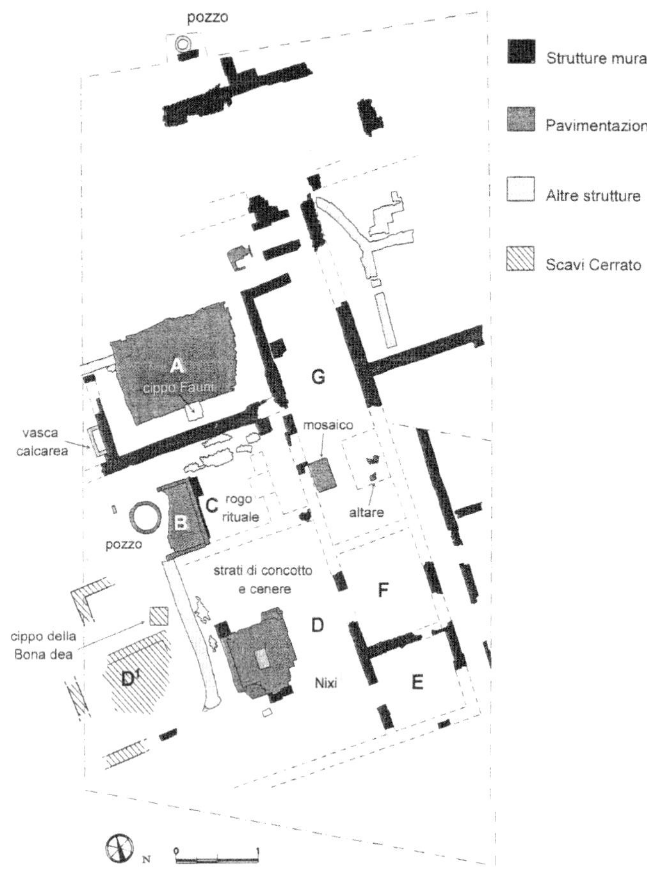

Fig. 1. Pianta del santuario di *Forum Cornelii* (da De Santis & Negrelli & Rigato 2009, 354).

e sul contesto di rinvenimento al II sec d.C., rappresenta l'unica raffigurazione oggi nota dei *Nixi*[49] e contribuisce a spegnere il dibattito relativo al genere di queste divinità. Sempre in occasione dell'ultima campagna di scavo è stato rinvenuto anche un nuovo altare dedicato ai *Fauni*[50]. Le strutture emerse sono state interpretate come i resti di un santuario dedicato alla Bona Dea, sulla base delle analogie planimetriche e strutturali con altri santuari archeologicamente noti dedicati a questa dea[51]. Lo scavo ha comunque restituito numerosi votivi dedicati a diverse divinità: Minerva, Mercurio, Iside, *Fauni*, *Nixi*. In età repubblicana gli edifici di culto erano organizzati in uno spazio rettangolare articolato in due aree con al centro del complesso una vasca calcarea; nella prima età imperiale si assiste a un primo organico intervento di ristrutturazione che vede la disposizione di una serie di ambienti attorno a un grande vano quadrangolare semiaperto (vano D)[52], in cui è stato rinvenuto il gruppo statuario dei *Nixi*. Nelle fasi successive le ristrutturazioni si concentrano prevalentemente nell'area nord, con la creazione di un grande ambiente rettangolare (vano A)[53], dove è emerso il cippo dedicato ai Fauni. Il vano C[54] è stato invece riconosciuto come un *Brandopferplatz* (rogo votivo), fulcro della funzionalità cultuale del santuario. Le ristrutturazioni dell'area santuariale si susseguirono fino agli inizi del III sec d.C. e sembrano essere dovute ad atti di evergetismo privato[55]. Il complesso santuariale si configura quindi come un importante nucleo cultuale votato alla fertilità, abbondanza, salute e al parto[56].

Il secondo santuario (fig. 2) è quello di Monte S. Martino[57], localizzato su un

49 De Bernardo Stempel 2013, 77.
50 'Il materiale epigrafico è inedito': De Santis, Negrelli & Rigato 2009, 350, nota 112.
51 De Santis, Negrelli & Rigato 2009, 318.
52 De Santis, Negrelli & Rigato 2009, 320–3.
53 De Santis, Negrelli & Rigato 2009, 323.
54 De Santis, Negrelli & Rigato 2009, 322.
55 De Santis, Negrelli & Rigato 2009, 323.
56 De Santis, Negrelli & Rigato 2009, 351.
57 Bassi 2003, 7–20; 2005, 248–71; 2011, 385–411; Ciurletti ed. 2007; Ciurletti 2002, 17–94; 2007,

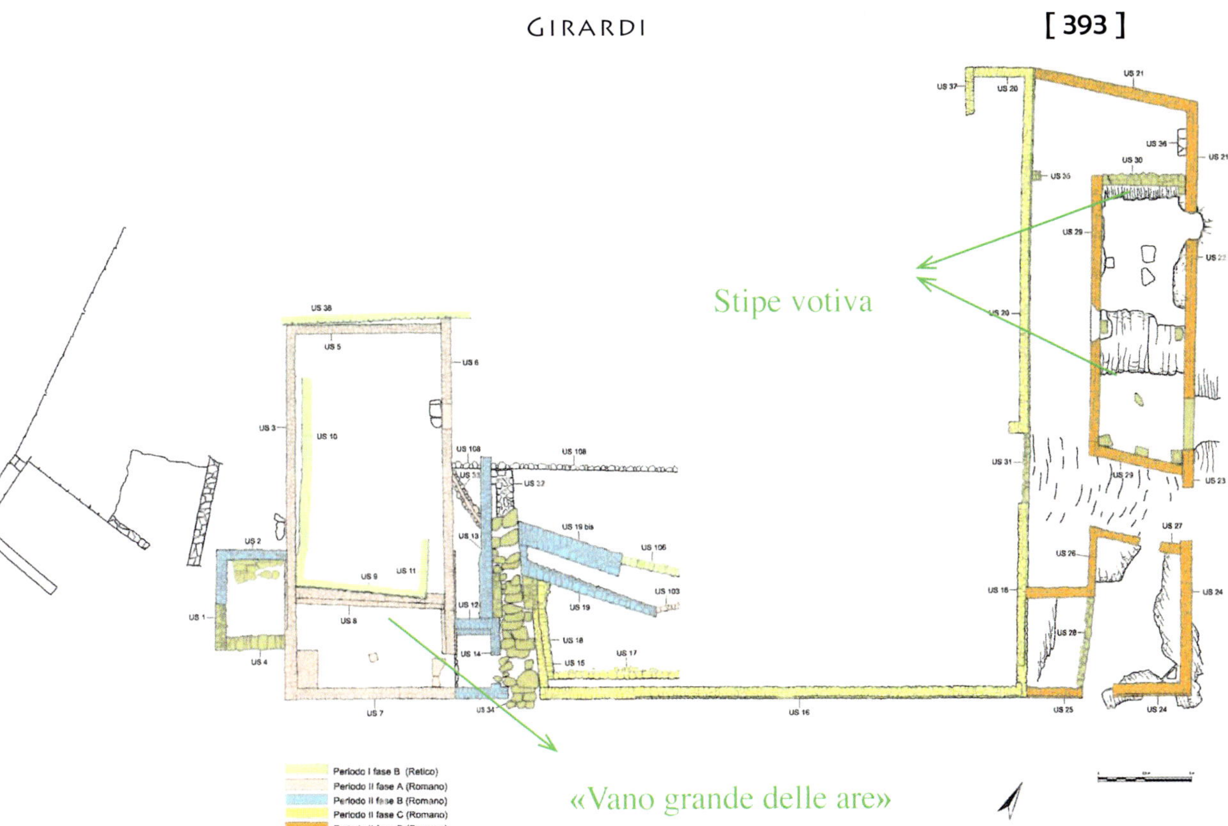

Fig. 2. Pianta del santuario di Monte S. Martino (da Ciurletti 2007, 48, rielaborata da C. Girardi).

ampio pianoro ad un'altezza di 843 metri sul livello del mare, a nord ovest della cittadina di Riva del Garda[58] (Trento). La prossimità del sito al lago di Garda – l'antico *Benacum*[59], che in età romana costituiva un'importante via di comunicazione[60] – favorì la frequentazione del santuario non solo da parte delle popolazioni locali ma anche da commercianti e viaggiatori. Il ritrovamento di *Brandopferplätze*, tipici luoghi di culto delle popolazioni retiche[61], testimonia come il sito fosse già frequentato durante la seconda età del Ferro. L'area dell'Alto Garda apparteneva, a quell'epoca, al gruppo culturale Fritzen-Sanzeno[62], ma sono ravvisabili fenomeni di contaminazione culturale tra i diversi gruppi limitrofi come i Cenomani e i Camuni. E' probabilmente durante la seconda metà del I secolo a.C. che l'area, in origine un luogo di culto all'aperto, si arricchisce di strutture architettoniche in muratura; un muro perimetrale correva lungo

17–94; Valvo 2007, 343–50.

58 *municipium* di *Brixia.*

59 Buonopane 1997, 17–52.

60 L'esistenza di un porto nell'antica *Ripa* (oggi Riva del Garda) è documentato dalla presenza di iscrizioni menzionanti il *collegium nautarum B(rixianorum)* (*InscrIt*, X, 5, 1065; 1070).

61 Bassi 2011, 390. Sui Brandopferplätze si veda anche il recente contributo di Anne-Lise Pestel [Pestel 2015].

62 Bassi 2011, 385.

i lati ovest, sud ed est, mentre il lato nord, in corrispondenza di un dirupo roccioso, ne era probabilmente privo; attraverso una gradinata posta sul lato sud si accedeva al grande cortile scoperto. Sebbene i dati relativi alle prime campagne di scavo siano scarsi, si possono riconoscere almeno due fasi: una più antica riguardante l'area sud ovest e una più recente, relativa ai vani lungo il lato est. In questi ultimi (vani C ed E) è stata riconosciuta una stipe votiva[63] che ha restituito diversi manufatti[64], tra i quali due laminette decorate a sbalzo con motivo a spina di pesce e una serie di statuette fittili e in piombo raffiguranti Minerva, Venere, una divinità femminile in trono e una maschile non identificabile. In uno dei vani del santuario, denominato 'vano grande delle are' sono state rinvenute due are, una integra[65] e una frammentaria, recante sulla cimasa una dedica a divinità plurali femminili. L'iscrizione[66], incisa in *scriptio continua*, con caratteri latini ma in lingua preromana con contaminazioni[67] latine, recita:

> PRAV[- - -]P̣ABVS *vel* PRAV[- - -]ṚABVS | SAVETPREAMMAVTVR |
> AVCATACIVS ASV | PREAMVICLASTA.

Sia per la collocazione nella parte finale della prima riga, sia per l'utilizzo della desinenza propria del dativo/ablativo femminile plurale della terza declinazione, il frammento [- - -]P̣ABVS oppure [- - -]ṚABVS, sembra possa essere riconducibile a un teonimo imprecisato di una divinità plurale, o a un epiteto della stessa. L'integrazione in *[Mat]rabus* potrebbe sembrare la più immediata, ma l'ipotesi risulta essere poco sostanziata, se si considera che in *Cisalpina* non vi sono attestazioni di *Matres* o *Matrae*. Sarebbe forse più prudente orientare l'integrazione verso un epiteto, preceduto dal nome della divinità; necessario è quindi uno sguardo al panorama teonimico dei dintorni: nella vicina Riva del Garda è stata recentemente scoperta (nel 2006) una dedica alle *Iunones*[68], anche se va puntualizzato che in *Cisalpina* le dediche alle *Iunones* sono tendenzialmente prive[69] di epiteti; da Calvagese (*ager Brixianus*) proviene la dedica ai *Fati Dervones*[70]; da Castel Toblino l'iscrizione *Fatis Fatabus* menzionata in precedenza. Allargando il raggio chilometrico ma rimanendo comunque nell'area dell'*ager Brixianus*, troviamo a Manerbio[71] e a Calvisano[72] due dediche con l'iscrizione *Matronabus.* Considerando gli

63 Bassi 2011, 248–71.
64 Bassi 2003, 18; 2005, 257–67.
65 *InscrIt*, X, 5, 1090: *L(ucius) Tre(bonius / mellius) Primus / et Bitumus Sec(undus) / Luppisi / Mainiali / fecerunt*; Valvo 2007, 344–5; *SuppIIt* 25, 2011, pp. 222–3, ad nr. (A. Valvo).
66 *InscrIt*, X, 5, 1091; EDR091091 (G. Migliorati); Tibiletti Bruno 1983, 99–109; *SuppIIt* 25, 2011, p. 223, ad nr. (A. Valvo).
67 Anche sull'intonaco di uno degli ambienti del santuario furono rinvenuti graffiti, ora purtroppo scomparsi, in entrambe le lingue (Paci 1993, 112). Esempi di bilinguismo si ritrovano anche a *Tridentum* in un contesto databile tra la tarda età repubblicana e quella flavia (Bassi 2004, 9).
68 *AE* 2008, 588: *Iunonibus / L(ucius) Licinius Firmu(s) / v(otum) s(olvit) l(ibens) m(erito);* Bassi 2008, 48–54.
69 Se non si considera l'epiteto *Augustae* di tre iscrizioni veronesi (*CIL* V, 3238; 3239; 3240) e di una proveniente dall'*ager Brixianus* (*InscrIt*, X, 5, 838).
70 *CIL* V, 4208: *Fatis / Dervonibus / v(otum) s(olvit) l(ibens) m(erito) M(arcus) Rufinius / Severus*; Migliorati 2008, 167–74.
71 *CIL* V, 4159: *Matronab(us).*
72 *CIL* V, 4137; *InscrIt*, X, 5, 841: *Matronabus.*

esempi citati, ritengo sia forse preferibile riconoscere le *Fatae* nelle divinità menzionate nell'iscrizione frammentaria, considerando innanzitutto la diffusione delle dediche ai *Fati/Fatae* nella zona e in secondo luogo la scelta frequente di affiancare un epiteto al nome di queste divinità. Altre iscrizioni[73], in gran parte frammentarie e pertinenti all'area del santuario, sono state rinvenute, a un centinaio di metri sud-est dal santuario, riutilizzate nelle strutture di un insediamento[74] del V–VI secolo, caratterizzato dalla presenza di diversi edifici con funzione residenziale[75]. In corrispondenza dell'estremità ovest dell'*edificio 1* dell'abitato venne costruita, a partire probabilmente dal VIII/IX secolo, una chiesetta dedicata a S. Martino, demolita poi nel 1750.

In assenza di evidenze archeologiche, un ulteriore passo che può essere intrapreso per tentare di localizzare i luoghi di culto delle divinità plurali è quello di seguire alcuni indizi[76]: particolari concentrazioni di iscrizioni sacre in una determinata area, la presenza di stipi votive, la riutilizzazione delle pietre in un'area geografica limitrofa, l'eventuale presenza di iscrizioni menzionanti cariche sacerdotali oppure strutture sacre. Un esempio è dato dal materiale epigrafico rinvenuto a Suno[77] (Novara) che solo da recenti studi, ad opera di Giovanni Mennella[78], è stato possibile ricondurre alla pieve di San Genesio. Le epigrafi si trovavano infatti murate nella chiesa e furono estratte fra il 1843 e 1877, informazione questa sconosciuta a Mommsen, che non fece controlli autoptici in quella località e che si avvalse solo di trascrizioni inviategli da informatori locali[79]. La presenza di una decina di dediche sacre – tra cui l'unica attestazione in *Cisalpina* delle *Fortunae*[80] e una dedica alle *Matronae*[81] – di tre are anepigrafi, e di iscrizioni menzionanti personale addetto al culto, tutte provenienti dalla medesima area, ha indotto Mennella a ipotizzare la presenza in questo luogo di un 'santuario rurale'.

Conclusioni

L'aspetto che accomuna i santuari discussi è la presenza, al loro interno, di culti dedicati a entità divine diverse [tabella 1]. E' possibile che in alcuni momenti si siano venerate contemporaneamente divinità diverse, ma, vista la frequentazione secolare dei santuari, è altresì probabile che vi sia stata una successione temporale dei vari culti. In entrambi i santuari attestati archeologicamente sono ravvisabili diverse fasi di frequentazione a cui corrispondono ristrutturazioni ed ampliamenti, inoltre vi sono tracce di *Brandopferplätze* imputabili, almeno nel caso del santuario di Monte S.

73 Paci 1993, 11–126; Bassi 2001, 237–42; Valvo 2007, 346–9.
74 Bellosi, Granata & Pisu 2011, 157–66.
75 Bassi 2005, 253.
76 Chevallier 1983, 485.
77 *Regio* XI, *ager Novariensis*.
78 Mennella 1999.
79 Mennella 1999, 97.
80 *CIL* V, 8929 = *AE* 1999, 782 : *Fortunab(us) / [-] Sertor[ius* (?) - - -] | - - - - - - ? ; Mennella 1999, 99–100; Boccioni 2006, 80.
81 *CIL* V, 6575 add p. 1087: *Matronis / et Dis Deabus. T(itus) Maius Iustinu(s) / pro se suisque / v(otum) s(olvit) l(ibens) m(erito)*; Mennella 1999, 104–5.

Martino, a pratiche cultuali epicorie. Come si evince dalla tabella 2 le strutture sacre dedicate alle divinità plurali sono alquanto modeste: *arae*, *aediculae* e piccoli tempietti (*compita* e *teguria*). Solo nel caso dell'*aedes* alle *Iunones*, menzionato nell'iscrizione di Aquileia insieme a un portico, a un muro di cinta e a una *culina*, è forse possibile pensare a una struttura cultuale un po' più articolata.

Tre sono i casi di ristrutturazione di una struttura sacra testimoniati dall'uso dei verbi *restituere*, *reficere:* il *compitum* di Foresto dedicato alle *Divae Matronae*, quello di Verona ai *Lares* e l'*ara* alle *Vires* di Aquileia.

Ricoprono un particolare interesse due dediche con indicazioni sull'utilizzo del luogo di culto: nell'iscrizione da Castel Toblino si fa riferimento a una somma di denaro di 200 sesterzi donati per la tutela del *tegurium* ai *Fati* e alle *Fatae*, mentre nell'iscrizione da Correggio la dedicante sancisce che è possibile restaurare e abbellire il luogo di culto e vi si possono praticare sacrifici, ma non possono essere compiuti atti ai danni delle divinità lì venerate.

Nella maggior parte dei casi l'esatto luogo di ritrovamento delle iscrizioni è purtroppo ignoto, e questo ci impedisce di ragionare sulla posizione del luogo di culto all'interno della topografia della città. Rimane pertanto insoluto il quesito relativo al posto che occupavano le divinità plurali, anche in relazione ad altri culti, all'interno degli insediamenti urbani. Per quanto riguarda invece la zona Piemontese è emerso che la devozione delle *Matronae* si svolgeva anche lungo i percorsi stradali vallivi, che erano scanditi da piccoli sacelli devozionali.

Tabella 1: santuari attestati archeologicamente e ipotizzati

Luogo	**Divinità plurali**	**Alte divinità**
Forum Cornelii	*Nixi*	*Bona Dea* *Fauni* *Minerva* *Mercurius* *Isis*
Monte S. Martino	*Fatae* ?	*Minerva* *Venus*
Suno	*Matronae* *Fortunae*	*Hercules* *Iuppiter* *Mercurius* *Victoria*

Tabella 2: strutture sacre menzionate in iscrizioni

Tipo di struttura sacra	Altri annessi	Azione	Luogo	*Regio*
compitum		*restituere*	Foresto	XI
compitum			Piacenza	VIII
compitum	*valvae* *limes*	*reficere*	Verona	X
aedes	*signa III* *porticus cum maceris* *culina*		Aquileia	X
tegurium			*Ager Brixianus*	X
ara			*Opitergium*	X
ara			Aquileia	X
ara			Correggio	VIII
aedicula			Verona	X

BIBLIOGRAFIA

Banzi, E. 1999 *I miliari come fonte topografica e storica. L'esempio della* XI Regio (Transpadana) *e delle* Alpes Cottiae. Roma, École Française de Rome.

Bassi, C. 2001 'Nuove testimonianze epigrafiche da Monte S. Martino (Riva del Garda) e Tridentum', *Epigraphica*, 63, 236–44.

Bassi, C. 2003 'Il santuario romano di Monte S. Martino (Riva del Garda) nel contesto dei culti di origine indigena del territorio benacense', *Santuari e luoghi di culto nell'Italia antica* (Atlante tematico di topografia antica, 12), ed. L. Quilici & S. Gigli, 7–20. Roma, *L'Erma* di Bretschneider.

Bassi, C. 2004 'Osservazioni sulla conoscenza della scrittura in Trentino durante l'età romana', *Archivio Veneto*, s.V, CLXII, 5–27.

Bassi, C. 2005 'La stipe votiva di Monte S. Martino (Riva del Garda)', *Stipi votive delle Venezie. Altichiero, Monte Altare, Musile, Garda, Riva. Corpus delle stipi votive in Italia, Regio X, XIX*, edd. G. Gorini & A. Mastrocinque, 249–71. Roma, Giorgio Bretschneider Editore.

Bassi, C. 2008 'Una dedica alle *Iunones* da Riva del Garda (Trentino)', Sartori, ed., 43–59.

Bassi, C. 2011 'Onomastica e affermazione dell'identità: il caso di Monte S. Martino nel contesto del territorio dei Benacenses', *Identità e autonomie nel mondo romano occidentale. Iberia-Italia – Italia-Iberia. III Convegno Internazionale di Epigrafia e Storia Antica* (Epigrafia e antichità, 29), ed. A. Sartori & A. Valvo, 385–411. Faenza, Fratelli Lega Editori.

Bellosi, G., A. Granata & N. Pisu 2011 'La chiesa dell'abitato in altura di Monte S. Martino, Comune di Riva del Garda', *Nuove ricerche sulle chiese altomedievali del Garda*. 3° Convegno Archeologico del Garda (Gardone Riviera, 6 novembre 2010), ed. G. P. Brogiolo, 157–66. Mantova, SAP.

Bertacchi, L. 2003 *Nuova pianta archeologica di Aquileia*, Udine, Edizioni del Confine.

Boccioni, S. 2006 'Fortune in Cisalpina', *ACME –Annali della Facoltà di Lettere e Filosofia dell'Università degli Studi di Milano*, 49.2, 71–92.

Bolla, M. 2009 'Testimonianze archeologiche di culti a Verona e nel territorio in età romana', in *Verona storico-religiosa. Testimonianze di una storia millenaria*, ed. P. A. Carozzi, 3–23. Verona, Edizioni Fondazione Centro Studi Campostrini.

Boscolo, F. 2013 '*Magistri e ministri* in un'iscrizione veronese dell'anno 1 a.C', *Epigraphica*, 75, 439–47.

Bruns, G. 1934 'Tugurium', *RE* SVIIA, 1, 778–81.

Buonopane, A. 1987 'Donazioni pubbliche e

fondazioni private', *Il Veneto nell'età romana, I. Storiografia, organizzazione del territorio, economia e religione*, ed. E. Buchi, 289–310. Verona, Banco Popolare.

Buonopane, A. 1997 'Il lago di Garda e il suo territorio in età romana', *Ville romane sul lago di Garda*, ed. E. Roffia, 17–52. S. Felice del Benaco (Brescia), TP Editore.

Buonopane, A. 2001 'Sevirato e augustalità ad Aquileia: nuovi dati e prospettive di ricerca', *Aquileia dalle origini alla costituzione del Ducato longobardo. Storia, amministrazione, società*. Atti del Convegno Internazionale (Antichità Altoadriatiche LIV), ed. G. Cuscito, 339–73. Trieste, Editreg.

Calzolari, M. 1984 '*CIL* XI, 944. Precisazioni sulla provenienza della lapide', *Epigraphica* 46, 219–25.

Chevallier, R. 1983 *La romanisation de la Celtique du Pô. Essai d'histoire provinciale*, Roma, École Française de Rome.

Chisté, P. 1971 *Epigrafi trentine dell'età romana*, Rovereto, Museo civico di Rovereto.

Cimarosti, E. 2012 *Le iscrizioni di età romana sul versante italiano delle* 'Alpes Cottiae' (Sylloge Epigraphica Barcinonensis, 1). Barcelona, Galerada.

Ciurletti, G. ed. 2007 *Monte S. Martino. Fra il Garda e le Alpi di Ledro. Il luogo di culto (ricerche e scavi 1969–1979)*, Trento, Giunta della Provincia Autonomia di Trento, Soprintendenza per i Beni Archeologici.

Ciurletti, G. 2007 'Il Monte S. Martino. Un sito archeologico tra preistoria ed età moderna', in *Monte S. Martino. Fra il Garda e le Alpi di Ledro. Il luogo di culto (ricerche e scavi 1969–1979)*, ed. Ciurletti G., 17–94. Trento, Giunta della Provincia Autonomia di Trento, Soprintendenza per i Beni Archeologici.

Ciurletti, G. 2002 'L'area cultuale di Monte San Martino (Tenno/Riva del Garda)', *Kult der Vorzeit in den Alpen. Opfergaben – Opferplätze – Opferbrauchtum / Culti nella preistoria delle Alpi. Le offerte – i santuari – i riti*, I – II, ed. L. Zemmer-Plank, 721–34. Bolzano, Athesia.

De Bernardo Stempel, P. 2013 'Celtic and other indigenous divine names found in the Italian peninsula', *Théonymie celtique, cultes,* interpretatio *– Keltische theonymie, Kulte,* interpretatio. X Workshop F.E.R.C.AN., Paris 24–26 Mai 2010, ed. A. Hofeneder & P. de Bernardo Stempel, 73–96. Wien, Verlag der Österreichischen Akademie der Wissenschaften.

De Ruggiero, E. 1900a 'Culina' *DE* II, 2, 1294.

De Ruggiero, E. 1900b 'Compitum' *DE* II, 1, 562–3.

De Ruggiero, E. 1895a 'Aedes, Aedicula' *DE* I, 139–202.

De Ruggiero, E. 1895b 'Ara' *DE* I, 594–606.

De Santis, P., C. Negrelli & D. Rigato 2009 '*Forum Cornelii*: *Nixi Dii* fra archeologia ed epigrafia', *Opinione pubblica e forme di comunicazione a Roma: il linguaggio dell'epigrafia.* Atti del Colloquio AIEGL – Borghesi 2007, ed. M. G. Bertinelli Angeli & A. Donati, 317–60. Faenza, Fratelli Lega.

Finocchi, S. 1978 'Luoghi di culto e insediamenti romani fra Foresto e Bussoleno', *Segusium*, 13–14, 5–18.

Fontana, F. 2004 'Topografia del sacro ad Aquileia: alcuni spunti', *Aquileia dalle origini alla costituzione del Ducato longobardo. Topografia, urbanistica, edilizia pubblica* (Antichità Altoadriatiche 8), ed. G. Cuscito & M. Verzár-Bass, 401–24. Trieste, Editreg.

Forlati Tamaro, B. 1958 *Iscrizioni lapidarie latine del Museo civico di Oderzo*, Milano.

Girardi, C. 2015 'Le divinità plurali del Noricum attraverso le testimonianze epigrafiche. Appunti di una ricerca in corso', *Culti e religiosità nelle province danubiane, Atti del II convegno internazionale, Ferrara, 20–22 novembre 2013,* ed. L. Zerbini, 57–70. Bologna, Casa editrice Emil di Odoya.

Häussler, R. 2015 'A landscape of resistance? Cults and sacred landscapes in Western Cisalpine Gaul', Trans Padum...usque ad Alpes. *Roma tra il Po e le Alpi: dalla romanizzazione alla romanità. Atti del Convegno, Venezia 13–15 maggio 2014*, ed. G. Cresci Marrone, 261–86. Roma, Edizioni Quasar.

Häussler, R. 2013 'De-constructing Ethnic Identities: becoming Roman in Western Cisalpine Gaul', *Creating Ethnicities & Identities in the Roman World* (BICS supplement), ed. A. Gardner, E. Herring & K. Lomas, 35–70. London, Institute of Classical Studies, University of London.

Landucci Gattinoni, F. 1986 *Un culto celtico nella* Gallia Cisalpina. *Le* Matronae-Iunones *a sud delle Alpi*, Milano, Jaca Book.

Landucci Gattinoni, F. 1994 'Le *Fatae* nella *Cisalpina* romana', *Culti pagani nell'Italia settentrionale*, ed. A. Mastrocinque, 85–95. Trento, Università degli Studi, Dipartimento di Scienze Filologiche e Storiche.

Marini Calvani, M. 2000 *Aemilia. La cultura romana in Emilia Romagna dal III sec. a.C.*

all'età costantiniana. Catalogo della mostra, Venezia.

Mastrocinque, A. 1991 'Culti di origine preromana nell'Italia settentrionale', *Die Stadt in Oberitalien und in der Nordwestlichen Provinzen des Römischen Reiches*, ed. W. Eck & H. Galsterer, 217–26. Mainz, Zabern.

Mennella, G. 1998 'Itinerari di culto nel Piemonte romano', *Archeologia in Piemonte. L'età romana*, ed. L. Mercando, 167–79. Torino, Allemandi.

Mennella, G. 1999 'Il santuario rurale di Suno', *Epigrafia e territorio*, 5, 97–116.

Mennella, G. & L. Lastrico 2008 'Le *Matronae-Iunones* nell'Italia settentrionale: anatomia delle dediche', *Continuity and innovation in religion in the Roman west*, vol. 2 (Journal of Roman Archaeology Supplement 67.2), ed. R. Haeussler & A. C. King, 119–30. Portsmouth, Rhode Island.

Migliorati, G. 2008 'L'epiteto *Dervones* nell'iscrizione *CIL* V, 4208 da Calvagese (Brescia)', Sartori, ed. 167–74.

Modonesi, D. 1995 *Museo Maffeiano di Verona. Iscrizioni e rilievi sacri latini*, Roma, 'L'Erma' di Bretschneider.

Murgia, E. 2013 *Culti e romanizzazione. Resistenze, continuità, trasformazioni*, Trieste, Edizioni Università di Trieste.

Paci, G. 1993 'Nuova iscrizione romana da Monte S. Martino presso Riva del Garda', *Archeologia delle Alpi* 1, 111–26.

Pascal, C. B. 1964 *The Cults of Cisalpine Gaul*, Bruxelles, Latomus.

Pestel, A.-L. 2015 'Du Brandopferplatz at temple romain. Romanisation de lieux de culte protohistoriques et réorganisations territoriales dans les Alpes centrales sous le Haut-Empire', *Hypothèses 2014. Travaux de l'École doctorale d'Histoire*, 18, 201–12.

Pistarino, V. E. 2014 L(ocus) d(atus) d(ecreto) d(ecurionum): *la concessione degli spazi pubblici nelle comunità cittadine dell'Italia romana*, Tesi di Dottorato, Alma Mater Studiorum – Università di Bologna.

Raoss, M. 1964–1967 'Locus', DE IV, 3, 1460–833.

Rigato, D. 2008 'Testimonianze della religiosità "celtica". Il caso della *regio octava*', Sartori, ed., 225–74.

Sartori, A., ed. 2008 *Dedicanti e* cultores *nelle religioni celtiche,* VIII Workshop F.E.R.C.AN., Gargnano del Garda (9–12 maggio 2007) (Quaderni di Acme, 104). Milano, Cisalpino.

Tarpini, R. 2002 'Un culto di origine preromana nella bassa pianura tra Modena e Reggio Emilia. Note a margine dell'iscrizione *CIL* XI, 944', *Pagani e Cristiani. Forme e attestazioni di religiosità del mondo antico in Emilia*, vol. II, ed. C. Corti, D. Neri, P. Pancaldi, 51–80. Bologna, Edizioni Aspasia.

Tibiletti Bruno, M. G. 1983 'L'iscrizione epicorica di Monte S. Martino (Riva del Garda)', *Beni culturali nel Trentino. Contributi all'archeologia*, 99–109. Trento, Provincia Autonoma di Trento.

Valvo, A. 2007 'Testimonianze epigrafiche', *Monte S. Martino. Fra il Garda e le Alpi di Ledro. Il luogo di culto (ricerche e scavi 1969–1979)*, ed. G. Ciurletti, 343–50. Trento, Provincia Autonoma di Trento.

Wissowa, G. 1900, '*Compitum*', *RE* 1900 IV, I, 792–4.

Zaccaria, C. 2001-2002 'Alla ricerca di divinità "celtiche" nell'Italia settentrionale in età romana. Revisione della documentazione per le Regiones IX, X, XI', *Veleia* 18–19, 129–64.

Zerbini, L. 1990 'Munificenza privata nelle città della Regio X', *Annali dei Musei Civici di Rovereto*, 6, 23–61.

XXI

THE CULT OF HERCULES IN CENTRAL-EASTERN TRANSPADANA (REGIO XI)

TWO CASE-STUDIES FROM LAUS POMPEIA (LODI VECCHIO, LODI) AND CEDRATE (VARESE)*

Paola Tomasi

This chapter analyzes the religious landscape of the cult of Hercules in the central-eastern part of regio XI, *through the reappraisal of the epigraphic evidence. Two complementary case studies (Cedrate and Laus Pompeia) show the significant role played by inscriptions in the reconstruction of the sacred landscape. The recently unearthed archaeological remains from Cedrate provide the missing monumental backdrop to CIL V 5558: this is particularly noteworthy because it offers an occasion to revisit the* communis opinio *about the very modest architectural appearance of rural shrines. Conversely, in Laus Pompeia the inscriptional body of evidence highlights the pivotal role of the findspot of the inscriptions as a means of pinpointing the original cult site when the pertinent archaeological remains no longer survive.*

THIS chapter analyzes the religious landscape of the cult of *Hercules* in the central-eastern part of *regio XI*. After a reappraisal of the epigraphic evidence, the paper will focus on two case studies, highlighting the interplay between inscriptions and their archaeological context.

1 Hercules in central-eastern Transpadana: General overview of the epigraphic testimonies

A reconsideration of the epigraphic material will allow us to outline the geographical provenance and distribution pattern of cult places, the nature of the cult, and the social make-up of the devotees.[1] Table 1 summarizes some relevant information pertaining

* The research has been funded by MIUR (Ministry of Education, University and Research) within the framework of PRIN 2009 (Research Project of National Relevance), entitled *Ancient Rome and the Transpadana: acculturation processes, infrastructure, systems of territorial and administrative organization.*

to each inscription.[2] For each source the geographical context[3] is highlighted, and the monument type (when known) is given with archaeological details; as regards the textual elements, the table focuses on the main structural elements of votive inscriptions.

1.1 The deity's profile

The dedications to *Hercules* are generally consistent with the expected syntax of votive inscriptions, which consists of theonym, dedicant (identified by name), and consecration formula (votive and/or generically devotional).[4] The great majority of inscriptions commemorate the fulfillment of a vow, and they superficially resemble each other in their repetitive use of typical formulae and abbreviations such as *vslm*.[5]

In a similar way the epigraphic materials do not offer a wide range of epithets: in a large majority of the texts, the deity is addressed only by the theonym in the simple dative, usually spelled out in full, at the beginning of the inscription,[6] without any epithet expressing the god's connotations.[7] Inscriptions of this type do not provide much information about the aspect of the god that is revered or the motives for setting up the inscription.[8] We shall therefore focus on the inscriptions that depart from this textual structure. By paying closer attention to the dedications that deviate from the usual pattern, we are able to infer a multifaceted range of traits of *Hercules*. The god's

1 On methodological issues, such as the parameters to be taken into account when analyzing votive inscriptions, see Mennella-Lastrico 2007, 125–7; Haeussler 2014, 323–4.

2 A detailed description and discussion of each document is beyond the scope of this paper: for further bibliography on each inscription, cf. the EDR entry. For texts not included in EDR, relevant bibliography is provided. When necessary, further clarifications are given: for example, I follow Reali's (1989, 238 no. 54) reading on CIL V 5642, and EDR124854 on Giussani 1931, 65–6.

3 On the *ager Comensis* I follow Sartori (1967–68) and Reali (1989; 2010, 93–4); hence CIL V 5688 has been attributed to the *ager Comensis*, not *Mediolanensis*. Differently in Mennella 2003, 483 n. 6.

4 Explicit consecration of the dedication to the god (*sacrum*) in CIL V 5606, 5768, 6349; *donum* in AE 2009, 417.

5 *VSLM* in CIL V 5467/8, 5498, 5507–08, 5528, 5533–34, 5559, 5561, 5593, 5606, 5694, 5703, 5718, 5721, 5723, 5743, 5645, 5759, 5767–69, 5686–87, 6346–48, 6350–52, 6356; SI 844; EDR124748; EDR137490. Variation: *V(otum) l(aetus) l(ibens) m(erito), v(oto) s(oluto) d(edit) l(aetus) l(ibens)*: CIL V 5520. *V(otum) l(ibenter) m(erito) s(olvit)*: CIL V 5521. *D(onum) p(osuit) l(ibens) m(erito)*: CIL V 5466. *Donum* and *VSLM* in AE 2009, 417. *VSLM* with specification *ex voto* in CIL V 5632. Only *v(otum) s(olvit)* in CIL V 5642; EDR124888; CIL V 6344, 6345, 6349. Just *v(otum)* in CIL V 5724; only *voto* in CIL V 5510. *Voto suscept(o)* in CIL V 6357. *Voto [sol]uto* in EDR124854. Unspecified circumstances in CIL V 5742, 5688, SI 724. Devotional act funded *de re sua*: CIL V 5693. On the nuances of the concept of *votum* and the communication between the dedicants and their gods via the contemporary audience, see Sartori 1992b, 425–6.

6 *Herculi* is the incipit in almost all of the epigraphic monuments. It appears in second position when paired with *Volkano* (CIL V 5510). It precedes *Quadrivis* (EDR124748). In only three instances does the theonym follow the dedicant's name and/or personal details: EDR124748, CIL V 6348, 5694.

7 CIL V 5466, 5507, 5521, 5528, 5533, 5558, 5559, 5561, 5632, 5642, 5686–88, 5694, 5703, 5718, 5721, 5723, 5742–43, 5767, 6345, 6347–48, 6350–52, 6363; SI 724, EDR124854, EDR124877, EDR137490, AE 2009, 417. Shortened forms, such as *Hercul(i)* in CIL, V 5467/8, *Hercli* in CIL V 5498, *Herc(uli)* in CIL V 6349.

8 Noteworthy nonetheless are grammatical peculiarities such as *Hercli* (CIL V 5498) or *Erquli* (CIL V 5510), which signal a popular devotion; attention should be paid also to the abbreviated formula *HLM* and variations (CIL V 6344, 6346), attested only in Laus Pompeia.

epithets in the votive inscriptions depict a multifunctional deity.[9]

The most frequent epithets are *Invictus* and/or *Victor*:[10] *Hercules* was revered as the god of strength, audacity, and triumph. Likewise alluding to the idea of an undefeated power is the matching concept of the tangible results guaranteed by *Hercules'* invincibility, which is conveyed by the epithet *Inpetrabilis*, either alone or paired with *Invictus/Victor*.[11] In other instances, *Hercules* is qualified as *Iuvenis*.[12] These lexical choices portray *Hercules* as an effective and powerful god who is especially invoked to preserve the vigour associated with youth, and is therefore particularly apt to be worshipped, as their protective deity, by *collegia iuvenum*, such as the *Modiciates Ioveni*.[13] Consistent with this conceptual framework is the god's connotation as a healer, clearly detectable in some dedications.[14]

Some epigraphic testimonies attest a combination of Celtic background and Roman religious understanding:[15] a couple of epithets, such as *Mertronnus* and *Anteportanus*, make reference to the local Celtic-speaking community in combination with the Roman idea of the protection of doors, gates, and passages.[16] Syncretism is attested also by the epithet *Ovanius*, which has been tentatively explained as a reference to a Celtic deity assimilated to *Hercules*: the dedicant wanted to express a particular local or personal *interpretatio* of a pre-Roman, autochthonous deity, but instead of setting up a dedication to that god, the dedicant decided to call this deity *Hercules Ovanius*.[17] The topographical aspect of the cult is clearly denoted also by epithets derived from toponyms, such as *Hercules Laudensis* in *Laus Pompeia* (*v. infra*).

9 The god's multifarious profile has been suggested as a plausible explanation for the wide popularity of Hercules in this area, as he was easily assimilated to pre-Roman indigenous deities: see Jaczynowska 1981, 631; Sartori 1992a, 81. A historical synopsis of the development of the cult of Hercules in Boscolo 2003, 267.

10 CIL V 5769, 5759, 5593, 5606, 5645, 5724 (and possibly CIL V 5520). CIL V 5508 is debated: Scuderi (2012, 139 n. 42) reads *Vic(tori)*, whilst EDR suggests a different text. In scholarly debate the epithet *Invictus* has been interpreted either as the mark of a fully Roman cult, or as a reminiscence of a previous autochthonous Celtic hero (*interpretatio romana*): cf. Reali 1989, 239–40.

11 Just *Inpetrabili*: CIL V 5768; *Invicto Inpetrabili*: CIL V 5769.

12 *Herculi Iuveni*: CIL V 5520, 5693. On this latter inscription see the different interpretation in Jaczynowska (1978, 94: inscription pertaining to the cult of young Hercules), and Passerini (1953, 164, 166–7), followed by Ginestet (1991, 250: inscription related to the local *collegium iuvenum*). The reference to youth was suggested in CIL V 5606 where Hercules' name is followed by *Conservatori Iuventia/rum*, interpreted by Scuderi (2012, 136 n. 13) as a reference to a tutelary deity of a collective entity. As *Hercules Conservator* he was revered as protector from any evil or danger that might befall the dedicant in other areas as well, such as the central Balkans: see Gavrilovic 2008, 145.

13 CIL V 5742: cf. Bitto 1973, 49; Jaczynowska 1978, 94; Ginestet 1991, 250; Resnati 1995, 60; Sartori 1995, 132. According to Gaviraghi (1955, 19, 35–6), *Modiciates* is a Celtic tribe name still in use during the Roman era. On *collegia iuvenum* in the Milanese area, see Boscolo 2003.

14 The consecration formula *pro salute* indicates reverence for Hercules as a god of health or welfare or as a personal protector: CIL V 5534 (*pro inpetrata salute*), 5558 (*pro salute*); in CIL V 5645 *salvo patrono* could point to the god's medical role. This protective aspect of the deity is also revered in the central Balkans, Dalmatia, Dacia, Gaul, and Britain: see Gavrilovic 2008, 144–6, 149.

15 On Hercules and Ogmios, see Pascal 1964, 165; Jaczynowska 1981, 654; Bauchhenß 2008, 92–3; Haeussler 2008, 195–6.

16 CIL V 5534. See Passerini 1953, 208; Sartori 1992b, 83; 2009, 47; De Bernardo Stempel 2009, 174; Scuderi 2012, 137–8.

17 SI 844; cf. Scuderi 2012, 139, n. 40.

Hercules appears to be mostly worshipped alone; in one case there is a clear association with another deity,[18] whilst in another[19] it depends on the preferred expansion of the abbreviation *Quadr*(...) that follows *Herculi*. In the latter case, if we read *Herculi Quadr*(*ivio*) or *Herculi* (*et*) *Quadr*(*ivis*), then this inscription should be listed among the testimonies to the association of the cult of *Hercules* with Celtic deities, here the *Quadriviae*; the dedicant would thus have made a vow to Hercules in his capacity of protector of roads and travellers.[20]

1.2. Cult places and devotees' social make-up

By attending to the geographical provenance of the inscriptions and to the dedicants, we can assess who used epigraphy, and recognize personal aspects of religious devotion. The inscriptional evidence pertaining to the cult of *Hercules* from the central-eastern *Transpadana* is predominantly extra-urban. Epigraphy seems to be widely used in rural areas:[21] the cult of *Hercules* is frequently attested in rural settlements and country shrines, and this also resulted in the frequent use of the local granite (*serizzo*), which dominates the record.[22] The only urban exception is *Mediolanum*,[23] while there are no testimonies from *Comum*, *Ticinum*, or *Bergomum*[24]. The cult of *Hercules* is mainly attested in rural communities and dispersed settlements (such as *vici* and *pagi*)[25].

Hercules was worshipped by male individuals and by communities. Collective

18 *Volkano et Erquli* in CIL V 5510. The association of these two deities has been interpreted as proof that 'ambedue siano divinità celtiche, travestite con nome romano': Passerini 1953, 209.

19 EDR124748.

20 Cf. Zoia 2013, 454–9. The other reading is *Herculi Quadr*(*atario*): despite being a hapax, this epithet remains intriguing, and it is not far from the semantic area of *Hercules Saxanus*, worshipped in Germania inferior; this epithet could hint at a possible facet of the cult of Hercules related to a quarry or a stone-cutters' workshop.

21 The vast majority of all Mediolanum's votive monuments come from the *ager*: 127 instances out of 152 inscriptions: Zoia 2014, 3. The abundance of epigraphic evidence of religious character from the countryside in Lombardy led to the apt definition 'terra di culti' by Sartori 1992b. On the concept of 'rural sanctuaries', cf. Sartori 1992b, 80–3.

22 15 instances out of 30 preserved monuments. On the frequent occurrence of *serizzo* within the *ager mediolanensis*, see Zoia 2013, 461. The persistent preference for this material is mirrored by the difficulty in assessing the chronology: the corresponding type of votive monument (fairly standard altars: cf. Sartori 1992b, 427, 433; Zoia 2014, 5–6, 16–8 for further archaeological details) is continuously repeated over the period (Sartori 2009d, 118 = Sartori 2014, 188). Since many instances do not give many personal details that would pinpoint or at least narrow down a possible date, nor is there a specific pattern in terms of consecration formulae or deities, this results in a broad chronological span in many cases (Zoia 2014, 3–4, 19, 22). Chronological inferences could be made on the basis of palaeography (e.g. the 3rd–4th century AD is inferable from the rustic lettering in CIL V 5521: cf. Sartori 2000, 158 no. 4; but see also Sartori 2009b, 465; for carving done at two different times in CIL V 5533, cf. Sartori 2009a, 45; possibly 1st century AD based on the 'Celtic' background in CIL V 5534: cf. Sartori 2009a, 47; Sartori 2009c, 571.

23 CIL V 5677, 5768, 5679; EDR 124748. A reference to Hercules, paired with *Telamon*, is borne by an epistylium, the small lettering of which probably indicates that the text served as the caption for a mythical episode displayed on the sculptural representation above it: cf. Sacchi 2012, 190, 192–3, no. 98.1–2. *Hercules* was the second most popular deity in the Milanese area after *Iuppiter*: cf. Passerini 1953, 208; Gaviraghi 1955, 36; Boscolo 2003, 267; Sartori 2009, 465.

24 Scuderi 2012, 144. Cf. Reali 1989, 238 no. 54.

25 Scuderi 2012, 137, 143.

devotees are either *cultores*,[26] unspecified *vicani*,[27] or are specified in geographical terms.[28] These examples illustrate how cults allow us a better understanding of social organization in rural areas. The latter is intertwined with the religious aspect of the Romanization process: the cult of *Hercules* appears to be associated with town-like *vici*, and so demonstrates continuity with pre-Roman territorial administration, and this fact attests in turn 'il perdurare di una religiosità epicorica spontaneamente espressa nell'*interpretatio* romana'.[29] Moreover, the location of these *vici* is characteristic of well-travelled areas, associated with a thriving economy based on animal husbandry, and so it depicts Hercules as the protective deity of traders and travellers.[30] This feature is intertwined with the social make-up of the devotees and the motivations that led them to appeal to this god[31].

When devotees are not specified by name, unanimous participation is conveyed by a generic allusion to other worshippers involved in the act of propitiating the god.[32] Only two dedications remain anonymous due to the unsatisfactory state of preservation of the inscription.[33] By taking into account the onomastic patterns, we can deduce that worshippers who deployed inscriptions must have consisted to a substantial extent of sub-elite persons:[34] as well as the cases where low social status can be established or reasonably inferred,[35] we often encounter unusual names or irregular polyonymy,[36]and dedicants who identified themselves by a single name only.[37] In addition, some records show orthographic anomalies/misspellings,[38] or irregular lettering.[39] Moreover, the

26 CIL V 5593.
27 CIL V 5528. Possibly *vicani Montunates*: see Scuderi 2012, 137. On the *vicani* as dedicants of votive inscriptions, cf. Reali 2010.
28 *Vicani Votodrones* in EDR124888. See Zanella 1952 on this toponym.
29 Scuderi 2012, 137. Cf. Jaczynowska 1981, 631.
30 See Mastrocinque 1991, 217–9.
31 Scuderi 2012, 137, 143–4.
32 *Cum suis*: CIL V 5686, 5561, 5718, EDR124877. The formulaic expression is emphatically enhanced by *omnibus* in CIL V 5769, 5703. *Pro se et suis*: CIL V 5606, 5686.
33 SI 724 and EDR124854.
34 Scuderi 2012, 139, 141.
35 CIL V 5534, 5558, 5521, 5466, 5723, 5498, 5645, 5688, 6344.
36 CIL V 5759, 5743, 5534, AE 2009, 417, SI 844, CIL V 5467/8, 5632, 5703, 5718, 5687; for CIL V 5724 cf. Passerini 1953, 208 n. 8; Resnati 1995, no. 68; Scuderi 2012, 141 n. 71; unusal onomastics in CIL V 5743, 5508, 5510, EDR137490. Unclear in CIL V 5520. Regular *tria nomina* in the following instances: CIL 5507, 5466 (but uncertain reading), 5510, 5498, 5561, 5642, 5694, 5721, 5645, 5688, 5743, EDR124748, EDR 137490. Regular polyonymy is prevalent in *Laus Pompeia* (CIL V 6344–46, 6348–52, 6356–57). Possible *tria nomina* in CIL V 5606, but *evanidus et lectu difficillimus* (in the CIL lemma).
37 CIL, V 5521, 5533–34, 5559, 5693 (Scuderi 2012, 137 n. 17 reads *p*(*osuit*) and not *P*(*ublius*)),5723, 5759, SI 844.
38 Diplography in CIL V 5703; *Hercli* pro *Herculi* in CIL V 5498; *Opetatus* pro *Optatus* in CIL V 5508; *Erquli* pro *Herculi* in CIL V 5510; *Ioveni* pro *Iuveni* in CIL V 5742 (on this specific vocalism, cf. ThLL VII 2, c. 732, 75 s.v. *Iuvenii*); *Eufemus* pro *Euphemus* in CIL V 6347.
39 E.g. CIL V 5718 (cf. Resnati 1995, 57, no. 38) and CIL V 5521 (cf. Zoia 2014, 8). Mixed lettering (capital and rustic) in CIL V 5498, 5528, Zoia 2013: cf. Zoia 2014, 9. Poorly arranged text in CIL V 5528 (cf. Zoia (2014, 7). On the Celtic nomen *Mogetius* (CIL V 6350), cf. Delamarre 2007, 134; De Bernardo Stempel 2008, 69; 2009, 175; Tomasi 2014.

devotees' names sometimes highlight the incipient/ongoing Romanization process.[40]

As regards the arrangement of the structural elements of the votive inscriptions, the theonym is usually the incipit, and the overwhelming majority of the epigraphic material falls within the following textual pattern: 'theonym + dedicant + fulfillment of a vow'.[41] After this, the most frequently attested combination is 'theonym + fulfilment of a vow + dedicant', and variations of this pattern.[42] Rarer are texts constituted only by 'theonym+dedicant',[43] 'theonym+fulfilment of a vow',[44] or just the theonym.[45] Less well attested is the reverse pattern, where the dedicant's name precedes the theonym,[46] showing in these cases that self-representation was at least as important as communication with the deity.[47] Sometimes, in order to highlight the act of worship, the inscriptions state the nature of the votive monument.[48] Personal details, such as voting tribe or other geographical reference,[49] professional occupation,[50] municipal offices or priesthoods,[51] are scarcely mentioned.[52] When they do occur they, as is to be expected, appear after the dedicant's name, and, unsurprisingly, they are chiefly attested among higher-ranking persons, with regular tripartite onomastics, and especially among the

40 CIL V 5534, 5533, 5559, 5467/8, 5687, 5686, 6350.

41 Attested in: CIL V 5767, 5559, 5467–5468, 5498, 5507, 5510, 5521, 5528, 5561, 5593, 5606, 5718, 5721, 5723, 5743, 5759, SI 844, AE 2009 417, EDR124888, EDR137490, CIL V 5642, 6345, 6346, 6351 (followed by *LDDD*), 6347, 6349, 6352; hypothetical (since the deity's name is missing) in CIL V 6356 and 6357 (with mention of restoration of a *sigillum* and *ara*). Variation ('theonym+object of the dedication+dedicant+fulfillment of a vow') in CIL V 5769. The only instance where the votive intention is not explicit (CIL V 5466) falls into this pattern as well. For comparisons with the general votive epigraphic landscape of Mediolanum, see Zoia 2014, 9–10, 22–3.

42 'Theonym + fulfillment of a vow + dedicant' in CIL V 5533, 5724 (followed by *LDDD*), 6645 (followed by *salvo patrono*), 5687, 5703, 6350. Variations include 'theonym+fulfillment of a vow + dedicant + fulfillment of a vow + other dedicants' (in CIL V 5508 but the text is debated; CIL V 5520); 'theonym + half formula of the fulfillment of a vow + dedicant + half formula of the fulfillment of a vow' (in CIL V 6344), 'theonym + motivation for putting up the dedication + dedicant + fulfillment of a vow' (CIL V 5534); 'theonym + motivation for putting up the dedication + dedicant + euergetic deed' (CIL V 5558).

43 'Theonym + dedicant' in CIL V 5742, EDR 124877.

44 'Theonym + fulfillment of a vow': EDR 124854.

45 'Nomen tantum' in SI 724.

46 'Dedicant + theonym + fulfillment of a vow': EDR124748, CIL V 6348, 5694.

47 Sometimes the same result was achieved in a more subtle way: e.g. in EDR137490 it is noteworthy that the dedicant's name is carved in larger lettering than the theonym, enhancing the visibility of the devotee. See Sartori 2014, 188. On other layout strategies, such as an hourglass arrangement of the text (e.g. CIL V 6348; AE 2009, 417), see Zoia 2014, 7–9, 23. On the interesting case of a dedicant with abbreviated name (spelled *C(aius) Vir(ius) Maxi(mus)* in CIL V 5561 and 5249 set up to *Iunones* and *Matronae*), as a deliberate choice to engage the reader's complicity in identifying the dedicant in a small community, cf. Sartori 2009, 705; Zoia 2014, 24.

48 CIL V 5768: *aram*; CIL V 5769: *Aram | constituit*; CIL V 6357: *huic / arae*. On the euergetic deed in CIL V 5558 and 6357, *v. infra*.

49 Voting tribe (*Oufentina*) or geographical provenance (*Mediolanensis*) attested in CIL V 6345, 6351, 6349, 6348, 6347, 6348, 6346.

50 Professional occupation is possibly attested by the *cognomen* of the dedicant in CIL V 6350 (*mercator*).

51 The sevirate is frequently attested: CIL V 5768, 5688, 6356, 6351, 6349, 6348, 6347. One *pontifex* (CIL V 6345) and one *sacerdos Laurens Lavinas* (CIL V 6357). Two *decuriones*: CIL V 5768, 6349; one *aedilis* (CIL V 6347), one *quaestor* (CIL V 5768), and one *curator aerari* (CIL V 6348).

52 On the intrinsic conciseness of religious inscriptions and their audience, esp. in *regio XI*, see Sartori 1992b, 426, n. 11, 427.

dedicants from Laus Pompeia. This leads us to examine our first case-study.

2. Laus Pompeia's sacred landscape: the river sanctuary of H(ercules) L(audensis) M(agnus) by the Adda river

The systematic survey of Laus Pompeia's epigraphic corpus (carried out within the editorial framework of the *Supplementa Italica*) has led to an assessment of the distinctive features of this river sanctuary, drawing attention to, among other aspects, the unique character of the worshippers in terms of social rank and geographical provenance.

These worshippers stand out because of their socio-economic position, which is generally higher than the rest of the devotees whom we have discussed above. Consistent with this is the fact that we are here predominantly dealing with marble inscriptions, usually of high-quality craftsmanship[53]. Moreover, the assessment of these devotees' social status is intertwined with the analysis of the sevirate, since many of them were *VIviri*;[54] some of them are *sexviri nude dicti* (CIL V 6347, 6348), but others are distinguished between *iuniores* (CIL V 6349, 6351) and *seniores* (CIL V 6349). This indication, combined with the fact that the city where the office was held is usually specified (when not clearly deducible from the place where the inscription was set up),[55] demonstrates that Laus Pompeia is to be listed among the cities with two types of sevirate (*iunior* for freeborn and *senior* for freedmen), as has been established for other cities in Cisalpine Gaul (Mediolanum, Vercellae, Augusta Taurinorum, Brixia).[56]

Many dedications to Hercules were set up after authorization was granted by the local *ordo decurionum*, and this indicates that the cult place was public ground.[57] This often occurs in cases where the devotees' provenance is stated:[58] in fact, the inscriptional evidence not only often displays the dedicants' social status, but does not omit to mention their origin too. The dedicants often identify themselves as *Mediolanenses*, either by declaring it directly,[59] or by mentioning the *Oufentina tribus*.[60] This demonstrates the close relationship between Mediolanum and Laus Pompeia, a constant feature from antiquity onwards.[61] At the same time, it sheds light on the god's local profile, who is likely to have been understood as the protector of trade and traders. This is consistent with the cult site's location, near a river harbour and commercial emporium, and leads

53 CIL V 6346, 6349, 6350–52: further archaeological details in Tomasi 2014, 284, 286, 287–8.

54 This is consistent with a more general pattern of élite and cults in Cisalpine Gaul, where inscriptions show *seviri* and *Augustales*' preference for 'una cultualità locale o interpretata': Mennella 2003, 483.

55 Cf. e.g. CIL V 6351. Cf. Tomasi 2014, 287–8.

56 Further discussion in Tomasi 2014, 272, 286–8.

57 This circumstance is marked by the formula *LDDD* in CIL V 6345–46, 6351, 6357. See Bassignano 2006/2007, 323–35; Granino Cecere-Mennella 2008, 287-300; Tomasi 2014, 271. Another dedication set up *LDDD* in CIL V 5724.

58 In three out of four instances, dedicants are not from Laus Pompeia: perhaps as foreigners they were particularly keen to display the authorization they had been granted. See Tomasi 2014, 271.

59 CIL V 6344–46, 6348–49.

60 CIL V 6347, 6351. Geographical provenance of the dedicants undeclared in CIL V 6350, 6352, 6356, 6357.

61 See Tomasi 2014, 254, 259–60, 264–5.

us to understand the cult place as an economic site that facilitated a dynamic exchange between people from different cities.[62]

In the Adda sanctuary Hercules was honoured with the local epithet *Laudensis*, sometimes followed by *Magnus*,[63] and his attributes were the traditional *clava, arcus et pharetra*, carved on the sides of CIL V 6351. Aside from the local name and the topographically conspicuous location by the Adda river (Fig.1), we unfortunately do not know much about this sanctuary. The inscriptions are the only remaining religious signs of this cult site: there are no archaeological remains of the sanctuary. As a consequence, we cannot assess its degree of monumentalization, i.e. it is impossible to outline how the natural sanctuary, with the conspicuous presence of the river, was turned into an architectural one, or to define how the sacred space was demarcated from the profane one. Therefore, we also cannot evaluate how the individual social agent may have experienced the sacred landscape, or how this experience may have been shaped and influenced by architecture. It is possible, however, to draw inferences about how the site was developed and turned into a sacred landscape from some clues in the inscriptional evidence and the literary sources: this case-study highlights the importance of the provenance and positioning of epigraphic materials as a key element for addressing the religious landscape constituted by temples and shrines. In this respect, the findspots of the epigraphic testimonies can play a pivotal role in a contextual analysis: the findspot is fairly certain for all of them;[64] and on the basis of this fact two further instances should be ascribed to this sanctuary, even though the theonym is not specified.[65]

Sometimes the *fortuna* of the monument provides an 'archaeological memory' of the physical appearance of the sacred landscape: for example CIL V 6349 was reused as a 'base per un'acquasantiera' in the Chiesa della Maddalena (Lodi), located in the present-day 'via del Tempio'.[66] This toponym hints at a certain degree of monumentalization of a topographically conspicuous environment. This clue is confirmed by Ciriaco d'Ancona: after visiting Lodi in 1430–1431, he reports that he had seen *vestigia non vulgaria* of the then still-existing *aedes* to Hercules.[67] Further, we can deduce the antiquity of this cult site from CIL V 6357 where we read *vestustate corruptam* as the motivation that justifies the restoration commemorated in the inscription.

62 Significant in this respect is the cognomen *Mercator* in CIL V 6350 and the fact that *L. Valerius Secondinus*, from Milan, was *sevir iunior* and *sevir* in Vercellae (CIL V 6351).

63 *H(erculi) L(audensi) M(agno)* in CIL V 6344; *Herculi L(audensi)* in CIL V 6346. See Tomasi 2014, 283–4.

64 Findspot attested by literary sources: CIL V 6344–45, 6347–50, 6352, 6356–57; inferable from the text: CIL V 6346, 6351.

65 CIL V 6356–57: cf. Tomasi 2014, 291. In CIL V 6348 the lettering of the theonym possibly indicates that it was carved when the inscription had already been set up: see Sartori 1992a, 81; 1992b, 428–9, n. 18 and Tomasi 2014, 285–6. We do encounter the theonym in all the other dedications: CIL V 6344–6352.

66 Cf. Tomasi 2014, 286.

67 Montevecchi 1939, 80–2; Tomasi 2014, 271, 274.

3. The sacred landscape of Cedrate. CIL V 5558 and its archaeological context: a new rotunda temple to Hercules?

Unlike the sanctuary of Hercules in Laus Pompeia, it is possible to reconstruct, to some extent, the physical appearance of the sacred landscape of this second place of worship. Cedrate (Varese) has recently drawn scholarly attention due to the discovery of a fragmentary Roman cornice block that still preserves traces of ancient painting, embedded in a modern building in Via Arconti (Fig. 2).[68] The shape suggests that the fragment belonged to a rotunda temple (Ø 9 m).[69] To identify the ancient functional

Fig. 1. *Ager Laudensis*: the Adda river is a prominent feature of the territory. The arrow points to Lodi (map after Tomasi 2014, 268).

68 'Reimpiegato come barbacane allo spigolo di un edificio, in via Arconti-angolo via dell'Asilo, con la parte decorata non in vista': Caramella 2010–2012, 187.
69 Further details in Caramella 2010–2012, 187.

Fig. 2. Cornice block found in via Arconti, Cedrate, now preserved in Museo Civico Archeologico di Villa Mirabello in Varese; picture from Caramella (2012, 185).

Fig.3. CIL V 5558 from Cedrate, now in Museo della Società Gallaratese di Studi Patri (picture from Caramella 2012, 189).

context of this architectural element, the adoption of an interdisciplinary approach proved to be invaluable, and led to the reappraisal of the area's epigraphic evidence.

A notable number of inscriptions from the province of Varese relate to the cult of Hercules,[70] notably two inscriptions from Cedrate. CIL V 5558 (Fig. 3) stands out because it provides a glimpse of the circumstances that led to the dedication. Not only does the text detail the dedicant and the motivation of the votive inscription (*pro salute Fulviorum*), it also commemorates one of the very few attested euergetic deeds:[71] the restoration of a temple and a statue of Hercules under the supervision of *Eutyches*, *ser(vus) vil(icus)*, in the lands owned by the *gens Fulvia*.[72] Judging by the shape of the monument, the *signum* was probably placed above the inscription. As regards the temple, the recently discovered cornice block (Fig. 2) has been interpreted as part of the remains of the temple restored by *Eutyches*. Combining the information provided by the epigraphic document and the archaeological evidence, the following (Fig. 4) hypothetical reconstruction of the building has been proposed. This is particularly noteworthy because it offers an occasion to revisit the *communis opinio* about the very modest architectural appearance of rural shrines.[73]

70 CIL V 5466–67, 5498, 5507–08, 5510, 5520–21, 5528, 5533–34, 5558–59, 5561, 5593, 5606, 5632; Mastorgio 1985, 91; SI 844, AE 2009, 417.

71 The only other one is CIL V 6357.

72 Cf. CIL V 5557 (dedicated to *Silvanus* by another *servus* of the Fulvii). The presence of an epigraphic workshop in Gallarate has also been proposed on the basis of these two finds coming from the same centre, though with different finishing: Zoia 2014, 17.

73 Sartori (2009, 703) on the present inscription: 'più probabilmente si sarà trattato di un tempietto o

Fig. 4. Architectural hypothesis of the *Hercules'* rotunda temple, attested by CIL V 5558 (picture from Caramella 2012, 191).

Concluding remarks

The examples discussed above show what a significant role is played by inscriptions as testimonies of cult. They have been chosen for their complementary paradigmatic value in the reconstruction of the religious landscape. On the one hand they highlight the difficulties in our record: in Laus Pompeia we have only inscriptions without any extant archaeological context *in situ*; in Cedrate we have fragmentary archaeological remains embedded in a modern context. On the other hand, they attest to the necessity of a multidisciplinary approach in order to better understand the context in which people employed epigraphy to communicate with their deities. The recently unearthed archaeological material from Cedrate provide the missing backdrop to an already known inscription, and enable us to reconstruct the precise location and visibility of the inscription in the privately-built temple; conversely, the body of evidence from Laus Pompeia highlights the importance of the findspot of the inscriptions as a means of pinpointing the original cult site when the pertinent archaeological remains no longer survive.

di un'edicola'.

TABLE 1

Corpus of the epigraphic materials related to the cult of *Hercules*. Inscriptions are arranged by their territorial modern administrative clusters; the current province is bracketed and should be understood as following: VA= Varese; MB=Monza Brianza, CO=Como; LC=Lecco; LO= Lodi. Max. dimensions are given in the following order: height, width, depth.

no	Source	Geographical context	theonym and epithet	dedicant(s)		formula, dedication	monument type
				one //	more than one		state of preservation
1	CIL V 5767, EDR124093	Milano, **Mediolanum**	Herculi	X		VSLM	ara?, periit
2	CIL V 5768 = ILS 3435a, EDR124094	Milano, **Mediolanum**	Herculi Inpetra(bili) sacr(um)	X		VSLM	ara, marble(?), periit
3	CIL V 5769 = ILS 3435; EDR124095	Milano, **Mediolanum**	Herculi In|victo Inpetrabi[li]		*cum suis omnibus*	VSLM	ara, periit
4	*Epigraphica* 2013; EDR124748	Milano, **Mediolanum**	Herculi <et> Quadrivis *vel* Herculi Quadr(ivio) *aut* Herculi Quadr(atario)	X		VSLM	ara, serizzo 100x54x41,50
5	*Archivo Storico Lombardo* 1897; Sacchi 2012; EDR124769	Milano, **Mediolanum**	[---Herc]ules Telamo[n---]				Epistylium 135x70x52
6	Sartori 2014; EDR 137490	Milano, **Mediolanum**	Herculi	X		VSLM	ara, serizzo, 90x43x30
7	CIL V 5759; AE 2002, 585; EDR124721	Desio (MB), **Mediolanum**	Herc|uli In|victo		X	VSLM	ara?, periit
8	CIL V 5742; AE 2002, 585; AE 2003, 769; EDR124704	Monza, **Mediolanum**	Herculi		X *Modicia|tes Ioveni*	?	ara,serizzo 48x62x47
9	CIL V 5743; AE 2002, 585; EDR12405	Monza, **Mediolanum**,	Herculi	X		VSLM	ara, periit (serizzo)
10	CIL V 5606; EDR124636	Castelseprio (VA), **Mediolanum**	Herculi | Invicto sacrum (+Conservatori Iuventia|ru[m?---])		X *pro se et suis*	VSLM	ara, serizzo, 106x56x41
11	Giussani 1927, 152; Giussani 1929, 89-90; EDR124877	Castelseprio (VA), **Mediolanum**	Hercul[i- - -]		*cum suis*	?	ara, lapis, 16x35x37

no	Source	Geographical context	theonym and epithet	dedicant(s)		formula, dedication	monument type
				one	// more than one		state of preservation
12	CIL V 5693; EDCS-05100848 [Bitto 1973, 52, 54]	Vertemate (CO), **Mediolanum**	Herculi Iuveni	X		*p(osuit?) de re sua*	periit
13	Giussani 1931, 65-6; EDR124854	Monate (VA), **Mediolanum**	He[r]c[u]li	?	?	*voto*	ara, lapis, 78x51x8
14	CIL V 5593; EDR124623	Sumirago di Caidate (VA), **Mediolanum**	Herculi | Invicto Deo		X *cultores*	VSLM	ara, marmor pario, periit
15	CIL V 5528; EDR124564; AE 2009, 411	Crugnola di Mornago (VA), **Mediolanum**	Herculi		X *vicani*	VSLM	ara, serizzo, 95x44x28
16	Giussani 1931, 71-2; EDR 124888	Somma Lombardo (VA), **Mediolanum**	Her[c]uli		X - *vicani Votodrones*	VS	ara, serizzo, 126x65x38
17	CIL V 5534; EDR124570	Arsago Seprio (VA), **Mediolanum**	Herculi Mertronno Anteportano	X (*Rusticio*)		*pro inpe(trata?) sa(lute?* VSLM	periit
18	CIL V 5533; EDR124569	Arsago Seprio (VA), **Mediolanum**	Herculi	X		VSLM	ara, serizzo 95x45x30
19	CIL V 5559; EDR124593	Cedrate di Gallarate, (VA), **Mediolanum**	Herculi		X	VSLM	periit
20	CIL V 5558;AE 2009, 411 EDR124592	Cedrate (VA), **Mediolanum**	Herculi	*Eutyches ser(vus) vil(icus)*		*pro salute Fulviorum, signum r[es] titu/it*	ara, serizzo, 108x52x37
21	CIL V 5520; EDR124556	Sesto Calende (VA), **Mediolanum**	Herculi I(uveni?)	X		*v(otum) l(aetus) l(ibens) m(erito) v(oto) s(oluto) d(edit) l(aetus) l(ibenter).*	ara, marble, 106x46x35
22	AE 2009, 417; EDR124857	Sesto Calende (VA), **Mediolanum**	Herculi	X		*donum,* VSLM	ara, gneiss, 107x54x38
23	CIL V 5521; EDR124557	Sesto Calende (VA), **Mediolanum**	[Herc]uli	X		VSLM	tabula, gneiss, 40X50,
24	SI 844; EDR124736	Sesto Calende (VA), **Mediolanum**	Herculi Ovanio	X		VSLM	periit
25	CIL V 5507; EDR124543	Besozzo (VA), **Mediolanum**	Herculi	X		VSLM	periit
26	CIL V 5508; EDR124544	Besozzo (VA), **Mediolanum**	Herculi vic(tori)		X	VSLM	periit

no	Source	Geographical context	theonym and epithet	dedicant(s)		formula, dedication	monument type
				one // more than one			state of preservation
27	CIL V 5510; EDR124546	Besozzo (VA), **Mediolanum**	Volkano et Erquli	X		voto	periit
28	CIL V 5466; EDR124512	Angera (VA), **Mediolanum**,	Herculi	X		*d(onum) p(osuit) LM*	ara, lapis (limestone) 97x56x40
29	CIL, V 5467/8; EDR124513	Angera (VA), **Mediolanum**	Hercul(i)	X		VSLM	ara, pietra d'Angera, 87x38x32
30							
31	CIL V 5723; AE 2002, 585; EDR124688	Villasanta (MB), **Mediolanum**	Herculi	X		VSLM	periit
32	CIL V 5498; EDR124536	Brebbia (VA), **Mediolanum**	Hercli	X		VSLM	ara, serizzo, 91x49x35
33	CIL V 5561; EDR124595	Gallarate (VA), **Mediolanum**	Herculi		X, *cum suis*	VSLM	ara, serizzo 85x43x29,
34	CIL V 5694, EDCS-05100849	Figino (CO), **Mediolanum**	Her|culi	X		VSLM	periit
35	CIL V 5721; AE 2002, 585; EDR 124686	Biassono (MB), **Mediolanum**	Herculi	X		VSLM	ara, serizzo 108x57x44
36	CIL V 5703a (p. 1085), EDCS-05100859, Reali 2010, 94)	Valle Guidino (MB), **Mediolanum**	[Her]culi		X, *cum su{u}is omnibus*	VSLM	ara serizzo 79x39x23
37	CIL V 5718; EDR124684	Lomagna (Co), **Mediolanum**	Herculi		X *cum suis*	VSLM	ara serizzo, 116,50x57x46
38	CIL V 5724; EDR124689	Vimercate (MB), **Mediolanum**	Herc(uli) Invic(to)	X		*v(otum)*, LDDD	periit
39	SI 724, EDR092131	Introbio (LC), **Bergomum**	Herculi	?	?		ara, lapis, 37x24 x3
40	CIL V 5642 (p.1085); Reali 1989, 238 no. 54; EDCS-05100796	Castelmarte (CO), **Comum**	Herculi	X		VS	ara, serizzo 67x38x22
41	CIL V 5632; EDCS-05100786	Tradate (VA), **Comum**	Herculi	X		*ex voto* VSLM	periit
42	CIL V 5645; Reali (1989, 239 no. 57); EDCS-05100799	Longone al Segrino (CO), **Comum**	Herculi In|victo	X		VSLM, *salvo patrono*	periit
43	CIL V 5687; EDCS-05100841 [Bitto 1973, 54]	Fino Mornasco (CO), **Comum**	Herculi	X		VSLM	periit
44	CIL V 5686; EDCS-05100841 [Bitto 1973, 54]]	Fino Mornasco (CO), **Comum**	Herculi		X, *pro se et suis*	VSLM	periit

no	Source	Geographical context	theonym and epithet	dedicant(s) one	dedicant(s) more than one	formula, dedication	monument type state of preservation
45	CIL V 5688; EDCS-05100843 [Bitto 1973, 54]	Fino Mornasco (CO), **Comum**	Herculi		X	*sacrum*--- (missing text)	periit
46	CIL V 6344; Tomasi 2014, 283-4	Chiesa della Maddalena, Lodi, ad ripas Abduae, **Laus Pompeia**	H(erculi) L(audensi) M(agno)	X		VS	periit
47	CIL V 6345; Tomasi 2014, 284	Chiesa della Maddalena, Lodi, ad ripas Abduae, **Laus Pompeia**	Herculi sacrum		X	VS LDDD	periit
48	CIL V 6346; Tomasi 2014, 284	Chiesa della Maddalena, Lodi, ad ripas Abduae, **Laus Pompeia**	Herculi L(audensi)	tria nomina		VSLM LDDD	Marble base, 90 x 27 x 26
49	CIL V 6347; Tomasi 2014, 284-5	Chiesa della Maddalena, Lodi, ad ripas Abduae, **Laus Pompeia**	Herculi	X		VSLM	periit
50	CIL V 6348; Tomasi 2014, 285-6	Chiesa della Maddalena, Lodi, ad ripas Abduae, **Laus Pompeia**	Herculi	X		VSLM	statue base, 46x43x31
51	CIL V 6349; Tomasi 2014, 286-7	Chiesa della Maddalena, Lodi, ad ripas Abduae, **Laus Pompeia**	Herc(uli) sac(rum)		X	*vot(um) s(olvit)*	small column, white marble, 97,5x30x17,5
52	CIL V 6350; Tomasi 2014, 287	Chiesa della Maddalena, Lodi, ad ripas Abduae, **Laus Pompeia**	Herculi	X tria nomina		VSLM	cippus, red Verona marble 68,5x43x34
53	CIL V 6351; Tomasi 2014, 288	Chiesa della Maddalena, Lodi, ad ripas Abduae, **Laus Pompeia**	Herculi		X	VSLM, LDDD	ara, marble 91x37,5x30
54	CIL V 6352; Tomasi 2014, 288	Chiesa della Maddalena, Lodi, ad ripas Abduae, **Laus Pompeia**	Herculi	X		VSLM	marble, statue basis, 90x24x20,5
55	CIL V 6356; Tomasi 2014, 291	Chiesa della Maddalena, Lodi, ad ripas Abduae, **Laus Pompeia**	?	X		VSLM	periit

no	Source	Geographical context	theonym and epithet	dedicant(s)	formula, dedication	monument type
				one // more than one		state of preservation
56	CIL V 6357; Tomasi 2014, 291	Chiesa della Maddalena, Lodi, ad ripas Abduae, **Laus Pompeia**	?	X tria nomina	*sigillum / cum ara huic / arae superposuît / et scriptur(am) eius / vestutate corrupt(am) renovavit Voto suspect(o) LDDD*	ara, lapis 110 x 51.5 x 47

BIBLIOGAPHY

Bassignano, M.S. 2006/2007 'Concessioni di suolo pubblico nel mondo romano', *Atti e Memorie dell'Ateneo di Treviso* 24, 323–35.

Bauchhenß, G. 2008 'Hercules in Gallien – facts and fiction', Haeussler & King, editors, vol. 2, 91–102.

Bitto, I. 1973 'L'età romana', *Storia di Monza e della Brianza*, I, *Le vicende politiche dalla preistoria all'età sforzesca*, 25–67. Milano, Edizioni Il Polifilo.

Boscolo, F. 2003 'Iuvenes a Mediolanium e dintorni', *Studi Trentini di Scienze Storiche* 82, 257–68.

Caramella, L. 2010–2012 'Il dono di *Eutyches* a Ercole', *Sibrium* 26, 183–201.

Claassen, W. J. 1956–1979, ThLL, VII, 2, col. 732, s.v. Iuvenii.

De Bernardo Stempel, P. 2008 'Continuity, *translatio* and *identificatio* in Romano-Celtic religion: the case of Britain', Haeussler & King, editors, vol. 2, 67–82.

De Bernardo Stempel, P. 2009 'La ricostruzione del celtico d'Italia sulla base dell'onomastica antica', *L'onomastica dell'Italia antica. Aspetti linguistici, storici, culturali, tipologici e classificatori*, ed. P. Poccetti, 153–92. Rome, École française de Rome.

Delamarre, X. 2007 Nomina Celtica Antiqua Selecta Inscriptionum. *Noms de personnes celtiques dans l'épigraphie classique*, Paris, Editions Errance.

Dozio, D. 1999 'Vimercate e il suo territorio', *Notizie dal Chiostro del Monastero Maggiore* 63–64, 133–200.

Gaviraghi, C. 1955 *Le epigrafi romane di Monza*. Monza, Modernografica.

Gavrilovic, N. 2008 'The cult of Hercules in the central Balkans', Haeussler & King, editors, vol. 2, 143–52.

Ginestet, P. 1991, *Les organisation de la jeunesse dans l'Occident romain*, Bruxelles, Latomus. Collection d'etudes latines, 123.

Granino Cecere, M. G. & G. Mennella 2008 'Le iscrizioni sacre con la formula LDDD e la gestione dello spazio santuariale da parte delle comunità cittadine in Italia', *Le quotidien municipal dans l'Occident romain. Actes du colloque tenu à Clermont-Ferrand et à Chamalières du 19 au 21 Octobre 2007*, ed. C. Berrendonner, M. Cébeillac-Gervasoni & L. Lamoine, 287–300. Clermont-Ferrand, Presses Universitaires Blaise-Pascal.

Haeussler, R. 2008 'The Civitas Vangionum: a new sacred landscape at the fringes of the Roman Empire?', Haeussler & King, editors, vol. 2, 185–216.

Haeussler, R. 2014 'Differences in the epigraphic habit in the rural landscapes of Gallia Narbonensis', *Öffentlichkeit – Monument – Text. XIV Congressus Internationalis Epigraphiae Graecae et Latinae 27. – 31. Augusti MMXII*, ed. W. Eck, P. Funke, M. Dohnicht, K. Hallof, M. Heil & M. G. Schmidt, 323–46. Berlin, De Gruyter.

Haeussler, R. & A.C. King, editors 2007–2008. *Continuity and Innovation in Religion in the Roman West*, JRA Supplementary Series 67, 2 vols. Portsmouth, Rhode Island.

Jaczynowska, M. 1978, *Les association de la jeunesse romaine sous le Haut-Empire*, Wroclaw-Warzawa-Krakòw-Gdansk, Zakł Narod. im. Ossolinsk.

Jaczynowska, M. 1981 'Le culte de l'Hercule romain au temps du haut empire', *ANRW*, 17, 2, Berlin-New York, 631–61.

Mastrocinque, A. 1991 'Culti di origine preromana nell'Italia settentrionale', *Die Stadt in Oberitalien und in den nordwestlichen Provinzen des Römischen Reiches*, ed. W. Eck & H. Galsterer, 217–26. Mainz, Philipp von Zabern.

Mennella, G. 2003 'Culti ufficiali ed élite in Cisalpina: appunti da un database epigrafico', *Les élites et leurs facettes: les élites locales dans le monde hellénistique et romain*, 481–502. Rome, Presses Universitaires Blaise-Pascal.

Mennella, G. & L. Lastrico 2007 'Le Matronae-Iunones nell'Italia settentrionale', Haeussler & King, editors, vol. 1, 119–30.

Giussani, A. 1927 'Iscrizioni romane e preromane del territorio comasco, varesino e ticinese', *Rivista Archeologica dell'Antica Provincia e Diocesi di Como* 92–93, 137–69.

Giussani, A. 1929 'Nuove iscrizioni romane e cristiane del territorio comasco e varesino', *Rivista Archeologica dell'Antica Provincia e Diocesi di Como* 96–98, 81–92.

Giussani, A. 1931 'Nuove iscrizioni romane di Como Varese Milano Cojra', *Rivista Archeologica dell'Antica Provincia e Diocesi di Como* 102–104, 1931, 62–76.

Passerini, A. 1953 'Il territorio insubre in età romana', *Storia di Milano*, I, 1–298.

Reali, M. 1989 'Le iscrizioni latine del territorio comense settentrionale', *Rivista Archeologica dell'Antica Provincia e Diocesi di Como* 171, 207–96.

Reali, M. 2010 'Le "microcomunità" insubri: localismo o integrazione?', *Pluralidad e integración en el Mundo Romano. Atti del Colloquio Italia–Hiberia/Hiberia–Italia. El mundoromano, modelo dei integracion social y cultural (Pamplona-Olite, 2008)*, 91–106. Pamplona, Eunsa.

Resnati, F. 1995 'Le iscrizioni latine della Brianza orientale e della Martesana', *Rassegna di Studi del Civico Museo Archeologico e del Civico Gabinetto Numismatico di Milano. Notizie dal Chiostro del Monastero Maggiore* 55–56, 35–119.

Sacchi, F., 2012 Mediolanum *e i suoi monumenti dalla fine del II secolo a.C. all'età severiana*. Milano, Vita e Pensiero.

Sartori, A. 1992a 'L'Alto Milanese, terra di culti', *Mélanges de l'École Française de Rome – Antiquité* 104, 7790.

Sartori, A. 1992b 'Epigrafia sacra e appariscenza sociale', in *Religio deorum. Actas del Coloquio Internacional de Epigrafía. Culto y sociedad en Occidente (Tarragona, 1988)*, M. Mayer & J. G. Pallarés editors, 423–34. Sabadell (Barcelona), Editorial AUSA.

Sartori, A. 1995 'Ercole Silva e le sue epigrafi: un interesse distratto', *Cinisello Balsamo. Duemila anni di trasformazioni nel territorio*, Quaderni d'Archivio. Comune di Cinisello Balsamo, 117-142. Assessorato alla Cultura Cinisello Balsamo, Centro di documentazione storica.

Sartori, A. 2000 'Le epigrafi romane del Museo di Sesto Calende', *Museo Civico di Sesto Calende. La raccolta archeologica e il territorio*, ed. M.A. Binaghi & M. Squarzanti, 155161. Gallarate, Assessorato alla Cultura di Sesto Calende (VA).

Sartori, A. 2009a *Le epigrafi di Arsago Seprio*. Gallarate, Comune di Arsago Seprio (VA).

Sartori, A. 2009b 'Età romana e altomedievale. Le pietre iscritte di Sesto Calende', *Alle origini di Varese e del suo territorio*, R. C. De Marinis, S. Massa & M. Pizzo editors, 463–6. Roma, L'Erma di Bretschneider.

Sartori, A. 2009c 'Le pietre iscritte di Arsago Seprio', *Alle origini di Varese e del suo territorio*, R. C. De Marinis, S. Massa & M. Pizzo editors, 567–72. Roma, L'Erma di Bretschneider.

Sartori, A. 2009d 'Epigrafi', *Pinacoteca Ambrosiana. Tomo quinto. Raccolte Archeologiche Sculture*, 51125. Milano, Electa.

Sartori, A. 2014 *Loquentes lapides*. Milano, Bulzoni editore.

Scuderi, R. 2012 'Testimonianze epigrafiche del culto di Ercole nella Transpadana centro-orientale', *Il paesaggio e l'esperienza. Scritti di antichità offerti a Pierluigi Tozzi in occasione del suo 75° compleanno*, R. Bargnesi & R. Scuderi editors, 135–51. Pavia, Pavia University Press.

Tomasi, P. 2014, 'Laus Pompeia', *Supplementa*

Italica, 27, 237–331. Roma, Quasar.

Volontè, P. 1902 'Marmi scritti dell'epoca romana tuttora esistenti in Varese e nel suo circondario', *Rivista Archeologica dell'Antica Provincia e Diocesi di Como* 46, 91109.

Zanella, S. 1952, 'Sul significato etimologico del nome dei Votodrones', *Rassegna Gallaratese Storia Arte*, 810.

Zoia, S. 2013 'Un Ercole itinerario o lapicida?', *Epigraphica* 75, 1–2, 452–61.

Zoia, S. 2014 '*Tra devozione e autorappresentazione: forme e contenuti dell'epigrafia sacra romana', Fonti per lo studio delle culture antiche e medievali*, ed. M. Malatesta, D. Rigato & V. Cappi, 1–42. Bologna, Dipartimento di Storia Culture Civiltà – DiSCi. DOI 10.6092/unibo/amsacta/3764.

XXII

DIVINE NAMES FROM LATIN INSCRIPTIONS OF ISTRIA: SOME CONSIDERATIONS

Alexander Falileyev

In this paper I am going to consider the divine names attested in Latin inscriptions from Istria. I will concentrate on those which are frequently labelled as Celtic. Indeed, the divine name Sentona, for example, was already analysed as Gaulish by A. Holder in his Alt-celtischer Sprachschatz, *and this view has been shared by a number of researchers ever since. I will discuss this and some other divine names attested in the area against the background provided by the corpus of Latin inscriptions in the region and will also apply distributional factors to show that the situation is less straightforward than is accepted in some of the modern publications.*

1. The data

THE starting point for this discussion is the listing of the divine na`me *Sentona* as Celtic in Holder's *Alt-celtischer Sprachschatz.*[1] The reasons are clear, as the name undoubtedly may have a Gaulish etymology. Indeed, Gaulish **sentu-* 'path, road' (cf. Old Irish *sét*, Old Breton *hint*, Welsh *hynt* 'id.', all to PIE **sent-* 'go') is well known. It is found in Celtic geographical names as, possibly, in the place name *Sentice* (Dueña de Abajo in modern Spain); the ethnic name *Sentii* interpreted as 'the people who live near the path', 'who know the path' or 'those who control the road';[2] and Gaulish personal names, cf. *Sentos*, *Sentamos*, etc.[3] The morphological configuration of the divine name is certainly Gaulish.[4] It is not surprising, therefore, that the Celtic linguistic affiliation of the divine name *Sentona* is accepted by a number of scholars,

1 Holder III, 1503.

2 See Sims-Williams 2006, 110–1; De Bernardo Stempel 2000, 93; 2009, 161–2, 170; DCC 202–3; Delamarre 2012, 236–7.

3 Delamarre 2007, 166; cf. Delamarre 2005, 48; De Bernardo Stempel 2008, 87; 2014b, 270 with further references.

4 See most recently on this morphological model Lambert 2013, 120; De Bernardo Stempel 2013, 74 with further references. It was applied here possibly by analogy, but see Sims-Williams 2015, 326 for *sentu- / sento-* in Gaulish compounds and the thematization of the former. I note that P. De Bernardo Stempel (2014a, 92) and elsewhere explains the vocalism of *Cremona* < **kremu-* by accentual reasons. For the place-name see also De Bernardo Stempel 2000, 93 or 2009, 163 and cf. DCC 110–1 for certain scepticism in its analysis.

most recently by Jufer and Luginbühl, who list only one attestation, CIL III 3026, and Delamarre, who admits its Celtic or Illyrian provenance.[5]

Holder himself catalogues three attestations of *Sentona*, in the Latin inscriptions CIL III 3026, 1075, and 1076. All of them are from the Istrian peninsula in modern Croatia, and it is noteworthy that all the known attestations of this divine name are located in the same area, remarkably in just a very small number of settlements.[6] Although they are, geographically speaking, from a relatively minute region, it should be noted that in prehistory the peninsula was occupied by different peoples, reflected in the map of the region in the Roman times. Most of Istria was inhabited by the population known as the Histri, while a smaller, eastern part was occupied by the Liburnians, whose area also extended further south along the Adriatic coast. Although these groups, as the archaeologists maintain, were very distinctive in both Early and Late Iron age,[7] our knowledge of the language or languages they spoke is totally insufficient, as the data at our disposal are entirely onomastic. As far as the personal names are concerned, it is now believed, following the seminal works by Untermann, Alföldy and particularly Katičić, that we deal here with the North Adriatic anthroponymic province; and various further specifications, as Istro-Venetic, Venetic-Istrian-Liburnian, Dalmato-Istrian or Liburno-Istrian, have been applied.[8] The interrelationships within this complex are difficult, if possible at all to estimate, and the associations of the onomastic data with the languages spoken in various parts of the province are impossible to approximate. As for the ancient geographical names in the North-Eastern Adriatic area, or rather areas, for obvious reasons their analysis does not allow any far-reaching conclusions on the

Fig. 1. Dedication to Sentona (CIL III 2910).

5 Jufer & Luginbühl 2001, 62; Delamarre 2007, 166. On the notion of 'Illyrian', used in the past in conjunction with the area to be analysed here (cf. e.g., Whatmough 1937, 103–4), and which is hardly relevant for the present discussion, see Falileyev 2014a, 111–2 (with further references) and Falileyev 2013a; for this term occasionally applied in some recent discussions of the data from the Istrian peninsula see Šašel Kos 1999, 67 fn. 19.

6 These are modern Labin, which accounts for four examples (CIL III 2910; CIL III 2909; CIL III 10075; Matijašić 2005, 201–2), Katuni near Boljun (ILJug 448) and Plomin (CIL III 2900; CIL III 2901; CIL III 3026 (probably, found in Trsat, ancient Tarsatica) and CIL III 10076).

7 See, e.g., various contributions in Dimitrijević, Težak-Gregl, Majnarić-Pandžić 1998; Batović 2005.

8 E.g., Untermann 1961, 172–90; Katičić 1976, 179. See Rendić-Miočević 1989, 729–35 ('Neke karakteristike histarske onomastike', originally published in *Građa i rasprave* 10, Pula, 1982) and Križman 1991 for the data from the peninsula, and Kurilić 2002 for 'Liburnian' personal names. Both works contain necessary further references. Cf. also Stifter 2012, 260 for the term 'Paravenetic' (cf. 'para-Celtic', on which see Sims-Williams 2007, 310) and the discussion of the 'Iggian' layer of names which also belongs to this anthroponymic province, cf. also De Bernardo Stempel 2014b, 273–4. For the languages of the Northern Adriatics see Zaccaria 2009, 81–2, 90–7 with references, and for the peninsula in particular see Crevatin 1991.

languages used.[9] It is most probable, though, that the dialects spoken were Indo-European of the *centum-* type. Later, in Roman times the two parts of the peninsula belonged to Italia (Regio X) and to the province of Dalmatia, with the river Arsia (modern Raša) as a border (Fig. 2).[10] Consequently, Plomin (ancient Flanona), and Labin (ancient Albona) as well as Trsat (ancient Tarsatica) are located in the area associated with the Liburnians, and not the Histri. The position of Boljun, as Professor R. Matijašić has kindly reminded me, is ambivalent: the ethnic line between Liburnians and Histri might have been in the area, so it can be attributed to both peoples.

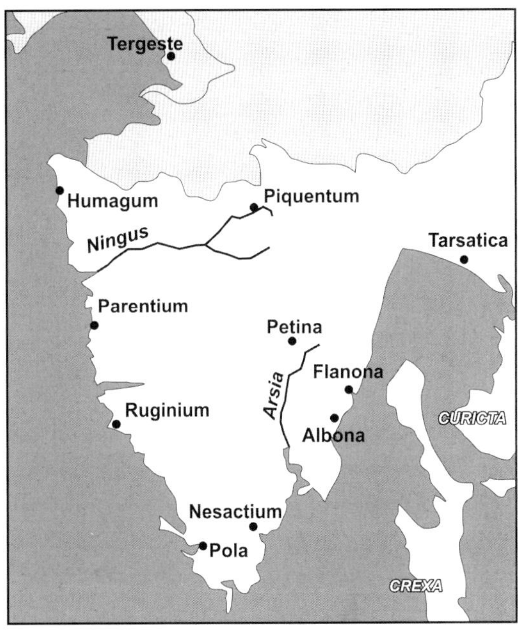

Fig. 2. Map of Istria in Late Antiquity.

The distribution of the divine name *Sentona*, which makes a notable geographically restricted cluster, is important, and it was clearly seen by the historians, who *en masse* considered it as the epichoric goddess, Liburnian,[11] or simply local,[12] to refer just to the most recent publications. Generally, modern historians seem to be united in their view that the divinity is not foreign to the area, and there are no Celtic linguistic references in their works. The third way in dealing with *Sentona* is advocated by De Bernardo Stempel,[13] who discussed it under the heading 'keltische Theonyme mit lateinischer Parallelbenennung'. She refers to the standard work on this subject by Šašel Kos referred to above, where its Liburnian provenance is stated, and adds:

> 'es ist aber nicht zu verkennen, daß etymologische Grundlage (gall. *sentu-* 'Weg'), Wortbildung (theonymisches Suffix kelt. *-onā*), typologisch / semantische Parallelen (festlandkelt. *Ritona* < **rit(u)-onā* 'Furtgöttin') wie auch die norische Entsprechung selbst eine sprachlich keltische Interpretation nahelegen'.

Before turning to the discussion of *Sentona*, we can note that Holder also considers a divine name *Ica*, as 'Name einer Quellnymphe bei den Liburnen',[14] and

9 For early toponymics of modern Croatia see most recently Šimunović 2013. For various layers of early geographical names on the peninsula see a useful survey in Matijašič 1994, 17–9. That the language of the Histri was not Celtic has been acknowledged for ages, cf. Whatmough 1937, 103–4. For the number of difficulties in the discussion of geographical names in the area formerly called "Illyrian" see Falileyev 2013a, 298–301.

10 The bibliography on the Istrian peninsula in Roman time is immense; see e.g., references provided in Buršić-Matijašić 2007. For the river name cf. Doria 1972, 34, 37; Šimunović 2013, 177; Repanšek 2014, 815–6.

11 Šašel Kos 1999, 75; Matijašić 2005, 201; Sanader 2008, 162.

12 Degrassi 1970, 618; Girardi Jurkić 2010, 88–90. Cf. also Rendić-Miočević 1989, 729.

13 De Bernardo Stempel 2004, 202.

14 Holder II, 16. Prümm 1954, 785 admits its Celtic and Illyrian affiliations.

the Celtic linguistic affiliation is accepted in some recent scholarly publications.[15] Again, linguistically speaking such an approach is totally unproblematic as there is unquestionably Gaulish **ico-*, although its meaning and etymology are still disputable.[16] The word (or words, if we deal here with homonyms) is reflected both in place-names, e.g. *Iciacum* (Yssac-la-Tourette?), *Iciniacum* (Theilenhofen), *Iciodorum* (Issoire?), *Icorigium* (Jünkerath), etc.,[17] and personal names e.g., *Iccius*, *Icelus*, *Icorix*, etc.[18] It is also significant that there are Celtic divine names with **ico-*, e.g., *Icauna* and *Iccona*,[19] and that the Gaulish personal name *Ica* is attested in Lezoux.[20] What is remarkable as far as the divine (not personal) name *Ica* is concerned, is its distribution. It is found only in two inscriptions from the Istrian peninsula, one from Plomin / Flanona,[21] and the other from Pula (ancient Pola).[22] Some scholars maintain, although very tentatively, that the masculine counterpart of the divine name, *Icus*, is attested in the Latin inscription from ancient Aenona (modern Nin to the north of Zadar) in Liburnia.[23] The inscription dated to the first half of the 3rd century reads *Iovi Sab/asio Iico / L(ucius) Plotius / Eperastus / v(otum) s(olvit) l(ibens) m(erito)*,[24] and this parallel with the evidence from the Istrian peninsula has been suggested already by its editors. However, this is not altogether clear if this instance should be considered in this discussion, and therefore should be treated quite cautiously. It may be noted in parenthesis that the name of the dedicant in this inscription is not Celtic.[25] Therefore, at our disposal there are two safe dedications to the (feminine) deity *Ica / Ika*, one from the Histrian part of the peninsula, the other from the Liburnian, to which the attestation from Aenona may be added, although with obligatory caveats. Again, it is not surprising that for the ancient historians the divinity is epichoric: Histrian and Liburnian,[26] Liburnian,[27] or simply local.[28] This view is accepted by some linguists.[29]

The third divine name known exclusively from the epigraphy of the Istrian

15 E.g. Delamarre 2007, 108.
16 See DCC 20–1 with further references.
17 See Sims-Williams 2006, 80; DCC 133–4; Delamarre 2012, 163; Falileyev 2013b, 77–8.
18 Evans 1967, 351–3; Delamarre 2007, 108–9; Falileyev 2013b, 78. Cf. also de Bernardo Stempel 2014b, 269.
19 De Bernardo Stempel 2004, 216; 2013, 81–2; cf. Lambert 2013, 116.
20 The name is noteworthy as masculine, not feminine, see Evans 1967, 352; for Gaulish masculine names in *-a* see recently Falileyev 2014a, 121–4 and the references cited there.
21 CIL III 3031: *M(arcus) / Vipsanus / M(arci) l(ibertus) / Faustus / Icae / v(otum) s(olvit) l(ibens) m(erito)*.
22 ILJug 415: *Ikae Aug(ustae) / sac(rum) / Vesiduc(us) / v(otum) s(olvit) l(ibens) m(erito)*.
23 Thus Šašel Kos 1999, 66; Sanader 2008, 163 (with a misprint in her reference).
24 ILJug 916; see further references in Sinobad 2010, 198.
25 For which see Alföldy 1969, 110, 193; it was suggested that he was of the Oriental origin (Sinobad 2010, 174).
26 See Šašel Kos 1999, 70 who also comments on toponym *Ika* near modern Rijeka in Liburnia and argues against the 'Nymphic' associations advocated by Holder, see above. For this overlap between two territories see also Matijašić 2005, 202.
27 Sanader 2008, 163; Sinobad 2010, 174. Degrassi 1970, 617 tentatively admits its Liburnian origins, but in no way insists on this point.
28 Girardi Jurkić 2010, 91; cf. also Rendić-Miočević 1989, 729.
29 Cf. De Bernardo Stempel 2004, 216.

peninsula which was thought by Holder to be Celtic is (Seixomnia) *Leucitica.*[30] It is attested in a single inscription from the area of Rovinj (ancient Arupinium, later Ruginium), and the texts reads as Seixomniai | Leuciticai | Polates.[31] This instance at least looks Celtic rather than 'Illyrian' (i.e. epichoric) for Whatmough, who refers to the Gaulish divine name *Leucetius* in his discussion of this example.[32] More definitive in its linguistically Celtic interpretation is Delamarre, who derives *Leucitica* from **leucī-tec(v)ā* and interprets it as 'Blanche-Belle'.[33] This interpretation cannot but remind us of the name *Leucimara* attested in Celeia, which has been considered Gaulish by several scholars as well, although its linguistic analysis entails a number of difficulties to the effect that it may be premature to consider it Celtic.[34] As for Delamarre's treatment of *Leucitica*, technically speaking it is rather unattainable, and this approach, additionally, shares a number of obvious difficulties with that applied to the analysis *Leucimara*. It should be taken into consideration that the stem **leuk´-* has a pan-IE status and is surely reflected in the idioms spoken at least in the surrounding areas.[35] It is also very important that *-*eu*- is preserved in this form, while in Celtic it is normally reflected as *ou*, with a number of exceptions caused or explained by various factors.[36] In this respect one may note that the neighbouring Venetic occasionally preserves **eu*, cf. e.g., Ven. te[.]u[.]t[a] < **teuteh*$_2$, and there are numerous explanations for the emergence of *ou*, and the 'Iggian', according to Stifter, seems to conserve the original PIE diphthong.[37] As for the Histrian and Liburnian '*Namenlandschaften*', it is difficult to make any conclusions, but it is not impossible that **eu* was also preserved.[38] Accepting that it is the sole and only attestation, it is certainly more rewarding to take *Leucitica* for Histrian as has been claimed by a number of scholars. If it is to be viewed as a geographical epithet, as some scholars maintain, it brings us at any rate outside of the Istrian peninsula[39]. For the latter case, moreover, the following suggestion of De Bernardo Stempel should be considered:

30 Holder 1896–1910, II, 195; Celtic or Illyrian for Prümm 1954, 785.

31 CIL V 8184.

32 Whatmough 1937, 164. For *Leucetius* see Evans 1967, 359; Lambert 2013, 116, 121.

33 Delamarre 2007, 116.

34 CIL III, 5265; see e.g., Evans 1967, 359; Delamarre 2007, 116 for its Celtic linguistic attribution, and Sims-Williams 2015, 314 where the author rightly expresses doubts on its Gaulish affiliation.

35 IEW 687–9; cf. De Vaan 2008, 305 for Italic languages. See also Lejeune 1993, 94–6.

36 See Sims-Williams 2007, 313; 2012, 157 and the references provided for the discussion of *Leucetius* above. De Bernardo Stempel 2009, 161 admits preservation of **eu* in Celtic place-names in Liguria, but for the present author both *Leucumellus* and *Neviasca* she quotes in this respect are not Celtic. For *Leucumellos* see De Bernardo Stempel 2009, 155, 162, who takes it for Celtic and also provides references to publications where it is considered Ligurian. It is also analysed as Celtic, but differently, in Delamarre 2012, 176.

37 See Lejeune 1974, 110–1 (note also Venetic *louki* (gen. sg.) equated with Lat. *lūcus*, cf. Lejeune 1993, 96–7) and Stifter 2012, 254.

38 Cf. Untermann 1961, 187. In this respect, perhaps, see the discussion of *Leucina Orfa* (Parentium in the Histrian part of the peninsula, CIL V 402) in Križman 1991, 113, and note abundant attestations of *C(a)eunus* in Liburnia (Kurilić 2002, 128).

39 E. g. Untermann 1961, 187; Degrassi 1970, 618; Sanader 2008, 162. See particularly Šašel Kos 1999, 71–2 for a comprehensive discussion, which *inter alia* considers a possibility to analyse it as a geographical epithet; for possibly non-Celtic *Leuconum* (and its localisations) see DCC 166; Šimunović 2013, 187. On the termination *-ai* and its possible significance in this inscription see Girardi Jurkić 2010, 85, 89. See also Zaccaria 2009, 87–8.

'even when a linguistically Celtic adjective is appended as epithet of appurtenance – e.g. *Leucimalicos* – to a Classical Mediterranean theonym – e.g. *Mars* –, it only means that the worshipper of Mars involved in the specific dedication had some interest vested in the locality of **Leucimèllon*; accordingly, the deity itself [...] does not tell us anything about the ethnicity, religion or language of the dedicant'.[40] Used in conjunction with epichoric *Seixomnia* and certainly difficult linguistically, *Leucitica* thus remains exceptionally problematic as far as its alleged Celticity is concerned, and there are a number of formal grounds to consider it therefore non-Celtic.

Fig. 3. Ruins of Nesactium.

Latin and Greek inscriptions of the Istrian peninsula preserve several other divine names. Apart from typically Roman deities like Asclepius or Fortuna, or probably epichoric divine cults in a Latin guise (e.g. *Terra Histria*), these dedications mention a number of local gods, such as *(H)eia*, *Melosocus*, *Nebres*, *Iutossica*, or *Aitica*. It has been noted that the female divine names in this area significantly prevail over the male, and various explanations of this phenomenon have been offered. The divinities of the peninsula have been thoroughly studied, and at least to my knowledge, only two divine names attested solely in this area – *Ica*, *Sentona* (and the highly suspicious (Seixomnia) *Leucitica*, which should be excluded from the present discussion) – have been treated by some linguists as Celtic although epigraphists and historians unanimously take them for epichoric.[41] As for the divine name *Trita* recorded on the altar from Nesactium (Fig. 3, close to Pula) in the 'Histrian' part of the peninsula which has apparently never been discussed from this point-of-view, it should be allowed that it may of course trigger certain Celtic associations. It is notable that the divine name *Tritus, -a* is not attested in Gaulish, although the corresponding personal name – with a perfect Celtic and Indo-European pedigree – is certainly well known.[42] As the name is trivial from the point of its prehistory, and as similar and historically cognate anthroponyms are known in various languages, there is no need to label all of its attestations as Celtic. In fact, the corresponding anthroponym – in its attestations throughout the 'Illyrian' world – has

40 De Bernardo Stempel 2013, 76. For the analysis of the toponym cf. also De Bernardo Stempel 2014a, 91 and for a different interpretation, which, however, does not affect the present discussion, Delamarre 2012, 176.

41 Bibliography of the scholarly discussions of the divine names is immense: see Degrassi 1970; Šašel Kos 1999, 63–80; Matijašić 2005; Sanader 2008; Girardi Jurkić 2010 where further references are provided. See also Zaccaria 2000 who treats epichoric cults of the area without their further linguistic differentiation and just opposes them to Latin. In regard of *Aitica* note Matijašić 2005, 203 for the possible readings *Amitica* or *Avitica*; the latter reading may generate some Celtic associations, but see below.

42 Evans 1967, 378–80; Matasović 2009, 390.

long been considered as indigenous.[43] It is also noteworthy that the component is found in a compound name *Tritaneria* attested solely in a Latin inscription from Municipium Riditarum in Central Dalmatia (east of modern Šibenik in Croatia) which is most certainly local.[44] Taking the divine name *Trita* for epichoric, which seems absolutely reasonable,[45] we, unfortunately, cannot go any further: as Šašel Kos, who rationally considers it Histrian, has noted, 'an attempt to explain the etymology of the name of the goddess would be quite uncertain, and it is unclear whether the names such as Tritus and related names, especially frequent in Liburnia and the Delmatae, could in any way be considered theophoric, since probably they are derived from the numeral three'.[46] In any event, the argument presented here is quite sufficient to exclude this example from the further discussion as well, which leaves us with just two divine names – *Sentona* and *Ica* / *Ika* – the linguistic attribution of which deserves attention. The question now is which side should we take. To accept their Gaulish origins on the basis of linguistic analysis one should have some Celtic-speaking individuals (to avoid the usage of the word *Celts* in this context) settled or at least being present in the region. To find them, several layers of analysis need to be undertaken.

2. Celtic presence in Istria? Archaeological, historical and place-name evidence.

Firstly, it is notable that historians and chroniclers of antiquity left no mention about the settlement of the Celts (or Gauls or Galatai, etc.) or linguistically Celtic tribal names in this area. The Tectosagi plundered the Histrians before settling in Pannonia,[47] but this campaign could hardly had an influence on the spiritual life of the Histri and Liburnians of the peninsula.[48] Generally, and it must be repeated once again, there is no positive evidence about the settlement of Celtic-speaking population in the area in

43 See Rendić-Miočević 1989, 811; Kajanto 1982, 356–7. For the excellent discussion of the 'Liburnian' *Tritus* see Kurilić 2002, 143. Cf. also Falileyev 2007, 146 for *Tritio* attested in Dacia, which is certainly not Celtic despite the attempts to consider it as such. I note that Delamarre (2007, 185) lists Dalmatian attestations of the personal name *Tritus* as Celtic, which seems totally unnecessary. I hope to demonstrate elsewhere that personal names in *Nant-* in Eastern Adriatics are epichoric, too.

44 CIL III 2796 *Vendo / Tritaneri/a Pinsi f(ilia)*; see also Rendić-Miočević 1989, 788. For the second part of the name, which at face value also finds certain Celtic parallels, see Falileyev 2014a, 124–7. For *Vendo* cf. Katičić 1976, 180, who takes it and *Tritaneria* for the names characteristic of the Delmatae.

45 Rendić-Miočević 1989, 730; Matijašić 2005, 202; Girardi Jurkić 2010, 84; but see also De Bernardo Stempel 2004, 211.

46 Šašel Kos 1999, 73. A Celtic attribution of the divine name *Iria* (for which see Šašel Kos 1999, 70–1) advocated by X. Delamarre (2009) – for Celt. **ir-* see most recently De Bernardo Stempel 2014b, 271 – does not seem attractive and is most probably coincidental.

47 Pompeius Trogus 32.3.

48 The sources for the early history of the peninsula are usefully collected and commented on in Križman 1979; see also Vedaldi Iasbez 2001 for the discussion of historical sources relating about the Celtic presence in Adriatic area. The passage 'From Strabo (7.5.3) we learn that during the third and second centuries the Celts advanced towards the southeast at the expense of the Histri, who were their neighbours on the coast' (Guštin 2005b, 53) is not clear for me, cf. Matijašič 1997, 203: 'Istria was not directly affected by the barbarian invasions'. For the episode in Livy (41.1.8) relating to the 3,000 Celtic soldiers of Catmelus in the war of the Romans against the Histri in 178 BC, see recently Šašel Kos 2014, 391–2.

the ancient authors. As far as archaeology is concerned, scholars are unanimous that there is no evidence at all for Celtic presence in the area during the Iron Age, although there are plenty of records pointing to it to the north and east of Istria. The territory of the peninsula, nonetheless, has finds of artifacts associated with the Celts or their influences, but these are only sporadic.[49] However, the archaeological evidence is secondary in our search for the speakers of Celtic in antiquity, and place-names of a given area provide us with more definitive information.[50] It is noteworthy in this respect that all recent works on Celtic place-names of Europe in antiquity leave the Istrian peninsula totally blank.[51] Still, references to Celtic origins of a number of place-names of the peninsula occur in travel-guides and particularly in internet publications – thus, for example, *Umag* in the north-western part of the peninsula is sometimes discussed in conjunction with Gaulish **magos* 'plain, field' or 'market'. The place-name, first attested in the Ravenna Cosmography as *Humago*, *Umago* is certainly linguistically difficult,[52] but definitely is not Celtic, as it was regarded, for example, by such a renowned Celticist as Joshua Whatmough.[53]

Unfortunately, this 'Celtic' approach to the analysis of the ancient geographical names of the peninsula sometimes creeps into modern academic publications. Thus, for example, Delamarre admits that the name of the island *Canta* is possibly Celtic, i.e. 'round island'.[54] There is of course no doubt that Gaulish **canto-* 'circle, rim, border' is well attested in toponyms, and Delamarre in fact finds a perfect parallel to the name of this island in Welsh – he quotes *Ynys Gaint*, the name of the island close to the Anglesey shore in Northern Wales. It is not at all clear that all examples normally treated under this Gaulish head-form indeed belong here, see the discussion of Common Celtic **kanti-* 'together with' by Matasović, which considers Gaulish *Cantio-rix* and British *Cantium* 'Kent'.[55] Notwithstanding that, a Celtic etymology of the name of the island in the vicinity of the Istrian peninsula is certainly feasible, at face-value of course. It should be borne in mind, however, that the same component has been attested in Venetic, and therefore it is not surprising that the place-name has been considered as straightforwardly Venetic.[56] Venetic or not – and we have next to nothing at our disposal to offer any judgement on the language of the Histri and their relationship with that of the Adriatic Venetes – it certainly finds parallels in the local onomastic (although not toponymic) landscape and

49 See e.g., Mihovilić 2001, 271–2; Buršić-Matijašić 2007, 603. For the 'Celtic' archaeology of the wider area see Zaninović 2001; Guštin 2005a; 2005b; Džino 2008.

50 See Falileyev 2014b, 9ff., where further bibliography is cited.

51 See Sims-Williams 2006, 207; Koch *et al.* 2007, map 17/6; and DCC *passim*.

52 *Rav. Cosmog.* 4.30–1; 5.14. For various attempts to clarify it see Crevatin 1991, 65 with further references; listed among 'Illyrian' (= local) geographical names in Doria 1972, 31.

53 Whatmough 1937, 103.

54 Delamarre 2012, 102.

55 Matasović 2009, 188. Cf. DCC: 13 with further references

56 Doria 1972, 28; cf. also Crevatin 1991, 63 for other non-Celtic (and pre-IE) linguistic associations. For some aspects of the analysis of Venet. *canto-* see Prosdocimi 2009, 90, and for Venetic personal names cf. Untermann 1961, 151 or Lejeune 1974, 317 (index). For the personal name *Cantia*, which is well attested in Northern Italy, see Alföldy 1969, 72 and for the *Cantii* of the Istrian peninsula of the Roman times in Tassaux 1983, 222.

therefore is most probably indigenous.

There is another problem in dealing with this nesonym. The geographical name is attested only once:

> *Colchi, qui cum Absyrto venerant, timentes Aetam illic remanserunt oppidumque condiderunt, quod ab Absyrti nomine Absorin appellarunt. Haec autem insula posita est in Histria contra Polam, iuncta insulae Cantae.*
>
> The Colchians who had come with Absyrtus, because they were afraid of Aeetes, stayed there and founded a town, which they named Absoros from Absyrtus's name. This island is located in Histria, opposite Pola, joined to the island of Canta.[57]

The localization of the island is thus controversial, as it cannot be *contra Polam* if Absoros is to be identified with modern Osor on the island of Crexa, and *vice versa*. If it is not identified with the Brijuni Islands, as some scholars suggest,[58] its other localizations, for instance as Curicta, may bring this island to the area inhabited by the Liburnians. The most troublesome aspect, however, is purely philological, as the spelling of the nesonym remains difficult, and, on balance, this geographical name should not be considered as a 'Celtic survival' in the north-western Adriatic.

The Brijuni or Brionian islands, known as *Pullariae* to Pliny,[59] form the archipelago of which Veliki Brijuni is firmly associated with the name *Brivōna*, which certainly invokes Celtic linguistic associations, in view of a number Gaulish place-names such as *Briva Isarae* (Pontoise), *Brivas vicum* (Brives), *Brivas* (Brioude), *Brivodurum* (Briare), all examples from Gaul. These go back to Gaulish *brīuo/ā-* 'bridge', which is attested, apart from toponymy, in Endlicher's Glossary (Gaulish *brio* gl. *ponte*), and epigraphy *briuatiom* (Naintré).[60] Although a possibility that the name of the island is based on the appellative cannot be ruled out ('the island linked with the mainland by the bridge', 'the island looking like a bridge', 'the island with the bridge' *vel sim.*), generally it does not seem very likely. Some interpretations of 'Lepontic' (acc. sg.) *Pruiam,* which is traditionally associated with the Gaulish data may in theory offer a more appropriate meaning for the discussion of the nesonym,[61] but its sole attestation in the inscription from Vergiate and the ongoing dispute on its semantics do not allow for any far-reaching conclusions. Moreover, it must be noted that the name is first attested in comparatively late sources – *Briona* (AD 543), *Brevona* (6th century) – and the reconstruction of the underlying form as **Brivona* is not secure at all. It should also be borne in mind that its linguistic Celticity was never seriously entertained, and in the scholarly literature it is viewed

57 Hyginus *Fab.* 23.

58 E.g. Crevatin 1991, 63; for these islands see below, and for the difficult passage, Rossignoli 2004, 351–3. For *insula Absortium* (Pliny *NH* 3.140) see Križman 1979, 246. For the Greeks in the North Adriatic area see Zaccaria 2009, 80, where further bibliography is provided. I am extremely grateful to Professor R. Matijašić for the discussion of the Hyginus passage with me.

59 Pliny *NH* 3.151; see Križman 1979, 247.

60 See DCC 12; 82–3; Sims-Williams 2006, 54–5; Repanšek 2014a, 241–2. Cf. De Bernardo Stempel 2009, 155 for the data from Italia.

61 See in particular Eska & Mercado 2005, 163–4.

as indigenous.[62] One may also note that at least at face value the same morphological model applies to other indigenous geographical names of the area, for which see below. At the same time it must be acknowledged that *Brione* in Val de Torre and similar looking geographical names elsewhere in Italy has been traced to Gaulish **briga*, but nowadays at least some of these as well as *Brivio* (Como), etc., are normally analysed to contain Gaulish *brīuo/ā-* 'bridge'.[63] They are never used to denote the island, though.

These two geographical names were considered by Crevatin in his lengthy discussion of the pre-Roman toponymy of the area, and this distinguished author aptly refrained from marking any of them as Celtic.[64] However, at face value even more of these place-names could be considered Celtic. Thus, the toponym *Mutila* is attested by Livy, who names it as an *oppidum* of the Histri;[65] it is associated with the area of modern Medulin in the south-western part of the peninsula[66]. It may remind us of a number of place-names, the linguistic Celticity of which is not totally unproblematic, nonetheless. Indeed, according to De Bernardo Stempel, *Mutina* (modern Modena in Italy) is Celtic, 'the Foggy (town)', **mut-īnā* (< IE **meut-*),[67] but there are certain reservations against this linguistic affiliation.[68] Even more obscure is the etymology of the ancient name of Leithaprodersdorf in modern Austria, *Muteno.*[69] Apart from these difficulties in identifying the stem, it should be considered that the morphological configuration of *Mutila* is troublesome from a Celtic linguistic standpoint. Certainly, there is no need to refer to Gaulish to explain this place-name, and its etymology and linguistic attribution remain unknown.[70]

The ancient name of Labin in the Liburnian part of the peninsula is well attested in ancient sources (*Alvona*, *Albona*) and cannot but remind of Gaulish *albo/ā-* 'white', well attested in ancient Celtic onomastics, both place- and personal names, for instance, *Albion* 'Britain', *Albiorix*, etc., and traced to PIE *h_2elb^h-.[71] However, it is clear that not all instances in *alb-* in Europe are Celtic: one may consider here the cognate Lat. *albus*, for example, and similar looking river names have been considered 'Old-European'.[72] It is not surprising that the name has been analysed as local; for the morphological model

62 Cf. Doria 1972, 31; Crevatin 1991, 63.
63 See Pellegrini 1981, 54–5.
64 Crevatin 1991, 60–75.
65 Livy 41.11.
66 See a thoughtful discussion by R. Matijašić (1999–2000, 93–102) for the possibilities of its localization.
67 De Bernardo Stempel 2000, 92.
68 See e.g., Sims-Williams 2006, 205 and other opinions on its linguistic attribution referred to in De Bernardo Stempel 2000, 86.
69 See DCC 166 for various approaches, including Celtic, none of which could be taken as final, and the bibliography cited there.
70 Crevatin 1991, 66. For *mutil-* in the ancient languages of Italy see Bourdin & Crouzet 2009, 464–5. On the chain *Mutila* (>) *Metilinum* (attested in 1156) > *Medolino* > *Medulin* see Matijašić 1999–2000, 95, who takes this evidence as inconclusive.
71 See e.g., Evans 1967, 301–4; Delamarre 2007, 16–7; Matasović 2009, 29; Delamarre 2012, 44–5; Repanšek 2014a, 251.
72 See DCC 6, 41-2; Sims-Williams 2006, 239. For the distribution of the underlying protoform see IEW 30–1; De Vaan 2008, 32. The place-name is listed as 'Illyrian' (= local) in Doria 1972, 31.

see the name of the neighbouring *Flanona* (modern Plomin).[73] And, finally, Crevatin notes a number of place-names in **-ācum* which are attested in various medieval sources, e.g., *Capriaca* (AD 1035), *Maraga* (AD 1332), *Mauriaca* (AD 1035), and this must certainly ring a bell for an expert in Celtic toponymics.[74] However, in this respect one should particularly note the discussion of the place-names with this suffix in Italy by Pellegrini. Two points are important for the present investigation. First, place-names with this suffix are found in Central Italy, where Gaulish speech was unknown. Secondly, and more importantly, it is argued that word formations with the guttural suffix are attested in Venetic.[75] Moreover, as Russell formulated it, 'it appears that the Gaulish suffix *-āko-* was borrowed into the Latin of Gaul and utilized as a LN suffix in Gallo-Latin and Gallo-Romance where it became so productive that even Germanic PNN were used as bases'.[76] Therefore, these examples are difficult to use as the secure evidence of Celtic place-names in the area, as well as the river name mentioned in the Ravenna Cosmography as *Argaone* and safely identified with modern Dragonja near Piran in north-western Istria.[77] There is no doubt, that the component **argo-* 'bright, shining' (to PIE **$h_2$erg´-* 'bright, white') is attested in Celtic geographical names,[78] but it is obvious that the river name, sometimes considered as 'Old European', could have been coined in any of the Indo-European 'centum' languages spoken in the area.[79] Detailed discussion of the river-name, which is not Celtic, has recently been offered by Repanšek.[80]

It is clear that in these and presumably many other cases we deal with the 'long arm of coincidence', to use Sims-Williams' coinage.[81] We have next to nothing of the evidence for languages spoken in the area in pre-Roman times (and no picture whatsoever of the linguistic situation on the peninsula in Roman times),[82] there is no possibility for any detailed discussion of the place-names. Moreover, there is an enormous difficulty in attaching linguistic labels to them, as *Sprach-* and *Namenlandschaft*en quite often do not coincide, and a research of the toponymy in the huge geographical area formerly known as 'Illyrian' does not allow for far-reaching conclusions.[83] It is more-or-less clear,

---

73 Illyrian in Doria 1972, 31; Liburnian in Crevatin 1991, 62. Note that Matijašić (2005, 201) calls both of them 'Liburnian', which seems to be not simply a geographical reference. See also Křižman 1979, 244; Šimunović 2013, 167–8 where more references are provided.

74 Crevatin 1991, 94–5; on place-names in *-āko-* see the classical work Russell 1988 and, recently, Lambert 2008, 133–7. Cf. also Lambert 2013, 116–7. For very frequent place-names in *-an-* of the peninsula see Matijašič 1994, 19–21 with further references.

75 Pellegrini 1981, 59–62; on Venetic data see Russell 1988, 159–61. Note, however, that the Celtic inscription from Todi in Umbria is also geographically isolated.

76 Russell 1988, 142; LN = Local names, PPN = personal names.

77 *Rav. Cosmog.* 4.36.

78 See Matasović 2009, 41–2. Delamarre 2012, 60 discusses hydronyms Argona, Arguna and l'Argen in modern France which he takes for Celtic. See also Sims-Williams 2007, 329–30 for the river-name *Argita* in Ireland.

79 For the distribution of PIE **$h_2$erg´-* see IEW 64-5; for its Italic congeners see De Vaan 2008, 53; for its 'Old European' affiliations see references in DCC 8.

80 Repanšek 2014.

81 Sims-Williams 2006, 26; cf. Falileyev 2014b, 34–9.

82 Although multilingualism cannot be of course denied, see e.g., Matijašič 1997, 206.

83 See Falileyev 2013a; 2013b, iv–v.

however, that the hypothesis regarding the linguistic Celticity of the geographical names of the Istrian peninsula cannot be regarded as attractive. Therefore, both archaeological observations and the toponymic data at our disposal do not point to the presence of the Celtic-speaking individuals on the peninsula in prehistory. This is not altogether surprising, and, as Sims-Williams notes, 'there is no reason why the area of Celtic place-names must have been originally continuous; Celtic speakers may have passed through some areas too swiftly to affect the toponymy. The Celtic groups that eventually reached Galatia via Delphi illustrate this: they left no toponymic (or archaeological) traces behind them in Greece'.[84]

3. Celtic personal names in Istria?

The situation may have changed in Roman times. Divine names of Celtic linguistic affiliation are attested in such faraway provinces as Dacia, where we find dedications, for example, to *Rosmerta* and *Sirona*, and the Roman deities have such Celtic epithets as *Camulus*, *Bussumarus* or *Bussurigius*. These cults were brought to the province by settlers from Gaul, Germania, Noricum and Pannonia, and also from Britain, Northern Italy and Galatia, indeed 'ex toto orbe Romano', as Eutropius put it. It is not surprising therefore that hand-in-hand with the divine names of Celtic linguistic origin, the Latin inscriptions of Roman Dacia contain a considerable number of personal names of unquestionably Celtic provenance as *Abuccia*, *Adcobrovatus*, *Deiotarus*, *Ibliomarus*, *Ivonercus* or *Samognatius*.[85] It is logical, for that reason, to have a search for the names of Celtic linguistic provenance in the Latin inscriptions of the Istrian peninsula.

This task is considerably eased by the excellent research of Croatian epigraphists. Križman's monograph on Roman names in Istria was certainly a milestone.[86] Personal names in the inscriptions unearthed since the 1990s have been discussed by Matijašić, Starac, Kurilić, Girardi Jurkić, to mention just a few scholars. As a result, we have at our disposal a reliable corpus of personal names of the Istrian peninsula in antiquity, but the list does not contain a single attestation of an anthroponym which could undoubtedly be considered linguistically Celtic, and, significantly, the texts of the inscriptions themselves also do not have any 'Celtic' associations. It may be noted nevertheless that some scholars still maintain that a number of the names attested in inscriptions of Roman Istria are in fact Gaulish. Thus, for example, Crevatin considers several examples from the peninsula, which he places into two sub-groups, 'tipo celtico' and 'probablimente celtici',[87] of which the first contains three names. *Bona* is attested in Pula (ancient Pola),[88] and notwithstanding the fact that G. **bono*-, *bon(n)ā*- does exist, this is most probably

84 Sims-Williams 2006, 305, cf. Falileyev 2014b, 49–132 for the distribution of Celtic place-names in Eastern and Central Europe.
85 For examples from Roman Dacia see Falileyev 2007, s. vv.
86 Križman 1991.
87 Crevatin 1991, 76–7.
88 CIL V 8156 *Bona Tit/acia Q(uinti) f(ilia)*.

Latin.[89] *Boicus* from Roč,[90] is appropriately treated by Alföldy among northern Italian names in *-icus*,[91] and should also be excluded from the present discussion. The second name combination on the inscription – *Boicus Avitus* – may of course trigger some considerations among Celtic lines, but this is altogether not necessary at all,[92] and, moreover, Roč is located quite in a distance from the area where we find allegedly 'Celtic' dedications.

Fig. 4. CIL III 10075.

The last name in Crevatin's sub-group, *Boninus*, deserves special attention. It is found in the inscription from Labin which has a dedication to *Sentona* (Fig. 4), and the text reads as *Geminus / Boninus / Hostiducis / Sentonae / v(otum) s(olvit) l(ibens) m(erito)*.[93] There is nothing conspicuously Celtic in the name, and although *Boninus* may have some distant 'Celtic' associations, it is certainly not Gaulish.[94] *Hostidux*, as Kurilić informs us, is found only in Liburnia, and its two attestations come from Albona / Labin. Therefore we cannot but agree with this author that the name should be treated as 'Liburnian'.[95] Most probably, it may be analysed among the 'hospitality' names in Northern Italy of various linguistic attributions (e.g., Venetic *Hostihavos* or Lepontic *Uvamokozis*),[96] but of course this suggestion can only be conjectural. Generally, as Šašel Kos has aptly commented on the dedicants of this inscription, 'obviously this was an autochthonous family'.[97] The fact that *Sentona* was venerated by dedicators with local names and of local origin, as well as the observation that not a single altar discussed here does contain an anthroponym of Celtic provenance,

89 See Falileyev 2007, 59–62 for various treatments of the Gaulish data, where further references are provided. It is also considered there that quite a few similar looking instances are non-Celtic in origin. For this particular inscription see Untermann 1961, 85 and Brouwer 1989, 245 where the name is aptly treated as Latin.
90 CIL V 433 C(aius) Boicus Silvester and C(aius) Boicus Avitus.
91 Alföldy 1978; cf. Untermann 1961, 78; Rendić-Miočević 1989, 731.
92 For the tradition of associating *Boicus* with the Celtic ethnic name *Boii* (for which see DCC 10, 77) see Križman 1991, 113. For *Avitus*, which may have a perfect Celtic etymology but is in many cases Latin (cf. Lat. *avītus* 'belonging to a grandfather, ancestral', Kajanto 1982, 80) and associated with the migrants from the Apennine peninsula, see Falileyev 2013b, 17–8. Note a possible reading of the divine name *Aitica* attested at the peninsula as *Avitica* by Matijašić (2005, 203).
93 CIL III 10075.
94 See above on *Bona*. The name has been treated as Venetic (Alföldy 1969, 67) and Liburnian (Kurilić 2002, 128). Cf. also Untermann 1961, 85.
95 Kurilić 2002, 130.
96 Which go back to PIE *g^hosti- (IEW 453), see valuable observations in Prosdocimi 2009, 135–42; Marinetti & Solinas 2014, 83–4; cf. also Križman 1991, 127, and additional Venetic and Celtic data in Falileyev 2015b.
97 Šašel Kos 1999, 75.

may be also important although of course not definitive for the present discussion.[98]

The second of Crevatin's sub-group, 'probablimente celtici', contains only two names from the inscriptions of the peninsula. Ironically, in fact they are more promising as far as their Celtic linguistic affiliation is concerned. *Arius*, which is attested twice in an inscription from Poreč (ancient Parentium),[99] is found *inter alia* in Gaul and Lusitania where it is aptly considered Celtic.[100] Although indeed it has a perfect Celtic etymology and is undeniably Celtic in many of its attestations, in case of Parentium, as well as in many others, it is likely to be non-Celtic.[101] The name *Castus* is attested twice in Pula and in a Christian inscription from Poreč (Parentium).[102] The name has long been analysed as Celtic; note that *Castus* who participated in the Third Servile War (73–71 BC) on Spartacus' side has been suggested to be a Gaul. At the same time *Castus* may well be Latin, cf. a Latin adjective meaning 'morally pure, guiltless, pure, chaste, pious'. One may remember here the name of the Roman general Lucius Artorius Castus; the Artorii family have roots in Italy, potentially of Messapic or Etruscan origin. It is not surprising therefore that Ellis Evans maintained that 'PN Castus is probably Celtic as well as Latin',[103] and its attestations beyond the borders of the 'traditionally Celtic-speaking world', unless there are other indications, are normally considered non-Celtic[104].

There are several more names in the epigraphy of the peninsula which were not considered by Crevatin but which allow a linguistically Celtic analysis, at least in theory. Some of them are without doubt meaningful in a Celtic linguistic context, but are certainly non-Celtic in origin,[105] while anthroponyms in *gal-* are also irrelevant for the present discussion.[106] Such names as *Macer* and *Macrinus,* although considered Gaulish in several academic publications, are definitely non-Celtic.[107] A more interesting case is that of *Abudius* which is recorded in several Latin inscriptions from Parentium / Poreč, and *Abudia Publia* is known from the epitaph from Pula.[108] The name has been analysed

98 Cf. in this respect the important research of Šašel Kos 2008.

99 CIL V 45: *L(ucius) Arius L(ucii) f(ilius) Proculus and T(itus) Arius L(ucii) f(ilius)*.

100 See Delamarre 2007, 26; De Bernardo Stempel 2013, 88–9; cf. Evans 1967, 141 for similar-looking names.

101 See e.g., Campanile 2008, 965–7 for this Venetic-Celtic correspondence, which he takes as a loan from Celtic, cf. Marinetti & Solinas 2014, 79. In respect of the Istrian aristocratic *gentes Arrii* cf. Salomies 1996, 124 and see further Untermann 1961, 143–4, Alföldy 1969, 61–2.

102 Pula: *Marcia M(arci) f(ilia) Casta and C(aio) Octavio C(ai) f(ilio) Casto f(ilio)*; Poreč: *Castus et Ursa pedis centum fecerunt*; see references in Križman 1991, 82.

103 Evans 1967, 331. Kajanto 1982, 251 notes that its 'frequency in Celtic areas is low'.

104 See the discussion in Falileyev 2013b, 44, with further references. For Dalmatia see Alföldy 1969, 172, where it is noted that the name is well attested in Italia. For certain Northern Adriatic parallels see Campanile 2008, 970.

105 As e.g., *Oppius* (for its attestations see Križman 1991, 67), *Silus, -o* (Križman 1991, 74, 94) or *Verecundus* (Križman 1991, 96). For discussion of the names see Falileyev 2012, 124–8; 2013b, 124; 2007, 151 respectively with further references. Note that *Op(p)ii* are very much at home in Liburnia, see Kurilić 2002, 120; Katičić 1976, 179.

106 L. Gallus, Galla, Galus, Gallio, see Križman 1991, 57, 85; for discussion see Falileyev 2013b, 70–1.

107 For the attestations in the epigraphy of the peninsula see Križman 1991, 87–8 and for linguistic discussion of the names see Falileyev 2013b, 85–6.

108 E.g., CIL V 216, 328, 329. See Križman 1991, 44; Matijašić 2007, 270.

as Celtic, and various possibilities of its linguistic analysis have been suggested.[109] Indeed Celtic in origins or just allowing a Gaulish linguistic interpretation[110], it is certainly unlikely that the vice admiral of the Ravenna fleet Titus Abudius Verus,[111] who is mentioned in these inscriptions, may have been responsible for the inventing of linguistically Celtic divine names, which, as should be repeated, are unknown outside of the area.

At this point we may be reminded of a very valuable observation elegantly summarized by Sims-Williams in conjunction with a slightly different line of research:

> While simple names such as *Cassius*, *-a*, listed by Holder, Evans and Delamarre, may sometimes be Celtic, or at least 'cover' Celtic names, it would be confusing to map them as definitely Celtic names. By contrast, one can be confident that compound names such as *Cassivellaunus* and *Vercassivellaunus* are Celtic and so these provide a secure sample for geographical examination.[112]

Ironically, *Cassius* in indeed attested in several inscriptions of Roman Istria, but at least to my knowledge there has been no attempt to explain these attestations as Celtic.[113] Notably, not a single compound Celtic personal name is attested in the inscriptions of the peninsula.

4. Conclusions: Istria as a 'Celtic-free zone'

Therefore, the inevitable conclusion from these observations is that there are at present no confident traces of Celtic personal names found in the inscriptions of the Istrian peninsula of the Roman era. To this it must be added, that there are no apparent extra-linguistic grounds to suspect that any of the bearers of Latin names in the area was a migrant from a traditional 'Celtic-speaking area', be it Gaul or the British Isles. A possibility that the cults were introduced by a single Celtic-speaking passer-by should be dismissed as totally improbable, and also due to the fact that the divine names are totally unknown outside of the region and quite popular inside a limited area. As we have seen, there is no evidence, direct or otherwise, which may enable us to trace Celtic-speaking people in the area in prehistory. Indeed, they are not mentioned in historical sources, there is not a single geographical name in the region which unambiguously could be labelled as Celtic in origin, and archaeologists, whatever frameworks they belong to, unanimously claim the absence of settlements of those who they call 'Celts' in the region. The multifaceted analysis in this paper suggests that the Istrian peninsula should be pronounced a 'Celtic-free zone'. As there is no evidence of speakers of early Celtic idioms in the region, the hypothesis that the two divine names – *Ica* / *Ika* and *Sentona* – attested on several occasions in Latin inscriptions, and which are found only

109 Delamarre 2007, 209; Falileyev 2013b, 1.
110 'A *nomen* hardly found outside Aquileia and Istria', Salomies 1996, 121.
111 For *Abudii* in Roman time Istria see Tassaux 1983, 216.
112 Sims-Williams 2012, 155; cf. also the map of distribution of compound Celtic personal names in Europe given as Figure 1 on p. 159. The Istrian peninsula is left there notably blank.
113 For the attestations see Križman 1991, 51 and for the Cassii in Roman Istria, see Tassaux 1983, 204–5.

in this area, are Celtic, should be rejected, and these divinities must also be considered indigenous by name. It has been noted by Šašel Kos that 'hypothesized Celtic influences in the indigenous Histrian cults cannot be proved on the basis of extant dedications'.[114] In view of what is said above, it can be added here that there is no need at all to consider this hypothetical influence, and it is almost certain – until new evidence comes to light – that we deal here with the 'long arm of coincidence'.

These conclusions are of importance for Celtic studies insofar that now we should exclude divine names *Ica / Ika* and *Sentona* from the Gaulish 'pantheon'. This also presupposes that personal names in *Sent-* (at least some and in the Adriatic area) must not be analysed as detheonymic Celtic;[115] also note in this respect that 'while the *gens Sentia* is very well documented in Aquileia and northern Italy, it is only rarely attested in Pannonia', and Noricum provides just one example.[116] In a somewhat wider perspective, the research has shown that the Istrian peninsula should be treated as a 'Celtic-free zone', a situation, which does not cause surprise and is certainly known in other parts of the continent.[117] Generally, this is certainly quite a disappointing *finale* for a paper presented at the F.E.R.C.AN workshop, but the compilation of the definitive corpus at which this project is aimed requires also a consideration of negative results of investigation. Furthermore, *Ica / Ika* and *Sentona* should not, as I think, be considered in F.E.R.C.AN project under the rubric 'Significatio indigena non Celtica',[118] as the term 'Celtic' could hardly be applied here at all in view of what has been said above and is totally irrelevant. The fact that they do look Celtic is not important – the divine names *Alban*, *Dura*, *Kamulla* or *Sali* at face value could easily be etymologized as Gaulish, but as they belong to the Kassites, the ancient Near Eastern people who gained control of Babylonia in the second millennium BC, such undertaking would be really outrageous. As Sims-Williams observes:

> The fact that the name or a similar one can be found in authoritative-looking works such as Holder's *Alt-celtischer Sprachschatz* is no guarantee that the name really is Celtic and often leads to circular arguments. It is also perilous to argue that a name must be Celtic because a plausible Celtic stem can be found in the Indo-European and Celtic etymological dictionaries, for many names are open to multiple etymologies.[119]

In fact, the purely linguistic procedure in the discussion of divine names in our and

---

114 Šašel Kos 1999, 67.

115 For that see De Bernardo Stempel 2008, 87.

116 Šašel Kos 2008, 291. For *Sentius* in Dalmatia see generally Alföldy 1969, 119. On *Recus Sentius*, a local from Nedinium (modern Nadin in the region of Zadar) see Sinobad 2010, 162 and 198 with references.

117 These are indicated in the maps published in Sims-Williams 2006, Koch et al. 2007, DCC; cf. also Falileyev 2014b, *passim*.

118 See De Bernardo Stempel 2013, 77 (with further references), where pre-Celtic divine names in the areas inhabited by the Celts are discussed. The classification system was estimated as "intricate" in Toorians 2014, 255, who also aptly notes in regard of the title of this contribution that "'Celtic and other indigenous' seems to cover virtually everything".

119 Sims-Williams 2012, 151.

plenty of other cases, particularly away from the areas which may – with all possible caveats – be labelled as 'traditionally Celtic-speaking', becomes really secondary, and the *faux amis* should be excluded from the discussion of *Alt-celtischer Sprachschatz.*[120]

On a more positive note, it may be suggested that the analysis presented here now firmly roots *Ica*, and particularly *Sentona*, into the landscape of 'Liburnian' linguistics. This is problematic due to our present knowledge of the language or even languages spoken by the Liburni. However, it is not impossible that the divine name *Sentona* may well go back to Liburnian **sent-*, as the morphological model seems to be attested in this idiom at least as the topoonomastic evidence prompts us. One could only theorize whether it is a reflex of the same PIE **sent-* 'go' as the Celtic forms referred to above,[121] or it goes back to PIE **senh*$_2$*-* 'bereiten' *vel sim.*[122] There is no way, however, to discuss the etymology of Liburnian **sent-*, probably belonging to *o*-stems, as it is accepted in modern historical linguistic studies, for the semantics of the word remains unknown. Indeed, we have no idea about the cult of the divinity, and iconography of the dedication is not supportive at all in this respect. Thus, the only detail known to us comes from the altar in Labin, which has not been properly published. It has been surveyed by Matijašič in the following manner: 'serpent whose tip of the tail extends over the lower right corner of the central epigraphic panel',[123] which is certainly valuable, but not very helpful for our purposes. The same is true also of *Ica / Ika*, and there are a great deal more PIE stems which may be nominated as candidates for etymological analysis,[124] and it is not at all clear in what language it was coined. Therefore, the present study indeed has enlarged the Liburnian lexicon, at least by one item, although its (or their) meaning and etymology must remain by default as not identified. As for the 'mythology' of the inhabitants of the Istrian peninsula, and, to be more precise, its pre-Roman component, this remains obscure. As it has been observed for Celtic, 'the etymology of divine names is already problematic enough and we should ask ourselves constantly how etymology relates to semantics and meaning. And again, how do such linguistic insights relate to mythology?'[125] The situation with the study of the deities of the Histri and Liburni in this respect is much harder and certainly less rewarding.

What is evident, however, is that particularly in difficult topo-onomastic landscapes one should insist on abandoning the practice of declaring any Celtic-looking form as linguistically Celtic unless there are solid formal linguistic grounds for that, as well as

120 See, e.g., Sims-Williams 2012, 155; Falileyev 2013b, 8–11, 42, 88–9, 108, 111–2, 121–2, 134, 150; 2014b, 86–7; 2015a for a number of examples.

121 IEW 908, cf. Old High German *sint* 'way, journey' or Lat. *sentio* 'to sense, feel' (for Italic see De Vaan 2008, 554), Balto-Slavic **sent-* 'think', etc.

122 IEW 906, cf. Hitt. *šanh-* 'to seek', Old High German *sinnan* 'to strive after'. See Kloekhorst. 2008, 720–1 for the PIE form.

123 Matijašič 2005, 202. The text reads as *[S]entonae / Miliotoc[--] / Nossicae / Sex. Patalicus*. See also Girardi Jurkić 2010, 90 who prints *Nassicae*.

124 For various attempts to compare it with the IE name for 'horse' see Križman 1991, 127–8; this connection was aptly considered doubtful by Šašel Kos (1999, 70). As far as the root-etymology is concerned, there are by far better PIE candidates, e.g., **h*$_1$*ei-* 'to go' (IEW 293-6) or **h*$_2$*eik´-* 'aufspießen' (IEW 15), but any discussion on this subject is by default pointless.

125 Toorians 2014, 258.

reasons of an extra-linguistic nature. Particularly this is important in the areas inhabited by the speakers of languages which are now known exclusively from onomastics. This, of course, contributes to circular arguments, as highlighted by Patrick Sims-Williams (see above), but otherwise one may be accused not only of inaccurate linguistic analysis and mistreatment of historical (in a wide sense) sources, but also of making the indigenous people or peoples of the area incapable of naming geographical objects, or gods in this case, in their own idiom or idioms.[126]

BIBLIOGRAPHY

Alföldy, G. 1969 *Die Personnennamen in der römischen Provinz Dalmatia*. Heidelberg, Carl Winter.

Alföldy, G. 1978 'Ein „nordadriatischer" Gentilname und seine Beziehungen', *Zeitschrift für Papyrologie und Epigraphik* 30, 123–6.

Batović, Š. 2005 *Liburnska kultura*. Zadar, Matica hrvatska.

Bourdin, S. & S. Crouzet 2009 'Des Italiens à Carthage ? Réflexions à propos de quelques inscriptions du tophet de Carthage', *L'onomastica dell'Italia antica*, ed. P. Poccetti, 443–94. Rome, École française de Rome.

Brouwer, H. H. J. 1989 *Bona Dea: the sources and a description of the cult*. Leiden, New York, E. J. Brill.

Buršić-Matijašić, K. 2007 *Gradine Istre. Povijest prije povijesti*. Pula, Zavičajna naknada Žakan Juri.

Campanile, E. 2008 'Sui rapporti onomastici fra Celti e Veneti', *Latina & Italica. Scritti minori sulle lingue dell'Italia antica*, vol. II, ed. E. Campanile & P. Poccetti, 963–73. Pisa, Roma, Fabrizio Serra editore (first published in *AION* 9 (1970), 41–51).

Crevatin, F. 1991 'Storia linguistica dell'Istria preromana e romana', *Rapporti linguistici e culturali tra i popoli dell'Italia antica* , ed. E. Campanile, 49–109. Pisa, Giardini.

De Bernardo Stempel, P. 2000 'Ptolemy's Celtic Italy and Ireland: a linguistic analysis', *Ptolemy. Towards a linguistic atlas of the earliest Celtic place-names of Europe*, ed. D. Parsons & P. Sims-Williams, 83–112. Aberystwyth, CMCS.

De Bernardo Stempel, P. 2004 'Die sprachliche Analyse keltischer Theonyme', *Die Kelten und ihre Religion im Spiegel der epigraphischen Quellen*: Akten des 3. F.E.R.C.A.N. Workshops, ed. J. Gorrochategui & P. De Bernardo Stempel, 197–225. Vittoria Gasteiz, Servicio Editorial Universidad del País Vasco.

De Bernardo Stempel, P. 2008 'I nomi teoforici del Celta antico. Individuazione, classificazione, divinitá venerate e cronologia relativa', *Dedicanti e cultores nelle religioni celtiche*, VIII Workshop F.E.R.C.AN, ed. A. Sartori, 73–104. Milano, Cisalpino.

De Bernardo Stempel, P. 2009 'La ricostruzione del celtico d'Italia sulla base dell'onomastica antica', *L'onomastica dell'Italia antica*, ed. P. Poccetti, 153–92. Roma, École française de Rome.

De Bernardo Stempel, P. 2013 'Celtic and other indigenous divine names found in the Italian Peninsula', *Théonymie celtique, cultes, interpretatio = Keltische Theonymie, Kulte, interpretatio*: *X. workshop* F.E.R.C.AN, ed. A. Hofeneder, P. de Bernardo Stempel, 73–96. Wien, Verlag der Österreichischen Akademie der Wissenschaften.

De Bernardo Stempel, P. 2014a 'Livelli di celticità linguistica nell'Italia settentrionale', *Les Celtes*

126 The investigation underlying this contribution, including my research stay in Istria in September 2014, would have been impossible without the help of Professor R. Matijašič of the University of Pula, Croatia. I am also grateful to Professor Matijašič for his comments on the earlier version of this paper, which were extremely beneficial. The discussion following the oral presentation at Lampeter workshop was very helpful, as well as that with Dr L. Repanšek of the Slovenian Academy of Sciences, who unfortunately did not attend the event. I would like to thank Ms N. Tighinean for drawing the map reproduced here, and Dr V. Kos, Head of Narodni Muzej Labin (Croatia) for his kind permission to publish the photos of the inscriptions preserved at the museum. All usual disclaimers apply.

et le Nord de l'Italie, ed. O. Barral *et al.*, 89–102. Dijon, Éditions Universitaires de Dijon.

De Bernardo Stempel, P. 2014b Review of *Personal names in the Western Roman world* (Berlin 2012), *Zeitschrift für celtische Philologie* 61, 266–78.

Degrassi, A. 1970 'Culti dell'Istria preromana e romana', *Adriatica praehistorica et antiqua, Miscellanea Gregorio Novak dicata*, ed. V. Mirosavljević *et al.*, 615–32. Zagreb, Universitas Studiorum Zagrabiensis.

Delamarre, X. 2005 'Les noms du compagnon en gaulois', *Studia Celtica Fennica* 2, 47–52.

Delamarre, X. 2007 *Noms de personnes celtiques dans l'épigraphie classique*. Paris, Errance.

Delamarre, X. 2009 '*Iria, (*Īryā)* "L'Opulente, La Fertile" (Ligurie, Galice, Dalmatie)', *Veleia* 26, 345–8.

Delamarre, X. 2012 *Noms de lieux celtiques de l'Europe ancienne*. Paris, Errance.

De Vaan, M. 2008 *Etymological dictionary of Latin and the other Italic languages*. Leiden, Boston, Brill.

Dimitrijević, S., T. Težak-Gregl, N. Majnarić-Pandžić 1998 *Prapovijest*. Zagreb, Napried.

Doria, M. 1972 'Toponomastica preromana dell'alto Adriatico', *Antichita Altoadriatiche* 2, 17–42.

Džino, D. 2008 'The Celts in Illyricum - whoever they may be: the hybridization and construction of identities in Southeastern Europe in the fourth and third centuries BC', *Opvscvla Archaeologica* 31, 49–68.

Eska, J. F. & A. O. Mercado 2005 'Observations on verbal art in ancient Vergiate', *Historische Sprachforschung* 118, 160–84.

Falileyev, A. 2007 *Celtic Dacia. Personal names, place-names and ethnic names of Celtic origin in Dacia and Scythia Minor*. Aberystwyth, CMCS

Falileyev, A. 2012 *Selecta Celto-Balcanica*. St. Petersburg, Nestor.

Falileyev, A. 2013a 'Pannono-Illyrica', *Sovremenniye metody sravnitelno-istoricheskikh issledovanij*, ed. V. Kazaryan, 298–306. Moscow, University.

Falileyev, A. 2013b *The Celtic Balkans*. Aberystwyth, CMCS.

Falileyev, A. 2014a 'Gaulish word for 'thin' and some personal names from Roman Siscia', *Studia Celtica* 48, 107–37.

Falileyev, A. 2014b *In search of the Eastern Celts. Studies in geographical names, their distribution and morphology*. Budapest, Archaeolingua.

Falileyev, A. 2015a 'Where linguistics fails: towards interpretations of some divine names in the Roman Danubian Provinces', *Culti e religiosità nelle province Danubiane*, ed. L. Zerbini, 167–76. Bologna, I libri di Emil.

Falileyev, A. 2015b 'K interpretatsiyi odnogo venetskogo antroponyma', *Imja kak kvant lingvisticheskogo i istoriko-kulturnogo analyza*, ed. T. Mikhailova & F. Uspenskij, 54–9. Moscow, Maks-press.

Girardi Jurkić, V. 2010 'Posebnosti autohtonih kultova u rimskoj Istri', *Godišnjak - Akademija nauka i umjetnosti Bosne i Hercegovine. Centar za balkanološka ispitivanja* 39, 81–98.

Guštin, M. 2005a 'The Adriatic Celts and their neighbours', *Celtic Connections*, vol. 2, ed. W. Gillies & D. W. Harding, 111–24. Edinburgh, University of Edinburgh.

Guštin, M. 2005b 'Celts on the margin of the northern Adriatic', *Celts on the margin: Studies in European cultural interaction*, ed. H. Dobrzańska et al., 49–55. Kraków, Institute of Archaeology and Ethnology of the Polish Academy of Sciences.

Evans, D. E. 1967 *Gaulish Personal Names*. Oxford, Clarendon.

Jufer, N. & T. Luginbühl 2001 *Les dieux gaulois*. Paris, Errance.

Kajanto, I. 1982 *The Latin Cognomina*. Roma, Bretschneider.

Katičić, R. 1976 *Ancient Languages of the Balkans*. The Hague, Mouton.

Kloekhorst, A. 2008 *Etymological Dictionary of the Hittite Inherited Lexicon*. Leiden, Boston, Brill.

Koch, J. T. in collaboration with R. Karl, A. Minard and S. Ó'Faoláin 2007 *An Atlas for Celtic Studies: Archaeology and Names in Ancient Europe and Early Medieval Ireland, Britain and Brittany*. Oxford, Oxbow Books.

Křižman, M. 1979 *Antička svjedočanstva o Istri*. Pula, Čakavski sabor.

Křižman, M. 1991 *Rimska imena u Istri*. Zagreb, Latina et Graeca.

Kurilić, A. 2002 'Liburnski antroponimi', *Folia onomastica Croatica* 11, 123–48.

Lambert, P.-Y. 2008 'Three notes on Gaulish', *Celtic and other languages in Ancient Europe*, ed. J. L. García Alonso, 133–44. Salamanca, Ediciones Universidad de Salamanca.

Lambert, P.-Y. 2013 'Le statut du théonyme gaulois', *Théonymie celtique, cultes, interpretatio = Keltische Theonymie, Kulte, interpretatio: X. workshop* F.E.R.C.AN, ed. A. Hofeneder & P. de Bernardo Stempel, 113–24.

Wien, Verlag der Österreichischen Akademie der Wissenschaften.

Lejeune, M. 1974 *Manuel de la langue vénète*. Heidelberg, Carl Winter.

Lejeune, M. 1993 '"Enclos sacré" dans les épigraphies indigènes d'Italie', *Les bois sacrés*, ed. O. de Cazanove & J. Scheid, 93–101. Paris, De Boccard.

Marinetti, A. & P. Solinas 2014 'I Celti del Veneto nella documentazione epigrafica locale', *Les Celtes et le Nord de l'Italie*, ed. O. Barral *et al.*, 75–87. Dijon, Éditions Universitaires de Dijon.

Matasović, R. 2009 *Etymological dictionary of proto-Celtic*. Leiden, Boston, Brill.

Matijašič, R. 1994 'Toponomastica e archeologia dell' Istrie', *Annales* 5, 17–27.

Matijašič, R. 1997 'L'Istria tra l'antichita classica e la tarda antichita', *Arheološki vestnik* 48, 203–18.

Matijašić, R. 1999–2000 'Smještaj Mutile i Faverije (Liv., 41, 11, 7) u svjetlu topografije južne Istre', *Opuscula Archaeologica* 23-24, 93–102.

Matijašić, R. 2005 'The iconography of indigenous cults in northern Liburnia', *Akti VIII. Međunarodnog kolokvija o problemima rimskog provincijalnog umjetničkog stvaralaštva*, ed. M. Sanander and A. Rendić Miočević, 201–4. Zagreb, Golden marketing-Tehnička knjiga.

Matijašić, R. 2007 'O nalazu kasnoantičkih tijesaka u Poreču 1997', *Opuscula archaeologica* 31, 265–81.

Mihovilić, K. 2001 'L'Istria tra Celti e Roma', *I Celti nell'Alto Adriatico*, ed. G. Cuscito, 261–75. Trieste, Editreg; Aquileia (Udine), Centro di antichità altoadriatiche.

Pellegrini, G. B. 1981 'Toponomastica celtica nell'Italia settentrionale', *I Celti d'Italia*, ed. E. Campanile, 35–65. Pisa, Giardini.

Prosdocimi, A. 2009 'Note sull'onomastica di Roma e dell'Italia antica', *L'onomastica dell'Italia antica*, ed. P. Poccetti, 73–151. Roma, École française de Rome.

Prümm K. 1954 *Religionsgeschichtliches Handbuch*. Rom, Päpstliches Institut.

Rendić-Miočević D. 1989 *Iliri i antički svijet*. Split, Književni krug.

Repanšek L. 2014 'Fluvius Argao, quis in sinum Argo fluit?', *Indoevropejskoie yazykoznanije i klassičeskaja filologija* 18, 814–20.

Repanšek L. 2014a 'Two notes on Old Celtic Morphology', *Acta Linguistica Petropolitana* 10/1, 239–54.

Rossignoli, B. 2004 *L'Adriatico Greco: culti e miti minori*. Roma, L'Erma di Bretschneider.

Russell, P. 1988 'The Suffix *-āko-* in Continental Celtic', *Études Celtiques* 25, 131–73.

Salomies, O. 1996 'Contacts between Italy, Macedonia and Asia Minor during the Principate', *Roman Onomastics in the Greek East. Social and Political Aspects*, ed. A. Rizakis, 111–27. Athens, Research Centre for Greek and Roman antiquity.

Sanader M. 2008 'O antičkim kultovima u Hrvatskoj', *Vjesnik za arheologiju i povijest dalmatinsku* 101, 157–86.

Sims-Williams, P. 2006 *Ancient Celtic Place-Names in Europe and Asia Minor*. Oxford, Blackwell.

Sims-Williams, P. 2007 'Common Celtic, Gallo-Brittonic and Insular Celtic', *Gaulois et Celtique Continental*, ed. P.-Y. Lambert & G.-J. Pinault, 309–54. Genève, Droz.

Sims-Williams, P. 2012 'Celtic personal names', *Personal names in the Western Roman world*, ed. T. Meißner, 151–66. Berlin, Curach Bhán.

Sims-Williams, P. 2015 'The Celtic Composition Vowels *-i-* and *-u-*', *Mélanges en l'honneur de Pierre-Yves Lambert*, ed. G. Oudaer, G. Hily & H. Le Bihan, 313–32. Rennes, TIR.

Sinobad M. 2010 'Jupiter i njegovi štovatelji u svjetlu epigrafskih izvora na području Hrvatske', *Opuscula archaeologica* 34, 145–228.

Stifter, D. 2012 'On the linguistic situation of Roman-period Ig', *Personal names in the Western Roman world*, ed. T. Meißner, 247–65. Berlin, Curach Bhán.

Šašel Kos, M. 1999 *Pre-Roman divinities of the Eastern Alps and Adriatic*. Ljubljana, Narodni Muzej Slovenije.

Šašel Kos, M. 2008 'Celtic divinities from Celeia and its territory: who were the dedicators?' *Dedicanti e cultores nelle religioni celtiche*, VIII Workshop F.E.R.C.AN, ed. A. Sartori, 275–303. Milano, Cisalpino.

Šašel Kos, M. 2014 'Cincibilus and the march of C. Cassius Longinus towards Macedonia', *Arheološki vestnik* 65, 389–408.

Šimunović, P. 2013 'Predantički toponimi u današnjoj (i povijesnoj) Hrvatskoj', *Folia onomastica Croatica* 22, 147–214.

Tassaux, F. 1983 'L'implantation territoriale des grandes familles d'Istrie sous le Haut-Empire romain', *Problemi storici ed archeologici dell'Italia nordorientale e delle regioni limitrofe dalla preistoria al medioevo*, ed. G. Bandelli, 193–229. Trieste, Università degli studi di Trieste, Civici musei di storia ed arte di Trieste.

Toorians, L. 2014 Review of *Théonymie celtique, cultes, interpretatio = Keltische Theonymie,*

Kulte, interpretatio (Wien 2013), *Zeitschrift für celtische Philologie* 61, 255–8.

Untermann, J. 1961 *Die venetischen Personennamen*. Wiesbaden, Otto Harrassowitz.

Vedaldi Iasbez, V. 2001 'I Celti in area altoadriatica nelle fonti letterarie greche e latine' *I Celti nell'Alto Adriatico*, ed. G. Cuscito, 71–86. Trieste, Editreg; Aquileia (Udine), Centro di antichità altoadriatiche.

Whatmough, J. 1937 *The Foundations of Roman Italy*. London, Methuen & Co.

Zaccaria, C. 2000 'Testimonianze epigrafiche dei culti greco-romani nell'area adriatica settentrionale in età romana. Bilancio e problemi', *Les cultes polythéistes dans l'Adriatique romaine*, eds Ch. Delplace & F. Tassaux, 171–92. Bordeaux, Ausonius.

Zaccaria, C. 2009 'Forme e luoghi della "mediazione" nell'Italia nordorientale romana',

XXIII

A SACRED RIVER LANDSCAPE WITH A SANCTUARY THE WORSHIP OF RIVERS IN THE SOUTH-EASTERN ALPINE AREA

Marjeta Šašel Kos

Presumably all rivers in antiquity were sacred, and indeed the cults of many rivers in the south-eastern Alpine area are well documented. A significant role was played by the Savus River (Sava); the god Savus was worshipped along the entire course of the river. A sanctuary erected for him and the goddess Adsalluta at a site above rapids and between two dangerous waterfalls has recently been re-excavated. All the altars dedicated to Adsalluta alone, as well as to her and Savus, must have originated from the sanctuary, although some were discovered elsewhere. Interestingly, an altar was dedicated to a divinity of the sources of the Savus, Savercna, where a small chapel must have stood in antiquity. Most of the river names are pre-Celtic, but the names of two river deities – if not Celtic – may be related to the local Celtic population: Aquo and Neptunus Ovianus.

An outline of the waterscape

IT is not only landscapes that have resulted from interactions between natural environment and complex cultural practices, but also waterscapes with sacred places along rivers and lakes. In defining a landscape or waterscape, religion has always played a prominent role. All rivers in antiquity were presumably sacred, and indeed the cults of several rivers in the south-eastern Alpine area are well documented. Next to mountains, rivers have always been the one of the most distinctive geographical features of every landscape and, in terms of traffic, they retained a significant role even after the construction of roads, despite rapids, waterfalls, and other impediments. Rivers have always decisively conditioned human life and their importance cannot be overemphasized. River cults are well attested from the Late Bronze Age onwards,[1] and they were deeply rooted throughout the Iron Age and Roman period, long after the Christian Church was established as the official religion.

Most of the evidence for river cults, partly epigraphic and partly archaeological, comes from the Roman period. Rivers created a chain of sacred sites and consequently a specific

1 Torbrügge 1970–1971; Hansen 1997.

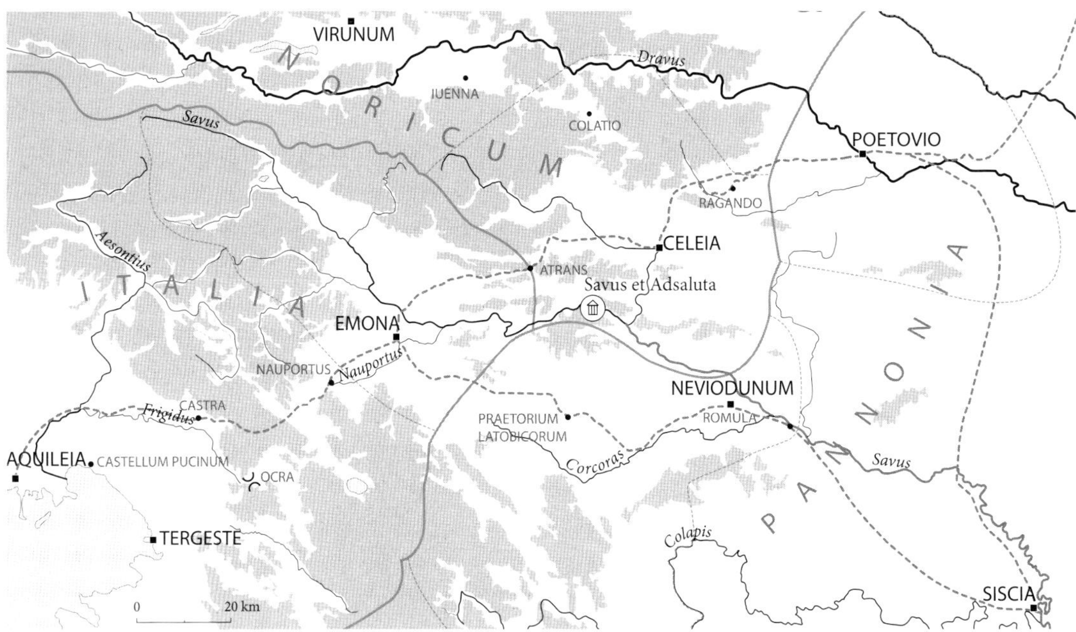

Fig. 1. South-eastern Alpine region with the main rivers (computer graphics: Mateja Belak).

sacred waterscape and landscape. Sacred sites were linked to the dangerous sections along the river course and were also located at significant crossings or other landmarks. Along the rivers, river gods and water divinities were undoubtedly worshipped in many sanctuaries and chapels, yet only one temple has been archaeologically identified and explored to date in the south-eastern Alpine and northern Adriatic regions that could be linked to particular water deities.[2] This is the sanctuary of Savus and Adsalluta by the hamlet of Sava near Podkraj opposite Hrastnik, situated above the rapids in the Sava River (Fig. 1), as well as between two dangerous waterfalls between Hrastnik and Trbovlje, where navigation was severely hindered.[3]

The main rivers that have always given significant imprint to these regions are the two large rivers, the Sava (Savus) and the Drava (Dravus), which both empty into the Danube. The names of these rivers linguistically belong to the Old European onomastic layer.[4] There are four other rivers of certain importance, which are all tributaries of the Sava: the Ljubljanica (Nauportus), of great economic and logistic significance although relatively short (41 km), the Kokra (Corcac), the Kolpa/Kupa (Colapis) and the Krka (Corcoras). These are the rivers which are mentioned in ancient sources. The Savinja, which is not mentioned, had a significant impact on Roman Celeia because it frequently flooded the town, causing considerable damage and eventually reducing it to a much smaller settlement. Celeia was an important centre both in Celtic and Roman Noricum, possibly a seat of a Tauriscan king, and later one of the most flourishing Norican

2 Jovanović 1998; Krajšek & Stergar 2008.
3 Dular 2009.
4 Šimunović 2013, 202–9; despite Delamarre 2012, 250, who regarded the Timavus as probably Celtic.

municipia.[5] Attempts at identifying the Savinja with Adsalluta have all failed, mainly because Adsalluta was worshipped at one particular place, that is, in her sanctuary above the Sava rapids, which was far from the Savinja. The last to be mentioned is the Voglajna, a small torrential river (35 km long), which empties into the Savinja at Zagrad not far from Celje and often inundates the valley to the east of the town.

It has been suggested that the river was called the 'Aquo' in antiquity;[6] however, only the name of a deity, Aquo, has been epigraphically attested. There is not much doubt that the deity's name referred to a stream, hence the Voglajna would be the most likely river to be considered in this case. Dedications to Aquo are carved on two small altars of the 2nd century AD, discovered at the late Roman fortified settlement of Rifnik near Šentjur, on a hill about 570 m high, above the Voglajna in the region of Celeia.[7] The altars must have been brought there as construction material for an early Christian basilica from the beginning of the 5th century AD. Originally, they were probably erected close to the Voglajna stream, at some sacred place, grove, or a shrine dedicated to the river god. As monuments of the pagan religion, they may have been deliberately used for building the Christian basilica.

One of the altars was erected by two dedicators, C. Stat(utius?) Masclus and Publicius Ianuarius, both bearing cognomina typical of the indigenous inhabitants of Celeia and its territory. The name Ianuarius, when borne by the native population, was very likely a Latinized form of a Celtic name with the root of *Ian-*,[8] and Masclus, too, is a name typical of Noricum. It could be interpreted as the so-called "Deckname", perhaps concealing a Celtic name.[9] The gentilicium of Masclus was Statutius rather than Statius,[10] because the family of the Statutii is well documented at Celeia and Šempeter, while the Statii have not been attested to date in Noricum.[11] The ancestors of Publicius Ianuarius probably belonged to a family of a municipal freedman or a public slave of Celeia. The dedicator of the second altar erected to Aquo was one Abascantus, a slave of a man who was a Roman citizen, and whose name was abbreviated as L. T() P(), indicating that he was easily recognizable.[12] That the dedicators were local people is understandable, as this river greatly threatened them by dangerous flooding. The name Aquo has been interpreted as of Celtic or perhaps a pre-Celtic origin, which was Latinized and possibly adapted to the popular etymology, and most probably reflected in the modern name of the stream, Voglajna.[13] However, according to a recent analysis, the Celtic origin of the

5 Šašel Kos 2014; Lazar 2002.

6 Šašel 1980.

7 Šašel 1980; cf. Šašel Kos 1999, 135–6.

8 Cf. Mócsy 1959, 176; Alföldy 1977, 257–8; Kakoschke 2012, 453–4.

9 Cf. CIL III 4761, 4880, 5040, see Lochner von Hüttenbach 1989, 101; Kakoschke 2012, 507–8.

10 Thus hypothetically supplemented by Šašel 1980, 62 no. 1 = AE 1974, 488 = ILLPRON 1837: *Aquoni sacr(um) / C. Stat(ius?) Masclus / et / Public(ius) Ianuar(ius) / v. s. l. m.*; in AE the gentilicium remained unsupplemented.

11 See ILJug 374; Alföldy 1974, 126.

12 Šašel 1980, 62 no. 2 = AE 1974, 489 = AE 1975, 672 (misleading) = ILLPRON 1839: *Aquon[i] / Abascantu[s] / L. T() P() s(ervus) / v. s. l. m.*; L. Trosius Propincus, for example, is known from a tombstone found in Celeia, CIL III 5274 a = ILLPRON 1724.

13 Šašel 1980.

name is unlikely, as is also the derivation of the modern river name Voglajna from the name Aquo.[14]

At Celeia (at the Mariborska Avenue in Celje), a recently discovered sacred pond with a supposed simple Celtic shrine from the mid/late 1st century BC was situated very near a favourable river crossing at the Voglajna, where most probably a permanent bridge had been constructed during the late La Tène period, before the coming of the Romans. This seems to have been a sacred site that coexisted with the Celtic *oppidum* along the Amber Route at the foot of Miklavški hrib, one of the major settlements of the Taurisci who inhabited southern Noricum. Towards the end of Tiberius' reign, the sanctuary would have been replaced first by a smaller Roman ambulatory sanctuary with an open-air *cella* and later by its more elaborate version, indicating an early 'Romanization' of the local elite, which at Celeia should not have been at all surprising. The sacred site with a 'sacred pond' was located on a gravel bar between the river courses of the Savinja and Voglajna, and possibly also the Hudinja,[15] but in the late Flavian period, at the time of the construction of the Celeia forum, it ceased to exist, having been transformed into a residential area.[16] Several epichoric gods were worshipped in the town, but the cult of none can be linked to the sacred site.[17]

Due to limited epigraphic evidence, not all river cults have been documented. Next to Aquo, altars were erected to Savus and Dravus, and two were dedicated to Dravus and Danuvius together. One of these two is known from Mursa (at Tenja near Osijek),[18] and the other from Poetovio,[19] where another altar was probably erected only to Dravus,[20] and a third one to Dravus and Genius legionis.[21] Colapis is depicted, together with the god Savus and with the personification of Siscia in the middle, on gold coins and silver medallions of Gallienus, as well as on the *antoniniani* of Probus (Fig. 2). These coins were minted at Siscia (Sisak),[22] where the Kupa flows into the Sava. The divinity of the Nauportus River has not been attested to date, but it is indicative that the god Laburus (a pre-Celtic name), elsewhere unknown, was worshipped at the site of the rapids in this river, at Fužine on the outskirts of Ljubljana.[23] This was actually the only obstruction in the otherwise well navigable river.

Two rivers flow into the Adriatic: the Aesontius (the Soča/Isonzo) and the Timavus (the Timava/Timavo). The river Aesontius is only mentioned in the late classical literary sources, although in the Peutinger Table a *mansio* Ponte Sonti is noted, between

14 Repanšek 2016, 45.
15 Jure Krajšek, personal communication.
16 Gaspari, Krempuš, & Novšak 2007: the sanctuaries have been excavated in 2003–2004; cf. Lazar 2011, 24–5; Gleirscher 2014, 141–3.
17 Šašel Kos 1999, 131–51.
18 CIL III 10263 = HD057338 = lupa 5260; see also Rendić-Miočević 2012, 295–7.
19 AIJ 266; HD068553; Rendić-Miočević 2012, 297–8.
20 AIJ 268; HD068554.
21 AIJ 267; HD057337 = lupa 8809; Piccottini 1970, 240.
22 Alföldi 1931, 47, nos. 14 and 2; Webb 1933, Probus nos. 764–6; Ostrowski 1991, 58 and fig. 60; cf. Rendić-Miočević 2012, 300–1.
23 CIL III 3840 + p. 2328,188 = ILS 4877 = EDR152825.

Fig. 2. *Antoninianus* of Probus with the personification of Siscia and the gods Colapis and Savus on each side (courtesy of the Coin Cabinet of the National Museum of Slovenia).

Aquileia and the settlement at Fl. Frigido, later Castra (Ajdovščina).[24] The river was worshipped as the god Aesontius, who is invoked on several small altars.[25] According to a modern 'folk etymology', his name has erroneously been associated to the well-known Celtic god Aisos/ Esus,[26] but it is doubtful if Aesontius ever reminded Celtic and Roman local and non-local population of the god Esus. The formerly proposed Celtic etymology, according to which the river name would be derived from the Celtic root *is-*, 'water',[27] is obsolete, and the name should rather be attributed to Old European or possibly Venetic.[28]

In contrast, the Timavus (the Timava/Timavo) was mentioned several times in classical sources and despite its very short course (merely 2 km), was one of the most remarkable landmarks in the hinterland of Tergeste, and an ancient sacred site. The river gave name to a lake near the area where it flows into the sea, Lacus Timavi, and to the mansio Fonte Timavi, located at the distance of 12 miles from Aquileia, and near the place where the river has its sources.[29] As a god, Timavus was widely worshipped also outside the area of the river, which sheds an interesting light on the significance of his cult.[30]

It should be mentioned that as much as other divine names, the names of the rivers, too, have always been popular also as personal names. The name of an auxiliary soldier from Paternion in Noricum was Ambidrabus;[31] the Ambidravi were settled in Upper

24 *Tab. Peut.* 3.5–4.1.
25 See, e.g., Inscr. Aqu. 96; Vedaldi Iasbez 1996.
26 On Esus: De Bernardo Stempel 2010.
27 Hopfner 1927, 996.
28 See Vedaldi Iasbez 1994, 113, with citations.
29 A sanctuary of Diomedes and sacred groves of Artemis and Hera are associated with this area; Zaccaria 2009.
30 See, e.g. ILS 3900 = Inscr. It. X 4, 318; Buora & Zaccaria 1989.
31 CIL III 4753 = HD053753 = lupa 2207.

Carinthia. From the territory of Celeia, not far from the Neviodunum area, a tombstone mentioning one Titus, son of Ambisavus, came to light.[32] Esontius as a *signum* is documented on the lid of a sarcophagus for a boy from Aquileia, L. Lusius Ingenuus (*Have Esonti*).[33] Timavus was a *signum* of an unknown boy or a man from Aquileia (*Timavi ha[ve]*).[34]

A sacred river's source described by Pliny the Younger

Pliny the Younger vividly describes the sources of the river Clitumnus, present-day Clitunno in Umbria, in a letter to his friend Voconius Romanus.[35] He was Pliny's literary friend and correspondent from Saguntum (Hispania), known mainly from Pliny's letter.[36] Pliny's account is most interesting for the understanding of a sacred waterscape:

> Have you ever seen the source of the Clitumnus? [...] There is a fair-sized hill which is densely wooded with ancient cypress; at the foot of this the spring rises and gushes out through several channels of different size, and when its eddies have subsided it broadens out into a pool as clear as glass. You can count the coins which have been thrown in and the pebbles shining at the bottom. [...] The banks are thickly clothed with ash trees and poplars, whose green reflections can be counted in the clear stream as if they were planted there. Close by is a holy temple of great antiquity in which is a standing image of the god Clitumnus himself clad in a magistrate's bordered robe; the written oracles lying there prove the presence and prophetic powers of his divinity. All round are a number of small shrines, each containing its god and having its own name and cult, and some of them also their own springs, for as well as the parent stream there are smaller ones which have separate sources but afterwards join the river. The bridge which spans it marks the sacred water off from the ordinary stream: above the bridge boats only are allowed, while below bathing is also permitted. The people of Hispellum, to whom the deified Emperor Augustus presented the site, maintain a bathing place at the town's expense and also provide an inn; [...].[37]

The Clitumnus springs and the sacred grove were famous in antiquity and often mentioned in Latin literature; they were visited, among others, by Caligula.[38] Several items in Pliny's description are of general interest and may be applied to other rivers in Italy and elsewhere. Throwing coins in sacred pools, river sources, lakes, as well as other sacred sites was most common in antiquity. Coins found in rivers can be an indication of a sacred site; a small hoard(?) of Celtic coins from the late 1st century BC, now lost, was supposedly found in the Gradaščica River, a tributary of the Nauportus

32 CIL III 13406 = HD067841.
33 AE 2004, 596; Zaccaria 2004, 173–4.
34 Zaccaria 2004, 173; interestingly, a young man from Dardania had a cognomen Timavius, *ibid.*
35 Pliny, *Ep.* 8.8.1–6.
36 Lippold 1961; Sherwin-White 1966, 93; 176–7; Gibson & Morello 2012, 150–4; 157.
37 From: Pliny, *Letters and Panegyricus* II, with an English translation by Radice 1969, 22–7. See now on this passage also Scheid 2015, 307–8.
38 Suet., *Cal.* 43.1. Other citations in the commentary by Sherwin-White 1966, 456.

(Ljubljanica) River;[39] a shrine there would well correspond to the sacred landscape described by Pliny. Some of the many coins recovered from the Ljubljanica, along with other possibly votive objects, may be linked to certain sacred places along the river that must have certainly existed,[40] but have not yet been identified with certainty.

Pliny then mentions, expectedly, the main sanctuary at the site and an ancient one, that of the god Clitumnus, with his statue placed in it.[41] Less usual may have been the prophetic competency that had been ascribed to the river god, indicating his polyvalent nature. Even less expected may have been the existence of so many other shrines in close proximity, each of them sheltering its own divinity with its own distinct cult, which sheds most interesting light on the intensity of a sacred landscape along a river. The mere proximity of these shrines indicates that in one way or another, these divinities and cults were interrelated.

In the Clitumnus River, the bridge that crossed it represented the border between sacred water and ordinary river course. Not the entire course of the Clitumnus was regarded as sacred, on the contrary, below the bridge and below the sacred area there was a public bathing place, which the city of Hispellum financed for its inhabitants, also keeping up an inn at the site. However, boats were allowed to navigate along the entire river course, perhaps not to obstruct the river traffic. In a similar way, a public bathing area, maintained at the expense of the town of Emona and organized on the initiative of its citizens, could also be hypothesized along the river Nauportus.

The central significance of the Savus

As has been emphasized, most of the rivers empty into the Sava. The river route could link also very distant regions and the Sava was part of such long-distance route and river traffic from the Adriatic to the Black Sea (and in the opposite direction), which began at the sources of the Ljubljanica (the Nauportus) at Nauportus (Vrhnika) and continued along the Sava and the Danube to the Black Sea. This was the legendary Route of the Argonauts, since according to a late version of the myth of Jason, the Argonauts would have returned with the golden fleece and Medea on their flight from Colchis along just these rivers.[42] On his way back to Greece, Jason allegedly first founded Nauportus, a flourishing Tauriscan and, since the mid-1st century BC, a Roman *emporium*; the story is recorded by Pliny the Elder.[43] The Romans established a large Roman *vicus* at Nauportus on the bank of the Nauportus River. The village, described as similar to a town (*municipii instar*) by Tacitus,[44] belonged to Aquileia; it was a fortified settlement.[45]

39 Šašel 1968, 569 (1992, 575); Kos 1977, 53 and 75.
40 Gaspari 2006.
41 An early Christian church, the so-called Tempietto del Clitunno, was not built at the site of the sanctuary, but near the town Campello sul Clitunno, not far from Spoleto.
42 Šašel Kos 2006.
43 *NH* 3.128.
44 *Ann.* 1.20.4.
45 Šašel Kos 1990; Mušič & Horvat 2007.

After its decline in the 2nd century AD, Jason was said to have founded Emona, an Augustan colony, the easternmost Italian city,[46] and one of the most important in the south-eastern Alpine area. The territory of Emona bordered on the northern Adriatic, Norican, and Pannonian regions. In both versions of Jason's myth, the significance of the Nauportus River is emphasized. The Ljubljanica empties into the Sava east of Ljubljana, below Podgrad near Zalog.

Occasionally rivers cut their beds through high hills creating narrow valleys with no space even for the tow paths; at certain sections this is also true of the Sava.[47] Navigation downstream was only hindered by rapids and waterfalls at some sections, while upstream it was impossible in certain areas, particularly from Zidani Most to Zalog near Ljubljana. There, boats had to be towed by draft animals along towpaths, built on the right bank of the river and even cut into the cliffs. Traffic along the river was busy until the construction of the southern railway in the first half of the 19th century. It was only then that the towpath, the so-called *Treppelweg*, controlled by the Austrian imperial bureau for river navigation (*k.k. Navigations-Amt*), was abandoned. Traffic along the Sava ceased when the railway from Zidani Most to Sisak was opened in 1862. The situation could be compared, *mutatis mutandis*, to that in antiquity, since even in the 18th and 19th centuries roads were in such poor condition that river transport was of far greater significance.

The name of the river Sava is of the Old European origin and is certainly pre-Celtic.[48] The god Savus was worshipped along the entire course of the river; an altar dedicated to him was found at Vernek opposite Kresnice in the territory of Emona,[49] the other was discovered at Andautonia (Ščitarjevo), to the southeast of Zagreb.[50] The god Savus is also invoked in a lead curse-tablet found in the river Kupa (the Colapis) at Siscia (Sisak), indicating that Savus' influence and impact were greater than expected, if only dedications from his altars were known. The curse-tablet, which is the first known one from the western part of the Empire, addressed to a river deity,[51] was written in vulgar Latin by a group of people who appealed to the god to drown their opponents in a legal process.[52] In this way they would be forever silenced and would not be able to testify against the writers of the curse. Significantly, at least some of the people mentioned in the tablet were from distant regions, and this highlights the importance of the river traffic in the Roman Empire. It has been suggested that one of those that should be silenced was Lic(i)nius Sura (H)isspan(us), who could hardly be identified with the Roman senator from Tarraco and a close friend of the emperor Trajan, L. Licinius Sura.[53] Despite long

46 Šašel Kos 2012.
47 Dular 2009.
48 Bezlaj 1961, 171–4; Šimunović 2013, 206–9.
49 RINMS 95.
50 AIJ 475 = CIL III 4009 + p. 1746; ILS 3908/9 = Šašel Kos 1999, 100 no. 12 = Knezović 2010, 188, fig. 2 (=*AE* 2010, 1239) = HD057335; Rendić-Miočević 2012, 298–300.
51 Marco Simón & Rodá de Llanza 2008, 173.
52 AIJ 557 = Marco Simón & Rodá de Llanza 2008 (= AE 1080) = HD027805; cf. Šašel Kos 1999, 100–1 no. 13.
53 Marco Simón, Rodá de Llanza 2008, particularly 182; however, the context would suggest a humbler

distance river traffic directed from Italy to the Danube, with Siscia playing a central role, and despite logistics needed for the Dacian wars, this would seem rather unlikely.

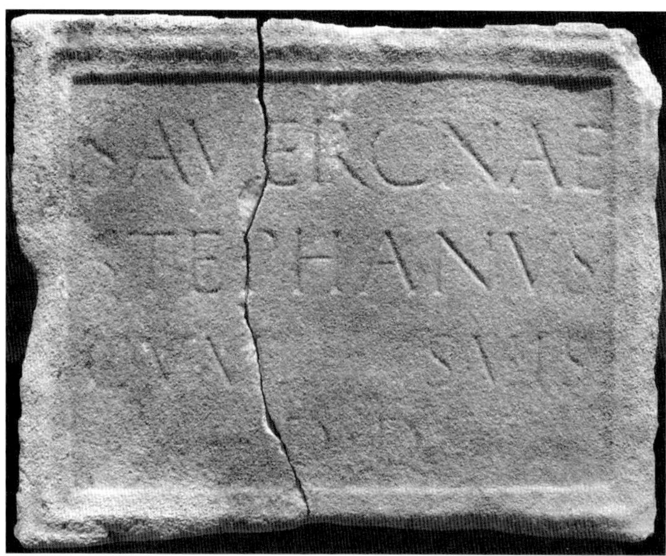

Fig. 3. Goddess Savercna (from Lovenjak 2007).

The Sava River has two sources, the Sava Dolinka and the Sava Bohinjka. In view of extreme scarcity of Roman inscriptions in the region of Gorenjska (Upper Carniola north of Ljubljana), it is most interesting that not far from the sources of the Sava Dolinka, a dedication to the goddess Savercna by one Stephanus was discovered some years ago (Fig. 3). In the village of Podkoren, built into a house, a moulded votive monument in the shape of a marble slab came to light, but clearly it must have originated from the nearby site called Zelenci, where the Sava Dolinka has its source. It could hardly be doubted that the goddess Savercna should closely be linked to the river Savus and to divine Savus. Milan Lovenjak who first published and interpreted the inscription, explained her name as Celtic, part of which may be linguistically related to the name of the goddess Vercana.[54] However, it has lately been demonstrated, that these two names are linguistically unrelated; the name Savercna could thus be ultimately derived from the river-name *Sawaro- and indeed be explained as the Goddess of the upper stream of the Sava.[55] A sacred place at Zelenci would be expected in any case; it has now been confirmed by this dedication. A small sanctuary or a shrine must have stood at the site, since no traces of any larger Roman-period settlement have been discovered to date in the area. Only a mountain track passed nearby, which linked the Emona territory with that of Virunum, leading to a *mansio* Santicum (Villach).

The second source of the Sava is the river Sava Bohinjka, its water coming from the Seven Lakes District within Triglav mountains. As the Savica waterfall, it flows into Bohinjsko jezero (Bohinj Lake) at one end and flows out of it as a navigable stream at the other, joined by another stream. The Sava Dolinka and the Sava Bohinjka, join into the Sava at Lancovo above Radovljica not far from Bled. A Roman period small sanctuary, erected at what had very likely been a pre-Roman sacred site, was dedicated

milieu.

54 Lovenjak 2007 (AE 2007, 577 = AE 2008, 121); Lovenjak 2012; Vercana is attested in Germania Superior and Belgica: CIL XIII 7667, 4511.

55 Repanšek 2016, 46; there are other possible explanations.

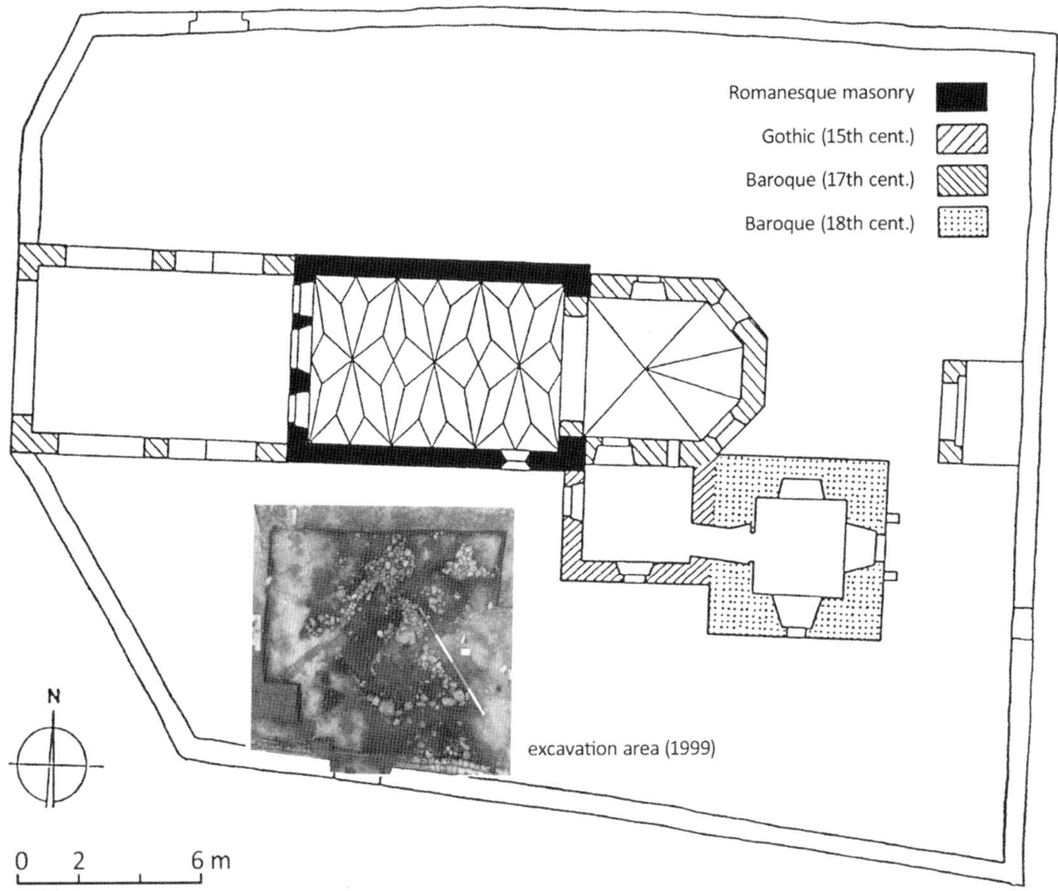

Fig. 4. Remains of a Celtic sanctuary near the church of St. John the Baptist at Bohinj Lake (from Josipovič, Gaspari & Miškec 2012).

to an indigenous, either Celtic or pre-Celtic, water deity. It must have been located close to the site where the river flows from the lake. There, at the very site of the sanctuary, a church dedicated to sv. Janez Krstnik (St. John the Baptist) is now located.[56] Recent rescue excavations confirmed Roman architectural remains close to the church (Fig. 4); among other small finds notably also 144 Roman coins ranging from the 1st to the 4th century AD have been discovered.[57] The excavators compared the architectural remains to several similar buildings, among others to the sanctuaries from Gaul, at Gournay-sur-Aronde and Villeneuve-au-Châtelot, as well as to the Norican Frauenberg.[58]

Another sacred site closely linked to the water worship in the region of Gorenjska is the rock-shelter Pod Gričo near Godič in the Kamnik area (the territory of Emona),

56 Josipovič, Gaspari & Miškec 2012.
57 Josipovič, Gaspari & Miškec 2012.
58 References cited in the quoted article.

which is the source of the brook Ribnik. The excavations in the early 90s of the last century revealed an eight-metre long corridor built of stone. Fine pottery, oil lamps, remains of silver votive tablets, as well as coins from the 1st to the 5th centuries AD have been discovered in the cave shelter, in addition to a large quantity of bones, mainly belonging to young animals. However, finds have not been analyzed yet.[59]

The sanctuary of Savus and Adsalluta

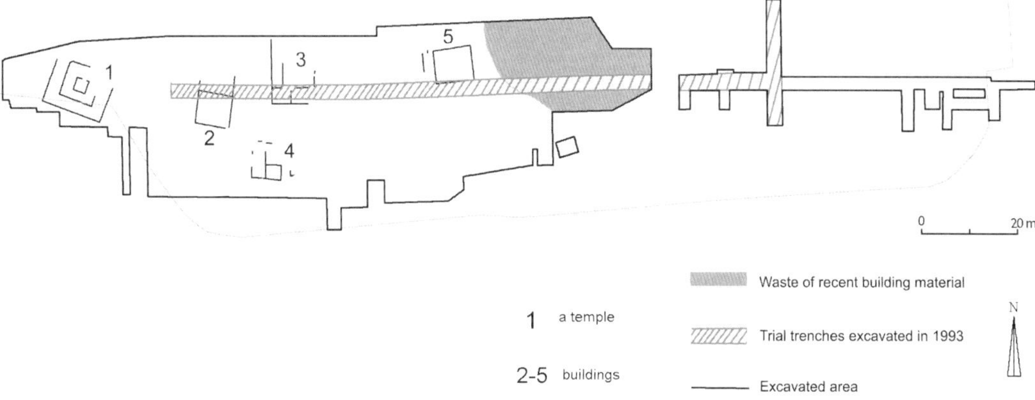

Fig. 5. Sanctuary of Savus and Adsalluta (from Krajšek & Stergar 2008, 247 fig. 3).

The central position along the Sava River belonged to the sanctuary of Savus and Adsalluta, located in the vicinity of the hamlet of Sava or Na Savi near Podkraj on the right bank of the river, opposite the railway station of Hrastnik. The sanctuary, built above the rapids in the Sava and situated between two dangerous waterfalls, was supposedly excavated already in 1917 by Walter Schmid.[60] Several years ago, due to the imminent construction of a gasoline station, modern rescue excavations revealed, in addition to the Roman ambulatory sanctuary, also a small Roman settlement at the site (Fig. 5).[61] It belonged to the administrative territory of the Claudian *municipium* of Celeia and hence to the province of Noricum.

Nine small altars dedicated to *Savus* and *Adsalluta*, or to *Adsalluta* only, were discovered long ago; this was a public cult and Adsalluta was several times invoked as Augusta. Regardless of her possible pre-Celtic origin, she was worshipped both by local Celtic Tauriscan population and by the Romans, particularly by the travellers along the river. As for her name, it has been suggested that it would have invoked to the Romans the association with the word *salus*, signifying health and well-being, and also worshipped as a deity, *Salus*.[62] More plausibly, Wolfgang Meid explained the name as

59 The cave shelter has not been published yet, see Knific 1997; Šašel Kos 2000, 32–3.
60 Schmid 1923–1924; Schmid 1925; the site was called Saudörfel or Savedörfel in German.
61 Jovanović 1998; Krajšek & Stergar 2008.
62 Šašel Kos 1999, 93–119.

being derived from the Proto-Indo-European root **sel-*, 'to jump', which in Latin resulted in *saltare*, *saltus*; however, he could not convincingly account for the double *ll*.[63] Lately, Luka Repanšek has persuasively interpreted the name Adsalluta as a Pannonian divine name; the geminate *ll* could be derived from **-ly-*, in a similar way as **ny* was regularly assimilated to **nn*. **Adsallu-tā* would mean 'the one connected to jumping' or even, 'the one connected to rapids or water-falls'.[64] Clearly, the Romans adopted her, reconciling her specific features to their own religious concepts, and she was worshipped in a Roman way. Her 'new' image undoubtedly influenced the beliefs of local population, which may have eventually resulted in cultic practices different from what they had been before the coming of the Romans.[65] Two more altars came to light at the site of the sanctuary, one without a dedication and one dedicated to Magna Mater, found during the latest excavations. The altar of Magna Mater sheds revealing light on the change of religious beliefs and worship in the sanctuary in the course of time.[66]

While most of the Adsalluta or Savus and Adsalluta altars were found at or near the site of the sanctuary, some came to light at the nearby places, reused as building material. However, since Adsalluta was a local deity closely linked to the sacred site, it may be assumed with the greatest probability that all of them originated from the sanctuary. If Savus alone were invoked on a reused altar, even if it were found in the vicinity of the sanctuary, its provenance would remain problematic, since the god was worshipped at several sanctuaries or shrines along the river.

Four of the altars have been found outside the area of the small Roman settlement with the sanctuary. The first was an altar dedicated to Savus and Adsalluta by one C. Memmius or Mammius.[67] It served as the base of the left lateral pillar in the gates leading to the graveyard of the church of sv. Jurij (St George) in Šentjur na Polju (near Loka at Zidani Most). Another altar was reused as the base of the right lateral pillar of the same gates, and was dedicated only to Adsalluta by L. Servilius Eutyches together with his pilots, *cum suis gubernatoribus*; both are now on display in the Sevnica Castle.[68] A small altar was discovered in 1910, during the demolition of the old church nave at Radeče near Zidani Most and is now built into the western wall of the new church. It was dedicated to Savus and Adsalluta by C. Iulius Iustus.[69] An altar erected to Adsalluta by C. Caecina Faustinus (Fig. 6), with no provenance noted in the inventory book, has been in the *lapidarium* of the National Museum of Slovenia since 1932;[70] there is not much doubt that it originated from the sanctuary.

Indeed, it may be significant that three of them, which had obviously been found long ago, were reused as building elements for two churches, and thus their pagan character

63 Meid 2005, 56 n. 77.
64 Repanšek 2016, 43–4; id., *Beiträge zur Namenforschung*, forthcoming; differently De Bernardo Stempel 2015.
65 For such processes in northern Italy, see Haeussler 2013, 251–77 and *passim*.
66 Lovenjak 1997, 67–8; Šašel Kos 2010.
67 AIJ 27 = ILLPRON 1875 = Šašel Kos 1999, 95 no. 1 = HD022287.
68 AIJ 26 = ILLPRON 1874 = Šašel Kos 1999, 98 no. 6 = HD022284.
69 AIJ 255 = Šašel Kos 1999, 95 no. 4 = HD057340.
70 CIL III 5135 = ILLPRON 1938 = Šašel Kos 1999, 98 no. 7 = RINMS 108 = HD066794.

neutralized. Although this cannot be proven, it can plausibly be argued that these four altars without provenance were originally placed in the sanctuary of Savus and Adsalluta, along with the other seven. Adsalluta was a local goddess, closely linked to the site of her sanctuary that had its 'raison d'être', since it was erected above the Sava River, at a site between two waterfalls, particularly the dangerous Beli slap (White Waterfall; Fig. 7),[71] and overlooking the rapids, where navigation was most dangerous. The 'Fury' of the Savus River was even invoked on a tombstone from Augusta Taurinorum (Torino) of a merchant L. Tettienus Vitalis, who was born at Aquileia and brought up at Emona.[72] Adsalluta was invoked to protect safe navigation along this section of the river. She can by no means be regarded as a personification of the Savinja River, which flows too far away from her sanctuary.

Fig. 6. Altar to Adsalluta by C. Caecina Faustinus (*RINMS* 108, photo Tomaž Lauko).

Other dedicators to Savus and Adsalluta, or to the goddess alone, included P. Antonius Secundus,[73] C. Cassius Quietus,[74] Secundio,[75] one C. C() A(),[76] and Ocellio, a slave of Castricius Marcellus.[77] The dedicators mostly belong to families from northern Italy,[78] particularly from Aquileia, where the Caecinae, Castricii, and Servilii are well attested. Members of these families came to live at Emona and later at Celeia, spreading from these two cities to other Norican and Pannonian towns. The dedicators attested on the Savus and Adsalluta altars must have mainly been travellers in transit, mostly merchants or staff in their service, who were active between Aquileia and Emona at the beginning of the fluvial route on the one side, and Celeia, Neviodunum, and Siscia on the other. They wished to secure the good will of the gods during navigation along the dangerous section of the river in the broad area of their sanctuary. Secundio and Ocellio probably belonged to local Celtic population, as both names were popular in Celtic provinces; they may have been employed by the merchants.[79]

71 Črešnar 2012.
72 ... *terras nec minus et maria impuri aqu(a)e Padi nec minus et Savi ira<m>*: CIL V 7047 + 7127 = EDR113494 with bibliography; Gabucci & Mennella 2003.
73 CIL III 5138= ILS 3907 = ILLPRON 1941 = Šašel Kos 1999, 96 no. 2 = HD026758.
74 CIL III 11684 = ILLPRON 1859 = Šašel Kos 1999, 96 no. 3 = HD066842.
75 CIL III 5134= 11680 = ILLPRON 1950 = Šašel Kos 1999, 97 no. 5 = RINMS 110 = HD066784.
76 CIL III 11685 = ILLPRON 1784 = Šašel Kos 1999, 99 no. 8 = HD057341.
77 CIL III 5136 = ILLPRON 1939 = Šašel Kos 1999, 99 no. 9 = RINMS 109 = HD066792.
78 Visočnik 2014, 285–7.
79 Secundio is known from northern Italy and Gallia Narbonensis, Ocellio (*ocellus* meaning a little eye

Fig. 7. Beli slap (White Waterfall) in the Sava River (from J. W. Valvasor, *Die Ehre deß Hertzogthums Crain*, IV. Buch, 1689, 607, fig. no. 99).

Worship of Neptune, Neptune Ovianus, Thana and Vidasus

The Castricii were no doubt a well-to-do family, to whom the traffic along the Sava River must have played an important role, as may be inferred from the fact that directly opposite the sanctuary of Savus and Adsalluta, at Klembas (or Klempas) near Hrastnik, an altar to Neptune was erected by another member of the family, C. Castricius Optatus.[80] Most probably, Neptune had his own small sanctuary or shrine on the left bank of the river. At Celeia, the Castricii belonged to the municipal upper class, since D. Castricius Verus Antonius Avitus was a town's *decurio*.[81]

Neptune was also worshipped by the Servilii family at the Aquileian *vicus* of Nauportus, evidently a merchant family, whose member (most probably a freedman) must have been the mentioned pilot L. Servilius Eutyches. L. Servilius Sabinus, inscribed in the voting tribe of the Aquileians, *Velina*, erected an altar to Neptune at the sacred site at Bistra near Nauportus (Fig. 8).[82] Neptune was regarded as a universal deity of seas, springs, and rivers, and of the power of water in general, not only among the Romans, but also among the Celts,[83] which is confirmed at Norican Celeia, where he played a central role and was worshipped by the entire population of Celeia.[84] A marble statue of

in Latin) from Raetia and in CIL XIII, OPEL, s.v.; Kakoschke 2012, 548; cognomina ending in *-io* were relatively common among Celtic population, cf. Kajanto 1965, 122; 239; 292.

80 CIL III 5137; ILLPRON 1940.

81 CIL III 5226 + p. 1830 (cf. ILJug 400); Wedenig 1997, C 16; ILLPRON 1686.

82 Šašel Kos 1990, pp. 150, no. 6, 155–156; the boundary between Aquileia and Emona ran east of Nauportus, Šašel Kos 2002.

83 Marco Simón & Rodá de Llanza 2008, 174.

84 CIL III 5197 = ILLPRON 1659 = Wedenig 1997, C 13 = Scherrer 1984, no. 334 = HD067022 = lupa 6736: *Neptuno / Aug(usto) sac(rum) / Celeiani / publice*; Šašel Kos 1999, 134–5.

Neptune was discovered at Cibalae (Vinkovci), which was located in the region between the Danube and the Drava, along the Bosut River, a left tributary of the Sava.[85]

Fig. 8. Dedication to Neptune by L. Servilius Sabinus from the sacred site at Bistra near Nauportus (CIL III 3778).

The significance of Neptune as a protector of merchants and river navigation is further illuminated by the altar of Neptunus Ovianus, found in 1898 during road works on the Krško–Sisak road, beneath the village of Čatež (the district of Krško), 21 m from the river Sava and 92 m from the Krka. The Krka (Corcoras) empties into the Sava near Brežice not far from Čatež (the *ager* of Neviodunum, Drnovo near Krško). The site of discovery is located on the road leading from Krška vas to Jesenice, along the former Roman road from Neviodunum to Siscia. It was dedicated by one Medus, a slave of the merchant C. Trotedius.[86] Carl Patsch supposed that Neptune had most probably been named after a locality, such as appears in an inscription on an amphora from Rome: *(Vinum) ex f(undo) Oviano n(ostro)*, or *n(ovo)*.[87] *Ovianus* must have been an indigenous epithet of Neptune, but not of course an Illyrian;[88] his epithet is etymologically unclear.[89] The Varciani, probably a mixed Pannonian and Celtic people, are known to have been settled in this region, that is, between Neviodunum and Andautonia.[90] The name *Medus* must be a local name, typical of this area, and indeed it has already been attested among the Varciani.[91] Trottedius, like

85 Rendić-Miočević 2012, 301–2.

86 Now in the *lapidarium* of the National Museum of Slovenia, CIL III 14354,22 = RINMS 136 = ILSl 59: *Medus / C(ai) Trotedi(i) / negotiator(is servus) / Neptuno / Oviano / [---]*. *Negotiator* in this case cannot be regarded as a cognomen (two cases cited by Kajanto 1965, 321), but as a profession of a merchant, especially in view of the dedication having been set up to Neptune, cf. also Mócsy 1974, 136.

87 CIL XV 4585; C. Patsch, *Jh. Österr. Arch. Inst.* 8, 1905, 140 and n. 20.

88 Thus Heichelheim 1942, 1907.

89 Repanšek 2016, 47.

90 Cf. Saria 1955; Pavan 1955, 517; Anreiter 2001, 143–4.

91 Not listed in the OPEL, but see Dobó 1975, 221, from Municipium Magnum in Dalmatia: *Vercaius Medi f(ilius) domo Varcianus*, from the *ala nova Claudia*. *Medu* is a feminine Celtic name from Noricum,

so many merchants active along the rivers Nauportus and Savus, came from northern Italy, where the *gentilicium*, elsewhere unknown, has twice been documented.[92]

A pair of deities related to water and similar to Savus and Adsalluta, is further known from Topusko, the Roman *Ad Fines*(?), where thermal springs were well-known in the early Roman period and most probably also in pre-Roman times. The site lies in the Kupa valley, at the juncture of this river with the Glina. There, several altars dedicated to Vidasus and Thana came to light; these divinities may have been linked either to the river(s), or to the thermal springs.[93] However, M. Ihm hypothesized that Vidasus could perhaps be related to a tributary of the Sava, called the Valdasus, mentioned in Pliny: *...inde XLV Taurunum, ubi Danuvio miscetur Saus; supra influunt Valdasus, Urpanus, et ipsi non ignobiles.*[94] This is unlikely on account of the distance between this river and the site of discovery of the altars. In any case, Vidasus and Thana were local, most probably Pannonian, deities; the name Vidasus could be linguistically compared to Silvanus, while Thana indeed is Diana.[95]

River cults are closely connected to the river traffic, which played a most significant role not only in antiquity but also during Middle Ages and well into the recent times. At Emona, an association of boatmen, *collegium naviculariorum*, was active during the Roman period,[96] and its members were undoubtedly worshippers of river deities. As is clear particularly from dedications to deities, whose worship was limited to a specific place, such as to Laburus, Adsalluta, or Neptune Ovianus, not the whole course of a river was regarded as sacred. Sacred waters may have been limited to sacred sites, and this is corroborated by Pliny's description of the Clitumnus. Boatmen were most probably aware when they entered sacred waters and acted according to the ancestral and well-established religious practices that mainly elude us.

BIBLIOGRAPHY

Alföldi, A. 1931 'Siscia. Vorarbeiten zu einem Corpus der in Siscia geprägten Römermünzen', *Numizmatikai Közlemények* 26–27, 1927–1928, 14–48.

Alföldy, G. 1977 'Die Personennamen in der römischen Provinz Noricum', *L'onomastique latine* (Colloques internationaux du C.N.R.S., N^0 564), ed. N. Duval, 249–64. Paris, Éditions du Centre National de la Recherche Scientifique.

Alföldy, G. 2011 'Eine umstrittene Altarinschrift aus Vindobona', *Tyche* 26, 1–22.

Anreiter, P. 2001 *Die vorrömischen Namen Pannoniens* (Archaeolingua, Ser. Minor 16), Budapest, Archaeolingua.

Bezlaj, F. 1956, 1961 *Slovenska vodna imena (Hydronymie slovène)* (Dela 2. razr. SAZU 9), I,

Lochner von Hüttenbach 1989, *s.v. Medulius* is sporadically used in Pannonia both as a *cognomen* and a *gentilicium*.

92 Also attested as Truttedius, cf. Solin & Salomies 1994, *s.v.*

93 AIJ 516–518; CIL III 3941.

94 *NH* III.148. Ihm 1896, 78.

95 Wilkes 1992, 246–7, regarded them as indigenous Diana and Silvanus (cf. Mayer 1948–1951); see also Cambi 2013, 84, and now Repanšek 2016, 46–7.

96 AIJ 178 = RINMS 46.

II, Ljubljana, Slovenska akademija znanosti in umetnosti.

Buora, M. & C. Zaccaria 1989 'Una nuova aretta votiva al Timavo da Monastero di Aquileia', *Aquileia Nostra* 60, 309–11.

Cambi, N. 2013 'Romanization of the western Illyricum from religious point of view', *Godišnjak/Jahrbuch – Centar za balkanološka ispitivanja* 42, 71–88.

Črešnar, M. 2012 'Beli slap in drugi pomniki plovbe po Savi med Litijo in Zidanim Mostom (Beli slap and other monuments of the navigation on the Sava between Litija and Zidani Most)', *Potopljena preteklost. Arheologija vodnih okolij in raziskovanje podvodne kulturne dediščine v Sloveniji*, ed. A. Gaspari & M. Erič, 337–46. Ljubljana, Didakta.

De Bernardo Stempel, P. 2010 'Celtic taboo-theonyms, *Góbanos / Gobánnos* in Alesia and the epigraphical attestations of *Aisos / Esus*', *Deuogdonion. Mélanges offerts en l'honneur du Professeur Claude Sterckx*, eds. G. Hily et al., 105–32. Rennes, Tir CRBC Rennes – 2 Université europ. de Bretagne.

De Bernardo Stempel, P. 2015 'Sprachwissenschaftlicher Kommentar zu den Götternamen *Savus* und *Adsalluta*', *Natur – Kult – Raum. Akten des intern. Kolloquiums, Paris-Lodron-Universität Salzburg, 20.–22. Jänner 2012* (ÖAI Sonderschriften 51), eds. K. Sporn, S. Ladstätter & M. Kerschner, 334–8. Wien, Österreichisches Archäologisches Institut.

Delamarre, X. 2012 *Noms de lieux celtiques de l'Europe ancienne (-500/+500)*. Paris.

Dobó, Á. 1975 *Inscriptiones extra fines Pannoniae Daciaeque repertae ad res earundem provinciarum pertinentes*. Budapest (4th edition).

Dular, J. 2009 'Sava v bronasti in železni dobi', *Ukročena lepotica. Sava in njene zgodbe*, ed. J. Peternel, 36–41. Sevnica, Javni zavod za kulturo, šport, turizem in mladinske dejavnosti.

Gabucci, A., & G. Mennella 2003 'Tra *Emona* e *Augusta Taurinorum*: un mercante di Aquileia', *Aquileia nostra* 74, 317–42.

Gaspari, A. 2006 'A possible multiperiod ritual site in the river Ljubljanica', *Studien zur Lebenswelt der Eisenzeit* (Ergänzungsbände zum Reallexikon der germanischen Altertumskunde 53), 7–17. Berlin, New York, W. de Gruyter.

Gaspari, A., R. Krempuš, & M. Novšak 2007 'Preliminary report on the discovery of a Late Celtic sanctuary and two Gallo-Roman temples in Celje (Slovenia)', *L'âge du fer dans l'arc jurassien et ses marges: dépôts, lieux sacrés et territorialité à l'âge du fer : actes du XXIXe colloque international de l'AFEAF* (Bienne, canton de Berne, Suisse, 5-8 mai 2005), ed. Ph. Barral *et al.*, vol. II, 835–40. Besançon, Presses univ. de Franche-Comté.

Gibson, R. K. & R. Morello 2012 *Reading the* Letters *of Pliny the Younger. An Introduction*. Cambridge, Cambridge University Press.

Gleirscher, P. 2014 'Eisenzeitliche Opferplätze und Heiligtümer im Südostalpenraum: Fakten, Thesen, Zweifel', *Rudolfinum* 2014, 132–48.

Haeussler, R. 2013 *Becoming Roman? Diverging Identities and Experiences in Ancient Northwest Italy*. Walnut Creek, California, Left Coast Press.

Hansen, S. 1997 'Sacrificia ad flumina – Gewässerfunde im bronzezeitlichen Europa', *Gaben an die Götter - Schätze der Bronzezeit Europas* (Bestandskataloge Bd. 4), ed. A. u. B. Hänsel, 29–34. Berlin, Museum für Vor- und Frühgeschichte, SMPK.

Heichelheim, F. 1942 'Ovianus', *RE* XVIII, 2, 1907.

Hopfner, J. 1927 'Sontius', *RE* III A 1, 996.

Ihm, M. 1896 'Keltische Flussgottheiten', *Archaologisch-epigraphische Mittheilungen* 19, 78–9.

Josipovič, D. A., Gaspari, & A. Miškec 2012 'Arheološko najdišče pri cerkvi sv. Janeza Krstnika v Bohinju (Archaeological site near the church of St John the Baptist at Bohinj)', *Potopljena preteklost. Arheologija vodnih okolij in raziskovanje podvodne kulturne dediščine v Sloveniji*, eds. A. Gaspari & M. Erič, 389–96. Ljubljana, Didakta.

Jovanović, A. 1998 'Podkraj, Hrastnik-Podkraj (no. 228)', *Varstvo spomenikov / Poročila* 37, 1996, 85–7.

Kajanto, I. 1965 *The Latin Cognomina* (Commentationes Humanarum Litterarum 36. 2). Helsinki, Societas Scientiarum Fennica.

Kakoschke, A. 2012 *Die Personennamen in der römischen Provinz Noricum* (Alpha-Omega, Reihe A, 262). Hildesheim, Zürich, New York, Olms-Weidmann.

Knezović, I. 2010 'The Worship of Savus and Nemesis in Andautonia', *Arheološki vestnik* 61, 187–202.

Knific, T. 1997 'Izkopavanja: 2. Godič', *Varstvo spomenikov* 36, 1994–1995, 234–5.

Kos, P. 1977 *Keltski novci Slovenije / Keltische Münzen Sloweniens* (Situla 18). Ljubljana, Norodni muzej Slovenije.

Krajšek, J. & P. Stergar 2008 'Keramika z rimskega svetiščnega območja v Podkraju pri Hrastniku

(The pottery material from the Roman sanctuary area at Podkraj near Hrstnik)', *Arheološki vestnik* 59, 245–77.

Lazar, I. 2002 'Celeia', *The Autonomous Towns of Noricum and Pannonia / Die autonomen Städte in Noricum und Pannonien. Noricum* (Situla 40), eds. M. Šašel Kos, P. Scherrer, 71–101. Ljubljana, Norodni muzej Slovenije.

Lazar, I. 2011 'The world of gods and religious life in Roman Celeia', *Religion in Public and Private Sphere* (Acta of the 4th Intern. Coll. The Autonomous Towns of Noricum and Pannonia, Annales Mediterranei), ed. I. Lazar, 23–37. Koper, Univerzitetna založba Annales.

Lippold, A. 1961 'Voconius Romanus', *RE* IX A.1, 698–704.

Lochner von Hüttenbach, F. 1989 *Die römerzeitlichen Personennamen der Steiermark*. Graz, Leykam.

Lovenjak, M. 1997 'Novi in revidirani rimski napisi v Sloveniji (Die neuen und revidierten römischen Inschriften Sloweniens)', *Arheološki vestnik* 48, 63–88.

Lovenjak, M. 2007 'Savercna – a new water goddess from the Slovenian Alps', *Epigrafia delle Alpi. Bilanci e prospettive* (Labirinti 107), eds. E. Migliario & A. Baroni, 351–63. Trento, Università degli Studi di Trento.

Lovenjak, M. 2012 'Saverkna – keltsko božanstvo izvira Save Dolinke? (Savercna – Celtic divinity of the source of the River Sava Dolinka?)', *Potopljena preteklost. Arheologija vodnih okolij in raziskovanje podvodne kulturne dediščine v Sloveniji*, eds. A. Gaspari & M. Erič, 385–8. Ljubljana, Didakta.

Marco Simón, F. & I. Rodá de Llanza 2008 'A Latin *defixio* (Sisak, Croatia) to the river god *Savus* mentioning *L. Licinius Sura, Hispanus*', *Vjesnik Arheološkog muzeja u Zagrebu* 41, 167–98.

Mayer, A. 1948–1951 'Die illyrischen Götter Vidasus und Thana', *Glotta* 31, 235–243.

Meid, W. 2005 *Keltische Personennamen in Pannonien* (Archaeolingua, Ser. Minor 20). Budapest, Archaeolingua.

Mócsy, A. 1959 *Die Bevölkerung von Pannonien bis zu den Markomannenkriegen*. Budapest, Akadémiai Kiadó.

Mócsy, A. 1974 *Pannonia and Upper Moesia*. London, Boston, Routledge & Kegan Paul.

Mušič, B. & J. Horvat 2007 'Nauportus – an Early Roman trading post at Dolge njive in Vrhnika. The results of geophysical prospecting using a variety of independent methods (Nauportus - zgodnjerimska trgovska postojanka na Dolgih njivah na Vrhniki. Rezultati geofizikalne raziskave z več neodvisnimi metodami)', *Arheološki vestnik* 58, 219–70.

Ostrowski, J. A. 1991 *Personifications of Rivers in Greek and Roman Art*. Warszawa, Kraków, Państwowe Wydawnictwo Naukowe.

Pavan, M. 1955 *La provincia romana della Pannonia Superior* (Atti della Accad. Naz. dei Lincei 352, 1955; Memorie [Cl. di Scien. morali, storiche e filol.], ser. 8, vol. 6, facs. 5), Roma [373–574].

Piccottini, G. 1970 'Dravus (1)', *RE Suppl.* XII, 239–40; 'Dravus (2)', 240.

Radice, B. 1969 Pliny, *Letters and Panegyricus* II, with an English transl. by Betty Radice (Loeb Classical Library 59). Cambridge, Mass., London, W. Heinemann.

Rendić-Miočević, A. 2012 'Rivers and river deities in Roman period in the Croatian part of Pannonia (Rijeke i riječna božanstva u rimsko doba u hrvatskom dijelu Panonije)', *Histria Antiqua* 21, 293–305.

Repanšek, L. 2016 *Keltska dediščina v toponimiji jugovzhodnega alpskega prostora*. Ljubljana, Založba ZRC.

Repanšek, L. 'Varia etymologica Pannonica', *Beiträge zur Namenforschung*, forthcoming.

Saria, B. 1955 'Varciani', *RE* VIII A,1, 363–5.

Scheid, J. 2015 'Natur und Religion. Zu einigen Missverständnissen', *Natur – Kult – Raum. Akten des intern. Kolloquiums, Paris-Lodron-Universität Salzburg, 20.–22. Jänner 2012* (ÖAI Sonderschriften 51), eds. K. Sporn, S. Ladstätter & M. Kerschner, 303–12. Wien, Österreichisches Archäologisches Institut.

Scherrer, P. G. 1984 *Der Kult der namentlich bezeugten Gottheiten im römerzeitlichen Noricum*. Unpublished thesis, Vienna University.

Schmid, W. 1923–1924 'Römische Forschung in Österreich 1912-1924. Die südlichen Ostalpenländer', *Bericht der Römisch-Germanischen Kommission* 15, 183–4.

Schmid, W. 1925 'Südsteiermark im Altertum', *Südsteiermark. Ein Gedenkbuch*, ed. F. Hausmann, 1–27. Graz, Ur. Mosers.

Sherwin-White, A. N. 1966 *The Letters of Pliny. A Historical and Social Commentary*, Oxford, Clarendon Press.

Solin, H. & O. Salomies 1994 *Repertorium nominum gentilium et cognominum Latinorum*, Hildesheim, Zürich, New York, Olms – Weidmann.

Šašel, J. 1968 'Emona', *RE Suppl.* XI, 540–78 (= 1992, 559–79).

Šašel, J. 1980 'Aquo, Aquonis, m., personifikacija in imensko izhodišče za potok Voglajna (Aquo, Aquonis, m., Personifizierung und Namensursprung für den Voglajna-Bach)', *Linguistica* 20 (In memoriam Milan Grošelj oblata) II, 61–6.

Šašel, J. 1992 *Opera selecta* (Situla 30). Ljubljana, Narodni muzej Slovenije.

Šašel Kos, M. 1990 '*Nauportus*: antični literarni in epigrafski viri (Nauportus: Literary and Epigraphical Sources)', in J. Horvat, *Nauportus (Vrhnika)* (Dela 1. razr. SAZU 33), 17–33 (pp. 143–59). Ljubljana, SAZU.

Šašel Kos, M. 1999 *Pre-Roman Divinities of the Eastern Alps and Adriatic* (Situla 38). Ljubljana, Narodni muzej Slovenije.

Šašel Kos, M. 2000 'Sacred Places and Epichoric Gods in the Southeastern Alpine Area – Some Aspects', *Les cultes polythéistes dans l'Adriatique romaine*, eds. C. Delplace, F. Tassaux (Ausonius Publ., Études 4), 27–51. Bordeaux, De Boccard.

Šašel Kos, M. 2002 'The Noarus River in Strabo's *Geography*', *Tyche* 17, 145–53.

Šašel Kos, M. 2006 'A Few Remarks Concerning the *archaiologia* of Nauportus and Emona: The Argonauts', M. Kokole, B. Murovec, M. Šašel Kos, M. Talbot (eds.), *Mediterranean Myths from Classical Antiquity to the Eighteenth Century / Mediteranski miti od antike do 18. stoletja*, 13–20. Ljubljana, Založba ZRC.

Šašel Kos, M. 2010 'Adsalluta and Magna Mater – is there a link?', *Celtic Religion across Space and Time (IX Workshop F.E.R.C.AN, Molina de Aragón)*, ed. J. Alberto Arenas-Esteban, 242–56. Toledo, Junta de Comunidades de Castilla-La Mancha.

Šašel Kos, M. 2012 'Colonia Iulia Emona – the genesis of the Roman city (*Colonia Iulia Emona* – nastanek rimskega mesta)', *Arheološki vestnik* 63, 79–104.

Šašel Kos, M. 2014 'Cincibilus and the march of C. Cassius Longinus towards Macedonia (Cincibil in pohod Gaja Kasija Longina proti Makedoniji)', *Arheološki vestnik* 65, 389–408.

Šimunović, P. 2013 'Predantički toponimi u današnjoj (i povijesnoj) Hrvatskoj (Pre-Roman place-names in present-day (and historical) Croatia)', *Folia onomastica Croatica* 22, 147–214.

Torbrügge, W. 1972 'Vor- und frühgeschichtliche Flußfunde. Zur Ordnung und Bestimmung einer Denkmälergruppe', *Bericht der Römisch-Germanischen Kommission* 50–51, 1970–1971, 1–146.

Vedaldi Iasbez, V. 1994 *La Venetia orientale e l'Histria. Le fonti letterarie greche e latine fino alla caduta dell'Impero Romano d'Occidente* (Studi e Ricerche sulla Gallia Cisalpina 5). Roma, Quasar.

Vedaldi Iasbez, V. 1996 'Una nuova aretta votiva all'*Aesontius*', *Aquileia Nostra* 67, 110–35.

Visočnik, J. 2014 'Foreigners in the area of Celeia', *Classica et Christiana* 9/1, 275–98.

Webb, P. H. 1972 *The Roman Imperial Coinage*, V 2, London 1933 (repr. 1972).

Wedenig, R. 1997 *Epigraphische Quellen zur städtischen Administration in Noricum* (Aus Forschung und Kunst 31). Klagenfurt, Geschichtsverein für Kärnten.

Wilkes, J. 1992 *The Illyrians*. Oxford, Cambridge, Mass., Blackwell.

Zaccaria, C. 2004 'Scelta dei *signa* onomastici e tradizioni religiose locali ad Aquileia', *Orbis antiquus. Studia in honorem Ioannis Pisonis*, eds. L. Ruscu et al., 171–8. Cluj-Napoca, Nereamia Napocae Press.

Zaccaria, C. 2009 '*Lacus Timavi*, *Fons Timavi*, e i *fontes calidi* dell'isoletta *ante ostia Timavi*. Alcune precisazioni terminologiche', *Histria Antiqua* 18/1, 273–82.

XXIV

ARCHAEOLOGICAL AND EPIGRAPHIC EVIDENCE FOR THE CELTIC PRESENCE IN THE UPPER TIMACHUS RIVER VALLEY (EAST MOESIA SUPERIOR)[1]

Vladimir P. Petrovic & Vojislav Filipovic

The aim of this paper is to shed some new light on the Celtic presence in the area of the Upper Timok (Timachus) River Valley in the east of modern Serbia, which is largely associated with the Scordisci. This region is situated on one of the major Trans-Balkan communication axes that linked the Danube basin with the territory of the Central Balkans and much further to the south with the Greek world and Aegean Sea. We shall predominantly discuss some recent archaeological discoveries that indicate the widespread presence of the Scordisci in the interior of Balkans, south of the Danube, before the Roman conquest. Furthermore, we shall deal with the rare epigraphic testimonies of the Romano-Celtic pantheon from the same area that point to the presence of the Celtic element in this region even after the establishment of Roman state and legal system.

THE movement of Celtic people from central to southern Europe took place over a long period of time, from the end of the 5th to the 3rd century BC. After the invasion and plundering of Macedonia and Greece in 280/279 BC, Celts finally settled in the broad valleys of the Danube and Great Morava Rivers.[2] From that period, they are known under the name of Scordisci.[3] Their material culture shows that they were actually a mixture between Celts and indigenous Paleo-Balkan tribes – Triballi, Illyrians, Dardanians, Moesians, Pannonians and others. According to classical writers, they settled along the Danube, Sava and Great Morava Rivers, and were divided into two tribes, the Great and Little Scordisci.[4] The Great Scordisci occupied the area along the

1 This paper is the result of the scientific projects of the Belgrade based Institute for Balkan Studies of SASA (num. 177012) and of the Belgrade based Archaeological institute (num. 177020) funded by the Ministry of Education, Science and Technological Development of the Republic of Serbia.

2 Popović 1994, 13.

3 Strab. 7.5.6 (c. 315-316); Iust. 32.3.6–8; Ath. 6.25, c. 234 a-c; Papazoglou 1969, 209–98.

4 Iust. XXXII 3.6–8; Ath. 6.25, c. 234 b. For the division of Scordisci into two tribes (Great and Little Scordisci), cf. Strab. 7.5.12.

Fig. 1. Bronze crossbow zoomorphic fibula from Banjska Stena by Zaječar.

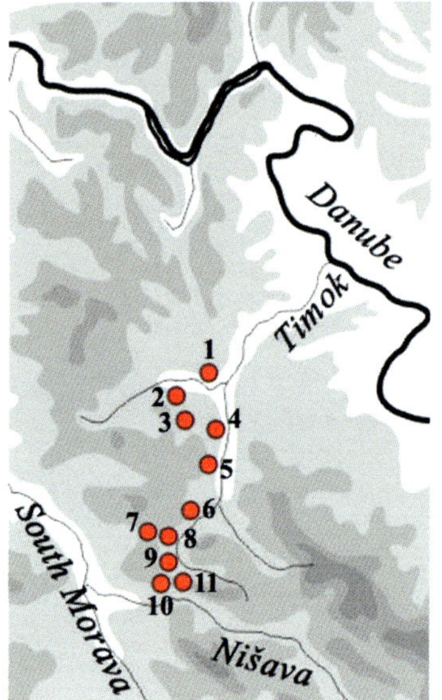

Fig. 2. Archaeological sites in the Upper Timok valley with the Eastern Celtic material. 1. Metovnica; 2. Banjska stena; 3. Višicina bašta; 4. Debelica; 5. Ravna – Timacum Minus; 6. Signal; 7. Ropalj; 8. Svrljig grad; 9. Niševac – Timacum Maius; 10. Gramada; 11. Prekonoška Cave.

Danube to the Great Morava River, while the Little Scordisci lived in the region from the Great Morava eastwards to the territory of the Triballi and Moesi tribes. That area constitutes the focus of our paper: the upper stream of the Timok (*Timachus*) River.

After the Delphi catastrophe, during the 3rd and the first half of the 2nd century BC, the Scordisci lived in relatively peaceful relations with their neighbours, but this is also a period of their expansion towards the south, which was, generally, a less populated part of the Central Balkan region.[5] Unfortunately, from this period, we do not have much information about their settlements. We only have several graves from the Karaburma necropolis near Belgrade and others in the Iron Gate region.[6] Among the limited archaeological evidence for Celtic presence in the Upper Timok River Valley, there is a bronze crossbow zoomorphic fibula with the upturned foot and knob shaped in the form of a hybrid animal from Banjska Stena by Zaječar (Fig. 1).[7] It seems that the form and fashion of this fibula was inspired by representations of the fish and the dragon. This type of fibula is quite rare in the Serbian Danube basin area, and only few examples were found at the sites of Dolna Dolina (Bosnia and Herzegovina), Pecica (Romania) and Kostolac (Serbia).[8] There are also three similar pieces in the northern Pannonian area, and it can be presumed that this type of fibula actually originated somewhere from the Pannonian plain. The fibula from the Timok River Valley represents the most eastern finding of this type, and may possibly indicate a Celtic presence in this area around the 4th century BC.[9]

Previous Yugoslav and Serbian scholars considered that the Scordisci inhabited only the lowland plains along the large rivers, and not the hills and mountains.[10] A large number of archaeological materials were discovered in the area around the upper stream of the Timok River during last ten years of

5 Popović 1994, 15.

6 Karaburma, a huge necropolis with settlement near Belgrade was investigated almost fifty years ago: Todorović 1972. The Celtic findings from the Pećine necropolis by Viminacium (Kostolac) have not been published so far. The findings from the Ajmana necropolis by Kladovo in the Iron Gate region are published in Stalio 1986, 27–50. For the early Celtic presence in the Central Balkan area, cf. Jovanović 1987.

7 Sladić 2002, 39, fig. 1.

8 Sladić 2002, 42-3.

9 Although this is the most eastern fibula of this type, it can have absolute chronological primacy due to its great similarities with specimens from the central Celtic areas (Alpine region).

10 Todorović 1968, 128; Popović 1994, 13.

intensive fieldwork and excavations (Fig. 2).[11] We consider it appropriate to add some previously known epigraphic indications of 'Celtic' religion from the Roman period that derive from the same area in order to point to the persistence of a definite Celtic element even in subsequent periods. All of the new archaeological data show that the Scordisci lived and controlled one of the main Paleo-Balkan communication lines, from the South Morava and Nišava Rivers in the south, to the Danube River in the north, which later became an important Roman line of communication *Naissus – Ratiaria* (Niš – Archar).[12]

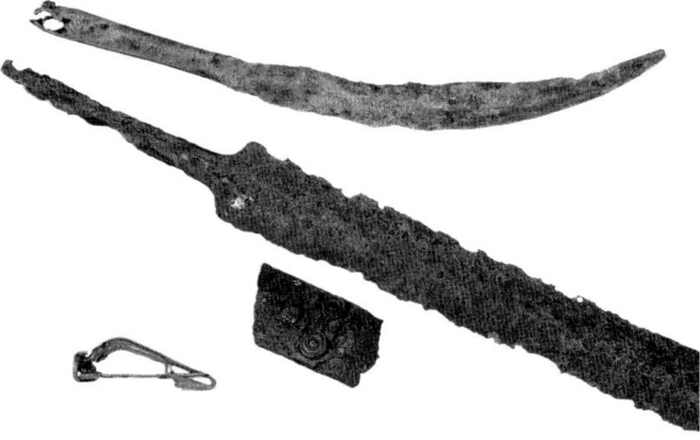

Fig. 3. Bronze fibula and iron sword and spear from the Debelica warrior grave.

The Celtic sites from the 2nd and 1st centuries BC are not numerous in the area of the Upper Timok River Valley, but all of them are positioned beside the river, i.e. the above-mentioned later Roman communication line. Sites, like Metovnica, Višicina bašta, Debelica (Fig. 3), Ravna, Signal, Svrljig grad, Niševac, Prekonoška cave and Gramada, represent solid evidence for the Celtic presence in this area, as well as directions of the proto-historic way from the Central Balkans towards the river Danube.

The main settlement in the area of Upper Timok River Valley is Svrljig fort with its surroundings, but also the key strategic stronghold at the Gramada saddle, where the mentioned communication line runs from the Niš basin to the Svrljig basin.[13] Thirteen silver drachmas of Apollonia and Dyrrhachium and two late La Tène fibulae could indicate the Scordisci's presence on the Gramada saddle, although there has not been any archaeologic research at this location so far. However, on the Svrljig fort we discovered a typical La Tène belt plate of the so-called Laminci type, as well as a dozen Celtic spurs.[14] The whole region of Svrljig is hilly and in this area, the Timok River passes through several large gorges. It could be supposed, based on the archaeological findings, that the upper stream of the Timok River was of major strategic importance for the Scordisci. This area could be connected with numerous Scordisci raids into the territory of Macedonia and Greece from the middle of the 2nd century BC.[15] After having been defeated in 100 and 85/84 BC by Marcus Minucius Rufus and Cornelius Scipio Asiagenus,[16] the Scordisci retreated from the southern part of their lands, but the Upper Timok River region was not disturbed.[17] Roman coins of the Republican period

11 Petrović, Filipović & Milivojević 2012; Bulatović-Kapuran-Jovanović 2011.
12 Petrović, Filipović & Luka 2014, 97–142; Petrović, Filipović & Milivojević 2012, 67.
13 Petrović, Filipović & Milivojević 2012, 75.
14 Filipović 2009, 176–177.
15 App. *Ill.* 5.
16 App. *Ill.* 5.
17 Popović 1994, 18.

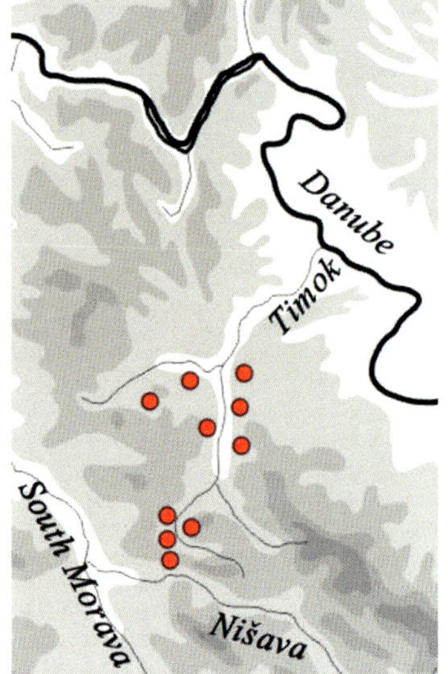

Fig. 4. Distribution of the Roman republican coins from the sites in the Upper Timok valley (2nd–1st century BC).

that were found all over the Timok River Valley (Fig. 4),[18] usually dating between the end of the 2nd and the first decades of 1st century BC, suggest that the Scordisci had good relations and a well-developed trade with the Roman Republic. At the beginning of the 1st century BC, Thracian and Dardanian tribes, without the Scordisci, penetrated into Greece and plundered the Dodona shrine. Soon after that, probably around 85 BC and encouraged by the Dodona plundering, the Scordisci together with the Thracian Maedi and the Dardanians plundered and burnt the sanctuary of Delphi. This raid triggered immediate Roman action, and a large Roman force under the command of Cornelius Scipio Asiagenus went deeply into the territory of the Scordisci. The written sources mention that Scipio almost destroyed the Scordisci, and those who survived were moved to the Danube and on its river islands.[19] It is interesting that the Republican coins after the 80s BC are not as widely represented as they had been in the area of the Morava and Timok River valleys. After the Roman military operations in 85 BC, the Scordisci lost their influence in the region while the centre of political and military power moved to the Dacian kingdom. In the period after the Dacian expansion over the former land of the Scordisci, we can notice a huge number of drachmas of Apollonia and Dyrrhachium.

Analyses of the hoards with the drachmas of Apollonia and Dyrrhachium have shown that the majority of coins originate from the last phase of minting, i.e. from *c.* 60–40 BC, but on this territory, we have only few findings of Republican *denarii* that can be dated to the end of 2nd and the beginning of 1st century BC.[20] This circulation of Roman coins could be interpreted as payments to Scordisci mercenaries who served in the numerous Roman wars.

The Scordisci were not explicitly mentioned in any literary source until 16 BC when they plundered Macedonia together with the Dentheletae.[21] In the meantime they had been exposed to the pressure and westward expansion of the Dacians, but were also mentioned as their allies, which may be dated to the 50s BC or slightly earlier. However, in spite of the Roman advances northwards, the Scordisci retained their independence, and in 12 BC they are mentioned as Tiberius' allies in his campaign against the Pannonian tribes. This suggests that between 16 and 12 BC they must have been somehow overpowered by the Romans,[22] but not conquered, which gave them the

18 Milivojević 2014.
19 App. *Ill.* 5.
20 Ujes-Morgan 2012, 374.
21 Dio. Cass. 44.20.3.
22 Vell. Pat. 2.39.3.

favourable status of allies of the Roman state. Probably around the end of the 1st century BC, the Timok valley was conquered by the Romans and incorporated into the Empire.

It is interesting that Pliny,[23] who left us a very detailed list of tribes that settled the Timok River Valley in the first half of the 1st century AD, does not mention the Scordisci at all, but he notes the presence of certain Timachi who may have been descendants of the Scordisci population.

Post-conquest Celtic presence in the Upper Timok River Valley

In general, the ethnic picture of the population of the Upper Timok River Valley during the pre-Roman period and in early Roman times was very complex. We must mention here the number of indigenous tribes of Thracian, Daco-Moesian, Celtic, Dardanian, and even Illyrian origin that were incorporated into the Roman state and legal order. The Dacian danger is certainly one factor that resulted in the very early establishment of a Roman military organization in the Timok River area. Other reasons would be, as far as it can be determined, the creation of a military command in Dardania at the time of Augustus (with Scupi/Skoplje or Naissus/Niš as headquarters) in order to secure the Danube border and the establishment of *praesidia* on the limes,[24] but also the transfer of the legions IIII Scythica and V Macedonica on the Danube and the organization of the Roman province of Moesia, probably during the early years of Tiberius' reign. The early military occupation of the region of the Timok River is further supported by the fact that the oldest military inscriptions in Moesia Superior originate from the triangle between the Timok, the Porečka reka and Cibrica Rivers.[25]

The oldest and most important traces of Roman military presence in the Upper Timok River Valley derive from Ravna (*Timacum Minus*), the camp of the cohort I Thracum Syriaca. This camp was probably erected during the reign of Vespasian when this unit, together with many other auxiliary detachments, was transferred from the East to the Danube region.[26] At the same time the cohors I Cretum settled in Niševac near Svrljig (*Timacum Maius*).[27]

After the Roman conquest, there are some traces of Celtic religion in the Upper Timok River Valley in the epigraphic sources. An interesting example is a dedication to Mars from Timacum Minus. In fact, from the text of this monument, discovered in 1940, which then disappeared, we can see that it was dedicated to Mars Campester, the Mars 'Protector of Camps'. The dedicant was the 2nd Cohort of Dardanians (*cohors II Aurelia Dardanorum equitata*), in honour to one of the emperors whose name is lost. The text of this inscription reads:

23 Plin. *HN.* 3.149.
24 Flor. 2.28.
25 Petrović 1995, 32.
26 Petrović 1995, 33.
27 Petrović & Filipović 2015, 33–9.

[Marti] Campestr[i coh(ors) II Aur(elia)] | [Dard(anorum)] Equit(ata) pro [salute] | [- - -].[28]

The epithet of Mars, Campester or Campestris, appears here for the first time on a monument from Moesia Superior.[29] The only other dedication to Mars Campester from the territory of today's Serbia comes from Sirmium in the neighbouring province of Pannonia Inferior, whose dedicant was Titus Flavius Aulus, a *beneficiarius consularis.*[30] Whatever the Latin roots of its name, the cult of Campester is originally Celtic and it was widespread in the Roman Empire by the Celtic horsemen involved in the military.[31] *Campestres* (usually in plural) are protectors of the camp (*campus*), which was designed for training and provided a space for equestrian parades. The presence of such camps has not yet been confirmed in Timacum Minus, although its existence seems evidenced by our dedication and cavalry unit that have been stationed there for a long time.

Conclusions

Concluding this paper, it is important to emphasize some notions that arise from the details considered above. The new archaeological material that derives from the area of the Upper Timok River Valley and that could be connected with the Scordisci, points to the importance of this region and a strong Celtic element in its ethnic identity. The Celtic component can be followed over a prolonged chronological framework, before and after the Roman conquest, and this requires that the territory, which was partly inhabited by the Scordisci, has to be enlarged south of the Danube to include the interior of the Balkans. This statement contradicts earlier conclusions in scholarship that were based on a much more limited basis of archaeological research. On the other hand, the data from literary sources must be more or less accepted with reservations. Only future archaeological research and new epigraphic testimonies will contribute to enlarge our knowledge about this interesting theme.

BIBLIOGRAPHY

Bulatović, A., A. Kapuran & I. Jovanović 2011 'La Tène Finds in the Vicinity of Bor'. *Zbornik Narodnog muzeja* 20.1, 119–28. Beograd, Narodni muzej u Beogradu.

Jovanović, B. 1987 'Istočna grupa', *Praistorija jugoslavenskih zemalja* V., ed. S. Gabrovec. Svjetlost i ANUBiH. Sarajevo, 815–54.

Milivojević, S. 2014 *Antički i srednjovekovni novac iz muzejske zbirke u Svrljigu*. Svrljig, Centar za turizam, kulturu i sport.

Papazoglu, F. 1969 *Srednjobalkanska plemena u predrimsko doba: Tribali, Autarijati, Dardanci, Skordisci i Mezi*. Sarajevo, Centar za balkanološka ispitivanja ANUBiH.

28 IMS III/2, 7 = ILJug 3, 1280 = GeA 438 = AE 1952, 189.
29 Petrović 2013, 265–70.
30 AE 1994, 1446.
31 Petrović 2013, 268.

Petrović, P. 1995 *Inscriptions de la Mésie Supérieure. Vol. III/2 : Timacum Minus et la vallée de Timok*, 1–158. Belgrade, Centre d'études épigraphiques et numismatiques.

Petrović, V. 2013 'L'inscription dédiée au Mars Campester de Timacum Minus (Provincia Moesia Superior)', *Keltische Götternamen als individuelle Option? / Celtic Theonyms as an Individual Option?* (Osnabrücker Forschungen zu Alterum und Antike-Rezeption, Band 19). ed. W. Spickermann, 265–70. Rahden/Westf., Verlag Marie Leidorf.

Petrović, V. P., V. Filipović & S. Milivojević 2012 *La région de Svrljig en Serbie orientale – préhistoire, antiquité et moyen âge*. Belgrade, Institut des études balkaniques de SASA et Centre culturel de Svrljig. Belgrade.

Petrović, V. P., V. Filipović & K. Luka 2014 'The Roman Road Naissus - Timacum Maius – Timacum Minus – Conbustica – Ratiaria', *Ratiaria Semper Floreat* Vol. I *(Ratiaria and its Territory Researches)*, ed. R. Ivanov, 97–142. Sofia, RSF Archaeological Trust.

Petrović, V. P. & V. Filipović 2015 'The First Cohort of Cretans, a Roman Military Unit at Timacum Maius', *Balcanica* XLVI, 33–9. Belgrade, Institute for Balkan Studies of SASA.

Popović, P. 1994 'The Territories of Scordisci', *Starinar* 43–44, 13–21. Belgrade, Archaeological Institute.

Sladić, M. 2002 'On Tracing Early Celtic Influences in Timocka Krajina'. *Balcanica* 32–33, 37–47. Belgrade, Institute for Balkan Studies of SASA.

Stalio, B. 1986 'Le site préhistorique Ajmana à Mala Vrbica'. *Djerdapske Sveske* 3, 27–50. Belgrade, Archaeological Institute.

Todorović, J. 1968 *Kelti u jugoistočnoj Evropi.* Beograd, Muzej grada Beograda.

Todorović, J. 1972 *Praistorijska Karaburma I – nekropola mladjeg gvozdenog doba*, Dissertationes et Monographiae XIII. Beograd, Muzej grada Beograda.

Ujes-Morgan, D. 2012 '1st Century B.C. Drachms of Apollonia and Dyrrhachium in the Territory of the Scordisci. A Prologue of the Roman Conquest of the Balkans', *Studia in honorem Iliae Prokopov sexagenario ab amicis et discipulis dedicata.* eds E. Paunov & S. Filipova, 367–87. Tirnovi, Faber Publishers.

XXV

MERCURIUS VALDIVAHANUS

Hartmut Galsterer, Alfred Schäfer & Patrizia de Bernardo Stempel

The threefold contribution scrutinizes, from the epigraphical, historico-archaeological and linguistic perspective, the votive dedication of a decurio *unearthed at the southern periphery of Cologne where it was reused for covering a 3rd-century cremation grave. Mercury's epithet, which is shown to be linguistically Germanic and related to the votive string* deo Requalivahano *in a dedication from the surroundings of Cologne, seems to express two of the usual qualities of the Roman Mercury, namely 'Leader and provider'. It is also at least possible, if not downright probable, that Milia Rhenas, the executor of the dedicant's testament, bore a Germanicized name.*

1. Die epigraphisch-historische Perspektive (HG)

BEI den archäologischen Untersuchungen in der südlichen Vorstadt des römischen Köln, am Waidmarkt und bei St. Georg, wo im Moment ein neues Wohn- und Geschäftszentrum entsteht, wurde 2010 ein Brandgrab freigelegt, das nach den Beigaben in das Ende des 3. Jahrhunderts zu datieren ist. Die blühende Vorstadt war damals bereits verschwunden, zerstört in den Germaneneinfällen dieser Zeit; die letzten Reste wurden wohl von den Kölnern selbst niedergelegt, damit sie nicht bei weiteren Plünderungszügen den Angreifern Schutz bieten konnten.[1] Nur die Tradition der Bestattungen in diesem stadtnahen Viertel an der römischen Nord-Süd-Strasse wurde wieder aufgenommen, wenn auch nicht mehr in der monumentalen Form wie früher, sondern meist in der Erde verborgen.

Ein gutes Beispiel hierfür liefert ein Anfang 2011 gefundenes Brandgrab,[2] je etwa 50 m westlich der Severinstrasse und südlich der Stadtmauer am Blaubach gelegen. Es handelt sich um einen in eine Planierschicht aus Bauschutt und Keramik des 3. Jahrhunderts eingelassenen Kasten aus Tuffstein, der annähernd 2 kg Leichenbrand und diverse Beigaben, darunter eine Münze des Probus enthielt. Am interessantesten war jedoch die Abdeckplatte des Kastens, eine Tafel aus lothringischem Kalkstein,

1 Schäfer 2011b.
2 Schäfer & Wieland 2011.

die eine siebenzeilige Inschrift aus erheblich früherer Zeit trägt. Da die Platte keine Spuren einer nachträglichen Bearbeitung zeigt, verwendete man sie demnach, wie man sie gefunden hatte, und ließ nach ihren Maßen den Kasten herstellen, vielleicht aus einem alten Fundamentblock, wozu Tuffstein gerne verwendet wurde. Woher die beiden wiederverwendeten Steine genau kamen, ist unklar. Doch wird man wohl auf die ruinierte Vorstadt am Verlauf der Severinstraße verweisen dürfen. Bemerkenswert ist vor allem der Text der Inschrift (der in der Zweitverwendung nicht mehr sichtbar war). Er lautet:

Mercurio
valdivahano
Milia rhenas
ex testamento
l carini sollemnis
dec ccaa ex
hs n iiii mil

Nach Auflösung der Abkürzungen ist dies:

> *Mercurio | Valdivahano | Milia Rhenas | ex testamento | L(ucii) Carini Sollemnis | dec(urionis) c(oloniae) C(laudiae) A(rae) A(grippinensium) ex | (sestertium) n(ummum) quattuor mil(ibus)*
>
> "Dem Mercurius Valdivahanus hat Milia Rhenas gemäß dem Testament des Lucius Carinius Sollemnis, Stadtrat der claudischen Kolonie am Altar der Agrippinensier, aus dem Erbe 4.000 Sesterzen für dieses Monument gestiftet".

Die Inschrift ist gut entworfen, mit in allen Zeilen fast gleich großen, relativ breiten Buchstaben. Nur in der dritten und vierten Zeile musste der Steinmetz zu so genannten Ligaturen greifen, das heißt dem Zusammenschreiben von Buchstaben, um eine Trennung zusammengehöriger Wörter oder Ausdrücke zu vermeiden.

Die Inschrift stammt ursprünglich aus dem sakralen Bereich und wurde dem keltischen oder germanischen Gott *Mercurius Valdivahanus* testamentarisch durch einen verstorbenen Stadtrat (*decurio*) Kölns gesetzt. Derartige Stiftungen wurden zwar normalerweise bei Lebzeiten vorgenommen, wenn man die „begünstigte " Gottheit um etwas bitten oder ihr für Hilfe danken wollte, doch wenn der Stifter selbst nicht mehr dazu kam, seine moralische Schuld abzulösen, oblag das selbstverständlich dem Erben. Bei der relativ geringen Summe von 4.000 Sesterzen, die Carinius Sollemnis ausgesetzt hatte, kann es sich nach den Vergleichszahlen (die allerdings hauptsächlich aus Nordafrika stammen, einer Provinz mit einem vielleicht viel höheren Preisniveau) nicht um einen Tempel oder gar ein größeres Heiligtum gehandelt haben, sondern vielleicht um eine Statue des Gottes oder ein kleines Sacellum innerhalb des Heiligtums.

Die Stiftung war also vielleicht bescheiden nach den Maßstäben Africas, doch muss dies nicht auch für Köln und sein Gebiet zutreffen. Die Vermögensverhältnisse der kölnischen Oberschicht sind uns zwar unbekannt; anzunehmen ist jedoch, dass die häufig im Reich belegte Summe von 100.000 Sesterzen als Mindestbesitz (*census*), der wohl vorwiegend in Immobilien nachzuweisen war, so oder ähnlich auch in Köln galt. Nach oben war dem Reichtum natürlich keine Grenze gesetzt. Bei einer ebenfalls in Nordafrika mehrfach belegten Rendite aus Grundbesitz von 5–6% wäre die obige Summe von 4.000 Sesterzen für einen ärmeren Dekurionen doch der erhebliche Teil eines Jahreseinkommens gewesen. Doch sind das wenig mehr als Spekulationen, da uns über die wirtschaftlichen Verhältnisse in Germanien wenig bekannt ist. Die Tatsache, dass nur wenige *Agrippinenses* in den Ritterstand oder gar in den Senat aufstiegen, könnte u.a. mit ihrem bescheidenen ökonomischen Status zusammenhängen.

„Empfänger" der Stiftung war der bisher unbelegte Gott Mercurius Valdivahanus. Aus vielen Inschriften vor allem aus den Rheinprovinzen sehen wir, wie die einheimischen Gallier und Germanen die Namen ihrer Götter – und damit ja wohl charakteristische Züge – mit einem römischen Götternamen zu „übersetzen" versuchten. Der Historiker Tacitus, der Germanien recht gut kannte, nennt dieses Verfahren *interpretatio Romana*. Man wird wohl nicht ganz fehlgehen, wenn man dem Gott *Valdivahanus* eine gewisse Beziehung zu Handel und Verkehr unterstellt. Ob dies jedoch die gesamte Bandbreite seiner Kompetenzen umfasst und ob nicht vielleicht andere, den Römern weniger genehme Züge, dabei unterdrückt wurden, ist unklar, da über die gallischen Götter, über den römischen „Leihnamen" und manchmal auch noch Tempelanlagen nichts bekannt ist. Der Rückschluss von P. de Bernardo Stempel, wonach der Beiname *Valdivahanus* etwa mit „Lenker" und „Fürsorger" zu übersetzen wäre, was nicht übel zum „Reisegott" Merkur passen würde, bedarf wohl noch weiterer Absicherung.[3] Im Kontext der aus Köln überlieferten Götterweihungen wird die Inschriftenplatte – auch statistisch – in die zweite Hälfte des 2. Jahrhunderts n. Chr. gehören.

Die Namen der in der Inschrift genannten zwei Personen sind in Köln bisher unbekannt, sonst aber nicht extrem selten. Milia Rhenas war die Testamentsvollstreckerin des Dekurionen Lucius Carinius Sollemnis.[4] Vermutlich war sie die Frau des Sollemnis und gehörte damit wohl zu derselben sozialen Schicht wie er, das heißt den „oberen Hundert" der Stadt, und war weiterhin – nach den zwei Namen, die sie trägt – auch römische Bürgerin, was auch durch ihre Stellung als testamentarische Vertreterin eines römischen Bürgers nahe gelegt wird.[5] Wenn sie auch die Frau des Sollemnis war, dürfte es in Köln wohl nicht nötig gewesen sein hierauf hinzuweisen, da man das sicher wusste, vor allem in einem Heiligtum, zu dem Carinius vermutlich schon vor seinem Tod Beziehungen hatte.[6]

Die Namensbestandteile der genannten Personen in der neuen Kölner Weihinschrift

3 Siehe Abschnitt 3. Zu Merkur vgl. Hupe 1997.

4 Es gibt keinen Grund, in Milia Rhenas einen Mann zu sehen, wie P. de Bernardo Stempel annimmt; siehe Abschnitt 3.

5 Nach ihrem Namen war sie keine Freigelassene, d.h. frühere Sklavin des Carinius.

6 Vergleichbar ist die Inschrift CIL XIII 2873 aus Alesia, wo zuerst der Stifter genannt wird, der alle Ämter bei den Haeduern und den Lingonen bekleidet hatte, dann der Empfänger, *deo Moritasgo*, das Stiftungsobjekt (eine Porticus), und schließlich der Name der Dedikantin, einer Tochter des Stifters.

sind selten, aber durchaus belegt. Ein Carinius Gratus ist in dem Nehalennia-Heiligtum von Colijnsplaat als ein *(mercator) allecarius*, also ein Händler mit Fischsauce bezeugt; da die Fischsauce, die *allec* genannt wurde, aus dem Mittelmeer stammte und über Rhone, Saone, Mosel und Rhein an den Fundplatz gelangte, um weiter nach Britannien verschifft zu werden, ergibt sich für Gratus so eine Beziehung zu Köln.[7]

Milius ist in Spanien, Rom und aus der Umgebung von Modena belegt, Rhenus in Gallien und auf einem der Täfelchen von Vindolanda (was für die Herkunft des dort genannten Sklaven wenig aussagt).[8] Rhenus ist der römische Namen des Reno, der nahe bei Modena und Bologna in den Po mündete. Weder Milia noch Carinius geben ihre Filiation an, was jedoch für die zweite Hälfte des 2. Jahrhunderts nichts mehr über ihren rechtlichen Status aussagt, da dies bei römischen Bürgern nicht mehr allgemein üblich war.

2. Mercurius Valdivahanus. Die archäologische Perspektive (AS)

Mit der Okkupation der keltischen und germanischen Gebiete kamen auch die Götter Roms in das eroberte Territorium.[9] Die indigene Bevölkerung der Nordwestprovinzen verehrte die neuen Gottheiten, wie Iuppiter, Iuno und Minerva, Merkur, Apollon oder Herkules, da sie in den jeweiligen göttlichen Wirkungskräften ihre eigenen Götter wiedererkannte. Ebenso konnte nach römischer Auffassung eine einheimische Gottheit in der Gestalt einer römischen Gottheit verehrt werden. In seiner Schrift *Germania* spricht Tacitus diesen Vorgang als *interpretatio Romana* an (Tac. *Germ.* 43, 13–17). Der Begriff steht für die römische Ausdeutung von keltisch-germanischen Gottheiten, von denen es ursprünglich keine Bilder (*nulla simulacra*) gab.[10] Hier soll der Blick auf die neue mediale Qualität der Götterwelt in den Nordwestprovinzen gelenkt werden: Nach römischem Vorbild wurden figürliche Darstellungen von Göttern in Stein gehauen, in Bronze und Blei gegossen, in Ton gebrannt oder in Bein gearbeitet. Das dauerhafte Werkmaterial trug zur Beständigkeit des provinzialen Pantheons bei. Auf den Weihemonumenten gaben lateinische Inschriften Auskunft über die Namen der verehrten Götter und die Personennamen der Stifter. Bildliche und schriftliche Medien waren nicht nur Teil der Kommunikation mit den Göttern, sondern richteten sich zugleich an ein Publikum. Der provinziale Götterhimmel war optisch präsent, haptisch erfahrbar und fest im religiösen Alltag integriert. Man muss diese Veränderungen in der Religion der römischen Nordwestprovinzen als fundamentalen Umbruch begreifen. Am Fallbeispiel eines Kölner Neufundes sollen einige Aspekte dieser religiösen Kommunikation auf lokaler Ebene erörtert werden.

7 AE 1973, 365.

8 *Milius*: AE 1978, 341; TVindol. II 347: *a Rheno Similis servo.*

9 Für Hinweise und Anregungen möchte ich P. de Bernardo Stempel, H. Bernhardt, C. Ciongradi, W. Eck, M. Euskirchen, H. Galsterer, R. Häußler, P. Noelke, W. Spickermann, M. Trier, J. Untermann und M. Wieland herzlich danken.

10 Schäfer 2011a.

2.1 Eine recycelte Weihinschrift aus der römischen Vorstadt der CCAA

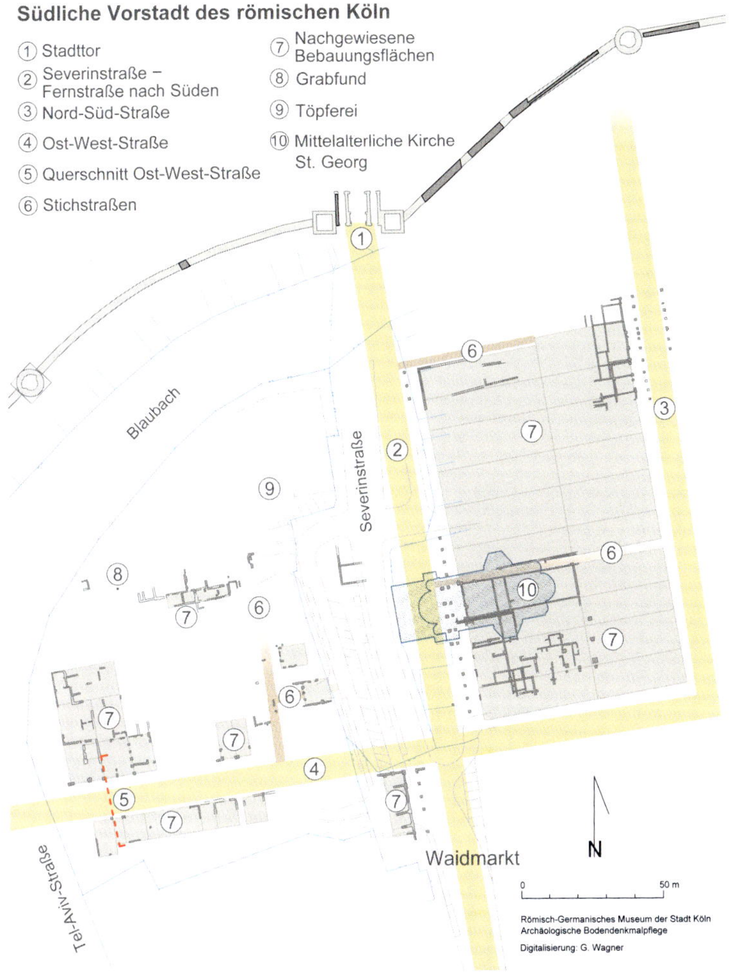

Abb. 1. Skizzierter Plan der südlichen römischen Vorstadt von Köln; Römisch-Germanisches Museum der Stadt Köln / Digitalisierung G. Wagner.

Anlässlich der Errichtung eines neuen Stadtquartiers am Waidmarkt in Köln fanden 2010/2011 bauvorgreifende archäologische Ausgrabungen des Römisch-Germanischen Museums statt.[11] Das Areal liegt direkt vor dem Südtor der steinernen Stadtmauer des römischen Köln, die seit den 80er Jahren n. Chr. entstand, nachdem die Siedlung im Jahre 50 zur Kolonie römischen Rechts erhoben worden war und den Namen *Colonia Claudia Ara Agrippinensium* (CCAA) erhalten hatte (Abb. 1).[12] Vor der Stadtmauer erstreckte sich die römische Vorstadt, deren Mittelachse die Fernstraße in Richtung Bonn bildete. Im ausgehenden 3. Jahrhundert n. Chr. gaben die Römer ihre Vorstädte wegen der Germaneneinfälle aus dem Rechtsrheinischen auf. Inmitten der Ruinen bestatteten die Bürger der CCAA ihre Verstorbenen wieder näher an der Stadtumwehrung. Ein Zeugnis dieser Umbruchzeit ist die Brandbestattung in einer Aschenkiste, die bei den jüngsten archäologischen Ausgrabungen am Waidmarkt entdeckt wurde. Das Brandgrab war in eine Erdschicht mit Bauschutt und Keramik des 3. Jahrhunderts eingetieft. Offenbar waren im Vorfeld der Stadtmauer Gebäude abgerissen und das Gelände eingeebnet worden, um Angreifern keine Deckung zu bieten und ein freies Schussfeld zu schaffen.

Die rechteckige Steinkiste aus Tuff (62 x 58 x 38 cm) enthielt fast zwei Kilo

11 Fundbericht 2010.018 des Römisch-Germanischen Museums der Stadt Köln. Technische Leitung der archäologischen Ausgrabungen: H. Bernhardt, M. Wieland; wissenschaftliche Leitung: T. Höltken, A. Schäfer. Einen Überblick zu den Ausgrabungsergebnissen gibt: Schäfer 2011b.

12 Trier 2010.

Abb. 2. Aschenkiste mit recycelter Weihinschrift als Abdeckplatte, RGM Inv. 2010, 95; Foto RBA d029044_2.

Abb. 3. Grabbeigaben aus der Aschenkiste vom Waidmarkt in Köln, ausgehendes 3. Jahrhundert n. Chr.; RGM Foto RBA d029045.

Leichenbrand sowie drei Bronzemünzen, ein Messer mit Eisenklinge und drei weißtonige Kännchen (Höhen 11–12 cm) (Abb. 2–3).[13] Außerdem fanden sich in der Aschenkiste drei Eisennägel, die vermutlich zur Konstruktion des Scheiterhaufens gehörten, und ein 6,5 cm langes Eisenstäbchen unbekannter Funktion. Zumindest die Keramikkännchen weisen keinerlei Brandspuren auf; somit handelt es sich um Grabbeigaben, die erst nach der Einäscherung des Leichnams in den Grabbehälter gelegt wurden. Der Zeitpunkt der Bestattung kann durch die Beigaben näher bestimmt werden. Kleine Kännchen mit seitlichem Ausguss gibt es von der ersten Hälfte des 3. bis zur Mitte des 4. Jahrhunderts n. Chr.; vor allem im späten 3. Jahrhundert sind sie häufig anzutreffen.[14] Trotz ihrer schlechten Erhaltung war eine der Münzen aus der Zeit des Kaisers Probus (276–282 n. Chr.) näher bestimmbar. Insgesamt datiert das Brandgrab in das späte 3. Jahrhundert. Damals war die südliche Vorstadt (*suburbium*) bereits aufgegeben.

Die Aschenkiste am Waidmarkt war mit einer Kalksteinplatte abgedeckt (65 x 60 x 10 cm). Erst bei der Öffnung des Grabes kam ein annähernd quadratisches Inschriftenfeld auf der Unterseite der Abdeckplatte ans Licht (55,5 cm x 56 cm). Augenscheinlich handelt es sich um einen wiederverwendeten Inschriftenstein (Abb. 4),[15] der ursprünglich in ein anderes Monument eingelassen war. Nach dem Formular ist es eine Weiheinschrift. Steinrecycling wie im Fall der als Grabdeckel genutzten Weiheinschrift wurde seit dem späten 3. Jahrhundert in Köln im großen Umfang und systematisch betrieben.[16] Da die Stadt keine Steinbrüche besaß, wurden in wirtschaftlich schwierigen Zeiten

13 Aschenkiste und Weiheinschrift, RGM Inv. 2010, 95; Erstpublikation Schäfer & Wieland 2011.
14 Naumann-Steckner 1997, 72.
15 Schäfer & Wieland 2011.
16 Ob die Tuffkiste aus einem älteren Werkstein umgearbeitet worden ist, kann nicht sicher entschieden werden. Die Werkspuren des Zahneisens und der geglättete Randschlag zeugen von keiner Zweitverwendung (Abb. 2). – Für das 4. Jahrhundert n. Chr. sind in den Nekropolen Kölns bergfrische Tuffhandquader nachweisbar. Kalksteine hingegen wurden zu dieser Zeit häufig recycelt; vgl. Schuler 2005, 408–10.

selbst den Göttern geweihte Steinmonumente als Baumaterialien wiederverwendet.[17] Ein Verstoß gegen geltendes Sakralrecht war diese Vorgehensweise nicht. Da die Weihemonumente zumeist auf persönliche Stiftungen zurückgingen, gehörten sie nicht, wie Geräte des rituellen Instrumentum oder ein dedizierter Opferaltar, zum unveräußerlichen Besitz einer Gottheit.[18]

Abb. 4. Inschriftenplatte mit einer Weihung an Mercurius Valdivahanus, RGM Inv. 2010, 95; Foto RBA d029044_1.

Die Inschrift der wieder verwendeten Kalksteinplatte ist sorgfältig gemeißelt und in sieben Zeilen gegliedert. Aufgrund der ausgewogenen Ordination des Textes fällt sogleich auf, dass die Buchstaben der ersten Zeile mit 5 cm Höhe etwas größer als die Buchstaben der übrigen Zeilen mit jeweils 4 cm Höhe sind. Der lateinische Text lautet nach Auflösung der Abkürzungen: *Mercurio | Valdivahano | Milia Rhenas | ex testamento | L(ucii) Carini Sollemnis | dec(urionis) c(oloniae) C(laudiae) A(rae) A(grippinensium) ex | (sestertium) n(ummum) quattuor mil(ibus).*

Der Adressat der Weihung wird zuerst genannt: Merkur, der aus römischer Sicht vor allem als Götterbote verstanden wurde. Hier trägt er einen einheimischen Beinamen *Valdivahanus*. Die Differenzierung der Buchstabengrößen sollte vielleicht die erklärende Funktion des Beinamens betonen, der eine bestimmte göttliche Kompetenz des in größeren Majuskeln geschriebenen *Mercurius* akzentuierte. Die Bedeutung des Doppelnamens *Mercurius Valdivahanus* erschließt sich vor allem im zeitgenössischen Wissenskontext. Aus epigraphisch-historischer und sprachwissenschaftlicher Perspektive schlagen H. Galsterer und P. de Bernardo Stempel in diesem Beitrag unterschiedliche Interpretationen vor.[19] Um die Aussage des Doppelnamens erörtern zu können, ist meines Erachtens eine Kontextualisierung des Inschriftentextes als auch der archäologischen Überlieferung notwendig.

Die neue Weiheinschrift aus der südlichen römischen Vorstadt von Köln geht auf testamentarische Verfügung zurück und reiht sich in die große Gruppe der lateinischen

17 Zum Steinrecycling im spätrömischen Köln: Galsterer & Galsterer 2010, 159–60, 416 Nrn. 172, 524; Gregarek 2005. Im Fundament einer so genannten *cella memoriae* aus dem 4. Jahrhundert n. Chr. in der nördlichen Vorstadt des römischen Köln sind Kalksteinspolien vermauert: Fundbericht des Römisch-Germanischen Museums der Stadt Köln 1996.15; Schuler 2005, 408–10.

18 Wissowa 1912, 385; 472–3.

19 Zum sprachwissenschaftlichen Ansatz vgl. De Bernardo Stempel 2005.

Inschriften mit der Formel *ex testamento* ein. Der Testamentgeber und damit der Stifter der Weihung heißt Lucius Carinius Sollemnis und war Stadtrat der *Colonia Claudia Ara Agrippinensium* (*CCAA*). Die gewählten Mitglieder dieses Rates stammten aus den vermögenden und angesehenen bürgerlichen Familien der Stadt. Etwa einhundert Dekurionen waren lebenslänglich im Amt, wenn sie sich nichts zu Schulden kommen ließen. Obwohl zwischen dem 1. und 4. Jahrhundert rund 1.000 Kölner Bürger zu den Vertretern des Rates (*ordo decurionum*) gehört haben müssen, kennen wir von ihnen nur eine verschwindend kleine Zahl. Namentlich bezeugt sind für die *Colonia* bislang zwölf Stadträte und Träger öffentlicher Ämter.[20] In der Zusammenschau der Götterweihungen aus Köln wird die Inschriftenplatte in die zweite Hälfte des 2. Jahrhunderts n. Chr. datiert.[21] Der Ratsherr Lucius Carinius Sollemnis zählt zu den frühesten bisher bekannten Vertretern des Kölner Dekurionenstandes. Darüber hinaus ist die wiederverwendete Steinplatte erst die vierte Inschrift aus Köln, in der die vollständige römische Stadttitulatur CCAA genannt wird.[22] Kölner Bürger verwiesen vor allem in der Fremde stolz auf ihre Heimatstadt. Innerhalb des Zentralortes musste man diesen Titel auf Grab- und Weihinschriften nicht eigens herausstellen, deshalb sind sie so selten.

Als ausführende Person des Testamentes wird in der dritten Inschriftenzeile Milia Rhenas genannt. H. Galsterer deutet den Personennamen als Witwe des Dekurionen Lucius Carinius Sollemnis. P. de Bernardo Stempel nimmt im Kontext eines germanischen Sprachmilieus die Namensformel eines Mannes an.[23] Hier sei darauf verwiesen, dass der zeitgenössische Leser des Lateinischen mächtig sein musste und daher die Namen im Kontext römischer Namensgebung sah.[24] Die meisten Rezipienten in der *colonia* dürften die weiblich klingende Form Milia Rhenas als Namen einer Frau verstanden haben. Dass der zweite Namensbestandteil Rhenas vermutlich vom Flussnamen Rhenus abgeleitet wurde und somit eine Herkunftsangabe sein könnte, widerspricht der lateinischen Kontextualisierung des Namens nicht.[25] Ordnet man die Kölner Weihinschrift in die Überlieferung der Votiveinschriften mit der Formel *ex testamento* ein, so sind zwei Aspekte hervorzuheben.

1. Weibliche Familienangehörige konnten ihre Beziehung zum Testamentgeber inschriftlich dokumentieren, selbst wenn sie am Ort von vielen Anwohnern gekannt wurden.[26] Auf diese Weise wurde auf ihre soziale Rolle als Ehegattin oder Tochter einer bestimmten Persönlichkeit verwiesen. Milia Rhenas ist somit nicht zwingend die Witwe des Kölner Ratsherrn. Möglich ist auch, dass es sich um eine Person ohne nähere

20 Eck 2004, 315–25.
21 Spickermann 2008, 130, 168–72.
22 Binsfeld 1960.
23 Siehe die Beiträge von H. Galsterer und P. de Bernardo Stempel.
24 Eck 2004, 284–94.
25 Siehe die Beiträge von H. Galsterer und P. de Bernardo Stempel.
26 *Gen(io) col(oniae) Mil(evitanae) / ex testamen/to P(ubli) Sitti Adiu/t[oris] aug(uris) inte/[gris] HS II m(ilibus) n(ummum) curante / Sittia Vitale fi[l(ia)]*; CIL VIII 8202 = CIL VIII 19980 = AE 2002, 1654. *Iunoni Reg(inae) / ex testamen[to] / M(arci) Valeri Ge[mi/n]i Val(eria) Hono/[r]ata fil(ia) et / Iun(ius) Gem[i/nu]s here[des] / [po]sueru[nt]*; CIL VIII 9753 (add. p 2046).

Verwandtschaftsbeziehungen handelt. Auffällig ist, dass Milia Rhenas sich selbst nicht als Erbin bezeichnet, wie es auf anderen Inschriften oft der Fall ist.

2. Die Ausführenden eines Testamentes wurden häufig erst an zweiter Stelle nach dem Testamentgeber genannt. Obgleich diese Reihenfolge keiner Regel entsprach, fällt doch die herausgehobene Stellung von Milia Rhenas auf, die gleich nach dem Theonym und noch vor dem Testamentgeber aufgeführt wird.

Wie darf man sich das Weihegeschenk an *Mercurius Valdivahanus* vorstellen, zu dem die Inschrift ursprünglich gehörte? Zwei seitlich überstehende Kanten zeigen, dass die Platte in ein Monument eingelassen war. Die in der letzten Zeile des Textes genannte Verfügungsumme von 4.000 Sesterzen wird wohl kaum für einen monumentalen Tempelneubau ausgereicht haben. Vielmehr ist an ein kleineres *sacellum*, etwa an eine Nischenarchitektur oder Erweiterung einer Kultstätte, und ebenso an eine Götterstatue aus Marmor oder Bronze zu denken.[27] Im letzteren Fall zierte die Inschriftenplatte dann vermutlich den hohen Sockel des Götterbildes. Solch ein Weihgeschenk war für die meisten Menschen im antiken Köln unerschwinglich. Die gestiftete Summe von 4.000 Sesterzen entsprach im 2. Jahrhundert n. Chr. einem mehr als dreijährigen Sold eines römischen Legionärs.[28] Der Betrag von 4.000 Sesterzen-Nummi steht für den noch glatteren, wohl tatsächlich gezahlten Betrag von 1.000 Denaren. Diese Summe entsprach damals, grob geschätzt, 3 kg Silbergeld.[29]

2.2 Mercurius Valdivahanus im Kontext der Merkurweihungen in Gallien, Germanien und der CCAA

In diesem Beitrag ist nun auf die einleitend formulierte Problemstellung zurückzukommen, die um den von Tacitus geprägten Begriff der *interpretatio Romana* kreist. Der Fokus richtet sich auf den Doppelnamen *Mercurius Valdivahanus*. Zugespitzt lauten die Fragen: Was macht ein germanisches Epitheton des Merkur in einer perfekten lateinischen Inschrift, die sich auf einen Stadtrat der CCAA bezieht? Ist für die Testamentsvollstreckerin wie für den verstorbenen Stifter eine besondere Nähe zum Kult des *Mercurius Valdivahanus* anzunehmen? Um diesen Fragenkomplex zu erörtern, bedarf es einer archäologischen Kontextualisierung der Kölner Inschrift auf überregionaler und lokaler Ebene.

In der bildlichen und epigraphischen Überlieferung der germanischen und gallischen Provinzen nimmt Merkur einen herausragenden Platz ein.[30] Im

---

27 Vgl. Duncan-Jones 1982, 162–3 Nr. 498 und 499.

28 Da es im Imperium Romanum regionale Preisunterschiede gab, wird hier die Soldentwicklung im römischen Heer als Vergleich herangezogen. Im 2. Jahrhundert lag der einfache Legionärssold bei 1.200 HS; Drexhage *et alii* 2002, 179.

29 In der Kölner Inschrift ist die Zähl-Einheit *nummus*, „Münze", auffälligerweise differenziert zu *HS N*, „Sesterzen-Nummus". Die Zuweisung ist in der zweiten Hälfte des 2. Jahrhunderts n. Chr. zweckmäßig, denn damals gab es zwei verschiedene Bedeutungen für *nummus*, entweder den alten Sesterz-Nummus oder den neuen Denar-Nummus; Mrozek 1978, 79–86.

30 Kuhnen 1996, 154–65; Hupe 1997, 139; Zelle 2000, 50–1; Klein 2003, 109; Spickermann 2003, 380–1; Spickermann 2008, 126, 187, 194, 206, 227.

Abb. 5. Weiherelief für Merkur aus Kalkstein, fortgeschrittenes 2. Jahrhundert n. Chr., RGM Inv. 40, 32; Foto RBA 54 806.

provinzübergreifenden Vergleich wird neben Iuppiter wohl keine andere Gottheit so häufig verehrt wie Merkur. Seine Bedeutung in Gallien und Germanien basierte auf einheimischen Gottesvorstellungen, die in der mittleren Kaiserzeit zumindest in Grundzügen noch präsent waren. Dass die Germanen eine Gottheit verehrten, deren Wirkungskreis aus römischer Sicht mit bestimmten Aufgaben des Merkur gleichgesetzt wurde, legt die ethnographische Schrift des Tacitus aus der Zeit um 100 n. Chr. nahe. Nach dem Zeugnis des römischen Historikers (*Germania* 9, 1) verehrten die Germanen unter den Göttern im höchsten Grade Merkur: *Deorum maxime Mercurium colunt* [...]. Bereits Gaius Iulius Caesar betonte im sechsten Buch seines Gallischen Krieges (*de bello Gallico* 6, 17) die Bedeutung des Merkur für die einheimische Bevölkerung: „Als Gott verehren sie besonders Merkur. Er hat die meisten Bildnisse, ihn halten sie für den Erfinder aller Künste, ihn für den Führer auf Wegen und Wanderungen, ihm sprechen sie den größten Einfluss auf Gelderwerb und Handel zu".

Bereits in der 2. Hälfte des 1. Jahrhunderts n. Chr. wird der Kult des Merkur durch eine relativ breite Denkmälerüberlieferung in Gallien und Germanien repräsentiert. Die Mehrzahl der Inschriften als auch der plastischen Denkmäler gehört dem späteren 2. Jahrhundert und der 1. Hälfte des 3. Jahrhunderts n. Chr. an. In den Nordwestprovinzen fällt der Höhepunkt der Produktion von Votivdenkmälern ganz allgemein in diesen Zeitraum. In der Forschung spricht man von einer Phase der intensiven Romanisation,[31] da die mediale Aneignung der Götterwelt nicht auf bodenständige Traditionen zurückzuführen, sondern als römische Innovation zu begreifen ist. Die Sprache der Weiheinschriften wurde vom Lateinischen dominiert. Der Opferritus für die Götter entsprach den Regeln römischer Kultpraxis. Gleichwohl konnte die Bedeutung einheimischer Götternamen in einigen Fällen Einfluss auf die bildliche Darstellung nehmen. Die Weiheinschrift für *Mercurius Valdivahanus* vom Kölner Waidmarkt stammt aus dieser Phase der größten Nachfrage nach Weihedenkmälern in der mittleren Kaiserzeit.

31 Spickermann 2008, 138–244.

Die bildlichen Darstellungen des Merkur entsprechen in Gallien und Germanien zumeist der römischen Ikonographie und unterscheiden sich nur in einigen Fällen von den italischen Zeugnissen. So wird der jugendliche, unbärtige Gott oft stehend (Abb. 5),[32] zuweilen auch auf einem Felsen oder Thron sitzend wiedergegeben. Er ist nackt oder trägt einen Mantel. Zu seinen Attributen als Götterbote gehören der Flügelhut (*petasus*) oder kleine Flügel, die auf dem Haupt sitzen. Manchmal trägt der Gott geflügelte Schuhe. Sein Heroldstab, der *caduceus*, zeichnet sich durch zwei achtförmig gewundene Schlangen aus. Ein Geldbeutel kann Merkur als Schutzgott der Kaufleute und des Handels kennzeichnen. Mitunter wird er in Begleitung von mehreren Tieren – Hahn, Widder, Ziegenbock, Schildkröte, Eber, selten auch Eidechse und Skorpion – dargestellt.

Verehrt wurde Merkur in einer Vielzahl von Heiligtümern, deren Spektrum von kleinen kapellenartigen Gebäuden bis zu größeren Tempelbezirken reichte.[33] Die geographische Verteilung der erhaltenen Bauinschriften und der archäologischen Befunde zeigen, dass vor allem große Teile der *Germania superior* und der nordöstliche Teil der *Gallia Belgica* mit einem Netz von Merkurheiligtümern überzogen gewesen sein müssen. In der Provinz *Germania inferior*, mit der Provinzhauptstadt des römischen Köln, wurde die Wahl der Gottheiten stark durch die bodenständigen Matronenkulte bestimmt.[34] Gleichwohl sind Merkurheiligtümer auf dem Gebiet der CCAA, wenn auch nicht so zahlreich, anzunehmen.[35] Bekannt durch eine Bauinschrift ist der Tempel für *Mercurius Augustus*, der sich innerhalb des Zentralortes befunden haben wird (Abb. 6).[36] Es handelt sich um einen größeren Baukomplex, der einen Tempel, einen Umgang und Nebengebäuden einschloss.[37] In der Zeit des Kaisers Titus (79–81 n. Chr.) wurde das Heiligtum gebaut oder bereits erneuert, denn die Weihung für *Mercurius Augustus* erfolgte sehr wahrscheinlich zum Wohl dieses Kaisers.[38] Da der Tempel in die Zeit des flavischen Herrscherhauses datiert, ist dessen Errichtung im Zusammenhang der großen Erneuerungsphase der Stadt im ausgehenden 1. Jahrhundert n. Chr. zu sehen. Der rheinseitige Stadtprospekt wurde damals mit monumentalen Sakralbauten, wie

32 Votivrelief für Merkur aus Kalkstein, gefunden am Georgsplatz in Köln 1940, RGM Inv. 40, 32; Schoppa 1959, 56 Nr. 43 Taf. 41; Hupe 1997, 166 Nr. 84.

33 Hupe 1997, 140; Klein 2003, 113–22.

34 Spickermann 2008, 184.

35 Noelke 1990, 100–1.

36 Bauinschrift aus Kalkstein, gefunden an der Nordostseite des Kölner Domes 1866, RGM Inv. 347; Schoppa 1959, 55–6 Nr. 42 Taf. 40; Galsterer & Galsterer 2010, 161–2 Nr. 174. Die Zuweisung der Bauinschrift nach ihrem Fundort zu einem mit Lisenen (Mauerverstärkungen) gegliederten Bau unter dem südwestlichen Ende des gotischen Chorumgangs ist zurecht abgelehnt worden. Bei diesem tief gegründeten, römischen Gebäude handelt es sich wahrscheinlich um eine Lagerhalle (*horreum*); Hauser 1993; 2003, 23. Der Fundort der Bauinschrift nahe der spätantiken Schenkelmauer, die die Rheinvorstadt in den Stadtmauerring einschloss, unterstützt die Annahme einer Verschleppung des Werksteins. In der Rheinstadtbefestigung des 4. Jahrhunderts waren recycelte Werksteine (Spolien) verbaut; Dietmar & Trier 2006, 45–6.

37 Übersetzung nach Galsterer & Galsterer 2010, 161: „Dem Mercurius Augustus. Zum Wohl des Kaisers Titus Caesar --- (ließ) --- den Tempel von Grund auf (errichten und) --- das Ziegelmauerwerk im Umgang und in den Gebäuden ---".

38 Eck 2004, 474–5.

beispielsweise dem Kapitol und einem nördlich angrenzenden Temenosbezirk mit Rundtempel, umgestaltet und erhielt auf diese Weise eine neue urbane Qualität.[39] Der Auftraggeber des Merkurtempels ist nicht überliefert. Eine öffentliche Baumaßname der Kolonie ist nicht auszuschließen. Dass der Tempel von einem Vertreter des römischen Stadtrates (*ordo decurionum*) oder vom Statthalter selbst dediziert worden ist, wird durch den Bezug auf den Kaiser durchaus wahrscheinlich. Die Weihung an *Mercurius Augustus* bezog sich zunächst einmal auf die Gottheit selbst. Durch das Epithet *Augustus* wurde das Wohl des Kaisers in die religiösen Handlungen eingeschlossen.[40] Der Kaiser ist gewissermaßen mit dem Gott assoziiert worden, wodurch die Dedikation in die Nähe des Herrscherkultes rückte. Die Verehrung des Kaisers dürfte integraler Bestandteil des Kultes für *Mercurius Augustus* im römischen Köln gewesen sein.[41]

Abb. 6. Bauinschrift eines Tempels für Mercurius Augustus aus Köln, Material Kalkstein, RGM Inv. 347; Foto RBA 27607.

Während die Bauinschrift für *Mercurius Augustus* sehr wahrscheinlich eine öffentliche Sakralarchitektur zierte, gehen die überlieferten Merkuraltäre aus Köln auf persönliche Weihungen zurück. Aufgrund ihrer sekundären Verwendung können diese Weihemonumente keinem bestimmten Heiligtum zugewiesen werden.[42] Hier seien drei Votivaltäre für Merkur aufgeführt. Ein Altar war wohl dem *Mercurius Venator* geweiht, dessen Beiname bisher nur einmal belegt ist.[43] Sehr wahrscheinlich ging der „jagende Merkur" auf lokale Gottesvorstellungen zurück. Ein weiterer Altar ist für *Mercurius Cissonius* überliefert (Abb. 7).[44] Das Hauptverbreitungsgebiet dieser Gottheit liegt im gallisch-germanischen Raum. Der keltische Funktionsbeiname dürfte auf die göttlichen Kompetenzen eines Transport- und Handelsgottes verweisen.[45] Der dritte Weihealtar ist als solcher kaum mehr kenntlich, da er in sekundärer Verwendung als Architekturglied umgearbeitet worden (Abb. 8).[46] Das Monument war dem *Mercurius*

---

39 Rathgens 1913, 17, 22; Kühnemann & Binsfeld 1965/66, 52–3; Hellenkemper 1972/1973; Thomas 1983; Irmler 2004; Spickermann 2008, 270.

40 Liertz 1998, 164.

41 Spickermann 2008, 85–7, 142.

42 Galsterer & Galsterer 2010, 157–64 Nr. 170–1, 173, 175–6.

43 Galsterer & Galsterer 2010, 163–4 Nr. 176.

44 Schoppa 1959, 57 Nr. 48 Taf. 45; Übersetzung nach Galsterer & Galsterer 2010, 162–3 Nr. 175: „Für Mercurius Cissonius hat Larinius Senilis sein Gelübde freiwillig und nach Verdienst erfüllt."

45 Van Andringa 2002, 135.

46 Schoppa 1959, 57 Nr. 47 Taf. 45; Übersetzung nach Galsterer & Galsterer 2010, 160–1 Nr. 173: „Dem arvernischen Merkur geweiht. Iulius --- (stellte das Altärchen) auf Befehl des Gottes (auf)."

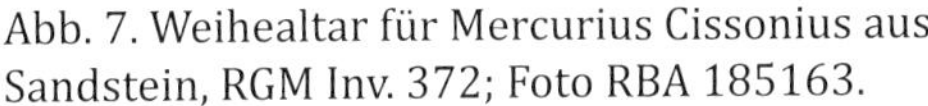

Abb. 7. Weihealtar für Mercurius Cissonius aus Sandstein, RGM Inv. 372; Foto RBA 185163.

Abb. 8. Weihealtar für Mercurius Arvernus aus Kalkstein, RGM Inv. 371; Foto RBA 185161.

Arvernus geweiht, einem Gott des gallischen Stammes der Arverner, der in der Gestalt des römischen Merkur verehrt wurde. Außer dem Kölner Exemplar stammen vier weitere Votivmonumente für diesen indigenen Gott aus der Provinz Niedergermanien und dem Dekumatenland.[47] Eine Weihung aus dem Stammesgebiet der Arverner selbst, deren Hauptheiligtum sich auf dem Puy-de-Dôme im französischen Zentralmassiv befunden hat,[48] richtet sich nicht an *Mercurius Arvernus*, sondern bezeichnenderweise an den *Genius Arvernus*.[49] Offenbar wurde der in der Auvergne beheimatete Gott mit einem römischen Ortsgenius (*Genius loci*) verbunden, da es sich um den in dieser Region dominierenden Gott handelte. In der Forschung spricht man auch vom *deus patrius*, von einem heimatlichen Schutzgott der Arverner.[50] In der Limesregion wurde dieser Gott ausschließlich dem Merkur gleichgesetzt.[51] Die *Mercurius Arvernus*-Weihung in

47 Van Andringa 2002, 137.

48 Hupe 1997, 107.

49 CIL XIII 1462.

50 Van Andringa 2002, 137.

51 Vgl. Hupe 1997, 162–3 Kat. 74 Abb. 1. Zum Phänomen der Identifikation von Gottheiten siehe das instruktive Beispiel einer Weihinschrift aus Mainz mit der lateinischen Formulierung *lares competales sive Quadriviae*; CIL XIII 11816 = 6731a und 6768. Die Gleichsetzung basierte darauf, dass die *lares competales* an den zentralen Straßenkreuzungen der Stadtbezirke Roms verehrt worden sind und die *Quadriviae* einheimische Wegegöttinnen waren. Der Stifter der Weihung war ein *beneficiarius consularis* namens Titus Flavius Castus, auf dessen persönliches Wissen die Göttergleichsetzung zurückging; vgl. Hainzmann & De Bernardo Stempel 2009; De Bernardo Stempel & Hainzmann 2010.

Abb. 9. Votivaltar für die Matres Aumenahenae, Köln RGM Leihgabe aus Privatbesitz; Foto RBA 149 448.

Köln bezieht sich auf eine Gottheit, die aus Gallien in die Provinzkapitale Niedergermaniens überführt worden ist.

2.3 Ein lokaler Gott in der CCAA

Auf der Grundlage der überregionalen und lokalen Überlieferung der Merkurweihungen ist auf die Bedeutung des Doppelnamens Mercurius Valdivahanus in der Kölner Inschrift zurückzukommen. Die erhaltenen Votivmonumente zeigen, dass der gewählte Beiname des Merkur bisher nicht anderweitig nachgewiesen ist. Ein Weihealtar aus Blatzheim, einer Ortschaft im Rhein-Erft-Kreis westlich von Köln, liefert die wohl engste sprachliche Parallele (Abb. 17):[52] *Deo Requalivah/ano Q(uintus) Aprian[i]us / Fructus ex im(perio) pro / se et suos v(otum) s(olvit) l(ibens) m(erito)*. Der Altar ist als dauerhaftes Zeichen für ein erfolgreich eingelöstes Gelübde an Deus Requalivahanus aufgestellt worden. Der zweite Bestandteil des Epitheton Requalivahanus entspricht dem zweiten Teil des Beinamens Valdivahanus. Die Endungen der beiden attributiv gebrauchten Adjektive gehen wahrscheinlich auf eine germanische Entsprechung -*vajano* zurück.[53] Das Weihemonument für Mercurius Valdivahanus bezieht sich auf den römischen Gott Merkur mit einer spezifischen germanischen Anrufung. In ihrer sprachlichen Analyse deutet P. de Bernardo Stempel den germanischen Funktionsbeinamen Valdivahanus darüber hinaus als „Lenker und Gedenker (Fürsorger)".[54] J. Untermann stellt dagegen zur Diskussion, dass der erste Teil des Kompositums Valdi- auf eine Variante von VALDU- "Wald" zurückgeht.[55]

Aus archäologischer Perspektive sind mehrere Aspekte herauszustellen:

1. Die beiden Votivmonumente für *Mercurius Valdivahanus* und *Deus Requalivahanus* stammen aus dem Territorium des römischen Köln.[56] Aufgrund der Fundorte und der vergleichbaren Komposita wird es sich nicht um transferierte, sondern sehr wahrscheinlich um ortsansässige Götter handeln, deren Verehrung auf Bewohner der CCAA und ihres Umlandes zurückging. Siedlungskern und Umland sind auch in religiöser Hinsicht nicht voneinander zu trennen, da das Zentrum die Götterkulte des Umlandes

52 Lehner 1918, 117 Nr. 243; CIL XIII 8512 = ILS 4737. Foto mit freundlicher Genehmigung des Rheinischen Landesmuseum Bonn, Inv. 3476.

53 Freundliche Mitteilung von J. Untermann mit dem Verweis auf: Neumann 1987, 106–7.

54 Siehe das Kapitel von P. de Bernardo Stempel.

55 Freundliche Mitteilung von J. Untermann mit dem Verweis auf: Scardigli 1989, 153–4.

56 Vgl. Eck 2004, 16–7.

an sich band und zugleich auf die Sakrallandschaft der Peripherie Einfluss nahm.[57]

2. Auf dem Territorium des römischen Köln finden sich die meisten Belege für die niedergermanischen Muttergottheiten.[58] Nach der Anzahl der inschriftlichen und figürlichen Zeugnisse sind zuerst die Matronen, dann Iuppiter Optimus Maximus, Merkur, Herkules und Diana zu nennen.[59] Matronennamen, wie die *Matronae Audrinehae*, *Matronae Gesahenae*, *Matronae Vallabneihiae* oder *Matres Aumenahenae* (Abb. 9),[60] waren einem großen Teil der Bevölkerung der CCAA und gewiss auch vielen ortsfremden Besuchern bekannt.[61] Auf dieser Grundlage konnte der Einzelne einen Götternamen wie *Mercurius Valdivahanus* in die Gruppe der lokalen Gottheiten auf dem Stadtgebiet des römischen Köln einordnen. Die im Ubiergebiet nachgewiesene enge Beziehung zwischen den bodenständigen Matronen und Merkur stützt eine solche Zuweisung.[62]

Abb. 10. Weihinschrift für Merkur aus Kalkstein, gefunden in St. Severin in Köln, RGM Inv. 25,811; Foto RBA 75046.

3. Wer heute eine antike Inschrift liest, tut dies in der Regel mit nur einem Sinne: mit den Augen. Wir lesen Texte so, wie wir uns Bilder anschauen. Im Altertum las man hingegen laut.[63] Beim lauten Lesen der Weihinschrift für *Mercurius Valdivahanus* nahm man den andersartigen Klang des Beinamens sogleich wahr, der sich bis auf seine Endung sehr deutlich vom Lateinischen unterschied. Sprachrythmus und Sprachmelodie des germanischen Epitheton *Valdivahanus* führten gewissermaßen zu einer spezifischen Anrufung des römischen Merkur. Der einzelne Betrachter des Weihemonumentes für *Mercurius Valdivahanus* konnte beim lauten Lesen frei entscheiden, ob er sich selbst an den Gott mit einem persönlichen Anliegen wandte. Entschied sich der Akteur im Rahmen einer solchen Kommunikation für den Gott, ist von einer Epiklese, einer Anrufung des Merkur zu sprechen.

4. Aus der südlichen römischen Vorstadt von Köln sind mehrere Weihedenkmäler für Merkur überliefert. Außer der Inschriftenplatte vom Waidmarkt (Abb. 4) ist ein Weiherelief vom Georgsplatz nahe der Kirche St. Georg zu nennen, das den jugendlichen, nackten Gott aufrechtstehend mit dem Botenstab und Flügelhut wiedergibt (Abb. 5). Ein

57 Zur Verbindung von Zentralität und Religion: Cancik *et alii* 2006.
58 Eck 2007; Spickermann 2008, 188–98; Biller 2010.
59 Ristow 1980.
60 Die Übersetzung der lateinischen Inschrift auf dem Votivaltar für die *Matres Aumenahenae* lautet nach Galsterer & Galsterer 2010, 135–6 Nr. 139: „Für die Matres Aumenahenae erfüllte Quintus Iulius Verinus sein Gelübde freiwillig und nach Verdienst."
61 Vgl. Neumann 1987.
62 Horn 1987, 47; Galsterer & Galsterer 2010, 160.
63 Leumann *et alii* 1977, 253; Chaniotis 2008.

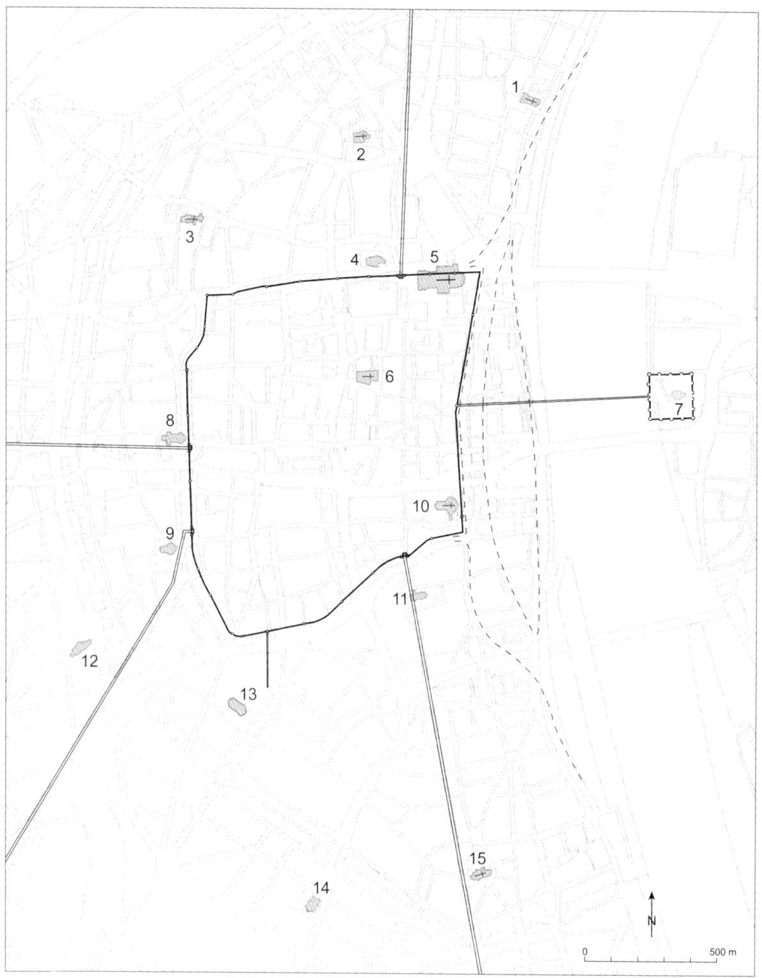

Abb. 11. Karte Kölns mit dem Verlauf der römischen Stadtmauer und der Lage ausgewählter Kirchen; 1 St. Kunibert; 2 St. Ursula; 3 St. Gereon; 4 St. Andreas; 5 Dom; 6 St. Kolumba; 7 St. Heribert; 8 St. Michael; 9 St. Mauritius; 10 St. Maria im Kapitol; 11 St. Georg; 12 St. Nikolaus; 13 St. Pantaleon; 14 St. Paul; 15 St. Severin; Römisch-Germanisches Museum der Stadt Köln / Zeichnung S. Haase.

drittes Weihemonument für Merkur wurde in St. Severin in sekundärer Verwendung entdeckt (Abb. 10).[64] Die Kirche St. Severin liegt an der römischen Fernstraße in Richtung Bonn und grenzt unmittelbar südlich an das Suburbium an (Abb. 11).

Der betreffende Inschriftenblock aus Kalkstein wurde wohl im 4. Jahrhundert in sechs oder sieben Platten zersägt, die zur Abdeckung von Steinsärgen dienten. Die lateinische Inschrift ist in einen Eichenlaubkranz eingeschrieben: *Primio | Celissi fil(ius) | curia(lis) gru(e)s duas | Mercurio | v(otum) s(olvit) l(ibens) m(erito)*. Die Übersetzung lautet: „Primio, Sohn des Celissus, Mitglied der Kurie, hat dem Merkur mit zwei Kranichen sein Gelübde freiwillig und nach Verdienst erfüllt."

Die Einlösung des Gelübdes bezeugt, dass Merkur die persönlichen Bitten des Stifters erhört hat. Zum Dank erhielt der Gott die versprochenen Kraniche. Ursprünglich übernahm der Inschriftensockel die Funktion einer Statuenbasis für die Bronzefiguren der beiden Zugvögel. Anzunehmen ist eine Gesamthöhe des Sockels von circa 1,60 m, eine Breite von circa 1 m und eine Tiefe von etwa 90 cm (Abb. 12).[65] Aufgrund der rekonstruierten Maße der Statuenbasis und der Lebensgröße der Kraniche von 115–130 cm wird es sich um ein monumentales Weihgeschenk gehandelt haben.

Das lateinische Wort für Kranich, *grus*, entspricht dem schnarrenden, trompetenden Ruf der größten Zugvögel Europas ("grrus grrus"), wenn sie im März und Oktober/

64 Galsterer & Galsterer 2010, 159–60 Nr. 172.
65 Gregarek 2004, 56–7; 2005, 142–3.

Abb. 12. Rekonstruktion des monumentalen Votivsockels für Merkur mit der figürlichen Darstellung von zwei Kranichen; nach GREGAREK 2004, 57 Abb. 22.

November in großen Schwärmen in V-Formation über die Lande ziehen.[66] Im ehemals gallisch-germanischen Raum sind Kraniche bis heute Boten des Frühlings beziehungsweise der herannahenden kalten Jahreszeit. Damit erschließt sich nicht nur eine Verbindung der Kraniche zum römischen Merkur, dem geflügelten Götterboten, sondern auch zu den bodenständigen Matronen. Die Ankunft der durchziehenden Kraniche verkündete sowohl den Beginn als auch das Ende des bäuerlichen Jahres.[67] In Niedergermanien sind die Kraniche daher mit den Fruchtbarkeitsgöttinnen, den einheimischen Matronen, inhaltlich verknüpft worden. Darstellungen von Kranichen finden sich auf Seitenreliefs von Matronensteinen.[68] Die enge Verbindung von Merkur und den Matronen auf dem Gebiet der CCAA geht anscheinend auf Vorstellungen der bodenständigen, agrarisch geprägten Bevölkerung zurück. Daneben werden sich die römischen Zuwanderer die Kulte schnell zu eigen gemacht haben, so dass eine Trennung nach der Herkunft der religiösen Akteure kaum mehr von Bedeutung war. Aufgrund seines Namens dürfte der Stifter der beiden Bronzekraniche – Primio, Sohn des Celissus – von einheimischer Abkunft gewesen sein.[69] In der Weihinschrift bezeichnete er sich selbst als *curialis*. Als Mitglied einer Kurie gehörte er zu einer Personengruppe, die sich zu einer Mahlgemeinschaft formiert hatte.[70] Die Teilnehmer waren wie eine religiöse Vereinigung organisiert, deren Zusammenhalt auf einem gemeinsamen Siedlungsraum, Wohnort oder verwandtschaftlichen Beziehungen gründete. Der ursprüngliche Standort des Kranichvotivs ist nicht bekannt. Die Statuenbasis dürfte nicht über eine allzu große Entfernung von ihrem Aufstellungsort nach St. Severin transportiert worden sein. Es liegt nahe, dass das Votiv für Merkur aus einem Heiligtum der römischen Vorstadt stammt.

Lokale Bezüge der Merkurverehrung in Köln erschließen sich auch im Giebelschmuck einer Aedikula aus Kalkstein, die angeblich in der Nähe der Severinstraße gefunden worden ist und damit aus dem Umfeld des südlichen Suburbium stammen würde (Abb.

66 Nowald & Dirks 2006.
67 Rüger 1987, 26.
68 Galsterer & Galsterer 2010, 160. Siehe auch den Nautenpfeiler aus Paris: Altjohann 2003, 67–79, Abb. 1.
69 Rüger 1987, 26–7.
70 Herz 2003, 141–5; Woolf 2003. Zu religiösen Vereinen allgemein: Egelhaaf-Gaiser & Schäfer 2002.

Abb. 13. Aedikula-Giebel für Merkur aus Köln, RGM Inv. 23, 61; Foto RBA 75 043.

13).[71] Im Giebelfeld ist ein figürliches Relief mit dem thronenden Merkur dargestellt. In seiner Rechten trägt der Gott den Heroldstab, während seine aufgestützte Linke vermutlich einen Geldbeutel hielt. Sein Oberkörper ist nackt und kräftig, sein Unterkörper wird von einem Mantel verhüllt, dessen Ende über den Rücken bis auf die linke Schulter geführt wird. Dargestellt ist nicht der knabenhafte Merkur, wie auf dem Weihrelief vom Georgsplatz (Abb. 5), sondern ein dem höchsten Gott Iuppiter angeglichener Gott auf dem Herrscherthron. Begleitet wird Merkur von der Glücksgöttin Fortuna mit Füllhorn und Steuerruder sowie vermutlich von Nemesis, der Schicksalsgöttin mit dem Ellenmaß. In den Zwickeln des Giebelfeldes befinden sich gelagerte Flussgottheiten. Im römischen Köln dachte der zeitgenössische Betrachter sicherlich zuerst an den Rhein (*Rhenus*), darauf an die Mosel (*Mosella*). Die beiden Flußgottheiten verweisen auf jenen Raum Galliens und Germaniens, in welchem Merkur eine besondere Verehrung zu Teil wurde. Seine dominierende Stellung im provinzialen Götterhimmel kommt in der herrschaftlichen Haltung auf dem Thron bildhaft zum Ausdruck. Eine Angleichung des Merkur an Iuppiter zeigt auch der Bildschmuck des Kranichvotivs (Abb. 12). Der Eichenlaubkranz, der auf der Vorderseite der Statuenbasis wiedergegeben wird, ist der Ikonographie des höchsten römischen Staatsgottes Iuppiter entlehnt.

Der Aedikula-Giebel für Merkur (Abb. 13 und 14) wurde aus einem Kalksteinblock gemeißelt. Mittel- und Unterteil der Votivnische sind separat gearbeitet und heute verloren. Die maximale Breite des Giebels beträgt 64 cm, die Höhe 25 cm und die Tiefe 19,5 cm. In die Sockelzone einer solchen Aedikula könnte die Inschriftenplatte mit der Weihung an *Mercurius Valdivahanus* eingelassen gewesen sein. Die Kalksteinplatte fällt mit ihren Maßen allerdings etwas zu groß aus (65 x 60 x 10 cm), um mit dem Merkur-Giebel in einem baulichen Zusammenhang stehen zu können.

5. In der südlichen Vorstadt der CCAA wird man mit einem oder mehreren

71 Ristow 1974, 139; Noelke 1990, 100 Abb. 15a; Hupe 1997, 68.

Abb. 14. Aedikula-Giebel für Merkur aus Köln, Detail, RGM Inv. 23, 61; Foto RBA 107 237.

Heiligtümern rechnen dürfen, in denen Merkur verehrt worden ist. Obgleich die überlieferten Weihedenkmäler aus sekundären Fundkontexten stammen, ist diese räumliche Zuordnung sehr wahrscheinlich. Insbesondere an kleineren Kapellen und Nischen dürfte der Kult des Merkur gepflegt worden sein. Die Einbindung in die nachbarschaftlich geprägte Gemeinschaft der städtischen Siedlung dürfte die Basis für die lokale Verehrung des Merkur gewesen sein. Darüber hinaus war ein Heiligtum für Merkur gerade im Umfeld des Suburbium sinnstiftend. Den Reisenden auf der Limesstraße stand es zur Wahl, als sie den Siedlungsgürtel der Stadt erreichten, ihre Ankunft mit dem Besuch eines solchen Heiligtums zu verbinden und dem Gott der Kaufleute und Reisenden für den gewährten Schutz zu danken.

6. Das Weihemonument für *Mercurius Valdivahanus* ist im Kontext lokaler Religionsausübung zu sehen, die sowohl zugewanderte römische Bürger als auch Angehörige der bodenständigen Bevölkerung auf dem Gebiet der CCAA zusammengeführt hat. Der Stifter des Weihemonuments für Merkur war Mitglied des Stadtrats. Für Lucius Carinius Sollemnis war Latein die maßgebliche Sprache, selbst wenn seine Familie ursprünglich auf ubische Vorfahren zurückginge. Da der Name Carinius in einer inschriftlichen Weihung aus Colijnsplaat in der niederländischen Provinz Zeeland überliefert ist, die sich gleichfalls an eine bodenständige Gottheit, die *Dea Nehalennia* richtet, ist eine ubisch-germanische oder keltische Herkunft des Kölner Dekurios nicht mit Sicherheit auszuschließen.[72] In jedem Fall ist es schwierig zu beurteilen, welche Bedeutung Lucius Carinius Sollemnis einer indigenen Sprache neben dem Lateinischen zumaß. Das Fortleben germanischer oder keltischer Namen muss nicht zwingend heißen, dass die Sprachen, auf die sie verweisen, noch lebendig geblieben waren.[73]

72 Weihung an *Dea Nehalennia* aus Colijnsplaat: *De(ae) | Nehalenniae L(ucius) Secundius | Similis et T(itus) Carinius | Gratus negotiatores | allecari v(otum) s(olverunt) l(ibentes) m(erito);* AE 1973, 365; vgl. de Bernardo Stempel 2004.

73 Eck 2004, 287.

Abb. 15. Weihealtar oder Statuenbasis für Merkur aus Sandstein, gefunden in Sechtem bei Bornheim, RGM Inv. 347; Foto RBA 33635.

7. Die ethnische Herkunft kann die Nähe des Kölner Dekurions zum Kult des *Mercurius Valdivahanus* nur bedingt erklären. Wichtig erscheint in diesem Zusammenhang die lokale Bedeutung des Merkur im südlichen Suburbium, dessen Kult für die Akteure so attraktiv gewesen ist, dass sie dem Götterboten und Schutzgott der Kaufleute und Reisenden persönliche Weihegaben hinterlegten. H. Galsterer nimmt in diesem Beitrag gleichfalls an, dass der Kölner Dekurio Carinius schon vor seinem Tod Beziehungen zum Heiligtum in der Vorstadt aufgenommen hatte.

8. Dass auch Frauen, insbesondere einheimische Ubierinnen an der Verehrung des Merkur aktiv teilnahmen, belegt ein Weihealtar oder eine Statuenbasis aus dem Territorium des römischen Köln (Abb. 15).[74] Der Weihestein wurde in Sechtem bei Bornheim gefunden. Das figürliche Relief der Hauptseite zeigt drei Personen, die an einem Altar ein unblutiges Opfer darbringen. Rechts und links des Altars steht je eine Frau, die mit einem hoch gegürteten Untergewand und einem Mantel bekleidet ist. Die größere der beiden Frauen zeichnet sich durch eine so genannte Matronenhaube aus, die ein einheimisch-ubisches Trachtelement der verheirateten Frauen ist. Gegenüber der Frau mit dem offenen langen Haar wird ihr der höhere soziale Rang zugewiesen. Diese Stellung kommt auch in ihrer Körpergröße bildlich zum Ausdruck (‚Bedeutungsgröße'). Die eigentliche Ausführung des Opfers kommt der verheirateten Frau zu. Die andere Frau am linken Bildrand nimmt gleichwohl an der sakralen Handlung teil. Die kleinere männliche Gestalt im Hintergrund, die einen gallischen Mantel übergeworfen hat, stellt einen Opferdiener dar. Die Inschrift des Weihesteins ist diesmal oberhalb der Opferszene eingemeißelt:

74 Yeo & Bauchhenß 1990; Galsterer & Galsterer 2010, 158–9 Nr. 171.

Mercurio Iul(iae) / Terti(a) et Nativa / v(otum) s(olverunt) l(ibentes) [m(erito)].

Die beiden genannten Frauen haben ihr gemeinsames Gelübde für Merkur dankbar erfüllt, da ihre Bitten erhört wurden. Im Bildschmuck des Weihesteins ließen sich die Stifterinnen bei der einmalig ausgeführten Opferhandlung wiedergeben und dokumentierten auf diese Weise dauerhaft ihr eingelöstes Gelübde. Der Weihestein ist als Erinnerungsmonument zu verstehen.

9. In Kenntnis des Weihesteins aus Sechtem bei Bornheim, der aus dem weiten Territorium der CCAA stammt, ist abschließend auf das Weihemonument für *Mercurius Valdivahanus* vom Kölner Waidmarkt zurückzukommen. Gemäß dem Testament des Stadtrats Lucius Carinius Sollemnis hat Milia Rhenas nicht nur das Weihemonument mit Hilfe des bereit gestellten Geldbetrages errichtet, sondern sicherlich auch das obligatorische Opfer vollzogen. Zur Errichtung des Weihemonuments für Merkur mit der germanischen Anrufung *Valdivahanus* gehörte eine Opferhandlung, die das Weihgeschenk in einem rituellen Akt übergab. Das Opfer selbst ging nicht auf bodenständige Rituale des Ubiergebietes zurück, sondern entsprach römischer Religionspraxis.

2.4 Zusammenfassung

Im Umfeld der südlichen römischen Vorstadt von Köln kam dem Kult des Merkur anscheinend eine besondere lokale Bedeutung zu. Für den Stadtrat Lucius Carinius Sollemnis war der Kult so attraktiv, dass er in seinem Testament Milia Rhenas beauftragte, dem Gott ein Weihedenkmal für 4.000 Sesterzen zu errichten. Möglicherweise handelte es sich um eine architektonisch gefasste Nische für ein Götterbild, in deren Sockel die Weihinschrift eingelassen war. Gemäß der persönlichen Entscheidung des Stifters wurde der römische Merkur mit einer spezifischen germanischen Anrufung, *Mercurius Valdivahanus*, verehrt. Eine besondere Nähe zum Kult des *Mercurius Valdivahanus* wird man gleichfalls der Testamentsvollstreckerin Milia Rhenas zusprechen dürfen. Ihr kam wahrscheinlich zu, das Weihegeschenk des Testamentgebers im Rahmen einer römischen Opferhandlung dem Gott darzubringen.

3. Mercurius Valdivahanus, deus Requalivahanus aus Blatzheim an der Neffel und die Deutung der neuen Inschrift aus dem Kölner Waidmarkt[75] (PdBS)

Die hier besprochene, sorgfältig gemeißelte Kölner Weihinschrift wurde im Februar 2011 auf der Unterseite der Abdeckplatte einer ungestörten und von Mitarbeitern des Römisch-Germanischen Museums der Stadt Köln ausgegrabenen Brandbestattung des späten 3. Jhs. gefunden.[76] Wahrscheinlich ist, dass die Kalksteinplatte mit der Votivinschrift in ein religiöses Denkmal eingelassen gewesen war, das sich im Umfeld des südlichen Suburbium der Kolonie befand. Dennoch weiß man nicht, ob zwischen dem mutmaßlichen religiösen Denkmal und der Bestattung / dem Bestatteten eine Beziehung bestanden hatte.

Der Text der Inschrift ist sehr deutlich (Abb. 16). Das lateinische Formular wird von den Entdeckern folgendermaßen aufgelöst:[77]

Abb. 16. Römische Weihinschrift für Mercurius Valdivahanus, Umzeichnung: Römisch Germ. Museum der Stadt Köln Inv. 2010, 95 / S. Haase.

Mercurio /
Valdivahano /
Milia Rhenas /
ex-testamento /
L(ucii)Carin^i Sollemn^is /
dec(urionis) C(oloniae) C(laudiae) A(rae) A(grippinensium) ex /
(sestertium) n(ummum) quattuor mil(ibus).

Daraus ergibt sich *primo visu* die folgende Übersetzung: "Dem Mercurius Valdivahanus (stiftete) Milia Rhenas aufgrund des Testaments von Lucius Carinius Sollemnis, Decurio von Colonia Claudia Ara Agrippinensium, mit viertausend Sesterzen".

Bei näherer Betrachtung der sprachlichen Form der Inschrift stellt man jedoch fest, dass deren indigene Elemente z.T. eindeutig germanisch sind, z.T. aber erst aus der Germanisierung einer bestehenden keltischen Vorlage hervorgegangen sind. Es zeigt sich ebenfalls – wie wir in §3.2 dieser Ausführungen en détail sehen werden –, dass der Testamentsvollstrecker und Ausführer der Stiftung trotz des Ausgangs *-a* seines Vornamens kaum eine Frau war, worauf *Rhenas* selbst an und für sich schon hinweist.

75 Mein Dank geht an Helmut Birkhan, Alfred Schäfer und Manfred Hainzmann, ohne deren Hilfe mein Beitrag nicht in dieser Form hätte entstehen können.

76 Näheres in Schäfer & Wieland 2011. Vgl. auch den Beitrag von H. Galsterer und A. Schäfer mit weiterem Abbildungsmaterial und de Bernardo Stempel 2014a.

77 Schäfer & Wieland 2011, 44.

3.1 Merkurs Beiname Valdivahanos und Devs Reqvalivahanos[78]

Bevor wir uns der Analyse des auf den unmittelbar vorausgehenden Dativ *Mercurio* bezogenen *Valdivahano* widmen können, müssen wir erst die Struktur und Etymologie der westlich von Köln belegten Votivformel *deo Requalivahano* untersuchen, die das gleiche zweite Kompositionsglied enthält. Die angesprochene *vahano*-Parallele wurde in Blatzheim a. d. Neffel "auf dem Emmerich" gefunden: Es handelt sich um die Inschrift *CIL* XIII 8512 (= *ILS* 4737, *n.v.*), "nunc Bonn in museo", die u.a. von Weisgerber (1968, 44) erfasst ist und folgendermaßen lautet (Abb. 17):

DEO · REQV^AL^IV^AH
ANO · Q · APRIANVS
FRVCTVS · EX · I^M^P · PRO
SE · E^T · SVOS · V · S ·L · M

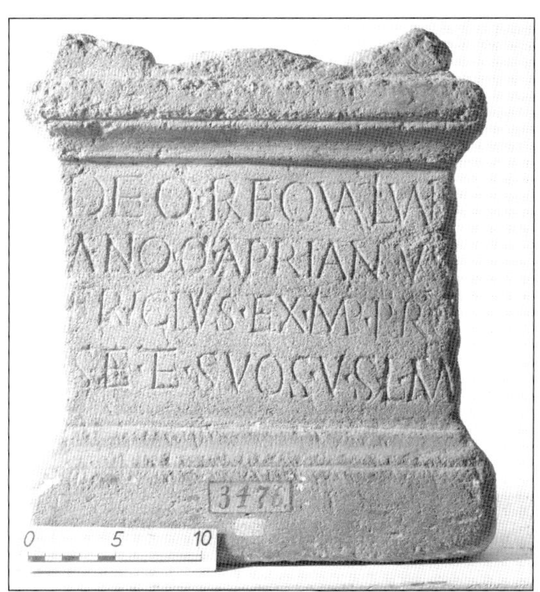

Abb. 17. Weihealtar für den Deus Requalivahanus aus Blatzheim; Foto Rheinisches Landesmuseum Bonn Inv. 3476.

Als Minuskeltranskription ergibt sich:

Deo Requalivah/ano
Q(uintus) Aprian<i>us / Fructus
ex imp(erio) pro / se et suos
v(otum) s(olvit) l(ibens) m(erito).

Der in seiner Originalform als *Reqvalivahanos* zu restituierende göttliche Titel ist schon lange und zu Recht mit der Finsternis in Verbindung gebracht und im Sinne eines Unterweltsgottes gedeutet worden, vgl. u.a. Simek: "am ehesten zu einem german. Wort *rehwaz 'Finsternis' zu stellen [...] Dies könnte auf einen Unterweltsgott deuten [...]".[79] Das geschieht aufgrund der indogermanischen Basis neutrius generis **reg*^{w}*os* 'Dunkelheit', die u.a. in armenisch *erek* 'Abend' und nicht zuletzt in ἔρεβος, dem griechischen Wort für das Dunkel der Unterwelt, fortlebt (*IEW*, S. 857). Im Germanischen erscheint dieselbe Basis aufgrund der ersten Lautverschiebung regelmäßig mit stimmlosem Labiovelar bzw. Velar in gotisch *riqis* – mit Genitiv *riqizis* (*GED*, R16) – und altnordisch *røkkr* 'Dunkel' (*AEW*, S. 456).

Der wiederholte Fund eines (dativischen) *-vahano* am Kölner Waidmarkt hat aber inzwischen gezeigt, dass der erste, frühgermanische Bestandteil des Kompositums

78 Hier und im Folgenden werden alle im Nominativ restituierten Götternamen mittels *kursiver Kapitälchen* wiedergegeben, während die einfache *Kursivschrift* unveränderten Belegformen vorbehalten ist. In derartig restituierten Nominativen werden dann auch die etymologisch ursprünglichen, noch nicht latinisierten Endungen eingesetzt, also *-os* und nicht etwa *-us* für die *o*-Stämme.

79 Simek 2006, 346 mit Literatur. Es sei am Rande angemerkt, dass dort das häufige Cognomen *Fructus* (*OPEL* II, S. 153) missverstanden und für einen Akkusativ Plural des lateinischen Appellativs *fructus* gehalten wird.

Requali- ist[80] und somit ein Suffix *-li-* enthält, das in der Indogermania zur Bildung von Adjektiven gebraucht wurde, wie z.B. in lat. *facilis*.[81] *Requali-* war also im Prinzip ein Adjektiv und bedeutete nicht bloß 'Finsternis', sondern 'zur Finsternis gehörend' oder 'finster'.

In dem wegen der früheren, überholten Segmentierung bisher ungedeutet gebliebenen Element *-VAHANOS* lässt sich das mittlere *-h-* nicht als keltische Fortsetzung eines indogermanischem **p* oder **s* erklären, somit weist es auf einen germanisch verschobenen stimmlosen (Labio-)Velar hin. Dieselbe Entwicklung vermag auch Matronennamensuffixe wie *-(an/in-)e(i)hae* < *-(an/in-)icae*, *-ahae* < *-acae*, *-ehiae* < *-eciae* zu erklären, zusammen mit dem neuen, aus der Metanalyse von Kompositis mit **ahwa+-inae* entstandenen Morphem *-henae*: Für sie alle braucht man nämlich nunmehr kein /j/ zu postulieren.[82]

Dementsprechend lässt sich *-VAHANOS*, gemäß einem freundlichen Hinweis von Helmut Birkhan, problemlos auf jenes schwache germanische Verb zurückführen, das im Althochdeutschen als *giwahanen* 'etwas erwähnen, sagen' und v.a. 'jemandes gedenken; denken an' (*AW*, S. 307) fortgesezt wird und denominal aus einem substantivierten Partizip der indogermanischen Verbalwurzel **wek*^{w}*-* 'sprechen' (*IEW*, S. 1135f.; *LIV*, S. 674) gebildet wurde. Wortbildungsmäßig handelt es sich um ein einfaches Nomen agentis mit Stammvokal *-o-*,[83] also 'der gedenkt' bzw. vermutlich – als Gott – fürsorgt.

Betrachten wir nun das Votivformular *Deo reqvalivahano* als ganzes, so kann es entweder als drei- oder als zweigliedrig verstanden werden. Im ersten Fall (a) hätten wir ein theonymisches Determinativ (*deus*)[84] gefolgt von zwei als getrennt zu verstehenden Epitheta, nämlich *Requali* als Dativ von *REQVALIS* 'finster' und *Vahano* als Dativ von *VAHANOS* 'fürsorgend'. Das Formular wäre demnach als 'dem finsteren und gedenkenden Gott' zu übersetzen. Alternativ (b) müßte auf das theonymische Determinativ *deus* eine Zusammensetzung *REQVALIVAHANOS* folgen, was aufgrund der *ordinatio* des Textes und der Verteilung der Worttrenner eher zuzutreffen scheint. Eine derartige Zusammensetzung würde demnach den Gott als einen 'dunklen Gedenker' beschreiben. Man sollte dabei allerdings anmerken, dass gerade die Bildung auf *–li–* des 1. Gliedes gegen hohes Alter und für eine rezente Zusammenrückung spräche. Denn die beschreibenden Determinativkomposita der Struktur {Adjektiv + Substantiv}, die schon für das Indogermanische rekonstruiert werden, enthalten im Prinzip nur Primäradjektive, meist mit Fugenvokal *-o-*.

Bevor unten in §3.3 auf den semantischen Inhalt beider Votivformulare näher eingegangen wird, kehren wir jetzt zum neuen *Valdivahano* zurück. Wir haben gesehen,

80 Stattdessen operierten frühere Etymologen – wie es sich aus Lehmanns *GED* (R16) ergibt – mit einer anderen und inzwischen überholten Segmentierung des Götternamens *Requalivahanos*.

81 Vgl. Krahe & Meid 1967, 88 §88; ferner *NWÄI*, S. 222ff.

82 Vgl. de Bernardo Stempel 2004, 183 mit Anm. 22. Daher ist u.a. Neumann 1987, 106–7 obsolet.

83 Krahe & Meid 1967, 58–9; *NWÄI*, S. 38 u. 44–5.

84 Der Terminus bezeichnet den Rang des erwähnten göttlichen Wesens (hier *deus* im Gegensatz zu *lar*, *genius*, *nympha* u.Ä.) und kann in Verbindung mit einem Beinamen den eigentlichen Namen (Theonym) der involvierten Gottheit vertreten, vgl. de Bernardo Stempel 2008a, 65–6.

dass das Element *(-)VAHANOS* eine Erklärung als thematisches Nomen agentis zu althochdeutsch *giwahanen* 'gedenken; denken' finden kann. Auch der *i*-Stamm *VALDI*- lässt sich problemlos als Nomen agentis bestimmen, und zwar mit der Bedeutung 'Leiter, Lenker' bzw. 'Herrscher'. Es gehört nämlich zum gesamtgermanischen Verb für 'leiten, lenken', das u.a. als gotisch *waldan*, altisländisch *valda* und — mit zweiter Lautverschiebung — als neuhochdeutsch *walten* fortgesetzt wird.[85] Der alte agentive *i*-Stamm erscheint im Altisländischen zum Nasalstamm erweitert, vgl. das Kompositionselement *-valdi* 'Herrscher', das als *jan*-Stamm u.a. im Adjektiv *sjalfvaldi* 'unabhängig < *selbstherrschend', in zusammmengesetzten Personennamen wie der 'sehr mächtige' *Alvaldi* und nicht zuletzt im Götternamen *Ívaldi* belegt ist.[86] Dasselbe Lexem **wald-* 'Herrscher' erscheint als Hinterglied in altgermanischen *o*-stämmigen Namenkompositis, die in der Römerzeit als Cognomina fungieren, wie u.a. - mit latinisierter Kasusendung - *Ragno(v)aldus /Rainovaldus* und *Rando(v)aldus* aus Germania superior.[87] Dazu zählt auch der 'Heereswalter' *Chariovalda*, ein von Tacitus erwähnter *dux Batavorum*,[88] dessen Name über Protogermanisch **Xariovaldaz* auf indogermanisch **Koryo-wald^h-o-s* zurückgeht. Dasselbe Lexem ist auch in vielerlei komponierten Namen aus späterer Zeit enthalten, darunter *Arnold, Friedwald, Gerwald* sowie - mit modernisierter syntaktischer Reihenfolge - *Waldemar, Walt(h)er* u.v.a.m.

Es gibt vier Gründe, die uns einen Anschluss an **walþu-*, das germanische Lexem für 'Wald',[89] verwerfen lassen: 1.) morphologisch, denn unser *VALDI*- ist *i*-stämmig, der germanische Wald aber *u*-stämmig; 2.) semantisch, denn eine unmittelbare Verbindung von Merkur und dem Wald ist nicht ohne weiteres gegeben, weder in der klassischen noch in der keltischsprachigen Antike, zumal *Viduco* jetzt als Eigenname des in Burdigala an Merkur dedizierenden *cives* (sic) *Lemovic(us)* aufgefasst wird;[90] 3.) syntaktisch, denn die hier vorgezogene Analyse impliziert eine größere Parallelität zwischen unseren beiden theonymischen Epitheta; 4.) und schließlich auch lautlich, denn zu der Zeit unseres Dokuments wäre der stimmlose Dental des dem 'Wald' zugrundeliegenden indogermanischen Etymons vermutlich noch nicht als stimmhafter Verschlusslaut wiedergegeben worden.

Somit ergäben sich für die Votivformel *Mercurio valdivahano* auch zwei Möglichkeiten der Analyse: a) als einfache Aneinanderreihung zweier Appositionen, 'der Lenker, der Gedenker', oder (b) als beschreibendes Determinativkompositum der Struktur {Substantiv$_1$ + Substantiv$_2$} wie in dem 'ein Seher, der ein Brahmane ist' bedeutenden altindischen Kompositionstyp *brāhmarṣi*. Die äußerst sorgfältige Ausführung der Inschrift vom Waidmarkt lässt allerdings die Interpretationshypothese

85 Vgl. Krahe & Meid 1967, 65ff.; *GED*, W24; *IEW*, S. 1111-2; *LIV*, 676-7.
86 *AEW*, S. 641 u. 288; Nedoma 2001, 46-7 §17.1.
87 Kakoschke 2006-2008, Bd. 2/2, 249-50 mit Bibliographie.
88 Kakoschke 2006-2008, Bd. 2/1, 236.
89 Kluge & Seebold 1989, 774; *EWD*, S. 1533; *IEW*, S. 1139f.
90 Ich berufe mich hier zum einen auf eine typologische Untersuchung der Epiheta und Epiklesen klassischer Gottheiten, die von Frau Dr. Milena Hienz de Albentiis (Bonn) im Rahmen des Projekts F.E.R.C.AN. durchgeführt wird, zum anderen auf *ILA-Bordeaux* 8.

(a) so gut wie verwerfen. Demgegenüber wird die Interpretationshypothese (b) dadurch gestützt, dass es im Germanischen gute Parallelen für den erwähnten indogermanischen Kompositionstyp gibt, in dem "Die beiden Glieder [...] das gleiche Objekt unter verschiedenen Gesichtspunten" bezeichnen.[91] Parallelbeispiele zu unserem *VALDIVAHANOS* als 'Lenker (und) Gedenker' wären der 'Freund (und) Gefolgsherr' im altenglischen *wine-dryhten* oder der 'Verwandte (und) Freund' in altsächsisch *māg-wini*, altenglisch *mæg-wine / wine-mæg*. Letzteres ist auch als Personenname *Mēguini / Mēguine* belegt.[92]

Wir können also davon ausgehen, dass der römische *MERCVRIVS* in Köln mit einem germanischen Funktionsbeinamen angerufen wurde, der die Gottheit zur gleichen Zeit als Lenker und als Fürsorger (wörtl. Gedenker) beschrieb und auf den wir inhaltlich in §3.3 näher eingehen werden.

3.2 Die Namen des Dedikanten und des Ausführenden der Weihung

Die erste Frage, die sich in diesem Zusammenhang aufdrängt, ist die nach dem Geschlecht des Ausführenden der testamentarischen Widmung im Auftrag eines Stadtrates von Köln, zumal in der Inschrift eine jener weiblichen Appositionen fehlt, die – wie *uxor, soror, filia, mater, nutrix* o.ä. – sonst üblicherweise das Verhältnis der agierenden Frau zum Verstorbenen spezifizieren.

Zwar könnte *Milia* der Eigenname einer Frau sein, der Zusatz *Rhenas* wirft aber bei einer derartigen – und keineswegs zwingenden – Geschlechtszuweisung gravierende Probleme auf:

1. In der Narbonensis und Italien ist ein Maskulinum *Rhenus* als Cognomen belegt, das zudem in Britannien als Nomen erscheint; dazu gehören auch die in Belgica, Lugdunensis und Pannonien gebrauchten maskulinen Ableitungen *Rhenicus, Rhenicius* und *Rhenanus*, sowie *Renicos* in Germania superior und *Rénnicus* in der Belgica.[93] Es handelt sich um eine hier als Cognomen umfunktionierte Herkunftsangabe, die auf der keltischen Version des bekannten Hydronyms beruht. Der ursprüngliche Name des Flusses war im Indogermanischen **Rei-no-s* 'der Fließende'; aus der einen Form ergaben sich aber – wegen der in historischer Zeit dokumentierten Zweisprachigkeit des betreffenden Gebietes – zwei Fortsetzungen, eine vollständig germanische *Rīnaz*, die im heutigen Flußnamen *Rhein* weiterlebt, und eine – davon unabhängige – keltische, nämlich *Rēnus*, die noch im Namen des italienischen Flusses *Reno*, unweit von Bologna, zu finden ist[94] und der Herkunftsangabe *Rhenus* sowie ihren Ableitungen zugrunde liegt. Eine etwaige feminine Herkunftsangabe dazu könnte aber nur ***Rhena* lauten, weil weder die keltische noch die lateinische Grammatik eine dentalstämmige Femininbildung bzw. -motion kennt.

91 Ilkow 1968, 19.
92 Ilkow 1968, 270-1.
93 *OPEL* IV, S. 29; *NPS*, S. 153; Kakoschke 2006-2008, Bd. 2.2, 261.
94 Vgl. De Bernardo Stempel 2000, 411. Belege in *DCCPIN*, S. 187.

2.1. Von einem mutmaßlichen *ā*-stämmigen Femininum **Rhena* könnte sich *Rhenas* nur als Rest des alten Genitiv Singular auf *-as* erklären lassen, d.h. als ein in unserem Kontext eher unerwarteter Archaismus.

2.2. Das Namenelement *Rhenas* müßte dann eine der allenthalben seltenen metronymischen Angaben darstellen.

2.3. Ein angebliches Metronymikon *Rhenas* würde die eher unerwartete Verwendung des auch ansonsten unbelegten **Rhena* als weiblicher Vorname statt als Cognomen voraussetzen.

Die Anhäufung von nicht weniger als drei unmotivierten Annahmen lässt nun selbst die einzig gangbare zweite Hypothese nicht ansprechend erscheinen und mindert somit die Wahrscheinlichkeit, dass der Testamentvollstrecker eine Frau gewesen sei, nicht unerheblich.

Demgegenüber suggeriert uns gerade das germanische Sprachmilieu, das an dem Beinamen Merkurs festgestellt wurde, eine alternative Möglichkeit, die alle Probleme zu lösen vermag: Die bei der Namenformel des Ausführenden der Weihung erscheinenden Endungen *-a* des Idionyms (*Milia*) und *-as* des Appositivs (*Rhenas*: keine Vatersangabe!) können nämlich problemlos die germanisch lautgesetzlichen Reflexe von **-o* bzw. **-os* darstellen. Bei dieser Annahme (3.) würden beide Elemente zusammen, also *Milia* plus *Rhenas*, die Namenformel eines Mannes ausmachen — ein Geschlecht, das bei einer derartig prominenten und aufwendigen Weihung keineswegs unpassender als das weibliche erscheint.

Im Einzelnen ließe sich das Idionym *Milia* als Germanisierung von *Milio* erklären. Ein *Milio* ist u.a. aus Aquincum /Pannonien als Vatersname eines keltisch benannten *Eburos* belegt, und derselbe Nasalstamm wird auch durch den u.a. in Germania inferior belegten *Milionius* vorausgesetzt.[95] Innerhalb des Keltischen scheint der betreffende Name zu dem nicht zuletzt aus Hispanien, der Narbonensis und Belgica bekannten Typ *Milus /Mila*, *Milo* zu gehören, der am ehesten zu einem "Semantem 'klein', kelt. **mīlo-* (aus [idg.] **mēlo-*) in air. *míl*, kymr. *mil* '(kleines) Tier'" zu stellen ist.[96] Die Voraussetzung ist zwar, dass der auslautende Vokal des Nasalstammes bei der Germanisierung zu *-a* umgewandelt worden wäre, aber man darf daran erinnern, dass auf *-a* endende Männernamen sich ohne weiteres unter den von Weisgerber (1968) der germanischen bzw. germanisierten Namenschicht zugeschriebenen Idionymen finden lassen, vgl. nicht zuletzt *Sidua* auf einem Soldatenstein (S. 153). Parallelen für den m.E. aus *Milio* germanisierten *Milia* bieten *Atissa eques* aus dem in Bad Kreuznach belegten, konservativeren keltischen *Attisso*[97] und das Cognomen von *L. Val(erius) Sera, miles* in Eisenberg, weil *Sera* sich als Germanisierung des auch (u.a.) in Germania superior

95 Kakoschke 2006–2008, Bd. 2.2, 491.

96 Meid (2005, 236–7), der auch alternativ an hypokoristische Rückbildung aus einem Personennamen wie *Miletumaros* 'groß an Zerstörung' denkt (Meid 2005, 237 u. 111); man beachte allerdings, dass das *-i-* bei letzterem erst kontextbedingt aus kurzem **e* entstanden ist. Vgl. auch *NPC*, S. 133 u. 237. *OPEL* III, S. 81.

97 Kakoschke 2006–2008, Bd. 2.1, 131 bzw. 136 (wofür *NPC*, S. 31, "*Terentius Atisso*" mit Vereinfachung der ersten Geminate anführt).

belegten lateinischen Cognomen *Sero* erklärt, von dem ebenfalls in derselben Provinz auch die Varianten *Serro* und *Serus* bekannt sind.[98] Von Männern getragene Cognomina wie *Magissa* und – mit germanisch spirantisiertem Velar – *Manchissa* könnten ebenfalls auf ursprüngliche Namen wie **Magisso* bzw. **Mancisso* (zu lat. *mancus* oder *Manca*?) zurückgehen.[99]

Das zweite Element der ersten Namenformel wäre – wie wir bereits gesehen haben – die für Männer wiederholt belegte, keltische Herkunftsangabe *Rhenus*, lediglich mit Germanisierung der etymologisch ursprünglichen Endung **-os* in *-as*.[100] Parallelen dazu liegen anscheinend in dem Namen des Töpfers *Oenias* aus Rheinzabern für den aus Noricum bekannten *Oinius* und, falls die entsprechende Kölner Inschrift echt sein sollte, in *Valgas* für den normalen lateinischen *Valgus* vor.[101] Auch der Name *Aduara[s?]* eines Dedikanten an die Muttergottheiten *Austriahenae* in Germania inferior wäre, wenn es sich um einen Mann handelte, hierher einzuordnen, denn die betreffende Variante scheint – mit Verschriftung der im ursprünglichen Kompositum **Ate-maro-* entstandenen Lenierungen – zu dem anderswo belegten keltischen *Admarus*[102] zu gehören.

Was nun Germanisierungen im Allgemeinen – und überhaupt den Fragenkomplex der Umgestaltung fremdsprachlichen onomastischen Materials – betrifft, ist es vielleicht nicht überflüssig, an einige onomastische Fakten zu erinnern:

1. Nicht alle Germanen trugen sprachlich germanische Namen, darunter der berühmte Germanenführer *Ariovistus*.[103] Dasselbe gilt sogar für diejenigen, die sich selbst als *Germ(anus/ana)* bezeichneten: Keltische Namen trugen z.B. *Maduhus Germ.* in Britannien und *Braetia Germana* in der Belgica.[104] Und dies gilt schließlich genauso nicht zuletzt für Kelten und Römer sowie im Prinzip für alle Völker bis zum heutigen Tage.[105]

2. Anpassungen der Namen an das Lateinische waren – wie bei den Kelten – auch bei den Germanen sehr beliebt. Dabei konnte entweder das gesamte sprachliche Zeichen involviert werden (Weisgerber [1968, 405] spricht sogar von "Namenromanisierung", weil in dem von ihm untersuchten Gebiet römisch-mittelländische Namenstämme ganze 78% der gesamten Namenbelege ausmachen), oder auch bloß die Kasusendungen. Daher weisen längst nicht alle indigenen Namen die je nach sprachlicher Zugehörigkeit zu erwartende Endung auf. Einen solchen Fall stellt nicht zuletzt die wiederholte

98 Die Belege in Kakoschke 2006–2008, Bd. 2.2, 322, 324 und 325; Kajanto 1982, 295.

99 Belege in Kakoschke 2006–2008, Bd. 2.2, 63 bzw. 70–1.

100 Zu der Struktur von Namenformeln im Allgemeinen vgl. de Bernardo Stempel 2010–2011, wo auf S. 92 auf Herkunftsangaben eingegangen wird.

101 Für die Belege vgl. Kakoschke 2006–2008, Bd. 2.2, 161 bzw. 423 mit Bibliographie; *NTS*, Bd. 6, S. 277; *NPC*, S. 144; Kajanto 1982, 242.

102 Kakoschke 2006–2008, Bd. 2.1, 65 und *NPC*, S. 12.

103 Dazu Ködderitzsch 1986, 201ff.

104 Insbesondere stellt *Maduhus* in *RIB* 1526 die Teilgermanisierung eines keltischen **Maducos* bei gleichzeitiger Latinisierung der ererbten Endung *-os* in *-us* dar, vgl. auch *NPC*, S. 122; Kakoschke 2006–2008, Bd. 2.1, 315. Für *Braetia* vgl. ebenda, S. 47, sowie Kakoschke 2010, 61.

105 Personennamen werden eben sehr stark Moden unterworfen. Außerdem hat „Die ausführliche Diskussion [...] inzwischen ergeben, dass die Übereinstimmung von archäologischer Kultur und Ethnos zwar möglich, aber doch eher die Ausnahme von der Regel ist": Fischer 2007, 313.

Dativendung *-o* von *-vahano* dar: Da die frühgermanische Dativendung eines thematischen Substantivs im Singular *-ai* lautete, wäre nämlich bei einer echtgermanischen Form ***Valdivahanai* oder zumindest ***Valdivahane* zu erwarten gewesen.[106]

3. Die Intensität der einzelnen Germanisierungen variiert je nach Milieu, Ort und v.a. Zeit, zumal nicht alle Lautwandelphänomene (Isoglossen) am gleichen Ort zur gleichen Zeit stattgefunden haben. Es genüge hier an theonymische Varianten wie *Bergviahenae* > *Berhviahenae* (für die Muttergottheiten **Bergusiacinae* zur keltisch benannten Erhabenen Göttin *Bergvsia*) oder *Ambiomarcae* > *Ambiamarcae* (für **Ambiobrogae*, 'Die um die Marken Wohnenden' Muttergottheiten, mit zusätzlicher lexikalischer Germanisierung des zweiten Kompositionsgliedes) zu erinnern.[107]

4. Partielle Germanisierungen sind u.a. in Personennamen wie *Hurmio* aus keltisch **Curmio* 'Der des Biers', *Hunatto* aus **Cunatto* oder den im Vokalismus angepassten *Namantabagius comes* aus Mainz zu sehen, die den in anderen Provinzen belegten keltischen *Curmillus*, *Curmisagius* bzw. *Cunetus*, *Cunit(t)us*, *Cunaito* und dem 'Feindesbrecher' *Namantobogios* zur Seite stehen.[108] Eine gänzliche Germanisierung scheint in *Iladecda* aus Germania superior (Dijon) vorzuliegen,[109] das sich problemlos auf keltisch **Ilótextos* aus indogermanisch **pelu-tekt-o-s* 'Vielbesitzer' zurückführen lässt. Besonders interessant in unserem Kontext ist auch jener *C. Challinius Paternus*, der zwischen 150 und 230 in Lechenich den Muttergottheiten *Lanehiae* widmet, denn beiden Namen enthalten ein germanisiertes keltisches /k/: Ihre Vorformen waren **Callinius* 'Der zum Wald Gehörige' und **Lánaciae*, entweder 'Die (mit guten Gaben) Angefüllten' oder 'Die zum Flachland Gehörigen'.[110] Selbst ein griechischer Name wie Σωτηρικός erscheint in Bern teilgermanisiert – und ebenfalls mit lateinischer Flexionsendung – als *Soterichus*, und *Scato* könnte in Mainz auf *Scot(t)o* zurückgehen.[111]

5. (Teil-)Germanisierungen keltischer Namen sind auch aus der indigenen Theonymie der germanischen Provinzen sehr gut bekannt. Stellvertretend sei hier vorerst auf drei Typen hingewiesen: i.) die Muttergottheiten, *Gesahenae* entweder für **Gesatenae* 'Die zum Stamme der – keltisch benannten – *Gēsates* Gehörigen', oder für **Gesacinae* 'Die zum – keltisch benannten – Gott *Gesacos* Gehörigen, mit phonetisch germanisiertem Suffix; ii.) die Matres *Mediotavtehae* für **Mediotouticae* 'Die zum mittleren Stamm(esgebiet) Gehörigen', mit – phonetisch gesehen – teilgermanisiertem zweitem Kompositionsglied und vollgermanisiertem Suffix (bei ebenfalls latinisierter Kasusendung!); iii.) die durchweg phonetisch germanisierte *Hlvdana* aus **Clutónā* 'Die Berühmte'.[112]

Die Germanisierung keltischer Namen war also kein allumfassendes Phänomen,

106 Vgl. Ramat 1988.
107 Weitere Details in de Bernardo Stempel 2005, 142.
108 Kakoschke 2006–2008, Bd. 2.1, 413, bzw. Bd. 2.2, 496 u. 137. Auf Germanisierung könnte auch der Vokalismus von *Tagamas* in Colijnsplaat zurückgehen, dem in Vindolanda eine konservativere Form *Tagomas* des Nominativs gegenübersteht, cf. *NPC*, S. 176 und Kakoschke 2006–2008, Bd. 2.2, 373.
109 Kakoschke 2006–2008, Bd. 2.1, 422.
110 De Bernardo Stempel 2005, 143 mit Bibliographie; Kakoschke 2006–2008, Bd. 1, 136.
111 Kakoschke 2006–2008, Bd. 2.2, 351 bzw. 300.
112 Vgl. de Bernardo Stempel 2005, 143 mit weiterer Bibliographie.

wenn auch in der betreffenden Region gar nicht so selten.[113] Jedenfalls war die Menge männlicher Namen auf *-a* im Römischen Reich doch so groß,[114] dass auch die damaligen Leser der Inschrift vom Waidmarkt kaum automatisch auf eine Frau hätten schließen können.

Was die Namenformel des eigentlichen Dedikanten angeht, so ist sie im Prinzip römisch. Dennoch dürfte zumindest der vermutlich darin enthaltene *Carinius* angesichts des Töpfers *Carinus* in Lezoux, von *Carinatius* und *Carinanus* in Narbonensis und Britannien, sowie der in der Keltiké recht verbreiteten Typen *Carilos /Carillus / Carilla, Carisius /Carissa / Carisso* u.dgl. (*NPC*, S. 58) als Deck- oder auch als echter Übersetzungsname in Bezug zu einer gallischen Vorlage (*Carinos*?) gestanden haben. Dasselbe gilt – wie schon 2004 erarbeitet[115] – für den an die Göttin *NEHALENNIA* dedizierenden *Carinius*.

Aus dem bisher Gesagten geht also hervor, dass der Handelnde in der neuen Kölner Inschrift vom Waidmarkt ein inzwischen Germanisch sprechender Kelte war, der, als Testamentsvollstrecker für einen römischen Beamten ebenfalls keltischer Abstammung fungierend, einer (gräko-)römischen Gottheit mit z.T. germanischer Anrufung huldigte.

3.3 Das Phänomen indigener Interpretationes und eine mögliche 'Explicatio Germanica'

Nachdem wir die formale Seite der Inschrift einigermaßen geklärt haben, können wir dazu übergehen, die inhaltliche Seite der Götternamen *VALDIVAHANOS* und *REQVALIVAHANOS* zu durchleuchten.

Obwohl *DEVS REQVALIVAHANOS* traditionell für den Namen einer selbständigen germanischen Gottheit gehalten wird, besteht eigentlich keine Evidenz dafür, dass es so sein muss. Im Gegenteil, der inzwischen zutage getretene *VALDIVAHANOS* als ebenfalls germanisches Epitheton des Merkur macht es viel wahrscheinlicher, dass das Votivformular *deo Requalivahano* lediglich einen 'theonymischen Stellvertreter' repräsentiert, eine Formel also, die, statt den echten Namen der Gottheit (d.h. das primäre Theonym) preiszugeben, bloß aus einem theonymischen Determinativ plus einem Beinamen besteht. Eine solche Struktur des Votivformulars ist ziemlich verbreitet in den indigenen Religionsvarianten des Römischen Kaiserreichs, vgl. u.a. *deae dominae Turibrigensi* als Stellvertreter für den theonymischen Dativ ***Ataicinae* in Santa Lucía del Trampal/E oder *deae Suli* anstelle von *Minervae deae suli* (d.h. 'des Auges') in Bath.[116] In dem vorliegenden Fall haben wir es mit einem Funktionsbeinamen zu tun, der vermutlich auch in diesem Falle Merkur selbst charakterisierte, wenn auch sein Name nicht explizit genannt und nur sein Götterstatus hervorgehoben wird.

Die Tatsache, dass es sich nicht um Latein handelt, spricht auch im Falle des

113 Zur Thematik vgl. Birkhan 1970; Rübekeil 2002. Eine rezente Bilanz bietet Schumacher (2007; englische Version 2009), der allerdings meine Beiträge von 1992, 2003 und 2005 nicht kennt. Die konkreten Lebensumstände, so wie sie aus Archäologie und Geschichte hervorgehen, erläutert Carroll 2001.

114 Man vergesse nicht, dass selbst viele der von Männern getragenen etruskischen und auch lateinischen Cognomina auf *-a* endeten.

115 De Bernardo Stempel 2004, insbes. 181–2.

116 Vgl. Abascal Palazón 1995, Jufer & Luginbühl 2001, 64–5, und die Bibliographie in Anm. 118.

MERCVRIVS begleitenden *VALDIVAHANOS* keineswegs gegen eine Deutung als Beiname. Es hat sich nämlich im letzten Jahrzehnt bezüglich der provinzialrömischen Religion folgendes herausgestellt:[117]

1) dass die sogenannte "Interpretatio Romana" nicht ausschließlich aus dem Phänomen der *Identificatio* bestand, also der Gleichsetzung eines göttlichen Wesens aus dem klassischen Pantheon mit einer bereits bestehenden indigenen Gottheit;

2) dass die von Römern oder Einheimischen vorgenommenen Gleichsetzungen (*Identificationes Romanae vel indigenae*) anderen Formen von Interpretatio gegenüber sogar die Minderheit darstellen;

3) dass die meisten Fälle von Interpretatio eigentlich aus fremdsprachlichen Erklärungen der Eigenschaften einzelner klassischer Gottheiten bestehen. Die durch das Phänomen der *Explicatio vel translatio barbarica* entstandenen fremdsprachlichen Beinamen klassischer Gottheiten hatten lediglich die Funktion, ausgewählte Figuren der mediterranen Panthea für ihre neuen, zentraleuropäischen Verehrer zu erschließen bzw. ihnen näherzubringen und in den Kult zu integrieren;

4) dass, wenn auch die keltische Sprache — meist in Form des Gallischen — als Vehikel der meisten einheimischen Erklärungen dient (*Explicatio vel translatio Celtica*), germanische Wiedergaben anderssprachiger Götternamen durchaus bekannt sind. Vgl. z.B. das Epitheton *LEVDINAE* für die 'zum Volke gehörigen' Muttergottheiten,[118] die *Celtice* als *OLLOTOTAE* und *Latine* als *MATRES OMNIVM GENTIVM* anderswoher bekannt sind. In derartigen Fällen sprechen wir dann von *Explicatio vel translatio Germanica*.

Die Vermutung, dass sich hinter *REQVALIVAHANOS* 'Finsterer Gedenker' und *VALDIVAHANOS* 'Lenker und Gedenker' lediglich germanische Umschreibungen von zwei bzw. eigentlich drei der Eigenschaften Merkurs verbergen, findet nun eine zusätzliche und nicht geringe Stütze in der Ähnlichkeit der verwendeten Beinamen mit einigen der keltischen Merkurparaphrasen: Der psychopompe Merkur wird auch in dem britannischen Votivformular *Mercurio deo andescocio* für 'the downleading Mercury' angerufen.[119] Als 'Sieger und Führer von Magna' wird derselbe Gott in der narbonensischen Weihung *deo Mercurio victori Magniaco vellauno* angerufen, während das Votivformular *deo Mercurio adsmerio* aus Aquitanien schließlich seine Eigenschaft als 'Fürsorger' unterstreicht.

Die hier vorgeschlagene Analyse der beiden Votivformeln vom Kölner Waidmarkt und aus Blatzheim als *explicationes barbaricae* des Merkur mithilfe germanischer Sprache gewinnt nicht zuletzt an Wahrscheinlichkeit, wenn man bedenkt, dass alle drei dort angesprochenen Facetten des Gottes, nämlich {Unterwelt}, {Führung} und {Fürsorge}, schon dem griechischen *HERMES* eigen waren, bei dem sie als Ἕρμης πομπαῖος bzw. ἡγήτωρ und χαριδώτης beschrieben wurden.[120] Ob es sich dennoch

117 Zu diesem ganzen Fragekomplex vgl. de Bernardo Stempel 2008a, 2008b sowie 2014b und forthcoming.

118 Vgl. de Bernardo Stempel 2005, 146.

119 In den Widmungen *(deo) Mercurio dubnocaratiaco* aus der Lugdunensis dagegen scheint *dubno-* eher die ‚Welt' zu repräsentieren, vgl. De Albentiis Hienz & de Bernardo Stempel 2013, 91–2.

120 Vgl. jeweils de Bernardo Stempel 2007a, 71; 2007b, 57; 2008a, 79; 2008b, 68 und 2010, 24. Weitere

bei den hier besprochenen germanischen Beschreibungen um einfache (Funktions-) Epitheta oder um echte, also kultisch festgelegte, unterschiedliche Epiklesen handelte, lässt sich freilich bei der vorläufigen Einmaligkeit der Belege nicht entscheiden.

BIBLIOGRAPHIE

Abascal Palazón J. M. 1995 'Las inscripciones latinas de Santa Lucía del Trampal (Alcuéscar, Cáceres) y el culto de Ataecina en Hispania', *Archivo Español de Arqueología* 68, 31–105.

Altjohann, M. 2003 ‚Cernunnos-Darstellungen in den gallischen und germanischen Provinzen', *Romanisation und Resistenz in Plastik, Architektur und Inschriften der Provinzen des Imperium Romanum*, ed. P. Noelke, 67–79. Mainz, Philipp von Zabern.

Bevilacqua, G. 2009 'Dediche ad Hermes', *Dediche sacre nel mondo greco-romano: Diffusione, funzioni, tipologie/Religious Dedications in the Greco-Roman World: Distribution, Typology, Use*, ed. J. Bodel & M. Kajava, 227–44. Rom, Institutum Romanum Finlandiae (Acta Instituti Romani Finlandiae 35).

Biller, F. 2010 *Kultische Zentren und Matronenverehrung in der südlichen Germania inferior* Rahden/Westfalen, Marie Leidorf.

Binsfeld, W. 1960 ‚Die Namen Kölns zur Römerzeit', *Mouseion. Studien aus Kunst und Geschichte für Otto H. Förster*, 72–80. Köln, M. Dumont Schauenburg.

Birkhan, H. 1970 *Germanen und Kelten bis zum Ausgang der Römerzeit*, Wien, ÖAW, SB philos.-hist. Kl. 272.

Cancik, H., A. Schäfer & W. Spickermann, Hrsg. 2006 *Zentralität und Religion. Zur Formierung urbaner Zentren im Imperium Romanum*. Tübingen, Mohr Siebeck.

Carroll, M. 2001 *Romans, Celts & Germans. The German Provinces of Rome*. Stroud, Tempus.

Chaniotis, A. 2008 ‚Konkurrenz und Profilierung von Kultgemeinden im Fest', *Festrituale in der römischen Kaiserzeit*, ed. J. Rüpke, 67–87. Tübingen, Mohr Siebeck.

De Albentiis Hienz, M. & P. de Bernardo Stempel 2013 'Apolls Epitheta – griechisch, lateinisch, keltisch bzw. keltorömisch: eine Typologie der Beinamen klassischer Gottheiten', *Geistes-, sozial- und kulturwissenschaftlicher Anzeiger der ÖAW*, Jg. 148/1+2 (2013 = Graekorömische und keltorömische Theonymik und Religion, Akten des XII. Internationalen F.E.R.C.AN.-Workshops Berlin 2012), 7–126.

De Bernardo Stempel, P. 1992 'A New Perspective on some Germano-Celtic Material', *Zeitschrift für celtische Philologie* 45, 90–5.

De Bernardo Stempel, P. 2000 'Keltische Ortsnamen', *Hoops' Reallexikon der Germanischen Altertumskunde*, Bd. 16, 407–13. Berlin / New York, Bibliopolis.

De Bernardo Stempel, P. 2003 'Continental Celtic *ollo*: Early Welsh *(h)ol(l)*, Olwen and Culhwch', *Cambrian Medieval Celtic Studies* 46 (Winter 2003), 119–27.

De Bernardo Stempel, P. 2004 ‚Nehalen(n)ia, das Salz und das Meer', *Anzeiger der Philosophisch-historischen Klasse der Österreichischen Akademie der Wissenschaften* 139, 181–93.

De Bernardo Stempel, P. 2005 ‚Götternamen in Germania inferior', *Keltische Götter im Römischen Reich*, Osnabrücker Forschungen zu Altertum und Antike-Rezeption Bd. 9, ed. W. Spickermann & R. Wiegels, 139–48. Möhnesee, Bibliopolis.

De Bernardo Stempel, P. 2007a 'Einheimische, keltische und keltisierte Gottheiten der Narbonensis im Vergleich', *Auf den Spuren keltischer Götterverehrung. Akten des 5. F.E.R.C.AN-Kolloquiums (Graz 2003)*, ed. M. Hainzmann, 67–79. Wien, ÖAW (MPK 64).

De Bernardo Stempel, P. 2007b 'Teonimia en las Aquitanias célticas: análisis lingüístico', *Auf den Spuren keltischer Götterverehrung. Akten des 5. F.E.R.C.AN-Kolloquiums (Graz 2003)*, ed. M. Hainzmann, 57–66. Wien: ÖAW (MPK 64).

De Bernardo Stempel, P. 2008a 'Continuity, *Translatio* and *Identificatio* in Gallo-Roman

Synonyme behandelt Bevilacqua 2009.

Religion: The Case of Britain', *Continuity and Innovation in Religion in the Roman West*, Supplementary series no. 67 to the *Journal of Roman Archaeology*, Bd. 2, ed. R. Haeussler & A. C. King, 67–82. Portsmouth: Rhode Island.

De Bernardo Stempel, P. 2008b 'More Names, Fewer Deities: Complex Theonymic Formulas and the Three Types of Interpretatio', *Divindades indígenas em análise /Divinités pré-romaines - bilan et perspectives d'une recherche. Actas do VII workshop FERCAN (Cascais, Mayo de 2006)*, ed. J. d'Encarnação, 65–73. Coimbra / Porto, Centro de Estudos Arqueológicos das Universidades de Coimbra e Porto.

De Bernardo Stempel, P. 2010 'Method in the Analysis of Romano-Celtic Theonymic Materials: Improved Readings and Etymological Interpretations', *Celtic Religion across Time and Space. Actas del IX Workshop F.E.R.C.AN. (Molina de Aragón, Septiembre 2008)*, ed. J. A. Arenas Esteban, 18–27. Toledo, Junta de Comunidades de Castilla-La Mancha.

De Bernardo Stempel, P. 2010–2011 'Zur Interpretation keltischer Inschriften im Lichte indogermanischer Namenformeln', *Incontri Linguistici* 33 (2010), 87–123 und *Incontri Linguistici* 34 (2011), 47–65 [2. Teil].

De Bernardo Stempel, P. 2014a 'Mercurius Valdivahanus aus dem Kölner Waidmarkt und deus Requalivahanus aus Blatzheim an der Neffel', *Beiträge zur Namenforschung* N.F. 49/1 (2014), 89–108.

De Bernardo Stempel, P. 2014b 'Keltische Äquivalente klassischer Epitheta und andere sprachliche und nicht-sprachliche Phänomene im Rahmen der sogenannten *interpretatio Romana*', *Zeitschrift für celtische Philologie* 61 (2014), 7–48.

De Bernardo Stempel, P. forthcoming 'Aspects of *Interpretatio*: *Identificationes* vs. *Explicationes vel translationes*', *Religious Individualisation in the Roman Empire*, ed. R. Häussler, T. King, F. Marco Simón & G. Schörner. Oxford: Oxbow.

De Bernardo Stempel, P. & M. Hainzmann 2009 ‚Die Namenformulare mit *sive* in römischen Inschriften', *Anzeiger der philosophisch-historischen Klasse der ÖAW* 144/1, 75–91.

De Bernardo Stempel, P. & M. Hainzmann 2010 '*Sive* in theonymic formulae as a means for introducing explications and identifications', *Celtic Religion across Space and Time. IX Workshop F.E.R.C.AN. Fontes epigraphici religionum Celticarum antiquarum*, ed. J. A. Arenas Esteban, 28–39. Toledo, Junta de Comunidades de Castilla-La Mancha.

Dietmar, C. & M. Trier 2006 *Mit der U-Bahn in die Römerzeit. Ein Handbuch zu den archäologischen Ausgrabungsstätten rund um den Bau der Nord-Süd Stadtbahn*, 2. Auflage. Köln, Kiepenheuer & Witsch.

Dodt, M. 2005 ‚Römische Bauten im südlichen Suburbium der Colonia Claudia Ara Agrippinensium', *Kölner Jahrbuch* 38, 433–733.

Drexhage, H.-J., H. Konen & K. Rüffing 2002 *Die Wirtschaft des Römischen Reiches (1.–3. Jahrhundert). Eine Einführung*. Berlin, De Gruyter.

Duncan-Jones, R. 1982 *The economy of the Roman Empire*, 2nd edition. Cambridge, Cambridge University Press.

Eck, W. 2004 *Köln in römischer Zeit*. Köln, Greven.

Eck, W. 2007 ‚Votivaltäre in den Matronenheiligtümern in Niedergermanien', *Kult und Kommunikation. Medien in Heiligtümern der Antike*, ZAKMIRA 4, ed. C. Frevel & H. von Hesberg, 415–33. Wiesbaden, Reichert.

Egelhaaf-Gaiser, U. & A. Schäfer, Hrsg. 2002 *Religiöse Vereine in der römischen Antike*. Tübingen, Mohr Siebeck.

Fischer, F. 2007 'Frühe Germanen am Rhein und Neckar', *Fundberichte aus Baden-Württemberg* 29, 311–25.

Galsterer, B. & H. Galsterer 2010 *Die römischen Steininschriften aus Köln*, Kölner Forsch. 10. Mainz, Philipp von Zabern.

Gregarek, H. 2004 ‚Monumentale Votive im römischen Köln', *Kölner Jahrbuch* 37, 45–60.

Gregarek, H. 2005 ‚Rediviva: Steinrecycling im antiken Köln', *Von Anfang an. Archäologie in Nordrhein-Westfalen*, ed. H. G. Horn, H. Hellenkemper, G. Isenberg & J. Kunow, 139–45. Köln, Philipp von Zabern.

Hauser, G. 1993 ‚Fragen zu einem römischen Tempel unter dem Dom', *Kölner Domblatt* 58, 313–42.

Hauser, G. 2003 *Schichten und Geschichte unter dem Dom. Die Kölner Grabung*. Köln, Kölner Dom.

Hellenkemper, H. 1972/1973 ‚*Delubrum martis* und die mittelalterlichen Überlieferungswege', *Kölner Jahrbuch* 13, 102–6.

Herz, P. 2003 ‚Matronenkult und kultische Mahlzeiten', *Romanisation und Resistenz in Plastik, Architektur und Inschriften der Provinzen des Imperium Romanum*, ed. P. Noelke, 139–48. Mainz, Philipp von Zabern.

Horn, H. G. 1987 ‚Bilddenkmäler des

Matronenkultes im Ubiergebiet', *Matronen und verwandte Gottheiten, Kolloquium der Göttinger Akademiekommission für die Altertumskunde Mittel- und Nordeuropas*, ed. G. Bauchhenß & G. Neumann, 31–54. Köln, Rheinland Habelt.

Hupe, J. 1997 ,Studien zum Gott Merkur im römischen Gallien und Germanien', *Trierer Zeitschrift* 60, 53–227.

Ilkow, P. 1968 *Die Nominalkomposita der altsächsischen Bibeldichtung*, Göttingen, Vandenhoeck & Ruprecht.

Irmler, B. 2004 ,Rekonstruktion einer Porticusordnung an der Rheinseite in Köln', *Kölner Jahrbuch* 37, 77–102.

Jufer, N. & Luginbühl, Th. 2001 *Répertoire des dieux gaulois*, Paris, Errance.

Kajanto, I. 1982 *The Latin Cognomina* (Societas Scientiarum Fennica, Commentationes Humanarum Litterarum 36, 2). Rom, Helsingfors.

Kakoschke, A. 2006–2008 *Die Personennamen in den zwei germanischen Provinzen*, Bd. 1, 2006; Bd. 2, 2008 (in 2 Teilbänden). Rahden / Westfalen, Bibliopolis.

Kakoschke, A. 2010 *Die Personennamen in der römischen Provinz Gallia Belgica*, Hildesheim u.a., Olms.

Klein, M. J. 2003 ,Von den Göttern verehren sie am meisten Merkur', *Die Römer und ihr Erbe*, ed. M. J. Klein, 107–28. Mainz, Philipp von Zabern.

Kluge, F. & E. Seebold 1989 *Etymologisches Wörterbuch der deutschen Sprache*, 22. Auflage. Berlin / New York, Walter de Gruyter.

Ködderitzsch, R. 1986 'Keltoide Namen mit germanischen Namenträgern', *Zeitschrift für celtische Philologie* 41, 188–213.

Krahe, H. & W. Meid 1967. *Germanische Sprachwissenschaft*, Bd. III. Berlin, Walter de Gruyter.

Kuhnen, H.-P., Hrsg. 1996. Religio Romana. *Wege zu den Göttern im antiken Trier*. Trier, Rheinisches Landesmuseum Trier.

Kühnemann, E. & W. Binsfeld 1965/66 ,Die Grabungen im Kapitolbezirk', *Kölner Jahrbuch* 8, 46–53.

Lehner, H. 1918 *Die antiken Steindenkmäler des Provinzialmuseums in Bonn*. Bonn, Cohen.

Leumann, M., J. B. Hofmann, A. Szantyr 1977 *Lateinische Laut- und Formlehre*, 5. Auflage. München, Beck.

Liertz, U.-M. 1998 *Kult und Kaiser: Studien zu Kaiserkult und Kaiserverehrung in den germanischen Provinzen und in der Gallia Belgica zur römischen Kaiserzeit*. Rom, Institutum Romanum Finlandiae.

Meid, W. 2005 *Keltische Personennamen in Pannonien*, Budapest, Archaeolingua.

Mrozek, S. 1978 'Les espèces monétaires dans les inscriptions latines du haut-empire Romain', *Les 'Devaluations' à Rome – époque républicaine et impériale*, ed. G. Vallet, 79–86. Rom, Collection de l'Ecole française de Rome.

Naumann-Steckner, F. 1997 *Tod am Rhein*. Köln, Asmuth.

Nedoma, R. 2001 *Kleine Grammatik des Altisländischen*, Heidelberg, Winter.

Neumann, G. 1987 ,Die germanischen Matronen-Beinamen', *Matronen und verwandte Gottheiten, Kolloquium der Göttinger Akademiekommission für die Altertumskunde Mittel- und Nordeuropas*, Beihefte der *Bonner Jahrbücher*, Bd. 44, ed. G. Bauchhenß & G. Neumann, 103–32. Köln, Rheinland & Habelt.

Noelke, P. 1990 ,*Ara et Aedicula*', *Bonner Jahrbücher* 190, 79–124.

Nowald, G. & H. Dirks 2006 *Kranichbegegnungen – Kranichwelten. Reportagen, Geschichten und Fakten entlang des westeuropäischen Zugweges*. Borken, Naturblick Verlag.

Precht, G. 2010 ,Der Grabbau vom Waidmarkt in Köln – ein Rekonstruktionsversuch', *Kölner Jahrbuch* 43, 607–22.

Ramat, P., 1988 *Introduzione alla linguistica germanica*, 2. Auflage. Bologna, Il Mulino.

Rathgens, H. 1913 *Die Kirche S. Maria im Kapitol zu Köln*. Düsseldorf, L. Schwann.

Ristow, G. 1974 ,Ein Giebel von einem Lararium', *Römer Illustrierte* 1, 139.

Ristow, G. 1979 *Religionen und ihre Denkmäler im römischen Köln. Zur Religionsgeschichte des römischen Köln*. 2. Auflage. Köln, Bachem.

Ristow, G. 1980 *Römischer Götterhimmel und frühes Christentum. Bilder zur Frühzeit der Kölner Religions- und Kirchengeschichte*. Köln, Wienand.

Rübekeil, L. 2002 *Diachrone Studien zur Kontaktzone zwischen Kelten und Germanen*, Wien, ÖAW, Phil.-hist. Klasse, Sonderberichte 699.

Rüger, C. B. 1987 ,Beobachtungen zu den epigraphischen Belegen der Muttergottheiten in den lateinischen Provinzen des Imperium Romanum', in: *Matronen und verwandte Gottheiten, Kolloquium der Göttinger Akademiekommission für die Altertumskunde Mittel- und Nordeuropas*, ed. G. Bauchhenß & G. Neumann, 1–30. Köln, Rheinland & Habelt.

Scardigli, P. 1989 ,Sprache im Umkreis der

Matroneninschriften', *Germanische Rest- und Trümmersprachen*, ed. H. Beck, 143–56. Berlin/ New York, De Gruyter.

Schäfer, A. 2011a ‚Religion in den Provinzen Roms', *Götterbilder – Menschenbilder. Religion und Kulte in Carnuntum, Landesausstellung Niederösterreich*, ed. F. Humer & G. Kremer, 23–9. Wien, Amt der NÖ Landesregierung.

Schäfer, A. 2011b ‚Planung am Reißbrett. Kölns römische Vorstadt', *Drunter und drüber: Der Waidmarkt. Schauplatz Kölner Geschichte*, 1, ed. M. Kramp & M. Trier, 35–41. Köln, Bachem.

Schäfer, A. & Wieland, M. 2011, 'Ein überraschender Grabfund: Aschenkiste und Weihenschrift', *Drunter und drüber: Der Weidmarkt. Schauplatz Kölner Geschichte* 1, ed. M. Kramp & M. Trier, 43–7. Köln, Bachem.

Schmidt, K. H. 1987 ‚Die keltischen Matronennamen', *Matronen und verwandte Gottheiten, Kolloquium der Göttinger Akademiekommission für die Altertumskunde Mittel- und Nordeuropas*, ed. G. Bauchhenß & G. Neumann, 133–54. Köln, Rheinland & Habelt.

Schoppa, H. 1959 *Römische Götterdenkmäler in Köln.* Die Denkmäler des Römischen Köln, Bd. 22. Köln, Der Löwe, H. Reykers.

Schuler, A. 2005 ‚Das nördliche Suburbium des römischen Köln', *Kölner Jahrbuch* 38, 245–431.

Schumacher, St. 2007 'Die Deutschen und die Nachbarstämme: Lexikalische und strukturelle Sprachkontaktphänomene entlang der keltisch-germanischen Übergangszone', *Keltische Forschungen* 2, 167–207.

Schumacher, St., 2009 'Lexical and Structural Language-Contact Phenomena along the Germano-Celtic Transition Zone', *Kelten am Rhein. Akten des 13. Internationalen Keltologiekongresses / Proceedings of the XIIIth ICCS (Bonn, Juli 2007)*, 2. Teil: Philologie, ed. St. Zimmer, 247–66. Mainz, Philipp von Zabern.

Simek, R. 2006 *Lexikon der germanischen Mythologie*, 3. Auflage. Stuttgart, Kröner.

Spiegel, E. M. 2008 ‚Eine augusteische Holzkohleschicht am Laurenzplatz in Köln', *Kölner Jahrbuch* 41, 273–82.

Trier, M. 2010 ‚Die Kölner Stadtbefestigung im Mittelalter und in der frühen Neuzeit', *Lübecker Kolloquium zur Stadtarchäologie im Hanseraum VII: Die Befestigungen*, ed. M. Gläser, 535–52. Lübeck, Schmidt-Roemhild.

Spickermann, W. 2003 *Germania Superior. Religionsgeschichte des römischen Germanien*, I. Tübingen, Mohr Siebeck.

Spickermann, W. 2008 *Germania Inferior. Religionsgeschichte des römischen Germanien*, II. Tübingen, Mohr Siebeck.

Untermann, J. 1989 ‚Sprachvergleichung und Sprachidentität: methodische Fragen im Zwischenfeld von Keltisch und Germanisch', *Germanische Rest- und Trümmersprachen*, ed. H. Beck, 211–39. Berlin/New York, De Gruyter.

Van Andringa, W. 2002 *La religion en Gaule romaine*. Paris, Errance.

Wissowa, G. 1912 *Religion und Kultus der Römer*, 2. Auflage. München, C. H. Beck.

Woolf, G. 2003 ‚Local cult in Imperial Context: The *Matronae* revisited', *Romanisation und Resistenz in Plastik, Architektur und Inschriften der Provinzen des Imperium Romanum,* ed. P. Noelke, 131–8. Mainz, Philipp von Zabern.

Yeo, E. & G. Bauchhenß 1990 ‚Ein weiterer Mercuriusaltar aus Bornheim-Sechtem', *Bonner Jahrbücher* 190, 125–37.

Weisgerber, J. L. 1968 *Die Namen der Ubier*, Köln und Opladen, Westdeutscher Verlag.

Zelle, M. 2000 *Colonia Ulpia Traiana. Götter und Kulte*. Köln, Rheinland Verlag.

XXVI

CORPUS-F.E.R.C.AN. GERMANIA INFERIOR PRELIMINARY CONSIDERATIONS AND INTENTIONS

Werner Petermandl

The proposed project aims to collect and analyse all Celtic divine names which are preserved in the inscriptions of the Roman Province Germania Inferior. This should lead to fundamental insights into the manifestation and development of the Gallo-Roman religion and shall at the same time contribute to the study of the process of what is commonly known as Romanisation. Moreover the project will provide deeper knowledge of the distribution of languages in Germania Inferior.

THE well-known, declared main purpose of the F.E.R.C.AN. project is to publish a Corups-F.E.R.C.AN. that will compile, edit and also analyse all the epigraphical sources of Celtic divine names. One part of this Corpus-F.E.R.C.AN. – the part that shall be presented here – will provide the material of the Roman province Germania Inferior. It will be carried out under the direction of Wolfgang Spickermann. It is the aim of this paper to give some insight into the main preliminary considerations and intentions of this project.[1]

Before getting down to that, however, some remarks shall be made about the very study area – the province Germania Inferior. First of all it has to be stressed that confining the chronological and local framework of the study area to a Roman province matches the structuring principles of the F.E.R.C.AN.-project. Moreover it is useful in a systematic and pragmatic sense and proves reasonable in other respects as well. It is evident that the religious situation in a territory was affected by the Roman political organisation. Furthermore this approach does not lose sight of the fact that the field of study is an artificial territory, which did not come into being naturally but was a result of the Roman conquest. Two more specific aspects can be put forward:

1. In Germania Inferior numerous records containing Celtic divine names were found. A linguistic analysis in a preliminary study on Germania Inferior could identify 22 proper Celtic divine names, including the epithets of Matronae. Additionally there

1 In order to get the necessary financial support an application was proposed at the "Österreichische Akademie der Wissenschaften" ("Austrian Academy of Sciences").

are 18 names combining Celtic and Germanic elements and furthermore 14 hybrid or obscure denominations. There are 304 epigraphic testimonials containing names classified as Celtic, 246 of which name Nehalennia. Also frequently found are Gabiae (12), Mercurius Gebrinius (11), Matronae Octocannae (9) and Suleviae (4). The numbers for the combined names are similar. Altogether there are also 304 epigraphic records. 264 of those testimonials come from votive inscriptions to the Matronae Vacallinehae. Also quite frequently attested are the Matronae Cantrusteihiae/Andrusteihiae (6), the Matronae Ambiamarcae (5), the Matronae Gesahenae (5) and the Matronae Albiahenae (4). It is striking that combined names are mainly found among the epithets of the Matronae.[2]

2. The specific situation regarding the population of the Lower Rhineland provides a very interesting field of research. The area was subject to massive migration and population changes. From the time of Caesar´s interventions there followed a completely new configuration of the population living there. A bulk of the population of Germania Inferior emigrated in large groups from the right bank of the Rhine. In the 1st century AD due to the stationing of legions a strong influx of people from north and middle Italy and the southern parts of Gaul followed. Furthermore auxiliary troops arrived from various parts of the Roman Empire. And, additionally, significant levels of immigration from the inner parts of Gaul of people benefitting from the Roman army´s economic power has to be taken into account. Since the 1st century AD, therefore, at least 3 different groups of population can be distinguished:

- Population living in this area before the Romans appeared. The so-called Germani Cisrhenani mentioned by Caesar (*B.Gall.* 2.3.4; 6.2.3; 6.32.1) are included in this group.
- Population keeping its group identities on an ethnical basis emigrating from the right bank of the river Rhine after Caesars interventions.
- Population coming from all parts of the Empire as a result of the Roman occupation and especially linked to the Roman army, in one way or another.

In this complex mixed population a uniform group identity did not exist. However, after the establishment of the two German provinces a very special Germano/Gallo-Roman society emerged, which was not founded on tribal identities but defined itself by its affiliation to urban settlements and *civitates* created by the Romans. In urban settlements mainly migrants from Italy and the inner parts of Gaul can be found. In the hinterland migrants from the right bank of the Rhine largely made up the population and it is evident how local elites in regional centres presented themselves in a Roman way (cf. e.g. the sanctuaries of Empel and Elst).[3]

Against this background it is especially interesting to examine the religious situation by investigating the appearance of Celtic divine names. Furthermore, it is likely that scrutinising Celtic divine names will also shed new light on the dispersion of languages throughout Germania Inferior.

2 Cf. Spickermann 2005, 139–146.
3 Cf. Spickermann 2008, 15–21.

The Corpus-F.E.R.C.AN. on Germania Inferior, of course, will follow the guidelines as outlined by M. Hainzmann.[4] That means it will consist of two volumes:

Volume 1 – "Celtic Divine Names and their Epigraphic Testimonials" – will be divided into two fascicles. The first fascicle will provide extensive commentaries on: a) all of the divine names (including theonyms, epithets etc.) found in Germania Inferior; that will be done in close collaboration with linguists; and b) the iconography linked to Celtic divine names in this very province.

The second fascicle will contain the "Catalogus Inscriptionum", the collection and new edition of the epigraphical sources in Germania Inferior presenting Celtic divine names or mixed names (about 600 testimonials). Due to the alignment to the Corpus-F.E.R.C.AN. guidelines each inscription will be presented with a majuscule as well as a minuscule transcription and a German and an English translation. In addition to the usual epigraphic data, such as material, date, place of discovery, relevant scholarly literature, etc. an extensive commentary will also be provided, as well as a photographic image of the object in order to record all iconographic details linked with the epigraphic testimonials of Celtic divine names. All this information will also be recorded in a database and made available on a special website.

It can be mentioned at this point that there is co-operation with CIL XIII. Due to the fact that the project leader W. Spickermann is one of the editors of the new edition of CIL XIII, all the existing material gathered for the CIL XIII edition is accessible to us. Conversely, work done within our project, such as new readings, for instance, will be directly utilised by the CIL XIII edition.

Volume 2 will also consist of two parts. Part 1 aims to glean and collect the archaeological evidence of the sites, where inscriptions with Celtic divine names were discovered. For the discussion of those inscriptions, it is of crucial importance to take into account the context of the material culture and to get the clearest picture possible what was going on at those places.

The second part of volume 2 will deal with the collected material on three levels, which shall here be summarised under the headings: a) facts, b) questions and c) further questions.

a) The tasks covered by "facts" will deal with the type of analysis that is just sorting the source material. An accurate collation is, indeed, an important prerequisite for further analysis and itself will offer new insights. We will especially focus on the following aspects:

- local distribution
- material background
- social distribution

b) The next category of analysis could be called "questions". We will especially be interested in the following questions. At least we will raise them and try to find out whether some answers are possible.

4 Hainzmann 2013, 5–21.

The first question will focus on the fact that the vast majority of our inscriptions belongs to the period after the middle of the 2nd century AD. Only very few inscriptions, can be dated with certainty to the time before 150 AD. Hence the question arises why those Celtic divine names appeared. First of all it needs to be clarified whether and to what extent old cult traditions survived despite the extensive migrations in this area. The aforementioned archaeological examination of the cult sites, where Celtic divine names were found, might shed new light on what really happened at those places. A different approach of our work will be to try to check the assumption that Celtic divine names were in many cases creations of a new Gallo-Roman religion.

Another question will deal with the motivation behind choosing deities with Celtic names. We want to ask whether the worshipping of Celtic divine names is a result of cultural resistance (i.e. a deliberate turning away from other cults) or it rather proves cultural fusion. What kind of role did Celtic divine names play for collective identities? Is there any indication or even proof that any religious change was deliberately brought about?

The third question, I want to point out here, concerns the population structure of the province relating to languages. By examining the local distribution of inscriptions with Celtic divine names we will try to improve our knowledge of the population structure of the province; i.e. the distribution of the Celtic language.

c) In the last category of analysis I previously referred to as "further questions" we hope to be able to make a contribution to two more general topics.

The first of these topics would be the development of religions. It is intended that our subject should provide an example of how religions can develop when the socio-political context is changing. At least it will be possible to demonstrate how flexible religion can be, despite its bond with tradition.

The second topic concerns the question of (self-)Romanisation. The revealed phenomena should be presented as an example of the Romanisation processes. In that context we would also like to highlight the fact that our study provides data for anthropological questions, dealing with cultural exchange, when different cultures collide. We believe that our material can, for instance, contribute to the topic of religion's political relevance, which particularly in current times is a subject for debate.

As a last point I would like to focus on terminology. As language and material culture do not necessarily overlap, ethnic assignments are highly problematic. Therefore, extreme caution needs to be exercised when assigning groups of population to the categories "Celts" or other. As the terms "Celts" or "Celtic" can be – and actually *are* – defined by language, material culture, local area, and denomination by ancient authors, this can lead to massive misunderstandings. In our project – for the sake of clarity – when we use terms like "Celts", "Celtic" and so on, we are only referring to the "Celtic" language or people speaking that language.

BIBLIOGRAPHY

Hainzmann, M. 2013 'In Erwartung des CORPUS-F.E.R.C.AN. – Ein Lagebericht', *Keltische Götternamen als individuelle Option? Celtic theonyms as an individual option? Akten des 11. internationalen Workshops „Fontes Epigraphici Religionum Celticarum Antiquarum" vom 19.-21 Mai 2011 an der Universität Erfurt*, ed. W. Spickermann in Verbindung mit L. Scheuermann, 5–21. Rahden (Westf.), Osnabrücker Forschungen zu Altertum und Antike-Rezeption 19

Spickermann, W. 2005 'Keltische Götter in Niedergermanien? Mit einem sprachwissenschaftlichen Kommentar von Patrizia De Bernardo Stempel', *Keltische Götter im Römischen Reich. Akten des 4. internationalen F.E.R.C.AN.-Workshops vom 4.–6.10.2002 an der Universität Osnabrück*, ed. W. Spickermann & R. Wiegels, 139–146. Möhnesee, Osnabrücker Forschungen zu Altertum und Antike-Rezeption 9

Spickermann, W. 2008 *Germania Inferior. Religionsgeschichte des römischen Germanien II.* Tübingen, Religion der römischen Provinzen 3

Index of theonyms and epithets

Topographic index

N.B.: pages 130-48 (King, Appendices 1 & 2) have not been indexed here.

Country codes: AT, Austria; BE, Belgium; BG, Bulgaria; BH, Bosnia & Herzegovina; CH, Switzerland; DE, Germany; DK, Denmark; EG, Egypt; EI, Republic of Ireland; ES, Spain; FR, France; GE, Georgia; GR, Greece; HR, Croatia; HU, Hungary; IT, Italy; LX, Luxembourg; MC, Macedonia; MN, Montenegro; NE, Netherlands; PT, Portugal; RO, Romania; SL, Slovenia; SR, Serbia; TN, Tunisia; TR, Turkey; UK, United Kingdom of Great Britain & Northern Ireland.